PARLIAMENTARY
PRACTICE
in
NEW ZEALAND

PARLIAMENTARY PRACTICE
in
NEW ZEALAND

Third Edition

by

DAVID McGEE, CNZM, QC

Clerk of the House of Representatives

© 2005 Office of the Clerk of the House of Representatives

Third edition published in 2005
by Dunmore Publishing Ltd
P.O. Box 25080
Wellington
books@dunmore.co.nz

First published 1985 by the Government Printer, Wellington
Second edition published 1994 by GP Publications, Wellington

National Library of New Zealand Cataloguing-in-Publication Data

McGee, David G.
Parliamentary practice in New Zealand / David McGee. 3rd ed.
Previous ed.: Wellington, N.Z. : GP Publications, 1994.
Includes bibliographical references and index.
ISBN 1-877399-06-X
1. New Zealand. Parliament—Rules and practice.
2. New Zealand—Politics and government. I. Title.
328.9305—dc 22

Printer: Keeling and Mundy, Palmerston North

PREFACE

This edition of *Parliamentary Practice in New Zealand* incorporates some 10 years of parliamentary experience of operating under the multi-party environment engendered by the adoption of the Mixed-Member Proportional (MMP) electoral system. As the last wholly first-past-the-post Parliament (the forty-fourth Parliament) was responsible for the adoption and first trial of the major changes in parliamentary procedure that attuned procedures developed for an essentially two-party system into ones designed for a multi-party system, a full decade of operating experience and adaptation to MMP has now elapsed. Most of the changes in procedure and practice described in this book have resulted directly from the parliamentary reforms adopted in the wake of that electoral reform. In particular, they have resulted in the explicit recognition of parties in the Standing Orders for the first time in the history of the New Zealand Parliament.

Of course, parties existed before MMP. However, the fact that their existence is now acknowledged in the House's rules makes it easier to describe how procedures work in practice as compared to a set of rules that studiously ignored parties but were not fully comprehensible without taking them into account. The major procedural changes adapting the House to MMP were agreed to in 1995. These have been followed by procedural refinements of a less substantial nature adopted in 1996, 1999, 2003 and 2005. The results of these procedural changes are set out in this book, together with the ensuing rulings by Speakers and other presiding officers interpreting the new rules and providing solutions for new sets of circumstances that have arisen. In addition, important contributions to explicating and forming parliamentary practice have been made by the House's select committees (particularly the Standing Orders Committee) in reports recommending procedures to be followed or describing practices adopted. These contributions are also noted as appropriate.

While there have been significant developments in the House's internal procedures since the last edition, statutory changes have been relatively less important in this period. The second edition described the new MMP electoral system. Changes since then have been to matters of detail rather than principle. The most significant legislative developments have been in the field of public finance, where the *Public Finance Amendment Act* 2004 has led to a considerable rewriting of the chapters on financial procedure. Other legislative changes of note relate to appropriation messages (now abolished), the reinstatement of business in a new Parliament, and oaths in Māori.

Case law, rather than internal change or legislation, has led to a considerable reworking of the chapters on parliamentary privilege. The material utilised includes New Zealand cases but also judicial contributions to this subject from Australia, Canada, India and the United Kingdom.

There are new chapters on the House's general power to inquire and on responses to adverse references made in the House (a procedure that did not exist in 1994). The chapters dealing with parties, the Business Committee and international treaties are substantially new and the chapters on select committees and legislation (primary and secondary) have been recast and expanded. Other chapters have been rewritten or revised depending upon the extent of the changes in the subject-matter with which they deal.

This book has been under active preparation for five years. Such a lengthy genesis has posed its own problems, as procedures have changed and thus necessitated the reopening of completed chapters. On the other hand, it has enabled me to submit the work for publication at a suitable time – while Parliament is dissolved and procedural development is in a temporary abeyance.

As with previous editions, a number of people have read draft chapters or portions of chapters and provided me with comment.

The critiques that I received on the financial chapters from Robert Buchanan (Assistant Auditor-General), Peter Lorimer (Senior Advisor in the office of the Minister of Social Development and Employment), Kevin Simpkins (formerly Deputy Controller and Auditor-General) and Ken Warren (Chief Accounting Advisor, the Treasury) were, without any exaggeration, indispensable. Their comments have saved me from many errors and have enabled me to treat this subject with a greater confidence than would otherwise have been justifiable on my part. While any errors that remain are mine, and I, of course, remain responsible for any challengeable interpretations that the text contains, I want to record my gratitude for their unstinting assistance.

Malcolm McDonald (formerly Legislation Coordinator in the Cabinet Office) provided me with extensive comments on the legislation chapters that were both timely and challenging. These chapters have benefited immensely from his contribution. David Henry (Chief Electoral Officer) and Simon Wall (Group Manager, Finance and Entitlements, Parliamentary Service) were kind enough to check the chapters on electoral matters and members' conditions of service, respectively. I am grateful for their painstaking assistance. Thanks also to Dr John Martin (Advisor (History), Parliamentary Service) for his comments and to the staff of the Parliamentary Library for their assistance.

Many staff in the Office of the Clerk have contributed to this edition: by reading and commenting on drafts (often more than once), providing suggestions for inclusion, and assisting with the task of proofreading and publishing the book. In regard to publication, the Ministry of Culture and Heritage and Dunmore Publishing have also provided valued assistance. The book is much the better for those contributions. But I would like to identify two staff for special mention: Milton Hollard (Clerk-Assistant (Research)) who, as well as providing extensive comment on the text and the references, has assisted in making the publication arrangements for the book, and Jo Shepherd (secretary to the Clerk of the House) who, since my own typing skills have not developed at all since 1994, has once again typed the entire manuscript of the book (probably several times over), including the feverish last fortnight, before it was transmitted to the publishers.

My thanks to all of those who have been involved for their help.

David McGee

October 2005

CONTENTS

Contents

Contents

Contents

CHAPTER 12: THE OPENING OF PARLIAMENT

CHAPTER 13: SITTINGS OF THE HOUSE

Contents

Contents

Contents

Contents

Contents

CHAPTER 28: ENACTMENT AND PUBLICATION OF ACTS

CHAPTER 29:   DELEGATED LEGISLATION

CHAPTER 30:   INQUIRIES

Contents

Contents

Contents

Contents

Contents

PRIMARY SOURCES

Appendices to the Journals of the House of Representatives. 1856 to the present.

Journals of the House of Representatives. 1856 to the present.

New Zealand Parliamentary Debates (compilation). 1854–66.

New Zealand Parliamentary Debates (Hansard). 1867 to the present.

Parliamentary Debates (Hansard) – Questions for Written Answer. 1989 to 2002.

Parliamentary Papers. 1999 to the present.

Standing Orders of the House of Representatives. Brought into force 20 February 1996. Amended 22 August 1996, 8 September 1999, 16 December 2003 and 2 August 2005. (Reprinted 2005.)

Votes and Proceedings of the House of the Representatives. 1854–56.

TABLE OF STATUTES

TABLE OF REGULATIONS AND
OTHER INSTRUMENTS

TABLE OF CASES

Bold numbers locate cases in this text.

SECONDARY SOURCES

Atkinson, Neill, *Adventures in Democracy – A History of the Vote in New Zealand.*
University of Otago Press, 2003.

Bain, Helen, "Making it on the list", *The Dominion*, 23 March 1999.

Barwick, Garfield, *A Radical Tory*. Sydney: The Federation Press, 1995.

Bassett, Michael, *Coates of Kaipara*. Auckland University Press, 1995.

Bassett, Michael, *Three Party Politics in New Zealand 1911–1931*. Auckland:
Historical Publications, 1982.

Bassett, Michael, *Sir Joseph Ward – A Political Biography*. Auckland University Press,
1993.

Bassett, Michael with King, Michael, *Tomorrow Comes the Song – A Life of Peter
Fraser*. Auckland: Penguin Books (NZ) Ltd, 2000.

Belshaw, Sheila M, *A Man of Integrity – A Biography of Sir Clifton Webb*. Palmerston
North: The Dunmore Press, 1979.

Burrows, J.F., *Statute Law in New Zealand*, Third Edition. Wellington: LexisNexis,
2003.

Cabinet Office, Department of Prime Minister and Cabinet, *Cabinet Manual* 2001.

Caldwell, J.L., "Election Manifesto promises: the law and politics" [1989] *New Zealand
Law Journal* 108.

Campbell, A.I.J., "Laying and Delegated Legislation" [1983] *Public Law*.

Campbell, Enid, "Oaths and Affirmations of Public Office" (1999) 25 *Monash
University Law Review*.

Campion, Lord, *An Introduction to the Procedure of the House of Commons*,
Third Edition. London: Macmillan & Co. Ltd., 1958.

Carr, Sir Cecil Thomas, *Concerning English Administrative Law*. Humphrey Milford:
Oxford University Press, 1941.

Caygill, Hon David, "Functions and Powers of Parliamentary Committees", Electoral
and Administrative Law Commission Seminar, Brisbane, 1 May 1992.

Chen, Mai, "The long arm of caucus", *The Dominion*, 8 October 1992.

Clarke, Peter, *The Keynesian Revolution in the Making 1924–1936*. Oxford: Clarendon
Press, 1988.

Cook, Rod, *Parliament: The Land and Buildings from 1840*. Parliamentary Service,
1988.

Dalton, Hugh, *High Tide and After – Memoirs 1945–1960*. London: Frederick Muller
Limited, 1962.

Dalziel, Raewyn, *Julius Vogel – Business Politician*. Auckland University Press:
Oxford University Press, 1986.

Dollimore, H.N., *The Parliament of New Zealand and Parliament House*,
Revised Edition. Wellington: Government Printer, 1973.

Elton, G.R., *England under the Tudors*. London: Methuen & Co. Ltd., 1955.

Evans, Harry, *ed., Odgers' Australian Senate Practice*, Eleventh Edition. Canberra:
Department of the Senate, 2004.

Freer, Warren, *A Lifetime in Politics – The Memoirs of Warren Freer*. Victoria
University Press: Wellington, 2004.

Gee, David, *Our Mabel*. Wellington: Milwood Press Limited, 1977.

Gilling, Bryan, *The Ombudsman in New Zealand*. Palmerston North: Dunmore Press Limited, 1998.

Gobbi, Mark, "Drafting Techniques for Implementing Treaties in New Zealand" (2000) 21 *Statute Law Review*.

Gobbi, Mark, "Making Sense of Ambiguity: Some reflections on the use of treaties to interpret legislation in New Zealand" (2002) 23 *Statute Law Review*.

Hallam, Henry, *The Constitutional History of England*. Two volumes. New York & London: Garland Publishing, Inc., 1978.

Hamer, David, *The New Zealand Liberals – The Years of Power, 1891–1912*. Auckland University Press, 1988.

Hannan, A.J., *The Life of Chief Justice Way*. Sydney: Angus and Robertson, 1960.

Harris, I.C., *ed.*, *House of Representatives Practice*, Fourth Edition. Canberra: Department of the House of Representatives, 2001.

Harris, Rodney, "International Issues – The Interaction Between International Law-Making and Domestic Implementation", address to the Fourth New Zealand Public Law Forum, Wellington, April 2002.

Hayward, Margaret, *Diary of the Kirk Years*. Queen Charlotte Sound & Wellington: Cope Catley Limited & A H and A W Reed Limited, 1981.

Heard, Andrew, "Constitutional Conventions and Election Campaigns" *Canadian Parliamentary Review*, Autumn 1995.

Herbert, A.P., *The Ayes Have It*. London: Methuen & Co Ltd, 1937.

Hurley, James Ross, "The Royal Prerogative and the Office of Lieutenant Governor: A Comment", *Canadian Parliamentary Review*, Summer 2000.

Iles, W., "New Zealand Experience of Parliamentary Scrutiny of Legislation" [1991] *Statute Law Review*.

Iles, W., "The Responsibilities of the New Zealand Legislation Advisory Committee" [1992] *Statute Law Review*.

Jackson, Keith, and McRobie, Alan, *New Zealand Adopts Proportional Representation – Accident? Design? Evolution?* Aldershot, England: Ashgate Publishing Limited, 1998.

Jennings, Sir Ivor, *The British Constitution*. Cambridge University Press, 1954.

Joseph, Philip A., *Constitutional and Administrative Law in New Zealand*, Second Edition. Brookers Ltd, 2001.

Joseph, Philip A., "Sampling the 'Wine Box'" [1994] *New Zealand Law Journal*.

Joseph, Philip A., "Report to the Standing Orders Committee on Natural Justice", September 1995, *Report of the Standing Orders Committee on the review of Standing Orders 1995*, I.18A, Appendix F.

Keir, D.L. and Lawson, F.H., *Cases in Constitutional Law*, Fifth Edition. Oxford University Press, 1967.

Keith, Sir Kenneth, "Governance, Sovereignty and Globalisation" (1998) 28 *Victoria University of Wellington Law Review*.

Laundy, Philip, *The Office of Speaker in Commonwealth Parliaments*. London: Quiller Press, 1984.

Laurie, Neil, "The Grand Inquest of the Nation – A notion of the past?" (2001) 16 *Australasian Parliamentary Review*.

Lawn, Geoff, "Format of Legislation and Access to Law" [1999] *New Zealand Law Journal*.

Leopold, Patricia M., "The Power of the House of Commons to Question Private Individuals" [1992] *Public Law.*

Lindell, Geoffrey, "Parliamentary Inquiries and Government Witnesses" (1995) 20 *Melbourne University Law Review.*

Littlejohn, C.P., "Parliamentary Privilege in New Zealand". Thesis submitted for the Degree of Master of Laws at Victoria University of Wellington, 1969.

Longdin-Prisk, M.L., "Setting Legal Limits to Government Borrowing" (1986) 12 *New Zealand Universities Law Review.*

McGee, David, "Members' bills or private bills?" [1999] *New Zealand Law Journal*

McGee, David, "Parliament and Caucus" [1997] *New Zealand Law Journal*

McIntyre, W. David, *ed., The Journal of Henry Sewell.* Two volumes. Christchurch: Whitcoulls Publishers, 1980.

McKay W.R., *ed., Erskine May's Treatise on the Law, Privileges, Proceedings and Usages of Parliament*, Twenty-third Edition. London: LexisNexis, 2004.

McLintock, A.H., *ed., An Encyclopaedia of New Zealand.* Three volumes. Wellington: Government Printer, 1966.

McLintock, A.H., *Crown Colony Government in New Zealand.* Wellington: Government Printer, 1958.

McLintock, A.H., and Wood, G.A., *The Upper House in Colonial New Zealand.* Wellington: Government Printer, 1987.

Malhotra, G.C., *Practice amd Procedure of Parliament (with particular reference to the Lok Sabha)*, Fifth Edition. New Delhi: Lok Sabha Secretariat, 2001.

Marius, Richard, *Thomas More – A Biography.* Cambridge, Massachusetts: Harvard University Press, 1984.

Marleau, Robert, and Montpetit, Camille, *House of Commons Procedure and Practice.* Ottawa: House of Commons, 2000.

Marshall, Geoffrey, *Constitutional Conventions – The Rules and Forms of Political Accountability.* Oxford: Clarendon Press, 1984.

Marshall, Geoffrey, *Constitutional Theory.* Oxford: Clarendon Press, 1971.

Marshall, Geoffrey, "Press Freedom and Free Speech Theory" [1992] *Public Law.*

Martin, John E., *The House – New Zealand's House of Representatives 1854-2004.* Palmerston North: Dunmore Press Ltd, 2004.

Mathieson, D.L., "Interpreting the proposed Bill of Rights (I)" [1986] *New Zealand Law Journal.*

Mukherjea, A.R., *Parliamentary Procedure in India.* Oxford University Press, 1958.

Mummery, D.R., "Freedom of Speech in Parliament" [1978] *Law Quarterly Review.*

Parliamentary Library, "Final Results 2002 General Election and Trends in Election Outcomes 1990-2002". 20 August 2002.

Peters, Graeme, "Employment Relations Bill secrecy doing a job on NZ", *The Evening Post*, 22 July 2000.

Redlich, Josef, *The Procedure of the House of Commons.* Three volumes. London: Archibald Constable & Co Ltd, 1908.

Reeves, W.P., *The Long White Cloud*, Fourth Edition. London: George Allen & Unwin Ltd., 1950.

Scott, K.J., *The New Zealand Constitution.* Oxford University Press, 1962.

Sinclair, Keith, *Walter Nash.* Auckland University Press, 1976.

State Services Commission, "Public Servants and Select Committees – Guidelines". February 2002, updated February 2004.

Sutherland, A., "Symbol of authority – The Mace in New Zealand", *Numismatic Journal*, (1947) Vol. 4, No. 1.

Tanner, George, "Legislation Drafting: Some Practical Issues", *New Zealand Law Society Seminar: New Legislation Guidelines*, 2001.

Tanner, George, "The Role of Parliamentary Counsel" [1999] *New Zealand Law Journal.*

Templeton, Hugh, *All Honourable Men – Inside the Muldoon Cabinet 1975–1984*. Auckland University Press, 1995.

Todd, Stephen, *ed.*, *The Law of Torts in New Zealand*, Third Edition. Wellington: Brookers Ltd, 2001.

Treasury, The, "Guidelines for Setting Charges in the Public Sector", December 2002.

Treasury, The, "Putting it Together – An Explanatory Guide to the New Zealand Public Sector Financial Management System", 1996.

Treasury, The, "Scoping the Scope of Appropriations", September 2005

Wilding, N., and Laundy, P., *An Encyclopaedia of Parliament*, Fourth Edition. London: Cassell, 1972.

Wilson, John, "The Status of the Caretaker Convention in Canada", *Canadian Parliamentary Review*, Winter 1995–96.

Wilson, J.O., "New Zealand parliamentary papers – changes in shoulder numbers", *New Zealand Libraries,* June 1974.

Wilson, J.O., *New Zealand Parliamentary Record 1840-1984*. Wellington: Government Printer, 1985.

Wilson of Dinton, Lord, "The Robustness of Conventions in a Time of Modernisation and Change" [2004] *Public Law*.

Wittke, C., *The History of English Parliamentary Privilege*. New York: Da Capo Press, 1970.

Woodward, Sir Llewellyn, *The Age of Reform*. Oxford: Clarendon Press, 1938.

Wright-St Clair, Rex E., *Thoroughly a Man of the World: A Biography of Sir David Monro, MD*. Christchurch: Whitcombe & Tombs, 1971.

ABBREVIATIONS

AC	*Appeal Cases* (law reports)
A & E	*Adolphus & Ellis* (law reports)
AIR	*All India Reporter* (law reports)
AJHR	*Appendix to the Journal of the House of Representatives* Preceded by a date signifying the session and followed by a reference number referring to a parliamentary paper.
All ER	*All England Reports* (law reports)
ALR	*Australian Law Reports*
BCLR	*British Columbia Law Reports*
Ch/ChD	*Chancery/Chancery Division* (law reports)
Car & K	*Carrington & Kirwan* (law reports)
cl.	clause
CLR	*Commonwealth Law Reports* (Australia)
Crim LR	*Criminal Law Review*
DLR	*Dominion Law Reports* (Canada)
ER	*English Reports* (law reports)
Esp	*Espinasse* (law reports)
Ex	*Exchequer* (law reports)
FCR	*Federal Court Reports*
Hansard Supplement	Parliamentary Debates (Hansard) – Questions for Written Answer
HC	House of Commons parliamentary paper printed by order of the House
HL	House of Lords parliamentary paper printed by order of the House
JHR	*Journal of the House of Representatives* Preceded by a date signifying the session.
KB	*King's Bench* (law reports)
Keny	*Kenyon* (law reports)
Littlejohn	Littlejohn, C.P, "Parliamentary Privilege in New Zealand" Thesis submitted for the Degree of Master of Laws at Victoria University of Wellington, 1969.
LQR	*Law Quarterly Review*
LR HL	*English and Irish Appeal Cases before the House of Lords* (law reports)
LR Ir	*Irish Law Reports*
LR PC	*Privy Council Appeals* (law reports)
LR QB	Law Reports, Queen's Bench (England)
May	Sir William McKay KCB ed., *Erskine May's Treatise on the Law, Privileges, Proceedings and Usage of Parliament*, Twenty-third Edition
M & S	*Maule and Selwyn* (law reports)
Mon LR	*Monash University Law Review*
Moo PC	*Moore's Privy Council cases* (law reports)

NLJR	*New Law Journal Reports*
NSWLR/LR NSW	*New South Wales Law Reports*
NSWSC	*New South Wales Supreme Court* (law reports)
NZAR	*New Zealand Administrative Reports*
NZ Jur (NS)	*New Zealand Jurist (New Series)* (law reports)
NZLJ	*New Zealand Law Journal*
NZLR	*New Zealand Law Reports*
NZULR	*New Zealand Universities Law Review*
OR	*Ontario Law Reports*
P	*Probate, Divorce and Admiralty Division* (law reports)
PD	*New Zealand Parliamentary Debates* (compilation) 1854-66
PL	*Public Law*
PLR	*Public Law Review*
PP	*Parliamentary Papers*
	Preceded by the year and followed by the reference number of the parliamentary paper cited.
QB/QBD/LR QBD	*Queen's Bench/Queen's Bench Division* (law reports)
Qd R	*Queensland Reports*
QSC	*Queensland Supreme Court* (law reports)
reg.	regulation
s.	section
Saund	*Saunders* (law reports)
Sch.	Schedule
SCR	*Supreme Court Reports* (Canada)
S.O.	Standing Order of the House of Representatives (see Appendix A.)
SR (NSW)	*State Reports (New South Wales)*
SASR	*South Australian State Reports*
Statute LR	*Statute Law Review*
St R Qd	*State Reports (Queensland)*
Tas SR	*Tasmanian State Reports*
TLR	*Times Law Reports*
Vol.	Volume of the *New Zealand Parliamentary Debates (Hansard)*, 1867 to the present
VP	*Votes and Proceedings of the House of Representatives, 1854-56*
VR	*Victorian Reports*
VUWLR	*Victoria University of Wellington Law Review*
WAR	*Western Australian Law Reports*
WIR	*The West Indian Reports*
WLR	*Weekly Law Reports*
ZR	*Zambian Reports*

INTERNET RESOURCES

The website of the Office of the Clerk (<www.clerk.parliament.govt.nz>) is the primary source of information about business before the House of Representatives. The features of this site include:

- the latest order paper
- details about the progress of bills through the House
- *Hansard*
- select committee business, including items open for submissions
- reports of select committees
- questions for written answer, and replies
- contact information for members of Parliament
- publications, including guides to parliamentary processes
- information on the arrangements for preparing and presenting reports to the House.

The following websites (as accessed at August 2005) also provide ongoing sources of information about Parliament and Government in New Zealand:

Audit Office	Office of the Controller and Auditor-General <http://www.oag.govt.nz> independent assurance over the performance and accountability of public organisations, including reports to Parliament
Bill of Rights advice	Ministry of Justice <http://www.justice.govt.nz/bill-of-rights/> advice provided to the Attorney-General on the consistency of bills with the New Zealand Bill of Rights Act 1990
Cabinet Manual	Department of the Prime Minister and Cabinet, Cabinet Office <http://www.dpmc.govt.nz/cabinet/manual/index.html> constitutional conventions, procedures and rules of Cabinet and central executive government
Cabinet Office circulars	Department of the Prime Minister and Cabinet, Cabinet Office <http://www.dpmc.govt.nz/cabinet/circulars/index.html> circulars addressing issues of interest to Ministers and departments, and setting out detailed guidance on central government processes

Cabinet Step By Step Guide	Department of the Prime Minister and Cabinet, Cabinet Office <http://www.dpmc.govt.nz/cabinet/guide/index.html> processes for developing and presenting proposals to Cabinet
Elections	Electoral Commission and Chief Electoral Office <http://www.elections.org.nz> election results, enrolment, registration of parties, and information about the electoral system
Estimates of Appropriations	The Treasury <http://www.treasury.govt.nz/appropriations/scoping/> guidance for departments for describing the scope of appropriations
Governor-General	Department of the Prime Minister and Cabinet, Government House <http://www.gg.govt.nz/> information on the role, functions and activities of the Governor-General
International treaties	Ministry of Foreign Affairs and Trade <http://www.mfat.govt.nz/support/legal/default.html> lists of international treaties, including treaties under negotiation
Law reform	Law Commission <http://www.lawcom.govt.nz> reports and publications on the review of areas of law that need updating, reforming or developing
Legislation	Parliamentary Counsel Office <http://www.pco.parliament.govt.nz> law drafting and public access to legislation
Legislation guidelines	Legislation Advisory Committee <http://www.justice.govt.nz/lac/> principles of process and content for the preparation of legislation
Ministers	New Zealand Government <http://www.beehive.govt.nz> information about Ministers and portfolios

Parliament buildings	Parliamentary Service <http://www.ps.parliament.govt.nz> information about the buildings, people and events at Parliament
Public finance	The Treasury <http://www.treasury.govt.nz/publicsector/#overviews> overview of the public sector financial management system
Public servants and political neutrality	State Services Commission <http://www.ssc.govt.nz/select-committees-guidelines> and <http://www.ssc.govt.nz/political-neutrality> guidelines covering principles of the relationships between public servants and select committees, and public servants and MPs
Regulations Review Committee Digest	Victoria University of Wellington, New Zealand Centre for Public Law <http://www.vuw.ac.nz/nzcpl> analysis of reports of the Regulations Review Committee
Speaker	Office of the Speaker <http://www.speaker.parliament.govt.nz/> information on the role, functions and activities of the Speaker, and determinations of services available to members of Parliament and Ministers

CHAPTER 1

THE PARLIAMENT OF NEW ZEALAND

The Parliament of New Zealand met for the first time on 24 May 1854 in Auckland. At that time the Parliament was officially styled "The General Assembly of New Zealand". It consisted of three bodies: the Governor, a Legislative Council and a House of Representatives. Only the House of Representatives, the elected component, has retained its unbroken membership of the Parliament under its original title, though it is now a much larger body – 120 members, as compared to 37 – than it was in 1854. (There are 121 members of the forty-eighth Parliament due to an electoral 'overhang' of one member.)

The Parliament of New Zealand today consists of the Sovereign in right of New Zealand and the House of Representatives.[1] The Sovereign was not originally mentioned as being part of the General Assembly. Legislation was consequently passed in 1953, on the occasion of the Queen's first visit to New Zealand, to remove any doubts about the Sovereign's power to give the Royal assent to bills.[2] The Sovereign's powers as part of Parliament are exercised by Her Majesty's representative, the Governor-General (who assumed that title in 1917). The Legislative Council (an appointive, rather than elective, body) was abolished on 1 January 1951,[3] thus leaving Parliament a single-chamber or unicameral legislature since that time.

THE SOVEREIGN AND THE GOVERNOR-GENERAL

The Sovereign has performed a number of acts as a constituent part of Parliament. These have included: giving the Royal assent to bills that have passed through the House; summoning and proroguing Parliament; delivering the Speech from the Throne at the opening of a session of Parliament; and sending messages to the House of Representatives.

The Governor-General, as the Sovereign's representative resident at the seat of government in New Zealand, naturally plays a more frequent part in the work of Parliament. The Governor-General is the representative of the Sovereign in the Sovereign's executive capacity as head of state. But the Governor-General also represents the Sovereign in respect of the Sovereign's legislative duties as a member of the Parliament of New Zealand. In this capacity the Governor-General summons, prorogues and dissolves Parliament, and gives the Royal assent to bills. If the office is vacant or the Governor-General is for any reason unable to perform the duties of the office, the Chief Justice performs them as Administrator of the Government.[4] (In the absence of the Chief Justice, the President of the Court of Appeal acts as Administrator.)

THE HOUSE OF REPRESENTATIVES

The House of Representatives is the popularly elected component of the Parliament, its members being elected for a three-year term. It is this body which is inevitably identified with the term "parliament", though it is in fact only a part of the Parliament.

This book is concerned with how that body is formed, what conditions apply to its membership, what rules it adopts for its procedures, what types of business it transacts and what is its legal relationship with persons and bodies outside Parliament.

---

[1] *Constitution Act* 1986, s.14(1).
[2] *Royal Powers Act* 1953.
[3] *Legislative Council Abolition Act* 1950.

[4] See generally, *Letters Patent Constituting the Office of Governor-General of New Zealand* (issued 28 October 1983 and amended in 1987).

FUNCTIONS OF THE PARLIAMENT AND THE HOUSE OF REPRESENTATIVES
The functions of the Parliament and of the House are not identical. Each constituent part of the legislature has a different role from the other. The Parliament of New Zealand has only one function, and that is to make laws. Whenever "Parliament" acts, its act has the force of law – as an Act of Parliament. There are communications between the Governor-General and the House of Representatives on other matters than laws, but the two constituents act together as Parliament only to make laws.

Originally this law-making function was confined to making laws for the "peace, order and good government of New Zealand"[5] (a common phrase at the time in legislative devolutions to colonial legislatures of the power to make laws). Following questions being raised as to Parliament's power to make laws having extra-territorial effect,[6] that is, *outside* New Zealand, Parliament itself extended this law-making provision in 1973 to the making of laws "having effect in, or in respect of New Zealand or any part thereof and laws having effect outside New Zealand".[7] The present legislative description of its law-making power speaks only of Parliament having "full power" to make law.[8]

The Governor-General, as the Sovereign's representative, has a much wider role to play than merely as a constituent part of Parliament. The Sovereign personifies the state and is head of the executive government – for example, appointing Ministers and formally performing many executive acts. But the House of Representatives too, apart from its role as part of the Parliament that makes laws, also performs other functions that are important in themselves though they do not lead to an action of the Parliament as such. Indeed only about half of the working time of the House is actually spent on its legislative function. However, the House does differ from the Sovereign in that the House of Representatives performs all of its functions under the aegis of the Parliament of New Zealand. The House of Representatives has no role outside the life of a Parliament and cannot function once that Parliament has been dissolved or has expired.

Every commentator on the House of Representatives will have his or her own ideas as to how its functions are to be described and classified. The House's role is not defined anywhere; it has been carved out by the members of the House, partly by the legal environment from which the House draws its power (including its "privileges"), partly by the expectations (including those of the early parliamentarians) of what members of Parliament "should do", partly by the initiative of members themselves in assuming functions that were open to them and partly by legislative conferment on an ad hoc basis (removal of judges, appointment of certain office holders, etc.). Nor is it necessarily the case that the House has an exclusive purchase on any of the functions it performs. It shares its legislative role and the finding of a government, for instance, with the Crown, and there are other means by which the Government may be scrutinised than just through parliamentary activity. With these qualifications, an outline of four major functions performed by the House is presented.

A legislature
The House of Representatives plays a part – manifestly the largest and most significant part – in the making of laws by Parliament. An Act of Parliament, a statement of law in its highest form, is a law agreed to by both the Sovereign or the Governor-General and the House of Representatives. The most visible part of the process by which a proposed law becomes law as an Act of Parliament is that part of its history in which it is processed by

---

5   *New Zealand Constitution Act* 1852 (UK), s.53.
6   *R v Fineberg* [1968] NZLR 119.
7   *New Zealand Constitution Amendment Act* 1973, s.2.

8   *Constitution Act* 1986, s.15(1). See Joseph, *Constitutional and Administrative Law in New Zealand*, especially Chapters 6, 13 and 14, for a discussion of legislative power.

the House. Only when it is agreed to by the House can it be submitted to the Governor-General for concurrence. When this is forthcoming and both parts of Parliament are of one mind on the matter, the proposed law is converted into law as an Act of Parliament.

The imprimatur of Parliament on a document, converting it from a piece of paper with no effect into a statement of rules of binding effect which will be enforced by the full might of the state, is important in a fundamental sense as providing a means by which binding rules (laws) can be recognised. Contributing to such a document is a primary function of the House and its committees.

The provider of a government

Neither Parliament nor the House governs the country in the sense of having direct control of the civil and military apparatus of state and making day-to-day decisions on the management and deployment of these resources. This is the job of the executive (the "Government") which carries on the government of the country by appointment of the Governor-General.

When the House first met in 1854 the executive authority within the colony was exercised much more personally by the Governor than is the case today. The Governor's advisers, those persons who carried out his wishes or "ministered" to him, were not members of Parliament but persons who owed their positions to their standing and personal relationships with the Governor.

For the first two years of Parliament's existence Ministers were chosen by the Governor not because they commanded the support of a majority of members of the House but for these other personal reasons. This severely limited the House's control and influence on the Government, for the ultimate means of such control – withdrawal of its support for the Government leading to the Government's dismissal – could not be brought to bear when other factors determined the composition of the Government. It was the endeavour of most of the early parliamentarians to achieve for New Zealand a "responsible" form of government – that is, one in which Ministers were answerable to, and subject to the full control of, the House for their official actions – to add to the "representative" form of government already conferred on the colony.

In 1856 the Governor, after consulting the Imperial Government, accepted that he would in future choose Ministers from among members of Parliament who could rely on the support of a majority of members of the House. Responsible government had been achieved.[9] It is on this principle that Ministers are appointed by the Governor-General today.

In effect, the House is an electoral college which translates the will of the people, as expressed at a general election, into a Government (a "Ministry") composed of a Prime Minister and Ministers. The member of the House who commands majority support from the other members is asked by the Governor-General to form a Government by taking office as Prime Minister and recommending to the Governor-General the appointment of other members as Ministers of the Crown. There is no legal or political necessity for this action to be ratified or confirmed by the House when it meets, though the justification for the choice of the Government is constantly tested throughout the life of the Parliament.

The House thus provides and sustains the Government from among its own members, and the Government, although appointed by the Crown, remains in office only for as long as it can maintain a majority in the House; that is, as long as it retains the confidence

---

[9] See Joseph, *Constitutional and Administrative Law in New Zealand*, Chapter 4, for the steps leading to responsible government.

of the House. In cases where no party has an overall majority in the House, a coalition government or a minority government sustained in office on the basis of agreements with other parties or members may be formed. But, whatever the precise arrangements, it is the political situation as represented by the members elected to serve in the House which determines who is to govern, not the whim or pleasure of the Crown. This is a fundamental convention of the constitution.

To scrutinise and control the Government

Though the Government is appointed from among members of the House depending upon the result of a general election, the House is not just an electoral college which disperses once its function of providing a Government has been fulfilled. The continuing support of the House is necessary to the continuance in office of the Government, and as part of that continuing support the Government must answer to the House for its stewardship of the executive functions of state. One of the principal means by which the House exacts from the Government explanations of official action it has taken is by the annual process of granting financial authority or supply to the Government. As a quid pro quo for the authority they consider necessary to carry on governing the country, Ministers must defend their policies and explain the administration of their portfolios to the House. Similarly, when Ministers ask the House to pass legislation, the House may hold them to account for their actions as part of the procedure of passing that legislation. Many of the procedures of the House are designed specifically to enable the House to play its part in the scrutiny and control of the Government. These include questions addressed to Ministers, general and urgent debates, and select committees of members investigating matters of governmental responsibility and regulations made by the Government under powers delegated by Parliament. Everything the House does potentially gives it the opportunity to probe and criticise the actions of the Government.

To represent government and the people

The final function of the House identified here reverts in part to the idea embodied in the Title of the original *New Zealand Constitution Act* – the idea of the representation of the views of the populace. The ideas of the Greek city-state, in which all the citizens met in conclave to express their opinions on affairs of state and listen to the opinions of others, are quite alien to those ideas derived from British constitutional practice on which the *New Zealand Constitution Act* was framed. They are also impracticable given the size and complexity of the modern state. New Zealand's constitutional theory proceeds on the basis that there is within the state a source of authority, the Crown, which carries on the government, but which calls its subjects into its presence in Parliament for the purposes of consultation and ratification. As all the subjects cannot attend in person, they attend through representatives (whether elected on a national or a local basis), and it is the task of these representatives to report what the inhabitants of the state feel and think about particular problems. It is also the task of the representatives to bind the persons they represent to the decisions of the Parliament to which they have been sent. As every person is symbolically present in Parliament through a representative, every person has a share in, and responsibility for, the actions of that Parliament, and is morally as well as legally obliged to obey its lawful dictates.

The House of Representatives, as the elective element of the Parliament of New

Zealand, fulfils this representative function. It permits members to report and give voice to national, provincial, local and individual views on matters of state. It also imposes on every inhabitant some responsibility for the ultimate decisions as to the law and policy according to which New Zealand is governed. It represents the governed to the Government and the Government to the governed.

THE DEVELOPMENT OF THE HOUSE OF REPRESENTATIVES

This book is concerned with the law applying to, and the procedures employed in, the House of Representatives. It is not a history of Parliament, and minimal background to the evolution of the present rules is given only when it is considered necessary so as to make them intelligible. Nevertheless, it may be useful to outline in general terms the principal phases which the House (in large part reflecting political and social changes) has passed through in its history.

1854–1856: The first two years of parliamentary democracy were something of a false start for the House. Though a representative institution (on the franchise then applying), it found that it could not control the Government, since the Government was not politically responsible to it but to the Governor. The steps by which responsible government was conceded to the colony have been adverted to above. In 1856 the House started afresh with a ministry appointed from among its members and holding office only as long as the ministry retained the confidence of the House.

1856–1890: This was a period of consolidation of parliamentary government in the colony. The House continued to function through a lengthy and difficult series of wars, and moved its meeting place permanently from Auckland to Wellington. Maori representation was firmly established in the House from 1867, and the House asserted its clear political pre-eminence over the Legislative Council. The council, indeed, started its long and ultimately terminal decline in this period. Elections became important means of changing the Government towards the end of this period.[10] Nevertheless, the House was not yet a "modern" legislature, largely because no comprehensive party system had developed. Such "parties" as there were were parliamentary-based alliances or factions that, while relatively cohesive in parliamentary terms, had little extra-parliamentary organisation. The history of this pre-party period can therefore be characterised somewhat as a calendar of "ins and outs", with much depending upon the actions of forceful parliamentary personalities.

1890–1935: In this period a much more recognisably modern Parliament did take shape. This largely resulted from stronger party organisations being formed to fight elections and return members on a party ticket, and was reflected in the House's procedural organisation taking on a firmer, more disciplined aspect. Under the influence of the stronger party approach to politics, the House adopted stricter debating and timetabling rules. This period too saw the advent of women's suffrage in 1893 and, much later, the first woman elected to the House.

The House was a more party-politically combative institution during this era, but it passed through periods of considerable instability reflective of outside social trends – the strength of the temperance movement, conflicting interests between rural and urban inhabitants, the surge of immigration after the First World War. Though party government was established, it was not yet stable party government.

1935–1996: This period represents perhaps the high point of two-party control of the House. With the election of a Labour Government in 1935, the country entered an

---

[10]　Martin, *The House – New Zealand's House of Representatives 1854-2004*, p.82.

extended phase in which the same party held power for a considerable period, followed by a further, even longer, period in which the other major party, National, held power. These two parties obtained a virtual monopoly of seats in the House during this era, and the House attuned its rules both explicitly and implicitly to reflect this situation. Not even the abolition of the Legislative Council in 1950 caused any significant interruption to what was from a parliamentary point of view a remarkably stable period of low-key adjustments in its rules.

1996 onwards: Towards the end of the two-party phase of the House's history a number of significant developments began to get under way, many of which were associated with the economic and governmental reforms introduced in New Zealand after 1984.

In 1985 the sitting pattern of the House, which had remained unchanged virtually from the beginning, was altered, and the full-time, round-the-year nature of parliamentary work was recognised. Select committees were conceded powers to conduct inquiries on their own initiative rather than having to have matters referred to them by the House. This is now second nature, but it was a major change in parliamentary culture in 1985. The longstanding arrangements for parliamentary administration which had not been the subject of serious examination for a century were completely overhauled, with a new body created to give members some executive responsibility for their own services for the first time.

In 1993, at a referendum, the country voted for a change to the electoral system, ushering in a proportional representation system and multi-party representation in the House from the 1996 general election onwards. In anticipation of this new political environment extensive changes to the House's procedures were adopted in 1995.[11] These procedures have continued to adapt in the light of the practical experience of operating in a multi-party, rather than a two-party, House of Representatives.

The year 2004 saw the 150th anniversary of the first meeting of the House. This was marked by a special sitting held on Monday 24 May 2004.[12] It also saw the completion of a project embarked upon at the time of the House's centenary, to write a history of the New Zealand Parliament. This work had commenced with the appointment of a parliamentary historian (Dr A H McLintock) and had seen the publication of two works: the first on the establishment of representative government in New Zealand[13] and the second on the nineteenth century Legislative Council.[14] In 2004 a comprehensive history of the House of Representatives throughout the first 150 years of its existence was published as a centrepiece of the celebrations organised to mark the House's anniversary.[15]

---

[11]   1993-96, AJHR, I.18A.
[12]   2004, Vol.617, pp.13179-213.
[13]   McLintock, *Crown Colony Government in New Zealand*.

[14]   McLintock and Wood, *The Upper House in Colonial New Zealand*.
[15]   Martin, *The House – New Zealand's House of Representatives 1854-2004*.

CHAPTER 2

ELECTORAL

THE ELECTORAL SYSTEM

The first elections for members of Parliament took place over an eight-month period in 1853 in time for Parliament to assemble for its first meeting in Auckland in the following year. The *New Zealand Constitution Act* 1852 (UK) did not prescribe in detail how the electoral system was to operate, leaving much of this to be determined by the Governor. This is in marked contrast to the present-day electoral legislation, the *Electoral Act* 1993, which is highly detailed and prescriptive in the electoral rules it sets out and is supplemented by only a small body of regulations made by the Governor-General.

New Zealand has employed three types of voting system in its history: simple first-past-the-post (FPP); a form of preferential voting system known as the second ballot; and the proportional representation system known as mixed member proportional (MMP). From the 1853 to the 1905 elections FPP was used. The candidate or candidates polling the highest number of votes in each constituency were automatically elected. Most constituencies were single-member electoral districts, electing one member, but the larger cities formed multi-member electoral districts from which the two or three highest polling candidates were elected to Parliament. Multi-member constituencies were abolished at the time of the 1905 election.[1]

For the 1908 and 1911 elections New Zealand employed the second ballot voting system.[2] Under this system the election was held as for FPP but only a candidate winning at least half the total valid votes cast in the electoral district was successful. Where no one won half of the votes a run-off election (the second ballot) was held one week later (two weeks in some rural constituencies) between the two top-polling candidates. The elections from 1914 to 1993 were again conducted under FPP in single-member electoral districts. At the 1996 election a new system of voting, MMP, was introduced. This is the present system employed.[3]

The MMP system

The MMP system combines members of Parliament elected from single-member electoral districts with members elected from nationally drawn party lists. It is designed to produce a legislature whose overall party composition is approximately proportional to the nationwide support for each political party contesting the election.

MMP was recommended for parliamentary elections by a Royal Commission which reported in 1986.[4] An indicative referendum was held in September 1992 at which voters were asked whether they wished to retain FPP or to change to another (unspecified) system. At that same referendum (and regardless of whether an individual voter wished to see a change in the voting system) voters were asked which one of four alternative forms of voting they would prefer to be adopted if there was a change in the system. A large majority of those voting favoured a change in the voting system, and the most clearly favoured option was MMP.

A further referendum was held on 6 November 1993 (simultaneously with the general

---

[1] *City Single Electorates Act* 1903.
[2] *Second Ballot Act* 1908.
[3] See generally, Atkinson, *Adventures in Democracy – A History of the Vote in New Zealand.*

[4] *Report of the Royal Commission on the Electoral System,* 1985-86, AJHR, H.3.

election of that year). This was a straight run-off between FPP and MMP. A majority of those voting (53.9 percent) favoured MMP.[5] Under the legislation governing the holding of the referendum,[6] this result was binding in that the vote for MMP automatically repealed the previous electoral law and a new electoral law was brought into effect (subject to a transitional period extending up to the next election due in 1996). This process of holding a binding referendum on a proposed alternative system that is fully prescribed in legislation was designed to satisfy the requirement of the law that certain important ingredients of the electoral system, known as "reserved provisions", can be amended or repealed only by a majority of the valid votes cast at a poll of all electors.[7]

In order to ensure that there is not a plethora of minor parties represented in the House, a threshold of five percent is set as a minimum proportion of votes that a party must ordinarily win nationally in order to be entitled to seats in the House. But the system, whilst ensuring party proportionality, also combines an element of constituency representation by providing that over half the members of Parliament are elected directly in single-member electoral districts (on a FPP basis). Thus, each voter has two votes: one for a constituency member and the other for a political party. Once the constituency members and their party affiliations are known, the membership of the House is topped up with candidates drawn from party lists to produce overall proportionality.

Electoral Commission

The 1993 legislation created a body to oversee the registration of political parties for the purposes of conducting the nationwide party vote. This body is the Electoral Commission.[8] In addition to registering parties, the commission carries out a number of other duties in regard to the electoral system, such as supervising parties' compliance with financial disclosure and election expenses requirements and allocating funding and time for election broadcasting. It has a general function of promoting public awareness of electoral matters by conducting educational and informational programmes and it reports to the Minister of Justice and the House on electoral matters referred to it by the Minister or the House.[9] The commission has assisted parliamentary select committees with their post-election reviews of general elections and their consideration of changes to the electoral law. However, the commission does not administer all aspects of the electoral system – the Representation Commission draws up electoral boundaries, the Chief Registrar of Electors (the chief executive of New Zealand Post Limited) is responsible for the registration of electors, and the Chief Electoral Officer (an official of the Ministry of Justice) is responsible for the actual conduct of elections, the supervision of candidates' election expenses and donations, and the application of the electoral law generally.

The Electoral Commission's membership consists of: the Secretary for Justice; the Chief Judge of the Maori Land Court; a judge or retired judge of the District Court, the High Court, the Court of Appeal, or the Supreme Court (who is appointed by the Governor-General from a list nominated by the Chief Justice and is automatically president of the commission), and a person appointed by the Governor-General to be its chief executive.[10] The commission's membership is supplemented for the purposes of its election broadcasting functions by two members nominated by the House, one to represent the Government and the other to represent opposition parties.[11] These latter two members can only be removed from office for just cause by the Governor-General acting on an address from the House.[12]

---

[5] See Jackson and McKoble, *New Zealand Adopts Proportional Representation*, for a detailed description of how MMP came to be adopted.

[6] *Electoral Referendum Act* 1993.

[7] *Electoral Act* 1956, s.189 (now *Electoral Act* 1993, s.268); 1991-93, AJHR, I.17A, p.5 (*Electoral Poll Bill*).

[8] *Electoral Act* 1993, s.4.

[9] *Ibid.*, s.5.

[10] *Ibid.*, s.8(1) to (3A).

[11] *Ibid.*, s.8(4).

[12] *Ibid.*, s.11.

The Electoral Commission must act independently in performing its statutory functions and duties and exercising its statutory powers.[13] For governance, reporting and accountability purposes the commission is classified as an independent Crown entity (a Crown entity that is generally independent of government policy).[14] In addition, the commission has taken steps to assert its independence from effective control by other regulatory bodies. Thus it has been established that the exercise of its statutory public information functions is not subject to an industry body effectively substituting its views for those of the commission.[15]

Review of the electoral system

Since 1981 a select committee has had electoral matters within its terms of reference. Until 1999 this was through an ad hoc Electoral Law Committee established in each Parliament. Since 1999 electoral matters have been linked with justice issues in the terms of reference of one of the subject select committees – the Justice and Electoral Committee.[16] This committee considers any electoral legislation that may be referred to it and through its estimates and review work may receive information on the administrative support available for the electoral system.

An interdepartmental committee of officials chaired by the Chief Electoral Officer takes an overall look at election administration. Following the 1999 election three separate governmental reviews of aspects of the electoral process were conducted.[17] The three major agencies concerned with elections (the Electoral Commission, the Electoral Enrolment Centre and the Electoral Office) report to the Justice and Electoral Committee after each election. Their reports form the starting point for the select committee to initiate an inquiry into the election. Officials from the Ministry of Justice (including the Chief Electoral Officer), the Electoral Commission and New Zealand Post Limited work closely with the Justice and Electoral Committee in helping it to carry out its work. The committee's report or reports lead directly to the preparation of amending legislation to remedy any defects in the electoral process that are identified.

In addition to the regular post-election review carried out by the Justice and Electoral Committee, the House was obliged to establish a committee as soon as practicable after 1 April 2000 to carry out a statutory review of the MMP electoral system.[18] This committee was required to report on the method by which New Zealand is divided into electoral districts, the provisions for Māori representation and whether there should be a further referendum on electoral reform. An ad hoc committee was established for this purpose, with a remit that went further than the terms of the statutory inquiry and included inquiring into the appropriate number of members of Parliament and whether there should be further legislative measures to support or enhance parliamentary representation of women or ethnic minorities. The committee, which was chaired by the Speaker, was required to reach its conclusions on the basis of unanimity or, if this was not possible, near unanimity, having regard to the numbers in the House.[19] The MMP Review Committee was unable to achieve unanimity or sufficient near-unanimity on a number of significant issues and supported the status quo in regard to most of the matters on which it could achieve consensus.[20]

COMPOSITION OF THE HOUSE

The House of Representatives, elected for the first time during the course of 1853, consisted

---

[13] *Ibid.*, s.7.

[14] *Electoral Act* 1993, s.4A; *Crown Entities Act* 2004, Sch.1.

[15] *Electoral Commission v Cameron* [1997] 2 NZLR 421 (Advertising Standards Authority attempting to substitute its views of an advertisement for the commission's).

[16] 1996-99, AJHR, I.18B, p.15; S.O.189.

[17] 1999-2002, AJHR, I.17C, pp.12-3.

[18] *Electoral Act* 1993, s.264.

[19] 2000, Vol.583, pp.1597-625.

[20] 1999-2002, AJHR, I.23A.

of 37 members. This figure was determined by Governor George Grey under powers delegated to the Governor. Parliament very soon took into its own hands the determination of the total membership of the House, and this has gone up and down (usually up) over the succeeding years. The current electoral legislation does not prescribe a total number of members. Instead, it prescribes a formula (based on there being 120 members) by which the total membership of the House is established. While 120 members is the norm this number can be exceeded or reduced in certain circumstances.

The House consists of members elected to represent general electoral districts, members elected to represent Māori electoral districts and members elected from lists submitted by political parties. Based on the 2001 census and the Māori electoral option exercised at that time there were 62 members for general electoral districts, seven for Māori electoral districts and 51 party list members for the 2002 and 2005 elections.

General electoral districts
There are 16 general electoral districts in the South Island.[21] The number of electoral districts in the North Island is calculated by dividing the general electoral population of the South Island (the total number of persons ordinarily resident there at the time of the last census, less the Māori electoral population) by 16.[22] The figure so obtained is known as the quota for the South Island. The function of the quota is to provide a degree of numerical equality in the electoral population of each electoral district. The general electoral population of the North Island is divided by the quota, thus giving the number of general electoral districts in the North Island.[23] (A fraction is rounded up or down for this purpose to the nearest whole number.) Thus the two islands each have numbers of general electoral districts that are equivalent to their general electoral populations. While there will always be 16 general electoral districts in the South Island, the number of such districts in the North Island will go up or down depending upon relative population movements between the islands and the number of Māori electoral districts that are created.

Māori electoral districts
Four Māori electoral districts were created in 1867 to provide Māori with parliamentary representation.[24] The number of Māori electoral districts remained at four until the 1996 election. There is now no set number of Māori electoral districts. The total number of Māori electoral districts is calculated from the Māori electoral population. This is the number of persons who have registered to vote in Māori electoral districts plus a figure to represent an appropriate proportion of the estimated number of persons of Māori descent who have not registered as electors at all or who are under 18 years of age.[25] The Māori electoral population is divided by the South Island's quota and the resulting figure gives the total number (over both the North and the South Islands) of Māori electoral districts.[26] (Again, fractions are rounded up or down to the nearest whole number.) The number of Māori electoral districts will therefore largely be determined by the number of Māori who choose to enrol to vote in a Māori electoral district. At the 1996 election there were five Māori electoral districts and this increased to seven for the 2002 election.

Party lists
The members elected from party lists are additional to the members elected from general and Māori electoral districts. Party list seats are awarded in accordance with a formula

---

21   *Electoral Act* 1993, s.35(3)(a).
22   *Ibid.*, s.35(3)(b).
23   *Ibid.*, s.35(3)(c).

24   *Maori Representation Act* 1867.
25   *Electoral Act* 1993, s.3(1).
26   *Ibid.*, s.45(3)(a).

designed to ensure that each party's total number of members is approximately equal to its share of the party vote for it at the election.

Generally these members will take the total number of members up to 120. However, this figure could be exceeded: if a party's constituency candidates win more seats than its national party vote entitles it to, it retains the seats it has won but is awarded no party list seats.[27] It may also not be reached: if a party's share of the vote entitles it to more party list seats than it has nominated candidates for, those seats are not filled.[28]

REDISTRIBUTION OF SEATS

Representation Commission
The job of dividing New Zealand into the ascertained number of electoral districts falls to a statutory body, called the Representation Commission, which meets every five years following each national census.

The Representation Commission was first established in 1887.[29] The creation of an independent commission to draw up electoral boundaries (work previously carried out by Parliament itself) has been called one of the most significant landmarks in New Zealand's electoral history. It became a model for the development of similar commissions in the United Kingdom and Australia.[30]

The Representation Commission for the purposes of determining the boundaries of general electoral districts consists of seven members. Four persons are members by virtue of their offices: the Surveyor-General, the Government Statistician, the Chief Electoral Officer and the Chairperson of the Local Government Commission (who does not have a vote). Two further members are appointed by the Governor-General on the nomination of the House, one to represent the Government and one to represent the opposition. The final member is appointed by the Governor-General as chairperson on the nomination of the members of the commission or of a majority of them.[31]

When the commission is determining Māori electoral districts, its membership is supplemented by three further members. One of these is the chief executive of Te Puni Kōkiri (the Ministry of Māori Development). The other two (who must each be Māori) are appointed by the Governor-General on the nomination of the House, one to represent the Government and one to represent the opposition.[32]

None of the commission's nominated members can be a member of Parliament.

Any political party to which a member of Parliament belongs, any independent member of Parliament and any party whose candidates obtained at least five percent of the votes cast at the last general election may make submissions to the commission.[33] Any party which obtains five percent of the votes will, by definition, have members of Parliament belonging to it.

The commission deliberates in private. It is accepted, however, that those commissioners nominated to represent government and opposition parties have a particular need to consult with and take advice from those that they represent. In general, the commission relies on their integrity and discretion. But it has adopted rules to guide commissioners in how consultation could proceed in an endeavour to achieve a workable balance between the need to consult and the need to maintain confidentiality.[34]

27 *Ibid.*, s.192(5).
28 *Ibid.*, s.193(4).
29 *Representation Act* 1887.
30 Atkinson, *Adventures in Democracy – A History of the Vote in New Zealand*, p.76.

31 *Electoral Act* 1993, s.28(1), (2), (5).
32 *Ibid.*, s.28(3), (4).
33 *Ibid.*, s.34.
34 1999-2002, AJHR, H1, Schedule D, p.15.

Boundaries

In principle, the commission attempts to draw electoral boundaries so that an equal number of electors is contained within each district. This will never be entirely practicable, so the commission is allowed to deviate from mathematical equality by drawing electoral boundaries for general electoral districts which contain up to five percent more or less of the general electoral population than the average for the districts within each island,[35] and to allow a similar percentage deviation by reference to the Māori electoral population for any Māori electoral district.[36]

The commission is obliged, when drawing new boundaries, to give due consideration to existing boundaries, community of interest, communications facilities, topographical features and any projected variation in the electoral population of the districts during their life. In the case of Māori electoral districts this includes community of interest among Māori people generally and members of Māori tribes.[37]

The commission publishes details of its provisional proposals in the *New Zealand Gazette*, and persons have at least one month from such publication to lodge objections to them. Objections received by the commission are also published, and the public is given at least two weeks to lodge counter-objections. The commission is obliged to consider these objections and counter-objections before coming to a final decision on boundaries.[38] But it may change its provisional proposals without regard to whether these have been the subject of objections.[39] Within six months of its being convened, the commission must deliver its final report to the Governor-General and publish it in the *Gazette*. No appeals or objections are possible after that point. The redrawn boundaries thereupon become the electoral districts for subsequent general elections until superseded by a new commission determination in five years' time.[40] Thus, depending upon the timing of the census and subsequent elections, one or two general elections will be fought on the basis of boundaries determined by each Representation Commission's report.

Any by-election occurring between the publication of the new boundaries and the next general election continues to be fought on the old boundaries.

ELECTORS

Registration

The first step towards securing the right to vote at an election is to register as an elector.

Registration within one month of becoming qualified to vote in an electoral district is compulsory.[41] All persons of or over the age of 18 years who are New Zealand citizens or permanent residents of New Zealand and have resided continuously at some time for not less than one year in New Zealand are qualified to register as electors. (A permanent resident is a person who is lawfully resident in New Zealand and who is not subject to any immigration restriction.[42]) The electoral district in which a person qualifies to register is that district in which he or she last resided continuously for at least one month or, where the person has never resided continuously for one month in any electoral district, the district in which he or she now resides or last resided.[43] A person is entitled to be registered in only one electoral district at a time. However, a person's registration in a new district in which he or she has recently become qualified to vote is not invalidated merely because that person remains registered in the old district (though the old registration must have been cancelled

---

[35] *Electoral Act* 1993, s.36.
[36] *Ibid.*, s.45(*l*).
[37] *Ibid.*, ss.35(3)(f) and 45(6).
[38] *Ibid.*, ss.38 and 45(8).
[39] *Timmins v Governor-General* [1984] 2 NZLR 298.
[40] *Electoral Act* 1993, s.40.
[41] *Ibid.*, s.82.
[42] *Ibid.*, s 73.
[43] *Ibid.*, s.74(1).

by the time of the next election to entitle that person to vote).[44] New Zealand citizens who have not been in New Zealand for three years and permanent residents who have been absent for 12 months (in each case other than through absence on a diplomatic mission or in the armed forces) lose their qualification to register as electors. Also disqualified as electors are certain persons detained in a hospital as a result of mental disorder or intellectual disability, persons detained in a penal institution and serving a life sentence, preventive detention or a sentence of more than three years' imprisonment, and persons who have been convicted of a corrupt electoral practice within the last three years.[45]

Registration is effected by making an application on the prescribed form to a registrar of electors (an employee of New Zealand Post Limited).[46] The registrar then includes the elector on the electoral roll for the appropriate electoral district. Electors who have registered by writ day for an election are included on the printed electoral roll produced for polling day. Electors who register after writ day do not appear on the roll but may cast a special declaration vote. No registration is permitted on polling day itself.

Māori option

A Māori, or a descendant of a Māori, may register as an elector of either a Māori electoral district or a general electoral district. A Māori may exercise the option of enrolling in either type of district when first qualifying and registering as a voter and may opt to transfer to the other type of electoral district at the time of each five-yearly census.[47] No transfer between rolls may be effected between censuses.[48] Between February and April 1994 there was a special opportunity to exercise the option to transfer between the rolls for the purposes of drawing boundaries for the new MMP system.[49] In regard to that special option to transfer, the Government was held to have had a duty to publicise the option at a level that was reasonable having regard to the position of Māori in society and the unsatisfactory number of Māori enrolled to vote.[50] This obligation to take adequate steps to publicise the option may apply in respect of the regular quinquennial option also.

Electoral rolls

In 2002 it was estimated that 94.17 percent of the eligible voting population had actually enrolled.[51] Enrolment in New Zealand compares favourably with enrolment rates achieved overseas.[52]

Lists of persons registered as electors are printed periodically on electoral rolls under the direction of the registrar of electors for each electoral district. The "electoral roll" for any district is technically a compilation of completed registration application forms held by the registrar of electors.[53]

Persons who can show that publication of their names and addresses could be harmful to their safety or the safety of their families may apply to the Chief Registrar for registration on an unpublished roll.[54] At the time of the 2002 election, for example, there were 6,508 persons on the unpublished electoral roll.[55] Such persons cast special declaration votes at an election.

REGISTRATION OF POLITICAL PARTIES

In order to obtain party list seats, a political party must first be registered with the Electoral Commission on the Register of Political Parties.

---

44   *Ibid.*, s.75.
45   *Ibid.*, s.80.
46   *Ibid.*, s.82(1).
47   *Ibid.*, ss.76 to 78.
48   *Ibid.*, s.79.
49   *Ibid.*, s.269(2).
50   *Taiaroa v Minister of Justice* [1995] 1 NZLR 411.
51   Information supplied by the Chief Electoral Officer, March 2005.
52   1999-2002, AJHR, I.7C, para.6.2.
53   *Electoral Act* 1993, s.3(1).
54   *Ibid.*, s.115.
55   Information supplied by the Chief Electoral Officer, March 2005.

Applications for registration of a party may be made by the secretary of the party or by any member of Parliament who is a current financial member of it.[56] A party may be registered with component parties;[57] that is, parties that are themselves members of the registered party or which have combined their memberships with another party for the purposes of registering with the commission. The commission may also register party logos for political parties (whether those parties are registered themselves or not).[58]

To be a registered party the party must have and maintain a current financial membership of at least 500.[59] (But the commission does not disclose any membership list made available to it. Membership of a political party is a matter for each individual to make known if he or she wishes to do so.[60])

The commission has power to deny registration of a political party proposing to use an indecent or offensive name or a name that is too long or is likely to cause confusion.[61] Subject to compliance with the formal requirements to provide the secretary's name and address, the commission advises its consent to registration in the *New Zealand Gazette* and approves an abbreviation for the name of the party, if one is sought.[62] The commission may cancel registration on the application of the secretary or of a member of Parliament belonging to the party where such an application is made on behalf of the party. It must cancel registration if the party's financial membership drops below 500.[63] There can be no registration of a political party during an election campaign (that is, after the issue of the writ).[64] At the time of the 2002 election there were 21 parties registered with the Electoral Commission (four of those were parties that were component parties of other registered parties).

Every registered party must make an annual return of the donations that it has received in terms of money or goods and services. The return must identify individual donors and the amounts that they have given and the individual amounts of anonymous donations.[65] Where a party believes that it has nothing to disclose in respect of the year in question it must submit a "nil" return, which is effectively advice to the commission that it received no donations.[66] The commission is charged with ensuring that parties submit returns of donations and with making the information available for public inspection.[67]

QUALIFICATIONS FOR MEMBERS

In principle, every person who is a registered elector and who is a New Zealand citizen is qualified to be a candidate and to be elected as a member of Parliament.[68] The fact that a person must be a registered elector to be a member of Parliament effectively imports the qualifications for registering as an elector (such as age and residence) and the disqualifications from registering (such as detention in a hospital for reasons of mental disorder, imprisonment and conviction for a corrupt practice) into the membership qualifications.

If a person is not qualified to be registered as an elector, but has nevertheless been registered, the person is not qualified to be a candidate or to be elected as a member of Parliament.[69] The election of such a person could therefore be challenged by way of an election petition. However, an election petition must be presented within 28 days of the declaration of the result of the election.[70] There is no way of challenging the validity of an election other than by means of an election petition.[71] If the fact that a

---

[56] *Electoral Act* 1993, s.63.
[57] *Ibid.*, s.67(1)(a)(iii).
[58] *Ibid.*, s.63A
[59] *Ibid.*, ss.66(1)(b) and 70(2).
[60] *Eleventh Compendium of Case Notes of the Ombudsmen*, 1998, Case No. W33807.
[61] *Electoral Act* 1993, s.65.
[62] *Ibid.*, s.67.
[63] *Ibid.*, s.70.
[64] *Ibid.*, s.64.
[65] *Ibid.*, s.214G.
[66] *Electoral Act* 1993, s.214K; 1996-99, AJHR, E.57, p.14.
[67] *Electoral Act* 1993, ss.214I and 214J.
[68] *Ibid.*, s.47(1), (3).
[69] *Ibid.*, s.47(2).
[70] *Ibid.*, s.231.
[71] *Ibid.*, s.229(1).

person was invalidly registered as an elector is discovered after the time for presenting an election petition has passed, it cannot be challenged by election petition. As no vacancy automatically arises by virtue of the fact that a sitting member is discovered to have been invalidly registered, it is likely that in such circumstances the person declared elected would remain as a member.

The qualifications for candidature and membership of the House are linked in the legislation. Nevertheless, it is conceivable that a person who is invalidly registered at the time he or she is nominated as a candidate qualifies to be registered before the result of the election is declared. It would seem that in these circumstances the election of that person would be void (unless, possibly, he or she re-registered before the election) since the defect in that person's registration at the outset would prevent that person being a valid candidate for election.[72]

There are a number of legislative provisions relating to membership of Parliament. These operate to disqualify persons who hold or have held certain offices from being members of Parliament. They operate whether the offices concerned are held at the time of election or are subsequently acquired.

The following are disqualified from being or becoming members of the House—
- members of the Representation Commission (while they hold office and for up to two years after ceasing to be members)[73]
- the Controller and Auditor-General[74]
- the Clerk of the House of Representatives and the Deputy Clerk[75]
- an Ombudsman[76]
- the Parliamentary Commissioner for the Environment.[77]

To be qualified for election, a candidate must be living. This is not as obvious as it may sound. There are jurisdictions in which a deceased candidate may be elected, in which case a vacancy immediately arises and is filled in the manner prescribed for filling vacancies.[78] In New Zealand, if a candidate for an electoral district dies after the close of nominations and before the polls have closed, the constituency election for that electoral district is aborted.[79] If a candidate who would have been successful dies after the close of the polls but before the declaration of the result, the candidate is not formally returned as a member and the writ is endorsed with that fact.[80] In all such cases a fresh election is held as if it were a by-election.[81] In the case of a party list candidate dying after submission of the list, the poll proceeds but the deceased candidate's name is entirely disregarded.[82]

CALLING AN ELECTION

The term of Parliament is three years, computed from the day fixed for the return of the writs for the previous election. At the end of this period, unless it has already been dissolved, Parliament expires.[83] In fact, except in 1943, Parliament has always been dissolved before it was due to expire, a step which is taken by the Governor-General issuing a proclamation on the advice of the Prime Minister. Dissolution (or the expiration of Parliament) sets in motion a train of events leading to the general election. The Governor-General, within seven days, issues a writ to the Chief Electoral Officer to make all necessary arrangements for the conduct of the general election.[84] The writ appoints a day by which candidates are to be nominated, a day for the poll to be held if there is

---

[72] Compare, for example, *Sykes v Cleary* (1992) 176 CLR 77.
[73] *Electoral Act* 1993, s.44.
[74] *Public Audit Act* 2001, s.8.
[75] *Clerk of the House of Representatives Act* 1988, s.9.
[76] *Ombudsmen Act* 1975, s.4.
[77] *Environment Act* 1986, s.5.
[78] See, for example, *The Economist*, 11 November 2000 (a candidate killed in a plane crash three weeks

before the election won a United States Senate seat).
[79] *Electoral Act* 1993, ss.153A and 153B.
[80] *Ibid.*, s.153C.
[81] *Ibid*, s.153E.
[82] *Ibid.*, s.153.
[83] *Constitution Act* 1986, s.17(1).
[84] *Electoral Act* 1993, s.125.

more than one candidate in an electoral district and the latest day for the return of the writ. Nomination day must be no fewer than 20 and not more than 27 days before polling day. The same day (which must be a Saturday) must be appointed for the poll to be held in each electoral district.[85] This was not always the case. Until 1881 European electorates (as they were then known) could hold polls on different days, and until 1951 polls took place in the Māori electorates on a different day from those in the European electorates. The latest day for the return of the writ is the same for each electoral district – the fiftieth day after the writ is issued.[86]

It is a matter for the Prime Minister to decide how long prior to the dissolution of Parliament an announcement is made that a general election is to be held on a particular day. In 1984 the announcement was only a matter of hours before dissolution with the election following one month later. In 1931 an election to be held on 2 December was only announced on 11 November, making it the shortest campaign on record.[87] This is legally an impossibly short period now. In 1996 the date of the election was announced almost five months beforehand.[88] The Prime Minister's advice is that a minimum of 43 days must be allowed between any public announcement of polling day and polling day itself.[89] For the 2002 election the period was 45 days and for the 2005 election it was 54 days.

In one circumstance the Prime Minister is obliged to signal in advance that an election is to be held. This is where it is desired not to hold a by-election to fill a vacancy that has arisen more than six months before Parliament is due to expire but within six months of the date when it is intended that an election actually be held. The House can, by a resolution carried by 75 percent of all members of the House, dispense with such a by-election but it must be informed beforehand by the Prime Minister that the general election is indeed to be held within the next six months.[90] A by-election that would otherwise have been held has been cancelled following such advice from the Prime Minister.[91] The Prime Minister is not obliged to disclose the exact date of the election in order to invoke the cancellation procedure (though this may be done), only the fact of the election's imminence.

(For restraints on governmental actions after the dissolution of Parliament see Chapter 7.)

THE ELECTION

Candidates
Constituency nominations
Any person who is registered as an elector and is a New Zealand citizen is qualified to be a candidate for an electoral district or from a party list.[92] Any agreement not to stand for election to Parliament is unenforceable as contrary to public policy.[93] Persons employed in the state services (which includes the education service and the police) who become candidates for election must be placed on leave of absence from nomination day for the election until the first working day after polling day.[94] If elected, a state servant is deemed to have vacated office as a state servant.[95] Candidates do not need to be qualified to vote in the electoral district for which they are standing for election, but a person cannot be a candidate for more than one district at the same general election.[96]

A person must consent to be nominated as a candidate. Any two electors registered in

---

85   *Ibid.*, s.139(1) to (3).
86   *Ibid.*, s.139(4).
87   Bassett, *Three Party Politics in New Zealand 1911-1931*, p.60.
88   1996, Vol.555, p.12541.
89   1999, Vol.578, p.17310.
90   *Electoral Act* 1993, s.131(b).
91   1996, Vol.555, pp.12541-62.
92   *Electoral Act* 1993, s.47.
93   *Peters v Collinge* [1993] 2 NZLR 554.
94   *Electoral Act* 1993, s.52.
95   *Ibid.*, s.53(2).
96   *Ibid.*, s.59.

an electoral district can nominate a candidate for election for that district.[97] A deposit of $300 must be lodged with the Returning Officer for each candidate. This is refunded if the candidate polls five percent or more of the total number of votes received by constituency candidates in the district.[98]

As an alternative to nominating candidates on a constituency-by-constituency basis, a registered party may lodge a single bulk nomination schedule with the Chief Electoral Officer. If a party uses this method of nominating candidates, no person may nominate as a candidate for that party on an individual basis. A bulk nomination is lodged by the secretary of the party and must be accompanied by a declaration by the secretary that each person nominated is qualified to be a candidate and by the deposit of $300 for each candidate nominated.[99] Most major parties use the bulk nomination system.

Party list nominations
In respect of candidates for election from party lists, the secretary of a registered party forwards a list of candidates to the Chief Electoral Officer by noon on the last day for the nomination of constituency candidates. Each candidate must consent to the inclusion of his or her name on the list. The list must set out the candidates in the party's order of preference for election.[100] A deposit of $1,000 (inclusive of goods and services tax) must be lodged along with the list. This deposit is refunded if the party receives at least 0.5 percent of the total number of all party votes cast at the election. However, the deposit is not refunded until the required returns of election expenses for the party have been made to the Electoral Commission.[101]

Registered parties are obliged to adopt internal procedures for selecting parliamentary candidates that ensure that provision is made for current financial members, or delegates elected or otherwise chosen by current financial members, to participate in such selections.[102] Precisely what such procedures should entail is undefined in the legislation. The candidates so selected do not themselves have to be current financial members or even members of the parties in whose interest they are nominated.

The Electoral Commission does not have any role in enforcing the requirement for parties to have democratic candidate selection procedures. The only form of redress for party members dissatisfied with their party's selection procedures would appear to be to bring court proceedings for compliance.[103] Nor is a party's candidate selection procedure a criterion for registration on the Register of Political Parties.[104] While the commission has been reluctant to give parties advice on questions of legal compliance with candidate selection requirements, it has developed a guideline definition of what is a current financial member for the purposes of participation in such selection.[105] In fact, each party has developed its own practices for drawing up its party list of candidates – some giving more emphasis to central control, others to regional participation in the decision-making and each with their own methods of achieving overall balance in the final party list.[106]

Campaign
How parties and candidates conduct their electoral campaigns is, within the constraints of the law against corrupt practices (for example, bribing, threatening or intimidating voters) and illegal practices (for example, restrictions on advertisements promoting candidates unless they make it clear that these are officially authorised), largely over to them.

---

[97] *Ibid.*, s.143.
[98] *Ibid.*, s.144.
[99] *Ibid.*, ss.146A to 146L.
[100] *Ibid.*, s.127.
[101] *Ibid.*, s.127A.
[102] *Ibid.*, s.71.
[103] 1995, Vol.550, p.9423; "NZ First faces action over

selection method", *The Dominion*, 27 September 1996.
[104] 1996-99, AJHR, I.24, p.111.
[105] 1999-2002, AJHR, I.7C, paras.8.11.1 and 8.11.3.
[106] See Bain, "Making it on the list", *The Dominion*, 23 March 1999.

School premises may be used free of any rental charge for the purposes of candidates' meetings,[107] and meetings at other venues within each electoral district will be held by candidates. Candidates are required to obtain express permission before entering onto defence property for any purpose during the campaign.[108] The shape, colour, design and layout of advertisements promoting a party or a candidate that are displayed in a public place or on private land must conform with prescribed conditions. These restrictions do not apply to newspaper and periodical advertising or to handbills and small posters.[109] Complaints that offences have been committed in respect of the campaign rules are made to the Chief Electoral Officer, who may deal with the matter informally or refer them to the police.[110]

No campaigning is permitted on polling day itself.

Most parties will publish election manifestos setting out their policy intentions should they become the Government or describing how they will act if their members are elected to Parliament. Promises made in election manifestos are not regarded as being legally binding,[111] though if an election promise was shown to be sufficiently seriously misleading it could conceivably constitute electoral fraud and therefore give grounds for challenging the election result.[112] However, this must be regarded as an extreme circumstance. Most importantly, the campaign, particularly nationally, will be fought out through the news media – print, radio and television.

Election broadcasting

Since the 1990 general election there has been a statutory regime governing parliamentary election broadcasting, including the provision of broadcasting services by the State-owned broadcasters Television New Zealand Limited and Radio New Zealand Limited. This regime does not apply in respect of a paid broadcast promoting the election of an individual candidate in a particular electoral district. Apart from this circumstance it is unlawful to broadcast an election programme, either during the election campaign or outside the period of the campaign, except as approved in terms of the legislation.[113] It is also unlawful to broadcast election programmes on television between 6 am and noon on a Sunday or Anzac Day or to broadcast such programmes at all on television or radio on Christmas Day, Good Friday or Easter Sunday.[114]

The allocation of time and money for election broadcasting has been carried out by the Electoral Commission since 1996 (the task was formerly discharged by the Broadcasting Standards Authority). For the purpose of carrying out its broadcasting duties the commission's membership is augmented by two members appointed on the nomination of the House. One is appointed to represent the Government, the other to represent opposition parties.[115] While there may be some preliminary consultation among the parties represented in the House about who these representatives will be, there is no formal consultation requirement under the legislation and ultimately the nominations are settled politically by decision of the House.[116]

Political parties

To qualify for the provision of an opening and closing address or for an allocation of broadcasting money for an election programme, a party must have been registered on the Register of Political Parties at the dissolution or expiration of Parliament and must

---

[107] *Electoral Act* 1993, s.154.

[108] "Who's not coming to dinner?", *The Independant,* *31 August 2005.*

[109] *Electoral (Advertisements of a Specified Kind) Regulations* 2005.

[110] See, for example, "ACT told to change election billboards or face $3,000 fine", *The Dominion Post,* 13 August 2005.

[111] See Caldwell, "Election manifesto promises: the law and politics" [1989] NZLJ 108.

[112] *Friesen v Hammell* (2000) 78 BCLR (3d) 317.

[113] *Broadcasting Act* 1989, s.70.

[114] *Ibid.*, s.79A.

[115] *Electoral Act* 1993, s.8(4).

[116] 1999, Vol.577, p.16346.

have advised the commission (by a date specified by the commission and notified in the *Gazette*) that it considers itself qualified to share in such an allocation.[117] A political party may join with other parties as a group of related parties to qualify for the allocation of broadcasting time and money.

The commission must, in allocating the facilities, time and money at its disposal, take into account: the votes the party received at the previous election; votes won at intervening by-elections; the number of members of Parliament belonging to the party; relationships with other parties; other indications of public support, such as opinion polls; and, finally, the need to provide a fair opportunity for each party to convey its policies to the public by television broadcasting.[118] Based on its consideration of these criteria, the commission divides the eligible parties into a number of categories treating each party within each category equally for the purposes of allocating broadcasting facilities, time and money.[119]

Opening and closing addresses

Both Television New Zealand Limited and Radio New Zealand Limited are obliged to provide time, free of charge, for the opening and closing addresses of political parties. In the case of a televised address this must be on one free-to-air channel with national coverage. For a radio address this must be on National Radio.[120] The broadcasts must be made between 7 pm and 9 pm and all closing addresses must be broadcast on the same night in the last week of the campaign. Advertisements must not be broadcast during opening or closing addresses or between different closing addresses.[121]

The Electoral Commission, after consultation with Television New Zealand Limited, Radio New Zealand Limited and the political parties involved, ascertains the amount of free time to be made available for such addresses and allocates this among the parties according to the general criteria for such allocations.[122] It also allocates, out of money appropriated by Parliament, funds to the broadcasters for them to produce opening and closing address programmes for the parties.[123]

Allocation of money for other election broadcasting

In each year in which an election is due, the commission receives notifications from political parties as to whether they consider that they will be entitled to an allocation of money to produce an election programme.[124] The Minister of Justice is obliged to notify the commission how much money Parliament has appropriated for the cost of producing election broadcasting programmes. If no appropriation is made, an amount equal to the amount appropriated for the previous election is deemed to have been appropriated. In fact, Parliament did not make any specific appropriation for producing election broadcasting programmes for the 1993, 1996, 1999 or 2002 elections and as a consequence the amount available for this purpose remained the same at those elections.[125]

The commission allocates the time and money available among the political parties who apply to it for an allocation. In making these allocations the commission is under distinct obligations to consult with both the broadcasters affected by its decisions and the political parties which have notified it that they believe they will qualify for an allocation of time or money.[126] In the case of the latter, this consultation must include the opportunity to meet with and be heard by the commission.[127]

The commission may stagger its decision-making on election broadcasting given the

[117] *Broadcasting Act* 1989, s.75(1).
[118] *Ibid.*, s.75(2).
[119] 2003, PP, E.57, pp.19-20.
[120] *Broadcasting Act* 1989, s.71.
[121] *Ibid.*, s.77A.
[122] *Ibid.*, ss.71A, 72 and 73.
[123] *Ibid.*, s.77A(5), (6).
[124] *Ibid.*, s.70A.
[125] 2003, PP, E.57, p.18.
[126] *Broadcasting Act* 1989, ss.75A and 76.
[127] *Ibid.*, s.76(2).

uncertainty of the date of the dissolution of Parliament. Thus, in 1999, the commission made an initial allocation of 90 percent of the time and money at its disposal before the date of the election became known. The unallocated 10 percent was used to allow for adjustments in respect of parties registering after the initial decisions were taken but in time to qualify for some allocation of broadcasting resources.[128] Special provisions apply expediting decision-making procedures if an early election is called.[129]

There is no appeal against the commission's allocation of broadcasting time and money. While it is conceivable that a court might be persuaded to intervene if the commission was clearly misinterpreting its legal powers, the commission has a wide area of discretion as to how it makes its allocations, and the short time-frame within which it must work makes it undesirable in the public interest for its task to be unduly inhibited.[130]

Political parties to which money is made available for the making of an election programme may expend that money only on the production costs of the programme or on purchasing broadcasting time for it.[131] A broadcaster may not discriminate between political parties in respect of the terms offered for broadcasting an election programme.[132] It is also possible that a broadcaster unjustifiably refusing access to a party for an election programme (for example, on discriminatory, arbitrary or unreasonable grounds) would be subject to judicial intervention.[133] A radio station has banned all election advertising rather than accept a particular advertisement that it did not agree with on political grounds.[134] Accounts for costs incurred in producing an election programme are submitted to the Electoral Commission for payment.[135] Broadcasters must provide the commission with a return showing all election programmes broadcast during the three-month period preceding polling day. These are available for inspection.[136]

Public information campaigns

The election broadcasting restrictions do not prevent non-partisan public information broadcasting about the election. This can take the form of advertisements placed by the Electoral Commission, the Chief Electoral Officer and other election officials or community service broadcasting.[137] In fact, both the commission and the Chief Electoral Officer run nationwide information campaigns designed to raise voters' general awareness of the imminence of the election and how votes are cast. The Chief Registrar of Electors sponsors advertising to encourage voter registration and individual Returning Officers place local advertisements advising of the location of polling places. Where such advertising is carried out within a statutory framework (as it is with the Electoral Commission), the advertising is not subject to effective control by other bodies performing private regulatory functions.[138]

News and current affairs programmes

News and current affairs broadcasting on the election is unaffected by the election broadcasting regime.[139] It is, of course, subject to the general broadcasting standards applying to all programmes. However, it has been held that in carrying out election

---

[128]   1999-2002, AJHR, I.7C, para.9.2.2.

[129]   *Broadcasting Act* 1989, ss.76C and 76D.

[130]   *Alton v Broadcasting Standards Authority* [1990] NZAR 571 (interim injunction refused).

[131]   *Broadcasting Act* 1989, s.74B(1).

[132]   *Ibid.*, s.79B.

[133]   See, for example, *R v (Pro-Life Alliance) v British Broadcasting Corporation* [2004] 1 AC 185 (broadcaster's decision to exclude offensive material upheld in that case).

[134]   "Iwi radio station bans all election ads", the *Dominion Post*, 3 September 2005.

[135]   *Broadcasting Act* 1989, s.74B(2), (2A), (3) and (4).

[136]   *Ibid.*, ss.79C and 79D.

[137]   *Ibid.*, s.70(2)(d), (e).

[138]   *Electoral Commission v Cameron* [1997] 2 NZLR 421 (Advertising Standards Authority could not control how Electoral Commission carried out its public information campaign).

[139]   *Broadcasting Act* 1989, s.70(3).

coverage, television companies (even private ones) are performing public functions and that programming decisions are susceptible to judicial review for unreasonableness.[140]

By-elections

By-elections are not subject to the provisions providing state funding for opening and closing addresses or for the allocation of money to produce election programmes.[141] However, the limited restrictions on the times and days on which election programmes may be broadcast on television and radio apply in respect of by-elections[142] and the general requirement that broadcasters offer identical terms to each party or candidate for election programmes also applies in respect of by-elections.[143]

Pre-election economic and fiscal update

Between 20 and 30 working days before each general election (10 working days if there is an early or snap election), the Minister of Finance is obliged to publish a report containing an economic and fiscal update prepared by the Treasury. The update must contain forecasts of movements in key economic data for New Zealand and projections of the Crown's financial position. These forecasts relate to the financial year in which the report is prepared and the two following years.[144]

The obligation to publish an official pre-election economic and fiscal update took effect in respect of general elections held after 1 July 1994. For the general election held in November 1993 the Government voluntarily published such a report.

Election expenses

For each constituency candidate at a general election, expenditure on certain defined election activities promoting the candidate's election in the three months preceding polling day is limited to $20,000 (including goods and services tax).[145] These activities (carried out by a candidate or with a candidate's authority) comprise: advertising, radio or television broadcasting and publishing materials such as notices, posters, pamphlets and billboards. To constitute an election activity the advertising or material must relate to the candidate in that capacity (and not to a person's capacity as a member of Parliament, for example) or must encourage or persuade voters not to vote for another candidate or party.[146] There is provision for apportioning expenditure on activities carried on both before and after the three-month period[147] and between two or more candidates where a single activity (for example, a joint advertisement) is intended to promote the election of more than one candidate.[148]

Within 70 working days after polling day, each candidate must submit to the Chief Electoral Officer a return of election expenses and details of all donations exceeding $1,000 made by persons to the candidate.[149] These returns must be retained by the Chief Electoral Officer and made available for public inspection.[150] The candidate's election deposit cannot be returned until this return of election expenses has been made.[151]

Registered parties are also limited as to the amount of election expenses that they may

---

[140] *Dunne v Canwest TV Works Limited*, unreported, High Court, Wellington, 11 August 2005 (injunction requiring that two party leaders be included in a programme).

[141] *Broadcasting Act* 1989, s.69A.

[142] *Ibid.*, s.79A.

[143] *Ibid.*, s.79B.

[144] *Public Finance Act* 1989, s.26T.

[145] *Electoral Act* 1993, s.213(2).

[146] *Ibid.*, s.213(1).

[147] *Ibid.*, s.213(4).

[148] *Ibid.*, s.214.

[149] *Ibid.*, s.210.

[150] *Ibid.*, s.211.

[151] *Ibid.*, s.144(4).

incur on specified election activities promoting the party in the three months leading up to polling day. Such activities comprise actions taken to promote a party and to encourage voters to vote for it or not to vote for another party.[152] The permitted party spending limit is $1,000,000 plus $20,000 (inclusive of goods and services tax) for each constituency candidate standing in the party's name. [153] Expenses incurred in respect of an election activity carried on both before and within the three months immediately preceding polling day may be apportioned so that only that proportion of the expenses relating to activities carried on within the three-month period are counted against the spending limit.[154]

Each party secretary must forward an audited return of election expenses to the Electoral Commission within 50 working days of the declaration of the result of the election.[155] The Electoral Commission may prescribe the precise form in which such a declaration is to be made, including requiring the categorisation of election expenses by particular activities.[156] No election deposit may be returned to a party until this return has been made.[157]

The failure of a candidate or a party to make a return of election expenses and the making of a false return by any candidate or party are offences. In addition, an elected member is liable to a fine for each day on which he or she sits or votes in the House while the return remains outstanding.[158] The House has ordered an inquiry into the disclosure of campaign spending by a party where concerns were raised as to whether it had made full disclosure.[159]

Administration of the election

The official responsible for conducting the election is the Chief Electoral Officer.[160] The Chief Electoral Officer is an employee of the Ministry of Justice and, as such, is under the direction of the Minister of Justice and the Secretary for Justice. However, a convention has developed that the Minister and the ministry do not provide directions to the Chief Electoral Officer in the discharge of that officer's electoral functions, though they may communicate their views on those functions.[161] The Chief Electoral Officer must designate a Returning Officer for each electoral district. Each Returning Officer, subject to the Chief Electoral Officer's control, makes the detailed arrangements for the conduct of the poll and the count of votes in each district. In practice, all Returning Officers follow detailed national standards and processes prescribed by the Chief Electoral Officer. State sector agencies are under an obligation to provide the Chief Electoral Officer with assistance in the conduct of elections,[162] and state servants together with other persons are recruited to perform duties as election officials. The Chief Electoral Officer establishes polling places (such as at schools and church halls) for voting in respect of each electoral district. At least 12 polling places must be established within each electoral district with access that is suitable for people with disabilities. Subject to this requirement, polling places may be established for a district even though they are actually located outside the district.[163]

Uncontested elections

If there is only one candidate nominated for an electoral district or if all candidates withdraw leaving only one candidate for the district, that candidate is declared elected and no poll is held for that seat (a party-vote poll will still be held).[164]

---

152 *Ibid.*, s.214B(1).
153 *Ibid.*, s.214B(2).
154 *Ibid.*, s.214B(4).
155 *Ibid.*, s.214C.
156 *Electoral Commission v Tate* [1999] 3 NZLR 174.
157 *Electoral Act* 1993, s.127A(4).
158 *Ibid.*, s.210(4).
159 1998, Vol.570, p.10966; 1996-99, AJHR, I.23, p.177 (found no intention to mislead in the election return).
160 *Electoral Act* 1993, s.18.
161 1999-2002, AJHR, I.7C, para.4.2.
162 *Electoral Act* 1993, s.20D.
163 *Ibid.*, s.155.
164 *Ibid.*, s.148.

A member has not been returned in this way since 1943, when two members who were overseas on war service were elected unopposed.[165]

Voting

In almost all circumstances there will be more than one candidate for election as the constituency member for the district, and, in any case, a party list vote needs to be held in every electoral district. A poll will therefore be held. Persons who are lawfully registered as electors in a district are entitled to vote at any election held in that district.

The ballot paper for a general election has two parts to it and an elector has two votes. On the left-hand side of the ballot paper a voter casts a party vote for the party of his or her choice. On the right-hand side the voter casts a vote for a candidate for the electoral district. Candidates are arranged on the ballot paper in alphabetical order. Party affiliations are printed next to the candidates' names. Where a registered party has a constituency candidate its party name appears on the party vote side of the ballot paper opposite to that candidate's name. Where a candidate for the electoral district (such as an independent) does not have a corresponding party standing for the party vote, the space on the party vote side of the ballot paper is left blank. Parties without individual constituency candidates are then arranged alphabetically on the party vote side of the ballot paper below parties with candidates.[166]

Voting is carried out in secret at a polling place on a Saturday between 9 am and 7 pm. The voter votes by placing a tick in a circle at the right of the name of the party or candidate (as the case may be) for whom the voter wishes to vote.[167]

Special voting

New Zealand first made provision for absentee or "special" voting in 1890 (for seamen). A general right to cast an absentee vote was introduced in 1905 and voting by post was first permitted in 1928.[168]

Regulations allow persons who will be absent from New Zealand or their own electoral district on polling day, or will otherwise be unable (for example, because of illness or infirmity) to vote at a polling place within the district, to vote by special vote.[169] This includes casting a special vote within a specified period before polling day (for example, where the elector is intending to go overseas shortly before the election). To cast a special vote, the elector must make a written application to an official authorised to issue special ballot papers.[170] Effectively, electors may vote at any polling place in New Zealand, though they are encouraged to vote at a polling place within their own electoral district.

Special ballot papers may be issued by electronic means to persons outside New Zealand (but the ballot paper must be returned by conventional means, including facsimile transmission).[171] Completed special ballot papers are sealed and deposited in a ballot box. A high proportion of special votes has been disallowed in the past mainly because the elector was not enrolled. For example, 15 percent of candidate and seven percent of party special votes cast at the 2002 general election were disallowed.[172] Special votes have also been disallowed through a voter voting for a constituency candidate in an electoral district in which the voter was not enrolled. Since the 2002 election a voter who votes for a candidate in an electoral district in which the voter is not enrolled has the party vote counted rather than the entire vote disallowed.[173]

---

[165] Atkinson, *Adventures in Democracy – A History of the Vote in New Zealand*, p.155.

[166] *Electoral Act* 1993, s.150 and Sch.2, form 11.

[167] *Ibid.*, s.168.

[168] Atkinson, *Adventures in Democracy – A History of the Vote in New Zealand*, pp.82-3, 135.

[169] *Electoral Act* 1993, s.172.

[170] *Electoral Regulations* 1996, reg.20.

[171] *Ibid.*, regs.45A, 47, 47A.

[172] 2002, PP, E 9, pp.446-7.

[173] *Electoral Act* 1993, s.178(5A).

Turnout

Turnout at New Zealand elections is traditionally high. A survey of elections held between 1945 and 1997 found that New Zealand, along with Iceland, had, at 89 percent, the highest turnout among countries where voting is not compulsory. Only some countries with compulsory voting scored higher (Australia's, for example, was 94 percent) and even countries with compulsory voting had lower turnouts than New Zealand's.[174] However, there is evidence of some decline in recent years. Average voting-age population turnout (not the same thing as registered voter turnout) was estimated at 80.4 percent in the four elections 1990–1999.[175] At the 2002 election registered voter turnout was 77 percent, probably the lowest authenticated figure since 1902. (Turnout at the 1978 election was officially recorded as 69.15 percent but the electoral rolls contained considerable duplication of electors. A more realistic estimate for turnout at that election is 79.86 percent.[176]) The overall turnout figure can also disguise considerable differences between the turnout of voters enrolled on the general roll as opposed to the Māori roll. Turnout of voters on the Māori roll was only 58 percent in 2002.[177]

Counting of votes

In respect of votes delivered to a Returning Officer before polling day (advance ordinary votes), the Returning Officer may, if authorised by the Chief Electoral Officer, conduct a preliminary count of such votes beginning after 3 pm on polling day.[178] The votes must be counted in a restricted area from which persons who enter (officials and scrutineers) may not leave without the Returning Officer's permission until the close of the poll and no information about the results of the count may be communicated to any non-authorised person.[179]

After the polls have closed, the manager of each polling place conducts a count of the votes cast for each candidate and for political party lists.[180] The aggregate totals from these preliminary counts are communicated to the Returning Officer for the electoral district and are entered into a national results system controlled by the Electoral Office. The results are fed to the media and placed on a website. Together with any advance vote totals, these form the basis of provisional election results released during the course of the evening of polling day. All ballot papers are then sent to the Returning Officer.

Over the next few days the Returning Officer for each district conducts a scrutiny of the rolls to ensure that there are no irregularities (such as a voter being issued with more than one ballot paper).[181] The Returning Officer then makes an official count of the votes from the various polling places in the district and counts any special votes remaining uncounted for the district, disallowing in all cases ballot papers that do not carry an official mark or do not clearly indicate the constituency candidate or the party for which the voter desired to vote.[182]

Scrutineers appointed by candidates or, where a party does not have an electorate candidate, the parties themselves may witness the counting (and any recounting) of the votes.[183]

Declaration of result and recounts

When the official count is completed the result is reported to the Chief Electoral Officer.[184]

---

[174] "Global Report on Political Participation by the Institute for Democracy and Electoral Assistance", May 1998, *Canadian Parliamentary Review*, Winter 1998-99, p.26.

[175] 1999-2002, AJHR, I.7C, Part 3 (Table 4).

[176] Wilson, *New Zealand Parliamentary Record, 1840-1984*, p.287.

[177] "Final Results 2002 General Election and Trends in Election Outcomes 1990-2002", Parliamentary Library, 20 August 2002.

[178] *Electoral Act* 1993, s.174C.

[179] *Ibid*, ss 174D and 174E.

[180] *Ibid.*, s.174.

[181] *Ibid.*, ss.175 and 176.

[182] *Ibid.*, s.178.

[183] *Ibid.*, ss.160, 174F, 175, 176 and 178.

[184] *Ibid.*, s.179(1).

As soon as practicable after receiving this information the Chief Electoral Officer must declare the results of the voting by notice in the *New Zealand Gazette*.[185] The results are also released to the media and published on a website.

Any constituency candidate may, within three working days of the public declaration of the result, apply to a District Court judge to conduct a recount of the votes cast for constituency candidates in that district.[186] If as a result of conducting the recount the judge finds that the original result was incorrect, the judge orders the Chief Electoral Officer to publish an amended declaration of the result.[187] Similarly, the secretary of any registered party may require that there be a judicial recount of party votes recorded on ballot papers in the electoral district and the judge may also order that the declared result of the party vote be amended.[188] Alternatively, the secretary of a party can seek from the Chief District Court Judge a national recount of party votes recorded in every electoral district. In this case a deposit of $90,000 (including goods and services tax) must be paid. A national recount is carried out by District Court judges in each electoral district under the Chief District Court Judge's direction. The deposit can, at the discretion of the Chief District Court Judge, be used to defray the costs of the recount.[189]

Return of the writ for constituency members

The Chief Electoral Officer, after declaring the result, and if satisfied that no application is to be made for a judicial recount, or, if there is a recount, after it has taken place, endorses on the writ the full name of every constituency candidate declared to be elected and the date of the endorsement, and transmits the writ to the Clerk of the House. The date endorsed on the writ is the date of the return of the writ, which should be (but is not always) within the time originally specified in the writ for its return.[190] The returned writ is, in effect, a certificate of election proving the right to membership of the House of the person named on it. It has been called the best available evidence that a person is a member of Parliament.[191] The elected candidate comes into office as a member of Parliament on the day after the date of the return of the writ.[192]

The House has, on being informed of an error on a returned writ, ordered an official (formerly the Clerk of the Writs) to attend the House in person with the original writ to amend it or correct it.[193] The Chief Electoral Officer now has power to correct an error in the name of a member as recorded on the writ.[194] A returned writ may also need to be amended if the result in an electoral district is overturned following an election petition to the High Court.

Party list returns

The results of the party voting on the ballot papers as declared by the Chief Electoral Officer are aggregated into national totals.

Where a party does not receive more than five percent of the total votes cast and no constituency candidate belonging to that party is elected for an electoral district, the votes cast for that party are entirely disregarded. If a constituency candidate belonging to a party that gains fewer than five percent of the party vote is returned for an electoral district, then that candidate's party also shares in the allocation of party seats, notwithstanding that the party failed to achieve the five percent threshold. The Chief Electoral Officer calculates

---

185 *Ibid.*, s.179(2).
186 *Ibid.*, s.180(1).
187 *Ibid.*, s.180(10).
188 *Ibid.*, s.180(2), (10).
189 *Ibid.*, s.181.
190 *Ibid.*, s.185.

191 *Forbes v Samuel* [1913] 3 KB 706, 719, 720, 725.
192 *Electoral Act* 1993, s.54(1)(a).
193 1882, JHR, p.4 (*Moeraki election return*); 1997, Vol.559, p.1117 (*Ilam election return*). Both returns described the member by the wrong given name.
194 *Electoral Act* 1993, s.186.

the number of party list seats in the new Parliament that every party achieving the five percent threshold of votes or electing a constituency member is entitled to.[195]

The mathematical methodology used to allocate party list seats is known as the Sainte Laguë formula after the political scientist who devised it. The application of this formula results in a near-proportional allocation of seats among the various parties entitled to party list seats. If a party has won more constituency seats than it is entitled to based on its share of the party vote, it keeps the constituency seats it has won and the size of the House is increased to that extent until the next election. This occurrence is referred to as an 'overhang'. The first overhang occurred at the 2005 general election when a party won four constituency seats but its share of the party vote would have only entitled it to three seats. The party seats to which each party is entitled are allocated by the Chief Electoral Officer to the candidates on each list in the party's order of preference. The same person may be a candidate in a constituency and also be included on a party list. Indeed this is common. A person who has already been elected for an electoral district is thus disregarded by the Chief Electoral Officer in allocating party list seats and the next candidate on the list is selected. If a party has not nominated enough candidates on its party list to take up all the seats to which it is entitled, those seats are not filled and the size of the House is reduced accordingly.

When the process of allocating party list seats is complete the Chief Electoral Officer declares the candidates to whom party list seats are allocated to have been elected and forwards to the Clerk of the House a return listing their full names.[196] These members come into office as members of Parliament on the day after this return is made.[197] The Chief Electoral Officer may correct an error in the name of a member on the list of members elected.[198]

Storage of ballot papers

Unused ballot papers are destroyed by the Returning Officers.

The ballot papers actually used at an election are packaged and forwarded by each Returning Officer to the Clerk of the House, who must retain the packages unopened for six months before they can be destroyed. (The legislation which requires the preservation of public records does not apply to such papers.[199]) A court of competent jurisdiction or the House itself may order any of the packages so delivered to the Clerk to be opened.[200] A "court of competent jurisdiction" is any court having jurisdiction over any matter in which the question of voting at an election is relevant.[201] Thus, the High Court on the trial of an electoral petition can order the opening of the packages, and the District Court has done so in the case of a prosecution for double voting.

DISPUTED ELECTIONS

Originally, the House was declared to be judge without appeal of the validity of election of each of its members.[202] Until 1880 persons questioning the validity of an election did so by means of a petition to the House that the House appointed a committee to try. In that year the House handed the trial of election petitions over to the courts.

Constituency seats

Election petitions complaining of the election or return of a member for an electoral district may be brought by defeated candidates or by electors of the district.[203] They may

---

[195] *Ibid.*, ss.191 and 192.
[196] *Ibid.*, s.193.
[197] *Ibid.*, s.54(2)(a).
[198] *Ibid.*, s.193A.
[199] *Public Records Act* 2005, s.6(a).
[200] *Electoral Act* 1993, ss.187 and 189.
[201] Mathieson, "Interpreting the proposed Bill of Rights (I)" [1986] NZLJ 130.
[202] *New Zealand Constitution Act* 1852 (UK), s.45.
[203] *Electoral Act* 1993, s.230(1)(a), (c).

also be brought by anyone "claiming to have had a right to be elected or returned at the election",[204] which appears to mean anyone at all on the electoral roll whether or not they offered themselves as candidates in that electoral district. Legal aid is not available for those involved in bringing an election petition.[205] An election petition must be presented to the High Court within 28 days of the public notification of the official results.[206] This requirement for a petition to be filed within a fixed, relatively short period of time of the result being announced is mandatory. In Australia it has been held to be an essential condition or jurisdictional requirement of any challenge to the election result. The time bar is designed to reflect the public interest in resolving expeditiously and with finality questions about disputed elections.[207]

The trial of an election petition takes place before three judges of the High Court named by the Chief Justice[208] under rules made for the purpose.[209] The trial takes place in open court and the court has jurisdiction to inquire into and adjudicate on any matter relating to the petition that it sees fit. It may direct a recount or scrutiny of some or all of the votes given at the election and, where another candidate claims to have been elected, may receive evidence rebutting that candidate's claim as if an election petition had been presented against that person's election.[210]

The decision of the High Court as to who was duly elected or whether the election was void is final and conclusive without any right of appeal.[211] The High Court (by majority if need be) certifies to the Speaker its determination as to whether the member whose election is in issue was duly elected, whether one of the other candidates was duly elected or whether the election in that district was void.[212] The court must also report on any allegations of corrupt or illegal practices that have been made in the petition and may also make a special report to the Speaker on any matters arising in the course of the trial that it considers should be submitted to the House.[213]

The Speaker presents the certificate and any accompanying report to the House. The House then orders them to be entered in its journals and gives any necessary directions for confirming or altering the return or for otherwise carrying out the determination.[214] If the original writ is required to be amended because the court certifies that a candidate other than the one originally returned was properly elected, the House may order the Chief Electoral Officer to attend with the writ and to amend it accordingly.[215] Where the court confirms the validity of the election of a sitting member, the court's certificate is merely entered in the journals without any other direction from the House.[216] No notice is required of a motion to enter the court's certificate in the journals.[217]

Party list seats

An electoral petition seeking a review of the procedures and methods used to allocate seats to political parties may be presented by the secretary of a party listed on the ballot paper. Such a petition must be presented to the Court of Appeal within 28 days of the declaration of the election of party list members.[218] The Court of Appeal then tries the petition. Any trial of an election petition relating to party list seats is concerned only with how the seats were allocated. No challenge to the fact that the vote of an elector was allowed or disallowed is permitted, nor may any allegation that corrupt or illegal practices have been engaged in at the election be made.[219]

---

[204] *Ibid.*, s.230(1)(b).
[205] *Legal Services Act* 2000, s.7(4)(b).
[206] *Electoral Act* 1993, s.231.
[207] *Rudolph v Lightfoot* (1999) 197 CLR 500 at 507, 508.
[208] *Electoral Act* 1993, s.235(1).
[209] *Electoral Act* 1993, s.234; *High Court Rules*, rules 796 to 818.
[210] *Electoral Act* 1993, s.236.
[211] *Ibid.*, s.242.

[212] *Ibid.*, s.243.
[213] *Ibid.*, ss.244 and 245.
[214] *Ibid.*, s.246(2).
[215] 1979, JHR, pp.44-5 (*Hunua election return*); 1987-90, JHR, p.693 (*Wairarapa election return*).
[216] 1982, JHR, pp.39-40 (*Taupo election return*).
[217] 1894, Vol.83, pp.18-9.
[218] *Electoral Act* 1993, ss.258 and 259.
[219] *Ibid.*, s.260.

The Court of Appeal determines whether the procedures used to allocate seats were correctly applied and consequently whether a valid return of members for party list seats has been made.[220] The court may make orders invalidating any candidate's return, declaring another candidate to have been elected or requiring the Chief Electoral Officer to repeat the allocation procedures for party list seats.[221]

VACANCIES

In addition to provisions disqualifying a person, otherwise qualified, from becoming a member of Parliament in the first place, there are a number of provisions that operate to disqualify a person who is already a member of Parliament from continuing to be a member and thus causing a supervening vacancy in the member's seat.

The following events cause the seat of a member of Parliament to become vacant:

Failing to attend the House.[222]
A member who fails, without the House's permission, to attend the House for one whole session of Parliament vacates his or her seat. Two members have lost their seats for failing to attend throughout a session.[223] The fact that a member who is in lawful detention stands in danger of losing his or her seat for not attending the House, is not a ground for relief against the consequences of that decision.[224] But disqualification on this ground is less likely to arise now given the longer parliamentary sessions (up to three years compared to up to one year formerly) throughout which a member would have to be absent to attract it and the House's more liberal rules on granting permission for members' absences. (See Chapter 3.)

Taking an oath or making a declaration or acknowledgement of allegiance to a foreign state, foreign head of state or foreign power or becoming, or becoming entitled to the rights, privileges or immunities of, a subject or citizen of a foreign state or power.[225]
These disqualifications are directly linked with the Oath of Allegiance that members must take before sitting or voting in the House. A violation of the allegiance proclaimed in the oath leads to the member's disqualification. It makes no difference that New Zealand has friendly relations with the foreign state or power concerned nor that New Zealand may share a Sovereign with the other country involved.[226] (In regard to a shared Sovereign, it may be doubted whether New Zealand does any longer share a Sovereign with those countries, for example, the United Kingdom, Australia and Canada, where the person of the Sovereign is the same. In New Zealand law the Sovereign is now Sovereign in right of New Zealand, a separate sovereignty from that of Her Majesty's other realms.) However, those self-governing states with special constitutional relationships with New Zealand – Cook Islands, Niue and Tokelau – are unlikely to be foreign states or powers to which the provision applies.

Dual nationality at the time of a member's election is not a disqualification, but voluntarily acquiring a foreign citizenship or the status attaching to a foreign citizenship subsequently may result in disqualification. Acquisition of a foreign citizenship or of the rights attaching to a foreign citizenship solely as a result of marriage does not disqualify the member.[227] Nor does a member who acquires another citizenship as a

---

[220] *Ibid.*, s.262(a), (b).
[221] *Ibid.*, s.262(c).
[222] *Ibid.*, s.55(1)(a).
[223] Thomas Fraser (Hampden) in 1862 and Patrick Charles Webb (Grey) in 1918.

[224] *Kunjan Nadar v State of Travancore-Cochin* AIR 1955 Travancore-Cochin 154.
[225] *Electoral Act* 1993, s.55(1)(b), (c).
[226] See, for example, *In re Wood* (1988) 167 CLR 145.
[227] *Electoral Act* 1993, s.55(2).

consequence of the member's birth in another country or because of another country's rules on acquisition of citizenship by descent thereby vacate his or her seat.[228] To incur disqualification a member must have taken some positive action to acquire the foreign citizenship concerned. A member who renews a passport or travel document issued to the member before his or her election does not thereby lose his or her seat,[229] though if the process of renewal involves taking an oath or making a declaration of allegiance to that foreign state, the member may incur a disqualification.

Becoming an honorary consul for a foreign state is not incompatible with membership of the House. A number of members have acted as honorary consuls for foreign states.[230] One member continued to act as an honorary consul after becoming a Minister.[231]

Ceasing to be a New Zealand citizen.[232]
This disqualification is the counterpart to the requirement that a person cannot be elected to Parliament unless he or she is a New Zealand citizen.[233] A member who subsequently loses his or her New Zealand citizenship also ceases to be a member of Parliament. New Zealand citizenship can be lost by voluntary renunciation.[234] A person can also be deprived of New Zealand citizenship where he or she acquires another citizenship and acts in a manner contrary to the interests of New Zealand or where the person originally acquired New Zealand citizenship fraudulently.[235] The mere fact that a person acquires a foreign citizenship does not affect that person's New Zealand citizenship, though a member voluntarily acquiring another citizenship would incur disqualification in any case.

Accepting nomination as, agreeing to be a candidate for election as, or agreeing to appointment as a member of Parliament of any other country or a governing body of any association of states exercising governing powers.[236]
Agreeing to become a candidate for election to a foreign legislature (whether at a national, state, territory or municipal level) automatically vacates a member's seat.

So too does agreeing to become a member of a governing body of an association of countries, states, territories or municipalities of which New Zealand is not a member which exercises governing powers. The instance of such an association given in the legislation itself is the European Union. Thus a member of Parliament agreeing to be a candidate for election to the European Parliament or to be appointed to the European Commission would thereby vacate his or her seat.

Conviction of a crime punishable by imprisonment for a term of at least two years.[237]
This disqualification applies regardless of the term of imprisonment to which the member is actually sentenced. If the crime of which the member is convicted carries a possible sentence of at least two years' imprisonment, the seat becomes vacant. A person who is discharged without conviction (which is deemed to be an acquittal)[238] would not be disqualified. In the United Kingdom a successful appeal against conviction was held to remove any incapacity to sit created by the conviction and, where the vacancy caused by the original conviction had not yet been filled, the court, in an endeavour to remove

---

[228] *Ibid.*, s.55AA(a).

[229] *Ibid.*, s.55AA(b).

[230] See, for example: *New Zealand Gazette*, 1 February 1945, p.1 (Czechoslovakia); 1950, Vol.289, p.518 (Panama); "MP will be Monaco's man in NZ", *The New Zealand Herald*, 5 February 2003.

[231] Sir Clifton Webb, first appointed as consul for Panama in 1944, continued in that role after becoming a Minister in 1949. See: Belshaw, *A Man of Integrity*

– *A Biography of Sir Clifton Webb*, pp.77-8; 1950, Vol.289, pp.518, 523.

[232] *Electoral Act* 1993, s.55(1)(ca).

[233] *Ibid.*, s.47(3).

[234] *Citizenship Act* 1977, s.15.

[235] *Ibid.*, ss.16 and 17.

[236] *Electoral Act* 1993, s.55(1)(cb).

[237] *Ibid.*, s.55(1)(d).

[238] *Sentencing Act* 2002, s.106.

all penalties flowing from the conviction, restored the member to office.[239]   In New Zealand, conviction creates an immediate vacancy rather than a continuing incapacity to sit (though serving a term of imprisonment thereby imposed may create an incapacity to sit).   Nevertheless, a successful appeal against conviction would seem to remove the justification for disqualification in the first place and the same principles for avoiding the loss of a member's seat, if this was still possible, may apply in New Zealand. A finding of contempt of court is not conviction of a crime and a member found in contempt does not vacate his or her seat.[240]

The registrar of a court in which a member is convicted is obliged to advise the Speaker of the conviction within 48 hours.[241]

Conviction of a corrupt electoral practice or being reported by the High Court in its report on the trial of an election petition to have been guilty of a corrupt practice.[242]
The same principles for avoiding disqualification in the case of a successful appeal of a conviction of a corrupt electoral practice as were discussed above in regard to conviction for a crime would seem to apply, if this is still possible.

Becoming a public servant.[243]
A member becoming a public servant thereby vacates his or her seat. Where a person continues to sit knowing that his or her seat has become vacant on this ground, he or she is, in addition to the loss of the seat, liable to a fine of $400 for each day the member sits.[244]

Resigning the seat by signing a written notice addressed and delivered to the Speaker.[245]
In the early days of parliamentary government in New Zealand, resignation was very common. (There were 46 resignations in the fourth Parliament between 1866 and 1870, out of a House of 70, including one member who resigned on two occasions during the course of that Parliament. One member resigned parliamentary seats on five occasions in the course of his career.[246]) Resignation subsequently became less common but has been increasing in frequency especially among party list members since the introduction of the MMP electoral system.

Members may, if they wish, pledge to resign in certain circumstances, such as if a majority of electors call on them to do so[247] or if they leave their party. But such pledges are not legally enforceable.[248] It is regarded as a contempt of the House for anyone to offer a financial inducement to a member to resign[249] or to attempt to procure a member to resign by threats or by using other improper means. But merely calling on a member to resign for a supposed breach of an election promise or for other reasons is part of political debate.

A member's reasons for resigning are no concern of the Speaker. Nor is the Speaker concerned with the circumstances that caused a member to resign (though if improper conduct was involved, the House may wish to inquire whether a contempt has been committed). The Speaker cannot refuse to receive a written resignation on the ground that the member has been subject to undue influence,[250] though the Speaker may privately counsel the member before the resignation is tendered.

A resignation must be unequivocal. It is direct advice to the Speaker that the member

---

[239] *Attorney-General v Jones* [2000] QB 66.
[240] 2004, Vol.616, p.12365; "Hon Dr Nick Smith MP – finding of contempt", Clerk of the House of Representatives, 6 April 2004.
[241] *Electoral Act* 1993, s.57.
[242] *Ibid.*, ss.55(1)(d).
[243] *Ibid.*, ss.55(1)(e).
[244] *Ibid.*, s.48.
[245] *Ibid.*, s.55(1)(f).
[246] Thomas Dick (City of Dunedin three times, Port Chalmers twice).
[247] Woodward, *The Age of Reform*, pp.95-6.
[248] 1996-99, AJHR, I.15B.
[249] 1998, Vol.574, p.14721.
[250] *Vikram Singh v Shri Ram Ballabhji Kajat* AIR 1995 Madhya Pradesh 140.

is resigning his or her seat. Resignation cannot be construed from a series of documents. It must itself be self-contained in a single notice.[251] Once a member has given the Speaker written notice of resignation, the notice takes effect according to its tenor. It cannot be withdrawn after it has taken effect. Unless postdated, resignation is effective immediately on receipt by the Speaker. At that point the member's seat becomes vacant. But members often give written notice of resignation to take effect on a future day. A postdated resignation could be withdrawn before it takes effect, whether the Speaker has already informed the House of its receipt or not. No formal steps to fill a vacancy caused by resignation are taken until the notice takes effect.

Member's election being declared void on an election petition.[252] (See pp. 26–8.)

Death.[253]
The registrar by whom a member's death is registered is obliged to notify the registration to the Speaker within 12 hours.[254]

Becoming mentally disordered.[255]
A member who is made the subject of a compulsory treatment order or is detained in a hospital under an in-patient order is subject to disqualification on the grounds of mental disorder.[256] The Speaker must be advised as soon as may be of either of those circumstances occurring.[257] A medical examination after not less than six months' detention must be made before the Speaker may declare the seat vacant for mental disorder.[258]

The occurrence of any one of these events causes the member concerned to lose the seat. But these are all events which must occur after the member's election in order to be relevant. They do not in themselves disqualify a person from seeking and securing election to the House in the first place (though some of them, such as New Zealand citizenship, are common to the rules qualifying a person for election to the House). In exceptional circumstances, Parliament has by legislation removed a disqualification that has been incurred so as to permit a member to remain in Parliament.[259]

All members vacate office at the close of polling day for the next election,[260] and these vacancies are filled at the ensuing general election.

FILLING VACANCIES

Determining that a vacancy exists
The responsibility for setting in train the machinery for filling a vacancy in the membership of the House rests with the Speaker. The Speaker is enjoined to act, without delay, to fill a vacancy (whether the vacancy is for an electoral district or arising from a party list) when satisfied that a seat has become vacant.[261] In most cases the Speaker makes the judgment that a vacancy exists unprompted on receiving the relevant information or formal advice. However, both the House and the courts may have a role in establishing or helping to establish for the Speaker that a vacancy in fact exists.

As far as the House is concerned the Speaker has indicated that before taking the

---

[251] 1996-99, AJHR, I.15B.
[252] *Electoral Act* 1993, s.55(1)(g).
[253] *Ibid.*, s.55(1)(h).
[254] *Ibid.*, s.58.
[255] *Ibid.*, s.55(1)(i).
[256] *Electoral* Act 1993, s.56; *Mental Health (Compulsory Assessment and Treatment) Act* 1992,

Part 2.
[257] *Electoral Act* 1993, s.56(1), (2).
[258] *Ibid.*, s.56(4).
[259] *Finance Act* 1941, s.37; *Electoral (Vacancies) Amendment Act* 2003, ss.4 and 5.
[260] *Electoral Act* 1993, s.54(1)(b), (2)(b).
[261] *Ibid.*, ss.129(1) and 134(1).

drastic step of declaring the seat of a sitting member to be vacant, the Speaker will give the member concerned leeway to argue to the contrary.[262] In a doubtful case this may involve the Speaker referring the matter to the Privileges Committee for consideration.[263] The Speaker's decision on whether a vacancy exists would then be informed by the report of the Privileges Committee and the House's consideration of that report. The Speaker has delayed taking a decision in such circumstances to permit the committee to report and the House to debate the report.[264] Ultimately, however, the statutory duty of determining whether a vacancy exists is the Speaker's, not the House's.[265]

It is conceivable that, in an appropriate case, a court of competent jurisdiction could declare that a member's seat had become vacant. This will arise most obviously in regard to electoral petitions where the High Court (for constituency members) and the Court of Appeal (for party list members) may declare a member's election void, thus establishing a vacancy. Indeed where the attack is on the validity of the member's election in the first place, this is the only means of establishing that there is a vacancy. A court has also considered the question of a vacancy arising subsequent to a member's election on specific statutory referral by Parliament. Thus the Court of Appeal was asked to certify if a particular member's seat had become vacant for bankruptcy.[266] But it is also conceivable that the question of whether a member was disqualified could arise for resolution incidentally by a court (for example, on a prosecution for sitting as a member after becoming a public servant, if there was a dispute as to whether the member had in fact become a public servant) or directly if a declaration as to the member's status was sought,[267] though the court might consider in the latter case that this was a matter for the Speaker or the House to determine, at least initially, rather than the court to rule on.

The House itself claims the power of determining the qualifications of its members to sit and vote in the House and a question relating to this may be considered by the House as a question of privilege. (See Chapter 46.) The House's determination of the right of a person to sit and vote in the House may lead the Speaker to initiate the provisions for the filling of a vacancy or confirm that there is no vacancy to fill.[268] No question as to the validity of the House's procedures arises from the fact that a member continues to sit and participate in its proceedings after incurring a disqualification.[269]

Electoral district vacancies

In the case of a vacancy arising among the members representing electoral districts, the vacancy is filled by a by-election.

The Speaker must publish a notice of the vacancy in the *New Zealand Gazette*.[270] The Speaker also advises the House of the vacancy, though if the House is not sitting at the time the vacancy arises, such advice may not be communicated until after the publication of the notice or, indeed, until after the vacancy has been filled. The Governor-General is obliged within 21 days of the publication of a vacancy notice to issue a writ to the Chief Electoral Officer directing that official to make all necessary arrangements for the conduct of a by-election to fill the vacancy.[271] This direction appoints a date (which must be a Saturday) for polling.[272] The Governor-General may by Order in Council postpone the issue of a writ for a by-election for up to 42 days after the publication of the vacancy.[273] A by-election has also been postponed for a few weeks by specific legislation.[274] The rules

---

[262] 2003, Vol.610, pp.7636, 7749.

[263] *Ibid.*

[264] *Ibid.*, p.7749.

[265] *Electoral Act* 1993, ss.129(1) and 134(1) (as amended in 2001).

[266] *Awarua Seat Inquiry Act* 1897.

[267] See, for example: *In re Wood* (1988) 167 CLR 145; *Sue v Hill* (1999) 199 CLR 462 at 568 (per Kirby J, dissenting).

[268] See, for example, 1996-99, AJHR, I.15B.

[269] *Vardon v O'Loughlin* (1907) 5 CLR 201; *In re Wood* (1988) 167 CLR 145.

[270] *Electoral Act* 1993, s.129(1).

[271] *Ibid.*, s.129(2).

[272] *Ibid.*, Sch.2, form 6.

[273] *Ibid.*, s.129(3).

[274] *Patea By-election Act* 1954.

for conducting a by-election and returning the writ are similar to those for conducting a general election. The main difference is that there is no party vote.

Party list vacancies

In the case of a vacancy arising among members elected from a party list, the vacancy is filled from the party list.

The Speaker publishes a notice of the vacancy in the *New Zealand Gazette*.[275] The Speaker also advises the House of the vacancy, as for a vacancy among constituency members. As soon as practicable after the publication of the notice the Governor-General must direct the Chief Electoral Officer to proceed to fill the vacancy.[276] The Chief Electoral Officer then asks the secretary of the party concerned if the next-ranked unelected candidate on the list of the party to which the member vacating the seat belonged (whether or not the vacating member still belonged to that party when the vacancy occurred) remains a member of the party. If he or she does, the Chief Electoral Officer then inquires of that person if he or she is still willing to be a member of Parliament. If that person is no longer willing to be a member or is no longer alive, then the next candidate on the list is approached and so on, until a candidate from that party's list is found who is still a member of the party and is willing to take up the vacant seat. If there is no such candidate willing to do so, the seat remains vacant until the next general election.[277] The Chief Electoral Officer declares the new member elected by publishing a notice in the *New Zealand Gazette* and files a return with the Clerk of the House or indicates that the vacancy cannot be filled, as the case may be.[278]

Vacancies not filled in certain circumstances

Where a vacancy occurs in the period between a dissolution of Parliament and the close of polling day, it is not filled.[279]

The House also has power to dispense with the holding of a by-election or the filling of a party list vacancy in two circumstances. These are if Parliament is due to expire within six months of the vacancy arising or if the Prime Minister informs the House in writing that a general election is to be held within six months of the occurrence of the vacancy. In either of these cases the House can, by a resolution passed by a majority of 75 percent of all members, direct that no steps be taken to fill the vacancy.[280]

It may be that where the procedure for filling a vacancy caused by the conviction of a member for a crime or corrupt practice has been put in train it could be cancelled by order of a court where that conviction is overturned on appeal.[281] (See pp. 29–30.) Otherwise, the standard procedures for filling a vacancy in the membership of the House can be set aside only by special legislation. This occurred in 1943 and 1987 when all by-elections were dispensed with for the remainder of those Parliaments.[282]

---

[275] *Electoral Act* 1993, 134(1).
[276] *Ibid.*, s.134(2).
[277] *Ibid.*, s.137.
[278] *Ibid.*, s.138.
[279] *Ibid.*, ss.129(4) and 134(3).

[280] *Electoral Act* 1993, ss.131 and 136; 1996, Vol.555, pp.12542-62.
[281] *Attorney-General v Jones* [2000] QB 66.
[282] *By-elections Postponement Act* 1943, s.2(1); *Electoral Amendment Act (No 2)* 1987, s.2.

CHAPTER 3

MEMBERS' CONDITIONS OF SERVICE

DESIGNATION OF MEMBERS

Members of the House of Representatives are known as "members of Parliament", abbreviated to "MP".[1] They have had this designation since 1907 when their previous abbreviated designation "MHR" was altered as part of a general set of changes to official titles consequent on the acquisition of Dominion status.[2]

ROLE OF MEMBERS

A member of Parliament holds a statutory office. Members are not (except for certain tax purposes) employees in an employment relationship, nor are they subject to any contractual obligations in regard to their duties.[3]

There is no prescribed description of the role of a member of Parliament. The office to which members are elected has a considerable amount of legal freedom guaranteed to it so that members themselves have the capacity to carry out the duties of the office as they see fit and indeed are able largely to define what the duties of that office are. The most visible aspect of the office is the ability to sit and vote in the House of Representatives after having taken the oath required by law.[4] Other parliamentary aspects of the office are the ability to participate in parliamentary proceedings conducted outside the House itself, such as serving on committees, presenting petitions, asking written questions and lodging notices of bills for introduction and motions for debate.

Members of Parliament are representatives for the citizenry both in relation to business transacted in Parliament and more generally, especially in dealings with organs of central, and even local, government. This applies both to the members elected to represent electoral districts and the party list members. All members to a greater or lesser extent make themselves available to assist with resolving individual problems, whether by making representations to a Minister or a department or simply taking the trouble to sift through the problem presented to them and giving advice on how it could be resolved. Electorate members have an obvious geographic focus for this work based on the electoral districts they represent. But most party list members assume a similar constituency focus for their work too, with their party allocating them responsibility for representing the party in a particular locality.[5] A survey in the early 1980s (when all members were constituency members) suggested that at least 30 percent of a member's time was spent on constituency work.[6] Indeed, members have been described as, first and foremost, local representatives, social workers and 'fix-its'.[7] Members may also assume profiles that cut across physical boundaries by cultivating roles as advocates for particular activities or groups, often with a nationwide profile.

Members are generally elected in a party's interest. They have strong obligations of loyalty to the party which nominated them and whose support they received to assist them

---

[1] *Electoral Act* 1993, s.27.
[2] *Parliamentary and Executive Titles Act* 1907; see Wilson, *New Zealand Parliamentary Record 1840–1984*, p.176.
[3] 1968, Vol.359, p.3777; *State Chamber of Commerce and Industry v Commonwealth of Australia* (1987) 163 CLR 329.
[4] *Constitution Act* 1986, s.11.

[5] See, for example: "Labour list MPs to set up shop in electorates", *The Dominion*, 26 November 1996; "Electorate jobs for Alliance MPs", *The Dominion*, 3 December 1996.
[6] Martin, *The House – New Zealand's House of Representatives 1854-2004*, p.299.
[7] Sinclair, *Walter-Nash*, p.86 (though this was written well before the advent of party list members).

to secure election. These obligations involve attending meetings of caucus and serving on caucus committees as well as participating in party activities generally, both in the locality that they represent and in other locations. Participation in political activities while holding office, even ministerial office, is inherent in the positions that members hold.[8] There will thus be strong expectations that, as members of a political party, members of Parliament will co-ordinate their political activities with those of their party and generally act in concert with the party in respect of matters of party political significance. Ultimately, if there are any differences, these are matters for the party and the individual members to resolve between themselves.

Statutory functions and disqualifications

Occasionally, statute may impose a particular role, duty or even disqualification on a member of Parliament *ex officio*. For example, the Speaker has a number of statutory duties arising out of holding that parliamentary office, most notably as chairperson of the Parliamentary Service Commission and as responsible Minister for a number of offices of state. (See Chapters 4 and 5.) Members elected for the Māori electoral districts automatically become members of the Māori Purposes Fund Board[9] and of the Ngarimu V.C. and 28th (Māori) Battalion Memorial Scholarship Fund Board.[10] The member representing Nelson is a member of the Cawthron Institute Trust Board.[11] The members who serve on the statutory Intelligence and Security Committee do so in their capacity as members of Parliament.[12]

Members have a statutory right to enter a prison and examine it and the condition of its prisoners. They may inform the manager of the prison of any matter that they observe and such information is to be recorded.[13] Prisoners are entitled to have access to a member of Parliament[14] and telephone calls between a prisoner and a member may not be monitored by the prison authorities.[15] Communications between members and persons subject to compulsory care under the intellectual disability legislation must not be withheld.[16]

An oath or declaration may be made before a member of Parliament.[17] Conversely, a member of Parliament may not be appointed as a member of a statutory entity or of a Crown entity company.[18] (Though, in respect of a statutory entity whose members are elected to it, a member of Parliament may be elected to office in the entity but is not entitled to any extra remuneration in respect of such service.[19]) However, members may be appointed to serve on the boards of other types of entity.[20]

But these statutory examples of a member's role are not numerous and do not amount to a comprehensive description of the role of a member of Parliament. As far as statute and parliamentary rules are concerned, such a description does not exist.

DUTIES OF MEMBERS

The fundamental obligation of a member of Parliament has been said to be "the duty to serve" and, in serving, to act with fidelity and with a single-mindedness for the welfare of the community.[21]

From time to time there have been suggestions that the House should be specific about

---

8   See, generally, *Vidadala Harinadhababu v N T Ramarao* AIR 1990 Andra Pradesh 20.

9   *Maori Purposes Fund Act* 1934-35, s.7(2)(c).

10 *Ngarimu V.C. and 28th (Maori) Battalion Memorial Scholarship Fund* Act 1945, s.4(2).

11 *Thomas Cawthron Trust Act* 1924, s.3(1)(a)(iii).

12 *Intelligence and Security Committee Act* 1996, s.7(4).

13 *Corrections Act* 2004, s.161.

14 *Ibid.*, s.69(1)(e).

15 *Ibid.*, s.114.

16 *Intellectual Disability (Compulsory Care and Rehabilitation) Act* 2003, s.58.

17 *Oaths and Declarations Act* 1957, ss.6(3) and 9(1)(g).

18 *Crown Entities Act* 2004, ss.30(2)(f) and 89(3).

19 *Ibid.*, ss.30(3) and 47(2)(b).

20 See, for example, *New Zealand Gazette*, 30 June 2005, p.2377 (member appointed to the Council of Legal Education).

21 *R v Boston* (1923) 33 CLR 386 at 400 (per Isaacs and Rich JJ).

members' duties and adopt a statement setting out a code of conduct or ethical principles that it expects its members to follow in carrying on their parliamentary and other roles. A number of Commonwealth legislatures, especially in Australia, have done this. In 1997 the Government Administration Committee in a special report sought the House's authority to carry out an inquiry that could have included consideration of whether a code of conduct was desirable.[22] No inquiry resulted from this report. Except in the case of financial interests, the House has not adopted any detailed ethical guidelines for its members, taking the view that advice about appropriate behaviour is primarily a matter for induction training and internal party discipline.[23] Ethical rules that apply to members tend to be ad hoc or indirect. Thus, a member who accepts or solicits a bribe commits a crime[24] and the House's contempt powers (for example, the rule concerning bribery) do set some rules for members that have an ethical content. (See Chapter 47.)

In the case of Ministers there are more developed conduct guidelines to which, as Ministers, they are expected to conform. Ministers on appointment take an oath or make an affirmation as members of the Executive Council promising to give their counsel and advice for the good management of the affairs of New Zealand.[25] The *Cabinet Manual* sets out guidelines on the public duties which apply to Ministers. Apart from being under an obligation to declare any personal interests in matters under consideration by Cabinet (see below), Ministers are restricted in the extent to which they may receive fees or gifts and are prohibited from engaging in activities that may be construed as endorsing a commercial product.[26] As occasion requires, ministerial guidelines may be issued by the Cabinet or the Prime Minister to deal with particular circumstances that have arisen (such as the conduct to be observed by Ministers involved in mayoral election campaigns[27]). However, these ministerial codes of conduct are political guidelines adopted by Governments to guide their own conduct. They have no statutory origin and are not regarded as being legally enforceable. Their significance depends upon the sense of commitment to public office held by Ministers and on their political responsibility to Parliament and public opinion.[28]

While no comprehensive statements of members' duties have been adopted, even as guidelines, the law does recognise that members, as the holders of a high public office, have duties of conduct that inescapably accompany that status. Insofar as these duties apply to the transaction of parliamentary business (in the House or at select committees) they are matters for the House itself, rather than a court, to supervise.[29] But in their dealings outside the House, whether with constituents, government officials, or lobbyists, members may still act in the capacity of members of Parliament.[30] If in these interactions they act in a way that brings their own personal interests into conflict with their public duties, the law may provide a counter to such an impropriety, for example, by holding a contract for a member's benefit to be void.[31]

MEMBERS' LENGTH OF SERVICE

The member with the longest-ever service in the House of Representatives is the Hon Rex Mason who was continuously re-elected as a member for Auckland constituencies from 1926 until his retirement in 1966. But even his length of service is eclipsed by that of Captain William Baillie, who was appointed to the Legislative Council in 1861 and died still a member in 1922, making him easily New Zealand's longest serving parliamentarian. (Appointment to the Legislative Council was for life until 1891 when a seven-year term

---

22 1996-99, AJHR, I.5B.
23 2002-05, AJHR, I.18B, p.23.
24 *Crimes Act* 1961, s.103(1).
25 *Oaths and Declarations Act* 1957, s.19.
26 *Cabinet Manual*, 2001, paras.2.46 to 2.77.
27 1995, Vol.550, p.9204.
28 *Vidadala Harinadhababu v N T Ramarao* AIR 1990

Andra Pradesh 20.
29 *Wilkinson v Osborne* (1915) 21 CLR 89 at 94; *R v Boston* (1923) 33 CLR 386 at 403.
30 *R v Boston, ibid.*
31 *Wilkinson v Osborne* (1915) 21 CLR 89; *Horne v Barber* (1920) 27 CLR 494.

was substituted but existing councillors retained their lifetime appointments. Baillie was the last of the life members.)

By way of contrast, Henry Jackson (Hutt) was a member for only just over one month in 1879, having been elected at a by-election just before Parliament was dissolved following the defeat of the Grey ministry in a vote of confidence. William Henry Cutten (Taieri) was re-elected to the House in 1878, some 23 years after having resigned his seat, the longest gap in service of a member of Parliament.

Traditionally the member with the longest period of continuous service (that is, service that is unbroken up to the present time) is regarded as the "Father of the House". Where members are elected at the same time, this accolade is accorded to the first of them to be sworn in as a member. The designation is entirely honorific. No duties or entitlements attach to it, though the first Father of the House, Hugh Carleton, the first member to be elected to the House in the staggered election of 1853, presided over the House when it assembled in 1854 until a Speaker was elected. Carleton was recognised as Father of the House until his retirement in 1870.[32]

ATTENDANCE OF MEMBERS

Penalties for failure to attend

Members are under obligations imposed by statute to attend meetings of the House; failure to do so can lead to penalties.

A member who fails to attend the House throughout an entire session without being granted leave of absence loses his or her seat, which thereupon becomes vacant.[33] A member who loses his or her seat in this way is eligible for re-election at the ensuing by-election. Two members have forfeited their seats under this provision – one who failed to attend throughout the 1862 session, and another who was court-martialled and imprisoned during the First World War for refusing to obey a superior officer, and who was thereby prevented from attending the House during one of the two sessions of Parliament held in 1918. A motion to grant the latter member leave of absence while he was in prison was defeated.[34] In 1942, when the Hon Walter Nash, the Minister of Finance, was appointed Representative in Washington, special legislation was passed to prevent his absence resulting in his seat becoming vacant.[35]

A member who is absent from the House for more than 14 sitting days in any session without leave of absence has a deduction of $10 made from his or her salary for every day (exclusive of those 14) during which the member has been absent. No expenses are payable in respect of any such day either.[36]

A member who persistently absents himself or herself from the House may be ordered by the House to attend. Failure to obey such an order would be a contempt.[37]

Leave of absence

The Standing Orders no longer require members to attend the House and the House does not have, and has no need for, any formal procedures for granting leave of absence or for recording members' attendances. If any member did require leave of absence so as to avoid a statutory penalty, this would need to be given by motion on notice.

A member who has been granted leave of absence for a period of time may return to the House and take his or her seat within that period. In these circumstances the remainder

---

[32] Martin, *The House – New Zealand's House of Representatives 1854-2004*, p.34.
[33] *Electoral Act* 1993, s.55(1)(a).
[34] 1918, Session I, JHR, p.24.
[35] *Overseas Representatives Act* 1942, s.3.
[36] *Civil List Act* 1979, s.20.
[37] 2002-05, AJHR, I.18B, p.81.

of the leave granted to the member is cancelled.[38]   Leave of absence may be granted to an elected member who has not yet taken the Oath of Allegiance and, therefore, a seat in the House, because such a person is a member of Parliament with all the privileges of a member except those of sitting and voting in the House.[39]

It is a well-established convention that members do not refer to the absence of members during the course of debates in the House.

The Speaker is permitted to waive the requirement that an independent member or the member of a party consisting of a single member be present within the parliamentary precincts to have a vote recorded in a case of the member's illness or other family cause of a personal nature or so as to enable the member to attend to other public business.[40]   This is not a general leave of absence; it merely enables a member's vote to be counted even though the member or the member's party is not within the parliamentary precincts.

Requirements for members to be present

There is no quorum in the House. The House's previous requirement for a quorum (15 members in a House of 99 members) was abolished in 1996.[41]   The House had not actually been counted out for want of a quorum since 1905.[42]   But though there is no quorum requirement, there must be a Minister present during all sitting hours of the House. If there is no Minister present, the sitting is interrupted and the bell is rung. If no Minister appears within five minutes of the bell being rung, the House automatically adjourns until the next sitting day.[43]   A sitting has been adjourned as a result of the absence of a Minister from the House.[44]   A motion to suspend the Standing Orders can only be moved without notice if at least 60 members are present at the time,[45] and in any case no decision can be reached on a personal vote if fewer than 20 members participate in it.[46]

(A quorum of half the membership of the committee is prescribed for a select committee meeting.[47])

PECUNIARY INTERESTS

It is a crime for a member of Parliament to accept or agree or attempt to accept a bribe in his or her capacity as a member of Parliament.[48]   This offence applies to bribes relating to business to be transacted in Parliament but it also extends beyond parliamentary business to other activities engaged in by members in the capacity of a member (such as constituency duties and *ex officio* statutory duties). Nor is the offence confined to actions that may be engaged in exclusively by members of Parliament. It can be committed by a member accepting or soliciting payment for an action which would be lawful if carried out by someone who is not a member of Parliament.[49]   Members of Parliament are required to conform to a higher ethical standard in matters pecuniary.

The House may treat the receipt or solicitation by members of bribes and the receipt of fees for professional services in respect of parliamentary business, as contempts.[50]   Thus a member who received payment for work he had done drafting two local bills was held to have committed a contempt, even though he had done the work before he entered Parliament.[51]   Members must be careful to keep their official and private capacities quite separate in their business dealings so that no misunderstanding may result.[52]   While

---

[38]   PD 1861-63, pp.736-7.
[39]   1887, Vol.59, p.359.
[40]   S.O.156(4)(d).
[41]   1993-96, AJHR, I.18A, pp.23-4.
[42]   1905, JHR, p.51.
[43]   S.O.38.
[44]   2005, Vol.624, pp.19676-7.
[45]   S.O.4(2).
[46]   S.O.152.
[47]   S.O.210(1).
[48]   *Crimes Act* 1961, s.103(1).
[49]   See *Attorney of Ceylon v De Livera* [1963] AC 103.
[50]   S.O.395(i) and (j).
[51]   1877, JHR, p.202.
[52]   1991, Vol.519, p.4541.

members may solicit funds for policies or programmes in return for their votes (known as "pork-barrel politics"), they may not seek a benefit for themselves or for other persons to whom they are related in return for their votes.[53] It has been suggested that a code of conduct regulating the dealings between members and officials and Ministers should be adopted.[54]

Registration of pecuniary interests

Many legislatures (either by statute or under their own rules) require members to make periodic returns of pecuniary interests for publication in a register. Proposals to establish a register of members' pecuniary interests in New Zealand have been discussed since at least 1986.[55] The failure to agree at that time on a parliamentary register led the Government of the day to establish its own register of Ministers' interests in 1990. (See p. 44.) In 2005 the House adopted Standing Orders (replacing proposals for legislation)[56] requiring members to make annual returns of their pecuniary interests for publication in a register.[57]

Contents of returns of interests
The interests that must be disclosed consist of information falling into two broad categories – matters which exist at the date on which the return must be made (assets and liabilities), and events which have occurred over the 12-month period preceding that date (activities). In no case is the actual value of any asset, payment, interest, gift, contribution or debt required to be disclosed.[58]

Those interests in the nature of assets and liabilities that must be disclosed are[59]—

- names of companies of which the member is a director or controls more than five percent of the voting rights relating to control of the company
- names of companies or business entities (entities operating for profit) in which the member has a pecuniary interest, but not including interests arising indirectly because a member has an interest in a company or entity that in turn has an interest in another company or entity[60]
- the name of any employer of the member (this does not include being a member or a Minister); a description of the main business activities of any company, business entity or employer so identified must also be given
- each trust in which the member has a beneficial interest
- the name of any organisation of whose governing body the member is a member or of any trust of which the member is a trustee if the organisation or trust receives or has applied to receive funding from the Crown, a Crown entity or a State enterprise (unless the organisation or trust is itself a government department, a Crown entity or a State enterprise)
- the location of each parcel of real property in which the member has a pecuniary interest, unless the member has no beneficial interest in that property
- each superannuation scheme registered under the *Superannuation Schemes Act* 1989 in which the member has a pecuniary interest
- each debtor who owes the member more than $50,000
- each creditor to whom the member owes more than $50,000.

---

[53] 2003, Vol.606, p.3551.
[54] *Report of the Controller and Auditor-General on Inquiry into Public Funding of Organisations Associated with Donna Awatere Huata MP*, November 2003.
[55] 1986-87, AJHR, I.18A.

[56] 2002-05, AJHR, I.22D, p.865 (*Members of Parliament (Pecuniary Interests) Bill*).
[57] S.O.164.
[58] Appendix B to the Standing Orders, cl.9.
[59] *Ibid.*, cl.4(1).
[60] *Ibid.*, cl.4(2).

In the case of debts outstanding, a description of each debt must be given. If the rate of interest charged on a debt is less than that currently prescribed by regulation as the notional rate of interest for tax purposes on employment-related loans, that rate must also be disclosed.[61] But a member does not have to disclose information relating to a debt outstanding (as a debtor or a creditor) between the member and the member's spouse or domestic partner or any parent, child, step-child, foster-child or grandchild of the member.[62] Nor is a member required to disclose short-term (under 90 days) debts for goods or services.[63]

Interests in the nature of activities in which the member has been engaged in the relevant preceding period are[64]—

- countries travelled to – the name, purpose of travel and details of who contributed to the travel or accommodation costs incurred must be given; however, where such costs were paid in full by the member himself or herself, or by the member's spouse or domestic partner, any parent, child, step-child, foster-child or grandchild of the member, or by the Crown, or by any other government where the primary purpose of the travel was in connection with an official parliamentary visit, the travel does not need to be disclosed[65]
- gifts with an estimated market value of more than $500 and the names of the donors of those gifts (if known or reasonably ascertainable by the member); gifts include hospitality and cash donations but do not include donations for election expenses
- debts of more than $500 owing by the member that were discharged or paid (in whole or in part) by some other person
- descriptions of each other payment received by the member for activities in which the member was involved (other than the salary or allowances of a member of Parliament).

The period covered by these "activities" is generally the 12-month period preceding the date on which the return must be made.[66] However, information given on any previous return does not need to be given again and only activities since a previous return need to be disclosed.[67] In the case of members on first being elected to Parliament at a general election, and in the case of members elected at a by-election or otherwise returned to fill a vacancy arising on a party list, the "activities" return is confined to the period commencing with their election or return to Parliament.[68]

Where a member is re-elected at a general election the period of the return extends back to the preceding 1 February to retain the continuity of returns from that member.[69] (But not in the case of members re-elected at the 2005 general election when the register first came into existence. Each member's returns are confined to the period commencing with polling day for that election.[70])

Timing and manner of making returns

There are two types of returns of interests that members must make – initial returns and annual returns.

An *initial* return must be made by all members as at the date that is 90 days after the date on which they take the oath or make the affirmation required of all members on taking their seats in Parliament.[71] Members have 30 days from that date to submit their

---

[61] *Ibid.*, cl.4(3).
[62] *Ibid.*, cl.5.
[63] *Ibid.*, cl.6.
[64] *Ibid.*, cl.7(1).
[65] *Ibid.*, cl.7(2).
[66] *Ibid.*, cl.8(1).

[67] *Ibid.*, cl.8(2)(a) and (e).
[68] *Ibid.*, cl.8(2)(h) and (d).
[69] *Ibid.*, cl.8(2)(c).
[70] *Supplementary order paper 381*, 2 August 2005; 2005, Vol.627, pp.22357-64.
[71] Appendix B to the Standing Orders, cl.2(1).

returns.[72] However, no initial return is required to be made if the general election or by-election at which the member is elected is held after 1 July or if the member is declared elected to fill a list vacancy after 1 July in any year.[73] In such cases the first or next return that the member makes will be the annual return due in the following year.

An *annual* return of pecuniary interests as at 31 January each year must be made by every member by 28 February that year.[74]

In all cases returns are made either on forms specially prescribed by the House or, in the absence of such prescription, in a form approved by the registrar.[75] The obligation to make a return by the due date falls on the member himself or herself. The registrar is not required to notify a member of the member's failure to transmit a return by the due date or to obtain a return from the member.[76]

Register of pecuniary interests

A register called the *Register of Pecuniary Interests of Members of Parliament* is established consisting of all returns transmitted by members.[77] The registrar is the Deputy Clerk or a person appointed by the Clerk of the House with the agreement of the Speaker.[78] The first registrar to be appointed is a former Ombudsman.[79] The registrar is required to compile and maintain the register and to provide advice and guidance to members in connection with their obligations to make returns of pecuniary interests.[80] A booklet communicating to members their obligations under the Standing Orders is to be produced.[81] However, the registrar is not required to notify members of their failure to comply with their obligations to make returns of their interests or of any errors or omissions in their returns.[82]

Publication of register

Members have 90 days from the date as at which an initial return must be made and one month from the date (31 January) as at which an annual return must be made to make their returns to the registrar. The registrar has 90 days from each of those dates to put the returns into a summary form that represents a fair and accurate description of the information that has been transmitted. These summaries are published on a website and in booklet form.[83]

The registrar must promptly provide a copy of the booklet to the Speaker, who presents it to the House.[84] It is then published as a parliamentary paper. The registrar is responsible for maintaining the information on the website and making it available for inspection at Parliament buildings during working hours. Copies of the summaries may be made.[85]

Apart from making information available to the Auditor-General for that officer to carry out the functions conferred on the office in regard to members' returns, the registrar must keep all other returns and information relating to individual members confidential.[86] At the dissolution or expiration of Parliament such information is to be destroyed except where the Auditor-General requires information relating to any individual to be retained for investigative purposes.[87]

Investigation and enforcement

The registrar must supply the Auditor-General with a copy of every return within 14 days

---

[72] *Ibid.*, cl.2(3).
[73] *Ibid.*, cl.2(2).
[74] *Ibid.*, cl.3.
[75] *Ibid.*, cl.10.
[76] *Ibid.*, cl.19.
[77] *Ibid.*, cl.11.
[78] *Ibid.*, cl.12.
[79] Hon Margaret Wilson, "Registrar of Pecuniary Interests Appointed", media release, 12 August, 2005.
[80] Appendix B to the Standing Orders, cl.13.
[81] 2002-05, AJHR, I.22D, p.865 (*Members of Parliament (Pecuniary Interests) Bill*).
[82] Appendix B to the Standing Orders, cl.19(2).
[83] *Ibid.*, cl.16(1), (2).
[84] *Ibid.*, cls.16(3) and 17.
[85] *Ibid.*, cl.16(4), (5).
[86] *Ibid.*, cl.18(2).
[87] *Ibid.*, cl.18(3).

of it being received by the registrar[88] and must disclose any information relating to the register in the registrar's possession that the Auditor-General requires for reviewing and inquiring into the returns.[89]

The Auditor-General reviews the returns and may inquire, either on the Auditor-General's own initiative or on request, into whether a member has complied with the obligations to furnish returns or whether the registrar has complied with the registrar's obligations under the Standing Orders. The Auditor-General may report to the House the findings of any inquiry carried out and may report on any other matter the Auditor-General considers it desirable to report on.[90]

It is a contempt of the House for any member knowingly to fail to make a return of pecuniary interests (initial or annual) by the due date[91] or knowingly to provide false or misleading information in such a return.[92] A complaint that a member has committed such a contempt is raised in the standard way for raising a matter of privilege. (See Chapter 48.)

Declaration of financial interests

Members who have a financial interest in business before the House are not thereby disqualified from participating in a debate on the matter, serving on a committee inquiring into it or voting on it. It is for members to judge whether they should participate in any of these ways when they possess a financial interest in the outcome of parliamentary proceedings.[93]

However, a member is required to declare to the House or to a committee a financial interest that he or she has in the outcome of parliamentary business before participating in consideration of it.[94] Failure to do so will constitute a contempt of the House[95] and can be dealt with as a matter of privilege. But the validity of the business transacted by the House or committee (for example, a question asked by the member) is not affected by the member's failure to declare a financial interest.[96] If a member does propose to refrain from participating in a particular item of business by not speaking and voting on it (recording a formal abstention is participating in its consideration), there is no obligation to disclose an interest. There is no obligation to disclose a financial interest where that interest is contained in the Register of Pecuniary Interests of Members of Parliament.[97] That register constitutes a standing declaration of financial interests.

Definition of financial interest

A financial interest that must be declared is defined as a direct financial benefit that might accrue to a member personally, or to any trust, company or other business entity in which the member holds an appreciable interest, as a result of the outcome of the House's consideration of a particular item of business.[98] A financial interest includes an interest that is held by the member's spouse or domestic partner or by any child of the member who is wholly or mainly dependent on the member for support.[99]

An obligation to declare an interest only arises where a benefit may accrue as the result of the outcome of the House's consideration of the business. A benefit could therefore generally accrue only from the House transacting business that has a legal effect. Passing legislation is the obvious example of this situation and a declaration must always be made

---

88 *Ibid.*, cl.14.
89 *Ibid.*, cl.18(1).
90 *Ibid.*, cl.15.
91 S.O.395(g).
92 S.O.395(h).
93 1993-96, AJHR, I.18A, p.82.

94 S.O.166(1).
95 S.O.395(f).
96 2005, Vol.624, p.19532.
97 S.O.166(2).
98 S.O.165(1).
99 S.O.165(2)(a).

of a benefit that would accrue to a member from legislation before the House. There are other situations in which the House participates in taking actions with legal consequences – such as disallowing regulations or recommending appointments – and any financial benefit resulting from these activities must also be declared. But in respect of most other business transacted by the House it is unlikely that any financial benefit could accrue as a result of the outcome of the House's consideration of the matter. Declaration of any interest that a member has in the subject is, in these circumstances, optional.

To constitute an "interest" at all, the interest must be a direct one. Thus a member who was a director of a company which provided mortgage broking services for a company which owned land affected by the proposal before the House was ruled to have had too indirect an interest to be affected.[100] The interest of members as policyholders in a large life insurance office has also been held to be too remote to be affected by this rule.[101]

The Speaker has ruled that the fact that an amendment might open up a business opportunity for a number of companies in which members have interests does not constitute a direct financial benefit to them. Such a business opportunity might or might not eventuate from the amendment becoming law. Entirely speculative interests cannot be direct financial benefits.[102]

Furthermore, a financial interest does not include an interest held by a member (or the member's spouse, domestic partner or dependent child) as one of a class of persons who belong to a profession, vocation or other calling, or who hold public offices or an interest held in common with the public.[103] Interests held in common with the public or vocational groups do not require to be declared.[104] So members did not have a financial interest in this sense in a payment of members bill[105] or in a bill dealing with members' superannuation entitlements,[106] and Ministers did not have a financial interest in a Minister's salaries and allowances bill.[107] Members who were farmers did not have financial interests in a bill providing payment for and the marketing of dairy produce[108] and a member who was a director or shareholder in a company operating within a particular industry did not have a financial interest in general legislation dealing with that industry. It is only if the member's company is singled out for special treatment in legislation that a financial interest could arise.[109] Private legislation is thus more likely to raise questions of financial interest than general legislation.

Declaring an interest

There is no particular means prescribed by which a financial interest must be declared. It can be done while speaking in debate,[110] by personal explanation[111] or on a point of order. In a select committee it could be done orally to the committee or in writing to the chairperson. In the case of the latter the chairperson is responsible for bringing it to the attention of the committee.

The obligation to declare an interest lies with the member who holds it; other members cannot impose an obligation on the member to take any action by alleging that a financial interest is held.[112] If a member holds a financial interest and fails to declare it, the issue becomes a matter of privilege. In this regard, if there is a dispute as to whether there is a financial interest the Speaker decides the matter and the Speaker's decision is final.[113] In

100   1977, Vol.411, pp.1133-4.
101   1990, Vol.506, pp.1358-9 (*Tower Corporation Bill*).
102   1998, Vol.574, p.14221-2 (*Accident Insurance Bill*).
103   S.O.165(2)(b).
104   1993-96, AJHR, I.18A, pp.82-3.
105   1892, Vol.78, p.624 (*Payment of Members Bill*).
106   1992, Vol.526, p.9413 (*State Sector Superannuation Bill*).
107   1900, Vol.112, p.386 (*Ministers' Salaries and Allowances Bill*).
108   1956, Vol.310, pp.2508-9 (*Dairy Products Marketing Commission Amendment Bill*).
109   1993-96, AJHR, I.18A, pp.82-3.
110   For example, 1995, Vol.549, p.8322 (*Waikato-Tainui Raupatu Claims Settlement Bill*).
111   For example, 1997, Vol.565, p.5845.
112   1998, Vol.574, p.14221.
113   S.O.167.

any subsequent consideration of the matter by the Privileges Committee, for example, the committee would be bound by the Speaker's finding on whether a financial interest existed.

Where the issue of whether members hold a financial interest arises at a select committee, the matter can be referred directly to the Speaker for decision by the committee itself or by any member. A committee has cautioned witnesses not to abuse their privileges as witnesses by making unsubstantiated allegations that members hold financial interests in the business before the committee.[114]

PERSONAL INTERESTS

Apart from pecuniary interests, the House has no formal rules requiring members to declare interests of a personal and non-pecuniary or non-financial nature that may be relevant to their participation in business before the House. However, it is likely to be in members' own political interests to make clear any personal interests that they have on matters under consideration by the House or a select committee (such as a relationship with someone else who may be affected by the outcome of the business under consideration), and to consider abstaining from participating in consideration of the matter if to do so may suggest impropriety on their part. (See Chapter 22 for members stepping aside from serving on select committees.)

MINISTERS' INTERESTS

Guidelines on Ministers' interests were first drawn up by a parliamentary select committee in 1956 following concern that a Minister may have allowed his official and business interests to be compromised.[115] These guidelines (known as the Harker rules, after the chairman of the select committee which prepared them) were replaced in 1990 by new guidelines on Ministers' interests announced by the Prime Minister. The guidelines are now contained in the *Cabinet Manual*. The guidelines are not parliamentary rules or conventions and the Speaker has no role to play in interpreting them.[116] Questions about their operation may be addressed to the Prime Minister, as long as such questions are not an attempt to pry into a member's private affairs and do not impute misconduct on the part of a Minister.[117]

There are a number of requirements set out in the guidelines. First, Ministers are obliged to declare at Cabinet or at a Cabinet committee any personal interest which conflicts with a matter under consideration by the Government. They are similarly expected to declare in the House any interests they may have in a matter which is under discussion. (In addition, Ministers are as equally subject to the House's rules on registering pecuniary interests and declaring financial interests as other members.) Secondly, Ministers are required to lodge with the Secretary of the Cabinet, as registrar, within two months of their appointment and at 31 December each year, a declaration of certain interests and assets that they hold. These declarations are subsequently presented to the House as a register of Ministers' interests and published as a parliamentary paper (B.4). Any major change in a Minister's assets during the year is to be notified to the registrar immediately. The types of interests that are required to be declared include: remunerated directorships or employment, ownership of shares and real property, and holdings of mortgage or debt instruments.[118] The register does not cover all assets and interests which a Minister may hold.[119] It is for Ministers to ensure that their returns are completed personally and are correct. The registrar facilitates the registration process, attempts to ensure consistency

---

114   1996-99, AJHR, I.22, p.382 (*Maori Reserved Land Amendment Bill*).
115   1956, AJHR, I.17 (Ministers' Private Interests Committee).
116   1991, Vol.514, p.1509.
117   *Ibid.*, p.1546.

118   *Cabinet Manual*, 2001, paras.2.52 to 2.55.
119   "Report for the Prime Minister on Inquiry into Matters relating to Te Whanau o Waipareira Trust and Hon John Tamihere", Douglas White QC, 20 December 2004, para.8.5.

between declarations, and clarifies information where this is unclear. But the registrar does not provide legal or accounting advice to Ministers or police the register.[120]

There are no set procedures on what happens if a Minister does not declare interests and assets within the rules. This would be a matter for the Prime Minister to consider.[121]

MEMBERS' REMUNERATION

The arrangements for determining the remuneration of members of Parliament have gone through a number of phases. For 30 years members voted expenses for themselves when passing the Government's annual estimates of expenditure. In 1884 provision was made in permanent legislation for the payment of an expense allowance to members. In 1892 this was converted into a salary (payable in monthly instalments) and a travelling allowance. Parliamentary salaries and allowances were fixed at intervals by further legislation until 1950. In that year, a new scheme for determining parliamentary remuneration was introduced under which a Royal Commission was to be set up after each general election to recommend changes to members' salaries and allowances. The commission's recommendations were implemented by statute or by Order in Council as the case required. These arrangements were suspended in 1974 and abolished in 1977.

Salaries and allowances are now paid to members of Parliament at rates fixed by a statutory commission.[122] Originally the commission was known as the Higher Salaries Commission. It was renamed the Remuneration Authority on 1 April 2003.[123] The moneys required to pay members' salaries and allowances are not required to be appropriated annually by Parliament, but are a permanent charge on the expenditure of the Government.[124] The Remuneration Authority has power to recommend different salaries and allowances for different office-holders, for the different electorates represented by members or for such other reasons as it considers justifiable.[125]

Remuneration Authority

The Remuneration Authority is a statutory commission that was first established in 1974 to determine the remuneration of a number of groups and individual office-holders. As well as determining the salaries, allowances and superannuation rights of members of Parliament, it carries out similar remuneration functions in respect of the judiciary and certain other statutory officers, including mayors and other elected members of local authorities. The authority has three members, each of whom is appointed by the Governor-General by Order in Council for a term not exceeding three years.[126]

The authority must review and issue a fresh determination for the positions within its jurisdiction (except in respect of superannuation) at least once every three years.[127] In practice, the authority has issued annual determinations of salaries and allowances for members of Parliament. Any person is entitled to make written submissions to the authority. The authority is obliged to facilitate the making of written and oral submissions by representatives of the persons to be covered by a determination it is proposing to make.[128] For this purpose, in respect of parliamentary salaries and allowances, a joint caucus committee (not a select committee), known as the Members' Services Committee, is invited by the authority to present its views to the authority on behalf of members of Parliament. When a determination is pending, the authority informs all members of their right to make individual submissions to it. The Members' Services Committee also invites members to communicate with the committee so that it can present members' views orally

---

120   *Ibid.*, para.8.8.
121   *Ibid.*, para.8.7.
122   *Civil List Act* 1979, s.16(1); *Remuneration Authority Act* 1977, s.12(1)(a).
123   *Remuneration Authority (Members of Parliament) Amendment Act* 2002, s.3.
124   *Civil List Act* 1979, s.16(3).
125   *Ibid.*, s.16(2).
126   *Remuneration Authority Act* 1977, ss.4, 5 and 6.
127   *Ibid.*, s.19(5).
128   *Ibid.*, s.21.

or in writing to the authority. The authority is also obliged, before making a determination relating to members' salaries and allowances, to consult with the Commissioner of Inland Revenue about the tax consequences of a proposed determination and with the Speaker and the appropriate Minister about the services provided to members and Ministers.[129]

Determinations of the authority are made known by a copy being delivered to the Speaker, the Prime Minister and the Leader of the Opposition, and by publication in the *New Zealand Gazette*.[130] A determination is deemed to be a regulation for the purposes of the *Acts and Regulations Publication Act* 1989 and is, therefore, published as a statutory regulation.[131] But a determination has effect in its own right[132] and is not subject to amendment or disallowance by the House. It is unlawful for any person to act contrary to a determination or to fail to observe the criteria or limits specified in it.[133]

Concern that the authority did not have a legislative mandate to oversee the administration of its determinations or issue formal guidance as to how they are to be applied,[134] has led to power being conferred on the authority to determine issues about how any provision of a determination is to be interpreted or applied, or is to operate.[135]

Salaries

In determining parliamentary salaries, the authority is guided by the general statutory criteria set out in its constituent legislation and by specific factors which it has identified as being applicable to members of Parliament.

The authority is obliged to have regard to the need—
- to achieve and maintain fair relativity with levels of remuneration received elsewhere
- to be fair to the recipient of the remuneration and to the taxpayer
- to recruit and retain competent persons for membership of the House.[136]

Further, the authority must take into account the requirements of the position and the conditions of service enjoyed by the person or persons in it, as compared to those of any comparable persons or group of persons.[137]

The job of a member of Parliament is a full-time occupation and salaries of members have been fixed on this basis for many years. In making its determinations, the authority has consistently pointed out that it is not its role to pass judgment on the performance of any member. Its task is to determine a rate for the job, no matter who holds it and irrespective of their performance in it.[138] It is for the electors to judge the performance of members of Parliament.

In 2003 the salaries of members were realigned on a total package basis, including in them the remuneration element of certain allowances formerly paid to members and deducting from them the value of other benefits paid to members (such as non-official air travel). This produced an appropriate level of salary as the basis for future determinations.[139]

Allowances

For allowances the authority only has jurisdiction to fix basic expense allowances and allowances for specified office-holders. These allowances are to reflect genuine expenses of members. They are not designed as remuneration. In 2003 the allowances were

---

129 *Ibid.*, s.17A.
130 *Ibid.*, s.16(1).
131 *Ibid.*, s.16(2).
132 *Ibid.*, s.14(1).
133 *Ibid.*, s.14(2).
134 *Report of the Controller and Auditor-General - Members of Parliament: Accommodation Allowances for Living in Wellington*, Interim Report, March 2001, paras. 4.04 and 6.05.

135 *Remuneration Authority Act* 1977, s.12(1)(bb).
136 *Ibid.*, s.18(1).
137 *Ibid.*, s.18(2).
138 See, for example, *Parliamentary Salaries and Allowances Determination* 1999, Explanatory memorandum.
139 *Parliamentary Salaries and Allowances Determination* 2003, Explanatory memorandum.

realigned to exclude any estimated remuneration elements and to provide a basis for the future.[140] The services provided to members by the Parliamentary Service are taken into account by the authority in fixing members' allowances.

Separate basic expense allowances have been determined for the Prime Minister, the Speaker and for members generally. The basic expense allowance is intended to cover out-of-pocket expenses incurred in carrying out parliamentary duties such as: entertainment, memberships and sponsorships, koha, donations and raffle tickets, gifts and prizes, flowers and wreaths, passport photos, clothing and grooming (for the Prime Minister only), briefcases and luggage, and meals.[141]

Period for which salaries and allowances are payable

The periods for which members' salaries and allowances are paid do not always coincide with the period for which the persons concerned hold office in law. The payment of salary and allowances to the Speaker and salary to the Deputy Speaker (formerly called Chairman of Committees) begins on the day of their respective appointments to office, and continues beyond the dissolution of Parliament until the first meeting of the next Parliament,[142] notwithstanding that the Speaker ceases to hold office on polling day[143] and the Deputy Speaker on the dissolution of Parliament.

The payment of an ordinary member's salary and allowance commences on the day after polling day at the election at which the member was elected (notwithstanding that that person does not in law become a member of Parliament until the day after the day on which the writ is returned or the Chief Electoral Officer makes a return of party list members who have been elected[144]) and ends on the polling day for the next general election.[145] The payment of salary to a Minister commences on the day of appointment as Minister. Members cease to draw an ordinary member's salary when they are appointed as Ministers.

A member who retires at a general election or is a defeated candidate at a general election receives a salary at the ordinary member's rate that is payable at the time of the election for three months after polling day. In the case of a Minister or a Parliamentary Under-Secretary who retires or is a defeated candidate at a general election, ministerial salary continues to be paid until that person formally resigns, which may be up to a month after the date of the election. On this resignation taking effect, the former Minister or under-secretary is paid the salary payable to an ordinary member for the unexpired period of the three months from the election.[146]

Similar provisions apply to a former Speaker and former Deputy Speaker who are unsuccessful candidates at the election. Their salaries and allowances as Speaker and Deputy Speaker continue until the new Parliament meets. When Parliament meets, they revert to the ordinary salary of a member for the remainder of the three-month period running from the election.[147]

If a member's election is overturned following an election petition, the salary and allowance payable to a member are still payable to that person for the period from polling day to the overturning of the election, since the ousted member was the member for that period. But where another person is declared elected in place of the originally returned member following an election petition, salary and allowance backdated to polling day are

[140]　*Ibid.*
[141]　*Ibid.*
[142]　*Civil List Act* 1979, s.17.
[143]　*Constitution Act* 1986, s.13.

[144]　*Electoral Act* 1993, s.54.
[145]　*Civil List Act* 1979, s.18(1).
[146]　*Ibid.*, s.18(3).
[147]　*Ibid.*

to be paid to the newly installed member, notwithstanding that that person was not, in law, the member for that period.[148]

Payment of salaries and allowances

The salaries and allowances payable to parliamentarians are paid fortnightly.[149] Members' salaries and allowances are payable, without specific annual appropriation, under permanent legislative authority.[149] As the payment of salary and allowances is made to a member under an Act of Parliament, the payment is mandatory and does not depend for its authority on any contract of service. It appears, therefore, that the payment cannot be waived.[151]

The salaries and allowances in force as at 30 June 2005 are set out in Appendix 1.

TAXATION

While members are in law neither employees nor self-employed, for tax purposes they are treated as employees and income tax is deducted from their salaries at source.[152] They cannot claim tax deductions for expenses as if they were self-employed.[153] Expenses paid to members for travel, accommodation, attendance and communications services are exempt from income tax if they are determined by the Speaker (for members) and the Minister for Ministerial Services (for Ministers)[154] but fringe benefit tax is payable on any element of personal benefit involved in such expenses.[155]

SUPERANNUATION

The superannuation rights of members differ depending upon whether or not they were members of Parliament on 30 June 1992, the date at which the Government Superannuation Fund was closed off to new members. Every person who was a member of Parliament on that date may continue to contribute to the parliamentary superannuation scheme established as part of the Government Superannuation Fund, for as long as they remain a member of Parliament. Once they cease to be a member by not being re-elected at a general election or by vacating their seat by resignation or otherwise, they also cease to be eligible to continue to contribute to the scheme and even if they subsequently return to Parliament they cannot rejoin it.[156] The parliamentary superannuation scheme will therefore, like the other schemes operated within the Government Superannuation Fund, gradually run down.

Members as at 30 June 1992

Those persons who were members of Parliament on 30 June 1992 and who remain continuously in office, may continue as contributors to the parliamentary superannuation scheme. (Though they also have the right to cease to contribute to the scheme and take a deferred pension or to receive a refund of their contributions.[157])

Contributions are payable at the rate of 11 percent of an ordinary member's salary. After 20 years' service, the rate of contribution is reduced to eight percent. The scheme provides a retiring allowance of one-thirtieth of the ordinary member's salary as at the date the retiring allowance first becomes payable, for every year of service up to a maximum of two-thirds of salary, plus one one hundred and twenty-eighth of salary for every year of service in excess of 20 years. The allowance is subject to cost-of-living adjustment. Up to 25 percent of the annual payment may be surrendered for a lump sum equal to 12 times the amount surrendered.

---

[148] *Ibid.*, s.19.
[149] *Civil List (Pay Periods) Order* 1982.
[150] *Civil List Act* 1979, s.2.
[151] 1968, Vol.359, p.3777.
[152] *Income Tax Act* 2004, s.OB1 (para.(a) of definition of **employment** and para.(b)(vi) of definition of **salary or wages**).
[153] 2002-05, AJHR, I.22A, p.432
[154] *Income Tax Act* 2004, s.CW25.
[155] *Ibid.*, s.CX11.
[156] *Government Superannuation Fund Act* 1956, s.82A(2).
[157] *Ibid.*, s.86FA.

The retiring allowance is payable only to former members who have served for not less than nine years (continuously or in separate periods) and who are at least 50 years of age. A member who retires from the House before attaining the age of 50 after serving for at least nine years does not begin to receive the allowance until he or she is 50 years old. However, a former member can surrender a proportion of the future allowance for an immediate cash payout. Members who serve for eight years or less receive a refund of twice the amount of their contributions on ceasing to be members. (Because a member's service is "rounded up" or "rounded down" to the nearest whole year depending on the date of election to the House, there can be no fractional parts of years served for superannuation purposes.) Any other former member can also elect to receive a refund of twice the amount of his or her contributions instead of receiving a retiring allowance.

A parliamentary superannuitant who again becomes a member of Parliament ceases to receive the retiring allowance during his or her new period in office. On the death of a member or a former member, the spouse of the member or former member receives an annuity at half the rate of the retiring allowance to which the deceased was entitled, payable until the spouse's death.[158]

The Remuneration Authority is empowered to consider and make determinations on the superannuation rights of members of Parliament who are contributors to the Government Superannuation Fund.[159] The authority is required to consult with the Government Superannuation Fund Authority and the Government Actuary before making a determination on parliamentary superannuation.[160] Any determination by the authority on parliamentary superannuation is made in the same form as its determinations on salaries and allowances. A determination may contain provisions which modify, or are to apply instead of, the provisions of the *Government Superannuation Fund Act* 1956.[161]

Members elected after 30 June 1992

No specific superannuation scheme exists for members of Parliament first elected to the House, or re-elected after a period of absence, after 30 June 1992. Nor is there any compulsion on such members to contribute to any superannuation scheme.

However, provision has been made for a public subsidy to be paid to any superannuation scheme registered under the *Superannuation Schemes Act* 1989 which a member chooses to join. The Remuneration Authority has the function of considering and determining the maximum amount that may be paid by way of subsidy to such a scheme in respect of each member and the contribution that the member must make to that scheme in order to become entitled to the subsidy. For this purpose the authority may express the subsidy as a monetary amount or as a percentage of an ordinary member's salary. The maximum amount that the authority fixes must be the same for all members.[162]

Under the authority's current determination, a member may receive a superannuation subsidy of 2.5 times the amount of the member's contribution to a registered superannuation scheme, up to a maximum amount of subsidy equal to 16 percent of an ordinary member's salary up to 31 October 2003 and 20 percent thereafter.[163] The maximum subsidy would therefore be payable (from 1 November 2003) if a member contributes eight percent of salary to a registered scheme. If a member contributes at a rate less than eight percent of salary, the subsidy payable reduces proportionately. The Crown's liability to any superannuation scheme to which a member elects to contribute is limited to the payment of the subsidy as determined by the authority.[164] The subsidy as determined by the authority

---

158 See generally, *ibid.*, Part 6.
159 *Remuneration Authority Act* 1977, s.12(1)(b).
160 *Ibid.*, s.17(2), (3).
161 *Ibid.*, s.17(1).

162 *Ibid.*, s.12(1)(ba), (2A).
163 *Parliamentary Superannuation Determination* 2003.
164 *Remuneration Authority Act* 1977, s.12(2B).

is paid out of public money under permanent legislative authority without the need for annual appropriation.[165]

TRAVEL, ACCOMMODATION, ATTENDANCE AND COMMUNICATION SERVICES

The travel, accommodation, attendance and communication services to be provided to members are determined by the Speaker. Such services to be provided to Ministers are determined by the Minister for Ministerial Services.[166] The Speaker must take into account any advice on such services given by the Parliamentary Service Commission, and both the Speaker and the Minister must consult with the Commissioner of Inland Revenue about the tax consequences of a determination and with each other about the services determined by each.[167] The services may be provided in kind or by the payment of money by way of reimbursement.

A determination of services by the Speaker and the Minister is published as a regulation,[168] but is not subject to amendment or disallowance by the House. The regulation may incorporate by reference all or part of any other document that sets out the services to be provided to members.[169] The current determinations incorporate by reference travel, accommodation, attendance and communications services available to members and Ministers that are set out in separate documents approved by the Speaker and the Minister respectively.[170] These documents[171] describe in detail the air travel entitlements of members, their ability to use taxis, rental cars and other forms of transport in New Zealand, their access to chauffeured cars, their right to reimbursement of Wellington and other accommodation expenses, and the entitlements to use telephones, faxes and the internet. (See Appendix 2 for the services for members determined on 23 October 2003.)

Where services are incorporated by reference in a determination the funding for those services is appropriated annually. Otherwise funding for members' services is provided under permanent legislative authority.[172]

OTHER SERVICES FOR MEMBERS

Apart from salaries and allowances and the travel, accommodation, attendance and communication services determined by the Speaker, members receive administrative and support services from the Parliamentary Service designed to assist them in the performance of their parliamentary duties. The moneys required to meet the cost of these other services must be appropriated annually. These administrative and support services are taken into account by the Remuneration Authority in fixing the rates of salaries and allowances payable to members.

The services to be provided to members are determined administratively by the Speaker each year after taking into account any advice and recommendations that are made by the Parliamentary Service Commission.[173] On receiving a written direction from the Speaker as to the services to be provided to members, the Parliamentary Service, under the direction of its General Manager, is responsible for providing those services.[174]

These other services either take the form of the allocation of resources in kind to members or the allocation of support funding to parliamentary parties and members for the parties and the members to determine how to use the funding.

---

[165] *Ibid.*, s.17(6).
[166] *Civil List Act* 1979, s.20A(1), (3).
[167] *Ibid.*, s.20A(2), (5).
[168] *Ibid.*, s.20A(8)
[169] *Ibid.*, s.20B(1)(c).
[170] *Parliamentary Travel, Accommodation, Attendance, and Communications Services Determination* 2003; *Executive Travel, Accommodation, Attendance, and Communications Services Determination* 2003.
[171] "Travel, Accommodation, Attendance, and Communications Services Available to Members of Parliament", signed by the Speaker on 23 October 2003; "Travel, Accommodation, Attendance, and Communications Services Available to Members of Executive", signed by the Minister for Ministerial Services on 23 October 2003.
[172] *Civil List Act* 1979, s.20B(4).
[173] *Parliamentary Service Act* 2000, s.8(1), (3).
[174] *Ibid.*, s.8(2).

Services in kind

Office accommodation

Members are provided with office accommodation for themselves and their executive secretaries in one of the buildings within the parliamentary complex. This is for the purpose of supporting members' parliamentary responsibilities. While these are necessarily wide and varied and can include support for matters having a commercial or business connection, such as a regional promotion, they do not extend to members carrying on a business from within the parliamentary complex.[175]

Office equipment

Office equipment, such as workstations and stationery, is provided for members' use in Wellington. Members are entitled to use parliamentary letterhead for their own correspondence.

Staff

Every member has the assistance of an executive secretary in Wellington and an out-of-Parliament secretary in their out-of-Parliament offices. These staff are employed by the Parliamentary Service.

Distribution of mail to members

Mail posted to members of Parliament is not free, and should be stamped like any other mail. However, the Parliamentary Service has agreed to pay New Zealand Post Limited for unstamped mail addressed to members of Parliament at Parliament House.

Each member has a personal bill box situated in the Bills Office, which is used for the distribution of bills and papers presented to the House and certain other official publications. Other material which is for distribution to members within Parliament buildings and is personally addressed to a member may be delivered through the normal parliamentary internal delivery system, provided it has been posted or hand-delivered to Parliament House.

Support allocation funding

Funding is made available annually to parliamentary parties and members to support their parliamentary operations. For party leaders' and whips' offices this funding can be utilised to employ staff or purchase services from external providers. For individual members, funding is provided to cover the costs of such matters as: postal services, photocopying and printing, periodicals and newspapers, out-of-Parliament offices (first established in 1984), advertising, office equipment, training courses and conferences. The support allocation funding cannot be used to fund types of expenditure that are covered by the expense allowance fixed by the Remuneration Authority. Members are not permitted to use the support allocation funding to initiate legal proceedings,[176] though it may be used in some circumstances to defend legal proceedings brought against the member in his or her capacity as a member of Parliament.

In all cases the bulk allocation of support funding allows the parliamentary parties and the members to decide how to use their allocations within any conditions attached to them, provided that the total amount of the allocated funding is not exceeded.

---

[175]   1998, Vol.568, p.9110.

[176]   "No public funding for Huata court case", *The Dominion Post*, 18 November 2003.

CHAPTER 4

SPEAKER OF THE HOUSE OF REPRESENTATIVES

THE SPEAKER

The Speaker of the House of Representatives is the highest officer elected by the House. Since the revision of the Order of Precedence in New Zealand in 1974, the Speaker is third in precedence, after only the Governor-General and the Prime Minister[1] (who is appointed to office by the Crown not by the House). On being confirmed in office, the person who is Speaker assumes the title "Honourable" (Hon) *ex officio*. During the course of this book there are a great many references to specific powers and duties of the Speaker. The purpose of this chapter is to deal with the Speaker's role from a general point of view.

Duties of the Speaker

The first task of the members of a newly elected Parliament, when they assemble for the first time following the general election, is to elect one of their number to preside over them.[2] The person so elected represents and embodies the House in its relations with the Crown. Indeed, this is the reason for the title of "Speaker": the need for the amorphous mass of commoners who came to Parliament to have one person who could report their opinions to the King and the Lords – who could speak for them. The Speaker was the House's orator. In New Zealand, the Speaker still performs this formal representative function by, on behalf of the House, laying claim before the Governor-General to the House's privileges, and by leading the members of the House into the Governor-General's presence at the commencement of each session to hear the Governor-General deliver the Speech from the Throne giving reasons for the summoning of Parliament. The Speaker also presents to the Crown addresses that are adopted by the House, and reads messages from the Crown to the House.

The Speaker is chairperson of the Parliamentary Service Commission and has principal political responsibility for the services and facilities provided to members of Parliament. (See Chapter 3.) Many of the House's contacts with overseas parliaments are carried on by, or in the name of, the Speaker who is president, *ex officio*, of the New Zealand branch of the Commonwealth Parliamentary Association and the New Zealand group of the Inter-Parliamentary Union. The Speaker announces the presence of parliamentary delegations or other distinguished visitors to the House. The Speaker also makes other formal communications to the House; for example, presenting reports to Parliament made by the officers of Parliament, and announcing and presenting any citizens'-initiated referendum petition that has been signed by at least 10 percent of registered electors.[3] The Speaker determines which portions of the proceedings of the House are to be reported in *Hansard* and in what form and under what conditions the report is made.[4] The Speaker is occasionally called upon to execute orders of the House.[5] The Speaker also has a number of statutory duties to perform in the case of vacancies in membership of the House[6] and the granting of exemptions to members of Parliament from attending court proceedings.[7]

---

[1]   *New Zealand Gazette*, 10 January 1974, p.5.
[2]   *Constitution Act* 1986, s.12.
[3]   *Citizens Initiated Referenda Act* 1993, s.21.
[4]   S.O.9; see, for example, 2002, Vol.602, p.54.
[5]   1981, JHR, p.40 (House's views on the 1981 Springbok tour to be communicated to the New Zealand Rugby Football Union).
[6]   *Electoral Act* 1993, ss.129 and 134.
[7]   *Legislature Act* 1908, ss.261 and 263.

The courts are enjoined to take judicial notice of the Speaker's signature on any document issued under the Speaker's statutory or Standing Orders powers.[8]

However, the chief duty of the Speaker is to chair the House, presiding over its deliberations, keeping order and determining points of procedure.

Speaker's position

The Speaker in New Zealand does not sever all links with a political party, as does the Speaker of the House of Commons. Nor is the Speaker guaranteed any continuity of office over more than one Parliament. There is no tradition of re-electing the member who served as Speaker in the preceding Parliament even if the Government changes following a general election as there is, for instance, in the United Kingdom. With two exceptions, throughout the course of the twentieth century all Speakers came from the governing, or a governing, party.[9] The member who is elected Speaker does not thereby become a non-party member of Parliament. However, the Speaker does not play a politically partisan role and exercises restraint in the speeches or comments he or she makes outside the House.[10] The Speaker must be prepared to assert an independence from the Government so as to ensure that the rights of all sides of the House are protected in the course of the parliamentary process.[11]

Whether the Speaker attends weekly party caucus meetings held while the House is sitting is a matter for the Speaker to decide. Practice has differed between Speakers of different parties and between Speakers of the same party. Speakers from the National party have generally not attended caucus.[12] On the other hand, Labour Speakers until recent years did attend caucus.[13] However, since 1984 most Labour Speakers have not attended caucus during sitting weeks.

The Speaker's vote is included in any party vote cast and the Speaker votes in a personal vote, though without going into the lobbies personally – the Speaker's vote is communicated to the teller from the Speaker's chair. As its presiding officer, the Speaker never participates in debate in the House. When the Speaker has charge of a local or private bill, another member moves the stages of the bill on the Speaker's behalf.[14] The Speaker may speak and vote in a committee of the whole House. Nowadays the right to speak in committee is usually exercised only when changes to the Standing Orders are under consideration or the Speaker is answering questions on the estimates of an office for which the Speaker is responsible. The Speaker may, and indeed often does, serve on select committees, such as the Officers of Parliament Committee and the Standing Orders Committee, but it would not be in keeping with the position for the Speaker to serve on a committee considering a party-politically contentious matter. Where the Speaker does chair a committee written questions relating to matters for which the Speaker has responsibility in that capacity, may be lodged.[15]

The Speaker's exalted position and the restraints it imposes as a consequence require members to treat the Speaker or any other temporary occupant of the Speaker's chair with respect and deference. Members are obliged to make an acknowledgment to the chair when entering or leaving the Chamber, or when crossing the floor of the House (except while voting).[16] The office of Speaker cannot be introduced into debate by members quoting the Speaker's views or otherwise referring to the Speaker during the course of

---

[8]   *Evidence Amendment Act* 1945, s.11A.
[9]   Speaker Statham from 1923 to 1935 was, at the time of his first election, an independent, "though with some pro-government leanings" (see Scott, *The New Zealand Constitution*, pp.59-60); Speaker Tapsell from 1993 to 1996 was a member of the opposition Labour party.
[10]   1982, Vol.448, p.4918.

[11]   See, for example, 1995, Vol.548, pp.7863-4.
[12]   Freer, *A Lifetime in Politics*, p.144.
[13]   Martin, *The House – New Zealand's House of Representatives 1854-2004*, p.276.
[14]   1990, Vol.510, pp.3514-5.
[15]   2001, Vol.592, p.9701.
[16]   S.O.81.

a speech.[17] Nor can the Speaker be attacked, except by a direct motion of censure of which notice has been given.[18] Any statement in the House reflecting on the Speaker either directly or indirectly is out of order; a suggestion of partiality on the part of the Speaker or any other occupant of the chair may constitute a contempt of the House.[19] Accusations against the Speaker that reflect on the Speaker in that capacity or in respect of an office held by the Speaker *ex officio* (such as chairperson of the Parliamentary Service Commission) may also constitute a contempt.[20]

The procession between the Speaker's office and the Chamber at the commencement and conclusion of each sitting is a regular feature of each parliamentary day, with the Speaker being preceded by the Speaker's assistant and the Serjeant-at-Arms carrying the Mace. The Speaker's route to and from the Chamber is blocked off by messengers to allow unimpeded passage while the procession passes along it.[21] The Speaker enters and leaves the Chamber via the Speaker's door to the left of the chair.

The Speaker may wear a full judge's wig, gown and tabs on formal occasions. This is a matter for the individual discretion of the occupant of the office. At the regular sittings of the House, the Speaker is less formally attired in a gown over ordinary clothing.

Administrative duties

As well as presiding over the House and chairing some select committees, the Speaker has a number of administrative duties.

The control and administration of the parliamentary precincts is vested in the Speaker on behalf of the House, whether Parliament is in session or not.[22] The Speaker may issue trespass notices relating to the parliamentary precincts and delegate the power to do so to other persons.[23] The Speaker has entered into a protocol with the Commissioner of Police regulating the exercise of police powers in the Parliament buildings and grounds.[24]

The Speaker is deemed to be the "responsible Minister" for a number of offices of state. These are: the office of the Auditor-General; the Office of the Clerk of the House of Representatives; the Office of the Ombudsmen; the office of the Parliamentary Commissioner for the Environment; and the Parliamentary Service.[25] During the House's consideration in committee of the estimates of these offices, the Speaker occupies the Minister's seat at the Table on the right of the chairperson, answering questions raised by members. The Speaker also attends the estimates hearings on the votes for these offices if requested by the select committee concerned. The Speaker's role in respect of each of these offices varies, with greater involvement in the administration of the Parliamentary Service than in that of the others.

The Speaker chairs, *ex officio*, the Parliamentary Service Commission,[26] a statutory committee of members which advises the Speaker on the nature of the services to be provided to members of Parliament. The commission meets approximately once each month. The Speaker determines the services to be provided by the Parliamentary Service[27] and the travel, accommodation, attendance and communication services available to members.[28] The administrative head of the Parliamentary Service, the General Manager, is directly responsible to the Speaker in carrying out his or her responsibilities.[29]

The Clerk of the House, as the principal officer of the Office of the Clerk, is directly responsible to the Speaker for the management of that Office.[30] The Controller and

---

[17] 1931, Vol.227, p.595.
[18] 1970, Vol.368, p.3202.
[19] 1982, AJHR, I.6, p.11.
[20] 1996-99, AJHR, I.15C.
[21] 1982, Vol.449, p.5215.
[22] *Parliamentary Service Act 2000*, s.26(1).
[23] *Ibid.*, s.26(2).
[24] *Policing functions within the parliamentary precincts – An agreement between the Speaker of the House*

of Representatives of New Zealand and the New Zealand Commissioner of Police, June 2004.
[25] *Public Finance Act 1989*, s.2(1).
[26] *Parliamentary Service Act 2000*, s.16(1).
[27] *Ibid.*, s.8.
[28] *Civil List Act 1979*, s.20A.
[29] *Parliamentary Service Act 2000*, s.11.
[30] *Clerk of the House of Representatives Act 1988*, s.16.

Auditor-General, the Chief Ombudsman and the Parliamentary Commissioner for the Environment also have a direct relationship with the Speaker concerning the management of their offices (known as offices of Parliament). However, in the case of the offices of Parliament and the Office of the Clerk, the Speaker does not control the discharge of the substantive duties carried out by the chief officers of those agencies. The Speaker's role is confined to the administration and expenditure of the offices concerned, not their professional and statutory duties, for which they are responsible to the House as a whole.

In respect of the Speaker's administrative responsibilities, the Speaker may be asked written questions.[31] But a point of order cannot be raised relating to the Speaker's administrative duties. A point of order must relate to a matter of order in the House and not, for example, to the administration of the building[32] or correspondence with the Speaker as chairperson of the Parliamentary Service Commission.[33]

Term of office

The Speaker assumes office on being confirmed by the Governor-General following the House's choice of Speaker being reported to His Excellency or Her Excellency.[34] (See Chapter 12 for the election of a Speaker.) The Speaker remains in office until the close of polling day at the next general election unless, by death or resignation, the office is vacated sooner.[35] The Speaker continues to hold office as chairperson of the Parliamentary Service Commission and continues to exercise the duties as the responsible Minister of the Office of the Clerk, the Parliamentary Service and the offices of Parliament until the new Parliament first meets.[36] The salary and allowances of the Speaker also continue to be paid until this time.[37]

DEPUTY SPEAKER

The Speaker's principal deputy is the Deputy Speaker. The first appointment of a Deputy Speaker by the House was made on 10 November 1992.[38] Until that time the House had, at the commencement of each Parliament, appointed a Chairman of Committees whose chief duty was to chair the committee of the whole House. When, at the Speaker's request or in the Speaker's absence, the Chairman of Committees assumed the Speaker's chair, the Chairman was known as the Deputy Speaker, but only for the period that he or she was actually chairing the House.

In 1992 this position was effectively reversed. The House now, by resolution, appoints a member to be Deputy Speaker.[39] The Deputy Speaker is a full deputy of the Speaker for all the purposes of the Standing Orders, whether actually presiding over the House or not. Thus the Speaker's Standing Orders' powers can be exercised by the Deputy Speaker during an adjournment of the House or a recess of Parliament.[40] The Deputy Speaker may also act for the Speaker in respect of the filling of any electoral vacancies that arise.[41] When the House goes into committee, the Deputy Speaker takes the chair as chairperson.

The appointment of the Deputy Speaker is usually made on the day of the State Opening of Parliament after the House has returned to its Chamber following the delivery of the Speech from the Throne.[42] For this purpose a notice of motion must be given on the previous sitting day and appear on the order paper. A party leader or a whip may not be appointed as Deputy Speaker.[43] The appointment of a Deputy Speaker may be for a fixed

---

[31] S.O.370(2).
[32] 1990, Vol.510, pp.3858-9.
[33] 1992, Vol.532, p.13236.
[34] *Constitution Act* 1986, s.12.
[35] *Ibid.*, s.13.
[36] *Parliamentary Service Act* 2000, s.18(3); *Public Finance Act* 1989, s.2(1).

[37] *Civil List Act* 1979, s.17.
[38] 1992, Vol.531, pp.12103-5.
[39] S.O.26.
[40] S.O.27.
[41] *Electoral Act* 1993, s.3(1).
[42] S.O.14(1)(e).
[43] S.O.30.

period and a Deputy Speaker may be removed from office by resolution of the House. Otherwise the appointment continues until the dissolution or expiration of Parliament.[44] The Deputy Speaker's salary and allowances continue to be payable until the first meeting of the new Parliament.[45] A vacancy in the office of Deputy Speaker is filled in the same manner as the initial appointment, that is, by resolution on notice.[46]

Whenever the Speaker is absent at the commencement of a sitting, the Deputy Speaker takes the chair without the need for any formal communication to the House.[47] Similarly, during the course of a sitting the Speaker and the Deputy Speaker share the task of presiding over the House. The Speaker has deliberately vacated the chair to allow the Deputy Speaker to rule on a matter in which the Speaker or the Speaker's electorate had an interest.[48] In the absence of the Speaker, the Deputy Speaker chairs the Parliamentary Service Commission.[49] Where there is a vacancy in the office of Speaker, the Deputy Speaker may exercise the statutory powers of the Speaker in regard to the parliamentary precincts, the Parliamentary Service and the Office of the Clerk.[50]

ASSISTANT SPEAKERS

Up to two members may be appointed by resolution of the House as Assistant Speakers.[51] These appointments may be made on the day of the State Opening of Parliament after that of the Deputy Speaker.[52] A party leader or a whip may not be an Assistant Speaker.[53] Often one of the Assistant Speakers is a member of an opposition party.

Assistant Speakers are deputies of the Speaker only in respect of the sittings of the House while they are actually presiding.[54] They cannot exercise the Speaker's statutory powers or any powers outside the House, though they may represent the Speaker on formal occasions such as receiving foreign dignitaries. Assistant Speakers hold office for the period named in the resolution appointing them or until the dissolution or expiration of Parliament, unless they are sooner removed from office by resolution of the House.[55] In the case of a vacancy (that is, if there are fewer than two Assistant Speakers at any one time), the House may appoint a new Assistant Speaker by resolution.[56] A special salary has been provided for Assistant Speakers since 1996.[57] This ceases on the dissolution or expiration of Parliament.

If the Speaker and the Deputy Speaker are absent at the commencement of a sitting, an Assistant Speaker may take the Chair.[58] During the course of a sitting, the Speaker, the Deputy Speaker and the Assistant Speakers share the task of presiding over the House between them.

TEMPORARY SPEAKERS

Any presiding officer may during the course of the sitting ask another member to preside over the House as temporary Speaker. This is done without any formal communication to the House and the temporary Speaker merely replaces the Speaker or other presiding officer in the Chair.[59] A temporary Speaker performs the duties and exercises the authority of the Speaker over the House while presiding,[60] except that a temporary Speaker cannot accept a closure motion.[61] A temporary Speaker cannot assume the chair at the commencement

---

44 S.O.29.
45 *Civil List Act* 1979, s.17.
46 S.O.31.
47 S.O.32.
48 1976, Vol.404, p.1552; 1993, Vol.535, p.15315.
49 *Parliamentary Service Act* 2000, s.16(2).
50 *Ibid.*, s.33.
51 S.O.28(1).
52 S.O.14(1)(e).
53 S.O.30.

54 S.O.28(2).
55 S.O.29.
56 S.O.31.
57 See now, *Parliamentary Salaries and Allowances Determination* 2004.
58 S.O.32.
59 S.O.33(1).
60 S.O.33(2).
61 S.O.137(4).

of a sitting or on the House resuming sitting following a report from the committee of the whole House.[62]

POSITION OF MEMBERS DEPUTISING FOR SPEAKER

While presiding over the House, the Deputy Speaker, an Assistant Speaker or a temporary Speaker is the Speaker and there can be no challenge to the validity or effectiveness of a decision taken by the House in the Speaker's absence. Likewise, a decision of a member deputising for the Speaker cannot be appealed to the Speaker.[63] When ruling on a matter arising in the House, a Deputy Speaker's, an Assistant Speaker's or a temporary Speaker's ruling is equivalent to that of the Speaker.[64]

The Deputy Speaker and the Assistant Speakers do participate in debates in the House, though less frequently than other members. It is a matter for their judgment as to which debates to take part in.[65] But it is the practice for a presiding officer not to speak in a debate over which that officer has been officiating.[66] It would be improper for a member when speaking in a debate to refer to his or her status as a presiding officer.[67] It would also be improper for other members to do so by way of debate.

---

[62] 1994, Vol.542, p.3697.
[63] 1925, Vol.208, p.468; 1928, Vol.218, p.577.
[64] 1980, Vol.429, pp.379-80.
[65] 1974, Vol.395, p.5580; 1992, Vol.531, p.12131;

2001, Vol.591, p.8396.
[66] 2001, Vol.591, p.8397.
[67] *Ibid.*, p.8398.

CHAPTER 5

ADMINISTRATION OF THE HOUSE

CLERK OF THE HOUSE OF REPRESENTATIVES

The principal permanent officer of the House is the Clerk of the House of Representatives. The Clerk is appointed by warrant by the Governor-General, on the recommendation of the Speaker made after consultation with the Prime Minister, the Leader of the Opposition and such other members as the Speaker considers desirable.[1] A Deputy Clerk is appointed in the same manner as the Clerk.

The Clerk notes all proceedings in the House; provides procedural advice to the Speaker and other members, and is responsible (subject to the Speaker's overriding responsibility) for all parliamentary printing such as the order paper, the journals, select committee reports and the official report of parliamentary debates, and for preparing and presenting copies of bills which have been passed by the House to the Governor-General for the Royal assent. The Clerk is the principal officer (chief executive) of the Office of the Clerk of the House of Representatives.[2]

When Parliament first meets after a general election, the Clerk administers the oath or affirmation to members and presides over the House for the election of a Speaker. Statute and the Standing Orders impose a number of other specific duties and functions on the Clerk. The Clerk has custody of all ballot papers used in general elections and by-elections, and is responsible, along with the Chief Electoral Officer, for destroying them after they have been held for six months.[3] The Clerk is also responsible for certifying that many of the procedures necessary in the promotion of a citizens'-initiated referendum have been followed. (See Chapter 41.) The Clerk may delegate any statutory or Standing Orders functions or powers to the Deputy Clerk or another officer of the House.[4] (The Clerk's functions of determining the precise form of an indicative referendum petition and certifying whether the petition has been signed by a sufficient number of eligible electors may only be delegated to the Deputy Clerk.[5]) The Deputy Clerk or a person appointed by the Speaker to act as Clerk may also perform the Clerk's Standing Orders functions.[6]

Office of the Clerk

The office of state supporting the Clerk of the House in the discharge of the Clerk's functions is known as the Office of the Clerk of the House of Representatives. The Clerk is responsible to the Speaker, on behalf of the House, for the efficient, effective and economical management of the Office.[7] Although not a government department, and therefore not part of the public service, the Office of the Clerk administers a vote containing appropriations for outputs associated with its activities. The Speaker is the responsible Minister for the vote which is administered in the same way as a vote administered by a government department.[8] The administrative and support services provided to the House by the Office and the funding for those services are subject to a triennial review by a committee appointed by the Speaker.[9]

---

[1] *Clerk of the House of Representatives Act* 1988, s.7.
[2] *Ibid.*, s.3.
[3] *Electoral Act* 1993, s.189.
[4] *Clerk of the House of Representatives Act* 1988, s.12; S.O.3(1).
[5] *Citizens Initiated Referenda Act* 1993, s.23(1).
[6] S.O.3(1).
[7] *Clerk of the House of Representatives Act* 1988, s.16.

[8] *Public Finance Act* 1989, s.2(1).
[9] *Parliamentary Service Act* 2000, s.20(1); "Resourcing Parliament, Report of the Review Committee on the First Triennial Review of Parliamentary Appropriations", 2002, PP, A.2(a); "Resourcing Parliament – Parliamentary Appropriations Review, Report of the Committee on the Second Triennial Review, 2004, PP, A.14.

Staff are appointed to the Office of the Clerk by the Clerk of the House and are employed under employment agreements negotiated with the Clerk. The Office is organised into four main divisions—

- a *House Office*, which provides support for the sittings of the House by producing the journals and scrutinising petitions and questions (through the Table Office) and distributing parliamentary papers, order papers and bills (through the Bills Office); the House Office also arranges the presentation of bills for the Royal assent, co-ordinates the Office of the Clerk's contribution to parliamentary education programmes and manages inter-parliamentary relations
- a *Select Committee Office*, which provides the staff and administrative and support services for the meetings of select committees
- *Reporting Services*, which is responsible for producing the official report of parliamentary debates (*Hansard*), parliamentary broadcasting and translation and interpretation services and maintaining the Office's website
- a *Corporate Office*, which provides information services, human resources and financial management support.

Journals

The Clerk is responsible for noting all the proceedings of the House by recording every motion considered by the House and the decision reached on it. The Clerk also records any other items of business transacted by the House, such as the presentation of a petition or the answering of questions; recording not what was said by individual members in a speech but what the House as a whole has decided. A similar note of the proceedings is maintained when the House goes into a committee of the whole House. The rough notes of proceedings made in the House are elaborated later and constitute the journals of the House, which are published by the Clerk.[10] Currently the journal is published on a weekly basis (as part of the *Parliamentary Bulletin*) and assembled at the end of each session into a sessional volume or volumes. The journal of the House is the official record of the proceedings of the House. It provides at least presumptive evidence of the business transacted by the House.[11]

Schedules are also compiled and bound with the journal, showing in a tabular form details of legislation dealt with by the House, papers and petitions presented to it, and select committees appointed. An appendix to the journal published from 1858 to 1999 contains select committee reports and other reports published by order of the House (*Appendix to the Journals of the House of Representatives*). (From 1854 to 1856 the journals and reports presented to the House were bound in one publication known as the *Votes and Proceedings*.) Since 1999, reports published by order of the House are published in an annual series, *Parliamentary Papers*. An appendix to the journal continues to be published but is confined to specifically parliamentary material such as select committee reports. (See Chapter 38.)

Records

The Clerk has custody of the journals and of all petitions and papers presented to the House and other records belonging to the House. These documents must not be taken from the

---

[10] S.O.8.
[11] *Evidence Act* 1908, s.30; *Baburao alias P B Samant v Union of India* AIR 1988 Supreme Court, 440.

House without the House's or the Speaker's permission.[12] The documents in the Clerk's custody include all evidence presented to select committees, which must be handed over to the Clerk when the committee's report is presented unless the House instructs a committee to retain confidential evidence in its own possession.[13] The House's papers and records as held by the Clerk can be seen by any member. Subject to any order of the House, they are also regarded as public documents and will be made available to other persons unless this would be contrary to the law. This would be the case, for instance, if a document was subject to a court order protecting its confidentiality or if it contained obviously defamatory material not protected by an order of the House. In these circumstances the Clerk would not disseminate the document beyond members.[14] Occasionally the House directs the Clerk not to disclose material in the Clerk's custody to any person,[15] and secret evidence in any event remains confidential unless the House authorises its release.[16] The Clerk also protects the material from possible damage or destruction and endeavours to maintain the privacy of personal information held. The Clerk must retain the original of all papers and records for at least three years before they may be disposed of.

The Chief Archivist may accept parliamentary records for deposit in Archives New Zealand.[17] Accordingly, before disposing of such documents, the Clerk must consult with the Chief Archivist.[18] Conditions for the deposit of parliamentary records may be agreed between the Clerk and the Chief Archivist.[19] An archiving policy has been agreed with Archives New Zealand providing for the transfer to it of parliamentary materials at the expiration of varying periods depending upon the class of documents involved and for the destruction of materials which are available in other forms. Parliamentary records (or any other records) do not become subject to the *Official Information Act* merely because they have been deposited with Archives New Zealand.[20]

SERJEANT-AT-ARMS AND THE MACE

The Serjeant-at-Arms is the officer of the House who is responsible for ensuring that visitors (known as strangers) admitted to the Chamber do not misbehave. For this purpose the Serjeant may require strangers who interrupt proceedings or who otherwise misconduct themselves in the galleries to leave.[21]

The Serjeant-at-Arms was originally a Royal officer with the power to arrest without warrant. The House of Commons in the fifteenth century induced the Crown to appoint such an officer to the House to enable it to order the arrest of persons who offended against its privileges. The symbol of the Serjeant's authority to arrest was the Mace he carried. In time the Mace came to be regarded as the formal corporate symbol of the authority of the House. To avoid removing the Mace from the House when an offender was ordered to be arrested, the Speaker began to issue warrants of arrest. Offenders are now arrested under the Speaker's warrant rather than by the authority of the Mace.[22]

The Serjeant-at-Arms is appointed by the Crown on the recommendation of the Speaker. Any person may perform the functions and exercise the powers of Serjeant at the direction of the Speaker.[23] The Speaker authorises a number of officers employed in the Parliamentary Service to perform the duties of Serjeant.

The Serjeant-at-Arms precedes the Speaker in the Speaker's formal procession, carrying the Mace on the shoulder to and from the House at the beginning and end of

[12] S.O.10.
[13] 1894, Vol.86, p.909.
[14] 1994, Vol.539 p.470.
[15] See, for example, 1996, Vol.557, p.14312 (Education and Science Committee proceedings on its inquiry into the sale of Tamaki Girls College).
[16] S.O.220(3).

[17] *Public Records Act* 2005, s.42(1)(a).
[18] S.O.11.
[19] *Public Records Act* 2005, s.42(2).
[20] *Ibid.*, ss.42(4) and 58.
[21] S.O.41.
[22] HC 34 (1967-68) (*Report of Select Committee on Parliamentary Privilege*).
[23] S.O.3(1).

each sitting, and also when the Speaker visits Government House to seek confirmation of election as Speaker (in this case, the Mace is held in the crook of the Serjeant's arm until the Governor-General's confirmation is forthcoming) and to present any address from the House. During a sitting with the Speaker or one of the Speaker's deputies in the chair, the Mace remains on the Table of the House. When the Speaker leaves the chair for the House to go into a committee of the whole House, the Mace is placed under the Table.[24]

While the Mace has become a corporate symbol of the House in New Zealand as well as in the United Kingdom, it is no more than that. The House had no Mace at all for the first 12 years of its existence, and although the absence of a Mace is not usual, it does not prejudice the continued sitting of the House or affect the validity of anything done at that sitting.[25]

The first Mace was presented to the House by its first Speaker, Sir Charles Clifford, in 1866, and was destroyed in the Parliament House fire of 1907. A temporary wooden mace was then used until, on 7 October 1909, the present Mace was donated to the House by the Prime Minister, Sir Joseph Ward, and his Cabinet. This mace was ordered from England at the Ministers' own expense. The Mace, which is a replica of the one used in the House of Commons, is made of silver gilded with 18 carat gold. It is 1.498 metres long and weighs 8.164 kilograms.[26]

REPORTING OF DEBATES

Hansard

When the House first met in 1854 there were no arrangements for the official reporting of debates. Debates were then, however, reported in the colony's newspapers in much greater detail than is the case today, and to assist the press some members took notes of speeches delivered by their friends which were later revised and submitted for publication.[27] Despite this there were numerous complaints from members of inaccurate reporting of speeches, and several times over the next 12 years the House expressed its view that full and accurate reports of its debates should be published under its authority. These demands became more insistent when Parliament moved from Auckland to Wellington, for members were extremely dubious of the capability of the Wellington press to report proceedings adequately. At the start of the 1867 session, the Government (on its own initiative) appointed an editor and a reporting staff to take down and report the speeches made in both the House and the Legislative Council.[28] The control of this staff and the arrangements for the publication of the debates were at first placed in the hands of a select committee composed of members of both Houses.

The expression *Hansard* derives from the name of the family responsible for arranging the private and official reporting of the British Parliament throughout most of the nineteenth century. The term was already widely used at the time official reports began in New Zealand, and is now used as a shorthand expression for the official report of parliamentary debates.

In 1885 the pre-*Hansard* parliamentary debates from 1854 to 1866 were published in an official series. All living members who could be traced were asked to supply any collected reports of speeches in their possession. Newspaper reports of speeches were

---

[24]   S.O.172.
[25]   1898, Vol.103, p.257.
[26]   Sutherland, "Symbol of Authority. The Mace in New

Zealand.", *Numismatic Journal*, (1947) Vol.4, No 1.
[27]   PD 1854-55, p.184.
[28]   1867, Vol.1, p.17.

consulted, as was the official record of proceedings made by the Clerk in the *Votes and Proceedings* and the journals. Even so, many of the speeches made in the two Houses during this period were wholly lost or could be recorded only in a much abbreviated form.[29]

An official report of debates is authorised to be made of such portions of the proceedings of the House and its committees as the House or Speaker determines.[30] The Clerk of the House is responsible for the making of the official report[31] and the staff engaged on this work are employed in the Office of the Clerk. Since 1996 all proceedings in committees of the whole House have been reported (previously only some 10 percent of proceedings were reported). Select committee proceedings are not reported comprehensively, although a recording of evidence is often taken and such recordings may be transcribed and published.[32] Secret sessions and sittings or parts of sittings from which strangers have been excluded are not reported.[33]

Form of the report

The form of the *Hansard* report is determined from time to time by the House or the Speaker.[34] *Hansard* is a report of speeches made in the House, not necessarily of all the business transacted there. A full record of the business transacted by the House, but without any of the reasons as expressed in speeches, is made by the Clerk for inclusion in the House's journals. If an item of business does not elicit any debate or words spoken about it, it may not be noted in *Hansard* at all, as happens, for example, with the presentation of petitions and papers.

Speeches are transcribed directly from digital recordings of the debate, with staff present in the Chamber beyond the Table of the House to monitor the debate by recording the sequence of speakers and any interjections. A transcript of the report is submitted to each member for correction, usually within two to three hours of the speech being made. The *Hansard* report is a report in direct speech of all speeches made in the House, sub-edited to omit repetitions and redundancies. Members are tied to what they have said in the House and may make only minor or grammatical alterations to the report. The meaning or substance of what was said cannot be altered in any way, though occasionally there may be controversy as to whether this has occurred.[35] The Clerk may bring to the Speaker's attention any attempt by a member to make extensive corrections to the transcript.[36]

Interjections are reported only if the member speaking replies to them or remarks on them during the course of his or her speech.[37] If the *Hansard* staff cannot identify the interjector themselves but have to rely on what they are told, they can confirm directly with the member that he or she was the source of the interjection.[38] Maps, documents, photographs, pictures or cartoons cannot be inserted in *Hansard* except by resolution of the House.[39] Nor does *Hansard* record which member objected if a request for leave is refused.[40] The Standing Orders formerly required that replies to written questions be recorded in *Hansard*. For this purpose a separate *Hansard* publication (known as the *Hansard Supplement*) was published from 1989 to 2002. Written replies are no longer published in *Hansard*.

Occasionally the House has (on notice having been given) ordered proceedings not

---

[29] PD 1854-55, preface.
[30] *Legislature Act* 1908, s.253A(1); S.O.9(1).
[31] *Clerk of the House of Representatives Act* 1988, s.3(e).
[32] S.O.232(1).
[33] S.O.40(c).
[34] *Legislature Act* 1908, s.253A(2); S.O.9(2).

[35] See Clarke, *The Keynesian Revolution in the Making*, p.67 (text of Budget speech apparently altered for inclusion in *Hansard*).
[36] 1960, Vol.323, p.1180.
[37] 1910, Vol.153, p.362.
[38] 1995, Vol.548, p.7623.
[39] 1898, Vol.103, p.526; 1905, Vol.133, p.108.
[40] 1995, Vol.546, p.6177.

to be reported in *Hansard*, as when the debate on the second reading of a bill (which had taken place the previous day and had been recorded by the *Hansard* reporters) was ordered not to be published.[41] In respect of speeches or parts of speeches given in Māori, an official English translation is published.[42] Like all speeches published in *Hansard*, the translation is subject to the approval of the member who gave the speech.[43] (See Chapter 16 for the translation of speeches.)

Hansard is published by order of the House.[44] An uncorrected transcript of each day's oral question period is available on the Office of the Clerk's website approximately two hours after the end of question time.[45] A corrected daily *Hansard* is available in print to members approximately one week after the debate takes place, and the daily reports are combined into publications with a pink cover (the *Hansard* "pinks"), containing one week's reports, for sale through bookshops. There is no copyright in *Hansard*.[46] Following a select committee recommendation, up to 25 copies of each *Hansard* pink are made available free to each member.[47] The pinks are bound into volumes and these volumes are numbered consecutively, beginning with number one in 1867. They are usually cited by the year, volume and page number. The official series of debates compiled for the years 1854–66 contains one or more sessions to each volume. *Hansard* is also available for public internet access.

Parliamentary Press Gallery
The gallery immediately above and behind the Speaker's chair is reserved for the use of accredited members of the Parliamentary Press Gallery. These members are representatives of newspapers, news agencies, radio stations and television channels supplying parliamentary news from within the Parliament buildings. Membership of the Parliamentary Press Gallery is granted by the Speaker on application by the chairperson of the Press Gallery (a member of the gallery elected by the other members).

As well as admittance to the press gallery in the Chamber itself, Press Gallery members may be provided with office accommodation and other facilities in Parliament House subject to rules made by the Speaker. Telephone rental and toll charges are payable by the news organisations represented in the Press Gallery. Members of the Press Gallery are permitted to dine at Bellamy's and to use the Parliamentary Library.

Press Gallery members may make a record of the proceedings in the House and at select committees, subject to control by the House, the Speaker or the committee concerned. The Press Gallery is subject to the general control of the Speaker, who from time to time makes rules for its members.[48]

BROADCASTING OF PROCEEDINGS

Radio
The House of Representatives was the first legislative chamber in the Commonwealth to have its debates broadcast. The first proceeding to be broadcast was the election of the Speaker on 25 March 1936.[49] Continuous sound broadcasts of the proceedings are made by Radio New Zealand Limited on its AM network as a condition of holding the

---

[41] 1888, JHR, pp.67-8 (*Contagious Diseases Bill*).
[42] 1990, Vol.508, p.2338.
[43] 1997, Vol.562, p.3193.
[44] S.O.9(3).
[45] 2002, Vol.602, p.54.
[46] *Copyright Act* 1994, s.27(1); *Copyright Act*

Commencement Order 2000.
[47] 1917, AJHR, I.11.
[48] "Rules of the Parliamentary Press Gallery", approved by the Speaker of the House of Representatives on 22 July 1999.
[49] *New Zealand Listener*, 28 March 1981.

licence for that network.[50] The conditions under which the broadcast is made are agreed between Radio New Zealand Limited and the Clerk of the House. Payments are made by the Office of the Clerk to reimburse Radio New Zealand Limited for the cost of providing the service.

The Standing Orders provide for the House's proceedings to be broadcast on radio during all hours of sitting.[51] But the occasional breakdown in a transmission does not affect the continuation of the sitting.[52] Broadcasting is discontinued during any period for which strangers have been ordered to withdraw from the Chamber.[53]

A microphone is attached to each desk in the Chamber, and microphones are provided at the Speaker's chair and the Clerk's seat at the Table. The microphones at the chair and at the Table are continuously "live" subject to a mute button by which they can be controlled by the presiding officer. The control of the other microphones is in the hands of a technician who observes proceedings from a booth at the far end of the Chamber. A member's microphone is activated by the technician when that member is called to speak by the Speaker. This system, introduced in 1975 to replace microphones suspended from the ceiling throughout the Chamber, was an endeavour to improve the quality of the broadcast by concentrating on the member speaking and cutting out background noise in the Chamber.

The parliamentary broadcast provides a strong primary signal to some 63 percent of the population. In secondary reception areas, listeners with a good-quality receiver or external aid should receive reliable reception. The broadcast is available to about 75 percent of the population if both primary and secondary areas are included.[54]

The live radio broadcast, as an extension of the debates in the House, is absolutely protected against legal liability arising in defamation.[55] The restriction on any unauthorised publication of a report or account of an inquiry before the Inspector-General of Security and Intelligence does not apply in respect of the broadcasting of parliamentary proceedings.[56]

In 1979, following a favourable recommendation by the Standing Orders Committee,[57] the practice began of using extracts from the parliamentary sound broadcast in news and current affairs programmes on radio and television. The use of such an extract from a speech has now become commonplace. In 1982 Radio New Zealand Limited, with the Speaker's concurrence, began to preserve material from the parliamentary broadcast in its sound archive. Since 1994, daily and weekly programmes summarising the work of the House have been broadcast on Radio New Zealand using funding provided by the Office of the Clerk.[58]

Television

The proceedings at the opening of Parliament were first televised in 1962[59] and are now regularly broadcast on television. In 1986 the House held an experimental telecast over the course of a week, during which its proceedings up to the end of question time were transmitted live to air and the remainder of the sitting was filmed and recorded and used for news programmes. Television cameras were subsequently admitted to the Chamber on special occasions, such as for the delivery of the Budget. In 1989 the Standing Orders Committee in a report to the House recommended that the proceedings of the House should be made available for television coverage. This recommendation has been reflected in the

---

[50] *Radiocommunications Act* 1989, s.177(2)(a).
[51] S.O.44(1).
[52] 1985, Vol.466, pp.7110-1.
[53] S.O.40(d).
[54] *Hansard Supplement*, 1989, Vol.2, p.1293.
[55] *Defamation Act* 1992, s.13(2).
[56] *Inspector-General of Intelligence and Security Act*

1996, s.29(6).
[57] 1979, AJHR, I.14, p.20
[58] "Covering the House", *New Zealand Listener*, 26 March 1994.
[59] Martin, *The House – New Zealand's House of Representatives 1854-2004*, p.268.

Standing Orders.[60] Any bona fide broadcaster may film in the Chamber.[61] The Serjeant-at-Arms should be informed beforehand so that any necessary administrative arrangements can be made, but formal permission is not necessary.

Any television broadcast of the House must maintain such standards of fairness as are adopted from time to time by the House.[62] Such a broadcast must also conform with general broadcasting standards. The House itself has not formally defined any rules for televising its proceedings, though the Speaker, drawing on past select committee recommendations, has done so.

The conditions under which the House may be broadcast are[63]—

- the broadcaster can decide which portions of the proceedings to film
- coverage should be medium range, concentrating on the Speaker and the member who has the call;　this means a head and shoulders shot of the member with the call, not a close-up
- an occasional general, wide-angle shot of the Chamber gradually returning to focus on the member speaking may be made
- interjections and interruptions from the gallery should not be covered (such incidents may be reported and tape of them used in legal proceedings[64])
- panning of the Chamber and close-ups are not allowed
- no extraneous matter, for example, graphics, other than the name of the member speaking, may be included in any broadcast.

The Serjeant-at-Arms will intervene if it becomes apparent that filming is occurring outside the rules. Broadcasters who offend against the rules may have their privilege of filming in the Chamber withdrawn. On one occasion when a complaint was made to the Speaker that a television news item had juxtaposed two statements by members made on different days so as to suggest that they were a direct exchange on the same day, the Speaker received a letter from the television company acknowledging its mistake and apologising for the error.[65] On another occasion when a television company deliberately broke the rules by filming a member who did not have the call, that company's operators were excluded from the Chamber for one week.[66]

In 2000 a satellite broadcaster began to transmit the House's proceedings live on one of its news channels each day until the end of question time, with rebroadcasts in the evening.[67]

The question of the House providing its own television broadcast of its proceedings has been discussed for two decades. In 2003 the Standing Orders Committee agreed that this be done under contract with a suitable contractor, providing a feed free to any broadcasters.[68] In 2004 the Government responded favourably to this recommendation and work commenced on a project to establish such a facility.

A live broadcast of the House is absolutely protected against legal liability arising in defamation.[69] The restriction on any unauthorised publication of a report or account of an inquiry before the Inspector-General of Security and Intelligence does not apply in respect of the televising of Parliament.[70]

Televising meetings of select committees is a matter for each individual committee to address. If the committee agrees, its proceedings can be filmed.

---

[60]　S.O.44(1).
[61]　1990, Vol.507, p.1828.
[62]　S.O.44(2).
[63]　2000, Vol.586, p.4970.
[64]　1997, Vol.562, pp.3805-8.
[65]　2000, Vol.586, p.4969-70.
[66]　2005, Vol.624, pp.19509-10.
[67]　2000, Vol.587, p.5408.
[68]　2002-05, AJHR, I.18B, pp.12-4.
[69]　*Defamation Act* 1992, s.13(2).
[70]　*Inspector-General of Intelligence and Security Act* 1996, s.29(6).

Stills photography

Stills photographs of the House at work exist from the nineteenth century, but they were still relatively exceptional, except on Budget day, until comparatively recently.

The liberalisation in regard to televising the House that has occurred since 1990 led to complaints that stills photographers were at a disadvantage compared to television broadcasters in that, while the latter had an open permission to film proceedings, the former had to seek individual permission on each occasion. Consequently, in 2000 the Speaker agreed to amalgamate the conditions for stills photography with those for televising the House. The same rules and conditions for the two now apply, but stills photographers must obtain the Speaker's express permission before using flashes.[71]

PARLIAMENTARY SERVICE

From 1854 onwards administrative services required in relation to the meetings of Parliament were devolved on to the Clerk of the House. There was a gradual accretion of such services in the nineteenth century (messengers, library, *Hansard* reporters, caterers) and into the twentieth century (executive secretaries, research units, security staff, out-of-Parliament secretaries and so on).

As early as 1868 the suggestion was made that the Speaker, perhaps as head of a commission of members, should be responsible for the legislative estimates.[72] Accordingly, the estimates for the House and the Legislative Council were, up to 1891, placed under the control of the respective presiding officers. In that year the House indicated that in future the estimates of expenditure for the legislature should be the responsibility of the Government[73] and after that date a Minister took charge of the legislative estimates, the first to do so being the Minister of Justice. In 1912, following a general reorganisation of the public service, a Minister was specifically designated to be responsible for drawing up and presenting to Parliament estimates of expenditure for the legislative service, though the two Speakers retained control of the staff employed in their respective departments. With the growth in size and diversity of legislative staff, the Speaker's administrative control diminished and the Minister in charge of the department (which was known as the Legislative Department) came to exercise a control over staff which was similar in most respects to staff control in government departments. This arrangement was maintained after the Legislative Council was abolished, and lasted until 1985.

On 1 October 1985 a new parliamentary agency, the Parliamentary Service, was created.

The Parliamentary Service is principally responsible for providing administrative and support services to the House and to the members of the House and for administering the payment of funding entitlements provided for parliamentary purposes.[74] As well as providing services to members of Parliament, the Parliamentary Service provides services to the other offices and departments of state that occupy accommodation in the parliamentary complex – Office of the Clerk, Parliamentary Counsel Office, Department of the Prime Minister and Cabinet, and Department of Internal Affairs (executive government support). The administrative and support services provided to the House and to members of Parliament and the funding entitlements for parliamentary purposes are subject to a triennial review by a committee appointed by the Speaker.[75]

---

[71] 2000, Vol.586, p.4970.
[72] 1868, AJHR, D.2.
[73] 1891, Vol.74, pp.723-30.
[74] *Parliamentary Service Act* 2000, s.7.
[75] *Parliamentary Service Act* 2000, s.20(1); "Resourcing Parliament, Report of the Review

Committee on the First Triennial Review of Parliamentary Appropriations", 2002, PP, A.2(a); "Resourcing Parliament – Parliamentary Appropriations Review, Report of the Committee on the Second Triennial Review, 2004, PP, A.14.

The General Manager of the Parliamentary Service is the administrative head of the Service.[76] The General Manager is responsible to the Speaker for carrying out the duties and functions of the service, for tendering advice to the Speaker and the Parliamentary Service Commission, for the general conduct of the service and for its efficient, effective and economical management.[77] The General Manager is also *ex officio* a member of the Parliamentary Corporation.[78] The General Manager is appointed for a term of five years by the Governor-General on the recommendation of a committee chaired by the Speaker and consisting of members of Parliament and the State Services Commissioner.[79]

The Parliamentary Service is not a department of the public service and is not part of the executive government at all.[80] It does nevertheless administer a vote containing appropriations for outputs as if it were a government department. The responsible Minister for the vote is the Speaker.[81] The staff employed by the Parliamentary Service are engaged in providing building maintenance, library services, security, reception, attendant services, party research, secretarial services and general administration. The majority of staff are employees on short-term contracts and work directly for members or parties. Core staff are generally employed on a permanent basis.[82] Many of the personnel provisions that apply to staff employed in departments of the public service apply to employment in the Parliamentary Service.[83]

Parliamentary Service Commission

The Parliamentary Service Commission is the body representing members which is responsible for advising and recommending to the Speaker the nature of the services to be provided to the House and its members and the criteria to be applied in allocating funding entitlements for parliamentary purposes.[84] Although it does not possess executive powers itself (these reside with the Speaker), it is the principal means by which consultations occur on the administrative and support services for Parliament. It provides a link between the Speaker's statutory responsibilities and the ongoing interests of members in resource allocation.[85] No major change in these is made without thorough discussion at the Parliamentary Service Commission or before it has indicated its general agreement to the course proposed. It must be consulted before the Speaker issues a determination of the travel, accommodation, attendance and communications services to be provided to members.[86]

The Speaker chairs the commission *ex officio*[87] and it consists of a number of other members of Parliament. The Leader of the House and the Leader of the Opposition (or members nominated by them) are automatically members of it. In addition, each recognised party is entitled to one member on the commission. Parties with 30 or more members which are not already represented on the commission through the Speaker, the Leader of the House or the Leader of the Opposition (which will usually be the case) are entitled to an additional member.[88] Apart from the Leader of the House, no Minister or parliamentary under-secretary can be a member of the commission.[89] Although it is not a select committee, service on the commission is regarded as service in the capacity of a member of Parliament.[90]

The commission meets regularly once each month and on other occasions as required. The Speaker, as chairperson of the Parliamentary Service Commission and political head

---

[76]   *Parliamentary Service Act* 2000, s.10.
[77]   *Ibid.*, s.11.
[78]   *Ibid.*, s.29(1)(b).
[79]   *Ibid.*, Sch.1, cls.1 and 4.
[80]   *Ibid.*, s.6(2).
[81]   *Public Finance Act* 1989, s.2(1).
[82]   2002-05, AJHR, I.19A, p.181.
[83]   *Parliamentary Service Act* 2000, Sch.1, cl.7.

[84]   *Ibid.*, s.14.
[85]   1999-2002, AJHR, I.22A, p.493.
[86]   *Civil List Act* 1979, s.20A(2).
[87]   *Parliamentary Service Act* 2000, s.16.
[88]   *Ibid.*, s.15(1), (2).
[89]   *Ibid.*, s.15(3).
[90]   *Parliamentary Service Act* 2000, s.15(6); 1996-99, AJHR, I.15C, pp.8-9

of the Parliamentary Service, inevitably plays a more involved role in the work of the Parliamentary Service than other members of the commission. The commission operates in a non-partisan way, endeavouring to ensure that services are delivered to members at the highest level and as efficiently as possible.[91] Its minutes or other papers are not normally released.[92] Written questions can be asked of the Speaker in respect of the Speaker's responsibilities for the Parliamentary Service and as chairperson of the Parliamentary Service Commission, but a point of order relating to this role is not permitted.[93]

The commission establishes committees as it sees fit.[94] It regularly establishes a House Committee, which decides the rules applicable to the use of members' catering facilities and the level of service to be provided.

Parliamentary Corporation

The Parliamentary Corporation was created in 2000, to facilitate transactions relevant to the duties of the Parliamentary Service and, in particular, to acquire, hold and dispose of interests in land and other assets.[95] The Parliamentary Corporation has wide powers to engage in transactions in respect of land and buildings.[96] The Bowen House lease is vested in the Parliamentary Corporation[97] and it must hold an interest in any land or premises before that land or premises can be added to the parliamentary precincts.[98] (See Chapter 11.)

The corporation consists of the Speaker (as chairperson), the General Manager and two members of the Parliamentary Service Commission appointed by the commission.[99]

Parliamentary Library

Soon after the first meeting of Parliament in 1854, members turned their attention to setting up a library. At first, library facilities were shared with the Auckland Provincial Council, which already had a collection of books, but in 1856 Parliament voted money for the purchase of further books and for the construction of a building in which to house them. The first librarian (who was also Clerk of the House) was appointed in 1858 but this post was not made into a separate full-time position until some time after Parliament and the library (then known as the General Assembly Library) moved to Wellington. For many years the General Assembly Library was the legal depository for all books published in New Zealand, a function performed by the National Library since 1985. However, there are still statutory obligations on local authorities to send copies of their annual plans to the Parliamentary Library.[100] In 1999 the House marked the centenary of the completion of the present Parliamentary Library building (the oldest building in the complex).[101]

From 1966 to 1985, the General Assembly Library was part of the National Library of New Zealand. On 1 October 1985 it became part of the Parliamentary Service.[102] It was renamed the Parliamentary Library on 1 January 1987 to reflect the abolition of the term General Assembly.[103]

The Parliamentary Library provides such library, information, research and reference services as are required by the General Manager for members of Parliament, officers of the House, officers of Parliament, staff of the Parliamentary Service and other staff employed within Parliament buildings.[104] The supply of works and broadcasts to members

---

91   *Hansard Supplement*, 1990, Vol.6, p.1497.
92   1999, Vol.577, p.17010.
93   1992, Vol.532, p.13236.
94   *Parliamentary Service Act* 2000, Sch.2, cl.8.
95   *Ibid.*, ss.27 and 28.
96   *Ibid.*, s.30.
97   *Ibid.*, s.24(1).
98   *Ibid.*, s.25(3).
99   *Ibid.*, s.29.
100   *Local Government Act* 2002, s.95(7)(b)(iii).
101   1999, Vol.578, p.17591.
102   See now *Parliamentary Service Act* 2000, Sch.1, cl.11.
103   *Constitution Act* 1986, s.27.
104   *Parliamentary Service Act* 2000, Sch.1, cl.12.

of Parliament by the Parliamentary Library does not breach any copyright subsisting in them.[105] The head of the library is the Parliamentary Librarian, who is an employee of the Parliamentary Service directly responsible to the General Manager.[106]

Bellamy's

The parliamentary catering and refreshment service is known as Bellamy's. The original Bellamy was John Bellamy, a deputy housekeeper at the House of Commons who made the first catering arrangements for members within the Houses of Parliament in 1773. These services were continued after Bellamy's death by his son.[107] John Bellamy's family ceased to have any connection with the House of Commons shortly before the New Zealand Parliament was founded, but the family name was used in referring to the catering arrangements established for members of Parliament in New Zealand. The name "Catering Department" was officially adopted in place of "Bellamy's" in 1945, but in 1951 the House reverted to the original and more popular name. At first, arrangements were made by outside caterers under contract for the session, but by 1880 a manager who combined catering duties with the position of custodian of the building was appointed, and meals and refreshments began to be provided in-house.

Meals are still provided in-house, but catering and refreshment services are now provided by a private catering firm under contract with the Parliamentary Service. Bellamy's provides breakfasts, lunches and dinners, and operates a bar. Bellamy's also caters for state and parliamentary luncheons and dinners and numerous other functions.

KAUMATUA

On 4 July 2000, the Speaker announced the appointment of a kaumatua to the Speaker.[108] The kaumatua renders advice and assistance to the Speaker as needed, such as at the opening of Parliament and other important formal occasions and events taking place within the precincts of Parliament. The kaumatua is the Speaker's adviser on the application of tikanga Māori to the proceedings of the House. Although not an employee or agent of the Office of the Clerk or the Parliamentary Service, the kaumatua gives advice and assistance to those organisations too.

---

[105] *Copyright Act* 1994, s.58.
[106] *Parliamentary Service Act* 2000, Sch.1, cl.13.
[107] Wilding and Laundy, *An Encyclopaedia of*

Parliament, p.39.
[108] 2000, Vol.585, p.3349.

CHAPTER 6

OFFICERS OF PARLIAMENT AND OTHER OFFICERS AND BODIES ASSOCIATED WITH PARLIAMENT

OFFICERS OF PARLIAMENT

The first officer of Parliament to be expressly created as such by statute was the Ombudsman (then known as a commissioner for investigations) when that position was established in 1962.[1] A second officer of Parliament was created in 1976 when the Wanganui Computer Centre Privacy Commissioner was established. This office was abolished on 30 June 1993. A third officer of Parliament, the Parliamentary Commissioner for the Environment, was created on 1 January 1987. An older position than any of these, that of the Controller and Auditor-General, became a formal officer of Parliament position on 1 July 2001.

Definition of officer of Parliament

There is no statutory definition or criteria established to identify an officer of Parliament. The status of officer of Parliament is one attached on an individual basis to particular positions. Nor is there any specific definition of what being an officer of Parliament entails in respect of powers, duties and functions flowing from the possession of that status. There are some common rules that have been developed for their relations with the House and for the funding arrangements for the officers, but in the main the powers, duties and functions of the officers are to be gathered from a consideration of the individual statutory provisions applying to each officer.

Nevertheless, some attempt has been made to define when it is appropriate to confer on an official the status of "officer of Parliament" because it is recognised that this should be done only after due deliberation and when it is appropriate given the nature of the official's duties. Conversely, if a position is to be established as an officer of Parliament it should be subject to the conditions that flow from being an arm of the legislative branch of the state, such as being outside the public service and not subject to the executive's control of its activities.

In an inquiry carried out in 1989, the Finance and Expenditure Committee set out five criteria to consider when the creation of an officer of Parliament was under investigation. The committee was of the view that—

- an officer of Parliament must only be created to provide a check on the arbitrary use of power by the executive
- an officer of Parliament must only discharge functions which the House itself, if it so wished, might carry out
- an officer of Parliament should be created only rarely
- the House should, from time to time, review the appropriateness of each officer of Parliament's status as an officer of Parliament
- each officer of Parliament should be created in separate legislation principally devoted to that position.[2]

These recommendations were endorsed by the Government of the day[3] and have formed

---

[1] *Parliamentary Commissioner (Ombudsman) Act 1962*, s.2(1).

[2] 1987-90, AJHR, I.4B.

[3] *Ibid.*, I.20, p.113.

the basis ever since for consideration of whether it is appropriate to make a particular position an officer-of-Parliament position.

In elaboration of these criteria, a committee considering a proposal for the creation of an officer of Parliament said that it was not an appropriate model for an official with an advocacy role, because an officer of Parliament must be seen to act impartially so as to retain the integrity and confidence of the whole House. The ability of an officer of Parliament to take a position on a matter of public controversy is thus necessarily inhibited. It was also considered inappropriate for an officer of Parliament to exercise executive responsibility and so become involved in the development of policies and services provided by the Government[4] or for officer-of-Parliament status to be accorded where the official's functions were confined to providing informational and related educational activities.[5]

Proposals to create officers of Parliament
Underpinning the recommendations made by the Finance and Expenditure Committee in 1989 was a recommendation that Cabinet adopt an instruction requiring consultation with the select committee on officers of Parliament (now the Officers of Parliament Committee) before it approves the drafting of legislation that includes the creation of an officer of Parliament. The Officers of Parliament Committee's terms of reference specifically include power to consider any proposals referred to it by a Minister for the creation of an officer of Parliament.[6] That committee has protested where a proposal to create an officer of Parliament reached legislative form in a bill without having been referred to it first.[7] It is also possible that such proposals may be made directly to committees that are considering bills without having been considered first by the Officers of Parliament Committee.[8] It has been accepted that it is for the House as a whole to come to a view on the creation of officers of Parliament and that it is desirable that there is a consensus on this in the House. Proposals made directly to a committee thus need to be assessed in this light. A proposal to create an officer of Parliament has been withdrawn by the Government where there was not consensus.[9]

OFFICERS OF PARLIAMENT COMMITTEE
One of the most important developments in ensuring a common parliamentary approach to the position of officer of Parliament was the creation of a select committee with a particular responsibility for the oversight of officers of Parliament. This committee was created in 1989 as a direct result of the inquiry carried out by the Finance and Expenditure Committee.[10] At first the committee was appointed on an ad hoc basis to examine the estimates of expenditure for officers of Parliament on referral from the Finance and Expenditure Committee. Since 1992 it has been one of the permanent select committees which are established at the commencement of each Parliament.[11]

The Speaker chairs the Officers of Parliament Committee *ex officio*.[12] Its size is determined by the Business Committee. All parties will be offered representation on it, though they may not be able to accept this. Apart from appointments of officers of Parliament, the committee's duties mainly involve considering the funding of the offices of Parliament but it also provides a central focus for the parliamentary relationship with officers. This does not by any means mean that officers of Parliament are not involved

---

4   1999-2002, AJHR. I.22A, p.893 (*Parliamentary Commissioner for Children Bill*).

5   2002-05, AJHR, I.22C, pp.1276-7 (*New Zealand Superannuation Amendment Bill*).

6   S.O.386(1)(c).

7   1993-96, AJHR, I.23C, p.127 (*Environment Amendment Bill*).

8   2002-05, AJHR, I.22C, pp.1276-7 (*New Zealand Superannuation Amendment Bill*).

9   1996, Vol.553, pp.11674-5 (*Environment Amendment Bill*).

10 1987-90, JHR, p.1678.

11 S.O.185(1)(b).

12 S.O.202(3).

with other select committees. The Auditor-General's staff provide services to all of the subject select committees when they are carrying out their financial and inquiry functions and the Auditor-General's reports may be directly relevant to topics under consideration by other committees. The Parliamentary Commissioner for the Environment's staff assist select committees on legislation and inquiries with environmental implications and the nature of that officer's duties means that there is frequent interchange with the Local Government and Environment Committee.

The Officers of Parliament Committee has a clear focus on the annual budget setting for offices of Parliament. (See Chapter 34.) But the estimates and financial reviews of offices of Parliament are allocated to subject select committees.[13] As well as its work on appointments and undertaking the work on pre-budget approval of funding for offices of Parliament, it is also the committee's duty to recommend to the House the appointment of auditors for each office of Parliament[14] and to consider proposals for the creation of a new officer of Parliament referred to it by a Minister.[15] It may develop or review a code of practice applicable to any or all officers of Parliament.[16] The committee has reported to the House on codes of practice which it has developed governing the provision of assistance to select committees by officers of Parliament and interaction with the House generally.[17]

PROCEDURES FOR THE APPOINTMENT OF OFFICERS OF PARLIAMENT

Officers of Parliament are appointed by the Governor-General on the recommendation of the House. Over time a convention has developed of inter-party consultation before a notice of motion endorsing the appointment of a person as an officer of Parliament is put to the House.[18]

Concern that the convention was not working as effectively as intended and that there was still too much departmental influence over the appointments, led the Standing Orders Committee in 1995 and 1996 to formalise the procedures under which consultations for appointments took place.[19] The procedures were further revised in 2002.[20]

The Officers of Parliament Committee is specifically charged with recommending to the House the appointment of persons as officers of Parliament.[21] The procedures followed vest the function of co-ordinating consultations for appointments (and reappointments) firmly in the hands of the Speaker working through the Officers of Parliament Committee. For this purpose where a new position is established and six months before the end of the term of office of an incumbent, the Speaker initiates consultations with representatives of all of the parties represented in the House through the committee. Where a party is not represented on the committee, the Speaker ensures that it is advised of the consultation and is able to have a representative attend meetings of the committee at which the appointment is discussed.

Members serving on the Officers of Parliament Committee are responsible for representing the views of their party colleagues on an appointment. However, any member of Parliament has the right to speak directly to the Speaker and the committee about an appointment. The relevant Minister is specifically advised of the consultation to be undertaken and invited to participate in it. The Minister of Justice has participated in an Ombudsman appointment, for example.[22]

Any member can suggest a name for appointment but, whether this is done or not,

13   1993-96, AJHR, I.18A, pp.41-2.
14   S.O.386(1)(b); 1999-2002, AJHR, I.22B, pp.1232-
      4.
15   S.O.386(1)(c).
16   S.O.386(2).
17   1993-96, AJHR, I.17B (Parliamentary
      Commissioner for the Environment); 1999-2002,
      AJHR, I.15A (Controller and Auditor-General).

18   1993-96, AJHR, I.18A, p.85 (Standing Orders
      Committee).
19   *Ibid.*, pp.85-6; *ibid.*, I.18B, pp.5, 36-7.
20   2002-05, AJHR, I.15A (Officers of Parliament
      Committee).
21   S.O.386(1)(d).
22   2002-05, AJHR, I.22B, p.967.

the committee will follow a rigorous selection process. A job description and person specification is prepared with assistance from the State Services Commission or a specialist adviser to the committee. The position is advertised and, in addition, the recruitment adviser will initiate a job search, as directed by the committee. The adviser helps the committee to assess applications and draw up a short list of candidates.[23] Candidates are interviewed by a subcommittee chaired by the Speaker which reports to the full committee for final endorsement. The cost of this process is charged to the office of Parliament concerned. Members are pledged to consider candidates for appointment in the light of the qualifications and qualities required by the relevant legislation and to use their best endeavours to find a person whose appointment can be supported by all parties.[24] No public comment on proposed appointees is made while consultations are continuing.

No proposal will be put to the House without the unanimous agreement of the committee unless the Speaker considers that total agreement is impossible, it is unreasonable to prolong the consultations and the public interest requires that an appointment be made forthwith. Even then the Speaker will only consent to this where, after extensive consultation, the Government and other major parties agree about the appointment but unanimous agreement cannot be reached due to the opposition of a party or parties representing a small minority of members of Parliament.[25]

A temporary appointment may be made on the Government's initiative while consultations are proceeding if the Speaker, in consultation with the committee, agrees that it is reasonable that this be done in any particular case.

When agreement has been reached on an appointment it is put to the House by means of a Government notice of motion in the name of the Leader of the House.

CONDITIONS APPLYING TO OFFICERS OF PARLIAMENT

Term of office
Officers of Parliament are appointed for fixed terms of office. In the case of the Auditor-General this is for up to seven years.[26] For the Ombudsmen, the Parliamentary Commissioner for the Environment and the Deputy Auditor-General this is for up to five years.[27] But all officers of Parliament (except for the Deputy Auditor-General) continue to hold office at the end of their terms until a successor has been appointed. The Auditor-General may not be reappointed to the position.[28] There is no prohibition in respect of the reappointment of other officers of Parliament.

Oaths
All officers of Parliament must, before entering upon the duties of the office, take an oath of office, in the form prescribed for each, before the Speaker or the Clerk of the House.[29]

Remuneration and funding
The salaries and allowances of officers of Parliament are determined by the Remuneration Authority and are appropriated under permanent legislative authority. Their salaries may not be reduced during the term of their appointment.[30]

The funding for the operation of the offices of Parliament is subject to special pre-

23 *Ibid.*
24 *Ibid.*, I.15A.
25 *Ibid.*
26 *Public Audit Act* 2001, Sch.3, cl.1(1).
27 *Ombudsmen Act* 1975, s.5; *Environment Act* 1986,

s.6; *Public Audit Act* 2001, Sch.3, cl.2(1).
28 *Public Audit Act* 2001, Sch.3, cl.1(4).
29 *Ombudsmen Act* 1975, s.10; *Environment Act* 1986, s.10; *Public Audit Act* 2001, Sch.3, cl.3.
30 *Ibid.*, s. 9; *ibid.*, s.9(1); *ibid.*, Sch.3, cl.5.

budget approval by the House on the recommendation of the Officers of Parliament Committee. (See Chapter 34.) The Speaker is the "responsible Minister" for each office of Parliament in respect of the offices' funding.[31] But the Speaker has no role in an officer's operational decisions. In this respect the officers are statutorily independent.

The auditors of offices of Parliament are appointed by resolution of the House.[32] The Officers of Parliament Committee is charged with making recommendations of auditors for offices of Parliament.[33] The House has appointed the Auditor-General as the auditor of the Ombudsmen and the Parliamentary Commissioner for the Environment and an independent auditor for the Auditor-General.[34] The latter appointment is reviewed every three years.[35] Before the Minister of Finance may issue any instructions to offices of Parliament and before any regulations may be made in respect of them concerning the information they must publish in respect of their activities or the non-financial reporting standards that they must comply with, the Minister must first provide the Speaker with a draft of such instructions or regulations.[36] The Speaker presents the draft to the House[37] and it is referred to the Officers of Parliament Committee for consideration.[38] The instructions or regulations can only be given or made after they have been approved by resolution of the House.[39]

Cessation and suspension from office

An officer of Parliament may resign from office by informing the Speaker in writing.[40] The Speaker informs the House of any such resignation that is received.[41]

An officer of Parliament may be suspended or removed from office only by the Governor-General on an address from the House on the grounds of disability affecting performance of the officer's duties, bankruptcy, neglect of duty or misconduct.[42] An officer may be suspended by the Governor-General while Parliament is not in session but such a suspension obtains only for a limited period after the next session commences during which time the House may consider the matter.

CONTROLLER AND AUDITOR-GENERAL

The Controller and Auditor-General is the state's auditor. The position was first established in New Zealand in 1878 absorbing functions from a number of audit officers. It became a full officer-of-Parliament position in 2001, with the first Auditor-General being appointed on the recommendation of the House early in 2002.[43]

Organisation of the office

The Auditor-General is a corporation sole with perpetual succession.[44] The Deputy Controller and Auditor-General is also appointed as an officer of Parliament,[45] and may exercise all of the functions, duties and powers of the Auditor-General.[46]

The Auditor-General employs the staff and engages the private-sector auditing firms necessary to assist the Auditor-General in carrying out the duties of the office. Staff are employed outside the public service. The office is organised into two internal business units. The office of the Auditor-General is responsible for strategic audit planning,

31   *Public Finance Act* 1989, s.2(1).
32   *Ombudsmen Act* 1975, s.31A; *Environment Act* 1986, s.26(1); *Public Audit Act* 2001, s.38(1).
33   S.O.386(1)(b).
34   2001, Vol.596, pp.12580-1.
35   2002-05, AJHR, I.22C, p.1097; 2004, Vol.622, pp.17664-5.
36   *Public Finance Act* 1989, s.82(1), (2).
37   *Ibid.*, s.82(3).
38   2002-05, AJHR, I.18C, pp.10-11.
39   *Public Finance Act* 1989, s.82(5).

40   *Ombudsmen Act* 1975, s.5; *Environment Act* 1986, s.6(3); *Public Audit Act* 2001, Sch.3, cl.1(3).
41   1992, Vol.525. p.8401; 1994, Vol. 543, p.4111.
42   *Ombudsmen Act* 1975, s.6; *Environment Act* 1986, s.7(1); *Public Audit Act* 2001, Sch.3, cl.4.
43   2002, Vol.598, pp.14655-61.
44   *Public Audit Act* 2001, s.10(1).
45   *Public Audit Act* 2001, s.11; 2002, Vol.601, p.16899.
46   *Public Audit Act* 2001, s.12(1).

setting auditing standards, allocating audits, overseeing auditors' performance, carrying out performance audits and special studies and inquiries, and for parliamentary reporting and advice. The second unit, Audit New Zealand, is responsible for carrying out annual financial report audits and providing assurance services to public entities.[47] Audits are allocated by appointment by the Auditor-General, though some audits of entities with a strong commercial focus are allocated on a contestable basis.[48]

Annual work plan

The Auditor-General is obliged to submit a draft annual plan to the House at least 60 days before the opening of each financial year. This draft plan sets out the Auditor-General's proposed work programme for that year along with the office's forecast financial statements.[49] To facilitate consideration of the plan, the Auditor-General sends an early draft of it to all Ministers and select committees in December with an offer to brief committees and discuss the plan with them if desired. Any comments received by the end of February are considered by the Auditor-General before the formal draft plan is presented to the House by the Speaker in March. Consideration of this draft is organised by the Finance and Expenditure Committee. The committee circulates it to other committees and co-ordinates their responses, which are forwarded to the Auditor-General by 30 April.[50]

The Auditor-General must take account of any such comments and comments from the Speaker before presenting a completed annual plan to the House. The plan must specifically identify any changes requested by the Speaker or the committees that are not included in the final work programme.[51]

Work of the office

The Auditor-General is the auditor of every public entity.[52] This includes auditing the Crown, public service departments, Crown entities, State enterprises, local authorities and a number of other public bodies.[53] The House has appointed the Auditor-General as auditor of the other officers of Parliament.[54] In total the office conducts over 3,900 annual financial reports (about 2,550 of these are of school boards).[55] The office must each year submit information to the House on its future operating intentions.[56] This information is referred to the Officers of Parliament Committee which communicates its views directly to the Auditor-General to enable a future operating plan to be finalised.[57]

Staff of the office of the Auditor-General work closely with select committees, especially in their estimates and financial review work. Staff have been seconded to select committees to provide technical support on other inquiries. The Auditor-General's office also carries out its own inquiries and reports directly to committees on them. A protocol for the provision of assistance to select committees by the Auditor-General has been adopted. This protocol sets out how decisions on the nature and level of such assistance are to be taken.[58]

The Auditor-General must present an annual report to the House[59] but may report to it at any time on matters arising out of the performance and exercise of the Auditor-

---

47   "The Auditor-General's auditing standards", Report of the Controller and Auditor-General, 3 May 2003.

48   2004, PP, B.28, p.97 (Controller and Auditor-General).

49   *Public Audit Act* 2001, s.36(1).

50   2002-05, AJHR, I.22A, pp.90-3.

51   *Public Audit Act* 2001, s.36(3), (4).

52   *Ibid.*, s.14(1).

53   *Ibid.*, s.5, Sch.1 and Sch.2.

54   2001, Vol.596, pp.12580-1.

55   "The Auditor-General's auditing standards", Report of the Controller and Auditor-General, 3 May 2003.

56   *Public Finance Act* 1989, s.45G(1).

57   2002-05, AJHR, I.18C, p.9.

58   1999-2002, AJHR, I.15A.

59   *Public Audit Act* 2001, s.37.

General's functions, duties and powers.[60] Each year the House receives three or four general reports from the Auditor-General on particular audits and inquiries that have been carried out into central government or local authority activities. The Auditor-General also has a general power to report to a Minister, a select committee, a public entity or any other person on a matter arising out of the discharge of the Auditor-General's duties if the Auditor-General considers it desirable to do so.[61] The Auditor-General's views must be sought by the Local Government Commission in its consideration of any reorganisation scheme.[62]

OMBUDSMEN

The position of Ombudsman was created in 1962 to investigate complaints relating to administrative decisions or recommendations made by government departments or other governmental bodies. The scope of the Ombudsman's remit was extended to include education and hospital boards in 1968 and local authorities in 1975. In 1982, extensive functions under the *Official Information Act* 1982 were added to the office's other tasks and these were extended into the local government area in 1987 and to school boards of trustees in 1994.[63] As from 1 January 2001 the Ombudsman is required to provide employees with information and guidance on making protected disclosures.[64]

The term "ombudsman" has been applied to industry complaints procedures in banking and insurance.[65] There is now a statutory prohibition on the use of the term without the permission of the Chief Ombudsman.[66] The Chief Ombudsman has devised criteria for considering applications for the use of the name that seek to avoid confusion between the parliamentary, recommendatory nature of an Ombudsman's work and the adjudicative, consumer complaints resolution process desired for industry procedures. Given the international and constitutional connotations of the title, permission to use it will rarely be given.[67]

There may be one or more Ombudsmen appointed as officers of Parliament, one of whom is to be appointed Chief Ombudsman.[68] A second Ombudsman was appointed for the first time in October 1975 and a third (for a two-year term, since renewed) in 2001. Temporary Ombudsmen may be appointed from time to time also. Holding or continuing to hold office as a District Court judge has been declared to be compatible with being an Ombudsman and an Ombudsman has been permitted to continue to hold office as a District Court judge during his term of office.[69] All Ombudsmen have equal authority in carrying out their work (the Chief Ombudsman's lead role is in respect of the administration of the Office of the Ombudsmen). A proposal for the appointment of "Deputy Ombudsmen" that would compromise this statutory equality has been rejected.[70]

The House may, if it thinks fit, make general rules for the guidance of the Ombudsmen in the exercise of their statutory functions. Such rules are printed and published as if they were statutory regulations.[71] Rules authorising the Ombudsmen to publish reports relating to their functions or to a particular case or cases have been made.[72]

Any committee of the House may refer a petition which it has before it to an Ombudsman for a report.[73] This has been done only rarely. An Ombudsman may report to the House at any time, but the Ombudsmen must report to the House on their activities at

60   *Ibid.,* s.20.
61   *Ibid.,* s.21.
62   *Local Government Act* 2004, Sch.3, cl.37(1)(c)(iii).
63   See Gilling, *The Ombudsman in New Zealand,* pp.51-2, 87-108.
64   *Protected Disclosures Act* 2000, s.15.
65   See, for example, *The Dominion,* 19 October 1994 (insurance and savings ombudsman appointed).

66   *Ombudsmen Act* 1975, s.28A(1).
67   2001, PP, A3, pp.27-32; 2003, PP, A.5, para.6.5.
68   *Ombudsmen Act* 1975, s.3.
69   *New Zealand Gazette,* 15 December 1994, pp.4421-2.
70   1999-2002, AJHR, I.15B.
71   *Ombudsmen* Act 1975, s.15.
72   *Ombudsmen Rules* 1989.
73   *Ombudsmen Act* 1975, s.13(4).

least once a year.[74] The House has held a specific debate on the Ombudsmen's report.[75]

The Ombudsman is an investigatory official. The office does not make final binding adjudications on issues, only recommendations, and it has no power to enforce its findings. This is seen as its strength. It seeks to persuade parties to a dispute to follow a reasonable course of action and resolve disputes without declaring a winner and a loser.[76] In most cases the prestige of the office is enough to lead any public agency to which a recommendation is addressed to comply with that recommendation. In an exceptional case where this did not occur the House criticised a body which rejected an Ombudsman's recommendations and called upon it to comply.[77] However, even in this case the body concerned was not under a legal obligation to comply.

As with other offices of Parliament, the Office of the Ombudsmen must each year submit information to the House on its future operating intentions.[78] The Officers of Parliament Committee conveys its views on the draft directly to the office so that the plan can be finalised.[79]

PARLIAMENTARY COMMISSIONER FOR THE ENVIRONMENT

The Parliamentary Commissioner for the Environment is an officer of Parliament appointed by the Governor-General on the recommendation of the House.[80]

The parliamentary commissioner has a wide-ranging role of inquiring into the actions of public authorities insofar as they might have an environmental impact, and auditing the procedures that public authorities themselves have in place for minimising any adverse environmental effects that might result from their activities.[81] The commissioner must report on the extent to which the Electricity Commission (Energy Commission) is meeting its governmental policy objectives and outcomes concerning the environment.[82] The views of the commissioner must be sought by the Local Government Commission on any reorganisation scheme it is considering.[83] The commissioner may appoint staff to assist in the exercise of the powers and functions of the office. These staff are employed under terms and conditions approved by the Speaker.[84]

The House or any select committee may request the commissioner to report on any petition, bill or other matter before it which may have a significant effect on the environment.[85] Under this provision, the commissioner has conducted an inquiry into planning for flood mitigation and reported the results to the House for a committee to utilise the report in an inquiry that it was conducting.[86] The House may also direct the commissioner to inquire into any matter with environmental consequences and to report on it to the House.[87] The commissioner and the commissioner's staff frequently assist select committees in their financial and inquiry work by acting as advisers to them.[88] A code of practice regulating the assistance that the commissioner may provide has been devised.[89]

The commissioner must submit information to the House on the office's future operating intentions,[90] and take account of the views of the Officers of Parliament Committee in finalising this plan.[91]

The workload of the office is determined by—

* the number of issues identified by the commissioner, the commissioner's staff,

---

74   *Ibid.*, s.29.
75   1999, Vol.576, pp.15799-812.
76   2003, PP, A.3A, para.6.6.
77   2004, Vol.619, pp.15085-91.
78   *Public Finance Act* 1989, s.45G(1).
79   2002-05, AJHR, I.18C, p.9.
80   *Environment Act* 1986, s.4.
81   *Ibid.*, s.16.
82   *Electricity Act* 1992, ss.172ZO and 172ZP.

83   *Local Government Act* 2004, Sch.3, cl.37(1)(c)(iv).
84   *Environment Act* 1986, s.11.
85   *Ibid.*, s.16(1)(d).
86   1987-90, AJHR, I.11A.
87   *Environment Act* 1986, s.16(1)(e).
88   2002, PP, C.12, pp.20-2.
89   1993-96, AJHR, I.17B.
90   *Public Finance Act* 1989, s.45G(1).
91   2002-05, AJHR, I.18C, p.9.

members of Parliament, and other individuals and groups, where these are considered significant in terms of their effects on the environment
- requests from the House and select committees
- environmental impact reporting required for Ministers and government agencies.[92]

The commissioner will become concerned with an issue only if no other government agency is already dealing with it or is capable of handling it.[93]

OTHER OFFICERS AND BODIES ASSOCIATED WITH PARLIAMENT

The House is involved in the appointment or removal of a number of other officers, apart from the officers of Parliament. These officers include the Representation Commission and the Electoral Commission, the Clerk of the House of Representatives and the Parliamentary Service Commission, and judges of the High Court, the Employment Court and the Environment Court who can be removed from office only following an address from the House. (See respectively, Chapters 2, 5 and 30.) There are also detailed parliamentary accountability requirements relating to Crown entities and State enterprises. (See Chapter 35.) Miscellaneous other officers and bodies with which the House has an association are dealt with below.

Abortion Supervisory Committee

This committee was established to keep under review the law on abortion and to perform administrative and licensing tasks under the relevant legislation.[94] (The committee has itself recommended that it be disestablished and that its functions be absorbed into health services regulation generally.[95]) The committee consists of three members (two of whom must be registered medical practitioners) appointed by the Governor-General on the recommendation of the House.[96]

Members of the Abortion Supervisory Committee hold office for three years but remain in office until their successors are appointed. They may be removed from office by the Governor-General only following an address from the House.[97] Vacancies in the membership of the committee arising by the death, resignation or removal of members are filled by the appointment of a successor by the Governor-General on the House's recommendation.[98] In that case the person appointed to the vacancy holds office only for the unexpired portion of the term of his or her predecessor, not for a three-year term in his or her own right.[99] Although it is not a Crown entity, the House has resolved that the committee should be subject to the House's financial review procedures.[100]

Association of Former Members of Parliament

In 1989, following the establishment of similar groups in the United States, Canada and Australia, a number of former members of Parliament established a group known as the Association of Former Members of the Parliament of New Zealand. The association is an unincorporated body with its own constitution. Membership is open to all former members of Parliament. The association charges its members an annual subscription and appoints a management committee from among its membership.

The objects of the association are: to encourage the continuance of associations and friendships formed while members of Parliament; to represent former members; to provide advice and assistance in appropriate cases to former members; and to arrange

[92]   1987-90, AJHR, I.19A.
[93]   *Ibid.*, I.19B.
[94]   *Contraception, Sterilisation, and Abortion Act* 1977, ss.10 and 14.
[95]   1999-2002, I.21A, p.11.
[96]   *Contraception, Sterilisation, and Abortion Act*

1977, s.10.
[97]   *Ibid.*, s.11.
[98]   *Ibid.*, s.12.
[99]   *Ibid.*, s.11(4).
[100]   1999, Vol.581, p.37; 2002, Vol.602, p.237.

functions and meetings to the benefit of parliamentary institutions.

The association holds an annual general meeting in Parliament House and its annual report is presented to the House by the Speaker.

Cawthron Institute Trust Board

The Cawthron Institute is an industrial and technical school, institute and museum set up under the will of Thomas Cawthron (1833–1915, a Nelson businessman and philanthropist) and a private Act of Parliament.[101] The member of Parliament for the electoral district of Nelson is an *ex officio* member of the Institute's trust board.[102]

Intelligence and Security Committee

The Intelligence and Security Committee is a statutory committee that was established in 1996 to exercise oversight and review of the intelligence and security departments – the New Zealand Security Intelligence Service and the Government Communications Security Bureau.[103]

The committee consists of the Prime Minister, the Leader of the Opposition, two members of Parliament nominated by the Prime Minister after consultation with the leader of each party in any government coalition and one member nominated by the Leader of the Opposition, with the Prime Minister's agreement, after consultation with the leader of each party not in government. The names of the nominated members must be submitted to the House for its endorsement as members of the committee. The committee cannot transact business until these members have been endorsed by the House.[104] As such membership is dependent on nomination by the Prime Minister or the Leader of the Opposition, as the case may be, it is not competent for the House to substitute its own nominees for appointment, though it may reject a nominee and vote on such nominations separately.[105] If it becomes apparent to the Speaker that the statutory requirement for consultation has not been carried out, the Speaker will rule any notice of motion seeking the House's endorsement out of order. It is therefore incumbent on the Minister lodging such a notice to satisfy the Speaker that the consultation has been carried out. Consultation in this context means more than merely informing other leaders of a decision that has already been reached; it means giving the person being consulted a real opportunity to be heard. But ultimately the matter is decided politically on the floor of the House.[106]

The committee can consider bills, petitions and other matters referred to it by the House.[107] The House has resolved that the committee consider the estimates and supplementary estimates for, and conduct a financial review of, each intelligence and security department. Bills are referred to the committee from time to time and the Clerk is obliged to refer any petition relating to an agency to the committee. The House usually orders that no select committee can examine an intelligence and security department.[108]

The proceedings of the committee are, subject to the legislation, to be conducted in accordance with the Standing Orders. Unless the committee unanimously resolves to the contrary, all proceedings are held in private.[109] The committee is serviced by the Department of Prime Minister and Cabinet.[110] Proceedings of the committee are privileged in the same manner as if they were proceedings in Parliament.[111] The committee is obliged to have regard to security considerations in any report it makes to the House.[112]

---

[101]   *Thomas Cawthron Trust Act* 1924.
[102]   *Ibid.*, s.3(1)(a)(iii).
[103]   *Intelligence and Security Committee Act* 1996, ss.5 and 6.
[104]   *Ibid.*, ss.7 and 8.
[105]   1997, Vol.560, pp.2023-4.
[106]   *Ibid.*

[107]   *Intelligence and Security Committee Act* 1996, s.6(1)(b).
[108]   See, for example, 2002, Vol.604, pp.1897-909.
[109]   *Intelligence and Security Committee Act* 1996, s.12.
[110]   *Ibid.*, s.13(7).
[111]   *Ibid.*, s.16.
[112]   *Ibid.*, s.18.

Judicial Conduct Commissioner

In 2004 provision was made for the appointment of a Judicial Conduct Commissioner. The commissioner's functions are to receive complaints about judges, conduct preliminary examinations of them and, in appropriate cases, recommend that a Judicial Conduct Panel be appointed to inquire into the conduct of a judge.[113] The commissioner is appointed by the Governor-General on the recommendation of the House. Before the House's recommendation is made, the Attorney-General must consult the Chief Justice about the appointment and advise the House that this has been done.[114] The commissioner holds office for such period (between two and five years) as is specified in the appointment.[115] The commissioner may only be removed from office within this period by the Governor-General acting on an address from the House for incapacity or misconduct.[116]

Legislation Advisory Committee

The Legislation Advisory Committee is an informal group of eminent persons (mainly, but not exclusively, lawyers) appointed by the Minister of Justice to advise the Government and, if it sees fit, Parliament on legislative proposals and legislative forms.[117] Guidelines issued by the committee have been endorsed by the Government as representing the drafting standards that legislation should generally follow.[118] The committee is available to departments to comment on particular legislative proposals they are developing to ensure that good legislative forms are employed. The committee may also comment on the wording of indicative referendum proposals.

The committee is a non-statutory body serviced by the Ministry of Justice.

Māori Purposes Fund Board

The Māori Purposes Fund Board administers the Māori Purposes Fund, which is responsible for promoting the health, education and economic welfare of Māori and for other matters in relation to Māori arts, language, customs and traditions.[119] Each member of Parliament representing a Māori electoral district is *ex officio* a member of the Board.[120]

New Zealand Business and Parliament Trust

The New Zealand Business and Parliament Trust was formed in 1991 as an educational charity. The Speaker is its president. It endeavours both to widen the experience and increase the knowledge of members of Parliament by assisting them to undertake periods of study with private-sector companies and to improve business people's understanding of how Parliament functions by arranging practical studies for them.[121]

The setting up of such a trust was inspired by the success of a similar organisation in the United Kingdom, the Industry and Parliament Trust. There were 44 corporate members of the trust at the end of 2001. The trust organises day-long study programmes held within Parliament House at which business people are introduced to the work of the House and of members of Parliament. In the first 10 years of the trust's existence 700 business people had been involved in the trust's study programmes with 588 of them having participated in seminars in Parliament House organised by the trust. By the end of 2001, 200 members of Parliament had participated in reciprocal study programmes, spending some five to 10 days with a company that is a member of the trust.

113   *Judicial Conduct Commissioner and Judicial Conduct Panel Act* 2004, s.8.
114   *Ibid.*, s.7; 2005, Vol.625, pp.20186-8.
115   *Ibid.*, Sch.2, cl.1(1).
116   *Ibid.*, Sch.2, cl.3.
117   On the work of the committee, see Iles, "The Responsibilities of the New Zealand Legislation Advisory Committee" (1992) 13 Statute LR, p.11.
118   *Cabinet Manual*, 2001, para.5.2.
119   *Maori Purposes Fund Act* 1934-35, ss.4 and 7(1).
120   *Ibid.*, s.7(2)(c).
121   *The National Business Review*, 31 October 1997.

New Zealand Lottery Grants Board

The New Zealand Lottery Grants Board is responsible for determining the proportions in which the profits of New Zealand lotteries are to be allocated for distribution among the various purposes to which lottery profits may be put.[122] The Prime Minister and the Leader of the Opposition are *ex officio* members of the board along with the Minister of Internal Affairs, who presides.[123] The Prime Minister and the Leader of the Opposition may nominate other members of Parliament to attend a meeting of the board in their stead. Such nominated members are regarded as full members of the board.[124]

Ngarimu V.C. and 28ᵗʰ (Māori) Battalion Memorial Scholarship Fund Board

The Ngarimu V.C. and 28ᵗʰ (Māori) Battalion Memorial Scholarship Fund Board administers a scholarship fund established in 1945. The fund provides educational assistance for Māori and for the study and promotion of the Māori language and Māori history, tradition and culture.[125] Each member of Parliament representing a Māori electoral district is *ex officio* a member of the board.[126]

Parliamentary Counsel Office

The House's closest working relationship with an outside body is that with the Parliamentary Counsel Office, which is the office principally responsible for the drafting of government legislation and for drafting amendments to legislation that is passing through the House. (See Chapter 26.)

The Parliamentary Counsel Office was founded as the Law Drafting Office in 1920 and given its present name in 1973. Its ministerial head is the Attorney-General (or, if there is no Attorney-General, the Prime Minister) and its chief executive is the Chief Parliamentary Counsel.[127] As well as drafting bills and amendments, the office compiles and supervises the printing and reprinting of statutes with any amendments which have been made to them. Since 1974 the Chief Parliamentary Counsel has also held the position of Compiler of Statutes, the chief officer of the compilation department within the office.[128]

The Chief Parliamentary Counsel is also responsible for the printing and publishing of statutory regulations. (See Chapter 29.)

Police Complaints Authority

The Police Complaints Authority (and a deputy to the Police Complaints Authority) was created in 1988 to receive and investigate complaints alleging misconduct, neglect of duty or other practices of the police, and to take action in respect of them in appropriate cases.[129]

The Police Complaints Authority, who must be a suitably qualified lawyer, is appointed by the Governor-General on the recommendation of the House for a term of between two and five years. The authority continues to hold office at the conclusion of this term until a successor is appointed.[130] It is the House's practice in recommending a person for appointment to specify in the resolution the term of the recommended appointment.

Where a vacancy occurs in the office while Parliament is not in session or one exists at the close of a session and the House has not recommended a successor, the vacancy may be filled during the recess by an appointment made by the Governor-General in

---

122 *Gambling Act* 2003, s.274.
123 *Ibid.*, s.272(2).
124 *Ibid.*, Sch.5, cl.3.
125 *Ngarimu V.C. and 28ᵗʰ (Maori) Battalion Memorial Scholarship Fund Act* 1945, s.7(1).
126 *Ibid.*, s.4(2)(c).

127 *Statutes Drafting and Compilation Act* 1920, ss.2(2) and 6.
128 *Ibid.*, s.6(4).
129 *Police Complaints Authority Act* 1988, s.12.
130 *Ibid.*, ss.4 and 5.

Council. Such an appointment lapses unless, before the end of the twenty-fourth sitting day following the appointment, the House expressly confirms it.[131]

The Police Complaints Authority may be removed or suspended from office by the Governor-General, on an address from the House, on the grounds of disability, bankruptcy, neglect of duty or misconduct.[132]

The same provisions for the appointment, suspension and removal of the deputy to the Police Complaints Authority apply as apply to the Police Complaints Authority.[133]

Radio New Zealand Limited

Radio New Zealand Limited was established as a Crown entity on 1 December 1995 to hold the public radio assets of Radio New Zealand.[134] Radio New Zealand Limited has a statutory charter setting out its principles and obligations.[135] The House is obliged to review the charter at five-yearly intervals.[136] The Commerce Committee carried out the first review for the House as part of its general inquiry function. In the absence of statutory guidance as to the object of the review, it adopted its own terms of reference to guide it in carrying out the review.[137]

Radio New Zealand Limited holds the licence to use the frequencies on which parliamentary debates are broadcast. (See Chapter 5.)

Reserve Bank of New Zealand

The Reserve Bank of New Zealand is responsible for formulating and implementing monetary policy and registering and regulating banks.[138] Any funding agreement between the Minister of Finance and the Governor of the bank relating to the income of the bank that is to be applied in meeting its expenditure must be ratified by resolution of the House in order to be effective.[139] Although not a Crown entity, the House has resolved that the bank should be subject to the House's financial review procedures.[140]

State Services Commissioner

The Governor-General may suspend the State Services Commissioner or a Deputy Commissioner from office for misbehaviour or incompetence. In this event a full state-ment of the grounds on which the suspension was effected must be laid before the House within seven sitting days of the suspension.[141] The matter is then in the hands of the House. If the House takes no action within 21 days of the statement being given to it, the commissioner is automatically restored to office. But if within that time the House resolves that the commissioner ought to be removed from office, then the Governor-General removes him or her from office as at the date of the suspension.[142]

Universities and tertiary institutions

Universities, colleges of education and polytechnics may not be disestablished unless the House has first passed a resolution approving the proposed disestablishment.[143]

---

131 *Ibid.*, s.7.
132 *Ibid.*, s.6.
133 *Ibid.*, s.8(2).
134 *Radio New Zealand Act* 1995; *Radio New Zealand Act Commencement Order* 1995.
135 *Radio New Zealand Act* 1995, s.7(1) to (3).
136 *Ibid.*, s.7(4).
137 1999-2002, AJHR, I.1B.
138 *Reserve Bank of New Zealand Act* 1989.
139 *Ibid.*, s.161(2).
140 1999, Vol.581, p.37; 2002, Vol.602, p.237.
141 *State Sector Act* 1988, s.16(3), (4).
142 *Ibid.*, s.16(4).
143 *Education Act* 1989, s.164(2).

CHAPTER 7

PARTIES AND GOVERNMENT

PARTIES

Political parties have long played a crucial role in New Zealand politics. A "party system" developed in the nineteenth century in the parliamentary sphere and in the country at large as political parties organised themselves and began to compete for office. Since the late-nineteenth century the composition of governments has been determined by the strength of the various parties' representation in Parliament. The party system helps both to formulate and to translate voter preferences into a parliamentary line-up of members. It helps to give some coherence to political action undertaken through parliamentary means, based on allegiances declared at the time of a general election.[1]

Although parties have occupied this leading role in New Zealand politics for over a century, they have received very little legal or official recognition until comparatively recently, having generally been regarded as private, voluntary bodies. This has changed significantly. The electoral system has, since 1996, been based explicitly on the existence and effective organisation of parties. Thus there are provisions in the law for the registration of parties, votes are cast for parties, not just for individual candidates, seats are allocated to parties on the basis of those votes, election broadcasting time and resources are provided to parties, and parties must disclose the funds donated to them.

Consequent on this overt change in the electoral system from a system that essentially ignored parties and focused on individual candidates to one that recognises parties as primary political actors, the House has radically changed its rules. In early 1996 (prior to the first general election under the new electoral system), the House introduced Standing Orders recognising political parties and explicitly determining many procedural rights on the basis of the party groups in the House.[2]

Recognition

Every party in whose name a member (constituency or list) was elected at the preceding general election or at a subsequent by-election is entitled to be recognised as a party for parliamentary purposes.[3] Recognition is claimed by informing the Speaker of the name by which the party wishes to be known for parliamentary purposes, the identity of its parliamentary leader and other office-holders, and its parliamentary membership.[4] In the period between a general election and the election of a Speaker, these details may be advised to the Clerk.[5] The fact that parties have entered into coalition must also be notified but even so the parties to a coalition remain separate parties for parliamentary purposes.[6] The name by which the party is known for parliamentary purposes need not be the same name under which the party is registered with the Electoral Commission.[7] The name by which it wishes to be known is the one used in all parliamentary publications, such as the journals and *Hansard*. Members who do not seek recognition as members of a party for parliamentary purposes are treated as independent members, regardless of what they may call themselves outside the House.[8]

---

[1] See Jennings, *The British Constitution*, p.31 *et seq.* for a characteristically forthright defence of the party system.

[2] 1993-96, AJHR, I.18A, pp.15-6.

[3] S.O.34(1).

[4] S.O.35(1).

[5] S.O.35(3).

[6] S.O.35(2).

[7] 1999, Vol.578, p.17299.

[8] S.O.34(4).

From this recognition as a party for parliamentary purposes flow a number of legal, procedural and funding consequences.

Legal consequences

Apart from in relation to the electoral system (where recognition depends upon registration with the Electoral Commission, not recognition by the House), there are still few express legal consequences flowing from party recognition. In regard to superannuation policy, attempts have been made from time to time to embody a mechanism for achieving political consensus in legislation based on the parties represented in Parliament. Provision was first made for party adherence to a political accord on superannuation in 1993.[9] It is now provided that before the Minister of Finance recommends the appointment of anyone to the Board of Guardians of New Zealand Superannuation there must be consultation with representatives of the other political parties in Parliament.[10] The leader of such a party may also notify that party's agreement to those parts of the legislation dealing with entitlements to New Zealand superannuation and the management of the New Zealand Superannuation Fund and may withdraw that agreement. Parties are listed in the schedule to the legislation as agreeing to the provisions on the basis of such notification. The schedule may have parties added to it or omitted from it by Order in Council as such parties agree to those parts or withdraw their agreement.[11] Parties are automatically omitted from the schedule if they are no longer represented in the House.[12]

Persons are nominated by the House to represent parties in government and parties in opposition on the Representation Commission (for the drawing of constituency boundaries) and on the Electoral Commission (for the allocation of election broadcasting resources). At least nominally, these are cross-party appointments. (See Chapter 2.)

Procedural consequences

The procedural consequences of recognition of a party for parliamentary purposes are myriad. In the Standing Orders "party" means a party recognised for parliamentary purposes in accordance with the Standing Orders.[13] It does not mean a party registered with the Electoral Commission (though the two concepts will often be identical).[14]

Procedurally, recognition as a party entails—

- the leader of the largest opposition party being recognised as Leader of the Opposition[15]
- parties, as far as practicable, occupying blocks of seats in the Chamber[16]
- representation on the Business Committee (in its own right if it has six or more members and on a shared basis otherwise)[17]
- where possible, the opportunity to participate in each debate[18]
- allocation of speaking time on items of business in proportion to party membership in the House[19]
- priority for spokespersons in debate[20]
- the right to vote by party[21]
- the right to exercise a proxy vote for its party members[22]

[9] *Retirement Income Act* 1993.
[10] *New Zealand Superannuation and Retirement Income Act* 2001, s.56(6).
[11] See: *New Zealand Superannuation (Political Commitment) Order* 2003; *New Zealand Superannuation (Political Commitment) Order* 2004.
[12] *New Zealand Superannuation and Retirement Income Act* 2001, s.72.
[13] S.O.3(1).
[14] 2002, Vol.599, p.15767.
[15] S.O.36.
[16] S.O.37(1).
[17] S.O.74(2),(3).
[18] S.O.102(a).
[19] S.O.102(b).
[20] S.O.102(c).
[21] S.Os 142 and 144.
[22] S.Os 155(4) and 156.

- membership of select committees in proportion to the party's membership of the House[23]
- right to make temporary replacements of its members on select committees[24]
- the right of the leader (provided that the party has a minimum of six members) to comment on ministerial statements[25]
- asking oral questions in proportion to the party's membership of the House[26]
- the leader of a party with six or more members having a longer speech on the Budget debate, the Address in Reply debate and the Prime Minister's statement debate.[27]

Funding

The parties recognised by the Speaker under the Standing Orders receive funding from the Parliamentary Service to help them to discharge their parliamentary duties. This funding consists of leader and party group funding based on a party's constituency and list membership, taking into account the number of a party's members who hold ministerial office and who are therefore entitled to funding in that capacity.[28] The policy under which such funding is made available is determined by the Speaker after consultation with the Parliamentary Service Commission.

Leader of the Opposition

The leader of the largest party not in Government and not in coalition with a Government party is entitled to be recognised as the Leader of the Opposition.[29]

The first true leader of the opposition has been identified as John Ballance in 1889.[30] However, in the more fluid political situation prior to the emergence of strong party organisations in Parliament other members were from time to time dubbed as "leader of the opposition" (often facetiously by their opponents).[31]

The office was first recognised by statute in 1933 when a special allowance was conferred on the holder. Although currently recognised in a number of statutes, it is not an office created by statute (nor is that of Prime Minister); it is a product of the conventions of the parliamentary system. The Leader of the Opposition is paid a special salary by virtue of the office.

The party which the Leader of the Opposition leads is known as the official Opposition and its members are seated immediately on the left of the Speaker's chair. As a parliamentary office depending upon recognition in the House, it is for the Speaker to determine any dispute as to who is the Leader of the Opposition.

Leader of the Opposition is a most important constitutional office, marked at the State Opening of Parliament, where the Leader of the Opposition and the Prime Minister flank the Governor-General as the Governor-General reads the Speech from the Throne. In no other instance is the peculiar strength of the parliamentary system of government so vividly demonstrated than in its recognition of the office of Leader of the Opposition. By this means the opposition is enlisted as an official Government-in-waiting.

The Leader of the Opposition or the Leader's nominee is an *ex officio* member of the Parliamentary Service Commission[32] and of the New Zealand Lottery Grants Board.[33]

---

[23] S.O.186(1).
[24] S.O.188(2).
[25] S.O.349.
[26] S.O.372(2).
[27] Appendix A to the Standing Orders.
[28] 1999-2002, AJHR, I.19C, p.259.
[29] S.O.36.

[30] Wilson, *New Zealand Parliamentary Record 1840-1984*, p.282.
[31] For example, Julius Vogel in 1867; see Dalziel, *Julius Vogel – Business Politician*, p.78.
[32] *Parliamentary Service Act* 2000, s.18(1)(d).
[33] *Gambling Act* 2003, s.272(2)(c).

The Leader of the Opposition is accorded a special status in regard to intelligence and security matters. The Leader is a member of the Intelligence and Security Committee.[34] The Director of the New Zealand Security Intelligence Service is obliged to consult regularly with the Leader of the Opposition in order to keep the Leader informed about matters relating to security.[35] The Leader of the Opposition must also be advised by the Prime Minister and the Attorney-General whenever an entity has been or is to be designated as a terrorist entity and must, if the Leader requests it, be briefed on the factual basis for the designation.[36]

The Leader of the Opposition initiates the debate on the Prime Minister's statement each year,[37] and is entitled to precedence on the opposition side of the House in participating in other major parliamentary debates.

Party leaders

Party leaders in the House include, by definition, the Prime Minister and the Leader of the Opposition. Other Ministers, including the Deputy Prime Minister, may also be party leaders if their party is in a government coalition.

Party leaders are by convention allocated a front-bench seat and will be accorded some precedence of recognition by the Speaker in calling members to speak. Those party leaders whose parties have six or more members may comment on a ministerial statement[38] and they have enhanced speaking times on the Budget, Address in Reply and Prime Minister's statement debates. Before regulations relating to electoral advertisements displayed in public places can be made, the contents of the regulations must be agreed to by at least half of the parliamentary leaders of the parties represented in the House and these must represent at least 75 percent of all members of Parliament.[39]

A court has refused to make an order making party leaders representatives of their parliamentary membership for the purposes of legal proceedings concerned with how members were to vote.[40] However, as those proceedings occurred before the introduction of the MMP electoral system and the consequent procedural changes recognising parties in the House (especially party voting), that judgment may not be a reliable indicator of the current position.

A special salary is payable to a party leader who receives no other special salary (such as a Minister or as Leader of the Opposition). This salary increases incrementally according to the number of members of the party. A salary is also provided for the deputy leader of each party whose members in the House number at least 25.[41]

The appointment of a leader of a party is entirely a matter for the party itself. The House has no role to play in it. The leader of each party must be specifically identified to the Speaker and will consequently be recognised as such by the Speaker.[42]

Whips

The whips are an essential and peculiarly parliamentary manifestation of the party system. The term "whip" (which is derived from the hunting field) indicates vividly the principal task of the holder of this office: to ensure that that member's party's supporters are present in Parliament to support a question when it is put to the vote.

The whips, especially a Government party's whips who need to maintain the

---

[34]   *Intelligence and Security Committee Act 1996*, s.7(1)(b).
[35]   *New Zealand Security Intelligence Service Act 1969*, s.4AA(3).
[36]   *Terrorism Suppression Act 2002*, s.20(5).
[37]   S.O.347.
[38]   S.O.349.
[39]   *Electoral Act 1993*, s.267B(1)(c), (d) and (2)(b), (c).
[40]   *Thomas v Bolger (No 1)* [2002] NZAR 945.
[41]   *Parliamentary Salaries and Allowances Determination 2004*.
[42]   S.O.35(1)(b).

Government's voting majority, are required to keep track of the movements of their members. If a member wishes to be absent from the House, he or she will be required to justify that absence to the whips. If a member cannot or does not bother to do this, and is absent nevertheless, the member can expect to be in trouble with the party for a breach of discipline. The whips carry out most of the tasks that enable parties to function as teams in the House, such as arranging the speaking order of their members and helping to smooth over personal and political differences within caucus. They possess certain powers under the Standing Orders such as holding proxy votes and making temporary replacements on select committees.[43]

The whips are the principal communicators between the parties represented in the House. The smooth running of the House depends to a large extent on the relationship which is built up between whips of different parties, and on the agreements and understandings which they reach with one another. Whips generally attend meetings of the Business Committee on behalf of their parties.

Whips first received additional remuneration by virtue of their office in 1961. A salary (increasing incrementally according to the number of members) is provided for one whip for a party with six or more members in the House and for two whips for a party with 25 or more members.[44] Parties can, of course, appoint as many of their members as whips as they wish, but no special remuneration is available beyond these one or two remunerated positions, as the case may be. The arrangements for the appointment of whips are internal matters for the respective parties to determine. The Speaker must be advised of the appointment of whips.[45]

Caucus

Meetings of members to discuss and co-ordinate parliamentary strategy were held even before a recognisable party system emerged. In 1872 Sir David Monro recorded attending a meeting which he termed a "species of caucus", at a private house.[46]

Each party represented in the House holds a regular meeting of its members of Parliament called a caucus. At these meetings parties discuss parliamentary and other political business. Caucus has been described as playing a necessary but subordinate role in the decision-making process, often making a particular contribution to policy formation.[47] A particular role of caucus is to agree on the tactics to be followed by party members in the House and at select committees.[48] Especially at meetings of caucuses of parties in government, proposals for appointments to public offices may be submitted to caucus for endorsement or consultation.

Depending upon each party's arrangements, caucus meetings may be attended by persons who are not members, such as the party president. Caucus meetings are held each Tuesday morning during sitting weeks (before 1996 they were held on a Thursday) and at less frequent intervals during adjournments of the House. Joint caucus meetings of

---

[43]   S.Os 155(4) and 188(2).

[44]   *Parliamentary Salaries and Allowances Determination* 2004.

[45]   S.O.35(1)(b).

[46]   Wright-St Clair, *Thoroughly a Man of the World: A Biography of Sir David Monro, MD*, p.271.

[47]   Martin, *The House – New Zealand's House of Representatives 1854-2004*, pp.236-7; see Sinclair,

Walter Nash, pp. 95, 164-7 for major policy changes adopted by caucus and not submitted for wider party endorsement until the following year and the contribution of caucus to the development of the social security reforms of 1938.

[48]   See, for example, Sinclair, *Walter Nash*, p.103 (caucus agreeing on what members could refer to in a debate)

parties in coalition have been held since at least as long ago as 1917.[49] However, the term "caucus" has taken on a wider meaning than simply referring to a party meeting; it is also used to refer collectively to all the members of Parliament belonging to a particular party without any connotation of a meeting being involved.

Committees of each caucus are often appointed to help formulate policy in particular subject areas. With the agreement of their Minister, departmental officials may attend meetings of such committees, especially those of a government party's caucus, in order to provide factual information. Officials are not permitted to provide personal comment on the merits of government or party policy to a caucus committee.[50] While departmental officials can assist caucus committees on matters within their (the officials') areas of expertise, they do not themselves provide secretarial or administrative services to the committees. These services are provided by employees of the Parliamentary Service who are engaged to give assistance to the party groups. A department which advertised for submissions for a caucus committee and offered its own premises for the receipt of such submissions has been criticised by a parliamentary select committee as having acted improperly in doing so.[51]

Caucuses and caucus committees are not governmental or parliamentary bodies; they are party bodies. Consequently documents prepared for caucus or caucus committees are not official information to which there is any public right of access, even where such papers are held by a Minister of the Crown.[52] However, such caucus information changes its status if it is attached to or incorporated in advice to Cabinet. It then becomes official information.[53]

Questions relating to caucus activities are not permitted in the House. The proceedings at party caucuses are not subject to the absolute legal protection that applies to proceedings in the House and at select committee meetings.[54]

Parliamentary party membership

The House itself is not concerned with who is or who is not a member of a political party. That is a matter which is relevant to the Electoral Commission. To be entered on the Register of Political Parties and thus enabled to compete for list seats, a party must establish to the commission's satisfaction that it has at least 500 current financial members who are eligible to enrol as electors.[55] If its membership falls below 500 its registration is cancelled.[56]

Party membership is also a matter about which there may be disputes between the party members themselves – such as over whether the party's membership rules (as an incorporated or unincorporated society) have been complied with.[57]

The House *is* concerned with the *parliamentary* membership of the parties, which are recognised for parliamentary purposes. These details must be advised to the Speaker.[58] The Speaker must also be informed of any change in a party's parliamentary membership.[59] A party's membership may change during the term of a Parliament by a member ceasing to be a member of Parliament (by death, resignation or disqualification), by other members

---

[49]   Bassett, *Sir Joseph Ward – A Political Biography*, p.243 (combined caucus meeting of Reform and Liberal parties); see, for a more recent joint caucus of National and New Zealand First parties, "Caucus meetings aim to cement coalition", *The Evening Post*, 18 November 1997.

[50]   *Cabinet Manual*, 2001, para.5.81.

[51]   1991-93, AJHR, I.19B.

[52]   *Sixth Compendium of Case Notes of the Ombudsman*, January 1985, Case No 117; *Ninth*, ibid., July 1989, Case No 1374.

[53]   1993-96, AJHR, A.3, p.26 (*Report of the Ombudsmen for the year ended 30 June 1994*).

[54]   See McGee, "Parliament and Caucus" [1997] NZLJ 137; approved in *Awatere Huata v Prebble* [2004] 3 NZLR 359 (CA) at [63], [64] (per McGrath J). See also *R v Turnbull* [1958] Tas SR 80 at 84.

[55]   *Electoral Act* 1993, s.63(2)(c)(vi).

[56]   *Ibid.*, s.70(2).

[57]   *Peters v Collinge* [1993] 2 NZLR 554.

[58]   S.O.35(1)(c).

[59]   *Ibid.*

being elected to Parliament in its interest, by a member resigning from the parliamentary party but continuing to sit as a member of Parliament, or by a member being expelled from the parliamentary party. The latter two occurrences raise consequential issues as to the members' ongoing status in the House. But in all cases parliamentary membership is determined entirely under the House's own rules, its Standing Orders.[60]

Resignation from the parliamentary party

Any member can leave the parliamentary party in whose interest he or she was originally elected. This would normally be effected by a letter resigning from the parliamentary party addressed by the member to the leader or whip of that party and a letter to the Speaker advising the Speaker of this. Without more, a member in these circumstances would be recognised as an independent for parliamentary purposes.[61] Alternatively, the member could join another parliamentary party already established in the House. In these circumstances the member advises the Speaker that he or she has joined that party with the agreement of its leader.[62] The member is then recognised as a member of that party and party numbers in the House are adjusted accordingly.

A member who has ceased to be a member of his or her original parliamentary party can also seek recognition by the Speaker as a member of another party not hitherto established in the House, provided that the new party is registered as a party by the Electoral Commission and that it has a minimum of six members of Parliament.[63] Such a party loses its recognition for parliamentary purposes if its number of members in the House subsequently falls below six.[64]

Finally, a member who stood as a constituency candidate in the preceding general election for a component party (that is, a party which is itself a member of a registered party or which has combined its membership with another party and registered the combined entity as a party) may leave the registered party and be recognised for parliamentary purposes as a member of that component party.[65]

When the Speaker receives advice that a member has left a party and is therefore an independent member or a member of another parliamentary party, the Speaker advises the House forthwith.[66] The Speaker acts only on advice received from a party leader that a party's membership has changed or on advice from a member that the member has left a party. It is not open to other members to give advice on behalf of another party or another member of such changes.[67]

From 21 December 2001 to 17 September 2005 (polling day for the 2005 general election) any member who resigned as a parliamentary member of the political party for which the member was elected automatically vacated his or her parliamentary seat.[68] This legislation (colloquially known as "party-hopping" or, in peculiarly New Zealand parlance, "waka-jumping" legislation) expired at the time of the general election in 2005.[69] No member resigned from parliamentary membership of their party during this period so as to trigger the legislation.

Expulsion from the parliamentary party

A party caucus may expel a member from membership.[70] How it does that is a matter for it rather than the House.[71] The leader of the party advises the Speaker of the change to

---

60 2004, Vol.619, p.14513.
61 S.O.34(4).
62 S.O.34(2)(a).
63 S.O.34(2)(b).
64 S.O.34(3).
65 S.O.34(2)(c).
66 See, for example: 1999, Vol.577, p.16860; 1999, Vol.580, p.19421; 2003, Vol.613, p.9837.
67 2002, Vol.600, p.15881; 2004, Vol.617, p.12554.

68 *Electoral Act* 1993, s.55A(2), (3)(a).
69 *Electoral (Integrity) Amendment Act* 2001, s.3.
70 For an example see *Peters v Collinge* [1993] 2 NZLR 554 (no legal challenge was made to the *caucus* decision in this case).
71 See Chen, "The long arm of caucus", *The Dominion*, 8 October 1992, as to whether a decision to expel from caucus may be subject to judicial review.

its party membership and the expelled member is henceforth regarded as an independent member.[72]

From 21 December 2001 to 17 September 2005 a more formal legislative expulsion procedure was available to parliamentary parties under the waka-jumping legislation which, if utilised, resulted in the expelled member losing his or her seat.[73] The expulsion procedure was used on one occasion to vacate a member's seat.[74] This power expired at the time of the 2005 general election.[75]

Suspension from the parliamentary party
The suspension of a member from a party caucus effects no change in that party's parliamentary membership.[76] For parliamentary purposes the suspended member remains a member of the party and the party's voting strength is not affected. There is no obligation on a party to notify the Speaker of a suspension. Whether it does so or not is entirely a matter for it.

GOVERNMENT
If he or she is not already Prime Minister, the leader of the political party which obtains a majority of seats in the House of Representatives is invited by the Governor-General to become Prime Minister and to form a Government. This is the essential feature of responsible government and is a cardinal constitutional convention. The action of the Governor-General in selecting and appointing a Prime Minister and a Government does not require any formal consultation with the House itself, nor does the Governor-General's choice of Prime Minister need to be confirmed by the House. In fact, the basis on which the Governor-General's choice is made – that the person concerned commands majority support in the House – should render formal confirmation or approbation by the House unnecessary.

If no one party has an overall majority of members of the House, the Governor-General still needs to find a member of Parliament to carry on in office as Prime Minister. For this purpose a coalition of parties sharing portfolios may be formed on the basis of a coalition agreement entered into between those parties. Its signatories may include party functionaries, such as the party president, as well as parliamentarians. Such an agreement generally sets out the political arrangements for forming and operating the coalition. It does not itself confer any legal rights or obligations; it operates purely at a political level. It has been described as a political manifesto as to how the coalition partners will act.[77] As a political document, accountability for it lies with Parliament. It may be the subject of questions, especially to the Prime Minister, insofar as it has implications for government business,[78] and has been the subject of a ministerial statement where a dispute arose under it between the coalition partners.[79] Although a coalition agreement itself (which is between political parties) is a political, rather than legal, document, the contents of the agreement or some of them may be approved by Cabinet and be promulgated by way of Cabinet Office circular.[80] The agreement may also be incorporated into government policy at a ministerial or departmental level.[81] In these circumstances the agreement's

---

72   2003, Vol.613, p.9837.
73   *Electoral Act* 1993, s.55A(2), (3)(b).
74   *Awatere Huata v Prebble* [2005] 1 NZLR 289;
      New Zealand Gazette, 19 November 2004, p.3749.
75   *Electoral (Integrity) Amendment Act* 2001, s.3.
76   2003, Vol.606, p.3257.
77   *South Taranaki Energy Users Association v South
      Taranaki District Council*, unreported, High Court,
      New Plymouth, 26 August 1997, at p.70 of the

transcript.
78   2000, Vol.587, p.5483.
79   1998, Vol.570, pp.11318-24.
80   *Cabinet Manual*, 2001, para.3.15.
81   See, for example, *Westhaven Shellfish Ltd v Chief
      Executive of Ministry of Fisheries* [2002] 2 NZLR
      158 at [28] (coalition agreement to be taken into
      account in approving fishing permits).

provisions take on the status of official governmental procedures and legal significance may attach to them.

The fact that parties have formed a coalition must be specifically advised to the Speaker.[82]

A Government, whether a single-party Government or a coalition of parties, might not command a majority of seats in the House but nevertheless be able to govern on the basis of agreements or understandings with other parties in the House short of a formal coalition. Such a Government is known as a "minority" Government. In a coalition Government, government is shared between the parties participating in the coalition. But a minority Government does not share power with the party or parties supporting it in office. The latter remain outside government. (However, there may be a minority coalition Government combining the elements of sharing power between parties as well as support from outside government.) A minority Government can remain in office for as long as it is able to avoid defeat in the House on questions of confidence. (See p. 94–9.)

Ministers of the Crown

The Prime Minister forms a Government by choosing some party colleagues to hold office as Ministers of the Crown and advising the Governor-General to appoint such persons accordingly. In a coalition, Ministers from two or more parties share the portfolios. Ministers almost invariably have one or more departments of state assigned to them to administer, although a Minister may be appointed without control of a specified department.

Ministers are appointed to the Executive Council, which is the body that tenders formal advice to the Governor-General and is presided over by the Governor-General. Many important legal powers are exercised by the Executive Council, in particular the making of most statutory regulations. It has been described as a conventional instrument for the formal making of subordinate legislation and a host of other routine administrative decisions.[83]

Most Ministers are also members of the Cabinet, a body which is chaired by the Prime Minister and meets apart from the Executive Council. While having few if any legal powers itself, it is the Cabinet which decides what advice is to be tendered to the Governor-General in the Executive Council and makes many other decisions of a political or administrative nature which are then implemented by Ministers in their individual capacities. It is thus the Cabinet, the meeting of those politicians charged with carrying on the Government, that makes policy decisions on behalf of the Government as a whole. These policy decisions are given legal authority by the Executive Council and translated into action by the Ministers themselves, as the political heads of the various government departments.

Some members of Parliament may be appointed as Ministers but not made members of the Cabinet. The decision as to whether a Minister should be a member of the Cabinet is made by the Prime Minister, though each party may have its own rules as to how these decisions are made (for example, by caucus electing the members of Cabinet).[84]

Ministers are entitled to the honorific "Honourable" (Hon) while they are in office. They lose this title when they cease to hold office, though the Sovereign may confer the title on former Ministers for life. Some senior Ministers, such as the Prime Minister, may be appointed as members of the Privy Council, in which case they use the title "Right Honourable" (Rt Hon). This appointment is for life.

---

[82] S.O.35(2).

[83] *FAI Insurances Limited v Winneke* (1982) 151 CLR 342 at 354 (per Stephen J).

[84] See, for example, Hayward, *Diary of the Kirk Years*, pp.96-9 for a description of the election of Cabinet in 1972.

By convention, Ministers are individually responsible to the House for their official actions and for the general conduct of their departments and officials. This is a political accountability. It is not limited to matters over which the Minister has legal control.[85] This responsibility is given its most obvious parliamentary form by way of questions to Ministers. These can relate to any public affairs with which the Minister is officially connected.[86] This goes far beyond matters for which the Minister has legal authority. It extends to matters over which the Minister may have no legal control but which, by virtue of accepting office, Ministers assume a political responsibility to answer for.[87] Some statutes contain provisions conferring a parliamentary accountability obligation on Ministers in respect of statutory functions which repose in them.[88] These provisions are either otiose or inadequate as statements of the accountability relationship between Ministers and the House. Such relationships rest on constitutional convention, not on legal rules.

Parliamentary Under-Secretaries

Since 1936 there has been provision for the appointment of Parliamentary Under-Secretaries. These are members of Parliament appointed by the Governor-General on the advice of the Prime Minister to assist particular Ministers in their departmental and parliamentary work. A Minister is able to delegate to his or her Parliamentary Under-Secretary any of the ministerial functions, duties and powers the Minister holds.[89]

A Parliamentary Under-Secretary may answer a question on behalf of a Minister in the Minister's absence.[90] Otherwise, a Parliamentary Under-Secretary cannot perform functions conferred by the Standing Orders on a Minister, such as taking charge of a Government bill.

Appointment of Ministers

No person may be appointed or hold office as a Minister of the Crown or as a member of the Executive Council unless that person is a member of Parliament.[91] A similar provision applies with respect to Parliamentary Under-Secretaries.[92] Ministers and Parliamentary Under-Secretaries automatically cease to hold their offices 28 days after ceasing to be members of Parliament.[93]

All members of Parliament cease to be members at the close of polling at the next general election following their election to the House.[94] Members (even those re-elected) do not come into office until the day following the return of the writ, in respect of electorate members, or the day following the forwarding by the Chief Electoral Officer to the Clerk of the House of a return of those elected, in respect of party list members.[95] There is thus a period of some two or three weeks following each general election when there are no members of Parliament in office and it would consequently not be possible to appoint new Ministers. This could prevent a rapid transfer of power to a new Government if this was desirable in the circumstances and also inhibit the urgent reconstruction of a Government that had been returned to power.

Provision has therefore been made in law for persons who were candidates at a general election to be appointed to office as Ministers of the Crown (but not as Parliamentary Under-Secretaries) even though they are not yet members of Parliament. It is provided,

---

[85] 2002-05, AJHR, I.22C, p.253 (*Public Finance (State Sector Management) Bill*).

[86] S.O.369(a).

[87] 1990, Vol.509, pp.2705-6.

[88] See, for example: *Land Transport Management Act 2003*, Sch.4, cl.4; *Gambling Act 2003*, Sch.4, cl.4.

[89] *Constitution Act 1986*, s.9(1).

[90] S.O.376(2).

[91] *Constitution Act 1986*, s.6(1).

[92] *Ibid.*, s.8(1).

[93] *Ibid.*, ss.6(2)(b) and 8(2).

[94] *Electoral Act 1993*, s.54(1).

[95] *Ibid.*, s.54(2).

however, that such appointees automatically cease to be Ministers if, within 40 days of their appointment, they have not become members of Parliament.[96]

While there is no express prohibition on the reappointment to ministerial office of a person who has lost office by failing to become a member of Parliament within 40 days, it would seem that such an appointment would be contrary to the general principle of law that Ministers must be members of Parliament.[97]

Resignation of Ministers

All Ministers may continue in office beyond a general election until they tender their resignations to the Governor-General or until 28 days after the election, whichever occurs sooner.[98] In the case of a Government which is defeated at a general election, all Ministers resign along with the Prime Minister. In the case of a Government returned to power at the election or which remains in office for a prolonged period as a caretaker Government because of extended coalition negotiations, the individual Ministers who did not themselves stand for re-election or who were defeated at the election may remain in office for up to 28 days afterwards. The other Ministers may be reappointed to office before the expiration of the 28-day period, on a caretaker basis if necessary. In the normal course of events, the resignation of an entire Government takes place when the election results for the seats in Parliament have been officially declared, some two weeks or so after polling day, though this period may be prolonged by coalition negotiations.

Caretaker conventions

Where a Government is defeated at a general election, its conduct during the period after the election (while it is holding over as the Government) is subject to certain constitutional conventions or understandings. These conventions were first expressed in the period following the defeat of the Government at the 1984 election.[99] The conventions applying to the Government following an election or a loss of confidence have now been given more expanded expression in the *Cabinet Manual*.[100]

Where, following the election, it is clear who the new Government will be, the care-taker Government is expected to act on the advice of the incoming Government on matters of significance, decisions on which cannot be delayed until the formal transfer of power (the situation in 1984 where the new Government wished to devalue the currency).

Where the election outcome is uncertain, or where during the term of a Parliament a Government loses the confidence of the House and continues to hold office until a new Government takes office or the House's confidence in it is re-established, the Government holds office in a caretaker capacity.

A caretaker Government has executive authority and carries on the normal business of government. However, it is not expected to make significant policy decisions, especially those with long-term implications, either by initiating new proposals or by changing existing policy. All such decisions should be deferred if possible. If deferral is not possible, temporary or holding arrangements may be put in place by the caretaker Government. If a significant decision cannot be deferred or resolved temporarily, consultation with other parties represented in Parliament must be undertaken to ascertain if a proposed course of action has the support of a majority of the House.[101]

[96]   *Constitution Act* 1986, s.6(2)(a).
[97]   *Chaudhuri v State of Punjab* AIR 2001 Supreme Court 2707 (attempted reappointment invalid).
[98]   *Constitution Act* 1986, s.6(2)(b).
[99]   Press statement issued on 17 June 1984 by the Hon J K McLay, Deputy Prime Minister and Attorney-General.
[100]   *Cabinet Manual*, 2001, paras.4.16-4.31.
[101]   *Ibid.*

Different considerations apply in respect of the immediate pre-election period.

In Australia a caretaker convention operates from the dissolution of Parliament until the election results are clear. In this period governments are required to avoid implementing major policy initiatives, making appointments of significance or entering into major contracts or undertakings. The principle is that important decisions that would bind an incoming Government should not be made.[102] It is accepted in Canada too that conventions operate to constrain the powers of the Government after Parliament has been dissolved for an election, though there can be dispute as to whether these constraints apply in a particular case.[103]

The *Cabinet Manual* states that in New Zealand, in the period immediately before a general election, the Government is not bound by the caretaker convention (unless the election has resulted from the Government losing the confidence of the House).[104] Nevertheless, it suggests, governments have chosen to restrict their actions to some extent in the period approximately three months before an election is due or from the date an election is announced, if this is within three months of the election date. Examples of the forms of restraint given are the deferral of significant appointments and limitations on government advertising.[105]

Given the statement in the *Cabinet Manual*, there is clearly no established constitutional convention requiring the Government to act in a caretaker capacity in the pre-election period. However, when Parliament is dissolved prior to an election a Government (even one with a majority in the House) is no longer meeting Parliament and accounting to it for the exercise of executive power. There would therefore appear to be a strong case for saying that a caretaker convention ought to apply from that point on to constrain the making of important decisions by the Government until the outcome of the election is clear.

Leader of the House

The Prime Minister is the leader of the Government in every sphere and through most of Parliament's history also played the role of a floor-leader in the House, deciding on the programming of government business and parliamentary tactics.[106] However, since 1978 another senior Minister has been appointed to the ministerial office of Leader of the House of Representatives and given particular responsibility for government business in the House. Because of the general precedence for government business in the House, the Leader of the House initiates many matters of a procedural nature. The Leader of the House determines the order in which government business will be taken, and is primarily responsible for the timing of the Government's legislative programme. The Leader attends meetings of the Business Committee to outline the Government's intentions with regard to the business to be transacted and suggests the sitting programme to be followed.

The Leader of the House or the Leader's nominee is an *ex officio* member of the Parliamentary Service Commission.[107]

---

[102] Harris, *House of Representatives Practice*, p.58.
[103] Compare, for example, Heard, "Constitutional Conventions and Election Campaigns" *Canadian Parliamentary Review*, Autumn 1995 and Wilson, "The Status of Caretaker Convention in Canada" *Canadian Parliamentary Review*, Winter 1995-96 (dispute over whether a contract for an international airport should have been entered into during this period).

[104] *Cabinet Manual*, 2001, para.4.14.
[105] *Ibid.*
[106] Though in 1931 on the formation of the National Coalition Government a separate Leader of the House was apparently appointed – see Bassett, *Coates of Kaipara*, p.169.
[107] *Parliamentary Service Act* 2000, s.15(1)(b).

Attorney-General

The Minister of the Crown principally responsible for providing legal advice to the Government is the Attorney-General. The Attorney-General is the ministerial head of the Crown Law Office. The chief executive of the Crown Law Office is the Solicitor-General.

The Attorney-General is responsible for reporting to the House on provisions in bills which appear to be inconsistent with the rights and freedoms contained in the Bill of Rights.[108] This must be done before the motion for the bill's first reading is moved.[109] The Attorney-General also usually chairs the Privileges Committee. Standing Orders provide that promoters must give the Solicitor-General notice of any private or local bill which affects the public revenues or the rights or prerogatives of the Crown or which affects a charitable trust.[110]

CONFIDENCE VOTES

A Government subsists in office because it possesses the "confidence" of the House. This is the ongoing basis of responsible government. The confidence of the House underpins any Government's right to hold office; constitutionally, except in a caretaker capacity, it cannot do so without that confidence. It is fundamental that a Government which has lost the confidence of the House must resign or seek a general election. A Government refusing to act appropriately in such a circumstance could, it has been suggested, be dismissed by the Governor-General.[111] Indeed the Governor-General may be obliged to do so to preserve constitutional government.

Strictly speaking, confidence is a negative (and somewhat circular) concept. A Government retains the confidence of the House for so long as it can avoid defeat on important parliamentary votes – those that involve a question of confidence. If a Government were defeated on such a vote, a new political settlement would need to be effected. This new settlement might take a number of forms. Another general election might be held with the defeated Government acting in a caretaker capacity up to the holding of that election; a coalition or a new coalition Government with a majority in the House might be formed; a party or coalition of parties might be commissioned to take office as a minority Government on the basis of understandings with other parties; or the defeated Government may be able to re-establish confidence in itself, having acted in a caretaker capacity in the meantime. (In any case where a new Government takes office, that new Government would itself continue in office only for as long as it retained the confidence of the House.) Whatever the new political settlement, demonstration of a loss of confidence in the Government is an event which demands a reconsideration of the basis on which the Government holds office. Until a new settlement has been effected, the defeated Government could continue in office only on a caretaker basis.

The question of the Government possessing the confidence of the House is not peculiar to a party system of government. It existed in New Zealand politics from the time of responsible government in 1856, long before there were recognisable parties in Parliament. Although legally the Prime Minister and the other Ministers are (on appointment by the Governor-General) carrying on the Sovereign's government, they are politically responsible to the House of Representatives in doing so, and are liable to dismissal, not legally by the House but at its behest, if they cannot maintain support there.

---

[108] *New Zealand Bill of Rights Act* 1990, s.7.
[109] S.O.266(1).

[110] Appendix B to the Standing Orders, cl.4(2)(a), (h).
[111] Marshall, *Constitutional Conventions*, p.27.

The advent of a party system introduced greater stability into government, for once elected with a majority it became unlikely that the Government would lose that majority otherwise than at a general election. Even so, there were times when general elections did not produce a clear majority for a single party and uncertainty over confidence matters ensued.[112] The means by which the retention of confidence in the Government is tested is by a vote in the House itself – a confidence vote. Not since 1928 has a Government been defeated on a confidence vote and thereby been obliged to resign. The adoption of proportional representation in 1996, and the consequent unlikelihood of a single party winning an outright majority of seats at a general election, has refocused attention on the need for each Government to retain the confidence of the House.

In practice, if a Government is facing inevitable defeat in a confidence vote it is unlikely to wait for that event to occur (as the Government did in 1928) before taking action to effect a new political settlement. In this way even if a Government has not been formally defeated in a confidence vote, it may be forced to recognise that defeat is inevitable, to act on the basis that it has occurred, and resign or seek new coalition partners, political agreements with other parties, or a new mandate at an election.

Definition of a confidence vote

The confidence of a House in a Government is a matter of political judgment. It is not a matter of parliamentary procedure on which the Speaker can rule.[113] Ultimately, it is a matter for the Governor-General in the exercise of the reserve powers of the office to judge whether a Government possesses the confidence of the House. This can involve making fine judgments on the legitimacy or effect of the actions of politicians in regard to their management of parliamentary affairs. It has been suggested, for example, that a Governor-General would be justified in refusing a Prime Minister's advice to dissolve Parliament and hold a general election if a motion of no confidence in the Government was under debate in Parliament, especially if the Government's capacity to win that vote was uncertain. The purpose of refusing to dissolve Parliament in these circumstances would not be to force the Government's resignation, but to allow Parliament to express its will.[114]

To be inherently regarded as a question of confidence of the House in the Government, a motion must be put before the House that raises the issue of the Government's survival in office. It is not enough that the motion raises an important issue. That might lead *the Government* to treat the motion as a question of confidence but does not inherently make it so.

A confidence vote must, by definition, be a party vote, with the party whips operating to ensure a turnout of members to support the Government. "Conscience" votes, where members are left to make up their own minds on an issue free of party discipline, cannot involve questions of confidence. But neither do most party votes. Governments may lose significant party votes without there being any necessity for them to resign or call a general election by virtue of the defeat. In 1983 the Government (a single-party majority Government) suffered a defeat on a major aspect of a bill on industrial law reform;[115] in 1998 a Government bill was defeated on its second reading;[116] and in 2001 the title of a Government bill was amended despite the Government voting against the amendment.[117] In none of these instances was the defeat indicative of the Government losing the confidence of the House in a constitutional sense.

---

[112]   See Bassett, *Three Party Politics in New Zealand 1911-1931.*
[113]   Marleau and Montpetit, *House of Commons Procedure and Practice,* p.37.
[114]   Hurley, "The Royal Prerogative and the Office of Lieutenant Governor: A Comment" *Canadian Parliamentary Review,* Summer 2000.
[115]   1983, Vol.455, p.4775 (*Industrial Law Reform Bill*).
[116]   1998, Vol.567, p.8195 (*Local Government Amendment Bill (No 5)*).
[117]   2000, Vol.589, p.7360 (*Apprenticeship Bill*).

But although not a resigning matter in itself, an important defeat could lead the Government to test its support in the House by a suitably worded motion intended to vindicate its decision not to regard the defeat as a defeat on a vote of confidence. A Government could also resign or seek a dissolution of Parliament after being defeated in the House even though the vote was not acknowledged as a matter of confidence before it occurred. In this case it would need to persuade the Governor-General that a dissolution was warranted.

Parliamentary procedure does, however, determine the circumstances in which a vote of confidence can be forced on to a Government. If the survival of the Government is to be tested at the instigation of the opposition, the Government's whole performance must be available for debate. There are only a few occasions in the House when the rules of debate permit a debate as wide-ranging as this to arise, thereby permitting a vote of confidence to be foisted on to the Government. An urgent debate, for example, where a *particular* matter is raised for debate, does not provide an opportnuity to raise a question of confidence.[118] While the Government cannot, except in one of those exceptional types of debates, be forced to face a vote of confidence, it can of its own accord at any time put its survival on the line by declaring any vote, no matter how narrowly based, to be a vote of confidence. This does not widen the scope of that debate but it does indicate how strongly the Government is committed to winning that particular vote, and what the political consequences of its defeat would be. Members then cast their votes on the motion knowing the possible consequence if the Government is defeated. These different types of votes of confidence are examined below.

Votes of confidence arising independently of the will of the Government
Express votes of confidence
There is no tradition in the House of Representatives, as there is in some other Parliaments, of the official opposition putting down a motion expressing want of confidence in the Government, and the Government then finding time to debate that motion – though this has been done on rare occasions.[119] Motions expressing want of confidence in the Government normally arise by way of amendment to other motions before the House, and, since amendments must be relevant to the motion which they seek to amend, such a broad amendment as a want-of-confidence amendment may only be moved to a motion which itself permits debate to be open-ended. There are only a few debates held each year on which the scope of debate is so wide that a motion or an amendment declaring that the Government has lost the confidence of the House is in order. Debates which permit a question of confidence to be raised are the Address in Reply debate (the first debate of each Parliament), the debate on the Prime Minister's statement (the first debate each year), the Budget debate and any Imprest Supply debate – that is, on at least four occasions each year. On these debates a motion or an amendment expressly raising a question of confidence can be, and often is, moved.

A question can arise as to how explicit the motion or amendment must be phrased to raise a question of confidence. In New South Wales (where confidence motions have statutory recognition) it has been suggested that the words "no confidence in the Government" do not have to be used in order to raise a question of confidence but that the terms of the motion must unmistakably convey the meaning that there is an absence of confidence in the Government. Thus a motion that the House "lacks confidence" in the Government would, for example, suffice. It was also accepted that a motion of no confidence in the Premier (Prime Minister) was sufficient to express no confidence in the Government but not a motion of no confidence in any other individual Minister.[120]

---

118   1998, Vol.570, p.10782.
119   1931, Vol.230, p.297; 1946, Vol.273, p.601.
120   Advice of the Crown Solicitor, New South Wales, 23 December 1999.

Implied votes of confidence

It has always been looked upon as fundamental to the survival of a Government that it be able to obtain the authority of Parliament to expend money, that is, to obtain supply. (Indeed the terms "confidence" and "supply" are often linked in agreements between parties regarding support on votes in the House and in political discourse generally.)

A denial of supply at any point at which a debate ranging over the whole field of government activity can arise, automatically raises a question of the confidence of the House in the Government. Votes on an individual Minister's estimates of expenditure do not automatically raise questions of confidence, as these are narrowly based questions.[121]

Unlike an express vote of confidence which emanates from the opposition, implied votes of confidence emanate inescapably from the Government. The Government cannot avoid asking the House for supply, for to do so would be to abdicate its responsibility as a Government. So the passing of the Budget and the granting of imprest supply inevitably raise questions of confidence. Even if no amendment is moved by the opposition expressly raising a question of confidence, any vote at the conclusion of the second and third readings of bills granting supply is a vote which tests the confidence of the House in the Government. It is also the practice to regard those provisions of a tax bill setting the annual tax rates (without which there could be no assessment to tax) as inherently raising questions of confidence.[122] Other provisions of tax bills are not inherently confidence matters.[123]

In respect of these issues – supply and annual rates of taxation – a failure of a Government to secure parliamentary support at all for their grant or imposition demonstrates a loss of confidence in the Government.

Votes of confidence arising by declaration of the Government

Even if no express or implied question of confidence arises as described above, it is open to *the Government* to declare that it will treat a vote on any issue before the House as a matter of confidence in itself and thus resign or seek an election if it is defeated. In 1929 the acting Prime Minister chose to interpret opposition criticism of the Government's failure to raise public service salaries as a question of confidence.[124] The vote on the motion before the House was taken in the knowledge that it was being treated as a question of confidence. A Government may also decide *ex post facto* that a defeat it has suffered involves a question of confidence and act accordingly. So, in 1891, a Government defeat on the vote on the election of the Speaker was treated by the Government as an indication that it did not have a majority in the House and it resigned.[125] The Government may itself take the initiative in proposing a question of confidence. In 1942 and in 1998, following reconstructions of the Government, the Government initiated and moved motions seeking positive expressions of confidence in itself. The motions were carried and in each case the Government continued in office.[126]

In each case it is a matter for the decision of the Prime Minister on behalf of the whole Government, rather than for an individual Minister, to decide if a matter is to be treated as a vote of confidence.[127]

Until 1962 the Standing Orders provided a minimum time-limit for speeches made on any motion or amendment declared by the Government to be a vote of confidence. A

[121] See Scott, *The New Zealand Constitution*, pp.56-7, for defeats on estimates

[122] 1998, Vol.573, pp.13199-200; 2004, Vol.622, p.17369 (*Taxation (Annual Rates, Venture Capital and Miscellaneous Provisions Bill*).

[123] 1998, Vol.573, pp.13199-200.

[124] Bassett, *Coates of Kaipara*, pp.157-8.

[125] Bassett, *Three Party Politics in New Zealand 1911-1931*, p.2.

[126] Bassett, *Coates of Kaipara*, p.267; 1998, Vol.571, pp.11806-41.

[127] See "Williamson backs down over shipping bill view", *The Dominion*, 29 June 1994.

number of motions which would not in themselves have raised a question of confidence in the Government, but which were declared by the Prime Minister of the day to do so, thereby had this minimum speaking time invoked for members debating the motion.[128]

Since the revocation of this Standing Order in 1962 there has been no procedural reason for a Government to declare an issue to be a question of confidence. Nor is there any political reason for it to do so as long as its parliamentary majority is secure. A Government might declare a matter to be a question of confidence if it is unsure of all its members supporting it on the issue before the House and it wishes to ensure their support by introducing another factor – the survival in office of the Government – into the equation. Members who vote against the Government where a question of confidence is involved know that they risk bringing down the Government. Thus, in 1897 a motion critical of the Premier was treated by the Government as a motion of no confidence. Several members who might otherwise have voted for the motion felt obliged to support the Government in these circumstances and the motion was defeated by six votes.[129] On the other hand, a Government may not wish unnecessarily to hazard its continuation in office by declaring a matter to be a question of confidence and thus risking its position. These are matters for political judgment. A Prime Minister can always be challenged as to whether a particular vote is to be treated as a question of confidence[130] or as to the general circumstances in which the Government will regard votes as confidence votes.[131]

CONSCIENCE ISSUES

Conscience issues are those decisions that the House takes free of the dictates of party loyalties and allegiances. Members are formally free of such loyalties and allegiances at all times and may vote in any way they please on any issue, but they tend to act in accordance with caucus decisions as part of their covenant with the electorate which returned them to the House as members of a political party.

In a sense, until the rise of parties, all votes in the House were conscience, or free, votes. But members did form parliamentary groups to give each other mutual support, and the continued support of a majority of the House on all major issues was essential to the continuation in office of the Government. Members therefore voted together on certain issues regardless of their personal predilections. It is undoubtedly true, however, that a party system subsumes personal choices in casting a vote in the House far more than the looser alliances of the nineteenth century did. Non-party voting survives for those issues like liquor licensing and gambling, which were regarded as too difficult ever to resolve into party matters, and for other issues (abortion and homosexual law reform, for example) that became public issues after the party system was established and were looked upon as being matters for the individual's own conscience to determine and not matters on which members should be bound by a collective decision of party colleagues.

The decision whether to treat a vote as a conscience issue is essentially for each party to decide in respect of its own members and depends upon the nature of the issue involved. The decision on what is a conscience issue may itself change over time as society's values themselves change.

The consequence in parliamentary terms of a matter being treated as a conscience issue is that a personal vote, rather than a party vote, may be held on it.[132] For this

---

[128] See, for example: 1903, Vol.124, p.454 (*Bruce Licensing Poll Validation Bill*); 1903, Vol.127, p.729 (*Preferential and Reciprocal Trade Bill*); 1904, Vol.129, p.734 (Government motion on the Land Question).

[129] Hamer, *The New Zealand Liberals*, p.210.

[130] See, for example: 1998, Vol.574, p.13704 (*Accident Insurance Bill*); 2001, Vol.590, p.8062 (*Electoral (Integrity) Amendment Bill*).

[131] 1998, Vol.571, p.11795.

[132] S.O.142.

purpose, the Speaker must be satisfied that the subject of the vote is to be treated as a conscience issue.[133] Usually, the fact that a matter is a conscience issue is known well in advance because the subject is one of those traditionally regarded as such over many Parliaments. But a conscience issue can arise out of the flow of debate (both public and parliamentary) on a subject not normally understood to be a conscience issue.[134] Applications for personal votes have been declined where there was no indication from the debate that the matter was being treated as a conscience issue.[135] (See Chapter 17.) As an alternative to a personal vote on a conscience issue, parties may divide their vote totals to reflect individual members' votes (a "split-party" vote).[136] In practice, whether a matter is to be treated as a conscience issue will have been discussed in advance at the Business Committee so that members are not taken by surprise by the holding of a personal vote.

Sometimes the initiation of conscience matters is left to a Member's bill rather than a Government bill. But the Government often brings forward its own legislation on a subject that is a conscience issue and then leaves a decision on its fate to the free votes of members. This was the case with a bill on contraception, sterilisation and abortion, drafted to implement the recommendations of the Royal Commission into the subject.[137]

The Government invariably makes the services of the Parliamentary Counsel Office available to members wishing to propose amendments to a bill which is subject to a conscience vote, for there is every likelihood that some members' amendments to such a measure will be carried into law. The alternation of speakers in a debate may also follow members speaking for and against the measure rather than a strict party rotation.[138] In any event, the Speaker has to exercise a greater personal discretion in calling members to speak to a question when the whips are not operating.[139]

Select committees may also take a lead from the House in their handling of a bill where the bill is being treated as a conscience issue in the House. Thus, a select committee has treated a bill as a conscience matter for the members of the committee, following an announcement in the House that the bill was a conscience matter.[140] In these circumstances, given that free votes are to be held on the details of the bill when it is returned to the House, the select committee is expected to confine itself to recommending drafting amendments rather than substantive amendments[141] and, where appropriate, presenting the House with an intelligible range of alternatives for it to choose from, rather than attempting to impose its own views. The fact that conscience issues can lead to results that are difficult to predict has led to criticism of them in respect of the quality of the law that is thereby produced.[142] However, criticism of poor-quality legislation is not confined to legislation passed as a conscience issue.

Conscience matters can be fractious, stimulating, moving and confusing by turns. But they remain a necessary safety valve to handle those issues which cannot appropriately be treated as party matters.

---

[133]   S.O.143.

[134]   1996, Vol.558, p.38.

[135]   *Ibid.* (appointment of Deputy Speaker); 1997, Vol.560, pp.2087-88 (*Compulsory Retirement Savings Scheme Referendum Bill*).

[136]   S.O.144(1)(b).

[137]   1977, Vol.412, p.2358 (*Contraception, Sterilisation, and Abortion Bill*).

[138]   1989, Vol.499, p.11487.

[139]   1976, Vol.405, p.2203.

[140]   1987-90, AJHR, I.1B, para.3 (*Casino Control Bill*).

[141]   1999-2002, AJHR, I.22B, p.42 (*Shop Trading Hours Act Repeal Amendment Bill*).

[142]   See, for example, 1996-99, AJHR, E.8, pp.4-6 (*Report of the Liquor Licensing Authority for the 12 months ended 30 June 1997*).

CHAPTER 8

COMMUNICATIONS WITH THE CROWN

The Sovereign and the House of Representatives together constitute the Parliament of New Zealand. There are, however, only a few formal occasions when these constituent elements of Parliament actually meet together. Under a system of responsible government, Ministers of the Crown are members of Parliament. They are therefore present in the House to communicate the Crown's desires to the legislature and to relay the legislature's views to the Crown. Nevertheless, there are formal methods by which the Crown communicates with the House and the House with the Crown. These formal methods of communication are respectively a message, which is the method by which the Crown conveys its views to the House, and an address, by means of which the House expresses its opinions to the Crown.

DIRECT INTERACTION

Direct interaction between the Sovereign or the Sovereign's representatives occurs at the opening of a new Parliament or a new session of Parliament. The Governor-General does not attend the first meeting of a new Parliament in person but empowers Royal commissioners (who are usually senior judges) to attend on the Governor-General's behalf and formally declare the opening of Parliament to the assembled members. After the House has elected a Speaker its members present their choice to the Governor-General at Government House for confirmation. The Governor-General also meets with members in the Council Chamber at Parliament House to declare the reasons for the summoning of Parliament – that is, to deliver the Speech from the Throne. If there is more than one session of Parliament, the Governor-General will deliver another Speech from the Throne to members. (See Chapter 12.)

The Governor-General formerly met with members in Parliament House at the end of each session in a prorogation ceremony that involved giving the Royal assent to legislation and then delivering a speech by way of a summing-up of the work of the session. But this ceremony was discontinued in the nineteenth century. One of the privileges claimed by the Speaker on behalf of the House at the opening of each new Parliament is the right to free access to the Governor-General whenever occasion may require it.[1] This is a right of the House in its corporate capacity led by the Speaker to address the Governor-General whenever necessary. The privilege is exercised by the presentation of addresses from time to time.

MESSAGES

The main occasion on which a message was formerly employed by the Crown was to recommend to the House that it make an appropriation of public money for the purposes of a proposal before it. Such a recommendation was an essential legal precondition to the House passing a bill appropriating public money or imposing a charge on the public revenue.[2] But this requirement was repealed in 2005.[3]

Members', local and private bills that affect the rights or prerogatives of the Crown

---

[1] S.O.23.
[2] *New Zealand Constitution Act* 1852 (UK), s.54;

Constitution Act 1986, s.21.
[3] *Constitution Amendment Act* 2005, s.5.

require the Crown's consent before they can be passed.[4] This consent is conveyed in a message.

It was formerly the Crown's practice to promulgate the fact that the Royal assent had been given to a bill by advising the House of this by message. That practice was discontinued in 1985. The Governor-General also formerly had the power to transmit bills directly to the House for its consideration,[5] and this power was also exercised by message. This power (last exercised in 1949[6]) was repealed in 1986. Other matters which might occasion a direct communication from the Governor-General to the House and which could give rise to the use of a message, include, for example, advice of the suspension of a senior official[7] or a reply to an address.

Obtaining messages

It is the Speaker's duty to ensure that the proper constitutional forms are observed and that no business that requires the consent of the Crown is transacted unless a message is first obtained.[8] But the Speaker has neither the obligation nor the power to obtain a message. The power to obtain a message lies with Ministers who are the Crown's responsible advisers and on whose advice the Governor-General sends a message to the House. The premature release of a message before its announcement to the House has been held to be a contempt of the House.[9]

For bills which require the Crown's consent, the Office of the Clerk identifies whether the rights or prerogatives of the Crown are affected. The Leader of the House is advised of such bills so that the Government can consider whether it wishes to facilitate those bills' progress by obtaining messages. In the absence of a message, a Member's, local or private bill affecting the rights or prerogatives of the Crown cannot be passed.[10]

Announcement to the House

The Speaker announces messages to the House by reading them out.[11] This is done at the first opportunity after receipt of the message. The announcement of a message can interrupt a debate but it cannot interrupt a member's speech.[12]

When the Speaker announces the receipt of a message from the Governor-General, members must stand in acknowledgement.[13] The Speaker then proceeds to read the communication to the House, starting with the Governor-General's name. Members may resume their seats as soon as the Governor-General's name has been read.[14]

The original copies of messages are retained by the Clerk as part of the records of the House. Under current arrangements they are transferred to Archives New Zealand after approximately six years.

ADDRESSES

An address may be presented to the Crown on any topic on which the House wishes to communicate its views. In the early Parliaments in New Zealand there were frequent addresses putting before the Governor the House's arguments on constitutional arrangements and government policy. With the advent of full responsible government, addresses of this kind are no longer employed, as the Ministers responsible for policy can be addressed directly in the House. However, there are a number of other types of addresses by which the House communicates or may communicate with the Crown.

---

4   1926, Vol.209, pp.917-8; S.O.309.
5   *New Zealand Constitution Act* 1852 (UK), s.55.
6   1949, JHR, pp.240-3.
7   *State Sector Act* 1988, s.16 (State Services Commissioner and Deputy Commissioner).
8   1909, Vol.148, p.1452.
9   1955, Vol.307, pp.2532-9.
10   1930, Vol.225, p.584; S.O.309.
11   S.O.168(1).
12   S.Os 168(2) and 133(d).
13   S.O.168(3).
14   1991, Vol.521, p.5913.

Address in Reply

The most well-known type of address is the Address in Reply, which is the House's response to the Speech from the Throne at the beginning of each session of Parliament. The form of the Address in Reply must itself be uncontroversial,[15] but it can be the subject of a "no confidence" amendment which, if carried, must be added to the text of the address.[16] The last time that a no confidence amendment was carried occurred in the Address in Reply debate in 1928.[17]

The Address in Reply debate is technically about whether an address should be presented to the Governor-General in reply to the Speech from the Throne. It is not about the text of the address. The actual text of the Address in Reply is prepared by the Speaker while the debate is in progress so that (on the assumption that no amendment to it is carried) it can be read to the House and adopted immediately at the conclusion of the debate.

Commending appropriations for offices of Parliament

For many years the Address in Reply was the only common form of address made by the House to the Crown. Since 1989, however, addresses have come to be used frequently to recommend appropriations for offices of Parliament.

In respect of offices of Parliament (the Auditor-General, the Office of the Ombudsmen, and the Parliamentary Commissioner for the Environment), the House approves estimates of expenditure before the Government's estimates are prepared and presented to the House. The method by which the House expresses its approval to proposed estimates for the offices of Parliament is by commending those estimates to the Crown in the form of an address. The address goes on to request that the expenditure be included as a vote in an Appropriation Bill for that year.[18] Any alteration to expenditure for an office of Parliament during the course of the financial year is handled in the same fashion.[19]

The detailed work of considering expenditure plans for offices of Parliament is carried out for the House by the Officers of Parliament Committee. Addresses embodying that committee's recommendations are then adopted by the House.

Royal occasions

The House adopts addresses from time to time to mark particular Royal occasions. A special address was adopted on the occasion of Her Majesty's presence in New Zealand in 1990, for example.[20] Addresses have also been adopted on the occasion of Royal births and deaths, and on the succession of a new Sovereign. Rather than adopting an address, the House may content itself with passing a congratulatory resolution.

Parliamentary occasions

An address was adopted at the special sitting held on 24 May 2004 to commemorate the 150th anniversary of the first sitting of the House.[21]

Removal of office-holders

The presentation of an address is an essential prerequisite to the removal of a number of office-holders. By law it is prescribed that superior court judges and the holders of a number of other important offices can be removed by the Crown only if an address from the House seeking the office-holder's removal has been presented first. This ensures

---

[15] S.O.169(2).
[16] *Ibid.*
[17] 1928, JHR, p.8.
[18] *Public Finance Act* 1989, s.26E(2).

[19] *Ibid.*, s.26E(5).
[20] 1990, JHR, pp.10-1.
[21] 2004, Vol.617, pp.13179-213.

the office-holder's formal independence from the Crown, because the Crown cannot of its own volition remove that person from office. The requirement that the House adopt an address and then present it to the Governor-General for action also ensures that the extreme step of removal would be taken only in a case of the utmost gravity. No one has been removed from office under these provisions in New Zealand. (See Chapter 30.)

Returns

Where the House wishes to obtain papers or documents that are in the Governor-General's hands, the presentation of an address is the appropriate method to seek them. In practice, this method is not now used, since members are able to question Ministers directly in the House about documents they wish to obtain.

Procedure for adopting an address

A motion that an address be presented may be moved after notice of it is given. The terms of the motion for an Address in Reply are specified in the Standing Orders,[22] otherwise a form of words appropriate to the subject-matter of the proposed address is devised. Most motions for addresses are proposed by Ministers as Government motions and dealt with as Government orders of the day. The motion for an Address in Reply is deemed to be a Government order of the day.[23] Notices of motion for addresses given by other members are Members' orders of the day. As with any Member's notice of motion they lapse one week after their first appearance on the order paper.[24]

A motion for an address (other than the Address in Reply) is debatable in the same way as for any other motion, with each member able to speak for up to 10 minutes. The motion is open to amendment.

Preparation of an address

The motion for an address asks the House to agree, in principle, to present an address to the Sovereign or the Governor-General. It may describe in detail or only in outline what the content of that address will be. But it is not the address itself. The address must still be prepared and endorsed by the House. It is the Speaker's duty to prepare an address whenever the House has agreed to present one.[25] The address as prepared by the Speaker must contain any words that the House in the resolution it has agreed to concerning the address has decided to include in the address.[26] Otherwise, as long as the wording of the address is consistent with the authorising resolution, the terms of the address are for the Speaker to determine. Apart from any words that the House specifically orders to be part of the address, an Address in Reply must not be controversial.[27] The chief opportunity for inserting controversial words into an Address in Reply arises on a no confidence amendment. Most other addresses are framed in non-controversial terms too, but they do not have to be non-controversial – for example, an address for the removal of an office-holder may be highly controversial.

Immediately or as soon as possible after a motion for an address has been agreed to, the Speaker reads the address that has been prepared to the House and puts the question for its adoption. There is no amendment or debate on this question.[28]

---

22   S.O.342(1).
23   S.O.64.
24   S.O.96(1).
25   S.O.169(1).

26   S.O.169(2).
27   *Ibid.*
28   S.O.169(3).

Presentation or transmission of an address

Addresses are presented or transmitted to the Governor-General by the Speaker on behalf of the House as part of the Speaker's representational role.[29] Strictly it is not necessary for the House by motion to direct the Speaker to present an address, but this may be done.

The Address in Reply is always presented with some formality by the Speaker in person. For this purpose the Speaker repairs to Government House, accompanied by the Serjeant-at-Arms with the Mace, the Clerk, the Deputy Clerk, the mover and seconder of the motion, and any other members who wish to be present. In presenting an address the address is read by the Speaker and then handed to the Governor-General, while the mover and seconder of the motion for the address stand at the Speaker's left hand. The Governor-General then makes a short formal reply to the address. In the case of the presentation of the address adopted by the House to mark the 150th anniversary of the first sitting of the House, the Speaker presented the address at a special function held in the banqueting hall in the Executive Wing of the Parliament buildings.[30]

Personal presentation by the Speaker is the formal manner of presenting any address to the Governor-General. However, an address may be transmitted in a less formal manner wherever the Governor-General approves this.[31] In respect of addresses relating to estimates for offices of Parliament, a less formal manner has been agreed between the Governor-General and the Speaker. These addresses are transmitted to the Governor-General privately on behalf of the Speaker.

If the address is to the Sovereign and the Sovereign is present in New Zealand, the address is presented to Her Majesty in person.[32] Otherwise the address is presented or transmitted to the Governor-General for communication to the Sovereign.[33]

Reply to an address

Any answer made by the Sovereign or the Governor-General to an address is reported to the House by the Speaker,[34] or it may itself be the subject of a message to the House. The Governor-General conveys any answer from the Sovereign to the House. Any reply is entered in the journals of the House.

---

[29] S.O.170(1).
[30] 2004, Vol.617, p.13213.
[31] S.O.170(2).

[32] 1990, JHR, p.11.
[33] S.O.170(4).
[34] S.O.170(3).

CHAPTER 9

SUMMONING, PROROGUING AND DISSOLVING PARLIAMENT

There are constitutional considerations which ensure that Parliament meets each year. The most important is the principle that Parliament does not grant supply to the Government for more than one year at a time. The latest date by which Parliament can meet in any year is 30 June, for this is the last day of the financial year and the annual appropriations made by Parliament in the Appropriation Acts for that year will consequently lapse. Parliament must therefore meet before then in order to give the Government interim spending authority (imprest supply). Other considerations of a financial nature relate to taxation. Income tax has its rates fixed on an annual basis. If no rates of tax are fixed there can be no assessment to tax, and much of the Government's revenue will consequently dry up. By granting only temporary authorities to the Government in financial matters, Parliament ensures that it must be called to meet at least annually to renew those authorities.

Political considerations also ensure that Parliament meets and that the House sits regularly. The House is the political forum of the nation. Although it is not the only place in which opposing political points of view can be expressed and Government actions tested and criticised, it is the highest institution in the land devoted to just such pursuits, and it is generally expected that it will meet fairly often and become a focus for political debate. Members of Parliament have important roles to perform in their own right in the business of legislating (which can only be carried out in Parliament) and in the ancillary business which is transacted by the House.

For these reasons, Parliament is summoned to meet regularly and the Crown's promise of calling a meeting of the newly elected Parliament is given in a proclamation issued in association with that which dissolves the old Parliament.

SUMMONING OF PARLIAMENT FOLLOWING A GENERAL ELECTION

Parliament meets when it is summoned to do so by the making of a proclamation by the Governor-General.[1] The proclamation identifies the time and place at which Parliament is to meet. The summoning of Parliament effectively breathes life into the House of Representatives which, although still in existence between Parliaments, can meet and transact business only while Parliament is in session. Because the House of Representatives is the working element of Parliament, the summoning of Parliament is really the calling of the House of Representatives into working mode.

By convention, after the Governor-General has issued a proclamation dissolving – that is, bringing an end to – the Parliament in being, and issued a writ to the Chief Electoral Officer to put in train the events leading up to the next general election, a proclamation is made summoning Parliament to meet for the first time after the election. The summoning of the new Parliament in association with the dissolution of the old is made as a token of the Crown's intention to preserve the continuity of the operation of parliamentary institutions in New Zealand. In respect of only one dissolution since 1860 has the date and time for the first meeting of the next Parliament not been appointed by a proclamation issued within a few days of the dissolution of the old Parliament. (No such

---

[1] *Constitution Act* 1986, s.18(1).

proclamation was issued in association with the dissolution of the fortieth Parliament in June 1984. This and other procedures surrounding the "snap" election of 1984 were the subject of subsequent inquiry.[2])

To be effective a proclamation summoning Parliament must be published in the *New Zealand Gazette* or read publicly by an authorised person in the presence of the Clerk of the House and two other persons.[3] In the case of the latter, the proclamation must subsequently be published in the *Gazette*.[4] No proclamation summoning Parliament has been made by this means.

Date of first meeting

Elections to the House of Representatives were held for the first time during 1853. In respect of the Parliament constituted following those elections, the *New Zealand Constitution Act* 1852 (UK) required the Governor to appoint a time for its first meeting as soon as convenient after the first writs were returned.[5] For subsequent Parliaments there was until 1987 no express statutory obligation on the Governor-General to summon a new Parliament to meet by a particular time, or indeed at all, except in the case of a proclamation of emergency, although a provision in the *Bill of Rights* 1688 declares that for the redress of all grievances and for the amending, strengthening and preserving of the laws, Parliaments ought to be held frequently.[6]

Since 1 January 1987 there has been an express statutory requirement for Parliament to meet not later than six weeks after the day fixed for the return of the writs for a general election.[7] The latest day for the return of the writ for an election is the fiftieth day after it is issued,[8] so the precise period after polling day within which Parliament must meet varies for each election depending upon how long before the election the writ was issued. As the writ is usually returnable some two to three weeks after the election is held, Parliament must effectively be summoned to meet within about two months of each general election.

This requirement for a relatively early meeting of Parliament following an election contrasts markedly with the practice followed up to the fortieth Parliament (1981–84) of allowing several months to elapse before Parliament met. For example, the thirty-eighth Parliament (1975–78) did not meet until almost seven months after the election, and delays of four to five months in Parliament meeting after an election were the norm.

Postponement of first meeting

The date appointed in the Governor-General's first proclamation as the day for the new Parliament to meet following the general election is not necessarily the day on which the new Parliament will actually meet. Between the making of that proclamation and the first projected meeting of Parliament, the Government may change as a result of the general election, and the incoming Government will have its own ideas and preferences for the timing of the first meeting of Parliament. Even if the same Government is returned at the polls it may wish to alter the date initially appointed for the first meeting of Parliament.

The day appointed for the first meeting of Parliament may thus be postponed by a proclamation proroguing Parliament.[9] For example, the day after Parliament was dissolved in 1972 a new Parliament was summoned to meet on 1 February 1973. However, on 17 January Parliament was prorogued and summoned to meet on 14 February instead. Parliament did, in fact, meet for the swearing-in of members and the election of a

[2]   See *Constitutional Reform – Reports of an Officials Committee*, February 1986.
[3]   *Constitution Act* 1986, s.18(3).
[4]   *Ibid.,* s.18(4).
[5]   *New Zealand Constitution Act* 1852 (UK), s.44.
[6]   *Bill of Rights* 1688, article 13.
[7]   *Constitution Act* 1986, s.19 (there is now a single writ for the election).
[8]   *Electoral Act* 1993, s.139(4).
[9]   *Constitution Act* 1986, s.18(2).

Speaker on 14 February 1973.[10] Such alterations to the date first nominated as the day for Parliament to convene are the rule rather than the exception, as the first proclamation summoning Parliament to meet plays a symbolic rather than definitive role in determining when the new Parliament will actually meet. Nevertheless, whatever date is eventually chosen for the first meeting of Parliament, it must be within six weeks of the return of the writ for the election.

Time of first meeting
The time of day appointed in the proclamation summoning Parliament varies depending upon what may be considered to be a convenient time for those concerned with the opening of Parliament. There is no presumption that the first meeting will be at 2 pm (the normal meeting time of the House).

Meetings of Parliament held shortly after the general election
Until the day named as the last day for the return of the writ for the election of members, not all electorates may have returned members (indeed, the return of a member is occasionally delayed beyond this date if a recount is necessary). Furthermore, until the results for each electoral district have been declared, the Chief Electoral Officer will not be able to allocate list seats.[11]

No new Parliament has met before the last day appointed for the return of the writs for elections to that Parliament, but the first meeting of the twenty-third Parliament in 1928 was held on the last day appointed for the return of the writs for the Māori electorates (the last date for the European electorates was six days earlier). In a sense this was the earliest meeting of a Parliament on record, although the ninth Parliament was summoned to meet in 1884 on the day following the last day for the return of all writs (European and Māori). The forty-sixth Parliament met on 20 December 1999. This was the fourth day after the latest day appointed for the return of the writs and the day following the actual return of the last writ to be returned.

Proclamations of emergency
There is an express statutory requirement for the Governor-General to summon Parliament to meet if a state of national emergency is declared while Parliament is dissolved or has expired. In this case, if Parliament is not already due to meet again within seven days from the date of the declaration, it must be summoned to meet within seven days of the last day appointed for the return of the writs for the general election.[12]

SESSIONS
Collections of sittings of the House may be grouped into sessions.

During the course of a session, the House will debate the Address in Reply, the Budget, and the estimates and supplementary estimates, and will pass other legislation. The sittings of the House during the session may be interspersed with adjournments, mostly for only a few hours until the next regular meeting of the House, but occasionally for periods of a week or a month or even longer. Although this is the traditional pattern of a session, the session can be as short or as long as the Government determines, through the exercise of the Governor-General's legal powers. It may, as in 1977 when Her Majesty the Queen opened Parliament, consist of only one sitting day. Conversely, it may be as

---

[10] *New Zealand Gazette*, 27 October 1972, p.2339; *ibid.*, 17 January 1973, p.65.

[11] *Electoral Act* 1993, s.191(1).

[12] *Civil Defence Emergency Management Act* 2002, s.67(1), (3).

long as the life of the Parliament if there is only one session held during the course of the Parliament.

Until 1984 there was usually one session of Parliament held in each calendar year during the course of each Parliament; though there were occasionally more than this when a special session was held, as in 1977 on the occasion of the visit of Her Majesty the Queen. It was exceptional for a session (like the ones of 1921–22 and 1941–42, for example) to extend over more than one calendar year. Since the 1984 session was brought to an end for a snap election, sessions have been more variable and lengthier. There were, for example, only two sessions in each of the three Parliaments after that. Since 1984 there has no longer been a presumption that a session will correspond with a calendar year. Since the forty-fourth Parliament (1993–1996) there has been only a single session lasting the entire life of the Parliament and this has now become the norm.

A session may be brought to an end by the exercise of the legal powers vested in the Governor-General. At the conclusion of a session Parliament goes into "recess" rather than the House merely standing adjourned (although the terms are often used synonymously).

PROROGATION

The grouping of the House's sittings into sessions is effected by the Governor-General proroguing Parliament and thus bringing the sittings of the House to a temporary conclusion (though this power is seldom used to terminate a session now). The legal power to prorogue Parliament belongs to the Governor-General.[13] The Governor-General exercises the power to prorogue by issuing a proclamation announcing the prorogation of Parliament. A session, therefore, lasts from the first sitting of the House following its being called together by the Governor-General until the prorogation of Parliament.

Prorogation brings the sittings of the House to an end. The House and its committees cannot meet following prorogation until Parliament is again specifically summoned to meet by the Governor-General. But Parliament as such is not brought to an end by prorogation. In this respect prorogation differs from dissolution, which not only brings the sittings of the House to an end but also brings Parliament to an end and precipitates a general election. Parliament may be prorogued immediately prior to being dissolved, although the modern practice is to dissolve Parliament without it having been prorogued first.

A proclamation proroguing Parliament does so only for a specified time, but this time may be extended by a further proclamation or proclamations. When the period of prorogation expires and Parliament meets again, the second session of that Parliament commences, and it in turn may be brought to an end by a further prorogation, and so on.

Publication of proclamation

A proclamation proroguing Parliament is made effective by being published in the *New Zealand Gazette* or by being publicly read, by a person authorised to do so by the Governor-General, in the presence of the Clerk of the House and two other persons. In the latter case, the proclamation must subsequently be published in the *Gazette*.[14] The 1986-87 session of Parliament was prorogued by the reading of a proclamation by the Governor-General's Official Secretary on the steps of Parliament House.[15] (Parliament was dissolved immediately afterwards.)

Prorogation is not directly communicated to the House. Indeed, the House has not

---

[13]   *Constitution Act* 1986, s.18(2).   [15]   *New Zealand Gazette*, 22 July 1987, pp.3425-7.
[14]   *Ibid.*, s.18(3), (4).

normally been sitting when Parliament is prorogued, as on its last intended sitting day each session the House adjourns for a week or so and is prorogued during the course of that week. This contrasts with the old practice when the Governor (until 1875) or commissioners appointed by the Governor (until 1887) attended Parliament in the Legislative Council Chamber to assent to bills and then prorogue Parliament in person. This procedure of personal attendance had been adopted to prevent the recurrence of such scenes as occurred at the conclusion of the first session of the first Parliament when the Governor's messenger with a prorogation notice was not immediately admitted to the House and the announcement of prorogation was delayed, making it doubtful whether the House had been validly sitting throughout the entire day.[16]

Accelerated meeting of Parliament during a recess
A recess must be brought to an end for Parliament to meet in the event of a declaration of national emergency being made. If Parliament stands prorogued when such a proclamation is made and is not due to meet within seven days from that date, it must be summoned by the Governor-General to meet within seven days of the making of the declaration.[17]

Opening of a session
The first meeting of Parliament following a general election, known as the Commission Opening, is also the opening of the first session of that Parliament. The first day of each subsequent session of Parliament (if any) is the day of the State Opening of Parliament.

DISSOLUTION
The Governor-General brings the life of Parliament to an end by issuing a proclamation dissolving it. The dissolution of Parliament is a legal power possessed by the Governor-General,[18] although constitutionally the Governor-General exercises this, like the other legal powers of the office, on the advice of the Prime Minister. A proclamation dissolving Parliament generates a course of events which leads to the holding of a general election.

Dissolution differs from prorogation in that it brings the life of Parliament, rather than just a particular session of Parliament, to an end. Whereas prorogation sends members away from Parliament with an indication that they, the same members, will be summoned to attend when Parliament next meets, there is no such indication with dissolution. A dissolution results in the termination (effective on polling day) of all membership of the House. To attend Parliament when it next meets, a member must be returned to Parliament anew by the process of election. The final or only session of each Parliament may be prorogued first and then Parliament dissolved, but it is now more likely that Parliament will be dissolved without first having been prorogued.

Publication of proclamation
As with a prorogation proclamation, a proclamation dissolving Parliament becomes effective on being published in the *Gazette* or on being publicly read by an authorised person in the presence of the Clerk of the House and two other persons. In the latter case it must then be gazetted.[19] The first Parliament to be dissolved by a proclamation read in this way was the forty-first Parliament in 1987.[20] Since the forty-third Parliament was dissolved in 1993 all Parliaments have been dissolved by a proclamation read on behalf of the Governor-General from the Parliament House steps or in Parliament grounds.[21]

---

[16]   VP, 1854, Session II, *Report of a Committee on the late Prorogation*; McIntyre, *The Journal of Henry Sewell*, Vol.II, pp.70-3, 333-3.

[17]   *Civil Defence Emergency Management Act* 2002, s.67(1), (3).

[18]   *Constitution Act* 1986, s.18(2).

[19]   *Ibid.*, s.18(3), (4).

[20]   *New Zealand Gazette*, 22 July 1987, pp.3426-7.

[21]   See, for example: *New Zealand Gazette*, 19 June 2002, pp.1741-2; *ibid.*, 11 June 2005, pp.3031-2.

Length of Parliament

Members elected at a general election are elected to the House for a period that extends to three years from the day appointed for the return of the writs for the general election.[22] This has been the case since 1879 with the exception of the 1935 election (when members were elected for four years). Unless Parliament is dissolved sooner, it expires at the end of its three-year term. The only Parliament to run its full legal course and then expire was the twenty-seventh Parliament of 1943–1946. The election of 1943 was held some two months earlier in the year than usual (September rather than November), causing the fact of Parliament's expiration in October 1946 to be overlooked. The validity of Acts assented to after the House had expired was upheld by the Court of Appeal in 1954.[23] The forty-second Parliament virtually ran its full course, since it was dissolved on 10 September 1990, the day on which it was due to expire in any case.

In the United Kingdom, the death of a Sovereign formerly caused an automatic dissolution of the existing Parliament. While it is questionable whether this rule ever applied in New Zealand, to remove any doubts on this score it was expressly provided in 1888 that the death of the Sovereign does not of itself dissolve Parliament. This remains the law.[24]

The maximum term of the first Parliaments was five years. This was reduced to three years in 1879. Since then the lives of Parliaments have been extended on four occasions, three of these being confined to the Parliament then in existence, and the other, although intended to apply to all Parliaments, being repealed before it could affect any future Parliament. The life of the nineteenth Parliament, elected in 1914, was twice extended for one year. It was finally dissolved in 1919. In 1934 an Act was passed extending the life of Parliament (including the Parliament then in being) from three to four years. The election of 1935 was fought while this provision was in force, so the members chosen at that election were elected for a term of four years. However, in 1937 the parliamentary term, including that for the existing Parliament, was reduced to three years. The life of the twenty-sixth Parliament, elected in 1938, was extended for one year in 1941, and in 1942 it was extended until one year after the end of the war, provided that the House, by resolution each year, approved of Parliament's continuance. No such resolution was passed and Parliament was dissolved in 1943.

The twenty-ninth Parliament, elected in 1949, was dissolved in 1951 as a result of the waterfront dispute (the first snap election since 1881, and the shortest of all New Zealand's Parliaments) and an election was held in September. This threatened to upset the normal calendar of November elections, and in 1954 the life of the thirtieth Parliament was extended by some four weeks to put the election timetable back on course.[25] The fortieth Parliament was dissolved in June 1984, some four months before it would otherwise have been expected to be dissolved and the forty-sixth Parliament was dissolved in June 2002, some three months earlier than might have been expected.

Two proposals for extending the term of Parliament from three to four years have been put to electors at referendums. In 1967 the proposal was rejected by some 700,000 to 300,000 votes, and in 1990 the majority against the proposal was one and a quarter million to 550,000.[26]

---

22   *Constitution Act* 1986, s.17(1).
23   *Simpson v Attorney-General* [1955] NZLR 271.
24   *Constitution Act* 1986, s.5(2).

25   *Electoral Amendment Act* 1953, s.6.
26   *New Zealand Gazette*, 12 October 1967, p.1792;   *ibid.*, 29 November 1990, pp.4505-6.

EXPIRATION

Expiration is the bringing of the life of the Parliament to an end by automatic operation of law rather than by the deliberate action of the Governor-General. Parliament expires three years from the day fixed for the return of the writs at the preceding general election unless it is sooner dissolved.[27] After the twenty-seventh Parliament expired in 1946, its expiration was not perceived at the time and a proclamation dissolving that Parliament was made and acted on. This was the only Parliament to expire. If a Parliament does expire, the procedures for the holding of a general election operate as if Parliament had been dissolved on the date of expiration.

EFFECT OF PROROGATION, DISSOLUTION AND EXPIRATION ON BUSINESS BEFORE THE HOUSE

Prorogation, dissolution or expiration bring the sittings of the House and the meetings of committees to an end and disable the House from further activity.

Historically, they also caused all business then before the House to lapse so that when Parliament resumed for its next session the slate had been wiped clean. This absolute effect has not been thought conducive to efficient parliamentary practice, and as long ago as 1886 a committee of the House recommended that a way should be found to avoid its effects in the case of prorogation.[28] A statutory means of avoiding the need for all unfinished business at the end of a session to be reintroduced and commence its passage through the House entirely anew in the succeeding session was first introduced in 1977.[29]

Prorogation now has no effect on any business then before the House or its committees. Such business does not lapse and may be resumed in the following session of the same Parliament.[30] (However, a sessional order of the House ceases to have effect on prorogation.)

On the dissolution or expiration of Parliament all business then before the House or its committees lapses. Following the dissolution or expiration of Parliament there is no business before the House. However, the House has the power, by resolution, to reinstate any business that has lapsed when it sits in the new Parliament.[31] This power to reinstate, if it is to be exercised, must be utilised in the first session of the new Parliament but reinstatement does not have to be effected at or by any particular time in that session nor does it have to be accomplished on only one occasion. The House can deal with reinstatement at any time in the session and on as many occasions as it finds needful. (See Chapter 14 for reinstatement of business.)

---

[27]   *Constitution Act* 1986, s.17(1).
[28]   1886, AJHR, I.10, p.1.
[29]   *Legislature Amendment Act* 1977.

[30]   *Constitution Act* 1986, s.20(1)(a).
[31]   *Ibid.*, s.20(1)(b), (2).

CHAPTER 10

THE BASIS OF PARLIAMENTARY PROCEDURE

Throughout this book the various types of business transacted by the House are examined. This chapter deals with the basis for the procedures which are employed by the House in considering its business – the sources of the rules which govern how the House goes about its work. These sources are: statute; Standing Orders; other orders of the House; rulings of the Speaker; and practice.

STATUTE
The authority for the existence of Parliament and the House of Representatives, the determination of who is to be a member of Parliament, and many other fundamental parliamentary rules are derived from statutes, principally the Constitution Act 1986 and the Electoral Act 1993. The privileges enjoyed by the House have a statutory basis.[1] These affect the House's legal relationship with the judiciary and with persons outside the House. In addition, statute law has erected a framework around which a great deal of the financial business of the House revolves. There are also many statutes directing that reports and regulations be laid before the House. Some enable the House to take action to disallow or amend such regulations.

Manner and form
If it is to make valid law, Parliament and the House must comply with any statutory condition of law-making that is addressed to them[2] - what is known as a "manner and form" provision. (The term "manner and form" is derived from the statute that formerly defined the scope of the legislative power possessed by colonial legislatures;[3] though a manner and form provision can apply to a legislature with unrestricted legislative power, such as the Parliament of New Zealand, as well as to legislatures without power to legislate on all subjects.)

Manner and form provisions are rare. They relate only to the procedure to be employed in enacting law (the legislative process), not to the substance of the policy that Parliament wishes to put into effect.[4] A manner and form provision exists where Parliament has statutorily bound itself or the House, as to the procedure to be employed in enacting law. There is no manner and form provision, for example, in a restriction applying to the Government or to a body outside the legislative structure.[5] Nor is a provision purporting to deprive Parliament of power to legislate at all on a matter, a manner and form provision. Such a provision can be overridden or repealed by subsequent legislation passed following the legislature's normal procedures.[6] The Attorney-General's obligation to report to the House on legislation that may be inconsistent with the fundamental rights and freedoms confirmed by the *New Zealand Bill of Rights Act* is not a manner and form provision. It is a legislative alert, designed to help members to debate legislation on a more informed basis. Any duty in relation to its discharge lies with the Attorney-General, not with the House. The judgment of whether there is an inconsistency and whether there is justification for the enactment of legislation remains with Parliament.[7]

The reserved provisions of the electoral law are obvious examples of manner and

---

1. *Legislature Act* 1908, s.242.
2. *Shaw v Commissioner of Inland Revenue* [1999] 3 NZLR 154.
3. *Colonial Laws Validity Act* 1865 (UK), s.5.
4. *Westco Lagan Ltd v Attorney-General* [2001] 1 NZLR 40 at [95].
5. *West Lakes Ltd v State of South Australia* (1980) 25 SASR 389; *Reference re Canada Assistance Plan* (1991) 83 DLR (4th) 297.
6. *Commonwealth Aluminium Corporation Limited v Attorney-General (Queensland)* [1976] Qd R 231.
7. *Mangawaro Enterprises Ltd v Attorney-General* [1994] 2 NZLR 451.

form provisions. Repeal or amendment of them can only be effected if the proposal for repeal or amendment is agreed to by 75 percent of the members of the House (or at a poll of electors).[8] Requirements that a particular provision of the law may be amended or a particular object achieved only by a "special" Act of Parliament may be manner and form provisions, requiring the special Act to be confined to that amendment or object. (See Chapter 25.) The granting of the Royal assent has been said to be another example of a manner and form provision.[9] A bill passed by the House of Representatives that did not receive the Royal assent would not become law.

Legislative fairness

The *New Zealand Bill of Rights Act* 1990 applies to acts done by the legislative branch of government.[10] It has been accepted that the House is therefore under a distinct legal obligation to observe the principles of natural justice in transacting its business.[11] The House has adopted Standing Orders designed to give expression to these obligations in a parliamentary context. (See Chapters 23 and 24 for natural justice before select committees and Chapter 39 for responses in the House.)

But while the House has in response to this obligation developed procedures designed to allow persons to respond in the parliamentary environment in situations in which their reputations or personal interests are engaged, the House's legislative decisions are of a different order from statutory decisions generally. The latter are subject to judicial review designed to ensure that they are made legally and reasonably. Different considerations apply to legislative decision-making. Decisions on legislation made by the House are not subject to review or control by the courts (except in the case of a manner and form provision, when what is in issue is whether a valid law has been created at all). The House exercises its legislative decision-making powers on political and policy grounds. For these decisions it and its members are responsible to the electorate, not to the courts.[12] The rules of procedural fairness for statutory decision-makers do not apply to bodies exercising purely legislative functions.[13] Furthermore, judicial review of particular actions taken by the House in its internal proceedings would be contrary to the House's privileges, which are themselves part of the general law.[14] (See Chapters 45 and 46.)

Duty to obey the law

The House is under the law, like every other person and body in New Zealand, and has a duty to observe any legal provision applying directly to it.

The Speaker has a special duty to ensure that the House observes any statutory requirements applying to it.[15] Speakers have emphasised that the House is bound by the law even though some aspects of the general law may not apply to proceedings in Parliament because of the privileges enjoyed by the House and its members in carrying out parliamentary business.[16] Indeed, as emphasised above, the law applying in Parliament is different to that applying outside Parliament. It is thus a difference in law that applies in a parliamentary context, rather than an absence of law.

The Speaker will always exercise any discretions vested in the Chair so as to promote legality.

In the case of statutory appointments to be recommended by the House, the statute may impose restrictions or requirements on who may be appointed or on the consultation to be undertaken. If these have not been complied with, the Speaker will rule a notice of

---

8   *Electoral Act* 1993, s.268.
9   *Westco Lagan Ltd v Attorney-General* [2001] 1 NZLR 40 at [91].
10 *New Zealand Bill of Rights Act* 1990, s.3(a).
11 1993-96 AJHR, I.18A, pp.79-80; Joseph, "Report to the Standing Orders Committee on Natural Justice", paras.3.1-3.15.

12 *Wells v Newfoundland* (1999) 177 DLR (4th) 73 at [59].
13 *Reference re Canada Assistance Plan* (1991) 83 DLR (4th) 297 at 319-20.
14 *Legislature Act* 1908, s.242(2).
15 1909, Vol.148, p.1452.
16 1989, Vol.497, pp.10262-3.

motion for the appointment out of order.[17] The Speaker has also ruled that an amendment restricting the scope of a motion so that it would have achieved less than was required by a statute (which required the House to set up a select committee) would not be in order, though an amendment extending the objects of the motion would be acceptable.[18]

Where a statute applies in relation to the House, all other forms of procedure are subservient to it.[19]

STANDING ORDERS

A provision now repealed[20] required the House to prepare and adopt from time to time Standing Rules and Orders for the conduct of parliamentary business. The Standing Orders adopted under this provision were subject to the Governor-General's approval. They were, in effect, a form of subordinate legislation over which the House did not have sole control. This is not the case now. The Standing Orders of the House, which form its basic code of rules of procedure, are adopted solely by the House and are no longer (since 1865) submitted to the Governor-General for approval. The Standing Orders are not intended to diminish or restrict the rights, privileges, immunities and powers otherwise enjoyed by the House.[21] These rights, privileges, immunities and powers are principally secured for it by statute.

The first committee appointed by the House was a committee to draft the Standing Orders. Following its report, the adoption of that report by the House, and confirmation by the acting Governor, the first Standing Orders came into effect on 16 June 1854.[22] Until that time proceedings had been regulated at the sole discretion of the Speaker.

Unlike their counterpart the Standing Orders of the House of Commons, which "assume a settled practice which they modify only in detail",[23] the House's Standing Orders are much more of a code of practice which set out the various procedures to be followed in considerable detail, although they do not (as would in any case be impossible to attain) purport to be exhaustive. In almost all circumstances when a point of procedure needs to be established, the first resort is to the Standing Orders of the House. There are some 400 Standing Orders. Each order may itself be divided into paragraphs and subparagraphs.

Standing Orders are, as the term implies, permanent rules of the House that remain in force until suspended or amended by a positive decision of the House. They apply to the House from Parliament to Parliament and do not require to be specifically readopted at the commencement of each new Parliament. The Speaker (or the Deputy Speaker or other member presiding) is responsible for ruling on any dispute as to the interpretation or application of the Standing Orders.[24]

Objects of Standing Orders
The Standing Orders are the basic detailed rules of the House providing for the conduct of its proceedings and for the exercise of its powers.[25]

While statutes affect House procedures fundamentally, they do so sporadically. But a prime object of the Standing Orders is to support and give effect to statutory requirements applying to the House. Thus the detailed mechanical provisions for electing a Speaker help to fulfil the House's duty, at its first meeting after a general election, to elect a Speaker.[26] The House's Standing Orders on financial procedure react to the financial business that

[17] 1997, Vol.560, p.2023 (consultation not carried out as required).
[18] 1989, Vol.497, p.10242.
[19] 2002, Vol.599, p.15690.
[20] *New Zealand Constitution Act* 1852 (UK), s.52.
[21] S.O.1.

[22] PD, 1854-55, p.94.
[23] Campion, *An Introduction to the Procedure of the House of Commons*, p.2.
[24] S.O.2.
[25] S.O.1.
[26] *Constitution Act* 1986, s.12.

statute requires to be placed before it[27] and the natural justice reforms introduced in 1996 give parliamentary expression to the House's statutory obligations to accord natural justice to persons whose interests are affected by its proceedings.[28] A significant number of the House's Standing Orders are statutorily related in this way (though not necessarily obviously so). Nevertheless, the House would require some of these procedural rules in any case (for example, rules on appointing a person to chair its meetings).

Standing Orders also represent political accommodations and allocations among the various parties and members of the House. This is particularly obvious since the 1996 changes to the Standing Orders which, for the first time, explicitly recognised parties in the formal rules.[29] The role of the Business Committee, the allocation of questions, speaking rights and committee memberships, and the seating arrangements in the Chamber are matters that are clearly related to the party complexion of the House. This influence of party complexion on the House was not, of course, new in 1996 but it is now openly acknowledged in the Standing Orders that were adopted in anticipation of a multi-party environment.

It has been said that the chief purpose of the rules of parliamentary procedure is to prevent members talking too much.[30] Certainly one of the principal purposes of the Standing Orders is to ration out parliamentary time – in absolute terms, or among the parties represented in the House, or between competing items of business. The Standing Orders prescribe the House's sitting times. They contain strict rules on overall time limits for debates and on the time for which individual members may speak. The House also has many rules providing what types of business have priority on what days and at what part of the day. These discriminate in favour of Government business in a legislative sense but leaven this by providing for regular accountability or scrutiny business (questions, general debates, etc.). The Standing Orders therefore perform a critical rationing function for a scarce parliamentary commodity – time.

Finally, the Standing Orders are designed to promote good outcomes by providing for the House to follow robust procedures before arriving at its decisions. The longstanding requirements for legislation to go through a number of successive stages, particularly the near-universal (since 1979) requirement for select committee consideration, helps to allow time for reflection and informed public input into the consideration of that legislation and so improve decision-making on the details of its final form. The more general procedural requirements for notice of motions to be given, for relevancy in debate and imposing restrictions on amendment, are also directed to this principle of good process leading (hopefully) to better outcomes.

No one of these objectives (statutory drivers, political accommodation, rationing scarce time, good process) predominates over the others. Even in the case of those rules that exist to facilitate statutory compliance by the House, the House makes choices about how it actually does comply with the statute. They each interact with one another, so that, for example, decisions on good processes to follow both temper and are tempered by political reality and the scarcity of House time.

Suspension of Standing Orders

A Standing Order may be formally set aside by a motion to suspend it. Suspension may be for an indefinite period (in which case it lasts until the end of the session), for a limited period,[31] or only in respect of a particular item of business.[32]

Suspension of the Standing Orders is not a frequent occurrence, as it is looked upon

---

27   *Public Finance Act* 1989.
28   *New Zealand Bill of Rights Act* 1990, s.27(1).
29   1993-96, AJHR, I.18A, pp.15-6.
30   A P Herbert, *The Ayes Have It*, p.40.
31   For example, 2003, Vol.608, p.5164 (Standing Order suspended for eight months).
32   For example, 2003, Vol.609, pp.6233-8 (allowing the introduction of an omnibus bill).

as a procedure to be adopted only in exceptional circumstances or as a precursor to an amendment of the Standing Orders. The motion may be moved with or without notice, but if it is moved without notice there must be at least 60 members present at the time it is moved.[33] A motion to suspend Standing Orders cannot interrupt a debate which is in progress and is not subject to amendment.[34] The suspension of Standing Orders can be moved while the House is sitting under urgency provided that the suspension is confined to the business for which urgency was taken.

Generally, a motion to suspend Standing Orders may be moved only by a Minister, but it can be moved by another member to permit some bill, clause or other matter of which the member has charge to proceed or be dealt with without full compliance with the Standing Orders.[35] This does not mean that other members may move the suspension of Standing Orders merely to obtain more favourable procedures for the passing of a bill or other matter of which they have charge. The bill or other matter must actually be prevented by a Standing Order from proceeding further. In this circumstance the member is then able to move a motion designed to remove whatever prevents the bill from proceeding or causes it not to be dealt with. Many suspensions of Standing Orders moved by other members are to permit a new clause to be incorporated into a local bill, notwithstanding that it is not within the objects of the bill as advertised.

A motion to suspend the Standing Orders must itself state the object or reason for the proposed suspension,[36] although it does not need to specify the particular Standing Orders which are to be suspended. Similarly, it is not essential (although it is desirable) that a motion state explicitly that the Standing Orders are to be suspended if it is clear that this is its intention.

There is no specified time limit on the debate on a motion to suspend the Standing Orders. Each member may speak for 10 minutes. The debate on such a motion is limited to the question of the suspension of the Standing Order or Standing Orders proposed to be suspended. Even where the specific Standing Order to be suspended is not identified in the motion, such a motion is not regarded as being for the suspension of all Standing Orders, only those which it is reasonably necessary to suspend to enable the House to proceed in the manner in which it is asked to proceed in the motion.[37] There can be no general discussion of the Standing Orders on a motion to suspend particular Standing Orders.[38]

Leave of the House

Although suspensions of the Standing Orders are comparatively rare, this does not mean that the House never finds it desirable to depart from the strict rules laid down in the Standing Orders. The House frequently, indeed daily, dispenses with the need to comply fully with the Standing Orders by granting "leave" for a matter to be dealt with in an informal way.

"Leave" means permission granted by the House (or a committee) to do something without a single member present dissenting.[39] The House, while it binds itself with Standing Orders, is ultimately master of its own procedures. If all members concur in an action, it would be absurd for the House to feel bound by its own rules to act differently. Therefore, if there is unanimous concurrence on a particular means of proceeding, the Standing Orders may be set aside without a motion to suspend them. But leave is not a means of imposing obligations on another member to do something, such as to table a document. If a member wishes to do something of this nature, the member can seek leave for himself or herself and should not have to react to leave sought by another member.[40]

---

33   S.O.4(1), (2).
34   S.O.4(3), (4).
35   S.O.5.
36   S.O.4(3).

37   1981, Vol.442, p.4310.
38   1903, Vol.125, pp.529, 601.
39   S.O.3(1).
40   1990, Vol.506, p.1291; 1999, Vol.580, p.19163.

There is no debate when it is proposed to the House that leave be granted to do something, for there is no motion before the House, although sometimes an explanation or elucidation of what is proposed is given on a point of order. If any member objects when the Speaker inquires whether leave is granted, leave is refused – each member of the House has a veto on the House proceeding informally. The Speaker decides in a general sense if there is an objection; no member is specifically identified as objecting to leave.[41]

The Standing Orders themselves require leave to be granted before certain things can be done. A member needs leave to make a personal explanation[42] and leave must be granted before a motion which has been proposed by the Chair can be withdrawn.[43] In these and other instances the concept of leave has been incorporated into the Standing Orders and must be obtained to comply with those Standing Orders. Usually, however, leave involves setting aside the Standing Orders and is an alternative to a formal motion to suspend the Standing Orders in cases where there is no objection to something being done.

The practice of obtaining leave is a very important one, for it is utilised on almost every sitting day to ease and expedite the business of the House, often as a result of discussions between the whips or at the Business Committee.

Standing Orders Committee
It had been the longstanding practice of the House to appoint a Standing Orders Committee to examine the Standing Orders as occasion required. However, after 1984 a Standing Orders Committee came to be regularly established in each Parliament. This arrangement of having a Standing Orders Committee has now been made permanent. A Standing Orders Committee is one of the select committees automatically established at the commencement of the Parliament.[44]

The committee is authorised to conduct a review of and report on the Standing Orders and the House's procedures and practices and to make such recommendations as it sees fit for the amendment, revocation or addition of Standing Orders or the alteration of any procedure or practice. The committee also considers and reports on any matter referred to it by the House or otherwise under the Standing Orders (for example, on petitions allocated to it by the Clerk).[45]

The committee usually contains representation from each party. It is almost invariably chaired by the Speaker. Its practice is to appoint the member of the committee with the longest service in the House (apart from the Speaker) as its deputy chairperson.[46]

The committee operates by endeavouring to find a consensus on its proposals rather than these being merely the recommendations of a majority of the committee. This does not mean that all sides of the House will be satisfied with the measures it suggests or even agree with them on an individual basis. Rather the committee works to produce an overall package of proposals which can be concurred in by the overwhelming majority of the House. This involves a process of give and take in the course of its deliberations.[47] But the principle of consensus on which it operates is not the same as the rule of unanimity or near-unanimity which binds the Business Committee. To the contrary, there is no presumption that every party in the House will agree with every recommendation for a change in Standing Orders. Often parties are obliged to accept what they regard as least-bad solutions.[48]

Amendment of Standing Orders
The Standing Orders or any Standing Order can only be amended or revoked on notice being

---

41   1995, Vol.546, p.6174-5, 6177.
42   S.O.350.
43   S.O.99(2).
44   S.O.185(1)(b).
45   S.O.7.

46   1996-99, AJHR, I.18B, p.18.
47   1991-93, AJHR, I.18B, para.9; 2002-05, AJHR, I.18B, p.5.
48   2002-05, AJHR, I.22D, p.865 (*Members of Parliament (Pecuniary Interests) Bill*).

given of a motion to effect this.[49] In fact, the House does not amend its Standing Orders without first having the subject considered in detail by a Standing Orders Committee.

Major amendments to the Standing Orders, after being reported on by the Standing Orders Committee, are considered by the House in a committee of the whole House, with the chairperson of the Standing Orders Committee (the Speaker) taking charge of them in committee, as a Minister does with a bill. They are formally adopted by the House when they are reported back to it after they have been fully considered and agreed to in the committee of the whole House.[50]

Less extensive amendments to the Standing Orders may be adopted by resolution of the House without consideration in a committee of the whole House.

The present Standing Orders were adopted in 1996 and amendments were made to them later in 1996, and then in 1999, in 2003 and in 2005. After the adoption of any amendments, the Standing Orders are reprinted and renumbered to incorporate the latest changes. Until 1974 the Standing Orders relating to private business were published in a separate volume from those relating to public business, but in that year both types of Standing Orders were incorporated into one volume which (with appendices) now contains all Standing Orders.

SESSIONAL ORDERS AND ORDERS OF CONTINUING EFFECT

While the Standing Orders are permanent orders of the House, the House from time to time makes other orders dealing with its procedures on a temporary or limited basis. The suspension of a Standing Order, in particular, is often accompanied by an order of the House directing that a different procedure be followed in respect of a particular matter but without giving that new procedure the permanence that its adoption as a Standing Order implies. In this way the House can experiment and trial new procedures before deciding whether to adopt them in the long term. This course was followed most notably with the House's financial procedures, which were made the subject of a one-year trial before being fully absorbed into the Standing Orders (with further changes introduced as a result of the experience gathered during the trial).[51]

In general, orders of the House affecting its procedures are regarded as being limited in their effects to the parliamentary session in which they are made. They are consequently known as sessional orders and cease to have effect on the prorogation of Parliament (or on the dissolution of Parliament if there is no prorogation).

But some orders of the House may be regarded as having a shorter or longer life than a session. For example, an order of the House may be made to give committees longer to report on particular estimates or financial reviews than is permitted by the Standing Orders. Such an order is spent when the business to which it relates has been dealt with.[52] On the other hand, some orders, even though they are not made into Standing Orders, may come to be regarded as having virtually permanent validity. In 1952 the House resolved that the then Valuation Department should present an annual report to the House on its activities.[53] A report was presented to the House under the 1952 order every year until 1989, when the obligation to present an annual report was made statutory. Another example of an order that has assumed a permanent aspect is that passed in 1962 adopting a form of words for the prayer with which the House begins each sitting.[54] This form of prayer is still used, although it may not be strictly binding on the Speaker.[55]

Orders of the House, even though they are not Standing Orders, are also sources of the rules of procedure that apply in the House.

---

[49] S.O.6.
[50] 1931, Vol.227, pp.544-5, 600.
[51] 1991, Vol.518, pp.4309-14.
[52] See, for example: 2002, Vol.602, p.308; 2002,

Vol.604, p.1796.
[53] 1952, JHR, p.82.
[54] 1962, JHR, pp.39-40.
[55] 1962, Vol.330, pp.337-8.

RULINGS OF THE SPEAKER

The Standing Orders require that in cases for which they do not provide, the Speaker is to decide, guided by previous Speakers' rulings and by the established practices of the House.[56] This provision replaced a previous injunction to Speakers to be guided by the procedures of the United Kingdom House of Commons so far as they could be applied to the House. The procedures of the House in 1854 were, of course, modelled closely on those of the House of Commons, and its procedures as they have developed since then have been heavily influenced by Commons' developments. This did not just occur as a result of the Standing Order injunction, but because of a natural tendency to draw on the experience of that larger and longer-established body. Many of the practices and procedures of the House of Commons are indeed themselves written into the Standing Orders of the House of Representatives.

The Speaker is constantly called upon to make rulings on the interpretation of Standing Orders or on problems which are not covered by the Standing Orders at all. From time to time, collections of the more significant Speakers' rulings (and those of the Speakers' deputies and of chairpersons in the committee of the whole House) are published as guidance for the future. Although there is no strict doctrine of binding precedent, Speakers naturally tend to follow the decisions of their predecessors unless the Standing Orders on which these decisions were based have changed, or unless the earlier rulings were quite plainly in error.

As well as decisions of former Speakers, recommendations of Standing Orders Committees (although not translated into Standing Orders) are also usually followed by the Speaker where they relate to matters within the Speaker's jurisdiction. Standing Orders Committees are composed of senior members of the House and their recommendations carry great weight. In some cases these recommendations are directed at how the Speaker or chairpersons should exercise discretions which are vested in them. The presiding officers invariably adopt these recommendations and apply them for the future,[57] though strictly speaking they are not bound to.

Points of order

Speakers' rulings usually arise following the raising of a point of order (although a matter on which the Speaker may make a ruling may arise extraneously). A member may raise a point of order at any time, and until the point of order is disposed of by the Speaker it takes precedence of the business then before the House.[58] A second point of order cannot be raised while the Speaker is already dealing with a point of order. How much discussion is permitted on a point of order is entirely up to the Speaker. The Speaker is not obliged to hear any argument at all on the point.[59] The member raising the point must put it tersely and relevantly, and other members whom the Speaker allows to contribute to the discussion must be equally concise.[60] It is not in order to interject while a point of order is being heard; a point of order must be heard in silence by the House.[61] Points of order must be raised at the time the matter of order to which they relate arises, and this rule is applied very strictly. If a member does not challenge a matter at once, the opportunity to raise a point of order on it is gone, even if the member was not present at the time the matter arose.[62] Speakers do not encourage the raking over of procedural disputes on matters which the House has already passed over.[63]

The point of order procedure is the method of raising matters of order – that is,

---

[56]   S.O.2.
[57]   See, for example, 1990, Vol.507, pp.1896-7.
[58]   S.O.84(1).
[59]   S.O.84(2).
[60]   S.O.84(3).
[61]   *Ibid.*
[62]   2003, Vol.611, p.8817.
[63]   1894, Vol.85, p.470.

matters on which the Speaker can rule in accordance with the Standing Orders, previous Speakers' rulings or the practice of the House. It is also a perfectly proper way of drawing the Speaker's attention to a procedural step that a member intends to take – for example, to move an instruction to the committee of the whole House or to move the recommittal of a bill.[64] But it is not a method of raising substantive issues that can and should be dealt with in the course of debate, and attempts to raise such matters in the guise of a point of order are deprecated by the Chair.

Once the Speaker has ruled on a point of order, the matter is settled and any attempt on the part of a member to question the ruling is highly disorderly.[65] Nor may a member comment on a point of order that has been decided, whatever the nature of the comment.[66]

PRACTICE

This is, as its name implies, all that lore of parliamentary procedure which is sanctified by being the manner in which things are consistently done, rather than that which is expressly laid down in the Standing Orders or by a ruling of the Speaker. For example, the practice of circulating two versions (provisional and final) of the order paper is just that, a practice, for the Standing Orders require only one version. Practice must be consistent with the Standing Orders or any other applicable order of the House. If challenged, it may be expressly blessed by the Speaker and, therefore, mature into one of the "higher" forms of parliamentary procedure, or it may be disavowed by the Speaker as wrong and thereby cease to be followed.[67]

One form which practice may take is the issue of guidelines, whether under the Standing Orders or otherwise. Guidelines were issued in 1987 to assist select committees in their general procedures.[68] The guidelines were not definitive interpretations of the Standing Orders, although the select committee issuing them attempted to ensure consistency with the Standing Orders. They have been used since then as an aid to meeting procedures. In 1992 it was recommended that the Standing Orders Committee at the time should, as part of its ongoing reviews of the operation of the Standing Orders, issue guidelines to select committees as to their general procedures.[69] This function was conferred on that Standing Orders Committee in its terms of reference.[70]

The Standing Orders Committee is itself an important source of practice. As well as its recommendations contributing to rulings of the Speaker, recommendations made by the committee as to how procedures are to be applied are, while current, accepted as representing the correct mode of proceeding. Where a statute provides for parliamentary business a recommended procedure for transacting that business may be made by the Standing Orders Committee. These procedures then become part of the House's procedures for dealing with that business, even though they may not (or may not yet) have been incorporated into the Standing Orders. Other committees concerned with particular business may themselves establish practice for the way in which that business is transacted.[71]

Consequently, it is important to record the practices which contribute to the operation of the House as well as the express rules introduced by statutes, the Standing Orders, other orders, and Speakers' rulings which, together with practice, form the basis of parliamentary procedure.

---

64   1985, Vol.462, pp.4652-3.
65   1985, Vol.465, p.6737.
66   1905, Vol.133, p.222.
67   1992, Vol.525, p.8938; 2003, Vol.612, pp.9024-9.
68   1987-90, AJHR, I.14A.
69   1991-93, AJHR, I.18B, para.26(a).
70   1993, Vol.539, p.26.
71   See, for example: 2002-05, AJHR, I.15A (Officers of Parliament Committee) – procedures for the appointment of officers of Parliament; *ibid.* I.22A (Finance and Expenditure Committee) – process for considering Auditor-General's draft annual plan.

CHAPTER 11

THE CHAMBER, BUILDINGS AND GROUNDS

MEETING PLACE FOR PARLIAMENT

The place at which meetings of Parliament are to be held is determined by the Governor-General (not by the House itself) and is indicated in the proclamation which summons Parliament to meet.[1]

The place appointed in the proclamation summoning Parliament for Parliament to meet is not expressed with any greater particularity than the city of Wellington. The Governor-General may, by a further proclamation, change the place appointed for the meeting of Parliament, if that place is unsafe or uninhabitable,[2] for example as a result of an earthquake. Changing the place of meeting by such a proclamation does not bring the session to an end. Except in these circumstances, once Parliament has met following a summons, the place of meeting cannot be changed during the course of a session. Parliament would need to be prorogued and a new session summoned for the meeting place to be altered.[3]

The first meetings of Parliament from 1854 onwards were held in Auckland in a building shared with the Auckland Provincial Council. The transport problems for members from outside the Auckland province were immense. It has been claimed that the South Island members spent nine weeks at sea on their way to attend the first Parliament.[4] These difficulties, combined with the relatively faster increase in population in the southern settlements, particularly in Otago, throughout the 1850s, resulted in strong pressure for Parliament to meet at a more central location, or for its meetings to rotate throughout the country. Implementation of a proposal to alternate the sessions of Parliament between Auckland and Wellington was postponed on the outbreak of the New Zealand wars, but the 1862 session was held in Wellington. In 1865 a permanent transfer of the seat of government from Auckland to Wellington was made following the recommendation of a commission appointed to study the matter. The site chosen for Parliament to meet was in Thorndon, Wellington, in the Wellington Provincial Council building, adjacent to the then Government House.

For more than 40 years the Legislative Council and the House of Representatives shared this site with Government House until the old Parliament House was destroyed by fire in 1907. The Governor moved to other accommodation to give the House a place to meet while a new building was being erected, and never returned to Parliament grounds, for shortly afterwards the present Government House in Newtown was completed. The General Assembly Library building had been completed in 1899 and work started on a new Parliament House adjacent to it in 1912. This was completed by 1922, but not to the original specification: as an economy measure, the southern section of the building was not proceeded with, and the old wooden Government House building was retained for use instead. As well as housing members, the new building accommodated Ministers' offices which were transferred away from their departments; "Parliament House thus became not only the home of Parliament but also the centre of the administration."[5]

The parliamentary buildings are still the centre of administration. Since 1979,

---

[1] *Constitution Act* 1986, s.18(1).
[2] *Ibid.*, s.18(1A).
[3] 1991-93, AJHR, E.31P, p.357 (*Law Commission: Final Report on Emergencies, December 1991*).
[4] Reeves, *The Long White Cloud*, p.182.
[5] Dollimore, *The Parliament of New Zealand and Parliament House*, p.44.

Ministers' offices have been established in an executive wing to Parliament House, popularly known as the Beehive because of its shape, which is situated to the south of the main Parliament House on the site of the old Government House building. Work on the Beehive was carried out between 1969 and 1980. In addition to ministerial offices, it contains part of the Department of the Prime Minister and Cabinet, and the parliamentary refreshment and catering rooms, better known as Bellamy's. Some further ministerial accommodation outside Parliament buildings has also been necessary owing to pressure on space in the Beehive. The main Parliament House building contains: the Chamber of the House of Representatives; the Council Chamber, the chamber of the former Legislative Council; select committee rooms, and offices for members and staff. A building connected to Parliament House and the Beehive, completed in 1981 for the Parliamentary Counsel Office, now houses the Parliamentary Press Gallery.

From 1991 to 1995, the House moved its meeting place to a temporary Chamber situated across the road from the Beehive at No. 3 The Terrace. This was to permit Parliament House and the library building to be strengthened against earthquake, refurbished (with an emphasis on restoring much of its original appearance), and further developed. Accommodation for members, their staffs and the parliamentary administration was provided in a building adjacent to the Chamber known as Bowen House. Parliament House was reoccupied in January 1996. Bowen House has been retained on a lease now vested in the Parliamentary Corporation.[6] It continues to accommodate members and staff and is linked by an underground walkway to the Beehive.

PARLIAMENTARY PRECINCTS

Together, the land occupied for parliamentary purposes – Parliament House, the library building, the Beehive, the Press Gallery building at the rear of the Beehive, and the land and premises subject to the Bowen House lease – constitute the parliamentary precincts both for legal and parliamentary purposes.[7] The House is empowered, by resolution, to vary the extent of the parliamentary precincts by adding to it or excluding from it land and premises. However, it cannot add land or premises unless the Crown or the Parliamentary Corporation already hold an interest in that land or premises.[8]

The ground on which Parliament House, the library, the Beehive and the Press Gallery building now stand comprises three distinct parcels of land set aside at different times as reserve for use for parliamentary purposes. The whole of that land is now vested absolutely in Her Majesty the Queen for parliamentary purposes.[9]

The Speaker is vested with the control and administration of the whole of the parliamentary precincts, on behalf of the House, whether Parliament is in session or not.[10] Between a general election and the first meeting of the House in a new Parliament, the person who was Speaker until the election continues to perform those functions.[11] In the case of a vacancy in the office of Speaker, the Deputy Speaker may perform the Speaker's functions.[12]

THE CHAMBER

The Chamber of the House is 19.83 metres by 13.12 metres. The Speaker presides at an ornate raised chair – a gift of the House of Commons in 1951 to mark the centenary of parliamentary institutions in New Zealand[13] – and the Clerk of the House is seated at an oblong table (the Table of the House) immediately in front of and below the raised chair.

---

6   *Parliamentary Service Act* 2000, s.24.
7   *Ibid.*, s.3; S.O.3(1).
8   *Parliamentary Service Act* 2000, s.25.
9   *Ibid.*, s.23.
10 *Ibid.*, s.26(1).
11 *Ibid.*, s.3.
12 *Ibid.*, s.33.
13 1951, Vol.296, pp.961-6.

On the Table are trays made of selected Samoan woods presented by the then Western Samoan Legislative Assembly in 1955.[14]

On either side of the Speaker's chair and the Table the members sit at desks arranged in three to five tiers in an irregular horseshoe shape, with the horseshoe divided at three points by gangways. One gangway at the far end of the Chamber leads beyond the bar of the House to an exit. The other two gangways are on either side of the Chamber. The one on the Speaker's right leads into a lobby known as the Ayes Lobby, and the one on the left leads into the Noes Lobby.

The members of Parliament who are members of the Government occupy seats on the Speaker's right. Those seats in the block nearest to the Speaker are occupied by Ministers, Parliamentary Under-Secretaries and whips. Other Government members occupy the seats at the far end of the Chamber beyond the gangway and, if necessary, some of the seats at the far end of the Chamber on the Speaker's left beyond the central gangway. Opposition members occupy seats on the Speaker's left. Although each member occupies an individual seat at what resembles an escritoire, the term "bench" (which is what members sit on in the House of Commons) is still used to refer to the seats occupied by Ministers (Treasury benches), the seats occupied by senior opposition members (front benches), the seats beyond the gangways on both sides of the House (cross benches), and to refer to non-ministerial members of Parliament generally (backbenchers).

The colour of the carpets and seats is green, a colour associated with the lower chamber of a legislature, which is what the House was until the abolition of the Legislative Council. Wooden plaques commemorating battlefields and campaigns engaged in by members of New Zealand's defence forces are affixed to the Chamber and gallery walls.

Ministerial advisers are able to converse with their Minister from a bench situated immediately to the right of the Speaker's chair. Immediately to the left of the chair there are seats available for former members of Parliament, heads of diplomatic missions and visiting members of overseas parliaments.[15]

Seating in the Chamber

The Prime Minister, Deputy Prime Minister, Leader of the Opposition and deputy to the Leader of the Opposition sit facing each other in recognised front bench seats. Their respective whips are seated immediately behind them. Other Ministers and members are allocated seats within the area of the Chamber occupied by the party to which they belong on a basis determined by the party. As far as practicable, each party occupies a block of seats in the Chamber, so that its members are seated contiguously.[16] A member who is under suspension from his or her party continues to be seated within the area of seating allocated to that party.[17] It is also a recognised practice that, if at all possible, every party leader should have a front-bench seat.

The Speaker resolves any disputes about seating that may arise.[18] This generally involves the Speaker determining which area of the Chamber particular parties are to have allocated to them if the parties themselves cannot agree on this. Within these areas the allocation of seats to individual members of each party is left to the party leaders and their whips, and the Speaker does not intervene.[19]

---

[14] 1955, Vol.307, pp.2313-6.

[15] See further, Dollimore, *The Parliament of New Zealand and Parliament House*, and Cook, *Parliament: The Land and Buildings from 1840*.

[16] S.O.37(1).

[17] 2003, Vol.606, p.3257.

[18] S.O.37(2).

[19] 1992, Vol.530, p.11441.

[20] S.O.80(1).

Conduct in the Chamber

It is the Speaker's duty to maintain order and decorum in the House.[20] But Speakers often remind members that they too share severally in that responsibility so that the House can function in an orderly manner without damaging its reputation. Speakers must also take account of the state of opinion among members in the standards that they seek to impose. Informal consultation, discussion at the Business Committee, and occasionally more systematic canvassing of members' opinions are means of gauging this.

In a reversal of the normal rules of courtesy, members must, when the Speaker rises, resume their seats. They must also be silent so that the Speaker can be heard without interruption.[21]

Members can, within limits, speak from seats that are not their own. But, except when speaking in debate or voting, members are expected to occupy a seat in the Chamber and not to move around it.[22] It is acknowledged, however, that some members (such as party leaders and whips) have duties to perform in the House that require them to move around the Chamber in the course of carrying out those duties and the seating requirement is relaxed in respect of them.[23]

Originally the seats that members occupied in the Chamber were intended to function as their offices because members did not have individual office space in the building. Even today they are still designed to facilitate members working on correspondence or other papers. Members have traditionally been permitted to read newspapers in the Chamber although these are no longer delivered to members at their seats as a matter of course. As technology has changed the use of other devices in the Chamber has been permitted too. There are a number of telephones installed, principally for leaders and whips. The installation of telephones and the use of electronic devices are subject to the Speaker's discretion.[24] The Speaker has, for instance, permitted members to use laptop computers in the Chamber provided these can be used silently and unobtrusively.[25] But cellphones are not permitted and must be turned off within hearing of the Chamber.[26]

Members are not permitted to drink or eat food in the Chamber (except water and inconspicuous confectionery such as peppermints).[27] Refreshment facilities are provided in the lobbies and it is to these that members must repair if they wish to consume food or beverages.[28] Knitting is permitted in the Chamber, but not by a Minister who is at the Table in charge of a bill in committee.[29]

Dress codes

The standard of dress of members is also regarded as a matter of order under the general control of the Speaker.[30] There are no fashion codes prescribed. The Speaker is expected to take issue with any member who is not dressed in appropriate business attire, whether the member is male or female.[31] Male members are regularly polled by the Speaker on their attitude to wearing a jacket and tie in the Chamber.[32] Currently, by an overwhelming majority, this is the preferred standard of dress.[33] There is no rule against the wearing of a hat;[34] indeed, a hat was a normal article of attire among nineteenth-century parliamentarians (a member has been sworn-in wearing a hat[35]) and a rule requiring members to take off any hat they were wearing only while actually speaking was revoked as recently as 1985. However, members cannot wear a hat with advertising or a message written on it for the purpose of making a "silent interjection" in the Chamber.[36]

---

21   S.O.80(2).
22   S.O.82.
23   1976, Vol.404, p.852.
24   1987, Vol.485, p.1679.
25   "MPs may bring laptops, but not to play games", *The Dominion,* 13 June 1997; 2003, Vol.608, p.5908.
26   2003, Vol.608, p.5741; 2004, Vol.616, p.12426.
27   1997, Vol.559, p.1061; 2003, Vol.609, p.6970.
28   2003, Vol.609, p.6970.
29   2003, Vol.608, p.5908.
30   2000, Vol.584, p.2594.
31   2002-05, AJHR, I.18B, p.23 (Standing Orders Committee).
32   1997, Vol.559, pp.1102-3; 2000, Vol.587, p.5776.
33   2002, Vol.604, p.2450.
34   1999, Vol.578, p.17631.
35   Dalziel, *Julius Vogel – Business Politician*, p.53.
36   1999, Vol.578, p.17631.

Maintenance of order

Any conduct or remark in the Chamber that is heard or comes to the attention of the Speaker may be dealt with by the Speaker as a matter of order. The Speaker, in the course of a debate, often requires members to withdraw unparliamentary expressions and sometimes requires them to apologise for having used those expressions.

Withdrawal from the Chamber

To deal with more serious breaches of order there are more potent weapons in the Speaker's armoury than merely requiring a member to apologise. In exceptional cases these may be resorted to. The Speaker has, on occasion, asked a member who has been persistently disorderly to withdraw voluntarily from the Chamber while a point of order or other matter is under discussion. This has helped to relieve tension and has obviated more serious steps being taken, but it depends on the co-operation of members.

In the absence of co-operation, or if the situation has deteriorated to such an extent that it is inappropriate to request a member to withdraw, the Speaker may order a member whose conduct is highly disorderly to withdraw from the Chamber for a period up to the remainder of the day's sitting.[37] Any member who is thus ordered to withdraw cannot re-enter the Chamber during the period of exclusion, but he or she is not suspended from the service of the House and can carry out other duties as a member, such as voting.[38] Where the Speaker uses this power to order a member to withdraw from the Chamber, the objectionable conduct which gave rise to the Speaker's action is dealt with finally by the order to leave the Chamber. The matter is at an end at that point. This contrasts with the situation where a member has defied the Chair and voluntarily left the Chamber rather than withdraw or apologise for unparliamentary remarks. In this case the matter is not at an end and the Speaker will deal with the member on his or her eventual return to the Chamber.[39]

The Speaker when excluding the member under this provision may name the period of exclusion. If the Speaker does not name the period, the member may make inquiries of the Speaker through the Serjeant-at-Arms as to the period of exclusion from the Chamber.[40]

Naming and suspension of a member

Whenever a member's conduct is so grossly disorderly that the Speaker considers that simply ordering the withdrawal of the member would not be adequate, the Speaker can "name" the member and thereby call on the House to pass judgment on the member's conduct.[41] The first member said to have been "named" in this way was Julius Vogel in 1887.[42] When a member is named, the Speaker says, "I name … [the member for …] for grossly disorderly conduct.". It is not possible to define what conduct will be regarded as grossly disorderly and so warrant naming. This will depend very much on the individual circumstances that confront a Speaker. But the Speaker has indicated that a member flagrantly defying the Chair can expect to be dealt with in this way.[43]

Where a member has been named, the House itself is asked to censure the conduct of the member and the Speaker accordingly states a question to the House immediately for the member to be suspended from the service of the House. This question is put without any amendment or debate.[44] If the motion is carried, the member is suspended for 24 hours, or for seven days if this is the second occasion on which he or she has been suspended in the same Parliament, or for 28 days if it is the third or more.[45] In each of the

37   S.O.85(1).
38   S.O.85(2).
39   2001, Vol.596, p.13100.
40   1985, Vol.468, pp.8862-3.
41   S.O.86.

42   Martin, *The House – New Zealand's House of Representatives 1854-2004*, p.98.
43   2001, Vol.596, p.13100.
44   S.O.87.
45   S.O.89.

two latter cases, the day on which the member is suspended is not counted as one of the seven or 28 days of suspension; it is additional to them.

If a member who is suspended refuses to withdraw voluntarily from the House at once, the Serjeant-at-Arms will be called on by the Speaker to enforce the House's direction. Should force prove to be necessary, the Speaker calls the House's attention to this fact and the contumacious member is automatically suspended from the service of the House for the remainder of the calendar year.[46]

Consequences of suspension
A member who is suspended from the service of the House suffers a number of disabilities during the period of suspension.[47] The member cannot—
* enter the Chamber (or the galleries[48])
* have a vote cast in a party vote
* vote in a personal vote
* give or exercise a proxy vote (though the member is still part of the party's membership in the House for the purposes of calculating how many proxies may be exercised for the party)
* serve on (or be replaced on[49]) a select committee
* serve as a member of the Intelligence and Security Committee[50]
* lodge an oral or a written question (but a question already lodged may be dealt with or asked on the member's behalf)
* lodge a notice of motion (but a notice already lodged may be dealt with on the member's behalf)
* lodge an application for an urgent debate (but an application already lodged will be dealt with and, if accepted, a motion may be moved on the member's behalf)
* submit an item for inclusion on a select committee's agenda (but an item already submitted may be dealt with by the committee).

Contempt of the House
Serious disorder in the House by members could also be held to be a contempt of the House; indeed ultimately the House's power to protect itself against disorder, whether by its own members or by strangers, depends upon its privilege to punish for contempt. (See Chapter 47.) The fact that the House has by its Standing Orders set out procedures for the disciplining of members for breaches of order does not prevent the House proceeding against a member under its privilege of punishing for contempt.[51] Thus, even though a member may have been suspended for grossly disorderly conduct, it is open to the House to hold that member in contempt in respect of that conduct and punish the member for it.[52] However, the fact that the member had already been suspended for the offence would be a relevant factor for the Speaker to consider in determining whether a question of privilege was involved and for the Privileges Committee and the House to consider in determining any punishment for the contempt.

Adjournment or suspension of the House for disorder
In addition to the powers to proceed against individual members, the Speaker has authority to adjourn the House or to suspend the House's sitting if the Speaker considers

---

[46]   S.O.90.
[47]   S.O.91.
[48]   1880, Vol.37, p.738.
[49]   S.O.188(3).
[50]   *Intelligence and Security Committee Act* 1996, s.10(1).

[51]   1986-87, AJHR, I.15; *Raj Narain Singh v Atmaran Govind, Speaker of the Uttar Pradesh Legislative Assembly* AIR 1954 Allahabad 319.
[52]   S.O.92.

it necessary to do so to maintain order.[53] The Speaker automatically resumes the chair in any case in which the chairperson temporarily suspends the proceedings of the committee of the whole House for disorder.[54] It is then up to the Speaker as to whether the House should be adjourned or suspended or whether the Speaker should otherwise deal with the disorder that had arisen in committee and declare the House in committee again.

After suspending a sitting the Speaker decides when the sitting will resume,[55] which may be at any time up to the time that the House would have adjourned in any case. If the Speaker adjourns a sitting the House stands adjourned until the next sitting day.[56] The power to suspend the sitting was last used by the Speaker in 1987, when the sitting was suspended for five minutes.[57]

Order in the committee of the whole House

The rules for maintaining order in the Chamber in a committee of the whole House are similar to those in the House itself.[58] The chairperson is responsible for keeping order in committee and has the same powers as the Speaker in the House to require a member to withdraw unparliamentary expressions and apologise for having uttered them.

The chairperson may also require a member whose conduct is highly disorderly to withdraw from the committee for a period fixed by the chairperson. In this case the period cannot exceed the time that the House spends in committee that day and does not apply whenever the House resumes during the course of the sitting (for example, to take a ruling from the Speaker). If the member has not been readmitted to the Chamber by the time the committee reports back to the House that day, the exclusion automatically lapses.

The chairperson may also name a member for grossly disorderly conduct. In such a case the proceedings of the committee must be immediately suspended and the fact of the naming reported to the House.[59] A committee of the whole House cannot punish a member; only the House can do that. Where the committee does report the naming of a member to the House, the Speaker institutes the same procedures as if the naming had been made by the Speaker in the House and immediately puts a question for the member's suspension.[60]

The chairperson may also temporarily suspend the proceedings of the committee of the whole House in any case of grave disorder.[61] In such a case the Speaker automatically resumes the chair.[62] It is then for the Speaker to determine what, if any, further action is required to be taken. Whenever the committee resumes sitting again after such a temporary suspension, its proceedings are resumed at the point they had reached when the sitting was interrupted by the suspension.[63]

Admission of officials to the Chamber

Officials are permitted to occupy seats on the right of the Chair to assist Ministers with business before the House or the seats on the right or left of the Chair to assist other members in charge of a bill before the House.[64] Officials are expected to conform to the dress standards required of members and otherwise to conduct themselves appropriately. Members are not permitted to refer to the presence of such officials in the course of debate or to approach them directly without the Minister's concurrence. If a member considers that an official is acting inappropriately this should be raised as a point of order or discussed privately with the Minister. On no account should the officials be directly accosted.[65]

---

[53] S.O 48(1)
[54] S.O.178(2).
[55] S.O.48(2).
[56] S.O.48(3).
[57] 1986-87, JHR, p.740.
[58] S.O.174.
[59] S.O.88.

[60] *Ibid.*
[61] S.O.178(1).
[62] S.O.178(2).
[63] S.O.180.
[64] 2001, Vol.594, p.10811.
[65] 1998, Vol.571, pp.12095-8.

From time to time the Speaker issues guidance for how officials should conduct themselves when occupying these seats.[66]

LOBBIES

The lobbies on either side of the Chamber are set aside for the exclusive use of members while the House is sitting. Strangers should not enter them during this time.[67]

The lobbies are used in a formal sense to transact business of the House when a personal vote is being held. But generally they are not a place of formal business, rather they are a place of retreat. Consequently, there are few, if any, rules as to how they may be used (food and beverages may be consumed there for example, but smoking is no longer permitted[68]). Indeed, formerly, the Speaker was not regarded as having jurisdiction over what occurred in the lobbies, except during a vote.[69] Now the Speaker's delegation of authority from the House to control admission runs as equally to the lobbies as to the Chamber and the galleries,[70] so disorder in the lobbies could be dealt with by the Speaker if necessary.

PRESS GALLERY

The press gallery is situated immediately above and behind the Speaker's chair. Admission to it is restricted to members of the Parliamentary Press Gallery. (See Chapter 45.)

PUBLIC GALLERIES

Around the sides of the Chamber and at the far end of the Chamber are public galleries. The gallery at the far end of the Chamber is known as the Speaker's gallery. Admission to it may, at the Speaker's discretion, be subject to stricter dress standards than the other galleries. Some 400 persons in total can be seated in the public galleries.

Admission to the galleries

The right to control access to its proceedings and determine the conditions under which such access is granted are aspects of the House's privileges.[71] (See Chapter 46.)

Conduct in the galleries

It is a condition under which strangers are permitted to be present at proceedings of the House that they do not misbehave or interrupt the business of the House. The Speaker and the Serjeant-at-Arms are authorised by the House to require any strangers who misconduct themselves or interrupt proceedings to withdraw from the galleries and the parliamentary precincts.[72] In committee, the chairperson has this authority also. The Speaker has ordered all strangers to withdraw from particular galleries when it was impossible to distinguish between strangers in those galleries who were misbehaving and strangers who were not.[73]

Other control over the behaviour of strangers in the galleries is exercised by means of the House's privilege to punish for contempt. A stranger wilfully interrupting the business of the House commits a contempt, which can be punished by the House as such.

Members are not permitted to converse with strangers from the floor of the House.[74] They must go out beyond the bar of the House if they wish to speak to visitors.[75] It is

---

[66] "Rules governing the admission of officials to the Chamber and Lobbies of the House of Representatives", 4 July 2000.
[67] 1910, Vol.153, p.360; 1913, Vol.164, p.240.
[68] 2000, Vol.582, pp.947-8.
[69] 1929, Vol.222, p.665.
[70] S.O.42.

[71] *New Brunswick Broadcasting Co v Nova Scotia (Speaker of the House of Assembly)* (1993) 100 DLR (4th) 212.
[72] S.O.41.
[73] 1977, Vol.414, p.3751.
[74] 1931, Vol.228, p.755.
[75] 1976, Vol.408, p.4344.

also a rule of debate that members in their speeches should not refer to the presence of strangers[76] or to what is happening in the galleries.[77] If members wish to express greetings to persons in the galleries they need leave of the House.[78] Amongst other things, these rules are designed to avoid any provocation of interruptions to the proceedings of the House by strangers present at the time. Strangers must refrain from encroaching into those parts of the House set apart for members while the House is sitting; that is, the floor of the House and the lobbies.[79] Members themselves may not bring strangers into those areas.

Celebrations in the galleries

The Speaker will permit contributions from the galleries in some circumstances. It is traditional when members make their maiden speeches for their families and supporters to be on hand to hear them and a wider latitude is given to persons in the galleries on these occasions. Less commonly, a group particularly affected by a piece of legislation (such as legislation effecting a settlement of a Treaty of Waitangi grievance) may wish to celebrate the occasion of the legislation passing. Speakers may permit this to occur.

The Speaker has set out the circumstances and conditions in which a contribution from the galleries may be permitted—

- prior permission of the Speaker is always required
- permission of the Speaker must be sought in writing
- permission will only be given for a contribution that is celebratory in nature and which relates to a speech or decision of the House
- usually the contribution will only be permitted between speeches, so as not to interrupt a member speaking, but on an occasion such as a maiden speech, if the member desires it, it can be permitted during a speech
- otherwise a celebratory contribution can take place only after the House's decision has been made; it can never be used to influence the House's deliberations on a matter
- karanga (welcoming call) and waiata (song) may be permitted but not anything in the nature of a speech (whaikorero)
- accompanying music is not permitted.[80]

THE PARLIAMENT BUILDINGS

The Parliament buildings contain the premises of a number of separate buildings: Parliament House, the Parliamentary Library building, the Beehive and the building occupied by the Parliamentary Press Gallery. It is not common to regard Bowen House as being part of the Parliament buildings but as it is part of the parliamentary precincts it is also under the control and administration of the Speaker. The Parliament buildings and Bowen House contain, as well as the Chamber, meeting rooms for select committees and caucuses, office accommodation for members, their staffs and parliamentary staff and other service areas necessary for a complex that has over 1,000 people working in it and through which approximately 100,000 visitors pass each year. The latter principally consist of tour parties conducted under the aegis of the Parliamentary Service. The buildings also contain reception areas which, with the Speaker's permission, may be used by groups from outside Parliament.

The buildings are used for parliamentary purposes as places of work. They are not

---

[76] 1934, Vol.238, p.68.
[77] 1990, Vol.506, p.967.
[76] 1934, Vol.238, p.68.
[77] 1990, Vol.506, p.967.

[78] 2001, Vol.593, p.9983.
[79] 1910, Vol.153, p.360.
[80] 1998, Vol.572, pp.12347-8.

places in which it is traditional or appropriate for persons to conduct demonstrations (unlike in Parliament grounds, for example). They are protected by security guards employed by the Parliamentary Service with the aim of safeguarding the personal security of members, staff and other persons who have resort to them to carry out parliamentary business or to observe proceedings. The Speaker exercises the powers of an occupier to exclude persons who act inappropriately in the light of these considerations. Occasionally, the House has resolved that certain persons be excluded from all or part of the buildings.[81] The Speaker, exercising control of the buildings on the House's behalf, has implemented these decisions under the powers possessed by the Speaker as occupier.

The Speaker has entered into an agreement with the Commissioner of Police as to the exercise of policing powers within the parliamentary precincts. The police liaise with the Parliamentary Service about operational policing functions and acknowledge the need to seek the authority of the Speaker to interview members within Parliament buildings.[82] The Speaker has also issued a protocol setting out the conditions under which reporters and associated camera and sound persons may have access to members for interviews and filming in the buildings[83] and supplemented this with a statement as to the new media's positioning within the buildings, especially when members are making their way to the Chamber.[84]

The courts have recognised the necessity, for its proper functioning, for a legislature, through its Speaker, to have control over the parliamentary precincts, including the power to exclude persons from the premises. It is for the House and the Speaker to judge whether in a particular case it is necessary to exclude an individual.[85] Usually the power to exclude a person from the buildings would be invoked by an official of the Parliamentary Service under delegation from the Speaker, rather than by the Speaker personally or by the Speaker at the behest of the House.

A number of different departments of state occupy accommodation in Parliament buildings: Office of the Clerk, Parliamentary Service, Department of Prime Minister and Cabinet and Department of Internal Affairs. (The Parliamentary Counsel Office, which was formerly located in the Parliament buildings, now occupies its own premises outside the buildings.) These may have their own workplace policies on various matters, particularly in relation to smoking. The Speaker has therefore prescribed a complex-wide smoke-free policy after being guided by a survey of members and staff opinion. Under this policy the entire complex is declared to be smoke-free.[86]

THE PARLIAMENT GROUNDS

The Parliament grounds are also part of the parliamentary precincts and are therefore subject to the Speaker's control and administration, but they are regarded as being in a different position to Parliament buildings as regards access and use.

The Parliament grounds are freely open to, and used by, the public.[87] Traditionally, they have been a place of resort for persons wishing to hold rallies, demonstrations and meetings, sometimes with and sometimes without, the prior permission of the Speaker. (This is so only insofar as pedestrian access is concerned; vehicular access is expected to be for the purposes of transacting business in the buildings and is subject to stricter controls, particularly for security reasons.) The law relating to criminal trespass does apply to the Parliament grounds. The Speaker is able to exercise the rights of an occupier

---

81 1981, Vol.442, pp.4315-6; 1992, Vol.528, pp.10626-31.
82 "Policing functions within the parliamentary precincts – An agreement between the Speaker of the House of Representatives of New Zealand and the New Zealand Commissioner of Police", June 2004.
83 "Protocol for filming and interviewing members in Parliament buildings", December 2004.
84 2005, Vol.625, p.20303.
85 *Zündel v Boudria* (2000) 181 DLR (4th) 463.
86 2004, Vol.621, p.16783.
87 *Melser v Police* [1967] NZLR 437 at 444.

to require persons to leave the grounds and can delegate this power to other persons.[88] Trespass notices are not generally issued by the Speaker personally; they are issued by members of the police or senior Parliamentary Service staff under powers delegated to them by the Speaker.[89]

The powers that the Speaker possesses as the occupier of Parliament grounds are conferred for the performance of a public function. Principally, these powers are entrusted to the Speaker to promote the effective functioning of the parliamentary system. They are explicitly conferred on behalf of the House.[90] But the Speaker and the Speaker's delegates must exercise the rights of an occupier in a manner that is reasonable having regard to the fundamental right of every person to assemble peacefully,[91] a right that applies within Parliament grounds. If a demonstration became disorderly or breached or threatened to breach the peace or to infringe unreasonably the rights of others (including those of the occupier to use the grounds), the Speaker would not be acting unreasonably in requiring the demonstrators to leave the grounds.[92] But in no circumstances should the right to assemble be abridged arbitrarily or without good reason. In exercising the occupier's powers the Speaker must: act in good faith, exercise the powers for the purposes conferred (as a public function) and not for an ulterior purpose (for example, party advantage), exercise the powers reasonably when balanced against the rights and freedoms of those affected, exercise the powers with due regard to others present in the grounds and others wishing to enter or use the grounds, and take into consideration the need effectively to operate, manage and control the property.[93]

The Speaker has acknowledged these constraints on the exercise of the occupier's powers and has declared that the powers will be used positively to facilitate the holding of demonstrations at the traditional venue of Parliament grounds provided that the manner of demonstrating is consistent with the Speaker's other duties to members and other persons using the buildings and grounds.[94] It is for the Speaker to judge in each case whether demonstrators are conducting themselves in a way which makes it reasonable to require them to desist or to leave.

The Speaker's expectations for the use of the grounds by demonstrators are—

- participants must assemble within and disperse from the grounds in an orderly manner, using the pedestrian ways so as to avoid damage to the lawns and flower beds and so as not to interfere with the flow of vehicular traffic
- participants must not mount the main steps nor interfere with the use of Parliament buildings by those entering or leaving it in the normal course of their business
- sound amplification equipment may be used, but never from the main steps of Parliament buildings without express permission; it must be directed away from the buildings and not operated in a manner disruptive to occupants of the buildings
- the size of any deputation from the group waiting upon a Minister or member is to be limited to six people
- participants are to conduct themselves in such a way as to avoid any breach of the peace
- no food may be prepared or sold within Parliament grounds, but there is no restriction on people consuming food that they may have brought with them
- without express authority to the contrary, no demonstration should last for longer than a normal working day, that is, eight hours

---

88   *Police v Beggs* [1999] 3 NZLR 615 at 623, 628; *Parliamentary Service Act* 2000, s.26(2).
89   *Hansard Supplement,* 1997, Vol.29, p.3832.
90   *Parliamentary Service Act* 2000, s.26(1).
91   *New Zealand Bill of Rights Act* 1990, s.16.
92   *Police v Beggs* [1999] 3 NZLR 615 at 627.
93   *Ibid.*, at 631.
94   1999, Vol.579, pp.18473-4.

- no vehicles may be brought on to the grounds as part of a demonstration
- no structure, such as a tent, may be erected.

Members are not prevented from taking part in demonstrations in the grounds or from addressing the crowds, but if they do so they must abide by the same rules as apply to the public.[95]

Organisers of demonstrations are asked to inform the Speaker's office or the Parliamentary Service management of the intention to hold a demonstration in Parliament grounds, particularly one of any size, so that appropriate arrangements can be made to facilitate it.

---

[95] *Ibid.*, p.18474; 2003, Vol.611, p.8439.

CHAPTER 12

THE OPENING OF PARLIAMENT

FIRST MEETING OF A NEW PARLIAMENT

Parliament meets according to the Governor-General's proclamation appointing the place and time for it to convene. Seven minutes before the time appointed in the proclamation summoning Parliament the House's Chamber bells are rung for five minutes and the members elected at the general election assemble in the Chamber of the House and await the Royal commissioners.[1]

Commission Opening

There are few times when both elements of Parliament, the Crown and the House of Representatives, come together to discharge their duties. The occasion of the opening of a new Parliament when the Parliament is declared open before the assembled members is one of them. In fact, neither the Sovereign nor the Governor-General attends this ceremony in person. Rather, they authorise Royal commissioners to attend on their behalf to declare Parliament open. Until the abolition of the Legislative Council, the commissioners opened Parliament from the Legislative Council Chamber. Now this task is performed in the House's own Chamber. There are three Royal commissioners, who are usually the Chief Justice or another senior judge as chief commissioner and two other judges.

At this time the House has no Speaker. Consequently, the Mace, being regarded as a symbol of the Speaker's authority, is not displayed. It is placed under the Table in the position it occupies when the Speaker leaves the Speaker's chair and the House goes into a committee of the whole House. The Clerk of the House, as a permanent officer of the House, occupies the Clerk's chair at the Table. At the appointed time the Usher of the Black Rod (an officer who, until the abolition of the Legislative Council, was a permanent official of that Council, but who now performs only ceremonial duties as the Governor-General's messenger in communications with the House) announces the arrival of the Royal commissioners, who enter the Chamber and occupy the chairs at the Table. At the same time the Clerk retires to the upper step to the left of the Speaker's chair. From that position the Clerk reads the Letters Patent by which the commissioners have been appointed and given the authority to act on behalf of the Governor-General.[2] Then the chief commissioner reads the proclamation summoning Parliament to meet. The chief commissioner also informs the House that the Governor-General will attend in person to declare to members the causes of Parliament being summoned to meet at that time – that is, to deliver the Speech from the Throne. Before this, however, it is necessary for the House to elect a Speaker, and the chief commissioner indicates that it is the Governor-General's wish that this should be done, and that the House's choice of Speaker should be presented to the Governor-General for confirmation. The Royal commissioners then withdraw.

---

[1]   S.O.12(a).   [2]   S.O.12(b).

SWEARING-IN OF MEMBERS

By law, no member is permitted to sit or vote in the House until that member has taken the Oath of Allegiance[3] or made an affirmation in substitution for the oath.[4] The terms of the oath and of the affirmation are set out in English by statute. For the swearing-in of members following the 1996 and 1999 elections an unofficial Māori language translation of the oath and the affirmation was prepared which those members who wished to do so could take in addition to the oath set out in the legislation. A number of members consequently took an oath or made an affirmation in Māori following their subscribing the oath or affirmation of allegiance in English. Statute now enables Māori language equivalents for all of the statutory oaths to be prescribed by Order in Council.[5] The first member to make an affirmation solely in Māori did so in 2004.[6]

The terms of the oath are:

> I, ..., swear that I will be faithful and bear true allegiance to Her Majesty Queen Elizabeth the Second, Her heirs and successors, according to law. So help me God.[7]

The equivalent in te reo Māori for the oath is:

> Ko ahau, ko....... e oati ana ka noho pūmau taku pono ki a Kuini Irihāpeti te Tuarua me tōna kāhui whakaheke, e ai ki te ture. Ko te Atua nei hoki taku pou.[8]

The affirmation is in these terms:

> I, ..., solemnly, sincerely, and truly declare and affirm that I will be faithful and bear true allegiance to Her Majesty Queen Elizabeth the Second, Her heirs and successors, according to law.[9]

The equivalent in te reo Māori for the affirmation is:

> Ko ahau, ko ......e kī ana i runga i te pono, i te tika, i te ngākau tapatahi me te whakaū anō ka noho pirihonga, ka noho pūmau ki a Kuini Irihāpeti te Tuarua me tōna kāhui whakaheke e ai ke te ture.[10]

(An equivalent in te reo Māori for the affirmation where it is taken in written form has also been prescribed.[11])

The oath or affirmation must be taken before the Governor-General or some person authorised by the Governor-General to administer it.[12] For the purpose of swearing-in members at the opening of a new Parliament, the Governor-General issues a commission to the Clerk of the House, giving the Clerk authority to administer the oath or affirmation. Consequently, when the commissioners have left the Chamber, the Clerk reads this commission to the House.[13] The Clerk then lays on the Table lists (taken from the returns

---

3   *Constitution Act* 1986, s.11(1).
4   *Oaths and Declarations Act* 1957, s.4(1).
5   *Ibid.*, s.30A.
6   Tariana Turia (Te Tai Hauauru).
7   *Ibid.*, s.17.
8   *Oaths and Declarations (Māori Language) Regulations* 2004, reg.4(1).
9   *Oaths and Declarations Act* 1957, ss.4(2) and 17.
10 *Oaths and Declarations (Māori Language) Regulations* 2004, reg.5(1).
11 *Ibid.*, reg.6(1).
12 *Constitution Act* 1986, s.11(2).
13 S.O.12(c).

forwarded by the Chief Electoral Officer) of the members who have been elected to the House[14] and invites members whose names appear on the lists to come forward, up to four at a time, in alphabetical order, to the left of the Table to take the oath or make the affirmation.[15] Provided that members subscribe the oath or affirmation in the terms prescribed, they may do so in any way that they declare to be binding on them.[16] For the oath, a standard edition of the Bible is generally used but there have been variations on this. Julius Vogel (who had been raised in the Jewish faith) was sworn-in in 1863 on the Old Testament while wearing his hat[17] and in 2002, Ashraf Choudhary, a Muslim, was sworn on the Koran.[18]

After having sworn or affirmed, members go to the other side of the Table and sign a roll of members. (For members affirming in Māori, the written form of the te reo Māori equivalent is used in the roll of members.)

When the swearing-in of members has concluded, the House proceeds to the election of a Speaker.[19]

Subsequent swearing-in of members

If any other members arrive after the election of the Speaker has commenced, the proceedings are interrupted and the member is invited to come forward to the left of the Table to take the oath or make the affirmation.[20]

In addition, there are often members who are unable to be present at the first meeting of Parliament, so they are not sworn-in on the same day as the other members. These members must be sworn-in at a subsequent sitting before they can take their seats in the House. Members elected during the term of the Parliament at by-elections or to fill party list seat vacancies must also take the oath or affirm before they can sit in the House. For the purpose of swearing-in members during the term of the Parliament the Governor-General issues a commission to the Speaker, giving the Speaker authority to administer the oath or affirmation which is required by law to be made before members can take their seats. It is also the practice for a similar commission to be issued to allow the Deputy Speaker to act in the Speaker's absence.

Any business in progress may be interrupted at a convenient time for a member to be sworn in.[21] All such members must present themselves at the bar of the House.[22] Members are called forward by the Speaker to the Table, at the right of the chair, for the purpose of being sworn-in.

The Speaker is entitled, indeed it is the Speaker's duty, to establish that a person appearing at the bar to take the oath or affirmation has been duly elected as a member of Parliament. The best evidence of this is a copy of the writ for the election endorsed with the member's name on it, in the case of a member elected to represent an electoral district, and the list of those candidates declared by the Chief Electoral Officer to be elected, in the case of party list candidates. The writ and an official list of members elected on a party list are required to be forwarded to the Clerk of the House by the Chief Electoral Officer.[23]

In the case of a by-election the member who has been returned may appear at the House before a copy of the writ has been seen by the Speaker. The Speaker has refused to admit a member when no notification of the member's election had been received.[24] It is

[14]   *Electoral Act* 1993, ss.185(1)(c) and 193(5)(b); S.O.12(d).
[15]   S.O.12(e).
[16]   *Oaths and Declarations Act* 1957, s.3.
[17]   Dalziel, *Julius Vogel – Business Politician*, p.53.
[18]   "MP swears on covered Koran", *The Dominion Post*, 27 August 2002.
[19]   S.O.12(f).
[20]   S.O.13(2).
[21]   S.Os 13(2) and 133(e).
[22]   S.O.13(1).
[23]   *Electoral Act* 1993, ss.185(1)(c) and 193(5)(b).
[24]   1858, JHR, p.83.

not essential, however, that the Speaker should actually receive a copy of the writ before a member can be admitted. On the occasion of a member appearing to be sworn-in before the writ had arrived, the matter was made the subject of a petition which was referred to a committee as a question of privilege. The committee established that the member had been elected and the Speaker administered the oath to him on the strength of its report. The writ (from Akaroa) was not in fact received until 12 days later.[25] It is now the practice for the Chief Electoral Officer to advise the Clerk of the House of the name of the person returned at a by-election by facsimile letter, and for the Speaker to read this letter (or a copy of the writ if it has been received) to the House immediately before swearing-in the member. In the case of the filling of a vacancy which arises among the members elected from a party list, the Chief Electoral Officer files a return with the Clerk of the House indicating who has been elected to fill the vacancy.[26]

Failure to take the oath

A person becomes a member of Parliament on the day after being returned for an electoral district or on a party list.[27] From that point on the person is a member of Parliament with the privileges and entitlements of membership of the House.[28] Failure to take the oath or make the affirmation prescribed by law does not affect one's status as a member of Parliament, but it does prevent the exercise of the most important incidences of that status, those of sitting and voting in the House of Representatives.[29] A member who has not been sworn cannot participate in proceedings of the House that require physical presence and cannot vote in any circumstances. Thus an oral question cannot be asked by or on behalf of an unsworn member, though an unsworn member may lodge a question for written answer.[30]

In practice, it is the Speaker's duty to enforce the requirement that members are sworn before participating in proceedings or voting.[31] The votes of members who attempted to vote before they had been sworn have been disallowed,[32] and an unsworn member's vote may not be included in a party's total in a party vote.[33] However, the validity of any proceedings of the House is not affected by the fact that a member who has not taken an oath participates in them.[34] The admission of a member to the House in order to take the oath or make the affirmation is regarded as an internal proceeding of the House within the exclusive cognisance of the House itself.[35] However, if there are any consequences outside the House that turn upon whether a member has taken the oath or affirmation, a court is entitled to make its own enquiry and determine whether a member has actually taken the oath or made the affirmation.[36]

Consequences of taking the oath

While any person taking an oath or making an affirmation is expected to do so in good faith, the oath or affirmation of allegiance is not a promise to refrain from advocating a republican or a different system of government. It is a promise of allegiance to the Sovereign established according to law. It is perfectly consistent with the oath for a person to hold views favouring an alternative form of constitutional arrangement, always provided that any change that they support is to be effected lawfully. (Advocating unlawful change to the constitution would be a crime in any case.) Nor is a breach of the oath or affirmation

---

25   *Ibid.*, pp.84, 94.
26   *Electoral Act* 1993, s.138(a).
27   *Ibid.*, s.54.
28   1887, Vol.59, p.359.
29   *Constitution Act* 1986, s.11(1).
30   1979, Vol.423, p.800.
31   Campbell, "Oaths and Affirmations of Public Office" (1999) 25 Mon LR 132 at 154.
32   1976, Vol.403, pp.9-10.
33   1994, Vol.539, p.53.
34   Campbell, "Oaths and Affirmations of Public Office" (1999) 25 Mon LR 132 at 154.
35   *Bradlaugh v Gossett* (1884) 12 QBD 271.
36   See, for example, *Haridarsan Palayil v Speaker of the Kerala Legislative Assembly* AIR 2003 Kerala 328.

in itself a crime. But a consequence of taking the oath or affirmation of allegiance is that it is inconsistent for a member to take a subsequent oath pledging allegiance to a foreign power. To do so will result in the member's seat becoming vacant.[37]

No new oath or affirmation following the demise of the Crown

It was formerly the law that all members were required to take fresh oaths or affirmations following the demise of the Crown (by the death or abdication of the Sovereign). This is no longer the case. The death or abdication of the Sovereign automatically transfers all obligations of allegiance to the Sovereign's successor, and no special action is required by members to effect this.[38]

ELECTION OF SPEAKER

The House must, at its first meeting, elect one of its members to be its Speaker.[39] It proceeds to the election of a Speaker after the swearing-in of members is completed.[40]

For the purpose of the election of a Speaker, the Clerk acts as chairperson.[41] It was formerly the practice of the Clerk, when calling on a member to speak during these proceedings, to stand and point to the member rather than call the member by name. Now the Clerk calls members to speak and deals with questions of order which relate to the election in the same way that a Speaker would, if the Speaker were presiding. But the Clerk proposes no question for debate on the election of a Speaker and no debate can arise concerning the election.[42]

Nominating a member

The Clerk calls for nominations for election as Speaker.[43]

Formerly candidates for election were proposed and seconded by other members. On election they traditionally showed a degree of reluctance to serve as Speaker and were escorted or led to the Speaker's chair by their proposer and seconder. Since 1996 this pretence of a 'reluctant' Speaker has been largely abandoned following the requirement that members who wish to be elected as Speaker must nominate themselves.

After the Clerk has called for nominations, any member, on being called by the Clerk, may propose himself or herself to the House for election as Speaker. If a member is absent from the Chamber, another member may make the nomination on that member's behalf provided that the consent to this course of the member to be nominated is produced in writing to the Clerk.[44]

Uncontested elections

If there is only one member nominated, the Clerk puts no question to the House; there can be no vote on the nomination, and the member is declared to be elected Speaker.[45] The member leaves his or her seat and approaches the Speaker's chair.

On reaching the chair, the Speaker-Elect (who is not Speaker until confirmed by the Governor-General) addresses the House from the upper step on the right of the chair, acknowledging the honour conferred by election to this position and advising the House of the member's hopes and aspirations for the discharge of the duties of Speaker. The Speaker-Elect then sits in the chair and the Serjeant-at-Arms lays the Mace upon the

---

[37] *Electoral Act* 1993, s.55(1)(b).
[38] *Constitution Act* 1986, s.5(1).
[39] *Ibid.*, s.12.
[40] S.O.12(f).
[41] S.O.15.
[42] S.O.16(2).
[43] S.O.15.
[44] S.O.16(1).
[45] S.O.17.
[46] S.O.21.

Table.[46] Members may then offer their congratulations.

The Government normally announces in advance of the first meeting of Parliament who is to be its nominee for the office of Speaker, and the person so nominated may be elected unopposed. In contrast to the practice in the United Kingdom, there is no tradition, if the Government changes, of re-electing as Speaker the member who held that post in the previous Parliament.[47] In modern times, the largest party in the House has usually provided the Speaker from among its ranks, although the Speaker from 1923 to 1935 was an independent when he was first elected as Speaker,[48] and the Speaker from 1993 to 1996 was drawn from the major opposition party.

Two members nominated

There may be two members who nominate themselves for election. There were two candidates for election in 1996, for example. Prior to this the last time there were two candidates (under a different system for electing a Speaker) was in 1923.

If there are two members nominated, a personal vote is held to determine which one is to be elected.[49] For this purpose the Ayes lobby is used for those voting for the member whose name comes first in the alphabet and the Noes lobby for those voting for the other member. (See Chapter 17 for personal votes.) No proxies are permitted for this vote.[50]

In the event of a tie on the vote the Clerk calls for further nominations,[51] which may include either or both of the members who were first nominated.

More than two members nominated

If more than two members are nominated for Speaker, members initially vote from their places in the House rather than by going into the lobbies as they do on a personal vote. The bells are rung for seven minutes and then the doors are locked.[52] Working alphabetically, members are then asked by the Clerk individually to rise in their places and state which of the nominated members they vote for. Members may record an abstention.[53] No proxy votes are permitted.[54] If, at the end of this process, any candidate has obtained an absolute majority of the votes of the members voting (that is, excluding any abstentions), that member is immediately declared elected.[55] Otherwise the member with the fewest number of votes drops out and the votes are taken again until only two candidates remain.[56] If the two candidates with the fewest votes have the same number of votes, the entire vote is taken again. If the two candidates with the fewest votes still have the same number of votes, the Clerk determines which candidate is to drop out by drawing lots.[57]

When, after this process, there are only two candidates remaining, the election is decided by a personal vote.[58] Again, no proxies are permitted.[59] In the event of a tie on the personal vote, nominations are called for again.[60]

In 2005, in a election held during the term of Parliament to fill a vacancy arising from the resignation of a Speaker, there were three candidates nominated and members voted from their places. This was the first time ever that there had been three candidates for Speaker. One candidate obtained an absolute majority of the votes cast on the first vote.[61]

Adjournment of the House following the Speaker's election

When the Speaker-Elect takes the chair and members have offered their congratulations,

---

[47] 1981, AJHR, I.17, p.40 (*Second Report of the Committee on the Electoral Law*).
[48] Scott, *The New Zealand Constitution*, p.60.
[49] S.O.18.
[50] S.O.20.
[51] S.O.18.
[52] S.O.19(1)(a).
[53] S.O.19(1)(b), (c).

[54] S.O.20.
[55] S.O.19(1)(d).
[56] S.O.19(1)(e).
[57] S.O.19(3).
[58] S.O.19(1)(f).
[59] S.O.20.
[60] S.O.19(2).
[61] 2005, Vol.623, pp.18945-6.

the House automatically adjourns under the Standing Orders so that the Speaker-Elect may seek the Governor-General's confirmation of the House's choice of Speaker. The next sitting of the House will be at the time at which the Governor-General has indicated that the Speech from the Throne will be delivered.[62] If an absent member is elected as Speaker, the House similarly adjourns at the conclusion of the election.

Confirmation

The House's choice of Speaker becomes valid and effectual when it is confirmed by the Governor-General.[63] The Governor-General has never refused to confirm a Speaker-Elect and it is almost inconceivable that this would occur.

The Speaker-Elect, accompanied by the Clerk, the Deputy Clerk, the Serjeant-at-Arms, carrying the Mace in the crook of the arm, and other members, presents himself or herself to the Governor-General at Government House either later on the same day as the election of Speaker was held or on the following day, but in any case before the House next sits. The Speaker-Elect informs the Governor-General of the House's choice of Speaker and asks for the Governor-General's confirmation of that choice. Immediately the Governor-General confirms the House's choice of Speaker, the Serjeant-at-Arms raises the Mace to the shoulder. Formerly a private occasion, it has become the practice for this ceremony to be held in the ballroom at Government House and for all members and their families or friends, together with news media, to be invited to attend.

The Governor-General may approve special arrangements for confirming the House's choice of Speaker and for the House's privileges to be claimed. For example, in the case of illness, the Speaker-Elect may not be able to attend on the Governor-General personally for these purposes.

Claiming the House's privileges

The Speaker's first duty as Speaker is to lay claim to all the privileges of the House, especially to freedom of speech in debate and to free access to the Governor-General whenever occasion may require it. The Speaker also asks that the most favourable construction be put on all the House's proceedings.[64] In these claims are echoes of days of conflict and suspicion between the Crown and Parliament. The claim of free access to the Governor-General is for the purpose of the House as a body, headed by the Speaker, to be able to present communications to the Crown by means of an address. It is not intended to give individual members, as members of Parliament, the right to make official approaches to the Governor-General that could cause the holder of that office political embarrassment. There were, in colonial times, numerous communications from the House when the Governor exercised a more personal control of the Government than is exercised today. Now such communications are more standard and formal. The claim for a favourable construction to be put on the House's proceedings is said to be made "merely by courtesy"[65] and is not of any practical significance.

The Speaker has claimed the House's privileges from the Crown since Speaker Munro, the second Speaker, did so in 1861. The House's privileges are part of the ordinary law. In general, they are those privileges enjoyed by the House of Commons on 1 January 1865.[66] The privileges of the United Kingdom House of Commons are also confirmed to the new Speaker on behalf of Her Majesty the Queen, but the privileges of the House of Commons, being part of the law and custom of Parliament, do not depend

---

62   S.O.22.
63   *Constitution Act* 1986, s.12.
64   S.O.23.

65   Campion, *An Introduction to the Procedure of the House of Commons*, p.62.
66   *Legislature Act* 1908, s.242.

for their existence on confirmation by the Crown. Confirmation is mainly ceremonial in nature, and the House of Commons would enjoy its privileges even if they were not confirmed. The House of Representatives' privileges, being statutorily based by reference to privileges once enjoyed by the House of Commons, would appear to be in a similar position and not to require the Governor-General's confirmation to be effective.

The Speaker must report to the House the Governor-General's reply to the claim to the House's privileges.[67]

Vacancy in the office of Speaker
The Speaker elected at the first meeting of the House holds office for the duration of that Parliament and ceases to be Speaker at polling day for the next election.[68] If during this term of office the Speaker becomes disqualified from membership of the House, or resigns from the House, the office of Speaker automatically becomes vacant, for the holder of this office must be a member of Parliament. The Speaker can resign office as Speaker at any time and remain as a member of Parliament. In 1972 the then Speaker resigned that office when he was appointed as a Minister of the Crown. In 2005 the Speaker resigned office and continued as a member for some four weeks before he resigned to take up a diplomatic appointment.

In the case of a vacancy arising in the office of Speaker during a Parliament, the House is obliged at its next meeting to choose another member as Speaker.[69] The Clerk reports the vacancy to the House when it meets. A Minister advises the House that it is the Governor-General's wish that it should proceed to elect a Speaker and present the Speaker-Elect to the Governor-General for confirmation. The House then proceeds to elect a Speaker in the same way as is prescribed for the election of a Speaker at the opening of Parliament.[70] Once a Speaker has been elected the House automatically adjourns until the next sitting day to permit the Speaker-Elect to seek the Governor-General's confirmation.[71] A Speaker elected during a Parliament does not again lay claim to the House's privileges. The Governor-General's confirmation of these at the beginning of the Parliament is regarded as lasting throughout its life.

STATE OPENING OF PARLIAMENT
The Royal commissioners, when opening Parliament, inform the House when the Governor-General will come to meet the House to declare to it the reasons for summoning Parliament. This is the occasion on which the Governor-General delivers the Speech from the Throne. It is known as the State Opening of Parliament. In fact, in delivering the Speech from the Throne the Governor-General is not opening Parliament; this has already been done by the commissioners. The Royal commissioners attend to open Parliament only once, at its first meeting following a general election. The State Opening of Parliament is thus the second day of the meeting of a new Parliament, though it is the first day of each subsequent session of that Parliament that may be held. Even where the State Opening occurs as the first day of the second and subsequent sessions of Parliament, the Governor-General's Speech from the Throne is not the instrument which actually opens the new session of Parliament. Parliament meets according to the Governor-General's proclamation summoning it to meet. When delivering the Speech from the Throne, the Governor-General is giving members the reasons for the opening of Parliament – an event which has, by then, already occurred.

---

[67]   S.O.24.
[68]   *Constitution Act* 1986, s.13.
[69]   *Ibid.*, s.12.
[70]   S.O.25(1).
[71]   S.O.25(2).

Members assemble

On the second day of a new Parliament and on the first sitting day of each subsequent session of that Parliament, members assemble in the Chamber at the time fixed by the Governor-General for the delivery of the Speech from the Throne. This may, but does not need to, coincide with the House's ordinary meeting time of 2 pm.

Prayers are read by the Speaker[72] who, in the case of the second sitting day of a new Parliament, has just been confirmed in office and consequently appears dressed as Speaker in the House for the first time. The Mace is in position on the Table. In the case of a new Parliament, the Speaker proceeds to report to the House both the Speaker's confirmation in office by the Governor-General and the Governor-General's reply to the House's claim to its privileges.[73] The House then awaits a message from the Governor-General requesting its attendance.[74]

Message from the Governor-General

The Usher of the Black Rod, on being commanded to do so by the Governor-General, comes from the Council Chamber, where the Governor-General's party has assembled, to the Chamber of the House to communicate the Governor-General's wish that the Speaker and members join the viceregal party. The door of the House's Chamber is locked as Black Rod approaches. Black Rod has to knock on it three times and is admitted only on the Speaker's command. The bar of the House is in a position which prevents Black Rod from advancing on to the floor of the House and is removed only with the Speaker's permission. The rituals of locking the door and putting the bar into position are designed to symbolise the House's independence of the executive, represented by the Crown's messenger. Once the bar has been removed, Black Rod advances into the centre of the Chamber and informs the House that the Governor-General desires its immediate attendance. On receiving this message the Speaker and members leave their places to attend on the Governor-General.[75]

Black Rod leads the Speaker's procession (the Serjeant, with the Mace, and the Speaker), the Clerks, the Prime Minister and the Leader of the Opposition, and the other members out of the Chamber, through the Grand Hall and into the Council Chamber and so into the Governor-General's presence.

Speech from the Throne

When the Speaker and the members have assembled in the Council Chamber, the Prime Minister presents to the Governor-General the speech which is about to be given. The Governor-General then delivers the Speech from the Throne.

The delivery of the Speech from the Throne is one of the principal state occasions. Ambassadors, judges, senior officers of the New Zealand Defence Force, the Mayor of Wellington and other dignitaries are invited to witness it. During the refurbishment of Parliament House and the consequent unavailability of the Council Chamber, the Speech from the Throne was delivered in the Banquet Hall in the Executive Wing in 1991 and 1993.

The Speech from the Throne is the Crown's explanation to members of the reasons for their being called together in Parliament at that time. It is primarily designed as an outline of the matters which the Government wishes Parliament to consider in the course of the forthcoming session. It is, therefore, an announcement of the Government's legislative programme, and members will be told in the speech that bills on various matters will be

---

72   S.O.14(1)(a).
73   S.Os 14(1)(a) and 24.
74   S.O.14(1)(b).
75   *Ibid.*

introduced in due course. The speech, in this regard, is a statement of present intention; it is not absolutely binding on the Government's future action. The fact that a bill has been mentioned in the speech as one it is intended to introduce does not mean that the Government must introduce it. Circumstances may change, causing the legislation to be abandoned before it is introduced, or its introduction may be postponed for that session. Nor does the absence of mention of a bill in the Speech from the Throne mean that such a bill cannot be introduced during that session. The Government can and does introduce bills that were not foreshadowed in the Speech from the Throne.

As well as dealing with legislation, the speech will refer to international and domestic affairs, particularly as they involve New Zealand and the policies of the Government. The Speech from the Throne is in the nature of a review of the state of the nation. The broad nature of the speech gives rise to a wide debate in the House shortly afterwards on the motion for an address to be made by the House to the Governor-General in reply to it.

After delivering the speech the Governor-General presents a copy of it to the Speaker. When the Governor-General has left the Council Chamber, members proceed back to their Chamber as part of the Speaker's procession.

As well as the Speech from the Throne being delivered by the Governor-General, it may be delivered by the Sovereign on any occasion on which she is present in New Zealand. Her Majesty the Queen has, in fact, delivered the speech at the State Opening of sessions of Parliament held in 1954, 1963, 1970, 1974, 1977 and 1990. The same procedures of the House as apply to a State Opening performed by the Governor-General apply to one performed by the Sovereign or indeed by the Administrator of the Government and by Royal commissioners should the latter be authorised by the Governor-General to perform these functions.[76]

Speech reported to the House
When the Speaker resumes the Speaker's chair, the Governor-General's speech is formally reported to the House by the copy given to the Speaker being laid on the Table of the House.[77] The speech is published in a special edition of the *New Zealand Gazette*, copies of which are made available to members.

Business transacted on returning from hearing Speech from the Throne
Following the formal business of reporting the Speech from the Throne, the Speaker goes through the House's items of opening business: the announcement of the presentation of petitions and papers and bills that have been introduced.[78] There are no questions for oral answer on this day.

While there are severe restrictions on the House transacting business on the day of the State Opening, the House may also wish to appoint its other presiding officers and this is specifically permitted.[79] If Government notices of motion for the appointment of a Deputy Speaker and Assistant Speakers have been lodged with the Clerk by 11 am on the day of the Commission Opening of Parliament they will appear on the order paper for the day of the State Opening and can be considered at this point before the House adjourns or the sitting is suspended for the commencement of the Address in Reply debate.[80] Similarly, if a notice of motion has been lodged, the House can deal with the reinstatement of business that had lapsed with the dissolution of the previous Parliament.[81] But the reinstatement of business does not have to be dealt with at this time. It can be attended to later as a Government (or Member's) order of the day.

---

[76] S.O.3(2).
[77] S.O.14(1)(c).
[78] S.O.14(1)(d).

[79] S.O.14(1)(e)
[80] *Ibid.*
[81] *Ibid.*

Adjournment of the House

After considering any Government notices of motion for the appointment of presiding officers and the reinstatement of business, the Standing Orders direct the House to adjourn or, if the sitting is in the morning, it may be suspended by the Speaker to permit the Address in Reply debate to commence later that day at 2 pm.[82] But it would be unusual for the Address in Reply debate to commence on the day of the State Opening of Parliament. The Speaker would exercise the power to allow the Address in Reply debate to commence on that day only after consultation with the parties represented in the House, possibly after convening the Business Committee if there was time for this.

ADDRESS IN REPLY

The Address in Reply debate is, along with the Budget, the most wide-ranging debate held each session. It is the first major debate upon which the House embarks in a new Parliament and in each new session of a Parliament if there is one.

The Address in Reply itself is adopted as an expression of the House's loyalty and fealty to the Crown and the Crown's representative, the Governor-General. Originally, when taking into consideration the Speech from the Throne, the House debated a motion for an Address in Reply to the speech. This motion answered, point by point, the matters raised in the speech. Debate in the House was not found to be a satisfactory way of considering, amending and redrafting a complex statement such as this, so from 1862 something akin to the present system was adopted. This involved debating a simple motion, that an Address in Reply to the speech be presented to the Governor-General. The details of the address were left to be settled later by a committee.

Nowadays the Address in Reply debate takes place on a simple motion, "That a respectful Address be presented to [His or Her] Excellency the Governor-General in reply to [His or Her] Excellency's Speech".[83] In this form it is not opposed. It does, however, provide a vehicle for a wide-ranging debate on the Government's economic or foreign policy, or indeed for any other matters which members wish to raise. It also permits motions expressing lack of confidence in the Government to be moved by way of amendment to the unexceptionable original motion.

Moving for an Address in Reply

The member who has the honour of moving the motion for the Address in Reply is a member of a Government party in his or her first term as a member of Parliament. The member may be chosen for this honour by the Prime Minister or by party colleagues, depending upon the party's or coalition's own internal arrangements. The motion for the Address in Reply may be seconded[84] and the seconder is similarly chosen from the ranks of first-term Government backbench members. If over the course of the sessions of a Parliament there are not enough first-term Government members to fill these slots, as there were not in the sessions of the Parliaments elected in 1966, 1969 and 1981, for example, Government backbenchers in their second or subsequent term who have not previously moved or seconded an Address in Reply are chosen. (However, as there is now generally only one Address in Reply debate in each Parliament there is no longer likely to be a problem in finding suitable members.)

It will be apparent that in moving the Address in Reply in the first session of a new Parliament the mover will also be making a first speech in the House – a "maiden speech". This is regarded as a singular mark of distinction. The mover and seconder may wear

---

[82]   S.O.14(2).
[83]   S.O.342(1).
[84]   S.O.342(2).

formal attire for the occasion (for example, clan tartan). The speeches are not expected to contain material of a highly partisan nature so that other members are tempted or provoked to interject. This does not mean that the speeches must be blandly non-controversial but that they are expected to describe the members' individual beliefs and approach to politics rather than to deal with matters in a party political context.

Address in Reply debate

The Address in Reply debate may commence at 2 pm on the day of the State Opening[85] but is more likely to commence on the third sitting day of a new Parliament and on the second day of any new session.

The debate on the Address in Reply always takes precedence over other Government orders of the day[86] and Government orders of the day take precedence over other orders of the day even on a Wednesday, while the Address in Reply debate is before the House.[87] The debate is accordingly set down as the first major item of business to be considered by the House each day until it is finally disposed of. (It may, however, be adjourned after it is reached on a particular day, thus enabling the House to proceed to business further down the order paper.) Following the speeches by the mover and seconder, the Leader of the Opposition, the Prime Minister and other party leaders may speak.

Leaders of parties with six or more members represented in the House may speak for up to 30 minutes each, members making maiden speeches (including the mover and seconder) for up to 15 minutes and other members for 10 minutes. The whole debate is limited to 19 hours, making it the longest debate that the House holds.[88] Question time operates as normal while the Address in Reply is running, but no general debate is held.[89] The entire debate should occupy about two sitting weeks. It is open-ended as far as relevancy is concerned.[90]

Maiden speeches

As well as the speech of the mover of the first Address in Reply motion of each Parliament having the added significance of being a maiden speech, this will also be the case with the seconder of that motion and with all other newly-elected members when they come to speak in the debate. This makes the character of the first Address in Reply debate of each Parliament rather different from that of any subsequent Address in Reply debate held in that Parliament.

In making their maiden speeches on the Address in Reply, members usually try to set out their hopes and aspirations for their careers as parliamentarians. They set out their personal beliefs and describe the character and problems of the electorate which has returned them to Parliament for the first (and in some cases the only) time. It is customary that other members do not interject in the course of a maiden speech and that the speech itself (being made under this privilege) will not be provocative.[91]

Those new members who are unable to participate (through illness or absence) in the Address in Reply debate and members elected during the course of a Parliament may make a maiden statement to the House at a later time.[92] (See Chapter 19.)

Amendments

An amendment raising a question of whether the Government possesses the confidence of the House, in the sense of whether it commands the support of a majority of members, is the archetypal Address in Reply amendment. On most occasions when a Government has

---

85 S.O.14(2).
86 S.O.344.
87 S.O.73(2).
88 Appendix A to the Standing Orders.

89 S.O.383(3).
90 1969, Vol.361, p.1449.
91 1977, Vol.410, p.289.
92 S.O.351.

fallen as a result of an adverse vote of confidence in the House, the defeat has been on an amendment proposed to the Address in Reply motion. (The last occasion was in 1928.)

Only amendments adding words to the Address in Reply motion may be moved.[93] The motion itself is uncontroversial because it is a necessary means of the House affirming its loyalty to the Crown. An amendment to the motion must take the form of a proposal that words be added to the address which the House will eventually adopt. In the case of a no confidence amendment, this will include words to the effect that the Government does not possess the confidence of the House. Were the Government to be defeated on such an amendment, it would be expected that the Prime Minister would resign or advise the Governor-General to dissolve Parliament so that a new election could be held.

Any amendment moved to the Address in Reply motion inevitably involves consideration and decision of the main question, as does any amendment moved to such an amendment. In 1981 not only was an amendment moved to an amendment (the first time since 1938) but also an amendment to the amendment to the amendment was proposed. Eventually, the Address in Reply motion was passed without any amendment to it being carried.[94] With the advent of a multi-party House multiple amendments to the Address in Reply motion have become more common. If an amendment is carried, the words so added must be included in the formal address presented to the House for its approval.[95]

Adoption of Address in Reply

When any amendments have been disposed of, the question is put on the motion that a respectful address be presented to the Governor-General in reply to the speech. Traditionally there is no vote against this motion.

When the motion has been carried, the terms of the address itself have to be agreed to by the House, for the House has hitherto been debating the principle of whether to have an address at all and not the details of that address. An address will, in fact, already have been prepared by the Speaker and this is brought before the House by the Speaker immediately after the motion for an address is passed. An Address in Reply must not contain any words or statements of a controversial nature (except where an amendment has been carried).[96]

The address usually thanks the Governor-General for the speech and gives assurance that the matters referred to in the speech will receive the House's careful attention. The Speaker reads the proffered address and then puts the question that it be agreed to, without any further amendment or debate being permitted.[97] Once the House has adopted the Address in Reply, it must then be presented to the Governor-General by the Speaker. (See Chapter 8.)

---

[93] S.O.343.
[94] 1981, JHR, p.48.
[95] S.O.169(2).

[96] *Ibid.*
[97] S.O.169(3).

CHAPTER 13

SITTINGS OF THE HOUSE

THE SITTING DAY

The regular days on which the House meets (its "sitting" days) are Tuesdays, Wednesdays and Thursdays.[1] The House can appoint other days as sitting days if it so wishes. Friday ceased to be a regular sitting day in its own right only in 1985. The House now sits on a Friday only when a previous sitting is extended under urgency into Friday. Saturday has never been a regular sitting day for the House. Sittings of the House on a Saturday occur occasionally when a previous day's sitting is extended. Monday is rarely used as a sitting day in its own right. Examples occurred in 1991 and 2000 when the House sat on Mondays to progress legislation[2] and in 2004 when the House held a special sitting on a Monday to mark the 150th anniversary of the first sitting of the House.[3]

Monday and Saturday sittings were more frequent occurrences in the past as the House endeavoured to get through all its business and allow members to return to their homes. In 1860 the House even went so far as to authorise the Speaker to appoint sittings of the House on either of these days for the remainder of the session if he thought fit.[4] Under the Standing Orders, there can be no sitting of the House on a Sunday, and a sitting of a previous day which lasts until midnight on Saturday is interrupted and adjourned in accordance with the provisions which apply to the regular adjournment of the House. If the House is in committee at 11.55 pm on a Saturday, the chairperson reports progress to the House preparatory to the House adjourning.[5]

THE WORKING DAY

As well as the days on which the House sits being available for the transaction of parliamentary business, business may also be transacted on a "working day" even though the House is not sitting. This opening up of the transaction of parliamentary business to non-sitting days enables parliamentary business to be transacted year-round.

A working day means—

... any day of the week other than—

(a)   a Saturday, a Sunday, Good Friday, Easter Monday, Anzac Day, Labour Day, the Sovereign's birthday and Waitangi Day, and

(b)   any anniversary or other day observed as a public holiday in a locality to which a particular local bill or private bill subject to procedures under these Standing Orders relates, and

(c)   a day in the period commencing with 25 December in any year and ending with 15 January in the following year.[6]

(15 January is not itself a working day.)

Government bills may be introduced,[7] select committee reports,[8] petitions[9] and papers[10] presented, and written questions lodged (in this case by 10.30 am)[11] on a working day. Where any deadline for performing an act (such as the time for a select committee to report to the House) expires on a non-working day, the act may be performed on the next working day.[12]

---

[1]   S.O.43(1).
[2]   1991, Vol.518, p.3661; 2000, Vol.586, p.4594.
[3]   2004, Vol.617, pp.13179-213.
[4]   1860, JHR, p.156.
[5]   S.O.46.
[6]   S.O.3(1).
[7]   S.O.275.
[8]   S.O.250(1).
[9]   S.O.360(1).
[10]   S.O.363(1).
[11]   S.O.373(1).
[12]   S.O.3(3).

SITTING HOURS

The regular sitting hours on Tuesdays and Wednesdays are from 2 pm to 6 pm and then from 7.30 pm to 10 pm. On Thursdays the regular sitting hours are 2 pm to 6 pm.[13] If a Monday, Friday or Saturday is appointed as a sitting day in its own right the sitting hours for a Tuesday apply.[14] But the House may also appoint special sitting hours for such a day.[15]

The House may alter the standard sitting hours prescribed for each day's sitting. An urgency motion is the most common means by which this is done, for, when urgency has been accorded a matter by order of the House, the normal time for the adjournment of the House is dispensed with and the House does not adjourn until consideration of that matter is completed. "Urgency" extends the sitting of the House indefinitely (but not beyond midnight on Saturday). The House may also resolve to change the sitting hours to a definite extent, as by resolving to meet or adjourn at a different hour from the one prescribed by the Standing Orders – for example, the House met at 4 pm following ceremonies for the interment of the Unknown Warrior.[16] The House also frequently gives the Speaker the power to determine the precise time at which a sitting should commence by ordering that it meet "on the ringing of the bell" (an uncertain time determined by the Speaker) where members are engaged at a state or parliamentary luncheon.

If a sitting of the House, as extended by urgency, lasts until beyond the time fixed for the commencement of the next sitting of the House, that next sitting day is lost altogether unless the House, before rising, appoints a new time for that next sitting. Examples of the House adjourning earlier than the time appointed for the conclusion of the sitting are legion. Usually they are instances of the House concluding its sitting a few minutes before the appointed time because it is not worthwhile going on to a new item of business with such a short time remaining. The House may also, on occasion, alter the sitting hours by pushing back the normal time for the adjournment to a later hour, as by ordering that for a period of time (for instance, until the end of the session) the House will sit to midnight on a particular day or days.[17]

The period of a sitting commences at the appointed time with prayers read by the Speaker and is terminated by the adjournment of the House, an adjournment that results either from a resolution of the House or by operation of the Standing Orders. The House rarely sits constantly throughout a sitting day. The sitting is suspended on Tuesdays and Wednesdays for one and a half hours between 6 pm and 7.30 pm,[18] and it may be suspended for other reasons such as to attend the Governor-General at the State Opening of Parliament, for disorder, or as a mark of respect to a deceased former member. A sitting day, if extended by urgency, may extend over a number of days and must be contrasted with a day on which the House sits. For example, in 2004 there were 85 sitting days but the House actually sat on 97 days. A sitting day is a fully self-contained period in the operation of the House, with a programme of items of business to be transacted within this period as prescribed by the Standing Orders.

The concept of a sitting day is now used to prescribe statutory or other time limits. For example, regulations must be presented to the House no later than 16 sitting days after they are made[19] and a notice of motion to disallow a regulation has automatic effect if it is not dealt with within 21 sitting days of it being given.[20]

---

[13] S.O.43(1).
[14] S.O.45.
[15] See, for example, 2000, Vol.586, p.4593.
[16] 2004, Vol.621, p.16865.

[17] 1974, JHR, p.517.
[18] S.O.43(2).
[19] *Regulations (Disallowance) Act* 1989, s.4.
[20] *Ibid.*, s.6(2).

SUSPENSION OF A SITTING

During its course, a sitting may be suspended for a period of time without being formally brought to an end by adjournment. This occurs under the Standing Orders and it can also occur by direction of the House or, in certain circumstances, by order of the Speaker. During the period of any suspension, the Mace is left in the Chamber (in committee, under the Table) to signify that the sitting has not ended. On the suspension of a sitting the bell is rung for 10 seconds to alert persons in the parliamentary complex to the fact that the House is no longer sitting.[21]

Standing Orders for suspension of sitting

The Standing Orders provide for a sitting to be suspended on Tuesdays and Wednesdays from 6 pm to 7.30 pm for dinner.[22] At 6 pm the Speaker (or, in committee, the chairperson) leaves the chair, the debate is interrupted[23] and the sitting is thereupon suspended. The House can, by leave, continue to sit during a time at which the sitting would otherwise be suspended if it wishes.[24]

The Standing Orders also provide for a sitting to be suspended when the House is sitting under urgency. Where the day on which urgency is taken is a Tuesday, a Wednesday, or (provided prior warning has been given to the Business Committee) a Thursday, there is an automatic suspension at 10 pm, that is, the normal time for the adjournment of the House on Tuesdays and Wednesdays. The sitting then resumes at 9 am on the following day.[25] If urgency is taken on a Thursday without prior warning to the Business Committee, the sitting is suspended at 6 pm until 9 am the following day. Thereafter, an extended sitting is suspended between midnight and 9 am, between 1 pm and 2 pm, and between 6 pm and 7 pm.[26] Where extraordinary urgency is taken, the sitting is not suspended at the normal time for adjournment nor at midnight, and the morning suspension is only between 8 am and 9 am. The sitting may therefore continue throughout the night. However, the sitting is suspended between 1 pm and 2 pm and between 6 pm and 7 pm under extraordinary urgency.[27]

Whenever a question is being put or a vote is in progress at the time for a sitting to be suspended, the suspension is postponed until after completion of the vote. If a closure motion has been carried, the suspension is deferred until the determination of the original question.[28] This includes putting the question on any amendments that may have been lodged[29] and so can considerably delay the suspension if there are a large number of amendments. Apart from this circumstance, no further question may be put after the time for suspension without the leave of the House.[30]

Order of the House for suspension of sitting

The House may agree to suspend a sitting by motion without notice or by leave. Sometimes the House does this as a mark of respect for the death of a former parliamentarian or other prominent person.[31] It often suspends its sitting a few minutes before 6 pm when it does not wish to start a new item of business just before the dinner break. If a motion to suspend a sitting is under debate at the time that the sitting would be suspended in any case, it lapses and the sitting is automatically suspended under the Standing Orders.[32]

---

[21] 2003, Vol.608, p.5457.
[22] S.O.43(2).
[23] S.O.133(c).
[24] 1901, Vol.119, p.1034.
[25] S.O.55(2)(a),(b).
[26] S.O.55(2)(c).
[27] S.O.57(2)(a).
[28] S.O.51.
[29] 1971, Vol.376, p.4733.
[30] 1960, Vol.322, p.704.
[31] 1987-90, JHR, p.1090 (Rt Hon Sir Arnold Nordmeyer).
[32] 1990, JHR, p.447.

Speaker suspending sitting

The Speaker has authority to suspend a sitting of the House if the Speaker considers that this is necessary in order to maintain order.[33] In this case the Speaker leaves the chair without putting any question and resumes it whenever he or she thinks it appropriate to do so.[34] If the Speaker does not resume the chair by 10 pm on a Tuesday or a Wednesday or by 6 pm on a Thursday, the House is automatically adjourned until the next sitting day. The Speaker also has authority to suspend the sitting on the day of the State Opening of Parliament to permit the Address in Reply debate to commence later in the sitting day.[35] (See Chapter 12.)

ADJOURNMENT OF THE HOUSE

Each day's sitting comes to an end with the adjournment of the House. Occasionally, the House adjourns for a longer period than to the next regular sitting day. The adjournment of the House never brings the session to an end. A session of Parliament is terminated by the Governor-General, not the House, though the House may adjourn for lengthy periods (such as over Christmas and New Year) within the course of a session. An adjournment of the House may be automatic, under the Standing Orders or pursuant to a previous decision of the House, or it may result from a motion which causes the House to rise at a particular time. These occasions for adjournment will be looked at in turn, as will other motions relating to the House's sittings, which are not adjournment motions in that they do not themselves cause the House to rise but rather govern the period for which the House will remain adjourned once it does rise.

When leaving the chair at the conclusion of a sitting, the Speaker rises and bows to both sides of the House. Members must also rise and remain standing until the Speaker has left the Chamber.[36] As on the suspension of a sitting, the bell is rung for 10 seconds when the House adjourns to let persons in the parliamentary complex know that the House has risen.[37]

Adjournment without question put

At the time for the conclusion of each sitting day, the Speaker interrupts the business in progress and leaves the chair. The House then stands adjourned until the time for its next regular or appointed meeting.[38] This adjournment occurs automatically under the Standing Orders and there is no debate on it.

To enable this adjournment to take place if the House is in a committee of the whole House, the chairperson must report the progress made by the committee to the House at five minutes before the time for the conclusion of the sitting.[39] It was formerly the case that, if there were still two or three minutes remaining after the chairperson had reported, there had to be a motion to adjourn to enable the House to rise early, but now the Speaker leaves the chair following the chairperson's report without any question being put, and the House stands adjourned.[40] Where the House concludes a piece of business within five minutes of the time for the adjournment of the House and the next business would require the House to go into committee, the Speaker does not call the next business and adjourns the House at that point.[41]

At the first sitting of the House following a general election, the House adjourns under the Standing Orders after it has elected a Speaker.[42] Other adjournments without a motion occur following the conclusion of business on the day of the State Opening

---

of Parliament and if the Speaker exercises the power to adjourn the House in the case of disorder. In these cases there is no motion to adjourn and, therefore, no question is proposed from the chair on which a debate can arise or a vote can be held. The House automatically adjourns until its next appointed sitting day.[43]

If a question is being put or a vote is in progress at the time at which the Speaker is required to interrupt proceedings and adjourn the House, the interruption is postponed until after completion of the vote. No further question may be put from the chair after that time except where a closure motion has been carried. If a closure motion has been carried any consequential questions necessary to determine the original question are put (and may be voted on).[44] Where the chairperson has accepted a closure motion and is in the process of putting the question on it to the committee at the time for reporting progress, determination of the question must be completed and, if carried, any consequential questions must also be put to the committee before progress is reported.[45]

Adjournment motions
An adjournment motion is a motion which, if carried, will bring the current sitting of the House to an end.

The adjournment of the House may be moved only by a Minister.[46] (In New Zealand the motion for the adjournment of the House cannot be moved by opposition members as a delaying or dilatory tactic.) No notice of an adjournment motion is required, even for one fixing a different time for the House to resume sitting than the time already prescribed.[47] An adjournment motion is debatable, and, unless the proposal for the adjournment is for the purpose of discussing a particular subject (as it is with arranged debates on foreign affairs, for example), the scope of debate on the adjournment is wide open. An adjournment motion is not a purely procedural motion; it is a motion on which members may raise any substantive matter.[48] The adjournment of the House cannot be moved so as to interrupt a debate in progress, although a debate may be adjourned so as to permit an adjournment motion to be moved.

An adjournment motion lapses if it is under debate at the time already appointed for the House to rise, as the House adjourns without a question being put at that time.[49] Where a vote is in progress at the time for the House to adjourn or a closure motion relating to an adjournment debate has been accepted, the question on the adjournment is put even though this is after the time for the House to rise.[50] But if the House is sitting outside normal sitting hours under urgency, it is possible to move the adjournment of the House to fix a new time for the next sitting of the House.[51] No special times are prescribed for speeches on adjournment motions, so the fall-back speaking time of 10 minutes for each member applies. It is not possible to move the adjournment of a debate on the adjournment of the House; the issue of the adjournment of the House must be decided one way or the other.

An adjournment motion may be a simple motion "That this House do now adjourn". In this case, if the motion is carried, the House will meet again on its next regular sitting day or on the next sitting day already appointed by any other order of the House. Alternatively, the motion itself may go on to prescribe expressly a date or time to which the House should adjourn, in which case, if it is carried, the House will meet on that day or at that time. The motion may provide for an indefinite adjournment, although there must be a mechanism by which the House can reassemble.

43 S.Os 14(2) and 48(3).
44 S.O.51.
45 1971, Vol.376, p.4733; 2003, Vol.613, p.10003.
46 S.O.47(2).
47 1889, Vol.64, p.565; 1904, Vol.131, pp.869-70;
1932, Vol.231, p.68; 2000, Vol.586, pp.4568-9.
48 1983, Vol.451, p.855.
49 S.O.49(1).
50 1987-90, JHR, pp.1230-1.
51 2000, Vol.586, pp.4568-9.

An adjournment motion may be amended provided that any proffered amendment is relevant to the motion, that is, if it relates to the period of the adjournment suggested in the motion.[52]

During the Second World War the House often adjourned until a fixed date, with power given to the Government to appoint an earlier day for the House to meet if it was necessary in the public interest.[53] The House has also used other variants for its adjournments, such as adjourning until a date to be determined by the Government and advised to the Speaker, who had to give members at least 14 days' notice of the day fixed,[54] and adjourning until a named date but with power vested in the Government to recall the House at an earlier date if this was necessary.[55] Standing Orders have now vested the power in the Speaker to order an earlier sitting of the House during an adjournment if circumstances warrant this.[56]

During adjournments, select committees may continue to meet. In fact, the object of an adjournment is often to allow an extended period, free from commitments in the House, in which select committees are able to make better progress with their work.

In rare circumstances the House uses adjournment motions as vehicles for special debates. These may be arranged debates on foreign affairs or economic policy which nominally take place on a motion for the adjournment of the House. The House also uses adjournment motions as a means of paying its respects on the occasion of the deaths of parliamentarians or former parliamentarians. It is the House's invariable practice to adjourn whenever a current member of Parliament or a former Prime Minister dies.

Motions regulating the period of adjournment

An adjournment motion always regulates the period of an adjournment, but so may other motions which are not themselves adjournment motions, since they do not bring the current sitting of the House to an end but determine how long the House will be adjourned for once it does rise. Such motions are usually identifiable by referring to the House's actions "at its rising".

The scope of debate on a motion regulating the period of adjournment, as opposed to an adjournment motion, is not wide open. Debate must be relevant to the question of adjourning for the period of time suggested in the motion, and debate on substantive matters cannot be introduced. The most significant type of motion regulating the period of the House's adjournments is the motion fixing the sitting programme for the year.

Adjournment until the ringing of the bell

A method of permitting an indefinite adjournment is for the House to adjourn "until the ringing of the bell" on the following sitting day. This leaves the decision of when the House will actually meet on that day in the hands of the Speaker. This device is employed when a state or parliamentary luncheon is to be held and it is desired to leave the precise time at which the sitting will commence to the Speaker's discretion.

Accelerated meeting of the House during an adjournment

Just as there is provision for Parliament to be called into session if a declaration of national emergency is made while Parliament is prorogued or dissolved, so must the

---

52   1904, Vol.131, pp.869-70; 1993, Vol.539, p.32.   55   1991, Vol.512, p.5.
53   For example, 1941-42, JHR, p.6.   56   S.O.53.
54   1982, JHR, p.88.

House reassemble if such a declaration is made during an adjournment and the House is not due to meet within seven days. For this purpose the Speaker must, by notice in the *New Zealand Gazette*, appoint a day for the House to meet. The day is not to be later than seven days after the date of the declaration. The House then meets and sits accordingly.[57] The House does not have to take any action in respect of the declaration which causes it to reassemble.

The Standing Orders also contain express authority for the House to be reassembled during an adjournment at an earlier time than the date to which it has been adjourned. This provision was adopted to cater for the situation which arose at the time of the Gulf War in 1991, when the only way for the House to meet early during a lengthy adjournment was for Parliament to be prorogued and a new session called. Now, if it appears in the public interest that the House should meet at an earlier time than that to which it stands adjourned, the Prime Minister may, after first consulting with the leaders of all other parties in the House, inform the Speaker of this fact.[58] The Speaker is then obliged to appoint an appropriate date and time for the House to meet, and to advise members accordingly.[59] If the House does meet in such circumstances the remainder of the projected adjournment is cancelled. The House could resolve on a new period of adjournment when it sits or resume sitting regularly from that point. On the first occasion on which this provision was used the House sat on the day in question and then resumed the previously appointed adjournment.[60]

URGENCY

From time to time it is necessary for the House to extend a sitting so that it can complete certain business before rising. The method by which this is done is by a motion for "urgency" to be accorded to that business. "Urgency" as a business tool has been available since 1903. It has become a key means of progressing Government business since 1929.[61]

Urgency is something that may be claimed only by the Government, although it need not be claimed exclusively for Government business. For instance, urgency has been taken for a local bill[62] and for a Member's bill.[63] An urgency motion is moved by a Minister without notice and is decided without amendment or debate.[64]

Time for moving

Urgency cannot be moved until general business has concluded.[65]

An urgency motion is not one of the events that may interrupt a debate.[66] Once the House has entered upon a bill or other item of business, it is too late to move urgency for that bill or business at that sitting.

Where the House is debating a bill at 6 pm when the sitting is suspended, urgency cannot be moved on the resumption at 7.30 pm, for the House continues with the same debate in the evening and an urgency motion in these circumstances would be an interruption of it. However, where a debate has been interrupted by an adjournment of the House and set down for resumption on the next sitting day, urgency can be moved before that debate is resumed on that future day.[67] The prohibition against interrupting a debate applies to interrupting a debate which the House has entered upon that day; it

57   *Civil Defence Emergency Management Act* 2002, s.67(2), (4).
58   S.O.53(1).
59   S.O.53(2).
60   1999, Vol.580, pp.19461-99 (deployment of peacekeeping forces to East Timor).
61   Martin, *The House – New Zealand's House of Representatives 1854-2004*, p.193.
62   2001, Vol.593, p.10314 (*Bay of Plenty Regional Council (Maori Constituency Empowering) Bill*).
63   2001, Vol.597, p.13965 (*Local Government (Prohibition of Liquor in Public Places) Amendment Bill*).
64   S.O.54(1),(3).
65   S.O.54(2).
66   S.O.133.
67   1976, Vol.403, p.706.

does not apply in respect of a debate which was interrupted by the House adjourning on a previous day.

Reasons for urgency

An urgency motion is not properly moved unless a reason for it of some description is given by the Minister.[68] The motion will be disallowed if a reason is not forthcoming before the question for urgency is determined. The motion can, however, be moved again.[69] If the absence of reasons is not perceived at the time, and the House agrees to the motion for urgency, there can be no re-opening of the apparent defect in the moving of the motion. Urgency, once accorded, comes to an end only by an event occurring subsequent to the House agreeing to the motion.[70] The reasons which the Minister gives are not required to be very detailed but they do require some particularity.[71] Merely to say that progress needs to be made is not sufficient,[72] and any bills to be introduced must be identified. But, reasons having been given, the Speaker is not the judge of their adequacy (unlike for extraordinary urgency); that is solely a matter for the House.[73]

Effect of urgency

Urgency enables the business for which it has been accorded (usually a bill or bills) to be completed before the House rises on that day. The sitting is accordingly extended for that purpose beyond the time for the normal adjournment of the House.[74] Urgency may be taken for a single stage of a bill, for one or more stages of one bill, for one or more stages of different bills, or for a combination of these.

A motion for urgency does not expedite consideration of a bill or other matter which the House has not already reached. Thus where a bill has been introduced or reported back from a select committee and set down for consideration on a future day (a three-day waiting period), it cannot be the subject of urgency until that day is reached. However, once the bill has been reached, urgency does enable the House to proceed with further stages of it which would not normally be taken on the same sitting day. Nor does urgency alter the sequence of business set out on the order paper. The urgency motion itself does not set out a binding order of business. It is indicative only and, subject to the order in which orders of the day stand on the order paper, it is open to the Government to introduce bills in a different order to that set out in the urgency motion and to take subsequent stages of bills in any order it pleases.[75] The Government may also move motions postponing business on the order paper so as to alter the sequence of business. But no other business (other than that for which urgency was accorded) may be transacted while urgency is current.[76]

Urgency does not enable the House to sit beyond midnight on a Saturday. If the sitting continues until then, the House adjourns.[77] The Standing Orders also provide for the sitting of the House to be specially suspended during urgency. On the day on which urgency is taken, these suspensions operate from the normal time for the House to rise (10 pm on Tuesdays and Wednesdays and 6 pm on Thursdays) to 9 am the following day, and thereafter from 1 pm to 2 pm, from 6 pm to 7 pm and from midnight to 9 am.[78] These suspensions begin to operate only after a sitting of the House has been extended by urgency. If urgency is taken during the course of an afternoon on Tuesday or Wednesday, the normal suspension from 6 pm to 7.30 pm applies on that day, because at the time the sitting has not been extended.

---

[68]   S.O.54(3).
[69]   1976, Vol.405, p.2019.
[70]   1978, Vol.421, pp.4042, 4047.
[71]   S.O.54(3).
[72]   1985, Vol.467, p.8181.
[73]   1998, Vol.569, p.10121.

[74]   S.O.55(1).
[75]   1998, Vol.569, p.10091; 2002, Vol.600, p.16085.
[76]   S.O.58.
[77]   S.O.55(2)(d).
[78]   S.O.55(2)(a),(c).

A special suspension applies under a procedure adopted in December 2003. The Business Committee may be advised by the Government of its intention to move for urgency on the next Thursday. In this case the Thursday sitting is suspended at 6 pm only to 7.30 pm and the House sits through to 10 pm before the sitting is suspended until 9 am the following morning.[79] This effectively converts the sitting into a Tuesday or a Wednesday sitting.[80]

In order to take advantage of this provision there must be a Business Committee meeting at which the advice is conveyed to it, though it is not necessary to specify in detail the business to be transacted and advice could be given about alternative programmes of business to be taken under urgency. The fact that such advice has been given to the committee is noted in the committee's minutes, but the taking of urgency is not a determination of the committee nor is the committee's agreement to it required. The fact that the Government has given such notice does not oblige it to utilise the notice and actually move an urgency motion. The Government may refrain from moving urgency that it has foreshadowed.

The suspensions of a sitting extended by urgency are automatic unless dispensed with by the leave of the House. In the case of a Monday sitting the rules for a Tuesday sitting apply unless the House has appointed different sitting hours for the sitting.[81] Consequently, if urgency is taken at a Monday sitting the first suspension is at 10 pm or such other hour appointed for the House to rise in the motion ordering the sitting.

Extraordinary urgency

Ordinarily, all-night sittings of the House cannot occur because the sitting, even under urgency, is suspended at the latest at midnight until 9 am the following day. But the House does have a procedure known as extraordinary urgency which, if taken, dispenses with the overnight suspension altogether and allows the House to continue its sitting with immediate effect and, if necessary, to sit through the night, breaking only between 8 am and 9 am, 1 pm and 2 pm, and 6 pm and 7 pm. At midnight on a Saturday the House adjourns.[82]

Extraordinary urgency is designed to facilitate the passing of a particularly urgent piece of legislation, such as Budget legislation or legislation to deal with the collapse of a commercial or financial organisation, or a matter involving state security.[83] An urgency motion may be moved from the outset as a motion for extraordinary urgency or, after urgency has been taken, a further motion for extraordinary urgency for some part of the urgency business that warrants it, may be moved.[84] As with ordinary urgency, there is no amendment or debate on a motion for extraordinary urgency, but the Minister moving it must inform the House of the nature of the business or the circumstances which warrant extraordinary urgency.[85] In this case, unlike for ordinary urgency, the Speaker has to make a judgment as to the justification for the Government asking for extraordinary urgency.[86] It would not be justified, for instance, if the legislation for which it was claimed was not designed to come into force immediately on enactment. Extraordinary urgency is particularly designed for use in connection with legislation for a tax change with immediate effect.[87]

The first use of extraordinary urgency was to pass legislation increasing excise duties at the time of the 1988 Budget.[88] The House sat until 1 am. The sitting was then

---

[79] S.O.55(2)(b).
[80] See 2004, Vol.617, pp.13424, 13469 for the first use of this procedure.
[81] S.O.45.
[82] S.O.57.
[83] 1984-85, AJHR, I.14, para.2.3.1 (*Report of the*

Standing Orders Committee, First report, July 1985).
[84] S.O.56(1).
[85] S.O.56(2).
[86] S.O.56(3); 1998, Vol.569, p.10121.
[87] 1998, Vol.568, pp.8581-2.
[88] 1987-90, JHR, p.771 (*Customs and Excise Amendment Bill*).

suspended, and at 9 am it was resumed to deal with other legislation for which ordinary urgency had been taken. Extraordinary urgency has been taken on a number of other occasions, always in association with tax measures.[89]

Termination of urgency

Urgency terminates when the business for which it has been accorded is completed. If this occurs before the normal time for the rising of the House, the House proceeds with business on the order paper until the normal time for it to adjourn. If the urgency business is completed after the normal time of adjournment, the House rises immediately, subject to considering any motion relating to its next sitting.

However, the House is not obliged, just because urgency has been taken, to process all the bills or business named in the urgency motion.[90] It has the opportunity to do so at that sitting (subject to the sitting ending at the latest at midnight on Saturday) but it does not have to do so. The termination of urgency and therefore of the sitting can be precipitated before all business has been disposed of. As no other business that was not included in the urgency motion can be transacted during urgency except by leave,[91] a positive decision to bring urgency to an end is always needed.[92] Urgency does not terminate inadvertently.

The Government may indicate to the Speaker that Ministers, in whose hands the remaining business for which urgency has been taken stands, do not intend to move motions in relation to that business. Urgency terminates at that point and if the House is sitting outside normal hours it adjourns.[93] The debate on a bill for which urgency was taken may be adjourned or, if it is in committee, progress may be reported, for this purpose. The Government may move a motion for the adjournment of the House while the House is sitting under urgency provided that the motion proposes a different time for the next meeting of the House to that at which the House would otherwise meet when it adjourns (in the latter case no adjournment motion is necessary anyway). The House always has the right, before rising, to fix the time for its next sitting.[94]

General

The occasional extended or all-night sitting which the House experiences occurs following the passage of an urgency motion. It was under urgency, for instance, that in 1991 the House sat from 2 pm on Tuesday 30 July until 11.30 pm on the following Saturday evening (a total of 67½ sitting hours) to pass legislation introduced following the delivery of the Budget.[95] This was the most extended sitting in modern times. The sitting day remained the same, Tuesday, despite the House sitting beyond midnight. To mark this fact the calendar showing the date in the Chamber is not altered until the House rises. The longest single sitting on record is that of Wednesday 24 July 1889, when the House sat for a total of 124¼ hours (from 7.30 pm on Wednesday 24 July to 10.30 pm on Friday 2 August, including three all-night sittings within that period) to consider electoral legislation.[96]

The proportion of the House's total sitting hours that are spent under urgency varies depending upon current political circumstances and the exigencies of the Government's legislative programme. In the forty-third Parliament (1990–93) urgency hours represented 30.25 percent of total sitting hours; in the forty-fourth Parliament (1993–96) 9.21 percent;

---

[89] 1991, Vol.517, p.3287 (*Finance (Revenue) Bill*); 1998, Vol.568, p.8581 (*Customs and Excise Amendment Bill*); 1999, Vol.577, p.16619 (*Stamp Duty Abolition Bill*); 2000, Vol.583, p.1984 (*Customs and Excise Amendment Bill*); 2002, Vol.598, p.14767 (*Customs and Excise Amendment Bill (No 5)*); 2003, Vol.608, p.5358 (*Customs and Excise (Alcoholic Beverages) Amendment Bill*).

[90] 1998, Vol.569, p.10121.
[91] S.O.58.
[92] 1997, Vol.565, p.6106.
[93] 1998, Vol.569, p.10121.
[94] 2000, Vol.586, pp.4568-9.
[95] 1991, Vol.517, pp.3215-660.
[96] 1889, JHR, pp.91-8.

in the forty-fifth Parliament (1996–99) 30.73 percent; in the forty-sixth Parliament (1999–2002) 13.12 percent; and in the forty-seventh Parliament (2002–05) 21.38 percent.

THE SITTING PROGRAMME

Parliament meets throughout the year to transact business. The only month that is regularly free of sittings of the House is January and even towards the end of that month a number of select committee meetings may be held. Since 1984 it has become the norm for an annual sitting programme to be drawn up in advance setting out the days that it is proposed that the House should sit during the year.

Business Committee recommendation

Until 1995 the proposed sitting programme was drawn up solely on the Government's initiative. It was usually announced by way of press release before Christmas and formally adopted by the House early in the new year. Since 1995, with the establishment of the Business Committee, the responsibility for recommending a sitting programme to the House has rested with the Business Committee.[97] The programme must be prepared on the basis that the House will commence its sittings no later than the last Tuesday in February and will sit in total for about 90 sitting days (30 weeks) during the course of the year.[98] In practice the House will often meet earlier in the year than this and sit for longer – in 2000, for example, the House sat for 34 weeks, the most on record.[99]

Planning for the annual sitting programme is built around the flow of parliamentary business that can be expected during the course of the year. Much of this results from the process of granting supply and conducting financial reviews. (See Chapters 34, 35 and 36.) Other considerations include: the debate on the Prime Minister's statement (a 14-hour debate which opens each year's sittings), the need to pass legislation fixing tax rates by 31 March, the popularity of 1 July as a commencement date for legislation (thus making it desirable that the House has a sustained period of sitting leading up to that date) and the need to pass annual legislation of a validating or confirming nature before the end of the year.

The Business Committee is obliged to report to the House with its recommendations for the sitting programme not later than the third sitting day in December or, if the House does not sit in December, not later than the sitting day before the House is due to adjourn for Christmas.[100] This is designed to permit the House to consider the sitting programme before the Christmas adjournment if it wishes to do so. In practice, the Leader of the House takes the initiative in drawing up proposals for the sitting programme. These are presented to the Business Committee in November and may be ready for report to the House well before the Business Committee's reporting deadline.

Adoption of the sitting programme

The Business Committee's recommended sitting programme is just that – a recommendation. It has no effect unless and until adopted by the House. Following the committee's report, the Leader of the House prepares a Government motion setting out a proposed programme of sittings. This usually follows (though it does not have to) the

---

[97] S.O.78(1).
[98] S.O.78(3).
[99] 2000, Vol.589, p.7517.
[100] S.O.78(2).

Business Committee's recommendation. It may be put to the House before Christmas or early in the next year.

A sitting programme adopted by resolution of the House sets aside the basic Standing Orders requirement for the House to meet on every Tuesday, Wednesday and Thursday throughout the year,[101] and obviates the need for the House to pass adjournment motions during the course of the year when it wishes to have more extended adjournment periods. The sitting days during the course of the period (up to the end of the year) that are described in the resolution become the House's sitting days and have effect subject to any subsequent decision of the House to the contrary.[102]

The form of the resolution setting out the programme has varied. It may prescribe the sittings by defining the adjournments the House is to take, requiring the House, on rising on certain defined days throughout the year, to adjourn for various periods. One problem with this approach is that if there is no such sitting day as that identified in the resolution for an adjournment (because a previous sitting has been extended by urgency and that day has been lost) there is nothing to which the resolution can apply and a specific adjournment motion must be passed before the House can rise for that period. An alternative approach is to list the individual sitting days in the resolution as far as possible.[103] This is the favoured method now.

In 2002, after the mid-year election, the House, following discussion at the Business Committee, adopted a new sitting programme to cover the period from September to December.[104]

Variation of the programme

A sitting programme that has been adopted by resolution can be varied by taking an unscheduled adjournment or by cutting out a planned adjournment. A variation to the programme is effected by a new motion on notice or by moving the adjournment of the House for a different period immediately before a planned adjournment.

---

[101]   S.O.43.
[102]   S.O.78(4).

[103]   See, for example, 2001, Vol.597, p.13916.
[104]   2002, Vol.602, pp.594-603.

CHAPTER 14

BUSINESS OF THE HOUSE

A warning bell is rung to announce the imminent sitting of the House. This consists of a 15-second ringing nine minutes before the time appointed for the House to assemble and then of a five-minute ringing commencing seven minutes before that time. The Speaker proceeds to the Chamber from the Speaker's office in a procession led by the Speaker's attendant and the Serjeant-at-Arms, carrying the Mace, aiming to reach the Chamber at the precise time for the commencement of the sitting. The Serjeant-at-Arms leads the Speaker into the Chamber through the door to the left of the Speaker's chair (known as the Speaker's door) announcing to members the Speaker's arrival as the Speaker's party enters. Members rise as the Speaker takes the chair, the Serjeant remaining standing with the Mace immediately to the left of the chair. The Speaker bows to the Government and Opposition sides of the House and then reads a prayer.[1]

PRAYERS

The first vote ever to be held in the House was over whether a prayer should be recited.[2] A majority of the House favoured this course and the prayer was read by a local clergyman who was apparently present in the expectation of such a course being followed by the House.[3]

The wording of the prayer has been altered on a number of occasions. The wording of the current prayer was adopted by resolution of the House in 1962,[4] but it is not written into the Standing Orders and is not regarded as binding on the Speaker.[5] It reads:

> Almighty God, humbly acknowledging our need for Thy guidance in all things, and laying aside all private and personal interests, we beseech Thee to grant that we may conduct the affairs of this House and of our country to the glory of Thy holy name, the maintenance of true religion and justice, the honour of the Queen, and the public welfare, peace, and tranquillity of New Zealand, through Jesus Christ our Lord. Amen.

The Speaker has used a Māori version of this prayer.[6] The fact that the House commences its sittings with a prayer, and what form that prayer takes, is a matter exclusively for it. The practice is not subject to scrutiny by a court or other body outside Parliament.[7]

Once the prayer has been read the Mace is placed on the Table by the Serjeant-at-Arms[8] and the business of the House may commence.

ORDER PAPER

The order in which the House transacts its business each sitting day is set out on an "order paper".[9] This is the House's agenda for the forthcoming sitting of the House. It is prepared by the Clerk for each sitting day so as to reflect the requirements of the Standing Orders as to the order of business to be transacted on particular days, any relevant decisions of

---

[1] S.O.59.
[2] VP, Session 1, 1854, p.3.
[3] "Mr Speaker at prayers in the House", *The Dominion*, 29 July 1950.
[4] 1962, JHR, pp.39-40.
[5] 1962, Vol.330, pp.337-8.
[6] 1994, Vol.545, p.5351.
[7] *Ontario (Speaker) v Ontario (Human Rights Commission)* (2001) 54 OR (3d) 595; "The Parliamentary Prayer", Human Rights Commission, 22 November 2004.
[8] S.O.59.
[9] S.O.60.

the Business Committee and any decisions of the House relating to particular business to be considered.[10]

More than one version of the order paper may be produced.[11] In fact two versions of each day's order paper are usually produced – a provisional order paper and a final order paper.

The provisional order paper for a Tuesday sitting is available on the parliamentary website on the previous Friday and is circulated in hard copy on the preceding day (or on Tuesday morning where Monday is a public holiday). The provisional order papers for Wednesday and Thursday sittings are available on the parliamentary website after the House adjourns on Tuesday and Wednesday respectively, and are circulated in hard copy on the mornings of the sitting days to which they relate. A provisional order paper is, as its title implies, subject to change and correction. This may result from the Government altering the order in which Government orders of the day stand,[12] which it has the right to do at any time up to the hard copy circulation of the final order paper. The provisional order paper may also change in the case of a Tuesday sitting due to the introduction of further Government bills or the reporting back of other bills during the course of Monday. Tuesday's final order paper incorporates such developments.

The order paper must be circulated as early as possible before the House sits.[13] The final version is printed at the same time as questions are processed on each sitting day and is usually available on the parliamentary website and circulated in hard copy about an hour before the House is due to sit.

The final order paper embodies the order of business to be followed by the House when it sits, and this can be departed from only by the House itself agreeing to do so. But if there is an error in the order paper, the Standing Orders prescribing the business to be taken at each sitting take priority and must still be followed.[14]

Supplementary order paper

As well as an order paper, supplementary order papers may be circulated by members, showing details of amendments they propose to move to bills at the committee stage.[15] These papers are supplements to the order paper only as a matter of form and have nothing to do with the order of business to be followed by the House at any particular sitting. (See Chapter 27.)

However, as a supplement to the order paper, a supplementary order paper must be dated according to a sitting day, for an order paper is produced only for a sitting day. It is irregular to circulate a supplementary order paper with a date that is not a sitting day, and such a paper must be withdrawn. For this reason a supplementary order paper with the next sitting day's date should be circulated only after the previous sitting concludes.

GENERAL BUSINESS

One of the major types of business transacted by the House each day is known as "general business".[16]

General business consists of a miscellaneous collection of business that involves announcements, formal motions, questions and some recurrent debates.[17] General business is the first type of business considered by the House at each sitting,[18] except where the Standing Orders expressly provide to the contrary, such as on Budget day. At the conclusion of general business the House moves on to consider orders of the day.

---

10   S.O.61(1),(2).
11   S.O.61(3).
12   S.O.65.
13   S.O.61(3).
14   1978, Vol.421, p.4259; 1985, Vol.467, pp.8218-9.
15   S.O.301.
16   S.O.62(a).
17   S.O.63(1).
18   S.O.63(2).

Orders of the day more closely correspond with the House's legislative outputs, that is, bills. Urgency cannot be taken until general business has concluded.[19]

The announcements that are made as part of general business consist of lists of petitions, papers and select committee reports presented and of bills introduced. These are read to the House by the Clerk. All of these are announcements of events that have occurred since the House last sat because in each case the actual presentation or introduction is accomplished by delivery of the instrument or advice to the Clerk by 1 pm that day. In addition, the Speaker may present papers during general business.[20]

Questions for oral answer follow these announcements as part of general business. These are questions lodged during the course of that morning, plus any urgent question accepted by the Speaker. (See Chapter 40.) Next, as general business, comes any debate on a matter of urgent public importance which a member has applied to the Speaker to hold and which the Speaker allows. (See Chapter 42.) On Wednesdays only, as part of general business, the weekly general debate is held. (See Chapter 42.) Finally, as general business, the House debates any report from the Privileges Committee which has been presented to it. This gives consideration of reports from the Privileges Committee a priority that does not attach to those of other committees. (See Chapter 48.)

ORDERS OF THE DAY

The principal items of business considered by the House each day are called "orders of the day". These are bills or other items which have been set down specifically for consideration by the House.[21] Bills or other matters are usually set down for consideration automatically pursuant to a provision in the Standing Orders but they may be set down by direction of the House, the Business Committee or by an individual member acting under a power conferred by the Standing Orders. Each order of the day stands in the name of a particular member. Orders of the day are sub-classified into Government orders of the day, private and local orders of the day and Members' orders of the day.[22]

Government orders of the day [23] consist principally of Government bills at their various stages. They also comprise Government notices of motion, which are notices of motion given by Ministers.[24] Certain other business that might not otherwise be considered to be Government business is also treated as a Government order of the day: the Address in Reply debate (even though moved by a backbench member of Parliament), the debate on the Prime Minister's statement (even though it is on a motion moved by the Leader of the Opposition), and the annual debate on Crown entities, public organisations and State enterprises (which for this purpose is put into the name of a Minister, often the Minister for State Owned Enterprises).

Government orders of the day have a general precedence of all other orders of the day.

Private and local orders of the day[25] consist exclusively of private and local bills at their various stages. Private and local orders of the day have precedence of Government orders of the day every second Wednesday.

Members' orders of the day [26] consist of Members' bills at their various stages and Members' notices of motion, that is, notices of motion given by members who are not Ministers.[27] They also consist of the reports of select committees on a briefing, inquiry, international treaty examination or other matter and reports of the Regulations Review Committee.[28] They do not include reports of the Privileges Committee (which are general

---

[19] S.O.54(2).
[20] S.O.363(2).
[21] S.O.3(1).
[22] S.O.62(b), (c), (d).
[23] S.O.64.

[24] S.O.3(1).
[25] S.O.66.
[26] S.O.68.
[27] S.O.3(1).
[28] S.O.251(3).

business), reports on bills, reports on estimates, supplementary estimates or financial reviews or reports on affirmative resolution notices of motion (the latter categories of reports have their own procedures for their consideration by the House). Nor do they include reports on petitions in the first instance. Reports on petitions are not set down as orders of the day at all unless the Business Committee specifically directs this, in which case the report would be set down for consideration as a Members' order of the day.[29]

Members' orders of the day have precedence over Government orders of the day every second Wednesday sitting, when they are taken immediately after private and local orders of the day.

Arrangement of orders of the day

The rules for the arrangement of orders of the day on the order paper differ between Government orders of the day, on the one hand, and other orders of the day, on the other.

As far as Government orders of the day are concerned, the Government may arrange them in any order it wishes on the order paper subject to any Standing Orders requirement to the contrary.[30] For this purpose the Leader of the House's office advises the Clerk during the course of the morning of each sitting day what is the order of the business (usually bills) to be debated that day. The final order paper is published to reflect this, with the orders of the day listed numerically. However, with the Budget debate, the Address in Reply debate and the debate on the Prime Minister's statement (which are all Government orders of the day), the Standing Orders require that they be taken ahead of all other Government orders of the day.[31] Consequently, while one of these debates is still before the House it is automatically listed as the first Government order of the day.

Private and local orders of the day and Members' orders of the day relating to bills are arranged in their respective groups on the order paper in descending order of the state of their progress through the House.[32] Bills for third reading have priority over other bills, and those awaiting their first reading are at the bottom of the list. Where debate on a bill at a particular stage has been interrupted, that bill takes precedence of other bills at the same stage.[33] (In the case of a bill introduced before 18 October 1999 the bill received a second reading before being referred to a select committee. The select committee report is therefore set down for consideration in its own right on the same basis as if it was a second reading debate.[34] Such bills are set down ahead of any other bills awaiting second reading.) In the case of interim reports on bills, consideration of the report is set down after bills awaiting their second reading.

The order in which private, local and Members' bills at the same stage stand on the order paper can be changed by the House, or by a member exercising his or her right to postpone an order of the day. The order can also be changed by determination of the Business Committee, which has the right to decide the order of business to be transacted in the House.[35] If the Business Committee exercises this power the order paper is arranged accordingly to reflect such a determination, which takes effect notwithstanding any Standing Order to the contrary.[36]

Setting business down as an order of the day

The Standing Orders provide that bills, following their introduction, are set down for first reading and, after each subsequent stage in their passing is complete, are set down for their next stage (as Government, private and local, or Members' orders of the day as the

---

[29] S.O.251(2).
[30] S.O.65.
[31] S.Os 326(1), 344 and 347.
[32] S.Os 67(1) and 69(1).

[33] S.Os 67(2) and 69(2).
[34] 2002, Vol.602, p.308.
[35] S.O.76(a).
[36] S.O.77(2).

case may be).[37] At each stage an order of the day is created for the consideration of the bill at the particular stage which it has reached. When members give notices of motions they wish to move, these are set down for consideration by the House as orders of the day.[38] The annual financial review debate on Crown entities, public organisations and State enterprises is set down as an order of the day.[39]

Most orders of the day are set down for consideration or further consideration on "the next sitting day". Setting business down for the next sitting day does not mean that it will actually be dealt with on the next day.[40] That will depend on what other business the House has before it and what priority that business is given. But business that has been set down as an order of the day will necessarily appear on the order paper and is business that potentially may be transacted by the House that day.

Reaching orders of the day

As orders of the day on the order paper are reached, the Speaker directs the Clerk to "call" them, which the Clerk does by reading the item as listed on the order paper. The appropriate motion is then moved by the member in charge of the order or the debate resumes at the point at which it was interrupted, as the case may be. Where the House has set business down as an order of the day at a particular time, other business is automatically interrupted at that time to enable the House to move on to the appointed order of the day.

Postponement of orders of the day

An order of the day may be postponed before it is reached. Postponement keeps the item of business on the order paper as an order of the day, though for consideration at a later time than that at which it was originally to be considered. Postponement may be to a later time on the same sitting day, thus altering the order in which business is to be considered, or it may be to a subsequent day. But in any event the period of postponement must be clear. It cannot be for an unspecified or indefinite time.

The member in whose name an order of the day stands has the right to have it postponed by informing the Clerk accordingly.[41] The member may nominate which day it is to be postponed to, otherwise it is postponed to the next sitting day. Such a notice is effective when the order paper shows the order of the day in its new position. The member can thus only effectively postpone an order of the day in this way by informing the Clerk before the final order paper is circulated. After that time business is transacted in the order set out on the order paper.[42] Where an order of the day has been postponed by the member in charge a note to this effect is recorded on the order paper.

An order of the day may also be postponed on motion.[43] Such a motion does not require notice and is moved immediately before the order of the day is called, since, if carried, it prevents the House reaching the order. The member in charge of the order has priority of call to move such a motion if the member wishes to do so, but any other member may move to postpone an order if the member in charge does not wish to. The question for postponement is put forthwith without any amendment or debate.[44]

Finally, the Business Committee has the power to postpone an order of the day in determining the order of business to be transacted in the House.[45] Where this occurs, a note to this effect is recorded on the order paper.

If an order of the day is postponed it becomes a new order of the day for the day or time to which it has been postponed.

---

[37]   S.Os 282, 292, 295 and 306.
[38]   S.O.95.
[39]   S.O.340(1).
[40]   1905, Vol.134, pp.312-3.
[41]   S.O.71(1)(b).

[42]   S.O.60.
[43]   S.O.71(1)(a).
[44]   S.O.71(2).
[45]   S.O.76(a).

Discharge of orders of the day

An order of the day may be discharged either before it is reached or on being reached. Discharge of an order of the day is a means of finally disposing of the business to which the order relates. In the case of a bill, the bill is regarded as having been withdrawn.

Automatic discharge

An order of the day is discharged if the member in whose name it stands (and no member on that member's behalf) fails to move a motion relating to it when it is called. In such a circumstance the order of the day is automatically discharged.[46] In addition, certain types of orders of the day are automatically discharged if they have not been considered by the House within a prescribed period of time. The order of the day for consideration of the report of an inquiry carried out by a select committee is discharged if it is not dealt with within 15 sitting days or within 15 sitting days of a Government response to its recommendations, as the case may be.[47]   Members' notices of motion lapse one week after their first appearance on the order paper[48] and the orders of the day for them are consequently discharged.

Discharge by the member

The member in charge of an order of the day has the right to have it discharged by informing the Clerk accordingly.[49]   Such a notice is effective on being received by the Clerk and the order of the day is consequently discharged at that point.

Discharge on motion

An order of the day may be discharged on motion.[50]   Such a motion does not require notice and is moved immediately the order of the day is called by the Clerk. Once the member in charge has moved a motion relating to the bill or other matter which is the subject of the order of the day, it is too late to move for the discharge of the order on that day.

A discharge motion may be a simple motion to discharge the order of the day or a motion to discharge the order for the purpose of referring the bill which is the subject of the order to a select committee. As a simple discharge motion if carried would remove the business from being before the House altogether, only the member in charge of the order or another member with that member's consent can move for its mere discharge.[51] If other members wish the business to be withdrawn from the House's consideration their proper course is to vote against the substantive motion on the bill or other matter, not to have the order of the day discharged.

But other members can move to have the order of the day discharged for the purpose of referring the bill or other matter to a select committee for consideration. If the member in charge wishes to do this that member has priority of call to move such a motion.[52] No discharge motion can be moved to refer a bill to a committee if the House has accorded urgency to the passing of the bill.[53] Nor can such a motion give instructions extending the select committee's terms of reference in considering the bill (though it may restrict them). If the committee's terms of reference are to be extended (for example, by widening the scope of permitted amendments or allowing the committee to meet at times it would otherwise be prohibited from meeting) this must be accomplished by motion on notice.

There is no debate or amendment permitted on a motion to discharge an order of the day.[54]

---

[46]   See, for example: 1987-90, JHR, p.1989 (*Abolition of the Death Penalty Bill*); 1994, Vol.545, p.5512 (*Far North District Council (Rating and Loans Validation) Bill*); 1997, Vol.561, p.3101 (*Urban Trees Bill*).
[47]   S.O.71(3).
[48]   S.O.96(1).
[49]   S.O.71(1)(b).
[50]   S.O.71(1)(a).
[51]   1924, Vol.204, pp.766-7.
[52]   1994, Vol.543, p.3954.
[53]   1999, Vol.580, p.19128.
[54]   S.O.71(2).

Business Committee
The Business Committee has no power to discharge an order of the day.

Accelerating consideration of orders of the day
Business is set down for consideration as an order of the day on a particular day. Most orders of the day are available for consideration each day (though in a particular order) by virtue of having been previously set down for consideration on the next sitting day. But some orders of the day are set down for consideration on days further ahead than this. Thus, bills introduced and bills reported from select committees are set down as orders of the day for their next stage on the third sitting day following.[55] The House may also appoint a future sitting day more than one day ahead for consideration of an order of the day, or an order of the day may be postponed by the member in charge to a day some time in the future.

In these circumstances only the House, by leave or on motion with notice, can accelerate consideration of the order of the day.[56] The House occasionally by leave dispenses with the three sitting day stand-down rule to allow bills to proceed to their next stage more expeditiously. Before leave is sought in such circumstances it is likely that the proposal will have been raised and discussed at a meeting of the Business Committee.

Reviving orders of the day
Where an order of the day has been discharged, whether automatically, by the member or by order of the House, it can only be revived by the House itself, either by leave or by motion on notice.[57]

In addition, there is an automatic revival of orders of the day not reached each day. The House does not expect to work its way through all the orders of the day on the order paper at one sitting. Sometimes, for example, the House will get no further than the first order of the day. Orders dealt with during the course of a sitting are set down as necessary when completed during the course of a sitting. Business interrupted at the adjournment of a sitting is expressly ordered by the Standing Orders to be set down for consideration on the next sitting day.[58] Orders not reached at all on any day are known as dropped orders. These have not been expressly ordered by the House to be considered on the next sitting day. However, they are carried forward to the following day's order paper and placed on it by the Clerk in accordance with the Standing Orders without an express order of the House.[59] They are then available for rearrangement by the Government if they are Government orders of the day. If they are private and local orders or Members' orders, they are set down in the same order as they stood on the previous day's order paper. Most orders of the day become dropped orders each day and are carried forward in this way from day to day until the House deals with them.

REINSTATEMENT OF BUSINESS
All business before the House or a committee lapses on the dissolution or expiration of Parliament.[60] In this way the new Parliament has a clean slate. It is not burdened with work in progress left over from the old Parliament and is able to set its own agenda.[61] However, as part of setting this agenda, the new Parliament may wish to pick up business that was under consideration in the old Parliament. It does this by reinstating that business.

Business which has lapsed may be reinstated in the next session of Parliament, that

---

55   S.Os 282 and 292.
56   See, for example, 2005, Vol.627, p.22028 (*Smoke-free Environments (Exemptions) Amendment Bill*).
57   See, for example, 1987-90, JHR, pp.1775-8 (*Abolition of the Death Penalty Bill*).
58   S.O.49(1).
59   S.O.70.
60   *Constitution Act* 1986, s.20(1)(b).
61   2002-05, AJHR, I.18B, p.15.

is, the first session of the new Parliament.[62] Only business which has lapsed because of the dissolution or expiration of Parliament can be reinstated, and that reinstatement can only occur in the following session of Parliament. If it is desired to revive business that was disposed of earlier in the Parliament or to revive business in the second or a later session of the new Parliament or even in a future Parliament, this cannot be accomplished by a reinstatement motion.

Reinstatement is effected by the House resolving in the next session that the business identified in the motion be reinstated.[63] Notice of motion is required. The House can reinstate all of the business it wishes to reinstate in a single motion or it can reinstate business on a piecemeal basis in several motions moved at different times (provided they are all moved in the first session of the new Parliament). An opportunity to reinstate business is provided on the day of the State Opening of Parliament. If a notice of motion for reinstatement is given by the Government on the previous sitting day (Commission Opening), the House can deal with any Government order of the day for reinstatement before adjourning that day.[64] But this opportunity does not need to be utilised. Reinstatement can be addressed at any later time. In order to give the House the opportunity to consider whether to reinstate business, proceedings of select committees that were confidential on the dissolution or expiration of the previous Parliament remain confidential for nine sitting days in the new Parliament.[65] If, within this time, that business is reinstated or readopted by the committee (in the case of business initiated by the committee itself) the confidentiality continues, otherwise it lapses at the end of the ninth sitting day.[66]

Reinstatement of an item of business automatically reapplies any obligation flowing from that item, such as the Government's obligation to respond to any recommendations in the report of a select committee that is reinstated as an order of the day.

If the House does reinstate any business, that business is resumed at the stage it had reached in the previous Parliament.[67] This means that if a bill that has been reinstated was subject to a stand-down period before it could be considered at its next stage (such as bills awaiting first reading and second reading that must remain on the order paper for three sitting days), the stand-down period continues to apply when the bill is reinstated. No time runs in respect of reinstated business between the dissolution or expiration of Parliament and the date that that business was reinstated. Thus, in calculating the 90-day period within which the Government must respond to recommendations in a select committee report that has been reinstated, the period between the dissolution and the date of reinstatement is excluded. A similar principle applies in regard to other reinstated business, such as the time for reporting back on bills and on financial review. In practice, however, the House may decide to fix an entirely new time-frame for reporting back on such business to take account of the hiatus in parliamentary activity resulting from the general election.

Reinstatement of business replaces the previous procedure of the outgoing Parliament carrying business forward to the new Parliament.

BUSINESS COMMITTEE

Establishment

With the move towards a multi-party environment in 1996 it was appreciated that managing parliamentary business would be a more complex matter than it had been in the past. In

---

[62]   *Constitution Act* 1986, s.20(1)(b).
[63]   *Ibid.*, s.20(2).
[64]   S.O.14(1)(e).
[65]   S.O.242(1).
[66]   S.O.242(2).
[67]   S.O.79.

particular, it became desirable that there be a forum in which discussions could be held among the parties represented in the House as to the organisation of the business to be transacted. In effect, the House needed an executive or management committee, on which all parties were represented, which could help to direct the flow of the House's work and spread information among members as to the management of that work. Thus (drawing on models from continental Europe) it was decided to establish a Business Committee to perform these functions.[68]

The Business Committee is a committee of the House but it is established in a different way from other select committees and its working practices are quite different. The Business Committee is convened by the Speaker who is *ex officio* the chairperson of the committee.[69] The convening of the committee involves more than just the Speaker appointing a date and time for its first meeting, it involves the Speaker establishing from the parties represented in the House, who are to be their members on the committee. These names must be given to the Speaker.[70]

Membership and participation

Explicitly, and more so than in respect of other committees, a member of the Business Committee is a party representative. Furthermore, membership of the committee is a fluctuating concept. It relates to each meeting of the committee rather than being an ongoing status. In practice, at the commencement of the Parliament parties each nominate a single member to represent them at meetings, but they are entitled to nominate another member at any other time.

Each party with six or more members is automatically entitled to representation on the committee.[71] In addition, parties with fewer than six members which are in a Government coalition are entitled to choose one member between them to represent them on the committee.[72] If there is only one party with fewer than six members that is in a Government coalition, that party is entitled to a representative in its own right. Finally, other parties with fewer than six members which are not in coalition and any independent members are entitled to choose one member between them to represent them on the committee.[73]

In practice, as was envisaged when the committee was conceived,[74] any party, whether formally entitled to a representative in its own right or not, is able to attend meetings of the committee and participate fully in its deliberations. Parties are often regularly represented by two or three members at meetings of the committee and other individual members attend and participate from time to time when a particular bill or other item of interest to them is under discussion. The committee operates an "open door" policy in regard to participation in its meetings by members, though its "core" membership, in addition to the Speaker, consists of the Leader of the House, the shadow Leader of the House and the party whips. It rarely hears from officials, though it has done so in order to help it devise special committee stage procedures for a complex piece of legislation.

The committee originally met regularly in the Speaker's own room and would often meet on more than one occasion each week. It now meets regularly in the Pacific room on the ground floor of Parliament House each Tuesday afternoon while the House is sitting. It does not generally need to meet more than once each week.

Basis of decision-making

The Business Committee is unique among the House's committees in that it does not

---

[68] 1993-96, AJHR, I.18A, p.20.
[69] S.O.74(1).
[70] S.O.74(4).
[71] S.O.74(2).
[72] S.O.74(3).
[73] *Ibid.*
[74] 1993-96, AJHR, I.18A, p.21.

vote on any matters before it. It can take decisions only on the basis of unanimity or, if this is not possible, "near-unanimity".[75] (The fact that the committee does not vote is one reason why it can be relaxed about its membership and the participation of members in its deliberations.) This requirement of unanimity or near-unanimity applies in respect of all business transacted by the committee.

Near-unanimity is specifically defined. Members represent and speak for their parties at the Business Committee. Each party's opinion as expressed at the Business Committee carries the weight of that party's representation in the House as a whole. If parties representing the overwhelming majority of members of Parliament agree at the Business Committee to a certain course of action, the dissent of one or two parties representing only a small fraction of the members of the House will not be taken to have prevented the committee from making a decision.[76]

The Speaker is made the judge of whether unanimity has been or can be reached and, if not, whether there is near-unanimity and thus an effective determination made by the committee.[77] Before concluding that near-unanimity exists, the Speaker must be satisfied that, having regard to their numbers in the House, a proposed determination is fair to all parties and does not discriminate against or oppress a minority party or parties.[78] The Speaker has held that there was near-unanimity, and therefore an effective decision made by the committee, where only a party representing four out of the 99 members of Parliament dissented from the proposal.[79] In practice, it is very rare for the Speaker to be called upon to make a judgment of this nature. Either agreement is reached or it is clear that there is not consensus and therefore the committee is unable to make a decision. But to participate in a decision, a party must actually attend the committee's meeting and express its view. Unanimity and near-unanimity is judged on the basis of the views expressed at meetings of the Business Committee. If a party representative does not attend, that party's views go by default.

Powers and functions
The Business Committee has the power to determine a number of matters. These are—
- the order of business to be transacted in the House[80]
- the time to be spent on an item of business[81]
- the allocation of the time spent on an item of business among the various parties[82]
- the speaking times of individual members on different items[83]
- authorising members absent from the precincts to be regarded as present for voting purposes[84]
- the size of each select committee[85]
- appointments of members to select committees[86]
- removing non-voting members from select committees[87]
- permanent changes to select committee membership[88]
- authorising committees to consider bills or supplementary order papers not otherwise referred to them[89]
- permission for committees to meet outside Wellington during a sitting[90]

---

[75]   S.O.75(1).
[76]   *Ibid.*
[77]   S.O.75(2).
[78]   S.O.75(3).
[79]   1996, Vol.557, p.14359.
[80]   S.O.76(a).
[81]   S.O.76(b).
[82]   S.O.76(c).

[83]   S.O.76(d).
[84]   S.O.144(3).
[85]   S.O.186(2).
[86]   S.Os 186(3) (full) and 187(1) (non-voting).
[87]   S.O.187(3).
[88]   S.O.188(2).
[89]   S.O.190(3).
[90]   S.O.194(a).

- setting petitions down for debate[91]
- allowing omnibus bills to be introduced[92]
- extending the reporting times of bills[93]
- omitting the committee stage of bills[94]
- deciding the order in which votes and financial reviews are to be considered and how long is available for considering them[95]
- deciding the order in which parties may ask questions.[96]

Where the Business Committee reaches agreement on one of these matters there is a Business Committee "determination" and, when it is published, it takes effect automatically. A determination does not require confirmation or endorsement by the House, it applies notwithstanding any Standing Order to the contrary.[97]

Following each Business Committee meeting, a draft of each determination made at the meeting is circulated to the members who attended for their confirmation as to the draft's accuracy. If there is no dispute as to the accuracy of the recorded determination, the determination is published by email to all members and listed in the *Parliamentary Bulletin*. Those determinations relating to business before the House are also noted on the order paper. A determination takes effect on publication and circulation to all members.[98] Email notification to members is effective for this purpose.[99] Determinations usually relate to how a particular bill or item of business is to be dealt with, but they can be more general and relate to how a class of business is to be dealt with.[100]

The Business Committee does not just discuss and deal with matters on which it has the power to make binding determinations. It discusses other matters too. These cannot result in binding determinations by the committee, but they may lead to leave being taken in the House after having been facilitated by discussion at the Business Committee and general agreement to the course of action proposed having been obtained there. Matters that may be discussed in this way consist of anything outside the formal powers of the committee as outlined above. Thus, such matters as extensions of proxy voting, relaxing the rules on giving notice of motion, expediting consideration of orders of the day, and committees meeting during urgency or at times prohibited by the Standing Orders may be discussed by the committee. A staple item on the committee's agenda is the forthcoming business of the House. For this purpose the Leader of the House is expected to outline the Government's intentions with its programme so that members will have a reasonable opportunity to prepare themselves for the debates likely to occur over the forthcoming week. The Business Committee also has the annual function of recommending (but not imposing) a programme of sitting days for the House to follow in the following year.[101] (See Chapter 13.)

While many Business Committee decisions are self-executing in the sense that they have automatic effect, the Business Committee is a committee of the House. Its decisions are therefore always liable to be countermanded by the House provided that the House follows the appropriate procedures to do so. Thus the fact that urgency, if taken, will override decisions on the order of business previously taken by the Business Committee, is not a reason that can prevent the House taking urgency if it is so inclined.[102]

---

91   S.O.251(2).
92   S.O.264(c).
93   S.O.291(2).
94   S.O.295.
95   S.O.341(3).
96   S.O.372(3).
97   S.O.77(2).
98   S.O.77(1).

99   2002, Vol.605, p.2802.
100   See, for example, Business Committee determination, 17 September 2002 (relating to the time limits for speeches on the first reading of Members' bills).
101   S.O.78.
102   1997, Vol.558, p.530.

ORDER OF BUSINESS ON PARTICULAR DAYS

The precise order in which business is transacted differs depending upon the day on which the House is sitting. In particular, Wednesday sittings have rules peculiar to them, for it is on alternate Wednesdays throughout the session that backbench members' business takes precedence of government business.

Tuesdays and Thursdays

On Tuesdays and Thursdays the House transacts general business first and, at the conclusion of general business, proceeds to Government orders of the day.[103] The precise time at which the House reaches Government orders of the day depends largely upon whether the Speaker has allowed an application for an urgent debate. If there is no urgent debate, Government orders of the day are likely to be reached between 3 pm and 3.30 pm. If there is an urgent debate they will not be reached until after 4.30 pm. A debate on a Privileges Committee report will also result in delay in reaching Government orders of the day, but such a debate is uncommon.

Wednesdays

On Wednesdays, general business is taken first. The general rule is then that private and local orders of the day and Members' orders of the day take precedence of Government orders of the day every other Wednesday.[104] General business on a Wednesday includes the general debate, so the time at which the House reaches orders of the day on a Wednesday will always be later than on other days. If no urgent debate has been allowed, orders of the day will be reached at or some time after 4 pm. If there is an urgent debate, orders of the day will not be reached until after 5.30 pm.

Government orders of the day are always taken ahead of other orders of the day, while the Address in Reply debate, the debate on the Prime Minister's statement and the Budget debate are still before the House. Precedence for private and local orders of the day and Members' orders of the day is, in these circumstances, postponed until the next free Wednesday, when alternation resumes.[105] In addition, no general debate is held while these debates are running.[106] Consequently, on Wednesdays in these weeks, the House will reach Government orders of the day at much the same time that it does on a Tuesday and a Thursday.

Other days

On any other day appointed to be a sitting day in its own right the rules for Tuesdays apply. General business is followed by Government orders of the day.[107]

---

[103] S.O.72.
[104] S.O.73(1).
[105] S.O.73(2).

[106] S.O.383(3).
[107] S.Os 45 and 72.

CHAPTER 15

MOTIONS

THE METHOD OF PROCEEDING

The casual radio listener tuning in to the parliamentary broadcast is almost certain to catch the House in the process of debating a matter; that is, discussing, in the form of speeches by individual members, a particular subject. The habitual method by which the House proceeds about its business is to have a proposition for consideration placed before it by a member, to consider that proposition by discussing its pros and cons and finally to decide whether a majority of the House agrees with it. There are other methods of proceeding which do not fall into this general pattern (including purely formal procedures such as the presentation of petitions and papers) and other ways of communicating information (such as by the question procedure and by making statements), but the overwhelming bulk of the House's work is transacted, in outline, in this way. This is, for example, the way in which the House considers legislation, both financial and general, during its passage; it is the method by which it considers reports from its select committees, and the method by which it gives instructions to itself or its members (like instructions to adjourn at a particular time or meet at a particular time), or to other persons (like instructions to attend at the House to produce certain information). The process of debate will be considered in this and the following series of chapters. The particular types of business transacted by the House in which the debating process is applied are considered in other chapters.

A proposition brought before the House for its consideration is called a *motion*. The Standing Orders and other rules of procedure regulate the proposing of motions to ensure that only one motion is under consideration by the House at any one time and that particular types of motions are moved in the House at particular times in the parliamentary day. Many motions require a preliminary step to be taken before they can be brought before the House. This involves giving the House warning of a member's intention to propose the motion – the giving of *notice* of motion.

NOTICE OF MOTION

The House requires, in respect of most types of motion, that it be given notice of a member's intention to move a motion.[1] In this way, members are informed of the text of the motion, which is printed on the order paper. Thus, members are able to think about the motion they are to be asked to agree to; they can consult persons known to be knowledgeable in the area dealt with by the motion; they have time to peruse books and articles on it or do other research of their own devising. Having been given notice of a motion means that they are not required to make a snap judgment as to its merits.

Giving notice of motion

Until 1985 the process of giving a notice of motion was an oral one which involved members rising in the House, stating their intention to move a motion on a future day and informing the House of the text of that motion. In 1985 the procedure of giving notice orally was abolished.

---

[1]   S.O.93.

A member now gives a notice of motion by delivering a written copy of the motion, signed by the member concerned, to the Clerk.[2] Such notices can only be lodged on a sitting day between 9 am and 10 am. There is no requirement for personal delivery by a member, and delivery is often effected by a staff member. A notice of motion may also be transmitted by facsimile letter. The notice must be signed by the member giving it or by another member on that member's behalf. A notice signed on behalf of a member by a person who is not a member of Parliament is not acceptable.

Form and content of notices

The rules for the form and content of notices of motion, which the Speaker applies in vetting notices, are set out in the Standing Orders. A notice is an inchoate motion. If adopted by the House it would express the House's will or opinion on a subject. It must, therefore, be drafted in a form suitable for such an expression of will or opinion by the House.[3] It must have an internal logic, even if one may disagree with the premises on which its conclusion is based. An entirely illogical and incoherent notice of motion is not permitted.

Only one issue may be raised for debate in each notice. This must be clearly indicated and supported only by such facts as are necessary to identify it.[4] The "one issue" requirement is always a difficult one to police. On the one hand, a notice juxtaposing criticism of a decision on school bursaries with one on housing war veterans would clearly not be in order because of the two disparate issues it raises. On the other hand, there may be a number of facets to an issue (such as criticism of lack of action on industrial retraining in a motion on regional unemployment) which makes any judgment on this aspect a question of degree. The inclusion of facts or supporting matter in the notice is limited to essentials. This is a reminder that the proper place to argue the case for the motion is in the subsequent debate, not in the motion itself.

All facts contained in a notice must be authenticated. This does not mean that they must be proved to be correct. The member must show to the Speaker an extract from a newspaper or report supporting facts which are stated in the notice. If this is done, the assertion will be accepted as having been authenticated.[5] The Speaker accepts evidence submitted at its face value as being submitted in good faith and does not go further to examine its validity. If it substantiates the statement of fact in the notice, it is accepted.[6] The underlying truth or falsity of the statement is a matter to be canvassed in the subsequent debate on the subject.[7] Not all assertions contained in notices are regarded as statements of fact which must be authenticated. The inclusion of a supporting assertion for the sole purpose of making clear to the House what it is being called upon to debate is not a statement of fact.[8]

The inclusion of the names of persons in notices of motion is deprecated unless this is strictly necessary to render the motion intelligible.[9] There is a similar rule regarding the inclusion of the names of persons in parliamentary questions. The extent to which members involve named individuals in their proceedings is, by and large, over to them, but the House requires that, in motions and questions at least, members should not introduce the name of a person unless it can be shown that this is essential to the point of the motion or question. Notices of motion cannot contain anything that would not be permitted in the course of debate.[10] Into this catch-all prohibition fall transgressions such as using unparliamentary expressions, and any other type of reference which would be ruled out

---

2 S.O.94(1).
3 S.O.97(1).
4 *Ibid.*
5 1979, Vol.422, p.179.
6 1982, Vol.445, p.1611.

7 1975, Vol.400, p.3912.
8 1981, Vol.437, pp.319-20.
9 S.O.97(2)(b).
10 S.O.97(2)(a).

of order if used in debate. It is specifically provided that a motion (and hence a notice of motion) cannot refer to a matter awaiting adjudication before a court of record.[11] (See Chapter 16.)

Publication of notices
A notice of motion is given so that members of Parliament will know of its existence. So, in respect of those notices which are accepted by the Speaker as being in order, copies are made available at the Table in the House when the House meets at 2 pm.[12] Photocopies of each day's notices are also made available for perusal by members of the Parliamentary Press Gallery in the Office of the Clerk at 2 pm. Once a notice has been made available at the Table it is set down as an order of the day for the next day on which the House sits.[13]

Notices of motion are printed on the order paper according to whether they are notices given by a Minister (known as Government notices of motion) or by a non-Minister (Members' notices of motion).

Government notices of motion
Government notices of motion remain on the order paper as Government orders of the day until dealt with or withdrawn. Whether and when they are dealt with depends upon the priority given to them by the Government in arranging its business on the order paper.

Many Government notices relate to the sittings of the House or the management of the Government's programme of business in the House. Others are of a congratulatory nature similar to many Members' notices. Occasionally a Government notice of motion will be given relating to an aspect of Government policy. Examples of this occurred in 1985 when a Government notice of motion was lodged urging the New Zealand Rugby Football Union not to accept an invitation for an All Black tour of South Africa, and in 2000 when the Government gave a notice of motion asking the House to take note of a select committee report on the closer economic partnership agreement with Singapore.[14]

Members' notices of motion
Members' notices of motion appear on the order paper for only a limited time. Unless they are debated sooner, notices given by non-Ministers are printed on the order paper for one week from the date of their first appearance on the order paper, that is, up to eight days from the date they are given.[15] An exception is made in the case of a notice for the disallowance of regulations given by a member of the Regulations Review Committee. Such a notice is not struck off the order paper after a week but remains there to be dealt with while the statutory provisions for disallowance of regulations continue to run.[16]

While a high proportion of Government notices of motion are dealt with by the House, very few Members' notices are. Those which are dealt with are considered because they fall into the category of non-controversial congratulatory or condolatory motions which the House by leave permits to be moved. Members' notices of motion, as Members' orders of the day, have too low a priority in the House's order of business to be reached in practice.

Notices of motions relating to the stages of legislation
No notice of motion is given for the introduction of Government bills, but a notice is required for the introduction of the other types of bills. For private bills this differs

---

[11] S.O.111(a).
[12] S.O.95.
[13] S.O.95; 2004, Vol.620, p.15736.
[14] *Order paper*, 28 March 1985; *order paper*, 7

November 2000.
[15] S.O.96(1).
[16] S.O.96(2).

slightly from the procedure already described, in that the notice takes the form of a petition presented to the House. (See Chapters 26 and 27 for the specific rules.)

A different means of giving notices of motion applies at the various stages of legislation. The Standing Orders require legislation to proceed in a particular way, and at each stage a different motion is moved. No oral notice of these motions is given. At the conclusion of each stage of a bill, the Speaker, on behalf of the House, sets the legislation down for consideration at the next stage on the next sitting day (although it will not necessarily be dealt with on that day) and the legislation appears on the order paper accordingly.

Because of the overwhelming preponderance of legislation in the business transacted by the House, this is the most common form in which notice of forthcoming business is given to members – merely a statement by the Speaker at the conclusion of a debate and a confirmatory note appearing on the following day's order paper.

Withdrawal of notices

A notice of motion can be withdrawn by the member who lodged it at any time up to its being made available to members in the Chamber at 2 pm. In such a case copies of the notice are not distributed by the Office of the Clerk. As an order of the day, a notice of motion once given may thereafter be withdrawn by the member informing the Clerk.[17] In any case, the member who gives a notice of motion is not obliged to move it when it is reached, and it disappears from the order paper if not moved by the member.

Motions not requiring notice

The general rule is that all motions require notice before they can be moved, but this is subject to any Standing Order or practice of the House to the contrary.[18] There are numerous exceptions to the requirement of notice. The general rule requiring notice is reversed altogether in the case of amendments (which are motions subsidiary to another motion), since notice is not obligatory for amendments.

In many instances the Standing Orders expressly provide that particular motions may be proposed without notice having been given, thus creating exceptions to the general rule. Certain other types of motion, although not expressly dealt with by the Standing Orders, have been ruled not to require notice. These are—
- motions altering the time fixed for the next sitting of the House[19]
- motions dealing with the meetings of select committees during the current sitting of the House.[20]

In addition to these types of motion, motions acknowledging communications to the House of a formal nature are moved without notice, subject to the Speaker's duty to ensure that this is appropriate. Thus, replies from the Crown to addresses are usually ordered to be entered in the journals by motions moved without notice.

Otherwise, leave of the House is necessary to dispense with the requirement of giving notice of motion.

MOVING OF MOTIONS

A motion is proposed to the House by a member *moving* it and thus formally putting the proposition that it contains before the House, so that ultimately it may be adopted or rejected. If the motion is one of which notice has been given, the Speaker (at the

---

17   S.O.71(1)(b).
18   S.O.93.

19   1932, Vol.231, p.68; 2000, Vol.586, pp.4568-9.
20   1927, Vol.215, p.560.

appropriate point in the sitting) will call upon the member who gave the notice to move it. In the case of a bill, the Speaker directs the Clerk to announce the particular stage of the bill which is to be debated, and then the Speaker invites the member in charge of the bill to move the appropriate motion. With other motions which do not require notice, the member seeking to move a motion (and in most of these cases only a restricted class of members, usually only Ministers, can move such motions) seeks the Speaker's permission to speak, often on a point of order or after intimating privately to the Chair what course is intended. Members wishing to move amendments must first seek the right to speak in the debate in the normal way.

If the mover of a motion has a right to make a speech in support of the motion (and not all motions are debatable), the motion is moved formally at the commencement of the speech. Where the terms of the motion are set out on the order paper, the member might not recite them at all in the speech, being content with informing the House that the motion is moved as set out on the order paper. A member is not obliged to read out the terms of a motion appearing on the order paper.[21]

If the member does intend to speak to the motion it is important that the member should proceed immediately to the speech after having moved the motion. Once the member sits down after moving a motion, the member's right to speak is ended.[22]

Moving on behalf of another member

It is permissible for a member to move a motion on behalf of a colleague who is absent from the Chamber, provided that the member has the authority of that colleague to do so.[23] For this purpose members do not have to state that they have authority to act on behalf of other members, but, if challenged, the Speaker will ask for an assurance that this is the case.

A member cannot move a motion on behalf of a colleague if the former could not move it in his or her own right. Thus, Ministers have an absolute authority to act for other absent Ministers;[24] but a non-Minister cannot act for a Minister – a Government motion must be proposed to the House by one of the Crown's responsible advisers. Conversely, a Minister cannot move a Member's bill on behalf of a member. While generally a Minister or member may act for another member only if the latter is physically absent from the Chamber, it is well established that a member can act for the Speaker in the Speaker's presence – for example, moving a local bill in the Speaker's name.[25]

Member absent

If a member gives notice of a motion and is absent from the House when the motion is reached and no one else rises to move it, the motion is struck off the order paper. If a member does not want to proceed with the motion on a particular day, it can be postponed.

Seconding motions

A seconder is not required to support any motion unless this is expressly required by the Standing Orders.[26] There is no instance of a seconder being required by the Standing Orders but the motion for an Address in Reply to the Speech from the Throne at the Opening of Parliament may be seconded.[27]

---

[21]   1992, Vol.531, p.12646.
[22]   1996, Vol.556, p.13643.
[23]   1906, Vol.137, p.19; 1997, Vol.558, p.96.
[24]   1904, Vol.129, p.2.

[25]   1990, Vol.510, p.3514.
[26]   S.O.98.
[27]   S.O.342(2).

QUESTION PROPOSED

Once a motion has been moved, the Speaker proposes a question to the House based on that motion.[28] This question is of an altogether different nature from the questions which members address to Ministers seeking information about government policy or the administration of a department. It is a question formulated by the Speaker which admits of one of two answers by the members of the House: yes, they agree with the motion, or no, they do not agree with it. An unequivocal yes or no is given by the House to every question (a tied vote means that the answer is no). What the House debates is that question: does it agree or disagree with the motion which has been moved?

The Speaker's propounding of the question puts squarely before the House the matter to be determined. It also forms a convenient break in the proceedings for the Speaker to consider whether the motion is in accordance with the rules of the House. The Speaker does have authority to propose a question, allow the debate to run on for a while, and then rule the motion out of order, but a ruling will normally be made at this stage if possible. The necessity to consider whether a motion is acceptable in terms of the rules of the House arises with all types of motions (Members' motions have already been subject to a vetting procedure so they are unlikely to raise any problems at this late stage) and applies particularly with amendments, which must comply with quite elaborate rules. It is at this stage in the proceedings that the Speaker will normally pause to consider the acceptability of the motion, and if the motion is considered to be out of order, the Speaker will rule accordingly instead of proposing the question.

Withdrawal of motion

The consequence of proposing a question is that the motion is no longer the exclusive property of one member. It now belongs to the House and cannot be withdrawn without the leave of the House.[29] In addition, where any amendment has been proposed to the motion, it is necessary for the amendment to be withdrawn before the motion can be withdrawn.[30] Although the mover of a motion loses exclusive power over it when a question on it is proposed, the mover's presence is still necessary if a motion is to be withdrawn by leave, whether at this or any later stage in the proceedings.[31] Even though the mover cannot kill the motion unilaterally after this stage, he or she retains the right to keep it alive.

---

[28]   S.O.99(1).
[29]   S.O.99(2).
[30]   1887, Vol.58, p.392.
[31]   1891, Vol.72, p.398.

CHAPTER 16

DEBATE

Following the proposing of the question on a motion, the issue is usually, but not invariably, thrown open for general debate. There are many types of motion which are not debatable at all and which even the mover of the motion cannot speak to. The House has decided that decisions on certain procedural questions must be made at once, without any debate. But each question proposed to the House is inherently debatable unless this right has expressly been taken away by the Standing Orders.

DEBATE ARISES AFTER QUESTION PROPOSED
Where the right of debate has not been prohibited, the one member who is unable to speak to the motion after the question on it has been proposed is the mover of the motion. The mover's time to speak is now over. A speech in support of a motion by the mover can be made only before the Speaker proposes the question. On sitting down, the mover's speaking rights are terminated and, the question having been proposed, the other members of the House now have the opportunity to speak to it.

In general, each member may speak only once to a question before the House.[1] The main exception to this is in committee where members may speak more than once, but there are other exceptions which are noted as appropriate. A new question or questions may arise during the course of a debate by the moving of an amendment or amendments, and members have a right to speak once to each such new question, even though they may have already spoken to the original or main question.[2] Members may also speak again in debate to correct a misrepresentation of their speech by a subsequent speaker.[3] (See Chapter 19.)

RESTRICTIONS ON THE LENGTH OF DEBATE
All debates in the House are subject to some time restraint. Time limits on speeches have been a part of parliamentary procedure since 1894. Before that, individual members were unrestricted in the length of time they could address the House – the record length of speech being that of Mr W L Rees, who spoke for some 24 hours in 1876 in a debate on whether the members of the Government were disqualified from membership of the House. The adoption of time limits at the end of the nineteenth century obviated for some time the necessity to adopt the more draconian procedures that the United Kingdom House of Commons was then forced to countenance in the face of obstruction by Irish members. But the House of Representatives with its highly developed system of restrictions on the length of debates now has a more formidable array of weapons available against deliberate time-wasting or obstruction than do most other legislatures. The restrictions that are employed are of two general types: those which impose time limits – whether on the length of a member's speech in a particular debate or the length of the whole debate – and those which limit the number of speeches that can be made in a particular debate. Usually these restrictions are employed concurrently.

---

[1] S.O.105.
[2] S.O.127.
[3] S.O.106(1).

TIME LIMITS

Individual speeches

Time limiting individual speeches was the original type of time restriction adopted in 1894. Appendix A of the Standing Orders sets out a comprehensive list of individual speaking times on particular debates.[4] In addition, the Business Committee has power to determine the speaking times of individual members on an item of business.[5] The committee may use this power in respect of a particular debate to be held in the House or in respect of all debates of a particular class. In both the forty-sixth and forty-seventh Parliaments, for example, it decided to vary the speaking times on the debate on the introduction of all Members' bills to accommodate the general time limits to the particular party alignments of those Parliaments.[6] There is a general rule that each member is entitled to speak for 10 minutes except where expressly provided to the contrary. But Appendix A does expressly provide for the time to speak in so many instances that falling back on this rule is the exception. To determine how long a member may speak to the question before the House, it is necessary to consider the type of debate involved. The shortest period allowed for an individual speech is five minutes (two minutes are permitted for a Minister to reply to comments on a ministerial statement), while the longest allowed an ordinary member is 15 minutes. The Minister of Finance in delivering the Budget and the Prime Minister in making the Prime Minister's statement are not limited in time at all, and extended times are prescribed for party leaders in other debates. The time limit of a speech on an amendment is the same as that on the original motion. Time taken up in interpreting a member's speech (whether the interpretation is rendered by the member or the official interpreter) is not counted against the time for the member to speak.[7]

The Speaker (in committee, the chairperson) is responsible for drawing the attention of members to when their permitted speaking time is up. This is done by a short ring on an electric bell, the Speaker's chair and the Clerk's seat at the Table being equipped with timing devices for the purpose. In general, the warning bell is sounded five minutes before the end of a 15-, 20- or 30-minute speech and two minutes before the end of a 10-minute speech. No warning bell is given in respect of a five-minute speech unless this is specifically requested. Other arrangements than these may be made if the member speaking or the whips desire them and the presiding officer agrees.

Time limits and points of order

As all individual speeches are limited in some way, members are jealous to protect their time from being eaten into by points of order (which are not speeches to a question and do not have a time limit of their own[8]). In general, a member has no right to claim an allowance for time lost in dealing with a point of order, but most Speakers do allow members extra time for such interruptions by not counting the time taken up on a point of order as part of the member's speech.[9] This is especially the case where the point of order is decided in favour of the member speaking. However, where points of order are raised because the member speaking is transgressing against the rules of the House, the Speaker might not be particularly generous in allowing extra speaking time in compensation.[10] A certain amount of flexibility is essential for the Speaker in this matter. On the one hand, if extra time were not allowed, a member's opponents could deny the member any speaking time at all by a constant series of spurious points of order. On the other hand, a member

---

[4]   S.O.117(1). References to speaking times are references to Appendix A of the Standing Orders.
[5]   S.O.76(d).
[6]   *Notice paper*, 29 March 2000; Business Committee determination, 17 September 2002.

[7]   1999, Vol.579, pp.17974-5.
[8]   1904, Vol.128, pp.175-6, 187.
[9]   1969, Vol.361, p.1146.
[10] 1962, Vol.330, pp.905-6.

who persists in speaking irrelevantly or using unparliamentary language cannot expect any concessions for time lost as a result of any disorder which ensues.

In committee, with its generally shorter speaking times, the practice has been for the clock to be stopped when a point of order is raised. The chairperson will subsequently decide whether the time occupied in determining the point of order is to be deducted from the speech. On the other hand, when the chairperson intervenes to point out that the member speaking is not being relevant, the clock is not stopped and the member loses that time.[11]

Time limits on the whole debate

There are a number of debates which have time limits imposed on them by specifying the number of hours that the debate may last. The Business Committee has power to vary these.[12] The debates subject to these time limits include the Address in Reply debate, the debate on the Prime Minister's statement and most financial debates, such as the Budget debate.

Where a debate is subject to a time limit, this time is taken to include any time expended on points of order arising during the course of debate, at least where those points of order arise directly out of that debate. So no extra time is added to the whole debate for time spent on points of order (time may be added to individual speeches made within the debate in accordance with the principles discussed above). Similarly, any time spent interpreting members' speeches is regarded as part of the debate and counts against the total time allowed for it.[13]

When the time allowed for a debate expires, the member speaking is immediately interrupted. There is no provision for an extension of the debate to permit that member's speech to be concluded.[14] Indeed, other members who might have expected to get the opportunity to speak may miss out altogether if a significant portion of debating time has been expended on points of order. In the case of the Budget debate, where there is provision for the Minister to speak in reply to the debate, the debate is interrupted 10 minutes before it is due to conclude and the Minister is given the opportunity to speak in reply.

RESTRICTIONS ON THE NUMBER OF SPEAKERS

In respect of most debates, except those subject to the overall time limits discussed above, there are restrictions on the number of speeches that may be made in the debate. This is the case, for example, with debates on the various stages of bills. Generally 12 speeches are allowed for each debate, although on the first reading of Members', private or local bills only seven speeches are permitted.

In such debates, even if a member does not use all of the individual speaking time available to the member, no extra speeches are allowed. This contrasts with debates that are subject to a simple time limit where time saved by individual members in speaking may permit more members to participate in the debate.

CALL

There are 120 members of the House. One, the Speaker, presides and does not take part in the debate. Another, the mover, has concluded his or her speech when the debate is thrown open to other members. There are, therefore, 118 potential candidates for the

---

11   1992, Vol.524, p.7893.
12   S.O.76(b).
13   1999, Vol.579, p.18503.
14   1986, Vol.472, p.3096.

privilege of speaking to the question before the House. In most cases the real number of potential speakers is likely to be much lower than this, because not all members will be present or will wish to take part in every debate. Only on the Address in Reply, Prime Minister's statement and Budget debates will significant numbers of members of the House participate in a debate. Even so, priorities of speaking in debate must be resolved. This is largely the job of the Business Committee and party whips within the framework of the House's rules on the order of calling members in debate.

Obtaining the call

When a member wishes to speak to a question, that member must rise and call to the Speaker. Once the Speaker has recognised the member by name the member has the floor and may proceed to speak.[15] If there is more than one member seeking the call, the Speaker exercises a discretion as to which of those members is selected to speak, and the member selected is then entitled to speak.[16] Such a rule of Speaker's discretion could continue to operate in a completely arbitrary fashion, with each member trying to "catch the Speaker's eye" but being entirely ignorant of what criteria (if any) the Speaker employed when making the decision as to who will be next to speak. In fact, the Standing Orders, Speakers' rulings and practices devised by the Business Committee have laid down ground rules for the exercise of this discretion of calling members to speak. Members are thus able to predict, fairly accurately, how the Speaker will exercise the discretion to call members in any particular instance.

Allocation of calls

Until the development of a multi-party environment with the change to the electoral system, New Zealand had had a two-party system in the House for some 60 years. In these circumstances the principle applied by Speakers in allocating calls to speak in debate was that contributions to a debate alternated between the two sides of the House.[17]

Vestiges of this principle are still applied in deciding on the allocation of calls, but in a Parliament with a number of different parties represented it is obviously no longer sufficient on its own as a criterion for the Speaker. Furthermore, the strength of party organisation in the House has led to a greater recognition of the party representative nature of a member's contribution to debate and the consequent need to recognise this explicitly in the rules. As a result, a new set of criteria to guide the Speaker in allocating calls was adopted in 1995 and set out in the Standing Orders.[18] The Speaker takes account of these criteria, but ultimately it is the Speaker's decision as to whom to call to speak in any particular instance. If, for instance, the call is given to a member by the Speaker in misapplication of those criteria, it cannot be taken away (although the member may, in these circumstances, voluntarily surrender it).[19] On the other hand, if a member who has been called does not have speaking rights at all because he or she has already spoken in the debate, the call is invalidly given and the Speaker will terminate the member's speech on becoming aware of this fact.[20]

Factors guiding the Speaker

In addition to the vestigial influence of the principle of calls alternating between the two sides of a question, there are four other factors that the Standing Orders require the Speaker to take into account in deciding whom to call to speak.[21]

---

[15] 1987, Vol.479, p.7804.
[16] S.O.101.
[17] 1936, Vol.245, p.279; 1948, Vol.280, p.597.
[18] S.O.102.
[19] 1991, Vol.516, p.2899.
[20] 1998, Vol.574, p.14422.
[21] S.O.102.

If possible, a member of each party should be able to speak in each debate
It is desirable that at least one member of each party should (if they wish) be able to
participate in each debate that is held. But, as recognised by the Standing Order, this will
not always be possible. On the first reading of Members', private and local bills only six
members can speak. In many other debates only 12 members can do so. Small parties and
independent members cannot expect to be represented in every debate. An independent
member, in particular, is regarded as $1/120^{th}$ of the House and this will guide the Speaker
in determining when to give the call to an independent, though that member's expertise
and particular interest in the subject under debate will also weigh in the balance.[22]

*Overall participation in a debate should be approximately proportional to party
membership in the House*
Party proportionality in participation in each debate is also desirable. But again only
very approximate effect can be given to this criterion, especially given the desire to be as
inclusive as possible in respect of party participation in a debate.

*Priority should be given to party spokespersons in order of size of party membership in
the House*
The leading spokesperson for each party should be called as early as possible in each
debate. This guides the order in which parties are given an opportunity to participate in
debates in the House.

*The seniority of members and the interests and expertise of individual members who wish
to speak*
The seniority of members and their interests and expertise come into play in the longer
debates such as the Budget and the Address in Reply debates and in debates on conscience
issues which are not being conducted along party lines. In the latter, the Speaker exercises
a more obvious discretion as to whom to call. But generally it is a matter for each party
to determine who represents it in any particular debate.[23]

Party arrangements

Allied with the factors guiding the Speaker in deciding how to exercise the discretion to
call members in a debate, is likely to be a set of arrangements between the parties as to
the sequence in which party members will be called. Indeed, if such arrangements do not
exist, the Speaker may suggest that they be devised so that members understand reasonably
accurately when they will be called upon to speak. Consequently, lists determining the
order in which parties will be called to speak on the various stages of bills are prepared
under the Speaker's direction. These differ depending upon the party make up of each
Parliament. They are adapted if party numbers change within the term of a Parliament.
The Business Committee too has the power to determine how the time for debate on an
item of business is to be allocated among the parties represented in the House.[24] It does
this consistently with the Wednesday general debate by approving a roster for several
weeks ahead setting out a sequential allocation of the speaking slots to be given to each
party in each debate. Parties may exchange these slots among themselves as is convenient
to them.

Apart from lists prepared by the Speaker and formal determinations by the Business

---

[22] 1998, Vol.574, p.14109.   [24] S.O.76(c).
[23] 2002, Vol.599, p.15690.

Committee, the party whips will often draw up speaking lists for longer debates. The Speaker will invariably follow these in giving the call. These pre-arrangements of speaking slots are seen as being a more efficient use of members' time than competing for a call in the Chamber at random. But the fact that a member is not on a party's speaking list does not deprive that member of the right to seek the call. On the other hand, the fact that almost all debates in the House are subject to some limitation rules means that not all members can speak on every occasion that they wish to. In this regard the Speaker will endeavour to see that each member gets a fair opportunity to speak while, at the same time, being fair to other members.[25]

Splitting calls

An individual speaking time (whether in a debate subject to an overall time limit or a debate for which there are a limited number of calls) may be shared between two members of the same party or between two members of different parties if both parties agree.[26] A party or the parties which wish to utilise this right inform the Speaker in advance and the Speaker in calling the first of the two members to speak in turn informs the House that the call is to be shared. Where members have shared a call in this way each is regarded as having spoken in the debate and cannot speak again.

Leave has been given for a member to complete the interrupted speech of another member who, because of illness, was not able to complete it herself.[27] The member completing the speech was not regarded as having spoken in the debate.

Speaking in the committee of the whole House

The criteria for the allocation of speeches in the House apply also to speeches in the committee of the whole House. But, in committee, members can speak more than once to the same question and debates are not subject to the overall restrictions in length that apply in the House.

MANNER OF SPEAKING

Physical arrangements for speaking

Members are allocated individual seats in the Chamber. While they are expected to address the House from those allocated positions, there is no rule requiring this and members may speak from another seat within the seating allocated to their party that is unoccupied at the time[28] or even come to the Table for the purpose.[29] The Minister or member in charge of a bill in committee, for instance, always speaks from a position at the Table immediately on the chairperson's right. Other members frequently speak from a position closer to the presiding officer's chair than their own seat, especially in committee.

Members must stand to speak in debate. But the Speaker may permit a member to speak from a sitting position if that member cannot conveniently stand by reason of sickness or infirmity.

---

[25]   1992, Vol.530, p.11440.
[26]   S.O.117(2).
[27]   2001, Vol.592, p.9608.

[28]   2000, Vol.586, p.4768.
[29]   1990, Vol.505, p.666; 1990, Vol.510, p.3560.

Forms of address

In debate a member addresses the Speaker, and the House only indirectly through the Speaker.[30] Members do not address each other directly. The origins of this practice are obscure, but it does, to some extent, assist in restraining quarrels or personal recriminations in the House by figuratively interposing the Speaker between members. Members may not address each other directly in the second person.[31] According to the rules of the House, references to "you" are taken to be directed at the Speaker and will be ruled out of order, for it is not in order to involve the Speaker in the debate.

It was formerly a rule that members could not refer to each other by their names but this rule was abolished when half of the House came to be elected from party lists and so had no electorates by which they could be referred.[32] Consequently, members can now refer to each other by name (or by electorate or position held if preferred). But this does not authorise total familiarity. A full name, title or position should be used, not just a member's given or Christian name.[33] Nicknames are not permitted as a form of address,[34] nor may members assign a title to a member's name.[35]

Debate in the House is a discussion among the members of the House present in the Chamber.[36] Unlike in select committees, where non-members of the House take part in the proceedings, only members take part in debates. For this reason members may not address remarks to,[37] or refer to the presence of,[38] persons in the gallery nor address persons outside the House.[39] The latter include persons listening to the radio broadcast of parliamentary debates. Members must address the Chair, not the "listener".[40]

LANGUAGES

English and Māori

Members may speak in English or in Māori.[41] Most contributions to debate are made in English, but to an increasing extent Māori is being used both in the Chamber and in committees, especially at the Māori Affairs Committee. The use of Māori in the Chamber is not by any means new. The first speech in Māori was made (through an interpreter) in 1868[42] and many Māori members spoke in Māori in the nineteenth and early twentieth centuries. The practice then was for the member to give his own interpretation or for an interpreter authorised by the Speaker to interpret the speech standing alongside the member for this purpose. As Māori was not at that time an official language, no extra speaking time was allowed to the member for the time spent interpreting a speech.

Interpretation

Māori was given official recognition in the House in 1985 and members have the right to use either language and are not obliged to give an interpretation of their remarks.[43] However, as not all members have competence in Māori an interpretation of speeches in Māori is provided. In many cases the member speaking Māori will provide this himself or herself, being entitled to speak for the extra time that this entails.[44] In these circumstances, no second interpretation of the speech is given by the official interpreter.[45] Members

---

30   S.O.103.
31   1996, Vol.554, p.12339.
32   1993-96, AJHR, I.18A, pp.25-6.
33   1996, Vol.553, p.11403; 1998, Vol.571, p.11820.
34   2002, Vol.599, p.15220; 2003, Vol.607, p.4164.
35   2000, Vol.585, p.3755.
36   1971, Vol.374, p.3410.
37   1997, Vol.562, p.3215.

38   1934, Vol.238, p.68; 2000, Vol.585, p.3764.
39   1976, Vol.405, p.1704.
40   1971, Vol.375, p.3495.
41   S.O.104.
42   1868, Vol.2, p.270.
43   1990, Vol.508, p.2336.
44   1999, Vol.579, pp.17974-5.
45   2001, Vol.593, p.9983.

who do give an interpretation of their speeches must be careful to do so accurately, otherwise they may be accused of deliberately misleading the House.[46] A member who gave an inaccurate interpretation of his remarks has cleared this up by way of a personal statement.[47] Otherwise an interpretation is given under the control of the Speaker. It can be given by anyone in whom the Speaker has confidence – even another member.[48]

But for the purpose of providing official interpretations interpreters are engaged by the Office of the Clerk. The official interpretation is given from a position immediately to the left of the Speaker after the member has finished speaking or pauses in the course of a speech.

An interpretation is not a polished version of what a member has said. It will always be somewhat rough and ready.[49] Given the different origins of the Māori and English languages there will always be differences over how to render one language into the other.[50]

The object of the interpretation is to enable members to have a reasonable, but not necessarily total, understanding of what is said. If the member speaking does not agree with the interpretation he or she is at liberty to give the member's own interpretation or clear up a misunderstanding on a point of order, but that member cannot control the interpretation that is given by the official interpreter. Such control is exercised by the Speaker on behalf of the House. Members often pause at relatively short intervals to allow the interpreter to give an interpretation but that is entirely over to them. If they speak for longer periods without a pause, the interpretation takes on more of the form of a summary of what they have said.[51]

It is not considered necessary to interpret from English into Māori.[52]

The interpretation in the House is the oral rendering of words used in debate in Māori into English.[53] The interpreter is not a translator providing an English version of documents written in Māori that may be relevant to the debate.[54] Translation is a different process and takes place off the floor of the House when a speech given in Māori is translated into English for inclusion in *Hansard*.

The interpreter, as a member of the staff of the Office of the Clerk, cannot be brought into the debate or appealed to to give assurances to the House about the accuracy of translations of documents presented to the House by Ministers or other members[55] any more than could any other official be appealed to in the course of a debate about a matter in issue between members.

Other languages

Only English and Māori have the status of official languages in the House, but other languages are used from time to time. This is particularly common in a member's maiden speech when Polynesian, Chinese, Dutch and other languages with a particular cultural or familial significance to the new member may be used. In these circumstances the members concerned provide their own interpretation and translation of the language that they have spoken.

Special arrangements have been made to employ sign language interpreters in the Chamber when a debate of particular significance to the deaf and hearing-affected community has been held.[56]

Occasionally, members employ foreign phrases in a speech. These may be French

---

46   *Ibid.*
47   2004, Vol.615, pp.11408, 11495.
48   2002, Vol.605, p.2886.
49   2002, Vol.603, p.982.
50   2004, Vol.615, p.11496.
51   1999, Vol.579, p.18503.

52   *Ibid.*; 2000, Vol.585, p.3716.
53   2005, Vol.623, pp.18734-5.
54   *Ibid.*, p.18731.
55   *Ibid.*, p.18739.
56   "Sign of the times", *The Dominion Post*, 23 June 2004 (*New Zealand Sign Language Bill*).

or Latin phrases that have not been fully absorbed into English. These are permitted in the course of debate and are treated in *Hansard* as terms of art, being published without any translation.

CONTENTS OF SPEECHES

In this section the rules which govern what a member may say, rather than how the member may say it, are examined.

Subject to these rules, how members use the call that has been given to them is a matter for them. They have absolute freedom of speech in debate and must exercise their own judgment as to how they use it. For instance, there is no rule that members must observe privacy principles,[57] though in practice members will often take care not to reveal personal details where this is inappropriate.

Relevance

The overriding principle as to what may be said is that all debate must be relevant to the question before the House.[58] Nevertheless, the particular rules detailed below – unparliamentary language, issues before the courts, and so on – are instances of material which is out of order despite the fact that it may be relevant and, therefore, on the face of it suitable for inclusion in a speech. In these cases, even though it is relevant, the particular reference is not permitted on other grounds of parliamentary policy.

What is relevant depends exclusively on the question before the House and whether the argument being advanced would make the House more likely or less likely to accede to it. In a few debates – notably the Address in Reply and Budget debates – the concept of what is relevant is virtually boundless. In these debates members may introduce almost anything without fear of being ruled irrelevant. With other debates the field is much narrower. At each stage of the passage of legislation, the concept of relevancy changes as the purpose of the House's consideration of the legislation changes. The question of relevancy is further considered as each different type of debate is looked at elsewhere in this work.

If a member persists in advancing irrelevant arguments the Speaker may, after publicly warning the member, terminate the speech.[59] The Speaker may also terminate the speech of a member who persists in repeating arguments which, though relevant, have been advanced earlier in the member's own speech or by other members in the debate.[60] This is known as "tedious repetition". An argument becomes tediously repetitive only if the Speaker serves notice that its repetition will be regarded as being so. In the absence of such a warning from the Speaker, the fact that other members find a member's speech tedious is immaterial.

Anticipating discussion

Members are not entitled to anticipate discussion of general business or an order of the day until that business or order is properly reached.[61]

In administering the rule against anticipating discussion, the Speaker must have regard to the likelihood of the business or order actually coming before the House for debate within a reasonable time.[62] If it is not likely to come on for debate in the near future, the Speaker may permit references to it. Applying this discretion, the Speaker has permitted

---

[57]   2003, Vol.612, p.8966; 2005, Vol.626, p.21195.
[58]   S.O.107(1).
[59]   S.O.107(2).
[60]   *Ibid.*
[61]   S.O.109(1).
[62]   S.O.109(2).

references to a select committee report on an alleged Budget leak, the debate on which had been adjourned and set down for resumption on a future day, after the Prime Minister was reported as saying that he did not intend to provide government time for the debate to be resumed. The Speaker concluded from this statement that there was no likelihood that the House would debate the matter again within a reasonable time, if at all, and, therefore, permitted members to refer to it although it was technically anticipating discussion.[63]

Quotations

Members are permitted to use quotations to illustrate or support points that they wish to make in the course of their speeches. Formerly a restrictive view of quotations was taken. Members were expected to give their own views on the measure under debate and the quotation of outside comment on the matter under discussion was prohibited. This is no longer the practice. Quotations are permitted provided that they are relevant to the subject of debate and are themselves inherently in order. Quotations must be as free from unparliamentary language as a member's own words;[64] indeed, effectively a member makes a quotation his or her own by incorporating it into the member's speech. So no improper reflections on another member can be made by means of a quotation from a letter or a newspaper.[65]

Members are under no obligation to disclose the source of a quotation used in debate[66] except when they quote from *Hansard*. In the latter case they must give the volume and page numbers from which they are quoting.[67] Similarly, members cannot be required to quote accurately or fully (although they must beware of deliberately misleading the House). Members naturally choose that portion of an article which best serves their argument and they are not obliged to read other portions which might not be so favourable, even in the face of the urgings of their opponents in the House.[68]

Official documents quoted

If a Minister, in the course of a speech, quotes from an official document, any member can require the Minister to lay that document on the Table.[69] The Minister is then obliged to table the document unless it is of a confidential nature. (See Chapter 38.) There is no obligation on members who are not Ministers to table a document from which they have quoted.[70]

References to the Sovereign or the Governor-General

Members must not use the names of the Sovereign or the Governor-General disrespectfully in debate or for the purpose of influencing the House in its deliberations.[71] This rule does not strictly apply to a Governor-General designate, such references being a question of taste. References to the Sovereign's representatives in her other realms are not excluded from debate, so references to actions of the Governor-General of Australia at the time of that country's constitutional crisis in 1975 did not contravene the rule.[72]

References to proceedings of a committee

References to the confidential proceedings of a committee are prohibited until those proceedings are reported to the House.[73] Effectively, this (at least temporarily) prevents references to what takes place at a select committee during consideration and deliberation and during the hearing of private or secret evidence. (Committees of the whole House

---

[63]   1977, Vol.412, p.2020.
[64]   1899, Vol.106, p.105.
[65]   1898, Vol.102, p.70; 1974, Vol.391, p.2467.
[66]   1970, Vol.367, p.1865.
[67]   1960, Vol.325, p.2959.
[68]   1973, Vol.383, p.1853.

[69]   S.O.368.
[70]   1972, Vol.381, p.2706.
[71]   S.O.114.
[72]   1976, Vol.403, p.689.
[73]   S.O.110.

conduct all of their business in public.) But this rule does not prevent a member referring to a bill or other business just because it happens to be before a select committee. It is information given to the committee in confidence and discussions at the committee among the members themselves behind closed doors that may not be referred to. The committee's public proceedings can be referred to if they are relevant to the matter before the House. Once the committee has reported, all of its proceedings (except secret evidence) can be referred to.

UNPARLIAMENTARY LANGUAGE

As well as the more technical rules already described, the House's debates are regulated in respect of matters which might otherwise be regarded as suitable to be left to the taste or discretion of individual members. Expressions used in debate may be ruled to be "unparliamentary" and be required by the Speaker to be withdrawn. The rules against unparliamentary language are designed to prevent personal invective and insults, and while they do not totally eliminate such exchanges, they do restrain members and provide a framework within which members' speeches can be judged and controlled. Members have absolute privilege in the law of defamation for words uttered by them in debate. No legal redress is possible to persons, whether other members or persons outside the House, who are defamed during a parliamentary debate, regardless of the motive of the member who made the statement. While a form of response is now possible, it behoves members to use this privilege of free speech responsibly, and one control mechanism which operates is the prohibition on the use of unparliamentary language. (See Chapter 39 for responses.)

Offensive or disorderly words

Members are not permitted to use any offensive words against the House.[74] In addition, the Speaker is required to intervene whenever any offensive or disorderly words are used in the Chamber, whether by the member speaking in the debate, or by another member by way of interjection or other comment.[75] In respect of comments which a member may make to a neighbour, it does not matter that it was not intended that the Chair (or another member, if another member objects and brings it to the Chair's attention) should hear what was said. If it is heard, it is within the jurisdiction of the Speaker, and if it is offensive or disorderly it must be withdrawn.

What is offensive or disorderly? There are some specific types of references which the Standing Orders hold to be unparliamentary – personal reflections and imputations of improper motives. These might equally be regarded as being offensive or disorderly; indeed, it may be very difficult to determine under which precise provision of the Standing Orders an expression is being ruled out of order.

Whether a particular phrase is offensive or disorderly depends upon the context in which it is used, and an expression acceptable in one context may be unacceptable in another.[76] A list of expressions ruled out of order each year is printed in the index to *Hansard*, as is a list of those expressions which have been challenged but allowed by the Chair to stand. Most such expressions will be found to be references to other members or parties. These may have been ruled to be unparliamentary because they could lead to disorder in the House, or because they are offensive in themselves, or because they are personal reflections.

---

74 S.O.113.
75 S.O.115.
76 1984, Vol.459, p.2273.

In determining whether an expression is disorderly or offensive, Speakers take account of the state of the House at the time it is uttered. The Chair does not like to be constantly intervening in a debate any more than a referee likes to be continually whistling up a football match. If the advantage rule can be applied to both pursuits, it will be. However, where there is a real chance that disorder will arise if a statement is allowed to pass, the Speaker will take action.[77]

Personal reflections

The Standing Orders specifically prohibit imputations of improper motives against a member, offensive references to a member's private affairs and all personal reflections.[78]

Imputations of improper motives cover allegations of any form of corruption. Members have a duty to expose anything in the nature of bribery or corruption on the part of other members, but they must not do this by making veiled suggestions in the course of debate.[79] Such allegations must be brought forward by giving notice of motion charging the member unequivocally with impropriety. Everything must be out in the open in the same way as must criticism of a judge, if such charges are to be bandied about in the House.

References to a member's private affairs are not automatically out of order. They are debarred only if they are strongly undesirable, insulting or offensive.[80] However, in judging whether something is offensive, the Chair will be guided to some extent by the reactions of the member to whom the remark is directed.[81] If that member does not object to it, it will generally be allowed to pass. Often, of course, personal references may be irrelevant to the question before the House, but, if relevant, reference may be made to a member's occupation or profession,[82] age or marital status,[83] or property,[84] provided this is not done in an insulting or injurious way. The Speaker generally prefers to discourage such references, however, as they tend to reduce the standard of debate, and repeated references could provoke retaliation and lead to disorder in the House.[85]

It is a well-established rule that members should not question the conduct or character of another member's spouse, partner or family member except where a member introduces his or her own spouse's, partner's or family member's conduct into the debate.[86] But if a spouse, partner or family member holds a political, commercial or public position separate from the relationship to a member, they may be referred to in debate. In these circumstances members must distinguish between quoting the spouse, partner or family member because of a position they hold and quoting them in the capacity of their personal relationship to the member.[87]

In each case in which a personal reflection is made the Speaker will rule it out of order if the member against whom it is directed objects. Otherwise, it would be ruled out of order only if it was offensive on the face of it.[88] An accusation of racism, for example, falls into this latter category and will invariably be ruled out of order if used to describe a member or party.[89]

Accusations of lying

It is a clear personal reflection to accuse another member of lying or of attempting deliberately to mislead the House.[90] Accusing a member of lying (whether the accusation relates to a lie alleged to have been told inside or outside the House) is a mode of

---

[77] 2000, Vol.584, p.3012.
[78] S.O.116.
[79] 1934, Vol.239, p.159.
[80] 1966, Vol.346, p.267.
[81] 1989, Vol.502, p.13428.
[82] 1913, Vol.163, p.870.
[83] 1969, Vol.364, p.3705.
[84] 1959, Vol.319, p.500.
[85] 1969, Vol.364, p.3273.
[86] 1938, Vol.252, pp.194-6.
[87] 1989, Vol.503, p.13892.
[88] 1997, Vol.564, p.4716.
[89] 1998, Vol.568, p.8393; 2001, Vol.595, p.11665.
[90] 1927, Vol.214, p.112.

expression that has been consistently ruled out of order.[91] If an accusation that a member had deliberately misled the House was correct, the member would have committed a contempt, and a member who believes that another member has misled or tried to mislead the House should raise this as a matter of privilege. That a member must not accuse another of lying does not mean that the correctness of that other's statements may not be questioned and it is in order to accuse a member of having misled the country.[92] But, while a member is at liberty to criticise another member, a member cannot (in debate) accuse another member of having made a statement (on any occasion) knowing it to be incorrect or untrue or impute a deliberate untruth to another member.[93]

References to the absence of a member

It is a convention of the House that members do not refer to the absence of other members from the Chamber (whether at that time or on a previous occasion).[94] This is not an absolute rule and can be overridden if the fact of absence is of sufficient importance to warrant reference to it.[95] This can occur if there is something intrinsic to the absence that makes it necessary to refer to it. But this does not mean that any member has the right to override the convention as a matter of choice. It is for the Speaker to decide whether such a reference is justified. It is not a breach of the convention to refer to the fact that a member did not speak in a particular debate[96] or to urge a member to take part in the debate currently under way.[97]

The convention also applies to references to the absence of members from a meeting of a select committee,[98] but a reference to the fact that a member was not a member of a particular committee and so did not attend its hearings is permissible.[99]

References to parties

The examples discussed above have been mainly of unparliamentary expressions directed at individual members, but many unparliamentary expressions are directed at groups of members – the Government or parties. It was ruled many years ago that as the Government consists of members of Parliament, a term cannot be applied to the Government which cannot be applied to members individually.[100] The Government was the first group within the House to have this principle extended to it, for it was the first group to coalesce within the House, but the principle extends equally to other groups or parties. Thus, allegations of corruption on the part of the Government or a party and offensive terms applied to a party are just as disorderly as allegations against or an offensive term applied to an individual member.[101] Allegations must be brought forward, if at all, in a formal motion.[102]

A type of allegation to which parties are particularly prone – although such an allegation against one member raises the same issues – is an allegation of outside domination by an influential group in the country such as farmers, trade unions or the brewing industry. In carrying out their parliamentary duties, members must be free to act in the best interests of the country as a whole, and suggestions of domination or direction from outside are unacceptable,[103] though, of course, members receive advice and are lobbied by sectional interests outside the House and, no doubt, take this into account in forming their opinions. A fine line has been drawn between suggestions that a party has been influenced in the policy it is pursuing by an outside body, which is in order, and a suggestion that it is being

---

[91]   1985, Vol.465, p.6716.
[92]   1995, Vol.546, p.6088.
[93]   1952, Vol.298, p.1188.
[94]   1961, Vol.329, pp.3168-9.
[95]   1970, Vol.368, p.3004.
[96]   1979, Vol.426, p.3220.
[97]   2000, Vol.583, p.2030.
[98]   1979, Vol.423, p.1143.
[99]   1985, Vol.462, p.4221.
[100]   1905, Vol.134, p.447.
[101]   1914, Vol.171, p.603; 2005, Vol.624, p.19625.
[102]   1892, Vol.76, pp.15-6.
[103]   1952, Vol.297, pp.475, 889.

dictated to by that body, which is not in order.[104] The term "pressure" is right on this line; any stronger term than this is regarded as insulting to members of the party at which it is directed, and is not permitted.[105]

References to persons outside the House

In general, there is nothing to prevent a member commenting in severe terms on the conduct of persons outside the House, though this may be done only if it is relevant to the debate before the House.[106] Indeed, it is the purpose of the absolute privilege of members to permit them to speak out freely where this is necessary in the public interest. Members have been exhorted to use this privilege responsibly with regard to persons who are unable to defend themselves in the Chamber or to vindicate their honour in a court of law, but largely this is left to the good sense of members themselves. However, if a reference to a person outside the House is regarded as so insulting by a section of the House that, were it to stand unchallenged, it might provoke disorder, that would be a ground for requiring it to be withdrawn.

Persons who claim to be adversely affected by a reference to them in the House may apply to the Speaker to have a response put before the House. (See Chapter 39.)

Withdrawal of unparliamentary language

If the Speaker considers an expression to be unparliamentary, the usual course of action is to direct the member to withdraw it. If the expression has been grossly insulting towards another member or if the member who has been ordered to withdraw is contumacious, the Speaker may also require that the member apologise to the House for the conduct. When ordered to withdraw a statement, a member must withdraw the expression without qualification or reservation.[107] If the member adds any words while withdrawing, the withdrawal is qualified and does not satisfy the Speaker's requirement.[108] Similarly, if a member is required to apologise, unless required to apologise in a certain way (for example, to refer to the injured member), the apology must be made without qualification.[109] When the Speaker has ordered a member to withdraw certain words and this has been done to the Speaker's satisfaction, those words are said to cease to exist and cannot be further alluded to by that member or by members speaking subsequently in the debate.[110] But because words have been withdrawn does not mean that they are expunged from the record. As they have actually been uttered they may be reported by the news media, for example. The words cease to exist for the purposes of debate in the House only, which continues with its business without further reference to them.[111]

If the Speaker considers that a member's conduct during a debate has been grossly disorderly and that the mere withdrawal and apology for an expression which has been used would not adequately reflect the gravity of the transgression, there are further disciplinary powers, such as ordering the member to leave the Chamber or naming the member, which may be invoked. (See Chapter 11.)

MATTERS CONCERNING THE ADMINISTRATION OF JUSTICE

The relationship between the House of Representatives and the judiciary is of the highest constitutional significance. It should be, and in general is, marked by mutual respect and

---

[104]   1979, Vol.428, pp.4742-3.
[105]   1968, Vol.357, pp.2376-7.
[106]   1979, Vol.424, p.2294.
[107]   1891, Vol.74, p.788.
[108]   1975, Vol.397, pp.1346-7.
[109]   *Ibid.*
[110]   1900, Vol.115, p.159.
[111]   1983, Vol.453, p.3018; 2000, Vol.585, p.3362.

restraint. Running through the concomitant practices of the judiciary and the legislature is the principle that what is under adjudication or discussion before one should not be discussed or adjudicated on by the other.[112] This does not mean that the same subject might not arise for resolution in a legal and in a political context. This may occur. But neither branch of government should thereby be led into reflecting on or criticising the actions of the other. They should respect their respective spheres.

On their part, the courts will not permit any challenge to be made to what is said or done within the House in performance of its legislative functions and protection of its established privileges.[113] Nor is it considered appropriate for courts to issue gratuitous criticisms of parliamentary proceedings.[114]

On the House's part, it has adopted a number of rules designed to maintain respect for the judiciary and to avoid members causing prejudice to any judicial proceedings that may be pending. Apart from these specific rules, members are required to exercise their privilege of free speech in Parliament responsibly and to respect the position of the judiciary in the judiciary's sphere of action, just as they would expect the judiciary to respect the privileges of Parliament.[115]

Unbecoming references to judges

Members are not permitted to use unbecoming words against any member of the judiciary.[116] This rule applies to the judge's conduct in presiding in court or when heading a Royal Commission or a Commission of Inquiry.[117] A succession of Speakers have held that members must not reflect on or speak disrespectfully of a judge.[118] This might occur, for example, by linking a particular court with the Government of the day – a clear case of questioning its impartiality – and this is not allowed to pass without intervention from the Chair.[119] A distinction must be drawn between disagreement with, and criticism of, a judgment delivered by a court on the one hand, and allegations directed at the judge that he or she has been consciously unfair or unjust on the other.[120] The House is the proper forum in which to consider the implications of a legal decision, and criticism may be made of the effects of a finding. There may also be criticism of a court system.[121] This is not only allowed; it is the duty of members, if they consider the public weal requires amendments to the judicial system, to advocate such changes. It is incumbent on the Speaker and members, however, to uphold the dignity of the judiciary and not to attack judges themselves.

Having said that, it is still the case that in exceptional circumstances the House does have a high constitutional duty to perform that would involve the criticism of a judge. To preserve the independence of the judiciary it is provided by law that a judge of the High Court (which includes all judges of the Supreme Court and the Court of Appeal) can be removed from office only by the Sovereign or the Governor-General, acting on an address from the House of Representatives.[122] In the exceptional case of such an address being moved in the House (and none ever has), the conduct of the judge concerned would be a relevant object of criticism. But if specific charges of such a nature as would call into question a judge's fitness to hold office are to be made in the House, they must be brought forward in a motion which can then be debated in the normal way.[123] Such charges cannot be made in the course of debate on another matter.

---

[112] 2001, Vol.590, pp.7802-3.
[113] *Prebble v Television New Zealand Ltd* [1994] 3 NZLR 1 at 7.
[114] *Hamilton v Al Fayed* [1999] 1 WLR 1569 at 1586 (per Lord Woolf MR).
[115] 1988, Vol.489, pp.4315-6, 4322.
[116] S.O.113.
[117] 1980, Vol.431, pp.1493-4.

[118] See for example: 1887, Vol.57, p.68; 1932, Vol.233, p.435.
[119] 1925, Vol.208, p.107.
[120] 1951, Vol.294, p.328.
[121] 1927, Vol.212, p.479.
[122] *Constitution Act* 1986, s.23.
[123] 1932, Vol.233, p.435.

Sub judice *rule*

The Standing Orders prohibit reference in any debate to any matters awaiting or under adjudication in a court from the time the case has been set down for trial or otherwise brought before the court, if it appears to the Speaker that there is a real and substantial danger of prejudice to the trial of the case.[124] This rule is commonly referred to as the "*sub judice* rule" and it also applies to such references in any motion or in any question to a Minister.

The purpose of the rule has been described as being to safeguard the interests of fundamental justice,[125] so that, for example, popular prejudice against a defendant is not excited through parliamentary statements. In the case of judge only and appellate proceedings it is extremely doubtful if any prejudice could arise from discussion of a case, whether in the House or elsewhere.[126] But there is another, and perhaps in a practical sense, more important strand to the rule. This is the implicit acknowledgment by the legislature that the proper forum in which to resolve legal disputes is the courts and that the legislature, above all other institutions, should take extreme care not to undermine confidence in the judicial resolution of disputes by intruding its views in individual cases. After all, if it is not satisfied with the outcome of the courts' resolution of a particular legal issue, Parliament always has the option of changing the law. In the *sub judice* rule the House applies more rigorous inhibitory standards to itself than is the case with news media reporting of judicial proceedings. This is not anomalous given the constitutional relationship between the House and the courts; the House and the news media are not in the same situation.[127] It is paralleled by the greater latitude that the news media has to criticise the House as compared to the courts.[128]

Scope of the sub judice *rule*

The House's *sub judice* rule takes effect in criminal cases from the moment a charge is made and in other cases from the time proceedings are initiated by filing the appropriate document in the registry or office of the court.[129] The restraint ceases when the verdict and sentence are announced or when judgment is given.[130] (It also ceases if the Attorney-General directs that summary proceedings be stayed, for in that circumstance there is no matter awaiting adjudication by a court.[131]) If notice of appeal is given, the restraint reapplies from the time of the notice until the appeal has been decided.[132] Preliminary inquiries by the police following a complaint being made to them cannot be excluded from comment if a legal action has not been instituted, but as soon as legal proceedings are commenced the rule applies.[133] Individual members cannot waive the application of the rule to legal proceedings in which they are involved.[134]

The *sub judice* rule applies only to matters before a court of record. Originally, a court of record was a court which maintained a record of its own proceedings. But the essential distinction between a court of record and other courts not of record came to be that a court of record possessed an inherent power to punish for contempt. In New Zealand the legislation which creates a court usually deals expressly with the question of whether the court is to be a court of record.

---

[124]   S.O.111(b).
[125]   1988, Vol.491, p.6244.
[126]   *In re Lonrho plc and others* [1990] 2 AC 154 at 209.
[127]   2003, Vol.609, p.6551; 2003, Vol.614, p.10353.
[128]   *Pepper v Hart* [1993] AC 593 at 638 (per Lord Browne-Wilkinson); *Hamilton v Al Fayed* [1999] 1 WLR 1569 at 1586 (per Lord Woolf MR).

[129]   S.O.112(1).
[130]   S.O.112(2).
[131]   *Summary Proceedings Act* 1957, s.77A(1).
[132]   S.O.112(3).
[133]   1975, Vol.400, p.3437.
[134]   1997, Vol.564, p.5239.

The following courts having jurisdiction in New Zealand are declared to be courts of record—

- Supreme Court[135]
- Court of Appeal[136]
- High Court[137]
- Courts Martial Appeal Court[138]
- Employment Court[139]
- Māori Appellate Court[140]
- Māori Land Court[141]
- Environment Court[142]
- District Courts (which include the Family Courts and Youth Courts)[143]

Reference to matters which are the subject of inquiry by a Royal Commission or a Commission of Inquiry is not out of order, as it is not a reference to a matter before a court of record.[144] Similarly, an inquiry by an Ombudsman is not within the scope of the rule.[145] Administrative tribunals set up under legislation to adjudicate on statutory rights created by the legislation are not courts of law at all.[146] Their proceedings do not fall within the scope of the *sub judice* rule.

Application of the sub judice *rule*

The House has not adopted a rule which leaves itself completely unable to intervene whenever a matter goes before a court, and the right – indeed the public duty – of the House to intervene in certain circumstances is recognised by the Standing Orders. The House expressly reserves to itself the right to legislate on any matter.[147] Notwithstanding the *sub judice* rule, a bill dealing expressly with litigation before a court may be introduced and proceeded with. The House's right to legislate on any matter is paramount.

Further, the *sub judice* rule is subject to the discretion of the Speaker.[148] This discretion is applied in the context of the purpose of the rule. The rule operates to ensure that nothing said in debate prejudices the decision of any court. It has been emphasised, for example, that it would be wrong to apply the *sub judice* rule to a generality of cases in such a way as to inhibit members in discussing penalties for offences. The House is not debarred from discussing possible or desirable penalties for drink or drug offences or any other type of offence merely because some cases involving such offences are currently before a court. To apply the Standing Order so generally would be to stultify debate in the House.[149] The law in general may be discussed, but not its application to a particular case that is before the court.[150] Where a Minister made a statement to the House of Commons about a finding that the Minister was in contempt of court,[151] the Speaker exercised his discretion to permit members to question the Minister on the statement, notwithstanding that notice of appeal against the finding had been lodged and the *sub judice* rule still applied.[152]

The *sub judice* rule is applied differently too depending upon the stage at which the matter under adjudication has reached. Thus all references to a criminal case are invariably excluded up to the point at which the verdict is reached. However, where only sentence is outstanding, while the rule continues to apply, there may be a less exclusionary

135   *Supreme Court Act* 2003, s.6.
136   *Judicature Act* 1908, s.57(1).
137   *Ibid.*, s.3(1).
138   *Courts Martial Appeals Act* 1953, s.4(6).
139   *Employment Relations Act* 2000, s.186(1).
140   *Te Ture Whenua Maori Act* 1993, s.50.
141   *Ibid.*, s.6(1).
142   *Resource Management Act* 1991, s.247.
143   *District Courts Act* 1947, s.3(1); *Family Courts Act* 1980, s.4; *Children, Young Persons, and Their Families Act* 1989, s.433.

144   1934, Vol.240, p.367.
145   1977, Vol.410, p.320.
146   *Proceedings Commissioner v Air New Zealand Limited* (1988) 7 NZAR 462 (Equal Opportunities Tribunal).
147   S.O.111.
148   *Ibid.*
149   1981, Vol.441, pp.3338-9.
150   1985, Vol.464, pp.5596, 5617.
151   *M v Home Office* [1992] QB 270.
152   House of Commons (UK) Debates (2 December 1991), vol.200, col.30.

approach. References to the case that do not obviously impinge on sentencing (such as, for example, the performance of other agencies involved with the convicted person or the victim) may be permitted in the interval between verdict and sentence.

There has been an increasing recognition in New Zealand, and in other Commonwealth legislatures with a similar rule, that judges are not so faint-hearted that any obscure remarks made in Parliament would cause them immediately to alter the judgment they would otherwise deliver in the case before them. Such a view would be grossly insulting to the judiciary. There is, nevertheless, a greater danger that remarks made in the House and widely reported could influence the minds of jurors engaged on a case. In administering the rule, Speakers have tried to adopt a realistic and worldly attitude by not excluding all discussion on matters of public interest merely because a court is seised of the matter, while maintaining the underlying purpose of the rule to avoid any real danger of prejudice to persons before a court and to maintain the separation of powers between the legislature and the judicature.

Other references to judges and judicial proceedings

Other questions affecting the relationship of the House and the judiciary do arise from time to time outside the categories of unbecoming references and the *sub judice* rule.

A particular instance is where judicial proceedings on a matter have concluded but the court has made an order for the suppression of the name of a party involved. Members have absolute privilege in the House for statements they make and cannot be held liable outside the House for a breach of such an order. But freedom of speech in Parliament is not a licence to flout the laws of the country. Members have been enjoined by the Speaker to treat their privilege of freedom of speech with the utmost respect and to use it only in the public interest. If a court has made a suppression of names order, this must be presumed to have been made for a good reason and should be observed by members unless the public interest impels them to act otherwise.[153] Ultimately, a member abusing the privilege of free speech in Parliament could be punished by the House itself if the abuse was serious enough for the House to treat it as a contempt. Further, documents tabled in the House will not (unless ordered by the House to be published) be distributed by the House authorities in contravention of an order of the court.[154]

Judges do appear before select committees from time to time to give evidence on matters with which they have a particular concern. In these circumstances there is no rule or convention which prevents members referring to the fact that a judge did appear before a committee.[155]

INTERJECTIONS

Strictly speaking, a member is entitled to be heard in silence.[156] A speech can be interrupted only by a point of order or a matter of privilege.[157] However, in practice, other members do not always sit listening to the member speaking in mute respect; they interject comments or questions of their own into the debate. This has become a well-established custom of the House, but interjectors do not have the floor, and the type and frequency of their interjections must be kept within bounds.

As an interjection is an attempt to contribute material to the debate, it is subject to all the rules that have already been discussed for the contents of members' speeches. An interjection must be relevant to the issue being debated. An irrelevant comment made

---

[153] 1988, Vol.489, p.4322; 1999, Vol.576, p.16210.
[154] 1994, Vol.539, p.470.
[155] 1984, Vol.457, p.477.
[156] 1932, Vol.231, p.362.
[157] S.O.132.

by way of interjection is disorderly and does not justify a reply from the member who is speaking.[158] The reason for permitting interjections at all is to enable members to elicit further information or to test the arguments being used by the member speaking. Interjections do not allow a member who does not have the floor to address arguments for or against the measure under discussion. Members can do this when called on to speak in their own right.[159] The Speaker will, therefore, often intervene if a member interjecting is tending to monopolise the time of the member speaking by putting forward arguments adverse to that member's views.

It has been said from the Chair that interjections must be "rare, reasonable and courteous" (although for "courteous", "witty" is tending to be substituted as a desideratum). A continuous series of interjections or a running commentary on a member's speech is out of order.[160] An interjection by way of contradiction is out of order,[161] as is a question to a member speaking to which that member takes exception.[162]

Members must stop interjecting when called to order by the Chair.[163] They may interject only from a seat in the Chamber, and must not make interjections while standing or leaving their seats or while moving around the Chamber. It is also disorderly for a member to change seats in order to facilitate interjection – for example, by moving nearer to the microphone of the member speaking or to a position more noticeable or distracting to that member.[164] Members have seats of their own in the Chamber but they often occupy another seat temporarily to discuss something with a colleague or even to speak in the debate from a seat nearer the Speaker's chair, and they may interject from any seat they happen to be sitting in, provided they did not move seats originally for that specific purpose. The occasional interjection from a member who is not sitting in his or her own seat may be passed off as being a subsidiary reason for sitting in that seat, but if the member embarks on a series of interjections the Speaker will be persuaded very soon that the member's motive for occupying the seat is the desire to interject, and the member will be ordered to stop interjecting or return to his or her own seat.[165]

Yielding

Another method of interjecting is the practice of yielding or giving way. This is based on the House of Commons practice whereby the interjector seeks to rise during the course of another member's speech with a question or comment relevant to a point made by that member. The member who has the floor may "give way" and resume his or her seat temporarily (or refuse to do so) so that the question can be asked or the comment made. The adoption of such a practice by members in the House of Representatives has been advocated occasionally.

If a member does yield to another, this can only be for the purpose of allowing the other to refer to matters raised by the member speaking. Yielding is a way of making an interjection, not a speech. It should only be for a brief period, after which the member with the call resumes speaking. Yielding is not a means of transferring the call or of developing a subject at length. If more than a reasonable time has been taken by the member who intervenes, the Speaker will interrupt and ask the original member to resume his or her speech.[166]

The time taken up by the member who interjects in this way is counted as part of the time of the member who gave way.[167]

---

[158]   1936, Vol.244, p.772.
[159]   1923, Vol.201, p.653.
[160]   1936, Vol.247, p.691.
[161]   1924, Vol.203, p.279.
[162]   1933, Vol.237, p.719.

[163]   1923, Vol.200, p.231.
[164]   1963, Vol.335, p.609.
[165]   1980, Vol.429, p.691.
[166]   1992, Vol.531, pp.12223-4.
[167]   1988, Vol.486, p.2266.

Recording of interjections

It is the member who is speaking who effectively decides whether an interjection will be recorded for posterity, because interjections are not recorded in *Hansard* unless they are responded to by that member. For this reason the wittiest and most effective interjections may be lost to posterity because they leave their object speechless.

Provoking interjections

A member speaking is under some obligation not to provoke interjections. If a member directs a constant series of questions to a member or to members present in the Chamber, the member is inciting them to disorder and may be asked to desist by the Speaker.[168] Members often ask questions, whether rhetorical or not, in the course of their speeches and they are not obliged to give members opposite an opportunity to reply there and then. Those members can seek the call and answer the questions later in the debate.[169] However, there does come a point at which the employment of this debating tactic tends to lead to disorder and the Speaker feels obliged to intervene. A member speaking cannot be required by the Speaker to give time for an interjection in reply to questions asked in the course of a speech, but the member can be told by the Speaker to make the speech in a different way in future.

VISUAL AIDS

Occasionally members bring into the Chamber objects they wish to use to add a visual impact to their speeches. The pair of bloomers held up by Miss Mabel Howard to emphasise a point about the cost of ladies' underwear is probably the most famous example.[170] Other members have introduced grocery items and charts. A member introducing a bill on drug misuse showed the House a stash can, a hookah pipe and other drug paraphernalia he wished to make illegal.[171]

Members are permitted to use appropriate visual aids to illustrate points made in their speeches, provided that these do not inconvenience other members or obstruct the proceedings of the House.[172]

The Speaker is the judge of whether such an object is appropriate and whether it is too inconvenient or obstructive. Members have been counselled not to trivialise Parliament by introducing inappropriate objects into the Chamber and the Speaker will refuse to permit an object to be used if, in the Speaker's opinion, it would lower the esteem in which the institution is held.[173] In judging whether an aid is convenient, the Speaker will generally require that it be confined to the desk of the member speaking. It is not permissible for another member to stand next to the member speaking holding something up.[174] The size of the object to be used will also be a consideration. The Speaker will not permit a demonstration to be staged in the Chamber.[175]

While members do not have to seek prior permission from the Speaker to use a visual aid, there are cases where the object will be visible on being brought into the Chamber before the member's speech commences. In these circumstances the Speaker's permission to bring the object into the Chamber in the first place must be obtained. This can be done privately.[176]

Any visual aid may be displayed only while the member is speaking and must be removed from the Chamber at the end of the speech.[177]

The Speaker will order the removal of more permanent visual displays; as when

---

[168] 1969, Vol.362, p.2522.
[169] 1970, Vol.367, p.2476.
[170] Gee, *Our Mabel*, p.155.
[171] "Ban on drug equipment considered", *The Dominion*, 26 November 1992.
[172] S.O.108(1).

[173] 1997, Vol.560, p.1755.
[174] 1997, Vol.559, pp.1382-5.
[175] 1997, Vol.560, p.1755.
[176] *Ibid.*
[177] S.O.108(2).

members pinned notices or pennants to their seats or to the sides of their correspondence trays and displayed them prominently over the course of a few days. The introduction into the Chamber of an object designed to make or illustrate a point in a member's speech is acceptable when it is reasonably necessary for that purpose, but objects introduced for the purpose of making a silent comment on issues, or that remain in the Chamber for a period of time, are not acceptable.[178]

INTERRUPTION OF DEBATE
There are a number of matters which may cause the House temporarily to lay aside a debate upon which it is engaged.[179] These matters do not necessarily permit the interruption of a member speaking. Most interruptions to a debate can only arise between speakers, not while a member is actually speaking.

Interjections, while in a sense interruptions to a member's speech, are, if properly made, contributions to the debate rather than interruptions of it. However, a member's speech or the debate is liable to be interrupted in other ways—
- the Speaker may be called upon to rule on a point of order[180]
- a matter of privilege may arise relating to the conduct of strangers present[181]
- the sitting may be suspended (at a regular time or for disorder)[182]
- a message from the Governor-General may be read to the House (this will only occur between speakers)[183]
- an unsworn member may take the oath or affirmation entitling the member to take a seat in the House (again only between speakers)[184]
- a motion may be made to exclude the press and the public from the galleries (but the moving of such a motion may not interrupt a member speaking)[185]
- a Minister may make a ministerial statement or a member may make a personal explanation or a maiden statement (also not so as to interrupt a member speaking).[186]

When a debate is interrupted by one of these events, the interruption is temporary as far as that sitting is concerned. When the interruption is concluded, the debate immediately resumes at the point it had reached.

ADJOURNMENT OF DEBATE
The adjournment of a debate also suspends the debate for a period. Usually where a debate is adjourned it is not intended to be resumed again until a future sitting day.

The most common way in which a debate is adjourned is when it is still running at the time appointed for the adjournment of the House or for the House to go on to other business. At the time for the adjournment of the House, any debate in progress is adjourned and it is set down for resumption on the next sitting day.[187]

Where the House has appointed a particular time for business to commence (which is not common) any debate in progress when that time is reached is automatically adjourned and set down for resumption on the next sitting day.

Motions for adjournment of debate
In addition to adjournment by the automatic operation of the rules of the House, a debate may be designedly adjourned, either to a later hour on the same day or to a future day, by a motion to that effect.[188] A motion for the adjournment of a debate is sometimes referred

[178] 1982, Vol.444, p.1070.
[179] S.O.133.
[180] S.Os 132(a) and 133(a).
[181] S.Os 132(b) and 133(b).
[182] S.O.133(c).
[183] S.O.133(d).
[184] S.O.133(e).
[185] S.O.133(f).
[186] S.O.133(g).
[187] S.O.134(2).
[188] S.O.134(1).

to as a dilatory motion, for it can be used to delay proceedings. However, its use in the House of Representatives as an instrument of prevarication has been severely curtailed owing to the fact that, if it is moved, the question on it is put forthwith and determined without amendment or debate.[189]

A motion for the adjournment of a debate can be moved only by a member who is called to speak in the debate. The member must therefore have speaking rights. A member who has already spoken to the question cannot move the adjournment of the debate. A member proposing to move the adjournment must do so immediately on being called to speak. The member cannot speak to the question and then move the adjournment, nor can the member preface the adjournment motion with an explanation of why it is to be moved. In the latter case the member is treated as speaking to the question and cannot move the adjournment of the debate. If the motion for the adjournment is defeated, the member may continue the speech. If the member does not continue in these circumstances, the right to speak is lost.[190]

Resumption of adjourned debate

A debate is resumed at the point it had reached when it was adjourned, whether that adjournment took place under the Standing Orders or on a motion.[191] The member who was speaking when the debate was interrupted or on whose motion a debate was adjourned has the right to speak first when the debate is resumed.[192] For this purpose, the member must seek the call when the debate is resumed, otherwise other members can be called to speak. If the member whose speech was interrupted does not exercise the right to speak first on the resumption of the debate, the speech is concluded.[193] The member who moved the debate's adjournment is not obliged to exercise the right to speak first, however, and may speak later in the debate if he or she wishes. That member does not need to declare an intention to do this when the debate resumes; the right to do so applies automatically.[194]

A member resuming the debate in these circumstances cannot again move its adjournment. The right to do that applies only when first being called to speak.

[189] *Ibid.*
[190] S.O.136.
[191] S.O.52.
[192] S.Os 52 and 135.
[193] S.O.52.
[194] 1985, Vol.468, p.8562.

CHAPTER 17

TERMINATION OF DEBATE

A debate terminates in one of five ways—
- the carrying of a closure motion
- the total number of speakers allowed in the debate having spoken
- the total time for the debate having expired
- no members with speaking rights wishing to speak
- all members having exhausted their speaking rights.

Once the debate has concluded, the Speaker "puts" the question to the House for decision (it having merely been "proposed" up to this point). The House decides the question first by a voice vote which is interpreted by the Speaker and, if this is not accepted as definitive, by more formal processes of voting known as party or personal votes.

CLOSURE

A closure motion is a motion which, if carried, brings the debate then in progress to an immediate conclusion even though there are still members who wish to speak in it. The closure motion in its present form was introduced in 1931, replacing a number of less potent weapons for the curtailment of debate. It is now a well-established aspect of parliamentary procedure; the fact that it was not used at all in the 1981 parliamentary session, for instance, was felt to be worthy of particular comment.[1] But because most debates in the House are now time-limited it is principally used in the committee of the whole House.

The closure motion is a motion moved by a member in the course of a debate asking the House to end its debate and proceed forthwith to decide the issue. The Speaker has to decide whether it is appropriate that a closure motion should be put to the House at that point. But it is the House, in voting on the closure motion, which decides if the debate should end, not the Speaker.

Moving the closure

The closure procedure is invoked by a member seeking the call in debate in the ordinary way and moving "That the question be now put".[2] In order to be in a position to move the closure motion, the member must be called to speak to the question under debate,[3] so only a member who still has a right to speak to the question before the House is in a position to move the motion. Once the member has been called to speak, the closure motion can be moved.[4] It may be moved from wherever the member happens to be sitting when called to speak.[5] The moving of a closure motion is itself treated as a speech and once it has been moved the member's right to speak has been exhausted, regardless of whether the motion is accepted by the Speaker or agreed to by the House.[6] But where, as in committee, a member may speak more than once to a question, there is nothing to stop the member moving the closure on the second or subsequent call that the member takes.[7]

The actual words that the member must use in moving a closure motion are prescribed

---

[1]   1981, Vol.442, p.4346.
[2]   S.O.137(1).
[3]   Ibid.
[4]   2000, Vol.586, p.4768.
[5]   2003, Vol.613, p.10014.
[6]   S.O.137(1); 1971, Vol.373, p.2376; 1985, Vol.468, p.8562.
[7]   2000, Vol.583, p.2365.

in the Standing Orders and the member must add nothing more to them either before or after moving the motion.[8] The member cannot, for instance, give reasons as to why the motion has been moved. If a member does add anything to the terms of the motion it is not properly moved and will be declined at that point.[9] Members have, from time to time, employed minor variations on the words of the motion set out in the Standing Orders. If this is appreciated at the time, the motion will be declined. But, notwithstanding that a motion may have been moved incorrectly, it will be allowed to stand if the House has agreed to it before objection is taken.

Restrictions on who may accept closure motions

Because the Chair is invested with an onerous discretionary authority as to whether a closure motion should be accepted, only certain presiding officers may accept the motion.

In the House, no temporary Speaker may accept a closure motion.[10] This means that only the Speaker, the Deputy Speaker or an Assistant Speaker may do so. Similarly, in committee, no temporary chairperson may accept the motion (though, on one occasion this power was conferred on a temporary chairperson).[11] In committee only the chairperson (who is the Deputy Speaker or an Assistant Speaker[12]) may accept the closure. Occasionally, if the Deputy Speaker or an Assistant Speaker is not available when the House is about to go into committee, the House appoints another member as acting chairperson. Such a member can accept a closure motion.

Limited-time debates

Where the Standing Orders prescribe the time allowed for a debate (whether by stating the time or limiting the number of speakers) or where the Business Committee has used its power to prescribe the time, no closure motion may be accepted.[13] To do so would frustrate the Standing Orders or the determination. This means that most debates in the House are not subject to closure motions, since limits are prescribed for them. But debates in committee are not subject to time limits, unless the Business Committee is able to agree on them, and so the closure is still frequently employed there.

Acceptance of closure motion

The Standing Orders leave the decision on whether to accept a closure motion solely to the Speaker (or other member presiding). The Speaker may accept the closure if, in the Speaker's opinion, it is reasonable to do so.[14]

In deciding whether to accept a closure motion the Chair will always have regard to the length of time spent debating the question and the number of members who have participated in the debate. The Chair will try to ensure that a party of large numbers gets an appropriate number of calls[15] and, if possible, that all parties have made a contribution to the debate.[16] However, this does not mean that overall proportionality in party participation in the debate must be achieved before a closure can be accepted. That is a relevant consideration, but does not bind the Chair in determining whether to accept a closure motion.[17] The degree to which members have been relevant or repetitious in the debate will also influence the presiding officer's decision.[18] Whether a closure motion is accepted or not will always depend upon circumstances. For example, the drafting

---

8   *Ibid.*
9   1958, Vol.318, pp.1600-1.
10   S.O.137(4).
11   *Ibid.*; 2000, JHR, p.690.
12   S.O.173(1).
13   S.O.137(2).

14   S.O.137(3).
15   1998, Vol.574, p.14109.
16   *Ibid.*, p.14085.
17   2001, Vol.594, p.11125.
18   1998, Vol.574, p.14109.

of a bill can influence the decision – a bill being considered in parts whose parts contain numerous subparts can expect a longer debate before a closure will be accepted than otherwise would be the case.[19]

If the Speaker or chairperson declines to accept a closure motion or if a closure motion is put to the vote and defeated, the debate continues. There is no rule preventing a closure motion which has been put to the vote and defeated being moved again, though in these circumstances it is unlikely that the Speaker or chairperson would accept another closure motion until reasonable further debate had ensued.[20]

The Speaker will not review a decision of a chairperson, in committee, to accept or refuse to accept a closure motion.[21]

Putting the closure motion

If the Speaker or chairperson decides to accept a closure motion, the presiding officer puts the question "That the question be now put" to the House for decision. This question is determined forthwith by the House or committee without any amendment or debate.[22]

Once a closure motion has been accepted, the House will usually agree to it. But this does not have to follow; the House may turn the motion down if members decide that they wish to continue the debate. This is no reflection on the Speaker. The Speaker in accepting a closure motion is not deciding to terminate a debate; the Speaker is giving the House an opportunity to do so. Although unusual, the House (or the committee) may turn this opportunity down.

Putting the question following agreement to the closure

If a closure motion is carried, the Speaker proceeds to put the question which the House has just ordered to be put. There is no further opportunity for amendment or debate.[23] Where an amendment has been moved or lodged before the closure motion is carried, not only is the question on the amendment put, so is any other question already proposed from the Chair. The House works its way back to the main question by putting the question on all intervening amendments that have been moved or lodged, and by deciding them without further amendment or debate.[24] The main question is then similarly decided forthwith. The Standing Order does not provide for a closure motion only in respect of an amendment, with further debate or amendment to the main question then following. This would defeat the purpose of the closure motion.[25] A closure motion, when agreed to, closes off all further debate on the main question too.

In both the House and the committee, any time for the sitting to conclude or be interrupted is deferred once a closure motion has been carried to allow these questions to be put.[26] Thus the House or committee may continue sitting after the time has arrived for the sitting to be suspended, or for the committee to report progress or for the House to adjourn, in order, in each case, to complete voting on questions consequential on the carrying of a closure motion.[27]

Amendments

Members are not denied the opportunity to have their amendments put to the House because a closure motion has been carried before an amendment to the motion has been considered. If a proposed amendment has been notified on a supplementary order paper

---

[19] 2003, Vol.607, p.4421.
[20] 2002-05, AJHR, I.18B, p.19.
[21] 1931, Vol.227, p.675; 1990, Vol.510, p.3735.
[22] S.O.138.
[23] S.O.139(1).
[24] S.O.139(2).
[25] 1991, Vol.520, pp.5203-4.
[26] S.O.51.
[27] 2003, Vol.613, p.10003.

(which most ministerial amendments in committee are) or is handed in to the Table before the closure motion is *accepted*, and is in order, it is put to the House for decision (without any debate) even though it has not been formally moved.[28] Conversely, after a closure motion has been carried, a member may not withdraw an amendment on a supplementary order paper or an amendment which has been handed in to the Table, without leave.[29]

LAPSE OF DEBATE

It is possible that a debate may terminate without the question on the motion being put to the House at all. This occurs when a motion lapses under the Standing Orders. Any motion for the adjournment of the House under debate at 10 pm (6 pm on a Thursday) lapses, for there is no occasion to put it to the vote when the time for the rising of the House has arrived in any case.[30] Motions to debate a matter of urgent public importance[31] and to hold a general debate on a Wednesday[32] also lapse at the conclusion of the time prescribed for them under the Standing Orders and no question is put on them at the end of the debate for the House to decide.

Furthermore, no question is put on the third reading of a bill, on an amendment in the committee of the whole House, on a motion to change a vote or on a motion that has the force of law, if a financial veto certificate has been issued in respect of it.[33]

REPLY

There is no longer any general right for the mover of a motion to speak for a second time in the debate as the concluding speaker in reply. This rule was abolished in 1999.[34] A right to speak for a second time in reply to a debate only exists where this is expressly provided in the Standing Orders. It is provided that the member in charge of the bill may speak in reply to the first reading debate on a Member's, a private or a local bill and also that the Minister may reply to the Budget debate.[35] In these circumstances the member or Minister is called upon by the Speaker to reply to the debate when the number of speakers allowed have spoken or the time prescribed for the debate has expired, as the case may be.

PUTTING THE QUESTION

The Speaker begins the debate on a motion by proposing a question based on it. At the termination of the debate for whatever reason (and except where the Standing Orders otherwise provide that the question lapses) the Speaker states the question again for the House and asks if the House agrees to the motion.[36] This is called putting the question. The debate is over once the question has been put from the Chair; no member may speak further to the question. Members must now express their opinion as to whether they favour the motion and a majority one way or the other decides the outcome, though members can abstain. Even if the time for the sitting to be adjourned or suspended has arrived, the adjournment or suspension, as the case may be, is postponed if the Chair is in the process of putting the question to the House at that time or if a vote has actually commenced.[37] This requirement for the House to complete its decision on a question that is in the process of being decided can only be set aside by leave.[38]

Dividing a question

If the question is complicated or it is convenient to vote on parts of it separately, it can be divided. But this must be done by leave; there cannot be a motion or amendment to

---

[28]   S.O.139(2).
[29]   1986, Vol.470, p.1052.
[30]   S.O.49(1).
[31]   S.O.381(2).
[32]   S.O.383(2).
[33]   S.Os 320(3), (4) and 321(2).
[34]   1996-99, AJHR, I.18B, pp.11-12.
[35]   Appendix A to the Standing Orders.
[36]   S.O.140(1).
[37]   S.O.51.
[38]   2000, Vol.586, p.4309.

divide a question. On occasion, the Speaker has suggested that it may be convenient to the House to vote on different parts of a question separately.[39]

Voice vote

What members are being asked to do when the question is put is to vote on the issue. The method by which the House votes initially on any question is by a vocal expression of opinion for or against the question – a voice vote.[40] The majority of voices decides "Aye" or "No" to the question,[41] and in most cases this method of deciding a question is sufficient. It is only in some instances that the House needs to take a further step to settle matters.

Having put the question, it is for the Speaker to decide whether the Ayes or the Noes "have it" – that is, which side is in the majority. (If the Speaker is not satisfied that members gave their voices in a way that confidently enables the will of the House to be deduced, the Speaker can ask the members to repeat the process by putting the question again.)

In determining whether the Ayes or the Noes have it, no decibel reading is taken; the Speaker uses intuitive judgment. Visitors in the gallery or radio listeners who have heard a question being put and have remarked on the different level of response from the two sides may doubt their own senses or, on occasion, assume that the Speaker is being perverse when it is announced that the apparently less vocal side "have it" following a testing of opinion in this way. The listener must not confuse vehemence with numbers. It is the Speaker's job to construe the sense of the House from the voices, not to register who can shout loudest.

The Speaker assumes that in all normal circumstances the Government will be in a majority and declares the result of the voice vote accordingly. In those cases where a vote is not being taken on party lines, the Speaker needs to make an instant assessment of the sense of the House from the strength of the voices, but these occasions are relatively few.

Call for a further vote

The Speaker's decision of where the majority lies is usually sufficient. The minority (if there is one, the House may be unanimous) acquiesces in the Speaker's decision and the motion is carried or defeated as the case may be. In some cases, however, the putative minority is not satisfied with this method of determining the matter and wishes to have a more formal testing of the waters. Members may, therefore, object to the Speaker's decision as to which side "have it" and call for a further vote to be held.[42] (To object a member must actually be present in the Chamber. There can be no objection by proxy.) It is incumbent on members who object, to make known their disagreement with the Speaker's decision at that point and to call for a further vote. If they fail to do so, the House goes on to its next business. Conversely, those whom the Speaker declares to be in a majority on the question do not have a right to call for a further vote just to test the position of other members in the House.[43] The right to challenge the Speaker's assessment of how the voice vote has gone lies only with those in the minority who believe that the decision of the House would be different if further tested.[44] The Speaker can refuse to allow a further vote if it is clear that a member calling for it was in the majority as declared by the Speaker on the voice vote.[45]

---

[39]   1997, Vol.560, pp.2023-4.
[40]   S.O.141.
[41]   S.O.140(2).
[42]   S.O.141.

[43]   1997, Vol.565, p.6102; 1999, Vol.580, p.19070.
[44]   1987, Vol.481, pp.9620-1.
[45]   1998, Vol.573, p.13599.

PARTY VOTES

Until 1996 if a more formal vote than a voice vote was required to resolve a question a "division" was always held. A division corresponds today to what is known as a personal vote. However, a new type of vote (known as a party vote) was introduced in 1996 based on a system used in the Netherlands[46] and this form of collective vote is now the method most commonly employed if members call for a further vote following a voice vote. (During the forty-seventh Parliament there were 3,544 formal votes held. Three thousand four hundred and twenty-eight of these were party votes and only 116 were personal votes.)

When a party vote is held votes are cast as a block by party representatives on behalf of each of the various parties recognised in the House. However, each member remains free to withdraw his or her vote from the party vote and to use it in a different way from that of the party.

Procedure for conducting vote

When members do not acquiesce in the Speaker's estimation of which side of the question has prevailed on a voice vote, the Speaker will ask members if a party vote is called for. If a member in the putative minority then calls for a further vote, a party vote is held.[47]

The Speaker directs the Clerk to conduct a party vote. For this purpose the Clerk calls on each party in turn, in order of their size, to cast its vote. (Parties with the same number of members are called in alphabetical order.) Each party is called on by its official name[48] and the call is directed to the leader of the party, or a member authorised by the leader of the party, to cast the vote.[49] In practice a whip or a member acting as whip casts the vote for each party. While parties are always invited to vote in order of size, if a party fails to vote when called (in which case no vote is recorded[50]) or votes and subsequently wishes to correct its vote, it can intervene while the vote is still in progress and record its vote even though by doing so it votes in a different order to that suggested by its size in the House.[51] A vote is cast from any seat that the member happens to be occupying, but cannot be cast from the floor of the House.[52] The whip or other member casting the vote stands in his or her place and responds to the Clerk by stating how the party casts its votes.

Following the casting of votes by parties, independent members are called on (in alphabetical order) to vote. Finally, if votes have not been cast for the total number of members of the House at this point, the Clerk will ask if there are any other votes. Members who wish to vote in a way that is contrary to their party (and have therefore consequently not been included in their party's vote) then have an opportunity to do so in person or by proxy.[53]

When all parties and members have had a reasonable opportunity to vote, the Clerk calculates the total of the Ayes, Noes and abstentions and hands the list to the Speaker. The Speaker can allow members more time to vote if there is some confusion or a mistake over a vote has occurred, so that the matter can be clarified rather than a dubious result being declared, but there is a limit to the indulgence that a Speaker will permit in these circumstances.[54] Once the Speaker is satisfied with the result, the Speaker declares it to the House.[55] The party vote is completed at that point.[56] Any error can be corrected subsequently only under the Standing Orders provisions for correcting errors or by leave of the House.

---

[46] 1993-96, AJHR, I.18A, pp.27-30

[47] S.O.142.

[48] 2000, Vol.586, p.4548.

[49] S.O.144(1)(a).

[50] 1997, Vol.561, p.2640.

[51] 1998, Vol.569, p.9778.

[52] 2001, Vol.593, p.10635; 2001, Vol.597, p.13650.

[53] S.O.144(1)(d).

[54] 1998, Vol.573, p.13564.

[55] S.O.144(1)(e).

[56] 1998, Vol.569, p.9778; 1998, Vol.573, p.13564.

Interjections during the conduct of a party vote are regarded as particularly serious since there is no debate in progress and they can therefore have no justification. In particular, members are not permitted to comment as the party votes are cast.[57] Indeed, the Speaker has suggested that interjections at this point, as well as promoting confusion, could, if intimidatory, amount to a breach of privilege.[58]

Participating in a party vote

A party vote is a collective vote cast on behalf of up to all members of the party concerned. "Zero" is not an acceptable vote; it is the absence of a vote. A party is entitled to decide not to participate in a vote but not to participate and cast no votes. In these circumstances the party is not recorded as having voted at all.[59]

The leader of the party or the senior whip of the party or any member acting for the time being in the House as leader or senior whip, holds a standing authority to exercise a proxy vote for all members of the party, subject to any express direction from a member to the contrary.[60] Members do not need to give their whip specific authority to vote on their behalf in a party vote. That is inherent in being a member of the party.

A party consisting of a single member and any independent member, may, in their absence, have their votes cast on their behalf by proxy. But the proxy may be exercised only if the member concerned is actually present somewhere in the precincts, or is attending a select committee meeting outside Wellington with the agreement of the House or the Business Committee or is absent from the precincts attending official business approved by the Business Committee, or has been granted leave of absence by the Speaker. Leave of absence can be granted for illness or other family cause of a personal nature or to enable the member to attend to public business in New Zealand or overseas.[61] For this purpose the Speaker may grant leave of absence on a case-by-case basis or generally, as the Speaker sees fit.

A party consisting of two members or three members may also have its vote cast by proxy if its members are absent from the Chamber, but in this case at least one of those members must be present somewhere in the parliamentary precincts at the time.[62]

Subject to these exceptions, in order to participate in a party vote, a party must have at least one member present in the Chamber when the vote is held.[63] This does not mean that a party vote must be actually cast by a member of that party (although this is usually the case); a whip of one party could be acting as the whip of another party.

When a member exercises a proxy for another party, the member does not have to state that a proxy is held. The member merely casts the vote.[64]

Party vote totals

To be included in a party's vote (or participate in any vote) a member must have been sworn in.

Parties may cast votes up to their total parliamentary memberships as advised to the Speaker.[65] Where a party has suspended a member from its caucus, its parliamentary membership has not changed and the party may continue to include the member in its party vote totals.[66] But where a party *expels* a member from its caucus, its parliamentary membership changes and so does its party vote.[67] In these circumstances the member becomes an independent member and is no longer included in a party's vote.

---

57   2000, Vol.586, p.4548.
58   1998, Vol.571, p.11946-7.
59   2000, Vol.586, p.4768.
60   S.O.155(4).
61   S.O.156(4).
62   S.O.156(3).
63   S.O.144(4).
64   1996, Vol.553, pp.11159-60.
65   S.O.35(1)(c).
66   2003, Vol.606, p.3257.
67   2003, Vol.613, p.9837.

A member who is suspended by the House may not be included in any party vote total,[68] though a suspended member is still part of the party's parliamentary membership and enters into the calculation of how many proxy votes the party may cast.

Absence of members

There are restrictions on the number of votes that may be cast for a party depending upon the absence of its members from the parliamentary precincts.

When a party vote is called any member present within the parliamentary precincts can automatically be included within the party vote total cast for that party.[69] (See Chapter 11 for the parliamentary precincts.) For this purpose any member attending a meeting of a select committee held outside Wellington with the Business Committee's agreement or attending any other official business approved by the Business Committee is deemed to be present in the precincts.[70]

Where a member attends a meeting of a select committee outside Wellington on a sitting day and is deemed to be present in the precincts, this deemed presence extends not just to the time that the committee is actually meeting but also for a reasonable period of time for travelling between Wellington and the meeting (both going to and returning from the meeting) regardless of the member's actual travel arrangements. (In the case of any dispute, the Speaker determines what is reasonable.) Outside this period the member's vote, if it is to be included at all, must be cast as a proxy.

From time to time the Business Committee determines whether members participating in ad hoc visits are to be regarded as present in the precincts for voting purposes.[71] The committee has determined that members travelling overseas on the official parliamentary travel programme funded through the Office of the Clerk are to be regarded as present in the precincts for voting purposes.[72]

Over and above the members who are actually or constructively present in the precincts, a party may include in its total vote properly authorised proxies.[73] But proxy votes may not exceed 25 percent of its total party membership in the House (rounded up to the nearest whole number).[74] Each party is allowed a minimum of one proxy vote.[75] Thus a party of 20 members can exercise proxy votes for five of its members (25 percent of its membership). It therefore needs to have 15 of its members actually or constructively present in the precincts in order to cast its full total of 20 votes in a party vote. If, for example, only 14 of its members were present it would have to reduce its party vote total to 19.

Split-party votes

A party vote is normally cast wholly on one side or other of the question (or as an abstention) but it can be distributed over the three options: Aye, No and abstention. This is known as a split-party vote.[76] (Until 2005 a split-party vote required leave. Now a party has the right to cast its votes on a split-party basis.)

Split-party voting has been employed as an alternative to holding a personal vote on a conscience issue since it saves time as compared to holding a full personal vote. Where a party does cast a split-party vote, the member casting the vote must deliver a list to the Clerk, immediately after the vote, showing the names of the members of the party voting

---

68   S.O.91.
69   S.O.144(1)(c)
70   S.O.144(3).
71   See, for example: 2001, Vol.597, p.13418 (Solomon Islands election observers); 2002, Vol.603, p.1391 (Battle of El Alamein commemorations); 2004, Vol.615, p.11077 (travel by members of a select

committee   not an actual committee meeting).
72   Business Committee determination, 2 March 2004.
73   S.O.144(1)(c).
74   S.O.156(2).
75   *Ibid.*
76   S.O.144(1)(b).

in the various options for voting.[77] This information is published in the journals and in *Hansard*.[78]

Members voting contrary to their party

Members voting on a question in a way contrary to their party's position have traditionally been described as "crossing the floor". This was originally a figurative reference to the fact that to vote contrary to one's party the member must have physically entered the division lobby on the opposite side of the Chamber to that being frequented by the member's party colleagues on that vote. Today members only vote by entering the lobbies on personal votes, which (as these are largely reserved for conscience issues) are not party matters in any case. The expression "crossing the floor" therefore no longer accurately expresses the physical form that voting contrary to one's party takes in the House. Nevertheless, it is a metaphor still often employed to describe a member who votes or may vote contrary to the position taken by his or her party on a particular question. Party or collective voting has not removed the ultimate right of a member to vote on any question as he or she sees fit. Members may still "cross the floor".

Consequently, the whip or other member casting the party vote must omit from the party's number any vote for a member who wishes to vote contrary to the party. The whip will usually have been advised or otherwise know of this beforehand. But in the absence of any prior indication from the member concerned the whip is entitled to presume that the party is able to cast the member's vote in the party's total. To withdraw that authority the member must take the initiative by "contracting-out" his or her vote from the vote for the party. If the whip does not know that a member wishes to vote contrary to the party position and casts a vote for all members of the party, it is incumbent on the member intending to vote against the party to raise a point of order so that the vote can be corrected. In any case, if a member casts a vote contrary to his or her party where the party has already voted its full strength, the inconsistency will need to be resolved by the Speaker before the result of the vote can be declared.

Sometimes a party may not vote its full strength because of the absence of a number of its members or because of dissidence within its caucus. Which of these alternatives represents the position may not be apparent, especially if no member actually votes against the party on the vote. But the Speaker is not concerned to know the reason why a party has not voted its full strength and will not entertain requests for an explanation from the party.[79]

A vote cast contrary to a member's party vote is cast after other votes have been cast (by proxy if desired).[80] (How such members are identified when they rise to cast their votes is a matter for the Chair. It could be done either by the members themselves or by the Chair.[81]) But there is no provision for a member who is voting on the *same* side of a question as his or her party to cast a vote separately from the party – for example, because the member wishes to emphasise some disagreement with or separation from the party. A member of a party voting on the same side of the question as the party participates in a party vote only by being included in the party's total.[82]

---

77 S.O.144(2).
78 S.O.144(5).
79 2003, Vol.606, p.3495.

80 S.O.144(1)(d).
81 2000, Vol.586, p.4718.
82 *Ibid.*, p.4720.

PERSONAL VOTES

If the issue on which a vote is to be held is a conscience issue, the alternative to a party vote is a personal vote.[83] A personal vote may also be held in addition to a party vote if the Speaker considers that a personal vote might make a material difference to the result.

Conscience issues

The Speaker is the judge of whether a particular vote is to be treated as a conscience issue. In these circumstances the Speaker may permit a personal vote to be held instead of a party vote.[84] (See Chapter 7.)

Matters which are to be treated as conscience issues and are therefore to be the subject of a personal vote will almost invariably have been discussed beforehand by the Business Committee and arrangements made to warn members in advance that the nowadays relatively unfamiliar practice of holding a personal vote is to occur. Members can then arrange to be present for the vote or can issue a proxy so that their position is reflected in the vote. It is regarded as highly undesirable to hold a personal vote without adequate forewarning being given to members that one is to occur. Apart from informal communications to members through their representatives on the Business Committee, the Leader of the House would normally include reference to forthcoming legislation being treated as a conscience issue in the Thursday business statement and the Speaker will announce to members in the House as early as possible that a personal vote will be held.[85]

Consequently, the Speaker will not be easily persuaded without advance warning that a personal vote should be held. If, for example, a debate on a matter follows normal party lines, it is most unlikely that the Speaker will accede to a request at the end of the debate for a personal vote to be held.[86] Nor is a personal vote on a matter outside the traditional range of subjects that are regarded as conscience issues likely to be permitted.[87] The fact that members have or are alleged to have views on an issue that differ from those of their parties is not a ground to treat the issue as a conscience issue. Conscience issues generally arise because parties do not have a position on an issue at all, not because members disagree with the party position. The party vote procedures (perhaps by employing a split-party vote) themselves cater for members who wish to vote contrary to their parties' positions.

Personal vote following party vote

The Speaker may also permit a personal vote to be held following a party vote if a member requests one and the decision on the party vote is so close that a personal vote may make a material difference to the result.[88]

The Speaker has emphasised that closeness on a party vote result cannot, by itself, be enough to justify holding a personal vote. Depending on party standings in the House, every party vote might be close.[89] A decision to permit a second vote, this time on a personal vote basis, could arise out of confusion as to the outcome of the first, although in this case the Standing Orders contain provisions for a second vote of the same nature as the first to be held[90] and the Speaker would have to be convinced that there were good reasons why, following an uncertain outcome from a party vote, a personal vote rather

---

83   S.O.142.
84   S.O.143.
85   See, for example: 1997, Vol.562, p.3468 (*Shop Trading Hours Act Repeal (Easter) Amendment Bill*); ibid., p.3831 (*Casino Control (Poll Demand) Amendment Bill*); 1998, Vol.574, p.14457 (*Gaming Law Reform Bill*).

86   1997, Vol.560, pp.2087-8 (*Compulsory Retirement Savings Scheme Referendum Bill*).
87   1996, Vol.558, p.38 (appointment of Deputy Speaker).
88   S.O.145.
89   1996, Vol.558, p.41.
90   S.O.153(1).

than a second party vote should be employed. Similarly, where the result of a party vote is clear, the fact that a number of members have voted against their parties is immaterial.[91]

Procedure for personal votes

If the Speaker agrees that a personal vote is to be held, the Speaker directs the Clerk to ring the bells. This is the same electronic bell that is rung before each sitting of the House. It is activated from the Clerk's chair at the Table and is audible all over the parliamentary complex, though the fact that the bells fail to ring in any part of the buildings does not invalidate a vote.[92]

After ordering the bells to be rung, the Speaker directs those members who are for the Ayes to pass to the right of the Speaker (that is, into the Ayes Lobby), those for the Noes to pass to the left (into the Noes Lobby) and members abstaining to come to the centre (that is, to the Clerk at the Table). The Speaker appoints a teller for each side.[93]

Tellers

The tellers are the members who act as poll clerks and actually record the vote cast by each member. There is a teller for each side of the question. The Speaker accepts volunteers who offer to serve as tellers. If there is no member wishing to act as teller for one side of the question, the Speaker immediately declares the result for the other side.[94]

A member who has accepted appointment as a teller and begun to act in that capacity must continue to act unless excused by the Speaker.[95] Other members are entitled to observe the work of the tellers in any part of the Chamber or the lobbies.[96]

Time for ringing the bells

The Standing Orders require the bells to be rung for seven minutes.[97] However, this has been found to be unnecessary where votes are followed in quick succession and members have already been able to make their way to the Chamber from the other parts of the parliamentary complex. This is the case, for instance, with votes consequent on the carrying of the closure motion, which are put without any further debate.[98] Consequently, the Speaker has a discretion to ring the bell for only one minute where a vote follows another vote without any intervening debate or other proceeding occurring.[99] While, principally, this provision for a one-minute bell is applied in respect of votes following a closure motion, it has also been applied, for instance, to a motion to refer a bill to a select committee, since such a motion follows immediately on the preceding question and is not debatable.[100] In all cases the Speaker exercises the discretion to permit a one-minute bell if there is likely to be no prejudice to members participating in the vote.

Locking the doors

The doors at either end of the lobbies and the doors at the far end of the Chamber are closed and locked on the Speaker's command when the bells have stopped ringing. The Speaker usually orders this to be done immediately after the seven minutes (or one minute, as the case may be) have expired but may allow the doors to remain open longer;[101] for example, if there is doubt as to whether the bells were operating in a part of the building. When the doors have been locked in this way, all entry to and exit from the Chamber and

---

[91] 2000, Vol.588, pp.6825-6 (*Resource Management Amendment Bill*).
[92] 1985, Vol.462, p.4606.
[93] S.O.146(1)(b).
[94] S.O.150.
[95] S.O.149.
[96] S.O.146(2).
[97] S.O.146(1)(a).
[98] S.O.139(2).
[99] S.O.148.
[100] S.O.286(1).
[101] S.O.146(1)(c).

lobbies is prevented. No further members can enter to cast a vote. They have missed the vote and their names cannot be recorded. While locking the doors is a necessary procedure designed to ensure that all members present when the vote is taken do vote and that no other members can enter subsequently and participate, failure to lock the doors adequately does not invalidate the vote or cause it to require to be retaken.[102]

Once the doors have been locked, the Speaker restates the question for the benefit of members who had arrived after it was first stated.[103]

Obligation to vote

Every member within the locked doors is obliged to vote or record an abstention.[104] (Only members who have taken the Oath of Allegiance may vote or have proxies recorded for them.[105])

If a member is locked in and inadvertently fails to vote, there is no procedure which permits that member to vote on a subsequent occasion or for the Speaker to amend the numbers to include the member.[106] The Speaker may amend the numbers only in the case of error or confusion concerning the result. A member's failure to vote may be an error on the member's part, but it is not an error in the carrying out of the vote. While the Standing Orders do not provide for any penalty for a failure to vote, a member who wilfully refuses to vote or record an abstention could be held to be in contempt of the House.[107] Where a member fails to vote through inadvertence, he or she should take the first opportunity to apologise to the House for the lapse.[108]

Vote follows voice

Members are subject to another obligation when voting in a personal vote. This obligation is expressed in the maxim: "vote follows voice". Members are bound to vote in any ensuing personal vote in the same way as they indicated orally when the question was put to the House at the conclusion of the debate. Members, having given their voices one way on this occasion, must give their votes in the same way in the personal vote.[109] Similarly, any member who challenges the Speaker's judgment of where the majority of votes lies on the voice vote has to vote consistently with that challenge in the subsequent personal vote.[110]

There have been a number of examples in New Zealand's parliamentary history of members who have given their voice with one side on the voice vote and then subsequently tried to vote with the other side. In these cases, on objection being taken, the Speaker has ordered the member's name to be recorded on the side of the question to which the member gave his or her voice, and the vote list is amended accordingly.[111] However, objection must be taken to the member's inconsistent action before the numbers have been announced by the Speaker; after that point the member's vote stands.

Other apparent inconsistencies are not formally held against members. A member may speak in the debate on one side of the question and vote on the other,[112] and a member is not compelled to vote for a motion or amendment which that member has moved.[113] A Minister has, for example, introduced a bill and indicated to the House in introducing it that he intended to vote against it.[114]

---

[102] 1985, Vol.462, p.4606; 1985, Vol.468, p.8858.
[103] S.O.146(1)(c).
[104] S.O.146(1)(d).
[105] *Constitution Act* 1986, s.11(1).
[106] 1979, Vol.427, p.4242.
[107] 1990, Vol.509, pp.2922-3.
[108] 1979, Vol.427, pp.4320-1.
[109] 1890, Vol.68, p.292.

[110] 1899, Vol.107, p.315.
[111] See 1860, JHR, p.160 for the first example of this occurring.
[112] 1876, Vol.21, p.379.
[113] 1888, Vol.62, p.198.
[114] 1991, Vol.515, p.2100 (*Smoke-free Environments Amendment Bill (No. 2)*).

Voting

A member votes by entering the appropriate lobby and declaring his or her name to the teller on duty or by approaching the Clerk at the Table and having the member's name recorded as an abstention.[115] The teller scores through that name on a vote list that has been preprinted with all members' names on it. Members do not wait until the bells have ceased ringing and the doors have been locked before beginning to cast their votes. Members vote while the bells are still ringing. The Speaker, who must also vote, does not leave the chair but asks another member to ensure that the Speaker's vote is recorded.

It is specifically provided that once a member has cast a vote or an abstention, the member must remain within the Chamber or the lobbies until the numbers are declared by the Speaker.[116] Members voting while the bells are ringing are voting with the doors to the Chamber and the lobbies still open. They are required to remain until the doors have been locked and all proceedings on the vote have terminated, at which point the doors are re-opened and members are free to leave if they wish. The vote of any member who fails to remain in the Chamber or voting lobbies until the result has been declared is disallowed.[117]

Order during a vote

During a personal vote there is considerable movement of members within the Chamber, and between the Chamber and the lobbies. Members move around and talk to each other in a way that would be unacceptable during the course of debate. The Speaker has warned members that this must not get out of hand and, in particular, that banter between members at this time must not degenerate into verbal intimidation of another member.[118]

Conclusion of the vote

When all members have cast their votes, the tellers sign the respective vote lists as an authentic record of the vote and deliver them to the Clerk at the Table, who checks them and hands them to the Speaker.[119] The tellers are obliged to satisfy themselves as to the numbers recorded before signing and parting with the vote lists.[120] If the lists are handed back to the Clerk before the doors have been locked, any member who has not yet voted may still do so.[121] To allow for this, the Clerk does not hand the lists up to the Speaker until the doors have been locked. The Speaker, on receiving lists that are properly signed, accepts them as correct unless there are good grounds to suggest that there has been an irregularity.[122] But a personal vote is not completed until the Speaker has actually announced the result to the House.[123] Up to this point the lists can be corrected on the tellers' authority. Thus, where, after the lists had been checked but before the result had been announced, it was realised that a member present had not voted, the member's name was added to the list when it was established which side he would have voted on.[124]

The Speaker announces the result of the vote to the House[125] and then directs that the doors be unlocked.

MAJORITY REQUIRED

All questions put to the House are decided by a majority of votes in favour of or against the question.[126] A simple majority of votes suffices, with abstentions (though recorded) ignored for this purpose.

---

[115] S.O.146(1)(e).
[116] S.O.147.
[117] *Ibid.*
[118] 1988, Vol.487, pp.3140-1.
[119] S.O.146(1)(f).
[120] 1985, Vol.468, p.9064.

[121] 1980, Vol.436, p.5600.
[122] 1985, Vol.468, p.9064.
[123] 1989, Vol.503, p.14139.
[124] 1992, Vol.525, pp.8799-800.
[125] S.O.146(1)(f).
[126] S.O.140(2).

However, a qualified majority of votes is required for changing certain provisions of the electoral law.[127] (See Chapter 2.) As well as these electoral law provisions, if a proposal is made for any legislative provision to be entrenched, a qualified majority of votes in favour of it must be obtained. A proposal for legislative entrenchment is a provision in a bill or an amendment to a bill that would provide that the provision or amendment could itself only be repealed or amended by a majority of more than 50 percent plus one of all members of the House. In this case the proposed provision or amendment must itself receive that same level of support for it to be adopted when it is considered at the committee stage.[128] If a proposal for entrenchment does not attain the qualified majority, it is lost.

If a party vote or a personal vote is tied, the question is lost.[129] There is no longer a casting vote vested in the Speaker.

ERRORS AND MISTAKES

It occasionally happens that errors occur in recording or tallying the numbers who have voted in a party or personal vote. If such an error is discovered before the results are declared by the Speaker, they are corrected by the Clerk or the teller. Errors discovered subsequent to the declaration of the result may be corrected by the Speaker.[130] Some errors may be more significant than a mere miscounting of the number of names struck through. Thus, a member has been recorded as having voted on both sides of a question. Where it has been established that the member concerned had in fact voted in only one lobby, the Speaker corrected the result accordingly.[131] Other errors may result from the numbers of the votes cast being misheard or miscalculated. The Speaker may use the Speaker's power to correct errors that occurred in committee.[132] (Where the error is identified before the committee has reported the bill on which the error occurred back to the House, the chairperson corrects it.)

If there is such confusion concerning the numbers reported that the Speaker feels unable to resolve it by ordering a correction, the Speaker may direct that a second vote be held.[133] But before taking this extreme action, the Speaker must be satisfied that there is a serious prospect that the count on the vote is indeed wrong. The mere circumstance of a door not being locked, for instance, is not a ground for a second personal vote to be held. There has to be a real element of doubt as to the numbers.[134]

There are other "errors" which cannot be corrected at all. For example, the circumstance of a member locked in the Chamber and forgetting to vote cannot be corrected by adding the member's name to the list.[135] Similarly, a member who enters the "wrong" lobby from whatever cause is bound by the vote actually given and cannot have his or her name struck off the list.[136] Members cannot have their votes altered by appealing to the Speaker to correct the vote list, whether their wish to do this results from initial error or second thoughts.[137] On the other hand, where a member had actually voted but his name did not appear on the list, the Speaker was able to order the list's correction.[138]

The "error" which the Speaker corrects or which can be corrected by a second vote must be an error connected with the administrative procedures for holding or recording a vote. It does not include an individual member's error or confusion as to the member's own vote. Such a correction can only be made if the House gives leave.

127　*Electoral Act* 1993, s.268.
128　S.O.267.
129　S.O.154.
130　S.O.153(2).
131　1978, Vol.419, p.1836.
132　1900, Vol.113, p.688; 1998, Vol.569, p.10092.

133　S.O.153(1).
134　1985, Vol.468, p.8858.
135　*Ibid.*, pp.9064-5.
136　1876, Vol.23, p.526.
137　1991, Vol.518, p.3691; 1992, Vol.532, pp.12815-6.
138　1887, Vol.58, p.295; 1994, Vol.542, p.3446.

RECORDS OF VOTES

The number of votes cast for each party in a party vote must be recorded in the journals.[139] The votes of independent members and members voting contrary to their parties are listed by name. In addition, where a party casts a split-party vote, the names of its members voting in the various categories must be recorded in the journals and in *Hansard*.[140] The results of all personal votes with the names of the members voting or abstaining must also be recorded in the journals.[141] The vote lists must also show if a vote or abstention was cast by proxy.[142] The name under which a member is recorded in the list is the name by which the member wishes to be known in parliamentary proceedings.[143]

Occasionally vote lists have been misplaced after the result has been announced in the House, in which case it has not been possible to print a list showing how members voted, only the numbers voting.[144]

PROXIES

Voting by proxy was first introduced in 1996 in substitution for the official recognition of pairing.[145] Proxy voting is a means by which a member who is absent from the Chamber and cannot vote in person has his or her vote recorded. A proxy vote cannot be recorded for a member who has not taken the Oath of Allegiance.[146] A proxy on a personal vote cannot be recorded if the member is actually present in the Chamber, but a member in a part of the House from which it is impossible to vote, such as in the gallery, can have a vote recorded by proxy.[147] A number of aspects of the proxy system are discussed above under party voting. (See pp. 204–207.)

Conferring proxies

A proxy is an authority given by one member to another authorising that other to cast a vote or record an abstention in the member's name.[148] The leader or whips possess a general proxy under the Standing Orders in respect of members of their party voting in party votes, though a member may withdraw this.[149] This general proxy does not apply on personal votes.[150] A proxy for a personal vote must be issued on an individual to individual basis. A proxy must be signed and dated by the member giving it, recording the member's name, the name of the member to whom it is given and stipulating the period or business in respect of which it is given.[151]

A proxy may be of an open nature applying to all business for an indefinite period and leaving it to the proxy holder to decide how to use it. A proxy does not have to direct the holder on which side of a question a member wishes it to be exercised, though, of course, it can and in the case of a proxy for a conscience issue it is likely to do so. The onus lies on the member giving a proxy to direct the proxy holder how to exercise it if the former sees fit to do so. If the member giving the proxy does direct how it is to be used, it must be exercised only as authorised by that member.[152]

A proxy cannot be transferred by the named holder to another member,[153] but a member is at liberty to give out more than one proxy. If any dispute arose as to overlapping proxies, the Speaker would decide which, if any, applied.

---

[139] S.O.144(5).
[140] *Ibid.*
[141] S.O.151(1).
[142] S.O.151(2).
[143] 1989, Vol.499, p.11114.
[144] 1886, Vol.55, pp.147-8; 1982, JHR, p.408.
[145] 1993-96, AJHR, I.18A, p.29.
[146] *Constitution Act* 1986, s.11(1).

[147] 2001, Vol.590, p.8154.
[148] S.O.155(1).
[149] S.O.155(4).
[150] 1998, Vol.573, p.13392.
[151] S.O.155(2).
[152] 1998, Vol.566, p.8013.
[153] S.O.156(1); 1998, Vol.569, p.10452.

Withdrawal or amendment of proxy

A proxy can be withdrawn or amended at any time by the member who gave it, provided this is done before it is exercised in any particular case.[154] It cannot be withdrawn retrospectively so as to invalidate its exercise in a particular vote.

Withdrawal or amendment of a proxy does not have to be effected in writing. It can be done orally, for example by telephone.[155] But in all cases it must be communicated directly to the proxy holder. It is not sufficient that a member has made public comments apparently inconsistent with the proxy or indicated to another member an intention to withdraw a proxy. Withdrawal of a proxy or any qualification to be placed on a proxy's exercise must be conveyed directly to the proxy holder.[156]

Disputes over proxies

If there is a dispute about whether a valid proxy exists or about the propriety of its exercise, the Speaker decides the matter, having examined the proxy if need be.[157] But proxy obligations are matters between the member giving the proxy and the member exercising it and the Speaker will not intervene at the behest of other members. The Speaker will accept the word of the member exercising a proxy if a question arises during a vote as to its proper exercise. Ultimately, if a proxy was deliberately misused this would constitute a contempt.[158]

RESOLUTION OF A QUESTION

When a question is put to the House and decided, whether on the voices or following a vote, it is said to be resolved in the affirmative (if carried) or passed in the negative (if defeated), as the case may be. Where fewer than 20 members vote or abstain on a personal vote no decision at all is arrived at[159] and certain decisions require a qualified majority of votes to be carried. (See p. 212.) If resolved in the affirmative, the question becomes a resolution or order of the House. The distinction between the two terms is that by a *resolution* the opinion of the House is expressed, while by an *order* the House expresses its will. Thus, abstract resolutions without legal effect or formal consequences may be passed by the House on any conceivable subject, but if the House wishes witnesses to attend at the bar of the House to give evidence with penal consequences for a failure to obey, it orders their attendance. In modern practice in the House of Representatives the two terms are used interchangeably, with a preference for "resolution". In principle, mere resolutions of the House do not have legal effect,[160] but statute may attach legal consequences to a resolution[161] or confer powers on the House which it exercises by passing a resolution (for example, recommending the appointment of certain officers).

All decisions of the House are recorded in the journals and are matters of public record. Occasionally, the Speaker is specifically directed by the House to convey a resolution or order of the House to a person at whom it is directed or who is specially affected by it. All members are at liberty to convey resolutions of the House to such persons as they consider should have them drawn to their attention.

RESCISSION OF RESOLUTION

Any resolution of the House may be formally rescinded. A resolution may be revoked even though it was passed many years ago. A motion for rescission of a resolution can be moved after notice has been given in the ordinary way.[162]

---

154 S.O.155(3).
155 1998, Vol.569, p.10452.
156 *Ibid.*, pp.10445, 10451-2.
157 S.O.156(1).
158 1998, Vol.566, p.8013.
159 S.O.152.
160 *Dyson v Attorney-General* [1912] 1 Ch 158

161 For example, *New Zealand Superannuation and Retirement Income Act* 2001, s.73(3) (if House resolves that the balance in the fund be allocated to individual retirement accounts, the Guardians must report on the best means of doing this).
162 S.O.100.

CHAPTER 18

AMENDMENTS

How a member speaks to a question before the House and what types of material the member is allowed and is not allowed to introduce into the speech have been considered. The question before the House is whether the motion which has been moved should be agreed to. Many members may be totally opposed to it. However, other members may have some, but not entire, sympathy with the motion. Are they then to vote for the motion in its present form as being less than perfect but better than nothing, or are they to oppose it in the hope that they can support an improved motion later? The answer is that ultimately, when the question is put to the vote, they may well have to decide between these two alternatives, but meanwhile another course is open to them – they could seek to have the motion amended.

Consideration of amendments to motions is integral to consideration of the motion itself. Members are not left without the alternative of altering the terms of a motion which is before them unless this right is expressly taken away from them by the Standing Orders. Just as the right to debate certain motions has been abolished, so also the right to propose amendments has been abolished in some instances (usually in respect of the same motions – restriction of debate goes hand in hand with restriction of amendment). It is necessary as particular motions are discussed to note where the right to propose an amendment has been taken away, just as it is necessary to consider the particular and special application of rules for amendments to different motions. This is especially the case when looking at the committee of the whole House's (and by extension each select committee's) consideration of bills, which is the most important manifestation of the right to amend a motion. Indeed a major reason for the existence of committee consideration of a bill is to enable amendments to it to be proposed. Particular rules therefore exist for dealing with amendments in committee on a bill. (See Chapter 27.) In this chapter the general rules governing the way in which amendments are proposed, the determination of whether they are admissible, the manner in which the House decides whether they are to be adopted, and their consequence for the future course of the debate will be considered. These general rules are subject to any specific Standing Orders provision dealing with how a particular amendment is to be dealt with.[1]

FORM OF AMENDMENTS

There is no particular form prescribed in the Standing Orders that an amendment must take. Since an amendment, if agreed to, will be embodied in a resolution of the House it must be in a suitable form for this purpose. An amendment completely lacking form will thus not be permitted. An amendment must describe precisely how the original motion or wording in the bill would be amended were the amendment to be carried. The precise verbal form that is used to express this is not critical as long as the effect is clear.

Common formulations of amendments are—

- to omit words from the motion
- to omit words and insert or add other words
- to substitute words

---

[1] S.O.118.

- to insert or add words
- to repeal or revoke earlier legislative provisions.

New words are said to be "added" if it is proposed to place them at the end of the motion or provision, otherwise they are said to be "inserted".

MOVING OF AMENDMENTS

Amendments may be moved by members until all amendments which members wish to propose have been adopted or rejected, when the House reverts to considering the original question as amended or as originally proposed if none of the amendments were adopted. No notice is required of intention to propose an amendment, but in the case of bills, Ministers and other members do often circulate supplementary order papers containing details of amendments they intend to move.

In debates in the House a member is able to move an amendment by being called to speak to the motion under debate. Different rules apply to the moving of amendments at the committee stage of a bill where members may hand them in at the Table and do not have to be called to speak first. (See Chapter 27.) Members lose their opportunities to move amendments entirely once they have spoken to a question.[2] It follows that the mover of a motion cannot move an amendment to it.[3] Furthermore, a member may move only one amendment to the same question.[4] When speaking to a question a member may move an amendment at any part of the speech, although the member's intention to do so is usually intimated to the House at the commencement of the speech.[5] The terms of the amendment must be put into writing, signed by the proposer and delivered to the Clerk at the conclusion of the speech.[6] Another member can sign the proposed amendment on behalf of the mover, provided the latter's authority has been given.[7] If the terms of the amendment as written differ from those as actually moved during the course of the speech, the amendment must be ruled out of order.[8]

ADMISSIBILITY OF AMENDMENTS

The Speaker or (in committee) the chairperson judges the admissibility of amendments.[9] An amendment is either in order or out of order. If it contains any element that is out of order this infects the entire amendment and it is inadmissible unless leave is given to sever the offending material from it.

Relevancy

The fundamental criterion for the admissibility of an amendment is a concept which runs through the consideration of the content of members' speeches: is the amendment relevant to the question it is proposed to amend? The House has settled down to debate a particular subject; a debate on a different subject entirely cannot suddenly be sprung on members. An amendment must be relevant to the question it is proposed to amend.[10] Amendments can be used to change the details of the proposition before the House, not the subject matter of the proposition itself. This fundamental rule of relevancy is a crucial point of difference with other legislatures that permit amendments to be "at large".[11]

The concept of what is relevant by way of amendment to the terms of a motion is linked to what is relevant in debating on the motion. The moving of an amendment cannot expand the area of relevancy in debate, although it may temporarily restrict it

2　S.O.131.
3　1888, Vol.60, p.300.
4　S.O.130.
5　1926, Vol.209, p.1204.
6　S.O.120.
7　2005, Vol.626, pp.21579, 21581.
8　1926, Vol.210, p.707.

9　1909, Vol.147, p.605.
10　S.O.119.
11　See, for example, *The Washington Post National Weekly Edition*, August 9 1999 (Pennsylvania legislature adopted an amendment to a banking bill instituting a Martin Luther King Day in the state).

while the House turns its exclusive attention to a narrower amendment. In debates such as those on the Address in Reply, the Budget and imprest supply, where relevancy is not a limiting consideration, there is a similar freedom in the scope of amendments which may be moved. For other subjects the area of debate and consequently of amendment is more restricted.

Direct negatives

As well as the requirement of relevancy, an amendment must not be a direct negative of the motion before the House. The proper course of action for a member directly opposed to a motion is to vote against it, not to try to amend it, although a member may propose a "wrecking" amendment designed to blunt its effectiveness. A motion could be completely reversed in meaning by the insertion of the word "not" before the main verb; this is not permissible. Amendments which seek to delete all the words in a motion after the word "That" often radically change the nature of the proposition before the House, but as long as they are relevant to the question and avoid the pitfall of directly negativing it, they are in order.

General compliance

An amendment, as a subsidiary motion, must not contain anything that is not permitted in motions generally or in debate on a motion. Thus the rules on motions and on the contents of speeches apply to limit the content of amendments, for a member cannot insert in an amendment something that would be unparliamentary if used in the member's speech debating it. (See Chapters 15 and 16.)

Amendments relating to statutory motions

Occasionally the House passes motions in fulfilment of statutory obligations or in the exercise of statutory powers. The most common examples of these are motions recommending the appointment of officers of Parliament and other statutory office holders. When playing its part in a statutory process, the House must comply with the applicable statutory conditions and the Speaker is diligent to ensure that this is done. In particular, the Speaker will not accept any amendment that is contrary to a statutory obligation placed on the House. So an amendment restricting (and thereby failing to fulfil) a statutory obligation will not be accepted, though an amendment going further than the statute requires will be.[12] Where nominations for statutory appointments are merely submitted to the House for its endorsement or rejection rather than being made on the House's recommendation, an amendment to substitute other nominations is not in order.[13]

QUESTION PROPOSED ON AN AMENDMENT

Assuming that the Speaker allows the amendment to stand as being in order, a question based on it is then proposed to the House just as is done on any other motion. The form of the question which the Speaker proposes on an amendment is prescribed in the Standing Orders.[14] The Speaker does not normally read out the full text of the amendment at this point. The question put to the House for it to determine is "That the amendment be agreed to". This question is decided by the House in the affirmative or in the negative, just like any other question proposed to the House.

---

[12] 1989, Vol.497, p.10242 (*State-Owned Enterprises Act* 1986).

[13] 1997, Vol.560, pp.2023-4 (*Intelligence and Security*

Committee Act 1996).

[14] S.O.121.

Restriction on second and subsequent amendments

There are further rules designed to ensure that the House moves logically through consideration of the question to be decided and does not repeat consideration of an issue on which it has taken a decision.

If the House has rejected an amendment to omit certain words, what it has done, in effect, is to carry a motion that these words should remain in or "stand part" of the question. These words have received the House's definite approbation and it is not in order to propose an amendment which contradicts a previous decision of the House declining to omit those words.[15] No further amendment at all may be proposed to those words. They then must stand part of the question. Similarly, if the House has agreed to an amendment which inserts or adds words, no amendment may later be proposed to those words.[16] Such words must also stand intact as having been agreed to by the House, though in either case further words may be added to them. In this way the House prevents a matter which has already been determined from being re-opened.

ORDER OF MOVING AMENDMENTS

There cannot be two amendments to the same question before the House at the same time. If an amendment has been proposed it must be disposed of by being adopted, rejected or withdrawn before a subsequent amendment can be moved (although the amendment itself can be amended).[17]

Since amendments must be considered in the order in which they relate to the main question, a member who has an amendment must take care to ensure that it is moved before another member proposes an amendment to a subsequent part of the question. For this purpose, a member with an amendment to be made at a point earlier in the motion than one which another member has announced or has sought to move may always claim the attention of the Chair, by rising on a point of order if need be.[18] A member who does not claim the attention of the Chair to an earlier-placed amendment loses the opportunity to move it when the question on the amendment to the subsequent part of the question is proposed by the Chair.

Amendments to amendments

While no further amendment to the main question may be proposed until an amendment is disposed of, the amendment may itself be amended: there may be an amendment to the amendment.[19]

Exactly the same rules apply for determining the admissibility of an amendment to an amendment as apply to an amendment to the main question. When an amendment is moved to an amendment, the first amendment is for the moment treated as the main question.[20] The second amendment is tested for relevancy to it, not for relevancy to the original question before the House.

Theoretically, an amendment to an amendment could itself be the subject of an amendment, and so on *ad infinitum*. During the debate on the 1995 Budget there were six amendments arising from the main question. The first was an amendment to the main question, the others were each an amendment to the preceding amendment.[21] Such examples of what has been likened to a Chinese puzzle, with each amendment being a box fitting inside another box,[22] are relatively uncommon.

---

[15]   S.O.122.
[16]   *Ibid.*
[17]   S.O.123; 1976, Vol.407, p.3884.
[18]   1924, Vol.204, p.359.
[19]   S.O.124.

[20]   1877, Vol.24, p.544.
[21]   1993-96, JHR, pp.869-75.
[22]   Campion, *An Introduction to the Procedure of the House of Commons*, p.178.

DEBATING AMENDMENTS

There can be only one live proposition under debate before the House at any one time. When an amendment is moved, it displaces the main question as the current issue for debate and the House debates the amendment rather than the main question (unless it also involves consideration and decision of the main question).[23]

An amendment is a new question, separate from the original or main question proposed to the House. This means that each member has the right to speak to it even though the member may already have spoken on the main question, since members have new speaking rights on any new question which arises.[24] (Though, in practice, restrictions on the overall length of the debate will usually prevent members exercising this right.)

The time limit of a member's speech on an amendment, or on an amendment to an amendment, is the same as the time limit applicable to the original motion.[25] Debate on an amendment is confined to what is relevant to that amendment, and no member – whether one who has already spoken on the main question or one speaking for the first time – can debate the main question when speaking to an amendment.[26] This is merely an application of the rules of relevancy to the debate. The question before the House is now the amendment; debate must be directed to the merits of that amendment. The House will eventually work its way back to the main question when all amendments have been disposed of, at which time those members who have not spoken to the main question may, if they wish, exercise their right to speak to it.

Amendments involving consideration and decision of the main question

There is a major exception to the rule that debate on an amendment must be confined to that amendment. This is wherever an amendment is of such importance in relation to the main proposition before the House that any determination of the amendment inevitably involves consideration and decision of the main question.[27] Where an amendment deals with a mere detail, debate must be confined to the merits of that detail, but where an amendment goes to the heart of the original motion and will, in effect, decide the main question, different considerations apply and members are allowed free rein to discuss the main question, even though the amendment is the question before the House.

One of the most common forms that an amendment to omit certain words and substitute others takes is to seek to omit all the words after the initial word "That" and substitute a new proposition adverse to, but still linked with, the original. This type of amendment is the prime example of an amendment which involves consideration and decision of the main question. If it were adopted, the whole substratum of the original question would be lost. Such an amendment provides the real battleground for debate on the merits of the original and the suggested alternative proposition. Accordingly, it is relevant to debate both the amendment and the main question in speaking to this kind of amendment.

While this is the typical type of amendment which involves consideration and decision of the main question, it is for the Speaker to decide in each instance whether an amendment is so wide in its terms or would be so pervasive in its effect if carried that its consideration involves consideration and decision of the main question. Amendments on major debates such as the Address in Reply, Budget and Imprest Supply debates inevitably fall into this category.

Apart from the effect on what a member may say in speaking to an amendment, the

---

23   S.O.128.
24   S.O.127.
25   Appendix A to the Standing Orders.
26   S.O.128.
27   *Ibid.*

categorisation of an amendment as one involving consideration and decision of the main question has important consequences for subsequent speaking rights. On the one hand, such an amendment confers new speaking rights on members who have already spoken to the main question. This is so with any amendment unless the right to speak to it has been expressly taken away by the Standing Orders. On the other hand, to speak to such an amendment is deemed to constitute a speech to the main question, and a member who speaks to an amendment involving consideration and decision of the main question cannot subsequently speak to the main question when it is returned to,[28] nor may that member move a subsequent amendment.[29]

WITHDRAWAL OF AMENDMENT

Just as with motions, a proposed amendment may be withdrawn. However, once the Speaker has proposed a question to the House on the amendment, withdrawal can be effected only with the leave of the House.[30] The moving of an amendment means that before the original motion can be withdrawn, any amendment to it must also be withdrawn.[31]

PUTTING OF THE QUESTION ON AN AMENDMENT

The rules for the putting of the question at the conclusion of the debate on an amendment and for determining the question on it are exactly the same as those for motions generally. Once the question on the amendment has been decided, the House reverts to considering the main question. For this purpose the Speaker restates the main question to the House. If the amendment has been agreed to, the Speaker proposes the question that the original motion "as amended" be agreed to.[32] If the amendment has been rejected, the original question is merely restated.[33]

---

[28] S.O.129.
[29] S.O.131.
[30] S.O.125.

[31] 1887, Vol.58, p.392.
[32] S.O.126(1).
[33] S.O.126(2).

CHAPTER 19

STATEMENTS

As well as speaking in debate, members do address the House on other occasions, such as asking questions or raising points of order. In particular, there are types of proceedings in which members may make statements to the House about matters of particular concern to those members. These statements are not debates – although they may arise out of a debate. They are a means, outside the normal rules for debate, for members to claim the attention of the House for subjects that are of national or personal importance and that the regular rules for debate would not provide opportunities to be raised.

The statements that members can make to the House are of the following kinds—
- the Prime Minister's statement
- ministerial statements
- correcting misrepresentations
- personal explanations
- maiden statements
- valedictory statements.

PRIME MINISTER'S STATEMENT

Until 1984 it was the invariable practice for each session of Parliament to be confined to one calendar year. Near the end of the year Parliament was prorogued and the next meetings of Parliament commenced with a new session and a State Opening of Parliament at which the Governor-General would deliver a Speech from the Throne. The first business of the session was for the House to hold a debate on the Speech – the Address in Reply debate. Thus each year's parliamentary sittings commenced with an extensive debate of a wide-ranging nature.

When, after 1984, the practice of proroguing Parliament at the end of the year ceased and sessions carried on uninterruptedly into the next year, there was no State Opening of Parliament each year and consequently no Address in Reply debate to open the year. To provide an opportunity for a wide-ranging opening debate each year regardless of whether the session is continuing, the concept of an annual statement from the Prime Minister (in years in which there is no State Opening of Parliament) was created, with such a debate arising on that statement.

Delivery of the statement

The Prime Minister must make a statement to the House on the first sitting day of each calendar year, reviewing public affairs and outlining the Government's legislative and other policy intentions for the coming year.[1]

No statement is made when the first sitting day is also the first day of the meeting of a new Parliament or the first day of a session of Parliament.[2] In either of these cases a State Opening and consequently an Address in Reply debate will be held. Also no Prime Minister's statement is made if an Address in Reply debate is still in progress when the House resumes in a new year.[3] An Address in Reply debate is regarded as being in

---

[1] S.O.345(1).
[2] S.O.345(2)(a), (b).
[3] S.O.345(2)(c).

progress if a Speech from the Throne has been made in one year and the Address in Reply is the next item of business to be considered by the House when it resumes sitting in the following year.

The Prime Minister's statement is made at 2 pm on the first sitting day.[4] There are no questions and no other general business is transacted on that day, although a member may be sworn in and the Speaker may give a ruling or make an announcement before calling the Prime Minister. The text of the statement that the Prime Minister intends to make must be given to each party leader by 10 am that day.[5]

There is no time limit on the length of the statement.[6]

Because the Prime Minister is delivering a prepared statement rather than engaging in a free debate, members are expected to exercise a greater degree of restraint with regard to their interjections than would otherwise be the case.[7]

Debate

Once the Prime Minister has finished delivering the statement a debate arises upon it immediately. For this purpose the Leader of the Opposition moves a motion relevant to the statement that has been made.[8] As long as this motion refers to the statement and is relevant to it, the precise terms of the motion are a matter for the Leader of the Opposition to determine. Frequently, the Leader of the Opposition will move a motion expressing lack of confidence in the Government. The Leader of the Opposition may speak for up to 20 minutes on moving the motion.

In the debate on the Prime Minister's statement party leaders are given the right to speak in order of the size of their party,[9] although they do not have to participate in this order if they wish to defer their speaking right to later in the debate. The leaders of parties with six or more members have up to 20 minutes to speak. Other leaders and all other members can speak for up to 10 minutes.[10] The 20-minute speaking times are personal to the Leader of the Opposition and the party leaders. Thus, while another member could move the motion for the debate in place of a Leader of the Opposition who was absent, that member would only have a 10-minute speaking time in the absence of leave to extend it.

The debate on the Prime Minister's statement is subject to an overall time limit of 14 hours. This time does not include the time spent in delivering the statement.[11] The debate on the statement is made a Government order of the day and automatically has precedence over all other Government orders of the day,[12] but it may be adjourned and the House may go on to other orders of the day before it has concluded. While the debate is before the House no Wednesday general debate is held[13] but on the second and subsequent sitting days of the year general business, including questions, is held. It is possible, if no other business intervenes, for the House to complete the 14 hours of the debate within the first sitting week but often the debate runs into a second week.

The debate on the Prime Minister's statement is a completely wide-ranging debate similar to the Address in Reply and Budget debates. As well as the initial motion moved by the Leader of the Opposition potentially raising a question of confidence, amendments moved during the course of the debate may do so too.

---

4 S.O.346.
5 *Ibid.*
6 Appendix A to the Standing Orders.
7 1999, Vol.575, p.14768; 2001, Vol.590, p.7527.
8 S.O.347.

9 1999, Vol.575, pp.14779-80.
10 Appendix A to the Standing Orders.
11 *Ibid.*
12 S.O.347.
13 S.O.383(3).

MINISTERIAL STATEMENTS

From the first session of the New Zealand Parliament, the practice of Ministers of the Crown making statements to the House on matters of public importance has been recognised. These were, and are, entirely unconnected with debate on a motion. A Minister, in making a statement, is not speaking to a question before the House, and the rules of debate do not apply.

In 1979 the procedure for the making of ministerial statements was expressly recognised in the Standing Orders for the first time. A Minister (including an Associate Minister) now has an absolute right to make a statement in the House, but not so as to interrupt a member who is already speaking.[14] So while a ministerial statement may interrupt a debate,[15] it cannot interrupt a member's speech. But this right to make a ministerial statement applies in the House only. If the House goes into committee to consider a bill, it may consider only that bill. A Minister needs leave of the committee to make a statement in committee.[16]

Circumstances giving rise to a ministerial statement

A ministerial statement must be for the purpose of informing the House of some matter of significant public importance which should be brought to the House's immediate attention.[17] Largely it is a matter of judgment for Ministers as to whether a matter is significant enough to warrant a statement. Ministerial statements were made on the outbreak of war and to keep the House informed of important events during the progress of the war. The commitment of substantial forces to peacekeeping duties, important events in neighbouring countries and natural disasters and civil defence emergencies have given rise to statements. Statements have also been made on other matters of lesser importance than these but which Ministers deemed worthy of announcement to the House in the form of a statement.

A Minister is the judge of whether a matter is important enough to justify a statement and no Minister is under an obligation to make one in the first place. There is no convention in New Zealand that such announcements will always be made in the House.[18] There have been criticisms of Ministers for making important policy announcements outside the House rather than by way of ministerial statement.[19] Questions as to whether important announcements should be made in the legislature arise in other countries too.[20]

Making the statement

The Minister making the statement is exhorted to provide a copy of it to the leader of each party before making it.[21] But failure to provide a copy does not prevent a Minister making the statement, nor is there any rule that a Minister can depart from this practice only in cases of national crisis.[22] Indeed some statements may not be in written form at the time they are delivered. It is entirely up to the Minister concerned how copies of a statement are distributed.[22]

The Minister has up to five minutes to make the statement, although this time may be extended by leave. The leader of each party with six or more members is then entitled to comment on the statement for up to five minutes each.[24] The House has on

---

14 S.O.348(2).
15 S.O.133(g).
16 2000, Vol.586, p.4272.
17 S.O.348(1).
18 2000, Vol.583, p.1659; 2002, Vol.603, p.1512.
19 See, for example, Hayward, *Diary of the Kirk Years*, p.157 (criticism of announcement of a wage and price freeze on television rather than in the House).

20 See, for example, "Arrivederci?", *The Economist*, 19 March 2005 (criticism of Italian Prime Minister for not announcing withdrawal of troops from Iraq in Parliament).
21 S.O.348(2).
22 1991, Vol.512, pp.587-8.
23 1989, Vol.496, p.9777; 1991, Vol.512, pp.587-8.
24 S.O.349.

occasion agreed to extend this right to comment to smaller parties.[25] Any member may be authorised to substitute for the leader in making this comment whether the leader is present in the Chamber or not. Finally, the Minister may reply to any comment for up to two minutes.[26]

While statements and the subsequent comments and replies are not part of a debate, the normal rules on the use of unparliamentary language are applied to them.

MISREPRESENTATIONS

The right of a member to make a statement correcting misquotations, misunderstandings or misrepresentations of an earlier speech made by the member arises directly out of debates in the House. Indeed it is in a sense a second speech in the debate and was formerly regarded as an exception to the rule that a member may speak only once to a question before the House.

A member who has spoken in a debate and whose speech is misquoted, misunderstood or misrepresented in some material part by a subsequent speaker in the same debate has the right to be heard again to explain the words used.[27] The member is thus given a second opportunity to address the House in the debate. The second opportunity, however, is very circumscribed. The member is confined to explaining how he or she has been misquoted, misunderstood or misrepresented. No new matter can be brought forward.[28]

This right (for so it is: a member does not need the leave of the House for it) is often called a point of misrepresentation and must be distinguished from the making of a personal explanation, with which it is closely related and which is dealt with below. A point of misrepresentation is much narrower than the making of a personal explanation, both in the occasions which give rise to it and in its permissible contents. Misrepresentation arises solely out of a debate in the House. It has no relation at all to any statements made outside the House.[29] It arises only in respect of statements which the member who claims to have been misrepresented made earlier in the same debate. A misrepresentation of what the member said in a different debate does not give rise to a point of misrepresentation.[30] But debates on the same bill at its different stages while it is passing through the House are treated as the same debate for this purpose and a misrepresentation of what a member said in debate at an earlier stage of the bill can be corrected at a later stage in the bill's passage.[31]

Time for correcting a misrepresentation

A member who has been misrepresented by a subsequent speaker cannot interrupt that speaker to correct a misrepresentation. The member must wait until the end of the speech of the member concerned.[32] As a point of misrepresentation arises as part of the debate on a question a member who has not corrected a misrepresentation before the debate concludes will have to seek leave to make a personal explanation. If the debate has been interrupted the member must wait for the bill to be resumed before correcting a misquotation. A member cannot correct a misrepresentation during consideration of another matter.[33]

Although a point of misrepresentation is primarily designed to give a member who cannot speak again in the debate an opportunity to clear up a misunderstanding concerning his or her speech, it may be that a member who has already spoken and who

---

[25]   2000, Vol.586, p.4019; 2002, Vol.603, p.1422.
[26]   Appendix A to the Standing Orders.
[27]   S.O.106(1).
[28]   S.O.106(2).
[29]   1969, Vol.360, pp.601-2.
[30]   1969, Vol.364, p.3628.
[31]   1891, Vol.71, pp.350, 367.
[32]   1901, Vol.118, p.171; 1913, Vol.162, p.243.
[33]   1987, Vol.484, p.1268.

has subsequently been misrepresented does have the opportunity to speak for a second time in the debate, and could deal with the point in that second speech. This will be the case in committee. In these circumstances the member can choose whether to take a point of misrepresentation or to seek a second call and deal with the point that way. The right to take a point of misrepresentation cannot be taken away from a member merely because he or she has the right to speak again.[34]

Interjections

The right to take a point of misrepresentation applies in respect of a misrepresentation of a material part of a member's speech. An interjector whose interjection is taken up by the member speaking and is misquoted has no right to correct this misquotation, for the interjector has not been misquoted as to a part of a speech, only as to an interjection. Members interject at their peril;[35] misrepresentation of what they have said by way of interjection is a risk that all interjectors run. They have no absolute right to correct a misrepresentation; all they can do is take the call and speak in the debate (if this is still open to them), or consider making a personal explanation.[36]

How a point is corrected

What a member may say in explaining words which have been misrepresented is very circumscribed. Basically, the member may state what was misrepresented and then state the actual words used in the speech, and leave it at that.[37] If possible, the *Hansard* proof should be used if it is available. If a member adds anything to a juxtaposition of the two statements – the misrepresentor's and his or her own – debatable material is being introduced, and the member will be called to order by the Chair.

PERSONAL EXPLANATIONS

A personal explanation is a statement by a member explaining a matter of a personal nature.[38] A personal explanation is not part of the debate on a question, although it may arise out of matters raised or mentioned in a debate.

A personal explanation is not made as of right. It is made only with the leave of the House.[39] It is designed to enable a member to explain to the House matters of a personal nature which reflect on the honour or integrity of the member, or are otherwise of some emotional import to the member. It is not designed merely as another channel to enable a member to take issue with a statement made in debate or outside the House on the grounds that it is mistaken or wilfully wrong. To use a personal explanation solely for the purpose of correcting a statement in this way is to come close to abusing the privilege and, as its use depends on the unanimous consent of the House, will prejudice its use by other members in the future.[40] In order that members can judge the merits of the request when they are asked to grant leave to a member to make a personal explanation, a member is expected to indicate broadly to the House, when seeking its authority, what the personal explanation is concerned with.[41] Once leave has been granted, the privilege cannot be withdrawn by motion in the House. Having been granted by the House unanimously, it would have to be taken away unanimously too.[42] But if a member makes comments in the statement that are impermissible the Speaker will intervene and ultimately, if the member misuses the privilege, the Speaker can terminate the statement.[43]

---

34 1973, Vol.383, p.1809.
35 2002, Vol.602, p.680.
36 1987, Vol.480, p.9265.
37 1966, Vol.347, p.1087.
38 S.O.350.

39 *Ibid.*
40 1977, Vol.413, p.2438.
41 1974, Vol.391, p.2161.
42 1976, Vol.407, p.3682.
43 1997, Vol.563, p.4285.

Time for making a personal explanation

There is no prescribed time at which a personal explanation must be made, for the House itself must decide unanimously in every instance in which a member seeks to make a personal explanation whether the member is to be granted permission to do so. It can therefore interrupt a debate.[44] However, interrupting the speech of another member to seek leave to make a personal explanation is strongly deprecated and members will often be told to wait until a speech ends.[45]

Although it is not part of the debate on a question, a personal explanation may be closely tied up with a debate currently in progress, and the fact that a member still has a right to speak in the debate is a matter which is a relevant consideration when members are asked to allow a personal explanation to be made.[46] It may be that members will feel that in these circumstances the member concerned should seek the call and make the personal explanation in the course of a speech, but this is entirely over to the House to decide when the member seeks leave for the personal explanation. There is no time limit within which a personal explanation must be made; it may refer to a statement or incident some months or years beforehand.[47]

Explanation must be personal to the member

The matter to be explained must be personal to the member seeking leave. A member cannot make a personal explanation on behalf of another member.[48] Personal explanations are used by Ministers when they have discovered an error in a reply which they have made to a question,[49] or in respect of any misleading statement which a member subsequently discovers he or she has made to the House. They are made by members who have been accused inside or outside the House of criminal conduct or improper practices, or where a member's word has been doubted or impugned.

As a personal explanation must be confined to matters personal to the member, a member cannot defend other persons during the course of making a personal explanation.[50] Nor can a personal explanation be used to attack or criticize other members or persons outside the House.[51] The Speaker will police the making of the statement to ensure that the member making the personal explanation does not go too far and strain the leave granted by the House.

Effect of statement

A member's personal explanation cannot itself be debated.[52] Furthermore, it is an axiom of the House that a member's word must be accepted without question, and the most formal way in which a member can give an assurance to the House is by making a personal explanation on a matter. Greater weight is therefore put upon assurances given to the House by way of personal explanation than upon remarks made in the course of debate.[53] A statement made to the House in a personal explanation is a formal statement, and if it is misleading can lead to a more ready presumption that the member deliberately intended to mislead the House.[54] A member who, in a personal explanation, denies having made a statement must have that denial accepted and cannot be challenged on the assurance that has been given.[55] This position obtains for as long as the member remains a member of the House even if the denial was made in a previous Parliament.[56]

---

44   S.O.133(g).
45   1997, Vol.560, p.1763.
46   1978, Vol.417, p.844.
47   1973, Vol.386, pp.3756-7.
48   *Ibid.,* p.3756.
49   2003, Vol.609, p.6544.
50   1892, Vol.78, p.2.
51   1997, Vol.563, p.4285; 2000, Vol.585, p.3906.
52   S.O.350.
53   1990, Vol.505, pp.347-8.
54   1986, Vol.476, p.5961.
55   1969, Vol.360, pp.886-7.
56   2000, Vol.584, p.3051.

If a statement made by way of personal explanation is not true, it could constitute a contempt. Therefore, any questioning of a statement made in a personal explanation is, in effect, an accusation of the member having committed a contempt. It should therefore be brought forward as a matter of privilege. On the other hand, a member who states something in the course of debate is engaging in the debate and can have the statement controverted as long as the controversion does not constitute a personal reflection.

Although members cannot impugn the reliability of a member's statement and cannot discuss any personal explanation once it has been made, they are not precluded from discussing the matter which was the subject of the personal explanation, providing that this is not done in such a way as to challenge the member's veracity.[57] No question can be lodged to a member about a member's personal explanation, although a personal explanation may be referred to in another question.

MAIDEN STATEMENTS

Most newly-elected members make their first or "maiden" speech during the Address in Reply debate following the opening of Parliament. But (because of illness, for example) a member may occasionally be prevented from participating in this debate and so members elected to fill vacancies arising during the course of a Parliament do not have any convenient debate in which to deliver the personal and wide-ranging address that is normally associated with a maiden speech. (See Chapter 12 for maiden speeches.)

For this purpose a member who has not (for whatever reason) made his or her maiden speech during an Address in Reply debate is permitted to make the equivalent address to the House as a maiden statement. The statement may not be made during the course of another debate. Subject to this limitation it is made at a time that the Speaker approves.[58] Normally the timing of such a statement is discussed in advance at the Business Committee. A member's intention to make a maiden statement, at the time approved by the Speaker, is advised on the order paper.

A member has up to 15 minutes for the maiden statement, the same time as the member would have had if he or she had been delivering a maiden speech in the Address in Reply debate.

VALEDICTORY STATEMENTS

At the last sitting of a Parliament before a general election is to be held retiring members have traditionally had an opportunity to deliver valedictory speeches on the motion for the adjournment of the House.

However, members may resign their seats during the course of a Parliament, either for reasons of ill-health or to take up other appointments, such as diplomatic positions. In these circumstances the House has developed the practice of giving leave for members to make valedictory statements on their last or near-last day of service in the House. As well as members who are resigning, individual members retiring at a general election have also resorted to the facility of a valedictory statement rather than waiting until the last sitting day and making a speech on the adjournment, especially where they are to be members of a parliamentary delegation and will be absent when the House adjourns.

Although at first regulated solely by leave, valedictory statements are now normally

---

[57] *Ibid.*

[58] S.O.351.

approved in advance by the Business Committee. They may be set down under its authority or with the leave of the House as an order of business shown on the order paper. Unless the House specifies one, no time is prescribed for a valedictory statement, this being left to the good judgment of the members concerned.

CHAPTER 20

COMMITTEES OF THE WHOLE HOUSE

COMMITTEES CONSISTING OF ALL MEMBERS

As well as considering and debating issues as a full House, the House establishes committees of members to give consideration to issues more conveniently. There are two types of committees that the House appoints: committees of the whole House, that is, committees of which all the members of the House are members (in this case the House forms itself into a committee), and select committees, that is, committees whose membership is confined to a limited number of members of the House. (See Chapters 21, 22, 23 and 24 for select committees.) There were formerly three distinct types of committee of the whole House: a Committee of Supply (for taking decisions on public expenditure), a Committee of Ways and Means (for taking decisions on taxation), and other committees of the whole House. The Committee of Supply and the Committee of Ways and Means were abolished in 1967.

There is a different committee of the whole House every time the House forms itself into such a committee. "Committee of the whole House" is only a shorthand expression for the different forms of proceedings that apply when the House goes into committee. Committees of the whole House sit in the Chamber of the House; they are said to meet "on the floor of the House".[1] As committees of the whole House consist of all members of the House and meet at the same venue as the House, it is physically impossible for the House to sit at the same time as a committee of the whole House.

The Speaker does not preside over a committee of the whole House. Indeed, this factor has been said to be the reason why the House of Commons originally adopted the practice of going into committee. Speakers were regarded by members with some suspicion as the King's or Queen's men who reported members' (sometimes less than complimentary) deliberations to the Sovereign. At a time when legal immunity for parliamentary proceedings had not been established this could be a dangerous matter for the individuals concerned. Going into committee to consider a matter without the Speaker in the chair was a means of maintaining the privacy of the Commons' proceedings from the Crown. ("Going into committee" has maintained something of this sense of deliberating in private even today.) This explanation of the origins of the committee of the whole House has been doubted on the ground that it ignores the fact that the Speaker, even though not presiding, always had a right to attend debates held in a committee of the whole House and to speak and vote there.[2] It may be that the practice originated from nothing more than a desire for more relaxed procedural rules for occasions when it was desirable that the whole House have an opportunity to participate in discussion of a matter that required detailed attention to its drafting and ready amendment of its text. This is close to the modern role played by the committee of the whole House.

The committee of the whole House is an extremely significant part of the operation of the House. Each year, for example, as much as a quarter or more of the total sitting time of the House is spent in committee.

---

[1] For a proposal that such committees meet elsewhere, see, 2002-05, AJHR, I.18B, p.10.

[2] Laundy, *The Office of Speaker in Commonwealth Parliaments*, pp.31-2.

THE HOUSE IN COMMITTEE

Consideration of a matter in committee is set down on the order paper as an order of the day like any other item of business to be considered by the House. When the order of the day is reached, the Speaker directs the Clerk to call it, which the Clerk does by reading its description from the order paper. The Speaker thereupon declares the House in committee on that business and immediately quits the chair. It was formerly the case that the Speaker proposed a question to the House on this point, "That the House do resolve itself into committee" and a debate was held on that question, but this does not happen now. There is no debate held on whether the House should go into committee. When an order of the day for consideration in committee is reached, the House goes into committee automatically.[3]

However, the House does not go into committee on an item of business where there are fewer than five minutes left before it would adjourn in any case. If business that would require the House to go into committee is reached within five minutes of the adjournment, the Speaker adjourns the House automatically.[4]

As the Speaker leaves the chair, the Serjeant-at-Arms removes the Mace from its position on the Table of the House and places it under the Table on brackets suspended from the underside of the Table for the purpose.[5] This signifies that the Speaker (or a member acting on behalf of the Speaker) is no longer presiding over the House. The presiding officer is the chairperson who sits in the Clerk's seat at the Table (though the Speaker may participate in the committee's proceedings like any other member of the House). Also seated at the Table on the chairperson's right is the Minister or other member principally responsible for the business before the committee and, seated on the chairperson's left, one of the Clerk's assistants who acts as clerk to the committee.

General rules for proceedings

A committee of the whole House may not adjourn its own proceedings.[6] An adjournment of the committee of the whole House would effectively adjourn the House. If the committee feels that it cannot proceed any further with the matter before it, its proper course is to report that fact to the House, whereupon the Speaker will resume the chair and the House will decide what is the next step to take on it. Nor may a committee of the whole House subdelegate the task which has been given to it by appointing a subcommittee to consider the matter or by referring it to a select committee.[7] If the House wishes to have a smaller group of members consider a matter, the House may refer that matter to a select committee. That is not a function of a committee of the whole House.

Although committees of the whole House do operate in a less formal way than the House itself, most of the formal rules that provide a background to the House's proceedings also apply in committee. Except where the Standing Orders expressly provide to the contrary, these general rules for the conduct of business apply in committee as they do in the House.[8]

Call in committee

The proceedings of the House in committee are principally differentiated from proceedings in the House itself by the fact that members make shorter and more frequent contributions to the debate. Unlike in the House, members may speak more than once to a question

---

[3]   S.O.171.
[4]   S.O.49(2).
[5]   S.O.172.

[6]   S.O.181.
[7]   2005, Vol.623, p.18723.
[8]   S.O.174.

before the committee.[9] This enables members to re-enter the debate to deal with points that have been raised earlier in the debate. This is a particularly important relaxation of debating rules from the point of view of the Minister in charge of the bill or business under consideration, because it enables the Minister to respond to questions or points made by members in the course of the debate. All speeches in committee are limited to a maximum of five minutes.[10]

CHAIRPERSONS

The Deputy Speaker is the chief presiding officer when the House goes into committee, presiding over each committee as chairperson.[11]

In committee, the chairperson performs the role played in the House by the Speaker. The chairperson is the sole judge of all matters arising in committee; for example, the relevancy of debate, the acceptability of amendments, whether there is tedious repetition and when to accept a closure motion. No individual member can appeal to the Speaker from a ruling of the chairperson.[12] If a ruling given by the chairperson is seriously disputed, a motion may be made that the chairperson report progress to take the Speaker's ruling on the matter. This motion is moved on a point of order. It is not subject to amendment or debate.[13]

It has been the practice, where the motion is moved in a case of genuine dispute, that it not be opposed, though there have been occasions on which it has been defeated.[14] The Speaker has warned members not to abuse the right to recall the Speaker to review a chairperson's ruling. Invoking it inappropriately or too frequently could bring the practice of the majority agreeing to the Speaker's recall into question.[15] Even when the Speaker is recalled to rule on a matter that has arisen in committee the Speaker's role is limited. Speakers have consistently ruled that they cannot alter a decision of the chairperson on a question of relevancy in debate or the admissibility of an amendment, whether or not they consider the chairperson to have been wrong. Such a decision could be reversed only by the House itself passing a motion following notice of that motion having been given.[16] In respect of other matters, the Speaker, if appealed to by the committee, will give guidance as to the proper procedure to be followed in a committee of the whole House.

Reflections on the actions of the chairperson or on any other member chairing the committee, such as inferring that the chairperson exercised rights that were not entitled to be exercised under the Standing Orders, are not in order.[17] Any questioning of the impartiality of the chairperson is regarded extremely seriously and may constitute a breach of privilege.

Other chairpersons

In the Deputy Speaker's absence an Assistant Speaker acts as chairperson of a committee of the whole House.[18] The Deputy Speaker and the Assistant Speakers are completely interchangeable as chairpersons and all exercise the full powers of the office. There cannot, for example, be any appeal from one chairperson to another chairperson. The only appeal from a ruling given in committee by whoever is in the chair is to the Speaker in the House if the committee decides to seek it. In practice, before the House goes into committee, the Deputy Speaker and the Assistant Speakers will decide between them who will preside and for what periods of time.

---

9   Appendix A to the Standing Orders.
10   *Ibid.*
11   S.O.173(1).
12   1881, Vol.40, p.97.
13   S.O.179.

14   2002, Vol.605, pp.2882-3.
15   1998, Vol.570, p.10675; 1998, Vol.573, p.13618.
16   1910, Vol.153, p.961; 1957, Vol.313, p.2118.
17   1913, Vol.167, pp.200-1.
18   S.O.173(1).

Temporary chairpersons

As in the House, the member presiding in committee may at any time ask another member to take over the duty of presiding over the committee. This is done without any formal communication to the committee; the member concerned simply takes the chair at the Table as temporary chairperson.[19] There is no restriction on who may take the chair as temporary chairperson, the decision lies with the chairperson who invites the member to do so. A whip has taken the chair as temporary chairperson.[20] A temporary chairperson is in the same position as any other chairperson except that a temporary chairperson cannot accept a closure motion.[21] In an exceptional case the House has given a temporary chairperson the power to accept a closure motion.[22]

Acting chairperson

Before the House can go into committee there must be a member present who can take the chair as chairperson. If neither the Deputy Speaker nor an Assistant Speaker is present at such a time it is necessary for the House to appoint a member as acting chairperson before the Speaker leaves the chair. This can be done by leave of the House, otherwise the Speaker will accept a motion for the appointment of an acting chairperson.[23] A member who has been appointed acting chairperson by the House exercises all the powers of the office while presiding, including that of accepting a closure motion. Appointment as acting chairperson in these circumstances endures only for the life of the particular committee of the whole House in respect of which it was made.

Participation in debate

When not occupying the chair, the extent to which a chairperson participates in debates or other proceedings of the House is entirely a matter for the member holding that office to determine.[24] In fact, it is not regarded as consonant with the office for the chairperson (who is also Deputy Speaker) to play a robust political role in the House.

An Assistant Speaker is less restrained in participating in debate in the House, although it is not regarded as good practice for an Assistant Speaker to debate in the House procedural issues that were dealt with in committee. If an Assistant Speaker is also the chairperson of a select committee, there is no practice which requires the Assistant Speaker to refrain from taking the chair on a bill which has been considered by that committee.[25]

MAINTENANCE OF ORDER

The maintenance of order in a committee of the whole House is the responsibility of the chairperson. (See Chapter 11.)

BUSINESS CONSIDERED IN COMMITTEE

There are different types of business that are considered in committees of the whole House and the precise rules for the conduct of the committee differ accordingly.

The most frequent use of a committee of the whole House is to consider a bill – the committee stage in passing legislation. (See Chapter 27.) The committee stage of the first or main Appropriation Bill of each financial year is the Estimates debate, when the committee goes through the various departmental votes seeking authority to spend money

---

19   S.O.173(2).
20   1995, Vol.550, p.9187.
21   S.O.137(4).
22   2000, JHR, p.690.

23   See, for example: 1982, JHR, p.298; 2004, Vol.616, p.11686.
24   1974, Vol.395, p.5580; 1992, Vol.531, p.12131.
25   1986, Vol.473, p.3496.

or incur expenses up to specified amounts. The Financial Review debate is held in a committee of the whole House. It is also the longstanding practice for major revisions of the Standing Orders to be considered in a committee of the whole House before their adoption by the House.[26] Finally, the House may conduct an examination of witnesses in a committee of the whole House.[27] (See Chapter 30.) The individual speaking times for these items of business and the particular rules applying to them are dealt with in the respective sections of this book.

INSTRUCTIONS

A committee of the whole House may consider only those matters which have been referred to it by the House.[28] Apart from the referral of particular items of business to the committee, the House directs and guides its committees by means of instructions. An instruction may relate to the scope of the business to be considered by the committee – by extending or restricting consideration of that business – or it may relate to the procedure that the committee is to follow in considering the business referred to it.[29]

An instruction must be relevant to the subject matter of the bill or other business that has been referred to the committee. It must not be foreign to it or destructive of it.[30]

An instruction must not be supererogatory – if the committee already possesses power to do what is in the instruction or is required by the Standing Orders to proceed in the same way as proposed in the instruction, the instruction cannot be given. An instruction must extend or restrict the committee's powers or require that they be exercised in a particular way and thus withdraw a discretion from the committee. An instruction must be supplementary to the task with which the committee is charged, not contrary to the functions of the committee as such. Thus an instruction seeking to permit the committee of the whole House to set up a subcommittee to report back to it and to embody the subcommittee's report in its own report to the House was not in order.[31] The question of setting up subcommittees is one to be dealt with by the Standing Orders, not by means of an instruction.

Most instructions relate to the way in which the committee is to consider a bill that has been referred to it. (See Chapter 27.)

Moving an instruction

An instruction can be moved on notice as a Government or Member's motion. But, in addition, an instruction may be moved immediately after the order of the day for committal (or further consideration) of the business to which it relates.[32] This is how an instruction is commonly moved. In this case no notice is required of the intention to move it. The initiative for moving an instruction at this time lies with individual members. Frequently, the Speaker will have received advance warning that a member intends to move an instruction, but this is not essential. What is essential is that the motion is moved before the House goes into committee.[33] But a member is not prevented from moving an instruction by the fact that a point of order is raised immediately after the order of the day is read; indeed a mover wishing to move an instruction usually attracts the Speaker's attention by taking a point of order and moving the motion on being called to speak to the point of order by the Speaker.[34]

A member can only move one instruction to a committee on any one occasion. The

---

[26] 1931, Vol.227, pp.544-5.
[27] S.O.175.
[28] S.O.176.
[29] S.O.177(1).
[30] 1931, Vol.227, p.436 (*Finance Bill*); 1993, Vol.534, p.14421 (*Taxation Reform Bill (No 6)*).

[31] 1933, Vol.236, p.896 (*Reserve Bank of New Zealand Bill*).
[32] S.O.177(2).
[33] 2000, Vol.582, p.902.
[34] *Ibid.*

Speaker will give preference to the member in charge of the business (usually a bill) if there is more than one member wishing to move an instruction on the same occasion, but there can be more than one instruction moved on each occasion provided that a later instruction is not inconsistent with a previous instruction already agreed to. An instruction given to a committee of the whole House on one day endures into a future day if the committee does not complete that business at one sitting and the House goes into committee on it again.

Debate on instruction

The debate on a motion for an instruction is restricted to the subject matter of the motion and may not extend to the principles, objects or provisions of the bill or other matter to which the motion relates. Debate must be solely directed to the power or restriction which it is proposed to address to the committee.[35] One particular type of instruction – to consider a bill clause by clause – is not subject to debate or amendment at all.[36]

Variation of an instruction

The House can vary or revoke an instruction. This can be done on notice as a Government or Member's motion or as a further instruction before the House goes into committee to consider the business again.

As a committee of the whole House consists of all members of the House, it can, by leave of the committee, vary the terms of an instruction given to it.[37] An instruction cannot be varied by a motion moved in committee.

Repetition of an instruction

An instruction cannot be repeated. Where the House has given an instruction or defeated a motion for an instruction on a bill or other piece of business, a motion for a similar instruction on that bill or business cannot be moved again in the same calendar year.[38]

REPORTS

The committee must report the results of its deliberations to the House, whether these are final[39] or interim (referred to as "progress" or "no progress").[40]

Motions to report

The chairperson may be directed by the committee to report to the House at any time during the committee's consideration of the matter before it. A motion to report progress may be moved to take the Speaker's ruling on a disputed point,[41] or it may simply be moved with the intention of bringing the committee's deliberations to an end.[42] In this latter case the member moves, "That the committee report progress". Only a member who has been given the call to speak in the ordinary way can move this motion; it cannot be done on a point of order.[43] A member who moves a motion for progress to be reported does this as an alternative to speaking to the question. When such a motion has been moved, the question on it is put at once without amendment or debate.[44] If the motion is lost, another member will be called to speak. If the motion is agreed to, further consideration of that business ends and the chairperson reports it to the House accordingly. Once reported, the business is then set down for resumption on a future day.

The member in charge of a bill before the committee may move a motion "That the

---

[35] S.O.177(3).
[36] *Ibid.*
[37] S.O.177(5).
[38] S.O.177(4).
[39] S.O.183(1).

[40] S.O.183(2).
[41] S.O.179.
[42] S.O.182(1).
[43] 1985, Vol.468, pp.8439-41.
[44] S.O.182(3).

committee report progress and sit again presently".[45] In this case too the question is put at once without amendment or debate.[46] If this motion is agreed to the business can be resumed later in the same sitting.

Obligation to report

The committee of the whole House must report back to the House five minutes before the sitting is due to end; that is, at 9.55 pm on a Tuesday and Wednesday and at 5.55 pm on a Thursday.[47] For this purpose the chairperson interrupts the business at that time and the Speaker automatically resumes the chair. If the Speaker is already in the chair five minutes before the sitting is to end to rule on a point of order which the committee has reported to the House in order to take the Speaker's ruling, or because of any other temporary suspension of the proceedings of the committee, the Speaker has the option of ruling on the matter there and then, or of deferring a ruling. In these circumstances, the Speaker declares the House in committee again so that the committee can complete the formalities of reporting to the House as if it were five minutes before the conclusion of the sitting.[48]

Occasionally, the chairperson may be required to report progress at a particular time for the House to go on to other business. This will occur whenever the House specifically orders a bill or debate to be held at a particular time.

Whenever a vote is in progress five minutes before the conclusion of a sitting or a question is in the process of being put and a vote results, the interruption of proceedings by the chairperson is postponed until after completion of the vote. No further question is put by the chairperson unless a closure motion has been carried, in which case all consequential questions may be put (and voted on) in order to determine the original question before the committee reports to the House.[49] Where there are many amendments to a question before the committee this can considerably prolong the sitting.

Manner of reporting

When the Speaker resumes the chair, the chairperson stands on the floor of the House to the right of the Speaker's chair, reports on each of the matters referred to the committee by the House and moves that the report be adopted. Where the committee has not fully considered a bill or other matter, the chairperson reports that the committee has made progress or, if the bill was not reached at all, no progress, as the case may be.[50] The Speaker repeats the committee's report to the House and then puts the question for its adoption. This question is not subject to amendment or debate.[51]

---

[45] S.O.182(2).
[46] S.O.182(3).
[47] S.O.50(1).
[48] S.O.180.

[49] S.O.51.
[50] S.O.183(2).
[51] S.O.184.

CHAPTER 21

SELECT COMMITTEES

Most large bodies find it convenient to refer issues to smaller groups of their members for detailed study and report back to the main body. Indeed it has been said that a legislature must function through its committees.[1] That is certainly true of the House of Representatives. For this purpose, as well as employing committees consisting of all its members to debate the details of legislation and Standing Orders changes (committees of the whole House) the House also employs smaller committees of members to carry out a wide range of parliamentary work. These smaller groups of members are known as select committees. The Business Committee, though a committee of the House, is not regarded as a select committee. Because it must make all of its decisions in accordance with a principle of unanimity, its membership and practices are more fluid than those of select committees and it is best considered *sui generis*. (See Chapter 14.)

It is in select committees that most of the intensive work of the House is carried on – whether of a legislative, financial, investigatory or scrutiny nature. It is in select committees too that the public is involved in the work of the House directly. By its nature, debate in the Chamber is confined to debate among members of Parliament. But select committee work is not conducted only by members of Parliament. It involves thousands of non-members each year – Government officials, members of public bodies, trade unionists, representatives of associations, and individual members of the public – who are themselves either the subject of some inquiry or scrutiny by a committee or, more often, who wish to contribute their knowledge and opinions to the subject under consideration by a committee. This interchange between parliamentarian and public, particularly as part of the legislative process, is the most distinctive feature of New Zealand's parliamentary system.

Select committees are established by the House[2] and are creatures of their parent body. They cannot have functions and powers that the House does not possess. Nor can they exercise functions and powers that have not been conferred on them by the House or which the House has directed them not to exercise. Their duty is to carry out work on behalf of the House and to communicate their conclusions to the House in the form of reports. The creation of select committees has been regularised in that the House has, by its Standing Orders, provided for the automatic establishment of particular committees at the beginning of each Parliament. In addition to those committees recognised in the Standing Orders, other committees are set up from time to time for particular purposes. These are often referred to as "ad hoc" committees. Thus a committee may be set up to carry out a particular task or for a limited time and go out of existence when it has performed that task or that time has expired. But most committees (whether regular committees or ad hoc) continue in existence for the duration of the Parliament.

FUNCTIONS OF COMMITTEES

The functions performed by select committees cover almost the entire range of functions performed in the House itself. Indeed, because of the pressures on House time, many

---

[1] *Attorney-General (Canada) v MacPhee*, Prince Edward Island Supreme Court, 14 January 2003 at [42].

[2] S.O.185(1),(2).

functions performed by committees are not performed in the Chamber or are performed there to a much lesser extent.

Legislation

With few exceptions, all bills which are introduced into the House are referred to select committees for study before they receive a first reading.

The functioning of select committees as part of the legislative process is one of the original functions that they came to perform after they were first set up in 1854. It is the single most important item of work which they perform and it is mainly through their performance of this task that the public participates in the parliamentary process.

A committee may be set up with the sole function of considering legislation that is referred to it,[3] but most committees combine a legislative function with other functions.

The proportion of time that each committee devotes to considering legislation as opposed to performing its other functions differs depending upon the committee's subject area. It can also differ markedly from year to year as legislative priorities change. The greater part of most committees' time is spent considering legislation, and for some this proportion can be as high as 90 percent of their meeting time. On the other hand, a committee which has a low legislative workload may devote perhaps only five percent of its time to legislation and concentrate its efforts on other select committee functions.[4] (See Chapter 27 for consideration of bills.)

Petitions

All petitions presented to the House that are in order are allocated by the Clerk to a select committee for consideration and report.[5] This does not generally open up as wide a field of inquiry as when a committee is considering a bill, but, on occasion, it can lead a committee into holding an extensive round of meetings and evidence-gathering.[6] (See Chapter 37 for petitions.)

Estimates and financial review

Each year select committees conduct both an examination of each government department's and office of Parliament's spending plans (estimates) and a financial review of the previous year's performance of each department, office of Parliament, Crown entity, State enterprise and of certain other public organisations. The Finance and Expenditure Committee allocates the estimates and financial review work to the various committees for these purposes. The estimates examination takes place in the period May-August, in the two-month period following delivery of the Budget. There may, in addition, be an examination of any supplementary estimates towards the end of the financial year. Committees have the period from the presentation of the department's annual report (September/October or rather later in an election year) to one week after the commencement of the House's sittings in the following year to conduct their financial reviews of departments. They have six months to conduct financial reviews of Crown entities, State enterprises and other public organisations. (See Chapters 34 and 36 for committees' financial work.)

---

[3] 2000, Vol.582, pp.1098-108 (Employment and Accident Insurance Legislation Committee); 2003, Vol.614, pp.10485-8, 10557-66 (Fisheries and Sea-related Legislation Committee).

[4] 1987-90, AJHR, I.14B, para.5.3 (*Report of the Business Committee on the Committee's Review of the Inquiry Function of the Subject Select Committees*); 1993-96, AJHR, I.18A, p.31 (Standing Orders Committee).

[5] S.O.361.

[6] 1970, Vol.370, pp.4930-1 (Lake Manapouri); 1987-90, AJHR, I.2B and I.2C (closure of rural post offices).

International treaty examinations

Select committees conduct examinations of international treaties with a view to drawing the attention of the House to any features of a treaty that the committee wishes to raise. In the first instance, treaties stand referred to the Foreign Affairs, Defence and Trade Committee which may allocate them to the committee whose terms of reference relate most closely to the subject-matter of the treaty. (See Chapter 43.)

Matters referred to a committee

The House may refer any particular issue to a committee for inquiry. This can occur because a statute requires that such an inquiry be undertaken by a committee, because of widespread public concern which the House wishes to address by requiring a committee to conduct an inquiry,[7] or in response to a request from the committee because the committee does not have the power to inquire into a matter which it has identified as needing attention.[8] (See Chapter 30 for statutory inquiries.) Often ministerial amendments to a bill which is before the committee are placed on a supplementary order paper and referred to the committee for it to study along with the bill. Indeed, in respect of substantial amendments it is expected that this be done.[9] In the case of the Privileges Committee, only issues specifically referred to it by the House as questions of privilege may be considered by it,[10] but it is unusual for a committee to be confined in its functions to considering only matters referred to it by the House (though this was the norm until 1985).

Apart from matters referred by the House, there are instances where the Standing Orders recognise that matters can be referred in other ways than by the House. Ministers can refer draft regulations, proposals for the creation of an officer of Parliament and amendments to Local Legislation bills to the appropriate select committees. The committees are obliged to consider and report on such proposals.[11] Further, in respect of regulations, any person aggrieved at a regulation's operation may complain to the Regulations Review Committee, and this complaint must be considered at the next meeting of the committee.[12]

Inquiries initiated by the committee

Matters referred to committees by the House are usually confined to legislation, estimates, financial reviews, treaties and petitions. The House refers relatively few other issues for select committee inquiry. This is largely because most select committees, within their subject areas of competence, have the power to initiate inquiries themselves. This is a major change; before 1985 most committees had no power to initiate inquiries and could work only on the basis of matters referred to them by the House. Subject select committees now have a general power to receive briefings on, or initiate inquiries into, matters related to their respective subject areas.[13] "Briefings" are in the nature of one-off meetings with experts in a committee's subject area, discussions with visiting parliamentary delegations or early information-gathering activities by a committee. "Inquiries" are more elaborate investigations of a topic, usually involving the receipt of evidence and culminating in a report to the House.[14]

When the committees were created in 1985 the subject areas of the committees were arranged so as to reflect the organisation of departmental responsibilities. They still maintain a close relationship between departmental responsibilities. But, since 1996, they are no longer tied to the policy or activities of Government. They extend to any

---

7   1989, Vol.497, pp.10004-16 (Agent Orange).
8   1991, Vol.518, pp.4308-9 (wholesale and retail electricity prices).
9   1993-96, AJHR, I.18A, p.56.
10 S.O.391(2).

11 S.Os 314(2) and 386(1)(c) and Appendix C to the Standing Orders, para.24.
12 S.O.316.
13 S.O.190(2).
14 2002-05, AJHR, I.18B, p.28.

matter falling within the generic subject area allotted to the committee.[15] If a committee wishes to initiate an inquiry falling outside its own subject-area it can ask the House for permission to do so.[16] Whether the other committees that the House establishes from time to time have authority to launch inquiries within the scrutiny areas allocated to them depends upon their precise terms of reference.

Some subject select committees are more readily able to utilise their powers to initiate inquiries than others. This results from the disparity in legislative work referred to committees. A committee may have little time left over from its heavy legislative commitments to devote to inquiry work. On the other hand, committees which work in subject areas that generate little legislation have much more opportunity to conduct major inquiries. (See also Chapter 30 for select committees' inquiry powers.)

Special functions

Apart from the general functions already referred to, committees may have special functions conferred on them. The Regulations Review Committee, for instance, carries out a scrutiny role in respect of regulations, drawing the House's attention to regulations with certain features and the Officers of Parliament Committee has administrative functions to discharge in respect of the offices of Parliament, such as recommending their funding and auditors and developing codes of practice for them.

TERMS OF REFERENCE

A select committee, being a creature of the House, may carry out only such investigations or functions which the House has empowered it to carry out. The committee's functions and special powers are set out in the Standing Orders or in the resolution appointing it, which is known as its order of reference, and this may be supplemented by further orders (instructions) enlarging or restricting its power or referring other matters to it for investigation.

When a bill stands referred to a select committee following its first reading, the motion moved by the member in charge of the bill nominating the committee to consider the bill may go on to confer special powers on the committee or instruct it as to how it goes about its task of considering the bill.[17] Thus, a committee has been ordered to return a bill to the House after having asked questions of officials and having been briefed on it. These were the only things it was empowered to do.[18] It is quite common for committees to be ordered to report bills back to the House by a particular date or to have conferred on them power to meet at times otherwise prohibited or restricted by the Standing Orders.

The scope of the committee's investigations and any special powers assigned to it can, therefore, be ascertained only by reference to its order of reference. The interpretation of a committee's order of reference is a matter for the committee itself to determine subject to any directions it may receive from the House.[19]

Instructions

As with a committee of the whole House, the House may give an instruction to one of its select committees extending or restricting its powers in regard to the consideration of business before it or requiring it to carry out that consideration in a particular manner. While there is an opportunity to give instructions to a committee as to how it is to conduct its proceedings when it is being set up or when business is being referred to it, there is no

---

[15]   S.Os 189 and 190(2).
[16]   See, for example, 1996-99, AJHR, I.5B (role of members of Parliament and their outside interests).
[17]   S.O.286(3).
[18]   1981, JHR, p.136 (*Social Security Amendment Bill*

(No 2)).
[19]   1984-85, AJHR, I.12C, p.147 (*Speaker's ruling, Public Expenditure Committee 1984, Report on Inquiry into Devaluation*).

subsequent opportunity to move instructions to it without notice. Select committees can only be subsequently directed in their conduct by motions of which notice has been given or of which notice has been dispensed with by leave.

An instruction to a select committee may relate to the substantive matters before the committee, giving it power to investigate matters not originally referred to it. This has happened when the scope of the inquiry which the committee was initially set up to carry out needed to be widened.[20] A committee may also suggest an amendment to its own terms of reference, such as inviting the House to extend them to enable it to consider whether a bill of wider scope than that before it is desirable, and to permit it to draft, circulate and hear submissions on a wider bill.[21] Instructions may also be given to a select committee on procedural matters, such as to allow it to meet at times that it was not originally authorised to meet at.

A select committee does not have the power to set aside an instruction by leave (as does a committee of the whole House).[22] However, when a power has been conferred on a select committee (as opposed to the committee being directed to do something) it is up to the committee whether or not it exercises that power.[23]

Terms of reference adopted by committees
In order to provide a focus for inquiries they decide to initiate and to assist groups who may wish to make submissions on them, committees usually draft and adopt terms of reference when they set out on an inquiry under their inquiry function. Provided the inquiry on which they have embarked is within the terms of reference conferred on the committee by the House, internally adopted terms of reference are for the committee's guidance only and no question of the committee acting outside those terms can be raised other than by committee members themselves at the committee.[24] Having adopted terms of reference for an inquiry, the committee may proceed to advertise them in the press and call for submissions, and may announce them at a press conference.[25]

TYPES OF SELECT COMMITTEES
There are 17 select committees established by the House pursuant to its Standing Orders. (A fuller treatment of the work of some of the specific committees is given elsewhere in this book.)

Subject select committees established by the Standing Orders
Thirteen subject select committees are established by the Standing Orders.[26] These committees and their subject area competencies are set out here.

Commerce Committee: business development, commerce, communications, consumer affairs, energy, information technology, insurance and superannuation.

Education and Science Committee: education, education review, industry training, research, science and technology.

Finance and Expenditure Committee: audit of the financial statements of the Government and departments, Government finance, revenue and taxation. The committee examines and reports on the Crown's financial statements and the Budget policy statement. It allocates estimates and financial review work to the other committees. (See Chapters 31, 34 and 36.)

---

20 1969, JHR, p.35 (Publicity Division Committee of Inquiry).
21 1982, AJHR, I.5, p.4; 1982, JHR, p.79 (*Domestic Violence Bill*).
22 1993-96, AJHR, I.18B, p.7.
23 2002, Vol.599, p.15303.
24 1984-85, AJHR, I.12C, pp.147-8.
25 1986-87, AJHR, I.3A, para.2.4.1.
26 S.Os 185(1)(a) and 189.

Foreign Affairs, Defence and Trade Committee: customs, defence, disarmament and arms control, foreign affairs, immigration and trade. The committee allocates proposed treaties to other committees for examination. (See Chapter 43.)

Government Administration Committee: civil defence, cultural affairs, fitness, sport and leisure, internal affairs, Pacific Island affairs, Prime Minister and Cabinet, racing, services to Parliament, State services, statistics, tourism, women's affairs and youth affairs.

Health Committee: health.

Justice and Electoral Committee: Crown legal and drafting services, electoral matters, human rights and justice.

Law and Order Committee: corrections, courts, criminal law, police and serious fraud.

Local Government and Environment Committee: conservation, environment and local government.

Māori Affairs Committee: Māori affairs. This committee has met in a specially dedicated committee room since 1922.[27] The room in which it currently meets (known as Maui Tikitiki a Taranga) is on the ground floor of Parliament House. It was dedicated in 1996 following the strengthening and refurbishment of Parliament House.

Primary Production Committee: agriculture, biosecurity, fisheries, forestry, lands and land information.

Social Services Committee: housing, senior citizens, social development, veterans' affairs and work and income support.

Transport and Industrial Relations Committee: accident compensation, industrial relations, labour, occupational health and safety, transport and transport safety.

These subject committees conduct the full range of business discussed above, considering bills, petitions, estimates, financial reviews, international treaties and other matters initiated by themselves or referred to them by the House.[28]

Other committees established under the Standing Orders

The Standing Orders establish four other select committees each Parliament.[29]

Officers of Parliament Committee: approves and recommends the budgets for the offices of Parliament (the Auditor-General, the Office of the Ombudsmen, and the Parliamentary Commissioner for the Environment).[30] The committee acts as the principal (though not the only) parliamentary contact for the officers of Parliament in their relations with the House. (See Chapter 6.)

Privileges Committee: considers and reports on any matters that may be referred to it by the House relating to or concerning the privileges of the House or its members.[31] (See Chapter 48.)

Regulations Review Committee: scrutinises all regulations and reports to the House on any matter relating to regulations.[32] This committee has, since it was first created in 1985, been chaired by an opposition member. (See Chapter 29.)

Standing Orders Committee: reviews the Standing Orders, procedures and practices of the House.[33] (See Chapter 10.)

Other committees established

The House may establish other select committees in addition to these 17 committees.[34] These other committees are established as the House decides that it needs them. In the

---

[27] 1922, AJHR, I.3B.
[28] S.O.190(1).
[29] S.O.185(1)(b).
[30] S.O.386.

[31] S.O.391(2).
[32] S.O.314.
[33] S.O.7.
[34] S.O.185(2).

forty-seventh Parliament one extra committee was established – the Fisheries and Sea-related Legislation Committee.[35] (The Standing Orders Committee became a committee established automatically under the Standing Orders on 10 February 2004.)

JOINT COMMITTEES

In bicameral Parliaments the two chambers often set up joint committees consisting of members of each chamber. In the nineteenth century the Legislative Council and the House of Representatives set up joint committees to study legislation or carry out inquiries on a number of occasions.[36] In 1950 the House established a committee on a bill and authorised it to confer with and agree a joint report with any similar committee established by the Legislative Council.[37]

In a unicameral Parliament, such as New Zealand's has been since 1951, a joint committee in these senses cannot be created. But occasionally the House has set up a committee whose membership consists of the members of two other committees. Such a committee, although termed a "joint committee", is in fact a distinct committee from the committees contributing to its membership. The last occasion on which such a committee was established was in 1970.[38] (See Chapter 23 for joint meetings of committees.)

---

[35]   2003, Vol.614, pp.10485-8, 10557-66.

[36]   McLintock and Wood, *The Upper House in Colonial New Zealand*, pp.198-200, 213-4.

[37]   1950, JHR, p.151 (*Capital Punishment Bill*).

[38]   1970, JHR, pp.47-8 (Lands and Agriculture Committee and Labour and Mining Committee).

CHAPTER 22

ESTABLISHMENT AND PERSONNEL
OF SELECT COMMITTEES

MANNER OF ESTABLISHING COMMITTEES

Select committees are established automatically by the Standing Orders or otherwise by the House on motion with notice. Seventeen select committees are established automatically at the commencement of each Parliament pursuant to the Standing Orders.[1] These committees cover the most important areas of work transacted by select committees. (See Chapter 21.) A motion to establish a select committee is only required if it is proposed to establish another committee outside one of these 17.

Debate

Where a committee is established by motion, each member may speak for up to 10 minutes on the motion. Debate must be confined to the subject mentioned in the motion and to reasons why the committee should or should not be established.[2] Other matters which are related to the subject proposed for consideration by the committee may be mentioned and suggested for inclusion in the motion. The motion to establish a committee is not the place for a debate on the merits of the matter proposed for consideration or for members to discuss in detail the questions which the committee will investigate,[3] though members may refer to what the committee can be expected to do.[4]

Amendment

Amendments which are relevant to any motion establishing a committee may be moved. An amendment may be designed to broaden or restrict the committee's terms of reference but it may not restrict those terms in a way that would conflict with the Standing Orders where a committee's terms of reference are prescribed by the Standing Orders (or with a statute in the rare cases where a statute prescribes terms of reference).

In general, the Business Committee appoints the members to serve on each committee. It is consequently not necessary for a motion establishing a committee to state the names of the members to serve on the committee (it was formerly obligatory that this be done). But this may still be done.[5] If the motion does deal with the personnel of the committee this subject is open to amendment. Amendments have been moved to omit the name of a member from the motion,[6] to omit the name of a member and substitute that of another member,[7] and to add a member to the nominated membership.[8]

LIFE OF COMMITTEES

Unless the House orders to the contrary, all select committees endure for the life of the Parliament.[9] This is the case with most select committees established by the House.

Committees appointed for a specified time or to perform a specified task go out of existence at the expiration of that time or on completion of that task by the presentation of their final report on it.[10] Usually such temporary committees are only established to consider a particular bill when it is not considered appropriate to refer the bill to one of

---

[1]   S.O.185(1).
[2]   1905, Vol.132, p.24.
[3]   1930, Vol.225, p.885.
[4]   1989, Vol.497, p.10229.
[5]   2000, Vol.583, pp.1597-8 (MMP Review Committee).
[6]   1967, JHR, p.88.
[7]   1969, JHR, p.31.
[8]   2000, Vol.583, p.1615.
[9]   S.O.185(3).
[10] Ibid.

the subject select committees. Temporary committees may also be appointed to conduct particular inquiries.[11] The peculiar characteristic of such committees is that they do not remain in existence until the end of the Parliament, as do most select committees appointed by the House.

SIZE OF COMMITTEES

The Standing Orders do not prescribe a standard size for each committee (from 1996 to 2004 a standard size of eight was prescribed). Rather, the determination of the size of each committee is left to the Business Committee.[12] In the absence of a Business Committee decision, the House would need to determine the matter itself.

The actual size determined for each committee depends upon the state of the parties represented in the House and their priorities as to which committees they wish their members to serve on. A constraining factor governing the size of individual committees is the need to ensure, as far as practicable, overall proportionality in party membership on the 13 subject select committees. The size of other regular committees is more flexible and the size of any special committee may be controversial and thus need to be determined, ultimately, by the House rather than the Business Committee.

The varying sizes of the respective committees can be illustrated by comparing the 13 subject committees established at the commencement of the forty-seventh Parliament in 2002. Three committees each consisted of 12 members, two of 11 members, one of 10 members, three of nine members, two of eight members, one of seven members and one of five members.

As part of its power to determine the size of each committee, the Business Committee may increase or reduce the size of a committee after having initially determined a particular size for it. Alternatively, the House may alter the size of a committee by motion on notice or by leave.[13]

MEMBERSHIP OF COMMITTEES

Overall proportionality

The general principle to be followed in determining the membership of select committees is that, overall, membership must, so far as reasonably practicable, be proportional to party membership in the House.[14] Thus, a party that holds half of the seats in the House should, if possible, have half of the available select committee memberships. This has been a formal rule of the House since 1996, although even before that select committee memberships had by convention tended to reflect the balance of parties in the House.[15]

There are a number of issues that arise from this general principle.

First, the total number of select committees is itself indeterminate. While the Standing Orders provide for 17 select committees to be established, the House may set up additional committees. Overall proportionality where the total number of committees is fluid, is impossible to achieve without constantly disrupting the memberships of established committees as new committees are set up. For this reason the obligation to achieve overall proportionality is taken to refer to the 13 subject committees, thus giving a finite goal. These are the general legislative and scrutiny committees which carry out the bulk of the House's committee work. Their overall membership must, as far as possible, be arranged on a party-proportional basis.

---

[11]   For example, 2000, Vol.583, pp.1597-625 (MMP Review Committee).

[12]   S.O.186(2).

[13]   See, for example, 2000, Vol.582, p.1071 reducing the size of the Māori Affairs Committee from 10 to nine members.

[14]   S.O.186(1).

[15]   1993-96, AJHR, I.18A, p.34.

Second, there is no standard size for a select committee. This means that the size of each individual committee can be adjusted in order to achieve overall proportionality.

Third, the obligation to maintain proportionality is a continuing obligation within certain limits. If a member of a committee leaves his or her party that member retains membership of the committee unless compulsorily replaced on it by the House or the Business Committee. In these circumstances the overall proportional balance on select committees may be distorted.

Initial appointment of members to committees

The House may appoint the membership of a select committee, either in the order establishing the committee (if there is one) or by a separate motion. Although the House still occasionally does appoint members to committees,[16] this is now comparatively rare. In practice, it is the Business Committee which appoints the members to serve on each committee established by the Standing Orders or by the House. The Business Committee may also fill any vacancy in the membership of a committee.[17] In carrying out this function at the commencement of a Parliament, the Business Committee's main concern is to agree which parties will be represented and in what numbers on the several committees, so as to achieve overall proportionality of party representation. Parties with only one or a few members cannot be represented on every committee, nor would they necessarily wish to be. However, each party will have particular committees that it wishes to serve on. The Business Committee will endeavour to agree on a formula for representation that accommodates such desires as far as possible. In addition, a particular effort is made to ensure that every party has the opportunity, if it wishes, to have a member on the Finance and Expenditure Committee given that committee's centrality to the House's budgetary and financial review work. Consequently that committee tends to have a larger membership than the other committees.

While the Business Committee formally appoints members to committees, it is normally concerned only with the party proportions on committees, not with the identity of the individual members who will serve on each committee. This is regarded as a matter for each party to determine according to its own internal arrangements and preferences. A convention has accordingly developed of the Business Committee not interfering in such matters. Thus, once the Business Committee has decided on how parties will be represented on committees, each party provides the names of its members who are to serve on each committee. These names are then formally endorsed by the Business Committee as the members appointed to the various committees.

No intimation to an individual member from the Business Committee that he or she is being appointed to serve on a select committee is necessary. Nor is a member's agreement to serve on a committee necessary. (These are matters left to each party to attend to in any case.) The member's appointment is embodied in a published determination of the Business Committee.

Non-voting members

Members may be appointed as non-voting members of committees. This practice developed so as to extend ongoing membership rights to members in suitable instances, but without destroying the party balances determined at the outset of the Parliament. In this way a small party unable to justify a full membership on every committee can

---

[16]   See, for example, 2000, Vol.583, pp.1597-625.   [17]   S.O.186(3).

participate in business of interest to it being transacted by a committee on which it does not have a full member.

While the House may confer the status of a non-voting member (before 2004 only the House could confer it), the Business Committee now has this power[18] and in practice all such appointments are made by it.

A non-voting member may not vote on any question put to the committee.[19] This means that the member cannot be a formal participant in any decision that the committee reaches, either by voting or by leave, where leave is a substitute for a decision that could have been taken by a vote. But where leave of the committee is mandatory in a particular circumstance and is not a substitute for a vote (for example, for agreement to meet on a Friday[20], to meet between midnight and 8 am[21], and to allow other members to participate in the proceedings[22]), a non-voting member's agreement to the proposal is as essential as any other member of the committee. A non-voting member does not count towards making up the quorum.[23] In all other respects (bar voting and the quorum) a non-voting member is a full member of the committee for the purposes for which he or she was appointed and is subject to replacement in the same way as any other member of the committee.

A non-voting member may be appointed permanently to a committee, for a limited time, or for the committee's consideration of a particular matter.[24] Generally non-voting members have been added to a committee's membership for consideration of a particular bill that has been referred to the committee. This sometimes has been done at the same time as the bill is referred to the committee.[25] More often it is done subsequent to the bill's referral. The House has appointed two non-voting members to a particular committee during its consideration of a bill.[26] Non-voting members have been appointed to a committee for consideration of particular estimates or the carrying out of a particular financial review.

Exceptionally, a member has been appointed as a non-voting member of a committee for all purposes.[27] In this case the House or the Business Committee must first agree to increase the size of the committee. The Business Committee may end a non-voting member's appointment where it has not otherwise lapsed.[28]

Vacancies in membership

Members who have been appointed to a select committee cannot resign from it. The House or the Business Committee can remove a member from a committee and replace the member with another member, but a member cannot simply take himself or herself off a committee to which the member has been appointed. Nor can the committee itself remove one of its members; only the House can do that.[29] But where a member dies or otherwise loses his or her seat (for example, by resigning from the House), a vacancy in the membership of the committee automatically arises. Such a vacancy can be filled by the House or by the Business Committee.[30] In filling the vacancy regard must be had to the need to maintain party-proportionality in the overall membership of select committees.[31]

Replacing members on select committees

Until 1972, replacing members on select committees could only be effected by the House

---

[18] S.O.187(1).
[19] Ibid.
[20] S.O.192.
[21] 1988, Vol.488, p.3395-6.
[22] S.O.211(1).
[23] S.O.210(2).
[24] S.O.187(2).
[25] 2001, Vol.591, p.8672 (*Shop Trading Hours Act*

Repeal Amendment Bill).
[26] 2000, Vol.589, p.7464 (*Injury Prevention and Rehabilitation Bill*).
[27] 2002, Vol.602, p.237.
[28] S.O.187(3).
[29] 2000, Vol.582, p.1071.
[30] S.O.186(3).
[31] S.O.186(1).

on motion with notice. In that year a new regime for making such changes to select committee personnel was instituted that allowed this to be attended to by the whips. The making of changes has now largely become an administrative matter dealt with off the floor of the House, rather than a matter of business to be transacted in the House itself.

A member cannot be replaced on a committee during any period for which that member is under suspension from the service of the House.[32] During such a period the suspended member cannot serve on any committee[33] and as no one can replace the member, the committee's effective membership is temporarily reduced by one. But a member who has been subjected to a lesser disciplinary process than formal suspension from the House, such as exclusion from the House or from a meeting of a select committee, may, in the case of the former circumstance, continue to serve on a committee, and, in the case of the latter, be replaced on the committee during the period of exclusion.

Changes made to the membership of a committee may be permanent changes made for the life of the committee or temporary changes for a limited time or for consideration of a particular matter.[34]

Permanent changes

Permanent changes may be made by the House itself but, more commonly, they are made by the Business Committee.[35] As party spokespersons change or for other reasons, parties from time to time wish to change their personnel on select committees. Such changes are formally effected by the Business Committee without it questioning any party's reasons for wishing to make the change. Only if it was proposed to vary the party proportions on a committee by replacing a member of one party by a member of another party would the committee exercise its own judgment on the proposal. Given the need for unanimity or near-unanimity in decision-making by the Business Committee, such a proposal would not be agreed to unless as a minimum both parties involved in the change were in agreement. Any such inter-party permanent replacements are also subject to the requirement to maintain overall party-proportionality on committees, although if the Business Committee was inclined to agree to the change this condition is likely to have been met in any case.

Changes approved by the Business Committee are actioned as Business Committee determinations.

Temporary changes

Temporary changes in the nature of replacements may be made by the House but this is extremely rare. Temporary changes may be effected under the authority of the leader or a whip of the party whose members are involved. Where two parties are involved the leaders or whips of both parties must agree to the change.[36] Temporary changes of this nature are not just common; they are invariable on days on which select committees are meeting as whips make arrangements to cope with the unavailability or indisposition of their members.

No question of varying overall party proportions on committees arises out of temporary changes. Where a permanent member has been temporarily replaced on a committee the permanent member is entitled to resume his or her place on the

---

32 S.O.188(3).
33 S.O.91.
34 S.O.188(1).

35 S.O.188(2).
36 *Ibid.*

committee at any time. If the member does so the temporary replacement is regarded as cancelled.

Temporary changes are advised to the clerk of the committee in writing by the whip or whips involved. They are effective, according to their tenor, when the advice is received. They are often given while the committee is actually meeting. It is sufficient that temporary replacement advices are received in the name of a whip, and a person acting as a whip may give them. They may also be signed on behalf of a whip by a person authorised by the whip. Only in cases of doubt that authority exists would a replacement advice be questioned.

Temporary replacements are announced to the committee by the chairperson and must be recorded in the committee's minutes.

Additional members

It is possible, once a committee has been established and its size fixed, for the House or the Business Committee subsequently to appoint an additional full member or members to the committee either on a permanent basis or for a particular item of business. The House has done this where parties have not had representation on a particular committee and it was desired to have them fully represented on the committee for consideration of a particular bill.[37]

Participation by other members

Any member of the House who is not a member of the committee can attend the committee's proceedings but can participate in them only with the leave of the committee.[38] This includes being given leave to vote if the committee is so inclined. But in the case of the Privileges Committee, while other members may attend its proceedings generally, they may only attend while it is deliberating with the specific leave of the committee.[39] If a member who is not a member of a committee attempts to participate in its proceedings without permission, the House could treat such a matter as a contempt.[40] A member attending a committee's proceedings in these circumstances who is disorderly may be excluded from the meeting by the chairperson.[41]

The member in charge of a bill before a select committee, if not already a member of the committee (when the member participates fully in that capacity), has the right to take part in any proceedings of the committee on that bill. But a member attending the committee in these circumstances may not vote on any question put to the committee.[42]

These rights to attend and, to a limited extent, participate in select committee meetings relate only to particular meetings. They do not extend ongoing membership rights, such as to receive committee documents and advices.

Nothing prevents members appearing before committees in another capacity and members often give evidence as witnesses to committees. A member has also acted as counsel (unpaid) before a committee.[43]

Disqualification of members

There are some circumstances in which a member is disqualified from serving on a select committee for a certain period of time or in respect of a particular item of business.

A member suspended from the service of the House is not able to serve on a select committee during the period of that suspension.[44] (See Chapter 11.) A committee may

---

37   See, for example, 1999, Vol.577, p.16320 (*Auckland Domain (Temporary Closure for APEC) Bill*).
38   S.O.211(1).
39   S.O.211(3).
40   1977, Vol.414, p.3127.
41   S.O.215(2).
42   S.O.211(2).
43   1986-87, AJHR, I.15, Annex B.
44   S.O.91.

itself exclude from its meeting one of its members for highly disorderly conduct. Such an exclusion is for the remainder of the meeting.[45] Furthermore, where a member of the committee participates in the committee's proceedings in another capacity, the member temporarily ceases to be able to participate as a member. This occurs, for example, when a member of the committee gives evidence to the committee.

Members may also be disqualified from serving on a committee for reasons of natural justice. In general, the prior stated views or conduct of a member are no disqualification for service on a particular committee or for consideration of a particular bill or other matter. Members are expected to make public declarations of their views and then to participate in the consideration of legislation that they have advocated or opposed. No concept of predetermination can apply to disqualify members carrying out their parliamentary duties, especially in the legislative sphere.

But where committees are investigating the conduct of particular individuals or activities (whether such an investigation arises out of the performance of a legislative function or out of a general inquiry function) with the potential to inflict damage on personal interests such as reputation or livelihood, committees are legally obliged to observe rules against bias.[46] The Standing Orders have given some content to this obligation in a parliamentary context. Thus, exceptionally, there are situations where a member's previous actions or statements mean that, in order to retain respect for the integrity of the select committee process, a member is prohibited by the House's own rules from serving on a particular inquiry.

A member who makes an allegation of breach of privilege or contempt cannot serve on any inquiry into that allegation, even if the member is a regular member of the Privileges Committee.[47] Where a member raises a matter of privilege on behalf of another member, that other member is also disqualified from serving on any Privileges Committee inquiry into it.[48] In these circumstances the member must be replaced on the committee.

"Apparent bias" on the part of a member may disqualify the member from serving on a committee. Apparent bias results when a member has made an allegation of crime or expressed a concluded view on any conduct or activity of a criminal nature, identifying a particular person as being responsible for that crime, conduct or activity concerned. In such circumstances, the member cannot serve on any select committee inquiry into that person's responsibility for or association with that crime, conduct or activity, nor may the member participate in any other select committee proceedings that may seriously damage the reputation of that person.[49]

A complaint of apparent bias may be made in writing to the chairperson of the committee concerned by any member of Parliament (whether or not a member of the committee) or by the person whose reputation it is claimed may be seriously damaged.[50] The chairperson must permit the member concerned to comment on the complaint. Having received such comment the chairperson decides whether the member is disqualified.[51] Whether the chairperson upholds the complaint or not, any member of the committee has a right of appeal to the Speaker against the chairperson's decision. This right of appeal is exercised by writing to the Speaker. If an appeal is made, the Speaker issues a decision in writing to the committee. The Speaker's decision is then final.[52]

The Speaker has emphasised that the rule on apparent bias is designed to prevent members serving on a committee if they have expressed decided views *against* a person whose reputation is in issue before the committee. It does not apply in respect of

---

[45] S.O.215(3).
[46] Joseph, "Report to the Standing Orders Committee on Natural Justice", para.6.1.
[47] S.O.398.
[48] 1996-99, AJHR, I.15C, pp.9-10.
[49] S.O.233.
[50] S.O.234(1),(2).
[51] S.O.234(3).
[52] S.O.234(4).

supportive statements. It is a specific, not a general, bias rule and must be construed accordingly. Concepts drawn from public law contexts may help to elucidate it but they cannot be used to construct a general set of rules on bias requiring the disqualification of members outside the scope of the Standing Order.[53] In particular, the rule is not a rule against predetermination in respect of the issues to be considered by the committee. Any resulting disqualification arises only from allegations of crime and not, for example, from allegations of breach of privilege.[54]

Though there are no general rules of bias to disqualify members from serving on select committees, members may in individual cases voluntarily step down from serving on a particular inquiry where their previous statements or involvements would compromise the integrity of any outcome of the inquiry. Thus, a member against whom a complaint of apparent bias was not upheld has stood down voluntarily.[55] Whether a member who has expressed views on a matter to be considered by a committee or who has a relationship that might render it inappropriate to serve on an inquiry[56] should stand down from the committee during its consideration of the matter is for the member to judge. For example, members who had signed a petition allocated to a committee of which they were members withdrew from participation in the committee's consideration of it.[57]

Financial interests

As with participation in proceedings in the House, members serving on a select committee are obliged to declare any financial interest that the member has in an item of business before the committee.[58] But this is an obligation to declare; it is not a disqualification from participating. (See Chapter 3.)

PRESIDING OFFICERS

Chairperson

Election by the committee

On a committee assembling for its first meeting, the committee's first duty is to elect a chairperson.[59] Until the committee has done this it is not in working mode. If it becomes clear during the first meeting that the committee is unable to elect a chairperson, the meeting is simply adjourned. The committee can transact no other business, nor can it decide when it will meet again. The Speaker convenes a further meeting of the committee.

For the election of a chairperson a procedure similar to the election of the Speaker is followed. The clerk of the committee acts as chairperson for the election of the chairperson of the committee and calls for nominations for election. Members nominate themselves for the office. If there is only one nomination that member is declared elected and immediately takes the chair. If two members are nominated a vote is held. If more than two members are nominated the clerk polls each individual member of the committee asking them in turn to vote for one of the nominees. If one member obtains the votes of an absolute majority of the members voting, that member is elected, otherwise the lowest polling member drops out until there are only two candidates remaining when a vote is held.

There are some conventions concerning the election of chairpersons. The Regulations

[53]   1996-99, AJHR, I.15A, Appendix 3.
[54]   *Ibid.*, I.15C, p.9.
[55]   2002-05, AJHR, I.6A, p.5 (Health Committee).
[56]   2002, Vol.598, p.14979 (Privileges Committee).
[57]   "Dalziel steps aside", *The New Zealand Herald*, 13 March 2004; 2002-05, AJHR, I.22D, p.644.
[58]   S.O.166(1).
[59]   S.O.202(1).

Review Committee has always been chaired by a member of the opposition since its creation in 1985. The Privileges Committee is usually chaired by the Attorney-General[60] and the Standing Orders Committee by the Speaker. There is no convention that overall party proportionality will be observed in the election of committee chairpersons. Most chairpersons are drawn from the ranks of the Government party or parties, though members from non-Government parties are also elected.

Appointment by the House

The Speaker is *ex officio* the chairperson of the Officers of Parliament Committee.[61] It is possible for the House, in establishing a committee, to designate a member as the chairperson. The House has done this with a committee that the Speaker was to chair.[62]

The House may be forced to appoint the chairperson of a committee where the committee is unable to elect the chairperson itself.[63]

Functions and duties

The chairperson performs a similar role in respect of chairing the committee that the Speaker does in chairing the House – calling on members to speak or ask questions, keeping order, ruling on disputed aspects of procedure and putting questions to the committee for formal decision. But the chairperson's role also extends to attending to more of the preparatory matters that are necessary for committee meetings, such as setting the proposed agenda. (See Chapter 23.)

In addition to the function of chairing the committee, the chairperson is a fully participating member of the committee in regard to the substantive business before it. In this latter regard the chairperson's role is radically different from the Speaker's since the Speaker does not participate in the debate on the business before the House other than to chair it in an impartial manner. The chairperson is bound to ensure that the House's rules and practices in regard to the conduct of select committee business are observed and to rule on their application with fairness and integrity. But the chairperson, as a member of the committee, is not an impartial figure as is the Speaker and may exercise discretions attaching to the office of chairperson in line with his or her own personal opinions on the merits of the substantive business before the committee, as long as this is done consistently with the House's rules and practices.

It is in the committee's interest to have a harmonious working relationship among members so that business can be progressed. Nakedly partisan chairpersonship does not promote this. Indeed, it is likely to be counterproductive. In practice, chairpersons carry out their duties in such a way as to endeavour to satisfy the interests of all members of the committee so far as practicable. Chairpersons also have a duty to represent the views and interests of the committee, both in authorised statements that they make to the House and the public and in less formal situations when arrangements for business that is to be considered by the committee may be under discussion.

Chairpersons must always be prepared to consider whether it is entirely appropriate for them to chair the committee or a particular meeting given other relevant factors or interests. Thus the chairperson of the Finance and Expenditure Committee indicated that he was reconsidering his position when he was appointed an Associate Minister. He referred the matter to the committee for consideration[64] and subsequently stepped down.

---

60 1996-99, AJHR, I.15C, p.10; the Attorney-General did not chair the committee in the forty-seventh Parliament.

61 S.O.202(3).

62 2000, Vol.583, pp.1597-625 (MMP Review Committee).

63 2000, Vol.581, pp.585-99 (Government Administration Committee), 601-20 (Education and Science Committee), 631-2 (Commerce Committee).

64 "Carter sees conflict in roles", *The Dominion,* 13 January 1999; 1999, Vol.575, pp.14927-8.

When the chairperson of the Māori Affairs Committee was appointed as a Parliamentary Under-Secretary he resigned the chairpersonship.[65] Where the chairperson is the member in charge of a bill which is before the committee or has another personal interest in a matter before it, the chairperson may decide to step aside from chairing the committee on that issue. This can be done either by being temporarily replaced on the committee or by the committee authorising the deputy chairperson to chair meetings while a particular item of business is under consideration.[66] (In the absence of the deputy chairperson, the committee may authorise another member to take the chair in these circumstances.) When a deputy chairperson or other member chairs the committee in this way the chairperson may continue to participate as a full member in the committee's business.[67] The House has itself authorised a chairperson to transfer the chairpersonship to another member while participating in the committee's work.[68] Otherwise the chairperson is obliged to chair a meeting at which he or she is present.

Suggestions are made from time to time that a chairperson should not chair the committee on a particular issue because of an alleged conflict of interest. Whether the chairperson does step down in any particular case is a matter for the chairperson to decide.[69]

Remuneration

The chairpersons of the 13 subject select committees and of the Regulations Review Committee enjoy a special salary by virtue of holding those offices.[70] No special remuneration is provided for the chairpersons of other committees. If a chairperson holds another office for which a higher salary is payable, he or she receives that salary rather than the chairperson's salary. Members cannot receive more than one parliamentary salary,[71] nor can they receive elements from more than one salary.

Removal from office

The chairperson can only be removed from office by the committee at a meeting of which at least seven days' notice is given of the intention to move a motion seeking the removal of the chairperson.[72] Notice of such a motion may be given orally at a meeting of the committee or in writing delivered to the clerk of the committee. If the latter, the clerk circulates a copy of the notice to all members of the committee immediately and automatically includes it on the agenda for the first meeting of the committee that is held at least seven days later. (Though if that meeting is being held on the authority of the House or the Business Committee to consider only specified business, a motion for removal must be deferred for consideration to the next regular meeting of the committee.)

Apart from through the formal removal process, a chairperson cannot be removed from office by the committee or have the rights of chairpersonship usurped by a motion to remove the chairperson from the chair.[73]

Vacancy

A chairperson may resign office at any time by advising the committee.[74] The chairperson also ceases to hold office if he or she is no longer a member of the committee, by

---

65   "Select committee reward for Mahuta", *The Dominion Post*, 6 August 2004.
66   S.O.204(1).
67   S.O.204(2).
68   2001, Vol.590, p.7865 (*Prostitution Reform Bill*); 2002, Vol.598, p.14484 (*Television New Zealand Bill*); 2002, Vol.602, p.616 (*Prostitution Reform Bill*); 2002, Vol.603, p.792 (*Smoke-free Environments (Enhanced Protection) Amendment Bill*).
69   See, for example: "Lobby wants O'Regan to step

aside", *The Dominion*, 19 November 1997 (*Casino Control (Moratorium) Amendment Bill*); 2002, Vol.598, p.14979 (Privileges Committee).
70   *Parliamentary Salaries and Allowances Determination* 2004, Sch.1.
71   *Ibid.*, cl.5(2).
72   S.O.202(2).
73   1992, Vol.526, pp.9031-2.
74   1978, Vol.417, p.765.

being permanently replaced on it or, of course, by ceasing to be a member of Parliament.

In all cases where a vacancy arises, the committee must, at its next meeting, proceed to elect a new chairperson.[75] The election procedure is the same as that followed when electing a chairperson at the first meeting. However, if a committee is unable to elect a new chairperson in these circumstances, the committee can continue to meet and function as a committee under the chairpersonship of the deputy chairperson.[76] The filling of the vacancy would be the first item on the committee's agenda each time it met until it was resolved, but the committee would not be disabled from transacting other business before it.

Deputy chairperson

At its first meeting, and immediately after the election of a chairperson, the committee must proceed to the appointment of a deputy chairperson.[77]

A deputy chairperson is appointed by the committee rather than elected by it, with the procedure being the same as with any other motion considered by the committee. Any member may move that a member of the committee be appointed deputy chairperson. This motion is subject to an amendment to substitute the name of any other member of the committee.

If a committee is deadlocked and unable to appoint a deputy chairperson this is not a disabling event, as with the failure to elect a chairperson at the first meeting. The committee proceeds to its next business. The question of the appointment of a deputy chairperson is placed first on the committee's agenda from meeting to meeting until it is resolved. A committee has informed the House by way of special report of its failure to appoint a deputy chairperson and sought guidance from the House.[78] The House has appointed deputy chairpersons to committees that were clearly unable to make the appointments themselves.[79]

The Standing Orders Committee's practice is to appoint the member of the committee with the longest service in the House as its deputy chairperson (the Speaker is chairperson).[80] Apart from this committee there are no conventions about who will be appointed to particular committee deputy chairpersonships. However, the accepted practice has been to appoint as deputy chairperson a member from a different party to that of the chairperson. Thus, a number of members from opposition parties are regularly appointed as deputy chairpersons.

The deputy chairperson automatically deputises for the chairperson in the chairperson's absence at the commencement or during the course of a meeting. The deputy chairperson also acts as chairperson if the chairperson is overseas and while there is a vacancy in the latter office.[81] When the deputy chairperson is deputising for the chairperson in these circumstances he or she performs the duties and exercises all the authority of the chairperson's office both while the committee is meeting and outside of committee meetings, such as in calling meetings and answering questions in the House addressed to the chairperson.[82] But a deputy chairperson is able to do this only while the circumstances relating to the absence of the chairperson obtain – that is, during a meeting, if the chairperson is absent, or otherwise while the chairperson is overseas, or if there

75 S.O.202(1).
76 S.O.203(1).
77 S.O.202(1).
78 1996-99, AJHR, I.22, p.295.
79 2000, Vol.581, pp.585-99 (Government

Administration Committee), 601-20 (Education and Science Committee), 631-2 (Commerce Committee).
80 1996-99, AJHR, I.18B, p.18.
81 S.O.203(1).
82 *Ibid.*

is a vacancy. At all other times the chairperson performs the duties and exercises the authority of the office exclusively and they cannot be usurped by the deputy chairperson. Thus, a deputy chairperson cannot, without leave of the House, answer a question in the House addressed to the chairperson during a casual absence of the chairperson from the Chamber.

Where the committee authorises the transfer of the chairperson's functions to a deputy chairperson during a meeting with the chairperson remaining as a participating member, the deputy chairperson performs the duties and exercises the authority of the chairperson during the meeting.[83]

The deputy chairpersons of the Regulations Review Committee and of the 13 subject committees are paid a special salary by virtue of the office.[84]

A deputy chairperson may be removed from office in the same way as may a chairperson – that is, at a meeting of the committee following seven days' notice having been given of the intention to move for the removal of the incumbent.[85] If the office becomes vacant the committee must at its first meeting after the vacancy arises proceed to appoint a new deputy chairperson.[86]

Other chairpersons

If neither the chairperson nor the deputy chairperson are present at the commencement of a meeting, but there is a quorum, the committee may elect a member to take the chair.[87] The clerk of the committee acts as chairperson for such an election. An acting chairperson elected in such circumstances chairs that meeting but performs the duties and exercises the authority of chairperson in respect of that meeting only.[88] The acting chairperson's election lapses when the meeting adjourns and that member has no further powers as chairperson outside the particular meeting in respect of which he or she was elected.

During the course of a meeting the chairperson or the deputy chairperson (if presiding) may ask another member to take the chair temporarily while they absent themselves from the meeting. In such a case the temporary chairperson performs the duties and exercises the authority of chairperson only for the period while he or she is actually chairing the committee.[89] Similarly, a member authorised to take the chair for a meeting at which the chairperson remains as a participating member exercises the authority of the chairperson only during that meeting.[90]

STAFF OF COMMITTEES

The Clerk of the House is the clerk of each committee.[91] In practice, this duty must be exercised by others on the Clerk's behalf. The Clerk may therefore authorise another person to be clerk of each particular committee.[92] Staff employed in the Office of the Clerk perform the duties of acting as clerks of committees[93] and are assigned to particular committees accordingly.

The clerk of the committee presides at the election of a chairperson and is responsible for the administrative arrangements that must be made for committee meetings, such as receiving notices of items of business that members wish to discuss, sending out notices of meetings, preparing draft agendas and drawing up minutes of the proceedings of each meeting. The clerk of the committee deals with the correspondence addressed to the committee, with guidance from the committee or the chairperson, as appropriate.

---

[83] S.O.204(3).
[84] *Parliamentary Salaries and Allowances Determination* 2004, Sch.1.
[85] S.O.202(2).
[86] S.O.202(1).
[87] S.O.203(2).
[88] *Ibid.*
[89] S.O.203(3).
[90] S.O.204(3).
[91] S.O.3(1).
[92] *Ibid.*
[93] 1988, Vol.488, p.3397.

Other staff are assigned to committees by the Clerk of the House depending upon the particular business under consideration by each committee. These staff are generally employed in the Office of the Clerk but may be drawn from related agencies such as the Parliamentary Library or be persons seconded to the Office of the Clerk for the purpose. The clerks of committees and these other staff together provide a range of support services to committees, including analysing submissions presented to committees, the drafting of reports, advising on procedural and jurisdictional aspects of a committee's work, helping to manage and co-ordinate the committee's work programme, and giving other information, research and administrative support which committees require from time to time.[94]

ADVISERS

Committees are empowered to seek the assistance of persons as advisers to help them with the work before the committee.[95] Advisers involved with committees in this way fall into a number of categories.

Officers of Parliament

Committees can ask an officer of Parliament to conduct an inquiry for it. Any committee may refer a petition, or any matter to which a petition refers, to an Ombudsman for report.[96] A somewhat wider provision exists in respect of the Parliamentary Commissioner for the Environment who may be requested to report to a committee on any petition, bill or other matter before it which may have a significant effect on the environment.[97] In these circumstances the officers are enlisted directly into the work of the committee.

Staff from the office of the Auditor-General are intimately involved in assisting committees to carry out their estimates and financial review work, providing briefings before a vote or department is examined and advice during the course of the examination. As well as assisting committees to carry out their financial business more effectively, the Auditor-General's staff may also be deputed to provide support on inquiries being undertaken by committees, and the office may carry out inquiries itself which it reports to committees to assist them with investigations they are making.[98]

The Speaker, at the request of any select committee, may require the Parliamentary Commissioner for the Environment to make staff available to advise the committee.[99] It has never been necessary to invoke this power. In fact the office of the Parliamentary Commissioner for the Environment has readily attached staff to committees either on the office's own initiative or at a committee's request to assist with bills, estimates, financial reviews or other inquiries which the committee was undertaking.[100]

The Officers of Parliament Committee has approved protocols for the provision of assistance to select committees by the Auditor-General and the Parliamentary Commissioner for the Environment.[101] These protocols describe the ways in which the officers may become involved with select committees in inquiries that the committees are undertaking or contemplating. They provide for the officers to consult with the committee concerned about the nature and extent of the assistance to be provided, and for the Officers of Parliament Committee to be consulted before an involvement that could lead to a commitment of more than six months duration or more than $20,000 in cost, is accepted.[102]

---

[94]   1996-99, AJHR, A.8A, p.4.
[95]   S.O.212(1).
[96]   *Ombudsmen Act* 1975, s.13(4).
[97]   *Environment Act* 1986, s.16(1)(d); 1987-90, AJHR, I.11A.
[98]   1991-93, AJHR, B.28, pp.18-9 (Controller and Auditor-General).

[99]   *Environment Act* 1986, s.14.
[100] 2004, PP, C.12, p.20.
[101] 1993-96, AJHR, I.17B (Parliamentary Commissioner for the Environment); 1999-2002, AJHR, I.15A (Controller and Auditor-General).
[102] 1999-2002, AJHR, I.15A, para.10.6.

Legislative drafters

For all Government bills the Parliamentary Counsel Office (the Inland Revenue Department in the case of tax legislation) undertakes the drafting of amendments which select committees wish to consider.

The Parliamentary Counsel Office is responsible to the Attorney-General but, nevertheless, provides advice and drafting services to select committees. It was formerly the case that a parliamentary counsel would attend all select committee meetings on the bill with which that counsel was involved, but this practice ceased some years ago and attendance is now generally limited to the consideration and deliberation phases of a committee's work. Even so, committees have experienced difficulties in securing the attendance of parliamentary counsel owing to competing demands on their (counsel's) time.[103]

The services of the Parliamentary Counsel Office are not available as a matter of course to select committees considering all bills. Committees must ask the Attorney-General if a parliamentary counsel will be made available to them to draft amendments which they wish to consider. While such assistance is taken for granted for Government bills and is virtually always forthcoming for private and local bills, it has been refused for a Member's bill.[104] If the services of the Parliamentary Counsel Office are not made available a committee can apply to the Clerk of the House for legislative drafting assistance to be made available from the Office of the Clerk.

Departmental officials

The principal source of advice available to committees considering Government bills comes from officials of the department of the Minister in charge of the bill. Sometimes a team of officials from more than one department provides this service. Such officials are, almost as a matter of course, accepted by the committee as advisers to it and attend the committee's proceedings at all times, including during the consideration and deliberation phases, unless specifically excluded. Although they are advisers to the committee, their primary duty as public servants lies to their respective Ministers and it is always a decision for Ministers as to whether to make officials available as advisers and who those officials will be.[105] It would be an exceptional event for a Minister to refuse departmental assistance on a Government bill for it is to the benefit of both the Government and the committee to have the participation of officials with a detailed knowledge of the measure, but even so the Government will have to consider what priority it gives to the legislation for which assistance is sought, given competing demands for officials' time.[106] If departmental assistance were refused, the committee would not be prevented from proceedings with the bill, but it might require other support to do so effectively.

Officials acting as advisers to committees on bills are regarded as doing so in support of ministerial accountability to Parliament and are ultimately subject to ministerial direction. They are expected to keep their Minister informed of their dealings with a committee and, as Ministers generally do not attend committees, can have a crucial role in preventing mutual misunderstandings arising between the Government and the committee on the progress of the bill.

Departmental officials provide information to the committee about the legislation and how it is intended to be implemented. They comment on evidence as it is received, if required, and after all the evidence has been heard they invariably produce a report for

---

[103] 1991-93, AJHR, I.23.
[104] 1996-99, AJHR, I.8A (*Conveyancers Bill* 1997).
[105] See generally, "Public Servants and Select Committees – Guidelines", State Services

Commission, February 2002, updated February 2004.
[106] 1996-99, AJHR, I.19A, p.157 (*Local Government Law Reform Bill*).

the committee summarising the submissions received and making their recommendations (with their Minister's endorsement) for amendments to the bill.

Although their primary duty is to their Ministers, they are officials of the committees that they are servicing. As well as observing the general confidentiality obligations applying to any parts of the committee's proceedings not held in public, they have obligations to act responsibly and in good faith towards the committee. They are expected to provide complete and accurate information to it, making it clear where (for example, because of a ministerial direction) they are unable to do so. Failure to be open with the committee in this way is an abuse of their position as advisers to the committee.

Departmental officials may, indeed must, keep their Minister and chief executive informed of their work for a committee. Where a committee asks a department to provide a governmental view on a matter it is implicit in such a request that consultation with other interested departments may be undertaken first as a matter of course. With other information requests where it may not be immediately apparent that inter-departmental consultation will be necessary, officials are expected to inform the committee before communicating committee proceedings to another department. In any case where in carrying out work for a committee consultation outside the public service will be necessary, the committee should be informed first.[107]

Departmental officials must not, without the committee's express authority, take action in a committee's name.[108] Not only is this a usurpation of the committee's authority, it is constitutionally inappropriate since departmental officials are employees of the executive, not the legislature.

On private and local bills officials are often invited by committees to play a similar role to that for Government bills. Subject to their Minister's agreement, they are likely to do so. They may be invited to act as advisers on Members' bills too, though such assistance has been denied by Ministers.[109] If the committee requests it, advisers may be engaged by the Office of the Clerk on Members' bills, otherwise the committee can proceed with no special advisory assistance.[110]

Other advisers

Committees often decide that they wish to obtain further assistance of an advisory nature beyond the range of support that is available within the Office of the Clerk or from officers of Parliament or departmental sources. This may be because, in relation to a particular inquiry, the committee requires the services of a person with a particular expertise or skill, because departmental assistance is not available (such as on a Member's bill), or because it is inappropriate to use departmental advisers (such as on an inquiry into a department's performance). Obtaining such assistance is not new – a professor of economics is recorded as having been enlisted as part of a committee's secretariat in 1931.[111] A member of Parliament (who was a doctor) has been used by a committee in an advisory role.[112]

In appropriate cases committees can obtain such assistance by appointing an adviser from a public body that is prepared to make its services available.[113] Occasionally a particular expert may donate his or her assistance. But in most cases where such assistance is necessary it will be engaged under contract with the Clerk of the House. Sometimes this assistance can be of an ongoing nature, such as the expert tax adviser position which has

[107] 1996-99, AJHR, I.16P.
[108] 1988, Vol.488, pp.3397-8.
[109] 1996-99, AJHR, I.8A (*Conveyancers Bill*); a decision later reversed see, *ibid.*, I.19B, p.194.
[110] 1999-2002, AJHR, I.22A, pp.19-20 (*Shop Trading*

Hours (Abolition of Restrictions) Bill).
[111] Bassett, *Coates of Kaipara*, pp.167-8.
[112] 2002-05, AJHR, I.22C, p.756 (*Human Assisted Reproductive Technology Bill*).
[113] 1996-99, AJHR, E.57, p.18 (Electoral Commission).

been available to the Finance and Expenditure Committee since 1992 for its consideration of tax legislation.[114] Generally, however, advisers are engaged ad hoc for a particular item of business before a committee.

The Speaker (as responsible Minister for the Office of the Clerk) has approved a protocol for the engagement of specialist advisers for select committees where this is to be funded from Vote Office of the Clerk.[115] This requires committees to notify the Clerk of the House formally of their need for specialist advice, setting out the reasons for the request and an estimate of cost. Such requests may be referred to the Speaker for approval. The method of selecting an adviser will differ depending upon the size and nature of the particular engagement, but a cost-effective, fair and transparent process must be followed. The adviser is engaged under contract with the Clerk of the House and the Office of the Clerk manages and monitors the performance of the contract. Where any adviser encounters a conflict or potential conflict of interest in carrying out his or her work this must be disclosed to the committee. It may then be necessary for the adviser to withdraw from the engagement or from parts of the committee's proceedings.[116] Whether a conflict exists and renders it necessary for the adviser to withdraw is ultimately a matter for the committee to determine.[117]

The role performed by the adviser for the committee is defined in the terms of the contract for the adviser's engagement and is subject to the ongoing control of the committee.

---

[114] "Finance committee to get own adviser", *The Dominion,* 10 March 1992

[115] 1996-99, AJHR, A.8A.

[116] 1999, Vol.577, p.16268 (*Taxation (Accrual Rules and Other Remedial Matters) Bill*).

[117] See, for example, "MPs unmoved by fish firm's cries of foul", *The New Zealand Herald,* 17 February 2003.

CHAPTER 23

SELECT COMMITTEE PROCEEDINGS

MEETINGS OF COMMITTEES

First meeting
The time for the holding of the first meeting of a committee after it has been established is determined by the Speaker.[1] (But where the House itself appoints a chairperson of the committee, the chairperson convenes the committee under the chairperson's power to decide when a committee will meet.)

The Speaker appoints a time for the first meeting that is within the regular meeting times for committees as set out in the Standing Orders. Members must have notice of the meeting at least one day ahead. The Speaker does not appoint a time for the first meeting that would otherwise require leave of the committee, such as during a sitting of the House. Where it is desired that the first meeting take place without a day's notice[2] or during a sitting,[3] the leave of the House is necessary to appoint the time for the meeting.

The Speaker advises all members of the committee in writing of the time appointed for the first meeting. Usually the arrangements for the first meeting are determined in consultation with the whips. It is irregular for any action to be taken in the committee's name before the committee holds its first meeting.[4] The only arrangements in connection with the business of the committee which may be made prior to its first meeting are those made by, or on behalf of, the Speaker for the purpose of convening that meeting.

Place of meeting
The first meeting of each committee is held in Parliament House.

A committee may meet at any place within New Zealand.[5] Committees can meet overseas if they are specially authorised to do so by the House.[6] The first committee to be given the authority to meet outside New Zealand was the Foreign Affairs and Defence Committee in 1989, which was authorised to meet with its counterpart committee in Canberra.[7]

In practice, most select committee meetings are held in Parliament House in Wellington or in the adjacent Bowen House building, which is within the parliamentary precincts. Nevertheless, committees have been increasingly willing in recent years to travel to other centres for the purposes of hearing evidence more conveniently from a number of witnesses where there are sufficient submissions to hear to justify this.[8] Where it is desired to meet outside the Wellington area (defined as comprising the cities of Wellington, Hutt, Upper Hutt and Porirua and the Paekākāriki/Raumati and Paraparaumu Wards of the Kapiti Coast District)[9] certain restrictions on meeting apply.

To meet outside the Wellington area during a sitting of the House, a committee needs the agreement of the Business Committee.[10] The Business Committee has indicated that it will agree to this only when a committee wishes to hear evidence, and not for the committee to transact other business in private (such as to deliberate on a bill) that could equally or more conveniently be transacted at Parliament House.

---

[1]   S.O.191(1).
[2]   1997, Vol.558, pp.641-2; 1999, Vol.581, p.154.
[3]   1999, Vol.581, p.154.
[4]   1981, Vol.439, p.2441.
[5]   S.O.193.
[6]   *Ibid.*

[7]   1987-90, JHR, p.1664.
[8]   1996-99, AJHR, I.22, p.560 (*Social Security Amendment Bill*).
[9]   S.O.3(1).
[10] S.O.194(a).

To meet outside the Wellington area at any other time requires the leave of the committee,[11] it cannot be done on the chairperson's authority alone.

Meetings held outside the parliamentary precincts are treated by the police in the same way as any other public meeting. (See p.273.)

Calling of meeting

Once a committee has held its first meeting and elected its chairperson, the arrangements for its subsequent meetings are a matter for it. The committee may itself appoint the times for subsequent meetings or it may leave this to be done by the chairperson.

In principle, the time for each committee's next meeting is decided by a resolution of the committee passed before the committee adjourns. In the absence of such a decision, the chairperson, by notice in writing, decides when the next meeting will be held.[12] An informal agreement among members of the committee about the time at which it will meet does not constitute an appointment of a meeting by the committee.[13] Generally, committees adjourn from meeting to meeting. A formal appointment of a meeting, whether by the committee or by the chairperson, relates only to the committee's next meeting, that is, to the time to which it stands adjourned. However, it is of obvious benefit to committee members to have a programme of meetings identified in advance. This is frequently done on a non-binding basis, though it can be done formally on a binding basis if the resolution of the committee appointing the programme clearly indicates this. In the latter case a variation of the programme (such as by the insertion of an extra meeting) can be made only by the committee.

In practice, most committees leave the calling of meetings in the hands of the chairperson as the most convenient mode of proceeding, but this practice is subject to general understandings with the members as to when the committee will meet. If there is no chairperson or deputy chairperson or they are both overseas, the Speaker exercises the chairperson's authority to call meetings of the committee.[14]

Notice of meeting

Notices to the members of the committee informing them of the committee's meeting time in accordance with the committee's or the chairperson's directions must be circulated by the clerk of the committee no later than the day before the meeting.[15] Such notices may be transmitted by email.[16] In practice, notices for the regular Wednesday and Thursday meetings of committees are despatched to members, if possible, at least two days before the meetings are to occur.

This requirement for notice at least one day in advance may be waived if all members of the committee or the leaders or whips of their respective parties agree.[17] This includes agreement from or on behalf of any non-voting members of the committee for any items of business to be transacted at the proposed meeting. In the case of a committee meeting which has lapsed or been adjourned because there is no quorum present and which it may consequently be possible to reconvene later in the day, agreement to waive notice is only required from those members who were expected to attend the aborted meeting.[18]

The notice of meeting must contain a summary of the items of business proposed to be dealt with at the meeting so far as notice of them has been given at that time.[19] The intention is that members must know what is likely to happen at a committee meeting

---

11   S.O.194(b).
12   S.O.191(2).
13   1988, Vol.493, p.7280.
14   S.O.191(3).
15   S.O.206(1).

16   2002-05, AJHR, I.18B, p.34.
17   S.O.206(2).
18   *Ibid.*
19   S.O.206(1).

on a given day and can consequently determine whether to attend and how to prepare themselves.[20] The notice describes the items, indicates any action proposed and attaches relevant papers, for example, a draft report. Notice of further substantive items of business to be dealt with that are received later than the circulation of the notice of meeting but in time to be included on the agenda for that meeting may justify a revised notice of meeting being circulated.

A schedule of the meetings of committees to be held is published to members by email and on the parliamentary website, the first edition of this becoming available on Friday of the preceding week.

Meeting times

The time appointed for the committee to meet does not need to be a particular time – it can be fixed by reference to an uncertain event. However, the time is always expressed in terms of a calendar day. Select committees "meet"; they do not "sit". The concept of a sitting day refers to the House's sittings, not a select committee's meetings, although a sitting day helps to define the particular times at which it is permissible for a select committee to meet. Consequently, references to the day on which a select committee is to meet are references to the calendar day, not to a sitting day.[21]

When the House is sitting, most select committees hold their regular meetings on Wednesday and Thursday mornings. At the beginning of the Parliament the Business Committee or the whips come to an informal arrangement as to which of the subject select committees will be "Wednesday" committees and which will be "Thursday" committees and will therefore be called to meet regularly on either of those days. Committees may meet at other times too during a sitting week in accordance with the Standing Orders but there is a strong understanding that meetings will not be called during the times that party caucuses meet – after 10 am on Tuesdays during sitting weeks. Committees are much freer in arranging meetings during adjournments but even here days on which parties have advised that they will be holding caucuses are avoided.

There are a number of other restraints on committee meeting times.

Sundays

The House is specifically precluded from sitting on a Sunday by the Standing Orders[22] and this absolute prohibition is taken to apply to select committee meetings too.

Fridays

In a week in which there has been a sitting of the House, a committee may not meet on Friday, except with the leave of the committee.[23]

This restriction was introduced when Friday sittings were abolished in 1985. It was intended to prevent the consequent freeing up of members for constituency work on Fridays being precluded by programmes of Friday select committee meetings being organised.[24] The House when referring a bill to a committee may confer power on it to meet on Fridays, notwithstanding that the House has been sitting that week. In these circumstances, the committee or the chairperson can appoint a meeting on Friday and the leave of the committee is not required. A subcommittee has also been authorised to meet on a Friday during sitting weeks to work on an inquiry it was carrying out for the full committee.[25]

20   1971, Vol.373, p.2080.
21   1991, Vol.515, p.2311.
22   S.O.46.
23   S.O.192.
24   1984-85, AJHR, I.14, p.8.
25   1991, Vol.513, pp.818-9.

Where a sitting of the House extends into Friday due to urgency, this does not authorise a committee to utilise its general power to meet while the House is sitting in order to meet on that Friday, without specific authority from the House to do so. The restriction on meeting on a Friday is a different restriction from the limited power committees have to meet during a sitting, and the latter does not override the former. Leave of the committee or distinct authority from the House is necessary in such a case.

Question time

A committee that is meeting in the Wellington area may not meet during question time.[26] If a committee is meeting outside the Wellington area (which it may only do during a House sitting with the Business Committee's agreement), this restriction does not apply as it would serve no purpose. Where a committee meeting has been appointed for a certain time and question time has not concluded by that time, the committee's meeting is automatically postponed until questions do end, subject to any leave being granted by the House for the meeting to proceed.

Sittings of the House

As well as during question time, there are some other restrictions on committees meeting while the House is sitting.

Before 1996 committees could not meet at all while the House was sitting (which includes the committee of the whole House since this takes place during a sitting of the House). Specific authority was always required from the House. Now select committees have some limited powers to meet during a sitting. For meetings outside the Wellington area, the Business Committee can authorise a select committee to meet during a sitting (that is, during the afternoon and in an evening).[27] For a select committee meeting in the Wellington area, whose members would otherwise have been expected to attend the House sitting, leave of the committee is essential for the committee to meet while the House is sitting.[28] Even then, such leave can only authorise the committee to meet after question time and up to 6 pm. A select committee cannot meet in the Wellington area after 6 pm on any day on which the House has sat (regardless of whether the House is actually sitting after 6 pm) except for the purpose of completing business in progress before the committee at 6 pm.[29]

The House, when referring a bill to a committee, may authorise the committee to meet while the House is sitting. This gives the committee, by resolution, and the chairperson, by appointment, power to convene meetings while the House is sitting during an afternoon. Leave of the committee is not required in such circumstances. Whether the committee or the chairperson, by notice, exercise such a power that has been conferred on the committee is a matter for them. There is no convention that a committee will not meet while the House is sitting under urgency, for example,[30] though it is likely that the whips will discuss compromises to committee meeting plans in these circumstances to accommodate members who have duties in the Chamber.

Evenings

A committee that is meeting outside the Wellington area (which it can do only with the agreement of the Business Committee or the leave of the committee itself) is unrestrained

26   S.O.195(1)(a).
27   S.O.194(a).
28   S.O.195(1)(b).

29   S.O.195(1)(c), (2).
30   2002, Vol.599, p.15303.

as to meeting during the evening. A committee meeting in the Wellington area on a non-sitting day is similarly unconstrained. But a committee meeting in the Wellington area on a day on which there has been a sitting of the House may not meet after 6 pm (except by leave for the limited purpose of concluding business in progress at 6 pm).[31] This restriction applies whether or not the House is actually sitting that evening, so it applies to prevent committees meeting on Thursday evenings even when the House adjourns at 6 pm. Only the House can release a committee from this restriction.

The House, when referring a bill to a committee, may confer on the committee power to meet during an evening on which there has been a sitting. In such a case the committee, by resolution, or the chairperson, by notice, may appoint a meeting for the evening and a meeting already in progress may continue after 6 pm.

After midnight
The Speaker has ruled that, unless all members of the committee are in agreement or the House specially authorises, committees should not meet between midnight and 8 am.[32] If it were otherwise, this would defeat the purpose of a major Standing Orders change introduced in 1985 that was to ensure that the House did not sit through the night except in extraordinary circumstances. There are no known examples of either the House or a committee giving permission for a select committee to meet after midnight.

Varying restrictions on meeting times
In referring a bill to a committee the House often varies the restrictions on meeting times imposed by the Standing Orders and allows the committee to meet on a Friday of a sitting week, during the sitting hours or during the evening on a sitting day, in the same way that it can meet at other times. Such a motion can be moved as part of the motion nominating the committee to consider the bill.[33] In practice, almost all variations to restrictions on meeting times are moved at this time since to do so then does not involve any extra debating time on the floor of the House (the debate being absorbed into the first reading debate).

But, in addition, the restrictions on select committee meeting times are subject to any other order of the House to the contrary, given either to a particular committee or in respect of a particular item of business, such as for a bill, subsequent to its referral to the committee. It is, however, improper for committees to anticipate the granting of such authority and to issue notices of meeting for a time that is prohibited under the Standing Orders. While it is permissible for members to be sounded out about the possibility of such a proposed meeting and for officials based in Wellington to be alerted to the possibility, no arrangements should be made for witnesses to attend before the authority of the House is obtained.[34]

The initiative (subsequent to a bill's referral to it) for a committee to have granted to it unlimited authority to meet during a sitting of the House or to meet at another prohibited time may come from the committee by way of a special report, or from the House itself.[35] A motion for a committee to have power to meet during the current sitting of the House does not require notice,[36] but a motion authorising a committee to meet during a future sitting does. The permission to meet might relate only to the consideration of certain business – for instance, to consider a certain bill – or it might be a power for a committee to sit on a particular day or days, without reference to the business to be transacted. The

31   S.O.195(1)(c), (2).
32   1988, Vol.488, p.3395-6.
33   S.O.286(3).

34   1993, Vol.537, p.16847.
35   1976, Vol.408, p.3975.
36   1927, Vol.215, p.560.

debate on such a motion is limited to the question of whether the committee should have the power to sit, and if it should not, then why not.[37] It is not an opportunity to debate the merits of business to be transacted by the committee at the meeting.

The fact that a committee is granted wider authority to meet than is conferred by the Standing Orders does not prevent it from meeting at any other time in accordance with the Standing Orders.[38] Such an authority widens the committee's powers; it does not take away powers the committee would otherwise have. Whenever a committee has been given wider power to meet it is for the committee to decide how and in what circumstances to exercise this power.[39] The fact that there is no apparently urgent business to transact at a meeting does not prevent it going ahead if the committee has power to meet and decides to exercise it.[40] It is a matter for the judgment of the committee.

Cancellation of meeting

Where the committee appoints the time for its next meeting the chairperson may not cancel the meeting,[41] nor alter the time for its commencement,[42] though this may be done on a "round-robin" basis with the agreement of all members of the committee or all members who can reasonably be contacted. The chairperson can cancel a meeting which has been appointed on the chairperson's authority.

Suspension of meeting

The chairperson may suspend a meeting in the case of grave disorder arising at the meeting.[43] The meeting resumes at the time that the chairperson, having given reasonable notice to members present at the time of the suspension, determines. As a meeting may not extend over separate calendar days,[44] if the meeting is to resume at all it must be later in the same day and before any time appointed for the meeting to adjourn in any case. If the meeting does not resume after it has been suspended by the chairperson, the chairperson appoints the time for a new meeting of the committee on a future day.

Other than in cases of grave disorder, only the committee can suspend its own meeting. In the case of a meeting that is scheduled to extend over the greater part of a day, times for the meeting to be suspended for lunch and dinner will usually be determined in advance and included in the notice of meeting. If the committee appoints the meeting it will include suspension times in the appointing resolution. But usually suspension times for a day long meeting (if discussed in advance by the committee at all) are discussed only informally and are included in the notice of meeting on the chairperson's authority. Whether the committee follows them or not is a matter for it to decide.

Adjournment of meeting

A select committee meeting concludes and the committee adjourns when—
- the committee has completed all of the business on its agenda, or
- the time appointed for the committee to adjourn arrives, or
- a time during which the committee is prohibited from meeting arrives, or
- the committee decides to adjourn.

While the chairperson of a select committee may suspend the meeting in a case of grave disorder, he or she may not adjourn it (nor may the chairperson of a committee of the whole House).

The committee may adopt formal meeting times in advance of a meeting but this is

---

37   1961, Vol.437, p.1287.
38   1976, Vol.408, p.4010.
39   2002, Vol.599, p.15303.
40   1990, Vol.510, p.3939.

41   1985, Vol.466, p.7006.
42   1991, Vol.518, p.4194.
43   See S.O.178(1) (committee of the whole House).
44   1988, Vol.487, p.2918.

unusual. Usually, while meeting times may have been discussed at a prior meeting, the advertised times for the meeting to last are published on the chairperson's authority and are indicative only. Thus, when the advertised time for the meeting to end is reached and the committee adjourns, this is because the committee has decided (perhaps implicitly) to adjourn at that point, not because adjournment is automatic. In such circumstances, while there is a presumption that the meeting will conclude at the advertised time, it is always open to the committee to resolve to continue to meet on.

On the other hand, where a committee meeting extends to a time during which a committee is prohibited from meeting, the continuance of the meeting comes into question and adjournment may be automatic. Thus, a committee meeting in the Wellington area cannot, even by leave, continue its meeting after 2 pm on a sitting day because committees are prohibited from meeting in the Wellington area during question time,[45] which commences at 2 pm or a few minutes thereafter. Adjournment at this time is thus automatic. In the case of a committee meeting at any other time when a sitting resumes (for example, at 9 am under urgency) leave of the committee would be required for the meeting to continue,[46] otherwise the committee must adjourn. (In all cases this is subject to any special permission from the House allowing a committee to meet at a time that is otherwise prohibited.) Although committees are not prohibited from meeting while meetings of caucus are taking place, there is a strong convention that any select committee meeting in progress when caucuses usually meet (after 10 am on Tuesdays in sitting weeks) will conclude and the committee will adjourn.

At midnight a committee adjourns unless leave of the committee is given to continue the meeting.[47] Even so, a meeting continued in this way could only be for the purpose of concluding within a reasonable time an item of business on which the committee was engaged at midnight, because meetings held on separate calendar days are, in principle, separate meetings rather than one continuous meeting.[48] Consequently, an extension of a meeting beyond midnight, even though all members are in agreement, could only be for a limited period of time. A new meeting of the committee would need to be appointed to resume business.

Any member of the committee can move that the committee do now adjourn. This motion can only be moved between items of business, not while an item of business is under consideration. (Though consideration of the item may itself be adjourned to permit a motion for the adjournment of the committee to be moved.) While there cannot be more than one adjournment motion moved between the same items of business, there can be subsequent adjournment motions moved during the continuance of the same meeting where the committee has transacted further business since it last rejected a proposal to adjourn. It is up to the chairperson how much discussion to permit on a motion to adjourn before the question is put to the committee. The fact that the committee had rejected a motion to adjourn earlier in the meeting would be a relevant factor to consider in the length of the discussion to permit on such a motion.

Joint meetings
A joint meeting is a meeting between two or more select committees, each of which retains its own separate identity as a committee. Such a meeting can be held without the express authority of the House, provided that the subject of the meeting is within the terms of reference of both participating committees. Where a joint meeting is to be held,

---

45 S.O.195(1)(a).
46 S.O.195(1)(b).
47 1988, Vol.488, pp.3395-6.
48 1988, Vol.487, p.2918.

the committees must resolve, by agreement between them, how they are to conduct their business (unless the House has determined this). Both committees must agree to the procedures to be adopted; the members at the joint meeting do not vote as one body on questions, unless each committee has agreed to operate in this manner.

A special type of joint meeting is the meetings that have been held between select committees and their counterpart committees in the Parliament of the Commonwealth of Australia and in a number of State Parliaments in Australia. Standard procedures for such meetings have been agreed between the Australian and New Zealand Parliaments. (See Chapter 43.)

SUBCOMMITTEES

Select committees have a general power to appoint subcommittees to help them perform their tasks.[49] They may do this to carry out or contribute to the consideration of substantive business before the committee or to discharge administrative or procedural functions.[50]

A subcommittee is a creature of the committee which appoints it and is wholly responsible to that committee. It can consist only of members who are members of the full committee. It does not report to the House; it reports to the committee.[51] It is then for the committee to endorse or reject its work as it sees fit and, if it is endorsed, the committee makes the subcommittee's conclusions its conclusions and takes responsibility for them. A committee may confer on a subcommittee any of the powers the House has conferred on it in respect of business it refers to the subcommittee (for example, the power to meet during an evening).

The rules for the conduct of business by a subcommittee may be prescribed by the committee, provided these are not inconsistent with the Standing Orders, for a committee cannot authorise a subcommittee to do something that it cannot do itself. Subject to any specific rules prescribed by the committee, the same rules for the conduct of business apply to the subcommittee as apply to the full committee.[52]

The committee may appoint the subcommittee's chairperson or leave that matter to the subcommittee. A subcommittee must have at least two members in order to be a subcommittee. The same formula for the quorum of a subcommittee applies as applies to the committee itself – at least half of the subcommittee's membership constitutes a quorum. More than one subcommittee of the same committee may meet at the same time provided that there are sufficient members of the committee available to service two such meetings, and a subcommittee may meet at the same time as the full committee provided that they both have a quorum.

The subcommittee's report is, in the first instance, brought to the full committee. Subject to receiving the committee's endorsement, it is then presented to the House as a report of the committee. Once a subcommittee established to carry out a particular task has made its final report to the full committee, it ceases to exist (though the committee may re-establish it if it sees fit).[53] Otherwise it is up to the committee how long the subcommittee remains in existence.

The chairperson of a subcommittee may have a question addressed to him or her,[54] and may, with the agreement of the subcommittee, make a public statement on the nature of the work before the committee.[55] The subcommittee may also make its proceedings available to any person for the purpose of receiving assistance on its consideration of a matter.[56]

---

[49]   S.O.199(1).
[50]   2004, Vol.619, p.14944; 2004, Vol.620, pp.15382-3 (Fisheries and Other Sea-related Legislation Committee), subcommittee appointed to suggest which witnesses (of 3937) should be heard in person.
[51]   1999-2002, AJHR, I.17B.

[52]   S.O.199(2).
[53]   1999-2002, AJHR, I.17B.
[54]   1977, Vol.415, p.3918.
[55]   S.O.243(1).
[56]   S.O.243(2).

A subcommittee's proceedings are open to the public during the hearing of evidence and subject to confidentiality at other times, in the same way as are the full committee's. (See pp. 275–80.)

QUORUM AND ATTENDANCE
The quorum of a select committee is half of the committee's membership, rounded-up if need be.[57] This relates to the committee's membership at any particular time. While the size of a committee is fixed by the House or the Business Committee, its membership may vary from time to time not just in personnel but also in number. If there is a vacancy on a committee its membership is consequently reduced and the quorum is reduced accordingly. Physical presence at the meeting is required for a member to count towards a committee's quorum (members are not permitted to participate in a committee meeting by videoconference in any case). A non-voting member of the committee is not counted as part of the quorum[58] and is left completely out of account insofar as its determination is concerned. A committee cannot proceed to transact any business unless a quorum is present. If there is not a quorum present within 10 minutes of the time appointed for a meeting, the committee stands adjourned.[59] The time for its next meeting is decided upon by the chairperson.

If a committee becomes inquorate during a meeting, the proceedings of the committee are suspended for up to 10 minutes. If by this time there is still no quorum, the committee stands adjourned.[60] The time for its next meeting is decided upon by the chairperson.

The members who attend a committee meeting are listed in the minutes.[61] However, it is up to members themselves whether they actually attend a meeting; there is no compulsion on them to do so. In practice, the party whips will endeavour to ensure that members are present at meetings so that the party's point of view is represented. In respect of larger parties this will involve arranging temporary replacements for members who are unavoidably absent. Replacing members is a more serious difficulty for smaller parties. Complaints may be made from time to time about the attendance record of particular members at committee meetings but this is not a matter over which committees themselves have any control.

GENERAL PROCEDURES OF SELECT COMMITTEES
Proceedings are conducted in select committees in a manner which is necessarily different from that on the floor of the House. First, the House is an assembly which transacts business mainly by its members making speeches. Members do not make formal speeches in select committees. They question witnesses and they discuss issues with each other across a table – quite different forms of proceeding. Secondly, proceedings in the House are confined to members; other persons do not participate in them. In contrast, one of the principal advantages of the select committee system is that it intimately involves people other than members by associating them directly with the consideration of parliamentary business. For both of these reasons it is not appropriate to have such elaborate rules for the conduct of proceedings in select committees as it is for those on the floor of the House. Select committees are conducted in a more informal manner and this relative informality is an important aspect of their mode of proceeding.

There are, nevertheless, a number of Standing Orders prescribing rules specifically for the conduct of business by select committees. Rules relating to the conduct of business

---

[57] S.O.210(1).

[58] S.O.210(2)

[59] S.O.210(3).

[60] *Ibid.*

[61] S.O.209.

generally by select committees are contained in Chapter IV of the Standing Orders. Rules relating to how particular items of business before select committees (bills, regulations, petitions, etc.) are to be dealt with are set out in the corresponding chapters of the Standing Orders relating to those types of business. Select committees have themselves developed common practices as to how business is conducted and these are recognised by the House as part of the general procedures of select committees.

But these specific rules are not as comprehensive for select committees as they are for the House itself and so they are supported by a framework of rules to which recourse can be had when no specific rule applies.

Consequently, it is provided that where there is no express provision in the Standing Orders or any practice of the House to the contrary, the same rules for the conduct of proceedings as apply to a committee of the whole House are to apply to select committees.[62] A committee of the whole House is itself enjoined to follow the House's procedures subject to any express rule applying to it,[63] so a select committee may have recourse for procedural guidance, first, to the particular rules applying to a committee of the whole House, and then to those of the House itself.

This does not mean that the Standing Orders relating to the House and to committees of the whole House are in effect for select committees, only that in the absence of more specific rules directly applying to a committee those Standing Orders may be applied by analogy to select committee proceedings. Some House rules (for example, the House's detailed time limits on speeches) can have no analogous application to select committees at all, while others may apply only imperfectly to the circumstances of a select committee meeting. Practices adopted by individual committees may be followed by agreement within those committees as long as they are not inconsistent with the Standing Orders, but they are not part of the general rules relating to select committees and they continue to apply for only as long as the members of the particular committee agree to observe them. (Such matters may relate to seating practices at a particular committee, for example.)

Ruling on matters of procedure

On matters of procedure, the chairperson of each select committee is in the same position as the chairperson presiding over a committee of the whole House. The chairperson deals with all points of order arising in the committee and the Speaker cannot interfere with the chairperson's decisions unless the committee decides to report to the Speaker to seek a ruling,[64] though the Speaker can, on a point of order, deal with general questions as to a committee's jurisdiction.[65]

This does not mean that all matters arising in a select committee are decided exclusively by the chairperson. If this were the case the chairperson would usurp the role of the committee in many instances. The chairperson is subject to control by the committee, although for convenience a great deal is left to his or her initiative. The chairperson of a select committee, being a participant in the substantive business transacted by the committee, has a much more active role in leading the committee than do the Speaker or the chairperson of a committee of the whole House who, in their respective spheres, confine themselves to keeping order and deciding procedural disputes. In each instance it is important to establish, therefore, whether the chairperson is deciding something for the committee as a presiding officer (such as whether an amendment is in order), in

---

[62] S.O.205.
[63] S.O.174.

[64] 1912, Vol.161, p.547.
[65] 1991, Vol.512, p.156.

which case the decision is final and cannot be reversed by the committee, or whether the chairperson is acting on behalf of the committee as its leader (such as in arranging the committee's agenda), in which case the committee could overrule the arrangements that have been made. While the power to make a decision on a matter may well rest with the committee (by a majority if need be), it may be that in practice the decision is made (at least in the first instance) by the chairperson on behalf of the committee.

When a procedural difficulty arises which the committee feels unable to resolve, the committee may ask the Clerk of the House to attend the committee to advise on the appropriate procedure.[66] It has also been a practice of long standing that select committees may instruct their chairpersons to consult the Speaker privately on matters of procedure. In this case the Speaker may give a private ruling for the guidance of the committee.[67] But, in any case, it is for the committee to authorise the seeking of advice or a formal ruling; the chairperson does not have the right to do so on his or her own initiative.

Procedural matters which arise in a select committee are not matters which can be raised as points of order in the House. They must be dealt with in the committee.[68] The House has no cognisance of anything that takes place in a committee until it is reported to it by order of the committee. Therefore, if it were desired to seek the Speaker's ruling in the House, the committee would have to direct the chairperson to present a report to the House accordingly.[69]

When the Speaker has ruled at the request of the committee, whether privately or in the House, that ruling is final and conclusive.[70] Rulings made by individual chairpersons within their authority are also final and bind the committee. But they are not precedents in the sense that Speakers' rulings are. They do not bind other committees and they do not bind chairpersons of the same committee when different items of business arise in the future, though in either case an earlier chairperson's ruling may be followed if a subsequent chairperson is persuaded that it is appropriate to do so.

Matters awaiting judicial decision

The House's rule against references to matters awaiting or under adjudication in a court of record applies also to the proceedings of select committees.[71] (See Chapter 16.) The chairperson of a select committee must have regard to the principles followed by the Speaker in applying the rule.[72] Thus, the chairperson could direct that a line of questioning be discontinued in order to prevent an infringement of the rule. Committees have accepted that reviews that they are carrying out may be more limited for the time being where relevant matters are before a court.[73] In one case an applicant for judicial review discontinued those proceedings so as not to inhibit a select committee's inquiry into the same matter.[74] But select committees have available to them the power of hearing evidence in private or secret and these are likely to be effective ways of avoiding any prejudice to legal proceedings that might otherwise arise.[75] The *sub judice* rule does not in any event prevent a committee deliberating on its report since this is always done in private.[76] A committee may also be able to delay presentation of its report until the legal proceedings are concluded so as to avoid prejudice arising. These procedures give select committees a potentially wider range of options to use to work outside the constraints of the *sub judice* rule than are available to the House.

66 1984, Vol.459, p.1892.
67 1977, Vol.414, p.3394.
68 1997, Vol.562, p.3715.
69 1926, Vol.209, p.744.
70 1913, Vol.165, p.511.
71 *May*, pp.751-2.

72 Harris, *House of Representatives Practice*, p.667.
73 1996-99, AJHR, I.21B, p.12.
74 *Ibid.*, I.10A, p.34.
75 *May*, p.752.
76 *Ibid.*

COMMITTEE'S AGENDA

In accordance with standard meeting practice, every committee has for each meeting an agenda setting out the business proposed to be transacted at that meeting and the order in which that business is to be transacted.

The agenda is prepared by the clerk of the committee under the chairperson's direction. There may be a number of items that it must contain because of previous decisions by the committee and notices of business given by members, but it is largely organised in a way that is at the discretion of the chairperson. The agenda is not formally adopted at each meeting. Committees generally follow it as it is laid before the committee, though it is open to a committee to vary the agenda as long as it does so in a way that is consistent with previous committee decisions and with the notices of business given by members.

Standard items on an agenda include: announcements of changes in committee personnel, confirmation of the committee's previous meeting's minutes and lists of papers to be formally received by the committee at the meeting. Alongside the items of business to be considered at the meeting it is usual to record the names and designations of the persons who are to participate in consideration of that item, whether as advisers or witnesses. An item designated "general business" is placed on the agenda (except where a meeting is restricted to considering a particular item of business). Under this item (often taken after other items of business) members can give notice of business they wish to have on the agenda at the next or a future meeting of the committee. They can also, if the committee unanimously agrees, raise under general business a matter for discussion at that meeting that was not on the agenda for the meeting. But "general business" is not an opportunity for members to raise for decision by the committee substantive items of business that require notice unless the other members of the committee concur in this.

Items of business

The committee's agenda shows the items of business to be transacted by the committee. This must be done with some particularity so that members are clear about what is to be considered. In principle, different types of proceeding on a bill, for example, such as being briefed on it by officials, hearing evidence, considering departmental and other reports, and deliberating on the bill should be separate items of business transacted at different meetings, though a committee may depart from this manner of proceeding if it sees fit. All items of business included on an agenda must have been advised to members in a notice of meeting circulated at the latest on the day before the meeting. No item may be included on the agenda (except with the leave of the committee) if it has not been advised in summary form in a notice of meeting.

Members of the committee may give notice of an item of business to be considered by the committee either orally at an earlier meeting of the committee (under the item "general business" or at any other time during the meeting that is acceptable to the committee) or in writing delivered to the clerk of the committee.[77] Notices of business given orally at a meeting and any notices of business received in writing by the clerk before 2 pm on the day before the next meeting of the committee is to be held, are included in the notice of meeting sent to members and must be placed on the agenda for that meeting or, if a longer period of notice is prescribed by the Standing Orders (such as the seven days' notice for removal of the chairperson), on the agenda for the first meeting after the minimum period of notice has expired.[78] The requirement to place such notices of business on the agenda

---

[77] S.O.207(1).   [78] S.O.207(2).

for the next meeting applies even when the committee has already set the agenda for its next meeting. But if the committee has been given special permission from the House to meet at a particular time at which it could not otherwise meet (for example, on a Friday) for the purpose of considering only a particular item of business, any notices relating to other business are placed instead on the agenda for the next regular meeting of the committee.

The right of any member of the committee to have business placed on its agenda is subject in all cases to that business being relevant to the committee's work. The chairperson has the power to rule whether a proposed notice of business is in order.[79] A notice relating to a subject that is outside the committee's terms of reference is not in order. Another reason why a notice may be ruled out of order is if it relates to an issue already determined by the committee earlier in the same calendar year. In any case in which a notice is ruled out of order it is not placed on the agenda. If it is already on the agenda when the chairperson rules on it, it is removed. In each case it is for the chairperson to decide if the notice which has been given is in order. Members do not have an untrammelled right to place items on the committee's agenda.

When the committee reaches an item on the agenda it can be deferred by the committee to later in the meeting or postponed to a future meeting, unless, in the latter case, it was specifically placed on the agenda for that meeting by an earlier decision of the committee. If this is the case, leave of the committee is necessary to postpone it. Once the committee has entered upon consideration of an item of business it is open to the committee to adjourn further consideration of it either until later in the meeting or to a future meeting. New items of business that were not on the committee's agenda can only be introduced, under general business, with the leave of the committee.

MANNER OF TAKING DECISIONS

Committees take decisions on the matters before them by resolving a question. This, in principle, is a similar process to that followed in the House, involving: notice, a member moving a motion, a question proposed by the chairperson, discussion on that question, the question being put by the chairperson and a vote being held. However, committees operate more informally than the House. Notice is not necessary in a number of instances and some of the other steps may be omitted if members concur in this.

Votes on questions put by the chairperson are given by members indicating from their seats by voice how they wish to vote. The chairperson then expresses the sense of the vote by stating whether, in his or her opinion, the "Ayes" or the "Noes" have it. At this point any member of the committee may require that a formal record of how members wish to vote be entered in the minutes, regardless of whether that member agrees or disagrees with how the chairperson has expressed the sense of the vote. It is the responsibility of a member to ask that the votes be formally recorded, otherwise the minutes will merely show that a decision has been taken without dissent.[80]

Where a vote is formally recorded, members are asked by the chairperson to indicate their votes individually. Their names for, against or in abstention on the question are recorded by the clerk and included in the minutes.[81] Where a series of votes is to be held, the committee may agree to a more informal practice than this for members' votes to be recorded. As long as these practices are clear this is acceptable.[82] Members must be physically present at the meeting to record a vote. There are no proxy votes at select committee meetings.

---

[79] S.O.207(3).
[80] 2002-05, AJHR, I.18B, p.37 (Standing Orders Committee).
[81] S.O.214.
[82] 2002-05, AJHR, I.18B, p.37.

Questions are resolved by a majority of the votes Aye or No. The House has on one occasion imposed on a select committee a requirement of unanimity or near-unanimity similar to the rule applying to the Business Committee because of the constitutional and political significance of the matters before it.[83]

MAINTENANCE OF ORDER

As in the House with the Speaker, the chairperson is responsible for maintaining order in a select committee. But this is a duty that is shared more equally with the members of the committee itself than it is in the larger gatherings of the House and the committee of the whole House.

On questions of dress and consumption of food and beverages, for instance, there is no reason why select committees (which operate far more informally than the House) should follow exactly the House's practices. Indeed, individual select committees may differ among themselves as to the standards that they apply. Committees conduct much of their business in public and there may appropriately be different rules for the public and private phases of their work – for example, as to consumption of food during a meeting. Ultimately, as matters of order, these are matters for the chairperson to determine after (as in the House) having taken due account of the views of members of the committee.[84]

A member of a committee (including a non-voting member in respect of that portion of the meeting for which he or she is a member) may be excluded from a meeting for highly disorderly conduct only on the order of the committee and not at the direction of the chairperson alone.[85] Such a motion may be moved at any time during the meeting of the committee. Although the decision to exclude the member is the committee's, it is solely for the chairperson to determine whether the occasion for the exercise of the power to exclude has arisen, that is, that the member has actually been guilty of highly disorderly conduct in the chairperson's opinion. Unless the chairperson rules that a member has been guilty of highly disorderly conduct, the committee cannot exclude the member. The House's rules for excluding, naming and suspending members do not apply to a select committee; a member can be excluded from a meeting only in accordance with the Standing Orders applying to select committee meetings.[86] The period for which the member is excluded from the committee meeting may not exceed the time of the remainder of the meeting held on that day.[87]

The chairperson may, on the chairperson's own authority, order any other member of Parliament present at the committee who is not a member of the committee to withdraw from the meeting if that member's conduct is disorderly.[88]

The meetings of a select committee are open to the public during the hearing of evidence, but any member of the public who is guilty of disorderly conduct can be ordered by the chairperson to withdraw from the meeting. This applies equally to witnesses and representatives of the press.[89] Furthermore, it is a contempt of the House for any persons to misconduct themselves before a committee,[90] so in serious cases of disorder persons may be proceeded against for a breach of privilege.

Suspension of meeting on account of disorder

The chairperson of a select committee may suspend the meeting of a committee for grave disorder in the same way as may the chairperson of a committee of the whole House. In

---

[83]   1999-2002, AJHR, I.23A, pp.10-11 (MMP Review Committee).

[84]   2000, Vol.584, p.2594.

[85]   S.O.215(3).

[86]   1988, Vol.487, p.2918.

[87]   S.O.215(3).

[88]   S.O.215(2).

[89]   S.O.215(1).

[90]   S.O.400(o).

the case of a suspension, the chairperson decides when the meeting will be resumed.

Order at meetings outside the parliamentary precincts

Meetings held outside the parliamentary precincts are in a different position from those held within Parliament House and the other areas under the Speaker's control. In the case of grave disorder arising at a meeting held outside the precincts, the chairperson's only option may be to suspend the meeting. A chairperson has closed a meeting of a committee in these circumstances on the ground that it was becoming unruly.[91] The committee could report the disorderly incidents to the House and let the House decide what action to take. The Serjeant-at-Arms has a duty of enforcing order at parliamentary proceedings held within the precincts, but not beyond them. A select committee meeting held outside the parliamentary precincts is no different from any other public meeting as far as the police are concerned. Ordinarily, the police would be unlikely to act to prevent interruptions by heckling or other means unless a breach of the peace or another offence seemed likely to occur.[92] However, the police may be delegated with power by the occupier of the premises in which a committee is meeting to remove trespassers. In this case, persons interrupting a meeting may be required to leave under trespass powers.

BROADCASTING OF PROCEEDINGS

The broadcasting of proceedings at meetings of select committees, whether by television or by radio, is a matter for the committee to decide upon should any request be made to it for permission to do so. Such requests are considered on their merits, having regard to the public interest on the subject matter and the privacy of individual witnesses.[93]

MINUTES

The clerk of the committee prepares minutes of each committee meeting.

Minutes are not a verbatim report of the meeting. They are intended principally to record decisions taken by the committee. For this purpose they are definitive. The confirmed minutes of a select committee meeting are conclusive evidence of resolutions passed by the committee.[94]

The minutes must show the names of the members of the committee present at the committee meeting.[95] This means only the names of members present as members of the committee (including non-voting members), not of other members present in the exercise of their general right to attend the meeting. It does not matter how long a member remained present at the meeting; if the member attended a meeting at all as a member of the committee the member's name must be recorded in the minutes relating to that meeting. The Standing Orders also require that the votes of members on questions put to the committee are to be recorded in the minutes if any member requires this.[96]

In practice, the minutes also record a number of other matters, such as: the time the meeting commenced and ended, apologies from members for non-attendance, notified replacements and details of the times or items to which the replacements relate, names and designations of other persons participating or present at the meeting as advisers and papers and documents presented to the committee or which witnesses or advisers undertake to provide.

---

[91] "'Unruly' hearing closed", *The Evening Post*, 24 February 1988.
[92] HC 308 (1968-69).
[93] 1996, Vol.556, p.13901.
[94] 1905, Vol.135, p.76; 2000, Vol.582, pp.1029, 1123.
[95] S.O.209.
[96] S.O.214.

Wherever practicable, draft minutes of the previous meeting are circulated to members with the notice of meeting for the next meeting of the committee and are confirmed or amended by the committee at that meeting.

CALLING FOR EVIDENCE

Provided that a committee remains within the terms of reference given to it by the House, the extent to which it hears evidence or canvasses for submissions is for it to decide. A committee may, by restricted terms of reference, actually be prevented from hearing witnesses, but this is most unusual. The whole point of most referrals of bills to committees for study is so that the proposal can be subjected to examination and criticism, and for this purpose the committees are able to collect information on the bills in the form of evidence. Similarly, committees will generally seek submissions on significant inquiries which they initiate. In the case of estimates and financial review examinations, scrutiny of treaties and most petitions, committees do not advertise for submissions, usually being content to hear from the departments, organisations or individuals directly concerned, supplemented by advice from staff assisting the committee.

Inviting submissions

The chairperson of a select committee has the power to invite any person to appear before the committee to give evidence or to produce papers and records that are relevant to the committee's proceedings.[97] The chairperson does not need to have been directed by the committee to exercise this power; the chairperson can do it of his or her own volition. But any action taken by the chairperson to request evidence is taken on behalf of the committee. It is not a general right to request information. Evidence can only be invited where it is relevant to a matter before the committee. Furthermore, it is only a power to request. Penal powers to enforce a request for evidence or the production of documents lie with the House and the Speaker. (See Chapter 30.)

Most commonly a chairperson exercises the power to invite evidence by initiating the process of advertising for submissions.

Advertising for submissions

Most select committees advertise for submissions on the bills and other matters which are referred to them. A committee cannot advertise for submissions in anticipation of a bill or other matter being referred to it.[98] Advertising for submissions, as with inviting submissions, may only be undertaken in respect of a matter that is before the committee.

The initial decision to advertise, and the form of the advertisement, may be taken by the chairperson. The advertisement is then placed on the chairperson's authority. In these circumstances the wording of the advertisement must not give the impression that all members of the committee participated in the decision to place it.[99] Placing an advertisement on the chairperson's authority is necessary where the committee is not due to meet for a little while and to wait for a meeting to authorise the advertising would lead to valuable time being lost for potential witnesses to prepare their submissions. In such a case the chairperson may consult with senior members of the committee before placing the advertisement.

Where the initial advertisement is placed on the chairperson's authority, it is for the committee when it next meets to endorse or repudiate the decision, as it sees fit.[100] If a

[97]   S.O.196(1), (2).
[98]   1996, Vol.555, p.12949 (*Adoption Amendment Bill (No 2)*).
[99]   2000, Vol.586, p.5168.
[100]   *Ibid.*

bill or other matter has been referred to a committee since it last met and no advertisement has been placed for it, the committee itself will decide the advertising arrangements to be followed in respect of it.

Extent of advertising

Most select committees advertise in newspapers for submissions on the bills and other matters which are referred to them. The extent of advertising coverage throughout the country depends upon the likely degree of interest in the subject under consideration. Advertising may be undertaken nationally or may be localised where there is only likely to be a local interest. In exceptional cases, further steps may be taken to publicise the committee's existence and its wish to receive evidence. Thus, on an electoral law inquiry, advertisements were placed in 37 newspapers and broadcasts made in Māori, Samoan, Tongan, Cook Islands Māori and Niuean, specifically inviting submissions to be made to the committee.[101] Often a committee will write to groups which it identifies as having a special interest in the subject under study[102] or even invite experts in the field to make submissions.[103] A committee has sought public feedback on its work through a dedicated website.[104] Witnesses may themselves make suggestions for what form of advertising is appropriate in a particular case.[105]

Advertisements often contain summaries of the subject-matter, normally a bill, on which submissions are being invited. These are not intended as a full substitute for potential witnesses studying the bill or other matter themselves. Rather, they are designed to alert the public to a matter which may be of interest to them. Summaries must be prepared as neutral statements of the contents of the bill or matter concerned.[106] Where a committee is advertising for submissions on an inquiry which it is about to undertake, it will normally publish the full terms of reference for the inquiry in the advertisement.

Closing date for submissions

The advertisement inviting submissions also names a date by which submissions should be made to the committee. This date may have been initially determined by the chairperson, but it is always a matter on which the chairperson is subject to direction by the committee. The date fixed for the closure of submissions on a bill will vary depending upon the need to pass the legislation by any particular time or if it is required to be dealt with before the House adjourns for the year. The standard time for committees to allow is between four and six weeks. A committee may begin to hear evidence before the lapse of the time fixed for submissions to be made, if submissions are received early enough for it to do this. Submissions received out of time may be heard by the committee if it so decides, but there is no guarantee of the committee accommodating a witness in these circumstances.

ACCESS TO EVIDENCE AND PROCEEDINGS

The general presumption is that a select committee hears the evidence submitted to it in public and conducts its other business in private.[107]

Public evidence

During the hearing of evidence on any matter by a select committee, the proceedings are open to the public, subject to the committee's right to hear evidence in private or in secret.[108] The House, in referring a matter to a select committee, could direct otherwise but

---

101   1980, AJHR, I.17, p.7.
102   1987-90, AJHR, I.4E, para.3.1 (*Reserve Bank of New Zealand Bill*).
103   2002-05, AJHR, I.6C, p.8 (inquiry into public health strategies related to cannabis use).
104   "Website set up for investigation into constitution",

The Dominion Post, 29 April 2005.
105   1996-99, AJHR, I.22, p.560 (community newspapers being suggested).
106   2000, Vol.586, p.5168.
107   S.Os 223 and 240(1).
108   S.O.223(1).

this would be extremely unlikely. The chairperson may order a member of the public who is being disorderly and any member of Parliament who is not a member of the committee, but who happens to be attending, to leave the meeting if their conduct is disorderly,[109] otherwise, in the ordinary way, any member of the public may attend a select committee meeting while the committee is hearing evidence.

A written submission may be released to the public by the committee at any time after the committee has received it.[110] Committees routinely authorise the release of written submissions at the meeting following receipt of the submission. Where a committee does not authorise release in this way, the submission automatically becomes available to the public when the committee hears oral evidence on the submission from the person who made it.[111] In any case, the person who made the written submission to the committee is at liberty to release it at any time.[112]

Private evidence

A committee may decide to hear (in the case of written evidence, receive) evidence as private evidence.[113] This means that the evidence does not become available to the public until the committee reports to the House on the bill or other matter to which the evidence relates.[114] Until that point it remains confidential to the members of the committee. It cannot be referred to even in the House.[115]

The suggestion that evidence be given in private may come from the committee itself, though it is more likely to come from the witness or potential witness. A witness may, before providing written evidence, ask that it be received by the committee in private. Wherever practicable, potential witnesses are informed that they may request this.[116] Before giving evidence and at any time while they are being heard, witnesses may apply to be heard in private. All witnesses are informed of their right to make such an application before they appear before the committee.[117] If a witness does ask to be heard in private, reasons must be given for making such a request.[118]

Where a committee becomes aware that evidence contains allegations against a person, it is always obliged to consider whether it would be best to hear the evidence in private so as to limit the evidence's potential damage.[119] Furthermore, a person against whom allegations are made in private evidence that is retained by the committee must be given a copy of it, if it is in writing, or otherwise adequately informed of it so that he or she has an opportunity of responding to the allegations.[120]

Apart from limiting damage to a person's reputation, other reasons that may persuade a committee to hear evidence in private include: where a matter is before a court and hearing the evidence in private will avoid any prejudice to the case, where the evidence is personally embarrassing and where commercial confidentiality is involved. The Regulations Review Committee has heard evidence on draft regulations in private to preserve their confidentiality at the policy development stage.[121]

Evidence may only be received as private evidence if the committee agrees by leave to receive it as such.[122] A single member's objection prevents it. Where a committee has agreed to hear oral evidence in private, the committee may require members of the public to withdraw from that meeting.[123] However, the committee is not obliged to exclude all members of the public from a meeting while private evidence is being heard and

---

[109] S.O.215(1), (2).
[110] S.O.218(1).
[111] S.O.218(2).
[112] S.O.218(3).
[113] S.O.219(1).
[114] S.O.219(3).
[115] S.O.110.
[116] S.O.221(1).

[117] S.O.221(2).
[118] S.O.221(3).
[119] S.O.235(1).
[120] S.O.238(1).
[121] 1996-99, AJHR, I.16X, p.35.
[122] S.O.219(1).
[123] S.O.219(2).

there may be a good reason why a particular person or persons should be allowed to remain present – for example, to hear at first hand an allegation that is to be made against them.[124]

Hearing evidence as private evidence gives that evidence a temporary confidentiality only, as no obligation of confidentiality attaches to it once the committee has reported to the House.[125] Until that time any unauthorised disclosure of the evidence would be a contempt.[126] It must be explained to a witness before he or she gives evidence that the confidentiality is only temporary and that if the evidence contains allegations that would seriously damage the reputation of a person it will be disclosed to that person.[127]

Secret evidence

A long-term means of according confidentiality to evidence that a committee is to hear is to hear it as secret evidence. The suggestion that evidence be given in secret may come from the committee or from a witness. An application may be made before providing written evidence for that evidence to be received as secret evidence. If practicable, witnesses are informed of their right to make such an application.[128] Before giving evidence and while giving it, a witness may apply to be heard in secret. Witnesses are informed of their right to apply to be heard in secret before they appear before the committee.[129] A witness asking to be heard in secret must give reasons for the request.[130]

As with private evidence, a committee can only declare evidence to be secret evidence by leave of the committee.[131]

Furthermore, a committee may only receive secret evidence in either of two sets of circumstances—

- where the committee believes that it can only obtain the information it wishes to obtain if it can assure the witness or other person in possession of that information that the evidence given to the committee will remain confidential,[132] or
- where the committee is satisfied that secrecy is necessary to protect the reputation of any person.[133]

As a committee must be unanimous before according secrecy, it is a matter for the individual judgment of each member of the committee as to whether either of these circumstances is satisfied and that, furthermore, secrecy is justified. In making this judgment, members are aware that secrecy is an exception to the strong presumption that any evidence presented to a select committee should be made publicly known so that it can be tested and criticised before it is accepted as an influence on the making of public policy. It may be that in these circumstances a committee will forego receiving certain evidence because it does not wish to agree to secrecy being accorded to it.

Where evidence is to be heard in secret, the committee must require all members of the public to leave the meeting unless leave is given for any person to remain present.[134] The committee may, by leave, permit any person to remain if there is good reason for this, such as if an allegation is to be made against that person. However, in the case of secret evidence it may be that allowing such a person to remain present or even disclosing the allegation to that person would defeat the purpose of according secrecy to the evidence in the first place (for example, in a situation involving domestic violence). Accordingly, a committee is given some discretion as to how it deals with an allegation against a person

---

[124] S.O.235(1).
[125] S.O.219(3).
[126] S.O.400(p).
[127] S.O.221(4).
[128] S.O.221(1).
[129] S.O.221(2).
[130] S.O.221(3).
[131] S.O.220(1).
[132] S.O.220(1)(a).
[133] S.O.220(1)(b).
[134] S.O.220(2).

made in secret evidence. If the evidence is retained by the committee, it must communicate it to that person only if it considers that the possible damage to the person's reputation outweighs any detriment that disclosure will cause to the witness who made the allegation (such as possible retribution).[135] This is the only possible exception to the principle that a person against whom an allegation is made in select committee proceedings must be informed of the allegation and given an opportunity to respond.

Long-term confidentiality attaches to secret evidence. Not only may it not be disclosed while the committee's inquiry is still under way (except to give a person a chance to respond to an allegation), it may not be disclosed even after the committee has reported, unless the House specifically authorises this.[136] Before giving secret evidence a witness must be informed by the committee that the evidence could be disclosed to a person against whom an allegation is made and also that the House has power to authorise its disclosure after the committee reports.[137] (See Chapter 24 for custody of select committee records.)

Proceedings other than evidence

The proceedings of each committee and subcommittee other than during the hearing of evidence are not open to the public and remain strictly confidential until the committee reports to the House.[138] A similar restriction applies in respect of the premature disclosure of the committee's report or draft report.[139] Such proceedings cannot even be referred to in the House until the committee reports.[140] An unauthorised disclosure of such proceedings would be a contempt of the House.[141]

Partly, this rule is designed to maintain any temporary confidentiality that is warranted for the contributions that may be made by others, such as the committee's advisers, to the committee's work. But it is also designed to facilitate members of the committee working together on the tasks that have been assigned to them, respecting each other's confidences and promoting frank and constructive contributions from them to the committee's work. Apart from the promotion of a productive work environment, premature release of a committee's proceedings is likely to be selective and not fully reflective of the work undertaken by the committee. These factors are held to justify the continuation of some restrictions on the public availability of certain committee proceedings prior to the committee reporting to the House.[142] However, the fact that committees (other than during the hearing of evidence) carry out their work in private has been criticised.[143]

Proceedings of committees that are confidential until the committee reports to the House include all proceedings relevant to the committee's work on an item of business still before the committee. This covers: members giving notice of business, notices of meetings circulated, papers circulated for consideration at a meeting, communications with witnesses and advisers about their appearance or attendance at a committee meeting and other formal communications with the committee. (See Chapter 24 for reports and draft reports.) Unauthorised disclosure of these proceedings may be treated as a contempt. For this purpose disclosure by the committee or by a member of the committee of proceedings to another member or to the Clerk or an officer of the House in the course of their duties, is authorised.[144] So members discussing select committee business among themselves (for example, in caucus) does not constitute a contempt.

Any disclosure of proceedings pursuant to the Standing Orders (for example, in order

---

[135] S.O.238(2)(b).
[136] S.O.220(3).
[137] S.O.221(4).
[138] S.O.240(1).
[139] S.O.241.
[140] S.O.110.
[141] S.O.400(p).

[142] 1997, Vol.562, p.3232; 2002-05, AJHR, I.18B, pp.43-4.
[143] See, for example, Peters, "Employment Relations Bill secrecy doing a job on NZ", *The Evening Post*, 22 July 2000.
[144] S.O.240(2)(a).

to fulfil natural justice obligations) is authorised.[145] Thus the Auditor-General, as adviser to committees on the estimates, may consult with outside persons to ensure that proposed advice to a committee is correct and, with the committee's agreement, may even disclose the nature of that advice to other persons if circumstances warrant it.[146]

Proceedings may also be divulged by the committee or a subcommittee to any person for the purpose of that person assisting the committee or subcommittee in its consideration of the matter.[147] This enables the committee to ask persons to comment on reports it has received that it does not wish to disseminate widely. Such comments are treated as private evidence (unless the committee declares them secret evidence).[148] The committee should always make this clear to such a person on sending the proceedings for comment.[149]

Matters no longer before the committee

While the House maintains restrictions on the disclosure of select committee proceedings that are current, there is no value in maintaining such restrictions in respect of business that is no longer before the committee or is not under active consideration by the committee.

All business before the House or a committee is automatically carried forward between sessions of the same Parliament.[150] But all business before the House at the dissolution or expiration of a Parliament lapses, though it may be reinstated in the first session of the next Parliament.[151] In order to preserve the confidentiality of business before select committees that has lapsed in this way until the House and the committees in the new Parliament have had an opportunity to consider whether they wish to reinstate or readopt business, confidential select committee proceedings remain confidential on dissolution or expiration, notwithstanding that they have lapsed.[152] This confidentiality then continues to obtain for the first nine sitting days of the new Parliament. It ceases if the business to which it relates has not been reinstated by the House or has not been readopted by the committee concerned by that time.[153]

There is also no point in maintaining confidentiality where a committee receives information or a communication relating to a matter on which it has already reported or where it receives a briefing or starts an inquiry which it subsequently discontinues. In either of these circumstances there is little likelihood that the committee will make a report to the House that makes the proceedings publicly available. Technically, therefore, they are likely to remain confidential to the committee until the end of the Parliament.

Consequently, it is now provided that where proceedings do not relate to business still before the committee, they may be disclosed.[154] The onus is on members to ensure that such matters are no longer covered by the confidentiality provisions of the Standing Orders before disclosing them.[155]

Matters of process and procedure

It has also been provided that members may disclose some current committee information where this relates only to process and procedure (such as the fact that a report is to be presented on a particular date or the appointment or non-appointment of advisers to the committee).[156] While such process matters may be disclosed, this does not extend to members revealing information about the substantive business before the committee or

145 S.O.240(2)(b).
146 1999-2002, AJHR, I.15A, paras.5.3 and 8.2.
147 S.O.243(2).
148 *Ibid.*
149 2002-05, AJHR, I.17D, pp.4 and 7.
150 *Constitution Act* 1986, s.20(1)(a).
151 *Ibid.*, s.20(1)(b).
152 S.O.242(1).
153 S.O.242(2).
154 S.O.240(3)(a).
155 2002-05, AJHR, I.18B, p.46.
156 S.O.240(3)(b).

that reflects or divulges the contents of a report or draft report of the committee or reveals a committee's findings.[157] Nor may a member disclose proceedings relating to process or procedural issues still under active consideration by the committee.[158]

Again, the onus is on any member making a disclosure of select committee information to ensure that it may properly be disclosed.[159]

Departmental officials

Where departmental officials are advisers to a committee they must take special care to ensure that information on select committee proceedings is not disclosed inappropriately. It is recognised that if committees ask for a Government point of view, this will necessarily involve inter-departmental consultation and, therefore, some sharing of select committee information with other departments that may not have adviser status with the committee. Disclosure is implicitly authorised in these circumstances. But where committees make simple information requests of a departmental adviser to the committee it may not be readily apparent to the committee that this will involve the adviser seeking assistance from another department. If this is the case, the advisory department is expected to seek the committee's agreement to involving the other department or departments in the select committee work that is being undertaken. Authority to consult outside the public service departmental structure is never implied. If a departmental adviser wishes to share select committee information with a Crown entity, a State enterprise or any other person outside the public service, the adviser should always seek the committee's agreement first.[160]

Chairperson's statement

Another authorised means of disclosing select committee proceedings before the committee reports to the House is by a public statement made by the chairperson. Such a statement can only be made with the agreement of the committee. It is confined to informing the public of the nature of the committee's consideration of a matter. A subcommittee can authorise its chairperson to make a similar type of statement.[161]

Such statements are made by chairpersons from time to time to announce the decisions made by committees as to how they propose to carry out their inquiries. A committee in deciding to conduct an inquiry, should always consider authorising the chairperson to announce this decision by means of a statement, even if detailed terms of reference for the inquiry have not yet been devised.[162] A chairperson's statement is not an appropriate means of announcing a committee's conclusions on the business before it, even its provisional conclusions. Conclusions should be communicated to the House by means of a final or interim report. Where a chairperson does make a public statement, other members may comment publicly on it and refer to the committee's proceedings insofar as they are disclosed in the statement. In the case of a statement announcing the decision of a committee to hold an inquiry, members are then free to talk about the committee's proceedings leading up to it taking that decision.[163] A chairperson can be asked a question in the House regarding any statement.[164]

The power to make a public statement under the Standing Orders applies only in respect of an item of business that is before the committee. It does not apply once the committee has presented its report on the bill or other matter concerned to the House (or, in the case of a subcommittee, to its parent committee). After a report has been presented

---

[157] S.O.240(3)(b)(ii), (iii).
[158] S.O.240(3)(b)(i).
[159] 2002-05, AJHR, I.18B, p.46.
[160] 1996-99, AJHR, I.16P; "Public Servants and Select Committees – Guidelines", State Services

Commission, February 2002, updated February 2004.
[161] S.O.243(1).
[162] 2002, Vol.602, p.545.
[163] *Ibid.*
[164] 1978, Vol.417, p.660.

to the House any person can comment on and disclose the committee's proceedings (except secret evidence); the chairperson is in no special position as compared to other members.[165]

WRITTEN EVIDENCE

As late as 1928 it was still regarded as irregular for select committees to receive written submissions. Giving evidence to committees was properly regarded as an oral process transacted in person.[166] But this view has radically changed. Written submissions may now be received by committees as evidence in their own right.

Written submissions are forwarded to the clerk of the committee and become part of the proceedings of the committee upon being received by the clerk on behalf of the committee.[167] Witnesses are normally asked to supply sufficient copies of their submissions for the members of the committee. A committee may make a written submission available for general release at any time after receiving it,[168] though where a witness requests that the evidence be received in private or secret the committee must consider the request before authorising the evidence's release.

A committee has a continuing obligation to give a witness reasonable access to any material or other information that the witness has provided to the committee.[169]

How many written submissions are received on an item of business depends upon the degree of interest in the bill or other matter. There may be no submissions received at all.[170] On the other hand, the select committee considering the *Employment Relations Bill* 2000 received 17,369 submissions (15,064 of these were in a standard form).[171] The submissions received by a committee are likely to be a mix of submissions from individuals, professional, sectoral and community groups (religious, health, political etc), and public sector organisations.

Return of written submissions

A committee is not obliged to accept a submission if it considers it inappropriate or undesirable that it should do so. It may return any evidence that it considers irrelevant to its proceedings, offensive or possibly defamatory.[172] It may also return a written submission which contains an allegation that may seriously damage the reputation of a person, if it is not satisfied that the evidence is relevant or considers that the risk of harm to the person concerned outweighs the benefit to the committee of receiving the evidence.[173] The committee itself cannot delete any material from a written submission but it can indicate to the witness that it will only receive the submission if it is resubmitted with the offending material omitted.

ORAL EVIDENCE

Many written submissions are made as a prelude to the witness giving oral evidence to the committee. Indeed, witnesses are asked to indicate in their submissions if they wish to appear before the committee in person in support of their submissions. While not all persons who make a written submission also wish to give oral evidence (thus regarding their written evidence as sufficient), it would be unusual for a person who had not made an initial written submission to appear before the committee to give evidence in person (though this can happen where the committee identifies a person who has not

165 1999-2002, AJHR, I.17B, p.3.
166 1928, Vol.219, p.572.
167 1987-90, AJHR, I.15D, para.7.
168 S.O.218(1).
169 S.O.222.

170 For example, 1992, Vol.530, p.11872 (*Local Legislation Bill*).
171 1999-2002, AJHR, I.22A, p.130.
172 S.O.217; 1987-90, AJHR, I.4E, para.3.1.
173 S.O.237(a).

made a submission but whom it wishes to hear from). Witnesses must always be given the opportunity to make a submission in writing before appearing before a committee to give oral evidence.[174]

While a witness's wish to appear in person before the committee will be met, if possible, committees are not obliged to hear all or indeed any of those wishing to appear in person. A committee's ability to do so depends upon the time constraints under which the committee is operating. It is a matter for determination by the committee as to whether it hears oral evidence at all or hears all of the witnesses wishing to give oral evidence on the matter before it.[175] A committee has appointed a subcommittee to help it make these decisions.[176] While committees do have to make hard decisions as to how many persons wishing to appear before them can be heard in the time available, it is most unusual for a committee to decide to hear no evidence at all in person.

Oral evidence is heard in committee meeting rooms in Parliament House, Wellington (sometimes by videoconference or teleconference) or on marae and at other venues out of Wellington where a committee agrees to travel to other centres.

Videoconference and teleconference

Committees may hear oral evidence by videoconference or teleconference if they choose to do so. Teleconferencing has been used for some years. Videoconferencing was first used on 17 April 2002 for evidence presented to the Standing Orders Committee. Following this a three-month trial was undertaken.[177] Permanent videoconference facilities are now established in Parliament House. Multiple simultaneous videoconference links have been employed in respect of a select committee hearing.[178]

These technologies are used to enhance the public accessibility of the select committee process, particularly for potential witnesses who cannot afford to travel to Wellington to present their submissions. But they are not intended to eliminate committee visits to other centres and regions. Where there are a considerable number of submissions to be heard in a particular region it will still usually be desirable for a committee to meet in a regional centre to hear from the witnesses in person.

Videoconferencing and teleconferencing are only available for the hearing of evidence.[179] They cannot be used for the transaction of committee business between members. Members must be present at the same physical location to participate in a committee's proceedings. A committee meeting conducted by videoconference or teleconference has the same parliamentary privilege status as any other select committee meeting. But a witness participating from an overseas location is subject to the law of that jurisdiction (which may itself confer a qualified privilege for evidence given to a foreign, that is, the New Zealand, legislature). Videoconferencing and teleconferencing are not considered suitable for hearing private or secret evidence, though a witness giving evidence by one of these means has the right to request it.

Particular categories of witness
Ministers
Ministers have a right to attend and take part in the proceedings of a committee considering a bill of which they have charge, but without being able to vote on any question.[180] As well as attending committee meetings as participating members (which is still uncommon apart

---

[174] S.O.216.
[175] 1999-2002, AJHR, I.22A, pp.19-20 (*Shop Trading Hours (Abolition of Restrictions) Bill*).
[176] 2004, Vol.619, p.14944; 2004, Vol.620, pp.15382-3 (*Foreshore and Seabed Bill*).
[177] "Parliament tries video-conferencing", *The Evening*

Post, 18 April 2002.
[178] 2002-05, AJHR, I.5C, p.41(links to Apia, Auckland and Christchurch).
[179] Speaker's letter to committee chairpersons, 1 May 2002.
[180] S.O.211(2).

from those committees, such as the Privileges Committee, of which Ministers are members in their own right), Ministers increasingly appear before committees as witnesses to give evidence and to submit to examination. Since 1994 Ministers have regularly attended the estimates examinations of the votes for which they are vote Ministers, leading a witness team consisting of the chief executive and other senior departmental officials.[181] Where a Minister did not wish to appear with the chief executive on an estimates examination, the meeting was postponed at the Minister's request to accommodate his wishes.[182] The Minister of Finance is expected to attend the Finance and Expenditure Committee's consideration of the Budget policy statement as a matter of course as the principal witness.[183] Less often, but still occasionally, Ministers give evidence to committees considering bills or other matters with which they are officially connected.

Other members

Members generally, including Ministers, may voluntarily appear as witnesses before select committees. They are not subject to the coercive powers of committees and cannot be directed to take an oath or to answer a particular question.[184] Apart from this limitation, where members do give evidence to committees they are treated in a similar manner to other witnesses. Members may give evidence to a committee of which they themselves are a member. In this case they change their status before the committee temporarily while they are witnesses because a member cannot simultaneously be a participating member of a committee and a witness to it. Thus, the chairperson of a committee can leave the chair to the deputy chairperson for the purpose of giving evidence to the committee.

Members often make submissions to the Standing Orders Committee and give evidence to the Privileges Committee. They occasionally give evidence to other committees too.[185]

Public servants

The government department whose Minister is in charge of a bill will provide officials to assist the committee but it may also make a formal submission to the committee on the bill. As a general practice the department whose Minister is responsible for the bill represents the Government's views to the select committee. A committee, of course, will accept a submission from any department. But the Government requires that departments wishing to make submissions on a Government bill should do so only with the express approval of their Ministers and of the appropriate Cabinet committee.[186] Select committees have occasionally sought the Government's approval for departments to be able to make individual submissions on measures before them. For instance, 13 departments made submissions on the *Public Finance Bill* 1989 after such an approach.[187]

Officials always appear before select committees as witnesses on estimates and financial review examinations and the relevant government department will be invited to make a submission on a petition within its area of responsibility.

The State Services Commission has issued guidelines for public servants appearing before committees as witnesses in their official capacity.[188] These emphasise that as witnesses public servants are acting on behalf of their Minister and to assist the Minister to fulfil the Minister's accountability obligations to Parliament. Officials are enjoined to keep Ministers informed about their appearances before select committees and not to

---

[181] See "Entertainment tax looks likely to stay in place", *The Evening Post*, 2 August 1994 (for the first appearance of the Minister of Finance following a Budget).

[182] *Hansard Supplement*, 2001, Vol.48, pp.1589-90.

[183] S.O.324(2).

[184] 2002-05, AJHR, I.18B, p.36.

[185] See, for example, "Mahuta won't commit to Labour yet", *The Dominion Post*, 5 October 2004 (member appeared before a committee to give evidence opposing a bill proposed by her party).

[186] *Cabinet Manual*, 2001, para.5.71.

[187] 1987-90, AJHR, I.4C, para.3.1.

[188] "Public Servants and Select Committees – Guidelines", State Services Commission, February 2002, updated February 2004, paras.14 to 30.

attempt to justify policy or suggest alternative policy proposals without explicit ministerial approval. Discussion of Government policy with a select committee is looked upon as the preserve of Ministers.[189] As Ministers are responsible to the House for bills which they are promoting and for the general administration of their departments, it is regarded as being ultimately a matter for them to determine which of their officials represents the department before a select committee.[190]

Officers of Parliament and officers of the House
The officers of Parliament (the Controller and Auditor-General, the Ombudsmen and the Parliamentary Commissioner for the Environment) and the Clerk of the House may give evidence to a select committee. They do so from time to time. No special authority from the House is required. Where an officer of Parliament who has been assisting a committee as an adviser is asked to give evidence to it as a witness, the officer's change of status from adviser to witness should be clearly identified.[191]

Judges
Whether judges ought or ought not, on constitutional or other grounds, to give evidence to a parliamentary committee on business before the legislature has been questioned.[192] Judges have occasionally given evidence to select committees, whether at the invitation of a committee[193] or on their own initiative.[194] A committee has devoted an entire report to a briefing it received (partly in public and partly in private) from the Principal Family Court Judge on the work of that court.[195]

A committee is quite likely to agree to hear a submission from the judiciary in private or even in secret and it has been argued that there is a convention that evidence received from members of the judiciary will be treated as private evidence.[196] But there is no requirement that this occur and, in fact, judges have been heard at public hearings of committees. It is in every case a matter for the committee to determine by leave. Where a judge does appear before a committee, it is not out of order to refer to this fact later in debate in the House, nor is there any convention that would prevent such a reference being made.[197]

Preliminary matters
Before appearing before a committee to give evidence, witnesses must be informed that they can ask to give evidence in private or in secret.[198] The clerk of the committee informs the witness of this in the correspondence confirming the arrangements for the witness to appear. Prior to appearing, the witness may raise any matters of concern relating to the evidence to be given with the clerk who will bring them to the attention of the committee.[199] Finally, a person who is to appear before a committee must be informed or given a copy of any evidence (other than secret evidence) or material in the committee's possession that contains an allegation that may seriously damage the reputation of that

[189] *Ibid.*; 2001, Vol.593, pp.10212-4.
[190] Wilson, "The Robustness of Conventions in a Time of Modernisation and Change" [2004] PL 407 at 419.
[191] 1999-2002, AJHR, I.15A, para.8.3.
[192] See Hanan, *The Life of Chief Justice Way*, p.212 (South Australian Attorney-General thought not; the judges themselves thought otherwise.)
[193] *Reports of select committees for 1996*, p.144 (President of the Court of Appeal on the *Taxpayer Compliance, Penalties, and Disputes Resolution Bill* 1996); 2002-05, AJHR, I.22C, pp. 854, 874 (Principal Family Court Judge on the *Care of*

Children Bill 2004).
[194] 1996-99, AJHR, I.22, p.858 (Chief District Court Judge on the *Land Transport Bill* 1997); "Judges question job law changes", *The Dominion Post*, 19 March 2004 (Employment Court judges on the *Employment Relations Law Reform Bill*).
[195] 1999-2002, AJHR, I.22B, pp.1328-33.
[196] 2002-05, AJHR, I.22B, p.672 (Justice and Electoral Committee).
[197] 1984, Vol.457, p.477.
[198] S.O.221(2).
[199] S.O.224.

person.[200] In this way, if possible, the person is given prior notice of any allegation so that in giving evidence the witness can reply to it.

Representation

Any witness is entitled to be accompanied by counsel.[201] The choice of counsel is a matter for the witness. But to appear as *counsel* a person must have been properly admitted to practice at the New Zealand bar, though need not necessarily be the holder of a current practising certificate.[202] A member of Parliament who is legally qualified may act as counsel before a select committee provided that the member is not remunerated for the work.[203]

The witness may consult counsel during the course of the meeting.[204] In addition, counsel has a number of procedural rights. Counsel may make written submissions to the committee on the procedure to be followed by it and, with the committee's agreement, may address the committee in person on this before the witness gives evidence.[205] During the witness/client's examination, counsel may intervene to object to a question on the grounds of relevancy or on any other ground.[206] Counsel has the right to ask that the committee hears from further witnesses when the witness/client's reputation may be seriously damaged by proceedings of the committee.[207] In addition to these procedural rights as counsel, it is open to a committee to concede counsel other procedural rights if it sees fit such as, for example, the right to examine or re-examine the witness/client.

While a witness has a right to be accompanied by counsel, a witness may seek the committee's agreement to be represented by any person. Although a committee is only obliged to permit representation by counsel it may, if it sees fit, permit representation by any other person, too. The procedural rights of such a representative is then a matter to be defined by the committee.

The appearance of counsel before the Privileges Committee is common. It is much less common before other committees and may attract comment from them. Only in exceptional cases should witnesses consider that they need to be accompanied by counsel.[208] In particular, chief executives of public bodies are expected to be able to represent themselves before select committees to answer questions about the organisation's performance without counsel, whatever their rights may be in this regard.[209] In-house legal staff from departments and corporations are regarded as appearing as part of the department's or corporation's team of witnesses rather than as counsel, unless they specifically request this status.

Order of hearing witnesses

The order of hearing witnesses is determined by the chairperson subject to any direction of the committee.[210] The scheduling of the witnesses' appearances before a select committee is arranged by the clerk of the committee under the chairperson's direction. Even after a schedule of witnesses has been prepared and advised to the committee, the chairperson can alter it, though the chairperson's decision to do this can be overturned by the committee.

---

[200] S.O.235(2).
[201] S.O.229(1).
[202] 1986-87, AJHR, I.15, Annex B.
[203] *Ibid.*
[204] S.O.229(1).
[205] S.O.229(2)(a), (b).
[206] S.O.229(2)(c), (d).
[207] S.O.229(2)(e).
[208] 1993-96, AJHR, I.18A, p.81.
[209] *Ibid.*, I.7A, p.26.
[210] S.O.225(1).

Conduct of examination

A witness is invited to the select committee table and seated at the opposite end from the chairperson, with members of the committee to either side. The chairperson announces the name of the witness to the committee and introduces the witness to committee members. At this point, if it is desired that the witness give sworn evidence, an oath or affirmation is administered by the clerk of the committee.[211] However, this is rare.

The witness's written submission will have already been distributed to the committee members. If it has not already been released by the committee, it becomes available at this point to the public.[212] It is the invariable practice to take the written submission as read rather than for the witness actually to read it to the committee. The chairperson invites the witness to make an opening statement by way of overall summary or emphasis prior to questioning beginning.

Witnesses are questioned in such manner as the chairperson, with the approval of the committee, directs.[213] Members may put questions to the witness through the chairperson,[214] though this is not taken to prevent a member addressing the witness directly if the chairperson permits this, as is normally the case. The chairperson may begin the questioning or invite another member to do so. Other members will then be called upon in turn to put any questions they have. Subject to control by the chairperson, a member may re-examine the witness on more than one occasion and put supplementary questions during examination by another member.

Relevancy

All questions put to a witness must be relevant to the matter which is under consideration by the committee, though they do not necessarily have to arise directly out of the written evidence or the opening remarks of the witness. As with all questions of relevancy, the chairperson is the sole judge. The chairperson is required by the Standing Orders to ensure that questions are relevant and that they seek only information that is necessary for the purposes of the committee's proceedings.[215] The chairperson will intervene if he or she perceives that the questioning is becoming irrelevant to the subject before the committee. In addition, the witness or counsel to the witness may object to a question on the ground that it is not relevant.[216] The chairperson, after hearing argument on the matter to the extent that the chairperson sees fit, decides if the question is relevant. If it is determined that it is, the question may be put to the witness again. If it is ruled not to be relevant, it is out of order.

Other objections to answer

Apart from relevancy, there are questions which it is not in order for a member to address to a witness in any circumstances. These include: questions which allege crime by identified persons,[217] make charges against the private conduct of members[218] or transgress the *sub judice* rule.[219] If a question of this nature is asked, the chairperson may rule it out of order on the chairperson's own initiative or following objection by other members, the witness or counsel.

A witness and counsel may also object to the witness having to answer a question on any other ground. In this case the witness must state the ground on which objection is taken.[220]

In the case of objection by a witness to answer on a ground other than relevancy, the

---

[211] S.O.231(2).
[212] S.O.218(2).
[213] S.O.225(1).
[214] S.O.225(2).
[215] S.O.226(1).

[216] S.Os 226(2) and 229(2)(c).
[217] S.O.200(1).
[218] S.O.201(1).
[219] S.Os 111 and 112.
[220] S.Os 227 and 229(2)(d).

committee, not the chairperson, decides whether the question should be asked. It may decide summarily that the question should not be pressed, otherwise it must consider, in private, whether to insist on an answer. In taking this decision it must have regard to the importance to its proceedings of obtaining an answer to the question asked.[221] It may be that the question is not important enough for the committee to insist on an answer from a witness, who is, after all, appearing voluntarily before the committee. It may be too that a witness's reluctance to answer is a result of the public nature of the examination and that any concerns could be assuaged by having the answer given in private or secret. The committee will consider this option too.[222] (Though, of course, the objection to answer may be made at a hearing that is already being conducted in private or in secret.) Committees have been urged not to insist on witnesses giving sensitive personal or commercial information in a public forum unless this is really necessary.[223]

Grounds for objection
There is no list (comprehensive or indicative) contained in the Standing Orders of the categories of circumstances in which witnesses may object to answering questions that are otherwise relevant. One likely ground on which a witness might object – self-incrimination – was acknowledged as a legitimate ground for objection in the report recommending the Standing Order on objections to answer.[224] While it is not listed as a specific ground for objection in the Standing Orders, it is a statutory ground for objection when evidence is being taken under oath.

A witness who is examined on oath before a select committee has a right to claim to be excused from answering any question which may be incriminating to the witness. If such a claim is made and the committee considers that an answer to the question is essential to its inquiry, it may report the matter to the House, which may then order the witness to answer the question. A witness who answers fully and faithfully after being directed to do so by the House is indemnified in respect of legal liability based on those replies, as those answers cannot be admitted as evidence against the witness in any civil or criminal proceedings (except for perjury).[225] But examination under oath is rare.

The State Services Commission, in its guidance to departmental officials appearing before committees as witnesses, suggests that officials should apply the criteria in the *Official Information Act* 1982 in considering their responses to the information requests that are made of them. For example, if information would have been made available under that Act, it should, as a matter of course, be provided to a committee if requested. While the Act does not constrain the powers of the House, and departments should never refuse to provide information on the ground that it does, that Act does identify categories of sensitive information which, the State Services Commission suggests, officials may object to producing. These are—

• protecting the security of New Zealand, or the international relations of the Government of New Zealand (including information given in confidence to the Government by governments of other countries)
• protecting the maintenance of the law
• avoiding endangering the safety of any person
• preventing serious damage to the economy of New Zealand
• protecting the privacy of individuals
• protecting commercially sensitive information

---

[221] S.O.228(1).
[222] S.O.228(3).
[223] 1991-93, AJHR, I.15, para.6.

[224] Joseph, "Report to the Standing Orders Committee on Natural Justice", para.8.12.
[225] *Legislature Act* 1908, s.253(1) to (4).

- protecting information that is subject to legal privilege
- maintaining constitutional conventions relating to the confidentiality of advice, ministerial responsibility and the political neutrality of officials.[226]

The State Services Commission also asks its officials to bear in mind a number of conventions that have developed, before responding to a committee's request for information—

- ministerial approval should be sought before providing information on the policies, administration and expenditure of a previous administration
- Cabinet papers should be treated as confidential to the Government, ministerial approval should be sought before such papers are released to a committee and the proceedings of Cabinet or its committees should not be divulged
- committees have accepted that it may be inappropriate to require the public disclosure of commercially sensitive information
- committees have not normally insisted on the presentation in public of information where this would infringe the privacy of individuals or of individual bodies, particularly where that information has been given in confidence
- departmental officials are entitled to refuse to disclose opinion or advice given to Ministers without the agreement of the Minister.[227]

Departments are also reminded that specific restrictions on the disclosure of information is contained in particular statutes. Whether these prevent the release of information to select committees is a legal question. (See Chapter 30.)

In any of these circumstances officials can be expected to object to answering a question or to producing information, at least in a public setting or without an opportunity to refer first to the Minister. It is always a matter for decision by the committee as to whether it will accede to any such objection. In Canada, the role of the public service as implementors and administrators of policy, rather than determinors of what that policy should be, has been seen as justifying some limitations on its obligations to respond to committees. For example, public servants have been excused from commenting on policy decisions made by the Government. It has also been said that "committees will ordinarily accept the reasons that a public servant gives for declining to answer a specific question or series of questions which involve the giving of a legal opinion, or which may be perceived as a conflict with the witness' responsibility to the Minister, or which is outside their own area of responsibility or which might affect business transactions".[228] The Australian Senate's Procedure Committee has acknowledged that that country's freedom of information legislation provides persuasive, though not binding, grounds for not producing information sought by a committee.[229]

Objection overruled

If the committee decides that it does require an answer (perhaps in private or in secret), it informs the witness accordingly.[230] The question is then put to the witness again. A witness who declines to answer a question in these circumstances may be held in contempt of the House.[231] The committee may report the failure to answer to the House for it to take such action as it deems appropriate.[232]

---

[226] "Public Servants and Select Committees – Guidelines", State Services Commission, February 2002, updated February 2004, para.22.

[227] *Ibid.*, para.23.

[228] Marleau and Montpetit, *House of Commons Procedure*, p.864.

[229] *Report of the Senate (Australia) Procedure Committee*, Third Report of 1992.

[230] S.O.228(?)

[231] S.O.400(u).

[232] S.O.228(4).

Conclusion of examination

When the examination concludes, the witness may be asked whether he or she desires to add anything to the evidence which has been given and will then leave the committee table. Often witnesses (especially departmental witnesses) agree to supplement their oral answers with written responses to questions asked of them during the examination but which require some research to answer adequately. Such questions for later written response are minuted and responded to subsequently in writing. Sometimes, too, the committee will supplement its oral examination of a witness with written questions to that witness. This is common in the case of estimates and financial review examinations. Such supplementary evidence is forwarded to the clerk of the committee for distribution to committee members.

Interpretation and translation

As in the House, English or Māori may be used in select committee proceedings.

In the Māori Affairs Committee's meeting room (Maui Tikitiki A Taranga) facilities for simultaneous interpretation have been permanently installed.[233] Interpreters employed by the Office of the Clerk provide the service at the request of the committee. Documents received by committees in one of the official languages may be translated into the other at the direction of the chairperson of the committee.

Interpretation and translation for non-official languages is not generally available. It is expected that a document submitted to a committee in another language will be accompanied by a translation into English or Māori. But special arrangements may be made in respect of an item of business of peculiar concern to a particular language group.[234]

RESPONDING TO ALLEGATIONS

A major procedural change made in 1996 was the adoption of procedures designed to bring to the attention of persons any allegations that are made against them that may seriously damage their reputations, and to give them a right to respond to such allegations. Committees, and in particular committee chairpersons, should be alert to preventing irrelevant and unnecessary personal allegations being made in the first place. Select committee hearings are not occasions for personal vendettas. Even if an allegation is made, committees have power to expunge irrelevant allegations from the committee transcript and to return such written evidence.[235] They are also obliged to consider seeking an order of the House permanently suppressing the evidence.[236] But such actions may not be enough to remove the stain of an allegation that has entered the public domain.

Serious damage to reputation

The right to be informed and the right to reply arise where an allegation is made against a person that may "seriously damage the reputation" of that person. (A person includes an organisation, such as a corporation.[237]) Whether an allegation may cause serious damage to reputation is a matter for the committee to assess in deciding whether it must activate the information or reply provisions of the Standing Orders. Where allegations are directed at someone, the committee will wish to hear a reply to those allegations, in any case, so

---

[233] "MPs get direct language versions", *The Evening Post*, 24 February 2000.
[234] 2002-05, AJHR, I.5C.

[235] S.Os 217 and 237.
[236] S.O.237(c).
[237] S.O.3(1); 1997, Vol.558, p.706.

that it can make informed conclusions on them. This is especially so when allegations are made against a public body, which is, by definition, under a public duty to account to the House. However, mere criticism, especially of a public body, is not seen as amounting to a serious damage to reputation and thus requiring the application of the reply provisions. In these cases it is a matter for the discretion of the committee as to whether it does apply them. There is thus a threshold test that must be applied by committees in determining if the rights to be informed and to reply that the Standing Orders confer are engaged at all. In the political environment of parliamentary proceedings a higher threshold for criticism applies than might operate generally. This does not mean that a committee will never or ought never to permit rebuttal of criticism not amounting to a serious damage to reputation. Committees do invite or accept rebuttal in these circumstances, not least so that they are better informed about the issues before them.[238] But committees are not *obliged* to do so unless the rebuttal Standing Orders are actually engaged.

Committees are therefore obliged to identify allegations in written evidence that may seriously damage the reputations of others and, if necessary, to take pre-emptive action by returning or expunging the evidence[239] or hearing the evidence in private.[240] Where it does receive such evidence, a committee must draw any allegations to the attention of those persons against whom they are made. In the case of a serious allegation made in advice received by the committee from one of its officials, the advice may be returned with a request that the allegation be expunged.[241]

Information on allegations

A person who is about to appear before a committee must be informed of, or given a copy of, any evidence or material in the committee's possession (other than secret evidence) that contains an allegation that may seriously damage that person's reputation.[242] It is then expected that that person, in giving evidence, will respond to the allegation. At the very least that person will thereby have an opportunity to do so. Anyone whose reputation may be seriously damaged by a committee's proceedings can request from the clerk of the committee a copy of all material, evidence (other than secret evidence), records or other information which the committee possesses concerning that person.[243] Such a request is considered by the committee and, if it considers it is necessary to prevent serious damage to that person's reputation, the material is provided to the person concerned.[244] It may, however, be provided in a different form to that requested so as to avoid undue difficulty, expense or delay.[245]

Where a serious allegation is received or made in public or in private, the committee is obliged to consider whether to expunge it from any transcript of the hearing[246] and whether to inform the person against whom the allegation was made, of the allegation.[247] In the case of an allegation made at a public hearing, merely expunging the evidence from the transcript without informing the person concerned and giving him or her an opportunity to respond is not likely to be an adequate means of dealing with the matter.

In the case of a serious allegation made or received in secret, the committee is also obliged to consider whether to return the evidence or seek to suppress it. If no such action is to be taken, it must then inform the person against whom the allegation was made of it, if it considers that the damage to that person's reputation outweighs any detriment to the witness who gave the evidence.[248] In the case of a witness who reasonably fears violence

---

[238] 1999-2002, AJHR, I.22B, pp.144-50.
[239] S.Os 217 and 237(a), (b).
[240] S.O.235(1).
[241] S.O.238(3)(a).
[242] S.O.235(2).
[243] S.O.236(1).

[244] S.O.236(2).
[245] S.O.236(3).
[246] S.O.237(b).
[247] S.O.238(1).
[248] S.O.238(2).

or other retribution from the person against whom the accusation was made, the committee may conclude that any damage to that person's reputation (limited in any case because the proceedings are secret) is outweighed by the personal danger disclosure would involve for the witness. This balancing of damage, however, applies only in respect of evidence given by a witness. If a serious allegation is made in secret by a member or by an adviser,[249] the person must be informed if the allegation cannot otherwise be satisfactorily suppressed.

Response

Where a serious allegation has been made against a person, that person must be given a reasonable opportunity to respond to the allegation by written submission and personal appearance before the committee.[250] The person (or counsel) may also ask the committee to hear evidence from further witnesses in that person's interest.[251] While the committee is obliged to consider such a request, it is not obliged to accede to it.

It may be that a person given an opportunity to respond to allegations made against him or her will decline to do so,[252] or will be content to make a written response rather than also appearing before the committee to answer the allegation. A person appearing before the committee to answer an allegation made against him or her is a witness before the committee. Where an allegation was originally made in private or secret, a response to it will be treated as private or secret evidence, as the case may be.[253] Even where the allegation was made in public, the person making a response can request to be heard in private or secret if this is desired.[254] The person can be questioned on the response after making it to the committee.

How the committee deals with allegations and responses in its report to the House is a matter for it. It may decide not to include mention of them at all. On the other hand, it may simply record them without adding any comment of its own.[255]

While the committee is obliged to give a person an opportunity to make a response, it and its members are not obliged to believe or accept the response that is made (or to believe or accept the initial allegation for that matter). If the matter is considered material enough to the committee's work, the committee may make findings indicating that it does not accept the responder's explanation – though if these are to be included in its report as adverse findings, that person must be given an opportunity to comment on them at the draft report stage. A committee has made a report putting on record a response to submissions made to it on a bill on which it had already reported. While it did not believe that the Standing Orders requiring it to seek a response had been engaged in that case, it nevertheless wished to ensure that all sides had an opportunity to put their views on record.[256]

EXPENSES

Witnesses are not reimbursed expenses incurred in appearing before a committee except with the Speaker's permission.[257] Committees, chairpersons or other persons may not give any promise or undertaking that a witness's expenses will be reimbursed without first obtaining the authority of the Speaker.[258] This will generally be given only where witnesses have had to travel to Wellington twice because of the committee's actions; for example, as a result of a last-minute cancellation of its meeting due to the House sitting under urgency. Where a committee invites a witness to give evidence for some special

---

[249] S.O.238(3).
[250] S.O.239(1)(a).
[251] S.Os 229(2)(e) and 239(1)(b).
[252] 1996-99, AJHR, I.19D, p.225.
[253] S.O.239(2).
[254] 1996, Vol.556, p.13901.

[255] 2002-05, AJHR, I.19B, pp.310, 335-52.
[256] 1999-2002, AJHR, I.22B, pp.144-50
       (*Telecommunications Bill*).
[257] S.O.230(1).
[258] S.O.230(2).

reason, the financial hardship of that witness may also be a good ground for reimbursement of expenses. A Government department has funded the preparation of a submission by private individuals on an inquiry being carried out by a select committee.[259]

OFFICIAL REPORTS OF PROCEEDINGS

Until the First World War it was common for shorthand reporters to attend meetings of select committees to take and prepare verbatim transcripts of the evidence heard. These were printed along with the committee's report and minutes, and published in the *Appendices to the Journals of the House*. This practice was considerably reduced as an economy measure during the First World War, and for many years afterwards a transcript of the evidence given to a select committee was rarely prepared.

Committees do have the power to decide to record evidence given at their meetings and, if they think fit, to have the evidence transcribed.[260] Recording and transcription, where desired, is arranged by staff of the Office of the Clerk. Where evidence is transcribed, a proof copy is provided to the witness who is given a reasonable opportunity to suggest corrections.[261] Corrections are accepted on the same basis as for the preparation of an official report of debates in the House. (See Chapter 5.) The committee may expunge evidence from the transcript that it considers to be irrelevant to its proceedings, offensive or possibly defamatory,[262] and also expunge any evidence that contains a serious allegation against a person that the committee is satisfied creates a risk of harm to that person not justified by the benefit to the committee from the evidence given.[263] (Though the fact that a committee has expunged evidence from a transcript does not mean that the evidence was not given on a privileged occasion. A committee cannot remove the protection that exists as a matter of law for proceedings in Parliament.)

Evidence that has been transcribed may be reported as an appendix to the committee's report or as a separate volume of evidence.[264] It has become the regular practice for the Finance and Expenditure Committee to include in its reports the transcript of the examination of some of its more important work, such as its examination of the Budget policy statement and the Reserve Bank of New Zealand's monetary policy statement. Other committees also do this from time to time. The House has also itself specifically authorised the publication of evidence tendered to a select committee.[265]

---

[259] *Hansard Supplement*, 2000, Vol.45, p.3934.
[260] S.O.232(1).
[261] S.O.232(2).
[262] S.O.217.
[263] S.O.237(b).
[264] See, for example, 1999-2002, AJHR, I.7B (containing the transcripts of evidence given on the inquiry into matters relating to the visit of the President of China to New Zealand in 1999).

[265] 1992, Vol.532, p.13286 (inquiry into contractual arrangements for flight inspection of aviation navigation aids).

CHAPTER 24

SELECT COMMITTEE REPORTING

TYPES OF REPORT

Select committees, as creatures of the House, make their reports to the House and through the House to the world at large.

Interim reports

All committees have power to make interim reports to the House to inform it of some of the committee's conclusions or of the progress of its investigations on the matter before it.[1]

The power has been used to give the public an indication of the substantial amendments to a bill before it which the committee had provisionally resolved upon. An interim report has also been presented as an opportunity for one last round of consultations with interested groups to canvass the acceptability of the committee's proposals.[2] A committee has used an interim report as a means of calling for submissions on an inquiry that it had initiated and giving details about how it proposed to progress the inquiry.[3]

When a committee makes an interim report, in principle, all prior proceedings of the committee relevant to the report that are not already publicly available become available on the presentation of the report,[4] though the committee may resolve to withhold some or all of them.[5]

Special reports

All committees may make special reports to the House. Special reports do not deal with the substantive issues before the committee but relate to requesting authority from the House to do something, seeking of guidance on a procedural issue, or merely informing the House of a matter that has arisen connected with the committee's proceedings.[6]

A committee has used a special report: to inform the House that it was unable to elect a deputy chairperson;[7] to acknowledge that the procedure for adopting a previous report had been flawed as not all members had seen a proposed amendment;[8] to announce that it had initiated a major inquiry;[9] and to correct a factual error contained in a previous report that it had presented.[10]

Since, unlike interim reports, special reports are not used to convey a committee's conclusions on the substance of the matter before a committee there is no presumption that all prior proceedings of the committee become publicly available with the report, though those proceedings of the committee directly relevant to the adoption of the special report do become available. Again, however, a committee can resolve to withhold details of its proceedings that would otherwise become available.[11]

Final reports

The committee presents its conclusions to the House in a final report on the bill or other matter which is the subject of the report. This does not mean that the committee will

---

[1]   S.O.244.
[2]   1987-90, AJHR, I.24A (committee on the *Maori Fisheries Bill*).
[3]   1999-2002, AJHR, I.21B, pp.361-70 (climate change).
[4]   2002-05, AJHR, I.18B, p.47.
[5]   S.O.240(4).
[6]   S.O.245.
[7]   1996-99, AJHR, I.22, p.295 (Internal Affairs and Local Government Committee).
[8]   *Ibid.*, p.547 (Social Services Committee).
[9]   *Ibid.*, I.24, p.140 (Finance and Expenditure Committee).
[10] 1999-2002, AJHR, I.21A, p.486 (Commerce Committee); 2002-05, AJHR, I.22D, p.407 (Foreign Affairs, Defence and Trade Committee).
[11] S.O.240(4).

always be able to reach firm conclusions on the substantive issues before it. Indeed, the final report may record the committee's inability to do so.[12] A committee may use its power to report for the purpose of conveying information to the House (such as the evidence it has heard) rather than to present conclusions as such. When a committee presents a final report on a bill or matter, that bill or matter is no longer in the committee's hands and it cannot deal further with it.[13] If the matter fell within the committee's general subject area terms of reference it could initiate a new inquiry.

Not every matter referred to a committee or every inquiry initiated by it will result in a final report. A bill or other matter referred by the House that has not been reported lapses at the end of a Parliament, though it may be reinstated. Any inquiry initiated by the committee that is uncompleted at the end of a Parliament also lapses, though it too may be readopted as an inquiry by the committee in the new Parliament. Proceedings on a bill or other matter that has lapsed in this way (including any draft report) remain confidential for the first nine sitting days of the new Parliament to give the House and the committee time to consider whether they wish to reinstate or readopt such business.[14] Whether they do reinstate or readopt it is a matter for the newly constituted House and committee to decide. Also, a committee may simply discontinue an inquiry it has initiated, whether from lack of interest in it or for any other reason.

Finally, the committee may fail to present a report within an applicable time limit on a bill. In these circumstances the bill is automatically withdrawn from the committee and returned to the House.[15]

Activities reports

Some committees have developed a practice of presenting periodic final reports of a miscellaneous nature called "activities reports". The Regulations Review Committee, for instance, presents an annual activities report. In these reports the committee describes the range of its activities in the period dealt with by the report. Many of the matters referred to are dealt with in more detail in other more specific reports that have already been presented to the House. An activities report can also assume some of the characteristics of an interim report, telling the House of the work in progress before the committee. Activities reports deal with many issues addressed by committees that may not warrant particular reports of their own. They enable the numerous issues dealt with by a committee over a period to be conveyed to the House in a convenient form.[16]

TIME LIMITS FOR REPORTING

Time for report fixed

If a time has been fixed for the presentation of the final report on a bill or other item of business, that report must be presented by the select committee on or before the day so fixed.[17] (The presentation of interim, special and activities reports is always optional.) A time may be fixed for a final report by the Standing Orders, by the House, by the Business Committee (for extensions of time only) or, exceptionally, by statute. A select committee cannot impose a binding time limit on itself, though it may adopt a work programme for a particular bill or item of business under which it tries to work to a timetable.

The Standing Orders prescribe the time for select committees to report on bills and in respect of a range of financial business.

---

12   1996 99, AJIIR, I.22, pp.313-7 (*Limits on Campaign Spending for Candidates in Local Body Elections Bill*); 1999-2002, AJHR, I.22A, pp.573-97 (*Electoral (Integrity) Amendment Bill*); *ibid*., I.22B, pp.667-75 (inquiry into New Zealand's adoption laws).

13   1980, Vol.429, p.523.
14   S.O.242.
15   S.O.291(3).
16   1987-90, AJHR, I.16.
17   S.O.249.

Six months is the standard reporting time prescribed for all bills referred to select committees. They must be finally reported to the House within this time.[18] But, the House, on referring a bill to a select committee may, and often does, vary this standard time by requiring the committee to report the bill within a shorter (or, exceptionally, longer) time-frame.

The Standing Orders prescribe standard reporting times for select committees on their estimates examinations (two months from the Budget),[19] and on their financial reviews of departments and offices of Parliament (within one week of the first sitting day in each year),[20] and on Crown entities, State enterprises and other public organisations (six months in each case).[21] The Finance and Expenditure Committee has specific reporting time obligations in respect of some of the financial business transacted by it: examination of the Budget policy statement (40 working days),[22] the fiscal strategy report and the economic and fiscal update (two months from the Budget),[23] and the annual financial statements of the Government (within one week of the first sitting day in each year).[24] A committee to which has been referred a notice of a motion for the approval of a regulation pursuant to a statute (an affirmative resolution) must report on that notice of motion no later than 28 days after the notice was lodged.[25]

It is always open to the House, in referring a matter to a committee, to fix a date by which the committee must report on it to the House. Exceptionally, statute may do this. In the case of the statutory select committee review of the MMP election system, the committee was required to report by 1 June 2002.[26] The statutory review by a select committee of the legislation implementing New Zealand's obligations under a United Nations Security Council resolution on terrorism had to be reported on by 1 December 2005.[27]

Where business that had lapsed is reinstated, that business is resumed at the same stage that it had reached in the old Parliament. However, if that business is subject to a reporting time limit, that time does not run between the lapse of the business and the date on which it is reinstated.

Failure to report within time fixed

A committee that fails to report within any time fixed for presentation of its final report is immediately in breach of its obligation to the House. The members of the committee can be ordered by the House to discharge their obligation to report, with the threat that if they fail to do so they will be in contempt of the House.

In the case of a bill, failure to present a report in time also means that the committee's task is at an end. The bill is automatically discharged from further consideration by the committee and is set down for its next stage in the House.[28] In the case of other business with a time limit for reporting which a committee fails to meet, the committee's obligation is not automatically discharged.[29] If the House in referring the matter has made provision for what is to occur if a committee has not reported, that provision applies. In absence of such a provision and in the absence of the House regularising the position by granting an extension, the Speaker determines when the committee must report and what the consequences are of its failure to do so.[30] The Speaker has ordered a committee which failed to report in due time on a financial review to report later in the week, failing which its task of review would be at an end and no report would be made at all.[31]

18 S.O.291(1).
19 S.O.330(2).
20 S.O.336(2).
21 S.O.336(3).
22 S.O.324(2).
23 S.O.327(2).
24 S.O.336(1).

25 S.O.317(2).
26 *Electoral Act* 1993, s.264(2).
27 *Terrorism Suppression Act* 2002, s.70(3).
28 S.O.291(3).
29 1999, Vol.577, p.16437.
30 *Ibid.*
31 *Ibid.*

Extensions to reporting time

The House may, on motion with notice or by leave, extend any time fixed for reporting by the Standing Orders or in a previous order of the House. The House frequently grants extensions to reporting times on bills including general extensions for bills held over from a previous Parliament.[32] It has also granted extensions to select committees for the financial reviews they were carrying out,[33] and to the Finance and Expenditure Committee in respect of financial business under consideration by it.[34]

In respect of bills, the Business Committee may extend (but not reduce) the time for a committee to report.[35] About one-fifth of all bills have their reporting times extended, often more than once, and the Business Committee is the most common means of effecting the extension. Select committees write directly to the Business Committee seeking an extension. The Business Committee will not grant an extension without hearing the views of the member in charge of the bill. These are given either in the select committee's letter or by way of a separate letter from the member in charge and considered by the Business Committee at the same time as the select committee's application for an extension. If the committee and the member are in agreement about an extension, the Business Committee will invariably grant it, though it may alter the length of the requested extension by increasing or decreasing it. If they disagree, the Business Committee will make its own judgment.

In practice, suggestions for extensions to the reporting time for any other business before a select committee will be discussed at the Business Committee before being raised in the House.

ADOPTION OF REPORT

Consideration

When the committee has heard all the evidence on the bill or other matter which it is prepared to hear, it begins the process of deciding upon its report to the House. The first stage in determining on the committee's report is known as the consideration stage. At this point the committee listens to comment from the committee's departmental or other advisers on the submissions heard by the committee. Papers and analysis may be called for by the committee from its staff and advisers. At the consideration stage (which may involve several meetings) the committee in a relatively informal manner discusses and reconsiders the details of the evidence and reports it has received. It does not take binding decisions as to the form of the report (though it may have a draft report before it), thus giving members an opportunity to discuss the matters among themselves and with colleagues. This stage in the formation and adoption of the committee's report also gives the committee the opportunity to invite comment on its provisional findings from persons who may be commented on adversely in the finalised report.

Draft report

Either as part of the consideration phase or arising from it, a draft report will be prepared for the committee to consider. In the case of a bill, this will be a draft of the select committee's commentary. The draft may be prepared by the chairperson or by any member of the committee, but it is usually prepared by the staff of the committee. It has the status of a draft report because it is prepared under the instructions of the committee

---

32   2002, Vol.602, p.54.
33   1999, Vol.581, p.37; 2001, Vol.597, p.14074.
34   1999, Vol.581, p.37; 2000, Vol.582, p.1342.
35   S.O.291(2).

and not merely on the personal initiative of a member of the committee or a member of staff. As such it is strictly confidential to the committee until the committee reports to the House,[36] when all the committee's proceedings (except secret evidence) will become publicly available. The disclosure of a draft report is a serious breach of privilege.[37] A draft report may be disclosed by the committee or by a member of the committee to another member of Parliament or to the Clerk and other officers of the House in the course of their duties.[38] The committee may also make it available to any person for the purpose of assisting the committee in its work by providing comment on the draft.[39] A draft report has been referred for academic peer review before being presented to the House.[40]

Adverse findings

If a committee provisionally determines to include in a report any findings that may seriously damage the reputation of a person to be named in the report, it must, as soon as is practicable, acquaint that person with the provisional findings and give him or her a reasonable opportunity to make a response to the committee on them.[41] That response can be made orally or in writing or both, as the committee determines. The committee is then obliged to take the response into consideration in making its report to the House.[42] It should be axiomatic that if a committee reaches the stage of considering making an adverse finding against someone, it will have heard from that person (or have invited that person to appear before it) earlier in its proceedings as a witness. If it has not, an adverse finding of any description can hardly be justified at all. It is also quite likely that an allegation may have been made against that person earlier in the committee's inquiries and the person given an opportunity to respond to it then. This is a separate process from considering whether to make an adverse finding against a person in the committee's report. The fact that a response may have been invited at an earlier stage of proceedings does not remove the obligation to give the person concerned an opportunity to comment before making an adverse finding in the report.[43]

The obligation to refer draft adverse findings for comment lies with the committee. But the chairperson has the interpretative responsibility of identifying findings that may be adverse and in respect of which the obligation may arise. Not all comments in a report which someone may consider objectionable will require to be referred for comment. In particular, the procedure is not an opportunity for a second comment on an issue just because a witness might disagree with the committee's view of it. It is a rule concerned solely with reputation. Bodies which are under recognised accountability obligations to Parliament, such as departments, Crown entities and State enterprises are in practice subject to a higher threshold test for adverse findings. The accountability relationships with these bodies means that they may be subject to select committee criticism or rebuke without necessarily being afforded an opportunity to comment on a draft report. Only if the criticism in respect of these organisations was of a particularly damning nature in respect of an identified individual would a committee feel obliged to acquaint them with it, though it may do so as a matter of discretion, rather than of obligation. A committee may always go further than the Standing Orders require and circulate its draft report for review as to its accuracy, even though it is not obliged to do so.

The committee must allow a reasonable opportunity for comment, though precisely how long it does allow is a matter for it. Generally one week (a committee's normal meeting interval) is the norm. But, if a committee is under a particular time constraint in

---

36   S.O.241(1).
37   1997, Vol.562, p.3232.
38   S.O.241(2)(a).
39   S.Os 241(2)(b) and 243(2).
40   1999-2002, AJHR, I.1A, pp.3-4.
41   S.O.247(1).
42   *Ibid.*
43   2002-05, AJHR, I.17D, pp.5 and 7.

reporting, a shorter response time will be necessary in that case. Any response received by a committee in these circumstances is strictly confidential to the committee until it reports to the House.[44] The committee should make this clear to any person who is invited to make a response to it.[45]

Having received comment on a draft adverse finding, the committee must take that comment into account in framing its report.[46]

At the highest level a comment on an adverse finding may cause the committee to change its mind entirely about its provisional conclusion and omit the finding or alter it to remove any adverse reflection. It may, on the other hand, not change the committee's mind at all or at least not materially. While the committee is obliged to take account of the comment in response, it is not obliged to reflect that comment in its report or even to refer to the fact that it sought it. However, it is usual for a committee report that contains findings seriously affecting a person's reputation to record the fact that that person's comment was sought, if only to put on record that the committee had carried out its obligation to do so. A committee may build the comment it receives into the text of its report if it sees fit, commenting on it in turn. Committees have also published the comments they have received as an annex to their reports.[47]

A committee's obligation to permit a response to adverse findings also applies where such findings are confined to minority views included in its report. In this case too it must take such a response into account in finalising the report.[48]

Deliberation

"Deliberation" is the point at which the committee goes through the bill or draft report before it and takes definite decisions by resolution or by leave in respect of these.[49] Deliberation must be specifically listed on the notice of meeting distributed to members as an item of business to be transacted, otherwise the committee can proceed to deliberate only by leave. Deliberation must take place before any report (interim, special or final) can be presented to the House. As with consideration, deliberation varies in the time it takes, though it is usually much shorter than consideration, often being confined to the formal endorsement of positions worked out during consideration. Deliberation is also confidential until the committee reports to the House.[50] While generally members of Parliament who are not members of the committee have a right to remain present during any part of a committee's proceedings, including deliberation, they must withdraw when the Privileges Committee goes into its deliberation phase unless that committee, by leave, permits them to stay.[51]

It is obviously desirable that the members participating in deliberation (and consideration) are the same members who listened to the witnesses giving evidence, but there is nothing to prevent members who have been absent from the hearings from informing themselves of the evidence placed before the committee and participating in deliberation.[52]

In the case of deliberation on a bill, the committee must consider the bill part by part and decide whether to recommend that the parts should remain part of the bill, with or without any amendments. Either before or after doing this, it considers the draft narrative commentary that will form part of its report on the bill and decides what the final form of the commentary will be. In the case of deliberation on an inquiry the committee will consider the draft report or successive draft reports before agreeing on a final report.

---

[44] S.O.247(2).

[45] 2002-05, AJHR, I.17D, pp.4 and 7.

[46] S.O.247(1).

[47] 1996-99, AJHR, I.7B, Appendices G-I; *ibid.*, I.21C, pp.331, 345-6; 1999-2002, AJHR, I.21B, pp.361-70.

[48] 2002-05, AJHR, I.22B, p.42.

[49] 1985, Vol.467, p.7984.

[50] 1997, Vol.562, p.3232.

[51] S.O.211(3).

[52] 1976, Vol.407, p.3169.

Minority or differing views

There is only one report presented to the House from a committee on each occasion it reports. That is the one adopted as the committee's report by a majority of the committee if need be. There is no "minority report".

But committees can in their reports indicate the differing views of the members of the committee.[53] These are often referred to as minority views, but they need not be minority views. There may indeed not be a majority/minority split on the committee at all; it may be equally divided on an issue. Thus a committee's report has consisted solely of a commentary setting out matters relating to consideration of the bill by the committee and then the respective parties' views. The committee itself was unable to agree on any amendments to the bill.[54]

The dissenting views of members were not at first recognised in select committee reports and for them to be revealed was looked upon as somewhat unusual, not to say improper.[55]

Summaries of minority or differing views are now commonplace in select committee reports. They are usually presented as the differing views of the parties represented on the committee (even when a party only has one member on the committee), but they may be presented as the views of individual members.[56] No member of the committee has the right to have differing views represented in the committee's report; the decision whether to do so is one for the committee to make.[57]

If the committee does decide to include differing views in its report, it cannot rewrite those views to express them in a way acceptable to a majority of the committee. That would misrepresent those views. Nevertheless, if a minority or a differing view is too objectionable or too lengthy, a majority of the committee might refuse to accept it for inclusion in the report altogether unless the minority or differing members agree to some rewriting of it. There can then be a trade-off.[58] Also, minority or differing contributions to a committee's report, like every other contribution, must be relevant to the subject of the report and must be free of unparliamentary language. In either of these cases the chairperson rules whether the contribution is wholly in order.[59]

For a member to release publicly a draft of a minority view intended to be presented to the committee for its consideration would prejudice the proper functioning of the committee process, and the Speaker has indicated that this could be treated as a contempt. Such a draft should be conveyed to the committee first.[60]

Amendments to bills are displayed in the reprinted bill as "unanimous" or "majority" once the bill has been reported to the House. This is done to facilitate a House process – majority amendments must be separately endorsed by the House on the second reading of the bill. They are not a means for committees to express the differing views of their members. That should be done in the committee's narrative commentary on the bill.[61]

Adoption of report

At the conclusion of deliberation the chairperson puts the question to the committee that the report be adopted.[62] Once the committee has adopted a report it must be presented to the House.[63] An original copy of the report is prepared (if it does not already exist) incorporating any final textual amendments agreed to by the committee. This copy may be in printed or manuscript form or partly one and partly the other. It is signed by

53   S.O.246.
54   2002-05, AJHR, I.22C, p.379 (*Foreshore and Seabed Bill*).
55   1867, Vol.1(Part II), pp.1167-9; see Dalziel, *Julius Vogel - Business Politician*, pp.77-8.
56   See, for example, 2002-05, AJHR, I.22D, pp.592-5 (*Relationships (Statutory References) Bill*).
57   2000, Vol.589, p.6893.
58   *Ibid.*, pp.6893-4.
59   *Ibid.*
60   1993, Vol.538, p.18335.
61   2002-05, AJHR, I.18B, p.37.
62   *Ibid.*, pp.48-9.
63   *Ibid.*

the chairperson[64] to authenticate that the report is as adopted by the committee. In the chairperson's absence it may be signed by the deputy chairperson or another member of the committee who has been authorised by the committee to do so.[65]

A committee can decide to report on more than one matter in the same report.[66] This course is often adopted with closely related subjects, such as with a bill and a supplementary order paper or petitions on the bill, which have been referred to the committee. It is also done with petitions of a similar nature.

Although the hearing of evidence on a matter is of critical importance in helping to shape a committee's conclusions, the report to the House embodies the opinions and policies of the members of the committee. It may or may not accord with the weight of the evidence received. (There is in any case no presumption that any decision will necessarily accord with the sheer weight of numbers of submissions received on it.[67]) Matters, particularly legislation, are considered by committees as part of a wider political programme. Parliamentary decisions are accordingly taken in this wider context. It is the case too that committees consist of only a small proportion of the House's membership and cannot themselves take final decisions on behalf of the House. It would not be reasonable for a committee to act as if it could. For these reasons, the committee's report may diverge from the preponderance of opinion expressed to it.

Languages

A report may be presented in the English language or the Māori language. A report presented in one language may be translated, under the Speaker's direction, into another language.[68] A select committee's report has been translated into Samoan, for example.[69] In 2004, for the first time, a select committee presented a bilingual report – that is, a report which had been deliberated on and adopted by the committee in both official languages.[70] In the case of a bilingual report both versions of the report are equally authoritative; one is not a translation of the other, regardless of the possible predominance of one of the languages in the preparation of the report as the committee's actual working language. In the case of an authorised translation of a committee's report, the authoritative version of the report is that in the original language.

Confidentiality of report

The report adopted by a committee is confidential to the committee until it is presented to the House in the same way as are the private proceedings of a committee and a draft report.[71] (See Chapter 23 for proceedings that are confidential.) Unauthorised disclosure of a copy of a report before its presentation may be treated as a contempt.[72] Disclosure by the committee or by a member of the committee of the report to another member or to the Clerk or an officer of the House in the course of their duties, is authorised.[73] This permits discussion of the likely outcome of a committee inquiry to be held in caucus and the necessary printing arrangements for the report to be put in train before it is formally presented.

Effect of adoption of report

Except where a committee is expressly making an interim report or a special report, once the committee has directed the chairperson to report to the House it has performed its

---

[64] S.O.248.
[65] Ibid.
[66] 1982, Vol.449, pp.5782-3.
[67] *Auckland City Council v Auckland Electric Power Board,* unreported, High Court, Auckland, 16 August 1993; *South Taranaki Energy Users Association v South Taranaki District Council,* unreported, High

[ ] Court, New Plymouth, 26 August 1997.
[68] S.O.366.
[69] 2002-05, AJHR, I.5C.
[70] Ibid., I.22C, pp.1063-76 (*Te Runanga o Ngati Awa Bill*).
[71] S.O.241(1).
[72] S.O.400(p).
[73] S.O.241(2)(a).

ultimate function in respect of the bill or matter before it and cannot afterwards reconsider the report. Events after that point must take their course. In respect of committees set up to consider one matter only, such as a special committee on a bill or a special committee set up to report on a particular topic, the committee ceases to exist as a committee when the House receives the report, and if the House wishes to give the committee further work to do it must first revive it. For permanent committees the adoption and presentation of a final report does not dissolve the committee as such, but it does take the particular matter which was the subject of the report out of the committee's hands.[74] (Though a committee may utilise its inherent power to initiate an inquiry to follow up on matters arising out of its consideration of the bill or other matter which was the subject of the report.[75])

PRESENTATION OF REPORT

When a report has been adopted it must be presented to the House within a reasonable time. The House may order a report to be presented if the chairperson does not act with despatch in the matter.[76] But the chairperson is justified in holding back a report for a few days so that the necessary arrangements can be made to have it in print in time for its presentation and so that an adequate check can be made as to its accuracy. It was unreasonable when a chairperson delayed for three months in presenting a report, but a delay of a week in presenting a report is quite acceptable.[77]

A report is presented to the House by the original copy being delivered to the Clerk by the chairperson. This may be effected on any working day but no later than 1 pm on a day on which the House sits.[78] (If the House sits on a non-working day – a Saturday – no report may be presented.) A list of all select committee reports presented since the House last sat is read out to the House by the Clerk at the time for the announcement of the presentation of reports of select committees (part of the first item of business each day).[79]

Reports from the Intelligence and Security Committee on bills and other matters referred to it by the House are presented in the same way as a report from a select committee. (Reports from the Intelligence and Security Committee on any of its other statutory functions are presented as papers in the same way as reports from any other non-parliamentary body.)

Committees may hold press conferences following a report's presentation to give greater publicity to their findings. Such press conferences are not formal proceedings of the committee and are not protected by absolute privilege.[80] Public comments made by individual members of the committee (even the chairperson) on a report are not protected by absolute privilege either.[81]

PUBLICATION OF REPORT

All select committee reports are published under the authority of the House.[82]

Bills are reprinted in a form which indicates the committee's proposed amendments together with the committee's commentary describing its consideration of the bill. (See Chapter 27.) Other reports presented by select committees are printed either at the time of or shortly after their presentation, or at the end of the session. It is obviously desirable for narrative reports to be in print at the time the committee reports to the House so that they can be made available at once. Short and formal reports by select committees are collected together at the end of the year or the end of the Parliament and compiled into

---

74   1892, Vol.77, pp.586-7.
75   See, for example, 1999-2002, AJHR, I.22B, pp.144-50 (report on statements made during consideration of the *Telecommunications Bill*).
76   1935, Vol.243, p.422.
77   1995, Vol.552, p.10603.
78   S.O.250(1).
79   S.O.250(3).
80   *May*, p.776.
81   1999-2002, AJHR, I.17B (Privileges Committee).
82   S.O.250(2).

a compendium of reports by each committee. Major narrative reports, if not already available, are published as soon as possible after their presentation to the House. In each case, the reports are included in the *Appendix to the Journal* with other parliamentary papers and are allotted a shoulder number with the prefix "I". All select committee reports are placed on the internet.

No copyright subsists in reports of select committees.[83]

CUSTODY OF SELECT COMMITTEE DOCUMENTS

When a select committee makes a final report to the House, its minutes, evidence and other documents relating to the subject of the report come into the possession of the Clerk of the House, who is the custodian of all records of the House and its select committees.[84] Unless the House makes an order instructing the committee to withhold certain evidence, all select committee documents must be handed to the Clerk. They can be seen by any member, subject to any express direction by the House to the contrary.

Secret evidence must also be delivered into the custody of the Clerk but is not available for perusal even by members unless the House expressly authorises disclosure.[85] While it is open to the House to remove the protection of secrecy that has been conferred on evidence by a committee, this will not be done lightly. As has been said by a committee of the Australian House of Representatives when considering a petition for the disclosure of confidential evidence:

> When confidentiality is requested and then given, and even more so when it is promised in advance and thus becomes a pre-condition for receiving information, a "contract" has been entered into between a committee and the provider of the information. Such a contract is not enforceable legally. The committee holds to the view that the House has a strong moral obligation to protect such a contract.[86]

Apart from secret evidence, which is automatically protected from release even after the committee reports, the House may itself order that evidence given to one of its committees not be released by the Clerk.[87] Where a select committee has retained evidence containing serious allegations against a person that it did not consider relevant to its proceedings or evidence that creates an unjustifiable risk of harm to a person, it is under an obligation to consider seeking an order from the House giving ongoing confidentiality to the evidence.[88] The House may subsequently lift any continuing confidentiality order by rescinding it if the conditions that led it to make the order no longer obtain.[89]

In the case of an interim report or a special report, the committee continues to retain custody of all select committee documents relating to the bill or inquiry, but any confidentiality applying up to that time to matters dealt with in the report is automatically lifted unless the committee decides to retain it.[90] Where business before a select committee lapses at the end of a Parliament, the Clerk maintains custody of the records relating to that business on behalf of the new Parliament's committee. These remain confidential for the first nine sitting days of the new Parliament. If not readopted as business by the new committee they then become publicly accessible.[91]

Documents in the custody of the Clerk as an officer of the House belong to the House of Representatives and are not official information. Nevertheless, it is the practice for virtually unrestricted access to be granted to such documents.[92] A set of documents

---

[83] *Copyright Act* 1994, s.27(1); *Copyright Act Commencement Order* 2000.
[84] 1894, Vol.86, p.909.
[85] S.O.220(3).
[86] *Report of the House of Representatives (Australia) Standing Committee on Transport, Communications and Infrastructure*, March 1989.

[87] 1996, Vol.557, p.14312; 1999, Vol.580, p.19755.
[88] S.O.237(c).
[89] 1999-2000, Vol.581, pp.247-8.
[90] S.O.240(4).
[91] S.O.242.
[92] 2002, PP, A3, p.32.

relating to each inquiry carried out by a select committee is lodged in the Parliamentary Library for this purpose.

RESPONSES TO RECOMMENDATIONS

The Government has been required to respond to recommendations in select committee reports on petitions since 1967. A general requirement for the Government to respond to recommendations addressed to it in select committee reports was introduced in 1986.[93] This requirement for a Government response applies in respect of reports made by committees on petitions, and in the discharge of their inquiry function (whether self-initiated or referred), including treaty examinations. It does not apply on bills, questions of privilege or the estimates and financial review reports made under the Standing Orders.[94]

The Government is required to respond formally to any recommendation addressed to it within 90 days of the report having been presented.[95] Where the 90 days expire on a non-working day, the response may be presented on the next working day. (While the Government must respond to the House within this period, whether it makes any earlier policy announcements related to the recommendations in the committee's report is a matter for it.) Where consideration of a report is outstanding at the end of a Parliament any obligation to respond lapses. However, if that report is reinstated in the new Parliament the obligation to respond is also reinstated. The 90-day period for a response starts to run again on the day of reinstatement.

Where a select committee report contains recommendations addressed to the Government, the Office of the Clerk sends a copy of the report to the Cabinet Office. The Cabinet Office asks the appropriate Minister to report on the recommendations and prepare a response. If the select committee's report suggests action that would require the Government to make a policy decision, the issue must be referred to the appropriate Cabinet Committee for decision in the normal way for any policy submission. Once any policy matters are finalised, the proposed response is submitted to the Cabinet Legislation Committee and then Cabinet for final approval.[96]

The response takes the form of a paper presented to the House by the Minister.[97] Responses are ordered to be published and are compiled in a parliamentary paper. There is no reason why the Government cannot make more than one response to the same report, especially where the issues are complex. In these circumstances the Government may, within the 90-day period, present what is effectively an interim response and follow up with a detailed response when it has considered the issue thoroughly. Thus the report of a working party set up to consider recommendations from the Regulations Review Committee on deemed regulations was embodied into a further response from the Government to the report.[98] While the Government's response to recommendations contained in a select committee report is intended to facilitate any debate on the report that is held by the House, the fact that the House does debate the report before a response is received does not obviate the obligation to present a response in due course.

Although not subject to the Standing Order, the Speaker has presented a response to a select committee recommendation in respect of an office for which the Speaker was responsible – the Office of the Clerk.[99]

Committees have, occasionally, when dissatisfied with a Government response or with the time that it has taken the Government to respond, conducted a further inquiry into the response itself and reported to the House on it.[100]

---

[93]   1985-86, AJHR, I.18A, pp.10-11.
[94]   S.O.253(2).
[95]   S.O.253(1).
[96]   *Cabinet Manual*, 2001, paras.5.75-5.78.

[97]   S.O.253(1).
[98]   1996-99, AJHR, A.5.
[99]   1987-90, AJHR, I.20, pp.35-6.
[100] *Ibid.*, I.16.

CONSIDERATION OF SELECT COMMITTEE REPORTS

Reports from select committees are set down for consideration as prescribed by the Standing Orders. Any report presented will appear on the order paper for the next sitting day. In the case of a report presented up to 1 pm on a sitting day this will be on the order paper for the following sitting day.

In the case of final reports on bills, the bill is set down as an order of the day (Government, private and local or Member's, as the case may be) for its second reading on the third sitting day following presentation.[101] The committee's report is considered when the House holds the second reading debate on the bill. In the case of a bill introduced before the end of the forty-sixth Parliament (October 1999) and which has (because of subsequent changes in procedure) already had a second reading when it is reported back from a select committee, the bill is set down for consideration of the report on the bill rather than for second reading.[102] Interim or special reports on bills are set down as orders of the day for consideration.[103]

A report from the Privileges Committee is set down for consideration as part of the next sitting day's general business.[104] Reports on briefings, inquiries, international treaty examinations and reports from the Regulations Review Committee (whether, in each case, a final, interim or special report), are set down for consideration as a Members' order of the day on the next sitting day.[105] Where a report is on a notice of motion (the affirmative resolution procedure), the report is set down for consideration along with the notice of motion (which will usually be a Government order of the day).[106]

Reports on estimates, financial reviews and other financial business are considered when those debates are held.[107] In the case of reports on petitions the Business Committee has the power to direct that the report be set down for consideration as a Member's order of the day.[108]

Reports on bills, questions of privilege, estimates, financial review and other financial business are debated in due course. But in practice, reports on briefings, inquiries, treaty examinations and petitions are unlikely to be the subject of a specific debate devoted to them. Consideration of reports of select committees on briefings, inquiries and treaty examinations do not have a high priority even as Members' orders of the day since they come after Members' bills on the order paper.[109] This means that they are most unlikely to be reached even on days on which Members' orders of the day have priority over Government orders of the day.

In the case of a report that does not require a Government response, consideration of the report is removed from the order paper 15 sitting days after it has been set down (or sooner if it is considered by the House earlier than this). A report that does require a response is removed 15 sitting days after the response is presented. In either case the order of the day for the consideration of the report is discharged when the period has elapsed.[110]

If orders of the day for consideration of select committee reports are reached, the House works through them as they stand on the order paper. As each order is reached the chairperson or, in the chairperson's absence, the deputy chairperson or some other member of the committee moves a motion to take note of the report.[111] If, when an order is reached, neither the chairperson nor any member of the committee is present, the order is discharged and the House proceeds to the next order.[112] In any debate on the consideration of the report on a bill, up to 12 members may speak, each for a maximum of 10 minutes. On other debates there is no prescribed limit to the number of speeches.

---

101   S.Os 251(1)(b) and 290(a).
102   2002, Vol.602, p.308.
103   S.Os 251(1)(b) and 290(b).
104   S.O.251(1)(a).
105   S.O.251(3).
106   S.O.251(1)(d).

107   S.O.251(1)(c).
108   S.O.251(2).
109   S.O.69(1).
110   S.O.71(3).
111   S.O.252(1).
112   1992, Vol.531, p.12581.

CHAPTER 25

CLASSIFICATION AND FORM OF LEGISLATION

Probably the most important business transacted by the House, and certainly the most significant in terms of the commitment of its time, is the process of passing legislation.

Supreme legislative power is vested in the Parliament of New Zealand, not in the House of Representatives alone. An Act of Parliament is a declaration of law made by the two constituent elements of Parliament – the Sovereign and the House of Representatives.[1] But it is in the House of Representatives and its committees that the effective work of passing legislation is carried out.

The next series of chapters examines the procedures whereby a proposed law (a bill) is introduced into, considered, and passed by the House of Representatives, and, once passed, is submitted to the Sovereign or the Governor-General, upon whose concurrence (the Royal assent) it becomes law. This chapter deals with the form which a bill takes and how it is classified as one of the four different types of bill recognised by the House. A bill's classification as one of these types determines the procedure for its consideration. Some of the principal components of a bill are described and some of the standard types of bill considered by the House are identified.

BILLS

Some of the early English Parliaments, when they had identified an injustice of general interest which they wished to correct, often employed the expedient of petitioning the King for action to remove the injustice. If the King and the King's Council agreed to the petition, a reply to it was drafted. This reply came to be regarded as a statute with the force of law. As this procedure grew, Parliament increasingly became a legislative assembly. Gradually, and possibly because on occasion the statutes as framed by the King and Council did not adequately meet the cases raised in the petitions, the members of Parliament developed the practice of drafting the law themselves and sending this instead of a petition to the King. All the King had to do then was to accede to it or reject it and there was no opportunity for it to be tampered with by the Royal officials after it had left the members' hands. The draft law was called a "bill". This is the name for a draft or proposed law which is before the House.

A proposal to change or add to the body of statute law in force in New Zealand comes before the House in a bill, which is a proposal that will take effect as law if the bill is passed. Once enacted by Parliament, the bill becomes an Act or statute and so part of the general law of New Zealand.

CLASSIFICATION OF BILLS

Until 1 November 1999, Acts of Parliament were categorised as either Public Acts or Private Acts.[2] This dichotomy was followed by the House, with bills being classified as either public bills or private bills (with further category divisions among public bills). In

---

[1]   *Constitution Act* 1986, ss.15(1) and 16.   [2]   *Acts Interpretation Act* 1924, s.5(a).

fact it was doubtful whether there was any legal significance to the distinction between Public Acts and Private Acts.[3]

The new interpretation legislation[4] does not make any distinction between types of Acts of Parliament. It no longer refers to Public Acts or Private Acts at all, though Acts are still numbered and bound in Public, Local and Private Act series depending upon the classification of the bill which became the Act. This change to the law has been reflected in the House's procedures, with the disappearance of the concept of a public bill and the consequent subdivisions within it.

The House now categorises each bill which comes before it into one of four categories—

- Government bills
- Members' bills
- local bills
- private bills.[5]

Each category of bill is of equal status with each other category as a proposed addition or amendment to the body of statute law in force in New Zealand. The differences between them are defined by two factors: the member in charge of the bill (Ministers for Government bills, non-Ministers for Members' bills), and the extent of their application (confined to a locality in the case of local bills, for the benefit of a limited class in the case of private bills). Government and Members' bills (and any Acts which result from them) may thus be regarded as of general application. Conversely, local and private bills are designed to be of limited application only. If they were not so limited they would not be local or private bills. Legislation has referred to a "special" Act of Parliament as the vehicle for amending the law or effecting a particular object.[6] It seems that such a provision requires that the bill for the Act to amend the law or effect that object must be confined to that amendment or object (and may, to that extent, be a manner and form provision), rather than that the bill must be of a particular type (Government, Member's, local or private). There is no type of "special" bill known to the House.

The consequence of classification in a particular category has application primarily in relation to the internal procedures of the House. Categorisation as one or other of the four types of bills defines the process that the House will employ in considering the bill and the procedures with which those promoting it must comply if it is to be introduced into and passed by the House. In particular, promoters of local and private bills must comply with a number of preliminary advertising and notice procedures before their bills may be introduced.

While as a formal instrument each bill is of equal status with each other, in practical terms Government bills are far more significant than the other types of bills because of the political and procedural advantages which attach to them. These enable Ministers to prepare, introduce and advance their legislative proposals far more readily than can other members. Non-government legislation, for example, is considered only at alternate Wednesday sittings. Consequently, substantially more Government bills are introduced into and passed by the House than any other kind of bill. As well as their numerical superiority, Government bills are intrinsically more far-reaching in their effects than are other bills.

The parliamentary procedures for a local bill or a private bill are more onerous than are those of a Government bill or a Member's bill, so there is nothing inconsistent

---

3   See Burrows, *Statute Law in New Zealand*, p.6.

4   *Interpretation Act* 1999.

5   S.O.254(1).

6   See, for example, *Foreshore and Seabed Act* 2004, s.14(2)(a) (public foreshore and seabed may be alienated by special Act).

from a procedural point of view in an important matter being dealt with by a local or private bill as opposed to a Government bill or a Member's bill. However, there has been a large relative movement away from legislation being promoted and enacted at the specific request of local authorities and individual suitors to the House in favour of most legislation being promoted for general public effect. This is particularly the case where public funding or important governmental functions are involved. The fact that a bill affects the rights of the Crown does not prevent it proceeding as a local or a private bill, although the Government in such cases can prevent its passage, for such a bill needs to be consented to by the Crown before it can be passed, and if such consent is not forthcoming the bill will lapse.[7]

Government bills

A Government bill is a bill dealing with a matter of public policy introduced by a Minister.[8] In 2004, 82 percent of the bills introduced into the House were Government bills and 96 percent of the bills passed started their lives as Government bills. They are thus overwhelmingly the most numerous and important of the bills dealt with by the House. The vast bulk of the legislation in force today was introduced into the House as Government legislation. Indeed a major function and expectation of Governments is the initiation and passing of legislation that implements their political programmes.

A member who is a Minister may introduce a private bill or a local bill but only a Minister may introduce a Government bill (this excludes also a Parliamentary Under-Secretary).

Members' bills

A Member's bill is a bill dealing with a matter of public policy introduced by a member who is not a Minister.[9]

There is no difference in the potential substance of a Member's bill and a Government bill. The essential distinction lies in the status of the member introducing the bill – the one being a non-Minister, the other being a Minister. There is a difference, however, in their relative numbers and even more so in their prospects for success. While all but a handful of the Government bills are eventually passed, few Members' bills make it into law. Prior to the end of the First World War the number of bills initiated by the Government was not substantially greater than the number initiated by other members. Since that time Government legislation has become much more preponderant.

For a long period after the Second World War the prospects of a Member's bill passing were extremely remote. In the 40 years up to the beginning of 1985 only three such bills were passed. Changes to the Standing Orders made in that year have redressed the balance somewhat in terms of Members' bills being introduced, and have increased the prospects for their becoming law. While there are still relatively few instances of this occurring, significant legislation has been enacted by this route.[10] In 2004 13 Members' bills were introduced as compared with 50 Government bills. Only five Members' bills became law.

Furthermore, ideas that were initially given a legislative airing as Members' bills have been adopted as government policy and subsequently enacted. The Hon Rex Mason's campaign for the introduction of decimal currency which he pursued through the introduction of a Member's bill on an annual basis from 1950 to 1956 eventually came to

[7]   S.O.309.
[8]   S.O.254(1)(a).
[9]   S.O.254(1)(b).
[10] For example: *Adult Adoption Information Act* 1985,

Homosexual Law Reform Act 1986, *Habeas Corpus Act* 2001, *Prostitution Reform Act* 2003, *Human Assisted Reproductive Technology Act* 2004.

fruition, though by means of a Government not a Member's bill.[11] Other Members' bills have had their provisions adopted wholesale and incorporated into Government bills – among them a bill on the publication of names in cases of sexual offences, the provisions of which were enacted as part of a Government bill.[12]

Apart from the more obvious examples, it is difficult to say to what extent Members' bills have directly and indirectly influenced legislation eventually introduced by the Government and passed into law.[13] An opposition Member's bill, for instance, may be produced in response to current Government policy in order to emphasise the contrast between the Government and the opposition's putative approach to the subject. Some are the result of individual initiative by members to highlight a perceived defect in the law and suggest a remedy. Others still are of a more speculative nature, to float an idea and gauge public reaction to it.[14]

A Member's bill may not deal with a matter that is properly the province of a private bill or a local bill.

Local bills

Until the abolition of provincial government in 1876, laws affecting only particular localities were dealt with by Provincial Councils. From 1876, these matters began to be brought before Parliament in Wellington, leading eventually to the recognition of local legislation as a separate category of bill.

Local bills are bills promoted by a local authority and are confined in their effects to a particular locality.[15] They may be introduced by any member, Minister or non-Minister. This does not affect their treatment by the House.[16] In 2004 one local bill was introduced and three local bills were passed.

Purpose

Local bills are intended to change or limit the effect of the general law in its application to the particular locality concerned. The need for local bills is thus closely connected with the provisions of the general law, particularly local government law.

A study by a select committee carried out in 1996 found that, while a number of local bills were promoted by local authorities to procure special powers to deal with unique situations (opening of a community centre, management of a museum, etc), the majority were concerned to validate irregularities that were inconsistent with local government legislation. Most of these irregularities were concerned with rating decisions made by local authorities.[17] In 1996 local authorities were given a general power to replace invalid rates.[18] This general power has largely obviated the need for local bills validating rates.

The conferring of wider powers on local authorities (the "power of general competence")[19] may also help to limit the need for local authorities to seek special powers by way of local Act.

The promotion of local legislation on an *ad hoc* basis has led to amendments being made to the general law by a Government bill so that all local authorities can take advantage of a well-conceived local reform. In 1982 enabling legislation permitted ratepayers to make lump-sum contributions to the capital costs of waterworks and drainage works. Schemes of this nature had been introduced by a few local authorities by means of separate local Acts. Their success led eventually to the Government introducing an amendment

---

[11] *Decimal Currency Act* 1964.
[12] 1980, Vol.430, p.937 (*Criminal Justice Amendment Bill*).
[13] See McGee, "Members' bills or private bills?" [1999] NZLJ 405.
[14] See Burrows, *Statute Law in New Zealand*, pp.39-40

for a discussion on the genesis of Members' bills.
[15] S.O.254(1)(c).
[16] 1888, Vol.60, p.350.
[17] 1993-96, AJHR, I.6A, p.2.
[18] See now *Local Government (Rating) Act* 2002, s.120.
[19] *Local Government Act* 2002, s.12(2).

to the *Local Government Act* 1974 permitting all territorial authorities to levy charges for such works by lump-sum contributions without the need for special local legislation each time.[20] In 1991 an amendment was made to the *Rating Powers Act* 1988 allowing councils to remit or postpone rates on property to be used for the construction of housing, or for industrial, commercial or administrative purposes. This general provision replaced a number of local Acts that had authorised individual local authorities to take this step. Those local Acts had inspired the general reform effected by the amendment.[21]

Promoter

Only a local authority may promote a local bill. While a bill may, in substance, be a local bill, if there is no local authority promoter a local bill cannot be promoted. A local authority is taken to be a body to which Parliament has given statutory authority to promote legislation affecting the inhabitants of its locality. Local authorities within the meaning of the *Local Authorities Loans Act* 1956 were expressly given this authority by statute.[22] Since the repeal of that Act and the inclusion of local authority borrowing powers in the *Local Government Act*,[23] a local authority that may promote a local bill is taken to be any local authority under general local government legislation such as the *Local Government Act* 2002 or the *Local Electoral Act* 2001 – that is, essentially, a territorial authority or a regional council. It also includes certain special-purpose authorities such as licensing trusts, administering bodies of reserves and museum trust boards. However, the fact that a local authority is promoting a bill does not automatically make it a local bill; the bill must in substance be a local bill.

Locality

A local bill may affect a particular locality only. The "locality" takes its meaning from the context of the bill. A bill dealing with a function carried out by a regional council will obviously extend over a wider area than one promoted by a district council. The concept of "locality" is greater in respect of the former than the latter. A local authority may promote a local bill only for an area which is within its jurisdiction. Occasionally, local bills have been jointly promoted where contiguous geographic areas were involved. A bill would not be regarded as relating to a locality where its effects are region-wide in respect of a function which is not generally administered as a regional matter. Such was the case with a bill designed to provide a site for Victoria University College because the college was to serve all the middle districts of New Zealand. The bill was consequently held not to be a local bill.[24]

Amending other Acts

Bills with the objective of amending general Acts must be introduced as Government or Members' bills and not local bills, even though they relate only to a particular district or locality.[25] This is the case too with a bill whose sole purpose is to amend a Local Legislation Act. Such bills must be distinguished from bills which, while not amending a general Act, seek to create an exception to it in respect of a particular locality, because this is one of the principal reasons for promoting local bills. Also, local bills may make incidental or consequential amendments to a general Act without losing their status as local bills as a result.

---

[20] *Local Government Amendment Act (No 2)* 1982, s.11, replacing four local Acts.
[21] *Rating Powers Amendment Act* 1991, s.6, replacing six local Acts.
[22] *Finance Act* 1978, s.2.
[23] By the *Local Government Amendment Act (No 3)* 1996.
[24] 1901, Vol.119, p.1184 (*Victoria College Site Bill*).
[25] 1903, Vol.124, p.438.

Proposed amendments to a local Act must be brought forward in a local bill, regardless of whether the bill is introduced by a Minister or a non-Minister.[26] Thus, where a Government bill contained a clause making a substantive (and not consequential) amendment to a local Act, the Speaker ordered that the clause be struck out of the bill as printed following its introduction.[27] Certain local matters, however, may be dealt with as matters of state policy and then proceed as Government bills (for example, legislation relating to the Auckland Harbour Bridge). A Government bill dealing with a matter of state policy can incidentally amend or repeal a local Act.[28] Subject to these exceptions, local legislation must be introduced in a local bill or in a Local Legislation Bill.[29]

Private bills

A private bill is a bill promoted by a person or body of persons for the particular interest of that person or body of persons.[30] In 2004 two private bills were introduced. No private bills were passed that year.

Purpose

In a society in which government activity touches almost every facet of life, it is not immediately obvious why there is a category of private bills. To find its causes one must look back to a time when legislative intervention was looked upon as a much more exceptional occurrence than it is today. When Parliament had not passed so many general laws it was necessary for persons to come to Parliament as suitors seeking parliamentary assistance for a change in the law to benefit their own circumstances. That assistance was sought in the form of legislation affecting only the individual suitor and not affecting the general public, which a general Act does. Apart from the possibility of obtaining a Royal grant, it was consequently "private" legislation. Private legislation was the only means of securing a divorce until a general divorce Act was passed in 1867 (although no one in New Zealand appears to have used this possible avenue to terminate marriage before the general Act was passed). Apart from the possibility of obtaining a Royal grant, it was the only means by which an inventor could protect the fruits of his or her ingenuity until a patents Act, passed in 1860, provided for the registration of inventions and their protection from exploitation without the patentee's permission.

Private legislation fills in the gaps left by the general law, for the benefit of individuals. Today there are fewer gaps to be filled in. There are now general statutes dealing with divorce and patents, and other subjects which have been dealt with in the past by private bills. There is, on the face of it, less need for persons to have resort to private legislation to deal with their own special circumstances, though the privatisation of some state activities has created a new demand for private legislation.

It remains the case, however, that there are occasions when legislation for the benefit of an individual or a small number of persons is necessary because there is no redress or remedy in any other way; and, in fact, the number of private bills which come before the House has not changed appreciably since the early days. Paradoxically, a demand for a private bill can arise to exempt an individual from the large volume of public legislation

---

[26]   1908, Vol.145, p.591.
[27]   1989, Vol.504, p.14723 (*Taxation Reform Bill (No 7)*).
[28]   1885, Vol.51, p.446.
[29]   S.O.273(1).
[30]   S.O.254(1)(d).

which may have failed to take account of individual circumstances. In 1982, a private bill was passed to permit a marriage to take place because, under the relevant general legislation, the two persons concerned were too closely related (through the adoption of one into the family of the other) to be able to marry legally.[31] Situations like this can give rise to applications to the House for private bills to alter the effect of general Acts on individuals.

Private bills commonly involve matters relating to private trusts – lands held on trust for community use, burial grounds or deeds of family arrangement.[32] Matters such as changes of the trustees administering an estate or a private trust, and the validation of scholarships and allowances provided by a private trust board, are matters for private, not general, legislation.[33] Some private bills relate to marriage within the degrees of relationship prohibited by the *Marriage Act* 1955. Bills relating to private schools are private bills. Bills dealing with the constitution of public schools are public bills unless they deal with matters relating to the school board peculiar to its personal capacity – for example, property rights under a trust or will – when they can proceed as private bills.

One of the most important uses to which private bills have been put is to facilitate reconstructions and amalgamations of individual banking corporations.[34] These latter examples show that private bills need not be intrinsically unimportant or trivial. They will never appear to be so to the parties promoting them in any case, but they need not be devoid of wider public significance to retain their private bill status.

Bills designed to inject state funding into corporations or other activities are general (Government or Members'), not private, bills. In this way, a bank originally created by a private Act of Parliament became liable to be dealt with by a Government bill when it was proposed that a state guarantee be given to it in legislation.[35]

In recent years a number of bodies have been restructured by legislation for sale or incorporation as private corporations. If the body being restructured is a public body (for example, a Crown entity or Crown-owned company) constituted by a general Act, then a Government or Member's bill is required to effect the restructuring.[36] But if the body is not of a public nature its restructuring or dissolution may be effected by a private bill even though the body is constituted under general legislation such as the *Companies Act* and amendment of a general Act is required.[37] Private bills have been used to reconstitute governance entities (runanga) which are to administer claims settlements made under public Acts.[38] A public corporation restructured by general legislation may be dealt with subsequently in a private bill.[39] A private bill can incidentally amend a general Act for the particular benefit of the person or body promoting the bill. It is a matter of policy for the House to decide whether to pass such a bill.[40]

Governmental functions that are dealt with by Government or Members' bills rather than private bills include the administration of justice, liquor licensing and the granting of diplomas for professional work.[41] In 1981, a bill seeking to require the Licensing Commission to hear and, if it saw fit, grant an application for a liquor licence from a

---

[31] *Papa Adoption Act 1982.*

[32] 1918, Vol.183, pp.1007-14.

[33] 1940, Vol.257, pp.1024-5, 1029.

[34] *ANZ Banking Group (New Zealand) Act 1979; Westpac Banking Corporation Act 1982; National Bank of New Zealand Limited Act 1994.*

[35] 1894, Vol.83, p.486 (*Bank of New Zealand Share Guarantee Act 1894, Amendment Bill*).

[36] See, for example: *Bank of New Zealand Act 1988; Maori Education Foundation (Abolition) Act 1993; Children's Health Camps Board Dissolution Act 1999.*

[37] See, for example, *Royal Society of New Zealand Act 1997.*

[38] See, for example: *Te Runanga o Ngai Tahu Act 1996; Te Runanga o Ngati Awa Act 2005.*

[39] See, for example, the legislative steps by which the Government Life Insurance Office (a government department) became the Tower Corporation (a private corporation): *Government Life Insurance Corporation Act 1983; Government Life Insurance Corporation Act 1987; Tower Corporation Amendment Act 1989; Tower Corporation Act 1990* (the latter a private Act).

[40] 1882, Vol.41, p.410.

[41] 1939, Vol.255, pp.44-5.

particular applicant, which under the general law it would be obliged to reject, was held to be a Member's bill. Although designed for the interest of one company, it affected the powers of a statutory body and dealt with a subject – liquor licensing – which had been consistently dealt with by general legislation.[42]

Relationship to general law

Private bills are required to have a preamble and this must address why the promoter prefers legislation if the objects of the bill could be attained by invoking the general law as it already exists.[43] This is a reminder that Parliament is reluctant to grant special legislative rights to private persons, unless there is a proven necessity. For example, while Parliament has, in general legislation, provided the machinery for the variation or revocation of trusts[44], it is also possible for the terms of a trust to be varied by private legislation. The promotion of a private bill is not prohibitively expensive; it may even be less expensive than applying to the court. However, having established a judicial procedure to deal with variations of trusts, Parliament is reluctant to create legislative exceptions to it for the benefit of individuals or small groups of persons unless compelling reasons can be advanced. In general, persons such as trustees must apply to the court where the law provides avenues for them to attain their objectives and not look to Parliament to play the role which has been given to the courts.[45]

Usually, if machinery exists under the general law to accomplish what the party (whether a trustee or not) wishes to effect, this is the course that must be followed. Private legislation should be a last resort because what is intended is impossible to effect without it, or because to proceed under the general law would be not merely inconvenient but impracticable or manifestly unfair in some way. Promoters must address themselves to this question at the outset of their bill, in its preamble and in the petition they must present to the House seeking the introduction of the bill.

DETERMINING A BILL'S CLASSIFICATION

All bills must show on their face which type of bill they are.[46] But this claim made by the promoter or the member introducing the bill is not conclusive; at best it enables the bill to proceed as if it were what it proclaims itself to be unless or until it is challenged. Formerly, if any doubt arose as to how a bill should be classified it was referred to a committee for examination of the matter. Now, if any question arises as to the character of a bill, the Speaker decides on the matter.[47] This may require that further progress on the bill be deferred until the Speaker has reached a decision.

The Speaker may make a determination on a question as to the bill's classification being raised on a point of order, on the Speaker's own initiative[48] or following a report from a select committee questioning the status of the bill or some of its provisions.[49] But the Speaker does not intervene until a bill is introduced.[50]

As the House has no concept of a "hybrid" bill falling into more than one of the four categories of bills, it may be necessary for the Speaker or the House to order that a bill be divided[51] or that a clause be omitted from it to reflect its proper classification.[52] In all cases the House can suspend its Standing Orders to permit a bill to proceed even though it contains provisions relating to more than one type of bill.

---

[42] 1981, Vol.438, pp.1352-7 (*Winton Holdings Licensing Bill*).

[43] S.O.259.

[44] *Trustee Act* 1956, s.64A.

[45] 1979, AJHR, I.16, pp.3-4 (*Okains Bay Maori and Colonial Museum Bill*).

[46] S.O.254(1).

[47] S.O.254(2).

[48] 1989, Vol.504, p.14723 (*Taxation Reform Bill (No 7)*).

[49] 1929, Vol.223, pp.1177-8 (*Petone and Lower Hutt Gaslighting Amendment Bill*).

[50] 1981, Vol.437, p.754.

[51] 1908, AJHR, I.7; 1908, JHR, p.46 (*Wellington Harbour Board Reclamation and Empowering Bill*).

[52] 1980, AJHR, I.19; 1980, JHR, p.171 (*Reynolds Hall Trust Bill*); 1989, Vol.504, p.14723 (*Taxation Reform Bill (No 7)*).

ADOPTION OF MEMBER'S BILL BY THE GOVERNMENT

As well as adopting the ideas contained in a member's bill for inclusion in its own legislation, the Government may formally take over a member's bill and convert it into a Government bill.

This can be done only with the consent of the member in charge of the bill.[53] If this consent is forthcoming, the Speaker must be notified in writing by the Minister who is taking charge of the bill, that it has been adopted by the Government.[54] The Speaker announces this fact to the House.[55] The bill is consequently listed among the Government orders of the day and treated thereafter as a Government bill.[56]

FORM OF BILLS

Where there are provisions requiring the inclusion of particular provisions in a bill, these must be observed, otherwise the bill will not comply with the Standing Orders. In respect of such provisions the House requires that any bill presented to it conform to the prescribed standards. There are now a number of such requirements and they are examined below. These are effectively drafting instructions to those preparing bills. The fact that a bill must be introduced in conformity with these requirements does not necessarily mean that any resulting Act will also contain them; the House may amend the bill by omitting them as the bill is being passed. But in fact this is quite unlikely. The object of specifically requiring that bills contain a minimum set of provisions is designed to improve the utility of legislation that has been enacted, as well as of legislation at the bill stage. However, there are relatively few formal rules requiring a bill to be drafted in one form rather than another.[57]

Nevertheless, although specific Standing Orders requirements are few, bills are expected to conform to a certain form and style in their presentation. In 1997, a number of format and drafting changes were instituted by the Parliamentary Counsel Office and in successive Parliaments since then the House has given authority for these to be made to bills already before it as these bills are reprinted during their passage through the House.[58] A more significant revision to the format in which bills are produced was undertaken in 1999 to coincide with the new *Interpretation Act* and consequent Standing Orders changes, the first major change in the form of bills since 1956. In this case too the House has agreed that bills introduced before the 1999 format changes were introduced should be amended to conform to them as they are reprinted.[59]

While a fairly wide latitude is given to those preparing legislation in deciding what form it should take, its form can be taken into account by the presiding officers in exercising discretions given to them by the Standing Orders, for example, in deciding whether to accept a closure motion.[60]

Preamble

A preamble recites the reasons which have led to the legislative provisions which are proposed in the bill.

It has been said that there is a difference between the preamble and the subsequent substantive provisions of a bill (or Act): "Parliament 'does' only what is set out in the enactment. The preamble may explain and justify; it may ... outline a whole political

---

53 S.O.271(1).
54 S.O.271(2).
55 1977, JHR, p.55 (*Evidence Amendment Bill*); 1999, Vol.580, p.19500 (*Taonga Maori Protection Bill*); 2000, Vol.582, p.799 (*Conservation (Protection of Trout as a Non-Commercial Species) Amendment Bill*).

56 S.O.271(3).
57 1989, Vol.498, p.10819; 2001, Vol.597, p.14010; 2003, Vol.607, p.4421.
58 1997, Vol.559, pp.869-79; 1999, Vol.581, p.37; 2002, Vol.602, pp.308-9.
59 1999, Vol.581, p.37; 2002, Vol.602, pp.308-9.
60 2003, Vol.607, p.4421.

philosophy, or … accept as given vast novel assertions; but it can never record what parliament has done."[61] Accordingly, if there is a preamble, it precedes the enacting words of the statute. But while a preamble may not enact law itself, it is one indication of the meaning of the enactment.[62]

Private bills are required to contain a preamble setting out the facts on which the bill is founded, the circumstances which gave rise to it, and, if there is an alternative to legislation, why legislation is preferred.[63] But in other types of bills preambles are not often employed. To a large extent the functions performed by the preamble have been taken over by the explanatory note. However, an Appropriation Bill always contains a preamble in the form of an address from the House to the Crown[64] and bills effecting Treaty of Waitangi settlements invariably contain preambles with extensive recitations of the background to the settlements.[65] If a bill is introduced without a preamble, one cannot be inserted by way of amendment to the bill,[66] but an existing preamble in a bill can be amended or omitted.

Enacting words

The preamble, if there is one, is followed by enacting words. This is a declaration testifying to the formal nature of the document as being intended by Parliament to have legislative effect.

The formula, which was adopted in 1999, reads: **The Parliament of New Zealand enacts as follows:**. If there is a preamble the words read: **The Parliament of New Zealand therefore enacts as follows:**.[67] The provisions of the bill follow this statement.

Title

This is the name by which the bill is commonly known and by which the resulting Act may be referred to in legal proceedings. The title of the bill (formerly known as the Short Title) is printed prominently across the top of the front page, and the first clause in the bill itself following the enacting words must be the provision giving the bill its title.[68] A bill may have two titles, one in Māori and the other in English.[69] The decision as to what title to use is a drafting decision made by the member introducing the bill. The Speaker cannot intervene unless it were to contain something of an extraordinary nature, such as an obscenity.[70] Many bills are designed to amend an Act already in force (known as "the principal Act"). In this case the first clause may go on to indicate this and describe the Act to be amended.[71]

A bill with the same title as another bill currently before the House or the same as that of a bill which has been before the House earlier in the same session is distinguished from that other by the addition of a number, "(No 2)", as part of its title. This number immediately follows the word "Bill". If "(No 2)" is not available because there is already a bill that has been assigned that number, the next available number is used, and so on.

Bills have been regularly held over or reinstated from session to session and from Parliament to Parliament since the 1970s. Consequently, it is not possible to number similarly entitled bills in a consecutive series each session or even each Parliament. Numbers assigned to the title therefore do not imply anything about the order in which

[61]   Elton, *England under the Tudors*, p.268.
[62]   *Interpretation Act* 1999, s.5(3).
[63]   S.O.259.
[64]   1982, Vol.446, p.2711.
[65]   See, for example: *Waikato Raupatu Claims Settlement Act* 1995; *Ngai Tahu Claims Settlement Act* 1998.
[66]   *May*, p.616.
[67]   S.O.255.
[68]   S.O.256(1).
[69]   For example, *Te Ture Whenua Maori Act* 1993/*Maori Land Act* 1993, s.1(1).
[70]   2001, Vol.597, p.14010.
[71]   S.O.256(2).

similarly entitled bills were introduced; they merely distinguish the different bills. Even so, distinguishing between bills with similar titles can be difficult. Consequently in recent years an attempt has been made to give bills unique descriptive titles rather than ones which largely duplicate the title of a bill already before the House. Appropriation bills and Imprest Supply bills are given titles that identify precisely the financial year, the subject (estimates, supplementary estimates, financial review) or the order (first, second etc.) of enactment in relation to the financial year in question. In the case of local bills the title or name of the local authority, and in the case of private bills the name of the person or the organisation promoting the bill, should be included in the title of the bill, thus helping to avoid any duplication of title.

Commencement

A bill must set out precisely when it is proposed that it come into force.[72] This rule reflects the legal rule that an Act comes into force on the date stated or provided for in the Act.[73] In principle, the commencement provision should fix a precise date.[74] But the commencement of legislation can be deferred for it to be brought into force by Order in Council where there are considered to be good reasons for doing so. In these circumstances the reasons for deferring the commencement of the legislation to an unspecified date are set out in the bill's explanatory note.[75] Any use of the power to defer the commencement of a bill's provisions other than for the reasons given in the explanatory note is likely to attract criticism.[76]

Until 1999 the commencement of a bill was invariably dealt with in the first clause along with the title. It must now be in a distinct clause devoted solely to that matter.[77] This is the second clause of the bill forming, along with the title clause, a bill's preliminary clauses that precede the first distinct part in the bill (if the bill is drafted in parts).[78]

There may be different provisions in the bill that come into force at different times. This must be indicated in the commencement clause with cross-references to those other clauses where the precise commencement details are set out.[79]

Temporary laws

Bills sometimes contain "sunset" provisions whereby the enactment is to remain in force for a limited time and is then to be wholly repealed or is to expire. Such a provision must be included as a distinct clause in the bill. It cannot be tagged on to another provision or annexed as a subclause in a clause dealing with other matters.[80]

Where only a single provision in the bill is subject to a sunset provision, the latter may be included in a separate clause or in a subclause as is convenient.[81] This requirement for a separate clause does not apply where a bill is inserting sections in another Act and those sections are to be subject to a sunset clause.[82]

Clauses

Clauses are the major building-blocks of a bill. Many old English bills and Acts set forth their provisions with little regard for the reader, providing no punctuation or breaks in the text. This form of drafting was never employed in New Zealand. All bills are divided into clauses (numbered consecutively in arabic numerals[83]) so that the subject-matter of a bill

---

72 S.O.257(1).
73 *Interpretation Act* 1999, s.8(1).
74 1993-96, AJHR, I.16K (Regulations Review Committee).
75 Tanner, "Legislation Drafting: Some Practical Issues", *New Zealand Law Society Seminar: New Legislation Guidelines*, para.18.
76 1999-2002, AJHR, I.17L (Regulations Review

Committee).
77 S.O.257(1).
78 S.O.3(1).
79 S.O.257(2).
80 S.O.260(1).
81 S.O.260(2).
82 S.O.260(3).
83 Some tax bills use a different, alpha-numeric, system.

can be constructed and arranged logically in the bill. A clause may in turn be subdivided into subclauses (arabic numerals in brackets), subclauses into paragraphs (lower case letters in brackets), and paragraphs into subparagraphs (small roman numerals in brackets).

While bills are drafted in clauses, these clauses become known as "sections" when the bill becomes an Act (and a subclause then becomes known as a subsection). For this reason a bill is drafted exactly as it would read if it became an Act. A reference in a clause to another clause in the same bill refers to that other clause as a section. Similarly the word "bill" is not used in a bill's text; when it refers to itself, a bill calls itself an "Act".

Printed above the text of each clause is a heading (formerly known as a marginal note when it was printed in the margin of the bill) which is really the title of each clause, describing as pithily as possible the clause's provisions. These headings are collected together and printed at the front of the bill as the contents of the bill. The headings may be used as indications of the meaning of the enactment.[84] They are subject to amendment as the bill is passing through the House in the same way as any other part of the text of the bill.[85]

As well as the title, commencement and temporary law clauses already discussed, there are a number of other different types of clauses that are commonly encountered.

If a bill needs to define words it uses so as to assist with its interpretation, this is often done in a distinct clause. Indeed sometimes there may be more than one clause dealing with interpretation issues.[86] Other distinct clauses that are often found in bills include: a purpose clause (declaring the objects that the bill is intended to achieve); an application clause (defining what persons or period or types of actions the bill's provisions are to apply to); and, where appropriate, a clause declaring that the Act is to bind the Crown (an Act does not bind the Crown unless it expressly states that it does[87]). Bills often also contain provisions authorising the making of delegated legislation. Such provisions are subject to the special scrutiny of the Regulations Review Committee. (See Chapter 29.)

Parts and other divisions

Most bills are divided into parts consisting of groups of clauses. Parts are numbered consecutively in arabic (formerly roman) numerals. Older Acts were sometimes divided into what were referred to as divisions or titles, which are similar to parts. A part may be divided into subparts. Other headings and subheadings without a formal division into parts may also be used to group together like clauses. Decisions whether to employ parts and headings (and also exactly when to use clauses, subclauses and the like) are essentially drafting decisions though they will be taken into account by chairpersons when deciding how long to allow for debate on the bill in committee.[88]

Schedules

A schedule of a bill, which may be in tabular form, is often employed as a convenient means of setting out provisions relating to repeals or amendments of previous Acts or other provisions of too detailed a nature to include in the main body of the bill. Any

---

[84]   *Interpretation Act* 1999, s.5(3).
[85]   1996-99, AJHR, I.24, pp.242-3.
[86]   For example, in the *Injury Prevention, Rehabilitation, and Compensation Act* 2001, 13 sections deal with interpretation.

[87]   *Interpretation Act* 1999, s.27.
[88]   2003, Vol.607, p.4421.

schedules of the bill are placed after the clauses.

A schedule has been described as an appendix to the bill, to which effect is given by a preceding clause in the bill.[89] The latter is almost invariably the case but a schedule has been added to a bill without any preceding clause giving effect to it.[90] A schedule of an Act is a full part of the Act and may contain very important provisions. Complaints have sometimes been made that matters included in a schedule should more appropriately have been included in the main body of the bill, but that is a matter for the House's judgment in deciding whether to agree to the schedule.[91]

Explanatory note

Every bill, when it is introduced, must contain a memorandum, known as an explanatory note, stating the policy that the bill seeks to achieve.[92] The explanatory note may also (and usually does) explain the individual provisions of the bill.[93] An explanatory note is an attempt to set out in non-legal or less formal terms the purport of the bill that has been presented to the House. It is regarded as a very important indicator of the meaning of the language used in the bill and also in the subsequent Act[94] even though in New Zealand (unlike in the United Kingdom)[95] it is not amended to reflect changes made to the bill as the bill passes through the House. In this regard the commentary produced by the select committee following its consideration of the bill supersedes the explanatory note in parliamentary terms.

The explanatory note of a Government bill is prepared by the Parliamentary Counsel Office and the department principally responsible for promoting the legislation. In all cases an explanatory note must be drafted in factual, not argumentative, terms.[96] While the note must not mislead the House, whether members agree with its assertions or accept them as correct is a matter for debate and is not something on which the Speaker can rule.[97] If the Minister in charge of the bill does become aware of a factual error in the explanatory note, the House should be informed and a correction tabled. An explanatory note that does not set out the policy of the bill or describe the nature of the changes to the law that the bill proposes to make has been criticised by the committee to which the bill was referred.[98]

A number of particular expectations have become established up as to the contents of the explanatory note. The Government has agreed to include in it the reasons for any provision empowering the making of deemed regulations[99] and to explain the reasons for proposing to defer the commencement of legislation to an unspecified date.[100] (See Chapter 29 for deemed regulations.) The Government has agreed that, as from 1 April 2001, any regulatory impact statement prepared in respect of a policy proposal presented to Cabinet will be included in the explanatory note to a Government bill giving effect to that policy proposal.[101] It is the established practice that the explanatory note will set out the reasons why a commencement date is to be set by Order in Council rather than in the

---

89 Harris, *House of Representatives Practice*, p. 340.
90 *Local Government Amendment Act (No 2) 1989*, Fourth Schedule; *Maori Reserved Land Amendment Act 1997*, Sch.5.
91 1998, Vol.574, p.14311 (*Accident Insurance Bill*).
92 S.O.258.
93 *Ibid.*
94 *Real Estate House (Broadtop) Ltd v Real Estate Agents Licensing Board* [1987] 2 NZLR 593.
95 *R (Westminster City Council) v National Asylum Support Service* [2002] 1 WLR 2956 at 4 (per Lord Steyn).
96 *May*, p.538.
97 2002, Vol.598, pp.14825-6 (*Customs and Excise Amendment Bill (No 5)*).

98 *Reports of select committees 1996*, p.535 (*Survey Bill*).
99 See 1999-2002, AJHR, I.16I; an explanatory note has been praised for listing the factors justifying use of deemed regulations, see *ibid.*, p.19 (*Apprenticeship Training Bill*).
100 1999-2002, AJHR, A.5; Tanner, "Legislation Drafting: Some Practical Issues", *New Zealand Law Society Seminar: New Legislation Guidelines*, para.18.
101 *Cabinet Office Circular*, CO(04)4, 19 November 2004.

legislation itself. Any departure from these reasons in exercising the power is likely to draw criticism.[102]

An explanatory note has also been used to convey the results of consultation carried out before legislation to amend the *New Zealand Superannuation Act* was introduced,[103] though it is the normal practice to do this in a separate report. It has been suggested that an explanatory note should explicitly identify any provision in a bill which authorises regulations to implement an international treaty by overriding New Zealand enactments.[104]

OMNIBUS BILLS

Early Royal instructions from the Sovereign enjoined Governors to take care, as far as was possible, to ensure that different matters were dealt with in different laws. Until recently there were no formal parliamentary rules requiring adherence to such a principle. However, there has been a huge development, especially since the 1970s, in the use of omnibus bills as a means of "fast-tracking" legislation through Parliament. The earliest established such omnibus bills were Statutes Amendment bills that made amendments to a large number of disparate statutory provisions of a minor or tidying-up nature. From the mid-1950s onwards Statutes Amendment bills have been divided into separate amending bills at the committee stage and passed into law as separate Acts. Statutes Amendment bills were and are subject to strong conventions that ensure cross-party agreement to their provisions.

But, beginning in the late 1970s a new type of omnibus bill, usually called a Law Reform (Miscellaneous Provisions) Bill, came into use. This bill also amended a number of disparate legislative provisions but it was not confined to minor, non-controversial matters. It was used as a vehicle to introduce and pass highly important and controversial legislation, sometimes of an entirely new nature from legislation already in force. By including a large number of provisions in the same bill, parliamentary consideration of the measure was severely truncated and interested parties found it difficult to identify provisions affecting them that were combined with other quite different provisions in the same bill.

In 1995 the Standing Orders Committee reacted to this development of defective legislative process by prohibiting Law Reform (Miscellaneous Provisions) bills and controlling the circumstances in which omnibus bills could be employed.[105]

Bills to relate to a single subject area

The principle for a bill introduced into the House is now that it must relate to one subject area only, except insofar as the Standing Orders provide otherwise.[106] This is a modern reaffirmation of the principles in the early Royal instructions already referred to. The Speaker is charged with the examination of each bill that is introduced to ensure compliance with this principle. The Speaker may order a bill to be discharged or to be amended as a condition of it proceeding so that it complies with the rule.[107] A Member's bill introduced to enhance access to official information and to amend the secrecy provisions of the tax Acts has been amended under this rule by the deletion of the latter provisions.[108] In the case of an omnibus bill that can be saved by being amended, the Speaker will normally give the member the option of choosing which provisions of the bill to excise so as to

[102] 1999-2002, AJHR, I.16L.
[103] *New Zealand Superannuation Amendment Bill* 2004, explanatory note (now the *New Zealand Superannuation and Retirement Income Act*).
[104] 1999-2002, AJHR, I.16H; *ibid.*, A.5.

[105] 1993-96, AJHR, I.18A, pp.49-51.
[106] S.O.261(1).
[107] S.O.262.
[108] *Access to Official Information Bill* 2000.

bring it within the Standing Orders, otherwise it will be entirely out of order.

The rule against omnibus bills is not automatically infringed by a bill amending more than one Act. A bill can make purely consequential amendments to a number of Acts affected by its provisions without thereby becoming an omnibus bill.[109] But if a bill proposes to amend more than one Act substantively (that is, other than consequentially) it is inherently an omnibus bill. Even if a bill does not amend more than one Act it may still be an omnibus bill if it deals with more than one substantively different subject. In each case a judgment needs to be made as to whether a bill is of an omnibus nature and making this judgment is not obviated by the technicality that no amendment of an already existing Act is involved.

Types of omnibus bills that are permitted

There are a number of standard types of bills which, though they are omnibus in nature, have become established as acceptable for consideration by the House. These are: Finance or confirmation bills; Local Legislation bills; Māori Purposes bills; Reserves and Other Lands Disposal bills; and Statutes Amendment bills.[110] Those types of bills are described below. The permissible contents of Local Legislation bills, Māori Purposes bills and Reserves and Other Lands Disposal bills are regarded as better defined than those of Finance bills, consequently matter more appropriate for inclusion in one of the former is to be included in one of those bills, rather than in a Finance Bill.[111]

Apart from these standard omnibus bills, it is possible to introduce omnibus bills in four circumstances.

1. A bill dealing with an interrelated topic that can be regarded as implementing a single broad policy may be introduced even though it amends several Acts.[112]

This exception is intended to permit a single bill to be introduced to effect an overarching set of reforms. Instances given by the Standing Orders Committee in 1995 were the companies reform legislation of the early 1990s, occasional customs legislation and the very common taxation reform legislation that is introduced.[113] The majority of permissible omnibus bills that are introduced fall under this exception.

2. A bill effecting similar amendments to a number of different Acts.[114]

Where, for example, statutory references need to be changed across the statute book, it is convenient that this be done by a single bill even though it will technically be an omnibus bill.[115]

3. An omnibus bill may be introduced if the Business Committee agrees to it being introduced.[116]

There are no criteria limiting the nature of a bill that may be introduced with the Business Committee's agreement but because of the rule of unanimity or near-unanimity applying to that committee,[117] a bill containing controversial provisions is most unlikely to obtain its approval for introduction. It may be that as a condition of its agreement the committee will require a particular provision to be omitted from the draft bill submitted to it for approval and insist on that provision's introduction as a separate measure. Notwithstanding this, a select committee has criticised the Business Committee's decision to allow a bill to proceed as an omnibus bill on the grounds that it contained substantial policy proposals that should have been introduced separately.[118]

Where the Business Committee does agree to an omnibus bill being introduced, a

[109] S.O.261(2).
[110] S.O.263(1).
[111] S.O.263(2).
[112] S.O.264(a).
[113] 1993-96, AJHR, I.18A, p.51.
[114] S.O.264(b).
[115] See, for example, the *Treasurer (Statutory References) Bill* 1997 amending references to the Minister of Finance to references to the Treasurer.
[116] S.O.264(c).
[117] S.O.75.
[118] 1999-2002, AJHR, I.22A, pp.49-50 (*Business Law Reform Bill*).

reference to this is included in the bill's explanatory note, thus making it clear on its face why it is able to proceed notwithstanding that it is an omnibus bill.

4. The Standing Orders may be suspended to permit an omnibus bill to be introduced. Where Business Committee agreement to the introduction of an omnibus bill cannot be obtained, it is always open to the House to suspend the Standing Orders to permit such a bill to proceed.[119] This has occurred on notice.[120]

Amendments of an omnibus nature

It is axiomatic, that as a bill cannot be introduced as an omnibus bill (subject to the exceptions already described), neither can a bill be turned into an omnibus bill by way of amendment as it is proceeding through the House, except by leave of the House or the suspension of Standing Orders.

In the case of a bill introduced as an omnibus bill, substantive amendments to it are confined to those Acts already proposed to be amended by it substantively unless the committee of the whole House gives leave for amendments to another Act to be inserted.[121] (This does not prevent amendments to other Acts of a purely consequential nature from being made[122] but an Act amended only consequentially in the bill as introduced cannot be amended substantively subsequently.) This exception for leave to amend Acts not amended by the bill as originally introduced does not extend to select committees,[123] except in respect of Statutes Amendment bills. The House has, by leave, occasionally given select committees power to make such amendments.[124] In the case of a Statutes Amendment Bill a select committee may, by leave, recommend a substantive amendment to an Act not amended by the bill as originally introduced.[125]

Any member, in the committee of the whole House, can require a clause to be struck out of a Statutes Amendment Bill, whether that clause was in the bill as it was introduced or whether the clause was inserted by a select committee.[126]

PARTICULAR TYPES OF BILLS

There are a number of types of general bills that are regularly introduced into the House. These bills may have particular parliamentary rules attaching to them or be defined by their special contents. In practice, these bills are invariably introduced as Government bills. Some of these bills are omnibus bills containing amendments to a number of different Acts already in force or dealing with a number of disparate subjects.

Appropriation bills

There may be three or more Appropriation bills relating to each financial year. The first or main Appropriation Bill is introduced on Budget day. The second reading of this bill constitutes the Budget debate. The bill contains the Government's main expenditure plans, and consideration of the estimates takes place at its committee stage. The bill must be passed within three months of the delivery of the Budget.[127] There is also one or more Appropriation Bill containing supplementary estimates of expenditure that must be passed before the end of the financial year.

The Appropriation (Financial Review) Bill is a bill introduced after the end of the financial year containing provisions confirming or validating financial matters in respect of that year, such as any unappropriated or emergency expenditure that may have been

---

[119] S.O.5.
[120] 2003, Vol.609, pp.6233-8 (*Business Law Reform Bill*).
[121] S.O.304(1).
[122] S.O.304(2).
[123] 2002-05, AJHR, I.18B, p.60.
[124] 2001, Vol.591, p.8613 (*Fisheries (Remedial Issues)*

Amendment Bill); 2003, Vol.609, p.6413 (*Volunteers Employment Protection Amendment Bill*).
[125] S.O.288(3).
[126] S.O.300(2).
[127] S.O.332(1).

incurred. This bill is the vehicle by which the House debates the Crown's financial position and holds its financial review debate.[128]

Apart from an Appropriation (Financial Review) Bill, an Appropriation Bill must relate only to the current financial year. It supersedes all Imprest Supply Acts still in force at the time it is passed. Grants of imprest supply merge into the appropriations made in an Appropriation Act. The introduction of an Appropriation Bill is accompanied by the presentation of estimates and other supporting information setting out how the amounts to be appropriated are to be charged to each vote.[129] (See Chapters 32, 34 and 36.)

Confirmation bills

A number of Orders in Council and other regulations have only temporary effect unless confirmed by Act of Parliament within a certain period of time. Consequently, there is usually at least one bill each year confirming subordinate legislation that has been made in the period since the last legislative confirmation was made. Such a bill may be an omnibus bill dealing with confirmation of a number of different instruments.[130] A confirmation bill is not an appropriate legislative vehicle for amending legislation. The task of compiling the bill is co-ordinated by the Parliamentary Counsel Office.[131]

Customs Acts Amendment bills

An omnibus bill called the Customs Acts Amendment Bill amending Acts dealing with customs and excise duties may be introduced. Sometimes this bill has been divided up into separate amending Acts at the committee stage, and on other occasions it has been passed as one Act.

Finance bills

Finance bills are bills containing miscellaneous provisions that do not warrant enactment in separate legislation and do not conveniently fall into any other category of legislation. There is no significance in the title "Finance Bill". The scope of debate on a Finance Bill is determined entirely by its contents.[132] While such bills were common at one time, they are rarely introduced now.

A Finance Bill may contain one-off provisions, such as validations and authorisations and repeals of spent enactments introduced as an omnibus bill.[133] It may not be used to make permanent amendments to legislation. These should be made in separate legislation or, if appropriate, in a Statutes Amendment Bill. Even in the case of validations and authorisations there may be another more appropriate "washing-up" bill in which the provisions can be included. If this is the case, one of those bills should be used rather than a Finance Bill.[134] A Finance Bill may not contain clauses in the nature of a private Act, such as ones relating to private trusts.[135]

A Finance Bill is introduced by a Treasury Minister.

Imprest Supply bills

There are two or three Imprest Supply bills each financial year. An Imprest Supply Bill authorises the expenditure of public money or the incurring of expenses or capital expenditure in anticipation of a formal appropriation by an Appropriation Act. A grant of imprest supply is a vote by Parliament to the Government of funds to keep the machinery

---

128 S.Os 337 to 339.
129 *Public Finance Act* 1989, ss.13 and 16.
130 S.O.263(1)(a).
131 1999-2002, AJHR, I.16H, p.24.

132 1987, Vol.485, p.1829.
133 S.O.263(1)(a).
134 S.O.263(2).
135 1940, Vol.257, pp.1024-5, 1029.

of state running until the Government's detailed expenditure proposals have been examined and approved.

An Imprest Supply Bill is passed before the financial year opens on 1 July to allow expenditure to continue until the main Appropriation Bill is enacted. Another Imprest Supply Bill is likely to be passed at the time of the passing of the main Appropriation Act to authorise expenditure not appropriated in that Act and which will be brought forward in an Appropriation Bill containing supplementary estimates to be passed before the end of the financial year. There may be a further Imprest Supply Bill depending upon the need for more interim appropriation during the course of the financial year.

An Imprest Supply Bill may contain provisions dealing only with temporary financial authority to continue public services. Other material would alter the nature of the bill and it would not then be subject to the procedures prescribed in the Standing Orders[136] for an Imprest Supply Bill. (See Chapters 32 and 34.)

International treaty bills

It has been estimated that a quarter of New Zealand's legislation is designed to give effect to international obligations which have been or are to be entered into by the Government.[137] The House now has procedures whereby multilateral treaties and some bilateral treaties are presented to it in draft and are subject to some parliamentary examination before they become binding.

There is no single form in which bills to give effect to treaty obligations are drafted.[138] However, where the treaty text itself is annexed to the bill, it is well-recognised that it is not for the House to seek to amend that text, which has its own independent origin.[139] As the object of such a bill is to implement a treaty, committees have also accepted that it is not open to them to amend the bill in a way that is inconsistent with the treaty.[140] It is for the House (as with Treaty of Waitangi settlement legislation) to decide whether to incorporate a treaty into New Zealand law and, if so, what form that incorporation will take.

Local Legislation bills

A Local Legislation Bill is a Government bill introduced by the Minister of Local Government containing provisions which otherwise would have been required to be the subject of separate local bills.[141] It is a permissible omnibus bill.[142] It enables small amendments to local legislation, which might not in themselves have warranted the promotion of a special bill, to be effected. It is the local bill equivalent of the Statutes Amendment Bill, though the provisions contained in a Local Legislation Bill are not solely confined to amending local Acts already in force; they may validate a technical illegality or confer a power on a particular local authority without reference to a principal Act.

Clauses are included in the bill by the Minister of Local Government on the application of local authorities.[143]

As well as containing local legislation clauses initiated by local authorities, a Local Legislation Bill can contain clauses repealing spent local Acts, spent Local Legislation Acts or spent provisions contained in a Local Legislation Act.[144] It is most unlikely that a local authority would wish to initiate a clause for any of these purposes (the local authority

---

[136]   S.O.317.
[137]   1993-96, AJHR, E.31X, para.7 (*Law Commission Report 34, A New Zealand Guide to International Law and its Sources*).
[138]   Gobbi, "Drafting Techniques for Implementing Treaties in New Zealand" (2000) 21 Statute LR 71.
[139]   *May*, p.609.

[140]   2002-05, AJHR, I.22A, p.169 (*Pitcairn Trials Bill*).
[141]   S.O.273(1) and Appendix C to the Standing Orders, paras.20 to 25.
[142]   S.O.263(1)(b).
[143]   Appendix C to the Standing Orders, para.20.
[144]   *Ibid.*, para.21.

which promoted the legislation may no longer exist, though if it does, it is likely to be consulted about the proposed repeal), so in the interests of tidying up the statute book the Minister of Local Government may include such provisions in a Local Legislation Bill on the Minister's own initiative.

A Local Legislation Bill is not divided into its constituent local bills at the committee stage; it is passed in a single enactment. Although at one time an annual bill on the legislative calendar, Local Legislation bills are infrequent now.

Māori Purposes bills

A Māori Purposes Bill may be an omnibus bill.[145] Such a bill makes tidying-up amendments to legislation relating to Māori affairs that do not warrant enactment as separate amending Acts. It can also effect miscellaneous authorisations, transfers and validations relating to Māori land and property. Provisions concerning Māori land and trusts that would otherwise require private legislation can be included in a Māori Purposes Bill.[146]

The Minister of Māori Affairs introduces the bill.

Reserves and Other Lands Disposal bills

Reserves and Other Lands Disposal bills are miscellaneous omnibus bills.[147]

They effect authorisations, transfers and validations of matters relating to Crown land and reserves and other land held for public or private purposes. They may also amend previous Reserves and Other Lands Disposal Acts. A Reserves and Other Lands Disposal Bill may not give effect to a deed of family arrangement; such a matter should be dealt with by a private bill.[148]

Where legislation is necessary for a step to be taken in respect of land held for public purposes, a Reserves and Other Lands Disposal Bill is an appropriate vehicle to use. Thus by law land may only be excluded from a national park by Act of Parliament.[149] A Reserves and Other Lands Disposal Bill is the appropriate means by which such exclusions are effected.

In general a Reserves and Other Lands Disposal Bill makes only the minimum provisions necessary for effecting the authorisation, transfer or validation concerned. Where more elaborate provision is necessary, separate legislation should be employed.[150] Land Information New Zealand assumes responsibility for liaising with local bodies, statutory authorities and Government departments about items for inclusion in such a bill. Matters are only included if they are identified as non-controversial and have the consent of all parties involved.[151]

Settlement bills

Bills to effect settlements of claims under the Treaty of Waitangi have become recognised as a particular type of bill.

Such bills embody conditions in deeds of settlement between the Crown and Māori. They invariably contain preambles setting out the background to the settlement. It has been accepted that it is not the House's task to amend settlement terms agreed by other parties unless those parties themselves agree.[152] As with international treaties such provisions have an independent origin.[153] Any amendment to the bill must also be consistent

---

[145] S.O.263(1)(c).
[146] 1918, Vol.183, pp.1007-14.
[147] S.O.263(1)(d).
[148] 1918, Vol.183, p.1008.
[149] *National Parks Act* 1980, s.11.

[150] 1996-99, AJHR, I.23, p.892.
[151] 2002-05, AJHR, I.22A, p.411 (*Reserves and Other Lands Disposal Bill*).
[152] *Ibid.*, pp.395-6 (*Ngati Ruanui Claims Settlement Bill*).
[153] *May*, p.609.

with its object – that is, the implementation of the settlement.[154]   It is for the House to decide whether to give effect to the settlement and, if so, what form that giving effect should take.[155]

Statutes Amendment bills

The Statutes Amendment Bill is the archetypal omnibus bill. It was the first type of bill, in 1955, to be divided up at the committee stage into separate bills that were then passed as individual enactments. Until that time Statutes Amendment bills had been passed as one Act. This practice is now invariable with Statutes Amendment bills.

A Statutes Amendment Bill consists entirely of amendments to other Acts of Parliament (this includes provisions repealing other Acts).[156] Unlike other bills, provisions are included in a Statutes Amendment Bill only if all other party spokespersons on a subject have indicated beforehand that they agree to the inclusion of the clause in the bill. This does not mean that the provision will inevitably be passed. Any member still has the right to object to a clause in a Statutes Amendment Bill at the committee stage. In such a case the clause is struck out of the bill.[157] This latter provision is intended to enforce the longstanding convention that a clause in a Statutes Amendment Bill that is objected to will be withdrawn.[158]

A select committee considering a Statutes Amendment Bill can with unanimous agreement add clauses to the bill amending Acts not already amended by the bill as introduced.[159] However, a committee has complained about requests being made to it by departments for additions to the bill. Cross-party support must always be demonstrated in the case of a provision in a Statutes Amendment Bill and late requests for amendment can undermine the goodwill that such a bill requires.[160] The Government has subsequently sought to reinforce this warning against making unreasonable demands for inclusion of provisions in a Statutes Amendment Bill.[161]

While amendments effected by Statutes Amendment bills must, by definition, be non-controversial, they can be significant. But provisions with significant policy implications should not be promoted by way of Statutes Amendment bills.[162]

Statutes Amendment bills are introduced throughout the parliamentary term. There may be more than one such bill dealt with in the same year.

Taxation reform bills

The practice has developed of introducing bills amending tax Acts in a package as taxation reform bills. Other legislation (such as accident compensation and social security) may be amended as part of the package where the Commissioner of Inland Revenue performs a collection or enforcement role in respect of it. Such tax bills are usually, but not invariably, divided up into their component amendment bills at the committee stage. There are often several taxation reform bills in a year.

---

[154] 2002-05, AJHR, I.22A, pp.395-6.

[155] 1996-99, I.23, p.624 (*Ngai Tahu Claims Settlement Bill*).

[156] S.O.263(1)(e).

[157] S.O.300(2).

[158] 1973, Vol.386, pp.5231-2.

[159] S.O.288(3).

[160] 2002-05, AJHR, I.22C, p.611 (*Statutes Amendment Bill (No 4)*).

[161] Cabinet Office Circular (CO(05)3), 28 February 2005.

[162] 1996-99, AJHR, I.24, pp.193,197.

CHAPTER 26

PREPARATION OF LEGISLATION

Bills undergo varying periods of gestation before they come before the House. The idea for legislation on a particular topic may originate in party meetings and result in a commitment being included in a party's election manifesto. An organisation set up to look after the professional interests of its members may lobby the Government successfully for a bill which helps the members in some way. The Law Commission or a committee of inquiry may recommend legislative changes in light of its investigations. A department or statutory body may suggest legislation arising from its experience in administering policies or programmes. In these, in combinations of these and in other ways, an idea which eventually results in legislation may be started.[1]

GOVERNMENT'S LEGISLATIVE PROGRAMME
Governments prepare an annual legislative programme by inviting requests from Ministers for bills to be included in the next year's programme towards the end of each year. The number of bids invariably exceeds the available drafting resources and likely parliamentary time. After discussion of the proposals by officials, ministerial groups led by the Leader of the House, and the Cabinet Legislation Committee, Cabinet endorses an intended programme for the year. Those bills that do make it on to the legislative programme are allocated a priority ranging from bills that must be passed as a matter of law (those dealing with appropriations, imprest supply, confirmation of regulations etc) to bills on which drafting may commence if time permits. The programme is not static; it is constantly reviewed and revised by the Cabinet during the course of the year. In some years as many as half of the Government bills introduced into the House were not in the Government's legislative programme initially.[2] It is not the practice for the Government to release details of the programme in advance[3] and the Chief Ombudsman has accepted that it may be kept confidential to Ministers and certain officials, on a need-to-know basis.[4]

PRE-LEGISLATIVE SCRUTINY BY THE HOUSE
Sometimes the House will be involved with legislation or proposed legislation before it is formally introduced in the form of a bill. The House spends over half of its sitting time considering bills. A similar proportion of the meeting time of select committees is devoted to considering bills. Even those items of House business not directly involving the consideration of bills – questions, urgent debates, select committee inquiries – can have legislative implications. There is no hard-and-fast distinction in the types of business the House transacts between legislative and non-legislative functions. Passing law is such an important feature of government that all roads may lead to it.

Thus, under their powers to initiate inquiries, committees may from time to time study what are effectively legislative proposals even before a bill has been drafted and introduced into the House. In September 1993 the Finance and Expenditure Committee initiated a study of the report of a working party on the reorganisation of income tax legislation. In its report the following year it recommended policy and format changes for

---

[1] See Burrows, *Statute Law in New Zealand,* Chapter 3, for a discussion of how ideas for legislation emerge.

[2] See Tanner, "The Role of Parliamentary Counsel"

[ ] [1999] NZLJ 423.

[3] *Hansard Supplement*, 1995, Vol.20, p.2419.

[4] *Ombudsmen Quarterly Review*, December 2001.

inclusion in the proposed legislation including amendments of draft legislation intended to satisfy objections that it was inconsistent with the *New Zealand Bill of Rights Act* 1990.[5]

The House may itself refer policy proposals to a committee for examination prior to legislation being prepared on the subject. This was done before the creation of the comprehensive accident compensation scheme. The recommendations contained in the report of the Royal Commission (the Woodhouse report) were referred to a special select committee for study and, based on this committee's recommendations,[6] a Government bill was prepared and introduced. In the case of the Bill of Rights a policy proposal containing draft legislation was referred to a select committee for consideration. Following this committee's report a bill, based on the draft but amended to reflect recommendations made by the committee, was introduced.[7] In other instances draft bills have been considered by a committee[8] or even prepared in the committee,[9] subjected to briefings by officials or the hearing of evidence, reported on by the committee and subsequently used as the basis for bills introduced by the Government and passed into law. Select committees have encouraged Governments to release exposure drafts of legislation for public consultation prior to introduction to the House where this can help to reduce the drafting resources that will be required during the select committee consideration of the bill.[10] This course has been followed on occasion.[11]

NEW ZEALAND BILL OF RIGHTS

The *New Zealand Bill of Rights Act* 1990 came into force on 25 September 1990. (It has no direct relationship to the *Bill of Rights* 1688 also in force in New Zealand.) The Act is designed to affirm, protect and promote human rights and fundamental freedoms in New Zealand, and to affirm New Zealand's commitment to the International Covenant on Civil and Political Rights.[12] For this purpose it identifies a number of important civil and political rights to which the protection of the Act is extended. The protection thus extended to civil and political rights by the *Bill of Rights Act* is additional to the protections existing under the general law, and is also subject to the former being in harmony with provisions of the general law applying in those areas. No other enactment is to be regarded as impliedly repealed or revoked or to be invalid or ineffective because it is inconsistent with the provisions of the *Bill of Rights Act*. Nor can a court decline to apply any provision of an enactment by reason of an inconsistency with the *Bill of Rights Act*.[13] On the other hand, where an enactment can be given a meaning that is consistent with the civil and political rights set out in the *Bill of Rights Act*, that meaning is to be preferred to any other meaning.[14]

The question of the relationship between proposals for new laws contained in a bill and the rights and freedoms set out in the *Bill of Rights Act* is obviously of importance for the House when it is dealing with a bill. The *Bill of Rights Act* effectively sets out a "checklist" of most of the important public law tests that could be devised for a proposed law. This does not mean that Parliament will never decide to legislate inconsistently with the *Bill of Rights Act*. It may, in an appropriate case, decide to do this if it considers that the circumstances warrant it. But Parliament should do this knowingly and only after considering carefully the relevant provisions of the *Bill of Rights Act*. These must in every case create a strong initial presumption of good practice that should be departed from only for compelling reasons.

---

5   *Reports of select committees 1994*, p.43.
6   1970, AJHR, I.15.
7   1984-85, JHR, p.819; 1987-90, AJHR, I.8C.
8   1976, JHR, p.616; 1977, AJHR, I.12, pp.22-4 (public finance).
9   1982, JHR, p.79 (domestic violence).

10   2002-05, AJHR, I.20C, pp.377-8.
11   See "Draft Patents Bill ready for comment", *The Independent*, 9 February 2005.
12   *New Zealand Bill of Rights Act* 1990, Long Title.
13   *Ibid.*, s.4.
14   *Ibid.*, s.6.

Reporting on inconsistencies

The Attorney-General is required to bring to the House's attention any provision in a bill that appears to be inconsistent with any of the rights and freedoms contained in the *Bill of Rights Act*. In the case of a Government bill this must be done on the introduction of the bill and, in any other case, as soon as practicable after the introduction of the bill.[15] A distinction is drawn between Government bills and other bills as to the time within which the Attorney-General must fulfil this duty because the Attorney-General, as a Minister, will have access to drafts of Government bills well before they are introduced and so is in a position to perform this task as soon as the bill is introduced. But in respect of other bills the Attorney-General will receive no more advance notice than any other member and a longer period for consideration of their provisions is needed.

In order to enable the Attorney-General to carry out this reporting function and also to ensure that, as far as possible, Government bills as introduced do not contain provisions inconsistent with the *Bill of Rights Act*, submissions to Cabinet committees on policy proposals and bills must include a statement on the consistency of the proposal or legislation with the Act.[16] (A similar statement is required addressing consistency with the *Human Rights Act* 1993.)

In addition, as part of the preparation of legislation, an examination of each draft Government bill is undertaken to determine if its provisions are consistent with the *Bill of Rights Act*.[17] The examination is carried out by the Ministry of Justice or, where a bill is to be introduced by the Minister of Justice, by the Crown Law Office. For this purpose the draft legislation must be provided to the ministry or the office at least two weeks before the meeting of Cabinet's Legislation Committee at which it is to be considered.[18] It is incumbent on the department which is promoting a bill to keep the Ministry of Justice informed of all background facts that are relevant to a judgment being made on consistency with the *Bill of Rights Act*. Thus a department has been criticised subsequently when it was learnt that it had failed to inform the ministry that legal proceedings had been issued on a matter dealt with in the draft bill.[19] Advice on a bill's consistency is formally tendered to the Attorney-General by the Ministry of Justice or the Crown Law Office. In the case of any difference of opinion between the Ministry of Justice and the Crown Law Office, the Solicitor-General may provide separate advice.[20] Nevertheless, regardless of the views of officials the legal responsibility for reporting an inconsistency with the Bill of Rights rests with the Attorney-General.

The results of the officials' examination are also reported to the Cabinet, which takes the political decision as to whether to introduce legislation that contains a provision inconsistent with the *Bill of Rights Act*.

Following protests that the advice from the departments on which the Attorney-General bases the decision whether to report an inconsistency was not made public[21] all such advice is now posted on the Ministry of Justice's website once the bill has received its first reading.[22]

In considering whether a bill contains provisions inconsistent with the *Bill of Rights Act*, the Attorney-General takes account of the balancing provision in the Act. This section contemplates that the rights and freedoms set out in the Act are subject to reasonable and justifiable limitations.[23] Only if the Attorney-General considers that a provision cannot be

---

15 *Ibid.*, s.7.
16 Cabinet Office Circular (CO(03)2), 18 February 2003.
17 Iles, "New Zealand Experience of Parliamentary Scrutiny of Legislation" [1991] Statute LR 165.
18 Cabinet Office Circular, op. cit.
19 1996-99, AJHR, I.24, pp.123-4 (*Taxation (Accrual Rules and Other Remedial Matters) Bill*).
20 *Hansard Supplement*, 1998, Vol.32, p.1169.
21 1999-2002, AJHR, I.22A, pp.133-4.
22 Hon Margaret Wilson, Attorney-General, Media Statement, 18 February 2003.
23 *New Zealand Bill of Rights Act* 1990, s.5.

justified under this section does the Attorney-General report that a provision is inconsistent with the *Bill of Rights Act*.[24]

The obligation to report to the House is a safeguard designed to alert members to legislation which may give rise to an inconsistency with the *Bill of Rights Act* and to enable them to debate the proposal on that basis.[25] It has been aptly described as a "watchdog" provision.[26] But the Attorney-General's obligation to report or to decide not to report is part of a parliamentary proceeding and cannot be reviewed by a court.[27]

Nor will the Speaker entertain any question of whether a bill is consistent with the *Bill of Rights Act*. The requirement to report to the House is a matter solely for the Attorney-General and it is for the Attorney-General, not the Speaker, to judge whether the occasion has arisen for the House's attention to be drawn to an apparent inconsistency.[28] Ultimately, it is for the House itself to determine whether it believes that a bill is inconsistent with the provisions of the *Bill of Rights Act* (on which it may reach a different conclusion to the Attorney-General) and, if it does consider that there is an inconsistency, that it nevertheless wishes to pass the bill. Indeed, when the House passes a bill in respect of which there has been a certification from the Attorney-General, it may be difficult to determine whether this is because the House or the select committee which considered the bill preferred a different legal opinion to the Attorney-General, or received evidence that put a new perspective on the *Bill of Rights Act* point, or has decided to go ahead with the bill, conflict or not.

DRAFTING

Parliamentary Counsel Office

Anyone can draft a bill for introduction but, in practice, as far as Government bills are concerned, bills (apart from tax bills) are drafted in the Parliamentary Counsel Office by specialist law drafters.[29] Because of the volume of legislation introduced into the House, the Government has on occasion employed private drafting services,[30] but even in these cases a parliamentary counsel will review the bill prior to introduction to the House. A parliamentary counsel attends meetings of the select committee when it is deliberating on a bill for which the parliamentary counsel is responsible. The drafting of the amendments to the bill which the committee proposes to include in its report is undertaken by the parliamentary counsel. Parliamentary counsel also draft all amendments to a bill proposed by the Government at the committee of the whole House stage. They do not normally draft amendments for other members though they may do this when authorised to do so by the Attorney-General. This happens when a bill is to be considered as a conscience issue and members' amendments have a high prospect of being carried or when it becomes apparent that a Member's bill is likely to be passed.[31]

The Parliamentary Counsel Office has a statutory responsibility to examine every local bill that is introduced into the House,[32] but in practice promoters of local bills and private bills consult the office before such bills are introduced in any case.

---

[24] 1992, Vol.528, pp.10621-3 (*Summary Proceedings Amendment Bill (No 3)*); 1999-2002, I.22B, pp.1400, 1405 (*Civil Aviation Amendment Bill*).

[25] *Mangawaro Enterprises v Attorney-General* [1994] 2 NZLR 451 at 457.

[26] *R v Poumako* [2000] 2 NZLR 695 at [66] per Henry J.

[27] *Mangawaro Enterprises v Attorney-General* op.cit. at 456.

[28] 1991, Vol.516, p.2968.

[29] *Statutes Drafting and Compilation Act* 1920, s.4(1)(a).

[30] *Hansard Supplement*, 1989, Vol.1, p.98.

[31] 1989, Vol.498, p.10932 (*Sale of Liquor Bill*); see Tanner, "The Role of Parliamentary Counsel" [1999] NZLJ 423.

[32] *Statutes Drafting and Compilation Act* 1920, s.4(1)(c).

Other drafters

Tax legislation is treated differently from other Government bills. Another agency can be authorised by Order in Council to draft tax bills[33] and in 1995 the Inland Revenue Department was authorised to draft such bills.[34]   Consequently, in respect of tax legislation, the Inland Revenue Department performs similar functions to those carried out by the Parliamentary Counsel Office in respect of Government bills generally. A select committee has recommended that this function be transferred back to the Parliamentary Counsel Office.[35]

For Members' bills, members may obtain drafting assistance from the Office of the Clerk, whose officers are familiar with drafting forms, or may obtain private assistance. The Parliamentary Counsel Office may be required to report upon such bills to the Prime Minister or the Attorney-General.[36] Otherwise that office becomes involved with Members' bills only if expressly authorised to do so by the Attorney-General. As with members' amendments to Government bills, this would occur only with Members' bills that were to proceed as conscience issues or otherwise with general support and which therefore had a likelihood of being passed into law. An increasing trend has been detected for the Government to direct that parliamentary counsel assistance be made available for Members' bills that gain political support.[37]

When a local authority decides that it wishes to promote local legislation, its first task is to draft the bill, for the bill must be available for inspection from the moment the first formal step is taken in respect of it. The drafting of the bill is a matter for the promoter to arrange. The Parliamentary Counsel Office does not normally draft local bills for local authorities, but the office may comment on and revise drafts submitted to it.[38] While there is provision for fees to be charged for this service, no regulations prescribing such fees have been made.[39]

Before initiating any proceedings, the promoter of a local bill should, after consulting parliamentary counsel, have finalised the draft of the bill to be introduced. The Parliamentary Counsel Office has a statutory duty to examine every local bill that is introduced into the House and to report to the Prime Minister or the Attorney-General whether the rights of the Crown are affected by it and whether there are any other matters connected with the bill that it considers should be brought to their attention.[40]

The responsibility for the drafting of a private bill lies with the promoter as it does for a local bill, but the Parliamentary Counsel Office will examine a draft of a private bill and offer its comments.

Drafting practice

Drafting practice must comply with any statutory or Standing Orders requirements governing the way in which a bill must be prepared. (See Chapter 25 for a discussion of these rules.) The Legislation Advisory Committee has recommended drafting practices to be followed in respect of particular bills and types of provision. Its guidelines have been endorsed by the Government as embodying good practice to follow.[41]   The Regulations

---

[33]   *Ibid.*, s.8A.
[34]   *Inland Revenue Department (Drafting) Order 1995.*
[35]   1996-99, AJHR, I.3I, pp.49-50.
[36]   *Statutes Drafting and Compilation Act* 1920, s.4(1)(d).
[37]   2002-05, AJHR, I.20B, p.302.
[38]   *Statutes Drafting and Compilation Act* 1920, s.4(2).
[39]   *Ibid.,* s.4(3), (4).
[40]   *Ibid.,* s.4(1)(c).
[41]   *Cabinet Manual,* 2001, para.5.2.

Review Committee has (in consultation with the Parliamentary Counsel Office) suggested standard clauses for use where a bill proposes to incorporate material by reference.[42] But drafting practice is largely determined by the practices followed by the Parliamentary Counsel Office. These vary from time to time as a result of conscious decisions that are formally adopted[43] and as a result of individual drafting decisions being absorbed into general practice. The Parliamentary Counsel Office seeks to reflect these practices in its drafting manual. Statute authorises the Chief Parliamentary Counsel to reprint Acts of Parliament in formats and styles that accord with the current drafting practice that is being followed in New Zealand.[44]

PRINTING

The member introducing a bill is obliged to provide printed copies to the Clerk for circulation.[45] This is an essential condition for the introduction of a bill,[46] otherwise the contents of a bill before the House would be known only to the member introducing it. In practice the obligation to provide copies of bills is discharged for the member by the Parliamentary Counsel Office and the Office of the Clerk. The Parliamentary Counsel Office is responsible for supervising the printing of Government bills.[47] The Office makes arrangements accordingly for printing Government bills for introduction as an internal governmental matter. The Office of the Clerk assumes responsibility for the printing of Members', local and private bills for introduction. Currently the Office of the Clerk does this by way of a service-level agreement with the Parliamentary Counsel Office whose printing unit thus produces all bills for introduction.

A member, when lodging a notice for the introduction of a Member's bill, must deliver a fair copy of the bill to the Clerk for printing.[48] In practice it is likely that a draft of the bill will already be in the Clerk's hands by this time. In the case of a private bill and a local bill, the deposited copies of the bill must be forwarded to the Clerk prior to its introduction.[49] Often the bill will be printed before the preliminary procedures on it commence so that a printed copy can be lodged in the court and available for inspection. But this is not obligatory, and a typescript copy can be used for this purpose.

The fees payable by promoters of local bills are intended to help to defray printing costs.

MEMBER IN CHARGE OF THE BILL

In the case of all bills, the name of the member who is to introduce and sponsor the bill during its passage through the House is printed at the top of the front page of the bill. This is the member in charge of the bill.

Government bills

In the case of a Government bill the member in charge is the Minister who the Government determines will introduce the bill. An Associate Minister who holds a ministerial warrant in his or her own right, may introduce a Government bill.[50] In the Minister's absence from the House at any stage of the bill's passage, any other Minister may act on the Minister's behalf.[51] If ministerial portfolios change (whether as a result of a reshuffle, a dismissal or

---

[42]   2002-05, AJHR, I.16G.

[43]   *List of Changes in Drafting Style to be effective 1 January 1997*, Parliamentary Counsel Office.

[44]   *Acts and Regulations Publication Act* 1989, ss.17A to 17F.

[45]   S.O.268(1).

[46]   But this has not always been the case: see Bassett, *Coates of Kaipara*, p.195 (bill introduced but no copies available).

[47]   *Statutes Drafting and Compilation Act* 1920, s.4(1)(b).

[48]   S.O.276(2).

[49]   Appendix C to the Standing Orders, cl.11(1).

[50]   1970, Vol.367, p.2136.

[51]   1904, Vol.129, p.2; *Constitution Act* 1986, s.7.

a resignation or, where a bill is reinstated, following a general election) the new Minister automatically becomes the Minister in charge of the bill and any subsequent reprint of the bill will show the new Minister's name. Even without a reshuffle the Government can transfer the responsibility of acting as Minister in charge of a bill to another Minister by advising the Clerk accordingly.

Members' bills
The member who introduces a Member's bill cannot be a Minister. A Parliamentary Under-Secretary may introduce a Member's bill.

If the member in charge of a Member's bill is appointed to ministerial office, the responsibilities of the member in charge of the bill must be transferred to a non-ministerial member (with that member's agreement), otherwise the bill must be withdrawn. A Member's bill cannot remain in the name of a Minister. Transfer of a bill is effected by advising the Clerk. If a member in charge is defeated or retires from Parliament and the bill is reinstated, this does not affect the ability of any select committee to which it has been referred to continue to consider the bill. But when the bill is set down for second reading it is necessary for a member to take charge of it if it is to proceed. In practice, consultations are held with members of the party of the former member to establish who might take charge of it. There is no presumption that the member's successor in an electorate seat will take charge of the bill, since Members' bills have no necessary connection with an electorate that the member represents.

Local bills
A local authority is entitled to ask any member to take charge of a local bill. Normally the member of Parliament for the locality involved is asked to take charge (whether a Minister or not). In larger local authority districts there may be more than one member of Parliament. In that case, the member for the centre of the district or the member for the area in which the promoter has its offices is usually selected, but there is no hard-and-fast rule. The fact that a member agrees to take charge of a local bill does not mean that the member supports the bill.[52] If the member in charge of a local bill ceases to be a member of Parliament, the member succeeding that member as the member for that electoral district is invited to take charge of the bill, since it is presumed that there is a territorial connection between the member in charge and the locality dealt with by the bill. If the new member does not wish to take charge of the bill, another member can do so.

Private bills
The promoter of a private bill must obtain the agreement of a member to introduce the bill. A Minister may introduce a private bill.

The promoter is entitled to ask any member to take charge of a private bill, and the fact that the member agrees to this does not imply that the member is necessarily in favour of the bill.[53] Normally, the promoter will ask the local member, where the promoter is an individual, or the local member for the district in which the company's or trust's head office is situated, where the promoter is a corporation. Where a private bill relates to land,

---

[52]   1976, Vol.408, p.4701.   [53]   1982, Vol.445, p.2217.

the appropriate member to take charge of the bill is the member for the area in which the land is situated and not, for instance, the member for the company's or trust's head office, which might be in an entirely different centre. In this case, if the member in charge ceases to be a member of Parliament, the member succeeding the member as the member for the electoral district is invited to take charge of the bill since there is a territorial connection between the member in charge and the subject matter of the bill. In other cases the promoter will be asked to nominate a new member to take charge of the bill.

PROMOTER

Local bills and private bills differ from Government bills and Members' bills in that in respect of the former types an organisation or person outside the House initiates the bill and takes formal responsibility for compliance with the House's rules relating to its passage. Although such bills must be introduced into the House by a sponsoring member, these outside bodies retain an "ownership" of the bills even after introduction for they may at any time withdraw their bills by advising the Speaker in writing.[54] Such an organisation or person is known as the promoter of the bill. If there is no promoter, there can be no local or private bill.

A local bill is promoted only by a local authority.[55] Each local bill must have a local authority promoter in order to be classified as a local bill. (See Chapter 25 for local authorities which may promote a local bill.)

Occasionally a local authority promoter may go out of existence after a local bill has been introduced or after all the preliminary steps have been taken in the promotion of the bill but before it is introduced.[56] In such cases the bill can proceed; it is for the select committee to which the bill is referred to recommend to the House whether it should be passed, and for the House to decide on the matter. Where the demise of a local authority is in consequence of a local government reorganisation there will usually be an identifiable successor to the local authority and the new authority can decide whether it wishes to proceed with the bill.

The promoter of a private bill is a person or body of persons (whether incorporated or not) who stand to benefit from the change in the law that is proposed in the legislation.[57] No one can be the promoter of legislation as the agent of another person, though an agent can act on behalf of a promoter in taking steps required by the Standing Orders and in executing the requisite documents. But all such actions must be taken in the *name* of the promoter, the person who is directly interested in the passage of the bill. The Standing Orders require the identification of the person who is the promoter at several stages.

In practice, promoters often do engage agents, such as solicitors, to arrange for the steps required to be taken in the promotion of private legislation to be attended to on their behalf.

A corporation incorporated outside New Zealand has promoted a private bill.[58]

SAME BILLS PROPOSED

A bill which is the same in substance as a bill which has received, or been defeated on, a first, second or third reading may not be proposed again in the same calendar year as it received that reading or was defeated.[59]

It was formerly a rule that Parliament could not repeal an Act passed earlier in the

---

54   S.O.274(1).
55   S.O.254(1)(c).
56   1989, Vol.502, p.13446.
57   S.O.254(1)(d).

58   See, for example, the *National Bank of New Zealand Bill* 1985.
59   S.O.265(a).

same session. This was a relic of the proceedings of the medieval English Parliament when all legislation passed in one session was regarded as part of one statute and, therefore, could contain no inconsistencies. The rule was abolished in New Zealand in 1858.[60] A bill to repeal an Act passed earlier in the same session or year may be introduced.[61] The rule against proposing the same bill is not engaged merely because a question on a bill was proposed from the Chair earlier in the year. If the question was never actually put to the House, for example, by the debate on it being adjourned and the bill being withdrawn, the bill has not received a reading or been defeated and another bill in the same terms is in order.[62]

The fact that a bill with similar provisions is already before the House when the second bill is introduced is irrelevant if the former did not receive a reading earlier in the calendar year.[63]

PRELIMINARY PROCEDURES FOR PRIVATE AND LOCAL BILLS
A further way in which local bills and private bills differ from Government bills and Members' bills is that an elaborate set of procedures is prescribed to be followed by promoters before such types of bills may be introduced into the House. These steps are designed to alert interested persons, and members themselves who may be particularly concerned, to the fact of the promotion of the bill. They are then enabled to make early representations to the promoter and other members or to prepare submissions for the select committee that will eventually consider the bill. Compliance with these preliminary procedures is a condition for the grant of the legislative privilege sought by the local authority or other person who is promoting the bill.

Preamble for private bills
A private bill must comply with a requirement as to its form which other types of bills are not required to meet.

The bill has to contain a preamble stating the facts on which it is founded and the circumstances which have necessitated it. An important requirement is that the preamble must deal expressly with a point which will be prominent in the consideration of the committee to which the bill is referred: that is, whether its objects could be attained otherwise than by legislation. If they could be, the preamble must state why legislation is preferred.[64] The preamble deals with this question only if the promoter in the petition for the bill has stated that there is an alternative remedy to legislation. If there is no real alternative, the point is not dealt with in the preamble. However, the promoter's failure to identify an alternative means of proceeding is subject to challenge, particularly when the bill is before the select committee. If there is a real alternative, and the promoter has not identified it and addressed it in the preamble, the committee may find that the preamble has not been proved and this will prejudice the chances of the bill proceeding.

Form of notices
The preliminary procedures for private bills and local bills require the promoter of the bill to give written notice of the intention to introduce the bill before it can be introduced.[65] This notice must be given on a number of occasions. Each notice is to be headed with the title of the proposed Act of Parliament.[66] The notice must then go on to state that

---

[60] *Interpretation Act* 1858, s.6.
[61] 1976, Vol.406, pp.2464-5 (*Foreign Travel Tax Repeal Bill*).
[62] 1976, Vol.407, p.3880 (*Sale of Liquor Amendment Bill (No 2)*).
[63] 2003, Vol.607, pp.4270-1 (*Resource Management Amendment Bill (No 2)*).
[64] S.O.259.
[65] Appendix C to the Standing Orders, cl.1.
[66] *Ibid.*, cl.2(1).

the promoter intends to promote the bill, describe its objects, give a postal address for the promoter or the promoter's solicitor or agent to which communications may be sent, and specify the address of the promoter at which the bill may be inspected, the address of the District Court at which it may be inspected and the dates during which it will be available for inspection.[67]

The description of the objects of the bill in the notices of intention to introduce it limits the scope of any amendments that may be recommended or made to the bill as it is passing through the House.[68]

Advertising

The promoter must advertise the notice of intention to introduce the bill in various newspapers at least once in each of two consecutive calendar weeks.

For a private bill this must be in a daily newspaper circulating in each of the cities of Auckland, Hamilton, Wellington, Christchurch and Dunedin.[69] In the cases of Auckland and Hamilton this can be the same newspaper. Where a private bill affects land or any interest in land, the notice must also be advertised in a daily newspaper circulating in the locality in which the land is situated, if that locality is outside the main centres.[70] For a local bill the notice must be advertised in a daily newspaper circulating in the local authority district.[71]

If no daily newspaper circulates in the locality in which the land affected by a private bill is situated or in the local authority district, the notice may be advertised in a daily newspaper circulating in an adjoining district or affixed to a public noticeboard.[72]

Delivery of notices to persons with a direct interest

As well as placing general advertisements, the promoter is required to serve the notice on persons who, to the promoter's knowledge, have a direct interest in the subject matter of the bill or in the exercise of any power proposed to be given by the bill.[73]

This could be a wide and onerous requirement if it was taken to apply to all interests generally. For example, in the case of a bill promoted by a company, its shareholders, creditors and employees could be said to have an "interest" in any actions it takes. However, the requirement of a "direct" interest is taken to imply an interest of a more restricted nature than this, such as a legal interest in property dealt with under the bill. Owners, mortgagees, lessees and occupiers of land or buildings transferred or otherwise dealt with by the bill must have notices served on them, but this is not required for persons with more remote or indefinite interests than these. Other types of interests that must be recognised by the service of notices are those concerned with family relationships which could be altered by legislation, such as an adoption or a marriage bill.

Delivery of notices to specified parties

Notice must also be given to a number of office-holders in certain cases.

In the case of the bill affecting the public revenues or the rights or prerogatives of the Crown, notice must be served on the Secretary to the Treasury and the Solicitor-General.[74] Where it is proposed to modify, restrict, repeal or amend the provisions of any general Act

---

67   *Ibid.*, cl.2(2).
68   S.Os 288(2) and 297(3).
69   Appendix C to the Standing Orders, cl.3(1)(a).
70   *Ibid.*, cl.3(1)(b).
71   *Ibid.*, cl.3(1)(c).
72   *Ibid.*, cl.3(2).
73   *Ibid.*, cl.4(1).
74   *Ibid.*, cl.4(2)(a).

of Parliament, notice must be given to the chief executive of any government department or agency charged with the administration of the Act.[75] A private bill can propose to repeal or amend a general Act incidentally to achieving its objects,[76] but most private bills seek to create exceptions to general Acts rather than to amend them. The Government department charged with administering the legislation which would be affected in this way must be specifically apprised of the promotion of the bill by being served a notice of it. The appropriate department on which to serve a notice can be ascertained from the note printed at the foot of each published Act of Parliament which identifies the department charged with administering the Act.

A notice must be given to the Commissioner of Inland Revenue in the case of a bill affecting liability under an Inland Revenue Act.[77] An Inland Revenue Act means: the *Estate and Gift Duties Act* 1968, the *Stamp and Cheque Duties Act* 1971, the *Gaming Duties Act* 1971, the *Goods and Services Tax Act* 1985, the *Land Tax Abolition Act* 1990, the *Child Support Act* 1991, the *Student Loan Scheme Act* 1992, the *Estate Duty Abolition Act* 1993, the *Income Tax Act* 1994, the *Tax Administration Act* 1994, and the *Taxation Review Authorities Act* 1994.[78] It also includes the *Income Tax* Act 2004. Notice must also be given to the chief executive of the New Zealand Customs Service where liability to excise duty or a related duty may be affected.[79]

In the case of a bill alienating or disposing of Crown land or proposing to exchange Crown land for other land, notice must be given to the Commissioner of Crown Lands.[80] Where land administered as a reserve, national park, conservation area or otherwise for conservation purposes is affected, notice must be given to the chief executive of the relevant department[81] and to the Registrar-General of Land if the bill relates to the transfer of title to land.[82]

Notice must be given to the Solicitor-General in the case of a bill affecting a charitable trust[83] and to the relevant registering authority if the incorporation or registration of any body is affected by the bill.[84]

Notices served on members
As well as the general advertising notices outlined above, the promoter must serve specific notice of the intention to promote a local bill on all members of Parliament for general or Māori electoral districts whose constituents may be affected by the provisions of the bill.[85] This requirement does not extend to list members as, although they may live in a locality affected by the bill, their mandate is not tied to a particular district. The chief executive of the local authority must certify that such members (by name) have been given notice. The certification must specify the date on which notice was given and be signed and dated.[86]

How notice is given
A notice to a person with a direct interest, to a specified person, or to a member of Parliament may be given in a number of ways.

It may be delivered to the person or to the office or department or agency concerned.[87] It may be posted or delivered by courier to the person's last known address or address for service or to the address of the department or agency concerned or by delivering it

---

75 *Ibid.,* cl.4(2)(b).
76 1882, Vol.41, p.410 (*Government Contractors Arbitration Bill*).
77 Appendix C to the Standing Orders, cl.4(2)(c).
78 *Tax Administration Act* 1994, s.3(1) and Schedule.
79 Appendix C to the Standing Orders, cl.4(2)(d).
80 *Ibid.,* cl.4(2)(e).
81 *Ibid.,* cl.4(2)(f).
82 *Ibid.,* cl.4(2)(g).
83 *Ibid.,* cl.4(2)(h).
84 *Ibid.,* cl.4(2)(i).
85 *Ibid.,* cl.5(1).
86 *Ibid.,* cl.5(2).
87 *Ibid.,* cl.6(1)(a).

to a document exchange which the addressee uses.[88] Finally, it may be communicated electronically (by facsimile or electronic mail).[89]

The notice may be included with another document provided that it is given reasonable prominence.[90]

Deposit and inspection

The promoter is obliged to make a copy of the bill available for inspection at a District Court and at the promoter's own premises. This must be done at the time of the appearance of the first notice advertising the intention to promote the bill.[91] This means on the day of the advertisement or on the next working day.

A private bill must be deposited at the District Court in or nearest to the locality in which the promoter's residence or registered office is situated.[92] In addition, if the bill affects land or any interest in land, it must be deposited in the District Court nearest to the locality in which the land is situated (if this is different from the promoter's residence or registered office).[93] In the case of a local bill the District Court in or nearest to the local authority district concerned is the place of deposit.[94]

Another copy of the bill must be deposited in the office of the promoter or (if a private bill) in the office of the promoter's solicitor or agent.[95] In the case of a local bill, the bill must also be deposited in a public library or service centre.[96]

A bill which has been deposited must remain available for public inspection during normal business hours, without fee, for 15 working days.[97] This excludes weekends, public holidays (national, and provincial in the locality to which the bill relates) and also excludes the period 25 December to 15 January.[98]

At the end of the period of deposit the copy lodged in the court must be certified by the judge, the registrar or the deputy registrar of the court and the copy lodged at the promoter's or other office must be certified by the promoter, the promoter's solicitor or agent or the promoter's chief executive.[99] The certificate is written directly on to the copy of the bill, not given separately from it. It must state the first and last whole days on which the copy was available for public inspection. The person certifying it signs over that person's designation and it is dated.[100]

The bill that is subsequently introduced into the House may differ from the copies that were made available for inspection only in respect of immaterial corrections such as of misprints or spelling mistakes or matters of form. If there is a material difference, the copy which was made available for inspection was not a copy at all and the Standing Orders have not been complied with. Whether the copy was a true copy ultimately is determined by the select committee when it considers the bill.[101]

Bills dealing with land

There are special requirements regarding bills which propose to take power to deal with any land. In these cases the copies of the bills made available for inspection must be accompanied by a description of the land (this may also be contained in a schedule in the bill) and a true copy of the plan of the land. The description and plan must be certified as correct by the chief executive of the department responsible for the administration

---

[88] *Ibid.*, cl.6(1)(b).
[89] *Ibid.*, cl.6(1)(c).
[90] *Ibid.*, cl.6(2).
[91] *Ibid.*, cl.7(1).
[92] *Ibid.*, cl.7(1)(a).
[93] *Ibid.*, cl.7(1)(b)(ii).
[94] *Ibid.*, cl.7(1)(b)(i).
[95] *Ibid.*, cl.7(2)(a),(b).
[96] *Ibid.*, cl.7(2)(c).
[97] *Ibid.*, cl.7(3).
[98] S.O.3(1).
[99] Appendix C to the Standing Orders, cl.8(1).
[100] *Ibid.*, cl.8(2).
[101] 1980, Vol.435, p.4898 (*Chatham Islands County Council Empowering Bill*).

of the *Cadastral Survey Act* 2002 (Land Information New Zealand) or any person to whom the chief executive delegates the power.[102] The plans are required to be drawn in a form specified by rules made under the Act. The plan must be lodged with the relevant Land Information New Zealand office and endorsed by the chief executive as having been approved for parliamentary purposes.[103] The officials of the court and of the promoter must certify that these documents have been available for inspection along with the bill.[104]

The description and the plan circumscribe the extent of land that may be dealt with by the bill. After it is introduced it is not possible for the bill to be amended to include land not encompassed within the description, although the legal description of the land contained in the bill may be corrected if it is found not to accord with the lodged description and plan. If the bill is subsequently amended to restrict the area of land dealt with in the bill, it is not necessary to lodge a further plan, though the select committee is likely to require further certification from the chief executive of Land Information New Zealand before it agrees to amend the legal description contained in the bill in any way.

A true copy of the plan is not required in three circumstances—

- where the land to be dealt with is wholly comprised in any certificate of title issued under the *Land Transfer Act* 1952 or any computer register created under that Act
- where the land has been previously dealt with and described in a statute, ordinance, proclamation, declaration, notice or Order in Council
- where the land to be dealt with is wholly comprised in a separate lot or other surveyed subdivision shown on a plan deposited in the relevant Land Information New Zealand office or lodged in the office of the chief executive.[105]

However, even in these latter cases a description of the land to be dealt with, certified as correct by the chief surveyor, must be made available for inspection along with the bill.

Fees

A fee of $2,000 (including goods and services tax) is payable by the promoters of all bills. It must accompany the documents forwarded to the Clerk.[106] The fee for a private bill is paid to the Speaker. It is held in a separate private bills' fees account administered in the Speaker's office and may be applied for such parliamentary purposes as the Speaker directs. The fee for a local bill is paid to the Clerk of the House. It is applied to defray the general administrative expenses incurred in respect of the promotion of local bills.[107] The fee must be paid before the Standing Orders can be certified as having been complied with. No fee is payable if the Standing Orders have not been complied with and the bill does not proceed to be introduced. The fee for a private bill may be refunded in whole or in part on the ground of hardship where the House so directs on the recommendation of the committee which considers the bill. In such a case the Speaker refunds the fee.[108]

Petition for private bill

A private bill is initiated for introduction into the House by a petition.[109] This is the only survival of the involvement of petitions, which formed the basis of some of the earliest statutes, in the passage of legislation. However, their involvement in private legislation is by way of a request made to the House and not, as was practised in the early English

---

[102] Appendix C to the Standing Orders, cl.9(1).
[103] *Ibid.*, cl.9(3).
[104] *Ibid.*, cl.10.
[105] *Ibid.*, cl.9(2).

[106] *Ibid.*, cl.13(1).
[107] *Ibid.*, cl.13(2)(b).
[108] *Ibid.*, cl.14.
[109] *Ibid.*, cl.15.

Parliaments, by way of a request made by the House to the Crown.

The promoter's petition is a request to the House that it introduce the legislation that the promoter wishes to see enacted. For this purpose the promoter must set out a statement of the reasons for the introduction of the bill and the objects it is intended to achieve. These reasons and objects should accord with the circumstances recounted in the bill's preamble. The petition must deal with why legislation is the preferred option if there is an alternative to legislation. The promoter also certifies in the petition that the appropriate advertising has been undertaken and notices given. A specimen form of petition is set out in Appendix C to the Standing Orders. The petition must in general conform to that specimen.[110]

Declaration for local bill

Before a local bill can be introduced the promoter must make a declaration to the House.[111]

The declaration requests that the bill be introduced. It must set out the reasons for the bill and the objects it is intended to achieve. If those objects could be attained otherwise than by legislation the promoter must state why legislation is preferred. The promoter certifies in the declaration that the advertising and notices required to be given by the Standing Orders have been undertaken. A specimen declaration is set out in Appendix C to the Standing Orders. The declaration must in general conform to that specimen.[112]

Examination by the Clerk

Each deposited copy of the bill, together with deposited copies of descriptions of land affected, as certified by the District Court and the promoter, along with copies of notices and other documents required by the Standing Orders must be forwarded to the Clerk.[113] These supporting documents are attached to the petition for a private bill or the declaration for a local bill, as the case may be.[114] The documentation must be lodged with the Clerk within six months of the first publication of the notice of the bill in order to remain effective.[115] Thus promoters have six months from taking their first formal step to promote a bill to complete the preliminary procedures.

The Clerk examines the bill, petition or declaration, and supporting documentation to ascertain whether the Standing Orders have been complied with.[116]

The examination of the petition or declaration and associated documents by the Clerk culminates in the Clerk endorsing the petition or declaration "Standing Orders complied with", if that is the case, and signing and dating the endorsement.[117] If on the other hand, in the Clerk's opinion the Standing Orders have not been complied with, the petition or declaration and the fee are returned to the promoter.[118]

It is not the Clerk's function, in making the examination, to determine whether the bill is actually a private bill or a local bill. However, in discussions with the promoter any doubts on the proper classification of the bill will be raised in an endeavour to settle this before the promoter takes steps to promote the bill. But if, nevertheless, after introduction, a question arises as to a bill's classification, the Speaker can determine it. The Clerk's certification that the Standing Orders have been complied with refers only to the procedural steps for advertising, inspecting, giving notice, paying fees and lodging documents; it is not a certification that the bill is a private bill or a local bill.

Once a petition for a private bill or a declaration in respect of a local bill has been

---

[110]   *Ibid.*, cl.16.
[111]   *Ibid.*, cl.17.
[112]   *Ibid.*, cl.18.
[113]   *Ibid.*, cl.11(1).
[114]   *Ibid.*, cl.11(2).
[115]   *Ibid.*, cl.12.

[116]   *Ibid.*, cl.19(1).
[117]   *Ibid.*, cl.19(2).
[118]   *Ibid.*, cl.19(3).

endorsed by the Clerk as complying with the Standing Orders the petition may be presented to the House, in the case of a private bill,[119] and notice may be given for the introduction of the bill, in the case of a local bill.[120]

Before 10 February 2004 (when the preliminary procedures for local bills were substantially amended), the Local Government and Environment Committee, rather than the Clerk of the House, determined whether the Standing Orders had been complied with. This examination took place after the bill had been introduced. In respect of local bills introduced before that date, this remains the case by sessional order.[121]

Effect of certification by the Clerk
The Clerk's certification that the Standing Orders have been complied with is essential for a local or private bill to be introduced. A bill lacking that certification can only be introduced on a suspension of Standing Orders.[122] But the Clerk's certification that Standing Orders have been complied with is not finally conclusive and can be challenged. If the select committee to which a bill is referred receives evidence which casts doubt on whether the Standing Orders have been complied with, it is expected to draw that matter to the attention of the House.[123] This can be done either in the committee's final report on the bill or by way of special report. If such a doubt is raised in this or in any other way, it is then for the Speaker to determine whether the Standing Orders have been complied with. If they have not, the House decides whether to set them aside to permit the bill to proceed.

INCLUSION OF CLAUSES IN A LOCAL LEGISLATION BILL
Local matters may be included in a Local Legislation Bill by a local authority applying to the Minister of Local Government for preliminary consideration and provisional approval of a clause or clauses.[124]

The promoter must first give a copy of the proposed provision to all members of Parliament for general or Māori electoral districts whose constituents may be, or are likely to be, affected by it, advising them in writing of the intention to apply for its inclusion in a Local Legislation Bill. The local authority must forward a draft of such clause or clauses to the Minister, with a certificate certifying that such members have been advised of the intention to apply to have it included in a Local Legislation Bill. The certificate must specify the date on which notice was given and be signed by the authority's chief executive.[125] Copies of the provisions and the required notices are served by personal delivery, letter post, courier, document exchange used by the member or by facsimile or electronic mail.[126]

The Minister may set a deadline by which such applications must be received where a bill is being prepared. Objections to the inclusion of provisions in a Local Legislation Bill on any grounds may be lodged with the Minister. Any objections received by the Minister in respect of a clause subsequently included in a Local Legislation Bill must be transmitted to the select committee considering the bill.[127] The bill is drafted in the normal way as a Government bill, consisting of clauses of which the Minister has provisionally approved and other clauses repealing any spent Local Legislation Act or spent provision in such an Act.[128]

Further clauses provisionally approved by the Minister after a Local Legislation

---

119 S.O.272.
120 S.O.273(2).
121 2003, Vol.614, p.10751.
122 1993, Vol.536, pp.16805-6 (*Te Runanga o Ngai Tahu Bill*).
123 2002-05, AJHR, I.18B, p.56.

124 Appendix C to the Standing Orders, cl.20(1).
125 *Ibid.*, cl.20(2),(3).
126 *Ibid.*, cl.20(4).
127 *Ibid.*, cl.22.
128 *Ibid.*, cls.21 and 23.

Bill has been introduced may be added to the bill by being placed on a supplementary order paper and referred by the Minister to the select committee on the bill.[129] This is an exception to the general rule that Ministers, or indeed any persons or bodies other than the House, may not refer matters directly to a select committee. The committee usually reports the supplementary order paper back to the House in the same report as its report on the bill. When the committee has reported the bill back to the House, it is no longer competent for the Minister to refer a supplementary order paper containing amendments to the bill to the select committee.

---

[129] *Ibid.*, cl.24.

CHAPTER 27

THE LEGISLATIVE PROCESS

STAGES IN THE PASSING OF BILLS

Bills pass through the following major stages in the House—
- introduction
- first reading
- select committee consideration
- second reading
- committee of the whole House consideration
- third reading.

(Bills introduced before the forty-sixth Parliament and held over to that and subsequent Parliaments had their second readings before referral to a select committee. These bills, on being reported from the committee are the subject of debate on the report.[1])

It is at these various stages that discussion on the substantive issues contained in the bill may take place. There are procedural issues that may arise within each, and there are procedural questions to consider as a bill passes from stage to stage, but it is only on the stages themselves that substantive issues may be debated.

All bills must have three "readings" by order of the House before they are passed.[2] "Reading" a bill is a reference drawn from early English Parliaments when not all members were able to read and copies of documents were, in any case, not readily available, so that the Speaker or Clerk would actually read or describe the bill to the House before the Speaker asked the members if they agreed to it. In those days a "reading" preceded the passing of the bill through each stage; now a reading follows it. However, the bill is not read in full each time. Once the House has agreed to read a bill, whether for the first, second or third time, the Clerk merely reads the title of the bill and this constitutes it being read.[3]

INTRODUCTION

Government bills

Time of introduction

A Government bill may be introduced on any working day or by 1 pm on any sitting day.[4] A bill has been introduced after 1 pm by leave where copies of it became available only after the House met.[5] In addition, an Appropriation Bill, an Imprest Supply Bill or a bill to which the House has accorded urgency may be introduced during a sitting (but not while a debate is in progress).[6]

This means that, apart from the period 25 December to 15 January, weekends and public holidays,[7] Government bills may be introduced during adjournments of the House. (A bill cannot be introduced while Parliament is prorogued, dissolved or has expired.) While bills cannot be introduced after 1 pm on a sitting day (unless they are included in an urgency motion), where the House sits into a subsequent day under urgency and then adjourns and does not sit again on that day, a bill could be introduced at any time during

---

[1] 2002, Vol.602, p.308.
[2] S.O.269(1).
[3] S.O.269(2).
[4] S.O.275.

[5] 1996, Vol.556, p.13890 (*Producer Board Acts Reform Bill*).
[6] S.O.281.
[7] S.O.3(1).

the remainder of that day. If the House does sit again on that day bills may be introduced in the period between its adjournment and 1 pm.

Procedure for introduction

When the Government intends to introduce a bill into the House, the parliamentary counsel (Inland Revenue Department drafter in the case of tax bills) arranges for a print of the bill to be obtained.

Introduction is effected by the Leader of the House informing the Clerk that it is the Government's intention to introduce a bill.[8] Advice is effected by the Leader's office delivering a written note to this effect identifying the title of the bill, the Minister in charge, and the bill's reference number. For the notice to be effective copies of the bill must also be delivered to the Clerk so that it can be circulated to members on introduction.[9] Where the House is sitting under urgency at the time that a bill is to be introduced copies of the bill must be available at the Table before it can be introduced.[10] Without leave, there can be no introduction of a bill without copies of it being made available for circulation to members. Leave has been given to permit a bill to be introduced even though copies of it were not available at the proper time.[11]

Members' bills

Giving notice

Unlike a Government bill, a Member's bill cannot be introduced without notice having been given at a previous sitting of the House. The member intending to introduce the bill must give a notice of intention to introduce it. Such a notice is given by delivery to the Clerk between 9 am and 10 am on any sitting day.[12]

The member is obliged to deliver to the Clerk a fair copy of the bill proposed to be introduced no later than the time at which the member gives the notice to introduce. The Clerk arranges on behalf of the member for sufficient copies of any bill that is introduced to be printed for the use of members, and for these copies to be circulated in members' bill boxes as soon as possible after the bill's introduction.[13]

Number of bills before the House

There was formerly no restriction on the number of Members' bills that could be introduced on the same day. Notices for the introduction of Members' bills were set down on the order paper in the order they were received by the Clerk. This led to unseemly and unnecessary queues by members to gain priority on the order paper.[14] The procedure has been altered to allow priorities to be determined by ballot rather than stamina. No significance is now accorded to the order in which notices are lodged.

The number of Members' bills that may be on the order paper awaiting their first reading on any one day is restricted to a maximum of four, and a ballot is held to determine which four bills these are to be. Where the debate on the first reading of a bill has been commenced and then adjourned the bill is not counted as a bill awaiting first reading. But any other bill on the order paper for its first reading is counted as one of the four even though the stand-down period for the first reading debate may not have concluded or the bill's order of the day may have been postponed to a future day. The number of Members' bill slots for new bills that are available each fortnight when Members' bills are debated thus varies from none at all to four depending upon how many Members' bills are already

8   S.O.275.
9   S.O.268(1).
10   1998, Vol.566, p.7938.
11   1996, Vol.556, p.13890 (*Producer Board Acts Reform Bill*).
12   S.O.276(1).

13   S.Os 276(2) and 268(1).
14   See, for example: "Parliamentary midnight stake-out ends with a deal, a smile and a drink", *The Dominion*, 21 November 1989; "Marbles save the day in private member's bill battle", *The Dominion*, 4 April 1990.

on the order paper. While a Member's bill slot could theoretically become available on any day, Thursday morning following a Wednesday on which Members' bills have been debated is the critical time for lodging notices for it is on this day that slots are likely to become available by the House having processed Members' bills at the previous sitting (by reading them a first time and referring them to select committees, defeating them or by starting the first reading debate on them).

Consequently each Thursday fortnight while the House is sitting members are likely to lodge notices of intention to introduce Members' bills which they have prepared. Often over 40 notices are lodged at this time. To determine which bills may proceed to introduction the Clerk conducts a ballot at midday. This ballot also determines the order in which the bills will proceed.[15] The Clerk is empowered to reject notices for the introduction of bills given by members where there are already four such bills on the order paper awaiting their first reading.[16]

The House has given leave for additional bills to be drawn in the ballot so as to bring the number on the order paper awaiting first reading to more than four.[17] This has occurred where some of the bills already on the order paper had been postponed and there was little business actually available for transaction on the next Members' day. The Business Committee monitors the amount of Members' business before the House to determine whether additional bills should be drawn in the ballot in this way.

Conduct of the ballot

In order to prevent members boosting their chances in the ballot by lodging multiple notices, it is provided that no member can be entered in the ballot in respect of more than one notice. A member who entered more than one notice would be invited to nominate which should proceed. Failure to nominate one by the time the ballot is held would lead to all notices from that member being rejected. Furthermore, only one notice is to be entered in respect of bills that are the same or substantially the same in substance. If similar bills are entered by different members, which Member's bill proceeds into the main ballot is itself determined by ballot.[18]

When a ballot is to be held, members are advised by email shortly after 10 am of the titles of the bills in respect of which notices have been lodged and are invited to be present in person or by representative at the ballot. The ballot is conducted in one of the offices of the Office of the Clerk in Parliament House at midday. Members are advised of the result of the ballot shortly thereafter.

Introduction by leave

The House may give leave for a Member's bill to be introduced without notice having been given and the bill having obtained a priority in the ballot. Members occasionally seek leave for their bills to be preferred in this way but they are rarely successful.[19] Where leave is granted to introduce a Member's bill it is treated as if it had been drawn in the ballot.[20]

Local bills

A local bill is introduced by a member giving notice of intention to introduce it. Such a notice is given by delivery to the Clerk on any working day or by 1 pm on any sitting day.[21] At the same time as giving notice the member must deliver to the Clerk a signed copy of the bill. The Clerk arranges on behalf of the member for sufficient copies of the

---

15 S.O.277(2).
16 S.O.277(1).
17 2005, Vol.625, p.20185; 2005, Vol.626, p.21123.
18 S.O.277(3).

19 See, for example, 2001, Vol.591, p.8659.
20 See: 1995, Vol.550, p.8974 (*Kerikeri National Trust Bill*); *ibid.*, p.9036 (*Arbitration Bill*).
21 S.O.278.

bill to be printed (if this has not already been done) and circulated to members as soon as possible after the bill's introduction.[22]

There are no restrictions on the number of local bills that may be introduced on the same day. Such bills are listed on the order paper in the order in which notice of them was received by the Clerk.

Private bills

The presentation of a petition for the introduction of a private bill constitutes the introduction of the bill.[23] A petition for a private bill may only be presented after it has been endorsed by the Clerk as complying with the Standing Orders.[24] There are no restrictions on the number of private bills that may be introduced on the same day. If the bill has not already been printed (often it will have been), the Clerk arranges for sufficient copies of the bill to be printed and circulated to members as soon as possible after the bill's introduction.[25]

CIRCULATION OF BILLS

Once a bill has been introduced it is circulated to members.[26] This is effected internally through the Bills Office. Following its introduction, copies of it are made available for sale to the public. Copies of Members' bills that are unsuccessful in the ballot are not available from the Office of the Clerk, though the member who has prepared the bill may make a copy of it available if he or she sees fit.

SETTING A BILL DOWN FOR FIRST READING

At the next sitting of the House following the introduction of a bill the Clerk announces the bill's introduction as an item of general business.[27]

Having been introduced, a bill is set down for its first reading on the third sitting day following its introduction.[28] During this waiting or stand-down period the bill is shown on the order paper as a Government, Members' or local and private order of the day (as the case may be) below other orders of the day and without an order of the day number. A line is printed on the order paper under other orders of the day and above such bills that are in this waiting period. Such bills are therefore said to be "below the line" and are not available for consideration without leave of the House.[29] On their third such appearance on the order paper, introduced bills are transferred "above the line". They may then be scheduled for their first reading if they are Government orders of the day, and they will be placed after other bills awaiting a first reading in the case of Members' and private and local orders of the day.[30]

Any report from the Attorney-General under the *New Zealand Bill of Rights Act* 1990 drawing the House's attention to a provision in the bill that is inconsistent with the rights and freedoms set out in that Act must be made before the first reading debate is held.[31]

WITHDRAWAL OF A BILL

A bill that has been introduced may be withdrawn.

In the case of local bills and private bills the promoters of such bills may withdraw them at any time. If there are joint promoters each must agree to withdrawal. Withdrawal

---

22 S.O.268(1).
23 S.O.279.
24 S.O.272.
25 S.O.268(1).
26 *Ibid.*
27 S.O.280.
28 S.O.282.
29 For an example of leave being given, see 2001, Vol.592, pp.9400-1 (*Hauraki Gulf Marine Park Amendment Bill*).
30 S.Os 67 and 69.
31 S.O.266(1).

is effected by notifying the Speaker in writing that the bill is to be withdrawn. The concurrence of the member in charge of the bill is not required. Withdrawal is effective on the day that the Speaker receives the letter notifying it. The Speaker informs the House at the next opportunity that the bill has been withdrawn.[32] The consequence of withdrawal of a bill is that it is discharged from further consideration by the House.[33] If the bill is before a select committee at the time of its withdrawal, it is at once discharged from the committee and no report is made on it. If a promoter wishes to bring a bill that has been withdrawn before the House again in the future the procedures for promoting a local or private bill must begin anew. (A promoter of a bill has been ordered by a court to apply to Parliament for leave to withdraw a bill. This was not regarded as an interference with parliamentary proceedings on the ground that the decision whether to accede to the request is still left to Parliament.[34])

In addition to withdrawal of a local bill or private bill by the promoter, an order of the day relating to a bill (Government, Member's, private or local) which is before the House may be discharged. This can be effected by the member in charge of the bill informing the Clerk accordingly, if this is done before the order paper for Wednesday on which the bill is to be debated is prepared[35] or on motion without notice, moved when the order of the day is reached.[36] A bill that is before a select committee is not an order of the day and cannot be withdrawn under these procedures.

The discharge of an order of the day relating to a bill is treated as equivalent to the withdrawal of the bill. However, unlike withdrawal of a local bill or private bill by its promoter, a discharged order of the day can be reinstated by a motion on notice.

REPORT UNDER THE *NEW ZEALAND BILL OF RIGHTS ACT*

Where the Attorney-General considers that a bill as introduced contains a provision which appears to be inconsistent with any of the rights and freedoms contained in the *New Zealand Bill of Rights Act* 1990, the Attorney-General is obliged to report such an inconsistency to the House. In the case of a Government bill this must be done on the bill's introduction. (A report has been presented before such a bill was introduced.[37]) In the case of any other type of bill it must be done as soon as practicable after the bill's introduction.[38] In all cases the Attorney-General must discharge this duty before the motion for the first reading of the bill is moved.[39] Thus at the time at which the House holds its first debate on a bill which has been introduced it will be aware of any provision which, in the Attorney-General's opinion, is inconsistent with the *Bill of Rights Act* and the debate on the bill can proceed on that basis.

The Attorney-General is not required to report on every bill certifying whether it is or is not consistent with the *Bill of Rights Act*, only on those bills which do, in the Attorney-General's opinion, contain an inconsistency.[40]

An Attorney-General's report takes the form of the presentation of a paper. This is presented in the ordinary way and ordered by the House to be published.[41] Where a bill is introduced under urgency, the Attorney-General may present the paper certifying any inconsistency at the time of introduction and move forthwith that the paper be published. There is no debate on such a motion.[42]

The paper must indicate what provision of the bill is considered to be inconsistent

---

[32] S.O.274(1); see, for example, 1998, Vol.570, p.10770 (*Southland District Reserves Vesting and Empowering Bill*).
[33] S.O.274(2).
[34] *Fairfold Properties Ltd v Exmouth Docks Company, The Times Law Reports*, October 15, 1990.
[35] S.O.71(1)(b).
[36] S.O.71(1)(a).
[37] *Future Directions (Working with Families) Bill* 2004.
[38] *New Zealand Bill of Rights Act* 1990, s.7.
[39] S.O.266(1).
[40] 1991, Vol.516, p.2968.
[41] S.O.266(2).
[42] S.O.266(3).

with the *Bill of Rights Act* and how it appears to be inconsistent.[43] The Attorney-General may also respond to challenges concerning the compatibility of proposed legislation with the *Bill of Rights Act* in other ways: for example, by participating in debates on the bill, by making a ministerial statement or by answering oral and written questions on the subject.[44] The Attorney-General's report relates only to the bill that is introduced. Thus where a bill was on its face consistent with the *Bill of Rights Act* but amended a provision in another Act which itself was inconsistent, no report was presented.[45]

The Attorney-General has no ongoing responsibility to report on a bill as it is proceeding through its various stages. Amendments, whether at the select committee or committee of the whole House stages, are not subject to a formal Attorney-General's report,[46] though the Attorney-General, the select committee and other members may address the issue of consistency with the *Bill of Rights Act* in considering whether to adopt amendments to the bill.

AMENDMENTS TO NEW ZEALAND SUPERANNUATION

On the introduction of any Government bill to amend the *New Zealand Superannuation and Retirement Income Act* 2001, the Minister of Finance (or other Minister charged with the administration of that Act) must bring to the House's attention the consultation process that was followed in the formulation of the proposed amendment. In particular, the statement that the Minister makes must include information on what consultation has taken place with political parties represented in Parliament that are listed in the Act or in any Order in Council made under the Act[47] as supporting the part of the Act that is to be amended and what consultation on the proposed amendment has taken place with the Guardians of New Zealand Superannuation. The statement must also describe the results of the consultation.[48]

Such a statement can be made by way of a ministerial statement, by the presentation of a paper to the House[49] or in the bill's explanatory note.[50]

FIRST READING

Debate

In initiating the first reading debate the member in charge of the bill moves "That the ... Bill be now read a first time"[51] and proceeds directly to speak to that motion.

The first reading debate is the House's first opportunity to debate the legislative proposal that has been put before it. The House may decide that it does not wish to spend further time considering the proposal and reject it out of hand. But most bills (and especially Government bills) are not rejected at their first hurdle and the first reading debate is looked upon as a prelude to sending the bill for detailed study by a select committee. It is therefore an opportunity for the Minister in the case of a Government bill to state to the House why the Government has introduced the bill and what it hopes that it will accomplish and to give a brief resumé of its provisions. It is an opportunity also for

43   S.O.266(1).
44   See, for example, *Hansard Supplement*, 2001, Vol.48, p.1702 (*Local Electoral Bill*).
45   1999, Vol.575, p.15251 (*Social Welfare (Transitional Provisions – Special Portability Arrangement) Amendment Bill*).
46   *R v Poumako* [2000] 2 NZLR 695 at [25], [66] and [96]; 2001, Vol.597, p.13349; *Hansard Supplement*, 2001, Vol.50, p.4172.
47   See *New Zealand Superannuation (Political Commitment) Order* 2003 and *New Zealand Superannuation (Political Commitment) Order* 2004.

48   *New Zealand Superannuation and Retirement Income Act* 2001, s.73.
49   *New Zealand Superannuation Act* 2001: *Minister of Finance's Statement on the Consultation Process followed in the formulation of the Amendments to the New Zealand Superannuation Act 2001 proposed in the Relationships (Statutory References) Bill*, presented pursuant to section 73 of the Act, 21 June 2004.
50   See *New Zealand Superannuation Amendment Bill* 2004, explanatory note.
51   S.O.283.

other members, and especially parties, to put on record their positions on the proposal or to reserve their positions until they have benefited from the information gleaned during the select committee's consideration of it. So while a first reading can lead to an "in principle" decision on the bill, it does not have to. It is perfectly consistent with the first reading process for judgment on the bill to be deferred to allow it to be given more detailed examination. The question of consistency or inconsistency with the *Bill of Rights Act* is always a legitimate debating point to be raised, especially during the first reading debate.[52] Indeed the Minister moving the first reading may deal explicitly with how the Government perceives that the bill's provisions relate to the *Bill of Rights Act*.[53]

One matter which it is obligatory for the member in charge to indicate in the speech is which select committee the member proposes to refer the bill to. Furthermore, if it is intended to give the committee any special powers or instruction (for example, allowing it to meet outside the hours prescribed in the Standing Orders or requiring it to report the bill back by a particular date) that must be specifically indicated in the speech too.[54]

The member in charge does not move a motion in respect of these matters in the first reading speech, though a written notice of the motion to be moved in respect of the special powers or instruction must be lodged at the Table immediately after the speech.[55] That motion is moved after the bill has been read a first time. At this stage the member in charge is advising members of his or her intentions with regard to the bill so that the first reading debate can proceed in full knowledge of those intentions. Members taking part in the debate are at liberty to comment on the appropriateness of the committee to which the bill is to be referred or on the powers or instruction to be given to it. If the member in charge fails to mention in the speech the committee to which the bill is to be referred, the Speaker will require this to be done before the debate proceeds.[56] If the member does not mention any special powers or instruction in the speech, a motion for these cannot thereafter be moved.[57] Further, if the member in charge does mention special powers in the speech, the motion for them must be in the same terms. So a Minister who indicated a particular date for reporting the bill back to the House in his speech could not move a motion with a different date without leave of the House.[58]

Amendments

An amendment to the motion that a bill be read a first time can be moved, but not an amendment that would extend the debate in a way that is not relevant to the first reading debate.[59] Thus, a want of confidence amendment would not be acceptable, nor is it acceptable to move an amendment relating to select committee consideration at this point, since there is a later procedure expressly dealing with that issue.

Conclusion of debate

The debate on a Government bill is limited to 12 speeches (including the Minister's), each of a maximum of 10 minutes duration. In the case of Members' and local and private bills there are six speeches (including the member in charge's), each of a maximum of 10

---

52 1990, Vol.511, pp.103-4; 1998, Vol.567, p.8268.
53 1990, Vol.511, p.593 (*Bail (Miscellaneous Provisions) Bill*).
54 S.O.284(1).
55 S.O.284(2).
56 1998, Vol.568, pp.8523-4 (*Ministry of Energy*

Amendment Bill (No 2)).
57 1997, Vol.561, pp.2726-9.
58 1997, Vol.562, p.3508 (*Taxation (Superannuitant Surcharge Abolition) Bill*).
59 1985, Vol.468, p.8981.

minutes duration. The member in charge then has five minutes to reply to the debate.[60]
The Business Committee has from time to time used its power to vary the speaking times
set out in the Standing Orders in respect of the debate on a Member's bill. Indeed this
is likely to vary from Parliament to Parliament depending upon the party composition of
the House. (For the forty-seventh Parliament there were two 10 minute speeches, eight
five minute speeches and five minutes for the member in charge to speak in reply.[61]) It
is understood that in all cases at least one of the members speaking in the debate on a
Member's bill will be from the same party as the member in charge.

At the conclusion of the debate the Speaker puts the question and this is decided in
the normal way. If the question for first reading is decided affirmatively (as it almost
invariably is with Government bills), the bill is read a first time by the Clerk. The Clerk
merely rises and reads the title of the bill.

If the debate on the first reading of a bill is interrupted by the adjournment of the House,
the debate is set down for resumption next sitting day. In the case of a Government bill,
when it is subsequently dealt with depends upon its position among the other Government
orders of the day. In the case of other bills it will automatically take priority over other
bills at the same stage.[62] The debate on the first reading of a bill could also be adjourned
by a motion to that effect. In this case, too, the adjourned debate would be set down as
an order of the day.

REFERENCE OF BILLS TO THE WAITANGI TRIBUNAL

There is a statutory provision for the House to refer any proposed legislation before it to
the Waitangi Tribunal, so that the tribunal may report on whether the provisions of the
legislation are in any way contrary to the principles of the Treaty of Waitangi.[63]

A bill before the House may be referred for report only by resolution of the House.[64]
Such a resolution requires notice of motion to be given first; a motion to refer a bill to a
body outside the House cannot be moved by way of amendment on the second reading
of a bill.[65] Referring a bill to the Waitangi Tribunal for report discharges any order of the
day in respect of the bill and discharges it from any select committee to which it has been
referred. Further parliamentary progress on the bill is arrested until the tribunal reports.

The tribunal's report on a bill referred to it is made to the Speaker. The Speaker then
lays it before the House.[66] Apart from formal referral of a bill to it by the House in this
way, the Waitangi Tribunal has no jurisdiction in respect of a bill before the House of
Representatives.[67]

It is, of course, always open to select committees themselves to give consideration to
whether the terms of a bill that has been referred to them is consistent with the principles
of the Treaty of Waitangi.[68]

REFERRAL OF BILLS TO SELECT COMMITTEES

With only limited exceptions every bill stands referred to a select committee for
consideration after its first reading.[69] This rule of near universal referral of bills to select
committees was introduced in 1979.

Appropriation bills and Imprest Supply bills are not referred to a select committee.[70]
These exceptions are more apparent than real. The contents of an Appropriation Bill
(estimates, supplementary estimates and financial reviews) are considered by select

---

[60] Appendix A to the Standing Orders.
[61] Business Committee determination, 17 September 2002.
[62] S.Os 67(2) and 69(2).
[63] *Treaty of Waitangi Act* 1975, s.8(1).
[64] *Ibid.*, s.8(2)(a).
[65] 1975, Vol.397, p.869.
[66] *Treaty of Waitangi Act* 1975, s.8(3)(a), (4).
[67] *Ibid.,* s.6(6)(b).
[68] 2002-05, AJHR, I.22B, Appendix C (*Supreme Court Bill).*
[69] S.O.285(1).
[70] S.O.285(2).

committees even though the bills, as the formal vehicles for debate in the House, are not. An Imprest Supply Bill is passed at one sitting, so there would be no opportunity for select committee consideration in any case (there are no more than three such bills each year).

The real exception to the rule that all bills are referred to select committees is bills to which the House accords urgency, in order to pass them through one or more of their stages.[71] A motion for urgency for a bill means that debate on that bill can continue until it is concluded, even though the time has come at which the House would otherwise have adjourned or moved on to other business. Urgency may be taken on a bill in respect of one stage of the bill only or it may be for the passage of the bill through its remaining stages after the select committee has considered it.

Occasionally a matter of such urgent importance arises that the Government considers it necessary to introduce and pass a bill through successive stages or indeed all its stages in one day. To do this it asks the House to accord urgency for the introduction and subsequent stages of the bill. If urgency is so accorded, the bill is exempted from the requirement of the Standing Order that it be referred to a select committee and no motion to refer the bill to a select committee will be accepted by the Speaker.[72]

In practice, some 95 percent of all Government bills introduced (and virtually 100 percent of all other bills) are now referred to select committees for study.

Determination of committee to consider bill

The member in charge nominates the particular committee to consider the bill in the motion for this purpose that the member must move after the bill is read a first time.[73] This will be the committee that the member in charge, in the member's first reading speech, indicated would be the committee to which it was proposed to refer the bill.

Which committee the member in charge nominates is a matter for that member. It will depend on the subject-matter of the bill and the workload of the committees. A bill does not have to be referred to any particular committee, even one whose terms of reference may appear to make it the most suitable. Nor does a bill have to be referred to a committee that is already in existence. A bill can be referred to a special committee to be established.[74] However, no committee can be established by the member in charge's motion at this stage. That motion can merely indicate that it is proposed to establish a committee to consider the bill. The committee must be established later by a motion of which notice has been given in the ordinary way. In practice, only a Government bill is likely to be referred to a special committee in this way, unless leave is forthcoming. It is possible that a Government notice of motion to establish the committee may be before the House as an order of the day at the same time that a Government bill is read a first time. On one occasion the order of the day for the establishment of such a committee was taken as the House's next business following the first reading of a bill that had been referred to a special committee to be established.[75] Otherwise, the Government will give notice of motion and the motion establishing the committee will be considered on a subsequent day.

Special powers or instructions

Provided that the member in charge described them in the first reading speech, the motion nominating the committee may also contain any special powers or instruction to be given to the committee in respect of its consideration of the bill.[76]

---

71 S.O.285(1).
72 1985, Vol.460, p.3048 (*Income Tax Amendment Bill (No 3)*).
73 S.O.286(1).
74 S.O.286(2).
75 1999, Vol.581, pp.106-18 (Committee on the *Accident Insurance (Transitional Provisions) Bill*).
76 S.O.286(3).

A motion referring a bill to a particular committee automatically engages the standard powers and obligations conferred on committees by the Standing Orders. In particular, these govern the times at which committees meet and must finally report back to the House on the bill (within six months), but they also include the general background rules about how committees conduct their business, interact with witnesses and take decisions. If it is desired to vary any of these rules, to confer extra powers on the committee or to constrain its examination of the bill in any way, that can be done in the motion moved by the member in charge at this time. (It can also be done subsequently by motion on notice but it is more convenient for the Government to do it at this point since it will not be further debatable. It is furthermore unlikely that any member in charge of a Member's bill will get a subsequent opportunity to move for such powers since Members' notices of motion have no particular priority.) The most common examples of instructions given to committees in such motions is to require them to report back earlier than the standard period of six months and the most common examples of special powers conferred on committees is to allow them to meet at times not otherwise open to them, for example, on a Friday in a sitting week.

Special powers or an instruction moved immediately after the first reading of a bill may relate only to the committee's consideration of that bill. They cannot extend the committee's terms of reference or powers generally. They can apply only in respect of the committee's consideration of the bill which was the occasion for them being moved.[77] Where a special committee is to be established, special powers can be conferred on it at this point, provided that those powers were mentioned in the member in charge's speech. Otherwise they can be conferred in the motion to be moved later establishing the committee.

Motion and amendment

Immediately after the bill is read a first time, the Speaker invites the member in charge to move the motion nominating the committee (which, if appropriate, will contain the special powers or instruction). If the member in charge adds anything to the motion not falling within these permissible matters, the extra words moved will be ruled out of order. Thus words explaining that it was intended to pass the bill by a certain date were ruled out of order as not being relevant to the select committee's terms of reference for consideration of the bill.[78]

Other members may object to the committee nominated by the member in charge on the grounds that another committee is more appropriate. They may also object to any conditions (especially those limiting the time that the committee may have to consider the bill) tagged on to the motion. During the first reading debate, when members were forewarned of the terms of the member in charge's motion, they were able to debate these matters. But they can also seek to amend the motion.

An amendment to alter the committee to which the bill is to be referred, or to change any further terms relating to the committee's order of reference added by the member in charge, may be moved provided that written notice of the amendment is handed in at the Table before the bill is read a first time[79] – that is, while the debate is still proceeding.[80] If no written copy of the amendment is handed in before the debate concludes, the amendment will not be accepted.[81] The Speaker puts any amendment of which notice has been given to the House for determination. If the member in charge does not propose

---

[77]   1997, Vol.558, p.671.

[78]   1998, Vol.569, p.9792 (*Local Elections and Polls (Processing of Votes on Receipt) Amendment Bill*).

[79]   S.O.286(4).

[80]   2003, Vol.606, p.4041 (*Local Elections and Polls (Processing of Votes on Receipt) Amendment Bill*).

[81]   2003, Vol.608, p.5350 (*New Organisms and Other Matters Bill*).

any special powers or instruction no amendment to the referral motion proposing these may be moved.

Neither the member in charge's motion nor any amendment to it are themselves debatable after the first reading debate concludes.[82] A motion nominating a particular committee to consider a bill has been defeated.[83] In this case the member was given leave to move a second motion nominating a different committee and this was agreed to. In the absence of the matter being disposed of immediately by leave, a motion nominating an alternative committee could be moved only on notice.

Transfer of bill to another committee

As the House orders a particular committee to consider each bill that has been read a first time only the House can transfer a bill from one committee to another.

A motion to effect this by rescinding the House's original order can be moved after notice has been given in the ordinary way. Alternatively, leave of the House could be given for this. Committees do occasionally raise the question of transferring a bill to another, in their view more appropriate, committee and may report to the House suggesting this.[84] Normally any proposal to transfer a bill to another committee will be discussed first at the Business Committee.

If a bill were to be transferred to another committee the standard six months' time limit for reporting would start to run anew from the date of transfer, but if any specific reporting date had been imposed on the former committee by the House that date would continue to apply to the new committee.

CONSIDERATION OF BILLS BY SELECT COMMITTEES

The House of Representatives has throughout its history made a regular practice of referring bills to select committees for detailed examination. Until 1979 this was done after second reading on an ad hoc basis. Approximately 30 percent of all Government bills (and virtually every other type of bill that received a second reading) were referred in this way. In 1979 a procedure of automatic referral of all bills (with limited exceptions) after their first reading was introduced. Between 1996 and 1999 the House reverted to its previous practice of referring bills after their second reading but in 1999 the House returned to referring bills after first reading. Given the importance of select committee consideration of bills it was considered that the House should take its "in principle" decision on legislation – that is, at the second reading of the bill – after the select committee had considered it and with the benefit of that consideration.[85]

Select committee consideration of a bill is not confined to looking at the details of the bill's drafting, as is, for instance, the committee of the whole House stage. Select committees are charged with examining bills which are referred to them to determine whether they should pass.[86] This is the fundamental question that is raised in respect of every bill introduced into the House and the select committee to which a bill is referred is expected to express its opinion on it. This does not mean that a select committee has the power to determine whether a bill should be passed or not passed. Only the House can do that. But select committees are not only authorised to express their opinions on that matter, they are enjoined by the Standing Orders to do so (though a committee may be unable to agree on whether a bill should pass).[87] A select committee's opinion on the passing of a bill results from the most minute study of the bill that any arm of the House makes.

---

82 S.O.286(1).
83 1996, Vol.553, pp.11597-8 (*Limits on Campaign Spending for Candidates in Local Elections Bill*).
84 See, for example, 1996-99, AJHR, I.22, p.297 (*Local Elections (Single Transferable Vote Option) Bill*).

85 1996-99, AJHR, I.18B, p.23 (Standing Orders Committee).
86 S.O.287(1)(a).
87 1999-2002, AJHR, I.22B, p.986 (*Police Amendment Bill (No 2)*).

As well as considering the question of the bill's passing, a select committee may recommend amendments to the bill.[88] While these must be relevant to the bill, they can be of fundamental importance and alter its shape accordingly (another reason to defer the "in principle" decision on the bill's passing until after select committee consideration).[89] Most motions nominating committees to consider bills contain no particular restriction or direction as to the committee's work. The committee may therefore exercise any of the powers given to it by the Standing Orders.[90] Sometimes the motion nominating the committee does go on to circumscribe the committee in its work. The committee must operate within any limitations laid down by the House when the bill is referred to it, and is always subject to subsequent direction by the House by means of an instruction.

PROCESS FOLLOWED BY COMMITTEES

Each committee is relatively free to organise for itself the performance of the legislative task it is given. All of the 13 subject select committees have bills referred to them at some time or other, as does the Regulations Review Committee. Even the Standing Orders Committee has had bills referred to it.[91] From time to time committees are established to consider particular bills. Committees are not obliged to discharge their task in any particular way unless the House specifically directs them to. They are not obliged, for example, to advertise for evidence or to hear witnesses. In 1979 the Standing Orders Committee, which recommended the new procedure of automatic reference of bills to select committees, remarked:

> The committee does not believe that select committees will find it necessary to subject all bills to elaborate study. While this must be a matter for each committee to decide for itself in the light of the bill it has before it, the committee envisages that there will be bills referred automatically to a committee under the new procedure which are so straightforward that they will require only the briefest consideration by the select committee.[92]

Most bills are referred to committees that are already in existence. Even so, it is irregular for the committee to take formal action in relation to a bill – such as advertising for submissions – before the bill is actually referred to it.[93] Nevertheless, the committee may have been informally advised by the Minister in the case of a Government bill that a bill is to be referred to the committee and it is quite proper for the committee to hold prior discussions on how the bill is to be processed once it is referred to the committee.

Briefings

Exceptionally a bill may be referred to a committee for it to receive only a briefing on the bill from the Minister in charge of it or officials from the Minister's department.[94]

In such a case the committee may not advertise for submissions or hear evidence. How, if at all, the committee considers such written communications as it may receive on the bill is a matter for it. But the committee may appoint advisers and receive reports from them on the bill, in addition to receiving briefings from the Minister and departmental

---

88   S.O.287(1)(b).
89   1996-99, AJHR, I.18B, p.23.
90   1990, Vol.511, p.127.
91   2002, Vol.602, p.114 (*Remuneration Authority (Members of Parliament) Amendment Bill*); 2003, Vol.612, p.9280 (*Members of Parliament (Pecuniary Interests) Bill*).
92   1979, AJHR, I.14, p.7.

93   1996, Vol.555, p.12949 (*Adoption Amendment Bill (No 2)*).
94   JHR, 1991-93, p.1243 (*Social Security Amendment Bill (No 6)*); ibid., p.1635 (*Social Security Amendment Bill (No 7)*); 2003, Vol.607, p.4311 (*Resource Management Amendment Bill (No 2)*).

officials. The committee still has the function of examining the bill to determine whether it should pass and the power to recommend relevant amendments to it.[95]

Advertising

The committee determines the extent of advertising for submissions to be undertaken on a bill. However, where a bill is referred to a committee at a time when it is not due to meet for some days and it is desirable not to lose the intervening time, the chairperson may, on behalf of the committee, direct the clerk of the committee to place newspaper advertisements calling for submissions by a particular time. But these steps are provisional and are subject to the ultimate authority of the committee which may repudiate or alter the chairperson's action.[96] It is normal practice for an advertisement to contain a concise neutral summary of the bill's provisions. These summaries are prepared by the committee staff subject to the final control of the committee.[97]

Where a bill is referred to a special committee that has been newly set up, the committee must meet and elect a chairperson before the calling of submissions can be arranged, and it is improper for anyone to act in the committee's name before that time.[98]

The extent of advertising that is undertaken will depend upon the perceived level of interest in the bill and the time constraints (if any) placed on the committee in considering the bill. Where the committee considers that a bill must be processed with despatch or the House has required that the bill be reported back within a matter of days, the committee may decide not to place any advertisements calling for public submissions.[99] A committee has decided not to call for submissions on a bill that it considered to be straightforward and uncontroversial.[100] But these situations are uncommon.

It has been suggested that the normal period to allow for submissions is a minimum of six weeks. This gives persons who wish to make submissions a realistic time to formulate their comments, even on a substantial bill. Shorter time-frames than this will be appropriate if the House has restricted the time for report by the committee or if the bill is of limited interest.[101] These are matters for determination by the committee. There are likely to be complaints from members and the public when a limited time-frame is allowed for a substantial bill.[102]

Although local and private bills have been the subject of preliminary procedures designed to draw attention to their promotion, it is still the practice for select committees to advertise for submissions on them in the appropriate locality.[103] Submissions are also requested from the promoters and any Government department with a particular interest in the subject-matter of the bill though the latter will often be appointed as an adviser to the committee and provide its input in that capacity.

Hearing submissions

The chairperson and the clerk of the committee organise a programme of hearings on the bill during which those who wish to appear before the committee give evidence. Witnesses can include members of Parliament themselves. The number of submissions received varies from none to many hundreds. In the case of the *Employment Relations Bill* 2000, there were 17,369 submissions received (including 15,064 "form" submissions).[104]

[95] S.O.287(1).
[96] 2000, Vol.586, p.5168 (*New Zealand Public Health and Disability Bill*).
[97] *Ibid.*
[98] 1981, Vol.439, p.2441.
[99] 1987-90, AJHR, I.4A, p.10 (*Taxation Reform Bill*); 1999-2002, AJHR, I.22A, p.482 (*New Zealand/Singapore Closer Economic Partnership Bill*).
[100] 2002-05, AJHR, I.22D, p.501 (*Medicines (Specified Biotechnical Procedures) Amendment Bill*).
[101] 2002-05, AJHR, I.18B, p.39 (Standing Orders Committee).
[102] See, for example, 1999-2002, AJHR, I.22B, p.1315 (*Social Security (Residence of Spouses) Amendment Bill* – 13 days allowed).
[103] 1986-87, AJHR, I.18A, para.4.4 (Standing Orders Committee).
[104] 1999-2002, AJHR, I.22A, p.130.

Even in the case of a local bill, the committee has received as many as 39 submissions.[105] In these circumstances, it is not always possible to oblige all persons who wish to appear in person before a committee. To some extent this problem can be met by "grouping" similar submissions and inviting witnesses to appear jointly before the committee even though they have put in separate submissions. Where consideration of a bill extended over a lengthy period and substantial amendments to the bill had been circulated on a supplementary order paper, a committee invited witnesses to make resubmissions to the committee on the bill and the amendments.[106]

But committees are not obliged simply to wait for people and organisations to initiate submissions. They can, if they consider it desirable, seek out submissions from groups that they consider may have particularly useful perspectives to contribute on the legislation before the committee. Thus the Finance and Expenditure Committee sought submissions on the *Public Finance Bill* 1989 from government departments, State enterprises and private sector financial institutions when it appeared that these groups were unwilling to make submissions or were unaware of the implications of the bill for them.[107] It has also been suggested that committees should more frequently invite the Minister in charge of a bill to appear before them to explain policy matters relating to their bills.[108] Committees do do this from time to time.[109]

Committees may meet anywhere in New Zealand[110] and have increasingly used this power to hear evidence at locations outside Wellington. But usually evidence is heard in a committee room in Parliament House where the witness appears before the committee in person or from a remote location using videoconferencing or teleconferencing facilities. At these hearings, witnesses elaborate on their written submissions and are questioned in turn by members of the committee. In this way the select committee process brings the legislator into direct contact with the citizen.

Opinions from other committees

A bill may relate to matters within the subject areas assigned to two or more committees. For this reason the committee to which such a bill is referred is empowered to ask any other committee for its opinion on a part, clause, schedule or other provision of the bill.[111] Any other committee which is asked for its opinion in this way may effectively treat the provision involved as if it had been referred to it by the House as a separate bill. It may call for submissions and hear evidence on the provision. When it reports its opinion to the committee which requested it, it can at the same time recommend amendments to the provision in question.[112]

The Regulations Review Committee has its own standing authority to report to any committee on a regulation-making power in a bill, on a provision in such a bill that contains a delegated power to make instruments of a legislative character, and on any other matter relating to regulations affecting a bill that has been referred to a committee.[113] Indeed, other committees frequently request the committee to examine specific issues (such as matters raised in submissions, questions about empowering provisions and assessing departmental advice) in bills before them.[114] The Regulations Review Committee makes its reports in correspondence with the committee on the bill and by its members and staff appearing personally before the committee. (See Chapter 29.)

---

[105] 1996-99, I.24, p.388 (*Marlborough County Council Empowering Act Repeal Bill*).
[106] 2002-05, AJHR, I.22C, p.744 (*Human Assisted Reproductive Technology Bill*).
[107] 1987-90, AJHR, I.4C, p.5.
[108] 2002-05, AJHR, I.18B, p.36 (Standing Orders Committee).
[109] See, for example, 1996, Vol.555, p.12663.
[110] S.O.193.
[111] S.O.289(1).
[112] S.O.289(2).
[113] S.O.314(3).
[114] 2002-05, AJHR, I.16I, p.18.

Private bills

The House, in passing private legislation, was formerly thought of as exercising a judicial as well as a legislative function.[115] This was especially the case when parties appeared in opposition to a measure before the committee considering the bill. However, now the consideration of private bills is merely a specialised form of legislation rather than the House sitting in judgment over parties to a suit. More often than not there is only one party in any case. The committee on a private bill conducts its proceedings much as any other select committee on a bill, although the promoter is more likely to be represented by counsel, which is not often the case with other committees. Reports are called for from interested government departments and evidence heard from any other person who wishes to offer it.

In the case of a private bill, committees are enjoined to examine the preamble to the bill to determine whether the statements set out there as justifying the bill have been proved to their satisfaction.[116]

Local Legislation bills

A committee considering a Local Legislation Bill is directed to consider whether, in its opinion, any clause included in the bill should more properly have been the subject of a separate local bill.[117]

Advisers and drafting

As well as hearing evidence from witnesses, committees also receive reports from their own advisers.

In all cases these will be provided by staff of the Office of the Clerk attached to the committee for the purpose. In addition, in the case of Government bills, staff from the department whose Minister is in charge of the bill are invariably accepted by the committee in the role of its advisers for the duration of its consideration of the bill. Departmental advisers will prepare a report for the committee summarising the evidence received and suggesting amendments to the bill. In the case of local and private bills, committees will usually seek similar support from the relevant department to help in their consideration of bills that are likely to become law. Occasionally, committees seek departmental involvement in the consideration of a Member's bill before them. Such assistance will only be rendered with the agreement of the Minister for the department concerned and is therefore problematic. A committee has been refused departmental assistance for a Member's bill.[118] Offices of Parliament also provide advisers from time to time to assist committees on bills, as do bodies such as the Electoral Commission on bills for which they have a particular expertise.

Other advisers may be engaged under contract with the Clerk of the House to assist the committee if they have a particular expertise or skill that is necessary for consideration of the bill before the committee. The Finance and Expenditure Committee has had a longstanding practice of engaging a tax adviser to assist it with the consideration of tax bills.

The drafting of amendments that a committee wishes to propose to a Government bill is undertaken by a parliamentary counsel who attends for the consideration and

---

[115] 1870, AJHR, A-30 (*Speaker's Memorandum*).
[116] S.O.287(2).

[117] S.O.287(3).
[118] 1996-99, AJHR, I.8A (*Conveyancers Bill*).

deliberation phases of the committee's work. The parliamentary counsel also drafts amendments to local and private bills before the committee. Whether drafting assistance will be forthcoming for amendments to Members' bills depends upon whether the Attorney-General will agree to make such a service available. This is normal for a bill being progressed as a conscience issue but may be refused in other cases.[119] In at least one case, departmental officials have drafted amendments for the member in charge of a Member's bill.[120] (This level of departmental involvement drew criticism from the committee as being inappropriate.) Committees can also obtain drafting assistance from the Office of the Clerk.

Bill of Rights Act

An important matter for select committees to consider is the relationship of the bill before them to the *New Zealand Bill of Rights Act* 1990. If the Attorney-General considered that the bill as introduced contained a provision inconsistent with the *Bill of Rights Act*, a report to this effect will have been made to the House and will consequently be available to the committee. But the Attorney-General's view that a bill is or is not inconsistent with the *Bill of Rights Act* is not conclusive and the House and a select committee are both free to come to a different view.

Committees may ask the Attorney-General or the Attorney-General's advisers to reconsider their initial view that the legislation was consistent (or was not consistent) in the light of submissions to the committee.[121] Whether the invitation to reconsider an initial view is acted upon is for the Attorney-General to decide. Advisers have reconfirmed their initial position in response to such a request.[122] Commonly, committees recommend amendments to the bill designed to reconcile the proposed legislation with the *Bill of Rights Act* where such issues are raised and require clarification. However, there are cases where a committee, while accepting that there is an inconsistency with the *Bill of Rights Act*, considers that the public interest justifies overriding a right or freedom given expression in that Act and that legislation containing such a provision should be passed nonetheless.[123]

Amendments

Select committees do not have, and have never had, the power to make amendments to bills; they have the power only to recommend amendments to the House.[124] Such amendments remain to be adopted (or not) by the House. Amendments recommended by a select committee are not adopted as part of the bill until the bill is read a second time by the House.[125] It follows that amendments proposed by a select committee to the title of a bill become effective at the time it is given a second reading. The new title is used to refer to the bill after that point.[126]

Admissibility of amendments

Although only recommendations, amendments proposed by select committees must be relevant to the subject-matter of the bill, be consistent with its principles and objects and otherwise conform to the Standing Orders and practices of the House.[127] Any recommended amendments must therefore conform with the rules that apply in respect of

[119] *Ibid.*

[120] *Ibid.*, I.23, p.836 (*Trade in Endangered Species Amendment Bill*).

[121] *Reports of select committees 1996*, p.230 (*Chemical Weapons (Prohibition) Bill*); 1996-99, AJHR, I.22, p.413 (*Evidence (Witness Anonymity) Amendment Bill*).

[122] 2002-05, AJHR, I.22C, p.909 (*Civil Union Bill*).

[123] For example, 1996-99, AJHR, I.23, p.853 (*Land Transport Bill*); ibid., I.24, pp.546-7 (*Crimes (Bail Reform) Bill*).

[124] S.O.287(1)(b).

[125] S.O.296.

[126] 1983, Vol.453, p.3101.

[127] S.O.288(1).

amendments offered in a committee of the whole House. If it is desired that a committee consider amendments that are outside the scope of the bill before it or are otherwise inadmissible, the committee must be specifically authorised by the House to do so.[128] Amendments proposed by a select committee that are inadmissible may be struck out of the bill by the Speaker before the bill is given its second reading.

In addition, in the case of local and private bills, the committee may not propose any amendment that is outside the scope of the notices advertising the intention to introduce the bill.[129] (But a widely drawn notice does not expand the scope of a bill – the bill's scope is still confined to its provisions.) If a committee adds a clause or makes an amendment to a local or private bill which is not within the scope of the advertised objects of the bill, it exceeds its powers. Where such an amendment is perceived as being out of order before the bill is read a second time, it will be struck out of the bill by the Speaker (though the Standing Orders may be suspended to allow the clause or amendment to stand). Alternatively, a bill may be referred back to the committee for it to amend its report and remove the offending clause or amendment. In the case of a Local Legislation Bill any new clause that the committee sees fit to recommend be added to the bill (unless it is in substitution for, incidental to, or consequential upon an existing clause) must first have been provisionally approved by the Minister of Local Government.[130]

The financial veto rule does not apply to amendments proposed in a select committee, though it can be applied by the Government to an amendment recommended by a select committee once the report has been presented, at any time up to the second reading of the bill.[131] An amendment which is the same in substance as an amendment already agreed to or defeated earlier in the calendar year, may be moved again only by leave or if notice of it has been given.[132]

The chairperson of the select committee rules on the admissibility of amendments. Amendments which would be out of order in a committee of the whole House (with the exception of the financial veto) are equally out of order in a select committee. (See pp. 376–82 for amendments that are inadmissible in the committee of the whole House.)

Consultation with promoters
In the case of private bills and local bills it is the practice for committees to consult with the promoter of the bill over proposed amendments. Promoters do not have a right of veto over amendments to their bills, though a promoter may withdraw the bill if dissatisfied with the outcome of the committee's consideration of it.

Amendments adopted unanimously or by majority
Once an amendment has been agreed to by the committee it is incorporated into the committee's report to the House. But committees are obliged to indicate in their report which amendments were adopted unanimously by the committee and which were adopted by a majority of the committee.[133] Amendments recommended by a majority of the committee must be specifically endorsed by the House.[134] They and any other amendments are deemed to be adopted when the bill is read a second time.[135] An amendment agreed in the committee on a voice vote is regarded as having been adopted unanimously though that does not necessarily mean that all members supported it. Only if a member requires that

---

[128] 2000, Vol.588, pp.6679-90 (*Crimes Amendment Bill (No 6)*).
[129] S.O.288(2).
[130] Appendix C to the Standing Orders, cl.25.
[131] S.O.321(1).
[132] S.O.208.
[133] S.O.288(4).
[134] S.O.294(1).
[135] S.O.296.

the votes or abstentions of members present be recorded for inclusion in the committee's minutes[136] is the amendment identified as having been adopted by majority.[137] Only *amendments* to the bill adopted by majority are identified in this way in the report. The fact that the committee agreed to a provision standing part of the bill by a majority vote is not specially shown in the report, though the committee may choose to draw attention to this in its commentary. Where only an abstention is recorded on an amendment without any member actually voting against it, the amendment is still regarded as having been adopted by a majority.

Amendments to Statutes Amendment bills are by convention adopted unanimously to complement the rule that, in a committee of the whole House, any member can veto a clause to the bill.[138] In addition, in the case of proposed amendments to Acts not amended by the bill as originally introduced, the committee is likely to seek assurances that each party in the House not represented on the committee consents to the amendments being added to the bill.[139]

Dividing a bill

Select committees have power to divide a bill and report the resulting bills back to the House as separate bills. This power arises where the bill referred to the committee is drafted in parts or otherwise lends itself to division because it comprises more than one subject-matter.[140]

When a select committee divides a bill, it may decide that it wishes to report only one or some of the newly separated bills to the House. It then retains the remaining bill or bills before it for further consideration.

Each new bill must have an enacting formula, title and commencement provision as must any bill introduced into the House. A bill that has been divided is reprinted as separate bills when it is reported to the House by the committee.[141]

REPORTING ON BILLS

When a committee has heard all the evidence submitted to it, or all the evidence it is prepared to hear, it considers reports from its advisers and draft amendments put before it and deliberates on the bill part by part or in any other way that it determines, adopting amendments to the bill's text as it sees fit. It also adopts a written text (the commentary) describing the process it followed and the conclusions that it has come to. These will constitute its final report to the House on the bill.

Prior to presenting its final report on the bill, the committee may have presented a number of interim or special reports on it.

Time for report

All bills must be finally reported back to the House within a specified time. This must be a date certain and not a time fixed by reference to some uncertain event. This applies too to any extension to the report-back date. It is possible for the House, when referring a bill to a select committee, to instruct the committee to report the bill to the House by a particular date. The committee must present its final report on the bill no later than that date. The committee may present as many interim or special reports on the bill as it sees fit but it must have finalised a report and presented it to the House within any time constraint imposed on it by the House.

---

[136]   S.O.214.
[137]   2002-05, AJHR, I.22B, p.489 (*Smoke-free Environments (Enhanced Protection) Amendment Bill*).
[138]   S.O.300(2).
[139]   1999-2002, AJHR, I.22A, pp.604-5; *ibid.*, I.22B, p.610.
[140]   S.O.290(1).
[141]   S.O.268(2).

The House often imposes time constraints in the motion moved by the member in charge of the bill nominating the particular committee to consider the bill.[142] Committees have occasionally protested at the short time-frames that they have been given to report back on a bill[143] and individual members often protest that not enough time has been allowed for a committee to do a thorough job of considering a bill. A time constraint imposed by the House is a major factor in the time allowed for the public to make submissions on the bill. Ultimately, disputes over the time for report are matters for the House to resolve. Where no time for the committee to report back on a bill is fixed in the House's order referring the bill to the committee, the Standing Orders impose a backstop reporting time of six months for the final report to be made.[144] The House has accorded a longer reporting time than six months for a committee to report.[145]

The time for report starts to run from the date of the sitting day on which the bill is referred (which may not be the same as the actual calendar day). In the case of a bill that is referred to a committee to be set up, time starts to run from the date the bill is referred even though this may be some time before the committee is actually set up. If a bill, having been referred to one committee, is subsequently transferred to another committee, the six months' reporting time starts to run anew from the date of transfer. Where a bill has been reinstated in a new Parliament, no time runs from the date on which the bill lapsed to the date on which it was reinstated. In all cases if the time for reporting the bill would expire on a non-working day (when no report can be presented in any case) the bill is regarded as due for report on the next working day.[146]

If a committee has not presented its final report on a bill by the time fixed in the House's order referring the bill or by the expiry of the six months provided by the Standing Orders, the bill is automatically discharged from further consideration by the select committee and is set down as an order of the day for consideration at its next stage in the House on the third sitting day following its discharge from the committee.[147] In the case of a bill referred after its first reading, this will mean that the bill is set down for second reading.

Extension of time

Many bills receive an extension to the initial reporting deadline assigned to them. Often bills receive multiple extensions. It is always open to the House to change a reporting deadline (by extending or contracting it), either by altering one that it imposed when referring the bill to the committee or by subsequently imposing one in lieu of the six months' deadline imposed by the Standing Orders. This may be done on motion with notice or, more commonly, by leave of the House. Following a general election the House has extended the deadline for reporting all bills.[148]

In addition, the Business Committee has power to extend reporting times for any bill.[149] The Business Committee cannot contract a reporting deadline. Committees that conclude that they cannot meet a reporting deadline write to the Business Committee and seek its agreement to an extension. The Business Committee has indicated to all select committees that it will not approve extensions without having been informed of the views of the member in charge of the bill on the proposal. Consequently, the committee's letter to the Business Committee either includes these views or is accompanied by a separate notification from that member setting them out. Failure to communicate them will invariably result in a decision on the extension application being deferred.

---

[142] S.O.286(3).
[143] 1996-99, AJHR, I.24, pp.753-4 (*Immigration Amendment Bill*).
[144] S.O.291(1).
[145] 2002, Vol.603, p.791 (*Hop Industry Restructuring Bill* – a seven-month deadline).
[146] S.O.3(1).
[147] S.O.291(3).
[148] 2002, Vol.602, p.54.
[149] S.O.291(2).

Usually, if the select committee and the member in charge are in agreement, the Business Committee will approve an extension, but occasionally, if it considers the extension sought to be unreasonably long or unrealistically short, it will substitute a date of its own. Where the select committee and the member differ over the extension, the Business Committee makes its own judgment of whether to grant one and, if so, for how long.

Form of report

A select committee's final report on a bill conveys two things to the House—

- it sets out in a narrative form (called a 'commentary') how the committee carried out its consideration of the bill and what its conclusions are with regard to the passing of the bill and any amendments that might be made to it
- if there are any recommended amendments, it indicates textually on a copy of the bill precisely what those proposed amendments are.

This form of reporting to the House was adopted following a Standing Orders Committee recommendation in 1995.[150] Previously select committee reports on bills had generally been confined to indicating textual amendments to bills without any supporting narrative describing the reasons for the committees' conclusions. These, insofar as they could be ascertained at all, appeared in the speeches of the members (especially the chairperson) when a report was debated in the House. Now select committee commentaries contain extensive material describing the committees' legislative work and discussing the substantive policy and drafting issues that confronted them in the course of considering particular bills.

Subject to it complying with any particular Standing Orders requirements,[151] how each committee's commentary is drafted is a matter for it to decide. Commentaries often describe the differing views of members or parties on the issues that have been considered. Indeed as there is no convention of collective responsibility attaching to committees, there is no expectation that committees should present unanimous views. Committees have therefore been urged to canvass the differing views of their membership in their reports.[152] Thus where a committee is divided on whether a bill should be passed, the majority opinions in favour of its passing have been described in the commentary party by party and then the minority opinions similarly set out party by party.[153]

Occasionally a committee may be evenly split on how to report a bill back to the House. In these circumstances the committee has reported the impasse and indicated that it was unable to make a recommendation on the future of the bill.[154] The committee, though split on the future of the bill, may be able to agree to present a report describing the differing views of its members or of the parties represented on the committee. Committee reports have done this even though the committee itself could make no recommendations.[155]

The fact that a select committee report records split views can make it unreliable as an aid to determining Parliament's intention where a question of statutory interpretation arises,[156] though the majority's view has been taken to represent the parliamentary intention.[157]

---

[150]   1993-96, AJHR, I.18A, p.44.

[151]   S.O.287(4).

[152]   1993-96, AJHR, I.18A, p.44.

[153]   1996-99, AJHR, I.24, pp.795-800 (*Paid Parental Leave Bill*).

[154]   1996-99, AJHR, I.22, p.314 (*Limits on Campaign Spending for Candidates in Local Elections Bill*); 1999-2002, AJHR, I.22B, p.986 (*Police Amendment Bill (No 2)*).

[155]   1996-99, AJHR, I.23, p.765 (*Social Security (Conjugal Status) Amendment Bill*); 1999-

2002, AJHR, I.22A, p.573 (*Electoral (Integrity) Amendment Bill*).

[156]   *Vela Fishing Ltd v Commissioner of Inland Revenue* [2001] 1 NZLR 437 at [129-131] (reversed on other grounds [2002] 1 NZLR 49).

[157]   As, for example, in *Norske Skog Tasman Ltd v Clarke* [2004] 3 NZLR 323 at [51] (per Anderson P and William Young J).

Majority amendments

Committees are obliged to distinguish in their reports between those amendments which were adopted unanimously by the committee and those adopted by a majority of the committee.[158] Amendments must be distinguished in the report in this way because the House will later be asked specifically whether it agrees to majority amendments.[159]

Reports on private bills

The committee's report on a private bill must indicate whether the statements contained in the bill's preamble have been proved to the committee's satisfaction.[160] If the objects of the bill could be attained otherwise than by legislation, the preamble must state why legislation is preferred.[161] This will be a crucial matter for the committee to address in deciding whether to recommend the bill's passage. The question of an alternative to legislation is an issue that must be confronted in the committee's report.

The preamble may be proved to the committee's satisfaction even though the committee decides to amend it. Only if the amendment were of a major nature would it be necessary for the committee to conclude that the preamble had not been proved. A finding that the preamble has not been proved does not automatically kill the bill, though it will obviously count against its passing.

Suitability of using Local Legislation bills

The committee considering a Local Legislation Bill must report on the appropriateness of using that bill as the vehicle for the particular legislative changes being proposed. A Local Legislation Bill is an alternative to having several local bills but if an amendment proposed for inclusion in it is of particular significance it may be more appropriate for the amendment to be introduced as a separate local bill. The committee is required to address this and report specifically on it.[162] It is likely that if the committee concludes that a clause of a Local Legislation Bill should more properly have been introduced as a local bill, it will recommend the omission of that clause from the bill.

Reports on associated topics

A committee can, in the same report, make a report on a bill that has been referred to it and on associated matters. That is a matter for the committee to decide. Conversely, a committee is not bound to bring reports on associated matters back to the House with a report on a bill. Bills are often reported back to the House along with linked petitions[163] or with supplementary order papers relating to the bill that have been specially referred to the committee.[164] In each case it is up to the committee whether to present one or separate reports.

PRESENTATION OF REPORTS

A select committee report on a bill is presented like any other select committee report by delivering it to the Clerk on any working day or before 1 pm on any day on which the House sits.[165]

It is the duty of the chairperson to present the report to the House within a reasonable

---

158 S.O.288(4).
159 S.O.294(1).
160 S.O.287(2).
161 S.O.259.
162 S.O.287(3).

163 For example, 1996-99, AJHR, I.24, p.252 (*Human Rights Amendment Bill (No 2)*).
164 For example, 1987-90, JHR, p.1490 (*Local Legislation Bill*).
165 S.O.250(1).

time of being directed to do so by the committee. This does not mean at once and a delay of up to a week in presenting a report is quite acceptable.[166] It is desirable in any case for the chairperson to refrain from presenting the report until the commentary has been printed and the bill reprinted to show the amendments which the committee has recommended. Ideally there should be no hiatus between presentation of the report and its availability for public dissemination in printed form though this always depends upon the size and amount of work to be done on the reprinted bill.[167] A delay in presentation by the chairperson to facilitate its reprinting before presentation of the report is therefore desirable.

REPRINTING OF BILLS

A bill must be reprinted to show the amendments recommended by a select committee and reprinted copies of it provided to the Clerk by the member in charge of the bill.[168] Bills are reprinted according to a standard style that indicates clearly on them any provisions that the committee has recommended be omitted from the bill and, conversely, provisions that the committee recommends for insertion in the bill. Occasionally this standard style is departed from in the interests of clarity. Thus, where the amendments recommended by a committee were so extensive that it would have been almost impossible to illustrate them by showing omitted and inserted material, the bill was printed "clean" to show it in the form that the committee recommended that it proceed. The amendments proposed by the committee were listed separately in a schedule.[169] In another case where a bill had been split out of another bill and extensively amended, it was also printed clean but this time with the addition of a "finding chart" that enabled the reader to identify the equivalent clause (if one existed) in earlier versions of the larger bill.[170]

On 1 January 1997 the Parliamentary Counsel Office adopted a number of changes in drafting style. On 8 September 1999 a number of Standing Orders changes affecting the format of bills were adopted and on 1 January 2000 the format of legislation underwent considerable change as a result of other design changes adopted at that time. Whenever bills introduced before any of these events are being reprinted, the Clerk of the House, in consultation with the Chief Parliamentary Counsel and the Commissioner of Inland Revenue (for tax bills) may make changes to the bill to ensure that it complies with the new Standing Orders and conforms to the new format. No such change can alter the meaning of the bill.[171]

Though reporting back a bill with amendment always involves reprinting it, the Speaker may agree to dispense with this requirement if only minor textual amendments are involved.[172] Thus, when committees recommended only a change to the date shown in the title in one bill[173] and the pluralising of a word in another,[174] the Speaker directed that the bills not be reprinted as this was not justifiable for such small amendments. Committees have occasionally reported a bill back without amendment but with a recommendation that the committee of the whole House make amendments to it where the amendments were not considered of sufficient importance to warrant reprinting the bill or, given the speed with which it was expected that the bill would proceed through the House, there would not be time to reprint it.[175]

A bill is not available for debate until copies of it, as reprinted, have been circulated to members.[176]

---

[166] 1995, Vol.552, p.10603 (*Hospitals Amendment Bill*).
[167] 2002, Vol.605, p.2704 (*Local Government Bill*).
[168] S.O.268(2), (3)(a).
[169] *Children and Young Persons Bill* 1986.
[170] *Taxation Reform Bill* 1990.
[171] 2002, Vol.602, pp.308-9.
[172] S.O.268(2)(c).

[173] 1986, Vol.472, pp.2850-1 (*New Zealand Mission Trust Board Empowering Bill*).
[174] 1991, Vol.517, p.3148 (*Invercargill Reserves Vesting and Empowering Bill*).
[175] 1987-90, AJHR, I.1, p.7 (*Tariff Bill* 1988).
[176] S.O.268(3)(c); 2002, Vol.605, pp.2704-5 (*Local Government Bill*).

SETTING BILL DOWN FOR SECOND READING

Once the committee's final report on a bill has been presented, the bill is set down for second reading on the third sitting day following.[177] An adverse select committee report on a bill – indeed one that recommends that the bill not proceed – does not kill the bill at that point.[178] It is still set down for second reading.[179] It is for the House to determine its fate when it next considers the bill. The bill will be available for debate as a Government, Member's or local and private order of the day depending upon which type of bill it is. An interim or special report on a bill is also set down for consideration as an order of the day on the third sitting day following.[180] In the case of bills that were introduced before 18 October 1999 (the date on which the forty-fifth Parliament was dissolved) and consequently had their second reading before referral to a select committee, the committee's report is set down for consideration by the House on the third sitting day following.[181]

The bill, at this stage, stands on the order paper as an order of the day for second reading. The order in which Government bills are taken is largely in the hands of the Government. Members', private and local bills are considered in the order prescribed by the Standing Orders. (See Chapter 14.) If the House has ordered that something be done before the second reading of a bill, that something must be done or the order of the House requiring it to be done must be rescinded before the second reading can take place. Thus, the Speaker would not permit the second reading of a bill to proceed where the House had ordered that a return be tabled before its second reading and the return had not been made to the House.[182]

When the order of the day for a bill's second reading is reached it is possible for any member to move to discharge it and for the bill to be referred back to a select committee for further consideration. There is no amendment or debate on this question.[183] If a bill is referred back to a select committee in this way, any recommended amendments will not have been adopted and so will not have become part of the bill, though, no doubt, the committee will take account of the work that has already been done when it considers the bill anew.

SECOND READING

The second reading of a bill is the stage at which the House is asked to adopt, in principle, the bill before it (including any amendments to it proposed by the select committee). While there may be changes to details after this stage, the House is being asked here to make a fundamental commitment as to the basic desirability of passing the bill at all.

When the order of the day for the second reading of a bill is reached, the Speaker calls upon the member in charge to move the motion "That the ... *Bill* be now read a second time".[184] While one member may act for an absent member in moving the motion, a non-Minister cannot move a motion in respect of a Government bill. The debate is limited to 12 speeches each of a maximum duration of 10 minutes.[185]

A much wider discussion on the bill is permitted at this stage than at any other, but members are still expected to discuss the main purpose and contents of the bill and matters reasonably related to it, and not to deal at length with matters not provided for in the bill.[186] While members should direct their attention to the bill as it is before them, they may indicate their intention to move amendments to the bill in the committee of the whole

---

[177] S.O.292(a).
[178] 1914, Vol.170, p.519.
[179] 1901, Vol.118, p.619.
[180] S.O.292(b).
[181] 2002, Vol.602, pp.308-9.
[182] 1901, Vol.119, p.715 (*Maori Lands Administration Bill*).

[183] S.O.71(1)(a) and (2).
[184] S.O.293.
[185] Appendix A to the Standing Orders.
[186] 1936, Vol.244, pp.837-8 (*Primary Products Marketing Bill*).

House, and it is legitimate for a member to state any reasons for this. However, a detailed debate on proposed changes to the bill is not permissible.[187] Members proposing to move amendments to their own bills usually place such amendments on a supplementary order paper for the information of members, and these may be circulated at any time, even before the second reading. If available at that time, a supplementary order paper may be referred to in general terms during the second reading debate, but not discussed in detail.[188] However, where a supplementary order paper is not only available but has itself been considered and reported on by a select committee, it can be discussed freely along with the bill.[189] Members should not refer to a supplementary order paper which has not yet been circulated, beyond making passing reference to its existence.[190] The question of the admissibility of amendments that members intend to move is a matter for the chairperson to deal with when the bill is considered in committee; it is not for the Speaker to rule on.[191]

Where the bill under debate is one amending an Act already in force (and most bills are of this nature), members may point out further amendments they think should be made to the principal Act but they cannot begin a debate outside the scope of the question before the House.[192] The fact that a bill is an amending bill does not make everything in the principal Act relevant in the debate. Only those sections of it directly affected by the amending bill and any of its other sections of general effect, such as the interpretation section, may be referred to.

Cognate bills

Sometimes the House has before it two or more bills on a related subject-matter – cognate bills. In the debate on one it may be very difficult to prevent debate spilling over to encompass the other or others. To deal with this, it may be agreed to take all the bills together for the purposes of discussion, permitting members to refer to all of the cognate bills on the order paper. At the conclusion of the debate the question for the second reading of each is put separately.[193] Cognate bills which have been dealt with in this way include similar bills establishing new universities and agricultural colleges and bills dealing with discipline in each of the branches of the armed forces. In practice, today, these matters are likely to be introduced in one omnibus bill.

The Standing Orders provide that the second reading debate on any Imprest Supply Bill may be taken together with the third reading of the main Appropriation Bill and with the second reading of an Appropriation (Supplementary Estimates) Bill.[194]

In every other case it is a matter for the leave of the House as to whether bills are treated as cognate bills.

AMENDMENTS ON SECOND READING

On the second reading of a bill members are asked to endorse the bill by giving it a second reading, but they may instead decide to defer a decision on it or decide definitively that it should not proceed. Deferral or defeat can also be effected by amending the question for the bill's second reading.

The question for the second reading of the bill is open to amendment in a way that is relevant to one of these objects. An amendment which merely seeks to add words to the motion does not do either of these things. Such an amendment would attach

---

[187] 1920, Vol.186, p.517 (*Gaming Amendment Bill*).

[188] 1922, Vol.197, pp.187-8 (*Post and Telegraph Amendment Bill*).

[189] 1983, Vol.452, pp.2219-20 (*Transport Amendment Bill (No 4)*).

[190] 1975, Vol.398, p.2175.

[191] 1991, Vol.512, pp.273-4 (*Finance Bill*); 2005, Vol.627, p.2228 (*Resource Management and Electricity Legislation Amendment Bill*).

[192] 1924, Vol.203, p.752 (*Legislature Amendment Bill*).

[193] 1961, Vol.328, pp.2666-7 (*Universities Bill*).

[194] S.Os 332(3) and 334(2).

conditions to the second reading and leave the House's decision unclear.[195] There must be an unequivocal decision reached if a bill is to be read a second time. Nor is it possible simply to move that the bill do not proceed.[196] If that is what members desire they should vote against the second reading.

An amendment cannot be moved at this stage to refer the bill to a select committee.[197] The Standing Orders provide appropriate procedures for the referral of a bill to a select committee and this cannot be done by a side-wind on the question for the second reading. Neither can an amendment propose to refer a bill to another body which is outside the control of the House.[198]

Amendments to defer second reading

A traditional deferral amendment is one to omit the word "now" and to add at the end of the question "this day three months", "this day six months", or any other specified time. The time must be specified and cannot be reckoned by reference to an uncertain event (such as "three months after the report of a Royal Commission"[199]). This type of amendment (which involves consideration and decision of the main question[200]) does not overtly defeat the bill, but it is intended to have the effect, if carried, of fatally postponing the second reading.

Adverse or reasoned amendments

An amendment moved on the question for the second reading may put forward an abstract proposition relating to the bill – what is known as a reasoned amendment.[201] The proposition will be unfavourable to the bill receiving its second reading that day, but it must offer an alternative to the second reading. An amendment declining to give a bill a second reading until certain amendments had been made to it and the money saved expended in other ways, was accepted because it offered an alternative course of action to the second reading. If it had merely confined itself to suggesting the striking out of certain parts of the bill this would not have been in order, because the committee of the whole House could have done this later quite consistently with the bill being read a second time.[202] While the proposition put forward in a reasoned amendment is an abstract one, it must be closely related to the bill under consideration or it will be ruled out as not being relevant to the question. Thus an amendment to substitute for the question for the second reading the words "this House views with grave alarm the Government's proposal to embark on a course of uncontrolled inflation" was ruled out of order. The amendment neither offered an alternative to the second reading nor was it linked with the motion.[203]

Public affairs amendments

An amendment relating to public affairs that is not required to be strictly relevant to the bill may be moved to the questions for the second reading of an Imprest Supply Bill and the main Appropriation Bill.[204] This permits an amendment raising a question of confidence in the Government to be moved in the course of those debates. (See Chapter 7.)

Superseded orders

If an amendment adverse to reading the bill a second time that day is carried, the bill becomes what is known as a superseded order. This does not in itself formally kill the

---

[195] 1994, Vol.542, p.3188 (*Appropriation Bill (No 2)*).

[196] 2000, Vol.582, p.963 (*Accident Insurance (Transitional Provisions) Bill*).

[197] 1959, Vol.320, pp.1625-6, 1647 (*Land Settlement Promotion Amendment Bill*).

[198] 1975, Vol.397, p.869 (*Hospitals Amendment Bill*).

[199] *Ibid.*, p.900.

[200] 1962, Vol.333, pp.3170-1.

[201] 1975, Vol.397, pp.899-900 (*Hospitals Amendment Bill*).

[202] 1886, Vol.56, p.186 (*New Zealand Loan Bill*).

[203] 1939, Vol.256, p.832 (*Reserve Bank of New Zealand Amendment Bill*).

[204] S.Os 323(3) and 326(2).

bill. All the House has decided is that it will not read the bill a second time on that day. The bill disappears from the order paper and effectively disappears from parliamentary consciousness, though it can be revived on a subsequent day by being placed on the order paper.[205] In most cases, however, a superseded order is treated as disposing of the bill for that session at least.

FINANCIAL VETO OF SELECT COMMITTEE AMENDMENTS

Any amendments recommended to the House by a select committee are subject to financial veto by the Government on the ground that they may have more than a minor impact on the Government's fiscal aggregates.[206] (See Chapter 31 for the giving of financial veto certificates.) A financial veto relating to amendments recommended by a select committee must be given (if it is to be given at all) before the amendments are agreed to by the House.[207] Thus a financial veto certificate in relation to select committee amendments can be given at any time between the presentation of the report and the House taking a decision on the second reading of the bill because it is at that point that the House is deemed to adopt select committee amendments.[208]

Where select committee amendments are the subject of a financial veto they are omitted from the bill.[209] The bill is reprinted with them deleted. Such amendments cannot be moved again in the committee of the whole House.[210]

ADOPTION OF SELECT COMMITTEE AMENDMENTS

The amendments recommended by the select committee in its report to the House are just that – recommendations. Unless the amendments are adopted by the House they do not become part of the bill which is to proceed to its committee stage. At the second reading stage the House decides whether or not to adopt the amendments. This is solely a matter that the House decides as part of its internal proceedings. The question of whether the amendments recommended by a select committee are appropriate for inclusion in the bill is not a matter on which a court can intervene or express an opinion.[211]

A select committee in its report on a bill must distinguish between those amendments which it is recommending with the unanimous agreement of its members and those which were adopted by a majority vote of the committee.[212] This distinction parallels the two-stage decision that the House makes before the amendments are adopted.

At the conclusion of the debate on the second reading of a bill there are one or two questions put to the House depending upon whether the committee recommended any amendments by majority. If there are no majority amendments the question for the bill's second reading is put and determined. If it is agreed to, the select committee amendments are regarded as having been adopted by the House.[213] But if there are majority amendments two questions are put. The first asks the House specifically whether it agrees to the majority amendments. There can be no amendment or debate on this question.[214] Following the determination of this question, the question for the bill's second reading is put.[215] If the House agrees to the majority amendments they, and any amendments recommended unanimously, are regarded as having been adopted by the House when the bill is read a second time.[216]

If the House does not agree with majority amendments but does give the bill a second reading, the bill is reprinted with the majority amendments removed.

---

[205]   1924, Vol.204, p.201.
[206]   S.Os 318(1) and 321(1).
[207]   S.O.321(1).
[208]   S.O.296.
[209]   S.O.321(1).
[210]   S.O.321(3).

[211]   *Ram Dubey v Government of Madhya Bharat* AIR 1952 Madhya Bharat 57.
[212]   S.O.288(4).
[213]   S.O.296.
[214]   S.O.294(1).
[215]   S.O.294(2).
[216]   S.O.296.

CONSIDERATION OF REPORT

In the case of a bill introduced before the dissolution of the forty-fifth Parliament (October 1999), the second reading of the bill preceded its referral to a select committee. Consequently, such bills that were held over to the forty-sixth Parliament (and then held over to or reinstated in any subsequent Parliament) have already been read a second time when they come to be reported back to the House. Instead of a second reading, these bills therefore are the subject of a consideration of report stage at which the member in charge moves a motion to take note of the committee's report. The debate is subject to the same rules as a second reading debate.[217] At the conclusion of the debate the question for majority amendments is put first if there are any. The select committee's recommended amendments are deemed to be adopted when the House agrees to take note of the report.

SETTING BILL DOWN FOR COMMITTEE STAGE

When the question for its second reading has been carried, the bill is ready to proceed to its next stage, which is consideration by a committee of the whole House. For this purpose it is set down for consideration in committee on the next sitting day.[218] This means that its committee stage becomes an order of the day. In the case of Government bills, the Government will determine when it is considered. Other bills stand on the order paper in the priority determined by the Standing Orders. (See Chapter 14.)

Dispensing with committee stage

The Business Committee has the power to dispense with the committee stage of a bill and determine that it should proceed directly to its third reading. If it so determines, the order of the day is altered and the bill set down for third reading accordingly.[219] The Business Committee may make such a decision at any time between the order of the day for the committee stage being set down and the committee stage being held. Alternatively, the House itself may give leave to dispense with a committee stage and proceed forthwith with the third reading of the bill. In the case of Imprest Supply bills and Appropriation bills dealing with supplementary estimates, no committee stage is held unless the Minister in charge of the bills requires there to be one so that an amendment can be considered or, in the case of supplementary estimates, a change to a vote has been recommended by a select committee.[220] These bills therefore generally proceed directly from the second reading to the third reading stage.

CONSIDERATION BY A COMMITTEE OF THE WHOLE HOUSE

Consideration of a bill by a committee of the whole House is known as the committee stage in the passing of a bill. The House goes into committee to give the bill's provisions detailed consideration. It has been called "the nuts and bolts stage" at which the bill is considered clause by clause or part by part to decide whether its detailed provisions properly incorporate the principles or objects of the bill agreed to on second reading.[221] Unlike a select committee, a committee of the whole House is not required to give its opinion on whether the bill should be passed. The principal function of the committee of the whole House is to make any amendments to the bill's text that may be found to be desirable before it proceeds to be passed by the House.

---

[217] 2002, Vol.602, pp.308-9.
[218] S.O.295.
[219] *Ibid.*

[220] S.Os 323(4) and 334(3).
[221] S.O.297(1); 1970, Vol.368, p.2805 (*Post Office Amendment Bill (No 2)*).

There is a different committee of the whole House every time the House goes into committee. "Committee of the whole House" is only a shorthand expression for the different forms of proceedings that apply at this stage of a bill's passage. Considering a bill in committee gives all members of the House an opportunity to participate, if they wish, in a detailed consideration of the bill and to move amendments to its text. Without the committee stage, only the handful of members who had served on the select committee considering the bill would have this opportunity.

As with the order of the day for the second reading of a Government bill, the time at which the order of the day for a bill's committal is reached is largely in the hands of the Government. Members', private and local bills are considered in the order prescribed by the Standing Orders. (See Chapter 14.) When the order of the day for going into committee on a bill, or for going into committee for further consideration of a bill, is read, the Speaker leaves the chair without any question being put and the House automatically resolves itself into committee.[222] This contrasts with the former position on the committal of a bill, where a motion was moved that the House "do resolve itself into a Committee of the Whole". The debate on this motion for going into committee was formerly a substantive stage in the passage of a bill on which the main debate took place. Now, where a bill is concerned, no debate is possible at this point; the House goes into committee automatically after dealing with any instructions.

Strictly, each bill awaiting consideration in committee should be committed separately, but if there are a number of bills for committal standing consecutively on the order paper, the House usually goes into committee on all of them at the same time. When a number of Government bills are committed together in this way, the Government can have them taken in committee in any order it chooses.[223] Unless advised otherwise by the Government, the chairperson will adhere to the order in which the bills were set out on the order paper.

INSTRUCTIONS

The task of a committee of the whole House on a bill is defined in the Standing Orders. Such committees are specifically given the power to make amendments that are relevant to the subject-matter of the bill, are consistent with the principles and objects of the bill and otherwise conform to the Standing Orders and practices of the House.[224] This power to make amendments defines the committee's major task on a bill. A committee cannot make an amendment which is not relevant to the bill before it or which the Standing Orders otherwise forbid it to make, unless it is specially authorised by the House to do so. The House gives such special power by means of an instruction.

As well as instructions relating to the subject-matter of a bill, an instruction may relate to the procedure to be followed by the committee while it considers the bill, for example, as to the order or manner of considering the bill's provisions. An unusual use of a procedural instruction was to direct the committee to take important decisions on the substance of the bill at the outset of the committee stage and to leave the detailed examination of the bill until after these decisions have been made, so that any amendments could be made in the light of the committee's "in principle" decisions. This approach can considerably simplify consideration of bills since only amendments that implement or are consistent with those initial decisions can then be moved.

When an instruction has been given in respect of a particular bill the instruction endures for any second or subsequent occasion on which the House resolves itself into committee to consider that bill and does not require to be moved again on those occasions.

---

[222] S.O.171.
[223] 1880, Vol.37, p.604.
[224] S.O.297(2).

Restrictions on instructions

While an instruction is designed to extend the committee's regular powers in respect of the way it can deal with a bill, it must not be completely foreign to the bill or it will not be a proper instruction.[225] This is particularly significant in the case of amendments. An instruction can be used to widen the scope for accepting amendments that would not otherwise be in order; it cannot be used to introduce a subject that is totally irrelevant to the bill.[226] Each bill (except an omnibus bill) must relate to one subject area only.[227] It is not possible to confer power on the committee by way of instruction to introduce a new subject that should properly form the subject of a distinct measure. This rule is designed to prevent entirely new matters being tagged on to a bill with which they have no connection. In such a case the Standing Orders would need to be suspended.[228] Furthermore, the fact that a bill has progressed a significant distance through the legislative process must be borne in mind in considering the width of any instruction that may be moved. The House has given the bill a first and a second reading; the principle of the bill as it has progressed so far cannot be destroyed by the device of introducing an amendment at the committee stage by way of an instruction.[229]

Moving of instructions

A member may move only one instruction in relation to the same bill.[230] (The general rules for moving and debating instructions are described in Chapter 20.)

PROCEDURE IN COMMITTEE

In committee on a bill the member in charge of the bill sits at the Table on the right of the chairperson. Departmental officials or other advisers sit behind the member in charge on the seats to the right of the Speaker's chair. Officials, while they may not come on to the floor of the House itself, are readily able to communicate with their Minister from this position while the committee stage is in progress. In the case of a Government bill, in the Minister's absence another Minister may act as Minister in charge, but this may draw protests from other members as an acting Minister is not likely to have the detailed knowledge of a bill's provisions required at the committee stage.[231]

A committee of the whole House goes through a bill's provisions sequentially. It may make amendments to any provision in the bill provided that these are relevant to the subject-matter of the bill, consistent with its principles and objects and otherwise considered admissible by the House.[232] The committee may order a clause or part to be divided. It may change the order of the clauses or parts set out in the bill.

Occasionally, the committee's task is radically redefined for it by way of an instruction. This can occur where it is desirable for the committee to reach some "in principle" decisions about alternative amendments before embarking on a detailed textual consideration of the bill. Rather than taking an in principle decision on a series of detailed drafts it may be easier to take such a decision on a short descriptive summary of each alternative and then, having taken that decision, come back to considering a single detailed draft that implements that decision. Where it is useful to tailor committee procedure in this way this has been done by instruction.

The select committee report on the *Sale of Liquor Amendment Bill (No 2)* 1999 set out a detailed blueprint for the procedure to be followed during the committee stage of

---

[225] 1993, Vol.534, pp.14421-2 (*Taxation Reform Bill (No 2)*).
[226] *May*, p.595.
[227] S.O.261(1).
[228] See, for example, 2001, Vol.591, p.8613 (*Fisheries*

(*Remedial Issues) Amendment Bill*).
[229] 1931, Vol.227, p.437.
[230] *May*, p.599.
[231] 1990, Vol.506, p.915.
[232] S.O.297(2).

that bill. It recommended that the committee stage be in two phases. The first would take a "themed" approach whereby the committee would make in principle decisions on 11 outstanding issues (minimum drinking age, opening hours, etc) on which various options had been identified (for example, age 18, 19 or 20 for the minimum drinking age). Once the committee had made decisions on these issues the committee stage would be interrupted while drafting proceeded to implement these decisions. For the second phase, the committee stage would resume on the usual basis to examine the proposed amendments to ensure that they properly implemented the committee's in principle decisions but with any attempt to reopen those decisions themselves being out of order. After discussion at the Business Committee, this procedure was adopted.[233]

A similar two-stage "themed" and "textual" approach to the committee stage was subsequently followed with another bill that required in principle decisions for a number of options to be taken before detailed drafting work could be undertaken.[234] Generally bills justifying this treatment involve conscience issues where there are multiple alternatives offered by way of amendment to their provisions.

Delegation of functions

A committee of the whole House has no power to delegate or transfer its functions to other bodies or organisations. The committee cannot refer a provision or proposed amendment to a select committee, and such a motion, if moved in committee, will not be accepted by the chairperson.[235] Similarly, the committee cannot refer a provision to the Government with a recommendation for amendment. The committee's job is to go through the bill and make its own decisions and it must discharge this task itself.[236] It cannot adjourn its own sitting, or the consideration of a bill, to a future sitting,[237] although it can report to the House what progress (or lack of progress) it has made and effectively ask the House to adjourn further consideration by the committee.

SPEAKING IN COMMITTEE

On most questions in committee on a bill a member may speak on up to four occasions for not more than five minutes on each occasion.[238] On the title clause, however, a member has only three opportunities to speak.[239] The member in charge is not subject to any limitation on the number of speeches he or she may make. Although the member in charge's individual speeches are subject to the same time limits as any other members', the member in charge may, at the chairperson's discretion, be called to take two consecutive calls, but not normally more than this.[240]

Except where otherwise provided, the same rules for debate apply in committee as apply in the House.[241]

ORDER OF CONSIDERING BILL

A bill's provisions are considered in committee in the following order[242]—
- the preamble (if there is one)
- the parts or clauses, other than the preliminary clauses
- the schedules (if any)
- the preliminary clauses, that is, the title and commencement clauses.[243]

Under the Standing Orders, if a bill is drafted in parts there is a presumption that the

---

[233] 1996-99, AJHR, I.24, p.473; 1999, Vol.579, pp.18556-8.
[234] 2000, Vol.583, pp.1926-51 (*Matrimonial Property Amendment Bill*).
[235] 1973, Vol.387, p.4704 (*Land and Income Tax Amendment Bill*).
[236] 1923, Vol.201, p.619 (*War Pensions Amendment Bill*).
[237] S.O.181.
[238] Appendix A to the Standing Orders.
[239] *Ibid.*
[240] *Ibid.*
[241] S.O.174.
[242] S.O.298(2), (3).
[243] S.O.3(1).

committee will consider it part by part.[244] The committee may be directed by the House by way of instruction to consider the bill in another way – such as clause by clause – or to consider provisions in another sequence. Alternatively, the committee itself may decide to consider the bill's provisions other than part by part.[245] Select committees in reporting a bill back to the House occasionally suggest that at the committee stage the bill's provisions be considered in a different order from that in which the bill is drafted.[246]

Debate

The chairperson begins the debate on each provision as it is reached, by proposing that the provision (preamble, clause or part, as the case may be) stand part of the bill.[247] In proposing the question on a provision the chairperson reads only its number.[248] Where no member of the committee wishes to speak to any provisions in the bill, the committee often allows the chairperson to put the question on the bill's provisions *in toto*, without reading each one separately. The proposing of each provision by the chairperson, without a motion from the floor that such provision stand part, is an exception to the general rules on the process of debate. In this case the motions are in effect deemed to be moved by the Standing Orders, and the chairperson is required to frame the necessary questions accordingly. Other motions may be moved in committee (such as for a new part or to amend a part, or to report progress to the House), but the basic work to be transacted by the committee is as prescribed by the Standing Orders and requires no mover to spark it off.

Debate on each provision must be strictly relevant to that provision and must be confined to it.[249] An amendment that is outside the scope of a bill does not permit the scope of debate on a provision to be widened.[250]

The debate terminates by the carrying of a closure motion or when no member wishes to speak. If no member does seek the call the chairperson puts the question on any amendments that have been lodged. Once the chairperson has begun to do this there can be no further debate.[251]

At the conclusion of the debate or after any amendments have been dealt with, the chairperson puts the question that the provision under debate stand part of the bill. In the case of a Statutes Amendment Bill (or a bill that was formerly part of a Statutes Amendment Bill that has been divided) any member has the right to object to a clause of the bill standing part of it. Objection is made at this point. Where there is objection, the clause is struck out of the bill.[252]

Preamble

If a bill does not have a preamble when it is introduced, one cannot be inserted by the committee of the whole House.[253] A preamble describes the circumstances that led to the bill's promotion; if there is to be one it should be prepared before the bill is submitted to the House, not concocted *ex post facto*. In practice, few bills (except private bills and treaty settlement bills) have preambles.

Consideration part by part

The effect of considering a bill in parts is to aggregate consideration of each clause within a part into one debate on that part, thus saving time in committee. The title clause and the commencement clause (the preliminary clauses) are not usually contained in a part

---

[244] S.O.298(1), (2).
[245] S.O.298(1)(b).
[246] 1987-90, AJHR, I.23A, p.49 (*Sale of Liquor Bill*); 1996-99, AJHR, I.24, p.473 (*Sale of Liquor Amendment Bill (No 2)*).
[247] S.O.300(1).
[248] S.O.299.
[249] 1924, Vol.205, p.728.
[250] 2004, Vol.621, p.16473 (*Parental Leave and Employment Protection Bill*).
[251] 1994, Vol.544, pp.4965-6.
[252] S.O.300(2).
[253] *May*, p.616.

at all, since their provisions relate to the whole bill. In these circumstances the first part of the bill commences with the third clause of the bill. Where the committee takes a bill part by part this includes any new parts to the bill set out as proposed amendments on a supplementary order paper.[254] But new parts to be inserted in the principal Act are not taken separately. These will be authorised by a clause in the bill which will be considered along with the part in which that clause is contained, not as a separate debate.[255]

Procedure on part-by-part consideration

The question proposed by the chairperson at the commencement of each part is "That part 1 (etc) of the bill stand part".[256] No separate question is proposed on each clause within the part, but amendments can be proposed to a clause, even to omit it entirely – something (as a direct negative) that would not be permitted if the bill was being considered clause by clause.

Debate may range widely over each part. There is no sequencing of clauses within each part for the purposes of debate when a bill is being taken part by part.[257] The chairperson generally allows a longer time for the committee to debate a part before a closure motion is accepted than would be the case on debating an individual clause and will permit a longer debate on a large part that contains numerous subparts than on a more confined part.[258]

In debating each part, any schedule or schedules of the bill relating to the part are debated along with the part.[259] At the end of the committee's consideration of all the parts, the questions on each schedule are then put separately but without any further debate.[260]

Consideration clause by clause

If a bill is not drafted in parts,[261] or if the committee is instructed by the House to do so, or itself decides to do so,[262] a committee considers the bill in sequence clause by clause.[263] The schedules of a bill are considered along with any clauses to which they relate.[264]

It is a matter for the judgment of the chairperson as to how long to permit for debate on each clause before accepting a closure motion.

Preliminary clauses

The Standing Orders require that every bill contain separate title and commencement clauses.[265] These clauses are known as the bill's preliminary clauses.[266] It is the practice not to include these clauses in a distinct part of the bill. Where a bill is considered part by part (which is the case with most bills), the preliminary clauses are debated together and are considered after all other provisions of the bill (including schedules) have been dealt with. The question on each clause is put separately.[267]

The debate on the title clause (formerly known as the Short Title) was previously different from the debate on the other clauses, not only in the different speaking rights that were attached to it but also in the scope of debate. In the Short Title debate, members were permitted to refer to all the clauses and schedules contained in the bill and were not restricted to that clause which is, after all, a very narrow clause. This wide debate on the title clause was abolished in 1992.

---

[254] 1991, Vol.512, p.319 (*Finance Bill*).
[255] 2003, Vol.611, p.8814 (*Smoke-free Environments Amendment Bill*).
[256] 1970, Vol.368, p.3167 (*Payroll Tax Bill*).
[257] 1998, Vol.569, p.10433 (*Electricity Industry Reform Bill*).
[258] 2003, Vol.607, p.4421 (*Resource Management Amendment Bill (No 2)*).
[259] S.O.298(2)(c).

[260] S.O.298(2)(d).
[261] S.O.298(1)(a).
[262] S.O.298(1)(b).
[263] S.O.298(3)(a).
[264] S.O.298(3)(b).
[265] S.Os 256(1) and 257(1).
[266] S.O.3(1).
[267] S.O.298(2)(e).

In principle, the debate on the preliminary clauses is limited to the elements of the clauses and any amendments that may be proposed to them.[268] The elements of the title clause, and thus the scope of the debate on it, are essentially limited to the bill's name.[269] However, members are accorded some latitude when debating the preliminary clauses at the end of the committee stage to summarise, and make concluding remarks about, the issues that they have raised during the committee's consideration of the bill.[270]

Although now usually considered towards the end of the committee stage, the title clause is still regarded as a significant clause because, if the committee rejects it, this is a definite expression of the committee's opinion against the bill. In such a case the committee either reports progress or goes on with the next bill before it (if there is more than one bill before the committee). The committee, when it comes to report, merely reports the rejection of the title clause, and the bill is dropped from the order paper.[271]

Schedules

The schedules are considered along with the parts or clauses to which they relate, though they are voted on separately.[272] They are subject to amendment on the same principles as the clauses or parts.

Postponement of provision

Subject to any direction by the House or any decision by the committee to the contrary, the member in charge of the bill has the right, as the bill is progressing through the committee, to require that consideration or further consideration of any provision of the bill be postponed.[273] (Thus any provision of the bill that is under consideration or is to be considered may be postponed.) The member is not confined to using this power for any particular reasons and does not have to give any reasons for doing so. However, it has been acknowledged that it is in the interests of good order for some reasons to be given to the committee either informally through the whips or by way of a short statement at the time the member raises a point of order to require the postponement.[274] The reasons given are not debatable. Any provision may be postponed by the member in charge in this way, including a new part offered by way of amendment by another member.[275]

The member postponing a provision can specify a special place in the bill for its consideration to be resumed. Alternatively, when a provision has been postponed, the committee may return to it when it by resolution decides. If the member does not specify when a postponed provision is to be resumed and the committee does not deal with this itself, a postponed clause or part is considered when all other remaining clauses or parts (as the case may be), other than the preliminary clauses, have been considered[276] and a postponed preamble or schedule is considered when all other provisions of the bill have been dealt with.[277] A provision postponed while the House is sitting under urgency may be resumed during that same period of urgency.[278]

Transfer of a provision

A provision may be transferred from one position in the bill to another.[279] Transfer is

---

[268] 1993, Vol.534, p.14901 (*Health and Disability Services Bill*); 1997, Vol.559, p.1493 (*Taxation (Income Tax Rates) Bill*).

[269] 1992, Vol.531, p.12129 (*Local Legislation Bill*).

[270] 2002-05, AJHR, I.18B, p.63; 2004, Vol.620, p.16022 (*Electricity and Gas Industries Bill*); 2004, Vol.621, p.16489 (*Parental Leave and Employment Protection Bill*).

[271] 1927, Vol.213, pp.1082-3 (*Legislature Amendment*

Bill (No 2)).

[272] S.Os 298(2)(c), (d), (3)(b), (c).

[273] S.O.298(1)(b).

[274] 2000, Vol.586, pp.4546, 4548.

[275] *Ibid.*, p.4546.

[276] S.O.298(4)(a).

[277] S.O.298(4)(b).

[278] 2000, Vol.586, p.4246 (*Employment Relations Bill*).

[279] *May*, p.602.

effected by a motion to this effect, moved when the provision is reached.[280] The intention to move for the transfer of a provision is included on any list of proposed amendments to the bill circulated to members. A part, clause, subclause,[281] or schedule[282] may be transferred to a new position in the bill.

Where the committee considers a provision out of sequence, either by leave or at the behest of the member in charge, this does not transfer that provision to a different position in the bill. Only a specific order of the committee to transfer the provision effects such a change.

Division of a provision

A provision may be divided into two or more separate provisions on motion.[283] Such a motion is taken at the end of the debate on the provision concerned but ahead of any amendments to it.[284] The intention to move to divide a provision is shown as a proposed amendment on any supplementary order paper circulated to members.

AMENDMENTS

Form of amendments

A proposed amendment may be framed as an amendment to the preamble or to a clause, a part or a schedule, or it may be a motion to add a wholly new clause, part or schedule to the bill. New provisions are considered in their numerical order in the bill.

A new provision to be inserted in the bill is distinguished by a letter after its number. New provisions added by the select committee to the bill as it was originally introduced are indicated in a similar manner. By the time the bill reaches the committee of the whole House provisions added by a select committee are not new provisions as far as the committee of the whole House is concerned; they are, by this time, an integral part of the bill having been adopted by the House at the second reading. The select committee may also have recommended that certain provisions be omitted and the bill may thus no longer include all of the clauses, parts or schedules it had when it was introduced. Therefore, by the time a bill reaches a committee of the whole House the numbering of its provisions may not be straightforward. The important thing, however, is that each provision is assigned a number or a number and letter which will enable it to be correctly and uniquely identified; the consecutive numbering of the bill can be tidied up when it is being prepared for the Royal assent.

Manner of lodging

A member may give notice of amendments he or she intends to move by lodging a written copy of them with the Clerk of the House, who then arranges for the amendments to be printed on what is known as a supplementary order paper.[285] This is a formal House document which is prepared in accordance with the Standing Orders. The parliamentary counsel responsible for drafting the bill arranges for the preparation of supplementary order papers containing ministerial amendments. Supplementary order papers may contain an explanatory note explaining the purport of the amendments they contain but there is no requirement for this.[286]

---

[280]   1990, JHR, pp.475-6 (*Health Research Council Bill*); 1991-93, JHR, p.1623 (*Crown Research Institutes Bill*); 1993-96, JHR, p.884 (*Land Transport Law Reform Bill*).

[281]   1996-99, JHR, p.408 (*Taxation (Remedial Provisions) Bill (No 2)*).

[282]   1991-93, JHR, p.2766 (*Privacy Bill*).

[283]   *May*, p.602.

[284]   1979, JHR, p.156 (*Electoral Amendment Bill*); 1993-96, JHR, p.809 (*Births, Deaths, and Marriages Registration Bill*).

[285]   S.O.301.

[286]   2002, Vol.602, pp.584-6 (*Social Security (Personal Development and Employment) Amendment Bill*); 2005, Vol.627, pp.22279-80 (*Resource Management and Electricity Legislation Amendment Bill*).

A supplementary order paper is circulated through the members' bill boxes or around the Chamber itself at a time decided upon by the Minister or member. Authority to circulate a supplementary order paper must be given explicitly by the member; it cannot be assumed by the Clerk.[287]

Where a member's proposed amendments are not placed on a supplementary order paper for circulation, six copies must be handed to the Clerk at the Table.[288] These copies are then available for perusal by other members.

Time for lodging

In general, there is no time at which proposed amendments must be lodged or circulated. They may be lodged at any time between the bill's introduction and the conclusion of the debate on the provision to be amended. Thus, supplementary order papers have been circulated as early as the introduction of a bill, and are occasionally themselves referred to a select committee for consideration. Once a closure motion on a question has been accepted by the chairperson no further amendments may then be lodged (though if the closure motion is defeated and debate continues further amendments may be lodged).

There is one time restriction which members must comply with otherwise their amendments will not be in order. In respect of any amendment which may have an impact on the Government's fiscal aggregates members must give notice of the amendment by lodging it with the Clerk at least 24 hours before the House meets on the day on which the amendment is to be moved.[289] But this requirement only applies if the bill in respect of which the amendment is proposed is actually set down for its committee stage on that day.[290] It does not apply, for instance, in respect of a bill introduced under urgency and passed through all its stages or to a bill that is before the House but which had not yet reached its committee stage and whose committee stage is expedited by urgency. In such cases members would not have had notice that the time limit for the circulation of amendments affecting the Government's fiscal aggregates was running against them.

An amendment is lodged with the Clerk for the purposes of the fiscal aggregates rule when the member gives authority for it to be circulated and thus made public.[291] An amendment cannot be "lodged" with the Clerk for this purpose if it is still to remain confidential. Authority to the Clerk to circulate an amendment can be given when the amendment is in proper form. Circulation can be effected as a supplementary order paper or in manuscript form.[292]

Moving amendments

A member who has a proposed new provision on a supplementary order paper is deemed to have moved it when called on to speak. If the member does not wish to move it, he or she should not accept the call. A member is not obliged to proceed with an amendment on a supplementary order paper,[293] though an amendment cannot be withdrawn without leave after a closure motion has been accepted.[294]

In the case of amendments to a part members do not formally move such amendments during the course of the debate on the part. The debate in committee is held entirely on the main question, that the part stand part of the bill. Members are able in speaking to this question to refer to any amendment on a supplementary order paper or amendment

---

[287] 2000, Vol.582, pp.1224-5.
[288] S.O.302(2).
[289] S.O.322(1).
[290] S.O.322(3).

[291] 2000, Vol.582, p.1224-5.
[292] *Ibid.*
[293] 1991, Vol.518, p.3677.
[294] 1986, Vol.470, p.1052.

in writing that has been handed in to the Table.[295]   But they cannot speak on matters outside the scope of the part by the expedient of handing in an irrelevant amendment; the chairperson still retains the right to maintain relevancy in debate. A similar rule applies in respect to amendments to a clause when a bill is being considered clause by clause.

ADMISSIBLE AMENDMENTS

A committee of the whole House may make amendments to a bill that are relevant to the subject-matter of the bill, are consistent with the bill's principles and objects and otherwise conform to the Standing Orders and to the practices of the House.[296] The permitted range of amendments that a committee may make to a bill can best be explored by considering what kinds of amendments are inadmissible on grounds of relevancy, inconsistency, direct Standing Orders prohibition or lack of conformity to practice.

INADMISSIBLE AMENDMENTS

Amendments outside the scope of the bill

An amendment that is not relevant to the bill is often described as being outside the scope of the bill. Such an amendment is inadmissible. The bill cannot be turned into something that it is not or that it did not start out as.[297]

Amendments outside the scope of the bill have been variously described as foreign to the bill,[298] outside its purview,[299] or not within the leave to introduce the bill granted by the House.[300] It is now provided in the Standing Orders that a bill must relate to one subject area only (except those omnibus bills that are specifically permitted).[301] Any attempt to introduce a second subject area into a bill would inevitably be outside the bill's scope in any case.

When a bill is introduced it defines its own relevancy; that is, the perimeter within which its details may be amended as a result of select committee proposals and by the committee of the whole House. A narrow view of the scope of a bill is not taken for the purpose of considering whether an amendment falls within it. If an amendment may be fairly associated with the clauses that are already in the bill, it is regarded as being within the scope of the bill.[302] The test for admissibility is confined to whether the amendment is relevant to the subject-matter of the bill, not whether it introduces new policy.[303]

Examples of amendments ruled out of order as irrelevant to the subject-matter of the bill include: an amendment to restrict liquor advertising when the bill dealt solely with the creation of a new type of liquor licence,[304] and an amendment requiring the Social Security Commission to comply with ministerial directions when the bill dealt only with the rules for the payment of benefits and their amounts.[305] In the latter case, an instruction was subsequently obtained from the House permitting the amendment to be made.[306]

In considering whether an amendment is within the scope of a bill, any purpose clause is a relevant aid to that consideration though it is not conclusive.

An amendment which is foreign to the provision which it seeks to amend is also out of order.[307] In such a case, if the amendment is within the scope of the bill, it can be moved as an amendment to a more relevant provision or as a new provision.

---

[295] S.O.302(1).
[296] S.O.297(2).
[297] 1997, Vol.560, p.1876 (*Trade in Endangered Species Amendment Bill*).
[298] 1892, Vol.78, p.537 (*Land and Income Assessment Bill*).
[298] 1890, Vol.69, p.256 (*Electoral Bill*).
[300] 1873, Vol.14, p.595 (*Provincial Officers Disqualification Bill*).
[301] S.O.261(1).

[302] 1987, Vol.485, p.1825 (*Finance Bill*).
[303] 2005, Vol.627, p.22281 (*Resource Management and Electricity Legislation Amendment Bill*).
[304] 1982, JHR, pp.383-4 (*Sale of Liquor Amendment Bill (No 2)*).
[305] 1977, JHR, pp.588-9 (*Social Security Amendment Bill (No 2)*).
[306] *Ibid.*, p.608.
[307] 1934, Vol.239, p.970 (*Customs Acts Amendment Bill*).

Amendments to omnibus bills

Omnibus bills are bills which deal with more than one defined subject area. They are generally prohibited by the Standing Orders,[308] though certain types of omnibus bills may be introduced.[309] Because of their scope, omnibus bills raise special issues as to the amendments permitted to be made to them.

In principle, the scope of an omnibus bill is defined by its contents when it is introduced just as with every other bill. However, in the case of certain kinds of omnibus bills, the Standing Orders themselves prescribe their subject scope. These omnibus bills are: Finance bills, confirmation bills, Local Legislation bills, Māori Purposes bills, Reserves and Other Lands Disposal bills and Statutes Amendment bills.[310] (See Chapter 26.) Amendments to these bills are relevant if they fall within the Standing Orders-defined scope of these bills even though their contents as introduced might be more limited.

Certain other omnibus bills are allowed to be introduced by the Standing Orders. These are defined not by reference to their subject-matter but by reference to the form that they take. Such bills are bills amending a number of Acts as part of the implementation of a single broad policy and bills amending a number of Acts in a similar way in each case.[311] Amendments to these types of omnibus bill are relevant if they conform to the pattern of amendments that the bills are effecting. Not everything in an Act being amended by such a bill is opened up for amendment. Only amendments relating to the interrelated topic implemented by the bill or which are of a similar nature (as the case may be) may be proposed.

Omnibus bills which the Business Committee agrees may be introduced[312] are of their own kind. Their scope can only be judged by their precise contents.

Omnibus bills by their nature may propose amendments to a number of different Acts when they are introduced. This is an intrinsic part of their omnibus nature represented in particular by Statutes Amendment bills. But the Standing Orders prohibit even omnibus bills being extended to amend other principal Acts not amended by the bill as introduced, without the leave of the committee of the whole House.[313] (Even where a committee may be prepared to grant leave for an amendment to another principal Act to be made, the amendment must still be within the scope of the bill, as defined by its contents.) A purely consequential amendment to another Act does not need leave.[314] But where an Act is only amended consequentially in the bill as introduced any later substantive amendment of that Act requires leave of the committee as if it was not amended at all by the bill as introduced.

Rather than leave of the committee being sought to propose an amendment to an omnibus bill to amend an Act not amended by the bill as introduced, the Standing Orders may be suspended to permit this to be done.[315]

Amendments of an omnibus nature

Every bill must relate to a single subject area (except for permissible omnibus bills).[316] No amendment which would introduce a second subject area into a bill may be made – for example, to make substantive amendments to another Act not amended by the bill as introduced. To do so would be to turn the bill into an omnibus bill. Such an amendment

---

308 S.O.261(1).
309 S.Os 263 and 264.
310 S.O.263(1).
311 S.O.264(a) and (b).
312 S.O.264(c).

313 S.O.304(1).
314 S.O.304(2).
315 2002, Vol.599, pp.15568-74 (*Sentencing and Parole Reform Bill*).
316 S.O.261(1).

may be outside the scope of the bill in any case. The Standing Orders may be suspended to permit an amendment of an omnibus nature to be proposed.

Amendments the same in substance as a previous amendment

No amendment may be proposed that is the same in substance as an amendment that was agreed to or defeated in the committee of the whole House earlier in the same calendar year.[317] The rule does not apply to an amendment where the question on the amendment was never actually put to the committee, for example, by it being withdrawn.[318]

The application of this rule received considerable attention during the committee stage of the *Electoral Amendment Bill* 1975. An amendment was moved proposing a number of electoral changes including an amendment to one of the reserved provisions which can be amended only by an affirmative vote of 75 percent of the members of the House. The proposed amendment obtained a simple majority but not the support of 75 percent of the members. It was declared lost. A further amendment was then moved similar to the first amendment in four of that other's five provisions but omitting the proposed change to the reserved provision. It was argued that this was substantially the same amendment as that which had already been negatived by the committee.

The Speaker, in ruling, held that it had been wrong to declare the first amendment to have been lost; only that part of it relating to the reserved provision had been lost. But he also held that the second amendment was not the same in substance as the first. It could only be the same if it had the same effect as the first. It was not substantially the same merely because it contained four out of the five points contained in the other. The important thing to consider was the effect of the words of the amendment, not their quantity, and the second amendment minus the critical proposed change to the reserved provision was a very different proposition to the first.[319] The effect of the amendment is what must be considered in deciding whether two amendments are substantially the same.

Where a select committee recommends amendments to a bill, their adoption or rejection by the House at the time the bill is read a second time does not preclude proposals for further amendment of those amendments in the committee of the whole House.

Amendments inconsistent with the bill or a previous decision of the committee

The second reading is the time to debate the principles of the bill. Amendments in committee which attack and seek to destroy the very principles already agreed to by the House at the second reading are not acceptable[320] nor are amendments that conflict with the provisions of the bill.[321]

Thus in a bill to implement an agreement, amendments inconsistent with the agreement (which must be taken to have been endorsed in principle when the bill was read a second time) are not permitted.[322]

No amendment which conflicts with a decision already taken by the committee on a provision or an amendment can be accepted. An amendment which has been lost in one part of the bill cannot be proposed again on another. Furthermore, when the committee has agreed that a provision shall stand part of the bill, it cannot propose to make an amendment later in its consideration of the bill which is inconsistent with that provision.[323]

---

[317]   S.O.265(b).

[318]   1976, Vol.407, p.3880 (*Sale of Liquor Amendment Bill (No 2)*).

[319]   1975, Vol.399, p.3055.

[320]   1992, Vol.530, p.11996 (*Union Representatives Education Leave Act Repeal Bill*).

[321]   1908, Vol.144, pp.668, 671-2 (*Second Ballot Bill*).

[322]   2002-05, AJHR, I.22A, p.169 (*Pitcairn Trials Bill*)

[323]   1974, JHR, pp.268, 315 (*New Zealand Superannuation Corporation Bill*).

Further, an amendment, even if not directly contrary to a previous decision of the committee, must be consistent with the pattern of the bill as it has come before the committee. Thus, it was not in order in a bill dealing with specific provisions applying to individual bodies to insert a clause of general application.[324] Nor could a new part containing substantive amendments to an Act be added to a bill when amendments to that Act had already been dealt with in an earlier part of the bill.[325]

It is, however, not part of the chairperson's job to redraft a bill so that it is logically consistent. A bill as it comes before the committee may have contradictory provisions. That is for the committee to correct by amending the bill if it sees fit; it is not for the chairperson to strike one of those provisions out of the bill. The chairperson merely rules on the admissibility of amendments offered in committee, not on the sense or consistency of the bill as referred to the committee.

Amendments which are frivolous, vague or lacking form
Amendments which are frivolous or vague or which lack legislative form are not in order.

An amendment to substitute the word "shall" for the word "may" in the title clause of a bill has been disallowed on the ground that it was frivolous. Normally the question of "shall" or "may" (the one being mandatory in connotation, the other permissive) would be a valid amendment, but not in the title clause which merely fixes a method of citation.[326]

Any amendment that is proposed to the title of a bill must be a serious or objective description of its contents. An amendment which is merely an attempt to criticise the contents of the bill will not be accepted.[327] Thus amendments to the title of a pensions confirmation bill describing it as "betraying" senior citizens and to a tariffs bill describing it as breaking international agreements, were not admissible.[328]

An amendment to a bill must be drafted with some precision; it is not an abstract motion. It is a form of words which may be embodied in law. If it is too vague it is not in order – as with an amendment providing that local authorities "were to have such resources as would enable them to engage adequate services and to operate adequate technical facilities, plant and equipment".[329] An amendment must conform to legislative forms by referring solely to the provision before the committee (and not to the bill as a whole), and proposing to omit, insert or add certain words to it. If a proposed amendment fails to do this it will not be accepted.[330]

The subject-matter of an amendment moved on the second reading of a bill may be moved again in committee provided it is put into proper form.[331]

Amendments to omit a clause or part
When a bill is being considered clause by clause, a motion proposing that a clause be omitted altogether is not an acceptable amendment. The proper course, if this is desired, is to vote against the question "That the clause stand part" when it is proposed by the chairperson.[332] However, it is usual to indicate on a supplementary order paper that it is proposed to omit a clause. Thus, supplementary order papers often show as a proposed amendment the omission of a clause. This is an amendment to the bill, although the mechanical process of omitting the clause is not accomplished by the moving of an

---

324 1987, Vol.485, p.1824 (*Finance Bill*).
325 1991, Vol.512, p.354 (*Finance Bill*).
326 1913, Vol.167, p.88 (*Legislature Amendment Bill*).
327 2001, Vol.597, p.13703 (*Human Rights Amendment Bill*); 2003, Vol.611, p.8269 (*Immigration Amendment Bill*).
328 1992, Vol.532, p.13128 (*Subordinate Legislation Bill (No 2)*); 2000, Vol.583, pp.2324-5 (*Tariff (Zero Duty Removal) Amendment Bill*).

329 1974, Vol.395, p.5224 (*Local Government Bill*).
330 1974, Vol.393, p.3540 (*New Zealand Superannuation Corporation Bill*).
331 1880, Vol.37, p.578 (*Property Assessment Bill*).
332 1996, Vol.555, p.12438 (*Tax Reduction and Social Policy Bill*); 1997, Vol.562, p.3518 (*Social Welfare Reform Bill*); 2002, Vol.604, p.1744 (*Climate Change Response Bill*).

amendment, but by voting against the question that the clause stand part. An amendment that is a direct negative of a clause in the bill is equivalent to an amendment to omit it and is also out of order.[333] However, clause by clause consideration of a bill is unusual now.

Usually, a bill is considered part by part. In this case, an amendment to omit a part is out of order.[334] But, on the other hand, an amendment to omit a clause is in order, for a clause is comprised within a part and its omission would not be a direct negative of the part. However, there can be no amendment to omit the only substantive clauses in a part or the single substantive clause in a two-clause part.[335]

Insertion of a preamble
A preamble cannot be inserted into a bill by way of amendment if the bill as introduced did not have a preamble.[336] But an existing preamble may itself be amended.

Amendment of a purpose clause
A purpose clause describes the objects that the bill is intended to achieve. Any amendment to this clause is limited to helping to describe those objects either by reflecting amendments made to other provisions of the bill as it has passed through the committee or by better expressing the original objects of the bill as it was introduced. Any proposed amendment to the purpose clause that is not linked in this way to the bill's provisions is out of order. The scope of a bill cannot be widened by the device of amending a purpose clause.

Amendments to deeds of settlement or agreements
No amendment may be made to a deed of settlement or other agreement set out or referred to in a bill except to correct typographical errors or to reflect changes to the deed or agreement made by the parties themselves.[337] A committee of the House cannot, by way of amendment to a bill, impose an agreement on parties that they have not reached themselves.

Deeds of settlement commonly embody a settlement between the Crown and Māori of a claim under the Treaty of Waitangi (though they are not confined to this subject). The task of a committee considering a bill to give effect to a settlement is to consider whether the provisions of the bill do give proper effect to the negotiated agreement. The committee could, for example, make amendments ensuring that the bill's provisions work in a technical sense.[338]

It is always for the House to decide whether to give legislative sanction to such a settlement or agreement.

Amendments to bills implementing treaties
Bills to incorporate international treaty obligations into domestic law often do so by including the text of the treaty in a schedule to the bill. No amendment may be made to the text of any international treaty or convention that is so contained in a bill except to correct any errors in transcription.[339] Such text has its own integrity as recording the agreement between the states which are parties to it. An amendment of the treaty or convention could be made only by any procedure prescribed by it. But the provisions of

---

[333]　1988, Vol.490, p.5638 (*Finance Bill (No 3)*).

[334]　1998, Vol.571, p.12084 (*Ngai Tahu Claims Settlement Bill*).

[335]　1991, Vol.518, p.3664 (*Finance Bill (No 2)*).

[336]　*May*, p.616.

[337]　2002-05, AJHR, I.22A, pp.395-6 (*Ngati Ruanui Claims Settlement Bill*); ibid, I.22B, p.959 (*Ngati Tama Claims Settlement Bill*); 2003, Vol.613, p.10180 (*Ngati Tama Claims Settlement Bill*); 2005, Vol.625, p.20204 (*Ngati Tuwharetoa (Bay of Plenty) Claims Settlement Bill*).

[338]　1996-99, AJHR, I.22, p.624 (*Ngai Tahu Claims Settlement Bill*).

[339]　*May*, p.609; 1996-99, AJHR, I.4A, p.5.

the bill giving effect to the agreement can be amended, for it is for the House to determine how or whether it gives legislative effect to international agreements.[340]

Select committee amendments subject to financial veto

Where a financial veto certificate has been given in respect of amendments recommended by a select committee the amendments are omitted from the bill and the certificate applies to prevent those amendments being moved again in the committee of the whole House.[341]

Amendments having an impact on fiscal aggregates

Amendments which may have an impact on the Government's fiscal aggregates must be lodged with the Clerk at least 24 hours before the House meets on the day on which they are to be moved. Failure to give notice in time means that they are out of order.[342] (See p. 375.)

The onus is on a member wishing to avoid the impact of the rule, to give 24 hours' notice.[343] If there is any doubt about the amendment's effect or a possibility that it may have a fiscal impact, an amendment lodged within the 24-hour time-frame will be ruled out of order.[344] The chairperson does not determine such a matter on a balance of probabilities; a possibility is sufficient. The Minister in charge of a bill often raises the issue on a point of order after receiving official advice, though it is finally for the chairperson to rule.[345]

Amendments subject to financial veto

An amendment that has been proposed may be the subject of a financial veto certificate before the question on the amendment is put.[346] (See Chapter 31 for the giving of financial veto certificates.) Such an amendment is out of order and no question is put on it,[347] though it may be debated along with the provision to which it relates. If the amendment consists of a new provision, the new provision may be moved and debated but at the conclusion of the debate (by closure or otherwise) no question is put on it.

Addition of provision fixing annual tax rates

A provision fixing annual tax rates can be in a stand-alone bill or it can be part of a general taxation bill. But if such a provision is to be proposed to the House as part of a general taxation bill it must be contained in the bill as introduced. A matter of such constitutional import as the fixing of the annual rates of taxation cannot be added to the bill by way of amendment. (See Chapter 33.)

Addition of new clauses to Local Legislation bills

No clause may be added to a Local Legislation Bill by the committee of the whole House unless the clause has been provisionally approved by the Minister of Local Government and reported on by a select committee.[348] A new clause moved at the committee stage which has not been through these processes is out of order. But this does not prevent the substitution of a clause for a clause already in the bill or the insertion of a clause incidental to or consequential on such a clause.[349]

---

[340] Marleau and Monpetit, *House of Commons Procedure and Practice*, p.657.
[341] S.O.321(3).
[342] S.O.322(1).
[343] 1993-96, AJHR, I.18A, pp.63-4.
[344] 1998, Vol.574, pp.14165-6 (*Accident Insurance Bill*);

2000, Vol.586, p.4553 (*Employment Relations Bill*).
[345] 1998, Vol.574, p.14166.
[346] S.O.321(2).
[347] *Ibid.*
[348] Appendix C to the Standing Orders, cl.25(1).
[349] *Ibid.*, cl.25(2).

Amendments outside the scope of local bill or private bill notices

Local bills and private bills are advertised as being designed to effect stated objects, and persons may be dissuaded from objecting to the passage of such a bill if they are satisfied with the advertised statement of objects. There is, therefore, a strict rule against a local bill or a private bill being amended while it is before the House in any way that is not within the scope of the notices advertising the intention to introduce the bill.[350] If such an amendment is not within the scope of the bill it would not be in order in any case, but the rule goes further than that and prohibits amendments relevant to the subject-matter of the bill but outside the advertised notices. (But the converse is not the case. A widely-worded notice does not extend the scope of the bill beyond the subject-matter contained in its provisions.) This restriction can be removed only by a suspension of the Standing Orders.

Where a local or private bill deals with land, it cannot be amended to encompass other land not contained within the legal description and the plan lodged for inspection along with the bill. But the bill can be amended to deal with land identified in the notices in a different way from that originally proposed.

Amendments that should be included in a local or private bill

A Government bill or a Member's bill can amend a local or private Act where this is consequential on the general legislative change being effected in the bill. But apart from consequential amendments, amendments to a local Act or a private Act should be made by a local bill or a private bill respectively.[351] No amendment of a private Act or a local Act may be proposed to a Government bill or a Member's bill, except where this is consequential on the other provisions of that bill.

Furthermore, no amendment that would require to be promoted by way of private or local legislation may be made to a Government or Member's bill. Thus amendments to a bill exempt individually identified establishments from the general smoke-free law, being for the particular interest or benefit of a person or body of persons, should have been promoted in private bills for that purpose. They were out of order as amendments to a Government bill even though relevant to the subject-matter of the bill.[352] (Amendments applying to all establishments of a particular type – generic amendments – were in order even though there were only a few such establishments.[353])

PUTTING THE QUESTION

Conclusion of the debate

At the conclusion of the debate on the provision before the committee, the chairperson puts the question on any amendments that have been circulated or handed in and then on the question that that provision stand part of the bill.[354]

The debate may conclude naturally or following the carrying of a closure motion. In the case of a natural termination of debate the chairperson pauses to ascertain if any member is seeking the call. If not, the chairperson commences to put the question. Once the chairperson starts putting the questions on any amendments, there can be no further debate on the provision.[355] When the closure is carried or the chairperson starts to put the questions on amendments it is too late for an amendment on a supplementary order paper or a manuscript amendment that has been handed in to the Table to be withdrawn by the member proposing it,[356] but it may be withdrawn by leave.[357]

---

[350] S.O.297(3).
[351] See, for example: 1907, Vol.140, p.59 (*Costley Training Institution Act Amendment Bill*); 1989, Vol.504, p.14723 (*Taxation Reform Bill (No 7)*).
[352] 2003, Vol.613, p.9977 (*Smoke-free Environments Amendment Bill*).

[353] *Ibid.*
[354] S.O.302(3).
[355] 1994, Vol.544, pp.4965-6.
[356] 1986, Vol.470, p.1052; 1994, Vol.540, p.1625.
[357] 1986, Vol.470, p.1052.

Manner and order of putting amendments

The member in charge of a bill has the right to have all amendments to a provision in that member's name put as one question.[358] These are dealt with after other amendments to that provision, unless the member in charge requests that they be dealt with first.[359]

Apart from the special rights of the member in charge of a bill, in principle, amendments should be dealt with in the order in which they occur in the provision concerned. But amendments can occur at the same place in a bill and their texts can overlap. If this occurs, an amendment from the member in charge (if not being taken together with other amendments from that member) is taken first.[360] If other members' amendments occur at the same place they are taken in the order in which they were lodged with the Clerk.[361]

The order in which amendments are dealt with can be significant in that a later amendment inconsistent with an earlier amendment that has been agreed to or defeated will be out of order. (See pp. 378–9)

The chairperson does not read out the full text of amendments when putting the question on them. It is incumbent on members to avail themselves of copies of amendments and study them.[362] But the chairperson will often give some description of the amendment by reference to its purport or sponsor, so that members can follow which amendment they are being asked to vote on.

RESOLVING THE QUESTION

The question that an amendment be agreed to or that a provision of the bill stand part is resolved in the same way as any other question – by voice vote, party vote or personal vote. An amendment must be agreed to by a majority of those voting in order to be adopted. However, where the question is whether an existing provision (even as amended) stand part of the bill, the provision *does* stand part of the bill even on a tie.[363] This is an exception to the general rule that on a tie the question is lost. If this rule were applied to the question that a provision stand part of the bill, the effect would be that the bill would be amended on a tied vote. Hence, the rule is set aside in this case.[364]

There are three circumstances in which a question is not determined by a simple majority of votes on a party vote or a personal vote, as the case may be, and where unanimous concurrence or a qualified majority must be obtained for the amendment to be agreed to or for the provision to stand part of the bill.

Clauses of a Statutes Amendment Bill

In the case of a clause of a Statutes Amendment Bill (or of any bill divided from a Statutes Amendment Bill) the chairperson, rather than putting a question, asks if there is any objection to the clause standing part. At this point any member may object to the clause standing part. If a member does so object, the clause is struck out of the bill.[365]

Reserved provisions

The repeal or amendment of one of the reserved provisions of the electoral law can only be made if the proposal for repeal or amendment is passed by a majority of 75 percent of all members of the House.[366] (See Chapter 2.) This does not apply in respect of the repeal of a reserved provision in a consolidating bill if that provision is at the same time to be re-enacted without amendment and the re-enacted provision is itself to be entrenched.[367]

A proposal for the "amendment" of one of the reserved provisions is regarded as

---

[358] S.O.303(1).
[359] S.O.303(3).
[360] S.O.303(2)(a).
[361] S.O.303(2)(b).
[362] 1998, Vol.573, p.13565.

[363] S.O.300(1).
[364] 1999-2002, AJHR, I.18B, pp.26-7.
[365] S.O.300(2).
[366] *Electoral Act* 1993, s.268(1).
[367] *Ibid.,* s.268(2).

including any provision extending or restricting the application of such a provision. It is not confined to an amendment making a textual change to a reserved provision. Such a proposal may be contained in a provision of the bill as originally introduced or as added to the bill following its consideration by a select committee. Alternatively, the proposal for amendment of a reserved provision may be contained in an amendment moved in the committee stage itself. In either case the proposal must be carried by the votes of 75 percent of the members of the House, otherwise it is lost.

The requirement for a special majority cannot be used to defeat any part of the question before the committee other than a reserved provision. So if a proposed clause consists of subclauses, one of which amends a reserved provision, and the question "That the clause stand part of the bill" is carried but not by a majority of 75 percent of the members of the House, the clause is not wholly lost. It stands part of the bill minus the subclause that amends the reserve provision.[368] The same rule applies to any amendment that contains a number of proposals, some of which amend reserved provisions and some of which do not. To avoid this problem arising, reserved provisions should be considered separately from other provisions if this is possible.[369]

It is not necessary for there to be a party vote or a personal vote which records 75 percent of the members voting in favour on every reserved provision. A question is decided in the first instance by a voice vote and proceeds to a party vote or a personal vote only if there are members who do not acquiesce in that decision. A vote decided on the voices is deemed to be carried unanimously by the House, and no question arises as to the numbers present.[370] Proposals to amend reserved provisions have been defeated, though they were supported by a simple majority vote of members.[371] There is only one instance of a reserved provision being amended by contested vote. This involved a repeal and replacement of the provision relating to the method of voting. The proposal was carried by a vote of 79 to 13, four votes more than the 75 percent majority of votes required.[372]

Proposals for entrenchment

The reserved provisions of the electoral law are themselves "entrenched" in law, in that they can only be repealed or amended if the proposal for repeal or amendment is supported by a 75 percent majority of members (or alternatively carried at a poll of electors).

Other than the reserved provisions, there are no other examples of provisions entrenched in law in this way, but proposals to entrench other subjects in legislation are made from time to time.[373][372] The House's Standing Orders require that before a proposal for entrenchment may be adopted, the proposal must demonstrate that it has the same level of support in the Parliament that is to adopt it as it proposes to require of any future Parliament that may wish to repeal or amend it.[374] Thus, a proposal that would require a 65 percent majority for amendment must be agreed to by the House in the first place by a 65 percent majority.[375]

This requirement for a qualified majority before a proposal for entrenchment may be carried applies in respect of a provision in a bill or an amendment to a bill that would require that it itself or any other provision can be amended or repealed only by a majority of more than 50 percent plus one of all members.[376] A requirement for a qualified majority below this threshold does not require to be carried in any special way.

The rule applies during the committee stage of a bill. Any provision or amendment

[368] 1975, Vol.399, p.3056 (*Electoral Amendment Bill*).
[369] *Ibid.*
[370] 1980, Vol.433, p.3513 (*Electoral Amendment Bill*).
[371] 1975, Vol.399, p.3056 (*Electoral Amendment Bill*).
[372] 1995, Vol.551, pp.10326-7 (*Electoral Reform Bill*).
[373] See, for example, the *Flags, Anthems, Emblems and*

Names Protection Amendment Bill 1990, cl.3 and cl.4 (New Zealand flag and national anthem not to be altered except by a 65 percent majority of members).
[374] S.O.267(1).
[375] 1993-96, AJHR, I.18A, p.57.
[376] S.O.267(2).

which proposes entrenchment in this way must itself be carried by not less than the majority which it proposes, otherwise it is lost. Before putting the question on such a proposal the chairperson draws the committee's attention to the fact that a qualified majority vote will be necessary for the proposal to pass.[377]

DIVIDING A BILL

A committee of the whole House now has inherent power to divide a bill into one or more separate bills and to report the bills back to the House separately. Until 1985 committees did not have this power and the power had to be specially granted each time by an instruction. For some 20 years from 1955 the only type of bill which was divided up into separate bills was the annual Statutes Amendment Bill, but increasingly from the early 1970s this power was taken for other bills too. It is now a very common occurrence for a bill to be divided at its committee stage either because it was introduced as an omnibus bill or because the bill's main provisions result in consequential amendments to other Acts and it is more intelligible to enact these as separate pieces of legislation.

The committee's power to divide a bill applies where a bill is drafted in parts or otherwise lends itself to division because it comprises more than one subject matter.[378] A supplementary order paper notifying members of the intention to move for the bill's division must be circulated.[379] Almost invariably such a supplementary order paper is prepared by the member in charge of the bill, but one could be prepared by any member. This "break-up" or "split-up" supplementary order paper must be separate from any other supplementary order paper that may be circulated notifying amendments that will be moved to the bill. It cannot itself contain amendments to the bill's substantive provisions; it must be confined to showing how it is proposed to divide the bill, setting out the enacting formula and title and commencement clauses for each new bill that is proposed.[380]

Any break-up supplementary order paper is taken at the very end of the committee stage when the bill has been fully considered by the committee.[381] This means that the committee's decisions on the title and commencement clauses of the bill are provisional up to this point, because they are liable to be countermanded or amplified by the amendments set out on the break-up supplementary order paper. The member who has circulated the supplementary order paper moves that the bill be divided in the manner set out on the supplementary order paper. This is a debatable motion and it is itself subject to amendment.[382] The debate is a narrow one confined to whether the bill should be divided. It is not an opportunity to recanvass the issues contained in the bill.[383]

If the motion to divide a bill is carried, the chairperson will report the several bills into which the bill has been divided back to the House as separate bills.

While it is generally no longer necessary to confer power on a committee of the whole House to divide a bill it may be necessary to do so in some cases. If it is desired that the committee should divide a bill that is not drafted in parts or which comprises a single subject matter (which all bills apart from omnibus bills are required to comprise), an instruction giving the committee power to divide is necessary. An instruction will also be necessary if it is intended to seek division of the bill before the whole bill has been considered. It is not competent for the committee to divide a bill earlier than this, even by leave.

Where division of a bill is effected following an instruction, circulation of a

---

[377] See, for example, 2004, Vol.621, p.17051 (*Foreshore and Seabed Bill*).

[378] S.O.305(1).

[379] *Ibid.*

[380] S.O.305(2).

[381] S.O.305(3).

[382] 1993, Vol.537, p.17235 (*Electoral Reform Bill*).

[383] 2001, Vol.595, p.11929 (*New Zealand Superannuation Bill*).

supplementary order paper is not required (though it is usually still done); the member in charge of the bill moves a motion to divide the bill following consideration of the parts or clauses that are to form a separate bill.

INTERRUPTION OF COMMITTEE STAGE

The committee stage of a bill may be interrupted by the time arriving for the committee to report progress (9.55 pm on a Tuesday and a Wednesday, 5.55 pm on a Thursday)[384] or by a motion to report progress being carried. Any member may move that the committee report progress.[385] This motion can be moved only by a member who has been called to speak to the question before the committee. It cannot be moved on a point of order.[386] Such a motion is put forthwith without amendment or debate.[387] If carried, the motion concludes the committee's consideration of the bill on that day. A member may also move that the chairperson obtain the Speaker's ruling on a matter of procedure. The question on this motion is also put forthwith without amendment or debate.[388] If carried, this motion temporarily interrupts the committee stage while the ruling is obtained.

Occasionally the Government moves to report progress in order to get on with other business on the order paper or to precipitate the conclusion of a sitting if the House is sitting under urgency. Where the House has gone into committee on several bills, an order to report progress on one of them does not dispose of them all, and the chairperson is obliged to go on with the others before leaving the chair.[389] However, it is usually (but not always[390]) the case when such a motion is carried that the committee intends the chairperson to leave the chair and report progress on all bills before it, and it is not necessary in such a case for a motion to be put separately and carried in respect of each.

If it is desired to consider the bill later in the same sitting, the member in charge of the bill may move that the committee report progress and sit again "presently".[391]

No other member may move to report progress in any way other than that prescribed in the Standing Orders.

CONCLUSION OF COMMITTEE STAGE

When all provisions of a bill have been considered and any motion to divide the bill has been dealt with, the committee stage of the bill is at an end. The chairperson informs the committee that the bill will be reported to the House with or without amendment, as the case may be, and, if the bill has been divided, states that the several bills will be reported. The chairperson then leaves the Table preparatory to the Speaker resuming the chair in the House. There is no question before the committee in these proceedings at the conclusion of a committee stage, the chairperson merely informs the committee of what is occurring pursuant to the Standing Orders.

REPORT OF THE COMMITTEE

Making the report

When reporting, the chairperson stands at the Speaker's right. The report is a single report which may relate to a mixture of completed and uncompleted bills. If consideration of a bill has been completed, the chairperson reports it to the Speaker with or without amendment as the case may be. Where applicable, the chairperson also reports that the bill has been divided into specified separate bills. On a bill which has not been fully

---

[384]   S.O.50(1).
[385]   S.O.182(1).
[386]   1985, Vol.468, pp.8439-41.
[387]   S.O.182(3).
[388]   S.O.179.
[389]   1911, Vol.156, pp.241-2.
[390]   For example, 1977, JHR, p.589.
[391]   S.O.182(2); 1988, Vol.495, p.8634.

considered, the chairperson reports that the committee has made some progress or (if a bill was not reached at all) no progress. The chairperson then moves that the report be adopted.[392]

Adoption of report

The Speaker puts the question that the report be adopted. There is no amendment or debate on this question.[393]

Once the report is adopted, the completed bills are set down for third reading and the uncompleted bills are set down for further consideration in committee on the next sitting day.[394] An uncompleted bill is set down for "further" consideration even where the committee has made no progress on the bill, for on the first occasion on which the House resolves itself into committee on a bill, the bill has been committed. When subsequently the House goes into committee on that bill, it is for further consideration by a committee of the whole House regardless of the extent of progress on the bill when it was last committed. Such a bill's committee stage is consequently listed on the order paper as "continued".

If the title of the bill has been amended, the amendment becomes effective from the moment the report is adopted by the House. Consequently, on the following day's order paper, where the bill appears for third reading, it will be referred to by its new title, and this is used in all future references to the bill.

RECOMMITTAL

It may be desirable, after a bill has been considered in committee and before it is read a third time, to give the bill's detailed provisions further consideration. A defect or an oversight may be discovered in the bill which can be put right only by an amendment to one of its provisions or the member in charge of the bill may wish to put forward further amendments to it. Amendments are not possible during the third reading of the bill but the House can order the bill's recommittal to a committee of the whole House for further consideration.

Moving for recommittal

A motion for recommittal of a bill may be moved when the order of the day for third reading is called by the Clerk.[395] The motion may be a general recommittal motion or it may limit the purpose of the recommittal in some way. Any member may move this motion. If there is more than one member wishing to move it, the Speaker gives priority to the member in charge of the bill.[396] Otherwise, the Speaker has given preference to a member who indicated that he wished to recommit the bill for a wider purpose than a competing member.[397] There can be only one such motion at each sitting at which a bill is reached, for the House will have taken a definite decision whether or not to recommit the bill on the first recommittal motion that is moved. If the motion is lost and the third reading is not completed that day, a further recommittal motion can be moved when the bill is next reached.[398]

A bill does not have to have appeared on the order paper for third reading for a recommittal motion to be moved.[399] It can be moved while the bill is being passed through all its stages under urgency.

A motion to recommit a bill is not subject to amendment or debate.[400]

[392]   S.O.183.
[393]   *Ibid.*
[394]   S.O.306.
[395]   S.O.307.
[396]   1994, Vol.543, p.3954 (*Maritime Transport Bill*).

[397]   1986, Vol.472, pp.2580-1 (*Homosexual Law Reform Bill*).
[398]   *Ibid.,* pp.2581-2.
[399]   1990, Vol.506, pp.861-2 (*Telecommunications Amendment Bill*).
[400]   S.O.307.

Effect of recommittal

If a bill is simply recommitted, it is referred back to the committee of the whole House for further study at large and the committee goes through it fully again as already described though it will do so this time in its amended form as a result of its first committee consideration. The order for recommittal may, however, go on to prescribe the purposes for which the bill has been recommitted. If it does so, the committee carries out only those tasks that it has been given to do.[401] But recommittal must be for a purpose connected with the business of the committee. There cannot, for instance, be a recommittal to enable the Government to consider a matter; the recommittal must relate to the bill's examination by the committee.[402] A bill may be recommitted for consideration of only one of its provisions or for consideration of specified amendments such as those notified on a supplementary order paper.[403] In such cases, the committee's work is confined to considering the provision or amendments referred to in the order for recommittal. The committee is not bound to accept any amendments referred to it for consideration; it can agree or disagree with them as it sees fit.[404] The committee can also reverse a decision taken by it when it previously considered the bill.[405] But it is not possible to recommit a bill in order to consider a new provision or other amendment which was ruled out of order by the chairperson when the bill was first considered in committee,[406] such a recommittal would be futile. Nor can a bill be recommitted to consider an amendment outside the scope of the bill. If it is desired that the committee reconsider a bill for the purposes of considering amendments outside its scope, an instruction must first be given to the committee authorising it to do this. Such an instruction (on recommittal) would require notice and is debatable.

Where a bill is recommitted for consideration of certain amendments, only those amendments (and any relevant amendments to them) may be moved. In such a case, when the amendments to a part (or clause if the bill is not drafted in parts) have been disposed of, the question is put that that part as amended stand part. When the committee of the whole House has fully considered a bill on recommittal, the bill is reported back to the House and is set down for third reading on the next sitting day.

SETTING BILL DOWN FOR THIRD READING

A bill fully considered by the committee of the whole House is set down for third reading on the next sitting day. The bill is reprinted if any amendments have been made in committee.[407] The bill is not reprinted if the third reading is taken immediately following the committee stage either because urgency has been taken for its entire passing or for its committee and third reading stages.[408] The third reading of a bill cannot be held until copies of the reprinted bill are available to members.[409] Leave has been given for a bill to proceed to its third reading without being reprinted where (in the case of a bill of over 2,000 pages) this was not regarded as necessary given the minor nature of the amendments and the cost involved.[410] The Speaker may dispense with the reprinting of a bill if the amendments are of a minor textual nature.[411] If the bill has not been reprinted since 1 January 1997 (in respect of drafting style changes adopted on that date by the Parliamentary Counsel Office) or 1 January 2000 (when the format of legislation underwent considerable change as a result of Standing Orders and design changes), it is reprinted in the new formats that were adopted on those dates.[412]

---

[401] 1913, Vol.165, p.789 (*Land Laws Amendment Bill*).

[402] 1926, Vol.211, p.201 (*Education Amendment Bill*).

[403] 1898, Vol.104, p.565 (*Old-age Pensions Bill*).

[404] 1898, Vol.102, p.412 (*Water-supply Bill*).

[405] 1880, Vol.37, p.606 (*Beer Duty Bill*).

[406] 1909, Vol.147, p.606.

[407] S.O.268(2).

[408] S.O.268(2)(a), (b).

[409] S.O.268(3)(b).

[410] 2004, Vol.616, p.11775 (*Income Tax Bill*).

[411] S.O.268(2)(c).

[412] 2002, Vol.602, pp.308-9.

The bill stands on the order paper as an order of the day awaiting its third reading. The order in which Government bills are taken is largely a matter for the Government to determine. Members', private and local bills are considered in the order prescribed by the Standing Orders. (See Chapter 14.) There is no three sitting day stand-down period before the third reading can be held, as there is between the report of a select committee and the second reading of a bill.

Referral to a select committee
When the order of the day for third reading is reached any member may move to have the order discharged and for the bill to be referred to a select committee for further consideration. There is no amendment or debate on this question.[413]

BILLS REQUIRING CROWN CONSENT
Members', local or private bills which contain any provision affecting the rights or prerogatives of the Crown cannot be passed unless the Crown indicates its consent to that provision.[414] If any question arises, the Speaker determines whether a bill affects the rights or prerogatives of the Crown.

This consent is communicated by way of a message from the Governor-General which is announced to the House by the Speaker. The message can be given at any stage before the bill's passing but it must be given before the bill can be read a third time. The Crown's consent to a bill passing includes agreement to any amendments that may be made to it during its passage. A separate message is not required for the amendments. Amendments may be made to a bill that convert the bill from one that would not otherwise require the Crown's agreement into one that does require such agreement. Such amendments may be made prior to any message being announced but, if the bill is to pass, a message must be forthcoming before the bill can be read a third time.

FINANCIAL VETO OF BILLS AWAITING THIRD READING
A bill awaiting its third reading is subject to financial veto by the Government on the ground that it would have more than a minor impact on the Government's fiscal aggregates if it became law.[415] (See Chapter 31 for the giving of financial veto certificates.) The financial veto may relate to the whole bill or to a particular provision or provisions of it.[416] To be effective it must be given before the third reading debate commences.

If a financial veto certificate relates to the whole bill, the third reading debate may still be held but at the conclusion of the debate the Speaker does not put any question on it and the bill will consequently lapse.[417] In the case of a financial veto certificate relating to a particular provision or provisions only, the bill may be amended (by being recommitted) to remove the provision or provisions objected to, in which case the bill proceeds normally. But, if it is not so amended, at the conclusion of the third reading debate no question is put on it and it lapses in the same way as if the financial veto certificate had applied to the whole bill.[418]

THIRD READING
When the order of the day for the third reading of a bill is reached, the Speaker calls upon the member in charge to move the motion "That the ... *Bill* be now read a third time".[419]

---

[413] S.O.71(1)(a) and (2).
[414] S.O.309.
[415] S.Os 318(1) and 320(1).
[416] S.O.320(2).

[417] S.O.320(3).
[418] *Ibid.*
[419] S.O.308(1).

Another member may act for an absent member but only a Minister may act for an absent Minister in charge of a Government bill. The debate is limited to 12 speeches each of a maximum duration of 10 minutes.[420]

The third reading debate is narrower in scope than the second reading debate. Members must confine themselves to the general principles of the bill as it has emerged from the committee of the whole House.[421] One of the principal uses of the third reading was formerly to record arguments that were advanced during the committee stage when that stage was not reported in *Hansard*. Now that the committee stage is subject to a full report, this is no longer the case.[422] Members may discuss amendments made to the bill by the committee and may allude to, but not discuss at length, amendments moved unsuccessfully in committee.[423] Amendments ruled out of order in committee by the chairperson cannot be discussed.[424] Any other matter which arose during the committee stage and which is relevant to the bill may be referred to. Although members may advance general arguments as to why the bill should or should not pass, they must confine themselves to matters contained in the bill[425] and may not go through the bill clause by clause and give detailed arguments on its contents.[426] The third reading debate is in the nature of a summing-up.

Amendments

The question for the third reading is open to amendment in any way that is relevant to the motion, for example, by deferring the third reading or declining to agree to it for a specified reason. It is not permissible to move an amendment to refer the bill back to a select committee. If this is desired it can be done by discharging the order of the day before the third reading debate commences.

Cognate bills

Where a bill has been divided at the committee stage, the several bills emerging from it may, at the option of the member in charge, be taken together for the purposes of debate on their third readings.[427] This is an option that is almost invariably exercised. The several bills are called on together for their third reading, the member in charge moves a single third reading motion and there is one debate instead of several. This option applies only in respect of bills divided by the committee of the whole House, not in respect of bills divided by a select committee (which often move through their subsequent stages quite independently of each other anyway). The option to take the third readings together applies to taking all of the several bills together. It is not an option to take some of them together and others separately. If the option is not exercised the bills are all dealt with separately.

Although there is a single debate, the question for the third reading of each bill is put separately at the conclusion of the debate. However, the third readings are often dealt with as one question unless it is intimated to the Speaker that members desire each bill or some of the bills to be voted on separately.

PASSING OF THE BILL

When the bill has been read a third time, it has been passed by the House.[428] Formerly a separate question was put after the third reading, asking the House to agree that the bill "do now pass", but the passing of a bill is now held to occur when the House agrees to its third reading. The bill is not yet law. It has been passed by one constituent of Parliament, the House of Representatives. It is now prepared by the Clerk of the House for submission for the Royal assent.

---

[420] Appendix A to the Standing Orders.
[421] 1961, Vol.329, pp.3922-3 (*Industrial Conciliation and Arbitration Bill*).
[422] 1998, Vol.568, p.8787 (*Social Security Amendment Bill (No 5)*).
[423] 1977, Vol.415, pp.4136-7 (*Human Rights*

[ ] *Commission Bill*).
[424] 1960, Vol.325, p.3009 (*Animals Protection Bill*).
[425] 1962, Vol.333, pp.3422, 3429 (*State Services Bill*).
[426] 1950, Vol.290, p.1225 (*Tenancy Amendment Bill*).
[427] S.O.308(2).
[428] S.O.310.

CHAPTER 28

ENACTMENT AND PUBLICATION OF ACTS

ROYAL ASSENT

Preparation of bill

When a bill (whether a Government, Member's, local or private bill) has been read a third time, it is prepared by the Clerk for submission to the Sovereign or the Governor-General for the Royal assent. The Royal assent to the measure is essential to transmute what, up to that time, is a proposal which has been agreed to by one branch of the legislature, into an Act of Parliament and, therefore, law.

For this purpose, after the bill's third reading, the Clerk arranges for it to be reprinted in the form of an Act as it was passed by the House.[1] The reprinted document no longer shows how the bill was amended as it passed through the House. Material struck out during its passage is not shown at all; there is no indication in the text as to what material has been added after the bill was introduced and what was in it originally. The bill is printed "fair", as it will read when it becomes an Act on receiving the Royal assent.

Amendments and corrections

Verbal or formal amendments to the text may be made by the Clerk during the reprinting process.[2] The main example of such a formal amendment is the renumbering of the clauses of the bill if, by amendment during the bill's passage, these no longer read consecutively. Any cross-references are corrected. Other clerical or typographical errors which are identified in the bill may also be corrected at this stage.

Finally, amendments are made to reflect any changes in drafting styles and legislative format made since the bill was introduced. Drafting changes were introduced on 1 January 1997 and 1 January 2000 respectively and Standing Orders changes on the format of legislation were adopted on 8 September 1999. The House has authorised the Clerk to make amendments in bills introduced before these dates to reflect these changes.[3] Such amendments involve removing Long Titles, converting Short Titles into title clauses, inserting commencement provisions in a separate clause and general changes to the layout and design of the document to conform to the new styles. Only bills introduced before the respective dates need such amendments to be made to them (bills introduced after those dates conform as a matter of course) and even in the case of bills introduced before those dates the opportunity may already have been taken to reprint them in the new format while they were proceeding through the House.

A print of a bill that is to be presented for the Royal assent is always checked within the Office of the Clerk and the Parliamentary Counsel Office before proceeding further. It may also be checked by the department whose Minister took charge of its passage.

Authentication of prints

The Clerk must authenticate two prints of the bill in its reprinted form.[4] (Occasionally a third print is authenticated if it is intended that the promoter of particular legislation should retain a copy of the bill with the Royal assent recorded on it.)

---

[1] S.O.311.
[2] S.O.312.
[3] 2002, Vol.602, pp.308-9.
[4] S.O.311.

The Clerk is charged by the House with presenting every bill which it has passed to the Sovereign or the Governor-General for the Royal assent.[5] But constitutional convention requires that in this, as in the exercise of the other constitutional and legal powers and duties of office, the Sovereign or the Governor-General acts only on the formal advice of a Government that is politically accountable to the House of Representatives. Consequently, after authenticating the two prints, the Clerk certifies that the bill has been passed by the House and is awaiting the Royal assent and delivers the bill to the Government for it to tender the formal advice to the Governor-General that the Royal assent should be given.

There are two steps in the tendering of this formal advice.

First, the Attorney-General certifies to the Governor-General that, in the Attorney-General's opinion, the bill contains nothing which requires that the Royal assent should be withheld. In the Attorney-General's absence, an Acting Attorney-General (if there is one) or the Solicitor-General gives the certification. Secondly, the copies of the bill are presented to the Prime Minister (or the most senior Minister available if the Prime Minister is absent from Wellington) for the Prime Minister to sign the formal advice to the Governor-General recommending that the Royal assent be given to the bill. Thus the legal act of assenting to the bill is the Sovereign's or the Governor-General's, but the political act of assent to a bill is the Prime Minister's, and the Prime Minister assumes political responsibility by formally tendering the advice on which the Crown acts.

Presentation of bill

It was formerly the practice for the Governor to attend Parliament House in person on the final day of each session and, before proroguing Parliament, to grant the Royal assent to any bills presented for assent at that time. An Appropriation Bill was traditionally reserved to be presented for assent after all other bills. Since 1875 the Governor has not attended in person to prorogue Parliament or assent to bills, nor is an Appropriation Bill any longer reserved for assent last.[6] Nowadays, when the Attorney-General's certification has been obtained and the Prime Minister's advice has been tendered, the Clerk causes the two copies to be presented to the Governor-General at Government House for the Royal assent. Traditionally, the Clerk presents the first bill passed after a new Governor-General has assumed office in person to the Governor-General. Bills are presented for the Royal assent strictly in the order in which they were passed by the House.

If the Administrator of the Government is in office, the bill is submitted to the Administrator for the Royal assent.

Giving of the Royal assent

A bill becomes law when the Sovereign or the Governor-General (or the Administrator) assents to it and signs it in token of such assent.[7]

The Governor-General completes the Royal assent to a bill by signing the two copies presented (and occasionally a third copy). Usually no particular formality is followed in the giving of the Royal assent. The Governor-General deals with bills submitted for the Royal assent in the same way as other state papers submitted for vice-regal attention. The

---

5   *Ibid.*

6   1958, Vol.318, p.1856.

7   *Constitution Act* 1986, s.16.

bill becomes law immediately it is assented to by the Governor-General, but its provisions might not immediately take effect. This depends upon whether it provides for its own commencement. If it does, it takes effect accordingly. If it does not, it comes into effect on the day after it receives the Royal assent.[8]

The Sovereign has given the Royal assent in person. Her Majesty Queen Elizabeth II became the first Sovereign to do so on 12 January 1954 when she assented to the *Judicature Amendment Act* 1954. Her Majesty has since assented to other bills passed while she has been present in New Zealand.

Refusal of the Royal assent

There is no longer explicit statutory recognition of a power to withhold the Royal assent, as there was in the previous law.[9] This was omitted in 1986 as being unnecessary. It was felt that to re-enact it then (when New Zealand's constitutional rules were being restated in modern terms) might suggest that a personal discretion was vested in the Governor-General. But even with the omission of any express statement of the power to refuse to give the Royal assent, it remains the case that a bill does not become law until signed by the Governor-General in token of assent.[10]

A refusal to assent would be a remarkable – indeed a unique – event in New Zealand. No bill presented to a Governor or a Governor-General has ever been refused the Royal assent in New Zealand, although two Acts were subsequently disallowed by the Sovereign (in 1855 and 1867) under a procedure which no longer exists.[11] In the United Kingdom, which has a comparable requirement for the Royal assent to be given to measures passed by the House of Lords and the House of Commons, the Royal assent has not been refused since 1707.[12] The constitutional principle that the Governor-General acts only on the advice of Ministers requires the Governor-General to accept that advice except in the most extraordinary circumstances.

Errors in Acts

Errors made in the course of preparing bills for the Royal assent have led to bills being assented to in a form which differed from the form in which they passed through the House. Such errors have included: failure to include an amendment made to the bill as it was passing through the House;[13] a printing error resulting in an incorrect figure being subscribed;[14] and a failure to correct a cross-reference.[15] In these circumstances, further legislation has been passed to correct the error made in preparing the bill for the Royal assent.[16] Until corrected, the law has been treated as being as assented to by the Governor-General in the incorrectly prepared bills. In one case the validity of the erroneous legislation was also specifically confirmed in the correcting legislation.[17]

In Australia, the Governor-General has rescinded a purported assent to an Act that did not include all of the material agreed to by both houses of the legislature in the print submitted for the Royal assent.[18] However, given that under that country's constitution the agreement of both houses is a requirement for enacting law, it may be that the bill as assented to was not a valid Act or at least not as regards the unagreed material. In

---

[8] *Interpretation Act* 1999, s.8.
[9] *New Zealand Constitution Act* 1852 (UK), s.56.
[10] See Burrows, *Statute Law in New Zealand*, p.4.
[11] Scott, *The New Zealand Constitution*, p.85.
[12] Marshall, *Constitutional Conventions*, p.22.
[13] 1872, Vol.12, pp.18, 222 (*Sharebrokers Bill*).
[14] 1996, Vol.553, pp.11302-3, 11483-5 (*Electoral Amendment Bill (No 3)*).
[15] *Supplementary order paper 315*, 7 December 2004, p.33 (*Public Finance (State Sector*

Management) Bill).
[16] *Sharebrokers Act Amendment Act* 1872, s.2 (correcting an error in the *Sharebrokers Act* 1871); *Electoral Amendment Act* 1996, s.2 (correcting an error in the *Electoral Amendment Act* 1995); *Crown Entities Act* 2004, s.201(1) (correcting an error in the *Crown Gas Amendment Act* 2004).
[17] *Crown Entities Act* 2004, s.201(2).
[18] House of Representatives (Australia), 21 June 2001, p.28261.

these circumstances the rescission of the Royal assent would merely acknowledge an already existing invalidity. Indeed this could be seen as an example of a situation in which the Royal assent is purportedly given to an instrument that has not been passed by the legislature at all. Thus, also in Australia, where the Governor-General gave the Royal assent to a bill that had not been passed by one house of the legislature, the assent was cancelled when this was discovered.[19] It would seem that in such circumstances the assent would be a nullity and that this would also be the case in New Zealand.

PROMULGATION OF ACTS

No special formalities are prescribed for promulgating the fact that the Royal assent has been given to a bill and that that bill is now an Act of Parliament. The Governor-General formerly advised the House by message of this fact and the message was read to the House by the Speaker but this practice was discontinued in 1985.

After the Royal assent has been given, the Clerk of the House deposits one of the assented copies with the registrar of the High Court at Wellington. The other is retained at Parliament House and eventually transferred to Archives New Zealand.[20] It is not necessary for the text of an Act to be published in the *New Zealand Gazette*,[21] although the fact that the Royal assent has been conferred is advised in the *Gazette*'s parliamentary notices section.

PUBLICATION OF ACTS

Following assent, arrangements are made by the Office of the Clerk and the Parliamentary Counsel Office to have the Act printed and made publicly available as soon as possible. The taking of official action in reliance on legislation which has come into force but not been made available to the public will inevitably raise questions as to the validity of that action. Access to the law is regarded as an aspect of the rule of law.[22]

A number is inserted showing the order in which the Act received the Royal assent, a legislative history showing the dates on which the bill passed through its principal parliamentary stages and was assented to is added, and a note made at the end of the Act showing which department is responsible for administering it. This latter note is intended to indicate which department would be concerned to initiate or promote an amendment to the legislation should one be contemplated. There is no such note to local or private Acts.

The Attorney-General may give directions as to the form in which a copy of an Act of Parliament is to be printed.[23] The Chief Parliamentary Counsel is responsible for carrying out the final checking of copies of Acts and for authorising their publication.[24] Loose copies of Acts are usually published within a week of the Royal assent having been given. They carry an imprint stating that they are published under the authority of the New Zealand Government.[25] They are sold on subscription and from retail outlets operated for the purpose under arrangements with the Crown. The Attorney-General has power to designate places where copies of Acts of Parliament are to be made available for purchase by members of the public,[26] and the Chief Parliamentary Counsel is required to make copies available for purchase at those places at a reasonable price.[27] But this does not prevent copies being made available for sale at any other place not so designated.[28]

---

[19] Harris, *House of Representatives Practice*, p.396.
[20] S.O.313.
[21] *Acts and Regulations Publication Act* 1989, s.17.
[22] *R (L) v Secretary of State for the Home Department* [2003] 1 All ER 1062.
[23] *Acts and Regulations Publication Act* 1989, s.7(1)(a).
[24] *Ibid.*, s.4(1)(a).
[25] *Ibid.*, s.4(2).
[26] *Ibid.*, s.9(1).
[27] *Ibid.*, s.10(1).
[28] *Ibid.*, s.9(2).

Acts of Parliament are bound into annual volumes of statutes (three or more volumes to a year) which are also made available for sale.

No copyright subsists in Acts of Parliament,[29] so the official publication of legislation does not preclude publication by any other person.

Following comments on a discussion document issued by the Parliamentary Counsel Office in September 1998 and a survey of users of legislation, the Government has initiated a project to provide greater availability of up-to-date legislation in different forms. This project (the Public Access to Legislation project) will integrate the systems and processes for the drafting of legislation with its publication in both printed and electronic form. The Crown will own and maintain an electronic database of legislation to be made freely available on the internet.[30] In the meantime free public access to statutes (and regulations), with amendments incorporated, is provided on an interim website of New Zealand legislation.

Reprints of Acts

Reprints of copies of Acts of Parliament in force are made from time to time as occasion requires. These arrangements are made by the Chief Parliamentary Counsel subject to such directions as the Attorney-General may give.[31]

Reprints are made in a format and style that accords with the legislative drafting practice that is being used in New Zealand at the time of the reprint.[32] Such practices change incrementally or as a result of the deliberate adoption of new styles and formats as occurred on 1 January 1997 and 1 January 2000.[33] When making such changes in an Act that has been reprinted, the reprint must indicate that such changes have been made and outline, in general terms, what those changes are.[34]

Comprehensive reprints of legislation in bound volume form were made in 1908 (the public law was completely repealed and re-enacted for that purpose), 1931 and 1957. Between 1979 and 2003 a progressive bound volume reprint of Acts of general application was carried out which eventually entirely replaced the 1957 reprint. Local and private Acts have not generally been included in any of these reprints. Reprints of statutes are now published in pamphlet form, focusing on best-selling titles that are frequently or heavily amended.[35] The reprinted statutes are available on the interim website of New Zealand legislation.

Evidence of Acts

Every copy of an Act of Parliament purporting to be printed or published under the authority of the New Zealand Government is, unless the contrary is proved, to be regarded as a correct copy of the Act and to have been published with authority.[36] A reprinted Act is, unless the contrary is proved, to be regarded as correctly stating the law enacted by the Act being reprinted.[37]

These provisions lay down only a presumptive rule for identifying statutes.[38] If there were genuine doubt as to the authenticity of the Act or its contents, reference could be made to the copies signed by the Governor-General and held at Parliament House (or Archives New Zealand) and the High Court.

---

[29] *Copyright Act* 1994, s.27(1); *Copyright Act Commencement Order* 2000.

[30] 2000, Vol.589, p.6967; see also Lawn, "Format of Legislation and Access to Law" [1999] NZLJ 418.

[31] *Acts and Regulations Publication Act* 1989, ss.4(1)(c) and 7(1)(b).

[32] *Ibid.*, ss.17A to 17E.

[33] 1997, Vol.559, pp.869-79; 1999, Vol.581, p.37.

[34] *Acts and Regulations Publication Act* 1989, s.17F.

[35] 2004, PP, A9, p.46.

[36] *Evidence Act* 1908, s.29(1).

[37] *Ibid.*, s.29A(1).

[38] Joseph, *Constitutional and Administrative Law in New Zealand*, p.522.

CHAPTER 29

DELEGATED LEGISLATION

Most of the legislation enacted each year is not made by Parliament directly. It is made by other persons or bodies under powers granted or delegated to them by Parliament and is generally known as delegated legislation. The forms which delegated legislation take are various. Orders in Council, proclamations, regulations, rules, notices, warrants and bylaws are how some of the instruments used to make delegated legislation are described. The most important of these instruments are known by the compendious term "regulations". Their common feature is that they are legal instruments made under powers delegated, directly or indirectly, by Parliament.

In contrast to the enactment of legislation by Parliament, there are no general procedures for the making of delegated legislation that ensure that it is subjected to public debate and scrutiny before it is made, though individuals uniquely affected by a regulation may have a legal right to be consulted before it is made.[1] In addition, statutes conferring the power to make regulations may contain specific provisions requiring notice of the intention to make a regulation to be given and allowing interested persons an opportunity to make submissions.[2] But such provisions are not common.

Generally too, neither Parliament nor the House has any part to play in the actual making of regulations. Parliament has played its part by passing the legislation conferring the power to make the regulations. The exercise of that power is in the hands of another authority.

PARLIAMENTARY REVIEW OF DELEGATED LEGISLATION

The importance of delegated legislation, the limited opportunities for prior scrutiny of it and the almost non-existence of any parliamentary role, led to an inquiry by a select committee in 1962. (The committee is known as the Algie Committee after its chairperson, Sir Ronald Algie.) In its report the committee recognised that in modern conditions the practice of delegating law-making powers is in many cases necessary in the interests of efficient administration. The committee did not agree that delegated legislation was wholly or even substantially bad in itself. It was rather an inevitable and necessary attribute of parliamentary government.[3] This fundamental acceptance of the need for delegated legislation has never been challenged.

Nevertheless, while accepting a necessary role for delegated legislation, the committee felt that steps should be taken to guard against its objectionable features. One of these steps was the establishment of a select committee, at first called the Statutes Revision Committee, with an express brief to report from time to time on regulations that it considered infringed certain criteria. The Statutes Revision Committee, however, was not a specialist delegated legislation committee. Throughout its life its work was dominated by the consideration of primary legislation. Bills of a technical legal character (which tended to include criminal, company and courts legislation) were invariably referred to it for consideration. As a result, scrutiny of delegated legislation was a minor and, until the last few years of its existence, almost entirely neglected aspect of its work.

---

[1] See Joseph, *Constitutional and Administrative Law*, pp.903-5.

[2] See, for example, *Securities Act* 1978, s.70(3).

[3] 1962, AJHR, I.18 (*Report of the Committee on Delegated Legislation*).

The increasing importance of delegated legislation and the apparent ineffectuality of parliamentary arrangements for dealing with it led to pressure for a more concentrated approach to it from the House. Consequently, in 1985, following a fresh look at possible arrangements,[4] the House determined to establish a select committee which was largely free of the burden of considering bills so that it could concentrate on scrutinising delegated legislation. This committee is known as the Regulations Review Committee, and it is the cornerstone of parliamentary oversight of delegated legislation.

At the same time as a specialist delegated legislation committee was established in 1985, the subject select committees were given power to initiate their own inquiries. In respect of regulations falling within their terms of reference they are able to examine any regulation that has been made. For the examination of a regulation on policy grounds a subject select committee, rather than the Regulations Review Committee, is the appropriate medium.

REGULATIONS REVIEW COMMITTEE
The Regulations Review Committee is a committee which the House by its Standing Orders establishes at the commencement of each Parliament.[5] The committee's principal task is to examine all regulations.[6] In addition, the committee may examine draft regulations referred to it by a Minister,[7] consider provisions in bills that are before other committees which relate to regulations,[8] consider any matter relating to regulations on which it wishes to report to the House[9] and investigate complaints about the operation of regulations that are made to it.[10]

The Regulations Review Committee was the first committee (in 1985) to be chaired by an opposition member, and it has now become an established convention that this should be so.[11] The committee meets regularly each week when the House is sitting and occasionally during adjournments too. In 2004 it held 30 meetings, for instance.[12] Included in its committee secretariat are legal staff from the Office of the Clerk to ensure that it has legal support of a high enough standard to enable it to carry out its tasks effectively.

The committee has taken the consistent line that it must strive to act in a bipartisan manner in conducting the scrutiny of regulations on behalf of the House. The House's purpose in setting it up was to ensure that the technical scrutiny of regulations was not neglected by the House. The committee is concerned with how policy is implemented in regulations, but not with the merits of that policy. It is for the House and for the subject select committees to address the policy aspects or merits of regulations. The committee will therefore not question the policy underlying regulations in the scrutiny that it carries out.[13]

The committee's role in respect of the varying aspects of parliamentary scrutiny of delegated legislation is examined in this chapter. (A digest of the committee's reports prepared under the auspices of the New Zealand Centre for Public Law is contained on the Victoria University of Wellington website.)

JUDICIAL REVIEW OF DELEGATED LEGISLATION
As delegated legislation involves Parliament conferring on another person or body legal power to make statute law, it is appropriate that the House be jealous in limiting the extent to which it gives such delegated authority and that it monitor closely its exercise. Since

4 1984-85, AJHR, I.5.
5 S.O.185(1)(b).
6 S.O.314(1).
7 S.O.314(2).
8 S.O.314(3).
9 S.O.314(4).

10 S.O.314(5).
11 1996-99, AJHR, I.16R, p.8.
12 2002-05, AJHR, I.16I, p.5.
13 1984-85, AJHR, I.5A, para.8.4; 1986-87, AJHR, I.16A, para.8.2; 1991-93, AJHR, I.16E, p.33; 1996-99, AJHR, I.16R, p.9; *ibid.*, I.16T, p.6.

the reforms effected in 1985 the House has endeavoured to make parliamentary control of delegated legislation more effective. But another, and longer-established, method of review of delegated legislation exists – that exercised by the courts.

The courts do not question the validity of a duly enacted Act of Parliament. But delegated legislation is subject to challenge in the courts on the ground of invalidity. As delegated legislation owes its existence to a statutory power, if its provisions are in excess of that power it is invalid and of no lawful effect. A regulation may also be invalid if a special procedure – for example, one involving consultation with interested parties – is prescribed to be followed before it is made and this procedure is not observed.

The courts' powers to review regulations to ensure that they are, or were, made in compliance with the enabling Act may themselves be cut down by Parliament. Provisions in Acts of Parliament which seek to inhibit the courts' power to rule upon the validity of delegated legislation may operate directly by prohibiting a court from reviewing the validity of regulations made under the Act, or indirectly by conferring the power to make delegated legislation in such wide subjective terms that it is difficult to put meaningful bounds on the delegated authority. These legislative practices are now generally regarded as undesirable, and are matters to which the Regulations Review Committee has regard in its work.

HUMAN RIGHTS REVIEW OF REGULATIONS

A regulation that is alleged to offend against the anti-discrimination provisions of the *New Zealand Bill of Rights Act* 1990 may be made the subject of a complaint to the Human Rights Commission. If the complaint cannot be satisfactorily resolved by the commission, civil proceedings may be brought against the Attorney-General before the Human Rights Review Tribunal.[14]

The Human Rights Review Tribunal may issue a declaration that a regulation is inconsistent with the freedom from discrimination guaranteed by the *New Zealand Bill of Rights Act*.[15] If such a declaration is made the Minister responsible for the administration of the regulation must report to the House, bringing the declaration to its attention and advising of the Government's response to it.[16]

Review of a regulation by the Human Rights Commission and the Human Rights Review Tribunal on anti-discrimination grounds may overlap with some of the grounds on which the Regulations Review Committee examines regulations.

DEFINITION OF REGULATIONS

Mention has already been made of the variety of instruments through which delegated legislation may be made. Those instruments which are subject to comprehensive requirements relating to their printing, publishing, scrutiny by the Regulations Review Committee and general control by the House are those falling within the statutory definition of "regulations".

Regulations are defined as—

(a) Regulations, rules, or bylaws made under an Act by the Governor-General in Council or by a Minister of the Crown:
(b) An Order in Council, Proclamation, notice, Warrant, or instrument, made under an enactment that varies or extends the scope or provisions of an enactment:

---

[14]   *Human Rights Act* 1993, s.92B(1)(b).   [16]   *Ibid.,* s.92K.
[15]   *Ibid.,* s.92J.

(c) An Order in Council that brings into force, repeals, or suspends an enactment:

(d) Regulations, rules, or an instrument made under an Imperial Act or the Royal prerogative and having the force of law in New Zealand:

(e) An instrument that is a regulation or that is required to be treated as a regulation for the purposes of the Regulations Act 1936 or Acts and Regulations Publication Act 1989 or this Act:

(f) An instrument that revokes regulations, rules, bylaws, an Order in Council, a Proclamation, a notice, a Warrant, or an instrument, referred to in paragraphs (a) to (e).[17]

Thus, not all proclamations or Orders in Council, for instance, are regulations. Acts of Parliament delegate powers to the Governor-General to be exercised by proclamation or Order in Council. These will often be regulations. But proclamations or Orders in Council made in the exercise of prerogative powers possessed by the Crown, or, though made under an Act, that do not vary or extend the scope or provisions of the Act (for example, orders or proclamations taking land under a power conferred by the Act) are not regulations. Nor are bylaws made by local authorities. (Bylaws made by local authorities are subject to a separate legal regime.[18]) As at 1 June 2001 there were 3,058 statutory regulations in force (as compared with about 700 Acts of Parliament).[19]

Regulations are sometimes referred to as secondary legislation as distinct from primary legislation enacted directly by Parliament. However, there has in recent years been a proliferation of types of delegated powers to make legislation and it is not always easy to classify delegated legislation in this way.[20] For example, regulations may themselves in turn delegate power to make legislation or to issue instruments of a legislative character, known as tertiary legislation. Instances of tertiary legislation are: bylaws (other than local authority bylaws), codes of practice, standards, guidelines, notices and directions. In general, tertiary legislation is not subject to the statutory and parliamentary controls applying to regulations.[21] Statute may specifically provide that tertiary legislation is not to be regarded as a regulation so as to avoid any doubt about the matter.[22] Other instruments may have only some of the characteristics of regulations and be exempted by statute from many of the other consequences (for example, in relation to their drafting and publication) that attach automatically to a full regulation.[23] What legal and parliamentary controls over delegated legislation apply to a particular instrument therefore depends on the precise nature of the statutory provision authorising (or ultimately authorising) its making. The Regulations Review Committee pays close attention to this aspect of any regulation-empowering provisions in bills before the House.

Only regulations as statutorily defined are within the purview of the Regulations Review Committee for examination.[24] Therefore a complaint to the committee about an instrument that is not a regulation cannot be pursued by the committee.[25] However, it is for the committee to decide whether an instrument falls within its jurisdiction.[26] The committee, in drawing matters of general significance to the attention of the House, can make recommendations about the institutional setting within which regulations are made. The unsatisfactory nature of the form in which some delegated legislation is made has attracted its attention.

The difficulties with the classification of delegated legislation have led to concerns both for potential users of delegated legislation and for scrutiny by the Regulations

---

17 *Regulations (Disallowance) Act 1989*, s.2.
18 *Bylaws Act* 1910.
19 *Hansard Supplement*, 2001, Vol.48, p.1630.
20 1996-99, AJHR, I.16R, p.6.
21 1980, AJHR, I.5, p.18; 2002-05, AJHR, I.16E, p.5.
22 *Securities Markets Act* 1988, s.36R (business and listing rules of a securities exchange are

not regulations).
23 1996-99, AJHR, I.16R, p.10.
24 S.O.3(1).
25 1999-2002, AJHR, I.16J, p.47.
26 2002-05, AJHR, I.16C, p.4 (committee decided a fisheries notice declaring stock subject to the quota management system was a regulation).

Review Committee. Accordingly, the committee has recommended that the definition of "regulations" in the *Regulations (Disallowance) Act* 1989 should be amended to follow the conceptual definition of "legislative instruments" in Australian legislation.[27] While not accepting that immediate legislative change is required, the Government has agreed to monitor the operation of the Australian legislation.[28]

PRIMARY LEGISLATION AUTHORISING REGULATIONS

Principles

Parliamentary control of delegated legislation ought, logically and effectively, to begin with close consideration and delimination of the provision that delegates the power to make such legislation in the first place. This power is contained in primary legislation. A first question for the House and its committees to address when presented with a proposal to authorise the making of delegated legislation is thus: is the power necessary and appropriate?

The Algie Committee in 1962 established that making delegated legislation is not, in principle, objectionable. The Regulations Review Committee has set out its view of the circumstances in which delegated legislation in its widest sense may be appropriate.

In the view of the committee, delegated legislation should be confined to matters of detail and the implementation of policy. It should not be the means of making policy itself. Specifically, the committee felt that primary, not delegated, legislation should be the means by which—

• an agency is established and has its functions defined
• substantive personal rights are created
• powers of search and seizure are created
• imprisonable criminal offences are created.[29]

These principles for using primary as opposed to delegated legislation have not been specifically endorsed by the House and are not rules that bind those preparing primary legislation or committees considering bills. However, they do provide a background against which proposals for delegated legislative powers can be judged in the course of the legislative process and are liable to be uppermost in the Regulations Review Committee's contribution to that process.

Power of the Regulations Review Committee to report on legislative proposals

In 1986 the Regulations Review Committee was given the power to report to any other committee on an empowering provision in a bill before that committee. This power to intervene in the legislative process has been considerably extended since then.

The committee may, in respect of a bill before a committee, consider and report to that committee on—

• any regulation-making power
• any provision that contains a delegated power to make instruments of a legislative character
• any matter relating to regulations.[30]

For this purpose the committee examines every bill that is introduced into the House. In 2003, for example, the committee made 11 reports to other committees on regulations

---

[27]   *Legislation Instruments Act* 2003 (Australia).   [30]   S.O 314(3).
[28]   2002-05, AJHR, I.16I, p.28.
[29]   *Ibid.*, I.16E, Appendix E.

issues in bills.[31] In making its reports the committee does not confine itself to a written report to the other committees. It also makes its staff available to those committees to present and explain the reports and answer questions from members of other committees that may arise.[32] The committee thus assumes an advocacy role in the legislative process for the delegated legislative principles that it has identified.

As well as having the right to intervene in the legislative process, the committee is often invited by other committees to comment on regulation-making powers either contained in a bill as introduced or to be introduced into the bill by way of amendment.[33] The committee has also been invited by another committee to comment on a regulation-making scheme in a proposed international treaty that was before the latter committee.[34]

The committee's reports to other committees are summarised or noted in its own periodical reports to the House.

Outcomes of committee reports
The committee's reports on regulation-making powers to other committees are merely recommendations to those committees. It is for the latter to decide whether to adopt them and recommend amendments to the bills to reflect them. They do not always do so. As subject select committees they are charged with considering the policy issues contained in bills; this is not the Regulations Review Committee's task. For this reason, they may come to a different conclusion from the Regulations Review Committee on a regulation-making provision – though the latter may ask the committee to reconsider the matter[35] and has shown some persistence in pursuing issues with Ministers even after its recommendations have been initially rejected by the committees to which they were directed.[36] There is no necessary inconsistency here, as finally it is a matter for the judgment of the House. But the ability of the Regulations Review Committee to focus committees' attention on regulations enables it to raise questions about their utility that may not otherwise arise, and has led to an increasing number of changes being made to legislation passed by the House. In 2001 it made 27 recommendations for bills to be amended, 23 of which were implemented in whole or in part.[37]

Regulation-making provisions
The section or sections in an Act of Parliament authorising delegated legislation to be made are known as regulation-making or empowering provisions. The Algie Committee recommended that the precise limits of the law-making power conferred by Parliament should be set out as clearly as possible in the empowering provision. Following this recommendation, a new standard formula for provisions authorising the making of regulations was adopted on the initiative of the then Chief Law Draftsman (Chief Parliamentary Counsel). The formula was designed to conform to the committee's ideal of a provision which set out the precise limits of the law-making power and left intact the courts' power to review the validity of regulations made under it.

No parliamentary body was specifically charged with keeping regulation-making provisions in bills under review for conformity with these principles. As each bill was referred to a select committee for consideration, it was open to the committee concerned to attend to any objections to regulation-making provisions that it contained. Inevitably, however, this was not a prominent part of each committee's consideration of the bills

---

31 2002-05, AJHR, I.16D, p.26.
32 *Ibid.*
33 *Ibid. (Border Security Bill)*; *ibid.*, I.22B, p.575 (*Health (Screening Programmes) Amendment Bill*).
34 *Ibid.*, I.22C, pp.699, 709-16.

35 1991-93, AJHR, I.16L, para.124.
36 1999-2002, AJHR, I.16I, p.38; *ibid.*, I.16J, pp.34, 40-1.
37 *Ibid.*, I.16J, p.34.

before it and no overall expertise about empowering provisions could be built up by one committee. The Regulations Review Committee now has the brief of commenting to other committees on such provisions.[38]

The committee examines bills to determine whether the delegation of Parliament's law-making power is appropriate and clearly defined and represents good legislative practice. While the committee's examination is not confined to the scrutiny grounds identified in the Standing Orders,[39] those grounds do provide a useful test: would regulations made under the empowering provision under review potentially transgress one of those grounds? The committee's examination also considers whether regulation-making powers infringe well-established principles applying to delegated legislation (for example, those set out in guidelines issued by the Legislation Advisory Committee). Legislative proposals that provide for matters of policy and substance to be enacted by regulations, for an Act itself to be amended by regulations (a Henry VIII clause), or for law-making powers to be delegated without provision for adequate scrutiny and control of the instrument exercising those powers, are all matters likely to receive attention from the committee.[40]

The grounds on which the committee has thus questioned the drafting of regulation-making provisions have been various. In some cases the committee's concerns have been about the process by which powers made under the empowering provision would be exercised. Where the exercise of powers would not be by regulations and the committee considered that it should be, it recommended accordingly.[41] On another occasion the committee considered that the regulations to be made under the empowering provision should be subject to express confirmation by Parliament given their significance (the fixing of levies).[42] Amongst other things, the committee has objected to: an empowering provision that would have allowed an Order in Council to override provisions of an Act;[43] a provision that was designed to oust the jurisdiction of the courts; a provision that would apply the provisions of one Act to another "with modifications" and one with retrospective effect.[44] Regulations containing any of these elements would constitute grounds on which the committee might draw them to the House's attention.[45]

Amendment or repeal of primary legislation by regulations

Parliament may delegate the power to amend or even repeal primary legislation by regulation. This type of regulation-making provision is commonly called a "Henry VIII clause". It has been said that this designation derives from that King's association with autocratic government and specifically because in 1539 Parliament gave him extensive power to amend statutes by proclamation. But it has been doubted whether this is truly justifiable, since Henry VIII ruled (1509 to 1547) well before the concept of parliamentary sovereignty was established.[46] Such provisions are in any case much older than that King's reign.[47]

The transfer of power from the legislature to the executive that a Henry VIII clause entails has led to such clauses being treated with suspicion as possibly constitutionally inappropriate.[48] The Regulations Review Committee has recommended that such powers should be delegated only in exceptional circumstances. It has accepted that in the case of transitional provisions in legislation a Henry VIII clause dealing with unforeseen contingencies arising during the implementation of a measure may be justified. But it has

---

[38] S.O.314(3)(a).
[39] S.O.315(2).
[40] 2002-05, AJHR, I.16I, p.18.
[41] 1990, AJHR, I.16.
[42] 1991-93, AJHR, I.16L, para.17.
[43] 1990, AJHR, I.16A, para.5.4
[44] 1991-93, AJHR, I.16E, para.4.4.

[45] S.O.315(2)(c), (f), (g).
[46] *Thoburn v Sunderland City Council* [2003] QB 151 at 13 (per Laws LJ).
[47] Carr, *Concerning English Administrative Law*, p.41 (quoting examples from 1383 and 1388).
[48] *Thoburn v Sunderland City Council*, op. cit.

been especially critical of using a Henry VIII clause to override legislative amendments made subsequent to the enactment of the clause.[49] It has also given detailed consideration to a special type of Henry VIII clause that allows statutory provisions to be overridden for the purposes of implementing international treaties.[50] (See Chapter 43.)

Other matters

The Regulations Review Committee has indicated that it will pay particular attention to regulation-making provisions authorising the making of deemed regulations. Deemed regulations are regulations not published with the general series of statutory regulations. The committee will need to be persuaded that such regulations are appropriate.[51] (See pp. 405–6 for deemed regulations.)

A further practice that the committee has indicated that it will pay attention to is the incorporation of material into regulations by reference. Incorporation by reference is a drafting technique which gives legal effect to provisions contained in a document without actually repeating those provisions or that document in the text of the legislation or regulation itself. Using such a technique can cause difficulties in accessing the law if the document is not readily available. It also means that as the document changes, the law effectively changes without any conscious parliamentary decision being made to alter it. The committee has indicated that it intends as a matter of course to scrutinise provisions in bills authorising this practice and to ask departments to demonstrate how regulations that incorporate material by reference comply with best-practice guidelines that have been issued by the Legislation Advisory Committee on the conditions under which this should be done[52] – for example, placing the document incorporated by reference on the internet so as to facilitate access to it. But the committee has also accepted that there may be circumstances in which such best-practice cannot be complied with because of copyright concerns.[53]

On a number of occasions the committee has recommended to the select committee on a bill that a regulation-making provision be amended to define with greater particularity both the object to be served by the regulations that the provision is to authorise and the power to be granted under it. Its concern with a commonly included general final paragraph in empowering provisions (that regulations may be made "for such other matters as are contemplated by or necessary for giving full effect to this Act") caused the committee to hold a special inquiry into that type of provision. The committee was able to satisfy itself that such a provision was acceptable and that its effect was truly limited to subsidiary and incidental matters.[54]

PREPARATION OF REGULATIONS

Drafting

Regulations are drafted in the Parliamentary Counsel Office. Some 40 percent of the drafting resources of that office may at any time be committed to drafting delegated legislation as opposed to primary legislation.[55] Most of the delegated legislation drafted by the office consists of statutory regulations, though the office also drafts other instruments (proclamations, some notices, etc.) that are not regulations. From time to time the Regulations Review Committee conveys its views on the drafting style of regulations to the Chief Parliamentary Counsel.[56]

---

[49] 1993-96, AJHR, I.16C.
[50] 1999-2002, AJHR, I.16H.
[51] 1996-99, AJHR, I.16R, p.20.
[52] 2002-05, AJHR, I.16G.
[53] *Ibid.*, I.22D, p.452 (*Legislation (Incorporation by*

Reference) Bill)
[54] 1990, AJHR, I.16, pp.2-5.
[55] 2003, PP, A.9, p.7.
[56] 1999-2002, AJHR, I.16I, pp.34-5.

Deemed regulations are not drafted in the Parliamentary Counsel Office. Indeed, one of the principal criticisms of such regulations (along with their unavailability) is the variable and often defective quality of their drafting. Deemed regulations are drafted by the department or agency responsible for making them.

Consideration of draft regulations

It is unusual for the House to have the opportunity to consider regulations before they are promulgated, but occasionally, when the House has a bill before it, the Minister produces a draft of regulations proposed to be made under powers to be conferred by the bill. This has happened with sets of draft regulations in the transport sector while the bills concerned were being passed through the House. In one case, proposed amendments to the bill enabled new regulations relating to seat belts and child restraints to be made, and appended to the supplementary order paper containing these amendments was a draft of the regulations proposed to be made under the powers sought. The supplementary order paper was referred to the select committee considering the bill, and the draft regulations were considered by it as part of its consideration of the bill.[57] In another case, by motion in the House, draft regulations were referred to the select committee then considering a bill to introduce a graduated licensing system and were considered by the committee along with the bill.[58]

Referral of draft regulations to the Regulations Review Committee

While formal referral of draft regulations to other committees is rare, there is provision under the Standing Orders for the Minister concerned to refer draft regulations to the Regulations Review Committee for its consideration.[59] This has now grown to be a significant area of work for the committee.[60] During the course of 1999, 21 sets of draft regulations were referred to the committee under this provision, the greatest number ever in a single year.[61]

Increasingly, and especially in the transport sector, the committee is being absorbed into the standard consultation process by having draft regulations referred to it. Since November 1998 all proposed land transport, maritime transport and civil aviation rules have been referred to it in draft by the Minister of Transport.[62] The committee may take the initiative in inviting a Minister to refer draft regulations which it has learnt about,[63] perhaps after being alerted by the receipt of a complaint.[64] In one case where there was a conflict of views within the Government itself as to the scope of draft regulations, the Minister referred them to the committee to seek its views. After the committee endorsed them with some recommended amendments, the Minister incorporated its recommendations into the final version of the regulations.[65] The committee has particularly urged Ministers to refer to it draft regulations that incorporate material into the regulations by reference.[66]

Generally, the committee has made it clear that it welcomes Ministers referring regulations for pre-promulgation scrutiny.[67] This is especially important where regulations, on their face, raise issues of trespass on personal rights and liberties. Pre-promulgation scrutiny can allow potential problems to be identified and resolved prior to the regulations being made.[68]

The committee regards its relationship with the referring Minister as an advisory one. For that reason if the draft of the regulations referred to it has not yet been publicly

---

[57]   1983, AJHR, I.5A (*Transport Amendment Bill (No 4)*).

[58]   1986-87, JHR, p.682 (*Transport (Law Reform) Bill*).

[59]   S.O.314(2).

[60]   1999-2002, AJHR, I.16J, p.32.

[61]   1996-99, AJHR, I.16X, p.35.

[62]   1999-2002, AJHR, I.16J, p.32.

[63]   1990, AJHR, I.16A, para.4.

[64]   1996-99, AJHR, I.16X, pp.40-1.

[65]   1987-90, AJHR, I.16A, pp.8-9.

[66]   2002-05, AJHR, I.16G, p.12.

[67]   1999-2002, AJHR, I.16J, p.32.

[68]   1996-99, AJHR, I.16X, p.42.

released, it may consider it appropriate to hear evidence from affected parties in private.[69] Generally, it does not hold extended hearings on draft regulations and may confine itself to a briefing from officials of the department concerned.

As with its scrutiny work generally, the committee will not comment on policy aspects of the draft regulations.[70]

The committee formally reports to the Minister on any draft regulations referred to it.[71] This does not preclude the committee subsequently reporting to the House in its periodic reports describing its activities, and it regularly does this. The committee has also conveyed its views on draft regulations to the select committee which was at that time considering a bill under which the regulations were to be made.[72] The committee may choose not to conduct a detailed scrutiny of draft regulations where there is insufficient time to do so satisfactorily, reserving such an examination for when the regulations are made.[73]

The fact that the committee has examined regulations in draft does not preclude a further review of the regulations by the committee when they are made.[74] Indeed the committee is likely to monitor whether any changes which it has suggested have subsequently been made to the final regulations. It may, where it has reported adversely on regulations, invite a Minister to refer any replacement regulations to it in draft. Thus, following criticism about fees regulations for identity services and codes of animal welfare, draft new regulations were referred to the committee for consideration.[75]

PUBLICATION OF REGULATIONS

Regulations made by the Governor-General in Executive Council are notified in the *Gazette* and then published in an official series first established in 1936.[76] Free public access to regulations is also provided on an interim website of New Zealand legislation. Eventually, this website will be superseded by an electronic database of New Zealand legislation (primary and delegated) available on the internet. (Regulations that are not published in this way – deemed regulations – are mentioned below.) The Chief Parliamentary Counsel arranges for reprints to be made of regulations incorporating any amendments to them that have been adopted since they were first made. Any regulations that are drafted outside the Parliamentary Counsel Office but which are required to be published in the official series must be forwarded to the Chief Parliamentary Counsel immediately after they are made so that that officer may arrange for their printing and publication.[77]

Instruments which are not regulations as defined may be published in the official series if the Attorney-General or the Chief Parliamentary Counsel so directs.[78] The Regulations Review Committee has recommended that amendments of instruments that are not regulations should be published in the official series if the original instrument was so published.[79]

These requirements are designed to ensure that regulations are published in a timely and easily-accessible form.

Deemed regulations

There are many legislative instruments which, although they are regulations, are exempted from these publication requirements and which are not submitted to the high-level internal governmental processes of endorsement by the Cabinet and at a meeting of

---

[69] *Ibid.*, p.35.
[70] *Ibid.*, p.42.
[71] S.O.314(2).
[72] 1991-93, AJHR, I.16L, paras.244 to 249 (*Health and Safety in Employment Bill*).
[73] 1999-2002, AJHR, I.16J, p.32.
[74] 1996-99, AJHR, I.16X, p.35.

[75] 2002-05, AJHR, I.16D, pp.16-8.
[76] 1996-99, AJHR, I.16R, p.13; *Acts and Regulations Publication Act* 1989, s.11.
[77] *Acts and Regulations Publication Act* 1989, ss.4(1)(b), 5 and 11(1).
[78] *Ibid.*, s.14.
[79] 1991-93, AJHR, I.16L, paras.168-72.

the Executive Council. Nor are such regulations drafted in the Parliamentary Counsel Office. These instruments have become known as "deemed regulations". In 1999 the Regulations Review Committee identified 50 statutes that authorised such regulations.[80] As regulations, they were subject to scrutiny by the committee but they could be difficult to identify and obtain and varied in the quality of their drafting. In general, the committee believed that deemed regulations suffered from inappropriate formats and lack of consultation and accessibility.[81] The committee consequently recommended that deemed regulations should be authorised only in defined circumstances when an exception to the traditional form of regulation is justified and that in any event they should be subject to explicit Cabinet endorsement. Furthermore, there are certain subjects which because of their importance (for example, taxation and criminal offences) the committee considered should never be dealt with by deemed regulations.[82]

In its responses to the committee's report, the Government agreed to alter certain of its internal procedures when a proposal to create a power to make a deemed regulation was under consideration. The new procedures were designed to require it to be clearly established that deemed regulations were justifiable. The Government did not accept that deemed regulations should be submitted to Cabinet for its endorsement. It did accept that deemed regulations should be published along with traditional regulations under the *Acts and Regulations Publication Act* 1989 unless there was good reason to the contrary. In such a case the instrument would be drafted in the Parliamentary Counsel Office. (Instances when a departure from this policy would be justified included regulations implementing internationally-promulgated standards which follow different formats from New Zealand legislation.) In response to the committee's complaints of difficulty of access to deemed regulations, a working party compiled and included in a report a list of all deemed regulations not published in the statutory regulations series. The Parliamentary Counsel Office has undertaken to keep this list up to date on the basis of advice from authorities making deemed regulations. Material from the Parliamentary Counsel Office has been made available to those drafting deemed regulations to help them to follow better-defined and more consistent drafting standards. Other preparation standards issued are to be addressed in guidance material to be prepared by the Legislation Advisory Committee.[83]

PRESENTATION OF REGULATIONS TO THE HOUSE

All statutory regulations must be laid before the House not later than the sixteenth sitting day after the day on which they are made.[84] This obligation applies as equally to instruments that are deemed to be regulations as it does to instruments that are regulations in their own right.[85] This is a general requirement specifying the time within which regulations must be presented to the House, but if there is a specific statutory requirement that particular regulations must be presented within a shorter time-frame (or may be presented within a longer time-frame), that provision prevails over the general provision.

In general, whether any failure to comply with a statutory requirement invalidates the process of which that requirement is part depends upon the view that the courts take of the consequences of non-compliance in the statutory context.[86] Factors identified by the court as relevant in making this consideration include: the degree and seriousness of the non-compliance, the potential consequences which may arise through the non-

---

[80]   1996-99, AJHR, I.16R, pp.6 and 13.

[81]   1999-2002, AJHR, I.16I, pp.19-20.

[82]   1996-99, AJHR, I.16R, pp.14, 16-7.

[83]   *Ibid.*, AJHR, A.5; *Further Government response to the report of the Regulations Review Committee on its* "Inquiry into instrument deemed to be regulations

– an examination of delegated legislation", presented 16 November 2000.

[84]   *Regulations (Disallowance) Act* 1989, s.4.

[85]   1999-2002, AJHR, I.16I, p.28.

[86]   *Wang v Minister of Internal Affairs* [1998] 1 NZLR 309 at 318.

compliance and whether prejudice has occurred or is likely to have occurred.[87] This test (formulated in respect of a statutory notice to an individual) has been applied by the court to test the validity of a *particular* regulation presented to the House out of time. In the circumstances of that case it was held that failure to present the regulations to the House within 16 sitting days did not invalidate them.[88]

But, it is suggested, while this is the appropriate test to apply to the *general* requirement that regulations must be presented to the House, it should not be applied to test the validity of particular regulations presented pursuant to that general provision.

Subject to any particular legislative variations, the presentation of regulations to the House is dealt with by one general legislative provision, which requires presentation within 16 sitting days.[89] There is no justification for reaching different conclusions on the effect of this provision in respect of its application to different regulations and in respect of its application of the same regulation to different persons. Yet if the factors identified above were applied to particular regulations, some regulations presented out of time might be found to be valid and others might be found to be invalid, and the same regulation found to be valid in its application on one occasion and invalid in its application on another occasion, regardless of the fact that the statutory provision requiring their presentation to the House is the same in all cases. Consequently, it is submitted, failure to comply with the general provision to present within time should have the same legal consequence as to validity, regardless of the particular regulation in question.

The requirement to present regulations to the House is something that is done with a regulation that has already been made; it is not a step in making the regulation in the first place. Although there is a general drafting practice followed of not bringing regulations into force until 28 days after they have been made, this practice is often departed from without any question being raised as to the legal effect of such regulations prior to their presentation to the House. Consequently, the view has generally been taken that presentation is one means of ensuring that publicity is given to a regulation that has already been made rather than being an essential step in making the regulation or in ensuring its validity or continuing validity (though this requirement has been described as a "feeble safeguard" given the large number of documents presented to the legislative).[90] Where the Regulations Review Committee has identified regulations as having been presented out of time, its comments have been limited to expressing its concerns that the failure to present the regulations may mean that they are not brought to its attention.[91] It is also clear that the House's power to disallow regulations is not dependent upon those regulations having been presented to it in the first place.

The statutory provision relating to presentation may in a particular case make presentation an essential condition for the validity or continuing validity of regulations made under it.[92] Thus, regulations increasing rates of social security and war pension benefits have, since 1983, been required to be laid before the House not later than 16 sitting days after they are made. The legislation formerly went on to provide that if they were not so laid within that time they automatically expired. When these sections were re-enacted in 1990, the provisions imposing automatic expiration of the regulations for failure to present them were omitted.[93] It was also formerly expressly provided that failure to present emergency agricultural regulations caused them to expire on the close

[87] *Ibid.*

[88] *Haliburton v Broadcasting Commission* [1999] NZAR 233.

[89] *Regulations (Disallowance) Act* 1989, s.4.

[90] Campbell, "Laying and Delegated Legislation" [1983] PL 43; Carr, *Concerning English Administrative Law*, p. 58.

[91] 1999-2002, AJHR, I.16B, pp.12-3; *ibid.*, I.16I, p.28.

[92] See, for example, *Metcalfe v Cox* [1895] AC 328 (ordinances not to be effectual until, *inter alia*, laid before Parliament).

[93] *Social Security Amendment Act* 1983, s.10; *War Pensions Amendment Act* 1983, s.4; *Social Security Amendment Act* 1990, s.3; *War Pensions Amendment Act* 1990, s.2.

of the sixteenth sitting day after they were made.[94]   There is a definite and significant contrast between the requirement to present such regulations and the general presentation requirement in the *Regulations (Disallowance) Act*.[95]

Where the statute under which regulations are made provides that failure to present the regulations within a certain time automatically invalidates them, the position is clear. But such a provision is exceptional (indeed there appear to be no such provisions currently in force). In the absence of a provision to that effect, it is submitted that the general obligation to lay regulations before the House (real and legally enforceable as the obligation undoubtedly is) should not be regarded as affecting the validity of the regulations. Any failure to comply (if relevant in a particular case) may, however, be taken into account by the courts in determining what penalty or relief to order in the case, especially if failure to present a regulation has been accompanied by failure to publish it generally.

Regardless of the legal effect of failure to present regulations to the House within the statutory time limit, failure to do so will inevitably attract criticism from the Regulations Review Committee.[96]

PARLIAMENTARY INVOLVEMENT IN MAKING REGULATIONS

Consultation with the House

Statute may require that, before a legal power can be exercised, there must be consultation with the House of Representatives. In regard to delegated legislation there is provision for consultation with the House and committees of the House before regulations relating to the reporting standards to be observed by departments, certain organisations and offices of Parliament may be prescribed.

Before any regulations may be made prescribing the non-financial reporting standards that departments, certain organisations or offices of Parliament must apply and the form in which that information must be presented to the House, the Minister of Finance must submit such regulations to the Speaker in draft.[97] The Speaker presents the draft regulations to the House as soon as reasonably practicable.[98] The Minister, after considering any comments of the Speaker or any committee of the House that considered the draft regulations, may amend the regulations relating to departments and organisations as the Minister sees fit.[99] The regulations may then be made. (See Chapter 35.) In the case of regulations relating to offices of Parliament, the regulations may only be made after they have also been approved by resolution of the House.[100]

Validation of regulations by statute

Some statutes provide for the making of regulations that will cease to have effect after a period of time unless they are "validated or confirmed" by an Act of Parliament passed within that time. Such regulations are subject to a statutory "sunset clause" whose effect can be avoided by Parliament confirming the regulations and giving them continuing force. To validate a regulation, however, as opposed to merely confirming it, potentially does more than avoid the lapse of the regulation under a sunset clause. It can also cure any other defect in the regulation or in the manner in which the regulation was made that would otherwise have led to the regulation being regarded as invalid.[101]

---

[94] *Agriculture (Emergency Powers) Act* 1934, s.27(6)(a) (repealed by the *Hop Industry Restructuring Act* 2003, s.13).
[95] *Haliburton v Broadcasting Commission* [1999] NZAR 233.
[96] 1999-2002, AJHR, I.16I, pp.19-20.

[97] *Public Finance Act* 1989, s.82(1), (2).
[98] *Ibid*., s.82(3).
[99] *Ibid*., s.82(4).
[100] *Ibid*., s.82(5).
[101] *Turners & Growers Export Ltd v Moyle*, unreported, High Court, Wellington, 15 December 1988.

Effectively, Parliament in validating a regulation ratifies it and adopts what has been done. The position is the same as if Parliament had itself made the regulation in primary legislation.[102] While to validate includes to confirm, it may go very much further than the latter process and can make an unlawful regulation lawful. However, as a matter of practice, the annual legislation validating and confirming regulations usually restricts the effect of any "validation" solely to preventing the regulation from expiring and thus leaves the regulation open to challenge on any other ground.[103] Such legislation, though it may be termed validating legislation, is in truth only confirmatory legislation.

The statutes that incorporate sunset clauses into their regulation-making provisions are dealt with below as aspects of Parliament confirming regulations in force, but when Parliament enacts legislation confirming the regulations it may take the opportunity to declare them to be valid also in a general sense. Indeed, the desire to remove any doubts about the validity of the regulations may be the main reason for introducing the legislation.[104]

Apart from regulations that are subject to sunset clauses, Parliament occasionally passes other legislation validating regulations about whose legality there is a serious doubt. In this regard the Regulations Review Committee has expressed concern at the retrospective validation of regulations that were made in breach of statutory consultation requirements. The committee will critically examine the reasons given for such a course. It has affirmed its belief that specific consultation procedures prescribed by statute should be strictly complied with.[105]

Confirmation of regulations by statute

There are a number of statutes which empower the making of regulations with immediate effect but which also require those regulations to be expressly confirmed by Act of Parliament within a period of time, otherwise the regulations will cease to have effect. In considering and passing a bill to confirm such regulations, the House is given the opportunity of debating the regulations concerned at all the stages involved in the passing of a bill, and members can express their views on the regulations' policy and drafting.[106] While retrospective, where this form of control operates it is of a very high order and of wide extent.

There are no particular types of regulations which must be made subject to this confirmation procedure. However, the Regulations Review Committee has suggested that there are four categories of regulation that should be considered as especially suitable for statutory confirmation—

* emergency regulations
* regulations imposing a financial charge in the nature of a tax
* regulations amending the empowering Act or another Act (Henry VIII clauses)
* regulations dealing with issues of policy under the authority of a broad empowering provision.[107]

The fact that regulations fall within one of these categories should indeed prompt a preliminary inquiry as to whether delegated legislation is appropriate at all, since the subject-matter of the regulations may be important enough for enactment in primary legislation. If a regulation-making power is appropriate, it is a matter for judgment as to whether statutory confirmation should be employed in any particular case. For instance

---

[102] *Boscawen Properties Ltd v Governor-General*, unreported, High Court, Wellington, 10 December 1993.
[103] For example, *Subordinate Legislation (Confirmation and Validation) Act* 2003, s.11; 1999-2002, AJHR, I.22A, p.877.
[104] 1988, Vol.494, p.8064 (*Primary Products Marketing Regulations Confirmation Bill*).
[105] 1996-99, AJHR, I.16G, pp.28-9.
[106] 1986-87, AJHR, I.16A.
[107] *Ibid.*, p.7; 2002-05, AJHR, I.16E, Appendix E.

it may not be appropriate to require confirmation in every case where regulations merely alter the details in a schedule to an Act. But where such alterations are not limited to minor corrections or updating, primary legislation or regulations subject to confirmation will be appropriate.[108]

The time for which regulations that are subject to confirmation may run before lapsing or expiring differs according to the precise provisions set out in the Act under which they are made. Some regulations lapse 12 months after they are laid before the House, unless confirmed by legislation passed within that time.[109] Others lapse on 31 December where they are made in the first half of the year, and on 30 June in the following year where they are made in the second half. This gives them an effective life of under a year before they must be confirmed.[110] Others have a slightly longer potential life before confirmation is needed by not expiring until dates in the following calendar year in all cases[111] or in some cases.[112] In one case, the regulations concerned remain in force until the end of the session in which they are made – an indeterminate period that may be shorter or longer than the other formulas.[113] (See Chapter 33 for Orders in Council relating to taxation that require confirmation or validation.)

Each year legislation is introduced to confirm regulations that would otherwise lapse. Insofar as it is possible, a variety of regulations made under different Acts will be confirmed in a single piece of legislation, often called the Subordinate Legislation (Confirmation and Validation) Bill, but this may not be possible if it is desired to validate or confirm a particular regulation urgently. There may therefore be more than one bill introduced each year for this purpose.

Confirmation is the House's opportunity to consider the policy which lies behind the regulations to be confirmed. It is not an exercise confined to examining regulations for conflict with delegated legislation principles. There is therefore no presumption that a confirmation bill will be referred to the Regulations Review Committee when it has been introduced. A confirmation bill dealing with regulations solely relating to producer boards, for example, would be likely to be referred to the Primary Production Committee, where the committee could hear evidence from growers opposed to the policy underlying the regulation – something the Regulations Review Committee avoids encroaching upon. But a confirmation bill dealing with a miscellany of regulations covering a number of subjects is likely to be referred to the Regulations Review Committee.

Regulations made by the House

Parliament usually delegates legislative powers to the Governor-General or Ministers, but it is perfectly competent for such powers to be delegated to the House itself and in one instance this has been done. It is statutorily provided that the House may make rules for the guidance of the Ombudsmen in the exercise of their functions.[114] Such rules are made by resolution of the House, and are printed and published as if they were regulations.[115] The House has made two sets of rules under this power, in 1962 and in 1989,[116] both relating to the publication of reports by the Ombudsmen.

---

[108] 1999-2002, AJHR, I.16J, p.35.

[109] For example, *Social Security Act* 1964, s.61H(3) (rates of benefit); *New Zealand Superannuation and Retirement Income Act* 2001, s.15(5) (adjustment of New Zealand superannuation).

[110] For example, *Electronic Transactions Act* 2002, s.14(4) (amending list of enactments to which Act applies – a Henry VIII clause); *Education Act* 1989, s.159(5) (domestic students' residence permits); *Animal Welfare Act* 1999, s.191(6) (codes of welfare).

[111] For example, *Wine Act* 2003, s.96(1), (2)

(wine levies).

[112] For example, *Maritime Security Act* 2004, s.78(8) (application of Act to a ship or port facility); *Gambling Act* 2003, s.319(4)(a), (b) (problem gambling levy).

[113] For example, *Primary Products Marketing Act* 1953, s.4(1).

[114] *Ombudsmen Act* 1975, s.15(1).

[115] *Ibid.*, s.15(3).

[116] 1962, JHR, pp.345-46 (*Ombudsman's Rules* 1962); 1987-90, JHR, pp.1150-1 (*Ombudsmen Rules* 1989).

Amendment of regulations by the House

The House has a general statutory power, by resolution, to amend any regulations or to revoke any regulations and substitute other regulations for them.[117] Such amendments or substituted regulations are advised to the Chief Parliamentary Counsel by the Clerk of the House, and are printed and published in the same manner as any other regulations.[118] They come into force on the later of any commencement date expressed in them or the twenty-eighth day after a notice advising of the revocation or amendment has been published.[119] Any member may give notice of motion to amend or substitute a regulation. Such a notice is set down as a Government or Member's order of the day, as the case may be. A notice for amendment of a regulation is subject to financial veto by the Government if the amendment or revocation would have more than a minor impact on the Government's fiscal aggregates.[120]

This amendment and substitution power gives the House a general authority to make regulations, but only in amendment or substitution for regulations that have already been made and not as an initiator of regulations in its own right. Any amended or substituted regulations made by the House must themselves, as delegated legislation, be within the terms of the empowering provision authorising the making of the regulations in the first place. The power has never been exercised.

Approval of regulations by affirmative resolution of the House

Statute may provide that certain types of regulations cannot come into force unless the House approves them or approves the Order in Council for their commencement. Effectively, the House is asked to approve the making of the regulations. This is known as the "affirmative resolution procedure" because unless the House positively approves of the regulations they will never come into effect. (The affirmative resolution procedure has also been applied to instruments that are not regulations, such as instructions as to the non-financial reporting standards of offices of Parliament.)

The affirmative resolution procedure was first introduced in respect of Orders in Council amending the lists of controlled drugs set out in the schedules of the *Misuse of Drugs Act* 1975. Where a substance is listed as a controlled drug, criminal penalties apply in respect of its supply or possession, depending upon its classification in those schedules. Substances are classified according to their risk of harm.[121] A "fast-track" means of responding to rapid developments in the illicit drug market, with the consequent need to include new substances in the schedules and reclassify others, led to the development of the affirmative resolution procedure whereby the schedules can be amended by regulations, but only following explicit parliamentary endorsement.[122] A similar procedure has been devised for altering the amount of a controlled drug in a person's possession that automatically raises a presumption that the drug is possessed for the purposes of supply.[123] The procedure has since been extended to other types of regulations.[124]

Typically, regulations subject to the affirmative resolution procedure can only come into force in accordance with a commencement order after the regulations have been

---

[117] *Regulations (Disallowance) Act* 1989, s.9(1).
[118] *Ibid.*, s.10.
[119] *Ibid.*, s.9(2).
[120] S.O.318(3).
[121] *Misuse of Drugs Act* 1975, s.3A.
[122] 1999-2002, AJHR, I.22A, pp.531-4 (*Report of the Health Committee on the Misuse of Drugs*

Amendment Bill (No 4)).
[123] *Misuse of Drugs Act* 1975, s.4(1B).
[124] *Dog Control Act* 2003, s.78B (breeds or types of dog that may be imported and must be muzzled); *Public Finance Act* 1989, s.82(5) (publication of information and non-financial reporting standards for offices of Parliament).

approved by resolution of the House.[125] Approval may be given only 28 days after notice of the regulations amending the schedules has appeared in the *New Zealand Gazette*.[126] Such regulations lapse if a motion to approve the commencement order is defeated or if no commencement order is approved within one year.[127] In the case of regulations prescribing the publication and non-financial reporting standards for offices of Parliament, the House must be consulted on the regulations in draft first and they may be made only after they have been approved by resolution of the House.[128]

The House has supplemented these statutory procedures by making its own rules for how a motion to approve a regulation or other instrument is to be dealt with.

A notice of motion to approve a regulation or proposed regulation under any statute stands referred to a select committee for examination. The Clerk allocates the notice to the most appropriate committee.[129] (A notice of motion may be given while any statutory waiting time is running. The select committee's examination of the commencement order and the statutory waiting time may run simultaneously.) The committee must report back to the House on the notice of motion no later than 28 days after it was lodged.[130] The depth of the examination carried out by the committee (in particular, whether it hears public submissions) is a matter for it. Inevitably its examination of the order must be carried out swiftly, otherwise the intent of the legislation to provide a fast-track amendment process would be defeated.

The House's rules provide that no motion to approve a regulation or proposed regulation may be moved until the committee has reported back on the notice of motion or 28 days have elapsed since the notice was given, whichever is the earlier.[131] During this time the notice of motion appears on the order paper with a note indicating that it cannot be dealt with until the occurrence of one of those events. When the committee does report on the notice, its report is set down for consideration together with the notice of motion.[132] If the committee reports back within 28 days the motion can be moved and dealt with at any time thereafter and if, for whatever reason, the committee fails to carry out its obligation to report within 28 days the motion can be moved in the absence of such a report. However, in any case, any time prescribed by statute must have elapsed since the original regulation was notified in the *Gazette* for the House's approval of it to be effective.[133]

The Health Committee in its consideration of controlled drugs orders has adopted a practice of requesting a briefing from the Expert Advisory Committee on Drugs before an order is made classifying a drug and then a further briefing when a notice of motion is lodged. Evidence from officials of other departments involved in the process may also be heard. The committee scrutinises the process followed by the expert committee in making the recommendations that led to the proposal to classify the drug. If the Health Committee feels that further consultation or examination is necessary it will undertake it.[134]

Where, in any case, the House is given power to approve the making of regulations,

---

[125]   See, for example, *Misuse of Drugs Act* 1975, ss.4(2) and 4A(1), (2).
[126]   *Ibid.*, s.4A(3); *Misuse of Drugs Amendment Act* 2005, s.34(3).
[127]   *Misuse of Drugs Act* 1975, s.4A(4); *Misuse of Drugs Amendment Act* 2005, s.34(4).
[128]   *Public Finance Act* 1989, s.82.
[129]   S.O.317(1).
[130]   S.O.317(2).
[131]   S.O.317(3).
[132]   S.O.251(1)(d).
[133]   See, for example, *Misuse of Drugs Act* 1975, s.4A(3) (28 days must have elapsed since the notification in the *Gazette*).
[134]   1999-2002, AJHR, I.22C, pp.510-16; 2002-05, AJHR, I.22D, p.540.

the House's approval of them does not exempt the regulations concerned from judicial scrutiny of whether they were made within the powers conferred by the empowering legislation.[135] It has been said, that if regulations have been approved by the House it will be more difficult to persuade a court to intervene on the grounds that the regulations are vitiated by being unreasonable.[136] On the other hand, judges may differ in the weight that they give to the fact that a regulation has received the prior approval of the House.[137]

As the initial examples of the affirmative resolution procedure involved Henry VIII clauses, the dangers of its proliferation for this purpose led the Regulations Review Committee to inquire into the principles regarding its use. The committee, in an interim report, expressed concern at the use of the procedure to amend primary legislation by regulation in areas that dealt with significant policy matters.[138] It has also protested at proposals to extend the procedure into new areas, though the subject select committee considering the matter may take a different view.[139]

Revocation or disallowance of regulations by the House

The House may have specific power conferred on it to revoke regulations in certain cases. Where these specific provisions apply, any disallowance by the House may be effected in accordance with their terms. There are currently no such provisions subject to this power.[140]

But the House does have a general power to disallow any regulations by resolution.[141] (Though it may not disallow amendments to regulations or substituted regulations that it has made itself.[142]) This power is not limited by time. The House does not have to exercise its general disallowance power within any particular time after the regulations in question have been made. Where the House does resolve to disallow regulations, those regulations cease to have effect on the day the disallowance resolution is passed or on such later date as may be specified in the resolution itself.[143] The disallowance of a regulation has the same effect as if the regulation had been revoked.[144] Thus it does not affect the validity of anything already done or any existing rights. Generally, the revocation of a regulation does not revive any legislation itself repealed or revoked by that regulation.[145] But in regard to disallowance this rule is changed. Where the regulation that is disallowed itself amended, repealed or revoked any Act or regulation, that Act or regulation is restored to force.[146] Any disallowance resolution is printed and published as if it were a regulation.[147]

Any member may give notice of motion to disallow a regulation. Such a notice is set down as a Government or Member's order of the day as the case may be. The first notice of motion to disallow a regulation that was given lapsed when Parliament was dissolved.[148] The first attempt to disallow a regulation that was debated by the House was defeated.[149] The House has simultaneously debated four motions to disallow regulations.[150]

A motion to disallow a regulation is a motion which, if passed, would have force

---

[135] *Hoffman-La Roche v Secretary of State for Trade and Industry* [1975] AC 295 at 341, 349, 354, 365 and 372.
[136] *Nottinghamshire County Council v Secretary of State for the Environment* [1986] 1 AC 240.
[137] See, for example, *Miah v Secretary of State for Work and Pensions* [2003] 4 All ER 702 at 34 (per Ward LJ) for "complete cynicism about the adequacy of parliamentary scrutiny of subordinate legislation of this kind".
[138] 2002-05, AJHR, I.16I, p.29.
[139] *Ibid.*, I.22D, pp.507, 514 (*Misuse of Drugs Amendment Bill (No 3)*).
[140] See, for a former example, *Civil Defence Act* 1983,

s.79(8) (repealed by the *Civil Defence Emergency Management Act* 2002, s.116).
[141] *Regulations (Disallowance) Act* 1989, s.5(1).
[142] *Ibid.*, s.5(3).
[143] *Ibid.*, s.5(2).
[144] *Ibid.*, s.7.
[145] *Interpretation Act* 1999, s.17.
[146] *Regulations (Disallowance) Act* 1989, s.8(1).
[147] *Ibid.*, s.10.
[148] 1991, Vol.512, pp.418-9.
[149] 1996-99, JHR, p.813 (*Disputes Tribunals Amendment Rules* 1998).
[150] 2002, Vol.598, pp.14573-99.

of law by virtue of the statute under which it is made. It is therefore a motion which is subject to financial veto by the Government.[151] If the Government considers that the disallowance that is proposed would have more than a minor impact on the Government's fiscal aggregates it may issue a financial veto certificate at any time before the motion is moved.[152] (See Chapter 31 for the issuing of financial veto certificates.) The consequence of the issuing of a financial veto certificate is that the motion is out of order and no question is put on it although it can still be moved and debated.[153]

Some instruments are made subject to the House's disallowance power though they are not subject to the printing and publication requirements that apply to regulations generally (deemed regulations).[154] The House's general power to disallow regulations may be abrogated in a particular case. Regulations amending the controlled drugs list and the list of restricted substances (which are subject to parliamentary approval before they can come into force) are not subject to disallowance.[155]

Automatic disallowance of regulations

In one case there is provision for the automatic disallowance of regulations. While any member of Parliament may give a notice of motion to disallow a regulation, there is no guarantee that this notice (or any other notice) will be considered by the House. Government orders of the day have a precedence that enables them to be considered, but Members' orders of the day do not, and a Member's notice of motion will lapse after seven days if it has not already been considered.[156]

In order to give members a real opportunity to utilise the disallowance power, it is consequently provided in the legislation that any notice of motion to disallow a regulation which is given by a member of the Regulations Review Committee and is not dealt with by the House, automatically takes effect on the expiration of the twenty-first sitting day after it was given.[157] Only a member of the committee at the time notice is given, including a member who is a full non-voting member of the committee, can give a notice subject to the statutory automatic disallowance procedure. A replacement or temporary member or a member made a non-voting member for a particular inquiry cannot give a notice that entails automatic disallowance.

Unless the member withdraws such a notice, the House must, within 21 sitting days of the notice being given, attend to it and dispose of it. The obvious way to dispose of such a notice is to debate the motion and vote on it at the end of the debate. But a financial veto certificate also disposes of the notice of motion. Where a financial veto certificate is given before the motion for disallowance is moved, no question is put on the motion at the conclusion of the debate and the motion is ruled out of order without a vote.[158] At that point the motion has been dealt with by the House. Otherwise a notice of motion that is undisposed of after 21 sitting days takes effect according to its terms. If, before this period has fully run, Parliament is dissolved or expires, the notice of motion lapses.[159] (In this case a new notice could be given in the next session of Parliament and the 21 sitting days would begin to run anew from that point.) As business does not lapse on the prorogation of Parliament, a notice given in one session will continue to run in the new session.[160]

To ensure that the House is aware that time is running towards automatic disallowance

---

[151] S.O.318(3); 1993-96, AJHR, I.18A, p.62 (Standing Orders Committee).

[152] S.O.320(4).

[153] *Ibid.*

[154] See, for example: *Food Act* 1981, s.111 (food standards); *International War Crimes Tribunal Act* 1995, s.61(3) (extension of Act to other tribunals); *Institute of Chartered Accountants Act* 1996, s.8 (rules made by the institute).

[155] *Misuse of Drugs Act* 1975, s.4(3); *Misuse of Drugs Amendment Act* 2005, s.33(3).

[156] S.O.96(1).

[157] *Regulations (Disallowance) Act* 1989, s.6(1)(a), (b).

[158] S.O.320(4).

[159] *Regulations (Disallowance) Act* 1989, s.6(1)(c).

[160] *Constitution Act* 1986, s.20(a); *Regulations (Disallowance) Act* 1989, s.6(1)(d) is now otiose.

of a regulation, the Standing Orders provide that a notice of motion for disallowance given by a member of the Regulations Review Committee does not lapse and is not to be removed from the order paper until dealt with by the House.[161]

A disallowance that occurs automatically on the expiration of 21 sitting days takes effect at that precise time or on any later date specified in the notice of motion for disallowance.[162] An automatic disallowance notice is printed and published as if it were a regulation.[163]

The power to initiate the automatic disallowance procedure that is vested in each member of the Regulations Review Committee does not depend upon the regulation concerned having been the subject of an adverse report from that committee. Nevertheless, it is assumed that those members would act in a manner that is consistent with the conventions attaching to that committee before initiating such a procedure.

COMPLAINTS RECEIVED BY THE REGULATIONS REVIEW COMMITTEE

The Standing Orders recognise that the Regulations Review Committee may receive complaints from persons or organisations aggrieved at the operation of a regulation. Any such complaint received by the committee must be placed on the agenda for its next meeting for the committee to decide whether, on the face of it, the complaint relates to one of the grounds on which the committee may draw a regulation to the attention of the House.[164] The committee must, unless it unanimously decides not to proceed with the complaint, give the complainant an opportunity to address the committee on the regulation.[165] In practice, the committee undertakes some initial investigation of complaints to establish if there is a case to answer before formally resolving whether to proceed with a more substantive inquiry.[166] Where, following its initial consideration, the committee considers that a complaint raises a *prima facie* case under one of the grounds for drawing a regulation to the House's attention, this is regarded as requiring a formal inquiry.[167]

It is obvious that a complaint has to relate to a regulation in force. But a complaint about a regulation that had not yet been made was still regarded as useful in focusing the committee's attention on it when it was eventually promulgated.[168] The number of complaints received by the committee varies. During the course of 1999 the committee received nine complaints and resolved to investigate five of them. In 2000 only two complaints were received. The main reasons why complaints are not pursued by the committee is that they relate to policy issues or relate to an instrument that is not a regulation as defined.[169]

EXAMINATION OF REGULATIONS

All regulations are examined by the Regulations Review Committee.[170] But this was never intended to lead to a process of public hearings and submissions in all cases. For this reason the committee has the discretion to decide how it goes about discharging its responsibilities to the House.[171] The committee and its staff peruse all new regulations as soon as possible after they have been made. All regulations are formally noted at the committee's regular meetings. If the committee has any concerns or wishes for further elucidation of a regulation, more details of the effects of the regulations are sought from

---

[161] S.O.96(2).
[162] *Regulations (Disallowance) Act* 1989, s.6(2).
[163] *Ibid.*, s.10.
[164] S.O.316(1).
[165] S.O.316(2).
[166] 1990, AJHR, I.16, p.26; 1991-93, AJHR, I.16L, para.195; 1996-99, AJHR, I.16X, p.62; 2002-05, AJHR, I.16A, pp.10-1.
[167] Caygill, "Functions and Powers of Parliamentary Committees", Electoral and Administrative Law

Commission Seminar, Brisbane, 1 May 1992, para.4.6.
[168] 1990, AJHR, I.16B, para.4.1.
[169] 1996-99, AJHR, I.16X, p.62; see *Making a Complaint to the Regulations Review Committee*, Office of the Clerk, for information on how to make a complaint.
[170] S.O.314(1).
[171] 1984-85, AJHR, I.5A, para.6.5.

the relevant Minister, department or other organisation. Often this will include obtaining a copy of any regulatory impact statement prepared in respect of the regulation.[172] Such inquiries may lead the committee to proceed to obtain further written information and may, in a few cases, result in a substantial inquiry involving the hearing of evidence and a report to the House.[173] In the course of 2004, 476 regulations were examined in this way.[174]

This sifting process may also identify a number of regulations raising related issues that can be considered and reported on together.[175] The comprehensive check on regulations carried out by the committee, supplemented by issues drawn to the committee's attention by complaints or by its consideration of draft regulations, alerts it to particular regulatory issues that require closer scrutiny.

Once the committee does decide to embark on an investigation, the fact that the regulation is revoked during the currency of the committee's consideration of it does not put an end to the committee's inquiry. The committee is obliged to consider whether to draw the House's attention to the regulation before it, and this duty can be discharged notwithstanding that the regulation is no longer in force. Revocation is relevant to the practical question of whether, in fact, the House's attention needs to be drawn to the regulation, but it does not obviate the question being asked at all.[176] But if a regulation is revoked before the committee resolves to conduct an investigation into it and the matter objected to is not included in new regulations, the matter is outside the committee's jurisdiction.[177]

GROUNDS FOR REPORT TO THE HOUSE

In carrying out its work of examining regulations (however they may have come to its attention) the Regulations Review Committee judges regulations against nine criteria set out in the Standing Orders. A regulation is not necessarily bad because it fails to conform to one of these criteria. But, if it does fail to conform, the committee must consider whether to draw the special attention of the House to the regulation by reason of that non-conformity.[178] The committee has a discretion as to whether it should draw the House's attention to a regulation even if it finds one of the grounds established. There may be good reasons for not drawing the House's attention to a regulation – such as if this would have no practical effect whatever – and the committee must always consider this.[179]

The committee has adopted the practice of making reports to the House informing it of its activities over a period (latterly annually). In this way the committee tends to inform the House of its consideration of all regulations that raised issues which it needed to address, even if the special attention of the House did not need to be drawn to them individually. A separate report drawing the House's special attention to a regulation is reserved for those few regulations which raise issues of particular significance.

One thing that the committee does not purport to determine is the question of whether the regulation is outside the legal authority delegated by Parliament – that is, if the regulation is *ultra vires*. Such a question is for the courts, not the House, to determine.[180] Indeed, the committee's grounds for examining a regulation are wider than those of a court.[181] From this it follows that while a court may have upheld the legality of a regulation, the committee is not precluded from inquiring further into it and examining its essential

---

172 2002-05, AJHR, I.16B, pp.7-8.
173 1987-90, AJHR, I.16A, para.5.3; 1990, AJHR, I.16, para.6; 1991-93, AJHR, I.16L, para.153; 1996-99, AJHR, I.16X, p.7; 2002-05, AJHR, I.16D, p.26.
174 2002-05, AJHR, I.16I, p.6.
175 1990, AJHR, I.16, para.3.2
176 1980, AJHR, I.5, p.18.
177 1991-93, AJHR, I.16E, p.37.
178 S.O.315(1).
179 1980, AJHR, I.5, p.6.
180 1984-85, AJHR, I.5A, para.8.4.
181 1996-99, AJHR, I.16R, p.9; 1999-2002, AJHR, I.16I, p.9.

fairness.[182] Nor is the committee concerned with how a regulation is being administered by a government department,[183] though the Ombudsmen or another committee may be interested in this as a question of maladministration. However, if a regulation is being applied inconsistently or unfairly this may suggest that there is a defect in the regulation on which there may be grounds for the committee to report.

The nine grounds on which the committee may draw the special attention of the House to a regulation are examined below.[184]

The regulation is not in accordance with the general objects and intentions of the statute under which it is made
This criterion comes closest to raising questions of *ultra vires*. Applying this ground to regulations involves construing the objects of the legislation authorising the making of the regulations in question. Thus, the committee took the view that the legislation under which the Reserve Bank was created was intended to constitute a central bank which advises the Government on and implements monetary policy. It was not the object of the Act to authorise the bank to engage in trading activities and so, the committee concluded, the House's attention should be drawn to regulations that did so authorise such activities.[185]

A particular concern of the committee has been regulations which impose fees. The committee takes pains to establish that a fee is clearly contemplated in the empowering legislation and that the fee is reasonable. The committee has put forward the view that a fee may be fixed at so high a level that it defeats the purposes of the Act and so is not in accordance with its objects and intentions. In the absence of clear statutory authority, if the fee recovered is greater than cost recovery for the service provided, there is a rebuttable presumption that Parliament could not have intended the holder of the delegated legislative power to be able to impose what is in effect a tax. This is especially the case where the "service" provided is effectively a monopoly.[186] (See also Chapter 33.) The committee considered that the provision of access to justice was among the general objects and intentions of statutes empowering the making of regulations that set civil court fees. Access to justice was so fundamental that a move to use fees to ration access would, in its view, require explicit legislative authority. Regulations were inappropriate instruments for implementing such a policy.[187]

In another case the absence of any effective risk assessment being made before health labelling requirements were imposed on certain food products led the committee to conclude that the statutory preconditions to such labelling were not satisfied. Acknowledging that the Minister had a discretion to impose such requirements, the committee insisted that there must be some evidence to justify them.[188]

Finally, powers to vary the commencement date of different provisions of an Act may provoke attention under this ground, if provisions of the Act that might be considered to be an integral part of the legislative package are not brought into force with the main body of the Act. In this case it may be that to bring into force parts of an Act, with the omission of important provisions, is to use the regulation-making power in a way that is not in accordance with the general objects and intentions of the Act.[189]

---

[182] 1986-87, AJHR, I.16, paras.4.1 and 4.2.

[183] 1999-2002, AJHR, I.16C, p.7.

[184] S.O.315(2)(a) to (i).

[185] 1987-90, AJHR, I.16, pp.13-5.

[186] 1990, AJHR, I.16B.

[187] 2002-05, AJHR, I.16H, pp.32-3.

[188] 1996-99, AJHR, I.16Q.

[189] 1999-2002, AJHR, I.16L.

The regulation trespasses unduly on personal rights and liberties

This was one of the original grounds for the scrutiny of regulations when a delegated legislation committee was first set up in 1962. It involves a two-part consideration. First, whether the regulations trespass against personal rights and liberties and, second, if any such trespass is "undue".[190]

Trespass on personal rights has been found to be a particularly applicable matter to consider with regulations which affect how persons are able to earn their living, for example, in cases where restrictions are placed on commercial enterprises. All laws in some respects inhibit freedom of action. Therefore, the fact that freedom is limited is not sufficient of itself to bring a regulation within this ground of complaint. The limitation must be balanced against the policy which is being furthered.[191] To enable it to do this, the committee has examined in some detail the technicalities of the subject matter of the regulations. Where regulations totally prohibited the commercial taking of rock lobster by diving or hand picking, the committee considered the purpose of the ban – the preservation of stocks – and compared this with the infringement of rock lobster fishers' rights to earn a living. It concluded on the evidence that a total ban went further than was necessary to protect stocks and did trespass unduly on personal rights and liberties. The committee suggested a closed season on taking rock lobster.[192] This suggestion was subsequently implemented by the Government.

The reference to regulations trespassing "unduly" on personal rights and liberties has been interpreted as implying that there be a serious infringement of personal rights or liberties before the regulation can be seen as objectionable. In the case of civil aviation fee regulations before it, the committee concluded that it could not be suggested that there should be no fee at all. There was no evidence to suggest that the fee levels reflected inefficiencies on the part of the ministry and such cross-subsidies between different forms of flying as could be identified were justifiable. The committee, therefore, found no breach in that case.[193] But with court fees, since access to justice is a fundamental right, regulations may more readily be regarded as unduly trespassing on personal rights and liberties. The committee has concluded that if court fees are set at a level that discourages potential litigants and that mechanisms such as legal aid, concession rates, and fee waivers are not available to a large section of court users, then there would be an undue trespass on personal rights and liberties.[194]

A relevant factor in determining whether regulations unduly trespass on personal rights and liberties is the policy of the Act under which the regulations are made. It may be the express policy of the legislation to place extensive restrictions on personal rights and liberties. Where this is the case, regulations that do nothing other than faithfully implement that policy are unlikely to be found to offend.[195]

The regulation makes some unusual or unexpected use of the powers conferred by the statute under which it is made

This is also one of the original grounds established in 1962.

If the empowering Act itself expressly contemplates what the regulations do, then it is very difficult to take the view that the powers conferred have been used in an unusual or unexpected way. In the case of the regulations authorising tertiary legislation setting requirements for the grant of pilots' licences, the principal Act specifically authorised

---

[190]   *Ibid.*, I.16G, p.8.
[191]   *Report on the Economic Stabilisation (Conservation of Petroleum) Regulations (No. 2) 1979*, presented on 10 July 1979.
[192]   1977, JHR, p.57.
[193]   1987-90, AJHR, I.16, pp.20-1.
[194]   2002-05, AJHR, I.16H, pp.32-3.
[195]   1999-2002, AJHR, I.16G, pp.8-9.

such stipulations to be made by tertiary legislation. Regardless of the committee's views on the desirability of such matters being dealt with under subdelegated powers, it could not be said that the regulations were open to objection on this ground. The committee did find, however, that in regulations dealing with a person's livelihood it would expect to find provision for appeals against refusals to grant or renew licences and that the absence of such provision was an unexpected use of the power.[196] On the other hand, if the empowering Act does not explicitly provide for the matter which is the subject of the regulations, the committee may take the view that the regulations make an unusual or unexpected use of the power. The committee found that it was unusual or unexpected to use a power to set fees and charges to implement an accreditation system for surveyors, where the empowering provision did not itself contain any reference to such a system.[197]

Where the empowering Act is drafted in very wide terms, it may be difficult to conclude that something has been included in regulations made under it that could not have been reasonably contemplated. For this reason the committee did not find a carless-days scheme and a weekend petrol sales ban to be unexpected or unusual uses of the powers conferred by the Act under which they were introduced. The width of the provisions in the Act led the committee to conclude that Parliament had intended to authorise the making of regulations going well beyond matters of administration.[198] This type of enactment, however, is very much the exception, otherwise the committee's scrutiny under this ground would be futile. Conversely, the width of the provision in the regulation can lead to the conclusion that it does make an unexpected use of the power. So regulations imposing fees for survey services on persons who did not receive those services, fell foul of this ground.[199]

The motivation behind the making of the regulations will often be an important consideration. When regulations were made principally by a desire to conform to Australian food-labelling standards (and this was not an object identified in the legislation) they were held to make an unexpected use of the power.[200] Another important consideration for the committee will be any explanation or justification that is given to the House for the regulation-making provision in the first place. Any use of the power that departs from such a reason or justification is prima facie unexpected. So where the explanatory note to a bill justified a power to bring legislation into force on different dates on the ground that regulations to implement the Act needed to be drafted, it was an unexpected use of the power to exempt a section from being brought into force because doubts had arisen as to its legal effectiveness.[201]

When a regulation authorises something to be done, the absence of adequate provisions for notice of the doing of that thing can lead to the conclusion that the power is being used in an unexpected way. Regulations which enabled the Government to limit the remuneration of a company's employees inescapably led to the assumption that notice of intention to invoke the regulation-making power would first be served on those affected. The extent of notice required will vary depending on the circumstances, but the total absence of a provision for notice was to make an unexpected or unusual use of that power.[202] In accordance with its general policy of looking critically at Henry VIII clauses, the committee has found that regulations overriding legislation passed subsequent to the Henry VIII clause made an unusual or unexpected use of that power.[203]

---

[196] 1980, AJHR, I.5, pp.20-1.
[197] 1999-2002, AJHR, I.16D, p.9.
[198] *Report on the Economic Stabilisation (Conservation of Petroleum) Regulations (No. 2) 1979*, presented on 10 July 1979.
[199] 1996-99, AJHR, I.16O.
[200] *Ibid.*, AJHR, I.16Q, p.13.
[201] 1999-2002, AJHR, I.16L.
[202] 1980, AJHR, I.5, pp.7-8.
[203] 1993-96, AJHR, I.16C, p.15.

The regulation unduly makes the rights and liberties of persons dependent upon administrative decisions which are not subject to review on their merits by a judicial or other independent tribunal

This ground principally relates to regulations conferring decision-making power on officials or bodies without making provision for a right of appeal or other review of the decision. Decisions taken under statutory powers are always subject to review by the courts to ensure that the statutory powers have been properly used, in the sense of being exercised within the express or implied terms of the statute. Judicial review can lead to an extensive and probing review of the original decision. But it does not permit the court to substitute its opinion on the merits of the decision for that of the person delegated with the statutory power to make that decision. For this reason judicial review is not necessarily an adequate alternative to conferring a right of appeal on which the merits of the decision can be re-examined. The committee will therefore look closely at regulations that do not contain appeal provisions in respect of administrative decisions taken under them.[204] The committee has recommended that regulations relating to domestic violence programmes should contain an appeal process so as to ensure that decisions made by approval panels were subject to independent analysis on their merits, particularly when a decision was made to remove an approval.[205]

The distinctive aspect of this ground, then, is that the committee looks for what is not in the regulations rather than for what is there.

The regulation excludes the jurisdiction of the courts without explicit authorisation in the empowering statute

Provisions in legislation ousting the jurisdiction of the courts to review action taken under the legislation (privative clauses) are no longer common, not least because they have been found to be an ineffective means of excluding the courts' jurisdiction. They are even less likely to be found in regulations. But regulations, while not expressly ousting the jurisdiction of the courts, may have this effect or tendency in practice and this has attracted the committee's attention. Thus the committee has reported on the timing of regulations concerning payments for kiwifruit and the effect that they would have on proceedings currently before a court.[206] The committee has rejected an argument that this ground of review would apply if increased court fees created a potential barrier to access to the courts.[207]

The regulation contains matter more appropriate for parliamentary enactment

This ground is relied on wherever the importance of the matter contained in the regulations suggests to the committee that it should have been enacted in primary legislation. The committee takes a pre-emptive approach in respect of this ground by subjecting proposed Henry VIII clauses to particular scrutiny in reporting to other committees on regulation-making provisions.

Regulations amending legislation, though authorised (as they must have been) by the empowering provision under which they are made, will still be scrutinised carefully by the committee. Such regulations may be justified, for example, where the legislation to be amended consists of lists of bodies in a schedule that requires to be constantly updated as new entities are created and old ones abolished.

One area that has been of particular concern to the committee on this ground has been

---

204   1991-93, AJHR, I.16C, para.7.7; 1999-2002, AJHR,   206   1991-93, AJHR, I.16I, pp.14-7.
    I.16E.   207   1999-2002, AJHR, I.16M, p.21.
205   1999-2002, AJHR, I.16E, p.6.

producer board regulations. The various producer board Acts commonly confer wide powers to make delegated legislation to regulate primary industries. But the committee has still baulked at the width of the rearrangements effected by regulations, taking the view that it was more appropriate for such sweeping changes to have been introduced by primary legislation, not by regulation.[208]

The regulation is retrospective where this is not expressly authorised by the empowering statute
In one case where this ground was considered, the committee held that a regulation that amended existing sharemilking agreements was not retrospective since the alterations it effected took effect from the date the regulation was made. The fact that the regulation altered the legal context in which agreements which had been negotiated would be played out was not sufficient to engage this ground. In any case the statute clearly authorised retrospectivity in this case.[209]

The regulation was not made in compliance with particular notice and consultation procedures prescribed by statute
A regulation made without compliance with prescribed notice and consultation procedures will be subject to legal attack before a court. It is not the committee's function to determine whether the Act's requirements in these respects have been complied with. But the committee may assume that consultation is required even if there is legal doubt about this, and then proceed to judge whether it considers such consultation as did take place was adequate. In assessing this ground the committee has referred to legal standards: that the party consulted must be adequately informed so as to be able to make an intelligent or useful response and that the consultor, while entitled to have a working plan in mind, must keep his or her mind open and be ready to change the plan and even start afresh.[210] But the committee may make its own value judgment as to whether, in the circumstances, it considers the consultation that did take place was adequate, regardless of whether it was legally sufficient.[211]

The committee has made particular recommendations for the principles to be followed for carrying out effective consultation before making deemed regulations. The Government responded that it would ask the Legislation Advisory Committee to consider these principles and produce guidance for consultation in respect of regulation-making generally.[212]

For any other reason concerning its form or purport, the regulation calls for elucidation
"Purport" is taken to mean the literal meaning of the words used in the regulation, rather than its practical effect which, insofar as it can be considered, would fall under one of the earlier grounds. The committee has stated that this ground is included to cover situations where the language used in the regulations is ambiguous or so complicated as to be unclear.[213] If the public is expected to comply with regulations, it is reasonable to expect them to be drafted in plain, unambiguous language and for their format to aid comprehension.[214] This ground could also be invoked if there is a defect apparent on the face of the regulations which needs to be corrected.[215] But findings of substantive unreasonableness are not appropriate under this ground of review.

Thus, the committee has drawn the House's attention to regulations where it considered

---

[208] 1987-90, AJHR, I.16, p.5; 1996-99, I.16X, pp.57-8.
[209] 1999-2002, AJHR, I.16G, pp.11-2.
[210] 1996-99, AJHR, I.16Q, p.14; 1999-2002, AJHR, I.16A.
[211] 1991-93, AJHR, I.16H, pp.12-6.
[212] 1996-99, AJHR, I.16R; *ibid.*, A.5.
[213] *Ibid.*, I.16K; 2002-05, AJHR, I.16K.
[214] 1996-99, AJHR, I.16X, p.23.
[215] 1977, JHR, p.145.

that they should have contained a clear statement of their scope and purpose and should have specified the criteria to be applied in exercising a discretion to grant permits to operators to transport persons to view marine mammals.[216] It also upheld a complaint about rules imposing standards of vehicle window glazing because it considered sections of the rules to be confusing and ambiguous.[217]

It is on this ground, too, that the committee has raised the question of the relationship between the regulation concerned and the *New Zealand Bill of Rights Act*, where the regulation might have had the effect of inhibiting an application for judicial review.[218]

OTHER MATTERS RELATING TO REGULATIONS

As well as its brief in respect of examining regulations, draft regulations and regulation-making provisions in bills, the committee is empowered to bring any matter relating to regulations to the notice of the House.[219]

This general authority has enabled the committee to conduct inquiries that fall outside the other specific powers it possesses. Significant exercises of this general power include its overall examination of regulation-making provisions when its consideration of individual provisions suggested that this was a desirable project. Among the important general reports it has made to the House are: the use of empowering provisions to override primary legislation (Henry VIII clauses);[220] on instruments deemed to be regulations;[221] on the constitutional principles to apply when Parliament empowers the Crown to charge fees by regulation;[222] on delays in bringing Acts of Parliament into force by Order in Council;[223] on the principles to be employed in determining when delegated legislation should be given the status of regulations;[224] and on the incorporation of material into regulations by reference.[225] The report on fee charging was used by the Controller and Auditor-General as a reference point in a review of revenue collected by departments from third parties.[226]

This wide power has also enabled the committee to follow up inquiries it has already conducted and to report to the House what, if any, amendments have been made to regulations to meet concerns expressed by the committee in earlier reports.

REPORTS

The Regulations Review Committee is unusual in that it formally reports both to the Minister who referred draft regulations to it for consideration and to select committees about provisions in bills before them, as well as to the House. However, in practice, the committee includes in its periodic reports to the House summaries of its reports to Ministers and other select committees, so that all of its work is eventually recorded and reported on to the House.

Reports from the committee are presented in the same way as other select committee reports. The committee's reports are set down as Members' orders of the day.[227] Like other select committee reports that are set down for consideration, there is little chance of its reports being debated, and the order of the day is discharged 15 sitting days after the Government's response to it is presented (if it requires a response) and 15 sitting days after being placed on the order paper in other cases.[228]

---

[216]   1991-93, AJHR, I.16C.
[217]   1996-99, AJHR, I.16K, p.15.
[218]   1991-93, AJHR, I.16L, para.162.
[219]   S.O.314(4).
[220]   1993-96, AJHR, I.16C.
[221]   1996-99, AJHR, I.16R.
[222]   1987-90, AJHR, I.16C.

[223]   1993-96, AJHR, I.16K; 1999-2002, AJHR, I.16L.
[224]   2002-05, AJHR, I.16E.
[225]   *Ibid.*, I.16G.
[226]   1993-96, AJHR, B.29[95c] (Controller and Auditor-General).
[227]   S.O.251(3).
[228]   S.O.71(3).

GOVERNMENT RESPONSE

As with reports from other committees, the Government is obliged to present a response on recommendations addressed to it in a Regulations Review Committee report within 90 days of the report being presented.[229]

The committee has shown that it will not be easily satisfied by a response that does not adequately address the matters contained in its report. It has written to the Minister concerned expressing its dissatisfaction with a Government response,[230] and on occasions has launched further inquiries because of the inadequacy of responses received to earlier recommendations. Following the committee's inquiry into geothermal energy regulations it protested that the Government response totally failed to address the issues it had raised.[231] Where the Government's response to a report on Reserve Bank regulations had been presented out of time, the committee reported that this delay had effectively circumvented the work of the committee, since in the meantime legislation had been introduced dealing with the point in issue. The committee also considered that the response had misunderstood the committee's concerns and was in any event inadequate.[232] The committee also issued a report following up the Government's response to its report on Henry VIII clauses, reiterating and elaborating on its views in respect of two of its recommendations that had been rejected by the Government.[233]

---

[229] S.O.253(1).
[230] 1991-93, AJHR, I.16E, p.38.
[231] 1987-90, AJHR, I.16, pp.3-4.
[232] *Ibid.*, pp.12-5.
[233] 1993-96, AJHR, I.16G.

CHAPTER 30

INQUIRIES

POWER TO INQUIRE

The House of Representatives enjoys the power to inquire into any matter that it considers requires investigation in the public interest. While the Parliament of New Zealand is solely a legislative body, the House of Representatives is not exclusively legislative in its functions, it is also inquisitorial. The House does use inquiries extensively as an aid to carrying out its legislative function (through select committees hearing evidence). But the power to inquire as a power existing independently of its legislative functions is recognised by the law as inherent in the House's nature as a representative and responsible legislature. As well as being inherent, it is also affirmed by statute as belonging to the House, since it was (and still is) a power possessed and exercised by the United Kingdom House of Commons on 1 January 1865 and is therefore confirmed as attaching to the House of Representatives too as a legal power.[1]

The House of Commons, its members, and other legislatures tracing their privileges to a similar root, have been called variously the "grand (or great) inquest (or council) of the nation" and the "general inquisitors of the realm", phrases (emanating from the writings of the great seventeenth century lawyer Sir Edward Coke) which express this general power to initiate inquiries into matters that members of Parliament deem worthy of their attention.[2] In Australia, the question has been raised as to whether the power to inquire is limited to being used *only* in aid of the legislative functions of that Parliament (which are themselves circumscribed by the Australian Constitution). However, it has been judicially acknowledged that even though the Commonwealth Parliament's legislative functions are constitutionally limited, there are no limits to the range of matters that may be relevant to its debates and other workings.[3] Furthermore, the fact that a legislature cannot validly pass legislation on a subject (and may thus be wasting its time in debating that subject at all) is no reason for judicial intervention to prevent the legislature considering that subject.[4] Thus, even a legislature with limited legislative functions may possess unlimited power to inquire or at least power that exceeds its legislative competence (though its ability to exercise coercive powers in aid of such inquiries may be inhibited). The better view in Australia today is that the Houses of the Commonwealth Parliament do have a general power to inquire into any matter that affects the public interest, read in its broadest sense, and that this power is not limited to that Parliament's field of legislative competence.[5]

In principle, the power to inquire possessed by the House of Representatives in New Zealand, as a House of a Parliament whose legislative powers are not legally or constitutionally limited at all, is untrammelled. However, that power and, more pertinently, the way in which it is exercised are potentially subject to restraint by any legislation applying to it.

[1] *Legislature Act* 1908, s.242(1).
[2] See, for example: *Morris v Burdett* (1813) 2 M & S 212 at 220 (per Blanc J); *Stockdale v Hansard* (1839) 9 Ad & E 1 at 115; *Howard v Gossett* (1845) 10 QB 359 at 405; *Wason v Walter* (1868) 4 QB 73 at 89 (per Cockburn CJ); *Egan v Willis* (1998) 195 CLR 424 at 475 (per McHugh J); *Canada (House of Commons) v Vaid* 2005 SCC 30 at 20.
[3] *Australian Capital Television Pty Ltd v Commonwealth of Australia* [1992] 177 CLR 106 at 142.
[4] *Rediffusion (Hong Kong) Ltd v Attorney-General of Hong Kong* [1970] AC 1136.
[5] Lindell, "Parliamentary Inquiries and Government Witnesses" (1995) 20 *Melbourne University Law Review* at 385-6; Laurie, "The Grand Inquest of the Nation – A notion of the past?" (2001) 16 *Australasian Parliamentary Review* at pp.176-83.

The nature of parliamentary inquiries

The principal mode of proceeding of a legislature consists of debate among its own members. Indeed, the word "Parliament" is derived from the French verb *parler* (to speak) and originally meant a colloquy or debate. A parliamentary inquiry, on the other hand, is generally understood to involve witnesses from outside the House giving evidence to members on the subject under consideration and being questioned by members in elaboration of that evidence. The main distinction between a debate and an inquiry is that the former is confined to members of Parliament expressing their views on a proposition (a motion), while the latter involves the gathering of information on a subject with a view to influencing future debate among members and may, and today usually does, involve non-members of Parliament participating in the proceedings. However, the oral and direct nature of both parliamentary debate and parliamentary inquiry was insisted upon until comparatively recently. In 1928 a New Zealand Speaker could still tell the House that all evidence given to a committee was supposed to be given in person and that it was irregular for a committee to receive written communications on a matter before it. Evidence was expected to be given orally and directly to the members of the committee.[6] This is no longer exclusively the case.

FORM OF INQUIRY

House

The first witness to give evidence to the House was James Busby, who had been British Resident in New Zealand from 1833 to 1840. He petitioned the House asking to be heard before certain land claims settlement legislation was passed. The House acceded to his request and he gave evidence on 1 August 1856 at the bar of the House before the House went into committee to consider the bill.[7] (Busby subsequently gave evidence at the bar on another occasion.[8]) However, members were already expressing the view that the floor of the House was not a convenient forum for hearing evidence and that a committee environment would be better suited for this. Consequently, proposals to hear evidence at the bar were sometimes rejected.[9] The last occasion on which an examination of a witness occurred at the bar of the House was on 17 July 1896, when the President of the Bank of New Zealand was examined on his refusal to answer questions put to him at a select committee inquiry into the bank.[10]

While it is competent, therefore, for the House to carry out an inquiry itself, it is an unwieldy body for this purpose and it is unusual for it to do so. More usually it delegates this function to a committee.

If it is proposed that a witness be heard at the bar of the House, the House must agree to this on a motion with notice. This motion appoints the time at which the examination is to be held. At the appointed time the witness is escorted to a position just inside the bar of the House by the Serjeant-at-Arms. Witnesses have been offered seats during such a hearing.

The examination of a witness at the bar is conducted by the Speaker with the approval

---

6   1928, Vol.219, p.572.
7   PD 1856-58, p.325.
8   PD 1861-63, p.351.
9   PD 1858-60, pp.384-9.
10 1896, Vol.93, Appendix.

of the House.[11] The witness may be permitted to address the House first, in person or by counsel. Whether or not the witness does address the House, the Speaker, and any member through the Speaker, may put questions to the witness.[12] In the examination of the President of the Bank of New Zealand, the Speaker himself put such formal questions to the witness as were suggested in the report of the select committee that led to the examination at the bar. Members were then permitted to send questions up to the Speaker, in writing, and the Speaker put them directly to the witness. At the end of the examination the witness was permitted to address the House.[13] In all cases the Speaker is the judge of the relevancy of the questions proposed to be asked of a witness.

Committees of the whole House
Committees of the whole House have also been employed to examine witnesses. The House of Commons conferred the power to summon witnesses on committees of the whole House as early as 1640, suggesting that the examination of witnesses by committees of the whole House had become established by then.[14] The first examination of witnesses in a committee of the whole House in New Zealand was conducted in 1860 as part of an inquiry into the outbreak of war in Taranaki.[15] However, the same objections apply to the practicable use of a committee of the whole House as an effective means of examining witnesses as apply to the House itself. Consequently, the examination of witnesses by committees of the whole House has also practically fallen into disuse.

Where an examination is held before a committee of the whole House, it is carried out at the bar of the House in the same manner as it would have been in the House. The examination of a witness is conducted by the chairperson, with the committee's approval.[16] The chairperson, and members through the chairperson, may put questions to the witness.[17]

Select committees
The House of Commons, from the early fourteenth century at least, has established smaller committees of members to consider issues in detail. The matters thus considered were often bills, but also included inquiries into other subjects. In 1341 a committee was established to investigate how the proceeds of a tax had been used, an early example of a public accounts inquiry.[18] While it is likely that most of these early committees were confined to members deliberating among themselves, many would have heard evidence from non-members, especially those inquiring into cases of disputed elections and breaches of privilege. Certainly by the reign of Queen Elizabeth (1558–1603) committees were regarded as indispensable parliamentary tools in gathering information.[19]

In New Zealand the House, at first on a case-by-case basis, specifically granted committees permission to examine witnesses on inquiries that the House had referred to them.[20] Soon the power to examine witnesses, indeed to summon witnesses, became an integral part of every committee's powers.

However, what the House's select committees did not have, until 1985, was a general power of inquiry. Select committees could only inquire into such matters as were referred to them by the House – bills and petitions in the main, but occasionally ad hoc topics referred on motion by the House to a committee for investigation. Before 1985, the Public Expenditure Committee (the predecessor of the Finance and Expenditure Committee) had

---

[11] S.O.159(1).
[12] S.O.159(2).
[13] 1896, Vol.93, p.301.
[14] Redlich, *The Procedure of the House of Commons,* Vol. II, p.207.
[15] PD, 1858-60, pp.284-306.

[16] S.O.175(1).
[17] S.O.175(2).
[18] Redlich, *The Procedure of the House of Commons,* Vol. II, p.205.
[19] *Ibid.*
[20] PD, 1854-55, p.97.

a limited power to initiate inquiries into matters arising from the public accounts. This was the only committee able to undertake inquiries on its own initiative.[21]

In 1985 a major change occurred when subject select committees were given the power to initiate inquiries themselves into most aspects of the activities of Government departments and related organisations. In 1995 this power was broadened from an exclusive focus on the scrutiny of departments and other public bodies to the ability to initiate inquiries into any matter relating to the subject area allocated to the committee.[22] The House's 13 subject select committees are now authorised by the Standing Orders to inquire into any matters that fall within their defined subject portfolios.[23] In the case of other select committees, their ability to carry out inquiries is governed by the terms of the Standing Orders or the resolutions under which they are established. A committee such as the Privileges Committee, for example, can consider and report only on a matter referred to it by the House,[24] while the Regulations Review Committee has a considerable amount of discretion as to the inquiries it may carry out in relation to delegated legislation.[25]

In its non-legislative exercise, the inquiry function of subject select committees has evolved into two forms: formal inquiries and briefings.[26] For formal inquiries committees usually prepare their own written terms of reference, advertise for and examine witnesses and prepare a report to the House. "Briefings" do not usually have established terms of reference, hear few witnesses and are unlikely to result in a report to the House. They are regarded more in the nature of members of the committee informing themselves about the subject-matter of the briefing.

Select committees, in their legislative, financial, treaties, petitions and general inquiry modes, are the House's principal vehicles for carrying out inquiries.

(See Chapter 23 for the conduct of the examination of witnesses before select committees.)

POWERS IN CARRYING OUT INQUIRIES

Power to obtain evidence
As most parliamentary inquiries are carried out by select committees, the effective performance of a committee's tasks depends upon the willingness of people in the community to share their knowledge and expertise with it, so that the committee can make its recommendations to the House after a full consideration of all the facts. Most people are only too willing to assist committees and it is extremely rare for a committee to meet with non-co-operation on the part of a prospective witness. Consequently, the arrangements for witnesses to attend a committee and for documents to be produced to it are made informally. But the House does possess powers to deal with cases of recalcitrance on the part of witnesses in order to ensure that the evidence which the House agrees that a committee must obtain can be obtained.

The power of the House to inquire into anything that it sees fit to inquire into has long been held to imply a concomitant power of compulsion in obtaining the information necessary to carry out the inquiry. Indeed these powers – the power to inquire and the power to obtain evidence coercively – have often been regarded as synonymous. It has thus been said: "The right to enquire draws with it the necessary means, the examination of witnesses, records, papers, enforced by the strong arm of parliamentary privilege."[27] In

---

21 1972, Vol.380, p.1749; 1984-85, AJHR, I.12C, Appendix 6.
22 1984-85, AJHR, I.14, pp.32-5; 1993-96, AJHR, I.18A, p.40; 1999-2002, AJHR, I.2A, Appendix D.
23 S.O.190(2).
24 S.O.391(1).
25 S.O.314.
26 S.O.190(2).
27 Hallam, *Constitutional History of England*, Vol.II, p.307.

parliamentary terms this may often be so, however, the House of Commons never claimed a privilege to administer an oath in aid of its inquiry power and it is not always the case that a body with a power to inquire also possesses a power to order production of evidence. It seems more accurate, therefore, to regard these as separate powers – with the power to secure evidence by requiring the attendance of witnesses and the production of documents supporting and usually (but not always) being co-extensive with the power to inquire.[28] It is also the case that while the power to obtain evidence may be co-extensive with the power to inquire, the likelihood that it will, if exercised coercively, involve intrusion into the rights of persons to security of person and property means that greater safeguards need to be built into the manner of its exercise by the House than is the case with the decision to hold an inquiry in the first place.

Summoning witnesses and documents
The power to summon witnesses and require the production of documents is not limited in its application to government bodies, public servants or other public agencies. It extends to ordering corporate and private bodies to appear before the House or a committee to give evidence and to produce to a committee documents in their possession that are relevant to the inquiry being prosecuted.[29] It was exercised by the House of Commons on four occasions between 1945 and 1991 in respect of private individuals who had or were thought to have evidence relevant to a parliamentary committee's inquiry. Up until 1991 in the United Kingdom no witness had refused to produce documents to a committee since 1835 and no witness had been found to be in contempt for refusing to respond to a summons since 1878.[30]

The procedures which the House employs for exercising its power to summon witnesses and obtain documents are for the House itself to determine as occasion requires. Such procedures are the mode of excercising a privilege (power) which the House possesses; they are not the creation of a privilege itself.[31] The House may exercise the power to summon witnesses and documents by ordering a person to attend at the bar of the House or at a committee for examination or to produce papers and records in the person's possession to the House or a committee. A motion for such an order requires notice. An order that papers and records be produced to the House is known as an order for a return. The power to order returns, however, is understood to be confined to ordering returns of papers of a public or official character.[32] (See Chapter 38.)

Persons, papers and records
The House may delegate to a committee the power to order witnesses to appear or documents to be produced.[33] Such a delegated power is known as the power to send for "persons, papers and records".[34] In 1640, for example, the House of Commons delegated this power to all committees of the whole House.[35] In New Zealand, the House did not at first grant its committees the power to send for persons, papers and records. Indeed, committees were expected to apply to the House for permission to examine witnesses at all, much less to coerce them by requiring their attendance. (Though whether committees

---

[28]   *Howard v Gossett* (1845) 10 QB 359 at 391, 405; *Egan v Willis* (1996) 40 NSWLR 650, especially per Mahoney P at 677-81.

[29]   *Aboriginal Legal Service v State of Western Australia* (1993) 9 WAR 297 at 314-5.

[30]   Leopold, "The Power of the House of Commons to Question Private Individuals" [1992] PL at 543.

[31]   *Harendranath Barua v Dev Kanta Barua* AIR 1958 Assam 160

[32]   *May*, p.263; *Egan v Willis* (1996) 40 NSWLR 650 at 663 (per Gleeson CJ).

[33]   See, for example, *Attorney-General (Canada) v MacPhee*, Prince Edward Island Supreme Court, 14 January 2003 at [41], [42] (a legislature functions through its committees).

[34]   *May*, pp.263, 757-8.

[35]   Redlich, *The Procedure of the House of Commons*, Vol. II, p.207.

actually refused to hear evidence from witnesses willing to appear voluntarily before them is not clear.) Committees wishing to have power to send for persons, papers and records had to make special application to the House to do so.[36] Gradually this position was relaxed and the House often conferred the power to send for persons, papers and records in the order establishing a particular committee.

In 1929 the House by its Standing Orders conferred the power to send for persons, papers and records on all select committees. This remained the position until 1999. It is thought that, at least in the twentieth century, an attempt to exercise the power was made only on one occasion – in 1996.[37] In 1999, in recognition of the fact that use of the power to send for persons, papers and records would be a serious infringement of civil liberties and that it must be exercised in a manner consistent with the right not to be subjected to an unreasonable search or seizure,[38] the House adopted new procedures governing its exercise. These are designed to ensure that the power is not used lightly – indeed is used only as a last resort in a case where the evidence is vitally necessary to the inquiry that is being carried out.[39] The procedures put in place by the House before the power can be exercised are the House's means of ensuring that the power is used in a lawful manner.

Committees with power to send for persons, papers and records
In effect, the pre-1999 position under which all committees possessed the power to send for persons, papers and records has been reversed. Select committees no longer have power to send for persons, papers and records unless this power is specifically delegated to them. The Privileges Committee is specifically delegated with the power by the Standing Orders.[40] The House may confer the power on other committees when they are established or subsequent to their establishment. No other committee has had this power delegated to it since the change in procedure in 1999.

Where a committee has the power to send for persons, papers and records it may, on its own authority, direct that any person be summoned to attend before it and be examined as a witness before the committee. It may also direct that any person be summoned to produce papers and records which are in that person's possession, custody or control and that are relevant to the committee's proceedings,[41] including papers in the possession of private bodies and individuals.[42] The chairperson of the committee is the judge of the relevancy of the papers and records to the committee's proceedings.

If such a summons for papers is directed to a Minister of the Crown, the Minister may refuse to disclose the document concerned as being a confidential state document.[43] In such a case, and in any other case in which a person who has been directed to produce a document by a committee with the power to send for persons, papers and records fails to do so, the committee may report the matter to the House to be dealt with by it.[44]

In the case of a ministerial refusal to produce a document on the grounds of confidentiality, the House, on receiving the committee's report, may order it to be produced, safeguarding the position if necessary by requiring it to be produced in secret.[45] A Minister's refusal to produce a document to a committee is not itself a contempt, but if the Minister refuses to comply with an order of the House for production, that refusal could be treated as a contempt. Where a committee reports the failure of any other person

---

[36] *Standing Rules and Orders of the House of Representatives*, No 78 (adopted 9 June 1854); see, for example, PD, 1854-55, p.118.
[37] 1996-99, AJHR, I.18B, p.16.
[38] *New Zealand Bill of Rights Act* 1990, s.21.
[39] 1996-99, AJHR, I.18B, pp.16-7.

[40] S.O.391(2).
[41] S.O.197(1).
[42] *May*, pp.263, 757-8.
[43] 1909, Vol.148, p.30.
[44] *Ibid.*, p.31.
[45] *Ibid.*, p.30.

to comply with a summons for production of documents, the House may treat that non-compliance as itself a contempt.[46] Alternatively, the House may give the person concerned a further opportunity to produce the document by ordering its production itself.

Even a select committee with the power to send for persons, papers and records cannot order the production of any paper which could not be ordered to be produced by the House.[47] Consequently, a statutory secrecy provision that applies against the House would also apply against a committee.

Furthermore, the fact that a committee has the power to send for persons, papers and records does not entitle it to summon members of Parliament to attend before it. Members may only be requested by a committee to attend before it, though any failure on their part to do so may be reported to the House for its information.[48] Ultimately, only the House can order a member to attend and give evidence to a committee.[49]

Committees not having power to send for persons, papers and records
In the case of committees not having the power to send for persons, papers and records (that is, most committees), coercive powers in respect of a potential witness can be exercised by the House itself on behalf of the committee. It is always open to a committee (for example, by way of a special report) to draw the conduct of a recalcitrant witness to the House's attention and seek the House's support for a summons to be issued directing the witness to co-operate with the committee. Whether the House sees fit to make such an order is a matter for it.

Apart from this, the House has delegated to the Speaker, in respect of committees that do not have the power to send for persons, papers and records, the power to require the appearance of persons and the production of papers. Any select committee may accordingly apply to the Speaker requesting the Speaker to issue a summons requiring the appearance of a witness or the production of papers and records in any person's possession, custody or control.[50] In the case of the proposed attendance of a member of Parliament, only the House itself can order attendance before a committee. It is therefore futile for a committee to apply to the Speaker if it is desired to force a member to attend the committee.

The Speaker will only entertain an application for the issue of a summons from the full committee and not from a subcommittee that it may have formed (though the summons may relate to the production of evidence to the subcommittee). The Speaker may agree to the issue of a summons if the Speaker is satisfied that this is necessary in all the circumstances (including that it is relevant to the committee's inquiry) and that the committee has taken all reasonable steps to obtain the evidence, papers or records concerned. The fact that the material required by the committee is subject to a statutory secrecy provision (whether or not that provision applies in respect of the House) is a relevant factor for the Speaker to consider in dealing with such an application.[51] If the Speaker is satisfied as to these matters, a summons will be issued.[52] The application to the Speaker from the committee for a summons and the Speaker's reply are dealt with in correspondence between the committee and the Speaker.

In agreeing to issue a summons the Speaker will exercise care to avoid any unnecessary impositions on witnesses. Thus, the Speaker has refused to agree to a person being summoned to provide multiple copies of evidence in that person's possession. It was unreasonable to require the witness by summons to provide more than a single copy of the evidence to the committee.[53]

---

[46] 1992, Vol.528, pp.10626-31.
[47] 1875, Vol.19, p.94.
[48] *May*, p.759; HC 588-I (1977-78) Appendix C, para.8.
[49] 2002-05, AJHR, I.18B, p.36 (Standing Orders Committee).

[50] S.O.198(1).
[51] 2002-05, AJHR, I.18B, p.31.
[52] S.O.198(2).
[53] 1999-2002, AJHR, I.7A, Appendix D.

Issue of summons

The Speaker is responsible for signing any order addressed to a person by the House, any order made by a committee with the power to send for persons, papers and records and any order made with the Speaker's agreement on the application of a committee, which, in each case, requires a witness's attendance or the production of evidence. The Speaker is also responsible for directing how such an order is to be served.[54]

Normally, such an order would be served by the Serjeant-at-Arms. Whilst a summons may be issued to anyone present in New Zealand regardless of their nationality, a summons is not issued to someone overseas and thus outside the jurisdiction of the Parliament of New Zealand.[55] A summons issued by the Speaker pursuant to an order of the House or at the behest of a committee must set out the time and place at which the person concerned must comply with it.[56] An order of the House may require the person to whom it is addressed to deliver documents in his or her possession to a specified official, such as the Clerk of the House.[57] In the case of a summons addressed to a witness who is in prison, the manager of the prison may be directed to bring the prisoner in custody before the committee, from day to day. While committees may examine witnesses at their residences, the prior consent of the House should be obtained before a committee proceeds to examine a witness in prison.[58]

Power to punish

The House possesses an inherent power to punish for contempt. The power to punish past transgressions or challenges to its authority can be seen as the ultimate safeguard to the power to inquire; that the House itself has the power to enforce compliance with the exercise of its role as "grand inquest of the nation". But the power to punish can be used in a more directly facilitative way in respect of inquiries, by being used to bring a witness or physical evidence before the House or a committee, rather than to punish for a past failure to attend before them. For the House to order that someone be taken into custody and brought to the bar of the House to give evidence is certainly a serious affront to the person concerned. Whether it is properly described as "punishment" may be a semantic point. It is nevertheless subsumed within the concept of the House's power to "punish".

(See Chapter 47 for the types of conduct that may be punished for contempt and Chapter 48 for the types of punishment open to the House.)

Oaths

Both the House and any committee of the House (a committee of the whole House or a select committee) have the legal power to examine any witness on oath.[59] A witness may make an affirmation in lieu of taking an oath.[60] This power dates from 1865 when it was specifically enacted into law. (As far as committees are concerned, it is not a privilege of the House derived from the United Kingdom House of Commons, since that House's committees did not gain this power until 1871.) Prior to 1865 neither the House nor its committees enjoyed any statutory power of examining witnesses on oath, though particular committees had been given such power.[61]

Where a person appears to be examined at the bar of the House, the House may, on motion without notice, order that that person take an oath or make an affirmation.[62] The Clerk of the House then administers the oath or affirmation.[63] A committee of the whole

---

54   S.Os 157(2)(b), 197(2)(b) and 198(3)(b).
55   *May*, p.764.
56   S.Os 157(2)(a), 197(2)(a) and 198(3)(a).
57   *Aboriginal Legal Service v State of Western Australia* (1993) 9 WAR 297 at 306.
58   1892, Vol.78, p.607.
59   *Legislature Act* 1908, s.252.

60   *Oaths and Declarations Act* 1957, s.4.
61   *Audit Act* 1858, s.19 (Audit Committee); *Private Bills Evidence Act* 1860, s.2 (committees on private bills).
62   S.O.158(1).
63   S.O.158(2).

House has no power delegated to it by the House to order a person to take an oath when being examined before it (though a witness could do so voluntarily). If it was desired to have such a power in any particular case, the power to order evidence to be given under oath would need to be conferred on the committee of the whole House by way of an instruction to it.

The House has given select committees a general authority to direct any person to take an oath or make an affirmation before giving evidence to them.[64] Disobedience to such an order could be treated by the House as a contempt. But a select committee cannot order a member of Parliament to take an oath before it (though a member can take an oath voluntarily). Only the House can exercise coercive powers over its members.[65]

An oath or affirmation before a select committee is administered by the clerk of the committee.[66] In all cases the oath takes the same form as the oath of a witness before a court, that is, a promise to tell the truth in the evidence to be given to the House or committee.

A person examined on oath before the House or a committee who wilfully gives false evidence is liable to the penalties of perjury, an offence which carries a maximum punishment of seven years' imprisonment.[67] In a prosecution for perjury in respect of evidence given to the House or a committee, a court may examine, and judge the accuracy of, evidence given in parliamentary proceedings. This forms a statutory exception to the principle that proceedings in Parliament cannot be examined before a court.[68]

PROTECTIONS FOR WITNESSES

Evidence protected

It is well established that no action, civil or criminal, will lie against a witness in respect of evidence given to the House or one of its committees. The position of witnesses is similar to that of members in respect of words spoken in parliamentary proceedings.[69] It does not matter whether the witness appears voluntarily or is summoned to appear before the House or a committee, the protection applies in either case.

By statute, witnesses examined under oath before the House or a committee enjoy the same protection at law from having their testimony impeached as do witnesses testifying under oath in the High Court.[70] Such evidence is absolutely privileged and cannot be used to support legal proceedings, civil or criminal, except a prosecution for perjury in respect of the evidence they have given. It is doubtful, however, whether this adds anything to the protection enjoyed by any other parliamentary witness under the general law.[71]

While no liability (apart from for perjury) can arise out of evidence given to the House or a committee, the extent to which parliamentary evidence may be used in legal proceedings to support or refute a cause of action arising out of events occurring outside the House is less clear. (This issue is discussed in Chapter 46.)

Even though evidence given to a committee may not itself be admissible in legal proceedings, it may alert the authorities or another party to a matter that they consider warrants further investigation. In this way a secondary process can arise leading to the potential liability of a witness, provided that the facts supporting the charge or legal action

---

[64] S.O.231(1).
[65] 1996-99, AJHR, I.4F, pp.4 and 5.
[66] S.O.231(2).
[67] *Legislature Act* 1908, s.252; *Crimes Act* 1961, ss.108 and 109.
[68] *Prebble v Television New Zealand Limited* [1994] 3 NZLR 1 at 10.

[69] *Bill of Rights* 1688, article 9; *Goffin v Donnelly* (1881) 6 QBD 307; *R v Wainscott* [1899] 1 WAR 77; *Prebble v Television New Zealand Limited* [1994] 3 NZLR 1.
[70] *Legislature Act* 1908, s.253(5).
[71] 1875, Vol.19, pp.355, 385, 387-8.

can be proved independently of the parliamentary proceedings.[72] No select committee can grant a witness immunity from potential liability arising in this way.[73] Neither can the House, short of passing legislation for the purpose. While the Attorney-General has the right to enter a stay of any criminal prosecution,[74] this would not prevent a civil action proceeding. It is specifically provided in law that no privilege against self-incrimination may be invoked by a Crown organisation (now subject to criminal liability under building and health safety legislation) as a ground for refusing to supply information to a committee.[75] However, this does not mean that the organisation's answer to a parliamentary committee could itself be used against it in legal proceedings.

For these reasons, committees have available to them the power to hear evidence in private or in secret[76] and can limit the possibility of incriminating evidence becoming widely known. Also, a witness's objection that to provide an answer to a question would be self-incriminating may be regarded by the committee as a justifiable reason to excuse the witness from answering the question.

Whether in any particular case they consider it justifiable to attempt to protect witnesses from the consequences of their conduct coming to public attention (possibly so that a witness will be more open with the committee), is a matter for the committees themselves to decide. In the administration of justice too the courts have acknowledged this problem. Evidence given in court can set in train a process of discovery that may effectively render the witness liable in respect of his or her testimony to the court.[77] On the other hand, it is not the function of a court to protect a witness from embarrassment or the risk of prosecution in respect of the witness's conduct outside the court.[78] Both courts and parliamentary committees must judge where the balance of interest lies in deciding how to conduct their proceedings.

Interfering with witnesses

It is a contempt of the House to intimidate, prevent or hinder a witness from giving evidence or giving evidence in full to the House or a committee.[79] The House is also concerned to protect witnesses against any adverse consequences being visited on them as a result of their giving evidence to the House or a committee. Anyone assaulting, threatening or disadvantaging a person on account of parliamentary evidence that that person has given may be held to be in contempt (apart from any criminal or civil liability that they may also thereby incur).[80] Thus, where a committee came into possession of facts that suggested a witness might have been penalised commercially as a result of evidence he had given to the committee, the committee made inquiries to determine if this had indeed occurred.[81]

In an extreme case, the House may instruct counsel to intervene in legal proceedings involving a witness where there is a danger that the witness's conduct before a parliamentary committee may be brought into issue.[82]

Natural justice

The *New Zealand Bill of Rights Act* 1990 applies to acts done by the legislative branch of government.[83] It has been accepted on behalf of the House that this means that the

---

[72] HC 101 (1938-39) para.16 (*Report from the Select Committee on the Official Secrets Acts*).

[73] 1993-96, AJHR, I.3C; Joseph, "Report to the Standing Orders Committee on Natural Justice", para.8.14.

[74] *Crimes Act* 1961, s.378.

[75] *Crown Organisations (Criminal Liability) Act* 2002, s.10(1)(d)(ii).

[76] S.Os 219 and 220.

[77] *Rank Film Distributors Ltd v Video Information Centre* [1982] AC 380 at 443.

[78] *Trustor AB v Smallbone* [2000] 1 All ER 811 at 821.

[79] S.O.395(t).

[80] S.O.395(v).

[81] "Privilege investigation", *The New Zealand Herald*, 16 March 1991; 1991-93, AJHR, I.15.

[82] See, for example, Senate (Australia) Debates (20 February 1991), pp.913-4, 965-6.

[83] *New Zealand Bill of Rights Act* 1990, s.3(a).

House and its committees are under distinct legal obligations in respect of how they carry on their proceedings.[84] The right of every person to the observance of the principles of natural justice by any tribunal or public authority with the power to make a determination in respect of that person's legal interests (such as matters affecting livelihood or reputation)[85] has particular application to the House and its committees. The House has accordingly adopted certain procedures designed to give expression to these principles in a parliamentary context. These go beyond giving procedural protections to witnesses. They apply to any person whose reputation may be affected by parliamentary proceedings.

In the House a right of response for persons who have been adversely affected by a reference to them in the House has been introduced and the circumstances in which a person may be held to be in contempt have been more clearly defined. (See Chapters 39 and 47.) In select committees a battery of procedures has been introduced providing for persons to be informed of allegations against them, to have access to information about themselves held by committees, to reply to allegations made against them, to be represented by counsel and to comment on adverse findings in a draft report before a committee makes such a report to the House. A rule on bias or prejudgment has also been introduced where a committee is inquiring into allegations of a criminal nature against someone. (These procedural protections are discussed in Chapters 22, 23 and 24.)

The Standing Orders Committee, in recommending these procedures, emphasised, however, that, in accordance with the House's privileges, it is solely for the House to decide how to apply them to its own proceedings and that that application takes place in a parliamentary not a judicial environment. In particular, it is for members to judge how much evidence to hear on a policy issue and to make up their own minds on it. The specific bias and allegation rules are concerned with protecting individual reputation only, not with excluding members on the basis of their expressed political positions.[86]

LIMITATIONS ON THE POWER TO INQUIRE OR OBTAIN EVIDENCE
While the power of the House to inquire is in principle untrammelled, there are potential limitations to its exercise and these must be considered. Potential limitations on the ability of the House to obtain all of the evidence that it requires must also be considered.

Statutory prohibition or inhibition
A statute might prohibit the House from conducting a certain inquiry or a certain type of inquiry. It would be an extraordinary step (akin to a legislative manner and form provision) for Parliament effectively to prohibit itself from conducting an inquiry. It is more likely that statutory provisions will be relevant to the way in which an inquiry should be conducted rather than that they would prevent an inquiry being conducted at all.[87] Even then, at the least a clear statutory intent is required for the House's powers to be formally limited.[88] In this regard any inquiry into criminal wrongdoing and an inquiry involving statutory secrecy provisions require particular consideration.

Inquiries into criminal wrongdoing
The House and its committees are not precluded by law from inquiring into criminal conduct or matters which might reveal evidence of crime. However, there would be a

---

[84]   1993-96, AJHR, I.18A, p.79; see also, Joseph, "Report to the Standing Orders Committee on Natural Justice", para.1.3.
[85]   *New Zealand Bill of Rights Act* 1990, s.27(1).
[86]   1993-96, AJHR, I.18A, p.80.

[87]   See 1999-2000, AJHR, I.2A as to whether parliamentary inquiries into tertiary education institutions were prohibited by law.
[88]   *Aboriginal Legal Service v State of Western Australia* (1993) 9 WAR 297 at 304.

potential breach of the *New Zealand Bill of Rights Act* 1990 if a person had been charged with a particular offence and a parliamentary inquiry into that person's culpability proceeded.[89] Such an inquiry could be regarded as unlawful and beyond the power of any committee established by the House.

In addition (and even when no charges are pending) the House has forbidden any select committee, without its express authority, from inquiring into or making findings in respect of allegations of crime by persons who are named or otherwise identifiable.[90] This prohibition applies in respect of an item of business referred to the committee (such as a petition)[91] as well as to an inquiry initiated by the committee. But it is not taken to prevent a committee, within its terms of reference, from inquiring into and making findings of a general nature as to alleged criminal wrongdoing by persons who are not named or otherwise identifiable.[92]

Similarly, committees are not prevented from inquiring into whether it is appropriate for certain positions to be held on public bodies by a particular person just because there are statutory offences that may have been committed by reason of holding those positions.[93] Nevertheless, before embarking upon any inquiry with criminal implications, select committees should take into account wider considerations of policy and fairness that might make it inadvisable for them to become involved (for example, the fact that police inquiries are under way[94]).

Secrecy provisions
A number of statutes provide that information provided to an official or body for the purposes of carrying out duties under the legislation are not to be disclosed except in limited circumstances. In some cases officials may be required to take an oath pledging to maintain the confidentiality of information that comes into their possession except insofar as disclosure is necessary for the purposes of carrying out their duties. The question can and has arisen as to whether these secrecy provisions apply so as to prevent the House or a committee requesting or ordering the production of such information and so as to give the witness or potential witness good legal grounds for withholding it in the face of such a request or demand.

Given the differing nature of the provisions involved, no single definitive answer can be given as to the effect of secrecy provisions on the House's power to obtain evidence relevant to an inquiry that it or a committee is conducting.[95] Some provisions appear to be absolute in their prohibition of disclosure;[96] others permit disclosure to any person with a proper interest in receiving the information;[97] and others combine the secrecy provision with a power to disclose for the purposes of carrying out the provisions of the Act (which may be taken to be implicit anyway).[98] A statutory secrecy provision expressly addressed to the House is binding, notwithstanding the House's general power to obtain information. In such a case it would be unlawful for the information to be disclosed to the House or a committee or for the House to use its coercive powers to obtain the information.

But statutory secrecy provisions do not normally deal expressly with their relationship to parliamentary inquiries and they must all be read in the context of the House's legal power and constitutional function of inquiring and obtaining evidence in its own discretion.

---

[89] Joseph, "Report to the Standing Orders Committee on Natural Justice", para.3.13 (citing *New Zealand Bill of Rights Act* 1990, s.25(a)).
[90] S.O.200(1).
[91] 2002-05, AJHR, I.22, p.691.
[92] S.O.200(2); see, for example, 1978, AJHR, I.12B (inquiry into pillaging on wharves).
[93] 1996-99, AJHR, I.7B, p.7.
[94] Leopold, "The Power of the House of Commons to Question Private Individuals" [1992] PL at 541.
[95] 2002-05, AJHR, I.18B, p.31.
[96] For example, *Fire Service Act* 1975, s.51B (fire service levies).
[97] For example, *Serious Fraud Office Act* 1990, s.36(2)(e).
[98] For example, *Tax Administration Act* 1994, s.81(3).

Consequently, the House's powers of obtaining information will not lightly be taken to be displaced.

In general, a statutory secrecy provision cannot be taken as applying as a matter of law to prevent the disclosure of information to the House or a committee unless this is one of the necessary intentions of the provision, for example, if disclosure in the course of a parliamentary inquiry (having regard to the safeguards that apply or can be imposed on the use or disclosure of such information outside Parliament) would render the secrecy provision nugatory.

Legal advice may need to be sought before responding to a committee's information request if a statutory secrecy provision is involved.[99] Given the variety of formulae to be found in legislation, it has been recommended that Parliament adopt a standard-form secrecy provision that makes it clear that it is not intended to apply against a select committee request for information and at the same time that the House spell out in its own procedures the interests that would warrant disclosure to it.[100]

No standard-form secrecy provision has yet been devised, much less enacted. But the House, in 1999, limited select committees' powers to send for persons, papers and records by, in general, requiring that such a demand be made through the Speaker, who must be satisfied that it is necessary for such information to be formally demanded.[101] This provides, though at a high level of generality, an opportunity for a parliamentary assessment of whether a committee's information request is justified in all the circumstances, including the existence of a secrecy provision.[102]

In the main, however, it is expected that committees and witnesses will work these issues through themselves on the basis of what is strictly necessary for the purposes of the inquiry. Committees are expected, even though they may not legally be bound by a statutory secrecy provision, to have regard to the values which the secrecy legislation is intended to promote and to exercise their powers consistently with those values if possible. Thus, information may in some circumstances be provided in secret or with particularly sensitive details obliterated.[103] A committee, recognising the sensitivity of the information to which it had sought access, has established protocols with the holder of the information defining the conditions under which the committee's adviser would inspect it and the use to which it would be put.[104] In addition, the chairperson can always, in controlling the relevancy of proceedings, guide members and witnesses away from raising matters that might cause difficulties with a secrecy provision.[105]

Thus, in all cases the committee's actual practices may be the means of resolving the potentially conflicting interests involved in the committee accessing information to which an element of statutory confidentiality attaches.

Charges against members

Select committees are prohibited by the Standing Orders from inquiring into or making findings about the private conduct of any member, unless specially directed by the House to do so.[106] The Privileges Committee is not subject to this restriction, since questions of privilege referred to it may by their very nature lead it into such inquiries. If any information is received by any other select committee (whether by way of an allegation or otherwise) suggesting reprehensible conduct on the part of any member, the committee may not proceed further with the information or allegation without the House's authority.

---

99   "Public Servants and Select Committees
     – Guidelines", State Services Commission, February
     2002, updated February 2004, para.23; 2002-05,
     AJHR, I.18B, p.31.
100 Joseph, "Report to the Standing Orders Committee
     on Natural Justice", paras.9.12-9.14.

101 S.O.198(2).
102 2002-05, AJHR, I.18B, p.31.
103 1993-96, AJHR, I.4A.
104 2002-05, AJHR, I.11A, p.183.
105 1996-99, AJHR, I.3I, p.10.
106 S.O.201(1).

It must, however, inform the member concerned of the information or allegation and give the member an opportunity to reply to it.[107]

If it is proposed that a committee be authorised to inquire into a member's conduct, the appropriate course is to give notice of motion to that effect.[108]

Self-incrimination

There is no general privilege for witnesses to refuse to answer questions in the course of parliamentary proceedings on the ground that to do so may incriminate them.[109] In respect of Crown organisations the fact that an answer may tend to incriminate the organisation is specifically excluded by statute as a ground for refusing to supply information requested by a parliamentary committee.[110] However, the danger of self-incrimination would be a valid ground for a witness to seek the committee's agreement to being excused from answering or at least to seek to reply in private or in secret. Whether the committee agrees to such a request is a matter for it to decide.

Intelligence and security agencies

The New Zealand Security Intelligence Service and the Government Communications Security Bureau are subject to the oversight of a statutory committee consisting of members of Parliament called the Intelligence and Security Committee. The Intelligence and Security Committee is not a select committee established by the House. Rather it is a statutory committee established under legislation passed by Parliament.[111] The legislation establishing the committee gives it the power to consider any bill or other matter relating to either intelligence and security agency that is referred to it by the House.[112] The House, by sessional order, enlists the committee into its procedures by providing: that it is to consider the estimates and supplementary estimates and to carry out the financial review of each agency; that bills and other matters relating to either of the agencies may be referred to the committee; and that petitions relating to an agency must be allocated to the committee by the Clerk. The House's power to inquire into the agencies is not removed by the legislation but the House has ordered that no select committee shall examine either of the agencies.[113] Intelligence and security matters are not within the terms of reference of any subject select committee. Consequently, an inquiry by a select committee into an intelligence and security agency is prohibited by order of the House, not by law.

Official information requests

Members of Parliament are among the principal users of the right of any member of the public under the *Official Information Act* to request official information held by a Minister or a department. However, requests for information made by the House, committees or members in the course of parliamentary proceedings (such as lodging questions for answer in the House or asking for information in the course of a select committee inquiry) are not to be regarded as requests for official information made under the legislation. Rather, they are information requests made under the inherent inquiry power of the House, a power that pre-dates the *Official Information Act*. If they were merely official information requests, the House's coercive powers to obtain the information that it deems necessary for it to carry out its inquiries would have been impliedly abrogated and superseded by the statutory grounds for withholding information set out in the Act. Question time in

[107] S.O.201(2).
[108] 2000, Vol.587, pp.5366-7.
[109] In the United States referred to colloquially as "taking the Fifth Amendment" since it derives from the Fifth Amendment to the Constitution.
[110] *Crown Organisations (Criminal Liability) Act 2002*, s.10(1)(d)(ii).
[111] *Intelligence and Security Committee Act 1996*.
[112] *Ibid.*, s.6(1)(b).
[113] 2000, Vol.582, pp.1265-75, 1378-84; 2002, Vol.604, pp.1897-909.

the House, for example, would be subject to the statutory limitations of the Act and to the arbitrament of the Ombudsmen. While it is well established that a clearly expressed legislative provision can abrogate the privileges of the House, the official information legislation is intended to promote, not restrict, the availability of official information. The House's entitlement to information exceeds that under the Act. Rather than the House's privileges having been abrogated, the Act is at pains to preserve the privileges of the House by permitting information to be withheld if to release it to other persons would constitute a contempt of the House.[114]

Consequently, the firm view of the House and its committees is that a request for information made by a parliamentary body is not an official information request and that it is for the House or its committees to judge whether the information should be made available to it, not the person or agency to whom the request is made.[115]

The State Services Commission acknowledges that the *Official Information Act* does not formally constrain the powers of the House, and instructs officials never to refuse to provide information to select committees on the grounds that the legislation permits this.[116] But, it points out, the statute does set out an accepted set of interests which may warrant the protection of information and these can be raised with a committee before responding to its information requests.[117] An Australian Senate committee has also acknowledged that the exemptions in that country's freedom of information legislation may be persuasive, though not binding, reasons for not providing documents to a parliamentary committee.[118] (See Chapter 23 for objections to answering questions.)

Ministers, in replying to questions, have occasionally used the grounds set out in the *Official Information Act* that justify withholding information by analogy as reasons for not providing all of the information sought in the question.[119] Whether to reply in this way is a matter for political, rather than legal, judgment. But it is axiomatic that if certain information must be disclosed under the *Official Information Act*, it should be given to the House in a reply to a question or to a committee in response to its request for information. To do less would be to treat the House or the committee contemptuously. Indeed, a committee has expressed surprise that Cabinet papers supplied to other persons were not provided to it though relevant to the issues before the committee.[120] It follows that Ministers and officials should be careful that, in using the legislation by analogy, they do not attempt to apply stricter disclosure standards to the House and committees than would be applied to the public generally.

In all cases the relationship between the House and the bodies subject to its scrutiny (principally government departments) is a constitutional one, not one that rests on the *Official Information Act*. Ultimately, the House's ability to obtain the information it requires rests on political will rather than legal principle.[121]

Other suggested legal inhibitions

It has been suggested that there may be other legal principles that can be invoked to resist an order of the House for the production of a document where a person asserts a privilege of a certain kind.[122] Thus, the power to order a return, being confined to a document of a public or official character, is said to raise the question of the availability of a claim

---

[114] *Official Information Act* 1982, ss.18(c)(ii) and 52(1).

[115] See, for example: 2002-05, AJHR, I.18B, p.31 (Standing Orders Committee); *ibid.*, I.22C, pp.56-7 (Commerce Committee).

[116] "Public Servants and Select Committees – Guidelines", State Services Commission, February 2002, updated February 2004, para.22.

[117] *Ibid.*

[118] *Report of the (Australian) Senate Procedure Committee*, Third Report of 1992.

[119] See, for example, *Hansard Supplement*, 2001, Vol.49, p.2838.

[120] 1999-2002, AJHR, I.22B, p.1352.

[121] 2002-05, AJHR, I.22C, p.238 (*Public Finance (State Sector Management) Bill*).

[122] *Egan v Willis* (1996) 40 NSWLR 650 at 693 (per Priestley JA).

of public interest immunity in respect of the production of such a document.[123] "Public interest immunity" is a rule of evidence protecting state documents from production in legal proceedings on the ground that such production would be injurious to the public interest.[124] If public interest immunity is available as a legal ground for resisting an order for a return, it has been said that a claim to immunity would be dealt with by the legislature itself analogously with how such claims in litigation are determined by a court. The legislature would be under the same duty as a court to balance the conflicting public interests between the legislature's desire to see the material and the executive's desire to maintain its confidentiality.[125] But this view has been vigorously contested, and it is difficult to see how it could be enforced.[126]

Another view is that public-interest immunity as a rule of evidence is confined to legal proceedings where disputes as to its operation can be determined by courts. It has no application as a "matter of law" to parliamentary inquiries, though the public interest that it promotes of maintaining confidentiality for state documents, where this is justified, may be a relevant consideration for the House, the Speaker or a committee to take into account in exercising their respective powers or making information demands. This view was upheld by the majority of the court in the only case in which this point was squarely in issue.[127] While acknowledging that a claim that production of evidence to a committee is not in the public interest is always a claim that should be considered seriously, it does seem unnecessary to complicate the judgment to be made by the House or committee with concepts drawn from the legal doctrine of public-interest immunity. In New Zealand, it has never been claimed that this doctrine formally applies to demands from the House for state documents. While this seems to be the correct position, it does not preclude the House and committees taking executive claims to secrecy seriously and formulating criteria for judging them. But these judgments are the legislature's to make in the exercise of its privileges. They are not applications of the public-interest-immunity doctrine.

A claim that legal professional privilege operates to limit a legislature's power to order production of a document has also been expressly rejected by a court.[128] However, the House has acknowledged that a legal opinion is the property of the person who commissioned it and that a select committee cannot expect the opinion to be furnished to it without the consent of that person.[129]

As well as public-interest immunity and legal professional privilege, other grounds on which it has been suggested that objections to the obligation to produce documents demanded by a resolution of the House could lawfully be made are individual privacy and the right to maintain confidentiality.[130] The legitimacy of these as valid legal grounds to resist production of documents to the House and, thus, as abrogations of the House's privilege to obtain information has never been claimed or conceded in New Zealand, though the need for individual privacy is often taken account of by committees in the way in which they organise their proceedings (for example, by taking evidence in secret). It is, it is submitted, a matter for the judgment of the committee concerned as to whether it accedes to an objection to produce evidence on either of these grounds.

---

[123] *Ibid.*, at 663 (per Gleeson CJ).
[124] See Joseph, *Constitutional and Administrative Law*, pp.614-22.
[125] *Egan v Chadwick* (1999) 46 NSWLR 563 at [142] (per Priestley JA).
[126] *Ibid.*, at [154] (per Meagher J).
[127] *Ibid.,* (per Spigelman CJ and Meagher J).
[128] *Ibid.*
[129] 2002-05, AJHR, I.18B, p.31 (Standing Orders Committee).
[130] *Egan v Willis* (1998) 195 CLR 424 at 505 (per Kirby J).

PARTICULAR TYPES OF INQUIRY

Removal of office-holders

In respect of a number of State office-holders it is provided that they may be removed from office (before their term expires in accordance with the applicable statute) only at the behest of the House of Representatives, by the House presenting an address to the Sovereign or the Governor-General seeking their removal. The office-holders who may be removed from office in this way are—

- a judge of the High Court (which includes all judges of the Supreme Court and the Court of Appeal)[131]
- a judge of the Employment Court[132]
- an Ombudsman[133]
- the Controller and Auditor-General and the Deputy Controller and Auditor-General[134]
- the Parliamentary Commissioner for the Environment[135]
- the Clerk of the House of Representatives and the Deputy Clerk[136]
- the Police Complaints Authority and the Deputy Police Complaints Authority[137]
- a member of the Abortion Supervisory Committee[138]
- a member of the Electoral Commission appointed on the nomination of the House for the purposes of allocating electoral broadcasting resources[139]
- a member of the Families Commission who is a High Court judge[140]
- the Judicial Conduct Commissioner.[141]

In all of these cases, the House may initiate the request for the removal of the office-holder only on stated grounds.

Thus, for a High Court judge the address may be moved only on the grounds of the judge's misbehaviour or incapacity to discharge the functions of the judge's office.[142] It seems that an address that sets out no grounds of complaint against a judge, reasons for removal or other justification would not be sufficient to justify the Crown removing the judge.[143] Furthermore, no judge may be removed from office unless a Judicial Conduct Panel has first reported to the Attorney-General that it is of the opinion that consideration of the removal of the judge is justified.[144] If a Judicial Conduct Panel does so report, the Attorney-General is obliged to consider whether to take steps to initiate the judge's removal by an address,[145] though if a judge has been convicted of a criminal offence punishable by two years' imprisonment or more, steps for removal may be initiated even without a panel recommendation.[146]

It is axiomatic that before proceeding to adopt an address for removal of an office-holder, the House or somebody responsible directly to the House will have carried out an inquiry to ascertain whether grounds exist and should be invoked for the House to request the removal of the office-holder in question. (In the case of a judge, a Judicial Conduct Panel will have made such a report.) This in turn will require the House to follow appropriate procedures guaranteeing that a fair and efficient process is followed before it makes a decision to adopt an address requesting the office-holder's removal. No process

---

131 *Constitution Act* 1986, s.23.
132 *Employment Relations Act* 2000, s.204.
133 *Ombudsmen Act* 1975, s.6(1).
134 *Public Audit Act* 2001, Sch.3, cl.4.
135 *Environment Act* 1986, s.7(1).
136 *Clerk of the House of Representatives Act* 1988, s.11(2).
137 *Police Complaints Authority Act* 1988, ss.6 and 8(2).
138 *Contraception, Sterilisation, and Abortion Act* 1977, s.11(3).
139 *Electoral Act* 1993, s.11(1).

140 *Families Commission Act* 2003, Sch.2, cl.10(5).
141 *Judicial Conduct Commissioner and Judicial Conduct Panel Act* 2004, Sch.2, cl.3.
142 *Constitution Act* 1986, s.23.
143 Hannan, *The Life of Chief Justice Way*, pp.52-7 (Crown declined to act on an address in South Australia on this ground).
144 *Judicial Conduct Commissioner and Judicial Conduct Panel Act* 2004, s.33(2).
145 *Ibid.*, s.33(1).
146 *Ibid.*, s.34(1), (2)(b).

for the removal of a judge or other statutory office-holder has ever been put in train by the House and no standing procedures for this purpose exist. Overseas Parliaments have referred proposals for removal for inquiry by an outside statutory body (either under general legislative authority or under ad hoc legislation) or have referred such proposals to a parliamentary committee for inquiry. Invariably the office-holder concerned is also permitted to address the House itself before a decision is taken.

Although the House has never proceeded on a motion to remove a judge or other office-holder, charges or allegations have been made from time to time causing some parliamentary response. It is a rule of the House that the conduct of a judge can only be raised before it by way of a notice of motion and not incidentally in the course of a debate.[147] Any such charge must also raise a strong *prima facie* case of conduct that would induce the House to address the Crown for the judge's removal if the notice of motion is to be accepted for consideration.[148] For example, to criticise a judge on the ground that he or she has committed errors, even gross errors, does not amount to raising allegations of misbehaviour that would justify removal.[149] On the other hand, a judge consistently making errors could demonstrate incapacity for the office. The House has referred allegations made against a judge to a committee for inquiry and report.[150]

Membership of the House

Until 1880 the House was, by statute, the sole judge of disputes as to the outcome of parliamentary elections. Disputed election petitions were tried by committees of the House. This function is now discharged by the High Court. However, questions can still arise from time to time as to whether a vacancy has occurred due to a sitting member becoming disqualified or otherwise ceasing to be a member. While the House no longer itself determines if a vacancy has arisen, its opinion on the matter, after inquiry by a committee, may be highly persuasive.[151] In 1897 when a question arose over the bankruptcy of a member (bankruptcy then being a disqualification), Parliament passed legislation providing for a special inquiry by the Court of Appeal to be held into the matter rather than the House making its own inquiry.[152] In 1997 when a question arose as to whether a member had effectively resigned her seat, the matter was inquired into by the Privileges Committee as a question of privilege.[153] In 2003 the Privileges Committee conducted an inquiry into whether a member had incurred a disqualification by applying for a foreign nationality.[154]

Inquiries of this nature are possible if the Speaker considers that a real doubt as to membership exists,[155] otherwise the Speaker acts on his or her own initiative. In all cases it is the Speaker who invokes the procedures for filling a vacancy that has arisen.[156] There is no longer any requirement for a direction from the House in the matter.

Statutory inquiries

Occasionally legislation ordains that a select committee inquiry be held. It is doubtful whether there is any legal means of enforcing such a provision, since its execution depends entirely on decisions taken in the course of parliamentary proceedings, which it is unlawful

---

147 1901, Vol.119, p.199.
148 1874, Vol.16, p.112.
149 *Daphtary v Gupta* AIR 1971 Supreme Court 1132 at para.68.
150 1874, JHR, pp.99, 146 (Ward Chapman inquiry report –no substance to allegations found).

151 2003, Vol.610, p.7749.
152 *Awarua Seat Inquiry Act* 1897.
153 1996-99, AJHR, I.15B.
154 2002-05, AJHR, I.17C.
155 *Ibid.*, p.5.
156 *Electoral Act* 1993, ss.129(1) and 134(1).

for any court to review. Nevertheless, the House is bound by a statutory obligation, just as it is bound by any other provision of the law, and the Speaker will attempt to see that such obligations are complied with.[157]

Statutes have provided for an inquiry into the application of the *Official Information Act* 1982 to State enterprises,[158] for a review of the MMP electoral system[159] and continuing provisions require five-yearly reviews of the charters of Radio New Zealand and Television New Zealand.[160] (The first review of Radio New Zealand's charter was discharged in 2001 by the Commerce Committee under its general inquiry powers.[161]) The House was required to establish a select committee as soon as practicable after 1 December 2004 to examine provisions of legislation designed to implement New Zealand's obligations under a United Nations Security Council resolution on terrorism. The committee was to report back to the House by 1 December 2005 stating whether the provisions should be retained, repealed or amended.[162]

In establishing a committee to carry out a statutory inquiry the House may, in addition, require the committee to carry out a wider (but not a narrower) inquiry than that required by the statute.

---

[157]   1989, Vol.497, p.10262-3.

[158]   *State-Owned Enterprises Act* 1986, s.31; 1990, AJHR, I.22A.

[159]   *Electoral Act* 1993, s.264; 1999-2002, AJHR, I.23A.

[160]   *Radio New Zealand Act* 1995, s. 7(4); *Television*

New Zealand Act 2003, s.12(4).

[161]   1999-2002, AJHR, I.1B.

[162]   *Terrorism Suppression Act* 2002, s.70(2), (3); 2005, Vol.623, pp.18557-66.

CHAPTER 31

PUBLIC FINANCE

Control of public finance has historically been at the heart of Parliament's constitutional pre-eminence. In England, government expanded from being virtually the prerogative of a King, funded out of the King's personal wealth, into a state function funded by public exactions. With this expansion and the need to broaden the tax base from its largely feudal origins there grew a dependence by the King and the King's Ministers, who were charged with carrying on the government, on Parliament, the body representing the subjects who contributed the funds that effective government now required. Parliamentary sanction was recognised as being a legal prerequisite to taxation being levied. The consent of taxpayers, at least in a representative capacity, was a practical necessity if civil strife was to be avoided and sums of tax productively raised. Furthermore, Parliament began to restrict what the proceeds of that taxation could be spent on by directing or appropriating that it be used only for particular ends (some of the earliest appropriations of taxation of the English Parliament were for wars with the Scots, for example). From the time of the restoration of the Crown in 1660, appropriating supplies to limited purposes defined by Parliament itself became the common practice. Parliament then started to demand to see the Royal accounts to satisfy itself that supplies appropriated to one purpose had not been used for another. Thus, public audit began to develop.[1] By the mid-nineteenth century a comprehensive system of parliamentary control of public finance had developed. When representative government was established in New Zealand this parliamentary control was reflected in the system of public finance that was put in place in the colony.

THE PUBLIC FINANCE PRINCIPLES
The fundamental public finance principles in New Zealand law are that taxation may be levied and public money may be expended only under parliamentary authority.[2] The rules for the receipt, payment and accounting for public funds derive from these principles of parliamentary authorisation.

Public finance could be seen in simplified terms as requiring all money received by or on behalf of the Crown (taxes, fees, rents, interest and so on) to be paid into a giant fund (formerly referred to as the Consolidated Fund) and all payments authorised to be made by the Crown (salaries, benefits, subsidies and so on) to be disbursed from this fund. Until 1989, with the qualification that there was more than one fund and that some departments were able to retain and reuse certain of their receipts without paying them into the fund, the New Zealand system worked very much like this. Each year Parliament authorised the Government through its departments to spend so much on various categories of expenditure (inputs) such as salaries, travel, operating costs and so on. The payments made in accordance with these authorities were drawn by the Treasury on moneys held in accounts at the Reserve Bank. While under some limited delegations small payments were made locally by departments, most payments were made centrally by the Treasury.

This system changed radically with the financial management reforms introduced

---

[1] See Hallam, *The Constitutional History of England*, Vol.II, pp.55-6.

[2] *Bill of Rights* 1688, article 4 and *Constitution Act*

1986, s.22(a) (taxation); *Constitution Act* 1986, s.22(c) and *Public Finance Act* 1989, s.5 (spending public money).

in 1989. Parliament no longer simply authorised the expenditure of public money to purchase the resources used by departments (although there is still an element of this involved). Parliament began to authorise the Government to purchase particular goods or services (called outputs) from its departments and from third parties. In some cases this authorisation is for the net cost of producing the output, taking into account any revenue the department expects to make in the course of producing it. Parliament also specifically authorises the Government to meet expenses associated with paying benefits, with borrowing and with capital expenditure and to incur certain other expenses.

The outputs supplied by departments and third parties are designed to contribute to outcomes which are desired by the Government. An outcome is a state or condition of society, the economy or the environment and includes a change in that state or condition.[3] An outcome thus represents some state or condition that the Government, as the promoter of expenditure proposals, wishes to promote. Information presented with the Budget must give an explanation of the link between each appropriation proposal and its intended outcome.[4] In the past the Auditor-General has expressed concern about whether the information presented to the House is sufficient to establish such links and whether, in any event, the asserted links can be measured and reported against satisfactorily.[5] Public finance reforms enacted in 2004 now require greater disclosure of the information needed to make informed assessments of these links.[6] Select committees, in examining the estimates, are also likely to enquire into the basis for the Government's view that the outputs being purchased will in fact contribute to outcomes.[7]

From a parliamentary point of view, the longstanding constitutional rule prohibiting the *expenditure* of public money without Parliament's authorisation is no longer adequate. The introduction of accrual accounting for the public sector means that income and expenditure are recorded in the public accounts in the time period to which each transaction relates and not necessarily when money is actually paid or received. Furthermore, the cost of an asset is spread across its estimated lifetime by depreciation rather than being fully recognised in the public accounts when it is acquired. Departments do not merely spend public money in cash terms. They also incur *expenses*, which must be recognised in their accounts with financial consequences that must be recorded as assets and liabilities in balance sheets. Consequently, the public finance legislation now goes further than merely prohibiting the spending of money without parliamentary approval, requiring such approval before a department may incur expenses or capital expenditure.[8]

BORROWING

Parliamentary control of the Crown's ability to borrow has historically been less developed than its control over taxation and spending. English Parliaments were concerned to prevent the monarch raising revenue by forcing "loans" on citizens. They were less interested in trying to control the Crown's power to borrow in general, perhaps on the basis that the Crown would effectively need parliamentary authority for a loan anyway if it was to have the means of servicing it. The general power of the Crown to borrow money is now, in New Zealand, a statutory one. It is unlawful for the Crown to borrow or for any person to lend money to the Crown except as authorised by legislation.[9]

---

3   *Ibid.*, s.2(1).
4   *Ibid.*, s.15(1)(a).
5   "Reporting Public Sector Performance", *Report of the Controller and Auditor-General, June 2001*, 1996-99, AJHR, B.29[99c], pp.45-56.

6   See, in particular, *Public Finance Act* 1989, s.45(2).
7   1999-2002, AJHR, I.22A, p.224.
8   *Public Finance Act* 1989, s.4(1).
9   *Constitution Act* 1986, s.22(b); *Public Finance Act* 1989, s.46.

In fact the Crown has, by statute, been given comprehensive general borrowing powers and powers to give security for such loans.[10] There is no limit to the amount of money the Crown may borrow in any financial year.[11] This legislative framework for the raising of loans means that there is no longer any special parliamentary involvement with the raising of individual loans and the House's involvement in debt management is minimal.[12] However, the Auditor-General makes a regular practice of commenting in detail on central government debt which is revealed in the various financial statements prepared by the Government.[13] The Finance and Expenditure Committee and individual members can, if they wish, probe further in this area.

Payment of principal, interest and other financing expenses on any loan is appropriated under permanent legislative authority.[14] No annual appropriation is required, although such payments are revealed in the estimates and in the Government's annual financial statements.

The House's authority is required for the issue of one type of security. State enterprises, if authorised by the House by resolution, may issue equity bonds which are deemed to be ordinary shares but carry no voting rights.[15] No such authority has been given by the House.

FINANCIAL YEAR

In England, the Crown's ever-growing need for finance led to the more frequent holding of Parliaments. This eventually resulted in a system of annual funding of government activity based on annual meetings of Parliament. New Zealand adopted an annual basis for its public accounts as soon as it obtained representative government, though there is no inherent necessity for adopting an annually-based system for public finance[16] – it is always a question of legislative choice.

At first, the financial year ran from 1 July to 30 June. This was altered to 1 April to 31 March in 1879. The financial year reverted to being from 1 July to 30 June in 1989. (There was a transitional quarter from 1 April to 30 June 1989 to bridge the gap between the different periods.)

CROWN BANK ACCOUNTS

The Crown (through the Treasury) operates Crown Bank Accounts.[17] There may be a number of bank accounts opened and operated on behalf of the Crown that are known collectively as Crown Bank Accounts. (Indeed, legislation may require a bank account to be opened for a particular purpose as a Crown Bank Account.[18]) By 2002, 96 Crown Bank Accounts had been established. Most of these are with the bank that is the Crown's principal financial transaction service provider,[19] though a few are with other banks (mainly overseas and in foreign currencies).[20]

With Treasury approval, government departments may open their own departmental bank accounts.[21] These accounts must be set up with the bank that is the Crown's principal transaction service provider unless the Treasury agrees to exempt a particular departmental bank account from this requirement.[22]

The Minister of Finance specifies the terms and conditions under which a Crown

10 *Public Finance Act* 1989, ss.47 to 65E.
11 1979, AJHR, B.1 [Pt.II], p.71.
12 Longdin-Prisk, "Setting Legal Limits to Government Borrowing" (1986) 12 NZULR 160.
13 1991-93, AJHR, B.1 [Pt.II], pp.68-77.
14 *Public Finance Act* 1989, ss.6(c), 60 and 61.
15 *State-Owned Enterprises Act* 1986, s.12.
16 *New South Wales v Commonwealth* (1908) 7 CLR 179 at 190 (per Griffith CJ).

17 *Public Finance Act* 1989, s.65R.
18 For example, *New Zealand Superannuation and Retirement Income Act* 2001, s.39(1).
19 Currently, Westpac Banking Corporation.
20 Information provided by the Treasury, 18 February 2002.
21 *Public Finance Act* 1989, s.65S.
22 *Treasury Instructions* 2001, para.6.5.2.

Bank Account is operated and either the Minister or the Treasury may give directions as to how a departmental bank account is to be operated.[23] All public money must be lodged in a Crown Bank Account or a departmental bank account.[24] Money may be paid out of a Crown Bank Account only pursuant to an appropriation, but money may be transferred between Crown Bank Accounts and departmental bank accounts without any appropriation being involved.[25] This system allows for the centralised management of cash held by the Government.

The Minister of Finance may close or suspend the operation of a Crown Bank Account or a departmental bank account,[26] except one required to be established by legislation. The Treasury's approval is specifically required before a department may close a departmental bank account.[27]

FINANCIAL RESPONSIBILITY OF THE CROWN

Parliament's consent to the expenditure of public money is often known as the granting of *supply*. The need for regular (annual) authorisation from Parliament for the expenditure of public money and the endorsement of tax rates is the single most important determinant of the House's sitting pattern. The financial business to be transacted by the House ensures that Parliament meets at least annually and defines the last day in each year (30 June) by which that meeting must take place. It also provides fixed points throughout the year by which certain business must be attended to. The question of whether sufficient financial authorisation exists to carry on government is always a matter that the Governor-General is entitled to seek assurances about from a Prime Minister before acceding to a request from the Prime Minister to dissolve Parliament for a general election. Indeed, a dissolution has been refused because supply had not been voted.[28]

The Crown has the duty to take the initiative in financial matters by presenting to the House of Representatives, at least on an annual basis, its proposals for public expenditure. This is a statutory duty.[29] But it is also a political duty. The Crown is charged with carrying on the government of the country. If the Crown's responsible advisers (its Ministers) were unable to take the initiative in financial matters because they did not have the confidence of the House, the continuance of the ministry in office would immediately come into question. At this point the House's financial procedures would become a matter of high constitutional significance. They are always so potentially.

The financial responsibility of the Crown is reflected in the House's internal rules permitting the Government to exercise a veto over legislative proposals that would have more than a minor impact on its fiscal aggregates if they were to become law.[30] Underlying this rule is the principle that those in office, and thus accepting responsibility for the Government's policies of economic and financial management, should not have fiscal decisions foisted upon them. The House of Representatives' alternative, if it wishes to change an important aspect of a Government's policy that those in office will themselves not change, is to change the Government, not to attempt to force Ministers to carry out, and thus accept responsibility for, fiscal policies with which they do not agree.

Although a Government cannot have fiscal policies foisted upon it, legislation (first introduced in 1994[31]) prescribes that Governments must pursue their policy objectives in accordance with the principles of responsible fiscal management. These principles include: reducing public debt to prudent levels and, once this has been achieved, maintaining it at those levels; achieving satisfactory levels of net worth; managing

---

23   *Public Finance Act* 1989, ss.65R(2) and 65T(1).
24   *Ibid.*, s.65U.
25   *Ibid.*, s.65V.
26   *Ibid.*, s.65W(3).
27   *Treasury Instructions* 2001, para.6.5.3.
28   1877, AJHR, A7; 1878, AJHR, A1, pp.3-4.
29   *Public Finance Act* 1989, ss 12 and 13.
30   S.O.318.
31   *Fiscal Responsibility Act* 1994.

prudently the Government's fiscal risks; and pursuing policies that are consistent with the reasonable predictability of tax rates.[32] The Minister of Finance is required to articulate the Government's fiscal policy and to identify how its objectives accord (or do not accord) with the principles of responsible fiscal management. These principles are not mandatory, they are statutorily ordained guidelines.[33] No legal sanctions are prescribed to deal with a failure to comply with them. Nevertheless, departures from them are expected to be temporary and must be fully explained by the Minister of Finance.[34] Thus, public opinion becomes the chief means of ensuring compliance with the principles.

The way in which the Crown must conduct financial transactions and the reporting which it must undertake are set out in considerable detail in the *Public Finance Act* 1989. This legislation recognises the central role of the Treasury in the management of the Government's financial business and in ensuring that financial statements that properly reflect that business are prepared. Finally, the *Public Audit Act* 2001 provides for the audit of the financial statements and accounts of all public-sector entities by the Controller and Auditor-General.

CROWN'S FINANCIAL VETO

The House reflects the principle of the Crown's financial responsibility through the procedure known as the Crown's financial veto, which has replaced a number of procedural rules that provided that only the Crown could initiate proposals for public expenditure.

The Crown's financial veto was introduced in 1996. It resulted from dissatisfaction with the operation of the House's previous appropriation rule, whereby bills or amendments involving an appropriation of public money were ruled out of order by the Speaker or chairpersons at various stages of the legislative process. It was felt that this rule operated capriciously, protecting some expenditure proposals but not others and having no application at all in regard to revenue. Where it did operate, it could operate too harshly, preventing members moving proposals that, even incidentally, involved the smallest amount of expenditure. The appropriation rule thus did not in any event protect the Crown's overall financial position and was a source of frustration in respect of the promotion of worthwhile projects involving small amounts of expenditure.[35]

The Standing Orders Committee, which recommended the new procedure of financial veto, recognised that it is the Government of the day that is responsible for the Crown's financial performance and position and that the Government needs to have control over the fiscal aggregates that determine that performance and position.[36] The financial veto procedure is designed to reconcile this principle of fiscal responsibility with the desire of individual members to promote policies that involve some amounts of expenditure.

Application of financial veto

The financial veto procedure permits members to promote any proposals regardless of their fiscal implications, but gives the Government a right to veto such proposals if, in its view, they would have more than a minor impact on its fiscal aggregates if they became law.[37] As such, it applies as equally to proposals with revenue implications as it does to those with expenditure implications.

The financial veto procedure applies to bills, amendments and motions. It also applies in respect of proposals to change a vote contained in an Appropriation Bill.

In respect of *bills* as a whole, the financial veto procedure applies only when a bill is

---

32 *Public Finance Act* 1989, s.26G(1).
33 1993-96, AJHR, I.3A.
34 *Public Finance Act* 1989, s.26G(2).
35 1993-96, AJHR, I.18A, p.61 (Standing Orders Committee).
36 *Ibid.*
37 S.O.318.

awaiting its third reading,[38] because it is only at this stage that the bill is in its final form.[39] This does not prevent the Government indicating earlier in the legislative process which provisions of the bill would cause it to exercise the financial veto, so that the House can remove or modify these if it chooses before the bill reaches its third reading.

Amendments are subject to financial veto at two points. Amendments recommended by a select committee may be vetoed before they are agreed to by the House on the bill's second reading.[40] There can be no financial veto of amendments proposed in a select committee itself. Otherwise, amendments can be vetoed when they are proposed, and before they are agreed to, in the committee of the whole House.[41]

There are two types of *motion* that are subject to the financial veto.

Any motion which, if passed as a resolution of the House, would have the force of law is subject to a financial veto.[42] Resolutions of the House do not have the force of law unless they are given such force by statute. Only certain resolutions of the House relating to statutory regulations have legal effect – for example, those disallowing, amending or substituting regulations.[43] The second type of motion that is subject to a financial veto is a motion to change a vote in an Appropriation Bill.[44] A financial veto may be applied to these types of motion before they are passed.

The Government's fiscal aggregates

A financial veto may be applied only to a proposal that has more than a minor impact on the Government's fiscal aggregates.

The term "fiscal aggregates" is defined as the Government's intentions for fiscal policy, in particular, for the following—

- total operating expenses
- total operating revenues
- the balance between total operating expenses and total operating revenues
- the level of total debt
- the level of total net worth.[45]

In contradistinction to the former appropriation rule, the financial veto procedure applies to changes in revenue as well as to changes in expenditure. Consequently, the House's previous rules imposing restrictions on members proposing increases in taxation have been abolished. The effects of proposals for tax changes are considered in applying the financial veto procedure.

There is no definition in dollar terms of what "more than a minor" impact on the fiscal aggregates means. This is a matter for the Government of the day to determine in the light of the circumstances of the time.[46] The Standing Orders Committee instanced bills or amendments whose main objective was not expenditure, but which would incidentally involve some cost in implementing or administering the proposal and small fiscally neutral transfers between votes, as falling into the category of having only minor impacts.[47]

Governments are expected to apply the procedure reasonably, although the ultimate judgment on whether to invoke it is theirs. Governments are able to take account of the cumulative effect of previous initiatives and proposals for the future in deciding whether to exercise the veto.[48] This means that the same proposal may be appraised differently at different times depending upon the overall fiscal situation.

---

[38] S.O.320(1).
[39] 1993-96, AJHR, I.18A, p.64.
[40] S.O.321(1).
[41] S.O.321(2).
[42] S.O.318(3).
[43] 1993-96, AJHR, I.18A, p.62; *Regulations (Disallowance) Act* 1989, ss.5 and 9.
[44] S.O.318(2).
[45] S.O.3(1).
[46] 1993-96, AJHR, I.18A, p.62.
[47] *Ibid.*
[48] *Ibid.*, pp.62-3.

The decision to invoke financial veto

How the Government makes the decision to invoke the financial veto is a matter for it. The Cabinet has issued instructions for the process to be followed by Ministers and officials in determining whether to invoke the procedure.[49]

The Minister of Finance and the Minister's office are designated as the primary points of co-ordination for the Government's exercise of the financial veto. All Ministers' offices and departments are enjoined to monitor House and select committee developments that affect their Minister's portfolio or vote and that may impact on the Government's fiscal aggregates or vote composition. They must alert the Minister of Finance's office as early as possible to any such developments or initiatives. The Treasury is responsible for co-ordinating advice to Ministers on the likely cost range of each non-ministerial parliamentary initiative that is identified. The decision whether to exercise the financial veto is made in the first instance jointly by the Minister of Finance and the Minister whose portfolio or vote is affected by the initiative.[50]

Any proposed amendment to a bill before a committee of the whole House that may have an impact on the Government's fiscal aggregates and any proposed change to a vote, must, under the Standing Orders, be notified at least 24 hours in advance by being lodged with the Clerk. If 24 hours' notice is not given, such an amendment is automatically ruled out of order regardless of its fiscal impact.[51] This provision for 24 hours' notice is designed to allow the Government to have some time to consider the likely fiscal impact of a proposed amendment or change to a vote. Otherwise an amendment might be moved without any notice at all, thus rendering appraisal of its effects on the fiscal aggregates difficult, if not impossible.[52]

Exercise of the financial veto

The financial veto is exercised by the Government certifying that it does not concur in a bill, amendment or motion because, in its view, the bill, amendment or motion would have more than a minor impact on its fiscal aggregates or on the composition of the vote.[53] The certificate is given in the name of the Government and is signed by a Minister of the Crown, who takes responsibility for it. Which Minister signs a certificate is a matter for the Government to decide.[54] Generally, it is signed by the Minister of Finance. Where there are several amendments to the same bill or proposed changes to the same vote, a single certificate can be issued in respect of the amendments or changes.[55]

In the case of an amendment proposed at the committee stage of a bill, the certificate cannot relate to part of the amendment, it may relate only to the amendment as a whole. In the case of a certificate relating to amendments recommended by a select committee, any certificate must relate to all of the amendments recommended.[56] But in the case of a bill awaiting third reading the certificate can be given in respect of the bill as a whole or in respect of a particular provision or provisions of the bill.[57] A certificate confined to a particular provision does not itself remove that provision from the bill, but it is open to the House (by recommitting the bill) to remove the provision to which the Government objects. The bill cannot be passed as long as that provision remains part of the bill and the bill remains subject to the certificate.[58]

A financial veto certificate must state with some particularity the nature of the claimed

---

[49] *Cabinet Manual*, 2001, paras.5.92-5.94; Cabinet Office Circular (CO(98)15), 15 October 1998; 1996-99, AJHR, I.20B, p.286.
[50] Cabinet Office Circular (CO(98)15), 15 October 1998.
[51] S.O.322(1), (2).
[52] 1993-96, AJHR, I.18A, p.63.

[53] S.O.318(1), (2).
[54] 2000, Vol.583, p.2062.
[55] 1993-96, AJHR, I.18A, p.64.
[56] S.O.321(1).
[57] S.O.320(2).
[58] S.O.320(3).

impact on the fiscal aggregates or on the composition of the vote and why the Government does not concur in the bill, amendment or motion to which it relates.[59]

Provided that the certificate complies with formal requirements by stating with some particularity the nature of the fiscal impact, the Speaker or chairperson will not permit the Government's judgment to be contradicted on a point of order. The Government, not the Chair, determines whether a proposal would have more than an impact on the Government's fiscal aggregates. But this does not prevent the Government's judgment being challenged by way of debate. The certificate is open to debate when the bill, amendment or motion to which it relates is next considered by the House.[60]

Delivery of the certificate

A financial veto certificate is given by delivering it to the Clerk.[61] It is effective at that point. It is announced to the House or the committee of the whole House by the Speaker or chairperson as soon as reasonably practicable. In the case of a certificate relating to select committee amendments to a bill, to a bill awaiting third reading or to a motion of which notice has been given, the Speaker announces it forthwith regardless of when the bill or motion is likely to be debated. In the case of amendments to a bill or changes to a vote, the chairperson announces a financial veto certificate at the outset of the consideration of the clause or part to which it relates if a certificate has been received by the chairperson by that time and, if received thereafter, as soon as one is received.

A financial veto certificate may be withdrawn at any time by the Government so informing the Clerk in writing.[62]

Effect of a financial veto certificate

A financial veto certificate prevents the bill, amendment or motion to which it relates being passed.

In the case of a bill, no question for its third reading can be put if a financial veto certificate has been issued in respect of it or if one has been issued in respect of a provision in the bill and that provision remains in the bill.[63] But the third reading debate may still be held.

In the case of select committee amendments, the amendments are omitted from the bill and cannot be again moved during the committee stage.[64] But the effect of the certificate may be discussed during the second reading debate on the bill.

In the case of a certificate relating to amendments at the committee stage, the amendments are out of order and no question is put on them,[65] though they can be debated during consideration of the clause or part to which they relate. Where a financial veto certificate relates to a new clause or a new part that has not yet been reached, the new clause or new part is out of order and no debate on it occurs. If a financial veto certificate relating to a new clause or a new part is lodged while debate on that new clause or new part is under way, the new clause or new part is out of order and debate on it terminates at that point.

In the case of a motion, including a motion for a change to a vote, the motion may be debated but no question is put on it at the end of the debate and it is ruled out of order.[66]

The issue of a financial veto certificate does not preclude the Speaker or chairperson ruling on the acceptability of a motion or amendment on general procedural grounds. If a motion or amendment is out of order in any case, it may not be moved or debated. In these

[59]   S.O.319(1), (2).
[60]   S.O.319(4).
[61]   S.O.319(3).
[62]   S.O.319(5).
[63]   S.O.320(3).
[64]   S.O.321(1), (3).
[65]   S.O.321(2).
[66]   S.O.320(4).

circumstances any financial veto certificate that has been issued is supererogatory. The fact that a certificate that is not needed has been issued does not permit a debate to take place that is prohibited on other grounds.

FINANCE AND EXPENDITURE COMMITTEE

A central role in the House's financial procedures is played by the Finance and Expenditure Committee.

The House has consistently appointed finance committees throughout its history, though they have generally been responsible for holding departments and agencies accountable for the expenditure of public money rather than playing a leading role in giving that authority in the first place. Thus, the House had an Audit Committee from 1858 to 1867 and a Public Accounts Committee from 1871 to 1962. In the latter year a new committee, the Public Expenditure Committee, took over the Public Accounts Committee's duties of investigating past governmental expenditure and financial transactions, and combined it with the role of examining the current year's estimates prior to the House making its annual appropriations. The other select committees were involved in this task by the committee referring individual votes to them for examination as part of the process.

The Finance and Expenditure Committee was first established in 1985 and took over the appropriation co-ordinating functions of the Public Expenditure Committee. At the same time, it was intended that much of the accountability work, that had previously been carried out almost exclusively by the Public Expenditure Committee, would be shared to a greater extent with the other subject select committees. Further Standing Orders changes in 1992, when the House's procedures were overhauled to take account of the financial management reforms effected in 1989, have emphasised that, while the Finance and Expenditure Committee is pre-eminent in the financial work carried out by select committees, the other committees have important responsibilities to fulfil in this respect too within their own subject areas. In 2000 the Finance and Expenditure Committee established a subcommittee to deal specifically with issues raised in reports of the Controller and Auditor-General. After receiving public briefings from the Auditor-General on the reports, it was intended to make suggestions to other committees about issues to follow up related to their own areas of responsibility.[67] However, this subcommittee was not re-established in the subsequent Parliament.

The Finance and Expenditure Committee is established at the commencement of each Parliament. In the 2002–05 Parliament it had 12 members drawn from six parties in the House. Its basic subject area of competence is audit of the Government's and departments' financial statements, Government finance, revenue and taxation.[68] Departments and institutions within its remit with an obvious significance in terms of economic policy and financial management include the Treasury and the Reserve Bank of New Zealand.

But the Finance and Expenditure Committee's leading role in the House's financial procedures does not depend on its subject-area remit. It results from the fact that the committee is the linchpin for the carrying out by all committees of their examinations of estimates (the making of the annual appropriations) and their financial reviews (the scrutiny of the past year's financial performance) of departments, offices of Parliament, Crown entities, public organisations and State enterprises. Following the introduction of the Budget or an Appropriation Bill proposing supplementary appropriations, the

---

[67]   1999-2002, AJHR, I.22A, p.225.   [68]   S.O.189.

estimates or supplementary estimates, as the case may be, stand referred to the Finance and Expenditure Committee. The committee then, as it sees fit, refers votes to the other select committees or retains them itself for examination.[69] The committee is not restricted to its own subject area in the votes that it decides to retain and may retain a vote dealing with another subject area if it wishes.

The Finance and Expenditure Committee is specifically required to make a report on the budget policy statement, on the fiscal strategy report and the economic and fiscal update and on the annual financial statements of the Government.[70] Half-year economic and fiscal updates and the statement on the long-term fiscal position are also referred to the committee.[71] It may, but does not have to, report on these statements. In addition, soon after 1 July each year, the committee must allocate to the other committees or retain for itself the task of conducting a financial review of the performance in the previous year and current operations of each department, office of Parliament, Crown entity, public organisation and State enterprise.[72] Again, the committee is unrestricted in the choices that it makes as to entities it will examine itself and those that it will allocate elsewhere.

As well as allocating estimates and departments for review, the committee takes a lead in how those tasks are discharged by committees. It issues a standard questionnaire to all departments on their estimates and has in the past prepared a questionnaire for the other select committees to use for their financial review work. These questionnaires suggest what information committees might wish to obtain from departments as a basis for carrying out their examinations. Carrying on a convention that developed with its predecessor, the Public Expenditure Committee, the committee expects to be informed of proposed changes to the presentation of financial information, particularly the estimates, before they are implemented. Failure on the part of the Minister of Finance to consult with the committee has led to criticism from the committee.[73]

The Minister of Finance is now required by statute to consult with the House before changing the format or content of information presented to the House with an Appropriation Bill.[74] Such proposals are referred to the Finance and Expenditure Committee, which co-ordinates the House's response to them.[75] The committee performs a similar role in regard to proposals to prescribe non-financial reporting standards for Ministers, departments and other organisations.[76]

In addition to its role at the centre of the House's financial procedures, the committee considers bills, petitions, treaties and other matters referred to it by the House.[77] The committee invariably holds a full public hearing, involving the Governor of the Reserve Bank, on each quarterly monetary policy statement issued by the bank. Most tax legislation is referred to the committee, and this can be a heavy burden. Any financial management legislation is inevitably referred to the committee. The committee made major reports on the 1989 public finance legislation (and on important amendments that were subsequently made to it), on the legislation reconstituting the Reserve Bank and on the fiscal responsibility legislation.[78] It has also made reports on other financial management issues, such as reporting by the Crown and its subentities[79] and on the format and layout of the Crown's financial statements.[80] In 1989, on referral from the House, it conducted a seminal inquiry into the officers of Parliament[81] and in 1998 it followed this up with an inquiry into the legislation applying to the Audit Office.[82]

69 S.Os 329 and 333.	77 S.O.190(1).
70 S.Os 324(2), 327(2) and 336(1).	78 1987-90, AJHR, I.4C; 1991-93, AJHR, I.4C; 1987-
71 S.O.328.	90, AJHR, I.4E; 1993-96, AJHR, I.3A; 2002-05,
72 S.O.335(1).	AJHR, I.22C, p.231.
73 1987-90, AJHR, I.19B, pp.221-2.	79 1991-93, AJHR, I.4A.
74 *Public Finance Act* 1989, s.18.	80 *Ibid.,* I.4B.
75 2002-05, AJHR, I.18C, pp.8-9.	81 1987-90, AJHR, I.4B.
76 *Ibid.,* p.10.	82 1996-99, AJHR, I.3E.

CHAPTER 32

APPROPRIATIONS AND AUTHORISATIONS

LEGAL AUTHORITY AND FINANCIAL AUTHORITY

There are two aspects to any governmental action involving the expenditure of public money – that is, to the incurring of expenses or of capital expenditure.

The first aspect is the legal authority of the Government or its agents to take the proposed action (in respect of which the expenditure or expenses are to be incurred) at all. This legal authority may be an inherent legal power possessed by the Government, it may be one conferred by statute, or it may be a combination of these.

The second aspect is the authority to expend public money for the purpose of performing that action should this be required. Ministers do not have authority to make payments out of public funds, even for activities that may otherwise be lawful, without parliamentary authority.[1] A payment made out of public funds without parliamentary authority is unlawful. Authority to expend public money can only be obtained by Parliament making an *appropriation* for the action which it is proposed to take or otherwise authorising the payment. An appropriation is a legislative provision which permits amounts of expenses or capital expenditure to be incurred for activities that fall within the defined scope of that provision. A financial authority for public money to be expended may be given separately than through an appropriation. Principally this occurs by means of a grant of imprest supply. However, such an authority lacks the specificity and accountability attendant on an appropriation. Consequently it is usually of temporary effect and is intended to be absorbed into the regular appropriation process.

Thus whatever the derivation of the Government's legal authority to perform an action, that authority is distinct from the appropriation enabling it to discharge financial liabilities arising from the action.[2] The two concepts of legal authority and appropriation can be linked if the provision of an appropriation is made a necessary legal condition of the activity in question;[3] for example, where a government contract was made "subject to" an appropriation being made by Parliament[4] and where a subsidy was made payable out of moneys standing in a particular account and insufficient funds had been appropriated to that account.[5] But even in such a case, there is still a conceptual distinction between the enabling authority and the spending authority, though the former may be defined by reference to the latter. However, defining the legal power to do something by reference to the financial authority to effect it is comparatively rare.

Sometimes the same statute provides, in separate sections, both the legal authority for the activity and for the appropriation. This type of appropriation is known as "permanent legislative authority". More often the statute conferring the legal authority on the Government to undertake certain activity does not make the appropriation itself but contains a section contemplating that Parliament will in the future (through its annual appropriations) make the appropriation necessary to discharge the financial obligations arising from that activity. In this case the need for an annual appropriation is made clear on the face of the legislation, but the effect is the same even if the statute is silent on the

1   *Public Finance Act* 1989, s.5; *R (Khan) v Secretary of State for Health* [2004] 1 WLR 971 at 91.
2   *Victoria v Commonwealth* (1975) 134 CLR 338 at 396.
3   *Commonwealth v Colonial Ammunition Co Ltd* (1924) 34 CLR 198 at 224-5.
4   *Churchward v R* (1865) LR 1 QB 173.
5   *Desailly v Brunker* (1888) 9 LR NSW (L) 536.

matter; an annual appropriation is still necessary to give any financial authorisation that is required to carry out the activity.

In any case where "expenses" are incurred under the authority of an appropriation this means expenses measured in accounting, not necessarily legal, terms.[6] However, any expenses incurred may well constitute legal liabilities too. Indeed the fact that a legal liability exists may be an important element in determining, in accounting terms, whether there is an expense needing to be recognised in the Crown's accounts, and thus requiring an appropriation.

EFFECT OF AN APPROPRIATION

An appropriation has only a limited effect. It is facilitative; it enables an expenditure to be made or a financial obligation to be satisfied that the Crown could not otherwise have made or satisfied. But while an appropriation enables the Government to spend public money and discharge its financial commitments, it does not require the Government to take those actions. An appropriation imposes no general duty on the Government to exercise the spending power thus granted,[7] nor does it in itself confer a contractual right to receive a payment.[8] A direction from Parliament that something actually be done is effected separately from the appropriation process.[9]

An appropriation does not enable the Crown, a department or anyone else to do something which they are not otherwise legally authorised to do; the existence of an appropriation does not make lawful something which is unlawful.[10] Thus, the fact that appropriations had been made in respect of certain departmental activities did not authorise the department to undertake those activities when they were not within the department's functions as defined in its parent legislation. The Auditor-General consequently refused to sanction expenditure on them even though there was an appropriation for them.[11] Nor does the fact that Parliament has appropriated funds for a particular purpose render disbursements pursuant to that appropriation immune from judicial review. The presumption is that Parliament in appropriating funds intends that they be used in a manner that complies with the legal principles developed by the courts to apply to anyone exercising a public power.[12]

It also follows from the requirement for an appropriation to be made before public money can be expended, that the fact that a statute has imposed an obligation on the Crown or its agents to pay money (for example, to pay benefits) does not in itself authorise that payment unless an appropriation for it has been made. For this reason statute now makes a standing appropriation allowing Crown liabilities to be settled.[13] But even apart from this provision the Crown is not excused from legal liabilities arising from statute, contract or otherwise, merely because no appropriation has been made to satisfy those liabilities. Judgment could still be entered against the Crown in these circumstances.[14] Nevertheless, formerly, parliamentary control of public expenditure was still emphasised since an appropriation was specially required to satisfy a judgment debt where no other legal appropriation for it existed.[15] In theory Parliament could have repudiated liability

6   *Public Finance Act* 1989, s.2(1).
7   *Archives and Records Association of New Zealand v Blakeley* [2000] 1 NZLR 607 at [70] and [79].
8   *New South Wales v Commonwealth* (1908) 7 CLR 179 at 190 (per Griffith CJ).
9   *R v Colonial Treasurer* (1878) 4 NZ Jur (NS) 47; *Awatere Road Board v Colonial Treasurer* (1887) 5 NZLR 372.
10 *Brown v West* (1990) 169 CLR 195; *R v Secretary of State for the Home Department, ex parte Fire Brigades Union* [1995] 2 AC 513 at 554 (per Lord Browne-Wilkinson); *Anning v Minister of Education*, unreported, High Court, Wellington, 26 April 2002.
11 1990, AJHR, B.1 [Pt.II], pp.18-22. The department's actions were validated by the *Ministry of Agriculture and Fisheries Amendment Act* 1990, s.2(6), (7).
12 *R v Criminal Injuries Compensation Board, ex parte P* [1995] 1 All ER 870 at 883.
13 *Public Finance Act* 1989, s.6(d).
14 *New South Wales v Bardolph* (1934) 52 CLR 455.
15 *Crown Suits Act* 1908, s.32.

by refusing to provide an appropriation to satisfy the judgment.[16] Now, however, it is provided that a judgment debt entered against the Crown following legal proceedings is sufficient authority for payment to be made even where Parliament has made no specific appropriation for that payment. A judgment debt against the Crown is subject to a standing appropriation under permanent legislative authority.[17]

PAYMENT OF PUBLIC MONEY

Money may only be paid out of a Crown Bank Account or a departmental bank account in accordance with an appropriation or other statutory authority.[18] Formerly there was a requirement for periodic certification from the Auditor-General before funds could be released. This was repealed in 2004 as being largely symbolic in an accrual accounting context and offering little practical check on public expenditure.[19]

The Treasury is required to report continuously to the Auditor-General on all actual expenses and capital expenditure incurred (whether under an appropriation or other authority) and to relate this expenditure to the amounts of authorised expenditure.[20] The Auditor-General may direct the Minister of Finance, the Treasury or a department, as the case may be, to stop payments out of a Crown Bank Account or a departmental bank account which the Auditor-General considers to be unlawful.[21] If the Auditor-General considers that expenditure has been incurred that was not lawful or was in excess of legal authority, the Auditor-General may direct the Minister concerned to report that belief to the House within 20 working days. But that Minister may also, in that report, set out the Minister's contrary belief about the legality of the expenditure, if the Minister holds one.[22] The Auditor-General, through the audit of public accounts, also checks for assurances that an entity has operated within the scope of an appropriation. In practice, this audit of appropriations or other authorities is the most important way in which the Auditor-General examines whether funds have been properly applied or committed.

In exercising these "controller" functions the Auditor-General is not concerned only with the existence of an appropriation or authority; the Auditor-General is also concerned to establish that the purpose to which any money to be paid from the Crown Bank Account is to be put is itself lawful. Where the proposed use of public money is not itself lawful, the Auditor-General may exercise the power to forbid payment, notwithstanding that there is an appropriation.[23] Where a legal obligation and an appropriation for a particular activity exist but it is likely that the amount appropriated will be exhausted, the Auditor-General has accepted a "letter of comfort" from the Minister of Finance and the Vote Minister as a condition of agreeing to the release of further public money for that activity.[24] A letter of comfort acknowledges the legal responsibility to continue to carry out the activity and is in earnest of the Ministers' intention to seek further appropriations from Parliament during the course of the financial year.

Whether the Auditor-General acquiesces in the release of public money on the basis of a letter of comfort is a matter for the judgment of the Auditor-General.

The Auditor-General's opinion is not conclusive of the validity of expenditure should

[16] *Rayner v R* [1930] NZLR 441 at 457-8.
[17] *Crown Proceedings Act* 1950, s.24(3).
[18] *Public Finance Act* 1989, s.65V(1).
[19] 2002-05, AJHR, I.22C, p.246 (*Public Finance (State Sector Management) Bill*); 2005, PP, B29[05a], pp.51-7 (Controller and Auditor-General).

[20] *Public Finance Act* 1989, s.65Y.
[21] *Ibid.*, s.65ZA.
[22] *Ibid.*, s.65Z.
[23] 1990, AJHR, B.1 [Pt.II], pp.18-22.
[24] See, for example, 1996-99, AJHR, I.21B, p.287.

it be subsequently challenged as not having been authorised.[25] If Parliament fails to pass detailed appropriations early in the financial year this can seriously compromise the Auditor-General's ability to carry out the controller function.[26] The House's financial procedures are now designed to ensure that detailed appropriations are made early enough in the financial year to prevent this occurring. The lack of specification for appropriations effected by way of imprest supply can undermine the effectiveness of the Auditor-General's role though this is ameliorated by the requirement (introduced in 2005) for continuous reporting to the Auditor-General on all expenses incurred.

DURATION OF APPROPRIATIONS

Permanent
Parliament is not limited to a particular period in specifying for how long an appropriation is to endure. In respect of some matters, the Act which provides for carrying on the activity goes on itself to authorise an appropriation for the purpose of that activity for an indefinite period. Expenditure of such a kind, permanent legislative authority, does not lapse (though the appropriation provision may, of course, be repealed). The exact proportion of total government expenditure which is permanently appropriated in this way varies each year. In the 2004/05 financial year it was 12.9 percent.[27] Permanent appropriations are not new phenomena. The *New Zealand Constitution Act* 1852 (UK) provided for defraying certain expenses without the necessity to seek an annual appropriation from Parliament. The expenses covered in this way included the salaries of the Governor and the judges, and of collecting state revenues.

Judges' salaries are an example of expenditure in respect of which there is still permanent legislative authority.[28] The placing of the authority to pay judicial salaries on a permanent basis rather than leaving them to be voted annually is of high symbolic importance as it demonstrates the independence of the judiciary from financial pressures. Parliament could, of course, repeal the section of the Act which makes judicial salaries a permanent charge on public funds, but to do that it must take a highly visible (and probably controversial) positive legislative action rather than merely omitting an item from the annual estimates. Other expenditure made under permanent legislative authority includes the salaries and allowances of Ministers and other members of Parliament;[29] the salaries of the Ombudsmen, the Controller and Auditor-General and the Deputy Controller and Auditor-General;[30] the government subsidy to various superannuation schemes[31] and the repayment of debt and the servicing of that debt.[32] Debt is payable under permanent legislative authority as an assurance to persons from whom the Government borrows that the sums required to discharge its liabilities will be forthcoming automatically each year. But the fact that permanent legislative authority for an appropriation exists does not preclude Parliament making appropriations for that activity on an annual basis if it sees fit.

While there may be good reasons for permanent appropriations in particular cases, in general permanent appropriations are deprecated as reducing Parliament's annual control of public expenditure.

All expenditure under permanent legislative authority must be reported to the House along with the annual estimates documents presented with the main Appropriation Bill.[33]

25   *Auckland Harbour Board v The King* [1924] AC 318.
26   1990-91, AJHR, B.1 [Pt.II], pp.16-7.
27   Information supplied by the Parliamentary Library, August 2005.
28   *Judicature Act* 1908, s.9A.
29   *Civil List Act* 1979, s.2.
30   *Ombudsmen Act* 1975, s.9(1); *Public Audit Act* 2001, Sch.3, cl.5.
31   *Government Superannuation Fund Act*, 1956, s.95.
32   *Public Finance Act* 1989, ss.6(c), 60 and 61.
33   *Ibid.*, s.15(3).

Annual

The standard appropriations are annual appropriations limited to the financial year to which the Appropriation Act under which they are made relates. They lapse at the end of that year.[34] These annual appropriations include money already spent and expenses already incurred that year under interim authorisations.[35] An Appropriation Act passed near to the start of the financial year enacts the main appropriations but there is usually a set of supplementary appropriations relating to the financial year made before the year closes. The majority of government expenditure is appropriated annually in these ways.

Multi-year

Rather than making appropriations annually or for an indefinite period, appropriations can be expressed to apply for a fixed number of years. In fact, Parliament has rarely done this. In the early years of responsible government there were two years (1857 and 1859) in which Parliament did not meet, and for these periods, in the expectation of a lengthy gap before Parliament would sit again, supply was voted for longer periods than 12 months. For a few years afterwards there was no automatic assumption that Parliament would meet every year and a section was inserted in the annual Appropriation Act allowing the Act's conditional extension for up to a further year if Parliament had not met sooner. The practice of including such a section in the Appropriation Acts ceased in 1865.

There is a provision in the public finance legislation contemplating that Parliament might make appropriations for more than one year – that is, a multi-year appropriation.[36] It is always open to Parliament in making an appropriation to express it to apply for any number of years. In that sense a provision contemplating multi-year appropriations is without legal significance. But it does acknowledge the existence of a new standard type of appropriation that may endure for up to five years.[37]

The first multi-year appropriation was made in the 1994/95 financial year to provide for the settlement of claims under the Treaty of Waitangi over the following five years. In the next year this multi-year appropriation was extended by a year.[38] Because of concern that multi-year appropriations are not subject to annual parliamentary scrutiny, a select committee has sought the Auditor-General's clarification of such a proposed appropriation and assurances that the risks to the Crown of the appropriation proving to be insufficient towards the end of the multi-year period were minimal.[39]

Akin to multi-year appropriations, although made outside the normal appropriation process, are funding agreements between the Treasurer and the Governor of the Reserve Bank concerning the income of the bank that may be applied in meeting its expenditure. These agreements are usually for five-year periods and are not effective unless ratified by a resolution of the House.[40]

INTERIM AUTHORISATIONS

Parliament could, before the financial year commences, decide upon the amounts to be appropriated for the coming year and appropriate them accordingly so that from 1 July the expenditure of public money could proceed on a settled basis. In practice, it has not been found possible to settle all the matters relating to a financial year before the year opens, and Parliament does not finish making the basic financial provision for the current year until some months of that year have elapsed. Indeed, until 1985 it was uncommon for

[34] *Ibid.*, s.10(1).
[35] *Archives and Records Association of New Zealand v Blakeley* [2000] 1 NZLR 607 at [72].
[36] *Public Finance Act* 1989, s.10(2).
[37] *Ibid.*, s.10(3).
[38] *Appropriation (1994/95 Supplementary Estimates) Act* 1995, s.7 and Third Schedule; *Appropriation (1995/96 Supplementary Estimates) Act* 1996, s.7 and Second Schedule.
[39] 1999-2002, AJHR, I.19B, pp.535-6.
[40] *Reserve Bank of New Zealand Act* 1989, s.161(2); see, for example, 2005, Vol.627, pp.21814-7, 21935.

parliamentary sessions even to commence before the beginning of a new financial year (at that time commencing on 1 April), thereby making it impossible to provide prospectively on an annual basis for public expenditure. Even when Parliament did meet some time before the financial year commenced, it showed no inclination to alter the usual cycle of financial business by making detailed appropriations prospectively.

In these circumstances an interim or temporary spending authority, called imprest supply, is used to confer authority to incur expenditures up to a specified limit[41] from 1 July (when the previous year's annual appropriations lapse) until new annual appropriations are made. In practice, other interim spending authorities may be necessary during the course of the financial year. These authorise expenses and capital expenditure separate from and ahead of any annual appropriations that are made.[42] Imprest supply is a distinct and separate spending authority from the appropriations made by the Appropriation Acts or other legislation.[43] Occasionally interim authority to incur such expenditures in advance of an Appropriation Act may be given by legislation other than imprest supply.[44]

An Appropriation Act when passed supersedes all Imprest Supply Acts applying to the financial year passed up to that time. The authorities conferred by an Imprest Supply Act merge into the annual appropriations made by the Appropriation Act. Imprest Supply Acts anticipate their temporary nature by expressly referring to the interim authorities which they make being charged in the manner to be set out in an Appropriation Act.[45] In this way they have been described as making "fictional" appropriations.[46] They then either expire or are spent when an Appropriation Act is passed. If no Appropriation Act were to be passed, the Imprest Supply Acts for the year would operate as distinct authorisations for expenses to be incurred and money to be paid on the bases set out in those Acts.[47]

An Imprest Supply Act does not specify in detail how the authorisations that it makes are to be exercised; it confers a general authority to spend up to a specified amount. This lack of information as to how the authority granted under imprest supply is to be used has been criticised by the Auditor-General as the constitutional equivalent of a blank cheque.[48]

However, no legal authority is unfettered. The Auditor-General's ability to question the lawfulness of the objects of expenditure incurred under imprest supply is unimpaired; an Imprest Supply Act, like an Appropriation Act, does not authorise expenditure on activities that it is not otherwise lawful for the Government or its agencies to incur. Furthermore, there may be extrinsic evidence of the purposes of the imprest supply authorisations that can be taken as factors in the legal definition of the scope of the authority given by an Imprest Supply Act. Thus the explanatory note to the bill may give information about how the authorisations are to be charged[49] and there must be a distinct Cabinet decision authorising the use of imprest supply for each particular purpose. The Treasury's obligation to report continuously during the financial year on actual expenses and capital expenditure incurred includes that incurred under the authority of imprest supply.[50] The Auditor-General is entitled to insist on a Cabinet decision being produced as authority for funds to be devoted to particular expenditure under the authority of an

---

[41]   1993-96, AJHR, I.19C, pp.41-2, 126-7 (insufficient imprest supply voted to cover the capital contributions needed for a transfer of assets between departments).

[42]   *Archives and Records Association of New Zealand v Blakeley* [2000] 1 NZLR 607 at [71].

[43]   *Ibid.* at [77] and [78].

[44]   See, for example, *New Zealand Public Health and Disability Act* 2000, s.113 (setting up of district health boards).

[45]   For example, *Imprest Supply (First for 2001/02) Act* 2001, s.8.

[46]   *Archives and Records Association of New Zealand v Blakeley* [2000] 1 NZLR 67 at [77].

[47]   *New South Wales v Bardolph* (1934) 42 CLR 455 at 479 (per Evatt J.); *Archives and Records Association of New Zealand v Blakeley* [2000] 1 NZLR 607 at [78].

[48]   1999-2002, AJHR, B.29[99c], p.87.

[49]   See, for example, *Imprest Supply (Third for 2001/02) Bill* 2001 (funding a capital injection into Air New Zealand Ltd).

[50]   *Public Finance Act* 1989, s.65Y.

Imprest Supply Act. In this way the Government takes explicit responsibility for how it uses imprest supply.

TYPES OF APPROPRIATION

Six types of appropriation are contemplated for the annual appropriations made by Parliament.[51] Separate appropriations must be made for each category of expenses or capital expenditure falling into each of these types. The appropriations are set out in detail in the estimates and other supporting information presented to the House in respect of each Appropriation Bill.[52] An appropriation made by any other Act is managed and accounted for in the same way as these types of appropriation.[53] Within each type of appropriation there are a number of separate appropriations. Each separate appropriation is limited in its scope and can be applied only to activities falling within the scope as defined.[54]

The six types of appropriation are—
* appropriations for output expenses
* appropriations for benefits or other unrequited expenses
* appropriations for borrowing expenses
* appropriations for other expenses
* appropriations for capital expenditure
* appropriations for expenses and capital expenditure to be incurred by an intelligence and security department.

The first four of these types of appropriation relate solely to operating expenditure.

Appropriations for output expenses

These are the payments for the cost of producing the goods and services which a department or third party is to supply to the Government to contribute to outcomes which the Government wishes to realise. They consist of policy advice, regulatory functions, inspection and administrative services and generally the "core" activities of government. They are organised into discrete groupings of similar products called classes of outputs. An appropriation may cover a single class of outputs or more than one class of outputs (known as a "multi-class output expense appropriation"). The output may itself be supplied by a government department or from a non-departmental source.[55]

Departmental outputs

How the Government decides what outputs it wishes departments to supply is a matter for it to determine. From 1993/94 to 2002/03, Ministers entered into annual purchase agreements with chief executives of their departments. These agreements specified the individual outputs which the department was to supply, defined the standards against which the department's performance in delivering those outputs was to be judged and identified the costs involved. While spoken of as agreements, they were not legally binding contracts as both parties to them (the Minister and the departments) were elements of the

---

[51] *Ibid.*, s.7(1).
[52] *Ibid.*, ss.14 and 15.
[53] *Ibid.*, s.11(2).

[54] *Ibid.*, s.9(1); for guidance in devising scope specifications for appropriations, see "Scoping the Scope of Appropriations", the Treasury, September 2005.
[55] *Ibid.*, s.7(3).

same entity – the Crown[56] – although they could form an element of a legally binding direction given by the Minister to the chief executive.[57]

From the 2003/04 financial year purchase agreements were replaced by outputs plans designed to provide detailed information about the service performance intentions of departments and to link these services explicitly with the outcomes set out in the department's longer-term statement of intent. Although still regarded as an agreement between the Minister and the chief executive and thus an accountability document in assessing the department's performance against the Government's expectations, there is less emphasis in output plans than there was in purchase agreements on the contractual nature of the relationship and more on the Government's strategic goals which the department is expected to contribute towards achieving.

Non-departmental outputs

Apart from outputs supplied by departments, the Government may obtain services from other organisations for which appropriations are made. The extent to which it does so will depend to some extent upon the organisation of the public sector – in particular the extent to which services are delivered by public service departments as opposed to Crown entities. A shift of appropriations from outputs supplied by departments to outputs supplied from non-departmental sources, particularly those supplied by Crown entities (which have been described as forming a "second tier" of government agencies), has been remarked.[58] Some of these organisations the Government may effectively control – for example, certain (but by no means, all) Crown entities – while others are entirely independent of the Government.

Crown entities must also prepare statements of intent setting out their medium-term intentions and providing an accountability base.[59] There may also be a purchase agreement between the Minister and the Crown entity or other provider specifying the outputs to be supplied. The management of such purchase agreements is often undertaken by the Minister's department on the Minister's behalf. Purchase agreements entered into between a Minister and a Crown entity may have legal force, unlike those between a Minister and a department.[60] Where outputs are supplied by a non-departmental entity which is not required by legislation to make a report to the House on its service performance (most Crown entities are now required to do so), the Minister for the vote must report on the performance of that entity in supplying the outputs.[61]

Appropriations for benefits or other unrequited expenses

These appropriations consist of transfer payments which do not require the recipient to provide any goods or services (outputs) in return for the payment. They consist mainly of the payment of benefits (such as social welfare benefits) to persons who have a legal entitlement to them. They also include any discretionary grants that are disbursed.

Appropriations for borrowing expenses

These appropriations consist of payments of interest or other financing expenses in respect of any loan or public security.

Appropriations for other expenses

Appropriations for other expenses include those expenses incurred by a department

---

[56] *Director-General of Social Welfare v Disputes Tribunal*, unreported, High Court, Whangarei, 23 February 1999.
[57] For example, under the *Defence Act* 1990, s.25(2) – see *Report to the State Services Commissioner by Douglas White QC and Graham Ansell*, December

[58] 1996-99, AJHR, I.20A, p.301.
[59] *Crown Entities Act* 2004, ss.138 and 139.
[60] 1996-99, AJHR, I.19A, p.233.
[61] *Public Finance Act* 1989, s.32A.

2001, para.18.

other than in the production of a good or service – for example, the costs of restructuring and losses incurred in selling or disposing of departmental assets at below market value. They include expenses incurred by the Crown (other than by a department) in the disposal or extinguishment of a Crown asset at less than fair market value, such as land or resources transferred in settlement of a claim under the Treaty of Waitangi.[62] However, if a Crown asset had no market value when sold or extinguished, any loss does not require an appropriation.[63] Grants to non-governmental organisations to develop their capacity rather than for the production of deliverable outputs, also fall under this category. Overseas development aid is appropriated under this type of appropriation. Other *ex gratia* payments and gifts that are made from time to time may be appropriated under the other expenses category too.

Appropriations for capital expenditure

These appropriations relate to the cost of assets acquired or developed by the Crown.[64] All capital expenditure on non-departmental assets and all equity or loan finance contributed by the Crown to non-departmental bodies or other persons is appropriated under this head. (Departments may incur capital expenditure from the proceeds of the sale of departmental assets or from disposing of their own working capital.)

Thus payments to provide for the purchase or development of capital assets (but not inventories) to be held as non-departmental assets are appropriated as capital expenditure. Such assets are regarded as part of the Crown estate (for example, State highways, national parks) but do not contribute to the production of outputs by a department. Any loan made by the Crown to another person or to the Government of another country must be charged as capital expenditure.[65]

Appropriations for expenses and capital expenditure to be incurred by an intelligence and security department

All of the above types of appropriations for expenses and capital expenditure are aggregated and appropriated separately for each intelligence and security department.

AGGREGATIONS OF APPROPRIATIONS

Although there are hundreds of individual appropriations made by Parliament in the Appropriation Acts, it is convenient for these appropriations to be grouped together for the purposes of administration and presentation. For this reason appropriations are grouped into votes. Each vote is made the responsibility of a designated Minister or Ministers and is administered by one department, though a department may administer more than one vote.[66]

In the case of the offices of Parliament – the Office of the Clerk and the Parliamentary Service – the Minister responsible for the respective votes administered by them is the Speaker.[67] Select committees, in their examination of the estimates, may seek explanations as to the need for the creation of a particular vote.[68]

TRANSFERRING APPROPRIATIONS

Though appropriations for classes of outputs are separate appropriations, transfers of amounts appropriated from one class of outputs to another class within the same vote can be made by Order in Council.[69] This procedure is used to deal with a small number

---

[62] See, for example, *Appropriation (1995/96 Supplementary Estimates) Act* 1996, s.9 (gift of pounamu to Ngai Tahu).

[63] 1993-96, AJHR, B.29 [95c], p.76 (Controller and Auditor-General).

[64] *Public Finance Act* 1989, s.2(1).

[65] *Ibid.*, s.65P.

[66] *Ibid.*, s.2(1).

[67] *Ibid.*

[68] See 1999-2002, AJHR, I.19B, pp.535-6.

[69] *Public Finance Act* 1989, s.26A.

of matters arising at the end of the financial year. They are usually confined to matters identified after the supplementary estimates have been prepared.[70]

The amount transferred by Order in Council cannot increase an appropriation for a class of outputs by more than five percent in any year, and the total amount appropriated for all classes of outputs in that vote must be the same. There can be only one transfer to a class of outputs under this power in any one year.[71] The Order in Council transferring appropriations between classes of outputs must be made before the end of the financial year.[72] A clause sanctioning such transfers must be included in an Appropriation Bill introduced in the next financial year.[73] This bill is usually called the Appropriation (Financial Review) Bill. However, a transfer of an appropriation by Order in Council is valid without the sanction of such legislation.[74]

LENDING

The Crown may lend money to any person or organisation if authorised by statute or this is otherwise necessary in order for the Crown to meet a legal obligation or properly perform a function.[75] The Minister of Finance may lend money if it appears to the Minister necessary or expedient in the public interest to do so and may lend money to a foreign Government for the purposes of economic development or otherwise to assist the inhabitants of that country.[76] Any such loans must be made from a capital expenditure appropriation or under other statutory authority.[77] Particular statutory authority is, for example, conferred on the Government to advance money to the Accident Compensation Corporation by way of loan or grant.[78]

EMERGENCY EXPENSES AND CAPITAL EXPENDITURE

Expenses and capital expenditure may be incurred to deal with emergencies. The Minister of Finance may approve the incurring of expenses or capital expenditure where any state of emergency or civil defence emergency is declared or any other situation arises that affects the public health or safety of New Zealand or any part of New Zealand and which the Government declares to be an emergency.[79] Public money may then be spent in accordance with the approval even though it has not been appropriated.[80]

There is no requirement for the emergency to have arisen after the passing of the Appropriation Acts, nor is there any limit on the amount which might be expended under this section (until 1953 there was a limit on the amount that could be expended in any year). The Minister may approve emergency expenses or capital expenditure even where Parliament has appropriated money for the same purpose. The expenses incurred for the purposes of an emergency or disaster affecting the public health or safety of New Zealand must be advised in the *Gazette* as soon as practicable.[81] All emergency expenses and expenditure must be included in the annual financial statements of the Government and in the following year's Appropriation Bill for confirmation by Parliament though this does not affect the validity of such expenditure.[82]

APPROVAL OF EXCESS EXPENSES AND CAPITAL EXPENDITURE

After Parliament has passed the Appropriation Acts for the current financial year, it may become apparent that, notwithstanding the supplementary estimates, the amounts

[70]　*Archives and Records Association of New Zealand v Blakeley* [2000] 1 NZLR 607 at [81].
[71]　*Public Finance Act* 1989, s.26A(1).
[72]　See, for example, *Public Finance (Transfers Between Outputs) Order* 2005.
[73]　*Public Finance Act* 1989, s.26A(2).
[74]　*Archives and Records Association of New Zealand v Blakeley* [2000] 1 NZLR 607 at [80].
[75]　*Public Finance Act* 1989, s.65K.
[76]　Ibid., ss.65L and 65M.
[77]　Ibid., s.65P.
[78]　*Injury Prevention, Rehabilitation, and Compensation Act* 2001, s.277(1).
[79]　*Public Finance Act* 1989, s.25(1), (2).
[80]　Ibid., s.25(4).
[81]　Ibid., s.25(3).
[82]　Ibid., s.25(5).

appropriated are insufficient to cover expenditure under a particular appropriation. The Minister of Finance has authority to approve the incurring of expenses or capital expenditure in respect of any appropriation in the last three months of the year in these circumstances. The Minister's approval must be given during the financial year or within three months of its end.[83]

The amounts which the Minister may approve under this provision in any financial year must not exceed $10,000 or more than two percent of the total amount appropriated for that appropriation, whichever is the greater amount.[84]

All such expenses or capital expenditure must be included in an Appropriation Bill for confirmation by Parliament (though its validity does not depend on confirmation).[85] A statement of such excess expenses or expenditure must also be included in the annual financial statements of the Government and in the financial statements of the department administering the vote concerned.[86]

UNAPPROPRIATED OR UNAUTHORISED EXPENSES AND CAPITAL EXPENDITURE

It is unlawful for expenses or capital expenditure to be incurred without appropriation or other authority from Parliament.[87]

Wherever any such expenses or expenditure is incurred any person or persons responsible may themselves incur liability for the illegality. However, it is likely, where the illegality was perpetrated in good faith (and not, for instance, dishonestly), that Parliament will wish to regularise the position, remove any legal liability arising, obviate recovery action being initiated in respect of any unauthorised payments that have been made, and provide for obligations that have been entered into to be satisfied out of lawfully appropriated funds.

Consequently, an Appropriation Bill (or other legislation) may seek to validate such expenses or expenditure.[88] Where validation of unappropriated expenses is sought by means of an Appropriation Bill, the Minister of Finance must present a report to the House setting out the amount of each category of expenses or capital expenditure so incurred and the explanation of the Minister responsible for those expenses or that expenditure.[89] A statement of such unappropriated or unauthorised expenses must also be included in the annual financial statements of the Government and in the financial statements of the department administering the relevant vote.[90]

Unless and until validated by Parliament, unappropriated or unauthorised expenses and capital expenditure remain unlawful.

[83] *Ibid.*, s.26B(1), (2).
[84] *Ibid.*
[85] *Ibid.*, s.26B(4), (5).
[86] *Ibid.*, s.26D.
[87] *Ibid.*, ss.4(1) and 26C(1).
[88] See, for example, *Appropriation (1997/98 Financial Review) Act* 1999, s.7 (validating an unquantified portion of expenses incurred in providing business capability improvement grants outside the scope of the appropriation for such grants).
[89] *Public Finance Act* 1989, s.26C(2).
[90] *Ibid.*, s.26D.

CHAPTER 33

REVENUE

As well as determining what it wishes to spend, Parliament has to decide how that spending is to be financed – that is, principally from taxation. This process was formerly known as "ways and means". In New Zealand a committee of the whole House called the Committee of Ways and Means would thus authorise the collection of taxes each year. That procedure was abolished in 1962. In practice, decisions on expenditure and revenue were never as divorced from each other as the separate parliamentary mechanisms of supply and ways and means might seem to suggest. In parliamentary terms this is especially the case now, with an elaborate system of financial reporting designed to give a complete picture of the Crown's financial position reflecting both revenues and expenditures, and the Crown's financial veto which replaces previous rules that differed depending on whether an appropriation or a taxation proposal was before the House with a financial rule that concentrates on the fiscal implications of the proposal.

Consequently, there are now relatively few specifically revenue-based or taxation-based parliamentary rules. This chapter outlines how authority is given for the Crown to raise revenue and to borrow and how this must be accounted for to the House.

ACCOUNTING FOR AND REPORTING REVENUE

All public money must be lodged in a Crown Bank Account or in a departmental bank account.[1] Certain sources of public money may be required to be lodged in a dedicated part of a Crown Bank Account as a separate fund.[2] "Public money" is all money received by the Crown (except money received in trust).[3] It does not include money received by Crown entities, State enterprises or local authorities. Departmental bank accounts receive disbursements from the Crown Bank Account to meet the costs of supplying their outputs. The revenue received from the supply of services by a department or from the sale of its capital assets is paid into a departmental bank account.[4] All investment income received by the Government must be paid into a Crown Bank Account.[5] Income received by a Crown entity must be held in a bank account established by the entity.[6]

Revenue must be accounted for by the Government as a component of the annual and monthly financial statements which the Government is obliged to prepare and publish.[7] The Finance and Expenditure Committee reports on the annual financial statements within one week of the first sitting of the House each year.[8]

The Minister of Finance must report annually to the House in the fiscal strategy report on the Government's long-term objectives for fiscal policy, including for operating revenues, and how these objectives accord with the principles of responsible fiscal management.[9] At least at four-year intervals a statement on the long-term fiscal position must be produced.[10] An annual economic and fiscal update must be made to the House. This must include fiscal forecasts and a statement of tax policy changes.[11] Government

[1] *Public Finance Act* 1989, 65U(1).
[2] See, for example, *Land Transport Management Act* 2003, s.8(1) (land transport revenue forms the national land transport fund).
[3] *Public Finance Act* 1989, s.2(1).
[4] *Ibid.*, s.65U(2)(b), (c).
[5] *Ibid.*, s.65I(3).
[6] *Crown Entities Act* 2004, s.158
[7] *Public Finance Act* 1989, ss.27 and 31A.
[8] S.O.336(1).
[9] *Public Finance Act* 1989, ss.26I to 26L.
[10] *Ibid.*, s.26N.
[11] *Ibid.*, ss.26O, 26Q, 26R and 26U.

decisions having a material effect on such forecasts must be disclosed to the fullest extent practicable. These reports stand referred to the Finance and Expenditure Committee for examination.[12] The committee must report to the House on the fiscal strategy report and the economic and fiscal update within two months of the delivery of the Budget.[13]

SOURCES OF REVENUE

Government revenue comes from taxation, sales of assets, investment income and receipts from third parties – for example, through fees or charges and in royalties on coal, minerals and petroleum.[14] Whenever possible, revenue from taxation is recognised as public money in the public accounts at the time the obligation to pay the tax arises – that is, when the income on which tax is payable is earned or when the good or service is consumed.[15] The Government may also borrow money.

TAXATION

Taxation must be authorised by Parliament either directly in primary legislation or by regulations authorised by such legislation. It is illegal for the Crown to levy money on its subjects without parliamentary authority.[16] This amounts to a constitutional principle and the courts may give effect to it by requiring taxes exacted under an unlawful demand to be returned to the taxpayer.[17]

The prohibition on taxation without parliamentary authority applies to a direct tax such as income tax and to indirect taxes, such as goods and services tax and customs and excise duties. While it is clear with such imposts as income tax and goods and services tax that a tax is involved and that therefore parliamentary authority is required, there can be a fine line between charges for governmental services, which the Crown may be entitled to make without express parliamentary authorisation, and an unlawful levy of money (whether this is termed a tax or is called a charge, a levy, a duty or a fee). A tax has been defined as any levy which is compulsory, for public purposes, and is legally enforceable.[18] The issue of whether the Crown or a department is seeking to recover a lawful charge or to impose an unlawful tax is most likely to arise when a charge is imposed by delegated legislation for the performance of a public duty. In these circumstances not only must the power to charge be authorised by the legislation under which any regulations are made,[19] but the actual charge imposed must also be reasonable having regard to the duty performed. The Regulations Review Committee has regarded it as a rebuttable presumption that any fees fixed by regulations above a cost recovery level are in the nature of a tax and that Parliament could not have intended them to be authorised solely by regulations.[20] Any such regulations will be subjected to close scrutiny to ensure that the charge is authorised and is justifiable.

In respect of a number of taxes there is special parliamentary involvement.

Income tax

Income tax was introduced in New Zealand on 1 April 1892.[21] It is the most important source of revenue available to the Government, accounting for some two-thirds of total Crown receipts. The liability to pay income tax is fixed by legislation

---

[12] S.Os 327(1) and 328.

[13] S.O.327(2).

[14] 1993-96, AJHR, B.29[95c], p.45.

[15] See 1999-2002, AJHR, B.11, p.52.

[16] *Bill of Rights* 1688, article 4; *Constitution Act* 1986, s.22(a).

[17] *Woolwich Equitable Building Society v Inland Revenue Commissioners* [1993] AC 70 at 172 (per Lord Goff of Chieveley).

[18] *Air Caledonie International v Commonwealth of Australia* (1988) 165 CLR 462.

[19] *Brocklebank v R* [1924] 1 KB 647.

[20] 1990, AJHR, I.16B, para.9.1.

[21] *Land and Income Assessment Act* 1891.

imposing a permanent charge to tax. However, the rates of income tax are not fixed on a permanent basis – at first by statute, subsequently by convention, they are fixed annually.

The income tax year runs from 1 April to 31 March.[22] This means that Parliament must pass legislation confirming the income tax rates that are to apply before the tax year commences on 1 April each year. In practice it often does this in legislation passed in the calendar year preceding the ending of the income tax year.

Until 1987 annual rates of income tax were set in Income Tax (Annual) bills which were introduced in each tax year and often debated in tandem with Income Tax Amendment bills, which contained amendments to income tax law generally. Since 1987 the practice has been to fix income tax rates by including a clause in an Income Tax Amendment Bill or in general taxation bills that are to be passed during the course of the year. But a clause fixing tax rates must be in such a bill when it is introduced; it cannot be added to it by way of amendment. The *Income Tax (Annual) Bill* 1991 was introduced and passed separately for this reason. Where the clause fixing tax rates is part of an amending bill, it is divided into a separate bill at the committee stage and passed as a separate measure.[23]

The annual taxing provision either fixes the rates of income tax by confirming the rates already in force or it fixes new rates by reference to a new schedule of tax rates which are to be substituted in the *Income Tax Act* 2004. The annual taxing provision itself, however, never contains the actual tables or figures of income tax rates. It legislates by reference to rates set out elsewhere.

The principle of an annual provision fixing rates of taxation is an important constitutional one. That part of any tax bill setting the annual rates of income tax is treated as a matter of confidence.[24] A proposal, announced in the 1979 Budget, that income tax rates should be subject to reduction by Order in Council, aroused strong opposition on constitutional grounds and was not proceeded with.[25] Even changing tax rules by regulation, with the consequent implications for tax liability, is looked at critically if it appears that Parliament is being asked to authorise the variation of tax by regulation.[26] The requirement for tax rates to be fixed annually, failing which there can be no assessment and liability to pay tax, is an extra assurance that Parliament will be called upon to meet every year.

Customs and excise

Customs and excise duties were initially the most important source of government revenue, accounting for 90 percent of tax receipts and 69 percent of total revenue in 1875–76.[27] They now account for about five percent of all Crown revenue.[28]

Customs duties

Customs duties are taxes levied on goods imported into New Zealand. The House has power to alter such duties by resolution. Generally, a resolution passed by a House of a legislature does not of itself alter the law[29] but a statute can delegate legislative power to the House of Representatives to be exercised by the passing of a resolution. For many years this has been the case in New Zealand in respect of customs duties. Provisional legal force is conferred on a resolution passed by the House for an alteration in the

---

22 *Income Tax Act* 2004, s.OB1 (definition of **tax year**).

23 See, for example, the *Taxation (Annual Rates of Income Tax 2001-02) Act* 2001 introduced as part of the *Taxation (Annual Rates, Taxpayer Assessment and Miscellaneous Provisions) Bill* 2001.

24 1998, Vol.573, pp.13199-200, 13209; 2004, Vol.622, p.17369 (*Taxation (Annual Rates, Venture Capital and Miscellaneous Provisions) Bill*).

25 1980, AJHR, B.1 [Pt.III], p.7; Templeton, *All Honourable Men*, pp.121-2.

26 2002-05, AJHR, I.22D, pp.222-3 (*Taxation (Base Maintenance and Miscellaneous Provisions) Bill*).

27 McLintock, *An Encyclopaedia of New Zealand*, Vol.1, p.661.

28 2004, PP, B11.

29 *Bowles v Bank of England* [1913] 1 Ch 57.

customs tariff,[30] thereby enabling changes to be made in rates of duty with immediate effect and so avoiding any delay that might otherwise occur by the need to pass amending legislation. Any motion for an alteration in the customs tariff is subject to the Crown's financial veto.[31]

Whenever the House resolves to amend the customs tariff no person may commence a legal action against the Crown, a Minister or any other person to whom powers have been delegated in respect of action taken to enforce the tariff as amended by the House's resolution. This legal protection subsists only until the end of the session in which the resolution was passed, by which time legislation must be passed to validate it. In the absence of such legislation, it then ceases to have effect.[32]

Such resolutions are not common now. Governments prefer to make such changes by passing a bill through all its stages at one sitting rather than effecting the changes in two bites, by a resolution and the subsequent passage of a confirming bill through the House. The last occasion on which such resolutions were passed was in 1970 when additional duties were imposed on tobacco and cigars imported into New Zealand.[33] The bill which ratified and revoked the resolutions was passed one month later, giving permanent effect to the amendments to the tariff.[34]

Alterations to the customs tariff may also be made by Order in Council. Such alterations expire at the close of 31 December in the following year unless they are expressly validated and confirmed by legislation passed before that time.[35] In the case of other customs orders which are not required to be validated and confirmed by legislation, the House may resolve that the order be revoked or varied, and if it does so resolve, the revocation or variation has legal effect, and any excess duty collected under the order must be refunded.[36] A motion to revoke or vary a customs order is subject to the Crown's financial veto.[37]

Excise duties

Excise duties are taxes levied on goods within New Zealand at some point before their final sale or supply to consumers. The principal goods on which excise duties are currently levied are petrol, tobacco and alcohol.

Orders in Council imposing excise duty or excise-equivalent duties or altering the rates of such duties are subject to confirmation by the House. An order made in the first half of the year expires at the end of that year, unless expressly confirmed by an Act of Parliament passed in that year. An order made in the second half of the year expires at the close of the following year, unless confirmed by Act of Parliament passed before the end of that year.[38] The House may also resolve to revoke or vary such orders. If it does so, the order is thereby revoked or varied and any excess duty that has been collected must be refunded.[39] A motion to revoke or vary an excise duty is subject to the Crown's financial veto.[40]

Goods and services tax

Goods and services tax was introduced on 1 October 1986. It is charged (at the rate of 12.5 percent) on the supply of goods and services in New Zealand.[41] It is not an excise duty, because it is levied at the point of sale or supply. No special parliamentary procedure is

---

30   *Tariff Act* 1988, s.12(1).
31   S.O.318(3).
32   *Tariff Act* 1988, s.12(1).
33   1970, JHR, pp.343-7.
34   *Customs Amendment Act* 1970.
35   *Tariff Act* 1988, s.11(1).
36   *Ibid.,* s.11(3).
37   S.O.318(3).
38   *Customs and Excise Act* 1996, s.80(1).
39   *Ibid.,* s.80(3).
40   S.O.318(3).
41   *Goods and Services Tax Act* 1985, s.8.

prescribed for the levying of goods and services tax. While goods and services tax is payable by the Crown,[42] no specific appropriation for the payment is required. General authority exists for the payment of goods and services tax in relation to the expenses or capital expenditure incurred in accordance with an appropriation or other spending authority.[43]

Road user charges

Road user charges are charges made for the licences needed by the operators of certain heavy motor vehicles. Rates of road user charges may be altered by Order in Council. Such an order has only temporary effect. Any order made on or before 30 June in any year expires on the close of the last day of that year, unless it is expressly validated or confirmed by an Act of Parliament passed in that year. Orders altering rates of road user charges which are made on or after 1 July expire on the close of the last day of the following year, unless expressly validated or confirmed by an Act of Parliament passed before the end of that year.[44] If such an order expires, the rates previously applying come into force again.[45]

Biosecurity levies

By Order in Council, levies may be made payable to the Director-General of Agriculture in order to fund, wholly or in part, a service provided or function performed by the Ministry in respect of biosecurity inspections. Such a levy order must be laid before the House as if it were a regulation.[46] Any such orders that are made in the first half of the year, if not already revoked, are deemed to be revoked on the close of 30 June in the following year, unless confirmed by Act of Parliament. Levies made in the second half of the year are deemed to be revoked on the close of 31 December in the following year, unless statutorily confirmed.[47]

Aviation levies

Levies may be imposed on holders of licences and permits to operate aircraft, aerodromes and other aviation services in order to fund the activities of the Civil Aviation Authority. The levies are made by Order in Council.[48] Such an order made on or before 30 June in any year expires on the close of that year unless it is expressly validated or confirmed by an Act of Parliament passed in that year. Orders made on or after 1 July expire on the close of the following year unless so validated or confirmed before the end of that year.[49] The expiry of such an order does not affect the liability to pay the levy prescribed while the order was in force.[50]

Wine levies

Levies may be imposed by Order in Council on wine and businesses producing wine in order to help defray the costs of establishing and maintaining wine standards in New Zealand.[51] Any levy imposed in the first half of the year expires on 30 June in the following year (if still in force) unless confirmed by Act of Parliament before then.[52] A wine levy made in the second half of the year expires on 31 December in the following year (if still in force) unless confirmed by Act of Parliament.[53] The costs of regulating the

---

[42]   *Ibid.*, s.7.
[43]   *Public Finance Act* 1989, s.6(b).
[44]   *Road User Charges Act* 1977, s.20(3).
[45]   *Ibid.*, s.20(4).
[46]   *Biosecurity Act* 1993, s.137.
[47]   *Ibid.*, s.138.
[48]   *Civil Aviation Act* 1990, s.42A.
[49]   *Ibid.*, s.42C(2).
[50]   *Ibid.*, s.42C(3)(b).
[51]   *Wine Act* 2003, s.89.
[52]   *Ibid.*, s.96(1).
[53]   *Ibid.*, s.96(2).

wine industry are to be recovered as far as possible out of fees and levies rather than by money appropriated by Parliament.[54]

Problem gambling levies

Levies (called "problem gambling levies") may be imposed on gambling operators by Order in Council to recover the costs of developing, managing and delivering an integrated problem gambling strategy.[55] Any such levy made in the first half of the year expires on 30 June in the following year, and any such levy made in the second half of the year expires on 31 December in the following year unless, in either case, the levy is confirmed by Act of Parliament.[56]

THIRD-PARTY REVENUE

Third-party revenue can arise from a number of sources. First, it may come from compulsory charges, penalties and fines. For example, 10 percent of the amount of every fine payable to a local authority as a result of a prosecution brought by the authority must be credited to a Crown Bank Account or a departmental bank account.[57] Statutory authority is required before a compulsory charge, a penalty or a fine may be imposed and the charge, penalty or fine must be levied in accordance with the terms of that authority.

Secondly, revenue is derived from fees and charges for the sale of goods and the provision of services, such as, for example, the sale of publications and the provision of translation services. No particular parliamentary authority is required for the Crown and departments to earn such income. The Crown is entitled to contract to provide a good or a service which it has no public duty to provide and which the recipient of that good or service chooses to accept on terms that include payment.[58] But the Crown is not entitled to demand or contract for payment for a good or service that it is obliged to provide, except in accordance with the statutory authority relating to the provision of that good or service conferred by Parliament.[59]

Both the Auditor-General and the Treasury have produced guidelines for charging for public-sector goods which departments should have regard to in setting user charges.[60] The Treasury guidelines are directed to charges for services for which the Government is a monopoly supplier when alternative sources of supply are not present or have not been identified. They are intended to promote efficiency, equity and fiscal issues.[61] However, there are acknowledged difficulties in applying these guidelines when fees are set at below full cost recovery rates or when the services to be provided contain a significant public-good component.[62]

Finally, the Crown may derive revenue from other miscellaneous sources and operating activities.[63] For example, unclaimed trust money, unclaimed money in departmental and other bank accounts and surpluses of the Public Trust may be paid to the Crown.[64]

---

[54] *Ibid.*, s.84(1).
[55] *Gambling Act* 2003, s.319(1), (2).
[56] *Ibid.*, s.319(4)(a), (b).
[57] *Public Finance Act* 1989, s.73; *Building Act* 2004, s.389(2).
[58] *China Navigation Co v Attorney-General* [1932] 2 KB 197.
[59] *Waikato Regional Airport Ltd v Attorney-General* [2004] 3 NZLR 1.
[60] 1993-96, AJHR, B.29[95c], pp.45-50 (Controller and Auditor-General); The Treasury, "Guidelines for Setting Charges in the Public Sector", December 2002.
[61] *Ibid.*, p.3.
[62] 1999-2002, AJHR, I16M, p.16 and App.E (Regulations Review Committee).
[63] See generally, 1993-96, AJHR, B.29[95c], pp.45-50 (Controller and Auditor-General).
[64] *Public Finance* Act 1989, ss.70 and 74; *Public Trust Act* 2001, s.43.

CHAPTER 34

THE PROCESS OF SUPPLY

The financial year runs from 1 July to the following 30 June. Supply – the appropriation or authorisation by Parliament of the sums of money required to carry on the government of the country – is made in respect of that year. Some of this supply is in place permanently under permanent legislative authority but the greater part needs to be authorised on an annual basis under the House's supply procedures. The process of granting supply involves the House taking action before, during and after the financial year to which the appropriations relate. So in any financial year the House is dealing with residual supply issues relating to the previous financial year, supply issues relating to the current financial year and preparatory supply issues relating to the forthcoming financial year.

OUTLINE OF THE SUPPLY PROCESS

In outline, the supply process involves: consideration of the Government's budget strategy for the coming year, an interim supply authority being given before the financial year opens, presentation, examination and approval of the Government's Budget and main estimates of expenditure, further temporary supply authorities being granted, approval of any supplementary estimates presented by the Government and, after the year ends, confirmation or validation of any unappropriated expenses or capital expenditure that were incurred.

The timetable for these processes as they relate to a particular financial year is—

Prior to the financial year commencing

August–September	Government's Budget preparations begin
November–December	*Economic and fiscal update* published (contains forecasts on which Budget decisions will be based)
December–March	*Budget policy statement* presented (sets out Government's Budget strategy)
May onwards	*Budget and estimates* presented (Government's main economic and fiscal policy proposals)
June	*Imprest supply* approved (interim spending authority to apply from 1 July)

During the financial year

July–September	*Budget and estimates* approved. Further *imprest supply* approved.
May–June	*Supplementary estimates* presented and approved (additions and variations to the main estimates approvals)

After the financial year ends

February-March	Excess expenditure or other expenditure not approved in the estimates or supplementary estimates, confirmed or validated.

(This is the standard time-frame for the process of supply but it is always liable to disruption by a dissolution of Parliament.)

Consequently, parliamentary consideration and authorisation of the supply required for each financial year commences before that financial year opens and does not conclude until well after that financial year has ended – occupying a period of some 18 months or more. This chapter examines the procedures employed to discharge these tasks. The House's confirmation or validation of excess expenditure or other unappropriated expenditure is integrated with the procedures under which the Crown and departments report to the House on their financial and operational performance. (See Chapters 35 and 36, where this aspect is dealt with in detail.)

BUDGET PREPARATIONS

The Budget is the collective name for a compendium of economic and fiscal measures announced annually by the Minister of Finance. It is a process rather than an event, involving the making of decisions, the preparation of documentation relating to those decisions and their release on "Budget day". Insofar as one event does signify the Budget, it is the Budget statement delivered to the House by the Minister in moving the second reading of the main Appropriation Bill[1] in which the main components of the Budget will be described.

The preparation of a Budget prior to its presentation to the House is almost exclusively a matter for the executive rather than the legislature. Rarely has the House itself been actively involved in making public expenditure decisions as part of Budget planning, as opposed to endorsing Budget proposals.[2] There are few statutory or Standing Orders obligations impinging on the process that Governments must follow in deciding what proposals are to be included in a Budget and in the executive's proposals for public expenditure that it presents to the legislature. Only in respect of the offices of Parliament is the House involved in devising estimates of expenditure itself. Statute provides some obligations relating to the conveying of a Government's intentions to the House (such as in the Budget policy statement) but the process followed in preparing a Budget is largely an internal matter for the Government to determine. Thus it is recorded that as late as the first Labour Government in 1935 it was rare for the Treasury even to report on Ministers' spending proposals, which were usually put before the Cabinet informally and on an ad hoc basis.[3] The arrangements followed by modern governments have tended to be increasingly sophisticated and take account of the overall economic and fiscal implications of individual spending proposals. The outline that follows represents that recently employed, linked in with the few extant statutory or House procedural requirements.[4]

Strategic phase

Formal preparations for a Budget begin as early as August in the preceding year when Ministers start to consider what the Budget strategy objectives will be. For this purpose, planning proceeds on objectives for the next three years. The Cabinet ultimately determines (usually by November) the relative importance of the outcomes that the Government wishes to achieve and agrees on what is to be included in the next Budget.

---

[1] *Public Finance Act* 1989, s.2(1).

[2] Though for an example see 1931, Vol.229, p.468 and Bassett, *Coates of Kaipara*, pp.167-8 (special economy committee set up to adjust public expenditure).

[3] Bassett with King, *Tomorrow Comes the Song*, p.159.

[4] This summary is drawn from "Putting it Together – An Explanatory Guide to the New Zealand Public Sector Financial Management System" published by the Treasury.

Half-year economic and fiscal update

An economic and fiscal update must be published in the November–December period (except where a pre-election update has been published in the last three months of the year). This update contains economic and fiscal forecasts for the current and the next two financial years.[5] This information is critical to the preparation of the Budget. The update stands referred to the Finance and Expenditure Committee[6], though the committee is not obliged to report on it.

Budget policy statement

Decisions taken during the strategic phase are embodied in a Budget policy statement which the Minister of Finance must issue by 31 March each financial year if Parliament is in session (which, unless an election is called at that time, it almost invariably will be). This means that, if the statement is ready, it can be released at the same time as the publication of the half-yearly economic and fiscal update. The Budget policy statement specifies the overarching policy goals that will guide the Government's Budget decisions, the policy areas the Government will focus on, and how the Budget will accord with the short-term intentions referred to in the most recent fiscal strategy report.[7]

The Budget policy statement stands referred to the Finance and Expenditure Committee.[8] The committee must report to the House on it within 40 working days of its presentation to the House.[9] The Minister of Finance, if requested, is expected to attend the committee for the purposes of its examination of the statement.[10] It is the invariable practice for this examination to be recorded and transcribed.

The first general debate held after the committee's report on the statement has been presented is devoted to considering the statement and the report. The chairperson of the Finance and Expenditure Committee (or, in the chairperson's absence, some other member of the committee) begins the debate.[11] There may be 12 speeches of up to 10 minutes each[12] in contrast to the usual one-hour general debate. But the debate is not a full Budget debate. Members must speak relevantly to the statement and the committee's report on it.[13]

The objective of issuing a Budget policy statement (which has been a statutory obligation since 1994) is to make more transparent the bases on which Governments make their Budget decisions. This objective is undermined when new initiatives with significant fiscal impacts are introduced late in the financial year, by way of the supplementary estimates. This can happen, for example, where the Government changes after a Budget has been delivered.[14]

Statements of intent

Each year departments must prepare information on their future operating intentions – known as statements of intent.[15] Statements of intent are presented to the House at the time of the Budget.[16] They are intended to provide information on the nature and scope of the department's functions and on what the department will be attempting to achieve over the next three years, explicitly linking the services which the department is providing for the Government (what the department does) with what the Government wishes to accomplish (its policy goals). Statements of intent are expected to identify the challenges the department faces in carrying on its business, both in terms of external factors, such as

---

[5]   *Public Finance Act* 1989, s.26S.
[6]   S.O.328.
[7]   *Public Finance Act* 1989, s.26M.
[8]   S.O.324(1).
[9]   S.O.324(2).
[10] S.O.324(3).
[11] S.O.324(4).

[12] Appendix A to the Standing Orders.
[13] 1995, Vol.547, p.6714.
[14] 1999-2000, PP, B.29[00c], para.3.710 (Controller and Auditor-General).
[15] *Public Finance Act* 1989, ss.38 to 42.
[16] *Ibid.*, s.39(1).

the international, national and sectoral outlook, and internal factors, such as its capability in terms of staff and other resources. The statements are also expected to explain how progress towards its achievements can be measured. While they are departmental documents they are developed with the Minister in charge of the department and must include any matters that the Minister wishes to include as a means to understanding the department and its operations.[17]

In respect of the immediate financial year, statements of intent must also set out detailed financial information on the department containing properly prepared forecast financial statements and statements of forecast service performance.[18] The department will be expected to report against these financial statements at the end of the year when they will be formally audited.

In the case of offices of Parliament there is a process of consultation with the House that must be followed in preparing each office's statement of intent. Before the start of each financial year each office must submit to the Speaker draft information about its future operating intentions.[19] This information is considered by the Officers of Parliament Committee, which may communicate its views directly to the office concerned.[20] Each office must then have regard to any such comments in preparing its final statement of intent.[21]

Crown entities and State enterprises are also obliged to prepare and publish statements of intent. (See Chapter 35.)

Preparation of the estimates

Priorities identified in the Budget strategy guide Ministers and departments in the preparation of submissions for matters to be included in the Budget. This involves preparing draft departmental budgets for the next three years complemented by output plans for the coming year. The output plans specify proposed departmental outputs, performance indicators in respect of those outputs and the expected costs of producing them.

Ministers and departments also prepare submissions on new policy initiatives that they wish to see included in the Budget and which will have an impact on revenue and expense levels. These policy proposals are considered by the Cabinet for consistency with the Government's overall strategy, particularly as set out in the Budget policy statement.

As part of the estimates preparation too, the levels of expenses on existing outputs and activities funded from each vote are updated. These levels (called baselines) are agreed for the current and the next two years on a rolling basis, giving the Government and departments some assurance about the expenditure levels they will enjoy over a three-year period. The baseline levels can be changed if Cabinet approves, though this will be done only in defined circumstances – such as, for example, if forecasts suggest that demand-driven expenditure is likely to change significantly. Failure to carry out a baseline update of a vote before preparing the estimates increases the likelihood that alterations to that vote will need to be made later in the financial year through supplementary estimates. In these circumstances the main estimates are less reliable as an indication of likely expenditure. This is considered an unsatisfactory basis on which to present estimates to the House.[22]

The decisions made as a result of these activities are consolidated into the estimates and other information to be presented to the House at the time of the Budget.

---

[17] *Ibid.*, s.40.
[18] *Ibid.*, s.41.
[19] *Ibid.*, s.45G(1).

[20] 2002-05, AJHR, I.18C, p.9.
[21] *Public Finance Act* 1989, s.45G(1).
[22] 1996-99, AJHR, I.19A, p.247.

Format of the estimates

The form in which the estimates are prepared results partly from the information that statute requires to be included in it. But, subject to this, its format is largely in the hands of the Minister of Finance as the Minister who is responsible for its preparation and presentation to the House.

It has been the practice for the Treasury to discuss significant changes to the format of the estimates with the Finance and Expenditure Committee in advance of their adoption. (See Chapter 31.) There is now also a statutory duty of consultation with the House over changes to the format of the estimates (including supplementary estimates) and the other supporting information that must accompany each Appropriation Bill. The Minister must submit any proposed change to the Speaker, who presents it to the House.[23] The proposal is referred to the Finance and Expenditure Committee which disseminates it to the other subject select committees and co-ordinates their responses. The Finance and Expenditure Committee then communicates its own views on the proposal and those of the other committees directly to the Minister.[24]

The Minister, in finalising any changes to the format of the estimates, must take into account any comments made by the Speaker and the select committees.[25]

Funding for offices of Parliament

The offices of Parliament are subject to a special process for the pre-budget approval of appropriations for their offices. This involves a parliamentary committee fixing their budgets before their estimates are formally presented to the House.

The officers of Parliament must submit to the House each year an estimate of expenses and capital expenditure to be incurred by their offices, together with a description of the classes of outputs to be produced, the revenue to be earned and other financial information.[26] In the case of the Auditor-General this information is incorporated in that officer's draft annual plan prepared for submission to the House.[27] The information is forwarded directly to the Officers of Parliament Committee. It is the committee's duty to recommend to the House an estimate of the expenditure of each office of Parliament for inclusion in a vote in an Appropriation Bill.[28] For this purpose the committee hears evidence from the officers themselves and calls for comment from officials of the Treasury. In determining what estimates to recommend, the committee is mindful of the criteria used by the Cabinet in considering departmental budget submissions.[29] Once it has made its decisions the committee reports to the House.

The House, in turn, recommends to the Governor-General, by way of an address, the estimates that are to be included for the offices of Parliament in the Appropriation Bill to be presented to the House for that year.[30] The House is not bound to follow the Officers of Parliament Committee's recommendations in making its recommendations for inclusion in the Appropriation Bill, though it invariably does so. Similarly, the Crown is not legally bound to include the recommended amounts in the Appropriation Bill, although it is an established convention that it will do so since Ministers have been a party to the address from the House recommending those amounts in the first place. On one occasion when the amount for an office of Parliament included in an Appropriation Bill differed from that recommended by the House, the Officers of Parliament Committee drew the discrepancy to the attention of the Prime Minister and the Minister of Finance, expressing its concern at the variation. The Ministers assured the committee that this had occurred as the result of an

23   *Public Finance Act* 1989, s.18(1), (2)(a).
24   2002-05, AJHR, I.18C, pp.8-9.
25   *Public Finance Act* 1989, s.18(2)(b).
26   *Ibid.*, s.26E(1).

27   *Public Audit Act* 2001, s.36.
28   S.O.386(1)(a).
29   1999-2002, AJHR, I.22A, pp.834-5.
30   *Public Finance Act* 1989, s.26E(2), (3).

administrative error and that there was no intention to infringe the rights of the House.[31]

Any alteration during the course of the financial year to the estimates so approved is subject to a similar procedure of recommendation by the Officers of Parliament Committee[32] and commendation by the House to the Governor-General by way of address.[33] Such altered estimates are included in the Appropriation Bill containing the supplementary estimates of expenditure.

The appropriations for outputs supplied by the offices of Parliament are included in separate votes administered by those offices. The Speaker rather than a Minister is responsible for these votes.[34] Each vote is examined by a subject select committee as part of the estimates examination in the same way as any other vote.

Budget secrecy

A constitutional convention of Budget secrecy has been acknowledged to exist protecting information from being required to be disclosured during the preparation phase of the coming Budget. The three-year cycle for expenditure projections may extend this convention of secrecy over an even longer period.[35] Certainly, premature disclosure of the Budget has important political implications, though it is not a question of privilege.[36] A British Chancellor of the Exchequer resigned after he personally disclosed the contents of the Budget to a journalist before delivering the Budget statement in the House.[37] In New Zealand the premature release of copies of the 1986 Budget (an error which the Minister had not made personally) led the Minister to offer his resignation. This was not accepted.[38] In 1977, allegations that Budget decisions had been disclosed to journalists before their presentation to the House resulted in a select committee inquiry being held. The committee could not identify if a leak had occurred.[39] An individual department's forecast report has been inadvertently released before the Budget, drawing strong criticism from the select committee examining the relevant vote.[40]

Although secrecy is accepted as applying to the preparation of a Budget, an assessment of any request for Budget information still has to be made as to whether disclosure of that information would prejudice the Budget's effective preparation and whether there are any countervailing public interest considerations favouring disclosure.[41] In general, however, the strong constitutional practice of Budget decisions being announced first in the House (subject to an embargoed Budget briefing or "lock-up" earlier that day) supports the constitutional convention that Budget decisions and information closely associated with those decisions are protected from disclosure until then.

FIRST IMPREST SUPPLY BILL

To start spending money or incurring expenses or capital expenditure in a new financial year, the Government must, before the year opens, obtain express parliamentary approval in the form of legislation. The Government's final demands for supply for the new financial year will not have been approved by the House by this time and, indeed, may not yet have been framed. Consequently, the Government asks for a general interim authority to spend public money and to incur expenses and capital expenditure. The request for interim authority is included in an Imprest Supply Bill.

The moneys to be spent and the expenses and capital expenditure to be incurred under the authority of an Imprest Supply Act are charged in the manner subsequently specified in the estimates which will show how the total financial authorities voted to the

---

[31] 1991-93, AJHR, I.21, pp.36-45.
[32] S.O.386(1)(a).
[33] *Public Finance Act* 1989, s.26E(5).
[34] *Ibid.*, ss.2(1) and 26E(4).
[35] *Ombudsmen Quarterly Review*, December 2001;
      Official Information Act 1982, s.9(2)(f).

[36] 1977, Vol.412, p.1587.
[37] Dalton, *High Tide and After*, pp.276-86.
[38] 1986, Vol.473, pp.3776-8.
[39] 1977, JHR, p.157.
[40] 1993-96, AJHR, I.19D, p.332.
[41] *Ombudsmen Quarterly Review*, December 2001.

Government (including those under imprest supply) are to be used. In the meantime the expenses and capital expenditure are charged as if such an Act had been passed.[42]

The Imprest Supply Act gives the Government financial authority for the new financial year. How long this authority lasts depends upon the amount the House grants, the rate at which the Government uses it, and the time it takes the House to pass an Appropriation Act making appropriations for the year. The first Appropriation Act for the year is passed within three months of the delivery of the Budget.[43] Therefore the first Imprest Supply Bill is designed to give at least sufficient supply from 1 July (the opening of the financial year) to the end of this period.

Introduction and passing

An Imprest Supply Bill is subject to specially prescribed procedures for its introduction and passing that differ from other Government bills.[44] In the first place, it may be introduced at any time during a sitting except during the course of a debate.[45]

Secondly, an Imprest Supply Bill is usually, but does not have to be, taken through all its stages at one sitting. The Standing Orders provide that this may happen and urgency is not necessary to permit it.[46] But a sitting is not automatically extended for the passing of an Imprest Supply Bill, so if there is not enough time remaining in the sitting day to pass the bill (three hours), it is necessary to take urgency so that the sitting can be extended, otherwise passage of the bill will be interrupted and resumed on a future day. Whether urgency is taken or not, an Imprest Supply Bill does not stand referred to a select committee.[47]

Following the bill's introduction, it is read a first time without any amendment or debate.[48] The Minister in charge of the bill (who may be, but is not necessarily, the Minister of Finance) then moves the second reading. As is the case with the Address in Reply and Budget debates, in practice there are virtually no limitations to this debate on the grounds of relevancy. The question for the second reading is open to amendment in the same way as other public bills and also to a "public affairs" amendment, by means of which a question of confidence in the Government can be raised.[49]

Each member may speak for up to 10 minutes on the second reading or on any amendment to that question, and the total debate is limited to three hours.[50]

The subsequent proceedings on the bill are then telescoped in a manner unique to it. The House does not resolve itself into committee except in the unlikely event that the Minister in charge of the bill wishes to propose amendments to it.[51] If this is the case, the House resolves itself into a committee of the whole House automatically. Where a committee stage is held, only the Minister's amendments (and any relevant amendments to them) are considered. When amendments to a part or schedule have been disposed of, the question is put that that part or schedule as amended stand part.

It is extremely rare for an Imprest Supply Bill to be amended. In the normal course, the House passes over the committee stage altogether and proceeds to the third reading, the question on which is put without any amendment or debate.[52]

The debate on the second reading of an Imprest Supply Bill may be taken together with the second reading of the Appropriation Bill dealing with the supplementary estimates.[53] In practice, this enables the first Imprest Supply Bill for the new financial year to be

---

42   *Archives and Records Association of New Zealand v Blakeley* [2000] 1 NZLR 607 at [75] and [77].
43   S.O.332(1).
44   S.O.270.
45   S.O.281.
46   S.O.323(1).
47   S.O.285(2).
48   S.O.323(2).
49   S.O.323(3).
50   Appendix A to the Standing Orders.
51   S.O.323(4).
52   S.O.323(5).
53   S.O.334(2).

debated along with the supplementary estimates for the current year as both bills need to be dealt with by 30 June.

THE BUDGET

The Budget statement is the Minister of Finance's speech in moving the second reading of the main Appropriation Bill.

The Budget statement has, since 1996, been delivered at 2 pm on a Thursday. (It was formerly delivered at 7.30 pm after the financial markets had closed.) It is regarded as the principal parliamentary occasion of each year. The time for delivery of the statement is prescribed in the Standing Orders.[54] The Budget must, by law, be delivered within one month of the opening of the financial year – that is, by 31 July – unless the House specifically resolves to the contrary.[55] In fact the Budget has tended to be introduced much earlier than this statutory deadline, indeed normally it is introduced before the financial year to which it relates has opened. Since the commencement of the financial year was shifted from 1 April to 1 July in 1989, the earliest Budget was delivered on 14 May in 1998 and the latest on 27 July in 1989. Governments tend to aim to present their Budgets to the House during the course of May.

The main Appropriation Bill

The main or first Appropriation Bill of each financial year contains the Government's comprehensive annual appropriation proposals. As with any Appropriation Bill special procedures apply to its passing.[56] In particular, its second reading debate gives rise to the Budget debate and its committee stage gives rise to the Estimates debate.

The main Appropriation Bill is introduced on a Thursday after the announcement of the presentation of any petitions, papers and select committee reports and of the introduction of any other bills. The day of the Budget and thus of the introduction of the main Appropriation Bill must be notified in advance to the House by the Government.[57] This is usually done by means of the Leader of the House's weekly business statement, though it is likely that the Leader will have previously advised the Business Committee.

The bill's introduction is announced by the Clerk and then the Minister moves that it be read a first time. There is no amendment or debate on this question.[58] At this point the Minister traditionally gives copies of the Budget statement to the Speaker, the Prime Minister, the Leader of the Opposition, other party leaders, the Clerk and the *Hansard* staff seated in the Chamber. Only one copy of the statement is given to each recipient.[59]

Budget statement

The House proceeds immediately to the second reading of the bill.[60]

The Minister moves the second reading of the Appropriation Bill and in speaking to that motion delivers the Budget statement.[61] This is not like any other second reading speech. It is the delivery of a prepared statement. Consequently, there are strong conventions against interjections because it is impossible for the Minister to reply to them. Similar courtesies of restraint are expected to be accorded the leaders of other parties who speak immediately following the Minister.[62]

In the speech the Minister reviews the international economic outlook, the performance

---

[54] S.O.325(1).
[55] *Public Finance Act* 1989, s.12.
[56] S.O.270.
[57] S.O.325(1).
[58] *Ibid.*

[59] 1992, Vol.526, p.9717.
[60] S.O.325(1).
[61] S.O.325(2).
[62] 2000, Vol.584, pp.2852-3.

of the New Zealand economy and the effectiveness of the Government's policies over the past year, and outlines the Government's proposed economic and fiscal measures to deal with the assessed situation of the country. The Budget, therefore, contains a number of announcements of economic and fiscal policy. But it may also contain announcements falling into the category of social policy changes. Among the more dramatic of Budget announcements are tax changes and, on one occasion, the revaluation of the currency[63], though there are few announcements of this nature in modern Budgets. Many of the measures proposed to be taken may be announced only in outline in the Budget statement. Further details of the proposed changes are then given in statements released by the responsible Ministers shortly after the statement has been delivered, and in due course legislation may need to be introduced to give effect to them. The Budget is concerned with much more than the expenditure proposals contained in the estimates and embodied in the main Appropriation Bill; it is concerned with the whole range of the Government's financial, economic and social policies.

In delivering the Budget statement the Minister is unrestricted as to the length of the speech.[64] A Budget occasionally has a sobriquet applied to it by which it subsequently becomes known – as with 'black Budget' (1958) and 'mother of all Budgets' (1991).

Budget papers

On concluding the Budget statement the Minister presents to the House a copy of the statement, the annual estimates and other supporting information,[65] the departmental statements of intent,[66] a fiscal strategy report,[67] and an economic and fiscal update.[68] The Minister then moves that these documents be published. There is no debate or amendment on such a question.[69]

The departmental *statements of intent* provide information on each department's future operating intentions for the next three financial years.

The *fiscal strategy report* states the Government's long-term objectives for fiscal policy. It must explain how those long-term objectives accord with the principles of responsible fiscal management. If the Government intends to pay less than the required annual capital contribution to the New Zealand Superannuation Fund, it must state this and the reasons for doing so in this report.[70]

The *economic and fiscal update* makes economic and fiscal forecasts for the financial year to which the Appropriation Bill relates and the two following years. It must include the annual capital contributions that are to be made to the New Zealand Superannuation Fund in those years.[71]

Statements of intent are used by select committees in the examination of the Estimates. The fiscal strategy report and the economic and fiscal update stand referred to the Finance and Expenditure Committee,[72] which must report on them to the House within two months of the delivery of the Budget.[73] The Finance and Expenditure Committee's practice is to examine the Minister on the fiscal documents and to combine this examination with its consideration of the vote relating to the Treasury. In this way it considers the economic and fiscal outlook together with the economic advice provided by the Treasury during the financial year and reports to the House accordingly.[74]

These documents and reports are available for debate on the third reading of the Appropriation Bill.[75]

---

[63]   Sinclair, *Walter Nash*, pp.272-3.
[64]   Appendix A to the Standing Orders.
[65]   *Public Finance Act* 1989, s.13(1), (2).
[66]   *Ibid.*, s.39(1).
[67]   *Ibid.*, s.26I.
[68]   *Ibid.*, s.26O.
[69]   S.O.367.

[70]   *New Zealand Superannuation and Retirement Income Act* 2001, s.44.
[71]   *Ibid.*, s.42(2), (3).
[72]   S.O.327(1).
[73]   S.O.327(2).
[74]   1999-2002, AJHR, I.22A, p.293.
[75]   S.O.332(2).

The Budget debate

The Budget debate opens following the presentation of the Budget papers with the Leader of the Opposition or the official Opposition's finance spokesperson speaking in response to the statement. Party leaders, in order of party size, are entitled to be called to speak first in the debate so the Leader of the Opposition is followed by the Prime Minister and other party leaders.

Party leaders of parties with six or more members are entitled to speak for up to 20 minutes. All other members are limited to 10 minutes.[76] Thus where the Opposition's finance spokesperson speaks first in the debate he or she is limited to a 10-minute call and the Leader of the Opposition takes the 20-minute call later in the debate. The debate takes precedence over all other Government orders of the day until it is completed.[77] While the debate must appear as the first Government order of the day on the order paper, this does not prevent it being adjourned after it is reached and other business transacted.[78] The total time allowed for the debate, excluding the Budget statement itself, is 14 hours.[79] This means that the debate ought to conclude by the end of the week following the delivery of the Budget if it is not otherwise adjourned. No Wednesday general debate is held while the Budget debate is in progress.[80]

As is the case with an Imprest Supply Bill, an amendment relating to public affairs may be moved on the question for the second reading of the main Appropriation Bill.[81] This gives the opposition parties an opportunity to move a widely framed amendment attacking the Government's policies. It also gives an opportunity for an express "no-confidence" motion to be moved. An amendment relating to public affairs does not need to be strictly relevant to the motion for the second reading of the bill. As relevancy is not a consideration on this type of amendment, an amendment is always treated as involving consideration and decision of the main question.

The Budget debate is unusual in that the Minister of Finance has a right to speak in reply to the debate for up to 10 minutes.[82] The Speaker therefore interrupts the debate 10 minutes before the 14 hours have expired and calls the Minister in reply. The Minister is not obliged to use this right.

Defeat of the main Appropriation Bill and therefore of the Budget would be a matter of extreme constitutional and political significance. It has even been suggested that the failure to pass an Appropriation Bill would cause all imprest supply authority to lapse unconditionally.[83] While this may not be the effect in law of the defeat of a Budget,[84] it does indicate how important such an event would be regarded. If an amendment expressly declaring no confidence in the Government is carried or the question for the second reading of the bill is defeated, a lack of confidence in the Government would have been demonstrated.

THE MAIN ESTIMATES

Estimates must be prepared for the main Appropriation Bill.[85] The estimates describe and support the appropriation proposals that the bill contains.[86] They identify the votes to which each appropriation relates, which Minister or Ministers are responsible for each vote, the department which administers it, and the type, amount, scope and (if a multi-year

---

[76] Appendix A to the Standing Orders.
[77] S.O.326(1).
[78] 1990, JHR, p.538.
[79] Appendix A to the Standing Orders.
[80] S.O.383(3).
[81] S.O.326(2).
[82] Appendix A to the Standing Orders.

[83] Barwick, *A Radical Tory*, pp.296-7.
[84] See, for example: *New South Wales v Bardolph* (1934) 42 CLR 455 at 479; *Archives and Records Association of New Zealand v Blakeley* [2000] 1 NZLR 607 at [78].
[85] *Public Finance Act* 1989, s.13(1).
[86] *Ibid.*, s.2(1).

appropriation is involved) the period of the appropriation.[87] (A Minister responsible for a vote may be a different Minister from the Minister responsible for the department which is administering the vote.) The estimates may also set out a range of other information about the appropriations.[88] The information in the estimates helps to determine the extent of the activities that may be lawfully funded out of the appropriations that Parliament makes.[89] In the case of the Budget and the main Appropriation Bill, the estimates (*Estimates of Appropriations for the Government of New Zealand*), known as the main estimates, are laid before the House by the Minister immediately after the Budget statement has been delivered.[90]

Along with the estimates the Minister must present further information supporting the main Appropriation Bill. This information gives additional information about the intended objectives of the appropriations, defines performance measures and forecast standards for each class of outputs and gives more comparative and forecast information about the proposed expenses and capital expenditure.[91]

In its schedules the Appropriation Bill specifies the names and amounts of the individual appropriations. While multi-year appropriations are fully specified in the bill, the annual appropriations are not. Parliament makes these appropriations by reference to the output descriptions and other information (especially that relating to the scope of the appropriation) contained in the estimates and other supporting information. The Appropriation Bill is therefore not intelligible without reference to its associated documents, which is why presentation of estimates is an essential part of introducing an Appropriation Bill.

The appropriations for the offices of Parliament are included in the Appropriation Bill and in the estimates, according to the address commending them made by the House to the Governor-General. (See pp.474–5.)

Examination of the main estimates

The task of carrying out an examination of the main estimates in detail falls to the House's select committees. An Appropriation Bill is not itself referred to a select committee, but the estimates are referred for scrutiny. The estimates stand referred to the Finance and Expenditure Committee immediately following the delivery of the Budget.[92]

Allocation of votes

It is the task of the Finance and Expenditure Committee to examine a vote itself or to allocate it to one of the other subject committees for examination[93] – that is, to one of the 13 select committees with subject area jurisdictions.[94] In recognition of the fact that a vote may have more than one responsible Minister and that appropriations may be made for multi-class output expenses, the Finance and Expenditure Committee is empowered to divide a vote for the purposes of estimates examination. Thus it may decide to allocate some only of the appropriations contained in a vote to another committee for examination.[95]

In determining what to allocate and which committees to make the allocations to, the Finance and Expenditure Committee is guided by its own workload, the significance of particular votes to the overall financial management of government and the subject areas of responsibility of the other committees. The committee is not obliged to consult with the other committees about the allocations it makes, though other committees have

---

[87]   *Ibid.*, s.14(1).
[88]   *Ibid.*, s.14(2).
[89]   1999-2000, PP, B.29[99c], para.5.010 (Controller and Auditor-General).
[90]   *Public Finance Act* 1989, s.13(1).
[91]   *Ibid.*, s.15.
[92]   S.O.329(1).
[93]   S.O.329(2).
[94]   S.Os 189 and 190.
[95]   S.O.329(2).

asked for an opportunity to comment when it is proposed to withhold from them a vote falling within their subject area.[96] The votes allocated include those relating to offices of Parliament which have been subject to pre-Budget approval by the Officers of Parliament Committee. In the 2005/06 financial year, the Finance and Expenditure Committee examined eight votes itself and allocated 61 votes to other committees for examination.

The Finance and Expenditure Committee resolves upon the allocations as soon as practicable after the Budget is delivered. It issues letters to all committees formally advising them of its decisions.

Standard estimates questionnaire

A preliminary action which the Finance and Expenditure Committee takes is to develop a standard estimates questionnaire which it forwards to vote Ministers as the initial step in the estimates examinations. Such a questionnaire was first developed in 1991 when the estimates examination was separated from review of financial performance. The committee receives advice on the form of the questionnaire from the Auditor-General.[97] The questionnaire focuses on the vote rather than departmental matters (which will be examined as part of financial review). It seeks information at a high level intended to supplement that contained in the estimates and supporting information presented with the Budget. It asks about critical issues affecting the vote and significant changes affecting appropriations contained in it, and for an elaboration of the mechanisms for evaluating the impact of outputs on outcomes. It may seek to identify matters which Ministers may be asked to elaborate on at the oral examination of the vote or provide pointers for the committee in targeting its examination. It is not designed to be burdensome.[98]

Committees to which votes are allocated may always supplement the standard questionnaire with questions of their own devising, but they do tend to follow it as the basis for their examinations.

Ministers are sent the standard questionnaire in respect of each vote that they administer by the Finance and Expenditure Committee some six weeks before the Budget and are requested to respond to the committee immediately after the delivery of the Budget statement – that is, before the vote's examination. These responses are distributed to the committees which are to examine the various votes. In addition to the questionnaire, other written questions on the estimates may be sent to the Minister or the department by the committee which is to examine the vote prior to the oral hearings on it. Such questions must be adopted by the committee in order to be transmitted for prior departmental response; individual members of the committee cannot send questions directly to the Minister or the department and make them part of the formal estimates process.[99]

Other estimates documentation

An essential information document that is required for the estimates examination is a copy of the departmental output plan specifying the outputs to be supplied by the department and the standards that are to be used to measure departmental performance. Committees have protested where a copy of the purchase agreement has not been made available to them in time for the estimates examination.[100] If a committee considers that the output plan (formerly purchase agreement) is deficient in any way, it may recommend that other matters be included in it.[101]

---

[96]   See, for example, 1999-2002, AJHR, I.19A, p.102.

[97]   1999-2002, AJHR, I.15A, para.4.

[98]   2002-05, AJHR, I.22D, p.189.

[99]   1987-90, AJHR, I.19A, p.188.

[100]   1996-99, AJHR, I.19A, p.79; *ibid.*, I.19C, pp.14-5.

[101]   1999-2002, AJHR, I.11A.

The statements of intent (which have absorbed department forecast reports) will also be considered by committees examining the estimates for any strategic commentary they contain, the adequacy of the performance measures specified and information relating to the department's objectives and operations.[102]

Officials and briefing

Officials from the office of the Auditor-General are available to assist committees with their examinations of the estimates. The Auditor-General consults with the Finance and Expenditure Committee each year to determine the general nature and extent of assistance to be provided on estimates examinations. Unless specific alternative arrangements are made, the assistance given to committees is as discussed with the Finance and Expenditure Committee and in accordance with the protocol in force for such assistance. The Auditor-General's assistance to each committee can extend to help in determining questions for each examination, reviewing evidence and compiling the report.[103] Before the oral examination commences, the committee will receive a written briefing from the Auditor-General's office on the vote it is to examine and may also have an oral briefing on that vote. These briefings will endeavour to draw the committee's attention to any unusual or unexplained features in the appropriations for classes of outputs and other appropriations that the vote contains. Briefings constitute advice to the committee and are confidential to the committee until it reports, unless the committee decides to reveal their contents to the Minister or department concerned to assist with the examination. An official from the Auditor-General's office may also be present during the committee's examination to assist the committee with any technical issues that may arise.

Other officials may also be appointed to assist the committee. For example, the office of the Parliamentary Commissioner for the Environment may act as an adviser to committees in respect of votes dealing with conservation and the environment.[104]

Hearings

Oral hearings will be scheduled as soon as practicable after Budget day. They may even start while the Budget debate is in progress.

Estimates hearings are conducted in public like the hearing of evidence on any other matter. A committee may, by leave, decide to hear some of the evidence in private, for instance if commercially sensitive information is to be disclosed.[105]

Formerly estimates examinations were almost exclusively directed to officials, with Ministers appearing only rarely. Now, to reflect the fact that appropriations are made to Ministers, the Minister responsible for the vote under examination is expected to attend and front the oral examination by the committee. However, the Minister will be accompanied by the chief executive of the department concerned and other officials who will also participate in the examination as required. Indeed, the fact that a chief executive did not appear even when the Minister did has drawn complaint from a committee.[106]

One area that can cause difficulty is the question of responsibility for appropriations for classes of outputs to be supplied by other entities. Chief executives of departments are not responsible for the outputs or financial performance of a Crown entity or a State enterprise, even though these may be wholly or partly funded through a vote administered by the department.[107] In order that the estimates examination is not stymied where a

---

[102]   1996-99, AJHR, I.19C, pp.32-3; 2002-05, AJHR, I.19C, pp.121, 147, 262, 364, 375 and 409.
[103]   1999-2002, AJHR, I.15A, paras.4 and 5.
[104]   See 1993-96, AJHR, I.19D, p.32.

[105]   1987-90, AJHR, I.19A, p.47.
[106]   1999-2002, AJHR, I.19A, p.101.
[107]   *Public Finance Act* 1989, s.36.

vote contains payments to Crown entities for non-departmental outputs, representatives of the Crown entity concerned may be invited to participate in the examination. (As comparatively few outputs are purchased from State enterprises the issue rarely arises with them.)

As well as asking questions orally of the officials appearing before the committee, committee members may ask the officials to prepare further detailed information in writing on matters which arise from the questioning. Indeed, in some cases this may be the only practicable means by which a reply can be given. These written replies to matters raised at the examination are delivered to committee members within a reasonable time after the conclusion of the examination.

Given the time constraints on the estimates examination, allowing responses to be given later in writing as a condition of the committee processing the vote referred to it, is a convenient mode of proceeding for all concerned. It is then incumbent on departments to provide the follow-up responses to members in time for the Estimates debate in the House, though this is not obligatory.[108]

Reports on votes

The Finance and Expenditure Committee and the other select committees examine the various votes to determine whether to recommend to the House that the appropriations contained in the vote be accepted.[109] The task of actually passing the estimates will fall to the committee of the whole House. At the conclusion of its examination of a vote, the select committee resolves whether to recommend the acceptance of the appropriations contained in the vote and draws up a report on it to the House. The committee may recommend that the House make changes to the appropriations made in the vote.[110] But the amounts contained in the estimates do not change as a direct result of select committee scrutiny.

Committees are required to report back to the House within two months of the delivery of the Budget.[111] (The House has extended this time where consideration of the estimates was disrupted by an early election.[112]) A committee has recommended that a vote be referred back to it where information that it had sought was not available by the time that it was obliged to report. The House subsequently referred the vote back to the committee for further examination.[113] A committee may report on a number of votes in the same report. These reports are expected to be concise, summarising the material provided in response to the written questionnaire and other significant written replies, and supplemented by material elicited during the oral examination.[114] A report on estimates is presented to the Clerk like any other select committee report.

Intelligence and security departments

Intelligence and security departments (the New Zealand Security Intelligence Service and the Government Communications Security Bureau) are in a special position in regard to their estimates. The statutory Intelligence and Security Committee may consider any matter in relation to an agency referred to it by the House.[115] Accordingly, votes relating to these departments are, by sessional resolutions of the House, examined by the Intelligence and Security Committee and are not subject to examination by a select committee.[116]

The committee's reports on its estimates examinations are presented to the House and dealt with as if they were select committee reports.

---

108 1979, Vol.424, pp.1831-2.
109 S.O.330(1)(a).
110 S.O.330(1)(b).
111 S.O.330(2).
112 2002, Vol.602, p.308.
113 1999-2002, AJHR, I.19A, pp.39-40; 2000, Vol.586, p.4895.

114 1984-85, AJHR, I.14, p.26 (Standing Orders Committee).
115 *Intelligence and Security Committee Act* 1996, s.6(1)(b).
116 See, for example: 2000, Vol.582, pp.1265-75, 1378-84; 2002, Vol.604, pp.1897-909.

The Estimates debate

The committee stage of the Appropriation Bill, the stage at which the main estimates are passed, is known as the Estimates debate. The Estimates debate is the House's consideration of the appropriations being sought by the Government in the votes set out in the main Appropriation Bill.[117]

The committee of the whole House may consider each vote contained in the schedules to the bill along with the elaboration of the vote in the main estimates and supporting information. The Minister responsible for the vote sits at the Table on the chairperson's right, and deals with questions which arise during the discussion. The Minister is assisted by officials who are seated in the Chamber on seats to the right of the Speaker's chair. One of the factors which sets the Appropriation Bill apart from other Government bills is that there is more than one Minister who is answerable for its contents. The Minister of Finance is the Minister in charge of the bill, but as its provisions cover the whole gamut of government activity, the House requires every Minister to be potentially answerable to it for the spending to be undertaken within a vote for which that Minister has responsibility.

Eight hours are allocated to the Estimates debate.[118]

Committee stage of the main Appropriation Bill

The order in which the committee of the whole House transacts its business when considering an Appropriation Bill is different from the order of business in committee on other bills. The committee stage is entirely devoted to the Estimates debate rather than to a consideration of the clauses and schedules of the bill. At the end of the total time permitted for the debate the provisions of the bill and any amendments will be put as one question without further debate.[119]

The Government has the right to select any day except members' Wednesdays for the Estimates debate. On such a day the Appropriation Bill is set down for consideration in committee.[120] The Government is also able to determine which votes are available for consideration each day and how long in total is to be spent on the Estimates debate each day. A note setting out this information must be printed on that day's order paper.[121]

Scheduling of the Estimates debate

Select committee examination and report by it of a vote is a prerequisite for that vote to be available for consideration during the Estimates debate.[122] As committees have two months from the Budget to make their reports on votes referred to them, the maximum time that a Government has to wait after the Budget before scheduling an Estimates debate is two months. Given the need to provide for eight hours of debate, the Estimates debate will occupy part of two or three sitting days. It has not been regarded as obligatory that written material called for by the select committee during its examination of a vote should have been delivered into the hands of members before the Estimates debate on that vote is held.[123] But where the committee has accepted a vote on the basis of an assurance that further material will be provided to members in time for the debate in the House, it is incumbent on Ministers and departments to ensure that such an assurance is observed. Estimates debates scheduled for votes have been postponed when it has been appreciated that written material asked for during the select committee examination has not been made available.

---

[117] S.O.331(1).
[118] Appendix A to the Standing Orders.
[119] S.O.331(4).
[120] S.O.341(1).
[121] S.O.341(2).
[122] 1979, Vol.424, pp.1831-2.
[123] *Ibid.*

The Government's determination of which votes are available for debate is also dependent on the availability of Ministers. As Ministers are often responsible for more than one vote, an attempt will be made to have all of a Minister's votes available for debate on the same occasion. A vote can be scheduled for the Estimates debate while an acting Minister is in charge of the department.[124] The Speaker is responsible for votes relating to the Auditor-General, the Office of the Clerk of the House of Representatives, the Office of the Ombudsmen, the Parliamentary Commissioner for the Environment and the Parliamentary Service.[125]

While the Government determines which votes are available each day and how long in total is to be spent on them, the Business Committee determines the order in which they are to be considered and how long will be spent on each vote.[126] In practice, the Business Committee leaves these matters to be agreed between the whips so that a detailed speaking list can be prepared dividing the overall time available between the parties and allowing any party to decide for itself the votes on which it wishes to make a contribution during the debate.

Consideration of the votes

As each vote is reached, the chairperson proposes the question "That Vote ... stand part of the schedule".[127] The Minister responsible for a vote under discussion must, if present in the Chamber, sit at the Table on the chairperson's right.[128] But another Minister may act for the responsible Minister in the latter's absence. However, as the scheduling of the debate is in the Government's hands, it is expected that the responsible Minister will attend the debate as part of the House's accountability process.[129] Where another Minister has responsibility for aspects of a vote, that other Minister may also participate in the Estimates debate from the Table. Members are entitled to make up to two five-minute speeches on each vote. The Minister responsible for the vote under discussion is not limited in the number of calls he or she may take. But the Minister is not normally allowed more than two consecutive calls (it is, in fact, entirely up to the chairperson whether the Minister is allowed even this number consecutively).[130] In practice, the whips' agreement on speeches in the Estimates debate will determine how many contributions are made by members on each vote.

Relevancy

Until 1972 the debate on the estimates was subject to a most important restriction: reference to policy was not allowed. This restriction was not the subject of a Standing Order; it was a rule which had been developed by successive chairpersons (supported by Speakers) as part of their inherent power to rule on relevancy in debate. In 1972 the Standing Orders Committee recommended that references to policy should be permitted at all times on the estimates.[131] This recommendation was immediately adopted by the chairperson at the time, and the discussion of policy as it relates to the vote under consideration has since then been freely permitted.[132] The change from a debate which was directed principally to examining the administration and expenditure of each department to one in which government policy may be debated has, as the 1979 Standing Orders Committee remarked, "changed the whole character of the estimates debate from an examination of items of expenditure to a general discussion ranging from items of detail to broad policy".[133]

---

[123] 1970, Vol.367, p.2059; 1978, Vol.418, p.1336.
[124] *Public Finance Act* 1989, s.2(1).
[125] S.O.341(3).
[126] S.O.331(2).
[127] 1988, Vol.492, p.7118.

[129] 2001, Vol.594, pp.10825, 10829-30.
[130] Appendix A to the Standing Orders.
[131] 1972, AJHR, I.19, p.11.
[132] 1972, Vol.379, p.1400.
[133] 1979, AJHR, I.14, p.10.

The 1985 Standing Orders Committee adopted the following statement of the scope of the debate:

> The normal rules of debate apply to consideration of the estimates; the main principle is that debate should be relevant to the matter which is contained in the estimate currently under discussion. On a main estimate it is in order to discuss the general policy which lies behind the demand for that particular sum of money … The purpose … is not to permit discussions of general policy … but to focus attention on the need to grant, reduce or refuse to grant particular items of expenditure.[134]

The Estimates debate is confined to the current spending plans as contained in the Budget papers and must relate to a matter for which an appropriation is contained in the estimates. It is no longer a vehicle for scrutinising and debating past performance (that is the purpose of the financial review debate).[135]

The rule of relevancy, that debate must be confined to the items in the vote under discussion, can be difficult to apply in respect of departments with control functions which extend over other areas of government, in particular the Treasury and the office of the Auditor-General. All ministerial spending proposals that are made to Cabinet are reported on by the Treasury, and the Treasury's functions in respect of the control of public expenditure and the formulation of economic policy can involve it intimately in the work of all other departments. This detailed involvement in another department may be discussed when the latter's vote is being considered, but not on the vote relating to the Treasury. The Minister on this vote can be asked general questions, and there can be a general debate on policies with which the Treasury has been involved, but specific questioning on another department's activities must be directed to the Minister for that department.[136] Similarly, issues relating to the policies and administration of a department must be raised when the vote relating to that department is being debated and not on the audit vote, even where reference to such matters is contained in an Auditor-General's report.[137]

Changes to the vote

During the Estimates debate on a vote any member may move to change a specified appropriation within the vote by a particular amount.[138] This is not an amendment to the question then before the committee; it is an independent motion moved during the course of the consideration of that question, though it is a proposed amendment to an appropriation contained within the vote and if it is carried it takes effect accordingly.

Traditionally, proposals to change a vote have taken the form of motions to reduce the vote as a means of expressing displeasure in the Minister or the department concerned. Token reductions of votes have been made from time to time.[139] The Government has itself agreed to or initiated the reduction of a vote.[140] Occasionally the select committee which has reported on the vote will recommend or indicate that it contemplated recommending a change in the vote.[141]

Debate on a motion to change a vote supersedes the original question, as it does on a normal amendment. When the motion to change the vote has been disposed of, debate resumes on the original question. However, such a debate is part of the overall time allocated for debate on that vote.

While most proposals for changes to a vote take the form of a reduction, they can

---

134   1984-85, AJHR, I.14, pp.24-5.
135   1993, Vol.537, p.17435; 1993, Vol.538, pp.18105-6, 18161; 1996, Vol.556, p.13745; 2003, Vol.610, p.7149.
136   1970, Vol.367, p.2581.
137   1972, Vol.379, pp.1531-7.
138   S.O.331(3).
139   Scott, *The New Zealand Constitution*, pp.56-7.
140   1890, Vol.69, p.919.
141   See, for example, 1993-96, AJHR, I.19D, p.32.

(since 1996) also take the form of an increase. Any proposal for a change is subject to the Crown's financial veto. (See Chapter 31.) If the financial veto is exercised in respect of a proposal to change a vote, the proposed change may be debated but no question is put on it at the end of the debate and it is ruled out of order.[142] A motion to change a vote is out of order if it may have an impact on the Government's fiscal aggregates and 24 hours' notice of it has not been given before the House meets on the day it is to be moved. But if the select committee has recommended the proposed change, notice is not required.[143]

A proposal to change a vote must specify the sum by which an appropriation contained in the vote is to be altered. Furthermore, as each output expense (or other type of appropriation) within a vote is a separate appropriation, a motion to change a vote must specify which output expense (or other type of appropriation) is to bear the reduction.[144] The debate is then confined to that appropriation.[145]

When moving to change a vote, members often wish to give reasons for the proposal. Such reasons are not part of the motion and are not stated by the Chair or recorded in the journals,[146] but, provided they are relevant to the vote under discussion, may be added by the mover and can be debated. A member cannot open up a discussion on a matter outside the limits of the vote by adducing wide-ranging reasons for a change. The chairperson does not state the reasons advanced by a member moving a change to the vote, and does not usually comment on them, but if they could lead to discussion travelling outside the vote before the committee, the chairperson might require the member to restate them more narrowly. For this reason a general statement of no confidence in the Government would not be acceptable as a reason for a reduction in a vote, but a statement of no confidence in the Minister then at the Table would be.

If a change to a vote is made, the Minister of Finance will present to the House an addendum to the estimates to reflect this change. This is so that the estimates documents accord with the legal appropriations that are made by Parliament through the Appropriation Acts. As the estimates are an elaboration of those appropriations it is of critical importance that there be no suggestion that they differ from the appropriations actually made by Parliament.

Adjusting estimates

Occasionally the Government itself will initiate changes to the votes and will prepare a supplementary order paper to amend the Appropriation Bill.

Where there are proposed amendments to the appropriations contained in the bill, these must be preceded by the tabling of further estimates adjusting the main estimates. In the case of proposals to adjust estimates relating to an office of Parliament, the proposal must first have been examined by the Officers of Parliament Committee and commended to the Governor-General by way of an address from the House.

Adjusting estimates may be examined by the Finance and Expenditure Committee. It is up to the committee as to whether it combines examinations of the main estimate with an adjusting estimate or reports separately on each. If it has already reported on the main estimate, a second, separate report on the adjusting estimate will be necessary.

Termination of the Estimates debate

At the conclusion of the eight hours allotted for consideration of the estimates, there are likely to be votes which have not yet been passed by the committee. The Standing

---

[142] S.O.321(2).
[143] S.O.322(1), (2).
[144] 1991, Vol.514, p.1743.
[145] *Ibid.*
[146] 1993-96, AJHR, I.18A, p.69.

Orders provide that in this case any remaining votes, together with the provisions of the bill and any amendments to the bill proposed by the Minister on a supplementary order paper, are to be proposed by the chairperson as one question and this question is to be decided immediately without amendment or debate.[147] There is no provision for dealing with amendments from other members that have not been proposed within the eight hours allowed for the debate.

PASSING OF THE MAIN APPROPRIATION BILL

The third reading of the main Appropriation Bill granting comprehensive annual appropriations must be completed within three months of the delivery of the Budget.[148] (This time limit has been extended where an early election dislocated examination of the estimates by committees.[149]) Effectively, given that the Budget must have been delivered by 31 July, this means the bill will be passed at the latest by 31 October, four months into the financial year. In practice, it has tended to be passed much sooner than this. This is a major improvement on the situation that obtained up to the 1990/91 financial year when, in the absence of a Standing Orders requirement, the main Appropriation Bill tended not to be passed until shortly before the end of the financial year to which it related.[150]

The normal rules of relevancy apply to the third reading debate. It is solely a spending bill, not a taxing bill, and a detailed discussion of economic policy is not permitted at this stage.[151] In addition, the debate may include reference to the content of the fiscal strategy report and the economic and fiscal update (presented at the time of the Budget) and the Finance and Expenditure Committee's report on those documents.[152] The question for the third reading is open to amendment but not in respect of an amendment that would postpone the third reading beyond three months of the Budget, as required by the Standing Orders. The debate may not exceed three hours and members are able to speak for up to 10 minutes each.[153] The debate may be taken together with the second reading of an Imprest Supply Bill[154] and it is the invariable practice to do this.

SECOND AND SUBSEQUENT IMPREST SUPPLY BILLS

When the main Appropriation Bill has been passed, the appropriation authority conferred by the first Imprest Supply Act lapses. The Government now has its principal, detailed appropriations as set out in the main Appropriation Act and the estimates. However, there will still be at least eight months of the financial year to run. Supplementary estimates adding to and adjusting the appropriations that have already been made will be presented later in the financial year. But, in order to give the Government a general authority to deal with spending issues relating to the current year that may have arisen since the main estimates were prepared and that will possibly arise before the presentation of the supplementary estimates, a second Imprest Supply Act is enacted immediately after the main Appropriation Act.

This second tranche of imprest supply is passed in tandem with the third reading of the Appropriation Bill. For this purpose the debate on its second reading may be taken together with the third reading of that bill.[155] The rules for the introduction and passing of the second Imprest Supply Bill are identical with those for the first bill. (See pp.476–7.) This second imprest supply authority lapses when the House enacts the Appropriation Act incorporating the supplementary estimates.

Normally there are two grants of imprest supply each financial year: the first given

---

147   S.O.331(4).
148   S.O.332(1).
149   2002, Vol.602, pp.308-9.
150   1990-91, AJHR, B.1[Pt.II], pp.12-3; 1991-3, AJHR, B.1[Pt.II], pp.16-7.
151   1979, Vol.427, pp.4287-99.
152   S.O.332(2).
153   Appendix A to the Standing Orders.
154   S.O.332(3).
155   *Ibid.*

before the financial year opens, which lapses with the passing of the main Appropriation Act, and the second given in association with that Act and lapsing with the supplementary estimates. But if there is an unexpected need for further spending authority arising ahead of the supplementary estimates, a third Imprest Supply Bill will be necessary.[156] The rules for the introduction and passing of such a bill and the time limits for debating it are identical with those for other Imprest Supply bills, but as there is no Appropriation Bill with which it can be linked for the purposes of debate, it is debated as a stand-alone piece of legislation.

SUPPLEMENTARY APPROPRIATIONS

The main Appropriation Act, appropriating the amounts set out in the main estimates, is the Government's chief financial authority for the year. However, the main estimates are presented to the House before or shortly after the start of the financial year and are passed within four months of it opening. During and after this time it may become apparent to the Government that the sums it has requested to be voted to it in the main estimates need to be altered. It is now generally expected that there will be a need for supplementary appropriations to be made by the end of the financial year. Indeed, this may be contemplated in the main estimates themselves.[157] Normally supplementary estimates make only technical accounting adjustments without any significant overall fiscal impact, but where the Government changes between the delivery of the Budget and the presentation of supplementary estimates, the expenditure initiatives authorised by the supplementary estimates can be very significant.[158] In considering supplementary estimates, select committees expect to have drawn to their attention changes in governmental priorities from the main estimates as opposed to merely technical adjustments.[159]

Supplementary appropriations are made by way of an Appropriation Bill introduced on the same day that supplementary estimates are presented to the House.[160]

Supplementary estimates

Supplementary estimates must be prepared for each Appropriation Bill that seeks supplementary appropriations. They set out how the amounts proposed to be appropriated are to be charged to each vote. Supplementary estimates are required to contain much of the information required for the main estimates except where this would be superfluous, in which case the supplementary estimates merely record any changes from the estimates previously presented.[161] The Auditor-General has in the past criticised some of the information given with the supplementary estimates as not clearly and understandably describing the purpose and reasons for the changes proposed to the main estimates.[162]

Just as the main estimates are an elaboration of the main Appropriation Bill, the supplementary estimates are an elaboration of the Appropriation Bill to which they relate.

Introduction of Appropriation Bill

Supplementary estimates are presented to the House on the day that an Appropriation Bill containing supplementary estimates is to be introduced. The bill may be introduced at any time as long as this does not interrupt a debate.[163] Alternatively, it may be introduced in the same way as any other bill. Although not invariable, the practice has been to introduce the supplementary appropriation bill on the same day as the Budget for the next financial year (that is, in May or June). There is no debate on the first reading of the bill.[164]

---

156 See, for example, *Imprest Supply (Third for 2001/02) Act* 2001 (capital injection for Air New Zealand).
157 1990, AJHR, B.7, p.356.
158 1999-2000, PP, B.29[00c], para.3.701-3.711 (Controller and Auditor-General).
159 1999-2002, AJHR, I.22B, pp.1087, 1219.
160 *Public Finance Act* 1989, s.16.
161 *Ibid.*, s.17.
162 2001, PP, B.29[01b], para.8.4 (Controller and Auditor-General).
163 S.O.281.
164 S.O.334(1).

Examination of supplementary estimates

No Appropriation Bill is referred to a select committee,[165] but any supplementary estimates relating to the bill do stand referred to the Finance and Expenditure Committee after the bill's introduction.[166] That committee can examine a vote contained in the supplementary estimates itself or refer it to any other subject select committee for examination.[167] It cannot divide a vote for examination in the supplementary estimates as it can on examination of the main estimates.

Although there is no report time prescribed, in practice the supplementary estimates examination is even more time-confined than the estimates examination because the bill has to be passed by the end of the financial year on 30 June. For this reason the Finance and Expenditure Committee does not always use its power to refer supplementary estimates to other committees. Often it carries out the examination itself, relying on Treasury officials to explain the supplementary appropriations but requiring the appearance before the committee of officials from other departments where necessary.[168]

Any committee involved in examining supplementary estimates resolves whether to recommend to the House the appropriations contained in the vote before it. Committees may also recommend changes to the votes.[169]

Further supplementary estimates

Just as the main Appropriation Bill may be amended by the presentation of adjusting estimates, an Appropriation Bill containing supplementary appropriations may be amended by the presentation of further supplementary estimates. (The amendments to the bill itself are set out on a supplementary order paper in the name of the Minister.) There can indeed be a succession of further supplementary estimates presented.[170] Further supplementary estimates stand referred to the Finance and Expenditure Committee. They could be referred by that committee to another committee but, in practice, are likely to be dealt with by it. (An alternative to amending the Appropriation Bill is to introduce another Appropriation Bill and present supplementary estimates in respect of it.)

Supplementary estimates debate

An Appropriation Bill containing supplementary estimates remains on the order paper until the supplementary estimates and any further supplementary estimates which relate to it have been reported to the House. When these have been reported to the House the supplementary estimates debate can be held.

The debate on the supplementary estimates in the House occurs on the second reading of the bill. Three hours are allowed for this debate with each member able to speak for up to 10 minutes.[171]

The debate must be relevant to the bill's provisions and deal with the appropriations that the Government wishes to supplement or vary; it is not another Budget debate. As it is the winding-up debate of the financial year, it may cover an overview of the policies for which the Government has sought appropriations in the financial year and of the Government's financial position at the end of the year.[172] There can be no "public affairs" amendment moved on the second reading of this bill. But the second reading of an Appropriation Bill containing the supplementary estimates may be taken together with an Imprest Supply Bill.[173] It is indeed the invariable practice to combine this debate with the

---

[165]   S.O.285(2).
[166]   S.O.333(1).
[167]   *Ibid.*
[168]   1990, AJHR, I.19, pp.73, 79.
[169]   S.O.333(2).

[167]   1990, Vol.508, p.2384.
[171]   Appendix A to the Standing Orders.
[172]   1992, Vol.526, p.9061.
[173]   S.O.334(2).

debate on the first Imprest Supply Bill for the following year which is likely to be ready for introduction at this time. A public affairs amendment can be moved on the second reading of an Imprest Supply Bill.[174]

Passing of Appropriation Bill

After the second reading of the bill the House proceeds immediately to its third reading unless the Minister wishes to propose amendments to the bill or a select committee has recommended a change to a vote and that change has not itself been the subject of a financial veto.[175] In either case a committee stage is held, where only the Minister's amendments (and any relevant amendments to them) or the amendment to the appropriation recommended by the committee, as the case may be, are considered. When amendments to a part or schedule have been disposed of, the question is put that that part or schedule as amended stand part.

There is no debate on the third reading or opportunity to move any amendment to the question.[176]

CONFIRMATION OR VALIDATION OF EXPENSES AND CAPITAL EXPENDITURE

Permanent legislative authority and the Appropriation Acts passed before the end of the financial year to which they relate, together with any transfers of appropriations made by Order in Council,[177] constitute the final appropriations and authorisations relating to that year. But some of those appropriations or authorisations contemplate that they are in part provisional in that they must be reported to the House and steps taken to seek parliamentary confirmation of them.

Emergency expenses or capital expenditure incurred under a state of emergency or civil defence emergency must be included in an Appropriation Bill for confirmation by Parliament.[178] Expenses or capital expenditure approved by the Minister of Finance in excess of existing appropriations must be included in an Appropriation Bill for the next financial year, for confirmation by Parliament.[179] In the case of Orders in Council transferring appropriations within a vote, a clause confirming the transfers must be included in an Appropriation Bill for the next financial year.[180] (See Chapter 32.) In no case is parliamentary *validation* of such expenses or capital expenditure involved required since the statute under which it is incurred provides legal authority for it. Thus the provision requiring the Government to seek confirmation of expenditure acknowledges that this does not affect the validity of the expenditure, of any Order in Council, or of any transfer.[181] But the requirement at least to seek subsequent parliamentary confirmation ensures that the House is appraised of the spending authority used by the Government under these provisions.

It is possible that expenses or capital expenditure may have been incurred without any appropriation or legal authority at all. In such a case unlawful expenditure has been incurred and, if the illegality is to be cured, parliamentary validation must be sought. (See Chapter 32.)

For all of these matters an Appropriation (Financial Review) Bill may be used as the legislative vehicle. An Appropriation (Financial Review) Bill is concerned solely with sanctioning, confirming or validating expenditure incurred in the previous financial

---

174 S.O.323(3).
175 S.O.334(3).
176 S.O.334(4).
177 *Public Finance Act* 1989, s.26A.
178 *Ibid.*, s.25(5).

179 *Ibid.*, s.26B(4).
180 *Ibid.*, s.26A(2).
181 *Ibid.*, ss.25(6), 26A(3) and 26B(5); *Archives and Records Association of New Zealand v Blakeley* [2000] 1 NZLR 607 at [80].

year.[182] (The procedures for considering an Appropriation (Financial Review) Bill are described in Chapter 36.) From time to time unlawful expenditure may also be validated by a Finance Bill[183] or other legislation.[184]

---

[182] S.O.337(1).
[183] See, for example, *Finance Act* 1976, s.2.

[184] See, for example, *Education Standards Act* 2001, s.84 (capital accommodation grants).

CHAPTER 35

REPORTING AND AUDIT

Concomitant obligations to the spending of public funds by public bodies arise. These involve making a report on the operational and financial consequences of the body's work and submitting to audit. These aspects of public reporting and public audit are some of the means by which the public sector accounts for its operations, first internally and then externally, to an auditor, to the House of Representatives and, through the House, to the wider public.

The Crown, departments, offices of Parliament, Crown entities, State enterprises and other publicly-owned organisations produce reports for transmission to the House each year. These reporting obligations may be discharged in a single annual report or, as with the Crown, in a number of different reports generated during the course of the year. The reports present a mix of information on financial and operational performance. Generally, a reporting entity is obliged to present financial statements that conform to legally prescribed standards, while the way in which it reports on operational performance is much more at its own discretion. Reporting is an essential tool in holding an agency accountable for its actions and performance. But it is only one aspect of this process and has to be supplemented by independent assessments made through the processes of auditing and reviewing the agency.

TYPES OF REPORTING ENTITY

The precise accountability obligations that arise depend upon the status of the body concerned and the specific terms of any statute applying to it.

There are six broad types of entity that are required to report to the House on their financial and operational activities: the Government itself, Government departments, offices of Parliament, Crown entities, State enterprises and other miscellaneous organisations. Apart from the other miscellaneous organisations, common financial reporting models apply to each of the types of entities. But there are individual differences in operation and control amongst those entities which fall into the category of Crown entities.

This chapter describes the reporting and audit obligations across the public sector. (Chapter 36 describes how the House considers the results of this reporting and auditing through the process of financial review.)

Government

The Government is defined as a separate reporting entity in New Zealand law. For this purpose the "Government reporting entity" is the Sovereign in right of New Zealand, and the legislative, executive and judicial branches of the Government of New Zealand;[1] in a broad sense central government (it does not include local government).

Departments

The principal administrative units into which the executive branch of government is divided are known as departments of state. These are bodies staffed by public servants,

---

[1]   *Public Finance Act* 1989, s.2(1).

funded by appropriations made by Parliament and under the political direction of a Minister (the portfolio Minister), who in turn answers to the House for the department's activities. Departments are at the core of the public sector. The exact organisation of each Government into departments is essentially a matter for the Prime Minister to determine. While there are still examples of departments that are created by statute,[2] strictly speaking this is unnecessary.[3] The practice today is to create and abolish departments under the Crown's prerogative or common law powers rather than by statute. However, named departments are expressly recognised in legislation (particularly in the *State Sector Act* 1988) and so administrative reorganisations usually entail consequential legislative amendments to these references. In many cases these can be effected by Order in Council and do not require primary legislation.

Relatively few departments actually have the word "department" in their titles. Many are known as ministries. Others, for example, the Treasury, have neither the word department nor the word ministry in their titles. There is no legal significance in these differences in nomenclature. Three departments (the Treasury, the State Services Commission and the Department of Prime Minister and Cabinet) have co-ordinating functions in respect of all departments. They are consequently often known as "central agencies". The official who heads each department is known as the "chief executive" of the department, though chief executives of certain departments may (by convention or by law) have another title too. For example, the chief executive of the Treasury is known as the Secretary to the Treasury. The functions and powers of each department are a mixture of legal provisions (statutory and common law) and of political and administrative decisions taken by the Government. In particular, statutes such as the *State Sector Act* 1988 and the *Public Finance Act* 1989 impose an overall framework of powers and accountability responsibilities for departments.

For reporting purposes a department is defined as a department or instrument of the Government, including any branch or division of such a department or instrument.[4] This clearly includes those departments that are listed in Schedule 1 of the *State Sector Act* 1988 – the departments of the New Zealand Public Service.[5] But there are other departments or instruments of the Government that are not part of the public service – for example, the New Zealand Defence Force and the New Zealand Police. These are also subject to the reporting requirements of the *Public Finance Act* 1989. In addition, the Office of the Clerk and the Parliamentary Service are deemed to be departments for the purposes of the *Public Finance Act*. An office of Parliament is not a department.[6]

Each department has a responsible Minister who is responsible for the financial performance of the department. This is reflected in the estimates. For public service and other government departments, the Prime Minister determines which Ministers perform these roles. The responsible Minister does not need to be the portfolio Minister, though this will usually be the case. For the Office of the Clerk and the Parliamentary Service, the Speaker is the responsible Minister.[7]

Offices of Parliament

Offices of Parliament comprise the Parliamentary Commissioner for the Environment, the Office of the Ombudsmen and the Controller and Auditor-General.[8] The Speaker is the responsible Minister,[9] and is therefore responsible for the financial performance, of each office of Parliament. (But the Speaker is not responsible for the performance of the

---

2   For example, *Conservation Act* 1987, s.5 (Department of Conservation).

3   "Departmental Statutes", Report 4 by the Legislation Advisory Committee, 1989.

4   *Public Finance Act* 1989, s.2(1).

5   *State Sector Act* 1988, s.27.

6   *Public Finance Act* 1989, s.2(1).

7   *Ibid.*

8   *Ibid.*

9   *Ibid.*

statutory duties cast on each officer of Parliament.) (See Chapter 6 for a discussion of offices of Parliament.)

Crown entities

Crown entities were first created as a financial reporting model in 1989 (they were then known as Crown agencies). By 2002 almost 100 types of body were described as Crown entities, with some of them (such as district health boards, boards of school trustees and reserves boards) comprising many individual Crown entities, making some 3,000 individual entities in total. As legislation created new bodies or abolished old ones, the number of Crown entities altered accordingly. Their heterogeneity and the fact that there were no common governance principles applying in respect of them (other than for financial reporting), led in 1998 to the commencement of a review of the principles that underpinned the roles and structures of Crown entities. This review culminated in legislation, the *Crown Entities Act* 2004, designed to provide a consistent framework for the establishment, governance and operation of Crown entities and to clarify their accountability relationships.[10]

Crown entities fall into one of five main categories.[11]

Statutory entities are bodies corporate established under legislation. They are listed in a schedule to the Act.[12] Statutory entities are in turn one of three types, depending upon the degree of control that may be exercised by the Government over them in a policy sense. *Crown agents* must give effect to government policy when directed to do so by the responsible Minister. Bodies of this type include: the Accident Compensation Corporation, district health boards, the Legal Services Agency and Transit New Zealand. *Autonomous Crown entities* must have regard to government policy when directed to do so by the Minister, but cannot be required to give effect to it. The Arts Council of New Zealand Toi Aotearoa, Guardians of New Zealand Superannuation and the New Zealand Symphony Orchestra are entities of this kind. *Independent Crown entities* are generally entirely independent of government policy. They often perform functions of a quasi-judicial nature. They include: the Broadcasting Standards Authority, the Commerce Commission, the Electoral Commission, the Human Rights Commission and the Law Commission.

The second category of Crown entities consists of *Crown entity companies*. These are companies incorporated under the companies legislation that are wholly owned by the Crown. They are listed in the Act.[13] The third category is *Crown entity subsidiaries* – any company that is controlled by a Crown entity. No comprehensive list of these is contained in the legislation. The fourth and fifth categories are respectively *school boards of trustees* and *tertiary education institutions* (universities, colleges of education, polytechnics, special colleges or wananga). Only a limited number of the governance rules set out in the *Crown Entities Act* apply to these latter two categories of Crown entity.[14]

In respect of statutory entities, Crown entity companies and Crown entity subsidiaries, the provisions of the *Crown Entities Act*, as supplemented or expressly modified by any other legislation applying to them (such as a parent act), govern their activities.[15] If there is any conflict between the legislation establishing an entity and the *Crown Entities Act*, the latter prevails.[16] There thus now exists a common legislative structure governing the basic governance of Crown entities as well as the general financial reporting provisions for them.

---

[10]   *Crown Entities Act* 2004, s.3.
[11]   *Ibid.*, s.7(1).
[12]   *Ibid.*, Sch.1.
[13]   *Ibid.*, Sch.2.

[14]   *Ibid.*, ss.5 and 6.
[15]   *Ibid.*, s.4(1).
[16]   *Ibid.*, s.4(2).

Ministerial responsibility

The responsible Minister for a Crown entity is the Minister expressed to have responsibility by any Act, or who is appointed by the Governor-General by warrant to have responsibility, or who is otherwise assigned responsibility by the Prime Minister. Essentially, responsibility is a matter for the Prime Minister to determine in allocating portfolios. But in the case of a Crown entity company, the Minister of Finance and any other shareholding Minister are statutorily declared to be the responsible Ministers.[17]

Responsible Ministers have a number of uniform duties and powers in respect of reporting by Crown entities. In respect of some Crown entities the Minister is expressed to be statutorily responsible to the House for the performance of the functions conferred on the Minister under the legislation.[18] But the precise legal powers and responsibilities (if any) of the Minister for the Crown entity concerned depend upon the terms of the legislation or other instrument under which the entity was created. This has led to conflict over the extent to which Ministers have the right to intervene (for example, through purchase agreements) to control the policies and operations of Crown entities.[19] The categorisation of Crown entities with their different obligations in regard to the observance of Government policy is an attempt to resolve ambiguities in this area.

Crown entities are obliged to prepare a statement of intent for the forthcoming year and at least the two following financial years.[20] These statements are intended to enable the Crown to participate in the process of setting the entity's medium-term goals, set these out for the House, and provide a base against which the entity's performance can be assessed.[21] To these ends each statement must contain key background information about the entity and its operating environment, its functions and operations, performance measures for assessing its operations and descriptions of how it intends to perform and manage the tasks that it undertakes.[22] A responsible Minister is entitled to participate in the drawing up of a statement of intent by specifying its form, commenting on drafts of the statement and directing the entity to amend provisions of the draft.[23] These processes can delay the finalising of a statement until any differences between the Minister and the entity have been resolved.[24]

The final statement of intent must be presented to the House no later than five working days after it is received by the Minister.[25]

The Government also has the right, through the Minister of State Services and the Minister of Finance acting jointly, to direct Crown entities to comply with specified requirements so as to support a whole-of-government approach in a particular area and to improve public services.[26] These directions (known as "whole of government directions") may be given to one or more categories of Crown entities (all statutory entities, all Crown entity companies or all school boards of trustees) or to one or more types of statutory entity.[27] Directions may not be given to Crown entity subsidiaries.[28] An example of a type of whole-of-government direction that might be given is a direction requiring that all Crown entities comply with e-government requirements. Ministers must, before giving a direction, first consult with entities to be affected by it and must present it to the House after it is given.[29]

A whole-of-government direction cannot come into force unless it has been presented.[30]

---

17   *Ibid.*, s.10(1).
18   See, for example: *Animal Control Products Limited Act* 1991, s.4; *Crown Research Institutes Act* 1992, s.6(1); *Southland Electricity Act* 1993, s.5.
19   See, for example, 1996-99, AJHR, I.21C, pp.369-70 (New Zealand Tourism Board).
20   *Crown Entities Act* 2004, s.139(1)
21   *Ibid.*, s.138.
22   *Ibid.*, s.141.
23   *Ibid.*, ss.145 to 148.
24   See, for example, "TVNZ delays financial forecasts", *The Independent*, 2 February 2005.
25   *Crown Entities Act* 2004, s.149(1).
26   *Ibid.*, s.107(1).
27   *Ibid.*, s.107(2).
28   *Ibid.*, s.107(3).
29   *Ibid.*, s.108.
30   *Ibid.*, s.108(2)(b).

It then stands referred to the Finance and Expenditure Committee,[31] which considers its subject area and decides, on the basis of its own and the other select committees' terms of reference, whether to consider it itself or refer it to another committee.[32] The Finance and Expenditure Committee or any other committee to which the direction is referred must report to the House on it no later than 12 sitting days after it has been referred.[33]

A whole-of-government direction does not require the approval or endorsement of the House. It comes into force 15 sitting days after it is presented to the House unless the House, within that time, resolves to disapply it.[34] Crown entities are obliged to give effect to a whole-of-government direction as soon as it comes into force.[35]

Regardless of the Minister's legal responsibilities in any particular case, the Minister's responsibility to answer questions in the House in respect of Crown entities is clear, although, as with State enterprises, there will always be complaints about how forthcoming Ministers have been in a particular case.

State enterprises

On 1 April 1987 a new type of public organisation called a State enterprise (popularly, though inaccurately,[36] referred to as a State-owned enterprise or SOE) came into existence. Originally 14 organisations were made subject to the State enterprises regime. They were designed to take over and carry on a large part of the Government's trading activities which had hitherto been run either within government departments, by ad hoc corporations or by other bodies. The concept of a State enterprise creates a standard model public trading organisation that may be registered as a company under the companies legislation[37] and into which those state activities which Governments wish to corporatise can be fitted. The governmental activities corporatised in this way in 1987 included airlines, airways, banking, coal, electricity, forestry, postal services, property services, shipping, telecommunications and tourism. There have been considerable changes in the categories of state trading activities since then, with many of the original State enterprises having been privatised and removed from government ownership entirely, and new entities made State enterprises. In 2004 State enterprises held total assets of $12 billion, or approximately 10.8 percent, of all Crown assets.[38]

The principal objective of every State enterprise is stated to be:

> ... to operate as a successful business and, to this end, to be—
> (a) As profitable and efficient as comparable businesses that are not owned by the Crown; and
> (b) A good employer; and
> (c) An organisation that exhibits a sense of social responsibility by having regard to the interests of the community in which it operates and by endeavouring to accommodate or encourage these when able to do so.[39]

State enterprises, as public bodies established by statute that take decisions which may adversely affect the rights and liabilities of private individuals, are, in principle, amenable to judicial review.[40] However, the courts have consistently held that the overriding consideration for a State enterprise is to act as a commercial entity; that is, to operate a successful business. State enterprises must "have regard to" the other three criteria set out

---

[31] S.O.384(1).
[32] S.O.384(2).
[33] S.O.384(3).
[34] *Crown Entities Act* 2004, s.109.
[35] *Ibid.*, s.110.
[36] See the *State-Owned Enterprises Act* 1986, s.2 *et seq.*

[37] *Ibid.*, s.30.
[38] Information supplied by the Treasury, May 2005.
[39] *State-Owned Enterprises Act* 1986, s.4(1).
[40] *Mercury Energy Ltd v Electricity Corporation of New Zealand Ltd* [1994] 2 NZLR 385.

in their statutory objective in carrying on their businesses insofar as a successful business is thereby promoted. But in the absence of fraud, corruption or bad faith on the part of a State enterprise justifying judicial review, the relationship between a State enterprise and its customers is similar to that between a commercial entity and its customers.[41]

As a commercial enterprise, a State enterprise is subject to receivership and in 2001 a receiver was appointed for the first time in respect of a State enterprise.[42] There is no government guarantee for State enterprises.[43] But State enterprises, as public entities, are subject to the jurisdiction of the Ombudsmen and to official information disclosure, and they are audited by the Auditor-General.

The rules of a State enterprise that is a registered company are its memorandum of association and articles of association or its constitution, if it has one. Otherwise the rules of the State enterprise are any documents comparable to these.[44] The rules (and any changes to them) must be laid before the House within 12 sitting days of their adoption.[45] A State enterprise's statement of corporate intent is drawn up in consultation with the shareholding Ministers, and the statements relating to the current and next two years must be presented to the House within 12 sitting days of being delivered to the responsible Minister.[46] The shareholding Ministers may, by written notice, require the board of a State enterprise to include in or omit from a statement of corporate intent matters relating to the objectives and policies to be followed by the enterprise. Whenever any such direction has been given, a copy of it must also be laid before the House within 12 sitting days.[47] Such statements have been described as essentially internal constitutional documents designed to ensure accountability to the shareholding Minister, rather than external constraints on their operations.[48] Contracts for the transfer of state assets to a State enterprise must be laid before the House within 12 sitting days of being entered into.[49]

Ministerial responsibility
The Minister of Finance and the Minister responsible for each State enterprise are together the shareholding Ministers for that enterprise.[50] Different Ministers may be made responsible for different State enterprises. Invariably a Minister for State Owned Enterprises is appointed to be responsible for State enterprises not specifically assigned to any other Minister.

The shareholding Ministers are responsible to the House for the performance of the functions given to them by the *State-Owned Enterprises Act* 1986 or the rules of the State enterprise.[51] There are examples in other legislation of statutory recognition of a Minister's responsibility to the House, but it is questionable whether such a provision is useful. The statute does not make Ministers responsible to the House for all of the activities of a State enterprise, only for the limited range of functions which are conferred on Ministers. The statutory provision could therefore be used as a means of denying responsibility entirely for State enterprise activities that do not fall within its terms. In fact, Ministers have not denied such a responsibility to the House in that they have accepted the responsibility to answer to the House for activities for which they, strictly, have no legal responsibility.

Principally, this exercise of ministerial responsibility to answer to the House arises in questions addressed to Ministers about the actions of State enterprises. Questions about the activities of State enterprises have not been challenged as being outside ministerial

---

41 *Ibid.; Auckland Electric Power Board v Electricity Corporation of New Zealand Ltd* [1994] 1 NZLR 551.
42 1999-2002, AJHR, I.19B, p.450 (Terralink NZ Limited).
43 2002-05, AJHR, I.19A, pp.337-8.
44 *State-Owned Enterprises Act* 1986, s.2.
45 *Ibid.,* s.17(1).
46 *Ibid.,* ss.14 and 17(2)(a).
47 *Ibid.,* s.13.
48 *Transpower New Zealand Ltd v Meridian Energy Ltd* [2001] 3 NZLR 700 at [67].
49 *State-Owned Enterprises Act* 1986, s.23(2).
50 *Ibid.,* s.2.
51 *Ibid.,* s.6.

responsibility, and have been consistently accepted since State enterprises were created.[52] The fact that a Minister does not have legal control over a certain action does not mean that the Minister has no responsibility to answer to the House for it.[53] Questions to Ministers about the activities of State enterprises are in order even when falling outside the Ministers' legal responsibilities.

Other organisations

There are other organisations that are not departments, offices of Parliament, Crown entities or State enterprises, but which nevertheless are required to prepare reports on their activities which are submitted to Parliament.

A handful of organisations which are not Crown entities have some of the financial reporting and controlling provisions of the *Crown Entities Act* applied to them. The organisations falling into this category are identified in a schedule to the *Public Finance Act*.[54] The Crown entity provisions which apply differ between these organisations: in some cases there is a requirement to prepare a statement of service performance; in others the provisions which relate to acquiring securities, borrowing, giving guarantees and engaging in derivatives transactions are applied.

The Reserve Bank of New Zealand and the Abortion Supervisory Committee are unique organisations. The Reserve Bank was specifically excluded from the reporting regime adopted for Crown entities when that was devised.[55] The bank has its own specific reporting obligations.[56] The Abortion Supervisory Committee reports directly to the House on its activities[57] although it is not classified as a Crown entity.

The House has, by resolution, consistently ordered that its financial review procedures should apply as equally to the Reserve Bank and the Abortion Supervisory Committee as it does to departments, offices of Parliament, Crown entities and State enterprises.[58] In 2003 the House extended this supervision to Air New Zealand Limited after the Government acquired a majority shareholding in that company.[59]

Many other organisations are statutorily obliged to report to a Minister so that the report can be presented to the House by the Minister. These organisations may not be publicly owned (they are often owned by their members) or administer public money (though they may have received some public funding). In these cases the requirement to report to the House is seen as a useful means of disseminating information about the organisation's activities, rather than as an aspect of public accountability.

REPORTING STANDARDS

Financial reporting

Financial statements must be prepared in accordance with "generally accepted accounting practice" (known as "GAAP"). This means any applicable financial reporting standards approved by the Accounting Standards Review Board or any accounting policies that are appropriate to the circumstances and have authoritative support within the accounting profession in New Zealand.[60] The board is authorised to approve such standards after engaging in consultation on them.[61] Such standards may be expressed to apply across-the-board to the Crown and all public-sector agencies or to particular agencies.[62]

52 1987, Vol.483, pp.617-8.
53 1990, Vol.509, p.2705-6.
54 *Public Finance Act* 1989, ss.45M and 45N and Sch.4.
55 1991-93, AJHR, I.4A, para.5.7.
56 *Reserve Bank of New Zealand Act* 1989, s.163.
57 *Contraception, Sterilisation, and Abortion Act* 1977, s.39.

58 1999, Vol.581, p.37; 2002, Vol.602, p.237.
59 2003, Vol.614, pp.10330-6.
60 *Public Finance Act* 1989, s.2(1); *Crown Entities Act* 2004, s.136(1).
61 *Financial Reporting Act* 1993 ss.24 and 26.
62 *Ibid.*, s.27.

The House may disallow or amend reporting standards determined by the board.[63]

The tasks of preparing and auditing financial statements are distinct tasks – the former performed by the reporting entity and the latter by the Auditor-General. The Auditor-General's audits are conducted in accordance with auditing standards published by the Auditor-General, which incorporate the auditing standards issued by the Institute of Chartered Accountants of New Zealand.[64] In forming an opinion on an entity's financial statements, the Auditor-General also evaluates the overall adequacy of the presentation of information in those statements.[65]

Non-financial reporting

In the case of departments, statute prescribes the types of information that must be included in each department's annual report. Information that is necessary to enable an informed assessment to be made of the department's performance during the year in review, must be presented.[66] Offices of Parliament must prepare similar reports.[67]

The general legislative obligation on departments to report on their operations does not elaborate in detail on the form that such reports must take. However, regulations may be made or the Minister of Finance may issue instructions to departments, offices of Parliament and miscellaneous organisations named in the *Public Finance Act* as to the non-financial reporting standards that they must apply and the form in which that information must be presented to the House.[68] Before any such instructions are issued or regulations made, the Minister must provide a draft of the instructions or regulations to the Speaker. The Speaker presents the draft to the House and it is considered by the Finance and Expenditure Committee (in the case of departments and other organisations) or the Officers of Parliament Committee (in the case of offices of Parliament). The respective committees are responsible for co-ordinating comment on the proposals from other committees and communicating this to the Minister.[69] The Minister must take account of any comments received from the Speaker or any committee before the instructions are issued or the regulations are made.

In addition, in the case of regulations or instructions applying to offices of Parliament, the regulations or instructions can only be made or issued after having been approved by resolution of the House.[70] For this purpose a notice of motion to approve the regulations or instructions stands referred to a select committee (likely to be the Officers of Parliament Committee).[71] The committee must report on the notice no later than the first working day 28 days after it is referred.[72] The motion to approve the regulations or instructions may not be moved until the report has been made or 28 days have elapsed, whichever is earlier.[73]

Where particular legislation specifies matters to be included in an entity's report, such matters must be addressed, but generally the extent of operational reporting, as distinct from financial reporting, is largely at the discretion of each department. Select committees expect departments to report against their key result areas and to attempt to evaluate their performance in terms of measurable and meaningful outcomes.[74] Select committees examining annual reports will expect to see those reports identify links between the output classes that departments produce and the desired governmental outcomes that these outputs are designed to contribute to.[75] Following a recommendation of the Government

63   *Ibid.*, s.33.
64   "The Auditor-General's auditing standards", Report of the Controller and Auditor-General, 3 May 2003.
65   2003, PP, B.29[03a], para.2.4 (Controller and Auditor-General).
66   *Public Finance Act* 1989, s.45.
67   *Ibid.*, ss.45F and 45G.
68   *Ibid.*, ss.80A, 81 and 82.
69   2002-05, AJHR, I.18C, pp.10-11.
70   *Public Finance Act* 1989, s.82(2) to (5).
71   S.O.317(1).
72   S.O.317(2).
73   S.O.317(3).
74   1999-2002, AJHR, I.20B, pp.40 and 137.
75   1996-99, AJHR, I.20A, pp.44-57.

Administration Committee, the State Services Commissioner has issued guidelines to chief executives on the format and content of annual reports.[76]

Crown entities are also required to prepare annual reports in accordance with statutorily prescribed standards, whether of a general nature[77] or in their own parent Acts. In addition, the Minister of Finance may prescribe non-financial reporting standards for Crown entities (except for school boards of trustees and tertiary education institutions). These instructions may be made in respect of Crown entities generally or certain categories or types of Crown entities.[78] However, before issuing an instruction to Crown entities on non-financial reporting standards, the Minister must submit the instruction in draft to the Speaker. The Speaker presents it to the House and it is referred to the Finance and Expenditure Committee. That committee co-ordinates comment on it from other select committees and communicates these to the Minister.[79] The Minister may issue the instruction only after considering any comments on the draft received from the Speaker or any committees that considered it and the Minister may amend the draft before issuing it, in the light of these comments.[80]

FINANCIAL STATEMENTS OF THE GOVERNMENT

The Treasury is responsible for preparing at the end of each financial year annual financial statements of the Government of New Zealand.[81] These are combined financial statements presenting a picture of the Government as a single reporting entity that includes the legislative, executive and judicial branches of government. The statements show the net worth of the Crown and enable comparisons to be made of changes in that net worth over time. The statements consolidate the revenues, expenses, assets and liabilities of all departments (including the activities they undertake on behalf of the Crown, such as making benefit payments), offices of Parliament and the Reserve Bank. From the 2003/04 financial year, so as to conform to changing financial reporting standards, they have also consolidated the revenues, expenses, assets and liabilities of Crown entities and State enterprises instead of just combining their net results.[82]

The Treasury must forward the annual financial statements to the Auditor-General by the end of August.[83] The Auditor-General must provide an audit report on the statements within 30 days of receiving them.[84] The annual financial statements are accompanied by a statement of responsibility signed by the Minister of Finance and the Secretary to the Treasury. This attests to the Minister's responsibility for the integrity of the statements and the Treasury's responsibility for establishing and maintaining a set of internal controls that allows the statements to be used with confidence as to their accuracy.[85]

The audit report on the annual financial statements is generally issued on the same date as the Minister and the Secretary to the Treasury sign the statement of responsibility. The audit report is therefore published along with the financial statements.[86]

The annual financial statements and the audit opinion must be presented to the House by the Minister not later than 10 working days after they are returned to the Treasury by the Auditor-General.[87] The Finance and Expenditure Committee is required to examine and report to the House on the Government's annual financial statements within one week of the first sitting day in each year.[88]

---

[76] *Ibid.*, I.3C; State Services Commission, 17 March 1998.
[77] *Crown Entities Act* 2004, ss.150 to 152.
[78] *Ibid.*, s.174(1), (2).
[79] 2002-05, AJHR, I.18C, p.11
[80] *Crown Entities Act* 2004, s.175.
[81] *Public Finance Act* 1989, s.27.
[82] 2003, PP, B.1 & B.6, pp.70-1.

[83] *Public Finance Act* 1989, s.30(1).
[84] *Ibid.*, s.30(2)(b).
[85] *Ibid.*, s.29.
[86] 2001, PP, B.29 [01b] (Controller and Auditor-General).
[87] *Public Finance Act* 1989, s.31(2).
[88] S.O.336(1).

A set of monthly financial statements must also be prepared, though these contain less detailed information than the annual statements and are without a formal audit.[89]

DEPARTMENTAL REPORTING

Departments and offices of Parliament are obliged to present reports on their financial and operational activities.

Financial reporting

The chief executive of a department is responsible to the responsible Minister for the financial management and financial performance of the department and for complying with any financial reporting requirements.[90] The chief executive must sign a statement of responsibility for the financial reports prepared for the department, testifying to their accuracy and consistency.[91]

Departments and offices of Parliament must, before the beginning of each financial year, prepare statements of intent describing their operating intentions for the coming year. (See Chapter 34.) These statements are presented to the House by the Minister of Finance immediately after the delivery of the Budget statement. They are part of the documentation on which select committees base their estimates examinations.

Departments and offices of Parliament must also prepare annual financial statements setting out their financial positions at the end of each financial year. These statements contain the information which is consolidated into the Government's annual financial statements. They must be prepared in accordance with generally accepted accounting practice. They must specifically include: information or explanations needed to reflect the department's financial operations and financial position, the department's forecast financial statements prepared at the beginning of the year, and statements of actual expenses and capital expenditure against appropriations administered by the department. They must also identify any unappropriated expenses or capital expenditure that has been incurred.[92]

The annual financial statements are audited by the Auditor-General. An audit report on each statement must be issued within three months of the end of the financial year.[93]

Operational reporting

All departments of the public service are under a general obligation to give to their Ministers an annual report on the operations of the department.[94] Such departments may also be required by specific legislation to prepare reports on their operations or particular aspects of their operations. These reporting obligations can be all discharged in the same report.[95] All such reports are presented to the House by the Minister. The Office of the Clerk, the Parliamentary Service and each officer of Parliament also present reports on their operations to the House. The annual report of each department or office of Parliament stands referred to the select committee which has been allocated the task of carrying out a financial review of that department.[96]

NON-DEPARTMENTAL REPORTING

Crown entities

All Crown entities are required to prepare financial statements at the end of each year

---

89   *Public Finance Act* 1989, s.31A.
90   *Ibid.*, ss.34 and 35.
91   *Ibid.*, s.45C.
92   *Ibid.*, s.45B.
93   *Ibid.*, s.45D.
94   *Ibid.*, s.43(1).
95   *Ibid.*, s.43(2).
96   S.O.335(2).

setting out a range of financial information about the entity.[97] These must be forwarded to the Auditor-General for audit within 90 days of the end of the financial year.[98] The Auditor-General is required to issue an audit opinion on them within four months of the end of the financial year.[99] The annual financial statements of each Crown entity are included in the entity's annual report, which is presented to the House by the responsible Minister.

The interests of the Government in Crown entities is included in the Government's financial statements.[100]

State enterprises

The *State-Owned Enterprises Act* 1986 requires each State enterprise to present to the House, through the responsible Minister, a range of documents on the future plans and past performance of the enterprise.

Within three months of the end of each financial year the board of a State enterprise must give a report to its shareholding Ministers on the operations of the enterprise and its subsidiaries and also deliver to them audited financial statements for the year.[101] This report is expected to provide clear comparisons of the State enterprise's performance against its statement of corporate intent.[102] The annual report is presented to the House. State enterprises are also required to give shareholding Ministers half-yearly reports on their operations.[103]

Other organisations

The board of directors of the Reserve Bank must prepare a report each year setting out the board's assessment of the performance of the bank and the Governor. The report stands referred to the House.[104] The Reserve Bank is also required to make an annual report to the Minister on its operations. This stands referred to the House too.[105] The Abortion Supervisory Committee is required to make an annual report to the House.[106] This report is forwarded to the Speaker who presents it to the House. A number of other bodies which are not departments, offices of Parliament, Crown entities or State enterprises are also required by specific legislation applying to them to prepare annual reports which must be presented to the House.

Reports on service performance

In respect of departments and Crown entities (except school boards of trustees and tertiary education institutions), their annual financial statements must contain a statement of service performance for each class of outputs. This addresses the performance of the department or entity in delivering those outputs, as compared with its forecast of performance included in its statement of intent.[107] But a school board of trustees, a tertiary education institution, a State enterprise and other public organisations that are not Crown entities are not required to produce such a statement of service performance. Consequently, where one of these latter entities is responsible for supplying any classes of outputs, its annual financial statements are not required to include a report on its actual performance as against its forecast performance in supplying those outputs.

To meet this reporting deficiency, it is provided that the Minister responsible for a vote containing an appropriation for classes of outputs for which expenses or capital

---

97   *Crown Entities Act* 2004, s.154.
98   *Ibid.*, s.156(1).
99   *Ibid.*, s.156(2).
100 *Public Finance Act* 1989, s.27(3)(a).
101 *State-Owned Enterprises Act* 1986, s.15.
102 1996-99, AJHR, I.21B, p.23.
103 *State-Owned Enterprises Act* 1986, s.16.

104 *Reserve Bank of New Zealand Act* 1989, s.53A(3).
105 *Ibid.*, s.163(3).
106 *Contraception, Sterilisation, and Abortion Act* 1977, s.39.
107 *Public Finance Act* 1989, s.45A (departments and offices of Parliament); *Crown Entities Act* 2004, s.153 (Crown entities).

expenditure are to be incurred other than by departments or offices of Parliament, must present a report on service performance in relation to those outputs comparing what was delivered to what was agreed to be delivered. The Appropriation Acts identify those classes of outputs that are subject to this reporting requirement. (Where the entity concerned is already required to produce its own statement of service performance, this obligation does not apply.) Such reports must be made to the House within three months of the end of the financial year.[108]

AUDIT

The Auditor-General is by statute the auditor of every public entity.[109] This includes the Government itself,[110] airport companies, Crown entities, departments, energy companies, licensing trusts, local authorities, local authority trading enterprises, Māori trust boards, marketing authorities, port companies, security and intelligence departments, and State enterprises.[111] It also includes a number of other entities not falling into these general categories, such as, for example, the Office of the Clerk, the Parliamentary Counsel Office, the Parliamentary Service and the Reserve Bank of New Zealand.[112] The Auditor-General also audits the other offices of Parliament on appointment by the House.[113] The House has appointed an independent auditor for a three-year term to audit the Auditor-General.[114] State enterprises may, after consultation with the Auditor-General, appoint a qualified person to be an additional auditor of the enterprise or of a subsidiary of the enterprise.[115]

The Auditor-General must, at least once every three years, publish, by way of a report to the House, the auditing standards that the Auditor-General applies or intends to apply to the conduct of audits and inquiries.[116] Currently the Auditor-General's standards incorporate (but are not limited to) the auditing standards issued by the Institute of Chartered Accountants of New Zealand.[117]

Audits are carried out by the Auditor-General or by auditors appointed by the Auditor-General.[118] These auditors may be staff of the Auditor-General from Audit New Zealand, a separate business unit within the Auditor-General's office, or suitably qualified private-sector auditors (both known collectively as "appointed auditors"). The Auditor-General and the appointed auditors must act independently in the performance of the Auditor-General's functions.[119] They have power to obtain information, to take evidence on oath and to inspect bank accounts, for the purposes of carrying out an audit.[120] The audits aim to obtain all information and explanations considered necessary to give a reasonable assurance that the financial statements do not have material misstatements, whether as a result of fraud or error.[121] The entity being audited is under an obligation to ensure that the Auditor-General has access to relevant documents at all times.[122] The Auditor-General has a discretion to disclose information received in the course of carrying out an audit where this is appropriate for the discharge of the Auditor-General's functions, duties or powers.[123] The Auditor-General is not subject to the *Official Information Act*.

The audit opinion is published along with the entity's financial statements. In forming the opinion the Auditor-General assesses the information presented in the

---

[108] *Public Finance Act* 1989, s.32A.
[109] *Public Audit Act* 2001, s.14(1).
[110] *Public Finance Act* 1989, s.29B.
[111] *Public Audit Act* 2001, Sch.1.
[112] *Ibid.*, Sch.2.
[113] *Public Finance* Act 1989, s.45F(1); 2001, Vol.596, p.12580; 1999-2002, I.22B, pp.1232-4.
[114] *Public Audit* Act 2001, s.38(1); 2001, Vol.596, p.12581; 2005, Vol.622, pp.17664-5.
[115] *State-Owned Enterprises Act* 1986, s.19(2).
[116] *Public Audit Act* 2001, s.23; "The Auditor-General's

auditing standards", Report of the Controller and Auditor-General, 3 May 2003.
[117] 2005, PP, B29[05a], p.19 (Controller and Auditor-General).
[118] *Public Audit Act* 2001, s.32.
[119] *Ibid.*, s.9.
[120] *Ibid.*, ss.25, 26 and 27.
[121] 2002, PP, B29[05a], p.19 (Controller and Auditor-General).
[122] *Public Audit Act* 2001, s.24.
[123] *Ibid.*, s.30.

financial statements and evaluates the overall adequacy of the information presented.[124] The opinion may be qualified due to a disagreement between the auditor and the reporting entity over the appropriate accounting treatment of a matter in the statements or due to a lack of information available to the auditor. In order to be able to issue an unqualified audit opinion, the Auditor-General has accepted letters of support from Ministers giving assurances regarding commitments of funds to Crown entities.[125] But not every failure to comply with accounting practice will lead to a qualified audit. Only if the failure leads to a material misstatement in the accounts will this be necessary.[126]

The Auditor-General may also (without qualifying the audit opinion) draw attention to any breach of the law that has been discovered or to any fundamental uncertainty about the outcome of a particular event material to the entity.[127]

The Auditor-General's audit opinion is issued in respect of each set of financial statements audited. In addition, the Auditor-General must report to the House at least once each year on matters arising out of the performance of the Auditor-General's functions, and may report also to the Government, select committees and other persons as the Auditor-General sees fit.[128]

Financial and service performance reporting

The Auditor-General's auditors also examine and report to the House on aspects of financial management and service performance management in the departments and entities which they audit. For financial management the aspects examined consist of the individual financial control systems operated, the financial management information systems employed to record, report and protect financial information, and the financial management control environment or "financial culture" which exists within the entity. Aspects of service performance management assessed, consist of the information and information systems for existing non-financial data and the planning processes, operational policies and quality assurance that the entity has in place.[129]

Performance audits

As well as auditing for probity and compliance with statutory obligations, the Auditor-General may carry out audits which seek to evaluate performance.[130] Such audits may examine whether the entity is operating effectively and efficiently, for example, by inquiring whether the outputs it produces are produced as efficiently as possible at the least cost to public funds and whether they are delivering their anticipated benefits. In this regard if an entity is required to adhere to an applicable policy, the audit examination is confined to establishing how effectively and efficiently the activities are being carried out consistently with that policy.[131] Thus the Auditor-General must accept the policy as a given in evaluating the entity's performance. But this constraint on performance audits applies to policies imposed on the entity by statute, by the Government or by a local authority. It does not apply where the policy is set by the entity itself being audited.

Performance audits may not be carried out into the Reserve Bank or any registered

---

[124] 2005, PP, B29[05a], p.20 (Controller and Auditor-General).

[125] 2001, PP, B.29 [01b], paras. 7.33-7.37 (Controller and Auditor-General).

[126] 2002-05, AJHR, I.21C, p.433 (failure to allocate funds properly not a material misstatement).

[127] 2003, PP, B.29[03a], paras.3.5 and 3.6 (Controller and Auditor-General).

[128] *Public Audit Act* 2001, ss.20 and 21.

[129] 2005, PP, B29[05a], pp.20-2 (Controller and Auditor-General).

[130] *Public Audit Act* 2001, s.16(1).

[131] *Ibid.*, s.16(4).

bank;[132] the Minister of Finance is empowered to initiate an assessment of the Reserve Bank's performance.[133] The Auditor-General is required to carry out a particular type of performance audit in respect of the Energy Commission (Electricity Commission), which must be the subject of an assurance audit on the appropriateness, adequacy, and accuracy of the information contained, or to be contained, in its annual report.[134]

Performance audit is an increasingly important aspect of public audit work and is seen as a means of promoting improvement in organisational performance. Consultation on the Auditor-General's annual plan may identify possible subjects for such audits, and briefings may be arranged for select committees on the audits that have been performed.

Finally, the Auditor-General is empowered to make any inquiry into how a public entity uses public resources even outside the annual audit of the entity.[135] This power is used for investigating high-profile allegations of impropriety or poor governance involving public entities or public money. Such inquiries are often initiated at the request of select committees or individual members of Parliament.[136] This type of work is not a feature of the mandate of Auditors-General in most other jurisdictions.

PUBLICATION OF REPORTS

The financial and operational reports prepared by the Government, departments, offices of Parliament, Crown entities, State enterprises and other organisations are submitted to the appropriate Minister who is responsible for presenting them to the House within the prescribed deadlines – within 15 working days after the audit report is provided by the Auditor-General for departments and offices of Parliament,[137] within five working days of receipt by the Minister in the case of Crown entities[138] and within 12 sitting days of receipt in the case of State enterprises.[139] Failure on the part of a reporting entity to prepare its report in accordance with the deadlines may attract parliamentary criticism, not least because the lack of a report to the House will hold up the House's work of financial review.[140] The Office of the Clerk, the Parliamentary Service, offices of Parliament and the Abortion Supervisory Committee submit their reports to the Speaker, who presents them to the House. Most, but not all (for example, State enterprises' reports), are published by order of the House as parliamentary papers. Individual reporting entities are responsible for publishing their reports and making them available to the public. Where, because Parliament has been dissolved or has expired, an annual report cannot be presented to the House within due time, the Minister must have the report published and have a note inserted in the *Gazette* advising the public where copies of it may be obtained.[141] Electronic publication is not, on its own, regarded as satisfying the statutory requirement to publish copies of the annual report.

In the case of financial statements of reserves boards, the Minister of Conservation forwards copies of the statements to each member of Parliament in respect of boards managed in that member's electoral district.[142] The annual report of the Department of Conservation must include information on the financial performance of reserves boards.[143] For financial statements of school boards of trustees, the Minister of Education forwards a

132 *Ibid.*, s.16(3).
133 *Reserve Bank of New Zealand Act* 1989, s.167; 1999-2002, AJHR, I.22A, pp.321-2.
134 *Electricity Act* 1992, s.172ZO.
135 *Public Audit Act* 2001, s.18.
136 See, for example: "Report of the Controller and Auditor-General on Certain Matters Arising from Allegations of Impropriety at Transend Worldwide Limited", December 2002; "Report of the Controller and Auditor-General on Inquiry into Public Funding of Organisations Associated with Donna Awatere

Huata MP", November 2003.
137 *Public Finance Act* 1989, s.44(1).
138 *Crown Entities Act* 2004, s.150(3).
139 *State-Owned Enterprises Act* 1986, s.17(4).
140 1991-93, AJHR, I.23B, pp.157-8; 1996-99, AJHR, I.21C, p.233; 1999-2002, AJHR, I.21A, p.177.
141 *Public Finance Act* 1989, s.44(2), (3); *Crown Entities Act* 2004, s.150(4); *State-Owned Enterprises Act* 1986, s.17(2A).
142 *Public Finance Act* 1989, s.45O(1), (2).
143 *Ibid.*, s.45O(4).

copy to each member in respect of any school situated in that member's electoral district.[144] The Minister of Education must also prepare an annual report on the performance of the schools' sector, which includes information on the supply of outputs by that sector.[145]

---

[144] *Education Act* 1989, s.87C(2).   [145] *Ibid.*, s.87B.

CHAPTER 36

FINANCIAL REVIEW

MONITORING AND CONTROL OF PUBLIC ENTITIES

Departments

The financial management reforms embodied in the *Public Finance Act* 1989 were designed in part to devolve much greater financial authority to departments and offices of Parliament. These now operate their own bank accounts and are responsible for making payments on their own authority rather than through offices of the Treasury. But departments still represent central government and they are subject to detailed requirements as to financial information and reports to be provided to the Treasury and, in particular, through Treasury instructions and other regulations, as to the accounting policies and practices that they must follow in their handling of public money.[1] The Treasury, the State Services Commission and the Department of Prime Minister and Cabinet as the central agencies take lead roles in co-ordinating and monitoring the policies and practices of departments under the political direction of the Cabinet. Departmental output plans can also provide a basis for an annual review of the performance of chief executives by the State Services Commissioner.

Non-departmental performance

Outside the departmental structure, the entities performing public functions are more heterogeneous. The internal governmental processes for monitoring their performance are consequently also more various. The decision on how to monitor such entities is essentially one for the Government to make.

Within the Treasury a particular unit, known as the Crown Company Monitoring and Advisory Unit (CCMAU), has been established to monitor the performance of State enterprises and a few of the more commercially oriented Crown entities. While the unit is operationally independent of the Treasury, it is responsible to the Secretary of the Treasury for its financial performance. CCMAU provides advice to the shareholding Ministers on the performance of the entities for which they have a responsibility and helps them to manage their relationships with the boards of those entities. Its annual report is included in the Treasury's annual report and its own performance is reviewed along with that of the Treasury's.[2]

Chief executives of government departments are not responsible for the outputs or financial performance of Crown entities or State enterprises, even where these organisations are funded wholly or partly through a vote administered by their departments.[3] However, through arrangements with Ministers who have responsibilities for Crown entities, State enterprises or other organisations, departments may be required to monitor the performance of these organisations and provide advice to their Ministers on them.

Thus, a department is likely to provide advice on appointments to Crown entities within the purview of votes administered by the department and to report regularly to Ministers on their funding and overall performance.[4] For example, one department with

---

[1]   *Public Finance Act* 1989, ss.79 to 81.
[2]   1999-2002, AJHR, I.20B, p.312.
[3]   *Public Finance Act* 1989, s.36.
[4]   1999-2002, AJHR, I.21A, p.177 (Vote Commerce).

nine Crown entities to monitor has established a special governance and monitoring unit for this purpose. The unit is responsible for ensuring that the department takes a consistent approach to its monitoring of Crown entities.[5] Departments that are discharging a monitoring role are expected to be proactive in this regard and to require regular reporting from the entity concerned. They should be aware of issues affecting the entities for which they have a responsibility and monitor their activities so as to enable their Ministers to carry out their responsibilities in an active and informed manner.[6] In conducting financial reviews on behalf of the House, committees are likely to probe how departments are monitoring the performance of Crown entities in their sector, notwithstanding the absence of legal responsibility.[7]

PARLIAMENTARY ACCOUNTABILITY

Parliamentary accountability for departments, offices of Parliament, Crown entities, State enterprises and other organisations can arise in a number of ways. The most obvious is through parliamentary questions, oral and written, that can be put to the responsible Minister. Even though there may be no legal responsibility for the actions of the entity concerned, a general political responsibility devolves on the responsible Minister to be the parliamentary mouthpiece through which the entity answers to the House. The performance of a department or other entity can also be the subject of debate on legislation relating to it, on the weekly general debate, in any urgent debate that the Speaker may accept, on the annual estimates, or occasionally on a special debate that may be held.[8] Select committees may receive petitions touching on their work and in any case have general power within their areas of subject competence to initiate inquiries into the performance and actions of all public-sector entities.

Although by these means the House and select committees can monitor the actions of public-sector entities and hold them accountable, a special accountability procedure known as financial review has been devised to be the parliamentary counterpart to the financial and operational reporting by these entities and to guarantee that some parliamentary attention is paid to them on an annual basis. The financial reviews that are conducted consist of select committee examinations of the entities (using, but not exclusively focused on, their reporting documentation) and of debates in the House. The procedures differ slightly between departments and offices of Parliament on the one hand, and Crown entities, State enterprises and other public organisations on the other.

GOVERNMENT'S FINANCIAL STATEMENTS

The Finance and Expenditure Committee is required to report to the House on the annual financial statements of the Government as at the end of the previous financial year.[9] These will have been presented to the House and thus become available to the committee about three months after the financial year ends. The committee must present its report within one week of the first day on which the House sits in the new year.[10] This first sitting is usually on a Tuesday in February.[11] Where a general election has supervened, preventing the committee doing its work in time, the House has extended the time for report.[12]

The Minister of Finance and the Secretary of the Treasury are the principal witnesses before the committee in its examination of the Government's financial statements. The committee's report forms one of the bases for the committee stage of the Appropriation (Financial Review) Bill.[13] There is nothing to prevent the committee reporting back to

---

5   *Ibid.*, I.20B, pp.173-4 (Department of Internal Affairs).
6   2002-05, AJHR, I.20A, p.223.
7   *Ibid.*, I.20C, pp.291-2.
8   For example, 1999, Vol.576, pp.15799-812 (report of the Ombudsmen).
9   S.O.336(1).
10 *Ibid.*
11 S.O.78(3).
12 1999, Vol.581, p.37 (extended to 6 April).
13 S.O.338(1)(a).

the House on the Government's financial statements before the Appropriation (Financial Review) Bill is introduced.

FINANCIAL REVIEW

The Finance and Expenditure Committee plays the leading role in co-ordinating the House's financial review process. The purpose of carrying out reviews is to determine whether the entity concerned has performed as promised – whether its actual performance, both in supplying services and in managing its balance sheet and other assets, is consistent with forecast performance.[14] It also involves considering how the entity is currently performing. Financial review involves a review by select committees of the annual reports and financial statements of departments, offices of Parliament, Crown entities, State enterprises and any other public organisation that the House resolves to make subject to the review procedures. For the forty-seventh Parliament the House resolved to extend these procedures to the Reserve Bank of New Zealand, the Abortion Supervisory Committee and Air New Zealand Limited.[15] (The Public Trust Office, which was previously declared to be a public organisation for this purpose, was dissolved on 1 March 2002.[16] Its successor, the Public Trust, is a Crown entity in its own right.[17]) The Education and Science Committee in 2001 decided to conduct staggered financial reviews of universities and other tertiary education institutions under its general inquiry powers.[18] This practice was continued by the committee in the succeeding Parliament.[19] The Standing Orders provisions for a debate on financial reviews do not apply to such education reviews.

Allocation of reviews

The Finance and Expenditure Committee is required, as soon after the commencement of the financial year as it thinks fit, to allocate to the subject select committees (or retain for itself) the task of conducting a financial review of the performance in the previous year and of the current operations of each individual department, office of Parliament, Crown entity, State enterprise or public organisation.[20]

For departments and offices of Parliament the Finance and Expenditure Committee may make this allocation at the same time as it allocates estimates for examination, though it may be unable to do this when an election is pending and it is clear that the responsibility for conducting the financial reviews will fall to the select committees to be set up in the new Parliament. Generally, there is some correspondence between the examination of estimates for which a department is responsible and the financial review of that department, but this does not have to follow. Nor will it always be possible, since estimates are allocated on the basis of votes rather than departments. As with estimates, other committees may express a view as to whether individual departments or entities should be referred to them for review.[21] But the matter is ultimately for the Finance and Expenditure Committee to determine.

In respect of reviews relating to the 2003/04 year the Finance and Expenditure Committee retained nine organisations for review itself and allocated 125 organisations to the other committees for review.

Preliminary information gathering

The financial review formally begins when the annual report of the department or entity

---

14   1996, Vol.553, p.11530.

15   1999, Vol.581, p.37; 2002-05, AJHR, I.19B, p.236; 2003, Vol.614, pp.10330-6.

16   *Public Trust Act* 2001, s.151(1); *Public Trust Act Commencement Order* 2002.

17   *Public Trust Act* 2001, s.13.

18   1999-2002, AJHR, I.2A.

19   2002-05, AJHR, I.22C, pp.107-12.

20   S.O.335(1).

21   1996-99, AJHR, I.21A, p.12 (Abortion Supervisory Committee).

is presented.[22] The annual report, statement of intent and output plan of the department or entity concerned are the basic materials on which each committee's work proceeds (though a financial review has proceeded even though the annual report had not yet been presented to the House).[23]

Formerly, these reporting documents were supplemented for departments by a standard financial review questionnaire developed by the Finance and Expenditure Committee and consistently used by the other committees. However, the standard questionnaire was discontinued in 1997 on the understanding that departments would provide the information previously sought in the questionnaire (key result areas, measurable milestones, expenditure variances, etc.) through their annual reports.[24] Nevertheless, each committee may develop its own questionnaire to issue to an entity that is to undergo review.[25]

Although a standard questionnaire is now rarely issued, committees often ask the entity concerned to provide further information on its operations, either before an oral examination by the committee commences or after it has concluded. Committees have criticised entities for failing to respond to such questions and for the poor quality of the responses received.[26] Only questions forwarded to the department or entity with the committee's authority are formally part of the review. Questions sent to the entity by members without being submitted first to the committee are not part of the review, they are merely individual information requests.

Following the gathering of such preliminary information, including the answers to questions that the committee requires, and before any oral examination of the entity, the committee receives a briefing from the Auditor-General's office on the entity's financial performance. The Auditor-General provides a written brief on each entity unless directed otherwise by the committee concerned. The audit officials may also remain present throughout the hearing of evidence to assist the committee at any point. Other advisers may also be appointed.[27]

Examination

It is entirely over to committees how they conduct the reviews that are entrusted to them. Because of the large number of reviews recurring each year (approximately 150 entities to be dealt with by the 13 subject select committees), it is not possible to conduct in-depth reviews of each one, each year. Indeed, financial review is not necessarily the place for an in-depth examination of any entity, since it operates within strict time-frames and is focused on recent performance. But issues identified in the course of carrying out a financial review may give rise to concerns that can be addressed by the committee utilising its inquiry powers to follow them up. Financial review is not intended to replace the committee's inquiry powers as far as public-sector scrutiny is concerned, though work previously performed through the inquiry function may be absorbed into it.[28]

Consequently, many financial reviews are completed on the basic documentation and the audit briefing without the need for an oral examination or a follow-up by written questioning. Where an oral examination is held, it is, as far as departments are concerned, focused on the chief executive and senior officials. Unlike the estimates, for which a Minister is responsible, the chief executive of a department is primarily responsible for answering to the committee for the performance of the department in fulfilling its objectives. Even in respect of reviews of non-departmental entities the focus is on the performance

---

[22] S.O.335(2).
[23] 2002-05, AJHR, I.21A, p.60.
[24] *Ibid.*, I.3C, p.4.
[25] *Ibid.*, I.21A, p.365.
[26] 1999-2002, AJHR, I.21B, pp.81 and 462.

[27] See, for example, 2004, PP, C.12, p.40 (Parliamentary Commissioner for the Environment acted as adviser for review of two departments).
[28] 1991-93, AJHR, I.18A, para.18.

of the entity, and the responsibility for this lies with the board and the management of the entity. However, a Minister has attended the select committee examination when critical questions of governance of the entity and the respective roles of the Minister and the board were in issue.[29] Exceptionally, committees may hear from other witnesses, as when justice-sector organisations were invited to make submissions on the financial review of the Ministry of Justice.[30] Normally, the time constraints under which committees conduct financial reviews preclude this, but any follow-up inquiry will inevitably open up the opportunity for other groups to give their perspectives. A committee may also combine a financial review with any other related business (such as a petition)[31] that may be before it.

As financial review is generally concerned with entities that are in the public sector rather than with companies listed on the stock exchange, usually no issues in regard to the insider-trading legislation arise. (Questions of commercial confidentiality do sometimes arise.) However, the financial review procedure can exceptionally be extended to a public organisation that is also a listed company. In an instance where this occurred (with Air New Zealand Limited), the committee conducting the financial review organised its proceedings in a way that avoided any infringement of the insider-trading provisions.[32]

As a result of the examination the department or entity may be asked (or may itself ask) to respond in writing to questions put to it. If there is an expectation of response before the committee reports, the department or entity will face criticism if it fails to do so.[33] Indeed, the report may be delayed in consequence. Committees may also criticise the quality of responses that they feel are inadequate.[34]

REPORTS ON FINANCIAL REVIEWS

Time for report
Following the committee's consideration of the documentation, receipt of an audit briefing and oral examination of the chief executive (where this is held), it reports the results of the review to the House.

In the case of departments and offices of Parliament these reports must be made within one week of the first sitting day in each year.[35] This is likely to be in February. Consequently, committees have some four to five months from the presentation of the annual report to complete their work. But this period includes the Christmas/New Year break. Every three years it also includes the likely time at which a general election is held. Consequently, the House occasionally extends the time allowed for reporting.[36]

For reviews of Crown entities, State enterprises and those public organisations that have been made subject to review, committees have six months from the date the entity's annual report is presented to the House to conduct the review.[37] The financial year of Crown entities is in general 1 July to 30 June.[38] The financial year of State enterprises is not statutorily prescribed and depends upon the enterprise's rules. Nevertheless, most annual reports are presented in the second half of the year and it is at that point that the six-month reporting time-limit begins to run.

Where a committee fails to report in time, its obligation to report is not discharged

---

[29] 1996-99, AJHR, I.21C, p.366 (New Zealand Tourism Board).
[30] 1999-2002, AJHR, I.20B, p.180.
[31] 2002-05, AJHR, I.21B, p.11.
[32] *Ibid.*, I.21C, p.35.
[33] *Ibid.*, I.20C, p.113; *ibid.*, I.21C, p.462.
[34] *Ibid.*, I.20C, p.157.
[35] S.O.336(2).
[36] 1999, Vol.581, p.37 (to 6 April); 2001, Vol.597, p.14074 (to 22 February).
[37] S.O.336(3).
[38] *Crown Entities Act* 2004, s.136(1).

immediately. (This contrasts with a failure to report on a bill in time, where the bill is automatically discharged from the committee.[39]) The obligation to report still remains. However, a committee cannot remain indefinitely in breach of an obligation to report. The House may therefore regularise the position by granting an extension of time.[40] In the absence of this happening the Speaker determines when the committee must report. Its failure then to do so in time means that its task is at an end. The Speaker has ordered a committee that had failed to report in time on its review of a Crown entity to present its report by the end of the current week.[41]

Nature of the report

Committees make a mix of narrative and formal reports on the results of their financial reviews. Where they do not feel it necessary to prepare a detailed narrative report, they present *pro forma* reports merely recording the fact that they have carried out a financial review of the department and that they have nothing to draw to the attention of the House. Usually these are cases where no oral examination was held. This does not mean that the process was not of value. Constant monitoring of the activities of departments was one of the main aims of the new select committee structure introduced in 1985. Financial review ensures that at least an annual interchange between a committee and the departments it is to monitor occurs, superficial as this may be in any particular case. If there are no apparent matters of concern to report, committees have pragmatically decided that they do not need to write a lengthy report each time to explain this. On the other hand, the financial review may reveal matters of concern that the committee considers need to be followed up in other ways, such as by the committee using its inquiry powers or by requesting the Auditor-General to investigate.[42]

Other reports on financial reviews may contain a range of information and comments gleaned by the committee while carrying out its work, together with recommendations for future action. Some of the issues raised as a result of the review have been of general significance. Thus, committees have discussed the relationship between the outputs produced by the department or non-departmental entity and the Government's desired outcomes. The entity's performance in delivering its outputs is discussed in the statement of service performance that is contained in its financial statements, but committees have often found it difficult to discern from these whether or not the Government's outcomes have been advanced. They have also complained of the difficulty of judging the effectiveness of outputs without information on their contributions to outcomes. Departments have therefore been asked to investigate ways of measuring this contribution in order to provide an indication of their effectiveness and have drawn praise where they have made progress in doing this.[43] The introduction of output plans with explicit links between outputs and outcomes was a direct response to this criticism.

Failure to make any statutory report in a timely fashion will inevitably be commented on, as will non-compliance with other reporting requirements, such as the need to report on equal employment opportunity initiatives[44] and to give reasons for any unappropriated expenditure that has been incurred.[45] The form of the annual report in its discretionary contents will also be commented on, such as a failure to give a breakdown of expenses or a clear explanation of how funds have been expended,[46] or a lack of detail about an

[39] S.O.291(3).
[40] See, for example, 2004, Vol.616, p.11907 (committee granted an extension to report on an entity).
[41] 1999, Vol.577, p.16437.
[42] See, for example, "New Zealand Trade and Enterprise: Administration of the Visiting Investor Programme", Report of the Controller and Auditor-General, December 2004 (initiated on the request of the Commerce Committee).
[43] 1999-2002, AJHR, I.20B, p.40.
[44] 1991-93, AJHR, I.23A, p.54.
[45] *Ibid.*, I.23B, p.196.
[46] 1999-2002, AJHR, I.21C, pp.347-8.

agency's business streams.[47]   The omission of a narrative from a department's report (though it technically met the State Service Commission's reporting guidelines) was criticised by a committee as diminishing the report's usefulness, and its reinstatement was recommended.[48]   Errors of fact in the annual report are likely to be the subject of comment.

Any illegality revealed in the materials before it will be focused on by the committee. Thus, a department that wrote off a debt without ministerial approval and so was in breach of the law was criticised in the committee's report on the financial review of that department.[49]

Where a committee has subsequently detected an error in a financial review report that it had made, it has presented a special report to correct this.[50]

APPROPRIATION (FINANCIAL REVIEW) BILL

The House's vehicle for considering the results of the investigations into the financial performance of the Government and Government departments that are conducted by the Finance and Expenditure Committee and the other select committees is the passing of the annual Appropriation (Financial Review) Bill.

The Appropriation (Financial Review) Bill is a Government bill containing provisions dealing exclusively with the sanction, confirmation or validation of expenditure incurred in the previous financial year.[51]   These comprise financial matters that occurred in the previous year and that are required by law to be included in an Appropriation Bill in the succeeding year: the confirming of transfers between classes of outputs that have been made by Orders in Council;[52] the confirming of excess expenses or capital expenditure approved by the Minister of Finance;[53] and the confirming of emergency expenses and capital expenditure approved by the Minister of Finance.[54]   The bill may also contain provisions validating illegal expenses or capital expenditure incurred in the previous financial year.[55]

Introduction, first reading and second reading

The Appropriation (Financial Review) Bill must be introduced before the end of March.[56] It is, in fact, usually introduced before the Christmas adjournment. There is no amendment or debate on the bill's first reading.[57]

As with any Appropriation Bill, the bill is not referred to a select committee after its first reading.[58]   It is set down as a Government order of the day for a formal second reading. There is no amendment or debate on the second reading of the bill.[59]

Financial review debate

The committee stage of the bill is the financial review debate. This is the House's opportunity to debate the Government's financial position as reflected in the Finance and Expenditure Committee's report on the Government's financial statements and to debate the previous year's performance and current operations of departments and offices of Parliament.[60]

The financial review debate must be held by 31 March,[61] by which time the select

---

[47]   2002-05, AJHR, I.21A, p.361.
[48]   1991-93, AJHR, I.23B, pp.134-5.
[49]   *Ibid.*, I.23A, p.191.
[50]   1999-2002, AJHR, I.21A, p.486; 2002-05, AJHR, I.22D, p.407.
[51]   S.O.337(1).
[52]   *Public Finance Act* 1989, s.26A.
[53]   *Ibid.*, s.26B.
[54]   *Ibid.*, s.25.

[55]   See, for example: *Appropriation (Financial Review) Act* 1993, s.3; *Appropriation (1997/98 Financial Review) Act* 1999, s.7.
[56]   S.O.338(5).
[57]   S.O.337(2).
[58]   S.O.285(2).
[59]   S.O.337(2).
[60]   S.O.338(1).
[61]   S.O.338(5).

committees' reports on their financial reviews of departments and offices of Parliament will all have been presented. Where committees have been given a substantial extension of their reporting time on financial reviews, the House has also extended the time within which the financial review debate may be held.[62]

The Government is entitled to select any day (other than a Members' Wednesday) for the financial review debate,[63] and to decide which financial reviews are available for debate on that day and how long is to be spent on the debate that day.[64] This information must be included on the order paper.[65]

Four hours in total is allowed for the financial review debate. The Minister responsible for the department or office of Parliament may make multiple speeches of five minutes each but not normally more than two speeches consecutively. Other members may make two speeches of five minutes each on each financial review.[66] In practice, the Business Committee[67] or the whips are likely to work out a suitable allocation of time among the parties from the overall time available for the debate and the order in which particular financial reviews will be considered.

At the commencement of the financial review debate (subject to any determination by the Business Committee or leave of the committee to the contrary), the committee considers the report of the Finance and Expenditure Committee on the annual financial statements of the Government.[68] It then turns to consider the financial reviews nominated by the Government for consideration that day.[69]

When the four hours for the debate have elapsed, the provisions of the bill and any amendments from the Minister in charge of the bill that are notified on a supplementary order paper are put as one question without debate.[70] No other amendments to the bill are permitted.[71]

Passing of the bill

When the report of the committee on the bill has been adopted, the bill is set down for third reading forthwith.[72] There is no amendment or debate on the question for the third reading.[73]

DEBATE ON CROWN ENTITIES, STATE ENTERPRISES AND PUBLIC ORGANISATIONS

The reports of committees on their financial reviews of Crown entities, State enterprises and public organisations are not debatable when presented to the House. But a debate of three hours during the course of each financial year is provided for the House to consider the performance and current operations of Crown entities, State enterprises and other public organisations.

The Government selects the day for such a debate to be held (it may extend over more than one day).[74]

The day selected may not be a Wednesday on which Members' orders of the day take precedence.[75] The Government also decides which financial reviews are available for debate and how long in total (up the maximum time for the debate) is to be spent on it that day. This information is advised on the order paper.[76] The Business Committee

---

62 2000, Vol.582, p.948 (extended to 2 May).
63 S.O.341(1).
64 S.O.341(2).
65 *Ibid.*
66 Appendix A to the Standing Orders.
67 S.O.341(3).
68 S.O.338(2).
69 S.O.338(3).
70 S.O.338(4).
71 *Ibid.*
72 S.O.339(1).
73 S.O.339(2).
74 S.O.341(1).
75 *Ibid.*
76 S.O.341(2).

may determine the order in which financial reviews are to be considered and how long is to be spent on each.[77]

The debate is usually held in the period April to June as financial review reports will have been presented by then. However, as reporting is a continuous process there will always be some entities' reports outstanding regardless of which date is chosen for the debate.[78] Leave has been given to debate an entity's performance even though the report relating to it had not yet been presented.[79]

On the day selected the debate is set down as a Government order of the day for consideration in committee of the performance in the previous year and the current operations of Crown entities, public organisations and State enterprises.[80] A Minister is nominated by the Government to take charge of the order of the day. The Speaker has an obligation to ensure that the Government provides time within Government orders of the day for such a debate and, if necessary, will interrupt other business on the final sitting day in the financial year.[81]

The debate does not have to be the first order of the day on the day it is held. When the order of the day for the debate is reached, the House resolves itself into committee to consider the financial reviews available for consideration.[82] Each member may speak on each review twice for five minutes each time. The Minister responsible for an entity has multiple five-minute speeches but not normally more than two consecutive speeches. The overall length of the debate is limited to three hours.[83]

A question is proposed on each financial review as it is raised, that the select committee's report on it be noted.[84] The debate covers both performance in the previous financial year and the entity's current operations. The history of the entity before the period covered by its annual report is outside the scope of the debate.[85] The annual report of the entity, its statement of intent and other documents presented in respect of the current and previous years can be referred to and used in the debate.[86] The responsibilities of the shareholding Minister for a State enterprise are within the scope of the debate and members can attack the Minister in that capacity, but not other aspects of the Minister's performance.[87]

---

[77]   S.O.341(3).
[78]   2004, Vol.617, p.13236.
[79]   *Ibid.*
[80]   S.O.340(1).
[81]   1995, Vol.548, pp.7863-4.
[82]   S.O.340(2).

[83]   Appendix A to the Standing Orders.
[84]   S.O.340(3).
[85]   1992, Vol.525, p.8603.
[86]   1993, Vol.533, pp.13510-1.
[87]   *Ibid.*, pp.13522, 13655

CHAPTER 37

PETITIONS

PETITIONING PARLIAMENT

The earliest legislative acts of the English Parliament were often transacted by the Commons petitioning the King that a certain amendment be made to the law, but petitions as a source of legislation soon disappeared from the picture, apart from their continued employment in the field of private legislation. In New Zealand, the only vestige of the petition's former role as a legislative element is similarly in the field of private bills, which are initiated in the House by the presentation of a petition from the promoter of the bill. Petitions for private bills have special rules applying to their form and content that are different from the general rules governing petitions to the House. (See Chapter 26.) In 1993 Parliament passed legislation permitting the presentation of petitions seeking the holding of referendums.[1] These statutory petitions are the subject of their own special rules. (See Chapter 41.) These special forms of petitions are a small minority of the total number of petitions received by the House each year.

The vast majority of petitions addressed to the House relate to a wide variety of public policy issues and private grievances. From its first meeting in 1854, the House, continuing an ancient right exercised in England, has admitted petitions seeking redress for an almost unlimited number of real or supposed wrongs done to petitioners, advocating amendments to the law or changes in government policy, or seeking public inquiries into some unsatisfactory situation. By petitioning the House, the citizen is able to express his or her opinion on a subject of some concern and address it in a public fashion to the country's legislators. The act of petitioning may or may not have any practical consequences but it does ensure that the petitioner's concerns are heard and given some consideration by those in authority.

The number of petitions presented to the House increased throughout the nineteenth century to a peak in 1906. It declined consistently from then until the mid-1980s, at which points the number of petitions presented to the House rose significantly.

However, these trends in the number of petitions presented to the House disguise other changes that have taken place in the way in which citizens have used the petitions procedure. In earlier days, the overwhelming number of petitions emanated from single petitioners with their own private grievances. While petitions from individuals seeking relief for a personal injustice are still common, they no longer predominate. Petitions now tend to relate to public issues and are promoted to demonstrate the strength of public feeling on the issue in the country at large or in a local community.

A further development has occurred with respect to this latter category of petitions on general public issues. Rather than promoting one petition with a large number of signatures appended to it to demonstrate its degree of support, those responsible for organising petitions often encourage the submission of many separate petitions on the same subject with only a few signatures to each one. Thus, for instance, in 1989 two campaigns objecting to legislation then before the House attracted more than 600 and 1,100 petitions respectively in the same terms. Such a development means that it is misleading to draw conclusions about the interest shown in presenting petitions to the House merely by comparing the number of petitions presented over time.

---

[1] *Citizens Initiated Referenda Act* 1993.

A further recently identified reason for petitioning the House is to demonstrate to an international body that the petitioner has exhausted all of his or her domestic remedies before applying to that body. One select committee has noted that the promoters of a petition had little interest in the parliamentary outcome of their petition other than to prove to the United Nations committee on human rights that they had sought relief domestically before applying to it. The committee expressed concern at the right to petition the House being used in this way.[2]

So important is the right of the citizen to petition the House considered to be that where Parliament creates legal remedies it often makes it clear in the relevant legislation that these remedies are not intended to qualify the ability to petition the House or to restrict the jurisdiction of any committee set up to consider such a petition.[3] Conversely, a body set up outside the House to provide an avenue of redress may be expressly excluded from taking account of the citizen's right to petition the House in deciding whether to exercise its own powers in respect of the matter. Thus, the Police Complaints Authority cannot decide not to pursue a complaint on the ground that the complainant could petition the House.[4]

PROMOTION AND CIRCULATION OF PETITION

A petition is usually initiated by a concerned individual or group of individuals who, having drafted the wording of the petition, sign it themselves and circulate it among other members of the public inviting them to subscribe to it. A corporation may petition the House. So may an unincorporated association, provided the association is adequately identified as a collective entity. Petitions which do not adequately identify an entity, such as, for example, a petition from teachers at a certain school or employees from a certain workplace, are not acceptable. These latter would have to be in the name of an individual on behalf of the other persons involved.[5]

The rules on the form and content of a petition are set out below.[6] A standard form of petition sheet is available from the Office of the Clerk, but provided that a petition complies with the rules on form and content it will be accepted whether it is on such a sheet or not.

The circulation of a petition among the public for the purpose of gathering signatures to it prior to its presentation in the House is not a proceeding in Parliament and the absolute protection from legal liability attaching to parliamentary proceedings does not apply.[7] The delivery of the petition to a member for presentation to the House, its presentation, and its subsequent publication in the ordinary course of parliamentary proceedings are so protected.[8]

Publication of defamatory material in a petition, other than in the course of parliamentary proceedings (for example, by delivering it to a member for presentation to the House), is not protected by parliamentary privilege. Nevertheless, given the significance of the longstanding right to petition the House (with its numerous statutory acknowledgements), it may be that publication to a member and to the public for the purposes of gathering signatures would be accorded qualified legal privilege. If so, it

---

2   1996-99, AJHR, I.24, p.564 (*Report of the Justice and Law Reform Committee on the petition of Banks and Banks-Foster*).

3   See, for example: *Treaty of Waitangi Act* 1975, s.9; *Citizens Initiated Referenda Act* 1993, s.59.

4   *Police Complaints Authority Act* 1988, s.18(1)(b)(v). See also: *Privacy Act* 1993, s.71(1)(g); *Health and Disability Commissioner Act* 1994, s.37(1)(e).

5   1991, Vol.513, p.1001.

6   A booklet describing the rules, *Petitioning the House of Representatives*, is available from the Office of the Clerk.

7   *Eleventh Report of the (Australia) Senate Standing Committee of Privileges*, June 1988; *Report of the (Western Australia Legislative Council) Select Committee of Privilege concerning the Petition of Brian Easton*, December 1992.

8   *Lake v King* (1667) 1 Saund 131.

would be protected from liability for defamation if such publication was not predominantly actuated by ill-will or otherwise improper.[9]

No authenticated records are kept of the number of adherents to each petition because individual signatures to a petition are not checked for authenticity and duplication. However, probably the largest petition ever presented to the House was that presented on 24 September 1985 objecting to the passage of the *Homosexual Law Reform Bill*.[10] There were three similarly worded petitions presented that day, with the largest claiming more than half a million signatures. Other petitions that have attracted a great deal of attention include those in favour of women's suffrage presented in 1893 (this petition was close to 300 yards long),[11] a petition seeking prohibition of the sale of alcohol presented in 1918 and signed by about one-fifth of the total population at that time,[12] and a petition against the raising of the level of Lake Manapouri in 1970 that led to extensive select committee hearings.[13]

FORM OF PETITION

A petition must conform with a number of rules designed to ensure that the document which it is proposed to place before the House is in fact intended for presentation to the House, is authentic, and is generally in a fit state to be received by that body.

Petitions must be addressed to the House of Representatives (or to "Parliament").[14] This is self-evident. A written statement addressed to the world at large is not a petition to the House, nor is a document addressed to the Governor-General or to a Minister of the Crown. For a petition to be received by the House it must indicate in its heading that it is intended for the House.[15]

Petitions must be in writing. This means they may be handwritten, typed, photocopied or otherwise duplicated or printed. They may be constructed partly by one of these methods and partly by another.[16] A petition written partly in braille has been accepted.

Where the original wording of a petition is erased or amended a question immediately arises as to whether the persons signing the petition signed it on the basis of its original wording or the altered wording. If the alteration is not significant, this will not be a material consideration. However, if the alteration is significant, those signing before the alteration was made will have agreed to a different proposition and cannot automatically be regarded as agreeing with the petition in its altered form. Thus the circumstances in which any alteration to the wording of a petition came to be made needs to be noted and explained by the person or persons promoting the petition. Any signatories to a petition before it was altered in any material particular should be invited to re-sign the petition, otherwise their signatures must be disregarded.

Request for action

A petition is not a statement in the abstract. Its whole purpose is that it seeks some relief for wrongs suffered, some amendment to the law or some change in government policy. In short, a petition seeks action. Thus, it is fundamental that a petition must ask the House to take some action in respect of its subject-matter.[17] It may be that the petition consists

---

9   *Defamation Act* 1992, s.19.
10 1984-85, JHR, p.797.
11 1893, JHR, *Schedule of Petitions Presented*, p.xvii;
    Martin, *The House – New Zealand's House of
    Representatives 1854-2004*, p.113.
12 1918, JHR, *Schedule of Petitions Presented*, p.xix.
13 1970, JHR, *Schedule of Petitions Presented*, p.583.
14 S.O.352.
15 1907, Vol.140, p.385.
16 S.O.3(1).
17 S.O.352.

of no more than this request. This is sufficient. There are no rules requiring petitioners to set out at length the grounds on which relief is claimed, but they must claim relief of some description. The request is, therefore, an essential ingredient in a petition, for it is by the request that the petitioner tells the House what he or she wants it to do in response to the grievance. A petition without a request for action is irregular and will not be received.

Signatures

There must be one person, sometimes known as the principal or chief petitioner, who takes responsibility for attending to the formal requirements involved in petitioning the House. The name and address of the principal petitioner must be entered on the petition. It is the principal petitioner to whom communications about the petition may be addressed.[18]

The text of a petition may be so long that the petition itself cannot be confined to one sheet of paper with appropriate space for signatures. It may therefore run on to additional sheets.

The persons subscribing to a petition must sign personally, except in the case of incapacity by sickness. A person signing on behalf of an incapacitated person should state this fact alongside the signature.[19] Petitions from corporations are signed by a duly authorised officer of the corporation. If the corporation is incorporated outside New Zealand, an authorised attorney may sign.[20]

Other than the principal petitioner, persons subscribing to a petition do not need to add their addresses, though they often do.

Continuation pages of signatures sometimes give rise to problems of authentication. Signatures may be written upon the petition or pages annexed to the petition (though they may not be pasted upon such pages or otherwise transferred to them).[21] But any pages annexed to the petition must at least have the request inscribed on them in full. The fact that a page containing signatures is annexed to the petition at the time of its presentation to the House does not in itself indicate that it was so annexed at the time those signatures were collected. Unless the page is itself headed with the terms of the petition, or at least the request, there is no indication that those who signed on that page were subscribing the petition at all. Continuation pages of signatures on blank sheets of paper are therefore not acceptable. On the other hand, signatures on the reverse side of a page headed with the request will be accepted.

Language of petitions

Petitions must be in the English language or the Māori language.[22] The Speaker may order that petitions presented to the House be translated and printed in another language.[23] Although petitions must be in English or Māori, that does not prevent promoters including a version in another language with the petition that they present.

CONTENTS OF PETITION

Petitions are required to be couched in respectful and moderate language.[24] Just as members' speeches must be free of unparliamentary language, so must the words of petitioners who are seeking to play a part in the proceedings of the House.

Petitions must not contain irrelevant statements.[25] The grounds on which relief is claimed need not be set out in the petition. But many petitioners do set forth the grounds for relief, at varying lengths. There comes a point, if these grounds are set out too fully, at which the petitioner is in effect giving evidence on his or her own petition in the petition

---

[18]   S.O.354.
[19]   S.O.355.
[20]   S.O.357.
[21]   S.O.356.

[22]   S.O.353.
[23]   S.O.366.
[24]   S.O.358(1).
[25]   S.O.358(2).

itself. Evidence supporting the petition should be reserved for the select committee which hears the petition; it is irrelevant to go into the evidence in the petition. It is also irrelevant to refer in the petition to a matter for which relief is not being claimed in the request for action. The petition may only set out the grounds for the request. Reference to unconnected matters can invalidate the whole petition.

CERTAIN PETITIONS NOT ACCEPTED
Apart from the rules on the form that a petition must take, there are certain types of petition that the House will not accept.

House's jurisdiction
There is an almost infinite variety of subjects on which petitions are presented, requesting (as they must) the House to take some action to ameliorate a problem. The receipt of such petitions by the House depends upon its competence to take action on the matter of complaint. As Parliament's legislative competence within New Zealand is untrammelled, there is no problem with this requirement as far as petitions seeking action within New Zealand are concerned. Petitions with the motive of reversing government policy can be received, for it is always open to Parliament to legislate for such a change. However, where action is requested to be taken outside New Zealand, different considerations apply.

Where the action called for outside New Zealand is merely an expression of New Zealand's foreign policy, petitions may clearly be addressed to such a matter. On the other hand, a petition calling for changes to the domestic law of a foreign state would not seek relief on a matter within the competence of the New Zealand Parliament and it is doubtful whether such a petition could be received. There have been no New Zealand examples of the acceptability of petitions being considered on such grounds. In the United Kingdom, a select committee did report that a petition from the people of the state of Western Australia seeking legislation to enable that state to withdraw from the Commonwealth of Australia was not a proper petition to be received, for, having regard to the established constitutional conventions, such a matter was not one for the United Kingdom Parliament to interfere in, except at the request of the Australian Government.[26] Similar considerations would apply to New Zealand's relations with foreign states and with those states with which it has a constitutional relationship (Cook Islands, Niue and Tokelau).

Petitions may be received from persons outside New Zealand. Indeed the Standing Orders contemplate that a petition may be received from a foreign corporation.[27] At the time of the passage of the *Western Samoa (Citizenship) Bill* 1982, a petition against the bill was presented on behalf of persons resident in Western Samoa[28] and the question of its receivability was considered. Most of the petitioners were, in fact, New Zealand citizens. However, regardless of whether they were New Zealand citizens, the petition, it was concluded, was receivable in any case as it related to a matter (New Zealand citizenship) manifestly within the legislative competence of the New Zealand Parliament. This view was followed with a petition on the same subject some 20 years later seeking to reverse the legislation.[29] Provided the subject of the petition is within the legislative competence of the New Zealand Parliament, the nationality or place of residence of the petitioners is irrelevant.

---

[26] *May*, p.933.
[27] S.O.357.
[28] 1982, JHR, p.190.
[29] 2002-05, AJHR, I.5C.

Petitioners with legal remedies

A petition on a matter for which the petitioner has not exhausted legal remedies is not permitted.[30]

This rule is directed at persons who have specific statutory rights to appeal or seek a review of the particular matter which is the subject of their complaint. A refusal of a resource consent by a local authority or an assessment to tax by the Commissioner of Inland Revenue gives the aggrieved citizen a statutory route to follow in each instance to challenge the decision. This must be utilised before a petition to the House should be considered. Not until all such appeal or review rights have been exhausted can a petition be received on a subject. Most appeal or review rights have time limitations within which the appeal or review must be brought. The Standing Order barring petitions only applies where such rights are still alive. A potential litigant who sleeps on these rights and allows the time limit to expire without invoking them no longer has such rights and is therefore not debarred by the Standing Orders from petitioning the House. However, he or she will undoubtedly have weakened the case for relief by acting in such a way, for the House is likely to be unsympathetic towards a petitioner who failed to use the appeal or review procedures without good reason.

Almost all administrative decisions can now be challenged by an application for judicial review of the decision. This is a general procedure, not a right of review of a particular proceeding. Nor does it involve a rehearing of the matter on its merits. It is concerned with the legality, rather than the merits, of the decision – for example, whether correct procedures were followed or whether improper factors were taken into account in reaching the decision. The fact that a petitioner could possibly apply to the High Court under these procedures does not preclude a petition to the House.[31] Nor does the Standing Order requiring petitioners to have exhausted their legal remedies require a petitioner or other person to embark on litigation of a speculative nature, such as launching a civil action for damages or other relief, before a petition may be received. Only where Parliament has prescribed a specific avenue for addressing the petitioner's complaint in legislation is the rule on remedies engaged.

But if a legal remedy for the subject-matter of the petition does exist, the fact that the person possessing the right to invoke that remedy is not the petitioner is irrelevant. The petition will still not be in order. Thus a person with a legal remedy cannot have the matter raised in a petition by the expedient of someone petitioning the House on that person's behalf.

The opportunity to make a submission to a select committee on a bill is not a legal remedy at all (although it may be regarded as a political remedy). Consequently, it is possible to present a petition relating to a bill before the House even though the petitioner could have made a submission on the bill.[32]

Finally, Parliament in creating alternative legal remedies has occasionally expressly saved the right to petition the House.[33] In such a case the statutory remedy does not preclude a petition on that matter, even though it has not been pursued by a petitioner with the statutory right to do so.

Petitions on matters within the Ombudsmen's jurisdiction

Petitions from persons who have not sought the Ombudsmen's assistance where the subject-matter of the petition is within the competence of the Ombudsmen, are not in order.[34]

---

[30]   S.O.362(a).
[31]   1989, Vol.499, pp.11081-2.
[32]   1989, Vol.502, p.13500.
[33]   See, for example, *Treaty of Waitangi Act* 1975, s.9 (claims to the Waitangi Tribunal).
[34]   S.O.362(h)

This prohibition was introduced in 1967, five years after the office of Ombudsman was created. It was clear that that office would deal with many complaints similar to those coming before the House by way of petition. Indeed, the creation of an Ombudsman could be one factor in the continued decline in the number of petitions with a sole petitioner seeking redress of a private grievance. The intention of a formal rule requiring petitioners to try the Ombudsmen first if their petitions are of such a nature that they could be dealt with by that office is not to deny in all circumstances the citizen's right to petition the House but merely to require that the statutory machinery, which has been specially erected for the resolution of such problems, is tried first. Conversely, the right to petition the House is not a ground on which the Ombudsmen can refuse to investigate a complaint.[35]

Petitions on a matter already dealt with

It is not in order to re-petition the House on a subject that has already been dealt with by an earlier petition, unless substantial and material new evidence is available that was unavailable when the earlier petition was considered.[36] This rule applies only to earlier petitions presented during the term of the current Parliament. Matters dealt with in a previous Parliament can be revisited by way of petition.

A petition which has been finally considered by the House cannot be reopened in the absence of compelling evidence. Furthermore, that evidence must be new; it must not be evidence that was available when the petition was first heard but which the petitioner or the petitioner's advisers decided not to use. A claim that new evidence exists must be substantiated to the Speaker's satisfaction before a similar petition is allowed to proceed.

The rule preventing the presentation of a second petition on the same subject operates only where the first petition has been finally dealt with by the House. Thus, where a petition is withdrawn without a report on its merits having been made, a subsequent petition with the same subject-matter is not prohibited.

Petitions relating to judges

There are restrictions on petitions relating to judges.

A petition cannot contain a reflection on the conduct of a judge.[37] Such reflections would not be permitted in the course of debate and cannot be introduced into the House in the form of a petition. Where the House does have a role to play in the removal of a judge (in the case of High Court judges) the appropriate method of initiating such a procedure is by giving notice of motion, not by petition, and a petition calling for the removal of a High Court judge from that office or another office that the judge holds by reason of being a High Court judge is not in order.[38]

PRESENTATION OF PETITIONS

Members' responsibilities

Petitions are presented to the House by members. No member is under a legal duty to present a petition, even one from a constituent of the member.[39] Nor does the House oblige a member to present a petition.[40]

Members are enjoined to take care that a petition which they are asked to present

---

35   *Ombudsmen Act* 1975, s.17(1)(a).
36   S.O.362(c).
37   1912, Vol.161, p.401.
38   1957, Vol.313, pp.1818, 1863-4.
39   *Chaffers v Goldsmid* [1894] 1 QB 186.
40   1983, Vol.451, p.925; 1989, Vol.502, pp.13500-1.

complies with the Standing Orders.[41] Members cannot divest themselves of the initial responsibility of scrutinising petitions. If they feel any doubt as to the authenticity of signatures, for instance, they would be abusing the confidence reposed in them by the House were they to go ahead and present the petition.[42] But members are not required to check, and vouch for, the authenticity of every signature on a petition.[43] In practice, most members consult the Office of the Clerk for advice on whether the petition is in order.

It was formerly a rule that petitions were presented by the member for the electorate in which the petitioner or principal petitioner resided or had his or her headquarters.[44] But, given that only about half the House is composed of electorate members, this is no longer the case. Petitioners are able to ask any member to present a petition on their behalf. If a petition is sent directly to the Clerk, the Clerk approaches the local electorate member to present it.

The fact that a member presents a petition does not signify that the member agrees with it. A member may not present a petition from himself or herself and cannot present a petition to which he or she is a signatory.[45] The presenting member must certify that he or she is presenting it.[46] It was formerly a custom that the Speaker did not present a petition, but this custom related to a time when the member presented the petition physically in the House. As this is no longer the case, the Speaker presents petitions like any other member.

Scrutiny of petitions

Petitions are often forwarded directly by petitioners to the Office of the Clerk, both in draft before the petitioners commence to promote them and when they have been completed. Other petitions may be given to members at various stages of their promotion. These are forwarded by the members to the Office of the Clerk. All petitions received by the Clerk are perused for compliance with the Standing Orders relating to the form and type of petitions that may be received. If a petition does not fully comply with these rules it may be possible for the petitioner to correct any defect and an endeavour is made to find a way to do this. In the case of a petition from an individual or few persons this may mean the petitioner creating a new petition that complies with the rules. In the case of a defective petition with a substantial number of signatures attached to it, it may not be practicable for the petitioner to contact the signatories again and get them to sign a new petition. Often, in such a case, a new petition is created referring to the fact that that number of persons had signed a (defective) petition on the subject.

In these ways most of the potential irregularities relating to petitions can be dealt with before their formal delivery to the Clerk for presentation to the House.

Method of presentation

A petition is presented by being formally delivered to the Clerk by a member. This may be effected on any working day or no later than 1 pm on a sitting day.[47] If the House is sitting under urgency no petitions may be presented until it adjourns. But when the House does rise after sitting under urgency, petitions may be presented up to 1 pm on that day if the House sits again that day or during the remainder of the day otherwise.

Acceptance of petitions

Most questions relating to the acceptability of petitions are resolved as part of the

---

41 S.O.359(1).
42 1889, Vol.66, p.271.
43 1983, Vol.451, pp.924-5.
44 1991, Vol.516, p.2494.

45 S.O.359(2).
46 S.O.359(1).
47 S.O.360(1).

interactive process of scrutinising petitions that involves petitioners, members and the Office of the Clerk. Any petition which the Clerk considers to be irregular is not accepted for presentation to the House and is returned to the member concerned.

Ultimately, the Speaker is the judge of whether a petition is acceptable. A petition may be ruled out of order by the Speaker even after it has been formally presented to the House. Indeed the select committee which examines a petition may comment on its acceptability,[48] and invite the Speaker to reconsider whether it complies with the Standing Orders (but no select committee may itself refuse to accept a petition).

Announcement of presentation
A list of petitions presented since the House last sat and which appear to be in order is compiled and is read out to the House by the Clerk at the time for the announcement of the presentation of petitions (part of the first item of business each day).[49] For this purpose petitions with the same or similar requests are consolidated, with only the names of the principal petitioner of each petition and the subject-matter of the request being read out. A note confirming each petition's presentation with a précis of the request is recorded in the *Parliamentary Bulletin*.

REFERRAL TO A SELECT COMMITTEE
A petition which is in order and has been presented stands referred to a select committee immediately. For this purpose it is allocated by the Clerk to the most appropriate select committee for consideration and report.[50] From that point on the petition is in the possession of the committee.

The House no longer has a specialist select committee to consider petitions. Until 1962 the House had two such committees, one dealing with petitions prepared by petitioners whose surnames began with the letters A to L, and the other for petitions from petitioners with surnames beginning with the letters M to Z. From 1962 to 1985 there was one Petitions Committee, although petitions could be referred to other committees too. In practice this committee had about half of the petitions referred to it.

Special committees established solely to examine a petition are rare. The last occasion on which a special select committee was set up to consider a petition was for the Lake Manapouri petition in 1970. If a special select committee is to be set up to consider a petition, this must be done on motion in the House; it is beyond the powers of the Clerk. The Clerk may only refer petitions to committees which have already been established. Subject to this restraint all select committees may have petitions referred to them unless their terms of reference specifically preclude this.

The Clerk will allocate a petition to the committee whose terms of reference relate most closely to the issue raised by the petition, without regard to whether it is politically appropriate or expedient for that committee to consider it. Any related business (such as a bill) that a committee currently has before it is a valid factor to take into consideration in deciding which committee to refer a petition to. But it is not appropriate to anticipate or speculate on business that might be referred to a committee in the future in deciding which committee to refer a petition to.

Given the common recent practice of petitions being addressed in support of or opposition to legislation before the House, it is usual to refer such petitions to the committee which is considering the bill, so that they can be dealt with at the same

---

48 2002-05, AJHR, I.22B, p.771.
49 S.O.360(2).
50 S.O.361.

time as the committee considers the bill. The House has ordered that the Clerk must allocate a petition relating to the New Zealand Security Intelligence Service or the Government Communications Security Bureau to the statutory Intelligence and Security Committee.[51]

A committee cannot refuse jurisdiction on a petition that has been referred to it, but it can recommend to the House that a petition be re-referred to another committee that it considers to be more appropriate to examine the petition.[52] A petition can be transferred by a committee to another committee if that other committee agrees to accept it. A committee has refused to accept the transfer to it of a petition before another committee.[53]

CONSIDERATION BY SELECT COMMITTEE

Once a petition has been referred to a particular select committee it is delivered into the custody of the clerk of that committee.

Form of committee's inquiry

The committee is required to deal with the petition and report it back to the House, but the extent of the consideration to be given to it is entirely over to the committee. There are certain well-established steps which a committee follows when it commences its consideration of a petition. All government departments which are considered to have some official interest in the subject-matter of the petition are sent a copy of its request and are asked to make a submission on it for the benefit of the committee. A department approached in this way may take the view that it would be more appropriate for another department to respond to the committee.[54]

The petitioner or principal petitioner is also asked if he or she wishes to tender any written evidence in support of the petition or, if the petition already fully sets out the grounds itself, if there are any written comments the petitioner wishes to add. Informal deadlines are set for the receipt of these written submissions.

A time is fixed for the petition to be heard. The petition and associated material are circulated to the other members of the committee before the meeting. The petitioner and the department may be shown copies of each other's submissions (if any) prior to the hearing if the committee decides to follow this course. The petitioner or principal petitioner, the member who presented the petition and the government departments involved are formally advised of the date and time of the hearing, and each department involved is asked to nominate an officer to attend. With the majority of petitions the receipt of evidence is confined to these persons or bodies. In the normal course no attempt is made to seek submissions from a wider audience, although committees may accept submissions from other persons or organisations not directly concerned with the petition.

However, on occasions committees will go beyond this in gathering evidence on petitions. In 1970 the public was specifically invited to submit evidence to the select committee considering the petition opposing the raising of the level of Lake Manapouri.[55] A select committee which had before it several petitions against the closures of post offices combined them for the purposes of its consideration and conducted an inquiry into the effects of post office closures on rural localities, travelling to those localities to hear evidence.[56] Another committee considering a petition seeking restrictions on liquor advertising received 54 written submissions on it and heard oral evidence from 10 parties.[57] A committee has engaged a specialist adviser to assist it with its consideration

---

51   1996-99, JHR, pp.115-7; 2000, Vol.582, pp.1265-75,   54   1987-90, AJHR, I.4D, p.4.
     1378-84; 2002, Vol.604, pp 1897-8.   55   1970, Vol.370, pp.4930-1.
52   2002-05, AJHR, I.22C, pp.614-5.   56   1987-90, AJHR, I.2B and I.2C.
53   *Ibid.*   57   *Ibid.*, I.1A.

of a petition.[58] The general rules applying to select committees, such as those forbidding a committee from inquiring into a specific allegation of crime, apply to any select committee during consideration of a petition.[59]

The rural post offices inquiry was a case in which the receipt of a number of petitions on a particular subject sparked off a wider inquiry than is normal with petitions. Consideration of petitions by select committees can inform and affect the performance of committees in their other roles of carrying out inquiries and financial reviews and in considering estimates.

Committees have an express statutory power to refer a petition, or any matter to which a petition refers, to an Ombudsman for report.[60] In such a case, the Ombudsman is required to investigate the matter referred (so far as it is within the Ombudsmen's jurisdiction) and to report back to the committee. Committees have made sparing use of their powers under this provision. A committee may also request the Parliamentary Commissioner for the Environment to report to it on any petition before the committee which may have a significant effect on the environment.[61]

Procedure before the committee

At the hearing before the committee, the member who presented the petition often introduces the petitioner to the committee but does not usually play any other part in the hearing. Whether a member who has signed a petition takes part in the committee's consideration of it is a matter for that member to decide. The committee cannot exclude the member, but the member may voluntarily stand aside.[62] The committee receives oral evidence from the petitioner and (if necessary) the government departments concerned. This supplements such written evidence as may already have been supplied. As is the case with other witnesses before select committees, after an address from the petitioner (witness), members of the committee, in turn, question the petitioner on the matter before them. This happens similarly with any departmental witnesses who give evidence. A petitioner or principal petitioner may be accompanied by associates who also comment or answer questions at the invitation of the committee.

In the case of petitions relating to a bill before the committee, consideration of the petition is not differentiated from consideration of the bill. The petition is akin to evidence on the bill and is treated as such by the committee. Where a petitioner desires to make a personal appearance in such a case, a hearing is arranged in the same way as it would be for any other witness.

Following the hearing of evidence, the committee considers and deliberates on the petition. (In some cases a committee might invite a witness to remain to assist it during its consideration of the petition.) Whether the committee proceeds to deliberate immediately is entirely over to the committee itself. Where the issues are complex, deliberation may be postponed. Deliberation is the final stage in the committee's examination of the petition. It is then that the committee determines the terms in which it will report back to the House on the petition. At the conclusion of the committee's deliberations, a report is adopted for presentation to the House.

REPORT

There is no prescribed form to which a report on a petition must conform. It is a matter for the committee to determine. In fact, most reports on petitions are presented in a similar

---

58 2002-05, AJHR, I.22B, p.38.
59 *Ibid.*, I.22C, p.691.
60 *Ombudsmen Act* 1975, s.13(4).
61 *Environment Act* 1986, s.16(1)(d).
62 See: "Dalziel steps aside", *The New Zealand Herald*, 13 March 2004; 2002-05, AJHR, I.22D, p.644.

form to reports on any other inquiries that the committee concerned may carry out.

A committee may report on more than one petition in the same report. This may be done, however, only if the petitions being reported on are associated with each other – for instance, because they are identical or relate to the same issue.

It is the practice to make a single report on a bill and on any petitions relating to that bill that have been referred to the committee. Thus, in 1989, in respect of the *Radiocommunications Bill* and the *Contraception, Sterilisation, and Abortion Amendment Bill*, the reports on those bills also included the committees' reports on, respectively, 604 and 956 petitions relating to the bills.[63] In reference to the latter bill, about which petitions were still being received as it was reported back to the House, the Speaker warned members that further petitions would not be in order as the House had finally dealt with petitions on the bill in receiving the committee's report on the first 956 petitions lodged on it.[64] Committees may also deal with petitions, and report on them, along with other related business that is before them.[65] A select committee's judgment on a petition, applying political criteria to it, may be different from that of a court on the same subject, applying legal criteria to it.[66]

The report is presented in the same way as any other select committee report, by delivery to the Clerk on any working day but no later than 1 pm on a day on which the House sits.[67] Its presentation is announced to the House by the Clerk at its next sitting along with any other select committee reports presented that day.[68]

Reports on petitions are not set down for consideration by the House on any particular day and specific debates on them are rarely held. The Business Committee has power to direct that a report on a petition be set down for consideration as a Members' order of the day.[69]

LAPSE OF PETITIONS

There are always petitions which have been referred to select committees but which, because of lack of time, have not been considered and reported back to the House by the end of the parliamentary session. At the conclusion of a Parliament all business before the House or its committees lapses or dies.[70] But such business can be reinstated in the next Parliament.

Where a petition lapses, a second petition with the same subject-matter as the one which has lapsed can be presented to a future Parliament.

RESPONSES TO RECOMMENDATIONS

Following the presentation of a report on a petition from a select committee, the Clerk of the House advises the petitioner or the principal petitioner, if more than one, of the nature of the committee's report.

Until 1967 there was no further parliamentary action required. The committees' reports were (and still are) binding on no one, and no one was required to answer for whether they were to be actioned. In that year, however, a Standing Order was adopted requiring the Government to report to the House on what action, if any, it had taken to implement recommendations made to it on petitions. This requirement for a government response has now been absorbed into the general rule that the Government must, not

---

63   1987-90, JHR, pp.2058-72, 2094-107; 1987-90, AJHR, I.11, pp.6-26 and I.13, pp.6-29.

64   1989, Vol.503, pp.13870-1.

65   2002-05, AJHR, I.21B, p.11 (petitions reported along with the financial review of the Abortion Supervisory Committee).

66   Contrast, for example, 1991-93, AJHR, I.26A (*Report of the Transport Committee on the Petition of*

Federated Farmers of New Zealand Incorporated), with *Federated Farmers of New Zealand (Inc) v New Zealand Post Limited*, unreported, High Court, Wellington, 1 December 1992.

67   S.O.250(1).

68   S.O.250(3).

69   S.O.251(2).

70   *Constitution Act* 1986, s.20(1)(b).

more than 90 days after a select committee report, report to the House responding to recommendations in the report directed to it.[71] This also applies to reports on petitions.

Whenever a select committee presents a report on a petition which includes recommendations addressed to the Government, the Office of the Clerk of the House sends a copy of the report to the Cabinet Office. The Cabinet Office then co-ordinates a consideration of the committee's report within the Government. This involves the appropriate Minister preparing a response to the recommendations for endorsement by the appropriate Cabinet committee and then by Cabinet.

Once a response has been agreed upon, the relevant Minister communicates it directly to the petitioner and presents it to the House.[72] Such responses are published as parliamentary papers in the *Appendices to the Journals of the House*. While only the Government is obliged to respond to recommendations in a committee's report on a petition, a local authority which took actions following a report on a petition invited the committee to review the actions it had taken. The committee accepted the invitation and used its power to initiate an inquiry to do so.[73]

In exceptional cases, a favourable recommendation from a committee on a petition can be the catalyst for the Government to agree to law changes or the paying of compensation to the petitioner.[74]

RECORDS OF PETITIONS

Petitions are held in the custody of the Clerk once they have been reported back to the House by the select committee to which they were referred. As House records they are subject to the same custody regime as any other records. (See Chapter 5.) However, petitions often contain the names and addresses of individuals. Accordingly, general access to such personal information attached to a petition is not accorded even after a petition has been reported to the House.[75]

---

[71]   S.O.253(1).
[72]   *Cabinet Manual*, 2001, paras.5.75-5.78.
[73]   1999-2002, AJHR, I.22B, pp.1106-21.
[74]   See, for example, "Former soldier to get compensation", *The Dominion*, 22 February 1997

($20,000 compensation paid following a committee's recommendation).
[75]   "Access to petitions", Clerk's Office policy; approved by the Speaker, 15 June 1988.

CHAPTER 38

PAPERS

In the Chamber of the House, in front of the Speaker's chair, there is a large Table at which the Clerk of the House sits when the Speaker is in the chair and from which the chairperson presides when the House resolves itself into a committee of the whole House. The numerous documents presented to the House during the course of each session by Ministers and the Speaker on behalf of government departments, public agencies and other organisations are physically laid on this Table (in a receptacle that was a gift from the Legislative Assembly of Western Samoa in 1955). They remain there until the end of the year. The documents that have been presented to the House are available for inspection by members, but the importance of presenting a document is figurative rather than physical. It is what the process of presenting a document to the House leads to, through its publication and wider circulation and through action by the House itself in relation to it, that is important. (Some statutes speak of documents being "laid" before the House, rather than "presented" to it. In modern parliamentary practice there is no difference between laying a document before the House and presenting it to the House.[1] The current preference is generally to refer to "presenting" a document to the House. A more colloquial term, with the same meaning, is "tabling" it.)

The House's collective term for the various documents presented to it is "papers". These consist of the annual reports of government departments, and the annual reports and financial statements of many other organisations created by Act of Parliament. They also include regulations made by the Governor-General or any Minister of the Crown under the authority of an Act of Parliament; indeed, this latter category comprises the largest single category of papers presented to the House. Finally, papers include miscellaneous letters, typescripts and photocopies of documents presented by members with the House's permission during the course of debates or other proceedings in the House.

REQUIREMENTS TO PRESENT PAPERS

Statute

The requirement to present a paper to the House most commonly arises because there is a statutory obligation to do so.

All statutory regulations must be presented to the House not more than 16 sitting days after the day on which they are made.[2] The annual reports of all departments must be presented to the House,[3] as must the annual reports of all State enterprises[4] and most Crown entities.[5] In addition, other organisations falling outside these general categories, such as the offices of Parliament, are required, under legislation applying particularly to them, to present an annual report to the House.

But the statutory requirements to present papers are not by any means confined to annual reports. There are many other types of document that statutes require to be laid before the House. These include ministerial directions and notices,[6] statements of intent[7]

---

[1] *R v Immigration Appeal Tribunal, ex parte Joyles* [1972] 3 All ER 213.

[2] *Regulations (Disallowance) Act* 1989, s.4.

[3] *Public Finance Act* 1989, s.44(1).

[4] *State-Owned Enterprises Act* 1986, s.17(2)(b).

[5] *Crown Entities Act*, s.150.

[6] For example, *Social Security Act* 1964, s.5.

[7] *Public Finance Act* 1989, s.39(1) (departments); *Crown Entities Act* 2004, s.149(1) (Crown entities); *State-Owned Enterprises Act* 1986, s.17(2)(a) (State enterprises).

and the Government's annual financial statements.[8] During the course of each year, Ministers present well over 1,000 papers to the House. Some 450 of these are regulations; the remainder are annual reports and miscellaneous notices and statements that statutes require to be presented.

In most instances of departmental and other annual reports that are required by statute to be presented to the House, the statute requires the report to be made in the first instance to the responsible Minister. Often the statute imposes a time limit for the submission of the report to the Minister. It may be expressly provided that the same Minister to whom the report is made must present it to the House, but usually it is merely understood that the Minister to whom the report is made will be the Minister who will present it to the House. In any event, one Minister may act for another in the exercise of statutory powers.[9]

The statute may also require presentation to be made to the House as soon as practicable or within a specified time after the Minister's receipt of the report.[10]

There are a few statutory officers or bodies with a close parliamentary connection who, in terms of the statutes governing them, report directly to the House without the mediation of a Minister. These reports are presented by the Speaker. The reports falling into this category are those of the Office of the Clerk, the Parliamentary Service Commission, the Parliamentary Service, the Ombudsmen, the Controller and Auditor-General, the Parliamentary Commissioner for the Environment and the Abortion Supervisory Committee.

Command

The Governor-General may command any Minister to present a report to the House. Before the statutory obligation to present an annual report was extended to all departments, it was traditional for some departments to be commanded to present an annual report. The only examples of reports presented by command of the Governor-General now are the reports of Royal Commissions or commissions of inquiry that are made from time to time.

Orders for returns

The House may order a paper (of a public or official nature[11]) that is in the possession of another person to be produced to it. Disobedience of such an order could be treated as contempt of the House. A paper produced in response to an order is known as a return. A number of returns were ordered by the House up to 1961, but since then the practice has fallen into disuse as information formerly obtained from the Government in the form of a return can be more conveniently elicited by way of a question in the House, from the departmental and other reports presented by Ministers or by way of an official information request. The House's power to order certain returns may be delegated to a select committee as the power to send for persons, papers and records.

Notice must be given of a motion for a return. Such a notice is set down as a Government or Members' order of the day depending upon whether it was given by a Minister or a non-Minister. Where the document that the House desires to have produced is in the hands of the Governor-General, its production is sought by means of an address.

---

[8] *Public Finance Act* 1989, s.31(2).
[9] *Constitution Act* 1986, s.7.
[10] For example, *Public Finance Act* 1989, s.44(1)(a) (departmental annual reports must be presented

within 15 working days).
[11] *Egan v Willis* (1996) 40 NSWLR 650 at 663 (per Gleeson CJ).

Other orders requiring presentation

The Standing Orders in one instance require the Government to present reports to the House rather than to present a document that already exists. The Government must, within 90 days of a select committee report being made to the House, present a paper responding to any recommendations contained in the report that are directed to it.[12] (In another instance, the Standing Orders acknowledge that the Government will present certain types of international treaties to the House.[13])

VOLUNTARILY PRESENTING PAPERS

During the course of a sitting any member, including a Minister, may seek leave to table a document.[14] This is done by raising a point of order. Members (except for the Speaker) do not have a right to table a document during a sitting of the House; they always require the leave of the House, and it is entirely up to members as to whether they object and thereby deny permission for a document to be tabled.[15]

The Speaker has reminded members that seeking leave to table a document is not an occasion for making a point; it is an opportunity to produce for the House a document (such as a letter) that other members may not have seen. Therefore, members should avoid seeking leave to table a document readily available from other sources, such as a newspaper extract.[16]

A member wishing to table a document must seek leave for himself or herself. A member cannot seek leave for another member to table a document.[17] In seeking leave a member must identify succinctly the document that it is desired to table. This must be done briefly, but accurately, so that members know precisely what they are being asked to agree to.[18] Subject to control of the length of the point of order by the Speaker, members are entitled to seek clarification of the leave that they are being asked to give and this can include obtaining assurances about the document's contents.[19] A member giving such an assurance must be careful to do so accurately, otherwise an implication that the member intended to mislead the House may arise.

If leave is given, this is a permission given to the member who sought leave to table the document concerned. It is not a direction from the House and the member is under no obligation to utilise the leave by tabling the document; it is entirely up to the member concerned whether he or she does table it.[20] Usually, the member concerned has the document in his or her possession in the House and immediately brings or sends it to the Clerk at the Table. Tabling is effected at the time of delivery to the Clerk. But the member, having been given leave, can table the document by delivering it to the Clerk at any time up to the adjournment of the House that day.[21] Leave to table endures during the remainder of the sitting during which it was given.

In tabling a document a member must be careful to deliver to the Clerk only the document in respect of which leave was granted. The Clerk will refuse to accept a document that is apparently outside the terms of the leave. If a member deliberately attempts to table a document that is different from the leave granted, a contempt would be committed.[22]

Leave is often sought to table a document during question time when a member is not satisfied that a Minister's reply conforms to information that the member possesses. Members may also seek leave to table documents at the end of a speech they have given, or following a personal explanation, to emphasise a point they have made or to verify

[12]   S.O.253(1).
[13]   S.O.387.
[14]   1982, Vol.443, p.328.
[15]   1978, Vol.417, p.811; 1992, Vol.531, p.12297.
[16]   1996, Vol.554, p.11689.
[17]   1990, Vol.506, p.1291; 1990, Vol.510, pp.3491-2.

[18]   1998, Vol.573, p.13062; 2003, Vol.608, p.5837.
[19]   1999, Vol.575, p.14854.
[20]   *Ibid.*; 2002, Vol.603, p.864.
[21]   1994, Vol.540, p.1568; 1997, Vol.558, p.673; 1999, Vol.575, p.14854; 2002, Vol.603, p.1187.
[22]   1999, Vol.575, p.14854.

facts they have stated. In all cases it is up to the House whether it grants leave for the document to be tabled, for one voice will prevent it.

Ministers generally present papers that they are statutorily bound to present, but they may also present other papers that they have no obligation to present, such as policy proposals set out in documents commonly referred to as white papers or green papers. Whether Ministers do present papers in respect of which there is no statutory obligation is a matter for them to decide. But it is expected that important documents will be presented as a matter of course.[23]

METHOD OF PRESENTATION

General
The Speaker or a Minister presents a paper to the House by delivering it to the Clerk on any working day or on a sitting day before 1 pm.[24] If the House is sitting under urgency, no papers may be presented until it adjourns. But when the House does rise after sitting under urgency, papers may be presented up to 1 pm on that day if the House sits again that day or during the remainder of the day otherwise.

A list of papers that Ministers desire to present in this way is forwarded to the Clerk from the Leader of the House's office each day. Supplies of printed copies of each paper for distribution to members are delivered to the Bills Office. The Clerk reads out the list of papers to the House at the time for the announcement of the presentation of papers, which is part of the House's first item of daily business.[25]

In the case of regulations, the Government arranges for bundles of regulations to be forwarded at intervals to the Clerk of the House for a record to be made of their presentation to the House.

Speaker
As well as presenting papers in the general way described above, the Speaker may and often does, present papers to the House.[26] Following the reading by the Clerk of the list of papers that are to be published by order of the House, the Speaker may announce to the House any paper or papers that the Speaker desires to present. It is in this way that the Speaker presents reports from the officers of Parliament.

Budget papers and estimates
Because of the special confidential nature of budget papers, the Minister, after delivering the Budget or introducing an Appropriation Bill, may present a paper relating to the Budget or the bill at that point in the sitting.[27]

Deemed presentation
In the case of a number of documents emanating from the Reserve Bank, statute provides that such papers "stand" referred to the House, thus effectively deeming them to have been presented without any further action.[28]

Official document quoted by a Minister
A Minister (or a Parliamentary Under-Secretary to the Minister whose measure is under

---

23   2000, Vol.587, p.5673.
24   S.O.363(1).
25   S.Os 364(1) and 63(1).
26   S.O.363(2).
27   S.O.367.

28   *Reserve Bank of New Zealand Act* 1990, ss.15(3) (policy statements), 53A(3) (performance of the bank and the Governor), 162E (final statement of intent) and 163(3) (annual report).

discussion[29]) who quotes from a document relating to public affairs must table that document if requested to do so by any member.[30]

When a member desires that the Minister who quotes from a public document should lay it on the Table, the proper time to require this is at the time the quotation is made. The member who requires the document to be tabled should thus raise a point of order immediately and not wait until the conclusion of the Minister's speech.[31] The Minister should comply with the requirement to table it as soon as it is made.[32]

If a Minister quotes from a copy of a document, it is the copy that is required to be presented to the House, not the original. Where a Minister has only an extract from an official document and quotes from that extract, it is the extract only that is required to be tabled. There can never be any question of a Minister having to go away and procure an original or a complete document for tabling; all that is required to be tabled is what the Minister physically possesses in the Chamber when the quotation is made.[33] When a Minister quotes from a page in an official document there is an obligation (if requested) to table that page, but there is no obligation to table the entire book or publication of which it is part.[34]

The document must be an official document: that is, a formal piece of writing connected with the government of the country, or which has passed between officers of the Government and Ministers, between one officer and another,[35] or between the Government and other persons.[36] It must emanate from within the Government. Thus, when a member of the public wrote a letter to a Minister about a bill before the House and the Minister quoted from that letter, the Minister was not obliged to table it as it was not an official document.[37] A Minister's personal note of discussions that have taken place is not an official document, for an official document must convey a message or memorandum from one person to another.[38] An official's note of such discussions that is passed on to the Minister would be an official document. If there is any doubt, the Speaker asks the Minister if the document that has been quoted from is an official document and accepts the Minister's reply.[39]

A Minister does not have to produce the document if the Minister states that it is of a confidential nature.[40] The Speaker accepts without demur a Minister's assurance that a document is confidential, though the fact that the Minister has quoted from it suggests that it can safely be made public and this makes it difficult for a Minister to resist a demand for its tabling.

Once an official document has been tabled, any member may see it.[41] Even though a Minister declines to table a document by reason of its confidentiality, the Minister may make it available privately to the member who asked for it.[42]

Members, other than Ministers, who quote from a document are under no obligation to table that document.[43]

RECORD OF PRESENTATION

All papers presented to the House by the Speaker or by Ministers are recorded by the Clerk in the journals. The notation shows the title of the paper and the reference number under which the paper will be bound (if it is to be bound) in any parliamentary series of papers. A similar record is made of papers tabled by leave or of official documents quoted

29   1971, Vol.374, p.3007.
30   S.O.368.
31   1951, Vol.295, p.89.
32   1980, Vol.429, p.573.
33   1979, Vol.422, p.397; 1998, Vol.570, p.11042.
34   House of Representatives (Australia) Debates (9 February 1999), pp.2193-4.
35   1901, Vol.119, pp.1017-8.
36   1970, Vol.365, p.669.
37   1968, Vol.358, pp.3294-5.
38   1973, Vol.388, p.5101.
39   1970, Vol.365, p.669.
40   S.O.368.
41   1893, Vol.79, pp.183-4.
42   1968, Vol.358, p.3607-8.
43   2003, Vol.614, p.10372.

by Ministers and tabled under the Standing Orders. These are also retained in the Clerk's possession as part of the records of the House and can be seen by any member.

PUBLICATION OF PAPERS

In the first years of parliamentary government in New Zealand, most papers presented to the House were not presented in printed form. The House would order the most important of the papers presented to it to be printed for the information of members and the public. The consequent delay in having a paper printed after its presentation to the House was irksome, and a committee of the House recommended that the Government have documents of importance that it intended to present to the House printed before the House met so that printed copies would be available immediately on presentation.[44] Even so, until 1863 all documents were presented in manuscript form, with their printing arranged later by the officers of the House. After that, papers began to be printed before presentation, but even by 1893 the majority of papers were still being presented in manuscript.[45]

Today, virtually every paper that is presented to the House is already in printed form. To reflect this fact, the House no longer orders papers presented to it to be "printed". It now orders them to be "published", with the consequent administrative and legal consequences which flow from such an order.

Motion for publication

Papers that are to be published by order of the House are identified to the Clerk in advance of their presentation by the Minister involved.[46] In practice, such papers are well known because they recur each year. Following the announcement to the House of their presentation, a Minister, usually the Leader of the House, moves, without notice, that the paper or papers on the list read out by the Clerk be published. There can be no debate on that motion.[47] Many, but not all, of the papers presented by the Speaker are also included in the motion for the publication of papers.

By such an order of the House the House directs that the paper concerned be published henceforth by the authority and under the control of the House.

Errors in papers

Occasionally, a report that has been presented to the House and ordered to be published is found to contain an error. No alterations can be made in any paper without the House's sanction after it has been presented.[48] If the error is serious enough, an erratum slip may be prepared. The erratum slip must itself be presented to the House and ordered to be published to make it part of the paper already presented to the House.

Parliamentary papers

When the House orders a paper to be published, the paper becomes known as a "parliamentary paper" and is thereby subject to the control and direction of the Speaker in regard to its printing and publication.[49] The Speaker may also direct that any paper presented to the House be translated and printed in another language.[50] The Office of the Clerk periodically issues a circular to government departments, Crown entities and other reporting organisations giving them information on the administrative arrangements to

---

[44] 1858, JHR, p.148.
[45] 1893, AJHR, I.6B (*Report of the Public Accounts Committee*).
[46] S.O.364(1).

[47] S.O.364(2).
[48] 1893, AJHR, I.6B, p.11.
[49] S.O.365.
[50] S.O.366.

be followed in preparing and presenting reports to the House. The information is also published on the parliamentary website.

From 1856 to 1999 parliamentary papers were bound in the *Appendix to the Journal* for the session in which they were presented. These volumes are a most valuable source for official reports that may not be preserved in a readily available form elsewhere. However, the sessional nature of the publication led to delays in its availability as sessions ceased to be confined to one year and came to extend to two or three years. Consequently, starting with the forty-sixth Parliament in December 1999, most parliamentary papers are published annually in a series known as *Parliamentary Papers.*

Classification of parliamentary papers

From the first production of the *Appendix to the Journal* in 1856, a grouping of parliamentary papers into broad subject divisions was followed. This was done by assigning to each parliamentary paper a "shoulder number" of a letter prefix followed by a numeral, printed on the top right-hand corner of the outside cover of the paper. The letter indicates the subject group (Finance, Communications, and so on) and the number identifies the particular paper within the group. A paper may also have a letter suffix following the numeral if it is closely related to a major paper in the series.

A review of the classification of papers was made in 1973. The class descriptions adopted then were—

A. Political and Foreign Affairs: foreign and defence policy and conferences, constitutional matters

B. Finance, Revenue, etc.:   financial and economic policy including Budget, government expenditure and debt, revenue collection, government banks, insurance, superannuation funds, building and friendly societies, etc.

C. Environment and Primary Production: the development and protection of land resources, primary industries

D. Energy and Works: power – electricity and gas; public works, conservation and use of water and soil

E. Welfare and Justice: education, social welfare, pensions, justice, prisons, liquor licensing and trusts, health, Māori and Pacific Island affairs

F. Communications: posts, broadcasting, and transport by sea, land and air

G. General: culture, trade, industry research, labour and employment, defence, police, etc.

H. Commissions, Royal Commissions: reports of commissions and committees of inquiry

I. Select committees.[51]

When the classes were revised, an attempt was made to iron out the large disparities in the number of papers falling into the then-existing categories, though there can still be considerable differences between the numbers in each category.

From December 1999 the sessional *Appendix to the Journal* consists solely of select committee reports (the "I" papers) together with other papers that have a close relationship with the operations of the House – such as Government responses to select committee recommendations and the Attorney-General's reports under the *New Zealand Bill of Rights Act*. These latter are part of a new "J" series of papers. The other papers published by order of the House are bound in the annual *Parliamentary Papers* volumes.

---

[51]   1973, AJHR, Introduction; see also Wilson, "New Zealand parliamentary papers – changes in shoulder numbers", *New Zealand Libraries*, June 1974, p.131.

Preparation and printing

The Speaker determines the standard size and style of parliamentary papers. The Office of the Clerk advises departments and other reporting entities of these requirements and publishes this information on the parliamentary website. The reporting entity provides the Office of the Clerk with copies of reports in a standardised paper size for binding and an electronic version of the report so that it can be published to the parliamentary website.

The Office of the Clerk allocates shoulder numbers for parliamentary papers. Most of these are the same from year to year, although in any year, as a result of recent legislation, a new body may be required to present a report to the House that it is desired to publish as a parliamentary paper, thus necessitating the allocation of a new shoulder number. Alternatively, an existing body may be abolished or may decide not to present its report as a parliamentary paper and the shoulder number formerly attached to its report may become vacant. As papers are already in print when presented to the House, shoulder numbers are allocated in anticipation of such presentation. The fact that a report bears a shoulder number does not make that report a parliamentary paper until it has been presented to the House and ordered to be published.

Where there is an obligation (statutory or otherwise) to present a report to the House, this is regarded as implying that the report should not be publicly disclosed before it is made available to the House. In exceptional cases the statute may provide that the report cannot be released before it is presented to the House.[52] The improper interception and publication of such a report or the breaking of an embargo with like effect could be treated by the House as a contempt,[53] but the House is unlikely to do this unless there are other aggravating features.[54]

As reports can now be presented to the House on any working day (which excludes only weekends, public holidays and the period 25 December to 15 January), the need to present the report to the House first is unlikely to hold up its general release. However, while Parliament is dissolved, has expired or is in recess it is not possible to present a paper. To avoid the public release of reports being unduly delayed during such a period, it is provided that a number of reports may be published in advance of their presentation to the House if Parliament is not in session during the period within which they must otherwise be presented.[55] The reporting entity concerned is responsible for ensuring that this is done. The reports must then be presented to the House as soon as the next session of Parliament commences.

Where there is no obligation to present a report to the House (such as most Royal Commission reports), the report or the contents of the report can be published before being presented.[56]

Distribution of papers

Limited supplies of each parliamentary paper (and of other papers presented to the House) are made available to members from the Bills Office. The annual reports of government departments and of many Crown entities are published each year as parliamentary papers in hard copy and on the parliamentary website. Regulations are not published as parliamentary papers but they are published in their own annual series under the direction of the Chief Parliamentary Counsel.[57] In respect of other papers presented to the House but not ordered to be published, the only official copy possessed by the House is the copy

52   *Conservation Act* 1987, s.6C(4) (New Zealand Conservation Authority).
53   1977, Vol.412, p.1587.
54   1987-90, AJHR, I.18B, paras.19 to 21.
55   *Public Finance Act* 1989, ss.31 (Government's annual financial statements) and 44 (departmental annual reports); *Crown Entities Act* 2004, s.150(4) (Crown entities' annual reports); *State-Owned Enterprises Act* 1986, s.17(2A).
56   1905, Vol.132, p.593.
57   *Acts and Regulations Publication Act* 1989, s.4.

physically presented to it. Such a paper is not bound as a parliamentary paper and its printing and publication are not subject to the Speaker's control.[58]

The department or agency responsible for any paper makes its own arrangements for general publication and public supply. All select committee reports are published under the authority of the House pursuant to the Standing Orders.[59]

LEGAL STATUS OF PAPERS PRESENTED TO THE HOUSE

Papers published by order or under the authority of the House
At common law it is no defence to an action for defamation that the statements that are complained of were published by order of the House.[60] Legislation providing protection for such publications was enacted in 1856 (following, in all material particulars, provisions in a United Kingdom statute, the *Parliamentary Papers Act* 1840).

These statutory protections are now contained in an amended form in the *Legislature Amendment Act* 1992. They extend to any "report, paper, votes, or proceedings" published by order or under the authority of the House of Representatives.[61] While this encompasses parliamentary papers, it has a much wider application than just to parliamentary papers as strictly defined, since it applies to any document in respect of which the House makes an order for publication or which is published under its authority. It thus applies also to such parliamentary publications as select committee reports, the journals, *Hansard* and order papers.

Persons (such as officers of the House) publishing parliamentary materials by order or under the authority of the House and persons who, though not acting under its direct authority, publish a copy of a report or proceedings published by or under the authority of the House, are entitled to have any legal action against them in respect of that publication stayed. This is deemed to dispose of the action finally.[62] Proof that the material was published under the authority of the House is made by the production of a certificate signed by the Speaker.[63] Proof of the correctness of a copy of the report is made by producing the copy together with an affidavit verifying the report and the correctness of the copy.[64]

These defences are not limited to actions for defamation; they apply in respect of any legal proceedings, civil or criminal. They extend protection to the distribution and reproduction of reports and documents ordered by the House to be published. They also extend protection to reports and documents that, though not ordered to be published, are circulated under the House's authority in the course of parliamentary business, for example, to members of Parliament. There are parallel statutory provisions conferring absolute privilege in defamation for the publication, by or under the authority of the House, of any document or of an official or authorised record of the proceedings of the House.[65] Absolute privilege in defamation also extends to the publication of a correct copy of any such document or record.[66] It seems unlikely that these provisions add anything to the protections conferred by the *Legislature Amendment Act* 1992.

The protection for parliamentary publications under the *Legislature Amendment Act* does not extend to the publication of extracts from such publications. Extracts were protected until 1992 when the relevant provision was omitted from the re-enactment of the protections that was then undertaken.[67] In respect of defamation, only a qualified

---

[58]   1970, Vol.369, p.4468.
[59]   S.O.250(2).
[60]   *Stockdale v Hansard* (1839) 9 A & E 1.
[61]   *Legislature Amendment Act*, 1992, s.2.
[62]   *Ibid.*, ss.4(1) and 5(1).
[63]   *Ibid.*, ss.4(1) and 5(2).
[64]   *Ibid.*, s.5(1).
[65]   *Defamation Act* 1992, s.13(3)(a) and (c).
[66]   *Ibid.*, s.13(3)(d).
[67]   Joseph, "Sampling the 'Wine Box'" [1994] NZLJ 292.

legal privilege applies in respect of the publication of a fair and accurate extract from, or summary of, such a publication.[68]

Neither the *Legislature Amendment Act* nor the *Defamation Act* expressly confer retroactive protection on publications. Where annual reports or reports of Royal Commissions are published prior to their publication being ordered by the House, they are not, at that time, published by order or under the authority of the House. Consequently, the statutory protections against legal liability would not appear to apply to protect any publication made before the House's order.[69]

While an order or authority of the House for publication protects against any legal action brought in respect of publication of the document or publication of copies of it, this does not amount to a prohibition of all or any examination of the contents of such a document in legal proceedings. The contents of a report or other document prepared outside Parliament may be examined in legal proceedings in which they are relevant, even where publication of them has taken place by order or under the authority of the House. Nor does publication of a report under the authority of the House immunise a body outside Parliament from judicial review based on actions taken in the course of preparing that report.[70] The protection afforded by the *Legislature Amendment Act* is directed to the legal consequences following from publication only. It has a narrower scope of operation than that which operates in respect of proceedings in Parliament protected by the *Bill of Rights* 1688. (See Chapter 46.)

Papers not published by order or under the authority of the House

Papers presented to the House but that are not published by order or under its authority are in a different position.

The mere presentation of a paper to the House does not give that paper any particular legal protection if it is used or circulated outside parliamentary proceedings.[71] This applies even to papers presented to the House pursuant to a statutory obligation. Thus, it has been held that it was no defence to an action in defamation (in respect of publication outside the House) that a report had been presented to the legislature under a statutory obligation, where the legislature made no order for the publication of that report. The fact of presentation and what was said in the legislature at the time of presentation were absolutely protected under the general principles of parliamentary immunity, but the contents of the report (not being a report emanating from the legislature) were not protected in respect of general use.[72]

Presentation of a paper to the House is communication of it to all members of Parliament. The Clerk will thus make it available to members as of right and normally to other interested persons too, such as members of the Press Gallery. But if the document contains material that it would be unlawful to publish, the Clerk may restrict access to members only. In these circumstances requests for access to the material are referred to the member who presented it.[73]

Members, in presenting a document, are not required to give any personal warranty about its contents, but the Speaker and the Clerk are entitled to take such steps as they consider proper to ensure that in handling the document they do not break the law.[74] Thus, access to documents subject to a court order protecting their confidentiality was denied (other than to members) until the House ordered their publication.[75] On another occasion

---

[68]   *Defamation Act* 1992, s.16(1) and First Schedule.
[69]   See *Isaacs & Sons Ltd v Cook* [1925] 2 KB 391 at 400 where the court expressly reserved any decision on that point.
[70]   *Ainsworth v Criminal Justice Commission* (1992) 175 CLR 564.
[71]   1994, Vol.539, p.470; 1997, Vol.558, p.718; 1997,

Vol.563, p.4019.
[72]   *Bruton v Estate Agents Licensing Authority* [1996] 2 VR 274.
[73]   1994, Vol.539, p.470.
[74]   1994, Vol.540, p.1029.
[75]   1994, Vol.539, p.470; 1993-96, AJHR, A.6 (wine-box documents).

where a tape had been presented to the House and the Speaker became aware that the tape might disclose the contents of a conversation in breach of the *Crimes Act*, he indicated that requests from non-members for access to the tape would be referred to the member who presented it.[76]

Where members or anyone else have access to documents presented to the House but not published by its order, the use of material from those documents outside parliamentary proceedings is at the members' or other persons' risk, as no protection from legal liability is available from parliamentary privilege or the *Legislature Amendment Act* 1992. The Speaker has circulated information to members and the press advising them of this position.[77]

PURPOSE OF PRESENTING PAPERS

The main purpose of presenting papers is to make them known to the world in the most public manner possible. The requirement that regulations and reports be presented to the House undoubtedly helps to draw them to the attention of members and of others who observe and report on parliamentary proceedings so that they can be examined and put to use. This aim has occasionally been made explicit in the legislation providing for presentation. Thus, a copy of a document executing a transfer of Crown assets to an educational institution must be presented to the House, and such presentation is itself deemed to be notice to any third party.[78] The value of formal promulgation of papers in this way in the House should not be overlooked, but the sheer volume of it makes it difficult for members and others to absorb its significance.

There are direct consequences in terms of the House's own procedures flowing from the presentation of papers. Regulations become available for scrutiny by the Regulations Review Committee; the reports presented by departments, offices of Parliament, Crown entities, State enterprises and other public organisations are available to select committees for reviews of their operations to be carried out;[79] and certain economic and fiscal reports stand referred to the Finance and Expenditure Committee.[80] In these and many other ways, the papers presented to the House contribute directly to the work that it and its committees carry out.

---

[76] 1997, Vol.558, p.718.
[77] 1997, Vol.563, pp.4019-20.
[78] *Education Act* 1989, s.206(5)(c). See also: *Crown Research Institutes Act* 1992, s.26(2)(c) (transfer of assets of Crown research institutes); *Southland Electricity Act* 1993, s.18(2)(c) (transfer of Crown assets and liabilities); *New Zealand Antarctic Institute Act* 1996, s.12(3)(b) (transfer of Crown assets and liabilities).
[79] S.Os 335(2) and 336(3).
[80] S.Os 327 and 328.

CHAPTER 39

RESPONSES

Members enjoy absolute protection from liability for things that they may say in debate. This freedom of speech is a necessary privilege designed to enable members to speak out in Parliament in the public interest without fear of legal repercussions. Although this is an essential adjunct of parliamentary democracy, persons outside the House who are the subject of strong criticism during the course of parliamentary debate have naturally felt aggrieved that the normal avenues of legal redress (such as an action for defamation) are not available to them to vindicate their reputations. Nor, until recently, did the House have a specific procedure for allowing such persons to put their side of the story, although it was always open to an aggrieved person to petition the House over the matter.

As a result of the expression of concern at this state of affairs, the House, in 1995, adopted a set of Standing Orders giving persons who are the subject of an attack that adversely affects them an opportunity to apply to the Speaker to have their response to that attack entered in the parliamentary record.[1] The procedure is similar, though not identical, to a procedure pioneered by the Australian Senate and subsequently adopted in a number of Commonwealth legislatures. It is not a right of reply. It gives a person a right to apply to the Speaker for a response to be entered in the parliamentary record. It does not guarantee that a response will be entered in all cases or entered in the precise form which the complainant might wish. In each case, it is for the Speaker to judge whether it is appropriate that a response be made and what the final form of that response will be.

ADVERSE REFERENCES

For the Standing Orders on responses to apply, there must be a reference in the House to a person that is capable of adversely affecting that person in some way or that has otherwise damaged the reputation of that person. In making an application to the Speaker for a response to be entered in the record, the complainant must claim to have been adversely affected or to have suffered damage to reputation as a result of the reference and the Speaker must take this into account in determining whether to allow the response.[2] The procedure is not a means for persons outside the House to engage in the parliamentary debate. Anyone is at liberty to use the normal media channels for that. Nor is it a means for the defence of a statutory office. It is an individual form of redress, not an official form of refutation (though a personal attack on the holder of an office can be responded to in that capacity). It exists to provide a means to redress reputational or other damage suffered as a result of parliamentary comment for which there would not otherwise exist a satisfactory avenue.

THE OCCASION OF THE REFERENCE

The most obvious occasion on which an adverse reference may be made to a person outside the House is during the course of a debate. The House has some rules controlling such references, but they essentially depend upon the judgment of the member making the reference. (See Chapter 16.) It is also possible that persons may be referred to in a motion

---

[1] 1993-96, AJHR, I.18A, p.81. [2] S.Os 160(1)(a) and 161(2)(b).

or in the course of a question. In each case the House requires that person be referred to by such means only if this is necessary to render the motion or question intelligible.[3]

Notwithstanding that a reference to a person in the course of a debate or in a motion or a question may be in order, if it is sufficiently damaging to a person's reputation or other interests it may be the subject of an application for a response.

The procedure is thus open to anyone who has been referred to in the House.[4] This does not necessarily mean that the reference must have been reported in *Hansard* (though if it is not, the Speaker will need to be satisfied of the authenticity of the supposed adverse reference). In the Australian Senate this has been taken to extend to references by senators speaking or otherwise using the procedures of the Senate, for example by tabling material. Thus the right to apply for a response has been applied in respect of an adverse reference in a paper tabled in the Senate.[5]

But the procedure is available only for adverse references in the House, not in select committees. Adverse references made at or to a select committee are the subject of their own response procedures. (See Chapters 23 and 24.)

COMPLAINANT

The right to apply for a response is conferred on any "person".[6] This includes any organisation,[7] such as, for example, a corporation.[8] A member of Parliament is not permitted to apply for a response; only persons outside the House can do so. In Australia it has been accepted that a person who is not a resident can apply under the equivalent procedures; the protection is not confined to citizens or residents.[9] Where a reference is made in the House to a person in an official capacity, an application in that capacity will be accepted. Otherwise an application must be made in a private capacity and not submitted on departmental letterhead.[10]

Normally, the person complaining will have been named in the House. But it is not necessary for the person to have been actually named if he or she has been referred to in a way that makes that person readily identifiable. But if no person is readily identifiable from the reference, a person cannot supply the identification by identifying himself or herself. The identification must arise from the reference, not be supplied by the complainant.

APPLICATION TO THE SPEAKER

An application for a response must be made to the Speaker in writing within three months of the reference having been made.[11] This is a strict time limit (though time does not run after Parliament is dissolved or has expired). The Speaker has no authority to extend it.

In the application, the complainant must expressly claim to have been adversely affected by the reference or to have suffered damage to his or her reputation as a result of it. The application must also contain a draft of the response which the complainant wishes to see entered in the parliamentary record and it must request this be done so that the Speaker is in no doubt what is intended.[12]

An application for a response may deal with more than one adverse reference. In one case a response dealt with thirty-one claimed references.[13] Furthermore, a single application may be made from more than one complainant if the adverse reference is to them both or if more than one adverse reference links them both.[14]

---

3   S.Os 97(2)(b) and 371(1)(a).
4   S.O.160(1).
5   *Reports of the Senate (Australia) Committee of Privileges*, Nos. 35 and 76.
6   S.O.160(1).
7   S.O.3(1).
8   1997, Vol.558, p.706.
9   *Report of the Senate (Australia) Committee of*

Privileges, No. 65.
10   *Report of the Members' Ethics and Parliamentary Privileges Committee (Queensland)*, No. 18.
11   S.O.160(1), (2).
12   S.O.160(1).
13   1996-99, AJHR, A.12.
14   *Ibid.*

CONSIDERATION BY THE SPEAKER

The Speaker may consult with the member who made the reference which is complained of.[15] Indeed, it is the invariable practice of the Speaker to refer any application to the member concerned for comment as soon as it is received.[16]

The reason for consulting the member is to allow the member to satisfy himself or herself that the procedures have been complied with and to comment on the form of the proposed response, for example, its succinctness and relevance. It is not for the purpose of the member making submissions as to the accuracy of the reference.[17] The Speaker is not concerned with this in any case. While the Speaker takes account of relevant comments made by the member who made the reference, and that member's comments may influence the form of the response that the Speaker allows, the member's comments themselves are not included in the response. The response is the complainant's response, not the member's comments on it.[18]

The Speaker may also correspond with the applicant during consideration of the application, to elucidate it and discuss any amendment to the form of the response that the Speaker wishes to see made.[19]

SPEAKER'S DETERMINATION

The Speaker determines whether in all the circumstances a response should be incorporated in the parliamentary record.[20]

The Speaker does not consider or judge the truth of the member's initial reference, nor of any response to it.[21] In either case any deliberate attempt to mislead the House (either directly or through the Speaker) could be treated as a contempt.

The Speaker considers whether the adverse reference is sufficiently serious to be capable of adversely affecting the applicant or damaging his or her reputation and thus warranting a response at all.[22] The Speaker will also consider the extent to which the comment complained of has already been addressed by being replied to subsequently in the debate. If it has been adequately dealt with as part of the debate, this may mean that a formal response is not required.

If the Speaker decides that no response should be entered in the parliamentary record, the Speaker must inform the applicant accordingly.[23] In such a case there is nothing to prevent any member on a suitable parliamentary occasion (such as the general debate) expressing the applicant's dissatisfaction at the original reference and defending that person's reputation. Nor does a rejection by the Speaker preclude a petition on the subject.[24] But it would not be in order to criticize the Speaker's decision on the application.

FORM OF THE RESPONSE

If the Speaker agrees that a response should be entered in the record, its form must still be settled. Where an attack on an individual's reputation is related to that person's official capacity, the response may be made in that capacity. But if an attack has nothing to do with an office that the person holds, a response in that capacity would not be permitted.

In determining the final form of a response the Speaker will take account of comments received by the member who made the reference.[25] The form of the response will depend to a large extent upon the initial attack. It must bear some relationship in length to the

---

[15] S.O.161(2)(a).
[16] 1997, Vol.558, p.706.
[17] *Ibid.*
[18] *Ibid.*
[19] S.O.161(2)(a).
[20] S.O.161(1).

[21] S.O.161(3).
[22] S.O.161(2)(b).
[23] S.O.162.
[24] 1997, Vol.561, pp.2532-3.
[25] 1997, Vol.558, p.706.

original reference. While it will often necessarily be longer than the attack, it must not be disproportionately so.[26] Material sent to the Speaker to support or authenticate a draft response is not included in the response itself unless it is necessary and strictly relevant to that response. The purpose of forwarding such material is to support a response being accepted for presentation, not to form part of the text of the response.

The Speaker cannot put words into the mouth of the applicant. The response must always be that of the person applying to make it. But the Speaker can refuse to allow a response to be presented unless it is amended to satisfy any objections to it that the Speaker has raised.[27]

PRESENTATION TO THE HOUSE

A response as approved by the Speaker is printed as a parliamentary paper and presented to the House by the Speaker at the time for presentation of papers.[28] On being ordered to be published by the House it becomes part of the permanent record of the House.

Normally, on presenting a response the Speaker makes no statement to the House. The response speaks for itself. However, the Speaker may add his or her own remarks if there is something that the Speaker considers should be conveyed to the House.[29] The Speaker has taken the occasion to inform the House of any significant procedural or interpretative issue that has arisen in the course of considering the particular application for response being presented. The fact that a response has been presented does not mean that members have to agree with it, nor does it preclude members commenting on the response on any suitable occasion. That is a matter for their judgment.[30]

---

[26]   *Ibid.*
[27]   S.O.163(2).
[28]   S.O.163(1).

[29]   1997, Vol.561, p.2532.
[30]   2004, Vol.621, p.16302.

CHAPTER 40

QUESTIONS

"Is it in contemplation by the Government to make any provision for reimbursing or compensating in land expenses incurred by families in bringing domestic servants to the Colony?" This question, addressed by Mr Hart to Mr Weld (a member of the Executive Council) on 22 June 1854, was the first question asked in the House of Representatives.[1] (The Government would give no undertaking on the matter.) Eighteen more questions were asked of Ministers that session in a procedure which was then entirely unrecognised by the Standing Orders and, indeed, was not clearly distinguishable from the ordinary motion procedure – questions at first being regarded as a form of motion. The practice ceased entirely the following year when there was no ministerial representation in the House. With the advent of responsible government in 1856, oral questions to Ministers were revived. As well as questions answered orally in the House, questions have, since 1903, been able to be lodged for written answer.[2] The practice has thus grown from such humble beginnings into a most important parliamentary industry, which saw nearly 60,000 questions answered during the course of the forty-seventh Parliament.[3]

Nowadays, on each sitting day, Ministers can be observed fielding questions from members on widely diverse subjects. The question period offers members an opportunity to put potentially embarrassing questions to the Government and obliges the Government to respond publicly to them. The importance attached to questions is indicated by the fact that a question period is set aside for them in the House each day. During this period members address questions to Ministers, and Ministers, having had previous notice of such questions, give replies which may then be tested by further (supplementary) questions. Ministers have to answer supplementary questions to the best of their ability, drawing on their own knowledge of the subject and any supplementary information on it which their departments may have provided in anticipation of a follow-up to the original question.

Unlike in certain other legislatures, no questions are asked without previous notice of the question having been given to the person (usually a Minister) who is to answer it. The period of notice required varies depending on whether the questioner wants an oral or a written answer, and what type of oral question is being addressed.

Questions are usually addressed to Ministers, but oral questions may be addressed to other members in certain circumstances. There are, however, many fewer questions to other members each year. Of the total number of questions answered each year, there are invariably more written questions than oral questions. For example, there were 21,900 of these lodged in 2003/04, compared to 1,051 oral questions.

TYPES OF QUESTIONS

Questions may be either for oral answer in the House itself or for written answer, in which case the reply to the question is not delivered in the House but is published electronically.

A question for oral answer to a Minister may be either an ordinary oral question (including a supplementary question) or an urgent question. Oral questions are lodged

---

1   PD, 1854-55, p.121.
2   Martin, *The House – New Zealand's House of*

Representatives 1854-2004, p.121.
3   2005, Vol.627, p.22383.

during the morning of the day on which they are to be answered. There can be up to 12 of them lodged each day. Urgent questions can be lodged at any time up to the end of the question period but these must meet a stringent urgency test in order to be admitted. Oral questions can be asked of non-Ministers. There is no restriction on the numbers that may be lodged. There are no urgent questions to non-Ministers. A question for written answer (which may be asked of Ministers and non-Ministers) is lodged electronically. The addressee has six working days to reply to it.

NOTICE OF QUESTIONS

The idea for a question in the House might originate in many ways. A report in a newspaper or other publication, a query from a constituent, a chance remark by an acquaintance, an orchestrated campaign to gather information on Government actions – all of these may spark off what becomes a question. The point at which an idea becomes a part of the proceedings of the House is when notice of the question is given to the Clerk of the House. There is no provision for the lodging of a joint question. Each question must come from a single member.[4] Any member of the House, including a Minister,[5] can lodge a question, except a member suspended from the service of the House. Questions can be lodged to any Minister. There is no roster of Ministers specifying on which particular days questions can be addressed to them. Nor is there any special period set aside for questions to the Prime Minister.[6]

A question lodged by one member may not be transferred into the name of another after it has been lodged.

Notice of oral questions

Members must give notice in writing of a question for oral answer. For this purpose printed forms are available (green for oral questions and white for urgent questions). The member inscribes a question on the form, signs it and delivers it to the Clerk.[7] Only 12 question may be lodged each day.[8] Occasionally, fewer than 12 may be lodged if a party does not utilise its allocation.

Notice of urgent questions

To lodge an urgent question, a member must furnish a copy of the question marked "urgent question" to the Clerk and a copy to the Minister to whom the question is addressed[9] (special forms have been printed for this purpose). It is the member's responsibility to have these two copies delivered within a reasonable time of each other, and a question cannot be asked, even if it is accepted as being urgent, if a copy has been submitted to the Clerk but not to the Minister.

Notice of written questions

For written questions, a system of electronic lodging and processing has applied since February 2003. Notices of questions for written answer may be lodged only in electronic form.[10] For this purpose members use a secured template system to communicate their written questions to the Office of the Clerk affixing an electronic signature to authenticate the question.

The Speaker may authorise the lodging of written questions in hard copy form in exceptional circumstances, for example, if there was a failure of the electronic system.[11]

---

4   1969, Vol.362, pp.1999-2000.
5   1988, Vol.495, p.8604.
6   See 1993-96, AJIIR, I.18A, pp.73-4.
7   S.O.372(1).
8   S.O.372(2).
9   S.O.379(1).
10   S.O.373(3)(a).
11   S.O.373(5).

Signing notices of questions

Every question must be signed by the member originating it or by another member on that member's behalf if this member is unavailable.[12] The Speaker relies on the integrity of members in these circumstances as to whether they have given authority for questions to be lodged in their names.[13]

In the case of notices of written questions, the notice must be signed by way of an electronic signature by the member or by another member on the member's behalf.[14] This takes the form of a timed and dated stamp identifying the user logged on to the system. It is not a replica signature. Only authorised users have log-on access to the system. It is not possible to lodge a notice unless the signature is affixed.

Electronic signatures may only be applied by members or under their direction. How members give authority for their signatures to be affixed is a matter for them. They may put in place systems whereby they entrust a staff member with affixing an electronic signature to a question in their name.[15]

It would be a contempt for any other person to attempt to mislead the House by impersonating a member through the use of that member's electronic signature.[16]

Party co-ordination

The party organisations within the House have members or staff appointed to oversee the lodging of questions by the members of the party, and all oral and some written questions pass through their hands before being submitted to the Clerk. This enables each party to co-ordinate its approach to question time and ensures that questions of significance to the party get priority. Indeed such party co-ordination is essential in respect of oral questions to Ministers since the 12 questions each day are allocated on a party basis. There are consequently no restrictions on how many questions may be lodged in the name of the same member provided the party has more than one question slot available to it. It is a matter for each party to decide how it utilises the question slots allocated to it each day.

TIME FOR LODGING NOTICES OF QUESTIONS

Oral questions

What are now referred to as oral questions were first devised in 1986. Before 1986 all questions for oral answer were lodged two or more days in advance. Between 1986 and 1995 a mixture of questions lodged two days in advance and questions lodged on the same day were permitted (the latter were called "questions of the day"). Since 1996 all oral questions have been lodged in the course of the morning of the day on which they are to be answered.

Notice of an oral question may be given between 10 am and 10.30 am on the day the question is to be asked.[17] When a sitting of the House is extended into a subsequent calendar day and the next sitting day is lost, there is no question time and consequently no oral questions. However, notices of oral questions are often lodged during the morning of such a day just in case the House rises before 1 pm that day and a new sitting day is held that would enable the questions to be asked. Where oral questions are lodged for answer on a day that does not eventuate as a sitting day because urgency extends the previous sitting of the House or the House decides to adjourn for a period, the lodged questions are lost altogether. They can, however, be resubmitted by members.

---

12 1973, Vol.384, p.2628.
13 1994, Vol.542, pp.2945-6.
14 S.O.373(3)(b).
15 2004, Vol.617, p.12621.
16 2002-05, AJHR, I.18A, p.8.
17 S.O.372(1)(b).

Urgent questions

There is no prescribed time by which an urgent question has to be submitted in order to be considered for answer at the next sitting of the House, though it would have to be lodged before the end of question time to be considered for answer at that sitting. Urgent questions have in fact been handed in at the Table during the course of question time itself and at least one has been accepted in these circumstances.[18]   However, the greater the member's delay in submitting a question once the member is in possession of the facts on which it is based, the less likely the Speaker is to be persuaded that it is, in fact, urgent.[19]

Written questions

Notices of questions for written answer may be given by 10.30 am on any working day during a session of Parliament.[20]   (The Speaker may extend this time in exceptional circumstances, for example, if there was a failure of the electronic system for lodging questions.[21]) A working day includes any day on which the House is sitting under urgency. But notices may not be given after the last day on which the House sits each year or before the first sitting day in the new year.[22] There is no limit to the number of written questions that may be lodged on a single day, nor is there a limit to the number that may be lodged by an individual member on any one day, though the Business Committee has asked members to show restraint and the Standing Orders Committee reviews the overall numbers of questions lodged from time to time.[23]

Questions for written answer may only be lodged in electronic form[24] and must be signed by way of an electronic signature by the member or by another member on the member's behalf.[25]   How the electronic signature is affixed is a matter for the member to decide as long as the member has authorised it. It does not have to be affixed by the member personally.[26]

PROCESSING OF NOTICES

Checking

When lodged with the Clerk, all questions are checked for compliance with the Standing Orders. If a question is not in order as lodged, it is returned to the member concerned or it may be accepted subject to amendment or authentication of a statement or quotation contained in it. Issues relating to the acceptability of a question can be raised with the Clerk at any time up to the commencement of question time.[27] These may lead to changes in the text of questions being made subsequent to their initial acceptance. The acceptability of a question can be challenged at any time up to its being asked in the House.[28] For example, circumstances may change after it is initially accepted or further information may become available indicating that it is in fact out of order.

Questions are not ruled out of order because they are ungrammatical.[29]   Editing changes to questions are not made lightly and relate only to questions of grammar or style on the same principles as apply to the editing of debates.[30]   Where a Minister transfers a question to any other Minister any consequential changes can be made in the text of the question.[31]

---

[18]   2000, Vol.588, p.6108.
[19]   1983, Vol.454, p.3750.
[20]   S.O.373(1).
[21]   S.O.373(5).
[22]   S.O.373(2).
[23]   2002-05, AJHR, I.18A, p.8.
[24]   S.O.373(3)(a).
[25]   S.O.373(3)(b).
[26]   2004, Vol.617, p.12621.
[27]   2003, Vol.606, p.3975.
[28]   1997, Vol.562, p.3705.
[29]   1975, Vol.397, p.1353.
[30]   1973, Vol.384, p.2625.
[31]   1998, Vol.566, p.7091.

Publication

When all notices of oral questions for that day have been lodged and checked, Ministers' offices are advised and copies of the questions are distributed to them through Ministers' boxes in the Bills Office. The text of oral questions is published on the parliamentary website at about 11.30 am, though questions are subject to further amendment if doubts about their wording arise subsequently.[32]

A list of each day's oral questions is printed on a paper circulated with the final order paper for that day. The text of the question as it appears on that paper is the official text to be answered in the House. Any change or discrepancy between the order paper and any earlier electronic version (including that published on the website) is irrelevant.[33]

Written questions are distributed electronically to the Ministers to whom they are addressed shortly after they have been accepted and are then published electronically on the same day they are received.[34]

Notices of urgent questions, because of the circumstances of their lodging, are not published at all.

ALLOCATION OF QUESTIONS

Until 1996 the order in which oral questions were listed for answer depended upon a set of conventions designed to ensure equity to all sections of the House. Questions from different parties were intermixed so as to give all parties some regular prominence in the order in which they stood. This was especially important as questions not reached that day were answered in writing. As all 12 oral questions are now answered each day this is no longer important, but a formal mechanism for determining how questions are allocated among the parties and the order in which they are set down for answer is now provided in the Standing Orders rather than relying on conventions. Consequently, the Business Committee is given power to determine the allocation and rotation of questions.[35]

The allocation of questions among the parties must be made on a basis that is proportional to party membership in the House.[36] However, for this purpose members who hold executive office (Ministers, Associate Ministers and Parliamentary Under-Secretaries) are excluded from the calculation of the number of questions available to Government parties.[37] Having made that calculation the Business Committee allocates question slots proportionately to parties over a cycle of several weeks.

The rotation of questions between the parties is similarly determined by the Business Committee in an endeavour to be fair to each party or independent member. An attempt is made to alternate between questions from Government party members and Opposition party members. Depending upon their size, each party will have an opportunity to lead off question time during the course of the cycle and will have to take its fair share of less prominent positions in the questions order. The Business Committee authorises the Clerk to issue a circular advising members of the allocation of question slots as each cycle concludes.

Parties are at total liberty to exchange slots with other parties or to surrender a slot to another party.[38] These arrangements are made privately between the parties with advice to the Clerk when a question is lodged in a different sequence from that on the roster prepared under the Business Committee's authority.

---

32 2003, Vol.606, pp.3975-6.
33 1996, Vol.555, pp.12748-9; 2003, Vol.606, p.3975-6.
34 S.O.373(3)(c)(i).
35 S.O.373(5).
36 *Ibid.*
37 1993-96, AJHR, I.18A, p.75.
38 *Ibid.*

TRANSFER OF QUESTION FROM ORAL TO WRITTEN

It is entirely over to the member who lodges a question whether to seek an oral or a written reply to it.[39] However, there are certain types of questions which are more suited to written answer. These comprise questions which require a long or technical reply or masses of statistical data which is better presented in writing or in tabular form. When, after an oral question has been submitted, it becomes apparent that too long or complex an answer is called for if a reply is to be given satisfactorily, the Minister may approach the member and seek agreement for the question to be transferred for written answer. This must be accomplished by leave of the House, and it must be the member who lodged the question (or a member acting on that member's behalf) who seeks such leave when the question is called. If leave is granted, the question is treated in every respect as if it had been submitted originally as a question for written answer.

Alternatively, a member may ask the question in the House and then have the reply, by leave, delivered in writing. This is different from the situation in which the question is not asked orally in the House at all but is forestalled by being transferred for written answer. A reply to an oral question which has been asked may be delivered in writing, but this does not alter the question's status as an oral question and it continues to be treated accordingly in all respects.

CONTENT OF QUESTIONS

The House has a number of rules relating to the content of questions. These have been considerably relaxed in recent years and are now much less prescriptive in nature than formerly. Nevertheless, rules on content are designed to give a formal structure to the process of asking questions. Most of these rules are reflected in the rules for the contents of answers to questions. The rules on content apply equally to all questions, including supplementary questions asked to oral questions. However, the nature of the process of asking supplementary questions makes them more difficult to enforce at this time.[40]

Conciseness

Questions must be concise.[41] This is an important consideration with oral questions, where the Speaker must endeavour to get through all the questions on the order paper without allowing question time to run on unduly. There is a working rule that a member may not include more than two legs to an oral question.[42] However, the requirement for a question to be concise does not necessarily mean that it must be short. It means rather than it must be "spare" and not contain any material not strictly necessary to the bare asking of the question. The application of the other rules relating to the content of a question, particularly those related to the factual content of questions, also contributes towards the aim of conciseness in questions.

Statements of facts and names of persons

Questions must not contain statements of facts and names of persons unless they are strictly necessary to render the question intelligible and can be authenticated.[43] Individuals should not be named in questions unless there is a need for the disclosure of the person's name. Questions designed to injure a named individual without any compensating need to disclose the name will not be accepted.[44] If it is necessary to name an individual, only

---

[39] 1975, Vol.401, p.4715.

[40] 1985, Vol.462, p.4549.

[41] S.O.371(1).

[42] 1997, Vol.559, p.1194; 1998, Vol.566, pp.7887-8.

[43] S.O.371(1)(a).

[44] 1986, Vol.470, p.1261.

relevant descriptive adjectives can be applied to that person (for example, identifying an office held).

The most common way in which factual statements are imported into questions is by way of quotations. The practice of members including in a question a quote from a source (most commonly a newspaper) is a longstanding and accepted one.[45] However, members are under two obligations if they do employ a quotation or make any other statement in a question. First, the quotation or statement must be truly necessary to the question being asked and, secondly, the member must provide authentication of it.

Whether the statement or quotation is necessary will depend upon the terms of the question itself.

One particular form of factual material that will be tested rigorously against the criterion of necessity before it will be allowed to be included in a question, is a statement that reveals facts that have been suppressed by a court order. If such an order is in force, members are enjoined to use the privilege of freedom of speech which they enjoy (and which enables them to override such an order with legal impunity) responsibly. To do otherwise would be to abuse their privilege.[46] In respect of a proposal to include such material in a question, the Speaker would have to be convinced that the public interest impelled the order to be disregarded to permit a question that did infringe a court order.[47]

Authentication

Members are not asked to verify the underlying truth of a quotation if they employ one;[48] but they must ensure that they are quoting accurately[49] and, if paraphrasing, that the paraphrase is a fair one.[50] However, if a statement is attributed to a member in a question and that member denies having made it, the question must be disallowed.[51] Such a denial can be made on a point of order; it does not have to be made by way of a personal explanation.[52] A question quoting another member which is challenged by that member can be resubmitted on a future day after having been authenticated, but it cannot be authenticated on the floor of the House.[53] Other statements of fact which a member includes in a question must be proved as accurate where any doubt arises.[54] The degree of inaccuracy determines whether a question inaccurate in some particular is altogether out of order or whether it can be asked subject to amendment.[55]

A member's duty to authenticate a statement or quotation is a duty owed to the Speaker, whose job it is to ensure that the Standing Orders have been complied with. It is not a duty owed to the House as such. A member is under no obligation to reveal sources to the House or to the Minister to whom the question is addressed by including such references in the question (indeed, such inclusion is discouraged as unnecessarily lengthening the question). But members using direct quotations are required to authenticate them to the Speaker as a condition of having their questions accepted.[56] Where a quotation is used, members must, on lodging their question, provide a copy of the newspaper or other document from which they are quoting.[57] A copy is not passed on to the Minister concerned as a matter of practice, although this will be done if the member makes it clear that this is desired, for example, by providing the Clerk with two copies for this purpose.[58]

Apart from direct quotations, authentication of factual content in a question is also required as a matter of course in respect of paraphrases of statements or reports referred to in the question, the name of any person mentioned in it, and figures or numbers set out in

45	1970, Vol.369, p.4078.	52	2001, Vol.596, p.13100.
46	1988, Vol.489, p.4322; 1999, Vol.576, p.16210.	53	1989, Vol.499, pp.11335-6.
47	1988, Vol.490, p.5257.	54	1975, Vol.397, p.1114.
48	1966, Vol.348, p.2464.	55	1975, Vol.396, p.538; 1999, Vol.580, p.19507.
49	1951, Vol.295, pp.156-9.	56	1995, Vol.549, p.8277.
50	1969, Vol.362, p.2076.	57	1977, Vol.414, p.3489.
51	1968, Vol.358, pp.2804-6.	58	1979, Vol.425, p.2786.

the question. Factual material falling outside these areas does not have to be authenticated when lodging a question. The responsibility for citing facts accurately in a question devolves on the member lodging it.[59]

Expressions

A certain number of expressions or figures of speech are not permitted in questions.

These are—

*   arguments
*   inferences
*   imputations
*   epithets
*   ironical expressions
*   expressions of opinion.[60]

Questions are, naturally enough, interrogatory in nature and are not a vehicle for a member to argue a point. This can be done in a speech. Arguments are, therefore, not permitted in questions. Nor are inferences or imputations. A member cannot hint at something (whether disreputable or not) in the text of a question. The member must come out and say what is meant, and then the question can be judged on the grounds of necessity, accuracy and authenticity. Questions must not contain epithets (these are in any case unnecessary, and only tend to lengthen a question) or ironical expressions, though, of course, the best of the latter may escape detection altogether. Such expressions could also be disallowed as not being necessary to render the question intelligible.

Questions must not contain expressions of opinion. The ban on a member injecting his or her own opinions into a question is intended to keep the member on the straight and narrow path of asking a question rather than indulging in debate on the issue. (Though the fact that the House does not wish to hear the opinion of a member asking a question, does not imply that it does not wish to hear the opinion of the member answering it. It may, and often does.)

Unparliamentary language

Standing Orders prohibit certain references in questions on similar grounds to those prohibited in debate. Discreditable references to the House or to any member of the House, or any offensive or unparliamentary expressions, are not permitted.[61] The rules against unparliamentary language in debate also apply in respect of questions. What is not permitted in the one, is not permitted in the other.

A member's personal explanation cannot be referred to or challenged in a question any more than it can be referred to or challenged in debate.

Seeking an opinion

Questions may seek an expression of opinion from the member to whom they are addressed, provided that that member has responsibility for the matter about which the opinion is sought.[62]

But a question may not seek a legal opinion.[63] A Minister is not a source of legal advice for members through the question process. Members are not prohibited by this rule from asking Ministers under what legal powers they or their departments are acting or purporting to act in particular cases. Such questions do not seek a legal explanation and

---

[59]   1995, Vol.549, p.8277.
[60]   S.O.371(1)(b).
[61]   S.O.371(1)(c).

[62]   1997, Vol.558, p.278.
[63]   S.O.372(2).

justification of the action taken; they seek the Minister's or the department's perception of its lawful authority for taking that action, and presumably in all cases one does exist. Indeed the rule of law requires that it do so.[64]

Repeating a question

There is no rule against repeating a question for oral answer. If members wish to use their limited allocation of questions to re-ask a question, they are entitled to do so.

But with regard to written questions there is no limit on the number of questions that may be lodged. Consequently a rule against repeating the substance of a question already answered or disallowed in the same calendar year was introduced along with the introduction of the system of electronic lodging of written questions.[65] This is intended to put some constraint on the unnecessary lodging of questions for written answer.[66]

Select committee and court proceedings

Finally, questions cannot refer to proceedings before select committees which are not open to the public (until the committee reports), or to a case pending adjudication by a court.[67] In respect of the latter, a question is not permitted about a case from the time proceedings are filed with the court or a prosecution is brought until the case is finally disposed of. (See Chapter 16 for the *sub judice* rule.)

URGENT QUESTIONS

Urgent questions are designed to cater for those situations that need to be dealt with by a question and reply in the House immediately, and for which the normal period of notice is inappropriate. With the development of questions lodged on the day that they are to be answered and notice periods of only some four hours, the need for urgent questions has been considerably reduced. Consequently, the Standing Orders Committee, as a guide to the Speaker, has recommended that an urgent question should only be accepted if it deals with a matter that has arisen since 10.30 am (the cut-off time for lodging oral questions).[68] Urgent questions therefore exist as a backstop to deal with a situation that suddenly arises.

When an urgent question has been submitted to the Clerk, it is for the Speaker to consider whether it should be allowed to be asked on the ground that it is one which, in the public interest, should be answered immediately.[69] For a member to be able to bypass the normal notice period for questions, there has to be a need inherent in the question for it to be answered on that day or before the member could obtain an answer by submitting it through the normal channels.[70] A classic instance is where some irrevocable course of events is about to happen – a demolition of a building or the sailing of a ship.[71] Questions are not accepted as urgent when they relate to something which has already happened. These, although they may be of great public interest, can be explored through the normal question system. The test for an urgent question is whether an important event is about to happen, not what has happened in the past. So a question asking whether the Prime Minister had that morning issued a request to the Rugby Union to call off the Springbok tour was not accepted as being urgent. Despite its obvious importance, it was exploring an event in the past. On the other hand, a question to the Minister of Police asking if he was considering giving the police authority to swear in special constables that day was accepted, because it was looking ahead to an important action which would be taken (if

---

64 See Joseph, *Constitutional and Administrative Law in New Zealand*, pp.212-3.
65 S.O.371(3).
66 2002-05, AJHR, I.18A, p.9.
67 S.O.371(4).
68 1993-96, AJHR, I.18A, p.74.
69 S.O.379(2).
70 1980, Vol.429, p.507.
71 1977, Vol.410, p.587.

taken at all) before the member could obtain an answer to the question in the normal course of events.[72]

A question does not become urgent merely because of the imminent departure overseas of the Minister to whom it is addressed. If the question relates to action to be taken at a conference which the Minister is to attend and which will be held before a question can be answered in the normal way, this may render the question urgent, for then the Minister's departure would not be unconnected with the question. If it is simply the case that the questioner prefers an answer to the question by the Minister before the Minister leaves, rather than an answer by an acting Minister, the question will not qualify as urgent.

Urgent questions must also conform to the rules with regard to content and ministerial responsibility. Once the Speaker reaches a decision on the acceptability of the question, both the member who submitted it and the Minister are informed. If the Speaker does not accept the question as being urgent, the member may resubmit it as an ordinary oral or written question.

AMENDMENT OF QUESTIONS

Where a question does not comply with the Standing Orders it is not accepted by the Clerk. However, the inadmissibility of a question or the inclusion of objectionable content can be inadvertently overlooked or not perceived at the time and the question accepted and published. For example, a Minister, on receiving notice of the question, may challenge it as being outside the Minister's area of responsibility. In these circumstances the acceptability of the question must be reconsidered.[73]

Even after a question has been initially accepted the Speaker has the authority to disallow the question.[74] In respect of a question for oral answer that appears on that day's list for answer, the Speaker would order its deletion only by a ruling given in the Chamber.[75]

Whether a question must be disallowed after having been accepted depends entirely on the extent of its non-compliance with the Standing Orders. For example, if the question contains an inaccuracy, it depends whether it is inaccurate to such an extent as to taint the whole question, in which case it will be ruled out, or whether it is inaccurate in respect of a minor detail only, in which case it may be allowed to stand.[76]

The Speaker has power to permit questions otherwise out of order if they are revised or amended to bring them within the Standing Orders.[77] If an infringement can be corrected by amendment of the question without prejudice to the Minister who has to answer it, the Speaker usually allows it to remain as amended. Thus the Office of the Clerk may negotiate the rewording of a question to ensure that it complies with the Standing Orders.[78] If the infringement is revealed on a point of order as late as the actual asking of an oral question in the House, the Speaker may still allow it to be asked subject to amendment, provided that this does not seriously prejudice the answer that the Minister may have prepared.[79] But it is also possible in these circumstances for the Speaker to order it to be deferred so that it can be asked with notice in a correct form.

QUESTIONS TO MINISTERS

For a question to a Minister to be admissible, there must be ministerial responsibility for the subject matter of the question.

---

[72] 1981, Vol.439, p.2454.
[73] 2003, Vol.606, p.3975.
[74] S.O.371(5).
[75] 1987, Vol.179, p.7793.

[76] 1975, Vol.396, p.538; 1999, Vol.580, p.19507.
[77] S.O.371(5).
[78] 2003, Vol.606, p.3975.
[79] 1989, Vol.496, p.9129.

A Minister may be questioned on public affairs with which he or she is officially connected, and on proceedings in the House or any matter of administration for which the Minister is responsible.[80] In practice, this gives a very wide scope for questions to be addressed to a Minister relating to matters for which he or she has ministerial responsibility.

Ministerial responsibility

Whether there is ministerial responsibility depends in each case on a consideration of the legislative and administrative circumstances surrounding the question.

In respect of the public service, legislation specifically declares that for a range of decisions relating to the recruitment, promotion, disciplining and discharge of individual employees, chief executives of departments are not to be responsible to their Ministers but are to act independently.[81] Ministers, therefore, cannot be asked questions relating to personnel actions taken in respect of identified public servants, though they are answerable for employment policies generally as they are followed in departments.[82] Only general information, for instance of a statistical nature, can be sought from Ministers about such matters. It is expressly provided too that the Director of the Serious Fraud Office is not responsible to the Attorney-General (the Minister responsible for the office) in regard to any decision to investigate any suspected case of serious or complex fraud or to take proceedings under the legislation.[83] It follows that the Attorney-General is not answerable in respect of such matters.

But the mere fact that a Minister has no legal control over a certain action does not mean that there can be no ministerial responsibility to answer a question about it. Ministers, by convention, are responsible to the House for their official actions and for the general conduct of their departments and officials.[84] They become answerable to the House for many matters over which they have no legal powers or in respect of the actions of public officials who are not subject to the legal control of Ministers. Legal responsibility and political responsibility are different things.[85] Thus, questions relating to actions taken by the State Services Commission in the course of carrying out its legal functions in regard to the appointment of a chief executive were held to involve ministerial responsibility.[86]

There has never been any doubt that questions may be put to Ministers regarding the activities of Crown entities. This is so regardless of the precise degree of legal control that Ministers exercise over the entity concerned. However, Ministers will often, in replying, make it clear that they are transmitting information from the entity concerned in response to the question, and do not have any legal or operational responsibility for the matters themselves.[87] Crown entities are under a general legal obligation to supply responsible Ministers with information relating to their operations and performance and thus to assist Ministers in fulfilment of Ministers' responsibilities to answer to the House.[88] But Crown entities may refuse to provide information, even to a Minister, to protect the privacy of a person (if this is justified) or to enable the entity to carry out judicial or statutorily independent functions with which it is entrusted.[89]

The creation of State enterprises in 1986, with Ministers' legal roles being, in the main, limited to those of shareholders in the listed enterprises, caused a reconsideration of the basis of ministerial responsibility for questions relating to their work. The Speaker has ruled that questions about the activities of State enterprises will be accepted. If a Minister

---

[80] S.O.369.
[81] *State Sector Act* 1988, s.33.
[82] 1989, Vol.501, p.12467.
[83] *Serious Fraud Office Act* 1990, s.30(1).
[84] 2002-05, AJHR, I.22C (*Public Finance (State Sector Management) Bill*).
[85] 1997, Vol.558, pp.484-5.
[86] 1990, Vol.509, pp.2705-6.
[87] 1997, Vol.558, p.484.
[88] *Crown Entities Act* 2004, s.133(1).
[89] *Ibid.*, s.134.

considers that a particular question does not disclose any ministerial responsibility, it is incumbent on the Minister to challenge the question's validity. The Speaker will not take the initiative in ruling out such questions.[90] In fact, Ministers have not challenged questions about the activities of State enterprises as being out of order on the ground of lack of ministerial responsibility, although they have often declined, in their replies, to provide as much information as the questioner has sought. As a matter of practice, questions about individual State enterprises on matters for which Ministers are not directly responsible are referred by the Minister to the enterprise concerned for a reply which the Minister then delivers, making it clear that the information was obtained from the enterprise (for example, by using the phrase "I am advised"[91]). If the State enterprise considers that the release of information could be prejudicial to it, it informs the Minister, who will then normally avoid releasing the information in the answer.[92] State enterprises have express power to refuse to disclose to Ministers information relating to individual employees or customers if the information would enable the employee or customer to be identified.[93]

Clearly Ministers have no responsibility for judicial decisions.[94] But, even so, Ministers can be asked to comment on judgments of courts where these have implications for official responsibilities which Ministers hold.

In practice, a wide view is taken of the concept of ministerial responsibility. There is no convention, for instance, (as there is in other legislatures) that Ministers are not answerable to the House for operational matters in the departments or agencies falling within their portfolio areas.[95] (Though a Minister may reply in those terms if the Minister chooses to.[96])

Where there is doubt about whether a question involves ministerial responsibility, it has been the practice for the Clerk to refer the question to the Minister concerned and, if the Minister denies any responsibility in that area, for the question to be disallowed.[97] The Minister is presumed to know best what matters he or she is responsible for, although ultimately, of course, it is the Speaker who decides whether to accept or reject a question.

Personal or party capacity

Questions cannot be asked of actions of a Minister in a personal or party capacity. They must relate to the portfolio which the Minister holds. A Minister cannot be questioned about a statement he or she has made if that statement was not made in respect of one of the Minister's own portfolios. Thus, only the Prime Minister is answerable in respect of the ministerial code on pecuniary interests. Other Ministers are not answerable in respect of their declarations under the code, as these do not relate to their portfolio responsibilities.[98] Nor is a question in order if it concerns the actions of caucus or seeks information about a party document.[99]

While the Prime Minister is answerable for all statements made as Prime Minister, the Prime Minister is not answerable for statements or actions taken purely in a non-ministerial capacity such as party leader (though this can be a hard distinction to draw).[100]

The coalition agreements negotiated between parties following general elections raise special issues of ministerial responsibility. Such agreements are agreements between *parties* and as such are not actions for which there is ministerial responsibility. But where

---

90   1987, Vol.483, pp.617-8.
91   1997, Vol.558, p.484.
92   1988, Vol.488, p.3964.
93   *State-Owned Enterprises Act* 1986, s.18(3); *Hansard Supplement*, 1993, Vol.16, p.6756.
94   1985, Vol.464, p.5594.

95   2003, Vol.611, p.8243.
96   2005, Vol.627, p.21957.
97   1978, Vol.418, p.954.
98   1991, Vol.514, p.1509.
99   1993, Vol.535, pp.15886-7.
100   2000, Vol.585, p.3768.

an agreement is endorsed by the Government which subsequently takes office as a basis for the structure of that Government and how it is to take decisions, questions relating to these matters may be put to any Minister who has responsibility for them. Thus questions to the Prime Minister and the Deputy Prime Minister about the 1996 Coalition Agreement's provisions on the division of Cabinet posts between the parties were permitted. On the other hand, questions asking the Deputy Prime Minister to comment on the change of leadership in the party of his coalition partner, were not. The latter related to his party leader, not his ministerial, role.[101]

One obvious area in which there is no ministerial responsibility relates to the policies advocated by opposition parties. Members (particularly Government members) may try to elicit comment from a Minister through the question system on items of opposition policy. Such moves usually fail because the question deals with an issue outside the Minister's responsibility. The Minister is obviously interested in such matters but has no official connection with them. This disentitles members to question the Minister on them directly.

But the fact that Ministers cannot be questioned in a party capacity does not prevent them giving a party perspective in their replies. Nor is it obligatory for Ministers to use any particular form of words in replying so as to distinguish their official from their party capacities, though it is advisable that they do so, so that they are not misunderstood.[102]

Associate Ministers

The House formerly followed a strict rule as to which Ministers could have questions addressed to them. A question could be addressed only to the Minister with principal portfolio responsibility for a particular matter. It could not be addressed to a Minister with subordinate responsibilities (Ministers designated as "Deputy", "Associate" or "Assistant" Ministers). While the latter could answer a question on behalf of an absent principal portfolio Minister, they were not questionable in their own right even on statements they had made within their own areas of responsibility. Their position, as far as questions were concerned, was the same as Parliamentary Under-Secretaries.

Now, following a Standing Orders Committee recommendation in 1995,[103] questions can be asked directly of Associate Ministers within the limits of any responsibilities formally delegated to them by the principal Minister. ("Associate Minister" is taken to include all subordinate Ministers, however designated, but not Parliamentary Under-Secretaries.)

For this purpose, early in the term of a Parliament and at such other times as may be necessary, the Leader of the House presents to the House a schedule showing which areas of responsibility Ministers have delegated to Associate Ministers. This schedule definitively determines the areas in which Associate Ministers are answerable. If delegated responsibilities change, the Speaker should be informed of this.[104] Not all Associate Ministers have any specific areas assigned to them.

Until these areas of responsibility are known, questions must be addressed to the principal Minister.[105] When the delegations are announced questions relating to them can be addressed directly to the Associate Minister or continue to be addressed to the principal Minister as the member lodging the question sees fit. But the principal Minister can transfer a question to an Associate Minister who has delegated responsibility. However,

---

101   1997, Vol.564, pp.5192-3; 2000, Vol.587, p.5483.
102   2000, Vol.587, p.5483.
103   1993-96, AJHR, I.18A, p.76.
104   2001, Vol.596, p.12886.
105   2000, Vol.581, p.322.

an Associate Minister can be questioned only about matters delegated to the Associate. An Associate Minister cannot be asked a question ranging across the whole portfolio in a way that the principal Minister can be.[106] Nor can an Associate Minister be questioned about statements the Associate makes on matters outside his or her delegated responsibility even where they relate to another part of the portfolio.[107]

Parliamentary Under-Secretaries

A Parliamentary Under-Secretary may reply to a question on behalf of an absent Minister.[108] However, a question cannot be addressed to a Parliamentary Under-Secretary in his or her own right as if the under-secretary were a Minister. Questions to Ministers must be addressed to Ministers of the Crown (including now an Associate Minister). A Parliamentary Under-Secretary may answer a question on behalf of a Minister, but can have a question addressed to himself or herself personally as a non-Minister only in respect of parliamentary proceedings of which the under-secretary has charge (for example, as the chairperson of a select committee), not in respect of the wider range of responsibilities for which Ministers are answerable. Thus, a question to a Parliamentary Under-Secretary relating to a statement the under-secretary had made was not allowed, even though the statement was made in respect of the Parliamentary Under-Secretary's official departmental duties.[109]

Transfer of questions between Ministers

A problem related to ministerial responsibility is: who is the proper Minister to answer a question? When members lodge a question they address it to a particular Minister, but it may transpire on closer examination that it is not that Minister but another Minister who has the responsibility to answer it. This is particularly likely to happen when a Minister holds more than one closely related portfolio. The classification of questions for which there is ministerial responsibility is a matter for Ministers to decide, and a Minister may, on informing the Clerk, have a question transferred to another Minister if it has been misdirected in the first place.[110] The arrangements for these transfers are made administratively between Ministers' offices and the Office of the Clerk, and the questions list and the parliamentary website are corrected accordingly.

A member cannot insist on a particular Minister or department dealing with a question. It may be transferred to another Minister without reference to the member who lodged the question if Ministers judge that its transfer is appropriate. If the member is dissatisfied with a transfer, the member has the right to withdraw it or to refuse to ask it.[111] Ultimately, however, the Speaker could refuse to allow a question to be transferred if the transfer would be an abuse; for example, where the responsibility for a subject was obviously held by a particular Minister.[112] This might happen, for instance, if the Minister concerned could be expected to have personal knowledge of an issue that it would not be likely that any other Minister would have.[113] In two known instances the Speaker has refused to permit the transfer of a question that was not inherently transferable.[114] This power to refuse to permit a question to be transferred has been called a "longstop protection" against abuse.[115] But, short of such an exceptional circumstance, the Speaker will not second-guess a ministerial transfer of a question, otherwise it would be the Speaker who was determining internal governmental arrangements rather than Ministers.

---

[106]   *Ibid.*
[107]   *Ibid.*, pp.621-2.
[108]   S.O.376(2).
[109]   1977, Vol.413, pp.2690-1.
[110]   1969, Vol.362, pp.2045-6.
[111]   1998, Vol.566, p.7091; 2005, Vol.623, p.18529.

[112]   1992, Vol.523, p.7583; 1994, Vol.539, p.316; 1996, Vol.555, pp.12594, 12748-9.
[113]   2000, Vol.581, p.322.
[114]   1998, Vol.573, p.13010; 2001, Vol.596, p.13150.
[115]   2002, Vol.598, pp.14893-4.

A Minister is under an obligation to transfer a question to the appropriate Minister if it has been misdirected. It is not satisfactory to reply to a question by saying that it should have been directed to another Minister. If that is so, the Minister should have arranged its transfer in the first place.[116]

A question can be transferred at any time up to the time at which it is asked.[117] While it is desirable that the Clerk be advised of a transfer as soon as possible so that this may be reflected in the questions list, transfers frequently take place after the initial publication of the list, whether electronically or in hard copy. The transfer of a question will often involve changes to its text to reflect the different Minister who is to answer it. Provided that these are consequential and do not involve substantive changes, they can be made without recourse to the member who lodged the question.[118]

Transfer of questions involving the Prime Minister

Objections to ministerial transfers of questions commonly arise in respect of questions addressed to the Prime Minister. Given the overall nature of a Prime Minister's responsibilities, every question for which there is any ministerial responsibility necessarily entails prime ministerial responsibility too. On this basis all questions could be addressed to the Prime Minister. But members are expected to, and do, address their questions to the Minister with direct portfolio responsibility, reserving questions to the Prime Minister for matters for which there is direct prime ministerial responsibility or for questions affecting the Government as a whole.

Where the Prime Minister considers that a question should be redirected to a Minister, the question is transferred to the Minister. There is no specific Prime Minister's question time. The Speaker has rejected suggestions that this permits the Prime Minister to avoid answering questions altogether. Prime Ministers cannot be seen to be continually avoiding potentially difficult questions and, in fact, this does not happen. During the course of 1998 up to August, for example, the Prime Minister answered an average of two of the 12 questions answered each day.[119]

QUESTIONS TO OTHER MEMBERS

As well as questions to Ministers, questions may be addressed to other members of the House (Government or opposition) but, as compared to questions to Ministers, in much more restricted circumstances.

A question to a non-Minister can be for oral or for written answer, except in the case of the Speaker, when it can only be for written answer.[120] Questions to non-Ministers are subject to the same rules regarding notice and contents as questions to Ministers.

Questions can be put to non-Ministers regarding any bill, motion or public matter connected with the business of the House of which the member has charge.[121] Only one matter may be raised in a question, not a number of items of business or a generality of issues. In respect of the Speaker, questions can relate only to any matter of administration for which the Speaker is responsible.[122]

The range of answerable questions to non-Ministers is much narrower than in the case of questions to Ministers. Apart from the Speaker, they must relate exclusively to proceedings in the House of which the member has charge, whereas a Minister, as well as being answerable for proceedings in the House, is answerable for his or her department

---

116 1987, Vol.483, p.224.
117 2000, Vol.582, p.1156; 2004, Vol.615, p.11366.
118 1998, Vol.566, p.7091; 1999, Vol.578, p.17300.
119 1998, Vol.570, p.11197.

120 S.O.370(2).
121 S.O.370(1).
122 S.O.370(2).

and for public affairs generally with which the Minister is officially connected. The Standing Orders do not, therefore, give members a general opportunity to cross-question each other over statements made outside the House on policy or procedural matters.

Examples of members who may be questioned under this provision include: members who have introduced a Member's bill, a local bill or a private bill, on whether they intend to take a stage of the bill on a particular day; members who have presented a petition, on whether they or the petitioners intend to appear before the committee or withdraw the petition; and, most often, chairpersons of select committees, on the procedure being followed by their committees. (A question to the chairperson of a subcommittee has also been permitted.[123])

Questions to select committee chairpersons

Questions to chairpersons of select committees can only relate to a matter of which the committee has charge, either because the House has referred it to the committee or because the committee has resolved to inquire into it.[124] Questions cannot probe about matters not before the committee or no longer before the committee.

References to proceedings in committees not open to the public are not permitted until such committees have reported to the House. After reporting to the House, the chairperson of the committee cannot be further questioned, because questions to non-Ministers can only be on a matter of which the member has charge, and once the committee has reported the matter is in the hands of the House. The chairperson is no longer answerable for it.

The responsibility of the chairperson of a select committee is only to chair the committee. In this capacity the chairperson can be asked questions about the process or procedure to be followed by the committee in respect of a matter that is currently before it – for example, the time of its meetings or the likely date of its report back to the House.[125] The chairperson is not answerable for the actions of other committee members or for their reasons for voting as they did in the committee,[126] nor for why he or she voted on a particular issue. Nor can the chairperson be questioned on his or her opinion of a matter before the committee. The chairperson's views on such a matter are of no greater or lesser significance than those of any other member.[127] Also a chairperson is no more questionable on general statements he or she may have made outside the committee as a member of Parliament than is any other member.

Where a chairperson makes a statement under the Standing Orders informing the public of the nature of the committee's inquiry,[128] questions on the statement may be asked even though the matter before the committee is not open to the public. However, such questions cannot seek the committee's reasons for directing or initiating the statement where these have been discussed at the committee and constitute confidential committee proceedings.[129]

Questions to the Speaker

Only written questions may be asked of the Speaker and then only in respect of matters of administration for which the Speaker is responsible.[130] The Speaker cannot be asked for procedural guidance by way of a written question. The proper way to raise a procedural matter is by a point of order in the House. The matters on which the Speaker can be questioned include the Speaker's duties as chairperson of the Parliamentary Service Commission, and as the "Responsible Minister" for parliamentary departments such as

---

[123] 1977, Vol.415, p.3918.
[124] 2000, Vol.582, p.1083.
[125] 2002, Vol.599, p.15371.
[126] 2003, Vol.611, p.8251.
[127] 1998, Vol.570, p.11008; 2000, Vol.582, p.1083;

2002, Vol.599, p.15371.
[128] S.O.243(1).
[129] 1978, Vol.417, p.660.
[130] S.O.370(2).

the Office of the Clerk, the Parliamentary Service, the Office of the Ombudsmen, the office of the Auditor-General and the office of the Parliamentary Commissioner for the Environment. In these latter cases, the Speaker's responsibility does not extend to answering for the performance of the officers' statutory duties, but only for the financial and administrative issues associated with their organisations. Regardless of the capacity in which the question is being asked of the Speaker, a question is addressed to "the Speaker". Where the Speaker chairs a select committee, the Speaker may be questioned in this capacity but, again, only by way of written question.[131]

PREPARATION OF REPLIES
The building-in of a period of notice gives Ministers and other members to whom a question is addressed an opportunity to prepare a considered response to the question. How the preparation of replies is organised is a matter for those Ministers and members themselves. In the case of Ministers this will usually involve the Minister's department preparing a draft or drafts of a reply and, in the case of oral questions, also providing the Minister with background information that will help the Minister to anticipate and deal with supplementary questions. Generally, such drafts and information can be withheld under the *Official Information Act* so as to allow Ministers to make their own decisions as to the most appropriate manner in which to answer parliamentary questions. Releasing a draft answer might lead Ministers to seek less assistance from departments in answering questions and thus diminish the quality of the information presented to the House. However, withholding such information will not always be justified. In a particular case there may be counterveiling public interest considerations requiring disclosure.[132]

In the case of questions to other members, it is up to the member concerned whether to seek assistance in the preparation of a reply. For questions to select committee chairpersons, the clerk of the committee will automatically offer assistance in preparing a reply.

QUESTION TIME
Oral questions are dealt with as the first substantive item of business transacted by the House each day.[133] The only items preceding it are the formal announcements by the Clerk of the petitions, papers and select committee reports presented that day and of any bills introduced. Therefore, questions are usually reached within a few minutes of the House assembling.

Until 1996 the length of question time was prescribed in the Standing Orders as 45 minutes (having been increased from 40 minutes in 1986). Now no time for questions is prescribed in the Standing Orders or even recommended by the Standing Orders Committee. There are 12 oral questions to Ministers each day and there may be urgent questions and questions to other members. The House deals with all oral questions set down for answer each day.[134] The time it takes to get through all of these questions (which includes supplementary questions) varies from day to day from between 45 minutes to over one hour.

Question time is particularly well-attended by most members. It is also the fastest-moving part of the proceedings, with relatively short contributions from a large number of members. Consequently, it can become disruptive at times. Strictly speaking, interjections are not permitted at question time (which is not a debate) but they do feature and will be

---

tolerated as long as they do not get out of hand.[135] The Speaker's chairpersonship is very much to the fore at question time; calling members to ask supplementary questions, making decisions about whether the questions and replies are in order, keeping members' questions as brief as possible, preventing disorderly behaviour and ensuring that the House gets through the questions before it without taking an inordinate amount of time over this.

ASKING ORAL QUESTIONS

When a question is reached, the Speaker announces the number of the question and calls on the member in whose name it stands to ask it. A question is asked by the member identifying the Minister to whom the question is addressed and reading it out as it is printed on the list of questions circulated to members in the House.[136] Questions are read out even though printed on the list so that people listening on the radio will be able to follow proceedings. For the same reason an English interpretation is given of a question lodged in Māori even though a translation is also printed on the list.[137]

Another member may ask the question on behalf of the member in whose name it stands if the latter is absent from the Chamber and has authorised that other member to do so.[138] Authority will be implied when members ask questions on behalf of absent members of their own party. But where a member acts for a member of another party, any authority must have been given expressly. A member asking a question on behalf of another member without authority risks committing a contempt of the House.[139] A question cannot be asked on behalf of a member who has not taken the Oath of Allegiance and who is, therefore, not entitled to sit in the House (an unsworn member is able to seek a written answer to a question, however).[140]

Withdrawal of questions

Members are not obliged to ask questions standing in their names and are quite free to withdraw a question simply by informing the Clerk. The question will then be deleted from the question list. If the list has already been circulated, the Speaker, if informed beforehand that a member does not wish to ask a question standing in the member's name, will not call it and will pass on to the next question on the list. Even when the question is reached and called, the member may still decline to ask it. No member can be compelled to ask a question standing in his or her name and no member can ask it on behalf of the member in these circumstances without the member's permission.[141]

Postponement of questions

A question may, with the leave of the House, be postponed.[142] A member may request that his or her question be postponed. Often this is done so that the Minister to whom it is addressed can be present personally in the House to answer it. Exceptionally, a Minister who wishes to answer a particular question personally will ask a member to agree to postpone a question so that the Minister can be present to give the answer rather than have another Minister answer. If leave to postpone a question is not forthcoming, the member can still withdraw it and resubmit it later. If leave to postpone is granted, the question is placed on the list of questions for the day to which it is postponed, for answer after other

[135]   1996, Vol.554, p.12077.
[136]   S.O.375(1); 1977, Vol.413, p.2528.
[137]   1999, Vol.578, p.17268.
[138]   S.O.375(2).

[139]   1996, Vol.553, p.11645.
[140]   1979, Vol.423, p.800.
[141]   1969, Vol.364, p.3577; 1989, Vol.501, p.12742.
[142]   1974, Vol.394, p.4830.

oral questions to Ministers that day.[143] A question may be postponed for more than one sitting day ahead.

Asking urgent questions

Urgent questions are dealt with immediately after oral questions to Ministers have concluded. If an urgent question has been accepted, then at the end of oral questions on notice the Speaker calls upon the member to ask it.[144] The member must then ask the question in the same form as it has been submitted to the Speaker[145] (it does not, of course, appear on the questions list) and it is answered in the normal way.

Asking questions to other members

Questions to non-Ministers are taken after questions for oral answer and urgent questions (if any) have been disposed of.[146] Another member may ask a question of a non-Minister on behalf of the member who submitted it if that member is absent.

REPLIES TO ORAL QUESTIONS

When the question is asked, the Speaker calls upon the Minister or member to whom it is addressed to answer it.[147] In the absence of the Minister, another Minister or a Parliamentary Under-Secretary may answer the question, prefacing the answer with an indication that it is being given on behalf of the Minister.[148] If an acting Minister has been appointed, then that Minister is the Minister for the time being and replies to a question in his or her own right and not on behalf of anyone. A reply may be in the English or the Māori language,[149] but it is not obligatory for a reply to a question asked in Māori to be given in Māori, or vice versa.[150]

A question to a non-Minister is personal to the member to whom it is addressed and another member cannot deliver a reply for him or her. In the absence of the member to whom such a question is addressed, the question is held over.[151] However, if the question is to the chairperson of a select committee who is absent from New Zealand or while there is a vacancy in the chairpersonship, the deputy chairperson can reply.[152]

Obligation to reply

A Minister cannot be forced to answer a question (unless the House orders the Minister to do so, in which case failure to answer could be punished as a contempt). An answer that addresses the question ought to be given if it can be given consistent with the public interest.[153] It may be refused if, in the Minister's opinion, the public interest would be imperilled by giving the information sought.[154] These are matters for the Minister to judge.[155] Certainly a refusal to answer at all would be wholly exceptional. (An unsatisfactory answer is not a refusal to answer.)

If a Minister does not wish to reply at all to a question, strictly the Minister should not respond to the Speaker's call when the question is asked. This is not a satisfactory way of indicating an intention not to answer, and the Speaker has indicated that Ministers in these circumstances should announce the refusal to answer by taking a point of order.[156] A Minister is not obliged to give reasons for refusing to answer, although it is preferable to do so.[157] The fact that a Minister does not intend to answer a question, or does not intend

[143] 1974, Vol.395, p.5363.	[151] 1978, Vol.420, pp.3311-2.
[144] S.O.379(2).	[152] S.O.203(1).
[145] 1933, Vol.236, p.480.	[153] S.O.377(1).
[146] S.O.370(3).	[154] 1892, Vol.78, pp.374-5.
[147] S.O.376(1).	[155] 1991, Vol.514, p.1241.
[148] S.O.376(2); 1963, Vol.336, p.1519-20.	[156] 1980, Vol.433, pp.3244-5.
[149] 1990, Vol.508, p.2336.	[157] *Ibid.*
[150] 1994, Vol.542, p.3325.	

to answer it on that day and wishes to have it postponed, does not abrogate the right of the member who lodged the question to ask it if he or she so wishes. The member would, of course, be met with no reply at all or with the reply that the Minister declined to answer it on that day.[158]

A Minister's response to a question that he or she does not intend to answer it is in fact a reply, unsatisfactory as it may be to members. Sometimes Ministers may be reluctant to give an informative response on a matter that is under negotiation or consideration by another body. A response in these terms is not, strictly speaking, a refusal to reply. Whether to respond in this way is a matter for ministerial judgment.[159]

However, Ministers are not expected to respond in an irrelevant manner; to do so is to act contrary to the spirit of the question process.[160] In such a circumstance the Speaker may allow more supplementary questions to be asked than would otherwise be the case. It is unparliamentary for a Minister to refuse to give information in a question to one member that the Minister is prepared to give to another member, and the Speaker has sought a further explanation from a Minister in such circumstances.[161]

Formerly, Ministers could not be asked for their opinions in questions. This rule has been abolished and Ministers can now be asked for an opinion on a matter for which they have responsibility. Though Ministers can be asked for their opinions, they are not obliged to give them in answering such a question or to respond to a hypothetical situation suggested in a question.[162] Whether they do so or not is a matter for them.

If the Minister thinks that a question is not in order, the Minister's proper course is to challenge it on a point of order and not to decline to answer it. The Speaker, not the Minister, decides whether it is in order.[163]

Form of reply

The Minister's reply must address the question asked. This involves a question of relevancy. The reply must be a direct response to the question; it cannot be a statement on an unrelated matter which it suits the Minister to introduce.[164]

Answering questions in the House is an important element in ministerial responsibility.[165] Ministers are therefore expected to take questions seriously and to give informative replies to them,[166] though how they go about answering questions is largely up to them.[167] Members cannot stipulate how Ministers must reply (for example, by insisting on a 'yes' or 'no' answer[168]), nor can the Speaker require a reply to be couched in one form rather than another.[169] Ministers in replying are not precluded from referring to newspaper reports that they have seen, rather than relying on official reports.[170]

The Minister's reply to a question is required to conform to many of the rules applying to questions. It must be concise and confined to the subject matter of the question asked.[171] It must not contain statements of facts and the names of any persons unless they are strictly necessary to answer the question.[172] Nor does a statement of fact in a reply require to be authenticated (as it would in a question).[173] The reply must be no longer than is necessary to answer the question adequately. But Ministers may add more than the bare facts in giving their replies. Any information which would supplement the reasons for the answer may be added.[174] Ministers must, however, confine themselves to giving information

[158]   1892, Vol.78, pp.374-5.
[159]   2001, Vol.592, pp.9009, 9101; 2002, Vol.603, pp.1182-3.
[160]   1991, Vol.521, p.5624; 2001, Vol.592, p.9170.
[161]   1994, Vol.542, p.3587; 2000, Vol.586, p.5168.
[162]   2004, Vol.615, p.11430.
[163]   1991, Vol.514, p.1241.
[164]   2001, Vol.595, p.11634; 2004, Vol.615, p.11495.
[165]   2004, Vol.620, p.15443.
[166]   1995, Vol.550, p.9423.
[167]   1997, Vol.558, p.484.
[168]   2004, Vol.617, p.12762.
[169]   2001, Vol.592, p.9009; 2002, Vol.603, p.1182.
[170]   1995, Vol.549, p.8728.
[171]   S.O.377(2).
[172]   S.O.377(2)(a).
[173]   2003, Vol.608, p.4959; 2005, Vol.627, p.22173.
[174]   1975, Vol.398, p.2070.

about matters for which they have responsibility. They cannot speculate about what may or may not be the effects of another political party's policy.[175]

Answers may not contain the plethora of expressions debarred from questions – arguments, inferences, imputations, epithets and ironical expressions[176] – and they must not contain any discreditable references to members or offensive or unparliamentary expressions.[177] Ministers may not, for example, make provocative remarks, such as commenting on the extent of the questioner's knowledge.[178] Ministers, in their replies, are also under the general constraint against referring to select committee proceedings not open to the public, and to cases pending adjudication in a court.[179]

The notes that Ministers use to answer questions are not official documents that, if quoted from, must be laid on the Table[180] but any other official document quoted by a Minister in answering a question can be required to be produced.

Adequacy of reply

While Ministers are required to "address" the question asked in their replies, whether the reply provided actually "answers" the question asked is a subjective judgment. It is no part of the Speaker's role to make such a judgment.[181] The test of adequacy is whether the answer addresses the question by being relevant to it.[182] Essentially, the House itself and public opinion (assisted by the news media and reports of parliamentary proceedings) are the judges of the adequacy of a reply by making a political judgment on the matter.[183] This is the position whether the criticism of a reply is directed to its accuracy in terms of facts asserted or its comprehensiveness in answering the question asked. (The Speaker does have a role in ensuring that it remains relevant to the subject matter of the question.)

Thus the Speaker cannot be appealed to on the ground that the reply is inaccurate.[184] A deliberate attempt to mislead the House would be a contempt and if a Minister discovers that incorrect information has been given to the House the Minister is expected to correct the record as soon as possible. But subject to these circumstances, accuracy or otherwise is a matter that may be disputed and the Speaker is not the judge of it. It is a matter for political criticism of the Minister concerned if members believe that a Minister has answered incorrectly.

Questions often have more than one leg to them. If this is the case, members cannot demand that a reply addresses every leg of their question. The Minister has the latitude to address one or other of the legs of a question and ignore others. This is a risk that members run in asking multiple questions.[185] It is also permissible for Ministers to answer questions that contain a premise or statement by disagreeing with or controverting the premise or statement.[186]

The widening of the scope of question time to permit members to ask Ministers for their opinions and to include hypothetical material in their questions has contributed to greater dissatisfaction with the replies to questions of much wider scope than formerly.[187] In essence, whether a reply emerges that answers the question satisfactorily, either in the questioner's view or even in any "objective" sense, is a matter for political discourse. No one person is imbued with the power to make such a judgment. Question time allows issues to be raised. It does not necessarily resolve them to everyone's satisfaction.

---

175 1993, Vol.534, p.14437.
176 S.O.377(2)(b).
177 S.O.377(2)(c).
178 1971, Vol.374, p.2813.
179 S.O.377(3).
180 1997, Vol.565, p.5769; 2000, Vol.586, p.5105.
181 2001, Vol.592, p.9172.

182 2005, Vol.625, p.20447.
183 2002, Vol.603, p.1622; 2003, Vol.608, p.5242; 2004, Vol.620, p.15448.
184 2004, Vol.616, p.11840.
185 *Ibid.*, p.11998; 2005, Vol.626, p.21043.
186 2005, Vol.623, p.18867.
187 2004, Vol.620, p.15448.

Follow-up to replies

Anyone giving inaccurate information in a reply to a question must correct this as soon as the error is appreciated. In the case of a reply to an oral question the appropriate procedure for correcting an answer is by way of a personal explanation.[188] Should leave be refused for this purpose (as has occurred on occasion), the Minister or member should write to the member who asked the question and to the Speaker, correcting the reply.

Where a Minister, in replying to an oral question, has promised to supply further information to the questioner, the Minister must follow up on this promise within a reasonable time. A member who does not receive the promised information can take this up with the Speaker.[189]

SUPPLEMENTARY QUESTIONS

Once the Minister has delivered his or her reply, members have an opportunity to ask supplementary questions at the discretion of the Speaker.[190] Supplementary questions are asked by members in their own right. They are not asked on behalf of other members.[191]

The Minister naturally does not know exactly what supplementary questions may be asked, but is not entirely in the dark. Supplementary questions may only be put to elucidate or clarify a matter raised in the original question or in the answer given to the question.[192] Supplementaries must be relevant to the original question asked; they are not an opportunity to ask questions without notice, which is a practice unknown in the New Zealand House of Representatives.

A supplementary question must conform to all the rules of content and form in respect of questions generally.[193] Members may ask only one supplementary question at a time[194] and any second element in such a question must be closely related to the first part and by way of a wind-off to the question being asked;[195] it may not be prefaced with a statement.[196] But it is more difficult to apply the detailed rules – for instance, on authentication – to oral exchanges on the floor of the House than it is to analyse questions submitted on forms in an office, and supplementary questions that would be disallowed as primary questions are inevitably allowed from time to time.[197]

Not all replies to questions provoke supplementary questions, although most do. Members wishing to ask a supplementary question rise in their places and seek the call. No member has a right to ask a supplementary question.[198] While it is entirely over to the Speaker as to whether supplementaries are permitted at all, in practice the House expects them to be asked and they are regarded as an integral, indeed vital, part of question time. As a matter of practice, the member who asked the original question is preferred first if he or she wishes to ask a supplementary question. If the questioner does not have a further question to ask, the Speaker will call any other member on the questioner's side of the House instead.[199]

After the member who asked the original question has had his or her turn, other members may ask supplementary questions.

While the Standing Orders repose the discretion entirely in the Speaker as to whom to call to ask supplementary questions and how many questions to permit on each question, in fact firm practices have evolved in the multi-party environment as to how this discretion is exercised.

Depending upon party sizes in the House, the Speaker allows each party a "quota" of

188	2003, Vol.608, p.5093.	194	1984, Vol.458, p.1401.
189	2003, Vol.609, p.6544.	195	1999, Vol.575, p.15343.
190	S.O.371(1).	196	1984, Vol.459, p.1786.
191	S.O.371(2).	197	1988, Vol.492, p.7082.
192	S.O.371(1).	198	1975, Vol.399, p.2682.
193	1985, Vol.462, p.4549.	199	1977, Vol.416, p.4995.

supplementary questions. Even if there are fewer than 12 questions lodged on a particular day the Speaker allows the same number of supplementary questions overall. Those questions can then be utilised by members of each party as they see fit. In this way parties choose how they wish to distribute their allocation of supplementary questions. They are not obliged to ask a supplementary question to every primary question just for the sake of it. (In fact smaller parties would not have enough supplementary questions to do this in any case.) Parties usually advise the Speaker in advance which primary questions they intend to ask supplementary questions to.[200] After giving preference to the member who asked the primary question, the Speaker calls members to ask supplementary questions in order of the size of parties. The Speaker endeavours to give all parties a chance to ask their first supplementary question before a party is allowed to ask a second supplementary question on that question.

In respect of an urgent question, supplementary questions are restricted to one question from the member asking the urgent question.[201] In respect of a question to other members, the Speaker exercises an unfettered discretion as to how many supplementary questions to permit.

REPLIES TO WRITTEN QUESTIONS

The member who has lodged a written question has nothing further to do to obtain the answer to the question. A question may be withdrawn by the member informing the Clerk at any time up to the receipt of the reply by the Clerk. After that time the question has already been answered and it is too late to withdraw it.

The reply to a written question must be lodged in electronic form with the Clerk.[202] The reply should be signed by way of an electronic signature by the Minister or one of the Minister's colleagues.[203] How the electronic signature is affixed is a matter for the Minister to decide as long as the Minister has authorised it. Thus a Minister's practice of authorising the affixing of his electronic signature by signing a hard copy of the reply was perfectly acceptable.[204]

The reply must be lodged with the Clerk no later than the sixth working day following the publication of the question.[205] This effectively gives one week for the reply to be prepared. A reply due on a particular day does not have to be lodged at any particular time on that day.[206]

Co-ordinated replies

There are a number of well-established governmental practices designed to co-ordinate replies to written questions. This is especially so where a question in similar terms is lodged to all Ministers and it is convenient for the Government to collect and collate information centrally or to respond with a single policy statement. Such questions might elicit a similar reply from all of the Ministers to whom they are addressed, or one substantive reply from one Minister and replies from the other Ministers merely directing attention to that substantive reply.

In the case of written questions addressed to the same Minister, the Minister may provide one amalgamated reply if this is warranted. But amalgamating replies cannot be used as a device to withhold information from the House, such as to avoid responding with disaggregated figures where this is material to the question asked.[207] The practice of

---

[200] See, for example, 2001, Vol.590, p.7600 when this practice began to develop.
[201] S.O.379(3).
[202] S.O.373(3)(a).
[203] S.O.373(3)(b).
[204] 2004, Vol.617, p.12621.
[205] S.O.373(4).
[206] 2003, Vol.608, p.5690.
[207] 2001, Vol.591, pp.8779-80.

amalgamating replies can only be resorted to where the questions concerned are themselves of a similar nature or are otherwise associated with each other. It is not acceptable to amalgamate replies to dissimilar questions into a single reply.[208]

Holding replies

As Ministers have only six working days to prepare replies to often complicated questions, a practice has developed of giving "holding" or "interim" replies in some cases and following up later with full replies. Technically these holding replies are the replies in terms of the Standing Orders and the later full reply is in the nature of a direct communication between the Minister and member concerned.[209] But Speakers have emphasised that holding replies should only be used exceptionally and every endeavour must be made by the Minister to follow up with the full reply as soon as possible thereafter.[210] Ministers have been reminded that giving holding replies should not become the norm. It is not acceptable to issue holding replies because a Minister's office has a large number of questions to deal with. A holding reply is only justified if a particular question will require considerable research to produce an answer.[211] If a Minister considers that this is the case, the Minister should say so in the initial reply. A Minister should not give a holding reply promising to supply the information and then follow up with a reply declining to provide it on the grounds of the expense involved. A promise having been given must be kept.[212] Nor should a holding reply be given where the Minister does not intend to follow up with a fully informative reply. It was thus wrong to give a holding reply and then some time later a short reply that could just as easily have been given in the first place.[213]

Contents of replies

The same rules as apply to the contents of replies to oral questions apply to replies to written questions. However, a written answer to a question is primarily a matter between the Minister and the member concerned, and the Speaker will not become involved in it unless it is brought to the Speaker's attention. The Speaker does not encourage this being done in the House, but will always consider objections by members to the replies they have received when they raise these with the Speaker in writing. In all cases, however, a member objecting to the contents of a reply must discuss it first with the Minister concerned to try to resolve any difficulties.[214] If the Speaker finds that a reply to a written question is not confined to the subject-matter of the question asked, or is otherwise out of order, it may be ordered to be amended and republished.[215]

Publication of replies

All replies are published on the parliamentary website on the third working day following the day on which they are lodged.[216] (The Speaker may relax this requirement in exceptional circumstances arising from the operation of the website.[217]) This delay in publication is to ensure that the member who asked the question has advice of the reply prior to its general publication.

Amended replies

If a Minister discovers that information provided in a written reply is incorrect, the Minister must, as soon as practicable, lodge an amended reply with the Office of the Clerk. This is then provided to the member and published on the parliamentary website. A Minister

---

[208]   2000, Vol.588, p.6851.
[209]   1995, Vol.546, pp.6366-7.
[210]   1995, Vol.547, pp.7195-6; 2000, Vol.582, p.872.
[211]   2000, Vol.582, p.1162.
[212]   2001, Vol.591, p.8913.
[213]   2000, Vol.586, p.5168.
[214]   1983, Vol.452, p.2013.
[215]   1983, Vol.450, p.388.
[216]   S.O.373(3)(c)(ii).
[217]   S.O.373(5).

should not merely correct an answer to an earlier question in replying to a subsequent question.[218] Where a Minister appreciates that there has been an error but needs further time to assemble the correct information, the Minister should still acknowledge the error immediately by lodging a further reply with the Clerk and provide a fully corrected reply in due course.[219]

---

[218] 2003, Vol.609, p.6121.   [219] *Ibid.*

CHAPTER 41

REFERENDUMS

Referendums have been used in New Zealand for more than a century as a means of making decisions on issues of public policy. The first national referendum in the country's history was held on 7 December 1911 on the prohibition of the sale of liquor.[1] The sale of liquor has been the most common subject to be submitted to a referendum. Until 1987 liquor licensing was subject to regular nationally organised referendums held at the time of each general election, as well as to local polls relating to the sale of liquor in particular localities. In 1949 three national referendums on social issues were held simultaneously (on off-course betting, sale of liquor and conscription).[2] Other legislation containing provisions for the calling of referendums or polls has included such matters as local authority loans and producer-board levies. As well as these standing legislative provisions, national referendums have been organised under special legislation from time to time on such subjects as betting, compulsory military training, compulsory retirement savings and the electoral system.

A referendum is an exercise in direct democracy, whereas the parliamentary system is the operation of a representative democracy. The two are not incompatible, but they raise separate issues. This work is not concerned with referendums generally. These are held under the terms of the legislation governing them and do not raise special issues for the parliamentary process. But there are two types of referendum that do have a special relationship to the parliamentary process – electoral referendums and citizens'-initiated referendums.

ELECTORAL REFERENDUMS

Binding referendums
Certain parts of the electoral system are entrenched in law by a requirement that any proposal for their amendment or repeal must be passed by a 75 percent majority of all the members of the House or carried by a majority of valid votes cast at a poll of the electors of the general and Māori electoral districts.[3] The provisions that can be altered only in this special way are known as reserved provisions. They are: the three-year term of Parliament; the constitution of the Representation Commission; the division of New Zealand into general electoral districts after each census; the electoral quota adjustment; the provisions that prescribe 18 years of age as the minimum voting age; and the provisions dealing with the method of voting.[4] The special majority provisions are not required for the repeal of a reserved provision in a consolidating Act if that provision is at the same time re-enacted without amendment and the re-enacted provision is also entrenched.[5]

The practice of the House in dealing with legislation that proposes to amend or repeal a reserved provision is dealt with in discussing the legislative process. (See Chapter 27.) The alternative means of effecting the amendment or repeal of a reserved provision is for this to be submitted to a referendum of electors. This can be done only by legislation. There is no general legislation providing the mechanism for a legally-binding electoral

---

[1] Atkinson, *Adventures in Democracy*, p.125.
[2] *Ibid.*, p.161.
[3] *Electoral Act* 1993, s.268(2).
[4] *Ibid.*, s.268(1).
[5] *Ibid.*, s.268(2), proviso.

referendum to be held, Parliament must pass special legislation for this purpose.[6] The only electoral referendum to be held in terms of the entrenched provisions of an Electoral Act was that held in November 1993 on the question of the voting system.

Legislation submitting a reserved provision to a referendum must be "binding", in the sense of self-implementing, if the amendment or repeal of a reserved provision is to be made by the electors rather than Parliament. Only if a referendum is binding in this sense has Parliament transferred the responsibility of making the change to the electors rather than shouldering it itself. Where Parliament does transfer responsibility for the change to the electors, no special majority of members is needed to pass the legislation providing for the referendum, even for provisions in the legislation that provide for the contingent repeal or amendment of reserved provisions (the contingency being the carrying of the proposal at the referendum). To constitute a binding referendum the proposal must spell out fully the details of the alternative system or systems under consideration.[7]

The November 1993 referendum was structured in this way. It was authorised by special legislation that applied many of the provisions of the *Electoral Act* 1956 to its conduct[8] and provided for the Chief Electoral Officer to declare whether the proposal was carried.[9] The proposal submitted to electors was a choice between the existing first-past-the-post system of electing members of Parliament and the alternative mixed member proportional system provided for under the contingent legislation.[10] That contingent legislation, the *Electoral Act* 1993, repealed five of the six reserved provisions (all except the provision for a three-year term of Parliament) and altered at least two of them in the provisions that it substituted. Had the legislation that became the *Electoral Act* 1993 not been made subject to a binding electoral referendum, those provisions would clearly have been required to be passed by a 75 percent majority of members.

The binding effect of the referendum was achieved by the enactment of a statutory trigger. The new electoral legislation was to be brought into force in stages, following the Chief Electoral Officer's declaration that the proposal favouring the introduction of a mixed member proportional system had been carried.[11] If the proposal had not been carried, the new legislation would have been automatically repealed.[12] In the event, the proposal was carried and the legislation took effect accordingly.[13]

Non-binding referendums

Apart from the 1993 referendum, four other referendums on electoral matters have been held. Legislation passed in 1967 and in 1990 made provision for electoral polls to be held on proposals to increase the term of Parliament from three years to four years.[14] These were not binding referendums. They contained no provisions automatically effecting the amendments to the law should the proposals have been carried. In each case it would have been necessary for Parliament to have passed further legislation giving effect to the electorate's wishes. In such a case it would have had to have done so by a 75 percent majority, notwithstanding the result of the poll, because it would be Parliament, not the electors, that was taking ultimate responsibility for making the law change. In the event, the polls favoured retaining a three-year term for Parliament.

An electoral referendum was held in 1992 to allow electors to indicate in principle whether they supported a change to the voting system and which of a range of alternative voting options they favoured.[15] This was an indicative poll with no automatic legislative consequences. Parliament gave effect to the results of the referendum in the *Electoral*

6   1999-2002, AJHR, I.22A, p.626.
7   1991-93, AJHR, I.17A, p.5.
8   *Electoral Referendum Act* 1993, s.3.
9   *Ibid.*, s.19.
10 *Ibid.*, s.2(2) and Schedule.
11 *Electoral Act* 1993, s.2(1), (2).
12 *Ibid.*, s.2(3).
13 *New Zealand Gazette*, 16 December 1993, pp.3753-4.
14 *Electoral Poll Act* 1967; *Term Poll Act* 1990.
15 *Electoral Referendum Act* 1991.

Referendum Act 1993 and the *Electoral Act* 1993. In 1999 a citizens'-initiated referendum was held on the size of the House of Representatives.[16] This was also a non-binding referendum.

Such non-binding referendums can now be held by postal vote under general legislation.[17]

CITIZENS'-INITIATED REFERENDUMS

A general legislative mechanism for citizens to initiate the holding of referendums (referred to as "referenda" in the legislation[18]) came into force on 1 February 1994. This involves the collection of sufficient signatures to a petition supporting the holding of a referendum and the delivery of that petition to the Clerk of the House. In respect of a petition that attracts the support of 10 percent of all registered voters, a referendum must then be held. This form of statutory petition is quite different from the ordinary petitions that individuals and groups frequently address to the House, and nothing in the new legislation affects the right to petition the House or the right of the House to deal with those types of petitions.[19] A petition that purports to be made under the legislation but that has not followed the statutory procedure may be presented to the House and dealt with as an ordinary petition.[20]

Scope of referendum

Any referendum held following the presentation of a referendum petition is indicative only.[21] It cannot by itself effect any change to the law or bind any person; it is intended to influence or persuade the Government, Parliament or some other constituency to implement or adopt the views it expresses. Because it is non-binding, a citizens'-initiated referendum is not an effective means of amending or repealing a reserved provision in the *Electoral Act*.

But while a citizens'-initiated referendum is not binding, there are few restrictions on the subject matter with which it may deal. There cannot be a referendum petition about a disputed parliamentary election result or about a disputed referendum result on an earlier citizens'-initiated referendum,[22] nor can a petition that is to the like effect to a citizens'-initiated referendum held within the previous five years be accepted.[23] With these limited restrictions, a citizens'-initiated referendum petition may be on any subject.

Proposals for petitions

A referendum petition cannot simply be circulated. To comply with the legislation it must go through a process of vetting and submissions designed to define the precise question that is to be offered to the judgment of the electors.

For this purpose any person wishing to promote a referendum petition must first submit a proposal for it to the Clerk of the House. The proposal must be accompanied by a draft of the petition and the fee payable, and give the name of the proposer, a New Zealand address where the proposer or the proposer's representative can be contacted and, where appropriate, the name of that representative.[24]

A referendum petition can be promoted by a natural person (whether or not an elector) and a body of persons (whether corporate or unincorporate). There may be joint promoters. Where the proposer is not a natural person, the Clerk will need to be satisfied

---

[16] *New Zealand Gazette*, 4 May 2000, pp.1018-9.
[17] *Referenda (Postal Voting) Act* 2000.
[18] The word "referenda" has been described as a piece of dog-Latin: Frank Haden, "Words", *The Dominion*, 18 April 1998.
[19] *Citizens Initiated Referenda Act* 1993, s.59.
[20] 1998, Vol.570, p.10997.
[21] *Citizens Initiated Referenda Act* 1993, s.3.
[22] *Ibid.*, s.4.
[23] *Ibid.*, s.11(2)(b).
[24] *Ibid.*, s.6.

as to the proposer's status, that it desires to promote a referendum petition and that the person claiming to represent it is authorised to do so. These matters can be established by a statutory declaration or by other sufficient proof being produced.

The prescribed fee that must accompany a referendum proposal is $500.[25] This fee, which includes goods and services tax,[26] is payable to the Clerk of the House of Representatives.

Advertising of proposal

If the Clerk is satisfied that the proposal is in order, its receipt is notified in the *Gazette* and such newspapers as the Clerk considers necessary. These latter will usually be newspapers circulating in the main centres. It is also the practice to notify receipt of the proposal in the *Parliamentary Bulletin* and to retain the notice in the bulletin while the proposal is open for submissions.

The notice includes the wording of the question that the proposer wishes to put to voters in the referendum and calls for submissions on that wording. At least 28 days must be allowed from the date of publication of the notice in the *Gazette* for persons to make comments on the question. They do this by sending three copies of their submission to the Clerk.[27] One copy of each submission received is sent to the proposer and one copy is made available at the Office of the Clerk for inspection.[28]

Withdrawal or cancellation of a proposal

A proposal for a referendum petition and any referendum petition itself may be withdrawn at any time by the promoter. In either case this is done by giving written notice to the Clerk of the House. Where this is done before the Clerk has determined the precise question to be included in the referendum petition (and the petition is therefore still at the proposal stage), no determination of a question is made at all.[29] Notice that a petition has been withdrawn at this stage is given in the *Gazette*. Where withdrawal is effected after the question has been determined (and the proposal has become a referendum petition), the Clerk is required both to notify the Governor-General and to publish notice of the withdrawal in the *Gazette*.[30] Withdrawal of a petition may be effected at any time before the writs for the holding of a referendum on it have been issued. In such a case no referendum is held.[31]

If the promoter dies or (in the case of a corporation) is dissolved or put into liquidation before the Clerk has determined the question on a proposal, no question is determined and the proposal is cancelled at that point.[32] If there is more than one promoter, the death or dissolution of one does not prevent the proposal proceeding. Once the question has been determined and the proposal becomes a referendum petition, the death or dissolution of the promoter does not automatically cancel it, although as there is no longer anyone in a position to promote it, it will lapse in due course.

Determination of question

The Clerk must consult with the proposer and may consult with any other person as to the determination of the precise question to be included in the referendum petition.[33] The Legislation Advisory Committee and the government departments most closely concerned with the subject matter of the proposed referendum are invited by the Clerk to comment

---

25   *Citizens Initiated Referenda (Fees) Regulations* 1993, reg.2.
26   *Ibid.*, reg.3.
27   *Citizens Initiated Referenda Act* 1993, s.7(1), (2).
28   *Ibid.*, s.8.
29   *Ibid.*, s.11(2)(a)(i).
30   *Ibid.*, s.22A(3).
31   *Ibid.*, s.22A(1), (2).
32   *Ibid.*, s.11(2)(a)(ii), (iii).
33   *Ibid.*, s.9.

as a matter of course. Cabinet has acknowledged that it is appropriate for departments to give the Clerk technical assistance in the task of finalising the wording of the question without commenting on the substantive merits of the proposal.[34] Any comments received as a result of this consultation are communicated to the proposer.

The Clerk, having taken account of the proposal, comments received on it, the consultation engaged in and such other matters as the Clerk considers relevant,[35] determines the precise question to be put to voters in the proposed referendum.[36] For this purpose the practice has been to allow the promoter to comment on a provisionally determined question, before making the final determination. There can be only one question to a referendum petition.[37] That question, as determined by the Clerk, must convey clearly the purpose and effect of the referendum and ensure that only one of two answers may be given to it.[38]

One of the intentions of the requirement that the Clerk determine the precise question is to ensure that the result of any referendum provides meaningful guidance to the Government and to Parliament as to the views of electors. But the Clerk cannot, in the course of determining the terms of the question, turn the proposal into something it does not purport to be (for example, the proposed referendum may not relate to action to be taken by the Government at all). The Clerk is obliged, in determining the question, to take reasonable steps to frame the question in a neutral way. But the subject of the proposal may not permit complete neutrality and in all cases the subject is chosen by the promoter.[39]

The determination of the precise question must be made within three months of receipt of the proposal.[40] Determination of the precise question is perfected when written notice of it is given to the promoter.[41] Notice of the question must also be published in the *Gazette* and in such newspapers as the Clerk considers necessary.[42] This is likely to be the same newspapers as those in which the receipt of the proposal was originally notified.

Forms for signatures

The Clerk must, as soon as practicable after determining the question, approve a form on which signatures to the petition are to be collected. For this purpose the Clerk may consult with the Government Statistician and such other persons as the Clerk thinks fit.[43] The petition itself must ask that an indicative referendum be held and it must specify the question, as finally determined by the Clerk, to be put to voters.[44] These details are incorporated into any form approved by the Clerk so that potential signatories know what they are being invited to sign. The form must contain spaces for the following details: the signature; the full name of the signatory; the signatory's residential address; and the signatory's date of birth.[45] The forms normally make provision for 10 to 20 persons to sign on each form.

When a form has been approved, notice of it is given to the proposer and published in the *Gazette* and newspapers.[46] This will often be done along with the notice advising of the precise question to be put to voters. The notice (or notices if published separately) must set out the precise question and the name of the proposer. It must also identify the proposer as the person who has been approved to use the wording which has been determined by the Clerk, as the person who will promote a referendum petition with that wording and as the person who is authorised to use the form that the Clerk has approved.[47]

[34]   *Cabinet Manual*, 2001, para.5.98.
[35]   *Citizens Initiated Referenda Act* 1993, s.10(2).
[36]   *Ibid.*, s.11(1).
[37]   *Ibid.*, s.5(2).
[38]   *Ibid.*, s.10(1).
[39]   *Egg Producers Federation of New Zealand v Clerk of the House of Representatives*, unreported, High Court, Wellington, 20 June 1994.
[40]   *Citizens Initiated Referenda Act* 1993, s.11(2).
[41]   *Ibid.*, s.13(1)(a)(i).
[42]   *Ibid.*, s.13(1)(b).
[43]   *Ibid.*, s.12.
[44]   *Ibid.*, s.5(1).
[45]   *Ibid.*, s.15(1).
[46]   *Ibid.*, s.13(1)(a)(ii), (b).
[47]   *Ibid.*, s.13(2).

Collecting signatures

When, but not before, the promoter of a referendum petition has received notification from the Clerk of the precise question to be put to voters and of the approved form, the promoter may proceed to promote the petition and collect signatures. All signatures must be on the approved form and will not count towards achieving the required number if they are not. It is the promoter's responsibility to arrange the printing and circulation of forms as approved by the Clerk.[48]

Signatories must, alongside their signatures, state their full names and addresses. They may, but do not have to, add their dates of birth.[49] Electronic signatures are not acceptable.[50]

The promoter has 12 months from the date of publication in the *Gazette* of the precise question determined by the Clerk to collect signatures to the petition. The petition must be delivered to the Clerk within this time if it is to proceed. If it is not so delivered, it lapses.[51] Persons who are invited to sign by the promoter or by the promoter's agents are not asked to endorse the promoter's substantive aims. The petition asks for a referendum to be held on a subject; it does not ask for support for any particular proposition. That is a matter to be addressed when the referendum is held if that stage is ever reached.

Expenditure in relation to a petition

No person (whether the promoter or not) may spend more than $50,000 on advertisements published or broadcast in relation to an indicative referendum petition, nor more than $50,000 on promoting one of the answers to the question to be given in any referendum that is held on it.[52]

Any person who commissions advertising promoting a referendum petition or supporting one side or the other in the referendum must file a return listing such advertising and its cost. This return must be made to the Chief Electoral Officer within one month of the petition lapsing or within one month of the result of the referendum being formally announced.[53]

The Chief Electoral Officer has no authority to publicise a referendum or to take steps to inform public debate about the question. Other public bodies (such as the Electoral Commission) have no general power to publicise referendums though they may be able to do so in respect of a particular referendum whose subject-matter falls within their area of responsibility.[54] Information about a referendum is therefore likely to be propagated only by the promoter or by anyone opposing the promoter's aims.

Scrutiny of petition

It is the Clerk's duty to determine whether a referendum petition has been signed by not less than 10 percent of eligible electors and that therefore a referendum will be held. An eligible elector is a person whose name appears on an electoral roll which is in force on the date on which the petition is delivered to the Clerk.[55] Consequently, to be successful, something over 270,000 eligible electors (in 2005 terms) must have signed the petition. The Clerk asks the Chief Registrar of Electors to preserve the electoral roll as at the date that the petition is delivered for the purposes of scrutinising the petition.

---

48 *Ibid.*, s.14.
49 *Ibid.*, s.15(1).
50 *Electronic Transactions Act* 2002, s.14 and Sch. (excluding *Citizens Initiated Referenda Act* from its application).

51 *Ibid.*, s.15(3), (5).
52 *Ibid.*, s.42.
53 *Ibid.*, s.43.
54 1999-2002, AJHR, I.7C, para.5.2.3.
55 *Citizens Initiated Referenda Act* 1993, s.2.

Forms used

The promoter must deliver the referendum petition and pages containing signatures to the Clerk together at one time. After delivery of the referendum petition to the Clerk no further pages or signatures may be added to it.[56] Any sent to the Clerk after this time are returned to the promoter.

The Clerk is required to disregard any signature that is not on a form supplied by the promoter and formally approved earlier by the Clerk. Such signatures do not count towards ascertaining the total number who have signed to the petition.[57] Minor alterations to the approved form do not disqualify the signatures (for example, where a signatory has written a comment on the form). On the other hand, it is critical that persons signing the form are aware of the precise question that has been approved and any substantive alteration to this (whether effected by the promoter or a signatory) will lead to the form being rejected. Where it can be presumed that the alteration to the question was made by a particular signatory, any earlier signatures (made when the question was unaltered) will not be disregarded.

Preliminary count of signatures

A preliminary count of all signatures on forms that have been approved is undertaken. The fact that a signatory may not have added his or her full name and residential address to the form is irrelevant for this purpose. All signatures are included for the purposes of determining which signatures may be checked to ascertain how many eligible electors have signed the referendum petition.[58] If, after this preliminary count, there are found to be fewer signatures than the number of eligible electors who would have been required to sign in order to force a referendum, the petition lapses and the Clerk notifies the promoter accordingly.[59]

Checking a sample of signatures

If the preliminary count reveals that there are sufficient signatures to suggest that it is possible that at least 10 percent of eligible electors may have signed, a sample of the signatures is checked to determine if this is in fact the case.

The sample to be checked is determined by the Clerk with the assistance of the Government Statistician. The sample to be taken must be such that it can, with confidence, be regarded as providing an accurate estimate of the result that would be obtained if all of the signatures were checked.[60] For the purpose of obtaining the sample to be checked the number of signatures on each form is ascertained and individual signatures at predetermined positions on some of those forms are identified. The signatures so identified are the ones to be checked against the electoral roll to determine if the signatory is an eligible elector. A relatively small number of the total number of signatures generally suffices to give a result that can be relied on with confidence. Where the result is likely to be close, a larger sample is taken to give greater comfort.

Having selected the sample, the Clerk gives the signature details to the Chief Registrar of Electors, who checks them against the electoral roll and reports the result of this check to the Clerk.[61] Many of the signatories will not be found on the electoral roll; for example, because they are from persons who are under 18 years of age or because they are from people visiting New Zealand on holiday. Also, where signatories did not give their full names or residential addresses, it may be impossible to establish that their signatures are

---

[56] *Ibid.*, s.15(4).
[57] *Ibid.*, s.16(1), (3).
[58] *Ibid.*, s.15(2).
[59] *Ibid.*, s.16(2).
[60] *Ibid.*, s.19(1).
[61] *Ibid.*, s.19(2), (3).

those of eligible electors. The check of the sample will also reveal the extent to which persons have signed the petition twice or even more times than this.

Determining if there are sufficient signatures
The Clerk, again with the assistance of the Government Statistician, considers the results of this check and determines whether the petition has indeed been signed by not less than 10 percent of eligible electors.[62] This consideration will involve making allowance for the likely number of ineligible persons who have signed the petition and for duplicate signatories. In any case, the Clerk must be satisfied that at least 10 percent of eligible electors have signed.[63] A public statement is issued when this matter has been decided.

Resubmission of petition
If the Clerk is not satisfied that the petition has been signed by 10 percent of eligible electors, the petition is certified as having lapsed and is returned to the promoter.[64] However, the promoter can, within two months, resubmit it to the Clerk for another check to be made.[65] For this purpose the promoter may continue to gather signatures to the petition while it is being checked by the Clerk[66] and may also include with the resubmitted petition any signatures gathered before it was first delivered to the Clerk but not submitted at that time.

The same procedure is followed in scrutinising a resubmitted petition as was followed in its initial scrutiny. This scrutiny is a completely new scrutiny and no regard is had to the results of the first scrutiny in determining whether the petition, as resubmitted, has been signed by 10 percent of eligible electors.

Presentation of successful petition to the House
If the Clerk is satisfied that a petition or resubmitted petition has been signed by at least 10 percent of eligible electors, it is certified as correct and delivered to the Speaker.[67] The Speaker, on receiving such a petition, must forthwith announce its receipt and present it to the House.[68] The first successful citizens'-initiated petition was presented to the House on 30 May 1995.[69] As a petition with its own statutory consequences, the House has no particular action to take in respect of it. Nevertheless, like all petitions presented to the House, a referendum petition is classified by the Clerk and distributed to the most appropriate select committee for consideration and report.[70]

Holding of the referendum
The presentation of a successful referendum petition to the House leads to the holding of an indicative referendum on the question set out in the petition. The referendum may be conducted either by personal voting as employed at a general election or it may be conducted by postal voting.

The decision whether to use personal voting or postal voting is made by the Government by Order in Council within one month of the presentation of the petition to the House.[71]

Date of the referendum
Regardless of the method of holding the referendum it must, in principle, be held within 12 months of the date of the presentation of the petition to the House.[72] More than one referendum may be held on the same day or during the same postal voting period.[73]

---

62 *Ibid.*, s.19(4).
63 *Ibid.*, s.18(2).
64 *Ibid.*, s.18(1)(b).
65 *Ibid.*, s.20(2).
66 *Ibid.*, s.20(1).
67 *Ibid.*, s.18(1)(a).
68 *Ibid.*, s.21.

69 1995, Vol.547, p.6841 (number of professional firefighters).
70 S.O.361.
71 *Citizens Initiated Referenda Act* 1993, s.22(2).
72 *Ibid.*, ss.22AA(1) and 22AB (2).
73 *Ibid.*, s.55; *Referenda (Postal Voting) Act* 2000, s.79.

Where a petition is presented within 12 months of the date by which a general election must be held, the Order in Council can itself fix the date of the election as the date for the referendum. Whether it does so or not, the House, by resolution, can in these circumstances require the referendum to be held on the same day as the general election.[74] If, after an Order in Council is made appointing a date for a referendum, a writ for a general election is issued, the order may be revoked and the date of the election appointed as the date of the referendum.[75] Finally, the House retains the right to postpone, but not cancel, a referendum. It can do this within three months of the presentation of the referendum petition by passing a resolution to that effect by a 75 percent majority of all members. Such a resolution must go on to appoint a new date for the referendum that is between 12 and 24 months after the petition was presented.[76]

Conduct of the referendum

Where an indicative referendum is to be conducted by personal voting, that voting is carried out in the manner prescribed by the *Electoral Act* 1993 for the taking of an electoral poll. Most of the electoral provisions are incorporated into the rules for the referendum.[77] Regulations have been made applying the general election provisions with modification and making detailed provision for the conduct of the poll.[78]

An indicative referendum may be conducted by postal voting under the provisions of the *Referenda (Postal Voting) Act* 2000. The Chief Electoral Officer is the Returning Officer for the purposes of such a referendum.[79] The voting period for postal voting extends over three weeks ending at 7 pm on a Friday.[80] The provisions of the *Electoral Act* 1993, as modified in their application to postal voting, are applied to the conduct of the referendum.[81] The Chief Electoral Officer notifies the results of a referendum conducted by personal voting in the *Gazette* and the Minister of Justice must, as soon as practicable, present these results to the House.[82] There are provisions enabling persons dissatisfied with the conduct of a referendum poll or the voting on it to apply to the High Court for an inquiry into its conduct within 20 working days of the declaration of the result.[83]

The voting papers used at a referendum (whether conducted by personal voting or postal voting) are disposed of in the same way as electoral ballot papers. They must be forwarded to the Clerk of the House and kept by the Clerk for six months before they may be destroyed.[84] The legislation requiring the preservation of public records does not apply to such papers.[85]

---

[74]   *Citizens Initiated Referenda Act* 1993, ss.22AA(5), (6) and 22AB(6), (7).
[75]   *Ibid.*, ss.22AA(7) and 22AB(8).
[76]   *Ibid.*, ss.22AA(3), (4) and 22AB(4), (5).
[77]   *Ibid.*, s.24.
[78]   *Ibid.*, s.58; *Citizens Initiated Referenda Regulations* 1995.
[79]   *Referenda (Postal Voting) Act* 2000, s.8(1).
[80]   *Ibid.*, s.30(1), (2).

[81]   *Citizens Initiated Referenda Act* 1993, s.24A.
[82]   *Referenda (Postal Voting) Act* 2000, s.40(2), (3).
[83]   *Citizens Initiated Referenda Act* 1993, ss.47 to 51G.
[84]   *Citizens Initiated Referenda Act* 1993, s.24 (applying, amongst other provisions, the *Electoral Act* 1993, ss.187 and 189); *Referenda (Postal Voting) Act* 2000, s.50.
[85]   *Public Records Act* 2005, s.6(a), (b).

CHAPTER 42

GENERAL, URGENT AND SPECIAL DEBATES

Each week the House sets aside one hour to hold a "general" debate which gives members free rein to raise matters they consider important. In addition, the House has a procedure whereby an event of particular importance can be raised for debate if the urgency of the situation requires this. The former is known as the general debate and recurs most Wednesdays automatically in accordance with the Standing Orders. The latter is known as an urgent debate and takes place as occasion requires, provided that the Speaker agrees that the matter which has occurred is appropriate for debate under that provision. From time to time other special debates are held outside those recognised and regulated by the Standing Orders.

GENERAL DEBATES

The general debate arises at each Wednesday sitting of the House following questions for oral answer and any urgent debate, if one has been allowed on that day.[1] If there is no Wednesday sitting of the House because Tuesday's sitting has been extended under urgency, then the general debate will be lost, although on occasion the House has, by leave, held a general debate in those circumstances.

The general debate is an opportunity for members to debate a miscellaneous collection of topics that would otherwise not, or probably not, come before the House for debate.

The potential width of the general debate is indicated by the motion that is moved to launch the debate: "That the House take note of miscellaneous business.".[2] During this debate members may raise any matters of concern to them.[3] This gives members an opportunity to refer to replies to questions that have been given, select committee reports, and Government responses to recommendations addressed to it in reports. In many cases the general debate provides members with their only realistic opportunity to focus on these matters on the floor of the House. For example, one general debate concentrated on a Member's notice of motion which censured the Speaker and which would otherwise not have been debated.[4] But a focus of this nature on business on the order paper is unusual.

Usually, each of the parties will ask its members who contribute to the debate to concentrate on a particular subject – the economy, housing, education, and so on – illustrating their points as need be with references to replies to questions given by Ministers. There is no reason (except coincidence) why the subject that each party is concentrating on should be the same, and this has led to criticism that the general debate is not one debate but a number. Proposals have been advanced for nominating one or two topics in advance as the subject matters for the debate, but no such proposals have yet been adopted.[5]

Form of the debate

There are 12 speeches, each of up to five minutes in length, provided for the general debate.[6]

In practice, the Business Committee agrees to a roster of speaking slots for general

---

1   S.Os 63(1) and 383(1).
2   S.O.383(1).
3   S.O.383(2).
4   1986, Vol.471, pp.19000-11.
5   1990, AJHR, I.18B, para.14.
6   Appendix A to the Standing Orders.

debates for several weeks ahead. This roster is designed to give each party its appropriate proportion of calls in the debate. In making this calculation Ministers are included in the proportions, unlike with the questions roster, as Ministers take part in the general debate on the same basis as other members. The roster also prescribes the order in which parties are called to speak in the debate so as to give each party a fair placing at or near the top of the list over a period of time.

No amendments are permitted to the motion that the House take note of miscellaneous business[7] and at the conclusion of the debate that motion lapses and no question is put on it.[8]

No debate held in certain weeks

The general debate is replaced by a debate on the Budget policy statement on the first Wednesday after the report of the Finance and Expenditure Committee on that statement has been presented.[9] In addition, on Wednesdays when the debates on the Address in Reply, the Prime Minister's statement and the Budget are still running, no general debate is held.[10]

DEBATES ON MATTERS OF URGENT PUBLIC IMPORTANCE

The House has a procedure whereby its pre-arranged business may be set aside so it can debate "a matter of urgent public importance". A debate on a matter of urgent public importance arises on a motion moved by a member to take note of that matter. Such a motion can be moved only with the Speaker's permission. The right to move such a motion is hedged around with conditions designed to ensure that it is not lightly conceded. Over the long term, approximately one in five applications for such a debate is successful. In 2004 there were 28 applications on separate subjects (some subjects attracted multiple applications) and six urgent debates were granted.

This section examines the steps that must be taken when applying to the Speaker for authority to stage such a debate, the criteria considered by the Speaker in appraising an application for one and the debate itself.

Applications for the debate

If a member wishes to move an urgent debate, the member must lodge a written application to do so at least one hour before the House meets or such lesser time as the Speaker may permit.[11] The written application must be handed to the Speaker or one of the Speaker's staff, or to the Clerk or one of the Clerk's staff for passing on to the Speaker. When delivered into one of these hands, it is regarded as having been received for the purposes of the Standing Order. It must not merely be left lying on a desk somewhere.[12]

In the written application the member sets out the matter which it is proposed should be discussed at the imminent sitting of the House. The statement or letter should deal with only one subject for discussion. If a member wishes to raise two subjects for debate, the member should lodge two applications. In the statement members may wish to elaborate on the bare statement of the matter proposed to be discussed so as to demonstrate to the Speaker why they consider that it falls within the scope of the Standing Order. It is, after all, for members to make out the case for an urgent debate, not for the Speaker to divine one.[13]

Every statement in a letter seeking an urgent debate must be authenticated in the same

[7]   S.O.383(1).
[8]   S.O.383(2).
[9]   S.O.324(3).
[10] S.O.383(3).

[11] S.O.380(1).
[12] 1976, Vol.407, p.3539.
[13] 2002, Vol.602, p.558.

way as statements in a notice of motion.[14] Applications that do not contain authenticating material will be disallowed on that ground whatever their merits.[15]

Unlike the lodging of urgent questions, no notice of the application is given to the Government by the member, and the fact that an application has been made is kept confidential by the Speaker. Nor is the member who has made an application informed of the Speaker's attitude to it prior to the Speaker formally ruling on it in the House. Most of the members of the House will, therefore, not know that an application is afoot (although if a matter of some importance has arisen they may surmise that an application has been lodged) and the remaining members who do know of it do not know whether it has been accepted. It is only when the Speaker rules on an application in the House that members are fully informed of the position.

An application may be withdrawn at any time before the Speaker rules on it in the House. In these circumstances, no reference is made to it at all by the Speaker.

Two or more applications received on the same day

There can only be one urgent debate on each day,[16] so if two or more applications for an urgent debate are received on the same day it may be necessary for the Speaker to choose between them. However, this will be necessary only if more than one of the applications meets the criteria for acceptance set down in the Standing Orders. If, out of two applications lodged, only one is acceptable to the Speaker as the subject of an urgent debate, the Speaker has no occasion to choose between them. The other is automatically rejected as not meeting the tests for acceptability in any case.

But if the Speaker does consider that two or more applications meet the criteria set out in the Standing Orders, then the Speaker is enjoined to give priority to the application which, in the Speaker's opinion, is the most urgent and important.[17] The Speaker makes this decision, not the members submitting the applications. Members may indicate in their applications their views of the relative importance of applications they may know are being submitted to the Speaker that day (if they do know of them) and the Speaker will take heed of such indications, but ultimately the Speaker decides their relative importance in such a case. Thus the Speaker has given priority to any application because two earlier urgent debates had been held on the other application and the House had not had an opportunity to debate the former.[18]

If two applications meet the criteria for acceptance and the Speaker is unable to distinguish between them on the grounds of importance and urgency, the Speaker will give preference to the application that was lodged first.[19] Any rejected application may be resubmitted on the following day[20] but there is no guarantee that it will be accepted for debate on that day, for by that time its relative urgency and importance will have changed.

Late applications

Applications for urgent debates must normally be lodged with the Speaker at least one hour before the House meets, which means by 1 pm on a sitting day. But the Speaker does have authority to allow a lesser period of notice than this[21] and an application can be lodged for consideration up to the time that the House actually meets.[22] However, an application received within one hour of the House sitting will be accepted only in exceptional circumstances.

---

14 1984, Vol.458, p.1086; 2000, Vol.585, p.3768.
15 2000, Vol.586, p.5030; 2002, Vol.604, p.1810.
16 S.O.382.
17 *Ibid.*
18 2005, Vol.625, pp. 20370–1.

19 1981, Vol.439, p.2010.
20 1982, Vol.444, p.1234.
21 S.O.380(1).
22 1997, Vol.562, p.3868.

An application can be lodged after 1 pm where the event on which the application is based occurs within one hour of the House meeting.[23] Thus when an announcement that an important State enterprise was to be sold was made at 1.30 pm, the Speaker accepted an application lodged shortly before the House met at 2 pm.[24]

Applications that cannot be accepted

Apart from the specific criteria set out in the Standing Orders against which an application for an urgent debate must be tested, there are a number of other factors that may cause an application to fail at the outset. Urgent debates are subject to specific rules before they can be allowed, but they are subject to a background of general rules within which the urgent debate procedure must fit.

The Speaker will not accept an application for an urgent debate from a Minister.[25] The reason for holding urgent debates is to allow members to raise for discussion actions taken by Ministers; urgent debates are not intended as a means for Ministers to generate discussions on matters of their own choosing. While it is true that opposition members lodge by far the greater number of applications, any member other than a Minister can do so and Government backbenchers are as entitled to lodge applications as any other member.

An application which otherwise would be acceptable will not be accepted if to do so would inevitably result in a breach of the rule against referring to a matter awaiting adjudication in a court.[26] Most applications involving the courts will fail in any event because there is no ministerial responsibility for judicial decisions. But even a decision with profound effects for the Government cannot be accepted if it is of an interlocutory nature and the matter under dispute is still before the courts. However, this does not mean that all matters that are the subject of legal proceedings are automatically debarred. Thus, the cancellation of an important contract could be accepted for debate even though it was known that there was a legal dispute over the propriety of the cancellation. The subject of the debate was the cancellation itself rather than the legal issues it raised.[27]

It is a well-established rule that charges of impropriety against other members must be brought forward in a substantive motion of which notice is given. The Speaker will not permit this rule to be circumvented by allowing an urgent debate to be held as a vehicle to raise such allegations.[28]

Finally, where an incident involving ministerial responsibility occurs at a select committee, it cannot be the subject of an urgent debate (and nor can a report of such an incident).[29] The proper time to debate what has happened at a select committee is when the select committee reports to the House. But the mere fact that a matter is referred to at a select committee meeting does not prevent a matter that occurred outside the committee being raised for urgent debate. In such a case, members would not be able to refer to what happened at the committee meeting, but neither would they be prevented from raising the matter itself. Thus the Speaker has advised members not to refer to select committee proceedings at all in their applications so that the different situations are not confused.[30]

Rules for acceptance of an application

An application for an urgent debate must satisfy three substantive criteria: it must relate to a particular case of recent occurrence; that case must involve the administrative or

---

[23] 1991, Vol.514, p.1368.

[24] 1990, Vol.507, p.2053.

[25] 1992, Vol.531, p.12499.

[26] 1985, Vol.463, p.5173; 1988, Vol.490, p.5512;
      2001, Vol.593, p.10022.

[27] 1999, Vol.579, pp.18710-1.

[28] 1990, Vol.507, pp.1529-30, 1622.

[29] 1993, Vol.536, p.16436.

[30] *Ibid.*

ministerial responsibility of the Government; and it must require the immediate attention of the House and the Government.[31]

Particular case of recent occurrence
In the application, the member must identify a particular matter for debate. It has been repeatedly emphasised that the alleged absence of action on the part of the Government is not a particular case of recent occurrence that can be raised for urgent debate.[32]

A particular case differs from the announcement of a situation which is the cumulative result of happenings over a period of time, such as unemployment statistics. An announcement of a particular level of unemployment relates to a continuing problem – the statistics being the reflection of a number of occurrences – and does not give grounds for an urgent debate.[33] The laying-off of particular workers, on the other hand, is a particular case for this purpose and could be ground for a debate, provided the other criteria, particularly ministerial responsibility, are satisfied. Nor can a particular case be construed out of an accumulation of information.[34] This may or may not demonstrate that a situation is deteriorating, but it is not a particular case. Allegations cannot constitute a particular case of recent occurrence.[35] There must have been some concrete event or announcement and not just newspaper speculation about it.[36]

The case must have been of recent occurrence. That is, the event must already have occurred. The urgent debate procedure is not a means of debating matters that may or may not happen in the future.[37] The event must have occurred recently. A member cannot sleep upon a matter and raise it weeks or months later. This does not mean, however, that the Speaker will never accept an application which is not raised at the first possible moment. (This contrasts with a matter of privilege which, to gain priority, must be raised at the earliest opportunity according to a strict definition.[38]) The fact that a matter is not raised as soon as possible argues against its acceptance by appearing to devalue its importance in the eyes of the member applying for a debate on it.[39] If it was not important enough to raise at once, how can it be important enough to set the House's business aside to debate it? But there may be good reasons why a matter was not raised immediately. Where a matter arose on Thursday evening, the fact that the member waited until the following Tuesday was not regarded as fatal by the Speaker, who took into consideration the early start to Friday's sitting (at that time the House sat at 9 am on Fridays) and accepted the application.[40] On the other hand, where a member waited a week before raising a matter based on documents he had received, the Speaker ruled that this was too long for it to be regarded as a case of recent occurrence. The member should have raised the matter when he received the documents.[41]

The requirement of "recent occurrence" relates to when the member became aware (or should have become aware) of the facts on which the application is based. Where the event to which certain documents related occurred some time in the past and the member discovered it only when receiving the documents, that was the point at which time began to run.[42] But by definition a member can only become aware of something when it becomes public. Time does not run against members when an event occurs in secret and no public announcement is made. In this case the public announcement is the particular case of recent occurrence for the purposes of an application for an urgent debate.[43]

The matter for debate must occur before the House meets at the sitting at which the

31 S.O.380(2).
32 1986, Vol.470, p.1336; 2000, Vol.582, p.1287.
33 1977, Vol.414, pp.3192-3; 1986, Vol.472, p.2623.
34 2005, Vol.625, p.20162.
35 1998, Vol.571, p.12002; 1999, Vol.575, p.14854; 2004, Vol.622, p.17228.
36 2000, Vol.586, p.5114; 2001, Vol.590, p.7727.
37 2000, Vol.589, p.7287.
38 S.O.392.
39 1982, Vol.444, p.1234; 2004, Vol.621, p.16301.
40 1977, Vol.413, p.2715.
41 1979, Vol.422, p.596.
42 *Ibid.*
43 2000, Vol.583, p.1659.

debate is to take place. A ministerial statement made at the commencement of a sitting does not give grounds for an urgent debate at that sitting (though it might justify such a debate at the next sitting).[44]

Members who expect an event to occur before the House meets may anticipate that event and lodge an application for a debate.[45] Provided that the event does actually occur before the sitting it can be considered for debate. Where an anticipated event does not occur, members usually withdraw the application. In those circumstances the application will inevitably fail since there has been no case of recent occurrence.

Involves the administrative or ministerial responsibility of the Government
An urgent debate is a way of holding the Government accountable for an action for which it is responsible; it is not a general debate. There must be distinct governmental responsibility for the particular case which it is sought to debate. The fact that there are implications for Government policy in what has occurred (which there will be in many instances) is not enough. There must be responsibility for what has happened, though this does not mean that the actor in the particular case that has occurred is necessarily a Minister or even an established entity.[46]

Where there is independence of Ministers in decision-making there can be no ministerial responsibility. The exercise of statutory powers by the Meat Producers Board to refuse to allow the export of certain meat, although of obvious significance to the Government, was held not to involve ministerial responsibility, as the Minister had no power to direct the board in this regard.[47] The exercise of powers by any statutory officer, where the powers are not subject to ministerial control, falls outside the scope of an urgent debate,[48] even where the officer is a public servant.[49]

Ministers have no responsibility for the decisions of courts. So an application to debate a High Court decision to grant an interim injunction effectively preventing the 1985 All Blacks' tour to South Africa was rejected on this ground.[50] Other applications to debate judicial decisions have also been rejected.[51]Nor can occurrences in respect of purely party matters, such as a manifesto commitment,[52] or a decision of caucus[53] be the subject of an urgent debate.

An urgent debate cannot be held on action taken by a select committee for the very reason that there is no ministerial responsibility for such a committee. Therefore, when an application was made to discuss the proceedings of a committee that was considering a bill, it was rejected on this ground.[54]

The concept of ministerial responsibility for a matter qualifying for an urgent debate is narrower than it is in respect of questions for oral or written answer; the latter encompass any matter relating to public affairs with which the Minister has an official connection. The fact that a question may be addressed to a Minister about a matter does not necessarily mean that the matter involves ministerial responsibility on which an urgent debate on it can be founded.

Requires the immediate attention of the House and the Government
The matter raised for debate must require the immediate attention of the House and the

---

[44]   1988, Vol.493, p.7408; 2000, Vol.586, p.5114.
[45]   1991, Vol.514, p.1368.
[46]   2002, Vol.600, p.15819 (Maori Television Service not yet established).
[47]   1979, Vol.425, pp.2568-9.
[48]   2001, Vol.591, p.8659 (Registrar of Electors).
[49]   1980, Vol.435, p.4974 (Examiner of Commercial Practices).
[50]   1985, Vol.464, p.5594.
[51]   2001, Vol.595, pp.11815-6.
[52]   1987, Vol.482, pp.10238-9.
[53]   1992, Vol.532, p.13272.
[54]   1977, Vol.414, pp.3846-7; 1998, Vol.573, p.13404.

Government. This criterion creates a hurdle designed to ensure that the matter is of such substance that it justifies the House spending a substantial part of its sitting in debating it. There are many recent occurrences which involve ministerial responsibility; the Government is continually making statements and taking action in one field or another. Without a requirement that the matter be of sufficient importance to require it to be debated immediately, the scope for urgent debates would be enormous. There must always be such an element of urgency as would warrant precedence being given to a debate on the matter.[55]

Inevitably, the Speaker's decision on whether a matter requires an immediate debate is liable to be somewhat impressionistic and the guidelines drawn from past decisions of limited value. Thus, while the release of a report has been accepted for debate,[56] this will be exceptional, especially where it will take time for the Government to work through the report's recommendations and make decisions on follow-up action.[57] Even where the event involves a new policy announcement, not every such announcement can give grounds for a debate. One that was held to satisfy the criterion was the announcement of a general policy on the sale of State enterprises. This related to an important aspect of policy towards all State enterprises and foreshadowed a possible future new development of considerable interest. Consequently it met the test for an urgent debate.[58] By way of illustration, the urgent debates allowed during 2000 included the following subjects: the cancellation of a contract for the purchase of F16 planes;[59] inquiries into a police shooting;[60] the purchase of a block of radio spectrum;[61] the dismissal of a Minister (though not all dismissals or resignations will justify such a debate);[62] and the Government's response to a bee-mite incursion.[63]

The Speaker does take account of attendant parliamentary circumstances in deciding whether an urgent debate is warranted. If there is another convenient parliamentary means available for debating the subject of the application, the Speaker takes that fact into account in deciding whether to accept the application.[64] In particular, if a wide-ranging debate such as the debate on the Address in Reply, the Prime Minister's statement or the Budget is before the House, this will count against accepting an application for an urgent debate though it does not in all circumstances preclude one being allowed.[65]

In all cases, if the matter which is sought to raise must soon come before the House in the form of legislation, this will be a factor telling against a special debate being held immediately.[66] But if there is no reasonably foreseeable opportunity for an important and controversial happening to be debated in the near future, this will weigh in favour of its being accepted for debate,[67] especially if legislative action is likely to be delayed by a lengthy adjournment.[68]

An application lodged before an adjournment but not able to be dealt with at that time (because the House was sitting under urgency) will be automatically considered by the Speaker when the House resumes, though it may in these circumstances have lost any intrinsic urgency by the delay. However, even in this case if the application relates to an important enough subject it may qualify for an urgent debate when the House resumes.[69]

[55] 1983, Vol.455, p.4113; 1998, Vol.572, p.12880.
[56] 1998, Vol.567, p.8210.
[57] 2003, Vol.610, p.7149.
[58] 1988, Vol.486, p.2235.
[59] 2000, Vol.582, p.1206.
[60] 2000, Vol.583, p.1965.
[61] *Ibid.*, p.2237.
[62] 2000, Vol.585, p.3315; 2004, Vol.617, p.12554 (debate declined).
[63] 2000, Vol.585, p.3588.
[64] 1996-99, AJHR, I.18B, p.31; 2000, Vol.584, pp.2987-8.
[65] 1984, Vol.459, p.1813.
[66] 1973, Vol.382, p.214.
[67] 1973, Vol.386, p.3834.
[68] 1991, Vol.513, p.1012.
[69] See, for example, 1998, Vol.567, p.8210.

Ruling by Speaker

The time at which a motion to take note of a definite matter of urgent public importance is moved is immediately after questions for oral answer have been disposed of and before the next business is embarked upon.[70] It is not possible to hold an urgent debate on the day of the State Opening of Parliament, as the Standing Orders prescribe specifically what items of business may be taken on that day.[71]

The Speaker rules on applications that have been lodged by informing the House what applications have been received and whether each application has been accepted or rejected.[72] In all cases the Speaker summarises the application in ruling on it. The Speaker does not read out the application in full.

Debate

Having ruled favourably on an application, the Speaker calls on the member to move that the House take note of the matter of urgent public importance. The member moving the motion has 15 minutes to speak, and so does the first member to speak to it. A further six members have 10 minutes each, making the total time available for the debate one and a half hours.[73] The second speaker in the debate is a Minister, regardless of who initiates the debate.[74] An urgent debate is designed to examine a matter of ministerial responsibility and, hopefully, elicit an explanation or response from the Government. A Minister is therefore given the opportunity to respond first in the debate. There is no amendment permitted to the question. At the conclusion of the speeches allowed for, the motion lapses and no question is put on it.[75]

SPECIAL DEBATES

Occasionally, the House holds special debates not contemplated by any of its regular procedures.

It was formerly the practice of the House to hold an annual foreign affairs debate and, less frequently, an economic debate. These debates have been discontinued for a number of years although proposals have been advanced for reviving the annual foreign affairs debate.[76]

Where special debates are held they often arise in substitution for an urgent debate that might otherwise have been held or that did not meet the criteria for such a debate but which the House desires to debate in any case. Thus, at the Government's initiative, the House held a special debate on the Crown's proposals for the settlement of Treaty of Waitangi claims. (The Speaker indicated that he would in any case have been prepared to accept an application for an urgent debate that had been lodged with him on this subject.[77]) In another case, applications for an urgent debate were withdrawn when the House agreed to hold a special debate on the subject.[78] Other debates quite unrelated to any urgent debate application have also been arranged.[79]

Often these debates are agreed to be held by leave of the House under the rules applying to urgent debates.[80]

---

[70] S.O.381(1).
[71] S.O.14.
[72] S.O.381(1).
[73] Appendix A to the Standing Orders.
[74] 1999, Vol.579, p.18714.
[75] S.O.381(2).
[76] 1996-99, AJHR, I.4A, pp.5-6 (*Report of the Foreign Affairs, Defence and Trade Committee: Inquiry into Parliament's Role in the International Treaty Process*).

[77] 1994, Vol.545, pp.5535-6, 5543.
[78] 1999, Vol.577, p.16520 (resignation of the chairman of the Fire Service Commission).
[79] 1997, Vol.562, p.3897 (on the report of the Commission of Inquiry into Taxation).
[80] *Ibid.*

CHAPTER 43

INTERNATIONAL RELATIONS

International relations have traditionally been seen as an executive, rather than a legislative, responsibility. Conducting relations with foreign states, making treaties and providing for the defence of New Zealand are quintessential executive functions in respect of which many of the Crown's legal powers are derived from the Royal prerogative rather than from statutes. Until comparatively recently the House devoted little attention to foreign affairs and defence issues. Policy on these subjects was largely bipartisan.

Much has now changed in these areas. Defence policy saw increasing politicisation in the 1980s with differences over defence relationships emerging particularly where nuclear weapons were involved. The wider diversity of views represented in Parliament through the MMP electoral system has given both foreign policy and defence policy higher public and political profiles.[1] At the same time the number of statutes passed by the New Zealand Parliament that have an international dimension has continued to grow both absolutely and relatively. It was estimated in 1998 that about 200 of the 600 to 700 New Zealand statutes are affected in one way or another by international law.[2] Quite apart from legislation implementing international obligations, the courts have been increasingly influenced in their approach to deciding cases under New Zealand law by what has been seen as the international dimension of law. It is well established that courts seek to interpret statutes in a way that is consistent with customary international law. But international obligations assumed by the New Zealand Government, though never legislated into New Zealand law, have also come to have important influences on the way in which courts interpret legislation.[3] Often these effects and linkages are not apparent on the face of the legislation itself, are expressed in expansive terms[4] or apply with surprising or unanticipated effects.[5] In these ways, the growth in importance of international law and international obligations as components of domestic law has to some extent been hidden from legislators and the public.

In 1998 the House adopted sessional orders (now incorporated into the Standing Orders) providing for some parliamentary scrutiny of treaties prior to them becoming binding international obligations.[6] These procedures, combined with the heightened political interest in foreign and defence policy, have led to international developments playing a greater part in the regular work of the House than was the case in the past.

PROCEEDINGS IN THE HOUSE

Special debates on foreign affairs used to be held by the House on an annual basis. But such debates ceased in the 1970s. However, an international event or commitment may be of such importance as to justify a specific debate or even a special sitting of the House. Thus in 1991, on the outbreak of the Gulf War, Parliament was summoned for a special

---

1   *Report to the State Services Commission* by *Douglas White QC and Graham Ansell*, December 2001, para.20.

2   Keith, "Governance, Sovereignty and Globalisation" (1998) 28 VUWLR 477 at 485.

3   Gobbi, "Making Sense of Ambiguity: Some reflections on the use of treaties to interpret legislation in New Zealand" (2002) 23 Statute LR 47.

4   For example: *Fisheries Act* 1996, s.5(a) (legislation to be interpreted, and all persons acting under it

to act, in a manner consistent with New Zealand's international obligations relating to fishing); *Extradition Act* 1999, s.11(1) (Act to be construed to give effect to extradition treaties).

5   For example, *Sellers v Maritime Transport Authority* [1999] 2 NZLR 44 (New Zealand regulations relating to the carrying of emergency equipment on vessels had to be read in the context of the international law of freedom of navigation on the high seas).

6   1998, Vol.568, pp.9419-43.

session. A debate on the war and New Zealand's contribution to it was held on the motion for an Address in Reply to the Speech from the Throne.[7] Provision now exists for the House to hold an expedited sitting during an adjournment.[8] This was utilised in 1999 when the House was recalled to debate the commitment of New Zealand forces to East Timor.[9]

An international commitment entered into by the Government may warrant the Speaker accepting an application for an urgent debate. Alternatively, a special debate may be arranged on the initiative of the Government or after representations from other parties.[10]

Foreign affairs, defence and trade issues can also be debated in the House during other debates of a general nature – the Budget, the Address in Reply and the Wednesday general debate – and during the estimates and financial review debates when the expenditure and performance of the Ministry of Foreign Affairs and Trade, the Ministry of Defence or the New Zealand Defence Force are under consideration.

An important means of exploring international issues on the floor of the House is by means of a question addressed to a Minister. This will usually be the Minister of Foreign Affairs and Trade or the Minister of Defence, but there may also be Ministers holding other portfolios with clear international roles, such as trade negotiations or disarmament and arms control. The expanded inquiry jurisdiction of select committees has given the subject select committees the opportunity, if they wish, to interest themselves in international developments of concern to New Zealand. Thus a committee has itself initiated an inquiry into a proposal which was likely to result in New Zealand becoming party to a treaty.[11]

FOREIGN AFFAIRS, DEFENCE AND TRADE COMMITTEE

The House has an external affairs committee – the Foreign Affairs, Defence and Trade Committee. This is one of the subject select committees established at the beginning of each Parliament. It considers bills, petitions, treaties and other matters referred to it by the House; conducts such estimates and financial review work as is allocated to it by the Finance and Expenditure Committee; and has within its subject areas of inquiry customs, defence, disarmament and arms control, foreign affairs, immigration and trade.[12]

Despite the high proportion of bills having international law implications, comparatively little legislation is actually referred to the committee. Such bills are generally dealt with by the committees operating in the particular subject areas concerned. The Foreign Affairs, Defence and Trade Committee deals with legislation relating to the departments concerned with foreign affairs, defence and trade and with other obviously internationally-related legislation such as that relating to diplomatic privileges, but tends to have a low legislative workload compared to most of the other subject select committees.

Its lower legislative workload gives the committee a greater opportunity to utilise its

---

7   1991, Vol.512, pp.1-53.
8   S.O.53.
9   1999, Vol.580, pp.19461-99.
10   1997, Vol.564, pp.5097-110 (framework convention on climate change); 2001, Vol.595, pp.11996-12017 (assistance offered as part of the response to the terrorist attacks of 11 September).

11   2002-05, AJHR, I.6D (Health Committee inquiry into proposal for a trans-Tasman agency on therapeutic products).
12   S.Os 189 and 190.

inquiry powers, and in this area of select committee work it has proved to be a most active committee. Since the reorganisation of the select committees in 1985, the committee has carried out major inquiries into: relations with China,[13] Canada,[14] and Tonga,[15] overseas development assistance,[16] the Anzac ship project,[17] the sale of educational services in New Zealand,[18] economic and trade linkages in the Asia-Pacific region,[19] Parliament's role in the international treaty-making process,[20] New Zealand's place in the world and role in Asia-Pacific security,[21] defence beyond 2000[22] and economic and trade relations with Australia.[23] At the direction of the House, the committee has also conducted inquiries into disarmament and arms control,[24] and the manufacture of the defoliant Agent Orange.[25]

In 1998 a most important responsibility was given to the committee – that of acting as the House's overall co-ordinator of the treaty examination process. In this regard, the committee plays a similar role to that performed by the Finance and Expenditure Committee in respect of the estimates and financial review processes. All treaties presented to the House for examination stand referred to the committee, which then decides which is the appropriate committee to examine them.

The committee regularly has allocated to it the votes relating to foreign affairs, defence and trade for estimates examination, and conducts the financial reviews of the departments concerned. It also has referred to it any petitions falling within the foreign affairs, trade and defence areas. As an aspect of its inquiry work, the committee sometimes meets with visiting politicians and officials from overseas and holds a debriefing session with members of Parliament on their return to New Zealand from attending international conferences or participating in observer missions.[26] The committee also receives briefings on matters of current interest from officials of the Ministry of Foreign Affairs and Trade and from non-governmental organisations.

TREATIES

As part of the Royal prerogative the Crown possesses the legal power to enter into treaties with foreign states on behalf of New Zealand. New Zealand's achievement of independent statehood with a capacity to enter into treaties in its own right occurred over an extended period of time, but the signing of the Treaty of Versailles on 28 June 1919 has been taken as significant. From that date New Zealand began to enter into treaties in its own right on a consistent basis and was treated as a separate party in respect of treaties that had previously been entered into on its behalf by the United Kingdom.[27] Appropriately, the pen used by the Prime Minister, William Massey, to sign the Treaty of Versailles is mounted in a display case in Parliament House.

The power of treaty-making as one of the prerogatives or inherent legal powers of the Crown does not derive from parliamentary enactment, although it cannot be exercised in a manner forbidden by or inconsistent with legislation.[28] Nor (unlike in a number of other political systems) does a treaty entered into by the Crown require to be ratified or endorsed by the House of Representatives.[29] A treaty is effective as a binding international

---

13 1986-87, AJHR, I.5A.
14 *Ibid.*, I.5B.
15 2002-05, AJHR, I.4C.
16 1990, AJHR, I.5B.
17 1991-93, AJHR, I.5A.
18 *Ibid.*
19 *Ibid.*, I.5C.
20 1996-99, AJHR, I.4A and I.4E.
21 *Ibid.*, I.4B.
22 *Ibid.*, I.4C and I.4D.
23 1999-2002, AJHR, I.4E.
24 1984-85, AJHR, I.19.
25 1990, AJHR, I.5A.

26 1996-99, AJHR, I.24, p.190 (East Timor).
27 *Ibid.*, A.263, p.10 (*New Zealand Consolidated Treaty List as at 31 December 1996*).
28 See, for example, *Yuen Kwok-Fung v Hong Kong SAR* [2001] 3 NZLR 463 at [18] (*Extradition Act* 1999, s.11(2) "is in effect a direction to the executive that in negotiating extradition treaties it is to ensure that the listed protections are incorporated" per Keith J).
29 Legislation to require parliamentary ratification of treaties has been rejected – 2002-05, AJHR, I.22A, pp.146-7; 2003, Vol.606, pp.3589-607 (*International Treaties Bill*).

obligation once it has been fully accepted by the Crown and has entered into force for New Zealand in accordance with its terms. (The precise means by which acceptance is signified differs depending upon the terms of the treaty.) However, while binding at an international level in New Zealand's relations with other states, longstanding legal doctrine inherited by New Zealand has held that a treaty is not in itself a source of law that can confer legal powers or duties on persons within New Zealand. Thus the Crown cannot change New Zealand law by the expedient of entering into a treaty. Only the New Zealand Parliament in enacting legislation can do that. Therefore, if the implementation of a treaty does have implications for New Zealand law, it will be necessary for the Government to ask Parliament to change the law to make it consistent with the treaty obligations. Otherwise it will be impossible to fulfil those obligations domestically.

In fact, New Zealand's treaty-making practice is to ensure that domestic law is compatible with a treaty's obligations *before* New Zealand becomes bound by it. (Indeed it has been asserted that there is a constitutional convention to this effect, though whether this is so remains doubtful.[30]) In many cases, no question of incompatibility between the treaty's provisions and New Zealand law will arise, because the treaty will not have legal effects within New Zealand – it may be designed to operate solely at an international level. In other cases the treaty's obligations may already be consistent with New Zealand law and no further action is required to ensure this. In yet others, legal powers may exist whereby the Government itself can make New Zealand law compatible with the treaty; for example, by using regulation-making power it already possesses or by changing its own policies and practices. But, finally, in some cases it may only be possible to assume the obligations in a treaty if primary legislation can be passed permitting this.

Even where it may be possible to implement a treaty through a variety of means – using existing laws and other non-legislative means, for example – it may, nevertheless, be preferable to enact new legislation for the purpose if the policy impact of the treaty is significant, or so as to ensure transparency and greater co-ordination of functions.[31] But, in general, legislation will only be resorted to where no viable alternative method is available to implement a treaty's policy objectives.[32]

Taking treaty action

The number of treaties entered into by New Zealand each year varies, but is substantial. Between 1990 and 1995, for example, New Zealand entered into an average of 30 treaties each year – 13 of a multilateral nature (that is, involving a number of other countries) and 17 bilateral treaties (that is, with one other party).[33] All treaties which have become binding on New Zealand are presented to the House and published as parliamentary papers.

Individual treaties vary greatly in their significance. Exceptionally, legislation may prescribe what provisions a treaty or a certain type of treaty must contain.[34] But this is rare. Furthermore, while consultation with interested parties in New Zealand is part of the process of considering whether to enter into a treaty and on what terms, there is generally little opportunity for general public participation in the treaty-making process, although interested non-governmental organisations are invited to participate in negotiations from

---

[30]   2002-05, AJHR, I.22A, pp.121, 125 (*Climate Change Response Bill*); *ibid.*, pp.147-8 (*International Treaties Bill*).

[31]   *Climate Change Response Bill* 2002, explanatory note.

[32]   Harris, "International Issues – The Interaction

Between International Law-Making and Domestic Implementation", p.9.

[33]   1996-99, AJHR, A.263 p.10 (*New Zealand Consolidated Treaty List as at 31 December 1996*).

[34]   *Extradition Act* 1999, ss.100 and 101 (provisions that must be contained in extradition treaties).

time to time or to join New Zealand Government delegations. However, occasionally, public input has been invited by the Government by way of public advertisement before negotiations on a treaty have begun.[35] Consequently, the Government has decided to provide the House and the public with more information on treaties under negotiation at an earlier stage and on a regular basis.[36] It now publishes an International Treaties List every six months, listing multilateral and bilateral treaties that are under negotiation. The list describes the treaties and indicates where further information about them can be obtained.

The Ministry also arranges briefings for the Foreign Affairs, Defence and Trade Committee and other committees on treaty negotiations that they express an interest in.[37]

These information and consultation processes have been supplemented by a parliamentary procedure of examination of treaties before binding treaty action (the final assumption of the treaty's obligations) is taken.

Presentation of treaties to the House

On 16 February 1998 the Government, in a paper presented to the House, agreed that it would present certain multilateral treaties to the House on a trial basis for limited examination before the treaties were finally ratified or agreed to.[38] This assurance to the House was recognised in a sessional order adopted by the House on 28 May 1998.[39] Since 8 September 1999 it has been recognised in the Standing Orders.[40] It was expressly reaffirmed by a Government statement on 28 February 2000[41] and is now recorded in the Cabinet's own treaty-making procedures.[42]

Multilateral treaties

The treaties that the Government has agreed to present for examination include those treaties that are to become binding on ratification, accession, acceptance or approval.[43] These are generally treaties to which there are a number of other parties – multilateral treaties. It is expected that in respect of such treaties, presentation to the House will occur after they have been signed by the Government (but before they become fully binding) though there is nothing to prevent a treaty being presented before the Government has signed it. Multilateral treaties which the Government wishes to withdraw from or to denounce are also to be presented for examination.[44] These latter, while rare, can be significant in their own right,[45] and in any case the act of withdrawing from a treaty is itself a treaty action requiring Cabinet approval. While, in principle, multilateral treaties are to be presented for parliamentary examination before they become binding, it is recognised that there may be circumstances in which a treaty must be entered into immediately in the national interest without the opportunity for prior parliamentary examination. Where this occurs, and an urgent multilateral treaty has become binding, the treaty is still to be presented to the House,[46] in this case as soon as possible after the binding treaty action has been taken.[47] The obligation to present treaties does not apply to reports which the Government is obliged to make to international organisations in complying with its existing treaty obligations.[48]

But even outside the strict terms of the Government's assurance as embodied in the

35 See, for example, *The National Business Review*, 9 April 1999 (public submissions invited on World Trade Organisation negotiations on agriculture and services).
36 *Hansard Supplement*, 2000, Vol.45, p.4053.
37 2002-05, AJHR, I.22A, p.149.
38 1996-99, AJHR, A.5.
39 1998, Vol.568, pp.9419-43.
40 S.O.387(1).
41 1999-2002, AJHR, A.5.
42 *Cabinet Manual*, 2001, para.5.83.
43 S.O.387(1)(a).
44 S.O.387(1)(c).
45 1996-99, AJHR, I.4E, pp.6-7.
46 S.O.387(1)(b).
47 *Cabinet Manual*, 2001, para.5.90.
48 *Hansard Supplement*, 1998, Vol.34, p.2072.

Standing Order, the Government may present treaties for examination. Thus, the Foreign Affairs, Defence and Trade Committee commented favourably in 2003 when the first status of forces agreement (with the Solomon Islands) was presented for examination. The major interest in the deployment justified its presentation, even though it did not fall strictly within the terms of the Standing Order.[49]

Bilateral treaties

Most treaties that the Government enters into are not multilateral, they are agreements with one other state; that is, bilateral treaties. Double taxation agreements are the most common form of bilateral treaty. If the bilateral treaty is subject to a process of ratification or post-signature acceptance, it will be presented to the House under the Standing Orders for examination.[50] But most bilateral treaties are not of this nature.

In the case of bilateral treaties, the undertaking from the Government to the House is that any major bilateral treaty of particular significance (as determined by the Minister of Foreign Affairs and Trade) will be presented.[51] The Government thus retains a large measure of discretion as to whether or not to present bilateral treaties for examination. In fact, most bilateral treaties entered into are not presented to the House for examination, though the proportion that is is increasing.

The Minister of Foreign Affairs and Trade has developed criteria for determining which bilateral treaties should be submitted to the parliamentary examination process. These criteria are—

- the subject-matter of the treaty is likely to be of major interest to the public
- the treaty deals with an important subject upon which there is no ready precedent (that is, it is an original treaty dealing with possibly a one-off situation)
- the treaty deals with an important subject and departs substantively from previous models relating to the same subject
- the treaty represents a major development in the bilateral relationship
- the treaty has significant financial implications for the Government
- the treaty cannot be terminated, or will remain in force for a specific period
- the treaty is to be implemented by way of overriding treaty regulations (that is, regulations that implement a treaty by overriding primary legislation)
- the treaty is a major treaty that New Zealand seeks to terminate
- the Foreign Affairs, Defence and Trade Committee indicates its interest in examining the treaty.[52]

Progress on bilateral treaty negotiations is included in the International Treaties List and in briefings given to the Foreign Affairs, Defence and Trade Committee. In the course of the forty-sixth Parliament (1999–2002), three major bilateral treaties were presented for examination.[53] A select committee with appropriate terms of reference can initiate its own examination of a bilateral treaty under its general inquiry power.

Amendments of treaties

Where the treaty that is being presented makes textual amendments to an existing treaty, the Government has been asked by the Foreign Affairs, Defence and Trade Committee to present a consolidated version of the treaty incorporating the amendments so that the amending treaty can be read intelligibly.[54]

---

[49] 2002-05, AJHR, I.22B, p.372.
[50] S.O.387(1)(a).
[51] S.O.387(1)(d).
[52] 2002-05, AJHR, I.22A, p.149.
[53] The closer economic partnership agreement with Singapore, amendments to the Australia/New Zealand joint food standards treaty and a New Zealand/Australia social security agreement.
[54] 1999-2002, AJHR, I.22B, pp.561-3.

National interest analyses

A critical accompaniment to the treaty that is presented to the House is a national interest analysis in respect of it. This is to be presented to the House at the same time as the treaty.[55]

Each national interest analysis must contain the following matters in respect of the treaty to which it relates:

- the reasons for New Zealand becoming party to the treaty
- the advantages and disadvantages to New Zealand of the treaty entering into force for New Zealand
- the obligations which would be imposed on New Zealand by the treaty, and the position in respect of reservations to the treaty
- the economic, social, cultural and environmental effects of the treaty entering into force for New Zealand, and of the treaty not entering into force for New Zealand (this does not require a full elaboration of all future domestic policy implementation)[56]
- the costs to New Zealand of compliance with the treaty
- the possibility of any subsequent protocols (or other amendments) to the treaty, and of their likely effects
- the measures which could or should be adopted to implement the treaty, and the intentions of the Government in relation to such measures, including legislation
- a statement setting out the consultations which have been undertaken or are proposed with the community and interested parties in respect of the treaty
- whether the treaty provides for withdrawal or denunciation.[57]

The Regulations Review Committee has urged the Government to include in the national interest analysis any material relating to the treaty that is to be incorporated into implementing legislation by reference rather than set out in it textually and to comment on how this is to be done[58] and for the justification for implementing a treaty by regulation to be addressed in the national interest analysis.[59] There is no requirement for the national interest analysis to identify the recommendations of the various government departments involved in devising policy towards the treaty, for example, by disclosing arguments that they may have advanced against New Zealand entering into the treaty.[60] However, there is nothing to stop the Government supplying more information than the national interest analysis requires.[61]

In the case of a multilateral treaty already entered into on the grounds of urgency, the national interest analysis must also explain the reasons why urgent action preventing prior parliamentary examination was taken.[62] Where the Government proposes to withdraw from or denounce a treaty, it is recognised that the Government's national interest analysis must be adapted from the matters set out above, since these are directed to eliciting reasons why a treaty should or should not be entered into in the first place, rather than why one should be abandoned. In these circumstances the national interest analysis is required to address those matters to the full extent that they are applicable.[63]

Given the importance of the national interest analysis to parliamentary examination of the treaty, the committee which examines the treaty is required to append the national interest analysis to its report so that it is readily and permanently available on the public record.[64]

The national interest analysis must fairly expose the case for and the case against entering into the treaty. (It would thus be expected that any contrary views expressed

[55]   S.O.387(2).
[56]   1999-2002, AJHR, I.22C, p.393.
[57]   S.O.388(1).
[58]   1999-2002, AJHR, I.16H, pp.27-8.
[59]   2002-05, AJHR, I.16G, p.11.
[60]   *Ibid.*, I.22D, pp.298-9.
[61]   *Ibid.*
[62]   S.O.388(2).
[63]   S.O.388(3).
[64]   S.O.390(3).

by government departments will be reflected in it, even if those departments are not identified.) The more information that can be put into it, the better parliamentarians and the public will understand the implications of the proposed treaty.[65] There have been criticisms that the case against has not always been adequately covered in the national interest analysis and that potential objections to a treaty are not revealed. As long as the national interest analysis makes the statements about the treaty set out in the Standing Order it will have complied with that Standing Order. It is then a matter for judgment as to whether it actually provides a justification for the treaty action in question.[66]

The Ministry of Foreign Affairs and Trade is responsible, on behalf of the Government, for presenting the treaty and the national interest analysis to the House.[67]

Select committee examination

On presentation to the House, the treaty and the accompanying national interest analysis stand referred to the Foreign Affairs, Defence and Trade Committee.[68]

The Foreign Affairs, Defence and Trade Committee is central to the treaty examination process and decides which committee a treaty should be referred to.

The committee considers the subject area of any treaty referred to it and, if that area is primarily within its own terms of reference, retains the treaty for examination. If, on the other hand, it is primarily within the terms of reference of another committee, it refers the treaty to that other committee for examination.[69] In this way all subject select committees are expected to share in the work of treaty examination. In recognition of the fact that time can be of the essence for treaty examination, the chairperson of the Foreign Affairs, Defence and Trade Committee is, by Standing Order, given the power to take this referral decision for the committee if it is not due to meet within seven days of a treaty being referred to it. In this case, if the treaty is clearly within the terms of reference of another committee, the chairperson may refer it to that committee for examination.[70]

The Standing Orders do not impose any time limit within which treaty examinations must be concluded. In the case of an urgent treaty, binding treaty action has, by definition, already been taken and so the committee's examination is retrospective in any case. But for most treaties the examination is, and is intended to be, prospective – giving the House an opportunity, if it wishes, to express a view on the appropriateness of the Crown entering into the treaty before it does so. In these circumstances the time that a committee has to carry out its examination before the treaty is ratified or otherwise accepted is obviously of critical importance.

Originally when the Government agreed to present treaties for examination it conceded that it would not proceed to take binding treaty action (except for urgent treaties) for at least 35 days (45 days over the Christmas break) after presentation of the treaty to the House.[71] As a result of a select committee recommendation in 1999, this concession has now been extended to 15 sitting days.[72] Committees have complained that they have insufficient time to conduct a proper examination.[73] Partly for this reason, most treaty examinations are carried out by committees on the basis of the national interest analysis, supplemented by briefings from departmental officials and material from committee advisers.

Only exceptionally does a select committee's examination extend beyond this. A committee has consulted the Regulations Review Committee on the proposed use of

---

[65]   1999-2002, AJHR, I.22C, pp.392-3 (Kyoto Protocol – national interest analysis of some 60 pages).
[66]   *Ibid.*
[67]   *Cabinet Manual*, 2001, para.5.87.
[68]   S.O.387(3).
[69]   S.O.389(1).
[70]   S.O.389(2).
[71]   1996-99, AJHR, A.5.
[72]   *Ibid.*, I.4E; *Cabinet Manual*, 2001, para.5.88.
[73]   1996-99, AJHR, I.24, p.648.

regulations under a treaty being examined by it.[74] With two important bilateral treaties presented to the forty-sixth Parliament, public submissions were called for and oral evidence heard on each, though with a short deadline for submissions.[75] In the case of another treaty on which the select committee invited public input, the committee received 35 submissions and heard 20 of these orally.[76] A committee has heard from a witness who approached the committee asking to be heard.[77] But the opening up of parliamentary treaty examinations to anything resembling the procedures for hearing evidence on bills is still uncommon.

However, the fact that the Government's assurance that it will not take binding treaty action in respect of a treaty lasts only for a maximum period of 15 sitting days does not mean that the Government will actually be insistent on ratifying the treaty immediately that the 15 sitting days expire. It may not be ready to do so for its own reasons. Indeed, from a parliamentary point of view, one way of looking at the 15 sitting days period is not that it represents a maximum time within which committees have to report, but that it is the minimum time which the Government must allow to elapse before it can take steps to implement the treaty, for example, by introducing legislation to make New Zealand law compatible with the treaty obligation that the Government wishes to assume. (See pp. 597–8 for the development of this convention.)

Treaties are generally presented to the House some time after they have been signed by the Government. Signing a treaty signifies an intention to ratify it and accept it as binding in the future. Though the Government may decide later not to ratify it, this would be unusual. Whether a treaty examination carried out by a committee alters the Government's intentions with regard to ratification is a matter for the consideration of the Government. Committees may seek the Government's agreement to keeping a treaty open for prospective committee examination for a longer period than 15 sitting days by asking the Government to defer taking binding action on the treaty, though there is no necessity for a Government to agree to do so. It is also open to a committee to continue with its examination of the treaty even after the Government has ratified or otherwise accepted it and it has become binding.

Report and consideration

Committees to which treaties are referred are required (though not within any particular time-frame) to report to the House on them,[78] and to consider whether to draw the attention of the House to the treaty on any of the grounds set out in the national interest analysis or for any other reason.[79] Committees are not required to state whether they agree with the proposal to enter into the treaty, though it is open to them to express their opinions on this if they wish to. In one case a committee has explicitly recommended against the Government entering into a bilateral agreement.[80] A committee has scrutinised the process followed in entering into the treaty for compliance with the *Cabinet Manual* procedures on treaties.[81]

The overwhelming majority of committee reports on treaties are quite brief and formal. The national interest analysis must be appended to the report.[82] A report on a treaty examination is set down for consideration as a Member's order of the day. It remains on the order paper for 15 sitting days or, if it contains recommendations

---

74 2002-05, AJHR, I.22C, pp.699, 709-10.
75 1999-2002, AJHR, I.4A (closer economic partnership agreement with Singapore); *ibid.*, I.22C, p.370 (agreement with Australia establishing a system for the development of joint food standards).
76 1999-2002, AJHR, I.22C, p.390 (Kyoto Protocol).
77 2002-05, AJHR, I.22D, p.364.

78 S.O.390(1).
79 S.O.390(2).
80 2002-05, AJHR, I.22C, pp.695-735 (agreement for the joint regulation of therapeutic products).
81 *Ibid.*, I.22D, p.365.
82 S.O.390(3).

addressed to the Government (only a few do), for 15 sitting days from the date that the Government's response is received.[83]   In practice, such reports are not reached for debate since Members' orders of the day for Members' bills take precedence over them.[84] However, the Government has initiated a debate on one treaty report by lodging its own notice of motion asking the House to take note of the report.[85]

LEGISLATING FOR TREATY OBLIGATIONS
Where a treaty will require legislation before it can be accepted as binding, treaty examination becomes the first step in an integrated process leading to legislative implementation of the treaty's obligations and then final acceptance of the treaty by the Government. Each step in the process informs or authorises the next step.

Allowing time for treaty examination
Treaty examination is conceptually different from legislative implementation of a treaty's provisions. Rather than considering only the domestic law implications of a treaty, in treaty examination the House, through its committees, requires the proposal to enter into the treaty to be justified as a matter of principle. The committee's conclusions on this (or the House's, if it chooses to express them) should, if possible, be available to the Government before it presents legislation to implement the treaty's obligations. For this purpose, such legislation is not as a matter of practice introduced until at least 15 sitting days after the treaty has been presented to the House for examination.[86] (However, preparatory work on the legislation within government, such as obtaining a legislative priority and drafting the bill, may proceed within this period.)

While it is highly desirable that the select committee will have completed its examination of the treaty and reported to the House so that this can inform and contribute to the Government's legislative proposals, the Government is free to introduce legislation when the 15 sitting days have expired.

Form of legislation
Where legislative action is necessary to implement treaty obligations, there is no standard form which this takes. In some cases legislation may be introduced to give direct effect to a treaty, with the text of the treaty included in a schedule to the Act. In such a case the treaty text itself becomes directly part of New Zealand's statute law. Where this method is adopted, it is accepted that no amendment to the schedule containing the treaty can be made by the House. But the clauses of the bill giving effect to the treaty are open to amendment, even if the effect of such an amendment would be to withhold legislative effect from the treaty or from part of it. (See Chapter 27 for inadmissible amendments.)

In other cases, wording taken from the treaty is used in the legislation, perhaps with some slight verbal or drafting changes so that it fits conveniently into the body of New Zealand law. (But the fact that the wording was drawn from the treaty may not always be readily apparent on the face of the legislation.) In yet other cases, the wording in the legislation relied upon to implement a treaty obligation may not be drawn from the treaty at all and may bear little textual resemblance to it. This is often the case where

---

[83]   S.O.71(3).
[84]   S.O.69(1).
[85]   2000, Vol.588, pp.6329-57 (report of the Foreign Affairs, Defence and Trade Committee on the

agreement between New Zealand and Singapore on a closer economic partnership).
[86]   *Cabinet Manual,* 2001, para.5.91.

New Zealand law is judged to be already compatible with a treaty obligation which the Government is proposing to enter into. Another legislative approach is to implement a treaty's obligations through delegated legislative powers that the Government already has or that are to be conferred on it. Legislative implementation of the same treaty may utilise more than one of these approaches.[87]

Regulations overriding statutes

Incorporation of treaty obligations by means of delegated legislation raises special problems of parliamentary scrutiny. These issues have been the subject of study by the Regulations Review Committee and response by the Government.[88]

In a number of instances (10 were identified by the committee) legislation permits treaties to be implemented by regulations that override or abrogate provisions of New Zealand law. This is an example of a type of Henry VIII clause and is contrary to the general principle that subordinate legislation should not override primary legislation.[89] (See Chapter 29 for Henry VIII clauses.) Some of these overriding regulation-making provisions are limited to overriding provisions of the same Act in which they are contained, others allow other specified Acts to be overridden, while some allow both the Act in which they are contained and any other Act to be overridden.[90]

The committee considered that any power for regulations to override a statute to implement a treaty obligation should be confined to the overriding of the Act in which the power is contained. The power should be clearly defined and identify precisely the provisions in the Act that can be overridden.[91] In all cases, overriding regulation-making power should only be granted by Parliament for technical matters or to deal with emergency situations. The committee instanced double taxation agreements and reciprocal child support agreements as technical agreements where overriding might be appropriate, and responding to United Nations obligations as emergency situations which would justify this power.[92] While, in general, the Government has accepted the committee's views of the principles to be applied, the Government has not accepted that in every case it will be possible to identify all legislative provisions that are to be overridden or to confine the overriding to the Act in which the power is contained.[93]

CONVENTION OF PRIOR PARLIAMENTARY EXAMINATION OF TREATIES

It is submitted that a constitutional convention has emerged that the Government will not (except in an emergency) take binding treaty action until the minimum period for parliamentary scrutiny of the treaty (15 sitting days from its presentation to the House) has expired.[94] (This is a narrower convention than the practice of first enacting legislation to make New Zealand law consistent with a treaty it is proposed to ratify – see p. 590.)

A constitutional convention is not like an Act of Parliament. Indeed, it is not enforceable as law at all. A constitutional convention is an important political practice that develops over the course of time and that is accepted as being binding on those who are parties to that practice. There may be dispute over whether a practice has developed into a convention and, since conventions are inherently imprecise, disagreement as to what the practice

---

[87]   See: 1993-96, AJHR, E.31X, pp.47-64 (*Law Commission: A New Zealand Guide to International Law and its Sources)*; Gobbi, "Drafting Techniques for Implementing Treaties in New Zealand" (2000) 21 Statute LR 71.

[88]   1999-2002, AJHR, I.16H; 2002, PP, A.5.

[89]   1999-2002, AJHR, I.16H, p.7.

[90]   See, for example, *Child Support Act* 1991, s.215(1)(a) (permitting regulations to override

the provisions of *any* Act in order to implement a reciprocal agreement with Australia).

[91]   1999-2002, AJHR, I.16H, p.22.

[92]   *Ibid.*, pp.18 and 29.

[93]   2002, PP, A.5.

[94]   See, for example, 1996-99, AJHR, I.4E, pp.2, 3 and 5 (*Report of the Foreign Affairs, Defence and Trade Committee on its examination of the treaty-making process).*

consists of and how it is to be applied in the light of the circumstances that obtain. It has been said that constitutional conventions possess a number of characteristics: they facilitate constitutional development without formal changes in the law, they co-ordinate the practices of government and provide means for co-operation between the organs of government (for example, between the executive and legislature), and they act as a restraining and modifying influence on the excercise of legal power. The most important conventions promote responsible government by ensuring that public affairs are conducted in accordance with the people's wishes as expressed through their representatives in Parliament.[95]

A political practice of parliamentary examination of multilateral treaties (except in emergencies) prior to them becoming binding commenced in 1998. This is recognised in the Government's responses to select committee recommendations for such a practice, Standing Orders changes implementing it and a state practice (supported by the Government's own internal arrangements, which select committees themselves are now monitoring[96]) of complying with it since then. In particular, parliamentary examination of a proposed treaty is subject to a quite different procedure and a different time-frame, to parliamentary enactment of any legislation to implement that treaty's obligations. The latter is part of the House's general legislative procedures; the former is part of its scrutiny function. A treaty is not of itself a source of law; legislation is.[97] The Government's own practices recognise this distinction between treaty and legislation by providing that any legislation needed to bring domestic law into compliance with a treaty is not to be introduced until after the treaty has been presented or the time for a select committee to report on it (15 sitting days) has expired.[98] Once the 15 sitting days have expired, the Government (if New Zealand law is compatible with the treaty's obligations) may take binding treaty action, whether or not the committee has actually reported back within that time and regardless of whether the House has debated its report.[99] The convention inhibiting the Government in exercising the treaty power applies only during the minimum examination period.

These arrangements have been settled practice since 1998, have been endorsed by successive Governments and were made a permanent part of its procedures by the House in 1999 (though the minimum time to be observed has been altered and there has been ongoing concern about its adequacy). Parliamentary scrutiny of treaties operates on a constitutional, rather than a legal, basis. There has been no change to the law of treaty-making, which remains essentially part of the Royal prerogative. The 1998 reforms represent a compact between the executive and legislative branches of government and were an acknowledgment of concern at the previous lack of parliamentary involvement in the treaty-making process. All parliamentarians now have the opportunity within the House's own procedures to contribute to consideration of any treaty which a Government is considering entering into in New Zealand's name.

In these circumstances, it is submitted that these executive and legislative practices which allow parliamentarians a limited period to examine a proposed multilateral treaty before the Government proceeds to ratify or otherwise accept it as binding, do amount to a constitutional convention.

JOINT COMMITTEE MEETINGS WITH AUSTRALIA

The House of Representatives has a well-established parliamentary exchange programme with the two Houses of the Commonwealth Parliament of Australia. In 1989 this was

---

[95] Joseph, *Constitutional and Administrative Law in New Zealand*, pp.270-1 and Ch.9 generally.
[96] 2002-05, AJHR, I.22D, p.365.
[97] See, for example, *R (European Roma Rights Centre)*

v Immigration Officer at Prague Airport [2004] QB 811 at 100, 101 (per Laws LJ).
[98] *Cabinet Manual*, 2001, para.5.91.
[99] 1996-99, AJHR, I.4E, p.3.

developed into the concept of joint meetings between parliamentary committees from the two countries. The aim is to hold two such meetings each year, one in each country. The meetings are working sessions on subjects chosen in advance on matters currently under examination by the committees or the legislatures. The arrangements for the meetings are formalised between the Speaker and the presiding officers of the Australian Parliament. The visiting legislature decides which of its subject committees will participate.

The first joint meeting was held in Wellington on 19 April 1989 between the then Foreign Affairs and Defence Committee and a subcommittee of the Joint (House and Senate) Committee on Foreign Affairs, Defence and Trade.[100] The Foreign Affairs and Defence Committee used this joint meeting to contribute towards the information it was gathering for an inquiry into overseas development assistance.[101] The exchange is not limited to foreign affairs committees, however. Each year, the Speaker writes to the subject select committees and invites each of them to make a submission if they wish to participate in the programme. The Speaker, after considering the bids they have made, selects the committee to participate that year on the basis of the items of common interest that it wishes to discuss.

As far as the participating New Zealand select committee is concerned, the House must authorise the committee to meet in Australia, as committees may only meet within New Zealand.[102] The House has also made a practice of passing resolutions specifically authorising the committee concerned (whether meeting in New Zealand or in Australia) to hold a joint meeting and empowering it to adopt such practices and procedures as are considered suitable for the conduct of the meeting.[103] Standard procedures for such meetings have been agreed between the presiding officers of the Parliaments and are adopted by the committees concerned at the outset of their series of meetings.[104]

The procedures generally follow the rules of the committee in whose country the meeting is being held. The host committee's chairperson presides and the visiting committee's chairperson acts as deputy chairperson. Votes are not taken. While the opening formalities of the meetings are held in public, subsequent sessions are held in private, subject to the right of any other member of the Houses of either Parliament to attend them. No transcript of the meetings is made, but a formal record of it is agreed by both committees. Subject to the agreement of the joint meeting, both the chairperson and the deputy chairperson may make public statements about the meetings prior to the committees reporting back to their respective Houses.[105]

Committees are expected to make a report to the House on their joint meetings.

INTER-PARLIAMENTARY RELATIONS

Members participate in two inter-parliamentary organisations with official support – the Commonwealth Parliamentary Association (CPA) and the Inter-Parliamentary Union (IPU).

Commonwealth Parliamentary Association

The CPA (founded in 1911 as the Empire Parliamentary Association) is a body with branches in most of the legislatures (at both federal and state levels) in the Commonwealth. Members of Parliament (and former members as associate members) are entitled to join the New Zealand branch. The Speaker is the *ex officio* president of the branch and the Prime Minister and the Leader of the Opposition its vice-presidents. The Clerk of the

---

[100] 1987-90, AJHR, I.5B.
[101] 1990, AJHR, I.5B, para.2.6.
[102] S.O.193.

[103] 1995, Vol.549, p.8224-5.
[104] 1987-90, AJHR, I.5A, para.4.
[105] *Ibid.*, Appendix A.

House acts as honorary secretary/treasurer. The CPA aims to promote understanding and co-operation among its members, and study of and respect for parliamentary institutions throughout the Commonwealth. It promotes conferences, seminars and publications towards these aims. Branches are organised on a regional basis, New Zealand being part of the Pacific Region. Many CPA activities are regionally based, with the Pacific Region collaborating with the Australian Region in regular conferences and seminars. In 2004 the Office of the Clerk assumed responsibility for providing a regional secretariat for the Pacific Region.

The New Zealand branch was host of the CPA annual conferences in 1950, 1965, 1979 and 1998, and has also staged other CPA conferences and seminars.

Inter-Parliamentary Union

Members are also entitled to join the New Zealand group of the IPU. The IPU was founded in 1889. It is an organisation consisting of groups formed by national legislatures. Its official languages are English and French. As with the CPA, the Speaker is the *ex officio* president of the New Zealand group and the Prime Minister and the Leader of the Opposition its vice-presidents. The IPU aims to secure and maintain the establishment and development of democratic institutions and international peace and co-operation. It promotes annual and ad hoc conferences and seminars. It also publishes information on parliamentary and other subjects.

Other international contacts

As well as participating in activities organised under the aegis of the CPA and the IPU, members engage in other international contacts at the parliamentary level. An official programme of parliamentary travel to be administered by the Office of the Clerk is drawn up each year under the Speaker's direction. Members participating in this travel programme are regarded as attending official business for the purposes of having their votes included in a party vote.[106] The programme covers both incoming and outgoing parliamentary delegations. Members participating in CPA and IPU activities are expected to report back to the annual meetings of the New Zealand branch of the CPA and the New Zealand group of the IPU respectively on their experiences. They may be invited to brief the Foreign Affairs, Defence and Trade Committee at its regular meetings. Following a suggestion by the select committee examining the relevant estimates that information obtained by parliamentary delegations should be more widely disseminated,[107] parliamentary delegations present formal reports to the House on their visits. These reports are published as parliamentary papers.

The Visits and Ceremonials Office of the Department of Internal Affairs is responsible for organising the provision of hospitality to incoming parliamentary delegations invited as part of the official travel programme. For this purpose, itineraries are arranged in consultation with the Speaker, the Office of the Clerk and the Ministry of Foreign Affairs and Trade.

---

[106]   Business Committee determination, 2 March 2004.   [107]   1991-93, AJHR, I.19C, p.159.

CHAPTER 44

EMERGENCY POWERS

There is no one definition of what constitutes an emergency and when emergency powers are justified. But there are statutes that make provision for action to be taken to deal with an emergency that has arisen in respect of a particular subject. The precise legal and parliamentary steps to be taken differ in each case, depending upon the provisions of the legislation.

An emergency that requires parliamentary action of some description will, of its nature, be an event of national significance, posing a serious threat to public safety or threatening the destruction of or damage to property. A severe earthquake or an outbreak of foot and mouth disease are the most obvious examples of this.[1] Whether or not a declaration of a state of national emergency has been made that requires that there be a special sitting of the House, the House will undoubtedly wish to give attention to any event of that nature by means of its regular procedures, for example, by means of an urgent debate.

SITTING OF THE HOUSE

Should an emergency, such as an earthquake, affect the meeting place of Parliament, there is legal power vested in the Governor-General to alter the place of meeting from that to which Parliament has been summoned to meet. Parliament is summoned to meet at such place as is appointed in the Governor-General's proclamation summoning it.[2] This is now usually expressed to be the city of Wellington. The House can alter its venue on its own authority, provided that it still meets within the city of Wellington. If, after Parliament has been summoned to meet, the place to which Parliament has been summoned becomes unsafe or uninhabitable, the Governor-General may, by proclamation, change the place at which Parliament is to meet.[3] This is done by a further proclamation. Such a proclamation does not prorogue Parliament and does not bring the session to an end.

If the House is adjourned at the time of an emergency and no question of its needing to meet outside Wellington arises, its meeting can be brought forward by the Speaker on being informed by the Prime Minister that the House should sit at an earlier time.[4] (See Chapter 13.)

In the case of a declaration of a state of national emergency made while Parliament is dissolved or prorogued or while the House is adjourned and is not due to meet again within seven days, statute requires that the House's reassembly be accelerated. In these circumstances Parliament must be summoned to meet within seven days of the last day for the return of the writ for constituency members if it is dissolved, and within seven days of the making of the proclamation if it is prorogued. If the House is adjourned at the time, it must sit within seven days of the making of the declaration at a time to be appointed by the Speaker by notice in the *Gazette*.[5]

Apart from any legal action that is required to be taken by the House in the event that an emergency occurs, there are a number of other relevant procedures that may be utilised when it assembles. The House could expect that the Prime Minister or another Minister

---

[1] 1991-93, AJHR, E.31P, para.1.12 (Law Commission, *Final Report on Emergencies*).

[2] *Constitution Act* 1986, s.18(1).

[3] *Ibid.*, s.18(1A).

[4] S.O.53.

[5] *Civil Defence Emergency Management Act* 2002, s.67.

will make a ministerial statement about a serious emergency, there will be an opportunity to ask oral questions about it and, if the Speaker agrees that it is important enough, an urgent debate on it could be held. In this way, whatever else is on the parliamentary agenda, members can, in the House, respond to a matter of serious import that has just arisen.

FORMS OF PARLIAMENTARY CONTROL

In a few circumstances the powers conferred on the Government or officials to deal with an emergency are regarded as so extreme that it is desirable that there be some parliamentary control to ensure that they are not abused. The House is only one means of control; another obvious means is the right to seek judicial review of the exercise of any statutory powers. The forms of parliamentary control include four elements: the right to be consulted in planning for emergencies, the right to be informed of an emergency, the need for the House in some circumstances to authorise the continuance of the emergency, and the power of the House to revoke or amend powers to deal with the emergency.

Planning for emergencies

The Minister of Civil Defence must, on behalf of the Crown, prepare a civil defence emergency management strategy. The strategy is designed to set out the Crown's goals in relation to civil defence strategy management, the objectives to be pursued to achieve those goals, and the measurable targets to be met to achieve those objectives.[6] Before completing the strategy the Minister must engage in a process of public consultation.[7] A copy of the completed strategy must be presented to the House.[8]

Once presented to the House, the strategy stands referred to the Government Administration Committee, which must report on it within 12 sitting days of its referral.[9] The strategy takes effect 28 days after it is publicly notified in the *Gazette* or on any later date specified in it.[10] But the House has the right to prevent it taking effect or to counteract it by resolving, within 15 sitting days of its presentation, not to approve it (the House's express approval for the strategy is not required).[11] A motion not to approve the strategy requires notice. A decision by the House not to approve the strategy would only be likely to be taken in the light of the report on it presented by the Government Administration Committee. If the House does resolve not to approve the strategy the Minister must complete a revised strategy. This is subject to non-approval by the House too.[12]

A strategy remains in force for 10 years or such lesser period specified in it.[13] It may be amended by following the consultation and approval procedure required for the strategy itself.[14]

A national civil defence emergency management plan that is consistent with the strategy may be made by Order in Council.[15] The plan must identify and provide for the hazards and risks to be managed at the national level, identify objectives and provide for the co-ordination of civil defence emergency management during a state of national emergency.[16] In drawing up the plan, the Minister must engage in a process of public consultation and must present the completed plan to the House.[17] The plan stands referred to the Government Administration Committee,[18] which may inquire into it as it sees fit. The plan (an Order in Council) is not subject to disallowance by the House.[19] A civil

---

[6]   *Ibid.*, s.31.
[7]   *Ibid.*, s.32(1).
[8]   *Ibid.*, s.32(2)(b).
[9]   S.O.385.
[10] *Civil Defence Emergency Management Act* 2002, s.34(1)(a).
[11] *Ibid*, s.35(1)
[12] *Ibid.*, s.35(2).
[13] *Ibid.*, s.34(2).
[14] *Ibid.*, s.36.
[15] *Ibid.*, ss.39(1) and 42.
[16] *Ibid.*, s.39(2).
[17] *Ibid.*, ss.41 and 43.
[18] S.O.385(1).
[19] *Civil Defence Emergency Management Act* 2002, s.38(4).

defence emergency management plan must be reviewed between five and 10 years after it is made.[20]

The right to be informed

The House must be informed immediately if it is then sitting, or as soon as it sits, of certain emergencies that have arisen.

This obligation is imposed on the responsible Minister in the case of a declaration of a state of national emergency (which could involve an earthquake or a flood) or the extension of such an emergency.[21] Similar obligations on the responsible Minister arise in respect of: a declaration of a biosecurity emergency (foot and mouth disease being an obvious example of this);[22] the authorising of the police to exercise powers in respect of an international terrorist emergency;[23] the grant of authority for the armed forces to provide assistance to the civil power in the time of an emergency (for example, to help the police, the prison service, or the civil defence authorities);[24] and when proclamations of a war emergency have been made and the armed forces mobilised.[25]

The House is informed of the emergency by a ministerial statement made by the relevant Minister. Any regulations that have to be presented are delivered to the Clerk before the House meets.

The obligation to inform the House of such a declaration having been made or authority having been given arises regardless of the fact that by the time the House sits the emergency may be over or the authority withdrawn. Thus, the House has been informed of the grant of authority for the armed forces to assist with the custody of prisoners even though the industrial action that led to the emergency was over by the time the House resumed sitting and the authority had never been exercised.[26]

Authority to continue or revoke an emergency

The House's authority is not required for a state of national emergency to continue in force. Nor is the affirmative approval of the House required in respect of a biosecurity emergency, although the House can by resolution revoke such a declaration at any time.[27] Any authority for the armed forces to assist the civil power lapses after 14 days unless the House agrees, by resolution, to extend it for such period as is specified in the resolution (the Governor-General may extend it if Parliament is dissolved or has expired).[28]

In the case of an international terrorist emergency, the authority given to the police expires when the incident ends or is otherwise dealt with. At the latest it expires after seven days.[29] The House has power to extend the authority, by resolution, for such period, not exceeding seven days, as it thinks fit (as does the Governor-General if Parliament is dissolved or has expired). But in no circumstances may the authority be extended beyond 14 days.[30] In addition, the House has the power to revoke an authority or an extension to such an authority at any time.[31]

Emergency regulations

It has been recommended that regulations which are of an emergency nature should be given a limited life, unless they are specifically confirmed by Act of Parliament.[32] The

---

20 *Ibid.*, s.46.
21 *Ibid.*, s.66(2).
22 *Biosecurity Act* 1993, s.147.
23 *International Terrorism (Emergency Powers) Act* 1987, s.7(1).
24 *Defence Act* 1990, s.9(7).
25 *Ibid.*, s.41(5).
26 1993, Vol.536, p.16547.

27 *Biosecurity Act* 1993, s.148.
28 *Defence Act* 1990, s.9(8).
29 *International Terrorism (Emergency Powers) Act* 1987, s.6(4).
30 *Ibid.*, s.7(2), (3), (4).
31 *Ibid.*, s.8.
32 2002-05, AJHR, I.16E, Appendix E (Regulations Review Committee).

only emergency regulations that are subject to statutory confirmation are biosecurity emergency regulations.

Biosecurity emergency regulations must be laid before the House within two sitting days.[33] They lapse if not confirmed by an Act of Parliament passed by the end of the year where they were made before 30 June in that year, or by the end of the following year where they were made after 30 June.[34]

In addition to this specific provision, the House has a general power to disallow any regulations or any provisions of regulations, and to amend or to revoke and substitute regulations.[35] These powers are not limited to regulations in respect of which the House possesses no other power of revocation or amendment. On the face of it, they apply to all types of regulations. It would therefore seem that they could be used in respect of emergency regulations (in the absence of any provision in the empowering Act to the contrary), notwithstanding that the emergencies legislation might make specific provision for revocation and amendment of regulations made under the relevant Acts.

EMERGENCY EXPENDITURE
Provision exists under permanent legislative authority for expenses or capital expenditure to be incurred to meet an emergency or disaster. This provision allows the Minister of Finance to approve such expenditure where any state of emergency or of civil defence emergency has been declared or any other situation occurs that affects the public health or safety of New Zealand or a part of New Zealand, and which the Government declares to be an emergency.[36] The Minister may then approve expenses or capital expenditure to meet the emergency even though no appropriation exists, and public money may be spent on it accordingly.[37] Any such expenses or capital expenditure must be included in the annual financial statements of the Government and an Appropriation Bill for subsequent confirmation by Parliament.[38]

---

[33] *Biosecurity Act* 1993, s.150(5).
[34] *Ibid.*, s.151.
[35] *Regulations (Disallowance) Act* 1989, ss.5(1) and 9(1).
[36] *Public Finance Act* 1989, s.25(1).
[37] *Ibid.*, s.25(2), (4).
[38] *Ibid.*, s.25(5).

CHAPTER 45

PARLIAMENTARY PRIVILEGE

THE NATURE AND PURPOSE OF PARLIAMENTARY PRIVILEGE

All legislative bodies enjoy certain legal privileges, powers and immunities. These privileges, powers and immunities may be set out in detail in a legal instrument, such as a constitution or a statute. But even where no single legal instrument of this nature exists (as is the case in New Zealand), the law implies privileges, powers and immunities as being inherent in any body operating as a legislature.[1] Compendiously, these privileges, powers and immunities are known as "parliamentary privilege".

Privileges for a legislature have been justified in law on the grounds: that a legislature must enjoy an autonomy from control by the Crown and the courts (an aspect of the constitutional separation of powers);[2] that it must possess certain powers to facilitate the carrying out of its functions; and that it, its members and others participating in its proceedings, must enjoy certain immunities, if the legislature is to discharge those functions effectively. The privileges that a legislature enjoys are not an end in themselves. They form part of a constitutional expression of parliamentary autonomy and are a means to achieving an end – an effectively functioning legislature able to operate in the public interest. Parliamentary privilege is thus designed to remove any impediments or restraints to the legislature going about its work and to enable it to deal with challenges to its authority in more indirect ways, such as attacks that affect its dignity and lower the esteem in which it is held.

The privileges, powers and immunities conferred on the legislature as parliamentary privilege inevitably involve the imposition of corresponding duties, liabilities and disabilities on other persons who are made subject to the exercise of those privileges or powers or who have those immunities invoked against them. The public interest in the promotion of the functioning of the parliamentary system of government and the maintenance of the separation of powers legitimates the derogation from any standards of legality that this may entail.[3] Nevertheless, the existence of other interests that may be infringed or abridged by the operation of parliamentary privilege justifies restricting the privileges to activities having a real connection with the operation of the legislature, and confining their scope in respect of such activities so as not to trespass on other rights unnecessarily.[4] Parliamentary privilege in New Zealand does not, for instance, confer any general legal immunity on members of Parliament (as opposed to particular immunities operating when they are functioning as legislators), and the exercise of the House's powers coercively outside the parliamentary environment must itself comply with general legal standards.

Necessity

Part of the rationale for parliamentary privilege is that certain powers and immunities are necessary for the transaction of parliamentary functions.[5] "Necessary" in this sense means that the privileges, powers and immunities are adapted to the needs or purposes of the legislature, and not that the legislature could not function without them.[6] Parliamentary

---

[1] *Kielley v Carson* (1842) 4 Moo PC 63.

[2] *New Brunswick Broadcasting Co v Nova Scotia (Speaker of the House of Assembly)* (1993) 100 DLR (4th) 212 at 265 (per McLachlin J).

[3] *Prebble v Television New Zealand Ltd* [1994] 3 NZLR 1; *A v United Kingdom 2002* (35373/97).

[4] *Re Ouellet (No 1)* (1976) 67 DLR (3d) 73 (privilege

did not apply to a press conference given by a member); *Canada (House of Commons) v Vaid* 2005 SSC 30 (no privilege of "management of staff").

[5] *May*, pp.75, 176.

[6] *Egan v Willis* (1996) 40 NSWLR 650 at 676 (per Mahoney P).

privilege consists of privileges, powers and immunities that are consistent or compatible with the purposes of the House and support its operations, but those privileges, powers and immunities do not have to be essential to its functions in particular instances. Indeed, the privileges, powers and immunities that the House possesses are an important factor in explaining why the House's functions have evolved as they have in the first place; there was no inevitability to this evolution of functions. Privilege therefore helps to define the type of legislature that New Zealand enjoys (for example, one having an inquisitorial role), rather than being wholly supportive or subsidiary to it or explicable only in terms of essentiality. Parliamentary privilege is an integral part of what the House of Representatives *is*. Without those privileges, powers and immunities or if they had taken a different form, there would have been a different House.

While necessity can help to elucidate the existence and extent of a particular privilege (and remains the legal justification for the privileges of some legislatures[7]), it is not the legal foundation of parliamentary privilege in New Zealand. That foundation has, since 1865, been firmly rooted in New Zealand's own statute law, which confers on the House of Representatives the privileges, powers and immunities already established at that time for the House of Commons of the Parliament of the United Kingdom.[8] Whether a privilege exists, and the definition of the scope of that privilege, are questions of law to be determined by a court by reference to the statute, rather than on any ground of necessity (though necessity may help to elucidate the statute). But, once the existence of a claimed privilege is established, it is for the House to judge whether it should be exercised in a particular case. The exercise of an established privilege does not have to be justified on a ground of necessity.[9]

ESTABLISHMENT OF PARLIAMENTARY PRIVILEGE IN NEW ZEALAND

By the time representative government was established in New Zealand by the *New Zealand Constitution Act* 1852, the United Kingdom House of Commons had evolved its privileges over the course of some six centuries.[10] Perhaps the best-known privilege was freedom of speech – a privilege designed to permit members to speak out freely in the House without fear of legal consequences. Another privilege was freedom from arrest – the House's claim to the service and attendance of its members overriding the legal rights of creditors or other persons to have members arrested or detained in civil (but not criminal) cases. Acting as a body, one of the privileges of the House was its power to punish for contempt persons who committed a breach of one of its privileges or who in any way interfered with it or its members in the execution of their duties. This was analogous to the power of any court of record summarily to punish persons who insulted or improperly interfered with its proceedings, and was partly justified as a power of the House of Commons on the ground that that House was part of a court of law, the High Court of Parliament.[11] It also helped to ensure the independence of the Commons from the courts. As the Commons could itself punish for contempt, it did not need to refer alleged cases of contempt to the courts to be dealt with (where the ultimate right of appeal was to the other Chamber of the legislature – the House of Lords), but could take action of its own volition to protect its authority and dignity.

In contradistinction to the House of Commons, the colonial legislatures created by legislation passed by the United Kingdom Parliament have not evolved out of a court.

---

7   For example, the Houses of the Parliament of New South Wales; see *Egan v Willis* (1998) 195 CLR 424.

8   *Parliamentary Privileges Act* 1865, s.4; now the *Legislature Act* 1908, s.242.

9   *R v Richards; ex parte Fitzpatrick and Brown* (1955) 92 CLR 157; *New Brunswick Broadcasting Co v Nova Scotia (Speaker of the House of Assembly)* (1993) 100 DLR (4th) 212; *Harvey v New Brunswick (Attorney-*

General) (1996) 137 DLR (4th) 142 at [71]; *Egan v Willis* (1998) 195 CLR 424 at 446; *Manley v Telezone Inc.*, Court of Appeal for Ontario, 6 January 2004.

10   See *May*, pp.78-92.

11   Though whether the House of Commons was ever part of a court has been doubted – see *Special Reference No 1 of 1964 (Keshav Singh's case* AIR 1965 Supreme Court 745 at 160 (per Sarkar J dissenting).

The New Zealand legislature is not and has never been a "court". Thus a reference to Parliament as "the highest court in the land" is, at least in New Zealand, a figure of speech (albeit a powerfully evocative one).

As a legislative body, in common with other colonial legislatures, the House of Representatives was invested by the common law with such privileges as were reasonably necessary to its existence and to the proper exercise of the functions it was called upon to perform. The main parliamentary privilege that the House of Commons possessed, but that the House obviously lacked, was the power to punish for contempt. It had been held in 1842 that colonial legislatures possessed no inherent power to punish for contempt.[12] If a colonial legislature wished to punish someone for a breach of privilege or for any other reason, it had to seek the aid of the courts; it could not inflict punishment itself.

Concern at the precise legal position in New Zealand regarding parliamentary privilege led the House, within months of its first meeting, to set up a select committee to inquire into what were or ought to be its privileges. The committee, in its report, recommended that legislation be passed to confer power on the House to preserve order in the Chamber and in the parliamentary precincts and to call for witnesses and papers, and that disobedience to such orders be made subject to punishment by fine or imprisonment. The committee also recommended exemption from service on juries and in the militia for members and clearer protections against liability for reports of speeches and other parliamentary publications.[13]

Legislation was subsequently enacted to implement many of these recommendations,[14] though, at first, not in respect of the power to punish for contempt. In respect of this power, there was considerable doubt as to whether a colonial legislature could, even by legislation, confer such a power on itself. If it was to be done, it was argued, the power had to be part of the grant of legislative power from the Imperial Parliament. However, in 1864 it was held by the Privy Council (in an appeal from the State of Victoria) that a colonial legislature was competent to confer on itself privileges equivalent to those possessed by the House of Commons, including the power to punish for contempt.[15] The New Zealand Parliament followed suit in the following year.

Statutory basis for privilege

The *Parliamentary Privileges Act* 1865 repealed the piecemeal legislative provisions for privilege that had been previously enacted and substituted one overarching definition of the privileges enjoyed by the House (and, at that time, by the Legislative Council). As re-enacted, this provision is still the basis of parliamentary privilege today in New Zealand:

> The House of Representatives … and the Committees and members thereof … shall hold, enjoy, and exercise such and the like privileges, immunities, and powers as on the 1st day of January 1865 were held, enjoyed, and exercised by the Commons House of Parliament of Great Britain and Ireland, and by the Committees and members thereof, so far as the same are not inconsistent with or repugnant to such of the provisions of the Constitution Act as on the 26th day of September 1865 (being the date of the coming into operation of the Parliamentary Privileges Act 1865) were unrepealed, whether such privileges, immunities, or powers were so held, possessed or enjoyed by custom, statute, or otherwise.[16]

While the provision does not make the House a court, it does give it attributes enjoyed by a part of a court (the House of Commons, as part of the High Court of Parliament).

---

12   *Kielley v Carson* (1842) 4 Moo PC 63.
13   1854, VP, Session I (1 August 1854).
14   See, for example, *Privileges Act* 1856 and

        Militia Act 1858.
15   *Dill v Murphy* (1864) 1 Moo PC (NS) 487.
16   *Legislature Act* 1908, s.242(1).

Many other Commonwealth countries have adopted the practice of originally defining their legislature's privileges by reference to those of the House of Commons. Many states and provinces define parliamentary privilege in a similar way.[17] Although the statutory provisions are not identical with New Zealand's, and the dates against which the Commons' privileges must be measured are always different, this does help to create a Commonwealth-wide body of precedent on the law of parliamentary privilege.[18]

The statutory base of parliamentary privilege in New Zealand has been supplemented by later statutes dealing with matters touching the privileges of the House. Privilege is part of the general law of New Zealand and is to be taken notice of judicially in all courts without being specially pleaded.[19] In ascertaining specific privileges enjoyed by the House it is necessary to establish the nature of the privileges enjoyed by the House of Commons so far as these have not been altered by British statutes passed since 1 January 1865 and in the light of changes in New Zealand law too, since that date. The leading work on the House of Commons' privileges to which reference is made is *Erskine May's Parliamentary Practice*, now in its twenty-third edition.

Immediately after being confirmed in office by the Governor-General, the Speaker lays claim, on behalf of the House, to the House's privileges which are thereupon confirmed by the Governor-General. This is a traditional proceeding only and is not an essential prerequisite to the enjoyment of the privileges conferred on the House by statute.

CLASSIFICATION OF PARLIAMENTARY PRIVILEGES

No attempt has been made in New Zealand law to codify or enumerate the privileges held by the House of Representatives. Any classification or list of them is therefore inherently subjective.

The types of privilege that have been recognised in New Zealand and that are discussed in this work are the following—
- freedom of speech
- freedom of debate
- exclusive control of the House's own proceedings
- control of reports of the House's proceedings
- control of the parliamentary precincts
- control of access to the sittings of the House
- power to inquire
- power to obtain evidence
- power to administer oaths
- power to delegate
- power to punish for contempt
- power to discipline members
- power to expel members
- power to fine
- power to arrest
- exemption from jury service
- exemption from liability for parliamentary publications
- freedom from arrest
- exemption from attending court as a witness
- right to have civil proceedings adjourned

---

[17]   See Marleau and Montpetit, *House of Commons Procedures and Practice*, pp. 61–2 (Canada); Harris, *House of Representatives Practice*, p. 708 (Australia); Malhotra, *Practice and Procedure of Parliament*, pp. 212–4 (India).

[18]   1987-90, AJHR, I.18B, para.11 (*Report of the Standing Orders Committee on the Law of Privilege and Related Matters*).

[19]   *Legislature Act* 1908, s.242(2); *Awatere Huata v Prebble* [2004] 3 NZLR 359 at [40] (CA).

- exemption from service of legal process
- power to determine the qualification to sit and vote in the House
- freedom of access to the Governor-General
- right to a favourable construction of the House's proceedings.

These privileges are discussed in detail in Chapters 46, 47 and 48 and in a number of other chapters of this book.

The privileges of the House do fall into two main categories: those that are in the nature of immunities from legal processes that would otherwise apply, and those that consist of a power to do something. The former privileges primarily operate in respect of individuals, usually members, but also other persons – officers, witnesses, petitioners – who participate in the work of the House. Freedom of speech, with the implications that flow from the proposition that nothing said or done in the House or in a parliamentary committee may be called into question in proceedings outside the House, is the most important form of immunity enjoyed. Freedom from civil arrest is relatively unimportant in New Zealand, but members do enjoy other immunities from legal process that have no direct connection with actions they have taken in Parliament (which freedom of speech always does) but that exist on the basis of a presumed priority for their parliamentary work over other legal commitments that have arisen. Though these privileges operate in respect of individuals, they exist for the benefit of the effective operation of an institution – the House of Representatives.

The privileges in the nature of powers are exercised collectively by the House or its committees. A major power is the power to punish for contempt. Any contravention of the privileges of freedom of speech or arrest or of the other immunities is unlawful and is known as a breach of privilege. As the privileges enjoyed by the House are part of the general law, the House can expect that if, in a case before a court, the possibility of a breach of privilege becomes apparent, the court, in simply applying the law, will take that fact into account and protect the House's privileges. (Though occasionally, to ensure that a court is sufficiently well-informed on such an issue, the House itself will seek to intervene in the proceedings to address legal argument to the court.) But, in addition to the courts' observance of privilege in the case of a potential breach, and in cases where a breach of privilege occurs outside a court, the House may itself take action to uphold its privileges by declaring that breach to be a contempt and then invoking its privilege of punishing for contempt. The punishments it may inflict range from imprisonment to requiring an apology.

CREATION OF NEW PRIVILEGES

The privileges enjoyed by the House of Commons in 1865 did not include the right to create new privileges. The House of Commons acknowledged, as long ago as 1704, that it had no power to create any new privilege not recognised by the known laws and customs of Parliament.[20] If a new privilege is to be created for the House of Representatives, as for the House of Commons, this must be accomplished by legislation. But the House has been at pains to declare that its privileges are not to be construed as having been diminished or surrendered because it has established procedures in its Standing Orders for their exercise.[21]

ABROGATION OF PARLIAMENTARY PRIVILEGE

Parliamentary privilege, as part of the law, is liable to be abrogated in whole or in part by

---

[20]   *May*, p.176.   [21]   S.Os 1 and 92.

legislation amending the law. Thus, the extent to which legal immunities flowing from the House's freedom of speech may have been overridden or modified by subsequent legislation has been questioned, and the House's power to inquire into particular bodies or insist on the production of certain evidence has been challenged, on the ground that these privileges are subject to other legal rules.

Parliamentary privilege is only part of the law. Though it is a (more or less) well-defined category of law, it is not self-contained and must coexist within the general corpus of legal rights, powers and immunities that are established and recognised by legislation and the common law. Since parliamentary privilege is of constitutional import, the public policy that it promotes is entitled to a high level of priority when it conflicts with other values protected by law.[22] But it is not a body of higher or fundamental law that automatically overrides all other law. It is, in principle, therefore, subject to statutory abrogation.

Clearly an express revocation by statute of an aspect of parliamentary privilege would be effective to abrogate it. However, such a provision is rare.[23]

Closely akin to express abrogation is a legislative direction to a court or other body outside Parliament to assess Parliament's enactments against a defined standard, such as an international convention. In such a case, the court or body will be obliged to make an objective judgment on what Parliament has done, an undertaking that would otherwise be illegitimate. In such legislation Parliament itself by its own direction requires a judgment to be made on the compatibility of its work with the prescribed standard.[24]

There have been claims that *only* an express provision in a statute is capable of abrogating parliamentary privilege.[25] But this seems too extreme a position to adopt. It has been accepted in a number of cases, for instance, that privilege will be surrendered if there is a necessary implication from a statute that this is so, for otherwise the statute would not work. A necessary implication has been defined (in the context of legal professional privilege) as one that necessarily, rather than reasonably, follows from the statutory provision in question. It is not a matter of a rule that it might have been sensible for Parliament to have abolished or that it might have abolished if it had thought about it. It is what the express language of the statute shows that the statute must have abolished.[26] Another way of approaching the question is to ask whether, if the privilege continues, an inconsistency is thereby produced or the statutory purpose is thereby stultified.[27] In this sense, parliamentary privilege must be subject to abrogation by necessary implication if otherwise the enactment would effectively be disapplied.

The creation of a criminal offence in regard to actions taken in the course of proceedings in Parliament[28] must, if that offence is to be prosecuted at all, to that extent set aside the freedom of speech protections that would normally operate to prevent anyone being held liable in legal proceedings for their parliamentary actions.[29] Where a statute provides for disqualification of a member on the basis of the member's parliamentary actions, judicial

---

[22]   *Prebble v Television New Zealand Ltd* [1994] 3 NZLR 1.

[23]   For Australian examples, see the *Parliamentary Privileges Act* 1987 (Australia) ss.4 and 6 (contempt), s.7(3) (power to fine) and s.8 (expulsion).

[24]   *Wilson v First County Trust Ltd (No 2)* [2004] 1 AC 816 (legislation to be judged for compatibility with human rights convention); for a possible New Zealand example, see *Human Rights Act* 1993, s.92B(1)(b) (complaint of discrimination under an enactment).

[25]   *Re House of Commons and Canada Labour Relations*

Board (1986) 27 DLR (4th) 481 at 490 (per Pratte J); *Harvey v New Brunswick (Attorney-General)* (1996) 137 DLR (4th) 142 at [70] (per McLachlin J).

[26]   *R (on the application of Morgan Grenfell & Co Ltd) v Special Commissioner of Income Tax)* [2003] 1 AC 563 at 45 (HL) (per Lord Hobhouse).

[27]   *B v Auckland District Law Society* [2004] 1 NZLR 326 at [59].

[28]   For example, *Crimes Act* 1961, s.108 (perjury).

[29]   *Prebble v Television New Zealand Ltd* [1994] 3 NZLR 1 at 10.

evaluation of them is unavoidable if the court is to scrutinise the legality of any claimed disqualification.[30] Thus, the Committee for Privileges of the House of Lords was of the view that a privilege attaching to peers was overridden by mental health legislation even though there was no express provision to that effect in the statute.[31] Apart from an express statutory direction or an implication arising as a matter of necessity, general words in a statute will not be taken to override parliamentary privilege,[32] nor will an implication arise indirectly because Parliament has created legal powers coextensive (or partially so) with parliamentary privilege.[33] Parliamentary privilege is always an important part of the constitutional background against which Parliament legislates.

On occasion, to make it absolutely clear that no abrogation of parliamentary privilege is to be implied, the statute may expressly declare this[34] or make it clear that the legislature is not within the purview of its provisions.[35] But such a provision is by no means essential to preserve parliamentary privilege.

While abrogation of parliamentary privilege by express words or by necessary implication must be rare, a subsisting privilege must still be applied in a contemporary legal context. This means that the way in which an admitted privilege can be exercised may be subject to modification. The principal contemporary means in which this may occur results from the *New Zealand Bill of Rights Act* 1990. That Act outlines a number of fundamental rights and freedoms that the House, in exercising its privileges (none of which are abrogated by the Act[36]) must observe.[37] Thus, notwithstanding the House's exclusive power to control its own proceedings, the right to natural justice confirmed by the Act[38] has led to substantial procedural changes designed to give effect to this value in a parliamentary context. The right to be secure against unreasonable search or seizure[39] is another obvious right that must be accommodated by the House in exercising its power to punish for contempt.

Abrogation of parliamentary privilege must be distinguished too from disputes over the interpretation of the scope of privilege. In 1986 the Supreme Court of New South Wales gave an extremely restrictive interpretation to the freedom of speech enjoyed by members of the Parliament of the Commonwealth of Australia (and by extension those of other Parliaments, including New Zealand's, with similar privileges).[40] This decision was not based on any claimed change in the law respecting parliamentary privilege. It was the court's view of the true meaning of that privilege. The decision led the Australian Parliament to pass legislation reaffirming the parliamentary view of the law.[41] As far as New Zealand is concerned, any difficulties that may have arisen from the New South Wales court's interpretation were avoided by the Privy Council in 1994 declaring that it did not represent the law in New Zealand.[42] However, there will always be interpretive problems arising in this as in other areas of the law, and a particularly restrictive interpretation of the scope of a privilege can, from a parliamentary point of view, be little different in effect to a legislative abrogation of that privilege. For this reason, the House will, in an

---

30 *Awatere Huata v Prebble* [2004] 3 NZLR 359 at [123] (CA) (per Hammond J) (reversed [2005] 1 NZLR 289 but without affecting the validity of this reflection as a matter of principle).

31 HL 254 (1983-84).

32 *Duke of Newcastle v Morris* (1870) 4 LR HL 668; *Aboriginal Legal Service v State of Western Australia* (1993) 9 WAR 297 at 304.

33 *R v Smith, ex parte Cooper* [1992] 1 Qd R 423; *Criminal Justice Commission v Dick* [2000] QSC 272.

34 See, for example: *Crimes Act* 1961, s.9(a) (power of arrest); *Copyright Act* 1994, s.225(1)(c) (privileges of the House).

35 For example, *Human Rights Act* 1998 (UK), s.6(3) (a "public authority" subject to the Act does not include either House of Parliament or a person exercising functions in connection with a proceeding in Parliament).

36 *New Zealand Bill of Rights Act* 1990, s.4(1).

37 *Ibid.*, s.3(a).

38 *Ibid.*, s.27(1).

39 *Ibid.*, s.21.

40 *R v Murphy* (1986) 5 NSWLR 18.

41 *Parliamentary Privileges Act* 1987 (Australia).

42 *Prebble v Television New Zealand Ltd* [1994] 3 NZLR 1 at 8.

appropriate case, seek to intervene in legal proceedings to ensure that a full argument on disputed aspects of parliamentary privilege is addressed to a court before it interprets the law in that case.

WAIVER OF PARLIAMENTARY PRIVILEGE

An issue linked to abrogation of parliamentary privilege is the extent to which parliamentary privilege, while continuing to subsist, can be waived or surrendered in a particular case, either by the House itself or by an individual, such as a member, who might otherwise be subject to it. (A rule of parliamentary privilege may apply to a person, even a member of Parliament, in a way that is adverse to his or her immediate legal interests.[43])

"Parliamentary privilege" is a term that covers an amorphous collection of legal rules applying in respect of the House. It is not possible, therefore, to give a single answer to the question of whether a privilege can be waived. In some areas of privilege (for example, relations between the Houses in a bicameral legislature), privilege clearly can be waived.[44] But even in the area of freedom of speech, where this question has arisen most acutely, there are a number of disparate elements to the privilege. It is not necessarily the case that the same answer would be given in respect of each element.

Parliamentary privilege is part of the general and public law of New Zealand. It is not necessary for it to be specially invoked by a litigant; courts are enjoined to take judicial notice of it themselves.[45] Parliamentary privilege cannot therefore simply be disapplied or (except by inadvertence) overlooked. Where a rule of parliamentary privilege (which is just another term for a rule of law) applies, it must contribute to the legal outcome in the matter under dispute – and perhaps contribute decisively to that outcome. However, those privileges that comprise powers vested in the House to do or control something, necessarily depend upon the House taking the initiative. If the House refrains from exercising such powers, even in a clear case (for example, by not punishing an obvious contempt) it is not waiving the privilege as such, though there is, in practice, very little difference between not invoking a privilege and waiving it in that instance.

With those privileges that consist of legal immunities, and thus involve legal proceedings, the question is likely to come into issue more pointedly.

It is a rule of law that proceedings in Parliament cannot be called into question or impeached in any court.[46] This rule does not depend upon who initiates legal action and it is therefore not impliedly waived because an individual member brings a legal action. A member initiating a legal action, for example, does not thereby open up his or her parliamentary conduct to judicial scrutiny.[47] The opinion has been expressed that this rule can be expressly waived, either by the House itself or by individual members in their own interest.[48] The House has, to the contrary, taken the firm view that this privilege is not subject to waiver; that, indeed, the courts lack the basic jurisdiction to review proceedings in Parliament and that neither the House nor individual members can confer such a jurisdiction on them.[49] This position has been impliedly endorsed by the Privy Council[50] and has been supported judicially in Australia.[51] Writers on Australian legislatures have also taken the view that this privilege cannot be waived in the absence of legislation[52]

---

[43] See, for example, *Rost v Edwards* [1990] 2 QB 460.
[44] *May*, p.921.
[45] *Legislature Act* 1908, s.242(2).
[46] *Bill of Rights* 1688, article 9.
[47] *Prebble v Television New Zealand Limited* [1994] 3 NZLR 1.
[48] *Television New Zealand Ltd v Prebble* [1993] 3 NZLR 513 at 525, 535 and 546.

[49] 1991-93, AJHR, I.15B; 1993, Vol.536, pp.16191-5; 1999-2002, AJHR, I.17B, p.6.
[50] *Prebble v Television New Zealand Ltd* [1994] 3 NZLR 1.
[51] *Rann v Olsen* (2000) 172 ALR 395 at [59] (per Doyle CJ).
[52] Harris, *House of Representatives Practice*, pp.718-9; Evans, *Odgers' Australian Senate Practice*, pp.69-70.

and this is the predominant view among other legislatures themselves.[53] Consequently, in the United Kingdom when it was desired to permit waiver in defamation proceedings for limited purposes it was necessary to pass legislation to allow this.[54]

The better view is that parliamentary privilege imposes a jurisdictional bar on a court questioning or impeaching proceedings in Parliament. This bar cannot be waived, either by individual members or by the House. In these circumstances legislation would be necessary to confer jurisdiction on a court to examine and make findings about matters otherwise inadmissible before it.[55]

ROLE OF THE COURTS

Parliamentary privilege is part of the general law of New Zealand and it is the constitutional duty of the courts to apply the law. In principle, therefore, parliamentary privilege may present issues on which the courts must rule in carrying out their duties. That is to say, an aspect of parliamentary privilege may become a justiciable issue before a court. However, it is of the nature of much parliamentary privilege that its object is to free the functioning of Parliament from judicial control. The resolution of justiciable issues of parliamentary privilege therefore requires that the courts do so in a way that is consistent with this ethos of non-intervention in parliamentary matters, for this ethos itself expresses the law. As was said in one case where the complaint was of a wrong done to the litigant in the course of the parliamentary process: "The remedy for a parliamentary wrong, if one has been committed, must be sought from Parliament and cannot be gained from the courts."[56]

Thus the courts do not sit in judgment on individual actions taken within the parliamentary process. But if the House seeks to project its power outside its proceedings (outside the "walls of Parliament") it must do so in a way that is lawful. In this respect exercises of parliamentary power are subject to judicial examination "not with tenderness, but with jealousy",[57] a proposition which ante-dates the establishment of parliamentary government in New Zealand. The *New Zealand Bill of Rights Act* 1990 provides a contemporary context for such jealous examination.

While the House, within its own sphere, is master of its proceedings and free of judicial control, the concomitant consequence of this freedom is that it is principally for the House to assert and enforce its own privileges. Parliamentary privilege does not give rise to a legal cause of action for which the courts will grant relief, any more than anyone can have a cause of action against the House in respect of the House's proceedings. On the one hand, while the courts will dismiss actions where the relief sought involves a direct attack on a privilege enjoyed by the House,[58] on the other hand, the court will refuse to give relief to an individual where the ground for the relief claimed is an alleged breach of privilege or contempt.[59]

This is not to say that the courts do not or should not rule on aspects of parliamentary privilege – they must do so insofar as these arise in a justiciable form in an issue before them. But the courts' role in regard to parliamentary privilege tends to be oblique. Where privilege arises it generally arises as a collateral issue in a dispute that is before the courts on other grounds.

---

[53] *Hamilton v Al Fayed* [2001] 1 AC 395 at 404.
[54] *Defamation Act* 1996 (UK), s.13 (by permitting the privilege of freedom of speech to be waived, the legislation to that extent abrogates the privilege).
[55] See, for example, *Special Commissions of Inquiry Amendment Act* 1997 (New South Wales) authorising the Governor, following a resolution of a House of the State legislature, to establish a commission to inquire into parliamentary proceedings.

[56] *British Railways Board v Pickin* [1974] AC 765 at 793 (per Lord Wilberforce).
[57] *Stockdale v Hansard* (1839) 9 A & E 1 at 214 (per Patteson J).
[58] *Dillon v Balfour* (1887) 20 LR Ir 600 (freedom of speech); *British Railways Board v Pickin* [1974] AC 765 (exclusive cognisance of its own proceedings).
[59] *Holden v Marks* (1995) 17 WAR 447.

A rule of parliamentary privilege (a rule of law) may be of legal significance as an element in a legal dispute and in this circumstance the court may need to make a finding in regard to it as a step in resolving that legal dispute.   Such questions can relate to the admissibility of evidence that may be given in the proceedings, the extent to which submissions may be addressed to the court or witnesses may be cross-examined, or whether a lawful excuse exists to prevent liability arising for conduct otherwise unlawful. Thus, while parliamentary privilege does not itself give rise to a cause of action, it may be a defence to an action, for example, by providing justification for using force that would otherwise be a trespass to the person.[60]   It may, in a legal context, be used "as a shield and not as a sword".[61]

Whenever parliamentary privilege impacts on a court's jurisdiction or powers, the court will need to ascertain the law relating to the parliamentary privilege in question, and apply it to the case before it in order to establish the extent to which the court or the parties to the litigation are constrained by that privilege or how the outcome of the litigation is otherwise affected by it.   In some circumstances the fact that a breach of privilege or a contempt of the House has or may be perpetrated will be significant (even determinative) of the legal outcome of the litigation, notwithstanding that this issue has arisen incidentally to the object of the litigation itself.

Parliamentary intervention in legal proceedings

The House itself is rarely, if ever, involved directly in legal proceedings as a party to an action.   It is also unusual for the House to be involved in legal proceedings as a party through one of its officers, such as the Speaker or the Clerk, though this is not unknown. A declaration has been sought against the Speaker on the treatment of evidence tendered to a select committee[62] and attempts have been made to persuade courts to inhibit the presentation of bills for the Royal assent with, for this purpose, the Clerk made a defendant in the actions.[63]   In these circumstances, as a party to the action, submissions will be directed to the court on behalf of the House on any aspect of parliamentary privilege that may arise in the proceedings.

But questions regarding parliamentary privilege may arise in legal proceedings to which neither the House nor its officers are parties.   While individual members of Parliament are often likely to be parties to such proceedings, this is either in a personal capacity or in the capacity of a Minister of the Crown, rather than as a representative of the House.   Indeed, the members' interests in the litigation may run contrary to the privileges of Parliament.   Also, a question regarding parliamentary privilege may arise in proceedings in which no member of Parliament is involved at all.[64]   Questions regarding parliamentary privilege, where they do arise, will therefore usually arise in litigation to which the House is not a party and in which it has no automatic opportunity to make its views known to the court.

---

[60]   *Egan v Willis* (1998) 195 CLR 424 (HCA); (1996) 40 NSWLR 650 (NSWCA).

[61]   *Combe v Combe* [1951] 2 KB 215 at 224 (per Birkett LJ quoting counsel referring to equitable estoppel).

[62]   *Queen v The Speaker of the House of Representatives*, unreported, High Court, Christchurch, 29 June 2004; 2002-05, AJHR, I.17F.

[63]   *Thomas v Bolger (No 2)* [2002] NZAR 948; *Westco Lagan Ltd v Attorney-General* [2001] 1 NZLR 40.

[64]   For example: *Hyams v Peterson* [1991] 3 NZLR 648; *Pepper v Hart* [1993] AC 593; *Wilson v First County Trust Ltd (No 2)* [2004] 1 AC 816.

In principle, there is nothing untoward with this situation. Parliamentary privilege as part of the general and public law of New Zealand is to be given effect to by the courts just as is any other part of the law.[65] But there are obvious dangers in a completely laissez-faire approach by the House to litigation involving parliamentary privilege. Litigants may overlook points of privilege, either through inadvertence or because they do not seem important to them.[66] The House can be expected to be more vigilant in such matters and to view their significance from a different or more pointed perspective. Even where a point of privilege is appreciated by the parties and is recognised as important in the litigation, there may still be value in the court hearing from the House so that a full argument can be presented. This can be of particular advantage to a court since the House's views will often be untainted by a concern for the outcome of the litigation as opposed to wishing to ensure that, whatever that outcome, parliamentary privilege is upheld. Parliamentary intervention in legal proceedings may thus be welcomed[67] or even sought by the courts.[68]

For these reasons, parliamentary intervention in litigation to which the House is not a party sometimes occurs.

In the United Kingdom, the Attorney-General has been invited to appear in proceedings to help the court when a question touching the privileges of the House of Commons arose in the course of argument.[69] Other interventions have occurred on the initiative of the House itself.[70] In Australia, the President of the Senate instructed counsel to seek leave to appear as a friend of the court in a criminal case in which evidence was tendered of confidential select committee hearings[71] and counsel has sought leave to appear on behalf of the Speaker of the House of Representatives in an action involving a person who had been a witness before a standing committee of the House.[72] In a case involving the privileges of the Nova Scotia House of Assembly, the Canadian Senate and House of Commons and nine other Canadian provincial legislatures intervened in the proceedings.[73]

In New Zealand, the Privileges Committee in 1988 suggested that, in an appropriate case, counsel instructed on the Speaker's own initiative or on the initiative of the House might appear as a friend of the court to argue any point of parliamentary privilege arising incidentally in legal proceedings.[74]

Counsel was first instructed in New Zealand litigation in 1989 (on the Speaker's initiative) in a defamation action involving a member of Parliament that raised questions of the extent to which the member's statements in the House could be used in the litigation.[75] The action was settled and never proceeded to a hearing. In 1992 and again in 1993 the House gave leave for counsel to be instructed to make submissions on issues of parliamentary privilege arising in a defamation action brought by a member against the state television channel.[76] The Attorney-General and Crown counsel (as *amici curiae*) appeared in the High Court, the Court of Appeal and, ultimately, in the Privy Council in the litigation.[77] Subsequently, the House has intervened in two other actions – one

---

[65] *Legislature Act* 1908, s.242(2).

[66] See, for an example, *News Media Ownership v Finlay* [1970] NZLR 1089 criticised in *Prebble v Television New Zealand Ltd* [1994] 3 NZLR 1.

[67] *Wilson v First County Trust Ltd (No 2)* [2004] 1 AC 816 at 54 (per Lord Nicholls).

[68] *Church of Scientology v Johnson-Smith* [1972] 1 QB 522.

[69] *Ibid.*

[70] *Pepper v Hart* [1993] AC 593; *Wilson v First County Trust Ltd (No 2)* [2004] 1 AC 816.

[71] *R v Murphy* (1986) 5 NSWLR 18.

[72] House of Representatives (Australia) Debates (19 and 20 February 1991), pp.898-9, 951-2.

[73] *New Brunswick Broadcasting Co v Nova Scotia (Speaker of the House of Assembly)* (1993) 100 DLR (4th) 212.

[74] 1987-90, AJHR, I.15B, pp.6-7.

[75] 1989, Vol.500, p.11754.

[76] 1992, Vol.525, pp.8814-5; 1993, Vol.536, pp.16191-5.

[77] *Prebble v Television New Zealand Ltd*, unreported, High Court, Auckland, 24 June 1992; *Television New Zealand Ltd v Prebble* [1993] 3 NZLR 513; *Prebble v Television New Zealand Ltd* [1994] 3 NZLR 1.

in which the Clerk of the House was a defendant concerning the submission of a bill for the Royal assent[78] and the other where a member was a defendant in a defamation action involving statements he had made in Parliament.[79] In another defamation action involving a member as a defendant, the Privileges Committee reported that it would have recommended that the House intervene in the absence of a settlement, since the likely defence to the action would have led to the court being invited to examine proceedings in Parliament.[80]

However, each decision to intervene is taken by the House on its merits. The Privileges Committee (which will invariably have such a proposal referred to it for consideration) has declined to recommend parliamentary intervention at too early a stage in litigation, preferring to keep the matter under review.[81] (The House did subsequently decide to intervene in that case.) The committee has also said that a decision to intervene should never be made lightly, and only when it is in the public interest to do so. The House does not intervene to protect its members – it intervenes to protect the House's privileges. Indeed, parliamentary intervention may be contrary to a member's litigation interest, for example, if parliamentary privilege prevents a member introducing evidence that would be to the member's advantage.[82] The committee has declined to recommend intervention when it considered that a full argument on the point of parliamentary privilege involved would be made by the parties themselves and that no extra value would be added by parliamentary intervention.[83]

Whenever the House does decide to intervene, it is the practice for the Attorney-General to be asked to represent the House's interests. In one case where the Attorney-General was a party to the proceedings, another counsel was instructed.[84] The Attorney-General may apply to the court for leave to intervene as a party to represent the public interest[85] or ask the court to appoint counsel to assist the court as *amicus curiae*.[86]

---

[78]   *Westco Lagan Ltd v Attorney-General* [2001] 1 NZLR 40.

[79]   *Buchanan v Jennings* [2001] 3 NZLR 71; [2002] 3 NZLR 145; [2005] 2 NZLR 577 (*sub nom Jennings v Buchanan*).

[80]   1999-2002, AJHR, I.17B, pp.5-6.

[81]   1996-99, AJHR, I.15D.

[82]   As it did, for example, in *Rost v Edwards* [1990] 2 QB 460.

[83]   1993-96, AJHR, I.15A.

[84]   *Westco Lagan Ltd v Attorney General* [2001] 1 NZLR 40.

[85]   *High Court Rules*, rule 81(e).

[86]   *Ibid.*, rule 438A.

CHAPTER 46

TYPES OF PRIVILEGES

There is no definitive list of the types of privileges enjoyed by the House. They are a collection of powers and immunities (often referred to as freedoms). This chapter discusses the specific powers and immunities enjoyed by the House, its members and other participants in the parliamentary process.

FREEDOM OF SPEECH

Everyone in New Zealand enjoys a general right of freedom of expression guaranteed by law.[1] Although the idea of freedom of speech is now regarded in this sense as a general or human right, it first appeared as a specific privilege of the members of the House of Commons rather than of the public generally.[2] "Freedom of speech" as enjoyed in a parliamentary context, while containing elements of such freedom of expression, is both older and more amorphous than this right. Indeed it is not possible to describe freedom of speech in parliamentary proceedings in specific terms as a single privilege of the House. Rather it is an idea that is expressed in specific legal powers and exemptions enjoyed by the House, its members and other participants in parliamentary proceedings.

The House's freedom of speech in debate is expressly mentioned in the Speaker's claim submitted to the Governor-General at the beginning of every Parliament.[3] It has been said that the first Speaker to lay claim to this freedom on behalf of the House was Sir Thomas More in 1523.[4] However, this has been disputed on the grounds that the principle precedes this date, More's contribution being merely to give expression to it,[5] and that More's claim was limited to asking the Crown to give a "favourable interpretation" to speeches made in the House rather than for freedom of speech in general. (A petition seeking recognition of freedom of speech in general was not addressed to the King until 1541.[6]) However, in the sixteenth century, seeking a favourable interpretation from the Crown of its proceedings was tantamount to the House claiming freedom of speech in general, given that infringements of freedom of speech were likely to emanate from the Crown anyway. Certainly since Sir Thomas More's time an express claim to freedom of speech has been made by each Speaker almost without exception. Though its precise effect was uncertain, consistently making the claim may have contributed to the growing acceptance that speech in Parliament ought to be free of legal repercussions. This principle is said to have been established by 1667.[7] Thus when the New Zealand Parliament was established a principle of freedom of speech was understood to apply in respect of its proceedings. A practice of expressly claiming the privilege was initiated in New Zealand in 1861.

The privileges connected with the House's freedom of speech have been seen as part of a set of rules reflecting the respective constitutional functions of Parliament and the courts, and specifically as aiming to avoid any conflict between their respective jurisdictions.[8] Thus the courts will uphold and refuse to question the House's control of its own internal proceedings and its exercise of its power to punish for contempt,

---

[1] *New Zealand Bill of Rights Act* 1990, s.14.
[2] Marshall, "Press Freedom and Free Speech Theory" [1992] PL at 41f.
[3] S.O.23.
[4] Marius, *Thomas More – A Biography*, pp.206-7.
[5] *Ibid.*
[6] Marshall, *op. cit.*

[7] Hallam, *Constitutional History of England*, Vol.I, pp.423-5 (citing *Eliot's* case).
[8] *Hamilton v Al Fayed* [1999] 1 WLR 1569 at 1587-8 (per Lord Woolf MR); *Wilson v First County Trust Ltd (No 2)* [2004] 1 AC 816 at [55] (per Lord Nicholls).

and will not visit legal liability on the contributions that members and others make to parliamentary debates and other proceedings (though these contributions may be legally relevant or admissible in legal proceedings). In these ways a principle of freedom of speech in Parliament is maintained.

While to assert freedom of speech in Parliament is not to say anything very specific about the precise legal position in any particular case, the principle is an important expression of legislative independence. Without it, the House's ability to proceed with a legislative programme and the scrutiny of the Government's activities would be subject to legal challenge and judicial control. Freedom of speech in the abstract entails that these activities are not justiciable.

EXEMPTION FROM LIABILITY FOR PARLIAMENTARY ACTIONS

General

There can be no legal liability for words spoken or actions taken in the course of parliamentary proceedings as part of those proceedings, except insofar as this protection may have been statutorily abrogated.[9] For most practical purposes, this specific exemption from legal liability now derives from a provision in the *Bill of Rights* 1688, though it predates its restatement there. The *Bill of Rights* is only a part of the wider compact between the legislative and judicial branches of Government, whereby their respective spheres of action are respected.[10]

The exemption from legal liability is wider in extent than just removing the possibility of legal liability arising out of a contribution to public debate made in Parliament; it also entails exemption from having to answer or account in legal proceedings for one's parliamentary contributions, even where personal liability is not in question. It is this latter aspect of the privilege that may be regarded as having been established (though not without some modern vacillations[11]) by the *Bill of Rights* and the political settlement out of which that legislation arose.

The ninth article of section 1 of the *Bill of Rights* declares: "That the freedom of speech, and debates or proceedings in Parliament, ought not to be impeached or questioned in any court or place out of Parliament." From this famous statement of parliamentary privilege flow a number of immunities which apply to the House, its members, and other participants in parliamentary proceedings. The basic concept underlying article 9 has been described by the Privy Council as "the need to ensure so far as possible that a member of the legislature and witnesses before Committees of the House can speak freely without fear that what they say will later be held against them in the courts". The important public interest, it went on to say, is to ensure that members or witnesses at the time of speaking are not inhibited from stating fully and freely what they have to say.[12] However, article 9 is also to be seen as only one of a collection of legal principles that give effect to the constitutional relationship between the legislature and the judiciary, though it is not itself a comprehensive statement of that relationship.

The protection expressed by article 9 is not conferred for the personal benefit of any individual, even a member of Parliament; it is conferred for the benefit of the parliamentary system. While freedom of speech may protect members and others from liability that would otherwise exist, it operates even-handedly and may equally prejudice a member in an individual capacity. This was the case, for instance, with a member who

---

[9]   See, for statutory abrogation, *Crimes Act* 1961, ss.108 and 109 (in regard to the crime of perjury).

[10]   1988, Vol.489, p.4322; *Prebble v Television New Zealand* [1994] 3 NZLR 1 at 7; *R v Parliamentary Commissioner for Standards, ex parte Al Fayed*

[1998] 1 WLR 669; 1999, Vol.576, p.16210.

[11]   See *R v Murphy* (1986) 5 NSWLR 18.

[12]   *Prebble v Television New Zealand* [1994] 3 NZLR 1 at 8.

was unable to give evidence of parliamentary proceedings to support his legal action when to have done so would have been in breach of article 9.[13]

House's disciplinary control and electors' democratic control

The freedom of speech expressed by article 9 is a freedom from legal liability and a freedom from having to account to bodies outside the House. Freedom of speech is not an exemption from liability to account to the House itself. Nor is it a freedom from having to account for one's parliamentary actions, ultimately, to the electors through the regular process of election. The fact that such a legal immunity exists does not prevent the legislature proceeding against its own members (or anyone else) for a breach of privilege or contempt.[14] Furthermore, the fundamental democratic right of free election to Parliament cannot be inhibited by parliamentary privilege. A political party does not breach privilege by withdrawing electoral support from a sitting member of Parliament on account of that member's actions, whether they occurred within Parliament or in the country at large.[15]

The privilege of freedom of speech is thus not a licence to be free of all restraint in how one conducts oneself. Rather, it is an assertion that the jurisdiction to exercise that restraint in a legal context belongs exclusively to the House during the period of the member's service as a member of Parliament, and belongs in a political context to the electors at the end of that service.

The House exercises restraint over its members prospectively by general rules, and retrospectively in dealing with particular incidents. Prospectively, the House's rules of debate impose constraints on what members may say and how they must conduct themselves – for example, that they must be relevant, that they may not refer to matters awaiting adjudication in a court, that they may not use "unparliamentary" language. These are general, internally imposed restraints on members' freedom of speech. They could not be imposed or enforced by the courts, but they can and are imposed by the House on its own members and are entirely unaffected by article 9, which is not directed to limiting the House's powers at all. Similar restraints in general rules apply to select committee proceedings and to other persons – officers, witnesses, petitioners – participating in parliamentary proceedings.

Any infringement of these general rules and any other particular conduct which the House on reflection considers to be an obstruction or impediment to the performance of its functions, is liable to be punished by the House as a contempt.[16] This is regardless of the fact that such conduct occurs in the course of parliamentary proceedings and is therefore exempt from legal liability. The exemption from accounting to a court for one's actions is not an exemption from accounting to the House; it is merely a manifestation of the fact that the exclusive jurisdiction for holding such actions to account lies with the House.

Criminal acts committed within Parliament

The principle of exemption from legal liability for parliamentary conduct does not mean that criminal acts are exempt from prosecution merely because they are committed in a parliamentary environment. Speech, uttered in debate or in evidence to a select committee, that would otherwise be subject to criminal liability will be exempt from legal sanction, but criminal actions taken in the face of the House or a committee are not part of their proceedings and are liable to be dealt with by the criminal law.[17] Thus persons protesting

---

[13] *Rost v Edwards* [1990] 2 QB 460.
[14] *Narasimha Rao v State* AIR 1998 Supreme Court 2120.
[15] *Peters v Collinge* [1993] 2 NZLR 554.
[16] S.O.399.
[17] *May*, p.117.

in the galleries of the Chamber or at select committee meetings are not participating in parliamentary proceedings and are not entitled to any protection from the criminal law on that account. Prosecutions for trespass and disorderly conduct have proceeded in such circumstances. Such incidents may also be dealt with by the House as contempts.

Freedom of debate

Article 9 declares that the "freedom of speech and debates or proceedings in Parliament" ought not to be questioned or impeached outside Parliament.

"Freedom of speech" has been described as permitting members to say what they wish to say, and "freedom of debate" to enable them to discuss any subject that they wish to discuss.[18] Freedom to debate any subject was formerly given expression in New Zealand by the *pro forma* first reading of a dummy bill (called the *Expiring Laws Continuance Bill*) – a bill not mentioned in the Speech from the Throne. This practice symbolised the right of the House to discuss any business it wished to discuss and not just business that the Crown invited it to transact. The practice of giving a *pro forma* first reading to a bill in this way was discontinued in 1985. It is still followed in the United Kingdom.[19] The priority given by the House's rules to the debate on the Address in Reply is another assertion of the House's right to decide what it wishes to debate rather than having to turn its attention immediately to the Government's legislative programme. Indeed this practice has even led to a challenge to the validity of legislation passed before a House has finished the Address in Reply debate, though such a challenge would itself appear to be a contradiction of the House's privilege to debate what it will, when it will.[20] In New Zealand, while priority is still given to the debate on the Address in Reply,[21] the debate is liable to be adjourned to permit other legislation to proceed before it is finished.

Freedom of debate in the sense of the House's ability to discuss whatever it wishes and to decide for itself when it wishes to discuss particular matters, is also part of the House's exclusive control over its own proceedings.

Proceedings in Parliament

Article 9 extends to protect "proceedings in Parliament" from external review.

Freedom of "debate" in article 9 may be seen as merely an identification of the most common and obvious occasion on which the privilege of freedom of speech is exercised. In this sense the addition of the phrase "proceedings in Parliament" to article 9 is understandable as extending the scope of the protection of freedom of speech from parliamentary debates to all other transactions of parliamentary business. By 1688 committee proceedings were well established as modes of parliamentary proceeding. Exchanges between members at such meetings might have been regarded as falling within the term "debate" (though not obviously so), but the examination of witnesses most certainly would not. The House would also have been aware that it had recently been established that no legal liability applied to the circulation of petitions to members of Parliament in the ordinary course of transacting parliamentary business.[22] Parliamentary business was thus coming to comprise a number of disparate activities and communications, many of which were not transacted on the floor of the House in the course of debate.

Article 9 makes it clear that these other modes of transacting parliamentary business are entitled to a similar protection from legal liability or examination as that which applies

---

[18] *Pepper v Hart* [1993] AC 593 at 638 (per Lord Browne-Wilkinson).

[19] *May*, p.289.

[20] *Namoi Shire Council v Attorney-General (New South*

Wales) [1980] 2 NSWLR 639 (the objection to the legislation on this ground was dismissed).

[21] S.O.344.

[22] *Lake v King* (1667) 1 Saund 131.

to parliamentary debates. Today, a much higher proportion of parliamentary business is "non-debate" and is transacted off the floor of the House than was the case in the House of Commons of the seventeenth century or even in the recent history of the House of Representatives itself. The extension of the privilege of freedom of speech and debate to proceedings in Parliament is therefore of critical importance to the effectiveness of that privilege given the way in which the House carries on its proceedings.

Meaning of proceedings in Parliament
The meaning of the term "proceedings in Parliament" has never been the subject of definition by legislation in the United Kingdom or in New Zealand, nor has its meaning been declared by the House. In Australia a definition of the term has been enacted,[23] and this statement is the most detailed official exposition of what proceedings in Parliament comprise, although even it is not intended to be comprehensive. The Australian legislation in respect of article 9 of the *Bill of Rights* has been accepted by New Zealand and English courts as representing a statement of the law in those countries too.[24] It thus may be taken to indicate the types of transactions falling within the term "proceedings in Parliament".

The Australian description of proceedings in Parliament is—

> ... ***proceedings in Parliament*** means all words spoken and acts done in the course of, or for purposes of or incidental to, the transacting of the business of a House or of a committee, and, without limiting the generality of the foregoing, includes—
>
> (a) the giving of evidence before a House or a committee, and evidence so given;
> (b) the presentation or submission of a document to a House or a committee;
> (c) the preparation of a document for purposes of or incidental to the transacting of any such business; and
> (d) the formulation, making or publication of a document, including a report, by or pursuant to an order of a House or a committee and the document so formulated, made or published.

Actions of the House, committees, members, officers, witnesses and petitioners which are either the transaction of parliamentary business themselves or which are directly and formally connected with the transaction of such business are proceedings in Parliament and are thus subject to the privilege of freedom of speech. This encompasses all actions taken by the House itself whether of a legislative or non-legislative nature. That does not mean that such actions automatically authorise otherwise unlawful activities to be perpetrated outside the House.[25] (Though an activity undertaken with the House's authority may be lawful when that same activity undertaken without the House's authority would be unlawful.[26]) Nor does it mean that the courts would necessarily enforce activities undertaken with the House's authority. But the House itself cannot be impeached or questioned for having taken them.[27]

Committee proceedings
Committee proceedings are as equally parliamentary as are proceedings on the floor of the House.[28] Such proceedings cover giving evidence orally and in writing to a committee and the advices and draft reports generated during a committee's work, provided that these are published in the course of the committee's proceedings. Publishing such documents outside the confines of the committee is not a proceeding in Parliament. Tendering a

---

23 *Parliamentary Privileges Act* 1987 (Australia), s.16(2).
24 *Prebble v Television New Zealand Limited* [1994] 3 NZLR 1; *Hamilton v Al Fayed* [2001] 1 AC 395.
25 See, for example, *Stockdale v Hansard* (1839) 9 A & E 1.
26 See, for example, *Legislature Amendment Act* 1992, ss.4 and 5.
27 *Hamilton v Al Fayed* [1999] 1 WLR 1569.
28 *Attorney-General (Canada) v MacPhee*, Prince Edward Island, Supreme Court, 14 January 2003.

committee's report to the House is a parliamentary proceeding.[29] But press conferences by the chairperson and members following the presentation of a report are not formal proceedings of the committee and are not protected.[30]

Although it is not a committee established by the House and its proceedings would therefore not normally be considered proceedings in Parliament, the proceedings of the statutory Intelligence and Security Committee are deemed to fall within the compass of article 9.[31]

Parliamentary documentation

Members draft and lodge questions, present petitions, give notices of motion and prepare bills and amendments. Many of these actions were formerly carried out on the floor of the House itself, but rule changes have enabled them to be executed administratively, and they now tend to be performed outside the Chamber. They nevertheless retain their essential quality as proceedings in Parliament. The statutory process of the Attorney-General examining and reporting on bills for conflict with the rights and freedoms confirmed by the *New Zealand Bill of Rights Act* 1990 has been held to be a proceeding in Parliament and thus exempt from judicial review as an internal legislative process of the House.[32]

Communications involving members of Parliament

By no means all actions of a member of Parliament constitute proceedings in Parliament. Proceedings in Parliament cover a much narrower range of activities than those performed by members generally, even actions performed in the capacity of a member.[33] While actions taken in or towards the House are proceedings in Parliament, actions taken in relation to constituents or other persons, or which constituents or other persons take in relation to the member, are usually not proceedings in Parliament. Thus, generally, communications between a member and the public, even a member's constituents, are not proceedings in Parliament.[34] A person sending information to an individual member is not engaged in a parliamentary proceeding. Such a communication is not a proceeding in Parliament,[35] unless the communication is directly connected with some specific business to be transacted in the House, such as the delivery of a petition to the member for presentation to the House, or was solicited by the member for the express purpose of using it in a parliamentary proceeding.[36]

Other than in these circumstances, no parliamentary privilege applies to a communication to a member of Parliament.

A communication's status after it has been received by the member depends upon the use made of it by the member. If the member takes some action in respect of it for the purpose of transacting parliamentary business, it may, at that point, become part of a proceeding (whether it is referable to a particular debate or not).[37] But, even so, that will not have any retrospective effect so as to afford protection in respect of the original communication to the member.

Where a member communicates with another member, such as a Minister, regarding parliamentary business (for example, forwarding an amendment to a bill before the House or a question that the member is contemplating lodging) this will be regarded as a proceeding

29   *New South Wales Branch of the Australian Medical Association v Minister for Health and Community Services* (1992) 26 NSWLR 114.
30   *May*, p.776; *Re Ouellet (No 1)* (1976) 67 DLR (3d) 73; 1999-2002, AJHR, I.17B.
31   *Intelligence and Security Committee Act* 1996, s.16.
32   *Mangawaro Enterprises Ltd v Attorney-General* [1994] 2 NZLR 451.
33   *Attorney-General of Ceylon v De Livera* [1963] AC

103; *Re Ouellet (No 1)* (1976) 67 DLR (3d) 73; *Crane v Gething* (2000) 169 ALR 727; *Rowley v Armstrong* [2000] QSC 88.
34   *Buchanan v Jennings* [2002] 3 NZLR 145 at [64].
35   *Rivlin v Bilainkin* [1953] 1 QB 485; *R v Ponting* [1985] Crim LR 321.
36   *Erglis v Buckley* [2005] QSC 25.
37   *Ibid.*

in Parliament.[38] But a member's action in releasing information outside the House attracts no parliamentary privilege,[39] even where the material released is a copy of a speech delivered in the House by the member[40] or a question submitted by the member.[41] Nor is a person (such as a journalist) who receives information from a member protected by any parliamentary privilege if that person publishes the information.[42] A letter to the Speaker raising a matter of privilege is a proceeding in Parliament, but circulating or disclosing the letter otherwise than in the course of the House's procedures for dealing with such a matter, is not.[43]

Statute may also forbid any interference with a person's right to communicate with a member of Parliament and with the member's right to communicate with that person.[44]

Qualified legal privilege

While not protected by parliamentary privilege, the law may accord a qualified legal privilege to certain communications. Qualified legal privilege affords a defence to actions for defamation. As has been said, this privilege has nothing but its name in common with parliamentary privilege.[45] Where qualified privilege applies, it protects proceedings from liability in defamation provided that the person who published the defamatory material was not motivated predominantly by ill-will towards the person defamed or otherwise took improper advantage of the occasion of the communication to defame that person.[46]

Qualified privilege attaches to a fair and accurate report of parliamentary proceedings. "Fair and accurate" does not mean verbatim – a good summary is enough. A report can concentrate mainly on one speech, but there must be some summary or acknowledgment of contrary views if these were expressed in the debate.[47] (However, no contrary views may have been expressed.) Nor do immaterial inaccuracies cause the protection to be lost.[48] But qualified privilege for a fair and accurate report does not apply where the publication is made in defiance of the House's rules on keeping proceedings confidential. Qualified privilege is not a licence to flout lawful orders.[49]

A qualified legal, not parliamentary, privilege may also apply to communications between members and constituents[50] and to a disclosure to the proper authority of a letter which contains otherwise defamatory material sent from a constituent to a member.[51]

Meetings of caucus

Meetings of party caucuses are not proceedings in Parliament. They are meetings which are attended by members of Parliament because they are members, and parliamentary business may be under discussion at such meetings, but they are not transactions of parliamentary business as such.[52] The absolute legal protection given by the *Bill of Rights* does not apply in respect of such meetings.

---

[38] HC 101 (1938-39); *Fowler & Rodrigues v Attorney-General* [1981] 2 NZLR 728.

[39] 1994, Vol.539, p.470; 1997, Vol.558, p.718; 1997, Vol.563, p.4019.

[40] *R v Lord Abingdon* (1794) 1 Esp 226; *R v Creevey* (1813) 1 M&S 273; *Suresh Chandra Banerji v Punit Goala* AIR 1951 Calcutta 176.

[41] *In re Satish Chandra Ghosh* AIR 1961 Supreme Court 613.

[42] *Re Clark and Attorney-General of Canada* (1977) 81 DLR (3d) 33.

[43] 1988, Vol.489, p.4436; 2003, Vol.609, p.6543.

[44] See: *Intellectual Disability (Compulsory Care and Rehabilitation) Act* 2003, s.58; *Corrections Act* 2004, ss.69(1)(e) and 114.

[45] Keir and Lawson, *Cases in Constitutional Law*, p.269; *Buchanan v Jennings* [2002] 3 NZLR 145 at [40]

(per Keith J).

[46] *Defamation Act* 1992, ss.16(1) and 19.

[47] See "Exam question leads to apology", *The Evening Post*, 30 January 1988 (the member who made the comments was not identified and contrary views were not given).

[48] See, generally, Todd, *The Law of Torts in New Zealand*, para.16.11.2(b)(i).

[49] *Defamation Act* 1992, s.17.

[50] *R v Rule* [1937] 2 KB 375; *Rowley v Armstrong* [2000] QSC 88.

[51] *Beach v Freeson* [1972] 1 QB 14.

[52] HC 138 (1946-47); *R v Turnbull* [1958] Tas SR 80; McGee, "Parliament and Caucus" [1997] NZLJ 137; *Awatere Huata v Prebble* [2004] 3 NZLR 359 (CA) at [63], [64] (per McGrath J).

Other proceedings

Actions taken by officers of the House in carrying out the orders of the House or its committees are also proceedings in Parliament.[53]

Persons delivering petitions to members, or written evidence and other material to a select committee, are engaged in proceedings in Parliament.[54] But circulating a proposed petition to the public for signature is not a proceeding in Parliament and no privilege attaches to it.[55] A report of what occurred in Parliament (other than the official report made under the House's authority) is not itself a proceeding in Parliament and is not protected by parliamentary privilege from any legal liability that may thereby arise, though other protections, such as a qualified legal privilege against defamation liability may be available.[56]

The fact that something occurred in Parliament House, even in the Chamber, does not thereby confer immunity on that action. It must still be a "proceeding in Parliament" in terms of article 9. Parliament House is not a sanctuary. The Speaker has reminded members that serious allegations made in the course of a private conversation in the Chamber may not be protected outside the House. The important test in determining whether they are proceedings in Parliament is the occasion on which they were used, not the place in which they were spoken.[57] The fact that a document is delivered within the parliamentary precincts does not immunise it from judicial scrutiny if it is not connected with any proceeding in Parliament.[58] Nor is a press conference protected just because it is held in the parliamentary precincts.[59] Similarly, any necessary legal approvals for the exhibition of films and videos to be shown within Parliament House must be obtained, unless the showing is confined to a meeting of a select committee.[60]

Application of article 9

Article 9 of the *Bill of Rights* is not confined to members in its effects. In fact, it does not refer to members or any other person at all; it refers to speeches, debates and parliamentary proceedings and prevents these occasions from being called into question. The main group of persons affected by this privilege is, incidentally, members, but other persons who take part in the House's proceedings are also within the provision.

The most obvious of these other persons are officers of the House who, in their official capacity, are constantly engaged in proceedings in Parliament. Also included are witnesses to select committees and petitioners to the House. The publication of defamatory words in a petition to members of Parliament, provided such publication is made in the ordinary course of proceedings, is not actionable.[61] Publication of defamatory material in a petition to members otherwise than in the ordinary course of proceedings is not protected.[62] It is open to the House, however, to refuse to accept a petition if it is abusive (petitions are required to be respectful and moderate in their language[63]), or to treat the publication of scandalous material in a petition as a contempt and to punish it as such.

It is well established that no action, civil or criminal, will lie against a witness in respect of evidence given to the House or one of its committees. The position of witnesses is similar to that of members in respect of words spoken in parliamentary proceedings.[64]

---

[53]   *Hamilton v Al Fayed* [1999] 1 WLR 1569 (Parliamentary Commissioner for Standards); *R(L) v Secretary of State for the Home Department* [2003] 1 All ER 1062 (Clerk of the Parliaments).

[54]   HC 624 (1977-78), App IV (disclosure of information to the House or a committee would not breach the *Official Secrets Act*).

[55]   *Eleventh Report of the Senate Standing Committee of Privileges* (Australia), June 1988; *Report of the Select Committee of Privileges* (Legislative Council, Western Australia), December 1992.

[56]   1988, Vol.489, pp.4315-6; 2003, Vol.613, p.10146.

[57]   1988, Vol.489, pp.4436-7.

[58]   *Rivlin v Bilainkin* [1953] 1 QB 485.

[59]   *Re Ouellet (No 1)* (1976) 67 DLR (3d) 73.

[60]   1989, Vol.498, p.10595.

[61]   *Lake v King* (1667) 1 Saund 131.

[62]   *Rivlin v Bilainkin* [1953] 1 QB 485.

[63]   S.O.358(1).

[64]   *Goffin v Donnelly* (1881) 6 QBD 307; *R v Wainscott* [1899] 1 WAR 77; *Prebble v Television New Zealand Limited* [1994] 3 NZLR 1.

It does not matter whether the witness appears voluntarily or is summoned to appear before the House or a committee, parliamentary privilege applies in either case.

Questioning or impeaching parliamentary proceedings

The *Bill of Rights* 1688 was passed to reflect in law a political settlement concerning the respective jurisdictions of the executive and the legislature.[65] Freedom of speech in Parliament was not created by the *Bill of Rights*. Rather, the dispute over its sphere of operation was settled by its crystallisation in a statutory provision. Although a settlement of executive and legislative powers, the legislation involved the judiciary too, by (amongst other things) prohibiting the executive from using the courts to undermine the legislature's freedom of speech.

Article 9 thus ordains that freedom of speech is not to be questioned or impeached outside Parliament.

It may be that at the time the legislation was passed there was considered to be little, if any, distinction between the injunction in article 9 that freedom of speech ought not to be "questioned" and that it ought not to be "impeached". The word "impeach" did not come to have a specific association with a charge at law until a century or so later. Legislative drafting was also prolix at that time. It tended to employ what we would today regard as synonymous terms but which to the drafters of the day, dealing with courts inclined to a more literal and formal interpretation of written provisions, were often words of genuine, though small, gradations of difference of meaning that are now lost to us.

For the seventeenth-century parliamentarians, article 9 was a declaration not only that they could not be held criminally or civilly liable for their actions in Parliament – something which would have been asserted to be the law in any case (though there had been notorious breaches of this principle) – but also that their parliamentary actions could not be used to support a cause of action against them, even one arising from events outside Parliament. If the latter were to be permitted, members would be answerable to the courts for their actions in Parliament. The application of article 9 thus goes much further than operating as a complete defence to a prosecution or to an action brought against someone in respect of their parliamentary actions. More often it will affect the evidence that can be tendered to the court, and limit the submissions that may be made to it, in respect of proceedings that have their origin outside Parliament.

Although it may not be an historically correct analysis of the phrase "questioned or impeached", this two-pronged modern meaning of article 9 is conveniently expressed by today's understanding of the two words. Freedom of speech is understood to be "impeached" where it is sought to make a member or another person liable in criminal or civil proceedings for what they have said or done in Parliament. Freedom of speech is understood to be "questioned" when it is sought to use what a member or another person has said or done in Parliament in criminal or civil proceedings in a way that involves a critical examination of that statement.[66] A New South Wales case which challenged this distinction and would have confined article 9 to the former class of case has now been discredited.[67] It is convenient, if unhistorical, to discuss article 9 in these terms.

---

[65] *Declaration of Right* 1688.

[66] Attorney-General's submission in *Pepper v Hart* [1993] AC 593 at 638 (per Lord Browne-Wilkinson).

[67] *R v Murphy* (1986) 5 NSWLR 18; declared not to represent the law in New Zealand (or the United Kingdom) in *Prebble v Television New Zealand Limited* [1994] 3 NZLR 1.

Impeaching freedom of speech – direct attack

Impeaching freedom of speech or proceedings in Parliament in the sense of holding someone liable for their parliamentary actions or speech means that article 9 confirms rather than adds to the recognised freedom of speech of members and others participating in parliamentary proceedings. Conduct in parliamentary proceedings cannot be the foundation of legal liability, either criminal or civil, except to the extent that statute has expressly or by necessary implication taken this immunity away. Thus the speech of a member of Parliament in a parliamentary debate cannot found an action for defamation[68] and documents held by a member that are part of a proceeding in Parliament cannot be subject to the compulsory process of a court.[69] Since 1688 this immunity from liability in respect of one's actions or speeches in Parliament has rarely been challenged and has come to be recognised as trite law.

Questioning proceedings – indirect attack

But the prohibition on "questioning" proceedings in Parliament in the sense of undertaking a critical examination of parliamentary proceedings so as to support legal proceedings arising from events outside Parliament, while not lacking the constitutional significance of its companion term "impeaching", is more elusive in its application.

The prohibition on a court questioning parliamentary proceedings is, in a constitutional sense, an assertion that goes to the separation of powers between the legislature and the judiciary. It has been said that its object is to avoid conflict between Parliament and the courts and that it consequently prevents condemnation by a court of what is said in Parliament because a court has no legitimate occasion to pass judgment on such proceedings.[70] It is wrong too for a court to make judgments on the quality or sufficiency of the reasons given in Parliament for the enactment of a particular measure or the transaction of particular business; that is a matter for Parliament.[71] In deference to this principle a court considered it would be improper for it to comment on a member's speeches in Parliament even where the body under review before it (possibly itself in breach of article 9) had done so.[72] This principle of non-intervention or non-intrusion by the courts in parliamentary proceedings is mandatory. Where a questioning of proceedings in Parliament would occur, it is not for a court to judge whether freedom of speech would actually be infringed in that particular case. The court's duty is to give effect to the principle as embodied in law.[73] The fact that there may be no attack on the propriety of a parliamentary statement also makes no difference. If a court is invited to examine it and draw inferences from it, it is inadmissible.[74]

The principle underlying article 9, from the point of view of those participating in parliamentary proceedings, has been seen as being to promote the freedom of their contributions to those proceedings, by ensuring that at the time they speak they are not inhibited from stating fully and freely what they have to say. Article 9 is thus designed to remove uncertainties about whether a member's (or witness's) statement may be

---

[68] *Dillon v Balfour* (1887) 20 LR Ir 600.
[69] *Crane v Gething* (2000) 169 ALR 727.
[70] *Hamilton v Al Fayed* [1999] 1 WLR 1569 at 1586 (per Lord Woolf MR).
[71] *Wilson v First County Trust Ltd (No 2)* [2004] 1 AC

816 at [117] (per Lord Hope) and [143] (per Lord Hobhouse).
[72] *Peters v Davison* [1999] 3 NZLR 744 at 765-7.
[73] *Rann v Olsen* (2000) 172 ALR 395 at [114], [124] and [125].
[74] *Rost v Edwards* [1990] 2 QB 460.

subsequently challenged in legal proceedings, and to give members and others confidence in making their parliamentary contributions that this will not be so.[75] Cases subsequent to the enunciation of this principle have emphasised this rationale as the basis for the extended operation of article 9.

Using parliamentary proceedings to support legal proceedings

There is therefore an inhibition on using speeches or proceedings in Parliament for the purpose of supporting a cause of action, even though that cause of action itself arose outside the House.[76] Article 9 means that the parties to litigation cannot bring into question anything said or done in the House by suggesting that the actions or words were inspired by improper motives or were untrue or misleading. This involves a prohibition on direct evidence, cross-examination, inferences or submissions having this effect.[77] Thus a court refused to allow a former Minister who was facing prosecution on a criminal charge to be cross-examined on remarks made by him in Parliament that appeared to contradict the evidence he had given to the court.[78] A judge has refused to admit extracts from *Hansard* where the purpose of putting them in evidence was to examine the motives of what had been said and done in the House.[79] It has been asserted that if a court were to be presented with two parliamentary statements and invited to infer that they were incompatible, that would be a breach of article 9.[80]

If the operation of parliamentary privilege makes it unjust for an action to proceed (for example, by preventing the introduction of evidence which is crucial to its defence), the court may order a stay of proceedings.[81]

Repetition

There is no "questioning" of proceedings in Parliament in a legal action that is based on a member having distributed a copy of his or her parliamentary speech to a newspaper or other publication.[82] Members therefore distribute copies of their speeches or other parliamentary contributions (such as questions they have asked)[83] at their own risk.

It has also been held that if a member subsequently refers outside the House to a speech he or she had made in Parliament in a way that can be interpreted as "adopting" or "effectively repeating" it, the speech can be examined in a court and support legal proceedings. In these circumstances, it is said, it is the member's own action that releases it for examination. The member was free from review at the time he or she made the original speech.[84] A member who merely acknowledges having made a speech, would not adopt or effectively repeat it in these circumstances and it could not thereby support legal proceedings. Cases of repetition or effective repetition thus may involve the use of evidence of parliamentary proceedings. Such use is not purely "historical" in the sense discussed below, since there may be serious dispute as to the meaning or effect of the words used in Parliament. In this case the justification for admitting the parliamentary material rests on the republication, or deemed republication, of parliamentary speech outside Parliament.

[75] *Prebble v Television New Zealand Limited* [1994] 3 NZLR 1 at 10.

[76] *Church of Scientology v Johnson-Smith* [1972] 1 QB 522 (attempt to show member's parliamentary speech evidence of malice in a comment made by the member on television); Western Australian Legislative Assembly, 29 October 2003, pp.12804-6 (personal explanation by member used to support disciplinary proceedings against member in his capacity as a lawyer).

[77] *Prebble v Television New Zealand Limited* [1994] 3 NZLR 1 at 10.

[78] *R v Jackson* (1987) 8 NSWLR 116.

[79] *Kable v State of New South Wales* [2000] NSWSC 1173.

[80] 1999-2002, AJHR, I.17B, p.4.

[81] *Prebble v Television New Zealand Limited* [1994] 3 NZLR; *Allason v Haines* [1995] NLJR 1576; *Hamilton v Greer*, unreported, High Court of Justice, Queen's Bench Division, 21 July 1995.

[82] *R v Lord Abingdon* (1794) 1 Esp 226; *R v Creevey* (1813) 1 M & S 273; *Suresh Chandra Banerji v Punit Goala* AIR 1951 Calcutta 176.

[83] *In re Satish Chandra Ghosh* AIR 1961 Supreme Court 613.

[84] *Peters v Cushing* [1999] NZAR 241; *Jennings v Buchanan* [2005] 2 NZLR 577; 2002-05, AJHR, I.17G.

But a member is not liable for the use that another person makes of the member's speech in Parliament (for example, reporting or repeating it), even though when the speech was made the member may have known that it was defamatory and was likely to be reported. To hold a member liable in these circumstances for even a forseeable repetition would defeat the member's freedom of speech.[85] However, the person defamed can have a response entered in the parliamentary record. (See Chapter 39.)

Collateral examination of proceedings

The fact that the House has expressed its view on a matter does not at all preclude a court making its own finding on that matter if it subsequently arises before it in judicial proceedings. It is no abuse of the process of the court or breach of parliamentary privilege to litigate a matter merely because that matter has also been considered by the House or one of its committees. Despite the fact that it has received parliamentary attention, the court must still make its own finding on the issue if it is relevant to the proceedings before it.[86]

It is thus conceivable that entirely different conclusions may be reached by a parliamentary inquiry into, and a judicial consideration of, the same matter.[87] The fact that such an inconsistent judicial conclusion implies a view about the parliamentary finding is irrelevant.[88] Indeed, an earlier parliamentary inquiry is not even persuasive, much less binding, on a court.[89] At the most, an earlier parliamentary inquiry would be relevant as part of the factual matrix out of which the legal proceedings before the court have emerged. But the court must be careful to make no finding on the parliamentary treatment of the matter.

Not all references to debates or proceedings in Parliament are contrary to the *Bill of Rights*. Evidence of proceedings in Parliament may be admitted before a court, provided that the evidence is used in a way that is consistent with article 9 and does not involve an examination of the propriety of the proceedings or of the motives or intentions of those taking part in the proceedings. Evidence of the occurrence of events or the saying of certain words in parliamentary proceedings, without any accompanying impeaching or questioning of proceedings, so-called "historical" use, is permissible.[90] Examples of historical uses which are not contrary to the *Bill of Rights* are: the use of parliamentary proceedings to prove material facts, such as that a statement was made in Parliament or made at a particular time or that it refers to a particular person;[91] the use to prove that a member was present in the House on a particular day;[92] and the proof that a report of a speech is fair and accurate and is thereby subject to qualified privilege in the law of defamation.

Statutory interpretation and judicial review

It is well established both in New Zealand law and in United Kingdom law that parliamentary statements and other materials may be used in aid of statutory interpretation.[93] In Australia use of parliamentary statements and material are themselves regulated by

---

85   *Suresh Chandra Banerji v Punit Goala* AIR 1951 Calcutta 176.

86   *Dingle v Associated Newspapers Ltd* [1960] 2 QB 405 at 410-1.

87   Compare, for example, 1991-93, AJHR, I.26A (*Report of the Transport Committee on the Petition of Federated Farmers of New Zealand Incorporated*) with *Federated Farmers of New Zealand (Inc) v New Zealand Post Limited*, unreported, High Court, Wellington, 1 December 1992.

88   *Rann v Olsen* (2000) 172 ALR 395 at [25], [80], [85] and [123].

89   *Hamilton v Al Fayed* [1999] 1 WLR 1569 (affirmed [2001] 1 AC 395).

90   *Prebble v Television New Zealand Limited* [1994] 3 NZLR 1.

91   *Ibid.*

92   *Forbes v Samuel* [1913] 3 KB 706; *Tranton v Astor* (1917) 33 TLR 383.

93   New Zealand cases are too numerous to require citation; the leading case in the United Kingdom is *Pepper v Hart* [1993] AC 593.

statute.[94] Such use is regarded in all jurisdictions as compatible with article 9, and occurs frequently, though if a court were to be drawn into comparing conflicting parliamentary statements and appraising them it could violate that provision.[95] However, this does not mean that a court will find all parliamentary statements or material equally valuable to it or, indeed, of any value at all.[96] Thus a court has declined to have regard to such material because a select committee was not unanimous in its views[97] and has ignored statements from members opposing the legislation that is in question.[98] In Australia, the interpretation legislation gives particular weight to the speech of the Minister moving the second reading of the bill.

It has also been stated that parliamentary proceedings may be used to assist in determining applications for judicial review, particularly by reference to ministerial statements to the House.[99] On the other hand, an attempt to construe an enforceable legitimate expectation from such a statement was rejected by one judge on the ground that to do so would infringe article 9.[100] The distinction may lie between, on the one hand, using a parliamentary statement in judicial review proceedings to establish precisely what the Government policy or position that is being reviewed is and, on the other hand, using the statement as itself giving grounds for review. A parliamentary statement made by a Minister can be introduced as evidence of the Government's position on a matter and that position can be criticised and (if need be) demonstrated to be unlawful. The announcement of the policy in Parliament is no different to its announcement by means of a letter.[101] But the parliamentary statement cannot in itself give grounds for relief (for example, by creating a legitimate expectation or being impugned as actuated by bias), for so to use it would be to impeach it and thus act contrary to article 9.

Court or place out of Parliament

The prohibition on speeches and parliamentary proceedings being called into question outside Parliament applies to such questioning before a court or in any "place" outside Parliament. Proceedings before a court are self-evident. The reference to any place outside Parliament, if taken literally, could be used to inhibit criticism or examination of Parliament on any occasion outside Parliament and thus unacceptably infringe the citizen's freedom of speech. There have occasionally been judicial statements of a rhetorical nature imputing this extreme meaning to the phrase.[102] Fortunately, these suggestions have not been taken seriously, either by the House or by the courts themselves.

It seems likely that what the parliamentarians of 1688 had in mind by the phrase was the jurisdiction of the councils previously established by Royal prerogative to exercise executive and judicial functions that were, in regards to the latter, in conflict with the jurisdiction of the common law courts. Members, in enacting the *Bill of Rights*, wished to ensure that these councils, as well as the regular courts, could not examine parliamentary proceedings. In a modern state these parallel, non-curial, executive and judicial functions are exercised by tribunals and other bodies established mainly by legislation. It is to such

---

[94] *Acts Interpretation Act* 1901 (Australia), s.15AB.
[95] *R v Secretary of State for the Environment, Transport and the Regions, ex parte Spath Holme Ltd* [2001] 2 AC 349 at 391-2 (per Lord Bingham).
[96] *P v National Association of Schoolmasters/Union of Women Teachers* [2003] 2 AC 663 at 37 ("in the usual hopeless attempt to obtain guidance from the Parliamentary debates" per Lord Hoffmann).
[97] *Vela Fishing Ltd v Commissioner of Inland Revenue* [2001] 1 NZLR 437 at [129-131].
[98] *Awatere Huata v Prebble* [2004] 3 NZLR 359 (CA)

at [89] (per McGrath J).
[99] HC 214-I (1998-99), paras 46 to 55; *Buchanan v Jennings* [2002] 3 NZLR 145 at [41] (per Keith J).
[100] *Thoburn v Sunderland City Council* [2003] QB 151 at 76 (per Laws LJ).
[101] *Wilson v First County Trust Ltd (No 2)* [2004] 1 AC 816 at [113] (per Lord Hope).
[102] See, for example: *R v Murphy* (1986) 5 NSWLR 18 at 29 (per Hunt J); *Pepper v Hart* [1993] AC 593 at 638 (per Lord Browne-Wilkinson).

bodies (as well as the courts) that the prohibition on questioning proceedings in Parliament is taken to be addressed today. Thus a statutory arbitrator has been held to be "a place out of Parliament" and thus bound to observe article 9, since the arbitrator was required to act judicially and in accordance with the law.[103] The Human Rights Commission[104] and the Ombudsmen[105] have accepted that they are bound by article 9 and have refused to investigate complaints that related to proceedings in Parliament. In Western Australia, the Legal Practitioners Complaints Committee and the Legal Practitioners Disciplinary Tribunal (both statutory entities) have also accepted that they are subject to the restraint against impeaching or questioning proceedings in Parliament.[106]

In 1978, following the report of a commission of inquiry which had been charged with investigating, amongst other things, public statements made by a member of Parliament (the "Moyle affair"), and the interpretation by the commission of its terms of reference as authorising it to examine statements made in the House, it was argued in a learned article that the commission had "acted in breach of article 9 of the *Bill of Rights* and thus (in this respect) in excess of jurisdiction".[107] At the time the commission of inquiry sat, Parliament was in recess and the matter was never raised as a matter of privilege in the House. Regardless of whether a breach of privilege was committed in that case, there would seem to be little doubt that a commission of inquiry or a Royal Commission does fall within the expression "place" in the *Bill of Rights*, and so is potentially subject to the restrictions of parliamentary privilege in carrying out its task.[108] For this reason, in 1980, the commission of inquiry into the marginal lands affair requested that the House give leave for it to refer to *Hansard* during the course of its inquiries.[109]

But the phrase "place out of Parliament" may not be restricted to bodies carrying out statutory functions. In 1978 the Press Council, which was set up by agreement between associations representing newspaper proprietors and journalists, refused to pursue a complaint against a member of Parliament in respect of a motion he had moved and a speech he had made in the House, which, it was alleged, seriously reflected on a newspaper and the probity and professional reputation of its editor. The council accepted legal advice that it could not inquire into the appropriateness of proceedings in the House, including a parliamentary question (it was in fact a motion that was involved in that case) or a discussion on it, and that if it did so it would be guilty of a contempt.[110]

The House has treated an attempt by the Legislative Council to examine a member about a speech he had made in the House to be a breach of privilege.[111]

THE HOUSE'S EXCLUSIVE RIGHT TO CONTROL ITS OWN PROCEEDINGS
One of the incidents of freedom of speech is the right of the House to control its own proceedings free of outside interference. It has been said that this right must be regarded as so essential a part of a legislature's procedure that it inheres in the very notion of being a legislative chamber in the first place.[112]

The House is said to have "exclusive jurisdiction" or "exclusive cognisance" over

---

[103] *New South Wales Branch of the Australian Medical Association v Minister for Health and Community Services* (1992) 26 NSWLR 114.

[104] "No Commission of Inquiry", Human Rights Commission, 17 October 2001 (select committee inquiry); "The Parliamentary Prayer", Human Rights Commission, 22 November 2004.

[105] *Ombudsmen Quarterly Review*, March 1996 (questions); 2002, PP, A.3, p.21 (questions).

[106] Western Australian Legislative Assembly, 29 October 2003, pp.12804-6 (though it was not conceded that they were actually questioning proceedings in that case).

[107] Mummery, "Freedom of Speech in Parliament" (1978) 94 LQR 276.

[108] In *Royal Commission into Certain Crown Leaseholds* [1956] St R Qd 225 it was accepted that a Royal Commission was bound by article 9.

[109] 1980, JHR, pp.204-5, 208.

[110] New Zealand Press Council: *Editor of the New Zealand Herald v Mr A G Malcolm MP*, decision published 31 August 1978.

[111] 1885, Vol.53, p.714.

[112] *Egan v Willis* (1998) 195 CLR 424 at 462 (per McHugh J).

how its proceedings are to be conducted; the conduct of those proceedings is not subject to examination elsewhere.[113] This right is not dependent on article 9 of the *Bill of Rights* (though it is clearly associated with it). Indeed in the leading cases on the right to control a legislature's proceedings none of the judgments refer to article 9 at all. The courts do not enforce or review internal parliamentary procedures – that is a matter for the House itself. Rather the courts as a matter of law recognise the House's internal decisions as being conclusive within that sphere.[114]

The House's internal rules – its Standing Orders – were originally required to be submitted to the Governor for approval before coming into effect, but this requirement was repealed in 1865 and the Standing Orders of the House are now a matter for the House alone to determine. It is solely for the legislature to decide what its Standing Orders and other procedures should be.[115]

In cases of alleged non-compliance with the House's rules of procedure, the courts disclaim all power to intervene. The Standing Orders are examples of the House giving orders to itself and it has exclusive authority to do this. Questions of this nature have arisen in cases in which it has been alleged that the legislature has passed a bill in contravention of its Standing Orders,[116] or has been induced to pass a bill by fraud or deceit and, therefore, contrary to its own rules,[117] and that in each case the validity of the resultant Act was thereby vitiated. The courts have declined to examine the internal proceedings of the legislature in such cases, referring litigants to Parliament itself for any redress. As has been said, "the remedy for a parliamentary wrong, if one has been committed, must be sought from Parliament, and cannot be gained from the courts".[118]

It is a matter for the House to decide what business to consider, legislation to pass, and resolutions to adopt.[119] This is so even though any resulting legislation will be invalid or ineffectual and the House will have been effectively wasting its time.[120] While, if a resolution is relied on as having legal significance in a particular case, a court must determine if it has the significance claimed,[121] the court will not allow itself to be drawn into giving relief (even of a declaratory nature) against the House for having adopted the resolution in the first place.[122] It is also exclusively for the House to decide how to discipline its own members, for example, whether to suspend or admonish them, and not for the courts to intervene in its decisions on such matters.[123] Reports to its committees on internal disciplinary matters by one of its officers are also regarded as being part of its internal proceedings and are therefore unsuitable subjects for judicial review.[124]

On the other hand, if a statute prescribes a mode of dealing with a matter, this is a case where Parliament has given an order to the House. The House and its members are subject to the law of the land as promulgated by Parliament, just as is everyone else in the state, and they must comply with any statute which applies to the House's proceedings, notwithstanding any Standing Order or practice of the House to the contrary.[125] Where the statutory mode of dealing with a matter is a prescription of the forms to be followed in enacting legislation (a "manner and form" provision), compliance with the prescription

---

[113] *Stockdale v Hansard* (1839) 9 A & E 1 at 233 (per Coleridge J); *Bradlaugh v Gossett* (1884) 12 QBD 271.

[114] Marshall, *Constitutional Theory*, p.8.

[115] *Ontario (Speaker) v Ontario (Human Rights Commission)* (2001) 54 OR (3d) 595.

[116] *Ram Dubey v Government of Madhya Bharat* AIR 1951 Madhya Bharat 57; *Namoi Shire Council v Attorney-General (New South Wales)* [1980] 2 NSWLR 639.

[117] *Hoani Te Heuheu Tukino v Aotea District Maori Land Board* [1941] AC 308; *British Railways Board v Pickin* [1974] AC 765.

[118] *British Railways Board v Pickin* [1974] AC 765 at

793 (per Lord Wilberforce).

[119] *Reference re Amendment of the Constitution of Canada (Nos 1, 2 and 3)* (1982) 125 DLR (3d) 1.

[120] *Rediffusion (Hong Kong) Ltd v Attorney-General for Hong Kong* [1970] AC 1136.

[121] *Stockdale v Hansard* (1839) 9 A & E 1; *Dyson v Attorney-General* [1912] 1 Ch 158.

[122] *Egan v Willis* (1998) 195 CLR 424; *Hamilton v Al Fayed* [1999] 1 WLR 1569.

[123] *In re Nalumino Mundia* [1971] ZR 70.

[124] *R v Parliamentary Commissioner for Standards, ex parte Al Fayed* [1998] 1 WLR 669.

[125] *Simpson v Attorney-General* [1955] NZLR 271 at 282.

is an essential condition of legal validity. A court must therefore satisfy itself that the prescription has been complied with, otherwise there will be no valid statute to apply.[126] (See Chapter 27.) However, even in such a case a court will accord the House a wide latitude to determine how the manner and form provision is to be applied in practice to the House's procedures.

Where no manner and form provision is involved, it was said in an English case that the House of Commons had the exclusive power of interpreting a statute (which allowed a member to make an affirmation rather than take an oath before taking a seat in the House) so far as the regulation of its proceedings within its own walls was concerned, and that even if that interpretation was erroneous the court had no power to interfere with it directly or indirectly.[127] Thus a court has held that it had no authority to review the discharge of the Attorney-General's function of drawing the House's attention to the provisions of any bill which appear to conflict with the fundamental rights and freedoms confirmed by the *New Zealand Bill of Rights Act* 1990, since this is a function discharged as part of a proceeding in Parliament. Any control of it therefore fell to be exercised exclusively by the House.[128] Similarly, with those rights and freedoms guaranteed by the Act, so far as they fall to be exercised within parliamentary proceedings, it is for the House to devise procedures and practices to give effect to them and to decide in individual cases how these are to be applied.

It has been emphasised, however, that in respect of proceedings outside Parliament a court could substitute its interpretation of the statute for that of the House's if it felt that the latter's was wrong, and protect such rights as flowed from this interpretation to the extent that they were exercisable outside the House.[129] The House's right to interpret how a statute applies to its own proceedings cannot affect one's status or the exercise of legal power outside Parliament.

EVIDENCE OF DEBATES AND PROCEEDINGS IN PARLIAMENT

Authority to refer to debates and proceedings

Historically, the House of Commons took a very restrictive view of attempts to report its debates or proceedings. Even though by the nineteenth century such reports had come to be tolerated and, indeed, officially produced and sanctioned,[130] it remained until 1971 a technical breach of privilege to report the House's proceedings.[131] If it was regarded as a breach of privilege even to make a report of the House's proceedings, to raise such proceedings before a court was potentially regarded as even more serious by the House of Commons, and any litigants who did so ran the risk of being held to be in contempt by it. Possibly for this reason, a practice began to develop of litigants petitioning the House for leave to refer to its proceedings where this was necessary in litigation in which they were engaged. By obtaining the House's prior agreement to their use, they insured themselves against the possibility that the House would hold them in contempt for referring to its proceedings without its permission.

This practice was not a means of securing release from the strictures of the *Bill of Rights* 1688. Any proposed use of materials that would involve impeaching or questioning proceedings in Parliament was unlawful and the courts, in applying the law, would prevent

---

126 *Westco Lagan Ltd v Attorney-General* [2001] 1 NZLR 40.
127 *Bradlaugh v Gossett* (1884) 12 QBD 271.
128 *Mangawaro Enterprises Ltd v Attorney-General* [1994] 2 NZLR 451.
129 *Haridarsan Palayil v Speaker of Kerala Legislative Assembly* AIR 2003 Kerala 328 (penalties imposed

for sitting and voting without having taken prescribed oath; court obliged to determine if oath taken in proper form).
130 *Wason v Walter* (1868) LR 4 QB 73 at 95 (per Cockburn CJ).
131 *May*, p.98.

it. But the courts would not forbid uses of parliamentary materials that were consistent with the *Bill of Rights*, and parliamentary authority for such materials to be used was never essential to their admissibility in legal proceedings. Rather, parliamentary authority was seen as an assurance for those persons using parliamentary materials that they would not come into conflict with the House of Commons for a breach of its privileges. The House of Commons, in 1980, formally abandoned the practice of litigants petitioning it for leave to refer to its proceedings, by giving a general authority for its proceedings to be referred to. The general authority specifically reaffirms the continuing applicability of article 9 of the *Bill of Rights* to any use of those proceedings.[132]

It is doubtful whether the practice of petitioning for leave to refer to parliamentary proceedings was ever truly applicable in New Zealand. The House of Representatives never took the restrictive view of the publication of its debates and proceedings that was formerly taken by the House of Commons and never considered it to be a breach of privilege to report or publish its proceedings (except secret sessions). Indeed, from its foundation it was concerned to encourage reports to be made of its proceedings. For example, New Zealand instituted an official report of parliamentary debates in 1867, while *Hansard* was not made an official report of the House of Commons until 1909.

Nevertheless, there were occasional petitions to the House seeking leave to refer to its proceedings. Indeed, in one early application for leave to produce as evidence a petition and minutes of the evidence on the petition, the House refused permission.[133] In later cases leave was invariably granted but there was no settled practice of litigants applying for leave in all cases.

Since 1996 the House has resolved any uncertainty for litigants by adopting the House of Commons' practice of giving a general leave for its proceedings to be referred to in legal proceedings and abolishing any requirement for its permission to be obtained.[134] At the same time, it made it clear that by granting a standing permission to refer to its proceedings it was not intending to waive or abrogate article 9 of the *Bill of Rights*, and it reiterated that any use of parliamentary proceedings in court must be in accordance with that provision.[135] It also made it clear that such permission was subject to any rule or order of the House extending confidentiality to its proceedings, such as the rules on confidentiality of select committee proceedings prior to their report to the House.[136]

Evidence by members

Members of Parliament are in no special position regarding the evidence that they may give of proceedings in Parliament, though they have entitlements to obtain exemption from court attendance as witnesses.[137] If the evidence which they give to the court is permissible in terms of the House's privilege of freedom of speech and particularly article 9, it is evidence that it is competent for a court to receive. If it is inconsistent with that privilege, then the fact that a member proposes to give it makes no difference; it is still inadmissible.[138] Nor does a member of Parliament have any parliamentary immunity from producing, or giving evidence of the source of, information received by the member, even if that information has been used in Parliament.[139] However, the court may take account of the wide functions of a member of Parliament in exercising a discretion whether to order production or to compel a member to give evidence.

---

132 *Ibid.*, p.105.
133 1880, Vol.37, pp.212-5.
134 S.O.401(1).
135 1993-96, AJHR, I.18A, pp.78-9; S.O.401(2).
136 S.O.401(3).
137 *Legislature Act* 1908, s.260 (Speaker) and s.261

(other members).
138 *Rost v Edwards* [1990] 2 QB 460.
139 *Reference re Legislative Privilege* (1978) 18 OR (2d) 529; *Attorney-General v Lightbourn* (1982) 31 WIR 24; *O'Chee v Rowley* (1997) 150 ALR 199.

The question has arisen as to whether a member of Parliament can be compelled to give evidence of proceedings in Parliament.

The Speaker of the Irish House of Commons was called to give evidence about what the plaintiff (a member) had said in Parliament. The court held that the Speaker was bound to answer as a fact whether the plaintiff had spoken but was not bound to disclose what he had actually said, though if the Speaker did give such evidence it would be accepted by the court.[140] The point in that case appears to have turned on the House's former prohibition of reporting its debates, which a court would not compel a witness to disobey. On this ground it is thus no longer relevant. In later cases courts have allowed members to refuse to give evidence of what had occurred in Parliament where they did not have the House's permission to do so.[141] But evidence of proceedings in Parliament has been given by members voluntarily without the express permission of the House. Providing such evidence is otherwise admissible in terms of article 9, the courts have held that it could be received by them. Even more, it was said that mere factual evidence of what has occurred in Parliament can be compelled from a member by a court.[142]

Clearly, evidence of proceedings in Parliament that is consistent with the House's freedom of speech can be given by members and neither the courts nor the House require that the House's express permission be obtained.

In the United Kingdom, the House of Commons' former practice of attempting to suppress reports of its proceedings has received acknowledgment from the courts in the sense that permission of the House has been regarded as necessary where a member objects to giving such evidence. The House's concurrence to evidence being given has been seen, in these circumstances, to be an aspect of its privilege of control over its own proceedings.[143] But in New Zealand (and Australia) a general practice of suppressing reports of proceedings has never been asserted. In these circumstances there seems to be no reason in principle why such evidence should not be compellable as a matter of the court's discretion, though the fact that the House has not been consulted would be a relevant factor for the court to take into account in exercising that discretion. It would be the case too that any confidentiality attaching to specific parliamentary proceedings ordered by the House or applying by virtue of the Standing Orders should be observed by the court both in exercising its discretion to compel evidence and in admitting evidence in the first place. It would certainly be the duty of any member giving evidence to object to giving evidence of confidential parliamentary proceedings. This point is expressly reserved by the House in its general permission for evidence to be given of its proceedings.[144]

If a member subject to the compulsory order of a court feels any difficulty in giving evidence of parliamentary proceedings, this can be raised with the House which, if it sees fit, can seek to intervene in the proceedings.

Evidence by parliamentary officials

In the case of evidence by parliamentary officials the House does have a special rule about its own proceedings being tendered in evidence to a court. This arises when it is desired that an officer of the House give evidence (in person or by affidavit) of parliamentary proceedings. (Indeed it may be that it was confusion with the House's interest in its own officers not tendering evidence about its proceedings without the House's authority that led litigants to begin petitioning the House for authority to refer to its debates even where it was not proposed that an officer give evidence.[145])

---

[140] *Plunkett v Corbett* (1840) 5 Esp 136.
[141] *Chubb v Salomons* (1852) 3 Car & K 75; *Royal Commission into Certain Crown Leaseholds* [1956] St R Qd 225 at 229.

[142] *Sankey v Whitlam* (1978) 142 CLR 1 at 35-8 (per Gibbs ACJ).
[143] May, pp.104-5.
[144] S.O.401(3).
[145] HC 102 (1978-79), Appendix, paras.1 to 5.

By Standing Order, the House has provided that neither the Clerk, any other officers of the House (which includes all staff of the Office of the Clerk[146]), nor any other person employed to make a transcript of proceedings before the House or any committee of the House, may give evidence of proceedings in Parliament without the authority of the House.[147] This Standing Order is directed solely to the manner in which evidence of parliamentary proceedings may be obtained. It does not prohibit the use of parliamentary proceedings before a court or other tribunal. Where such use is prohibited, that is dealt with by the *Bill of Rights* 1688.

Applications for officers to give evidence can be made by way of petition to the House or they can be dealt with on a motion for which notice is necessary. During an adjournment of the House, where it is not convenient to wait until the House will next sit, the Speaker may give authority on behalf of the House unless, in the Speaker's opinion, the matter should await consideration by the House itself.

Any evidence given by a parliamentary official must be consistent with the House's own rules on the disclosure of its proceeding.[148]

CONTROL OVER THE PARLIAMENTARY PRECINCTS
The House, through the Speaker, exercises such control over the parliamentary precincts as is necessary for the proper functioning of its work as a legislature. This control can include excluding persons from the parliamentary buildings. (See Chapter 11.)

POWER TO CONTROL ACCESS TO ITS SITTINGS
As an aspect of its privileges, the House possesses the power to control access to its sittings by regulating the attendance and conduct of members and non-members at sittings and excluding strangers if it sees fit.[149]

Proceedings in the House
The House's privileges include the power to effect (at least) the temporary removal of members insofar as this may be necessary to allow the House to conduct its business in an orderly fashion.[150] The House has rules for the maintenance of order and for the circumstances in which members can be excluded from the Chamber. (See Chapter 11.)

Strangers are normally allowed to be present during all sitting hours of the House. However, it is open to any member of the House to move, without notice, "That strangers be ordered to withdraw".[151] A debate, but not a member speaking, may be interrupted to deal with such a motion.[152] The motion is decided immediately, without amendment or debate.[153] If it is carried, the public galleries are cleared immediately, the broadcasting of the debates is discontinued, *Hansard* reporters and members of the press gallery withdraw, and no official report of the debate is made; a record only of the formal motions moved and questions put while strangers were excluded is noted by the Clerk for the journal.[154]

During the Second World War, the House occasionally went further than merely ordering the exclusion of strangers, and after strangers had withdrawn it sometimes ordered that the remainder of the sitting should be a secret session. Under regulations, it was an offence to publish a report or description of any of the proceedings of the House at a secret session in any newspaper, periodical, circular or other publication, or in any public speech, except a report or description officially authorised by the Speaker.[155]

---

[146] *Clerk of the House of Representatives Act* 1988, s.18.
[147] S.O.402.
[148] S.O.401(3).
[149] *New Brunswick Broadcasting Co v Nova Scotia (Speaker of the House of Assembly)* (1993) 10 DLR (4th) 212.
[150] *Egan v Willis* (1996) 40 NSWLR 650.

[151] S.O.39(1).
[152] S.O.133(f).
[153] S.O.39(2).
[154] S.O.40.
[155] *Parliamentary Secret Session Emergency Regulations* 1940; 1940, Vol.257, p.123. The regulations, made by Order in Council on 5 June 1940, were never published.

Members themselves were not able to discuss or comment in the House on what had been said at secret sessions.[156] However, anything said at a secret session could be repeated outside the House if it did not constitute giving information to the enemy, was not itself confidential and was not attributed as having been discussed at a secret session.[157]

The first secret session was held on 5 June 1940[158] and 17 further secret sessions were held during the war. In addition, the galleries were cleared on one occasion on the Speaker's own authority.[159] However, officials, such as the chiefs of staff, and even members of the press ("who were forbidden to report anything")[160] were admitted to some secret sessions.[161] The secret sessions regulations were revoked along with a number of other emergency regulations in 1947.[162]

Subject to any order of the House, the Speaker controls admission to the galleries and may make rules for the conduct of those admitted to them.[163]

The Speaker has ordered all strangers to withdraw from the galleries when the Speaker felt that the nature of the subject under debate warranted this.[164] The Speaker and the Serjeant-at-Arms may, as part of the power to keep order in the galleries, require strangers who interrupt proceedings or otherwise misconduct themselves to withdraw.[165]

Select committee proceedings

The admission to, and exclusion of members and strangers from, meetings of select committees is dealt with earlier, as are the circumstances in which reports of proceedings at select committees may be divulged before being reported to the House. (See Chapters 23 and 24.) The House will hold the divulging of select committee proceedings or a select committee report in a way that is contrary to the Standing Orders to be a contempt. (See Chapter 47.)

Official information

The House's privilege of keeping material confidential is recognised in those statutes that provide for access to information. Requests for such information or access may be declined if to release it would lead to a contempt of the House.[166] Amongst other things, this protects Ministers and their officials who have confidential select committee documents circulated to them in the course of their duties from having to disclose them and thereby commit a breach of privilege.

POWER TO HOLD INQUIRIES

The House has inherent power to inquire into any matter that it considers requires investigation. (See Chapter 30.)

POWER TO OBTAIN EVIDENCE

In support of its power to inquire, the House has power to obtain information and evidence by summoning witnesses and requiring the production of documents. This power may be delegated to a select committee as the power to send for persons, papers and records. (See Chapter 30.)

POWER TO ADMINISTER OATHS

The House and its committees have the power to administer oaths to witnesses. (See Chapter 30.)

---

[156] 1940, Vol.257, pp.135, 455.
[157] 1941, Vol.259, pp.287-8.
[158] 1940, Vol.258, p.546.
[159] 1942, Vol.261, p.930.
[160] Bassett with King, *Tomorrow Comes the Song – A Life of Peter Fraser*, pp.243-4.
[161] 1942, Vol.261, p.423; 1943, Vol.262, p.517.

[162] *Emergency Regulations Continuance Act* 1947, s.6.
[163] S.O.42.
[164] 1891, Vol.74, p.98.
[165] S.O.41.
[166] *Official Information Act* 1982, s.18(c)(ii); *Local Government Official Information and Meetings Act* 1987, s.48(1)(b); *Privacy Act* 1993, s.29(1)(i).

POWER TO DELEGATE

The House has always exercised a power to form committees of members and to delegate to those committees parliamentary functions and powers. The functions thus delegated include the examination of legislation, estimates, treaties and petitions and the conduct of inquiries. The powers delegated to committees are ancillary to carrying out these functions. These powers include disciplinary authority over members of the committee and authority to regulate access to committee proceedings. Coercive power to require persons to attend such committees and produce papers to them is no longer generally delegated to committees. Parliamentary committees have been described as extensions of the legislature, deriving their authority from it and, insofar as they act within the scope of the authority delegated to them, being every bit as "parliamentary" as the legislature as a whole.[167]

But the House may also delegate powers to individual members in their own right. It does so particularly with regard to the Speaker, who is given considerable power, both within the House and outside the Chamber, to make decisions that would otherwise have to be taken by the House itself. These delegated powers include the power to issue a summons at the request of a select committee requiring a person to appear before the committee or to produce documents to it. The House also delegates its powers to non-members. Principally these delegations relate to powers to be exercised by officers of the House, such as the Clerk of the House and the Serjeant-at-Arms, on its behalf. These delegated powers are exercised subject to the oversight of the Speaker on behalf of the House. But the House does not delegate the power to punish for contempt. (See Chapter 47.)

It is also doubtful how far, if at all, the House can delegate its functions, as opposed to its powers, to non-members and give them parliamentary authority, without legislative authorisation. Where the House has desired that another body or group of persons carry out its functions, it has legislated for this,[168] and the concept that officers of Parliament carry out functions on behalf of the House[169] is underpinned by legislation authorising those officers to carry out that work. (See Chapter 6.) It is likely, therefore, that an attempt by the House to delegate the carrying out of its functions to a body of non-members would not (in the absence of legislation) be recognised as according to the activities of that body the status of a proceeding in Parliament with the legal authorities and protections that are attendant on that status.

POWER TO PUNISH FOR CONTEMPT

The House's power to punish for contempt is discussed in Chapter 47.

POWER TO EXERCISE DISCIPLINE OVER MEMBERS

Members are exempt from being punished or disciplined by anyone outside the House on account of what they may have said or done in the course of parliamentary proceedings. But members are subject to being held accountable to the House for their conduct in parliamentary proceedings. Thus the House's rules of order in debate and its rules for disciplining and ultimately suspending members from service in the House and on committees subject members to the power that the House possesses to exercise disciplinary authority over its own members. (See Chapter 11.)

---

[167] *Attorney-General (Canada) v MacPhee*, Prince Edward Island, Supreme Court, 14 January 2003 at [41].

[168] *Awarua Seat Inquiry Act* 1897 (determination of membership of the House).

[169] 1987-90, AJHR, I.4B.

POWER TO EXPEL

The extent to which the House may have the power to expel members from the House and thus cause a vacancy to arise is discussed in Chapter 48.

POWER TO FINE

The House's possible power to fine members or others is discussed in Chapter 48.

POWER TO ARREST

The House's power to arrest or commit persons into custody is discussed in Chapter 48.

POWER TO CONTROL REPORTS OF ITS PROCEEDINGS

One of the incidents of freedom of speech is the power of the House to control the extent to which its proceedings may be reported. The House of Commons was, at one time, extremely suspicious of reports of its proceedings getting abroad, and treated such reports as technical breaches of privilege until as late as 1971. The House of Representatives has never been jealous to protect the confidentiality of its debates – indeed, quite the opposite – but it has consistently exercised the power to control the release of reports of its proceedings. Proceedings of committees have always been treated on a different basis from proceedings in the House itself as far as disclosure is concerned, for the House has taken the view that it should be the first body to learn of the deliberations and conclusions of its own committees. The report and certain other proceedings of a committee are confidential until the committee reports to the House. Disclosure of such matters before this time may be treated as a contempt.[170]

The House's proceedings have been broadcast on radio since 1936 and have been available for television broadcasting since 1988.

EXEMPTION FROM JURY SERVICE

The House of Commons has always claimed that its members are exempt from being required to serve on juries. In New Zealand the law goes even further than this and provides that members of the Executive Council and members of Parliament are not to serve on any jury in any court on any occasion.[171] Rather than being exempt from serving on a jury, members are now disqualified from doing so.

EXEMPTION FROM LIABILITY FOR PARLIAMENTARY PUBLICATIONS

At common law no privilege existed protecting any parliamentary publication from legal liability. It was thus no defence to a legal action that the document in respect of which the action related was published by order of the House.[172] In order to overcome this situation the United Kingdom Parliament in 1840 passed specific legislation protecting such publications from legal liability.[173] The New Zealand Parliament first passed equivalent legislation in 1856.[174] The present exemptions attaching to documents and extracts from documents published by order or under the authority of the House are set out in specific legislation.[175] (See Chapter 38.)

The House has also, since 1962, ordered that its proceedings be broadcast.[176] (Though proceedings have been broadcast since 1936, this was done without an order of the House

---

[170] S.Os 240(1), 241(1), 242(1) and 400(p).
[171] *Juries Act* 1981, s.8.
[172] *Stockdale v Hansard* (1839) 9 A & E 1.
[173] *Parliamentary Papers Act* 1840 (UK).

[174] *Privileges Act* 1856.
[175] *Legislature Amendment Act* 1992.
[176] S.O.44(1).

until 1962.) Re-broadcasts of extracts from debates are afforded qualified legal privilege in defamation.[177] The publication of an official report of proceedings (*Hansard*) was not initiated in 1867 by or under the authority of the House. Rather it was done on the Government's authority. Today it is carried out by order of the House under the control of the Speaker.[178]

Members of Parliament who publish outside the House copies of speeches they have made in the House are liable for any defamatory statements contained in the speech, subject to any legal privilege they may be able to claim.

Protection from liability for infringement of copyright is provided for anything done for the purposes of parliamentary proceedings or for the reporting of such proceedings.[179] In regard to use of copyright material in the course of parliamentary proceedings, it is likely that no liability would arise in any case.[180] Republication of documents generated in the parliamentary process (other than as a report of parliamentary proceedings) for commercial purposes or private gain is unlikely to be protected from liability.[181]

FREEDOM FROM ARREST

Members of Parliament enjoy freedom from arrest in civil process. The privilege of freedom from civil arrest runs from 40 days before the start of each parliamentary session to 40 days after its termination.[182] The 40-day period after the end of the session continues to run even though Parliament is dissolved[183] and even though the person claiming the privilege was a member of the old Parliament but is not a member of the new Parliament.[184]

The significance of this privilege has been considerably reduced by the practical abolition of imprisonment for debt in New Zealand. Legislation passed in 1874 abolished imprisonment for failure to pay a sum of money, except in very restrictive circumstances.[185] Nor are members immune from detention under an inpatient order in a case of mental disorder.[186]

A similar privilege of freedom from arrest in civil process applies to witnesses summoned to attend before the House or a committee; to witnesses in attendance upon the business of the House, and while they are coming to, or going from, the House on parliamentary business; and to officers in personal attendance on the House.[187]

Criminal matters

The privilege of freedom from arrest applies only to arrest in civil proceedings; it does not protect members from arrest in criminal matters or from detention under emergency powers.[188] There is no general immunity from the criminal law for members of Parliament in New Zealand. The only privilege that members enjoy in criminal matters is that words used by them in proceedings in Parliament cannot be made the subject of criminal proceedings or be used to support a prosecution. A court will therefore be concerned to ensure that a member has not been arrested on account of anything said in the House.[189] But otherwise a member convicted of a crime is in the same position as any other convicted person and will, in addition, lose his or her seat in the House if the crime carries a penalty of imprisonment for two years or more or if the member is committed to prison and is unable to attend in the House for a whole session without obtaining leave

---

177 *Defamation Act* 1992, s.16 and First Schedule.
178 *Legislature Act* 1908, s.253A; S.O.9.
179 *Copyright Act* 1994, s.59.
180 *Ibid.*, s.225(1)(c).
181 House of Representatives (Australia) Debates (18 February 2002), p.380.3.
182 *Goudy v Duncombe* (1847) 1 Ex 430; *In the matter of Pillalamarri Venkateshwarlu* AIR 1951 Madras 269; *Ainsworth Lumber Co v Canada (Attorney-General)* (2003) 226 DLR (4th) 9.

183 *Barnard v Mordaunt* (1754) 1 Keny 125.
184 *In re Anglo-French Co-operative Society* (1880) 14 Ch D 533.
185 See now *Imprisonment for Debt Limitation Act* 1908.
186 *Electoral Act* 1993, ss.55 and 56.
187 *May*, pp.126-7.
188 *May*, pp.119-21.
189 *In the matter of Pillalamarri Venkateshwarlu* AIR 1951 Madras 269.

of absence from the House.[190]   Indeed, the fact that a member who is lawfully detained stands in danger of losing his or her seat for not attending the House is no ground for a court to give relief against that detention.[191]   Although members have no freedom from arrest in criminal matters, the House expects to be informed of the arrest or detention of any of its members. This is done by the arresting or sentencing authority informing the Speaker of the circumstances by letter.[192] Quite apart from other rights to communicate from detention, a member who is detained is entitled to communicate with the Speaker on parliamentary business.[193]

Contempt of court

It has been said that members' immunity from arrest does not apply in respect of contempt of court.[194] This appears to depend upon whether the contempt is of a criminal (or "quasi-criminal") or civil nature .[195] Members are not exempt from being proceeded against for a contempt of court of a criminal nature and such proceedings are not a breach of privilege.[196] Members in New Zealand have been proceeded against for contempt of court and a member has been found to be in contempt.[197]

The distinction between civil and criminal contempt has been said to be that the former is brought to compel performance of a civil obligation, while the latter punishes conduct "which has about it some degree of criminality, some defiance of the general law".[198] In Australia, the commitment to prison of a member for failure to pay court costs awarded against him following a civil action was considered by a committee of the House of Representatives to be a breach of privilege, but this view has been challenged on the ground that commitment for costs is criminal in nature.[199]

EXEMPTION FROM ATTENDANCE AS A WITNESS IN LEGAL PROCEEDINGS

The *Legislature Act* 1908 (in provisions, most of which were first enacted in 1866) lays down detailed provisions dealing with the exemption of members and certain officers of the House (the Clerk of the House, the Deputy Clerk, the Clerk-Assistant, and the Serjeant-at-Arms[200]) from attending courts of law as witnesses during a session. These provisions are seen as having codified and superseded any exemptions that would have applied at common law. In no case, however, is the general power of the House to grant leave for its members or officers to attend court to give evidence limited or abridged by the statutory provisions.[201]

Members or officers not in attendance on the House

Any member who already has leave of absence from the House may be exempted from attending civil or criminal proceedings before the Court of Appeal, the High Court or a District Court, during a session or within 10 days of the commencement of a session, by the court concerned.[202] If applied for, exemption must be granted unless it appears to the court that "the ends of public justice would be defeated or injuriously delayed or irreparable injury would be caused to any party to the proceedings by the non-attendance".[203] There can be no exemption where the member or officer is a defendant in criminal proceedings.

[190]   *Electoral Act* 1993, s.55(1)(a), (d).
[191]   *Kunjan Nadar v State of Travancore-Cochin* AIR 1955 Travancore-Cochin 154.
[192]   1918, JHR, Session 1, p.2; 2003, Vol.613, p.9621.
[193]   *In re Ananda Nambiar* AIR 1952 Madras 117.
[194]   *Re Ouellet (No 1)* (1976) 67 DLR (3d) 73.
[195]   *May*, pp.121-3.
[196]   *Ibid.*
[197]   *Solicitor-General v Broadcasting Corporation of New Zealand* [1987] 2 NZLR 100 (radio and press statements by member relating to a person being tried

– no contempt found); *Solicitor-General v Smith* [2004] 2 NZLR 540 (pressure on litigants, criticism of a court and disclosure of court proceedings – contempts found).
[198]   *Stourton v Stourton* [1963] P 302 at 310.
[199]   Harris, *House of Representatives Practice*, pp.724-5.
[200]   *Legislature Act* 1908, Sixth Schedule.
[201]   *Ibid.*, s.269.
[202]   *Ibid.*, s.257.
[203]   *Ibid.*, s.259.

If exemption is granted, the member or officer is discharged from attending the court until an appointed time, which is at least 10 days after the end of the session.[204]

Members or officers in attendance on the House

In the case of members or officers in attendance on the House, exemptions from court appearances may be granted by the Speaker or the House itself. Once again, no exemption may be granted where the member or officer is a defendant in criminal proceedings.

If the Speaker is served with an order to attend a court, the matter may be submitted to the House for it to decide what action is to be taken. The House may make any order it thinks fit. In particular, it may resolve to exempt the Speaker from attending the court. If it does, the Speaker is exempted from attendance until 10 days after the termination of the session.[205] Speakers have been so exempted by the House on three occasions.[206] During an adjournment, the Speaker may sign a certificate that exempts the Speaker from attendance but in this case the matter must be submitted to the House at the first available opportunity.

Other members of the House who are required to attend court in civil or criminal proceedings during a session or fewer than 10 days before the commencement of a session may apply to the Speaker (or Acting Speaker) for exemption.[207] To claim exemption the member must apply to the Speaker certifying that it is necessary for the member to attend to parliamentary business and provide any other information that may be relevant to the Speaker's consideration of the application. The Speaker may seek the views of other parties involved in the proceedings and give them an opportunity to comment.[208] The Speaker must grant exemption unless justice would be defeated or injuriously delayed, or irreparable injury would be caused to another party.[209] But the length of time and the dates claimed for the exemption will be relevant considerations. An exemption granted at or near the beginning of a session (given the length of sessions nowadays) or for days on which the House will not be sitting, is unlikely to be justifiable, for instance.[210]

When the Speaker's certificate has been issued, the member is exempted from attending at the court until 10 days after the termination of the session.[211]

RIGHT TO HAVE CIVIL PROCEEDINGS ADJOURNED

At one time it was regarded as a breach of privilege merely to bring a civil action against a member of Parliament or the member's servant during a session. During the course of the eighteenth century such privileges were abolished by legislation, although the House of Commons (and by extension the House of Representatives) can still, in any appropriate case, treat as a contempt the bringing of legal proceedings against a member in respect of conduct in the House and punish it accordingly.[212] The privileges of members in New Zealand in respect of civil proceedings instituted against them depend now upon the provisions of the *Legislature Act*.

In 1872, it happened that a member's personal attendance at a civil action against him was not actually required by process of law (which would have entitled him to invoke the sections of the Act already considered to have the action postponed), yet it was desirable from his point of view that he attend the trial personally, which he was unable to do by the

---

[204] *Ibid.*

[205] *Ibid.*, s.260.

[206] 1906, JHR, p.66; 1977, JHR, p.394; 1987-90, JHR, p.552.

[207] *Legislature Act* 1908, s.261.

[208] "Service of proceedings on members of Parliament",

The Speaker, 9 November 2004.

[209] *Legislature Act* 1908, s.263.

[210] "Service of proceedings on members of Parliament", The Speaker, 9 November 2004.

[211] *Legislature Act* 1908, s.264.

[212] *In re Parliamentary Privileges Act 1770* [1958] AC 331.

necessity for him to attend the House.[213] Legislation was consequently enacted to enable members and officers in this situation to obtain a stay of the action.

Where a civil action against a member or officer is to come on for trial during the course of a session or 10 days before or 30 days after a session has ended, the member or officer may apply to the court, if he or she is not in attendance on the House, and to the Speaker, if he or she is, for the trial or hearing to be adjourned. Any such application must be supported by an affidavit from the member concerned. The court or the Speaker must grant the application unless irreparable injury would be caused to any party.[214] As with an application for exemption from attending court as a witness, on an application for an adjournment the Speaker may make inquiries in order to establish that an adjournment is justified. This may involve giving other parties an opportunity to comment. Also, as with an exemption, the stage of the session and whether the House will actually be sitting are relevant factors for the Speaker to consider in deciding whether irreparable injury would be caused to any person.[215]

Where such an application is granted, the trial or hearing is adjourned to a sitting of the court to be held at least 30 days after the end of the session.

EXEMPTION FROM SERVICE OF LEGAL PROCESS

The issue of court documents against members of Parliament (service of process) from courts other than the Court of Appeal, the High Court and District Court, is restricted. The service of process out of any other court, on any member or officer during a session or within 10 days before or 10 days after a session (except a summons or warrant on a charge of a criminal offence) is invalid and of no effect.[216] While members are not immune from the service of process out of the Court of Appeal, the High Court or a District Court, how and where such process is served is material in determining whether it constitutes an affront to the dignity of the House and should be treated as a contempt.[217]

POWER TO DETERMINE THE QUALIFICATIONS OF MEMBERS TO SIT AND VOTE IN THE HOUSE

The House of Commons has exercised a number of privileges in regard to its own constitution, such as the power to order writs to be issued to fill vacancies in its membership, trying controverted elections and determining the qualifications of members to sit or to continue to sit in the Commons. It is doubtful how far the first two of these powers have ever been possessed by the House of Representatives as an aspect of privilege, for the *New Zealand Constitution Act* 1852 (UK) provided, from the beginning of representative government, for how vacancies were to be filled and how disputed elections were to be determined (at first, by the House itself).

The power of determining the qualifications of its members to sit in the House, however, has been exercised on a few occasions. If there is a doubt whether a person claiming to be a member is entitled to take a seat in the House or if it appears that a member may have become disqualified from membership, the House may inquire into the matter. Thus, when a member appeared at the Chamber claiming to have been elected but without producing the returned writ, the House inquired into the affair as a matter of privilege. It was only on the House being satisfied that he had been elected, that he was admitted.[218]

Two of New Zealand's most famous parliamentarians have had their right to sit in the House challenged in exercise of this privilege. The question was raised as to whether

---

213   1872, Vol.13, pp.202, 227, 248-52.

214   *Legislature Act* 1908, ss.265(b)(ii) and 266.

215   "Service of proceedings on members of Parliament", The Speaker, 9 November 2004.

216   *Legislature Act* 1908, ss.257(1) and 267.

217   1990, AJHR, I.15, para.12; S.O.400(c).

218   PD, 1856-58, pp.559-60.

Sir George Grey had become disqualified by reason of his absence from the House, but a motion to refer this matter to a select committee for investigation failed.[219] Sir Joseph Ward's bankruptcy in 1897 (bankruptcy of a member was then a disqualification) caused the House to set up a committee to inquire into whether he was disqualified as a member.[220] In its report the committee recommended that the matter should be referred to the Court of Appeal for its opinion on the subject.[221] Because there was no machinery for this to be done, Parliament passed a special Act referring the question of Ward's bankruptcy to the court on a case stated.[222] The court certified that the seat had not become vacant.

In 1997 the Privileges Committee conducted an inquiry into whether a member had resigned from the House. The committee found that she had not resigned.[223] In 2003 a similar inquiry into whether a member had incurred a disqualification by applying for the citizenship of another country found that he had done so.[224]

While the power of the House to inquire into the qualifications of its members to sit in the House and, as an aspect of its exclusive control of its own proceedings, to admit to or exclude from its presence any person claiming to be a member remains, the House does not make legal determinations of membership of the House. Ultimately, this is a matter of law, which may be determined by a court of competent jurisdiction. Statutory procedures exist, for example, for determining disputed elections.[225] In the case of members who incur or may have incurred disqualifications, the Speaker, on being satisfied that a vacancy exists, must notify that vacancy in the *Gazette* and commence the process of filling that vacancy.[226] But, even so, it is not the Speaker who determines authoritatively that a vacancy has arisen; rather the Speaker's role is a consequential one. Whether a vacancy exists could be established independently of any action of the Speaker.[227]

The House may also suspend its members from service in the House. It has never exercised a power to expel a member. (See Chapter 48.)

FREEDOM OF ACCESS TO THE GOVERNOR-GENERAL AND FAVOURABLE CONSTRUCTION OF THE HOUSE'S PROCEEDINGS

The right to freedom of access to the Governor-General and the right that a favourable construction be put on the House's proceedings are two privileges specifically included in the Speaker's claim to the privileges of the House immediately after the Governor-General has confirmed the Speaker in office.[228] It may be that the claim to a favourable construction of its proceedings was part of the formation of a general principle of freedom of speech. (See p.617.)

Neither privilege has been regarded as being of practical importance in New Zealand, having been adopted, it has been said, "through the desire of our early parliamentarians to follow as closely as possible the procedures and precedents of the Commons".[229] However, in 1877 the House did protest that, contrary to its privileges, the Governor of the day had taken notice of its proceedings and used this as a reason for declining to follow advice tendered to him by his Ministers.[230] This could be significant if there was uncertainty over the confidence of the House in the Government in office.

The privilege of freedom of access also emphasises that individual members do not have a right of access to the Governor-General; only the House as a whole does, through its Speaker. The proper form that communications between the House and the Governor-General take is that of an Address. Otherwise advice to the Governor-General is tendered solely by the Crown's responsible advisers, its Ministers.

---

[219]   1895, Vol.87, pp.54-61.
[220]   1897, Vol.98, pp.122-40.
[221]   1897, JHR, Session II, pp.26, 53.
[222]   *Awarua Seat Inquiry Act* 1897.
[223]   1996-99, AJHR, I.15B.
[224]   2002-05, AJHR, I.17C.

[225]   *Electoral Act* 1993, Part 8.
[226]   *Ibid.*, ss.129(1) and 134(1).
[227]   2003, Vol.610, p.7749.
[228]   S.O.23.
[229]   *Littlejohn*, p.116.
[230]   1877, JHR, p.280.

CHAPTER 47

CONTEMPT

At common law a legislature such as the House enjoyed no power to punish for contempt, though it could take direct action to coerce persons into obeying its orders (such as to leave its presence or to attend a sitting).[1] It was doubt about the House's ability to take action itself to enforce or vindicate a breach of its privileges or to punish any other contempt shown to it that was the motivating factor behind a general legislative statement of the House's powers early in its life. With the enactment of the *Parliamentary Privileges Act* 1865, the House was empowered to take action against persons who breached its privileges or showed contempt to it in any other way, and to punish those persons itself, rather than being forced to rely exclusively or mainly on the courts for protection. The power to punish for contempt is the power to take direct action that is sanctioned by law. (The types of punishment which the House may inflict are considered in Chapter 48.)

APPLICATION OF THE POWER TO PUNISH FOR CONTEMPT

The power to punish applies in respect of breaches of privilege. Any breach of one of the privileges of the House can be punished by the House. However, by the very nature of these privileges it is unusual for the House to be involved in enforcing them (except those relating to disclosure of select committee proceedings). Breaches are more likely to be raised in the context of legal proceedings before the courts and, being part of the general law of New Zealand,[2] are recognised and applied by the courts as may be necessary even if not specifically raised by the parties to the litigation.[3] Cases of breaches of specific privileges do arise before the House but they are comparatively infrequent.

But as well as the House's power to punish for contempt extending to punishing breaches of specific privileges, the power also includes the power to punish any act which the House considers to be a contempt whether or not that act violates a specific privilege. The distinction between a contempt and a breach of privilege is not always clearly drawn; there is a tendency to refer to a "breach of privilege" when what is really meant is a contempt.

There are many acts other than breaches of privilege which, although they do not interfere with freedom of speech, freedom from arrest or the House's other privileges, nevertheless interfere with the work of the House or its members or are a serious affront to their dignity. Not being violations of a specific privilege of the House, the courts cannot protect the House against them unless they are also crimes or in some sense unlawful. But the power to punish for contempt held by the House extends to punishing these types of acts too. They are not breaches of privilege, but just as breaches of privilege may be treated as contempts and punished, so may any other acts which "obstruct or impede [the House] in the performance of its functions, or are offences against its authority or dignity, such as disobedience to its legitimate commands or libels upon itself, its Members or its officers".[4] These types of acts, along with breaches of privilege, may be treated as contempts and punished accordingly. "Contempt", then, is a term which may embrace all breaches of privilege as well as a great many other types of conduct that the House considers to be worthy of censure.

---

[1] *Fenton v Hampton* (1858) 11 Moo PC 347; *Egan v Willis* (1996) 40 NSWLR 650.

[2] *Legislature Act* 1908, s.242(2).

[3] *Awatere Huata v Prebble* [2004] 3 NZLR 359 (CA) at [40] (per McGrath J).

[4] May, p.75.

Definition of contempt

There is no formal legal definition of what constitutes a contempt. Ultimately, the House is the judge of whether a set of circumstances constitutes a contempt. This potentially open-ended nature of contempt has led to criticism of the lack of certainty for those indulging in conduct that might be treated as objectionable by the House. An attempt has therefore been made by the House to give greater definition to the types of conduct that it may decide constitute contempts. To this end, in 1996 a general statement defining contempt was adopted by the House together with a number of other particular statements of the types of conduct that may fall within the overall definition. It was emphasised, however, that these particular statements were not intended to be exhaustive and that new situations could arise which the House may wish to treat as contempts.[5] Its right to do so is declared to remain unimpaired.[6]

Using the contemporary edition of *Erskine May* as the model, the House has resolved that it may treat as a contempt—

> ... any act or omission which—
>> (a) obstructs or impedes the House in the performance of its functions, or
>> (b) obstructs or impedes any member or officer of the House in the discharge of the member's or officer's duty, or
>> (c) has a tendency, directly or indirectly, to produce such a result.[7]

Although the statement refers expressly to the House, members and officers only, contempt can also embrace conduct involving other persons, such as witnesses and petitioners, insofar as it has deleterious effects on their participation in the parliamentary process and thus obstructs or impedes the House.

This general statement gives a context and background within which the House judges whether a contempt has occurred, but the specific examples of the types of conduct that may constitute a contempt stand in their own right as presumed obstructions or impediments to the House or its members. There is no two-stage test for contempt against both the specific examples and the general definition.[8]

Exercise of the power

The House may declare particular conduct to be a contempt without any antecedent inquiry into it.[9] But, under the House's rules, a deliberative process is usually followed before arriving at such a finding. Thus it is invariably the Speaker who decides, in the first instance, if a matter of complaint falls within the definition of contempt, as concerning a breach of a recognised privilege, or by falling within one of those areas of conduct identified by the House in its Standing Orders, or as otherwise being potentially justified for treatment as a contempt even though there is no definitional precedent of that type of conduct. But, reverting to the reason why parliamentary privilege exists in the first place, it has been emphasised that the power to punish for contempt is not a power to punish for its own sake. It may justifiably be utilised only in case of need – the need to vindicate the House's position because of an obstruction or impediment to carrying out its constitutional functions. If there is no need to exercise the power (notwithstanding that facts that would otherwise support its exercise exist), the matter will not be pursued.[10]

The fact that a matter may have been dealt with as a breach of order does not prevent that matter being punished as a contempt if the facts justify this. There is no "double jeopardy"

---

5   1993-96, AJHR, I.18A, p.78.
6   S.O.1.
7   S.O.399.
8   1993-96, AJHR, I.15C, p.3.

9   See, for example, *May*, p.132 (member's untrue personal statement declared to be a grave contempt).
10 2001, Vol.590, p.7912.

rule in regard to breaches of order and punishment for contempt. (See Chapter 11.)

The view has also consistently been taken that the exercise of the power to punish, being vested in the House, is so significant a power and must be used with such deliberation that even the House cannot delegate it. It must be exercised by the House itself.[11] No committee, not even the Privileges Committee, has ever been delegated with the power to inflict punishment. But whatever action the House chooses to take, it must avoid acting in a disproportionate or unreasonable manner.[12] In Australia, a Senate committee has accepted that if a public servant refuses to answer a question or produce a document at the explicit direction of a Minister, the legislature's remedy should lie against the Minister and that it would be unjust to impose a penalty on the public servant in such circumstances.[13] If there is a personal culpability on the part of a witness, the House will proceed against the witness in a personal capacity, but political culpability should be addressed at the political level. By making such distinctions a legislature applies proportionality and reason in its proceedings.

The House's procedures for invoking the power to punish for contempt only after preliminary examination by the Speaker, inquiry by the Privileges Committee and endorsement by the House are designed to ensure that the power is used proportionately and reasonably. However, it is of the essence of parliamentary privilege that the House ultimately makes the judgment as to when to exercise its own privileges and there can be genuine differences of opinion as to whether an exercise in a particular case is justifiable.

The power to punish for contempt is a highly discretionary power and this discretion is much more commonly exercised to refrain from invoking it in circumstances where it may be justifiable, than the contrary.

EXAMPLES OF CONTEMPT

The House, in its Standing Orders, has given examples of the types of conduct that it may decide to treat as contempt.[14] These examples do not form a code of contempts, though it would be exceptional for a case not falling within them to be treated as a contempt.[15] It is always possible that a situation will arise that is not explicitly contemplated in these examples but which the House will wish to treat as a contempt. Some miscellaneous examples of conduct already identified as potential contempts, even though not falling within the specified examples of contempt, are described below. But to constitute a contempt such other conduct must fall within the House's overall definition of an act or omission obstructing or impeding the House or those executing the House's business.[16] If conduct does not have this quality, it cannot be a contempt.

The types of contempt recognised by the House are discussed below under several broad headings—

- breach of privilege
- attendance of members
- pecuniary contempts
- records and reports
- disobedience to the rules or orders of the House
- interference or obstruction
- misconduct
- punishing parliamentary contributions
- reflections
- other contempts.

---

[11] HC 588-I (1977-78) Appendix C, para.3; *Howard Gossett* (1845) 10 QB 359 at 393.
[12] *New Zealand Bill of Rights Act* 1990, ss.9 and 21.
[13] *49th Report of the Senate Committee of Privileges* (Australia), September 1994.
[14] S.O.400.
[15] 1996-99, AJHR, I.15C, pp 3-4.
[16] S.O.399.

Breach of privilege

The House may punish as a contempt a breach of one of the privileges of the House.[17] Because the privileges of the House (freedom of speech, freedom from arrest, exemption from legal process etc.) are part of New Zealand law, they should be observed in applying the law. The House may wish to be represented in legal proceedings in order to ensure that a point of parliamentary privilege is not overlooked and a court, in determining what the law is, may not agree with the House's view of the extent of its privileges.[18] But, given those inevitable tensions, a breach of privilege should be corrected or prevented in the same way as any other breach of law, by the parties concerned obeying the law, and, in the absence of them doing so, a court declaring and enforcing the law.

While the power to punish for contempt will not normally need to be invoked in such circumstances, it has been specifically affirmed by the House as remaining available to it,[19] and the House has, on occasion, reminded litigants that it remains an option, notwithstanding that the matter has also been dealt with in legal proceedings.[20]

Attendance of members

The House's Standing Orders imposing an obligation on members to attend the House and providing machinery for granting leave of absence were revoked in 1999.[21] However, it is still open to the House to resolve that a member who has absented himself or herself from parliamentary duties attend the House.[22] Failure to do so in response to such an order would be a contempt.[23] (See Chapter 3 for attendance of members generally.)

Pecuniary contempts

Disclosing financial interests

Members are under an obligation to disclose any financial interest that they have in the outcome of the House's consideration of any business before participating in consideration of that business.[24] (See Chapter 3.) Failure to disclose such an interest is a contempt.[25] In all cases it is the Speaker who determines whether or not the member actually has a financial interest. The Speaker's decision on this point is final[26] and is not subject to review or reversal by the Privileges Committee if an allegation that a contempt has been committed is referred to that committee.

Registration of pecuniary interests

Members are required to make initial and annual returns of pecuniary interests that they hold.[27] (See Chapter 3.) Knowingly failing to make a return by the due date specified for a return is a contempt.[28] It is also a contempt for any member knowingly to provide false or misleading information in a return of pecuniary interests.[29] While the Auditor-General has a review and inquiry role in respect of returns of members' pecuniary interests and may inquire into whether a member has complied with his or her obligations to make a return,[30] a report from the Auditor-General is not an essential prerequisite to alleging a contempt in regard to the registration of pecuniary interests. However, it would be difficult to establish grounds for an allegation of contempt without invoking or attempting to invoke the Auditor-General's involvement first.

17 S.O.400(a).
a19 *Ibid.*
20 *Reports of select committees 1996*, p.654; 1999-2002, AJHR, I.17A, pp.5-6.
21 1996-99, AJHR, I.18B, p.7.
22 2002-05, AJHR, I.18B, p.81.
23 S.O.400(r).

24 S.O.166(1).
25 S.O.400(f).
26 S.O.167.
27 S.O.164(1) and Appendix B to the Standing Orders.
28 S.O.400(g).
29 S.O.400(h).
30 Appendix B to the Standing Orders, cl.16.

Bribery

Any member who receives or solicits a bribe to influence the member's conduct in respect of proceedings in the House or at a committee commits a contempt.[31] Because of the serious nature of such allegations, members are not permitted to bring them up incidentally in debate but must raise them in the proper way as matters of privilege.[32] Also, given the seriousness of an allegation of bribery, the standard of proof needed to make it out is of a very high order. This is reflected in the Speaker's consideration of any matter of privilege that is raised.[33]

Such allegations are rare. In 1872 it was alleged that a member had been offered money to use his parliamentary position to advance the interests of a railway manufacturer. The allegation was not proven.[34] In 1912 an allegation was made that a member had been paid to support Sir Joseph Ward's Government in a crucial vote in the House. Though this allegation was referred to a committee for investigation, no evidence to support it could be found and the matter was dropped.[35] In 2003 an allegation that a member had solicited funds for herself or for other persons close to her, such as her children, in return for her vote, was dismissed by the Speaker for lack of evidence.[36]

It is a contempt to offer or attempt to offer a bribe to a member as an inducement to act in a certain way in the House or in a committee.[37] Though allegations of attempted bribery have been made on several occasions, there has never been a case where the payment and receipt of a bribe has been disciplined as a breach of privilege in New Zealand.[38] The Speaker has warned that a contempt would be committed if a member was offered payment to resign his or her seat.[39]

To constitute a contempt, any bribe offered or received must relate to the member's conduct in respect of business before the House or a committee or business to be submitted to the House or a committee.[40] But attempting to bribe a member in any capacity at all, whether in relation to parliamentary business or not, is also a crime.[41]

Professional services connected with proceedings

It is a contempt for a member to accept fees for professional services rendered by the member in connection with proceedings in the House or at a committee.[42]

This contempt will be committed whether or not the member concerned participates in parliamentary proceedings on the matter for which the member has received fees. Nor need there be any suggestion of corruption on the part of the member. The House is concerned to ensure that a member's judgment may not be influenced by a professional interest (other than an interest as a member of Parliament) which may be in conflict with the member's public duties. Whether there is a conflict or not, the House will not tolerate the appearance of one. For this reason members should be careful to keep their official and private capacities quite separate in their business dealings.[43]

Where a newly elected member, who was also a practising solicitor, received payment for two local bills he had drafted (even though he had done the work before he entered Parliament), the House found him to have acted improperly and fined him a sum equal to his professional fees.[44] In another case, a comment (later withdrawn) that a member had been paid for things that a trust wished him to achieve in Parliament appeared to raise a serious question of contempt. Acceptance of a payment for parliamentary services to be

[31] S.O.400(i).
[32] 1934, Vol.128, p.641.
[33] 2003, Vol.606, p.3551.
[34] 1872, Vol.13, p.533-9, 553-4, 582-4, 745.
[35] 1912, Vol.157, p.356.
[36] 2003, Vol.606, pp.3551-2.
[37] S.O.400(k).
[38] *Littlejohn*, p.144.
[39] 1998, Vol.574, p.14721.
[40] 1992, Vol.525, p.8612.
[41] *Crimes Act* 1961, s.103.
[42] S.O.400(j).
[43] 1991, Vol.519, p.4541.
[44] 1877, JHR, p.202.

rendered would be a potential contempt. However, on inquiry it was found that there was no evidence in that case that the payment in question was made, other than in recognition of past services to the trust rendered before the member was elected to Parliament.[45]

Advocacy by members of matters in which they have been concerned professionally
Closely akin to receiving fees for professional services is advocacy in respect of business with which the member has been professionally concerned.

This type of contempt is based on a House of Commons resolution of 1858 that "it is contrary to the usage and derogatory to the dignity of this House that any of its members should bring forward, promote or advocate in this House any proceeding or measure in which he may have acted or been concerned for or in consideration of any pecuniary fee or reward".[46] This is not taken to preclude members taking part in debates on matters (such as law suits) in which they have been professionally engaged.[47] A member was held to have acted contrary to its terms, even though the parliamentary action he took (presenting a petition) occurred five years after he had acted professionally in respect of the petition.[48]

Records and reports
The custody of the journals and of all petitions and papers presented to the House and other records belonging to the House is vested in the Clerk of the House. Such documents may not be taken from the House or its offices without an order of the House or permission of the Speaker.[49] To remove, without authority, any papers or records belonging to the House is a contempt.[50] Similarly, to falsify or alter any such paper or record will be treated as a contempt.[51]

It is also a contempt to publish a false or misleading account of proceedings before the House or a committee.[52]

A newspaper headline misrepresenting the purport of evidence given before a select committee was considered to be of such a "startling and inaccurate nature" that it would tend to lower the esteem in which the House was held and, therefore, amounted to a contempt.[53] (It stated that a witness had made a statistical claim that four members of Parliament were probably homosexuals, although this did not accurately convey the essence of the witness's evidence even as reported in the newspaper article.) In another case, a member complained that a newspaper article falsely accused him of attacking the integrity of the Speaker in a speech he had made in the House (which, if true, could in itself be treated as a contempt), but a motion to treat the article as a question of privilege was not proceeded with.[54]

But merely stating one's opinion of the effect of a committee's decision cannot amount to a contempt under this head (though if it was a serious reflection on the character of members of the committee it might constitute a contempt for that reason).[55] Only a statement that purports to be a factual description of parliamentary proceedings falls within this example of contempt.[56]

Disobedience to the rules or orders of the House
Any person who disobeys an order of the House directed to that person commits a contempt of the House.[57] Such an order would normally be a direction to attend the House

---

45 "Report for the Prime Minister on Inquiry into Matters relating to Te Whanau o Waipareira Trust and Hon John Tamihere", Douglas White QC, 20 December 2004.
46 *May*, p.137.
47 *Ibid.*
48 1877, Vol.27, pp.497-8.
49 S.O.10.
50 S.O.400(d).
51 S.O.400(e).
52 S.O.400(q).
53 1968, JHR, p.239.
54 1923, Vol.199, pp.36-9, 344-5.
55 See S.O.400(l).
56 2000, Vol.589, p.7497.
57 S.O.400(s).

or a committee to give evidence, or to produce to the House or a committee documents thought to be in that person's possession. The power to treat disobedience to such an order as a contempt directly supports the House's power of inquiry.

Orders to attend or produce documents

It is unusual for the House itself to make an order to attend or produce documents. If a committee has the power to send for persons, papers and records it may itself direct that a person attend before it to give evidence or that the person produce papers and records in that person's possession that are relevant to a matter before it.[58] Only the Privileges Committee inherently has this power.[59] In respect of other committees the power must be specifically conferred on the committee by the House. The current practice is not to confer the power. In such cases the Speaker may order any person to attend or produce papers in lieu of an order of the committee.[60] (See Chapter 30.)

Any failure to comply with the order of a committee having power to send for persons, papers and records or with the order of the Speaker may be treated as a contempt.[61]

Refusing to answer a question

A witness who refuses to answer a question as ordered to do so by the House or a committee may be held to have committed a contempt.[62] Witnesses have been held in contempt for refusing to answer a question in the House[63] and before a select committee.[64] Where a witness before a select committee does object to answering a question, the committee must, in private, consider the ground of objection and the importance of the question to its proceedings before deciding to insist on a reply.[65]

Premature publication of select committee proceedings or report

It is a contempt to divulge the proceedings or report (including a draft report) of a select committee or a subcommittee contrary to the Standing Orders.[66] In general, the proceedings of a select committee or a subcommittee, other than during the hearing of evidence, are confidential until the committee reports to the House.[67] This rule is designed to promote the better functioning of the committee process and to affirm that the House is entitled to first advice of the conclusions of its committees.[68] Speakers have warned members and journalists from time to time about the need to respect this rule.[69] (See Chapters 23 and 24 for the rules on disclosure of select committee proceedings and reports.)

Strictly speaking, only members, officials, advisers and witnesses are in a position to divulge a committee's proceedings, for it is only they who are privy to those proceedings. However, other persons or organisations who disseminate information which has been improperly disclosed to them are also considered to have committed contempt if they do so, and have been punished by the House accordingly.

In principle, all evidence heard by select committees is heard at public meetings and all written evidence received is made available to the public. Only if the committee takes special steps to protect evidence it has received from public disclosure can any question of contempt arise. Members have been found to have committed contempts by divulging select committee proceedings when they informed other persons who then gave the proceedings further publicity;[70] by writing a newspaper article disclosing evidence

---

[58] S.O.197.
[59] S.O.391(2).
[60] S.O.198.
[61] S.O.400(r), (s).
[62] S.O.400(u).
[63] 1896, Vol.93, p.336.
[64] 1903, Vol.125, pp.693-4; 1991-93, AJHR, I.15A.

[65] S.O.228(1).
[66] S.O.400(p).
[67] S.O.240(1).
[68] 1997, Vol.562, p.3232.
[69] *Ibid.*
[70] 1874, Vol.16, p.429; 1889, Vol.104, pp.179-92; 1900, Vol.113, pp.411-4; 1971, JHR, p.222.

given at a select committee hearing which was not open to the public, under the mistaken impression that it was open;[71] by revealing what had taken place at a select committee meeting during the course of a television interview;[72] and by revealing the contents of a select committee report before it had been presented to the House.[73] Members are liable to be held in contempt if they disclose in debate in the House proceedings which they are not authorised to repeat outside the committee.[74]

Members of the Parliamentary Press Gallery have been found to be in contempt in forwarding to their newspapers for publication confidential select committee evidence,[75] as have the newspapers which published such material[76] and a television channel in respect of a disclosure of select committee deliberations made during a programme.[77] In these cases, it was clear that the initial breach of confidence of the select committee proceedings was not made by these persons or parties but by some other person or persons, and in all of these cases the question of who initially divulged the proceedings to the journalists concerned has been raised, although it was not possible to establish who was to blame. It would have been possible in these circumstances for the House to hold the journalists or newspapers concerned guilty of contempt for refusing to divulge their sources, but, with one exception,[78] this has not been the way the House has proceeded. The House has invariably treated the publication of confidential select committee material by members or by other persons as a contempt in its own right, whether that material was obtained at first-hand or second-hand.

Interference and obstruction

The House regards as most serious any improper attempt to prevent, dissuade or inhibit anyone (member, officer, witness or petitioner) from participating fully in its proceedings. For the House to acquiesce in such conduct would be inimical to its effective functioning. It may be that an attempt to prevent participation may also be a crime (for example, a threat of assault), but it need not be, and in such cases the power of the House to punish for contempt may need to be invoked.

Members and officers

Interferences or obstructions of members or officers may be overt or covert: consisting of an assault, a threat or other form of intimidation or otherwise of an obstructing or molesting of a member or officer. In any case, if the action occurs in the discharge of the member's or officer's duties, it may be treated as a contempt.[79] One early complaint of a molestation of members was the sending of a spurious telegram to two Dunedin members which caused them to return south and needlessly absent themselves from the House.[80] The House took no action.

A ministerial adviser was found to have committed a contempt by molesting a member in the execution of his duty when he made an insulting remark to the member as the member was passing him in the Chamber on the way into a division lobby.[81] In another case a jocular remark directed by one member to another in the division lobby at which the latter took offence was held not to be a contempt.[82] The Speaker has warned members not to allow banter in the Chamber to get out of hand. If it tended towards verbal intimidation of members, it could ultimately constitute a contempt.[83] This is particularly

---

71 1974, JHR, p.525.
72 1976, Vol.404, p.832.
73 1999-2002, AJHR, I.17C.
74 1895, Vol.95, pp.701-16.
75 1901, JHR, p.154; 1903, Vol.125, pp.693-4.
76 1903, Vol.125, pp.693-4; 1971, JHR, p.222.
77 1976, Vol.408, p.4447.
78 1903, Vol.125, pp.693-4.
79 S.O.400(l), (m).
80 PD, 1864-66, p.929.
81 1974, JHR, p.463.
82 1929, Vol.222, pp.663-70; *ibid.*, Vol.223, p.35.
83 1988, Vol.487, pp.3140-1.

the case when a vote is in progress.[84] Members of the Parliamentary Press Gallery have been reminded not to impede the free access of members to the Chamber, and a protocol regulating approaches to members on their way to the Chamber has been drawn up as a result of complaints.[85]

A distinction must be drawn, however, between members or outside persons properly seeking to influence other members, and attempts to influence members' actions which are intimidatory and may be held to be contempts. All members, when they speak in debate, try to influence their fellow members; so do all lobbyists when they are advancing their interests.[86] Such conduct is perfectly proper. There is no contempt in respect of attempts to influence members, even by bringing pressure to bear on them (such as to withdraw support from them at the next election), unless there is a threat to do something which is improper in itself or which is of such an extraordinary or exaggerated nature that it goes beyond an attempt to influence the member and becomes an attempt to intimidate. So where a Bible-in-schools league accused a member of a breach of faith in failing to give total support to Bible reading in schools, and announced that a letter of his explaining his stance would be read at every league meeting held in Canterbury and equal prominence given to his vote against a bill then before the House on Bible reading, this was held to be a contempt as attempting to intimidate the member in his parliamentary conduct.[87]

If an article could have the effect of intimidating members in their parliamentary conduct, that is sufficient for a contempt to be made out. There does not need to have been any specific intention to threaten.[88]

Instituting legal proceedings against members or officers seeking to restrain them from carrying out their official duties could also constitute a contempt on this ground, provided that such proceedings related to actions that members had taken or intended to take as part of parliamentary proceedings (for example, seeking an injunction to prevent a member raising a matter in the House).[89] But in respect of their actions outside the House members are in the same position as any other citizen.[90]

Witnesses and others

A similar principle of protection from harassment operates in regard to witnesses. Any attempt to intimidate, prevent or hinder a witness from giving evidence in full to the House or a committee may be held to be a contempt.[91] Such intimidation or hindrance may take the same overt form as that relating to a member. It could also take a less overt form, such as the offering of a bribe to give false testimony, or the taking of legal action to prevent a witness from giving evidence at all or from producing all the evidence in the witness's possession.

Petitioners and counsel appearing before the House or a select committee are also entitled to be protected by the House from molestation or obstruction while discharging their duties. Such molestation or obstruction may be treated as contempt.[92]

Serving legal process in the precincts of Parliament

Persons come to Parliament buildings on sitting days to take part in or observe the transaction of parliamentary business. The House will hold the service or attempted service of legal process within the parliamentary precincts to be a contempt if this is done on any day on

---

[84] 1998, Vol.571, pp.11946-7.

[85] 2004, Vol.616, pp.12431-2; "Protocol for filming and interviewing members in Parliament buildings", December 2004.

[86] 1979, Vol.428, p.4718.

[87] 1905, Vol.134, pp.300-5.

[88] 1984-85, AJHR, I.6A, p.9.

[89] 1996-99, AJHR, I.15B, p.654; 2001, Vol.590, pp.7912-3.

[90] *Ibid.*

[91] S.O.400(t).

[92] *May*, p.152.

which the House or any committee of the House sits.[93] (The House or committee need not be actually sitting at the time service is effected; if such a sitting is held at any time on that day, a contempt is committed.) No contempt will be committed if the authority of the House or the Speaker to service of legal process is obtained beforehand. In practice, if a member is willing to accept service at Parliament House, the Speaker will give authority for process to be served. Service on a member in the Parliament buildings, even with the member's agreement, will be a contempt if the Speaker's authority is not obtained.[94]

The parliamentary precincts are those areas which are legislatively held for parliamentary purposes.[95] They include, as well as the Parliament buildings (the main building, library and executive wing), the Bowen House building.[96] Service of a subpoena on a Minister in his office in the Beehive (executive wing) has been held to be a contempt, as it was effected on a sitting day. It is well established that law firms make arrangements with the Crown Law Office for effecting service on Ministers.[97]

The limitation on serving or executing legal process within the precincts does not prevent police officers on duty within the Parliament buildings or grounds arresting persons who commit or are about to commit criminal offences, but a warrant for the arrest of a person should not be executed there without first obtaining the Speaker's permission.

Misconduct
Deliberate misleading of the House
It is a contempt deliberately to attempt to mislead the House or a committee, whether by way of a statement, in evidence or in a petition.[98] This example of contempt, while always potential, was given explicit recognition in 1963 when, following a political *cause célèbre* (the Profumo affair), the House of Commons resolved that a former member who had made a personal statement to the House which he subsequently acknowledged to be untrue had committed a contempt of the House.[99] It has been submitted that there is an established constitutional convention that Ministers should always tell the truth to Parliament as far as this is possible without harming national security.[100] Whether this type of contempt embodies a convention or not, regarding lying to the House as a serious transgression of parliamentary etiquette (quite apart from any moral considerations) has been said to be the only way for Parliament to keep a check on the executive.[101]

The contempt can be committed by anyone taking part in parliamentary proceedings. It consists of the conveying of information to the House or a committee that is inaccurate in a material particular and which the person conveying the information knew at the time was inaccurate or at least ought to have known was inaccurate.[102]

Members deliberately misleading the House
Most commonly allegations that there has been an attempt deliberately to mislead the House involve statements made by members in the House – whether by way of personal explanation, in the course of debate or in replying to a question.

There are three elements to be established when it is alleged that a member is in contempt by reason of a statement that the member has made: the statement must, in fact, have been misleading; it must be established that the member making the statement knew at the time the statement was made that it was incorrect; and, in making it, the

---

[93] S.O.400(c).
[94] (1991) 2 PLR 196 (Western Australian Royal Commission apologised for serving a subpoena in a member's office even though member had invited investigators to the office.)
[95] S.O.3(1).
[96] *Parliamentary Service Act* 2000, ss.23, 24.
[97] 1990, AJHR, I.15.
[98] S.O.400(b).
[99] *May*, p.132.
[100] *R v Ponting* [1985] Crim LR 321.
[101] *The Observer*, 16 September 1984.
[102] 1998, Vol.570, p.11042.

member must have intended to mislead the House. The standard of proof demanded is the civil standard of proof on a balance of probabilities but, given the serious nature of the allegations, proof of a very high order.[103] Recklessness in the use of words in debate, though reprehensible in itself, falls short of the standard required to hold a member responsible for deliberately misleading the House.[104] The misleading of the House must not be concerned with a matter of such little or no consequence that is too trivial to warrant the House dealing with it. A misunderstanding of this nature should be cleared up on a point of order.[105]

For a misleading of the House to be deliberate, there must be something in the nature of the incorrect statement that indicates an intention to mislead. Remarks made off the cuff in debate can rarely fall into this category, nor can matters about which the member can be aware only in an official capacity. But where the member can be assumed to have personal knowledge of the stated facts and made the statement in a situation of some formality (for example, by way of personal explanation), a presumption of an intention to mislead the House will more readily arise.[106]

As well as a deliberate misleading of the House arising from a remark in the House, it is conceivable that members could mislead the House by their actions: for example, from a deliberate misuse of a voting proxy, by delivering to the Clerk a totally different document from that which the member obtained leave of the House to table,[107] or by misrepresenting their authority to act on behalf of an absent member.[108]

Witnesses and petitioners deliberately misleading
Witnesses giving evidence to committees are under an obligation to be truthful, whether they are under oath or not. As with members, for a contempt to arise there must be some strong indication that there is an intention to mislead the committee. This can arise out of the nature of the evidence, if it can be presumed to be within the personal knowledge of the witness, or by the circumstances of its delivery, for example, if an answer is deferred and delivered in writing on a later occasion when it can be presumed to be a more considered reply than an immediate response.[109]

It is a contempt to present forged, falsified or fabricated documents to the House or a committee. The main form which such a contempt has taken in the United Kingdom is the affixing of forged or fictitious signatures to petitions. Any conspiracy to deceive the House or a committee in this regard will be held to be a contempt. There are no examples of these having occurred in New Zealand.

Correcting inaccurate information
It is not a contempt to make a genuine mistake and thereby give the House or a committee incorrect information. But it is incumbent on a member or any other person who has given misleading information on a parliamentary occasion to clear the matter up as soon as the error is appreciated. This applies even though the full correct information may not be available at the time that it is realised that an error has been made. Action to alert the House or committee should still be taken at that point with a full correction to follow later.[110]

In the case of a misleading statement in the House, for example, in reply to an oral question, a personal explanation is the invariable form that the correction takes.[111] Misleading information given by way of a reply to a written question is corrected by the

---

[103] 1980, AJHR, I.6, pp.6-7.
[104] 1982, AJHR, I.6, p.17.
[105] 1976, Vol.405, pp.2131-2.
[106] 1986, Vol.476, p.5961.
[107] 1999, Vol.575, p.14854.
[108] 1996, Vol.553, p.11645.
[109] 2002, Vol.598, p.14744.
[110] 1998, Vol.570, p.11043.
[111] 2003, Vol.607, p.5678.

Minister delivering an amended reply to the Clerk. In the case of misleading information having been given to a committee, a written correction of the information should be given to the committee if a personal appearance before the committee cannot be arranged or if the committee agrees that it is not warranted.

Misconduct in the presence of the House or a committee
Any other misconduct in the presence of the House or a committee may be held to be a contempt.[112]

Such misconduct may take the form of an interruption or disturbance to the proceedings of the House or of one of its committees. When a group of persons in the public gallery rose at the commencement of business and recited the prayer which the Speaker was about to read, they were held to have committed a contempt.[113] But if the Speaker has given permission for a celebratory contribution to be made from the galleries, there can be no question of contempt.[114] Members who conduct themselves in a disorderly manner may themselves be punished for contempt, notwithstanding that the Standing Orders contain specific procedures for disciplining members for breaches of order.[115]

Punishing parliamentary contributions
The House may punish members or others on account of their contributions to the House's deliberations, for example, if they attempt to mislead the House or a committee and in respect of breaches of order. But it is a contempt for anyone outside the House to punish anyone for what they have done in the course of parliamentary proceedings (it may also be a crime and an unlawful act to do so too).

Anyone who assaults, threatens or disadvantages a member on account of the member's conduct in Parliament or any other person on account of evidence given by that person to the House or a committee commits a contempt.[116] For this contempt to be established it is essential that the action directed to the member or witness is on account of what they have done in parliamentary proceedings.[117] If it is not, it is not a matter for the House to be concerned with, whatever its legal effect outside the House.

On two occasions conduct complained of as a contempt has amounted to challenging a member to repeat outside the House, without protection of privilege, what the member had said in the House. The absolute protection against actions for defamation afforded members by the *Bill of Rights* 1688 is to enable them to speak out in the House in the public interest without fear of legal repercussions. The disadvantage which may befall an individual unjustly attacked in the House is held to be outweighed by the greater public good of permitting full, free and frank discussion in the House (though that person may apply to the Speaker to enter a response). Any misuse of the right of freedom of speech is for the House to deal with by its own internal disciplinary proceedings, and anything that tends to impair freedom of speech by unduly inhibiting members in its use is viewed seriously by the House. Challenges to repeat outside the House words spoken in debate, with the implication that what was said was untrue and a misuse of parliamentary privilege, fall into this category and can constitute a contempt. But each case must be considered on its own merits, and depends on the form of the challenge. In one case, the person who committed a contempt by challenging the member to repeat his statement outside the House explained his action at the bar of the House and apologised for his unwitting breach.[118] In another case, where a firm issuing the challenge published it in a

---

[112] S.O.400(o).
[113] 1981, AJHR, I.6, p.3.
[114] 1998, Vol.572, p.12347.
[115] S.O.92; 1986-87, AJHR, I.15.

[116] S.O.400(v), (w).
[117] 1996-99, AJHR, I.15A.
[118] 1895, Vol.91, p.778.

letter and in the form of an advertisement accompanied by a strong attack on the member, breaches were held to have been committed, again unwittingly.[119]

But in debate it is not automatically out of order, much less a breach of privilege, to invite a member to say outside the House what the member has just said in it. The cases involving a contempt are confined to the issuing of formal challenges to the freedom of speech enjoyed by members. Nevertheless, persistently challenging a member to repeat comments outside the House so as to imply that the member is not telling the truth may itself become disorderly.[120]

A classic case of molestation of a member because of action the member had taken in the House occurred in 1872 when, because a certain person wished to make the member pay for the way the member had voted in a division, the person applied (as he was legally entitled to do) to purchase pastoral land held on licence by the member. The consequence of this application to purchase was that the land had to be offered for auction with no preference for the licensee, thus putting the member to inconvenience and potential expense. The House found the person to have committed a contempt by making the application to purchase, and induced him to withdraw it.[121]

Two Prime Ministers have been the subject of complaint in the House in respect of remarks they made about the way members had voted. William Fox in 1869 wrote to a member who was a serving officer in the Army after the member had voted against the Government, saying that the member must either resign his seat or his command. A committee appointed to consider the matter found that no contempt had been committed and this was endorsed by the House, but the House went on to pass a resolution reiterating that every member of the House, without exception, was entitled to speak and vote in the House according to the member's conscience.[122] In 1896 Richard Seddon made a veiled remark that he would not forget how two West Coast members had voted (they had voted against the Government on the previous day). The remark was complained of, but after some discussion the House dropped the subject.[123]

Legal proceedings against witnesses

The House of Commons in 1818 passed a resolution declaring that witnesses were entitled to its protection in any legal proceedings brought against them in respect of testimony given by them to the House or a committee.[124] Legal proceedings in such circumstances also constitute a breach of privilege by infringing the freedom of speech guaranteed to persons taking part in proceedings in Parliament by the *Bill of Rights* 1688. Legislation also provides a legal indemnity for parliamentary witnesses who incriminate themselves while giving evidence on oath.[125]

Reflections

Speeches or writings which reflect on the character or conduct of the House, or of a member in the member's capacity as a member of the House, may be treated as a contempt.[126] This is seen as a longstop means for the House to protect itself and its members against attacks which would lower it in public esteem and thus compromise its ability to function effectively. But it is not a means of inhibiting legitimate political debate. It has been emphasised that for any statement to constitute a contempt as a reflection it would have to allege corruption or impropriety of some description. Hard-hitting and contentious statements to which members might well object fall within the boundaries of acceptable

---

[119] 1931, Vol.229, pp.324, 365-78.
[120] 1992, Vol.531, p.12223.
[121] 1872, Vol.13, pp.78, 158-63, 187-92, 201.
[122] 1869, JHR, p.195.
[123] 1896, Vol.194, pp.478-82.
[124] *May*, p.151.
[125] *Legislature Act* 1908, s.253.
[126] S.O.400(n).

political interchange.[127]   It is also the case that as social mores change, the limits of acceptable comment change too. To accuse members of engaging in homosexual conduct when such conduct was not regarded as publicly acceptable (and indeed was still criminal) was regarded by the House at the time as a serious reflection on members. These days it is likely to be viewed very differently. All examples of comments reflecting on the House and members must be considered in this light; they are not indications that similar comments will contemporarily be regarded as contempts.

Reflections on the House
Speeches or writings which reflect on the character or proceedings of the House may be treated as contempts. The fact that the prohibition on publication of reports of its debates formerly applied by the House of Commons has never operated in New Zealand does not authorise reflections on members in their parliamentary capacity or on the propriety of the House's procedures.[128]

An article criticising the practice of pairing in the House was held to be a contempt as containing incorrect statements which falsely represented the proceedings of the House.[129] Reflections on members of the House in their capacity as members which do not identify the particular member or members who are the subject of attack may also be treated as contempts. Thus, where unnamed members of Parliament were accused of homosexuality and bisexuality, the person making the allegation (which she admitted was baseless) was found to have committed a contempt by tending to lessen the esteem in which the House was then held.[130]

Reflections on members
Speeches and writings reflecting upon the character or conduct of individual members in their parliamentary roles have been punished as contempts. To establish that a contempt has been committed on this ground, however, the words complained of must reflect on the member in the discharge of his or her duties in respect of some proceeding in the House or in a committee, and not merely arise out of the member's status as a public figure. It is not a contempt, for instance, if a member is attacked in respect of the discharge of his or her constituency duties, for although this is an integral part of being a member of Parliament, it is not an aspect of a member's work that is directly concerned with proceedings in the House. Similarly, most functions performed by Ministers are not performed as members of Parliament (other than introducing a bill and answering a question, for example) and do not involve any question of parliamentary privilege.[131] A reflection on the Speaker in his capacity as chairperson of the Parliamentary Service Commission was found to relate to his capacity as a member of Parliament because this is an *ex officio* position held by the person who is Speaker.[132]

To constitute a reflection on a member, it is not necessary that the words used against the member should amount to defamation as a matter of law.[133] Nor does the fact that a member may have good grounds for taking legal action for defamation preclude the member raising the reflection as a matter of privilege.[134]

A member is not bound to seek redress in the House only. If the remarks are defamatory, the member may bring an action for damages in the courts instead of or in addition to pursuing the matter of privilege[135] (though the fact that a member has taken action in the courts will be relevant for the House in considering what penalty to

---

[127]   2000, Vol.589, p.7497.
[128]   1938, Vol.251, p.909.
[129]   1982, AJHR, I.6, p.8.
[130]   1975, Vol.400, pp.3375-93.
[131]   1996-99, AJHR, I.15C, p.7.

[132]   *Ibid.*
[133]   *May*, pp.144-5.
[134]   1978, Vol.417, pp.1261, 1294.
[135]   See, for example, *News Media Ownership v Finlay* [1970] NZLR 1089.

impose[136]). Any member may raise a reflection on a member as a matter of privilege, even though the reflection is on another member.[137]

Reflections on members in their parliamentary roles have been found where a member was accused of perjuring himself in an election petition case,[138] where a report which was submitted to the House accused a member of not having told the truth in some statements he had made to the House[139] and where a member was accused of being in the pocket of the tobacco industry.[140] The House also found that the Attorney-General had been libelled in his place in Parliament and a contempt was committed when a newspaper editorial accused him of bringing forward a bill to further his claims to certain property.[141] No contempt was found where two members were accused of hypocrisy over atomic bomb tests, because the reflections did not concern the conduct of the members as members but related to statements made by them outside the House.[142]

Reflections on the Speaker and other presiding officers

Some of the most serious reflections on members that can be made concern those against the character of the Speaker or any other presiding officer – in particular, accusations that presiding officers have shown partiality in discharging their duties. Reporting on a question of privilege concerning a reflection on the Speaker, the Privileges Committee has said, "[The] Speaker is in a special position. Being the embodiment of Parliament, reflections upon [the Speaker's] character or conduct directly attack the very institution of Parliament itself, and have been dealt with accordingly here and in England". The committee refused to consider the reasons "why" the attack which was before it on that occasion had been made, confining itself to a consideration of "whether" such an attack had been made.[143]

Reflections upon the Speaker have been censured on six occasions, five on which members attacked the character or conduct of the Speaker, and one on which newspapers did so: in 1967, when the Speaker was accused in a newspaper article of racial prejudice;[144] in 1975, when a member wrote a newspaper article criticising the matter in which the Speaker was presiding over the House;[145] in the following year, when a member in a radio interview advocated the replacement of the Speaker and accused the Speaker of weakness;[146] in 1982, when a member in a press statement criticised the Deputy Speaker's failure to call him to speak in a debate and stated that it was difficult to believe that the Deputy Speaker was not affected by his politics in the line he had taken;[147] in 1987, when a member in a press statement made reflections on the way in which the Speaker was presiding over the House;[148] and in 1998, when a member accused the Speaker (as chairperson of the Parliamentary Service Commission) of selectively releasing personal information to disadvantage a political party.[149]

Other contempts

The examples of contempts set out in the Standing Orders are not exhaustive. A number of other circumstances have arisen which it has been acknowledged could amount to a contempt even though these do not fit clearly into the listed examples. But in all cases the conduct could only amount to a contempt if it obstructed or impeded the House or members in the course of their functions and duties or if it had a tendency to do so.[150]

---

[136] 1984-85, AJHR, I.6A, p.10.
[137] 1912, Vol.161, p.672.
[138] 1911, Vol.158, pp.748-68.
[139] 1911, Vol.156, pp.884-98.
[140] 1996-99, AJHR, I.23, p.723.
[141] 1877, Vol.24, pp.473-9.
[142] 1972, JHR, p.62.
[143] 1975, Vol.400, p.3295.

[144] 1967, JHR, pp.144-5, 249-50.
[145] 1975, Vol.400, pp.3295-312.
[146] 1976, Vol.407, pp.3157-69.
[147] 1982, AJHR, I.6.
[148] 1986-87, AJHR, I.15.
[149] 1996-99, AJHR, I.15C.
[150] S.O.399.

Abuse of the right of petition

In the United Kingdom, the submitting of a petition containing false or scandalous allegations against a person, the inducing of signatures to a petition by false representations and threatening to submit a petition against a member have been treated as contempts. There are no examples of abuses connected with the right to petition occurring in New Zealand and being treated as a contempt by the House of Representatives.

Advice to the House

There is no convention that the House will be advised of important policy announcements by Ministers.[151] But the circumstances in which prior publication outside the House of a matter to be submitted to the House can constitute a contempt has been considered on a few occasions.

If a document or statement (such as a departmental report) intended for first promulgation in the House is improperly obtained or intercepted and then published before its promulgation in the House, that may be regarded as a contempt.[152] But the Privileges Committee has recommended that the House not treat as a contempt the premature release of parliamentary papers presented to the House under statute.[153]

Where a Minister prematurely released the contents of a message to the House from the Governor-General containing the text of a bill His Excellency was transmitting to the House for introduction, it was held that a breach of privilege (contempt) had been committed.[154] (This method of introducing bills has been abolished.) On the other hand, it is no contempt for the Government to disclose in advance of any formal parliamentary steps the terms of a bill about to be introduced into the House. This may be a matter for criticism from members of the House who learn of a bill from the news media in advance of its introduction, but it is not a matter of privilege.[155] But where formal parliamentary steps have been taken in respect of a bill, such as notification to the Clerk that a bill is about to be introduced (or notice of intention to introduce having been given in respect of a member's or a local bill), to disclose or improperly abstract copies of such a bill after that time could be treated as a contempt.[156]

Miscellaneous

Other examples of acts that may have a tendency to obstruct or impede the House in carrying out its functions are: unauthorised use of the name of the House or its crest on an unofficial publication,[157] the placing of material in the bill boxes reserved for members in Parliament House without the Speaker's permission,[158] and improperly attempting to induce a member to resign from the House.[159]

LEGAL SIGNIFICANCE OF CONTEMPT

The power to punish for a contempt of the House is a power that inheres in the House. The power is exercisable only by the House itself. The courts do not punish for contempt of the House, nor do they enforce punishments meted out by the House. The fact that a contempt may have been or may be about to be committed does not give rise to a cause of action for which relief can be obtained from a court.[160] Contempt is an extra-judicial

---

[151] 2000, Vol.583, p.1659; 2002, Vol.603, p.1512.
[152] 1977, Vol.412, p.1587.
[153] 1987-90, AJHR, I.18B, para.21.
[154] 1955, Vol.307, pp.2532-9.
[155] 1892, Vol.77, pp.73-7.
[156] 1984-85, AJHR, I.14, p.17.

[157] *Hansard Supplement*, 2001, Vol.48, p.1680.
[158] 1903, Vol.124, p.571.
[159] 1998, Vol.574, p.14721.
[160] *Holden v Marks* (1995) 17 WAR 447; *Criminal Justice Commission v Nationwide News Pty Ltd* [1996] 2 Qd R 444.

proceeding, though, as it is a power possessed by the House pursuant to law, its lawful exercise by the House will be recognised and, if need be, vindicated by the courts (for example, as a defence against legal liability that would otherwise arise).

But apart from the fact that the power to punish for contempt is of legal significance as justifying actions that might otherwise be unlawful, the power can be legally significant in some other ways.

The fact that compliance with a request for official information or personal information held about an individual, if satisfied, would constitute a contempt of the House is a good ground for refusing to provide that information.[161] One obvious circumstance in which these provisions reinforce the House's privileges is in respect of confidential select committee information which is in the hands of a Minister or a government department and which otherwise might be obtainable as official information. Indeed, as far as official information is concerned, the legislation goes further than making the commission of a contempt a good ground for refusal to produce such information. It recognises that a positive obligation to avoid committing contempt can arise, by also providing that nothing in the legislation authorises or permits the making available of official information that would constitute a contempt of the House.[162] In reviewing decisions to withhold official information on the ground of contempt, the Ombudsmen and the Privacy Commissioner may be required to make judgments in accordance with the legislation as to whether a contempt would be committed were the information to be made available.[163]

Similar provisions apply to protect the House against contempt arising in the course of meetings of local authorities and committees of district health boards. In each case it is a good ground for the exclusion of the public from their meetings that admission would be likely to result in disclosure of information which would constitute a contempt of the House.[164]

Even apart from these explicit legislative significances, the fact that an otherwise lawful or unexceptionable decision or action may constitute a contempt can, it is submitted, itself imbue that decision or action with legal significance and may be a governing factor in whether the action can legally be taken or what decision should actually be made. Thus the Human Rights Commission has accepted advice that it should not embark upon an inquiry where to do so would inevitably lead it into committing a contempt of the House (such an inquiry may also have been unlawful on other grounds too).[165] It may also be the case that the fact that a contempt will result would be recognised by the courts as legally justifying other legal positions that are taken, for example, resisting inspection of documents in the course of legal proceedings where they are subject to parliamentary confidentiality, unless the permission of the House or the relevant committee is obtained first.[166]

In such ways (an aspect of comity between the legislative and judicial branches of government) the fact that a contempt of the House has been or may be committed can be significant in determining legal outcomes, without contempt giving rise to a cause of action itself.

---

[161] *Official Information Act* 1982, s.18(c)(ii); *Local Government Official Information and Meetings Act* 1987, s.17(c)(ii); *Privacy Act* 1993, s.29(1)(i).

[162] *Official Information Act* 1982, s.52(1); *Local Government Official Information and Meetings Act* 1987, s.44(1).

[163] See, for example, 2002, PP, A.3, pp.31-2.

[164] *Local Government Official Information and Meetings Act* 1987, s.48(1)(b)(ii); *New Zealand Public Health and Disability Act* 2000, Sch.4, cl.34(b).

[165] "No Commission of Inquiry", Human Rights Commission, 17 October 2001; Opinion of Dr G P Barton QC for Human Rights Commission, 28 September 2001, paras.33-40.

[166] See discussion, 1996-99, AJHR, I.16P, pp.12-4.

CHAPTER 48

PROCEEDINGS IN MATTERS OF PRIVILEGE

RAISING MATTERS OF PRIVILEGE

A complaint of a breach of privilege or of any other type of contempt, or any matter dealing with the privileges of the House, may be raised by a member in one of four different ways—

- with the Speaker
- on motion, following notice having been given in the normal way
- on the floor of the House without notice
- by petition.

These means of raising a matter of privilege are dealt with in turn below.

MATTERS RAISED WITH THE SPEAKER

The most common means of raising a matter of privilege is to raise it with the Speaker. Indeed, if the matter is to have precedence of other business in the House (and it is only if it does have precedence that it is likely to be dealt with at all), a member must raise the matter of privilege with the Speaker first. Until 1979, allegations of breach of privilege or contempt were raised orally in the House and accorded precedence if the Speaker ruled that a prima facie case of breach of privilege or contempt had been established. The Standing Orders were then changed. They now require members wishing to raise matters of privilege through the Speaker to raise them in writing first so that the Speaker can consider and deal with the matter in the first instance off the floor of the House.

A member alleging that a breach of privilege or contempt has occurred may put the allegation into writing and deliver it to the Speaker.[1] A member cannot (except in the special circumstances dealt with below) raise a matter of privilege on the floor of the House.[2] Any allegation must be formulated as precisely as possible, so that any person against whom it is made has a full opportunity to respond to it.[3]

Must be raised at the earliest opportunity

A matter of privilege must be raised with the Speaker at the earliest opportunity, otherwise it cannot be accorded any precedence over other business.[4] What is the earliest opportunity to raise a matter of privilege depends upon the nature of that matter. In general, a member must raise a matter of privilege with the Speaker before the next sitting of the House.[5] However, in the case of a matter involving the proceedings of a select committee a greater leeway than this is accorded. In the latter case it is recognised that it is desirable (though not essential) that a member contemplating raising a matter discuss it with the committee concerned first. The committee can then consider whether it wishes to take any action in regard to the matter. It may, indeed, be able to resolve it satisfactorily without any need for the Speaker's involvement at all.[6]

Consequently, in the case of a matter relating to the proceedings of a select committee, a member has until the commencement of the first sitting of the House following the day of the next meeting of the committee to raise it with the Speaker.[7] The member can in the

---

[1] S.O.392(1).
[2] 1988, Vol.492, p.6460.
[3] S.O.393.
[4] S.O.392(1).
[5] S.O.392(2).
[6] 2002-05, AJHR, I.18B, p.80.
[7] S.O.392(2).

meantime place the matter on the committee's agenda for its consideration. However, the member still retains the right to raise the matter with the Speaker by the next sitting of the House, regardless of the views expressed by the committee on the merits of the matter.

A matter of privilege that has been raised in a previous session but that has lapsed before being dealt with because of the prorogation or dissolution of Parliament cannot be raised again with the Speaker in the next session. Such a matter must, by definition, have already been raised at the earliest possible opportunity, and there cannot be another "earliest opportunity" to raise it.[8] It could be raised again only by giving notice of motion.

A matter arises when it comes to public notice or to the notice of a member, whether or not the member appreciates immediately that a breach of privilege may be involved. So when on 4 July a member raised a matter of privilege concerning a letter dated 25 March, he was held to have raised it at the earliest opportunity, for he had actually received the letter only the previous day.[9] Where a member becomes aware of facts that suggest that a breach of privilege or contempt has occurred but requires further time to establish this, the member may lodge a holding complaint so as to reserve the member's right to raise the matter and follow up later (or not, as the case may be) with fuller particulars.[10] For this purpose the Speaker will allow the matter to remain open for a reasonable period of time.

If a matter is not raised at the earliest opportunity, the Speaker will not certify that a question of privilege is involved.

Informing other members
The member raising a matter of privilege with the Speaker is under an obligation to forward a copy of the letter sent to the Speaker to any other member of Parliament who is implicated in it. This must be done as soon as reasonably practicable after the matter has been raised.[11] The Speaker's office checks that this requirement has been complied with if this is not apparent on the face of the letter sent to the Speaker.[12]

References to matters of privilege
Members are not under any duty to keep confidential a matter that they intend to raise or that they have raised with the Speaker.[13] The Speaker has deprecated the circulation of a letter that had been written to him raising a matter of privilege, but there is nothing to forbid this.[14] On the other hand, a member making public statements about a matter of privilege that has been raised with the Speaker and circulating copies of the letter would not be protected against any liability in defamation by the absolute privilege attaching to proceedings in Parliament.[15]

It is not in order to refer in the House to the intention to raise a matter of privilege or to refer to a matter that has already been raised with the Speaker.[16]

Speaker's role
The Speaker is required to consider the nature of the matter that has been raised and to determine whether a question of privilege is involved.[17] Formerly, the Speaker was required to rule whether a prima facie case of breach of privilege or contempt had been made out. This was changed in 1979. The change was not intended to alter the nature of

---

8   Ruling of the Speaker on a matter of privilege, 23
      August 1984.
9   1912, Vol.158, pp.242-6.
10   2001, Vol.592, p.9618.
11   S.O.395.
12   1996-99, AJHR, I.15C, p.10.

13   2004, Vol.615, p.10998.
14   1988, Vol.489, pp.4436-7; 1987-90, AJHR, I.15E.
15   1987-90, AJHR, I.18B, para.59; 1988, Vol.489,
      p.4436; 2003, Vol.609, p.6543.
16   1986, Vol.473, p.3805.
17   S.O.394(1).

the decision that must be made by the Speaker. The Standing Orders Committee (which considered the procedure for raising matters of privilege and recommended changes) felt that ruling that a prima facie case existed gave an unwarranted impression that the Speaker thought that a breach of privilege or contempt had actually been committed, and that a verbal change to a more neutral phrase such as that a question of privilege was involved was, therefore, desirable.[18] It is also the case that not all matters of privilege involve allegations that a breach of privilege or contempt has occurred – for example, a matter of privilege may relate to whether a member is qualified to sit in the House without any suggestion of a breach of privilege.

The Speaker is there to sort the wheat from the chaff, and to consider, on the evidence presented, whether the facts alleged could, if true, amount to a breach of privilege or contempt of the House or whether they do otherwise raise a matter seriously affecting the privileges of the House.

Where a matter of privilege involves the Speaker personally, Speakers have delegated the responsibility for ruling on it to the Deputy Speaker.[19]

Consideration by the Speaker

The Speaker is a judge of law. The Speaker does not inquire into the validity of evidence presented, and does not hold a full inquiry into the matter that is raised. These are the functions of the committee appointed to consider questions of privilege – the Privileges Committee.[20] The Speaker does appraise any evidence that is submitted with a complaint to determine whether it points to a reasonable, not a remote, possibility that a breach of privilege or contempt has occurred.[21]

Members affected by a matter of privilege may make representations to the Speaker about it.[22] Indeed, it is expected that any members who are implicated in a complaint of breach of privilege or contempt will wish to put their points of view forward for the Speaker's consideration. But it is incumbent on members to take the initiative in making such comments and the Speaker will delay making a decision on a matter of privilege only for a reasonable time in order to give an opportunity for this to occur. The Speaker has rejected a complaint from a member that he was not given sufficient time to respond when the Speaker waited one week before ruling and the member had twice been reminded by the Speaker's office that it was in his interest to comment.[23]

Where a matter of privilege relates to the proceedings of a select committee, the Speaker may have the benefit of the committee's views in the material forwarded by the member raising the matter. If not – either because the member has not raised it with the committee or has not communicated its views to the Speaker – the Speaker will invariably seek comment from the committee before ruling on it.[24]

Where a matter of privilege involves the conduct of a person outside the House, there is no obligation on the member raising it to inform that person, nor is there any obligation on the Speaker to give that person an opportunity to comment. However, if the person is aware that a matter of privilege is to be raised with the Speaker (because the member has informed the person or the member has made a public statement to that effect), any comments on the matter that the person wishes to make will be received and considered by the Speaker in determining the matter.

---

18 1979, AJHR, I.14, p.16.
19 1976, Vol.404, p.1552; 1987, Vol.479, p.7974; 1998, Vol.566, p.6688.
20 1980, Vol.433, p.3761.
21 *Ibid.*, pp.3673, 3761.
22 1989, Vol.500, p.12150; 2000, Vol.589, p.7499.
23 2000, Vol.589, p.7499.
24 2002, Vol.598, p.14743.

Determination by the Speaker

The Speaker determines whether, on the facts as alleged and the comments on those facts made by members or a committee, a breach of privilege or contempt could have occurred or another matter relating to the privileges of the House has arisen, having regard to the rules and precedents that exist describing the privileges of the House. The House cannot create new privileges, but original factual situations arise that may fall within already established categories of privilege or contempt. Initially, therefore, it falls to the Speaker to decide whether the matter that is the subject of complaint relates to one of the House's established privileges at all. If it does not, the Speaker will rule that no question of privilege is involved. In cases of genuine doubt and importance, the Speaker will allow the matter to proceed so that the House and the Privileges Committee can consider it in detail.

A factor that the Speaker is enjoined to consider in ruling on matters of privilege is the degree of seriousness of the matter that has been raised. The Standing Orders require that the Speaker should take account of the importance of the matter and not find that a question of privilege is involved if it is technical or trivial and does not warrant further attention.[25] Only if the conduct complained of can genuinely be regarded as tending to impede or obstruct the House in the discharge of its duties or is otherwise of some moment should the House bother to deal with it as a question of privilege.[26]

This does not mean that all matters of privilege which are trivial in themselves will be automatically rejected by the Speaker, for an incident, although unimportant in itself, may be important as a matter of principle. But it does require the Speaker to exercise judgment on the desirability of the matter proceeding further, having regard to its intrinsic worth. Thus, where a clear contempt had occurred by reason of the premature disclosure of select committee proceedings, the Speaker exercised his discretion to find that no question of privilege was involved since the chief executive of the department had already apologised and there was no reason to pursue the matter.[27] If there is no reason for the House to take corrective action because a matter has been resolved, the Speaker may hold that no question of privilege is involved even though it may be clear that a contempt has occurred.[28]

When the Speaker determines that no question of privilege is involved

If the Speaker considers that no question of privilege is involved, the Speaker makes this determination known by informing the member who raised the matter of the decision. This is done in writing and is copied to any other member involved. That is the end of the matter as far as the Speaker is concerned.[29] The member may still try to raise the matter by giving notice in the House, but no precedence of other business will be accorded to it. It is the Speaker's usual practice not to give reasons for determining that no question of privilege is involved, but merely to inform the member of the decision. In some circumstances, such as if the decision called for elucidation in some way, the Speaker may elaborate on the determination in the letter to the member, but this has been done only rarely.

If the member has publicly released details of the complaint to the Speaker, and these involve persons outside the House, those persons are also advised by the Speaker of the determination.[30] Otherwise, there would be no guarantee that persons against whom a

---

[25]   S.O.394(2), (3).
[26]   1982, AJHR, I.6, pp.17-8.
[27]   1988, Vol.488, pp.3396-7.

[28]   2001, Vol.590, p.7912.
[29]   1980, Vol.433, pp.3672-3.
[30]   2003, Vol.609, p.6543.

complaint had been lodged, and that had been publicly referred to, would be advised that the complaint had been dismissed.

As well as advising the member that no question of privilege is involved, the Speaker also has the authority to rule in the House if an important point is involved in the decision.[31] There have been a number of instances of Speakers having given guidance to members on the procedure to be followed in raising matters of privilege and on the substantive content of the type of privilege or contempt raised, even though determining that no question of privilege is involved in the instant case.[32]

When the Speaker determines that a question of privilege is involved

The Speaker's determination that a question of privilege is involved in the complaint is the authorisation for it to proceed to a full hearing before the Privileges Committee. For this purpose the Speaker reports the matter to the House at the first opportunity.[33]

Any member who is involved in a question of privilege must be informed by the Speaker that the Speaker intends to report the matter to the House before the report is made.[34] The member thus has an opportunity to be present in the Chamber when the Speaker reports and to respond to any immediate public comment on the ruling.

Normally, the Speaker reports to the House on a question of privilege in a ruling given immediately after prayers. There is no particular form this report must take but, in response to a request from the Privileges Committee, the Speaker attempts to express the ruling in terms that are sufficient to make clear the nature of any breach of privilege or contempt that is alleged.[35]

Once the Speaker has ruled that a question of privilege is involved, the matter automatically stands referred to the Privileges Committee.[36] There is no motion and no debate in respect of the matter.

MATTERS OF PRIVILEGE RAISED BY NOTICE OF MOTION

A member does not have to raise a matter of privilege with the Speaker. If it is wished that such a matter be given precedence of other business, the only way this can be achieved is by raising it first with the Speaker, when the procedures already discussed come into play. But a member can, if he or she wishes, give a notice of motion in the ordinary form raising a matter of privilege.[37] This may be done whether or not the member has already raised the matter with the Speaker and received a ruling that no question of privilege is involved. This method is the only way of reviving a question of privilege that lapsed in the previous session. A notice of motion alleging a breach of privilege or a contempt is not treated in any special way (at one time such notices were given precedence of other notices), and under the House's current procedures for dealing with notices is most unlikely to be dealt with at all. Such a notice must set out clearly what constitutes the breach and cannot contain any further material other than the bare charge or allegation that the member is making.[38]

Such a notice may seek to refer a matter to the Privileges Committee for inquiry or it may declare certain conduct to be a breach of privilege or contempt without any further inquiry. For the House to act in this way without a Privileges Committee hearing would be highly unusual, though the House of Commons has declared a former member's conduct to have been a contempt[39] and the House of Representatives has censured a member for remarks he uttered,[40] both without formal hearings.

31	1986, Vol.476, p.5961.	36	S.O.397.
32	See, for example, 2003, Vol.606, pp.3551-2.	37	1982, Vol.447, p.3981.
33	S.O.396(1).	38	1929, Vol.222, p.663.
34	S.O.396(2).	39	*May*, p.132.
35	1981, AJHR, I.6, p.3.	40	2000, Vol.585, p.3457.

MATTERS OF PRIVILEGE RAISED WITHOUT NOTICE

In one circumstance where a matter of privilege occurs in the House, it can be raised without notice. This is where the conduct of strangers present gives rise to a matter of privilege, for example, as a result of misconduct on their part.[41] In these circumstances the Speaker has discretion to deal with the matter in such a way as the Speaker determines and any debate in progress may be interrupted for this purpose.[42]

MATTERS OF PRIVILEGE RAISED BY MEANS OF PETITIONS

A petition was the recognised means of seeking authority to use extracts from debates or other reports or proceedings of the House in court. (See Chapter 46.) This form of petition is now obsolete as the House has granted a general authority to refer to its proceedings before a court.[43]

A petition alleging that a contempt has been committed has been received and allocated to the Privileges Committee.[44]

PRIVILEGES COMMITTEE

The select committee at the centre of determining matters relating to the privileges of the House is known as the Privileges Committee.

The Privileges Committee is established by the House at the commencement of each Parliament. Its brief is to consider and report to the House on any matters referred to it relating to or concerning parliamentary privilege.[45] The committee does not have the power to initiate inquiries itself; it works solely on the basis of issues referred to it by the House.

The committee's membership often includes senior members such as the Prime Minister, the Leader of the Opposition and the Leader of the House. The member who raised a matter of privilege with the Speaker alleging a breach of privilege or contempt may not serve on the committee while it is considering that complaint.[46] This does not preclude a member who raised a matter of privilege not involving an allegation of breach of privilege or contempt from serving on the committee inquiring into the matter. It is usually (though not invariably) chaired by the Attorney-General.[47] Its reports to the House carry great weight. The Standing Orders Committee has recommended that the committee's membership should remain fixed throughout any particular inquiry so that only those members who have heard the evidence on a complaint should deliberate on it.[48]

Powers

The Privileges Committee possesses the same powers and is subject to most of the same procedural rules as other select committees. However, in addition it has conferred upon it the inherent power to send for persons, papers and records.[49] This means that the committee does not have to apply to the Speaker and secure the Speaker's agreement to that power being exercised, as other committees must do.

The committee hears evidence in public. However, the nature of the task it has to perform inevitably results in it proceeding in a manner somewhat different from other committees. The committee is exempt from the prohibition applying to other committees that they may not enquire into, and make findings in respect of, the private conduct of members.[50] Indeed, the nature of its tasks often call upon it to do just that. The committee is often concerned with allegations made against members and other persons that they have

---

[41]   S.O.392(3).
[42]   S.O.133(b).
[43]   S.O.401.
[44]   1996-99, JIIR, Schedule of petitions presented, p.1367.
[45]   S.O.391(1).
[46]   S.O.398.
[47]   1996-99, AJHR, I.15C, p.10; 1998, Vol.567, p.8364.
[48]   1979, AJHR, I.14, p.16.
[49]   S.O.391(?).
[50]   S.O.201.

breached privilege or committed a contempt or, if the allegation is not specifically directed against an individual or individuals, that a breach of privilege or a contempt has occurred and that, by implication, the perpetrator ought to be identified and punished. In these circumstances the committee is called upon to conduct an inquest and to make findings, often adverse findings, against members and others. Therefore, it endeavours to act and to conduct its proceedings in accordance with normal judicial principles, including ruling on the standard of proof required to establish whether a contempt has been committed.[51]

Persons appearing before the Privileges Committee have long been permitted to have the assistance of their own counsel if they wish, well before this was a requirement of the Standing Orders.[52] Indeed, it is the practice for the committee to ask witnesses appearing before it whether they wish to be assisted by counsel, so that the matter is raised by the committee and the witness does not, by default, forego the opportunity to be so assisted. Counsel has been permitted to cross-examine other witnesses appearing before the committee.[53]

Scope of inquiry

The nature of an inquiry by the Privileges Committee has been described as *sui generis*.[54] Its proceedings do not fall into any general category of inquiries.

Once a matter of privilege has been referred to it, it is for the Privileges Committee to decide how deeply to investigate the matter and how widely to pursue possible offenders. In particular, once it is seised of a question of privilege, it does not regard itself as being confined to considering only issues referred to by the Speaker in making the ruling. The committee is charged with investigating the facts and reporting to the House if, in its opinion, a breach of privilege or contempt has been committed or if some other matter referred to it affects the privileges of the House. In this regard it is not limited by the precise formulation of any allegation of breach of privilege or contempt made by the Speaker in ruling on the matter.[55] However, before broadening an investigation into a question of privilege beyond the scope initially suggested in the Speaker's ruling, the committee must give notice to any member thereby affected.[56]

Findings

In making a finding as to whether a breach of privilege or contempt has occurred, the committee is bound by the same rules of natural justice as is any other committee making findings with a potential to reflect on reputation, and must acquaint any person whose reputation may be seriously damaged with its provisional findings and give that person an opportunity to comment.[57] The Privileges Committee, in addition, has found it necessary to establish the standard of proof necessary for an adverse finding on a question of privilege. In general, the committee has accepted that the civil law standard of proof on a balance of probabilities is appropriate when it is making decisions on matters of fact or drawing inferences from matters of fact. But in making findings of breach of privilege or contempt, the committee must consider the totality of the evidence and then ask itself if it is satisfied on the basis of compelling evidence that a breach of privilege or contempt has occurred. Only if it is should it make such a finding.[58]

Report

The committee presents reports on the questions of privilege referred to it.

51   1980, AJHR, I.6, pp.7-8.
52   See, for example, 1912, AJHR, I.7, p.3.
53   1980, AJHR, I.6, p.4.
54   *Dentice v Valuers Board* [1992] 1 NZLR 720 at 724.
55   1982, AJHR, I.6, p.8; 1996-99, AJHR, I.15A, pp.3-4.
56   1996-99, AJHR, I.15A, p.4.
57   S.O.247(1).
58   1996-99, AJHR, I.15A, p.5.

The committee has not shown itself averse to commenting on aspects of procedure in the House and the administrative arrangements for providing services to members where these subjects have arisen during the course of its inquiries.[59] Although it is the House that finally decides if a breach of privilege or contempt has been committed and, if so, whether any punishment should be inflicted, the most important determinant of the final outcome of a complaint of breach of privilege or contempt is the finding of the Privileges Committee. For this reason the committee becomes actively involved in working out the ultimate solution to the complaint – for example, by corresponding with and discussing a suitable apology with persons it considers to be in contempt and recommending punishments to the House where necessary.

The committee does not confine itself to a factual report to the House on the subject of the complaint, which it is then up to the House to devise means of acting on. It aims to present comprehensive findings and recommendations that the House can deal with in one bite.

Consideration of report

A report from the Privileges Committee is set down for consideration as general business.[60] This ensures that it has a priority for consideration by the House that is not accorded to any other type of select committee report. Consideration of a report from the Privileges Committee is taken on the sitting day following its presentation, after questions and any urgent or general debate.[61]

The debate on the committee's report takes place on a motion moved by the chairperson of the Privileges Committee. This may be a motion to take note of the report (the normal motion on the consideration of any select committee report) but, if the report contains recommendations (as it often will), the chairperson's motion may instead reflect those recommendations.[62] The debate is not subject to any overall time limit prescribed by the Standing Orders. Each member may speak for up to 10 minutes.

OUTCOME OF QUESTION OF PRIVILEGE

There are a number of potential outcomes from a question of privilege without the matter necessarily involving a finding that a contempt of the House has been committed and that the House will punish the contempt. The House's privileges relate to its legal position generally and the House may need to consider these in other contexts than just contempt.

Thus the outcome of a question of privilege may be that the House decides to become involved in legal proceedings so as to protect its view of its privileges or so that consideration of the effect of its privileges on a matter before a court is not overlooked.[63] On the other hand, consideration of a question of privilege may be a means for the House to form a view about the status of a member or of proceedings before Parliament. Thus, on a question of privilege, the House has decided whether a person has been duly returned as a member of Parliament[64] and whether a member's seat has been vacated by resignation or other disqualification.[65]

Most questions of privilege, however, do relate to allegations of contempt by members or by persons outside the House. Consequently, a finding that a contempt has been committed raises the question of what the House should do in response – whether it should invoke its power to punish for contempt.

---

59   1982, AJHR, I.6, pp.7-9.
60   S.O.251(1)(a).
61   S.O.63(1).
62   S.O.252.

63   1993-96, AJHR, I.15B; 1999-2002, AJHR, I.17A.
64   PD 1856-58, pp.559-60.
65   1996-99, AJHR, I.15B; 2002-05, AJHR, I.17C.

PUNISHMENTS

If it finds that a contempt has occurred, the House must decide whether to take any action to punish individuals who have been identified as having transgressed against it, or whether the offence is not worth further notice. If the House does decide to take the matter further, there are a number of options open to it regarding the types of punishment it may inflict or the means it may employ to express its displeasure. As well as using these means to "punish" an offender for contempt, the House may also use them to enforce its privileges by coercing someone to do something it wishes to be done – such as committing that person into the custody of the Serjeant-at-Arms so that he or she may be brought to give evidence before a committee. When the House uses its powers in this way, it is not "punishing" anyone for past transgressions, it is merely ensuring that no transgression – such as a failure to testify after being required to do so by the House – can occur. If the person concerned escaped from the Serjeant's custody in these circumstances, then a contempt would have been committed and the person concerned would be liable to be punished for contempt. However, the House may use its powers to secure compliance with its orders before there has been any disobedience to them, as well as inflict punishment for a contempt that has already occurred. Distinguishing between punishing for disobedience and taking action to induce compliance can be difficult.[66] But it is not necessarily relevant to make this distinction for a House enjoying by statute the privileges possessed by the House of Commons in 1865.

The punishments which the House may decide to inflict must be seen against the background of the human rights and fundamental freedoms confirmed by the *New Zealand Bill of Rights Act* 1990. Those civil rights that would seem to be particularly relevant in respect of punishment for contempt are: protection against unreasonable search or seizure,[67] protection against arbitrary arrest or detention,[68] and minimum standards of conduct to be observed in respect of a person under arrest or in detention.[69] In seeking to project its will beyond the internal proceedings of the House, the House must ensure that it acts in a way that is consistent with these rights.

Imprisonment

The ultimate power possessed by the House to enforce or vindicate its privileges is the power to imprison. This power has been used by the House of Commons on literally hundreds of occasions. It has been claimed that there were a "little less than a thousand" commitments between 1547 and 1810.[70] Imprisonment has never been resorted to by the House of Representatives[71] (or by the Legislative Council, which also possessed the power to imprison), although a proposal was made and debated in the House in 1896 that the President of the Bank of New Zealand, who had refused to answer certain questions put to him by a select committee, be imprisoned. The proposal was defeated and a fine imposed on the president instead.[72] A further proposal – that he be committed into the custody of the Serjeant-at-Arms until the fine was paid – was dropped.[73]

The power of the House of Commons to imprison persons by committing them into the custody of the Serjeant-at-Arms or any other person was well recognised by 1 January 1865, the date on which the House of Representatives acquired privileges similar to those enjoyed by the Commons in the United Kingdom.[74] In 1893, when all common law

---

[66] *Egan v Willis* (1998) 195 CLR 424 at 455 (per Gaudron, Gummow and Hayne JJ).

[67] *New Zealand Bill of Rights Act* 1990, s.21.

[68] *Ibid.*, s.22.

[69] *Ibid.*, s.23.

[70] Wittke, *The History of English Parliamentary Privilege*, p.137.

[71] *Littlejohn*, p.172.

[72] 1896, Vol.93, pp.327-34.

[73] *Ibid.*, p.334.

[74] *May*, pp.156-60.

crimes were abolished in New Zealand, it was specifically enacted that such abolition did not limit or affect the House's power to punish for contempt.[75]

The authority of the House to punish for contempt by imprisonment is not limited or affected by the courts' jurisdiction to grant a writ of habeas corpus in the case of an unlawful detention of any person.[76]

When Parliament is prorogued or dissolved, bringing the session to an end, any person then held in custody is automatically discharged.[77] The House cannot imprison a person beyond the session in which the committal was ordered.[78] This does not, however, prevent the House ordering that person's rearrest in the following session if it feels so inclined.[79]

Speaker's warrant

The commitment of any person into custody by order of the House is made under a warrant issued by the Speaker. There can be no arrest without warrant in New Zealand except with express statutory authority.[80] As there is no express statutory authority to arrest without warrant for breach of privilege or contempt, the Speaker's warrant is essential for a person to be taken into custody by order of the House.

There is no particular form that the Speaker's warrant must take. Warrants issued in other jurisdictions have merely stated that the person named in it has been found guilty of a contempt and is committed into custody for that reason, without stating the facts on which the finding of contempt is based.[81] On the other hand, the warrant may go on to set out, with some particularity, why the person is being arrested. The extent to which the courts are able to review warrants on the ground that they do not disclose any breach of a known privilege or that they are otherwise irregular has been judicially considered in a number of cases.

In the leading case on the committal by order of a legislature, the Australian High Court said that a court may examine the warrant if it specifies a ground of commitment in order to determine whether that ground is sufficient in law to amount to a breach of privilege, but if the ground appears to be consistent with a breach of an acknowledged privilege, that is conclusive. The court would not go behind the warrant even if it was stated in general terms.[82] On the other hand, the Indian Supreme Court (by majority) has advised that a general warrant committee for contempt could be inquired into to ascertain if there were grounds for that committal.[83] It may be too, that the civil right to be secure against unreasonable search and seizure[84] now imports a requirement for the Speaker's warrant to set out with sufficient particularity the grounds on which the arrest has been ordered. Failure to do so may itself be unreasonable and so vitiate the warrant.

Fine

Much doubt has been expressed about the power of the House to exact fines. This depends upon whether such a power was "held, enjoyed and exercised" by the House of Commons on 1 January 1865.[85] In fact, the House of Commons has not, since 1666, exercised the power it undoubtedly once had to fine, and the leading authority on the powers of the Commons does not explicitly claim this power as one currently enjoyed by that

---

[75] See now *Crimes Act* 1961, s.9(a), proviso.

[76] *Habeas Corpus Act* 2001, s.4(2).

[77] 1888, Vol.63, p.37.

[78] *Shri Susant Kumar Chand v Orissa Legislative Assembly* AIR 1973 Orissa 111.

[79] *Pandit MSM Sharma v Shri Sri Krishna Singh* AIR 1959 Supreme Court 395.

[80] *Crimes Act* 1961, s.315(1).

[81] *Speaker of the Legislative Assembly of Victoria v Glass* (1871) LR 3 PC 560.

[82] *R v Richards; ex parte Fitzpatrick and Brown* (1955) 92 CLR 157 at 162.

[83] *Special Reference No 1 of 1964 (Keshav Singh's case)* AIR 1965 Supreme Court 745.

[84] *New Zealand Bill of Rights Act* 1990, s.21.

[85] *Legislature Act* 1908, s.242(1).

legislature.[86]   Furthermore, in 1967 and in 1977 House of Commons' select committees recommended that legislation should be introduced to enable that House to impose fines,[87] thus implying that the power once held may have been lost.

The position in New Zealand is not as clear-cut as this may suggest.   It has been argued that "exercised" must be understood in the sense of "exercisable", and that on 1 January 1865 the power to fine was exercisable by the House of Commons even though it had not actually been exercised for 199 years.[88]   If a power is not used, it is not necessarily forfeited.   The House of Commons allowed its power of impeachment to fall into disuse for 170 years between 1450 and 1620 before reviving it.   There has not been a prosecution for impeachment since 1806 (though there was an attempt to invoke it in 1848) and the leading authority on the House of Commons regards it as having fallen into disuse or having become obsolete with the development of responsible government.[89]   However, it has never been formally abolished and an attempt was made in 2004 to revive it.[90] The same is true of the power of the Commons to suspend its members.   For nearly two centuries this form of punishment had not been imposed until the Speaker ruled in 1877 that it was still available to be used against a member.[91]

The contemporary edition of *Erskine May* in 1865 suggested that the Commons had the power to fine,[92] and it is against the position at that time that the House of Representatives' power to fine must be tested, whatever view of its powers the House of Commons takes today.   Another indication of contemporary thinking on the subject was the section of the *New Zealand Constitution Act* 1852 (UK) that required the House to draw up standing rules and orders, but that enjoined it not to subject any person who was not a member of Parliament to any "pain, penalty or forfeiture",[93] words that could clearly encompass fines.   The words of the *New Zealand Constitution Act* suggest that the House either had, or its draftsmen in 1852 believed that it had, power to fine its own members, and would, but for the express provision to the contrary, have had power to fine other persons too.   Acting on this hint the House, by its Standing Orders, made provision for fines to be imposed on members for breaches of discipline.   These remained in force until 1951 and were used to fine members on two occasions.[94]

That provision of the *New Zealand Constitution Act* was repealed in 1865 when the House acquired the wider powers of the House of Commons, and from that time on the House regarded itself as being free to fine strangers as well as members as a punishment for contempt.   Strangers have been fined on four occasions: the President of the Bank of New Zealand was fined in 1896 for refusing to answer questions before a select committee relating to customers' accounts;[95]   a member of the Parliamentary Press Gallery was fined in 1901 for publishing evidence given to a select committee before the committee had reported to the House;[96]   a newspaper was fined in 1903 for publishing select committee papers before the committee had reported to the House;   and its representative in the Press Gallery was fined for refusing to reveal the person from whom he had obtained the papers.[97]

In view of the conflicting opinions held on the existence of the power, it is doubtful whether the House today would ever seek to impose a fine.[98]   A few years after the last of

[86]   *May*, p.161.

[87]   HC 34 (1966-67), para.197;   HC 417 (1976-77), para.15.

[88]   *Littlejohn*, pp.46-54.

[89]   *May*, p.73.

[90]   See, "A Case to Answer.   A first report on the potential impeachment of the Prime Minister for High Crimes and Misdemeanours in relation to the invasion of Iraq.", produced for Adam Price MP, August 2004.

[91]   *May*, p.164f.

[92]   *Littlejohn*, pp.48-9.

[93]   *New Zealand Constitution Act* 1852 (UK), s.52.

[94]   1877, Vol.26, pp.98-103;   1881, Vol.40, pp.232-44.

[95]   1896, Vol.93, p.336.

[96]   1901, JHR, p.154.

[97]   1903, Vol.125, pp.693-4.

[98]   *Littlejohn*, p.190.

these fine cases, it was said by a Speaker that the House still had the power to fine,[99] but by 1929 a Standing Orders Committee was recommending that the power of the House to inflict fines and otherwise safeguard its privileges be supplemented by statute, thus suggesting that some doubts on this score had been expressed by that time.[100] Such a proposal has been repeated by a later Standing Orders Committee.[101] In Australia an express power to fine has been included in legislation.[102]

Censure

The House may consider that the conduct of a member or other person is deserving of its formal censure or rebuke, and may express its views accordingly. In the House of Commons the practice is for a formal reprimand or admonition to be made personally by the Speaker on behalf of the House, with the offender standing in his or her place in the Chamber, if he or she is a member, or at the bar of the House, if not. In New Zealand the Speaker has admonished a person at the bar of the House on a question of privilege,[103] but it has not generally been the practice for a rebuke to be administered in such a formal manner. The House, where it has felt that a member's conduct should be censured, has contented itself with coming to a formal resolution to that effect and leaving the matter at that. On at least two occasions members have been censured (on both occasions for criticising the Speaker) by the House adopting recommendations to censure them contained in Privileges Committee reports.[104] The House has also resolved to censure a member for remarks that he made without referring the matter first for inquiry by the Privileges Committee.[105]

Prosecution at law

Certain breaches of privilege or contempts may have wider significance than as breaches of parliamentary law; they may also be criminal offences. In fact, the House has quite often left actions that it could have treated as contempts to be dealt with by the courts in prosecutions for an offence. This has been the case with most disturbances in the public galleries that have resulted in arrests and charges of trespass or breach of the peace. The fact that a person has been charged with a criminal offence in respect of such an incident does not preclude the House taking its own proceedings against that person on the ground that the incident also constitutes a contempt, but usually the House has left matters of a criminal nature to be dealt with solely in the forum of a court.

Where a matter is raised as a question of privilege and, after considering it, the House concludes that a criminal offence may have been committed, it may (in addition, if it wishes, to punishing any contempt) direct that the offender be prosecuted in the courts for the offence. Such a prosecution is undertaken by the Attorney-General. In the only case in which such action was taken in New Zealand, the Attorney-General (who was the member who had been accused of improper conduct, so leading to the matter being raised in the first place) was directed by the House "to prosecute according to law for a libel on a member of this House in his place in Parliament".[106] The prosecution failed.

Impeachment

One of the powers possessed by the House of Commons in 1865 (though it had not been exercised since 1806) was the power to impeach. Impeachment was a prosecution by the

---

99   1911, Vol.156, p.898.
100   1929, AJHR, I.18.
101   1987-90, AJHR, I.18B, para.30.
102   *Parliamentary Privileges Act* 1987 (Australia), s.7;
      Harris, *House of Representatives Practice*, p.740.

103   1872, Vol.13, p.201.
104   1975, AJHR, I.6, adopted 1975, JHR, pp.203-6;
      1982, AJHR, I.6, adopted 1982, JHR, p.393-4.
105   2000, Vol.585, p.3457.
106   1877, JHR, pp.63-6.

House of Commons of a person (often a Minister who had fallen from favour) for "high crimes and misdemeanours". The trial took place before the House of Lords.

There is nothing in the *New Zealand Constitution Act* 1852 (UK) to suggest that this power had ever devolved on to the House of Representatives. Nor did the acquisition of the House of Commons' powers and privileges in 1865 alter this. The House of Commons' power was to accuse a person of high crimes and misdemeanours before the upper House, the House of Lords. It was not a power to convict a person. The Legislative Council in New Zealand did not enjoy any powers or privileges equivalent to those of the House of Lords; in fact, its privileges were also equated to those of the House of Commons.[107] In these circumstances there was no legislative chamber in New Zealand empowered to conduct a trial on impeachment. The proceeding could have no application in New Zealand. The abolition of all common law crimes in 1893[108] confirms the non-applicability of impeachment to New Zealand.

Suspension from the House

By its nature this is a punishment applicable only to members of the House.

The Standing Orders prescribe procedures whereby members may be suspended from the service of the House for breaches of order.[109] But the House may also suspend a member for contempt as a quite distinct exercise of its power of suspension from the summary procedure employed to deal with breaches of order.[110] The fact that the House utilises its procedures concerned with breaches of order does not mean that a member may not also be proceeded against for contempt if the member's conduct justifies it. But in those circumstances any earlier punishment inflicted by the House will be taken into account when considering what action to take over the contempt.[111]

Three members have been suspended from the service of the House for contempt after being found to have made remarks reflecting gravely on the conduct of Speakers in their capacity as Speaker. The Privileges Committee recommended that the members be suspended for varying periods, and those recommendations were adopted by the House.[112]

The rights forfeited by a member suspended under the disciplinary procedures of the Standing Orders are set out in the Standing Orders themselves.[113] (See Chapter 11.) These Standing Orders provisions do not apply in respect of a member suspended for contempt, but they may be taken to indicate, by analogy, the disabilities suffered by a suspended member. Such a member cannot enter the Chamber or voting lobbies, or any other part of the building from which the House specifically excludes the member. Nor can the member serve on or attend a meeting of a select committee or lodge questions or notices of motion.

Expulsion

One of the powers the House of Commons may employ in relation to its members is to expel them from membership of the House, with the result that the member's seat thereby becomes vacant. (Expulsion does not disqualify a member from being re-elected at the ensuing by-election.) There is no instance of expulsion occurring in New Zealand. Before the *Parliamentary Privileges Act* 1865 was passed, the House, on one occasion, refrained from proceeding with a motion to expel a member on the ground that it was

---

[107] *Parliamentary Privileges Act* 1865, s.4.
[108] *Criminal Code Act* 1893, s.5 (now *Crimes Act* 1961, s.9).
[109] S.Os 85 to 91.
[110] S.O.92.

[111] 1986-87, AJHR, I.15.
[112] 1976, JHR, pp.267-8, 655; 1987, Vol.480, pp.9169-82; 1998, Vol.567, pp.8358-81.
[113] S.O.91.

doubtful if the House possessed the power to expel.[114] With the acquisition of the House of Commons' privileges as at 1 January 1865, the legal situation changed. Even so, in 1877 the Speaker denied that the House had power to declare the seat of a member to be vacant: "the utmost extent to which the House can go, and this is very widely different from declaring a seat to be vacant, is to expel the member from its presence"[115] – that is, to suspend the member. The list set out in the *Electoral Act* 1993 of the events that cause a seat to become vacant does not include expulsion from the House.[116] However, this is not in itself a conclusive factor since the power to expel is seen as a self-protective power rather than a disqualification.[117]

In other jurisdictions with a link to the House of Commons' privileges it seems to be accepted that the power to expel a member still obtains by virtue of that link. Thus, in New South Wales it has been held that the legislature has inherent power to expel a member, this being seen as a self-protective power rather than a punishment.[118] The Australian House of Representatives has also expelled a member, though this power has now been expressly abolished by legislation.[119] The Canadian House of Commons still possesses the power to expel in reliance on an equivalent statutory link with the United Kingdom House of Commons' privileges. It may expel for any conduct it deems unbecoming for the character of a member. It has used the power on four occasions.[120] It has been held in Canada that the power to expel a member (both as a means of discipline and as a means to remove an unfit member from the legislature) is an undoubted privilege of the House.[121] Furthermore, the power of expulsion does not conflict with the electoral rights guaranteed under the Canadian equivalent of the *New Zealand Bill of Rights Act* since these are concerned with the qualification to be a member of Parliament rather than with the imposition of a restriction on a sitting member.[122] In India, expulsion in reliance on a similar link with the privileges of the House of Commons has been upheld as in the nature of a disciplinary control over members. The power could be used to expel for misconduct outside as well as inside the House.[123]

The Standing Orders Committee has recommended that any power to expel be abolished in New Zealand.[124]

Exclusion from the precincts

The Crown, as legal owner, permits the House to exercise control over the Parliament buildings and grounds. This control is vested in the Speaker.[125] But the House may, if it wishes, make orders relating to the presence of strangers in the galleries of the Chamber or anywhere else within the Parliament buildings. The power of the House to exclude strangers at any time from its presence (that is, from the galleries) is an aspect of its freedom of speech, and it has been held that control over access to the premises that it occupies is a necessary adjunct to the proper functioning of a legislature.[126]

In 1981, following an incident in the galleries at the beginning of a sitting, the House adopted a report from the Privileges Committee recommending that everyone who could be identified as having participated in the incident should be excluded from the precincts

---

[114] PD 1854-55, p.339.

[115] 1877, Vol.26, p.341.

[116] *Electoral Act* 1993, s.55(1).

[117] *Yeshwant Rao Meghawale v Madhya Pradesh Legislative Assembly* AIR 1967 Madhya Pradesh 95; *Anbazhagen v The Secretary, Tamil Nadu Legislative Assembly* AIR 1988 Madras 275.

[118] *Armstrong v Budd and Stevenson* (1969) 71 SR (NSW) 368 (doubted by McHugh J in *Egan v Willis* (1998) 195 CLR 424 at 479).

[119] Harris, *House of Representatives Practice*, pp.155 and 743.

[120] Marleau and Montpetit, *House of Commons Procedure and Practice*, pp.101 and 206.

[121] *Harvey v New Brunswick (Attorney-General)* (1996) 137 DLR (4th) 142.

[122] *MacLean v Attorney-General of Nova Scotia* (1987) 35 DLR (4th) 306.

[123] *Anbazhagen v The Secretary, Tamil Nadu Legislative Assembly* AIR 1988 Madras 275.

[124] 1987-90, AJHR, I.18B, para.31.

[125] *Parliamentary Service Act* 2000, ss.23 and 26.

[126] *Zündel v Boudria* [2000] 46 OR (3rd) 410.

of the House for 12 months.[127] The Speaker, in enforcing this order on behalf of the House, decided that the areas of the Parliament buildings from which the persons concerned were to be excluded were the public areas of the buildings and the areas used by members generally. The exclusion did not apply to rooms or suites allocated for the personal use of members or Ministers, or to the use of otherwise prohibited areas for transit in order to visit a member as an invited guest.

In another case, involving the director of a courier company refusing to answer questions before the Privileges Committee, the House ordered that courier companies with which he was associated be banned from making deliveries to the parliamentary complex.[128] The Speaker implemented this order by issuing instructions to that effect.[129]

Exclusion from the Parliamentary Press Gallery
Membership of the Parliamentary Press Gallery carries with it special responsibilities. Journalists who commit a contempt of the House are liable to have their memberships terminated or downgraded. One journalist had his status as a full member reduced to that of an associate member and his privilege of using Bellamy's withdrawn for disclosing confidential select committee materials.[130]

Apology
Most findings of contempt end with the offender tendering an apology, which the House accepts. In many cases the apology or expression of regret is tendered to the Privileges Committee during its investigation of the question of privilege. The absence of an expression of regret by an offender is a factor taken into account by the Privileges Committee in determining what action to recommend to the House.[131] In its report the committee acquaints the House with any apology or expression of regret and, if it thinks fit, recommends that the House accept the apology. If the House does so, the matter is then at an end.

In other cases there may have been no apology delivered to the Privileges Committee during its consideration of the matter. If the committee considers that an apology is called for, this view is included in its report for adoption by the House. The apology is then tendered by letter, usually to the Speaker, some time after the report has been received by the House. Failure to tender an apology when required to do so by the House could itself be treated as a contempt. The Speaker may read the letter of apology to the House, or may decide merely to present it to the House. Exceptionally, the House may order that the apology be tendered personally in the House. Thus, the House has ordered that a member attend in his place in the House and apologise for a contempt that he had committed.[132]

---

[127] 1981, Vol.442, pp.4315-6.
[128] 1992, Vol.528, pp.10626-31.
[129] Media release from the Speaker of the House of Representatives, 18 August 1992.

[130] 1984-85, JHR, 820-1.
[131] 1976, Vol.407, p.3157.
[132] 1998, Vol.567, pp.8358-81.

APPENDIX 1

PARLIAMENTARY SALARIES AND ALLOWANCES
(as at 1 July 2004)

Office	Yearly rate of salary ($)
Members of the Executive	
Prime Minister	317,200
Deputy Prime Minister	226,700
Each member of the Executive Council who is a Minister of the Crown holding one or more portfolios and who is a member of Cabinet	202,800
Each member of the Executive Council who is a Minister of the Crown holding one or more portfolios, but who is not a member of Cabinet	171,600
Each other member of the Executive Council	150,100
Each Parliamentary Under-Secretary	134,500
Officers of the House of Representatives	
Speaker of the House of Representatives	202,800
Deputy Speaker	144,900
Each Assistant Speaker	124,200
Leader of the Opposition	
Leader of the Opposition	202,800
Other Party Leaders and Deputy Leaders	
Each member of Parliament who is the Leader of a party—	
Base salary	124,200
plus	
For each additional member of the party up to a maximum of five	1,550
plus	
For each additional member of the party over five and to a maximum of 23	1,035
plus	
For each additional member of the party in excess of 23	520
Each member of Parliament who is the Deputy Leader of a party whose members in the House number not less than 25	124,200
Whips	
In respect of each party whose members in the House number not less than six,—	
One Whip	
Base salary	124,200
plus	
For each member of the party in excess of six up to a maximum of 24	1,035
plus	
For each member of the party in excess of 24	520
In respect of each party whose members in the House number not less than 25,—	
One Junior Whip	124,200
Plus, if a Whip referred to in one of the provisions under this heading *Whips* is also the Senior Government Whip	3,100

Office	Yearly rate of salary ($)
Chairpersons of select committees	
Each member of Parliament who is—	
(a) the chairperson of the Regulations Review Committee; or	
(b) the chairperson of a subject select committee specified in Standing Order 189	124,200
Deputy chairpersons of select committees	
Each member of Parliament who is—	
(a) the deputy chairperson of the Regulations Review Committee; or	
(b) the deputy chairperson of a subject select committee specified in Standing Order 189	116,440
Other members of Parliament	
Each other member of Parliament	113,300

Office	Yearly rate of expenses allowance ($)
Prime Minister	17,000
Speaker	16,000
Each other member of Parliament	12,815

APPENDIX 2

TRAVEL, ACCOMMODATION, ATTENDANCE AND COMMUNICATION SERVICES FOR MEMBERS OF PARLIAMENT
(approved 23 October 2003)

Part 1
Introduction and principles

1   **What does this document do?**
This document sets out the travel, accommodation, attendance, and communications services available to members of Parliament and their families.

2   **Who does this document apply to?**
This document applies to a person who is a member of Parliament while this document is in force.

3   **What period does this document apply to?**
(1)   This document applies to travel, accommodation, attendance, and communications services that take place on or after 1 November 2003.
(2)   This document continues in force until a new document is issued by the Speaker that sets out the travel, accommodation, attendance, and communications services available to members of Parliament and their families.

4   **Legal nature of this document**
This document is—
(a)   a direction by the Speaker to the Parliamentary Service to provide services to members of Parliament, and to administer funding entitlements for parliamentary purposes under section 7(1)(a) and (b) of the Parliamentary Service Act 2000; and
(b)   a specification of some of the services to which section 25 of the Civil List Act 1979 applies.

5   **Definitions used in this document**
In this document, unless the context otherwise requires, —
day means a period of 24 hours
family member includes a wife, husband, partner, or issue of a member
important official engagement means Royal, Vice-Regal, and State occasions
member means a person who is currently a member of Parliament
official function means any function to which the member may have been invited by reason of their status within a party but does not include political party functions or functions attended for personal reasons
parliamentary business means the undertaking of any task or function that a member could reasonably be expected to carry out in his or her capacity as a member of Parliament and that complements the business of the House of Representatives and includes any of the following:
(a)   attending a sitting of the House; or
(b)   attending a meeting of a select committee of the House of which the member is a member, or which the member is required to attend because of being in charge of a Bill or other matter under consideration by the committee or because of any other valid reason relating to the business of the committee; or
(c)   undertaking research or administrative functions that relate directly to the business of the House; or
(d)   attending meetings for the purpose of representing electors or explaining the application of policy or to receive representations; or
(e)   attending caucus meetings that are expressly for the purpose of enhancing the parliamentary process; or
(f)   attending meetings of his or her party; or
(g)   attending any ceremony or official function or national or international conference as a representative of Parliament or with the authority of the House
partner means a person in a relationship in the nature of marriage
party means a parliamentary political party whose members in the House include at least 1 member elected as a constituency or list candidate for that party

party leader means the leader of a party

primary place of residence means the place of residence that the Speaker determines, by written notice to the member, to be the member's primary place of residence in New Zealand

Speaker means the Speaker of the House of Representatives

Wellington commuting area means the cities of Wellington, Lower Hutt, Upper Hutt, and Porirua, and the Paraparaumu Ward of the Kapiti Coast District

whip, in relation to a member, means the whip of that member's party and, if the person is a member of a party whose members in the House number not less than 25, the junior whip

year means a financial year (1 July to 30 June).

6	**Cost-effective principle**

Wherever reasonably practicable, members should endeavour to use the most cost-effective alternative available.

7 **Evidence of costs incurred**

A person must produce evidence of costs incurred and a receipt to the Parliamentary Service before being entitled to be reimbursed for the cost of any entitlement under this document.

8 **Monitoring of aggregate expenditure by whips**

(1) Each whip must monitor, on a monthly basis, the aggregate expenditure by the members in his or her party, including expenditure in respect of members' families, in respect of the entitlements under this document.

(2) If excessive costs are being incurred by a party, a whip may advise any 1 or more members that the member should limit, or not incur, any further costs in that year.

9 **Alternative arrangements**

(1) This clause applies if—

(a) a member is entitled to a travel, accommodation, attendance, or communication service under this document in respect of a particular activity; and

(b) the cost to the Vote: Parliamentary Service of doing the activity in a different way is less than the cost to the Vote of the entitlement under this document.

(2) The member may ask the Speaker for approval to convert his or her entitlement under this document into the right to receive a service costing the lesser amount.

(3) The Speaker may give approval to the service costing the lesser amount being provided to the member if the Speaker is satisfied that the cost of the service represents a fair return for the service provided.

10 **Cost to be met from Vote**

The cost of any entitlement in this document is met fully from Vote: Parliamentary Service, except to the extent that—

(a) this document expressly provides otherwise; or

(b) the entitlement is met from Vote: Ministerial Services.

Part 2
Air travel

Domestic air travel

11 **Domestic air travel of members**

A member may travel by air at any time on scheduled air services throughout New Zealand.

12 **Domestic air travel of spouses and partners**

The spouse or partner of a member may travel by air at any time on scheduled air services throughout New Zealand, provided that the travel is not for the business purposes of the spouse or partner.

13 **Members who do not have a spouse or partner**

(1) If a member has neither a spouse nor a partner, the member may nominate to the Speaker a family member to become eligible for the entitlements of a spouse or partner under clause 12.

(2) If the Speaker approves that nomination, the entitlements in that clause apply to that family member as if he or she were a spouse or partner.

International travel on parliamentary business

14   International travel of members on parliamentary business

(1)   A member may travel by air on scheduled international air services if—

    (a)   the travel is for the purpose of undertaking parliamentary business; and

    (b)   the trip has been approved by the member's party leader and the Speaker.

(2)   The cost of the travel and accommodation is a charge against the funding for the party leader's office.

15   International travel of spouse or partner of party leader on parliamentary business

(1)   The spouse or partner of a party leader travelling under clause 14 may travel by air on scheduled international air services if—

    (a)   the primary purpose of the trip is to undertake parliamentary business; and

    (b)   the spouse or partner has been formally invited to undertake that parliamentary business in his or her capacity as the spouse or partner of a party leader; and

    (c)   the trip has been approved by the Speaker.

(2)   The costs of the travel and accommodation are a charge against the funding for the party leader's office.

16   Leader of Opposition's official international travel entitlement

(1)   The Leader of the Opposition may incur up to $50,000 in costs related to official international travel each year incurred by that member. The Leader may be accompanied by his or her spouse or partner and 1 official.

(2)   Official travel under this clause requires notification to the Prime Minister of—

    (a)   who is travelling; and

    (b)   where they are travelling; and

    (c)   the purpose of the travel; and

    (d)   when the travel will occur.

(3)   The costs of the air travel are a charge against the travel appropriation.

International air travel for private purposes

17   Private international air travel

(1)   This clause applies to a member who is also a member of the Commonwealth Parliamentary Association.

(2)   The member is entitled to a rebate on any international air travel undertaken by the member on a scheduled airline in accordance with the following rules:

    (a)   A rebate is payable in respect of expenditure incurred, or to be incurred, by the member personally, and a rebate is not payable where a member's fare is paid from public funds or from any other source.

    (b)   No rebate is payable in respect of any travel undertaken by the member for private business purposes.

    (c)   The amount of rebate to which a member is entitled is the appropriate percentage of the fare that applies to that member as calculated in accordance with the schedule below.

    (d)   The fare includes any tax and service fee payable in respect of the travel. It is calculated on the fare for the journey undertaken at the class of travel used. It does not include any amounts paid for cancellation fees or accommodation.

Schedule of rebates applicable

Number of complete Parliaments through which the member has served (if the member was elected at a general election)	Number of complete years of membership of Parliament (if the member was elected at a by-election or enters Parliament off a party list)	Percentage of fare payable by Vote: Parliamentary Service
Less than 1	Less than 3	Nil
1	3–5	25%
2	6–8	50%
3	9–11	75%
4 or more	12 or more	90%

18   International air travel of spouses and partners

(1)   A spouse or partner of a member is entitled to the same rebate on any international air travel undertaken by the spouse or partner on a scheduled airline as the member is entitled to under clause 17, provided that the travel is not for the business purposes of the spouse or partner.

(2)   The rules in subclause 17(2) apply equally to a rebate under this clause.

Part 3
Taxi, rental car, private car, rail, ferry and bus travel

19   Taxi travel

A member may use a taxi for travel—

(a)   between the member's primary place of residence and the local airport, when the member is on the way to undertake parliamentary business:

(b)   between the airport and the member's Wellington lodgings or Parliament House:

(c)   between Parliament House and the member's Wellington lodgings:

(d)   between the airport and the member's destination when on approved select committee or parliamentary business:

(e)   when the member is going to, or engaged on, other parliamentary business.

20   Spouse or partner taxi travel

The spouse or partner of a member, or a nominee approved under clause 13, may use a taxi provided that the travel is not for business purposes—

(a)   between the member's primary place of residence and the local airport:

(b)   between the airport and the member's Wellington lodgings or Parliament House:

(c)   between Parliament House and the member's Wellington lodgings:

(d)   between the nearest airport, Parliament House, or the member's Wellington lodgings and the location of an official function or engagement to which he or she is accompanying the member.

21   Rental cars for parliamentary business

A member may use a rental car if that use of a rental car is authorised by the member's whip as necessary for parliamentary business.

22   Rental cars for other travel

A member may use a rental car for other travel if a rental car is the only appropriate means, or is the cheapest means, of travel to enable a member to complete his or her journey between Wellington and his or her primary place of residence.

23   Mileage

(1)   A member may be reimbursed for mileage done when travelling on parliamentary business.

(2)   The rate of reimbursement is the rate agreed to by the Inland Revenue Department.

24   Rail, road, and ferry travel in New Zealand

A member, and the spouse or partner of a member, may at any time—

(a)   travel by rail and by ferry throughout New Zealand; and

(b)   travel by bus on all non-urban services.

Part 4
Self-drive cars and chauffeur driven cars

25   Self-drive cars

The Speaker, Deputy Speaker, and the Leader of the Opposition are each entitled to 1 self-drive car based at the member's primary place of residence.

26   Chauffeured car travel

(1)   The Speaker, Deputy Speaker, and the Leader of the Opposition may use a chauffeured car as if he or she were a Minister of the Crown.

(2)   This entitlement includes the use of chauffeured cars by those in subclause (1), and his or her spouse or partner, for personal reasons.

27 **Access to chauffeured car travel of party leader with 25 or more members**
A leader of a party with 25 or more members has the same entitlements to chauffeured car travel as the Leader of the Opposition.

28 **Access to chauffeured car travel of party leader with 13 to 24 members**
A leader of a party with between 13 and 24 members may use chauffeured cars for attendance at official functions.

29 **Access to chauffeured car travel of party leader with 6 to 12 members**
A leader of a party with between 6 and 12 members may use chauffeured cars for attendance at important official engagements if this has been agreed to by the Speaker.

30 **Deputy leader's access to chauffeured car travel**
The deputy leader of a party with more than 25 members may use chauffeured cars for attendance at official functions.

Part 5
Additional travel entitlements

Speaker and Leader of Opposition

31 **Travel expenses (Speaker and Leader of Opposition)**
(1) Both the Speaker and the Leader of the Opposition are entitled to have his or her travelling expenses paid in respect of each occasion on which the member is, in the course of travelling within New Zealand on parliamentary business,—
(a) absent from the Wellington commuting area; and
(b) at least 100 km from his or her primary place of residence and could not reasonably be expected to get home by conventional methods or where there is an issue of safety.
(2) The rate of the travelling expenses payable in respect of each occasion is a sum equal to the actual and reasonable cost of the expenses incurred, with a maximum of —
(a) $350 per day or part of a day; or
(b) $500 per day or part of a day if the occasion involves the attendance of the person entitled and the spouse or partner of that person at an official function—
   (i) that the person entitled attends by reason of the duties of his or her office; and
   (ii) that the person entitled is invited to attend, or is required to attend, primarily because of the office that the person entitled holds; and
   (iii) that the spouse or partner of the person entitled necessarily attends.

Dependent children

32 **Dependent children**
A child under 18 years who is dependent on a member may make 4 return trips each year between the member's primary place of residence and Wellington to be with his or her parent when that parent is engaged on parliamentary business. There is no limit to the number of trips for children under 5.

Part 6
Accommodation entitlements

33 **Non-Wellington accommodation expense reimbursement**
(1) A member may be reimbursed for actual and reasonable expenses incurred by the member while engaged on parliamentary business in respect of accommodation outside the Wellington commuting area.
(2) This is normally in instances when the member is at least 100 km from his or her primary place of residence and could not reasonably be expected to get home by conventional methods or safely.
(3) The rate of reimbursement is the sum required to reimburse the member for actual and reasonable net costs already incurred by the member in using that accommodation, except that the sum must not exceed—
(a) $160 if the accommodation is in commercial premises outside Auckland; or
(b) $180 if the accommodation is in commercial premises in Auckland; or
(c) $50 in the case of other premises.

34   **Wellington accommodation expense reimbursement**
(1)   A member whose primary place of residence is outside the Wellington commuting area may be reimbursed for actual and reasonable expenses incurred by the member while engaged on parliamentary business in respect of accommodation within the Wellington commuting area if—
    (a)   the member is not provided with a residence at the public cost; and
    (b)   the member uses, in the Wellington commuting area, when the member is in the Wellington commuting area for the purpose of carrying out parliamentary business,—
       (i)   accommodation owned by that member; or
       (ii)   accommodation rented by that member on a continuous basis for use in lieu of overnight accommodation; or
       (iii) accommodation in commercial premises; or
       (iv)   other private accommodation.
(2)   The rate of reimbursement is the sum required to reimburse the member for the actual and reasonable net costs already incurred by the member in using that accommodation.
(3)   The maximum amount that may be paid to any member under this clause in any year is $22,000 for a whip or party leader and $20,000 for any other member.
(4)   The maximum amount that may be paid to any member under subclause (1)(b)(iii) or (iv) in respect of any 1 night is—
    (a) $160 if the accommodation is in commercial premises; or
    (b) $50 in the case of other premises.

35   **Security system reimbursement**
A member who has a security system installed at his or her primary place of residence may be reimbursed for actual and reasonable costs associated with the security system up to the maximum of, —
    (a)   for installing the system, $400;
    (b)   for annual costs of monitoring and call-outs, $600.

Part 7
Communications

36   **Landlines**
(1)   A constituency member who is not a member of the Executive may have 4 landline rentals.
(2)   A constituency member who is a member of the Executive may have 2 landline rentals.
(3)   A list member who is not a member of the Executive may have 3 landline rentals.
(4)   A list member who is a member of the Executive may have 1 landline rental.
(5)   The member is entitled to incur the actual and reasonable costs of all associated costs (including rental and calls).

37   **Calls from parliamentary exchange**
All calls for Ministers' and members' offices from the parliamentary exchange are paid by the Parliamentary Service.

38   **Fax machines**
All members may use the communal fax machines within Parliament.

39   **Additional lines**
If a member needs any additional lines, the line charge is funded from the member's support allocation and the toll-call costs are met by the Parliamentary Service.

40   **Internet services**
(1)   Each member of Parliament may have high speed Internet service in the member's home and in an out-of-Parliament office. The particular service will be approved by the Speaker and may change with advances in technology.
(2)   The associated Internet service provider charges are paid by the Parliamentary Service.

41   **Cellular services**
(1)   Each member who is not a member of the Executive may have 1 cellphone.
(2)   All associated charges (other than the cost of international telephone calls provided for in clause 42) are paid by the Parliamentary Service.

42   **International toll calls**
(1)   The cost of international telephone calls, faxes, and cables, whether made from Parliament

Buildings or elsewhere, must normally be reimbursed by the member personally.

(2) However, the cost of international calls, faxes, and cables on parliamentary business may be charged to the Parliamentary Service if the claim is certified by the party leader or whip as being a charge incurred on parliamentary business.

43   Calling cards

(1) A member may be issued with a calling card.

(2) A calling card may be used only by a member on parliamentary business.

44   Other communication services

(1) A member may use other communication services that are funded from party and member support allocations.

(2) These are—

    (a)   use of pagers:

    (b)   photocopying:

    (c)   printing:

    (d)   postage:

    (e)   stationery supplies:

    (f)   signage and advertising.

Part 8
Attendance entitlements

45   There are no entitlements relating to attendance, previously known as the Day Allowance.

Part 9
Miscellaneous provisions

Use of operational resources

46   Use of operational resources

(1) A member is entitled to use operational resources for the purpose of undertaking parliamentary business.

(2) **Operational resources** means resources that are provided to assist members of Parliament and parliamentary parties in—

    (a)   discharging their responsibilities as legislators and elected representatives, including responsibilities determined by their parliamentary party:

    (b)   developing, researching, critiquing, and communicating policy:

    (c)   communicating with constituents or other communities of interest:

    (d)   establishing and operating out-of-Parliament offices:

    (e)   meeting the operational needs of each parliamentary party in fulfilling its parliamentary responsibilities.

(3) Operational resources are not provided, and may not be used, —

    (a)   for personal or private benefit; or

    (b)   in circumstances where provision has already been made by way of remuneration of the member, pursuant to a determination applicable to members of Parliament, under the Remuneration Authority Act 1977 or a determination made under section 20A of the Civil List Act 1979 (other than under this clause); or

    (c)   for soliciting subscriptions or other financial support for a political party; or

    (d)   for producing or distributing promotional or electioneering material by mail or other means of communication for the purpose of supporting the election of any person or the casting of a party vote for any political party; or

    (e)   for any work directly related to the administration or management of a political party; or

    (f)   for any work undertaken as a member of the Executive.

Members for part of year

47   Persons who are members for part of financial year

(1) This clause applies to a person who is a member for part but not all of a financial year.

(2) Any amount (or method of calculating an amount) in this document that is a maximum for a financial year applies to the person as if the maximum were reduced to the same proportion that the member's service as a member bears to a full financial year.

APPENDIX 3

STANDING ORDERS OF THE HOUSE OF REPRESENTATIVES

CHAPTER I

GENERAL PROVISIONS AND OFFICE-HOLDERS

INTRODUCTION

1   Purpose

These Standing Orders contain rules for the conduct of proceedings in the House of Representatives and for the exercise of powers possessed by the House. They are not intended to diminish or restrict the House's rights, privileges, immunities and powers.

2   Interpretation

The Speaker (or other member presiding) is responsible for ruling whenever any question arises as to the interpretation or application of a Standing Order and for deciding cases not otherwise provided for. In all cases the Speaker will be guided by previous Speakers' rulings and by the established practices of the House.

3   Definitions

(1)   In these Standing Orders, if not inconsistent with the context,—

amendment includes a new clause

Clerk means the Clerk of the House of Representatives or, if the office is vacant or the Clerk is absent from duty, means the Deputy Clerk of the House of Representatives or a person appointed by the Speaker to act as Clerk of the House of Representatives; and includes any person authorised by the Clerk to perform any of the functions or exercise any of the powers of the Clerk under these Standing Orders

clerk of the committee means the Clerk of the House of Representatives or a person authorised by the Clerk to be clerk of a committee

Crown entity means a statutory entity or a Crown entity company named or described in Schedules 1 or 2 of the Crown Entities Act 2004, and includes Crown entity subsidiaries

department means a department within the meaning of the Public Finance Act 1989

fiscal aggregates means the Government's intentions for fiscal policy, in particular, for the following:

(a)   total operating expenses:

(b)   total operating revenues:

(c)   the balance between total operating expenses and total operating revenues:

(d)   the level of total debt:

(e)   the level of total net worth

Government notice of motion means a notice of motion given by a Minister

leave, or **leave of the House** or **leave of the committee**, means permission to do something that is granted without a dissentient voice

Member's notice of motion means a notice of motion given by a member who is not a Minister

Office of Parliament means an Office of Parliament within the meaning of the Public Finance Act 1989

order of the day means a bill or other item of business that has been set down for consideration by the House

parliamentary precincts means the parliamentary precincts within the meaning of the Parliamentary Service Act 2000

party means a party recognised for parliamentary purposes in accordance with the Standing Orders

person includes an organisation

preliminary clauses means the title clause and the commencement clause

public organisation means any organisation (other than a Crown entity or a State enterprise) that the House resolves to be a public organisation

regulation means a regulation within the meaning of the Regulations (Disallowance) Act 1989

Serjeant-at-Arms means any officer appointed by the Crown, on the recommendation of the Speaker, to be the Serjeant-at-Arms to the House; and includes any person performing the functions or exercising the powers of Serjeant-at-Arms by direction of the Speaker

State enterprise means a State enterprise within the meaning of the State-Owned Enterprises Act 1986

Wellington area means the cities of Wellington, Hutt, Upper Hutt and Porirua and the Paekakariki/ Raumati and Paraparaumu Wards of the Kapiti Coast District

working day means any day of the week other than—

(a) a Saturday, a Sunday, Good Friday, Easter Monday, Anzac Day, Labour Day, the Sovereign's birthday and Waitangi Day, and

(b) any anniversary or other day observed as a public holiday in a locality to which a particular local bill or private bill subject to procedures under these Standing Orders relates, and

(c) a day in the period commencing with 25 December in any year and ending with 15 January in the following year

written or **in writing** means written by hand, typewritten, duplicated, or printed, or partly one and partly one or more of the others, and includes a communication transmitted in facsimile or otherwise electronically.

(2) References in the Standing Orders to the Governor-General, unless the context otherwise requires, are read as necessary as references to the Sovereign, the Administrator of the Government and Royal commissioners.

(3) Where a report or paper is to be presented by or on a particular day or within a limited period of time, it may, if that day or the last day of that period is not a working day, be presented on the next working day.

4   Suspension of Standing Orders

(1) A Standing Order or other order of the House may be suspended in whole or in part on motion with or without notice.

(2) A suspension motion may be moved without notice only if at least 60 members are present when the motion is moved.

(3) A suspension motion may not interrupt a debate and must state the object of or reason for the proposed suspension.

(4) An amendment may not be moved to a suspension motion.

5   Limitation on moving suspension

A member who is not a Minister may move a suspension motion only for the purpose of allowing a bill, clause or other matter in that member's charge to proceed or be dealt with without compliance with the Standing Order or other order to be suspended.

6   Amendment or revocation of Standing Orders

A Standing Order may be amended or revoked only by motion with notice.

7   Functions of Standing Orders Committee

The Standing Orders Committee—

(a) may conduct a review of the Standing Orders, procedures and practices of the House:

(b) may consider and report to the House on any matter relating to the Standing Orders, procedures and practices of the House:

(c) may recommend to the House the amendment, revocation or addition of any Standing Order or the alteration of any procedure or practice of the House:

(d) considers and reports to the House on any matter referred by the House or otherwise under Standing Orders.

JOURNALS AND RECORDS

8   Clerk to note proceedings

The Clerk notes all proceedings of the House. The Clerk's notes are published as the Journals of the House.

9   Official report

(1) An official report (known as *Hansard*) is made of those portions of the proceedings of the House as are determined by the House or by the Speaker.

(2) The report is made in such form and subject to such rules as are approved from time to time by the House or by the Speaker.

(3) The report is published.

10   Custody of Journals and records

The Clerk maintains custody of the Journals and of all petitions and papers presented and records belonging to the House. Such Journals, petitions, papers and records must not be taken from the House or its offices without an order of the House or the permission of the Speaker.

11   Disposal of records

The Clerk may, after consultation with the Chief Archivist, dispose of Journals, petitions, papers and records that are more than three years old.

OPENING OF PARLIAMENT

12   Proceedings on meeting of new Parliament

On the first day of the meeting of a new Parliament the business is as follows:

(a)   the House awaits the arrival of the Royal commissioners:

(b)   after the arrival of the Royal commissioners, the Clerk reads their commission:

(c)   when the Royal commissioners have withdrawn, the Clerk (or other person so authorised) reads the commission authorising the administration of the oath or affirmation required by law:

(d)   the Clerk lays on the Table lists of the names of the members elected to serve in the House:

(e)   members are called in alphabetical order to take the oath or make the affirmation required by law:

(f)   the House then proceeds to the election of a Speaker.

13   Further provision for swearing in of members

(1)   Members who are unable to take the oath or make the affirmation at the time appointed by Standing Order 12(e) and persons becoming members of Parliament subsequent to the general election, may take the oath or make affirmation by presenting themselves at the bar of the House.

(2)   The Speaker interrupts the business as convenient and calls the member to the Table for the purpose. If this occurs during the election of the Speaker, the Clerk interrupts the proceedings for the purpose.

14   Proceedings on day of State Opening

(1)   On the second day of the meeting of a new Parliament and on the first day of each subsequent session of Parliament,—

(a)   the Speaker reads prayers and reports the Speaker's confirmation in office and any other communication from the Governor-General:

(b)   the House awaits a message from the Governor-General requesting its attendance; on receiving such a message, the Speaker and members attend accordingly:

(c)   the Speaker reports to the House the Governor-General's speech and lays a copy of it on the Table:

(d)   the announcement of the presentation of petitions and papers or of the introduction of bills may be made:

(e)   Government orders of the day relating to the appointment of the Deputy Speaker and Assistant Speakers, and the reinstatement of business may be considered.

(2)   The Speaker may then suspend the sitting to permit the moving of the Address in Reply at 2 pm that day or the House may adjourn.

ELECTION OF SPEAKER

15   Clerk acts as chairperson

For the purposes of the election of a Speaker, the Clerk acts as chairperson and calls for nominations.

16   Nomination of members

(1)   Any member may, on being called by the Clerk, rise and nominate himself or herself for election as Speaker. A member who is absent may be nominated by another member for election as Speaker provided that that member's consent in writing to being nominated is produced to the Clerk.

(2)   No question is proposed on the election of a Speaker and no debate may arise in connection with it.

17   One member nominated

If only one member is nominated for election as Speaker, the Clerk declares that member elected.

18   Two members nominated

If two members are nominated for election as Speaker, the election is decided by a personal vote. In the event of a tie, the Clerk again calls for nominations.

19   More than two members nominated

(1)   If more than two members are nominated for election as Speaker,—

(a)   the bells are rung for seven minutes; after the bells have stopped the doors are closed and locked:

(b)   the Clerk states the names of the members nominated and calls on each member, in alphabetical order, to vote for one of the candidates:

(c)   members vote by standing in their places on being called by the Clerk and stating the name of the member for whom they vote; a member may abstain:

(d)   if a member receives the votes of a majority of the members voting, the Clerk declares that member elected:

(e)   otherwise, the member with the fewest number of votes is eliminated and the votes are taken again for the remaining members until their number is reduced to two:

(f)   when the number of members is reduced to two, the election is decided by a personal vote as provided in Standing Order 18.

(2)   In the event of a tie in any personal vote, the Clerk calls for nominations for election again.

(3)   Where, under paragraph (1)(e), there is more than one member with the fewest number of votes, that vote is taken again. If, after the vote is retaken, there is still more than one member with the fewest number of votes, the Clerk must determine by lot which member is to be eliminated.

20   No proxies permitted

On the election of a Speaker no vote may be cast, or abstention recorded, by proxy.

21   Election of Speaker

A member, on being elected by the House, takes the Chair as Speaker-Elect and the Mace is laid upon the Table.

22   Adjournment following election of Speaker

After electing a Speaker, the House adjourns until the time indicated by the Governor-General for the delivery of the Speech from the Throne. The Speaker-Elect seeks the Governor-General's confirmation as Speaker before the next sitting of the House.

23   Speaker to lay claim to privileges of House

On being confirmed by the Governor-General as Speaker of a new Parliament, the Speaker, on behalf of the House, lays claim to all the House's privileges; especially to freedom of speech in debate, to free access to the Governor-General whenever occasion may require it, and that the most favourable construction may be put on all the House's proceedings.

24   Speaker reports to House

The Speaker must report to the House the Governor-General's decision as to confirmation and the Governor-General's reply to the Speaker's claim to the House's privileges.

25   Vacancy in Speakership

(1)   When, during the term of Parliament, the office of Speaker becomes vacant, the Clerk reports the vacancy to the House at its next sitting and the House proceeds to the election of a Speaker as prescribed in Standing Orders 15 to 21.

(2)   After electing a Speaker, the House adjourns until the next sitting day. The Speaker-Elect seeks the Governor-General's confirmation as Speaker before the next sitting of the House.

OTHER PRESIDING OFFICERS

26   Deputy Speaker

The House appoints a member to be Deputy Speaker.

27   Powers of Deputy Speaker

The Deputy Speaker performs the duties and exercises the authority of the Speaker in relation to all proceedings of the House during a sitting and an adjournment of the House and during any recess of Parliament.

28   Assistant Speakers

(1)   The House may appoint up to two members to be Assistant Speakers.

(2)   An Assistant Speaker performs the duties and exercises the authority of the Speaker while presiding over the House.

29   Term of office

The Deputy Speaker and any Assistant Speaker hold office during the remaining term of Parliament unless the House otherwise directs.

30   Party leader or whip not to be presiding officer

No member who is the leader of a party or who holds office as a whip may be appointed Deputy Speaker or Assistant Speaker.

31   Vacancy in office

When a vacancy occurs in the office of Deputy Speaker or Assistant Speaker, the House appoints a new Deputy Speaker or Assistant Speaker.

32   Absence of Speaker

In the absence of the Speaker, the Deputy Speaker or an Assistant Speaker may take the Chair.

33   Temporary Speaker
(1)   The Speaker may, while presiding over the House, ask any member to take the Chair. The member, on being asked, may take the Chair as temporary Speaker.
(2)   A temporary Speaker performs the duties and exercises the authority of the Speaker while presiding over the House.

PARTIES
34   Recognition of parties
(1)   Every party in whose interest a member was elected at the preceding general election or at any subsequent by-election is entitled to be recognised as a party for parliamentary purposes.
(2)   Members who cease to be members of the party for which they were originally elected may be recognised, for parliamentary purposes,—
    (a)   as members of an existing recognised party if they inform the Speaker in writing that they have joined that party with the agreement of the leader of that party, or
    (b)   as a new party if they apply to the Speaker and their new party—
        (i)   is registered as a party by the Electoral Commission, and
        (ii)   has at least six members of Parliament, or
    (c)   as members of a component party in whose interest those members stood as constituency candidates at the preceding general election if they inform the Speaker in writing that they wish to be so recognised.
(3)   A party that has been recognised as a new party under paragraph (2)(b) loses its recognition if its membership falls below six members of Parliament.
(4)   Any member who is not a member of a recognised party is treated as an Independent member for parliamentary purposes.

35   Notification of party details
(1)   A party must inform the Speaker of—
    (a)   the name by which it wishes to be known for parliamentary purposes, and
    (b)   the identity of its leader and other office-holders, such as deputy leader and whips, and
    (c)   its parliamentary membership.
The Speaker must be informed of any change in these matters.
(2)   A coalition between two or more parties must be notified to the Speaker, but each party to the coalition remains a separate party for parliamentary purposes.
(3)   In the period between a general election and the House electing a Speaker, the matters specified in this Standing Order may be notified to the Clerk.

36   Leader of the Opposition
The leader of the largest party in terms of its parliamentary membership that is not in Government or in coalition with a Government party is entitled to be recognised as Leader of the Opposition.

CHAPTER II

SITTINGS OF THE HOUSE

SEATING AND ATTENDANCE
37   Seating
(1)   As far as practicable, each party occupies a block of seats in the Chamber.
(2)   The Speaker decides any dispute as to the seats to be occupied.

38   Minister to be present
A Minister must be present during all sitting hours of the House.
If a Minister is not present, the Speaker interrupts proceedings and the bell is rung for up to five minutes. Where no Minister appears, the Speaker adjourns the House until the time for its next sitting.

STRANGERS
39   Strangers may be ordered to withdraw
(1)   A member may move, without notice, that strangers be ordered to withdraw.
(2)   There is no amendment or debate on the question.

40   Effect of order that strangers withdraw
If the House resolves that strangers be ordered to withdraw,—
    (a)   all strangers must leave the galleries, and

(b)   all members of the parliamentary press gallery must leave that gallery, and

(c)   official reporters and attendants must leave the Chamber and no official report of the proceedings is made, and

(d)   broadcasting of debates ceases.

The Clerk makes a note of proceedings for the Journals of the House.

41   Strangers interrupting proceedings

The Speaker or the Serjeant-at-Arms may require strangers who interrupt proceedings or who otherwise misconduct themselves to leave the galleries and the parliamentary precincts.

42   Speaker controls admission

On behalf of the House, the Speaker controls admission to the Chamber, the lobbies and the galleries, and may from time to time issue rules setting out who may be admitted to those areas and governing their conduct there.

SITTINGS

43   Sittings of the House

(1)   The House sits as follows:

        Tuesday and Wednesday: 2 pm to 6 pm and 7.30 pm to 10 pm

        Thursday: 2 pm to 6 pm.

(2)   On a Tuesday and a Wednesday, the sitting is suspended at 6 pm until 7.30 pm.

44   Broadcasting

(1)   The proceedings of the House are broadcast on radio during all hours of sitting and are available for television coverage.

(2)   Any broadcast of the televised proceedings of the House must maintain such standards of fairness as are adopted, from time to time, by the House.

45   Appointment of Monday, Friday or Saturday as sitting day

Any other day (other than a Sunday) may be ordered by the House to be a sitting day. On such a sitting day, the sitting hours are as for a Tuesday unless the House provides otherwise.

46   No Sunday sitting

The House must not sit on a Sunday. Whenever a sitting extends to midnight or, in committee, five minutes before midnight, on a Saturday, proceedings are interrupted as provided in Standing Orders 49 or 50 respectively.

47   Adjournment of House

(1)   At the conclusion of each sitting the House adjourns until its next sitting day.

(2)   Any motion for the adjournment of the House may be moved only by a Minister.

48   Speaker may suspend sitting or adjourn House

(1)   The Speaker may suspend a sitting or adjourn the House if the Speaker thinks it is necessary to do so to maintain order.

(2)   Whenever the Speaker suspends a sitting, the Speaker decides when the sitting should resume.

(3)   Whenever the Speaker adjourns the House it stands adjourned until its next sitting day.

49   Conclusion of a sitting

(1)   Business before the House at the conclusion of each sitting is interrupted by the Speaker and set down for resumption on the next sitting day, but a motion for the adjournment of the House lapses.

(2)   Whenever the next business would require the House to go into committee within five minutes of the time for the conclusion of a sitting, the Speaker adjourns the House until its next sitting day.

50   Interruption when House in committee

(1)   Whenever the House is in committee five minutes before the time for the conclusion of a sitting, the chairperson interrupts the business and leaves the Chair.

(2)   On the Speaker resuming the Chair, the chairperson reports to the House the business transacted in committee. After the House deals with the report the Speaker adjourns the House until its next sitting day.

51   Interruption deferred when vote in progress

Whenever, at the time for the Speaker or the chairperson to interrupt business, a question is being put to the House or a vote is in progress or the closure is carried, the interruption of business is deferred until the question (in the case of the closure, the main question) is determined.

52   Resumption of business
Business interrupted by the Speaker or the chairperson for whatever reason is resumed at the point of interruption. A member whose speech was interrupted may speak first on the resumption of the debate. If the member does not exercise the right to speak first when the debate resumes, the member's speech is concluded.

53   Early sitting during adjournment
(1)   Whenever the House is adjourned and it appears to the Prime Minister desirable in the public interest that the House should sit at an earlier time than that to which it is adjourned, the Prime Minister, after consulting with the leaders of all other parties, may inform the Speaker that the House should sit at an earlier time.
(2)   The Speaker, on being so informed, decides on a day that is appropriate for the House to sit and notifies members accordingly. The House sits on the day determined by the Speaker.

54   Urgency
(1)   A Minister may move, without notice, a motion to accord urgency to certain business.
(2)   A motion for urgency may not be moved until after the completion of general business.
(3)   There is no amendment or debate on the question, but the Minister must, on moving the motion, inform the House with some particularity why the motion is being moved.

55   Effect of urgency
(1)   If the House agrees to accord urgency to business, that business may be proceeded with to a completion at that sitting of the House and the sitting is extended accordingly.
(2)   Whenever urgency has been accorded,—
    (a)   the sitting is suspended at the normal time for its conclusion and the House resumes at 9 am on the following day,
    (b)   despite paragraph (a), if the Government has advised the Business Committee of the intention to move on a Thursday to accord urgency to business, the sitting on that Thursday is suspended between 6 pm and 7.30 pm and between 10 pm and 9 am,
    (c)   a sitting that has been extended is suspended between midnight and 9 am, 1 pm and 2 pm and 6 pm and 7 pm, and
    (d)   on a Saturday, the provisions of Standing Order 46 apply.

56   Extraordinary urgency
(1)   An urgency motion may be moved as a motion for extraordinary urgency or, after the House has accorded urgency, a Minister may move, without notice, a motion to accord extraordinary urgency to some or all of the business being considered under urgency.
(2)   There is no amendment or debate on the question, but the Minister must, on moving the motion, inform the House of the nature of the business and the circumstances that warrant the claim for extraordinary urgency.
(3)   Extraordinary urgency may be claimed only if the Speaker agrees that the business to be taken justifies it.

57   Effect of extraordinary urgency
(1)   If the House agrees to accord extraordinary urgency to business, that business may be proceeded with to a completion at that sitting of the House and the sitting is extended accordingly.
(2)   Whenever extraordinary urgency has been accorded,—
    (a)   a sitting which has been extended is suspended between 8 am and 9 am, 1 pm and 2 pm and 6 pm and 7 pm, and
    (b)   on a Saturday, the provisions of Standing Order 46 apply.

58   No other business except with leave
Except where otherwise provided, whenever urgency or extraordinary urgency has been entered upon, no business, other than the business for which the urgency was accorded, may be transacted by the House except with leave.

BUSINESS OF THE HOUSE
59   Prayers and Mace
On taking the Chair at the commencement of each sitting the Speaker reads a prayer to the House and the Mace is placed upon the Table.

60   Order of business
At each sitting the House transacts its business in the order shown on the Order Paper.

61   Order Paper

(1)   The Clerk must prepare an Order Paper for each sitting day showing the business of the House in the order in which it is to be transacted.

(2)   The Order Paper is prepared in accordance with the provisions of the Standing Orders as to the order in which business is to be transacted and in accordance with any determination of the Business Committee.

(3)   The Order Paper is circulated as early as possible before the House sits. Two or more versions of the Order Paper may be circulated.

62   Types of business

The business of the House consists of the following:

(a)   general business:

(b)   Government orders of the day:

(c)   private and local orders of the day:

(d)   Members' orders of the day.

63   General business

(1)   General business is taken in the following order:

1.   announcement of the presentation of petitions, papers and reports of select committees and the introduction of bills

2.   questions for oral answer (including urgent questions)

3.   debate on a matter of urgent public importance (if allowed by the Speaker)

4.   a general debate (on Wednesdays only)

5.   consideration of reports of the Privileges Committee.

(2)   General business is held at 2 pm on each sitting day.

64   Government orders of the day

Government orders of the day consist of Government bills, the Address in Reply debate, the debate on the Prime Minister's statement, consideration of the performance and current operations of Crown entities, public organisations and State enterprises and Government notices of motion.

65   Arrangement of Government orders of the day

The Government decides the order in which Government orders of the day are arranged on the Order Paper, subject to any requirements in the Standing Orders that a particular debate be taken ahead of other Government orders of the day.

66   Private and local orders of the day

Private and local orders of the day consist of private bills and local bills.

67   Arrangement of private and local orders of the day

(1)   Private and local orders of the day are arranged in the following order:

1   third reading of bills

2.   committee stage of bills

3   second reading of bills

4.   first reading of bills.

(2)   Where the debate on a bill has been interrupted or adjourned, the bill is taken ahead of other bills at the same stage.

68   Members' orders of the day

Members' orders of the day consist of Members' bills, the consideration of reports of committees (other than those of the Privileges Committee) and Members' notices of motion.

69   Arrangement of Members' orders of the day

(1)   Members' orders of the day are arranged in the following order:

1.   third reading of bills

2.   committee stage of bills

3.   second reading of bills

4.   first reading of bills

5.   consideration of reports of committees

6.   notices of motion.

(2)   Where the debate on a bill has been interrupted or adjourned, the bill is taken ahead of other bills at the same stage.

70   Orders of the day not reached

Orders of the day that are not reached are, subject to the Standing Orders, automatically set down on the following day's Order Paper.

71   Discharge or postponement of order of the day

(1)   An order of the day may be discharged or postponed—

   (a)   on motion without notice, or

   (b)   by the member in whose name the order stands informing the Clerk accordingly.

(2)   There is no amendment or debate on the question to discharge or postpone an order of the day.

(3)   The order of the day for consideration of the report of a select committee is discharged if not dealt with within 15 sitting days or within 15 sitting days of the presentation of a Government response that relates to it, as the case may be.

72   Tuesdays and Thursdays

At a Tuesday and a Thursday sitting (and on any other day specially appointed by the House to be a sitting day) Government orders of the day are taken ahead of private and local orders of the day and Members' orders of the day.

73   Wednesdays

(1)   At a Wednesday sitting private and local orders of the day and Members' orders of the day alternate with Government orders of the day as to precedence.

(2)   Government orders of the day are always taken first on a Wednesday if the Address in Reply debate, the debate on the Prime Minister's statement or the Budget debate is before the House. In these circumstances private and local orders of the day and Members' orders of the day are taken first on the next Wednesday.

BUSINESS COMMITTEE

74   Business Committee

(1)   The Speaker convenes a Business Committee at the commencement of each Parliament. The Speaker chairs the Business Committee.

(2)   Every party with six or more members is entitled to be represented at each meeting of the committee by one member nominated by its leader.

(3)   Parties with fewer than six members, and which are in a Government coalition, are entitled to choose one member between them to represent them on the committee. Other parties with fewer than six members and Independent members are entitled to choose one member between them to represent them on the committee.

(4)   The names of the members nominated are to be given to the Speaker.

75   Basis of making decisions in Business Committee

(1)   The committee reaches decisions on the basis of unanimity or, if this is not possible, near-unanimity having regard to the numbers in the House represented by each of the members of the committee. **Near-unanimity** means agreement has been given on behalf of the overwhelming majority of members of Parliament.

(2)   The Speaker is the judge of whether unanimity is possible and, if it is not, whether a sufficient degree of near-unanimity has been reached for there to be an effective determination by the committee.

(3)   Before determining that near-unanimity has been reached, the Speaker must be satisfied that, having regard to the party membership in the House, the proposed determination is fair to all parties and does not discriminate against or oppress a minority party or minority parties.

76   Business of House

The Business Committee may determine—

   (a)   the order of business to be transacted in the House:

   (b)   the time to be spent on an item of business:

   (c)   how time on an item of business is to be allocated among the parties represented in the House:

   (d)   the speaking times of individual members on an item of business.

77   Determination of Business Committee

(1)   A determination of the Business Committee takes effect by its publication and circulation to all members of Parliament. A determination must be published and circulated on the Order Paper before any sitting of the House at which it is to apply.

(2)   A determination of the Business Committee applies notwithstanding any other Standing Order to the contrary.

78   Sitting programme
(1)   The Business Committee must recommend to the House a programme of sittings for each calendar year.
(2)   The recommended programme of sittings is to be made to the House not later than the third sitting day in the preceding December or, if the House does not sit in December, not later than the sitting day before the House is due to adjourn.
(3)   The recommended programme must require the House to sit first no later than the last Tuesday in February and to sit in total on about 90 days in the calendar year.
(4)   On being adopted by the House the sitting programme operates subject to any decision by the House to the contrary.

REINSTATEMENT OF BUSINESS
79   Reinstatement of business
Business that had lapsed with the dissolution or expiration of Parliament and which is reinstated by resolution of the House in the next Parliament is resumed in that Parliament at the stage it had reached in the previous Parliament.

CHAPTER III

GENERAL PROCEDURES

MAINTENANCE OF ORDER
80   Speaker maintains order
(1)   The Speaker maintains order and decorum in the House.
(2)   Whenever the Speaker rises during a sitting, members must sit down and be silent so that the Speaker can be heard without interruption.

81   Members to acknowledge Chair
Except when voting, members must make an acknowledgement to the Chair on entering and leaving the Chamber.

82   Members to be seated
Members must be seated when they are in the Chamber except when speaking in debate or voting.

83   Members to stand as Speaker leaves Chamber
When the Speaker is about to leave the Chamber at the conclusion of a sitting, members rise in their places and remain standing until the Speaker has left the Chamber.

84   Points of order
(1)   Any member may raise a point of order. A point of order takes precedence of other business until ruled on by the Speaker.
(2)   The Speaker may rule on a point of order when it is raised without allowing any discussion apart from that of the member raising the point.
(3)   A member raising a point of order and any member permitted by the Speaker to speak to a point of order must put the point tersely and speak only to the point of order raised. A point of order is heard in silence by the House.

85   Disorderly conduct
(1)   The Speaker may order any member whose conduct is highly disorderly to withdraw immediately from the House during the period (up to the remainder of that day's sitting) that the Speaker decides.
(2)   Any member ordered to withdraw from the House may not enter the Chamber but may vote.

86   Naming of member
The Speaker may name any member whose conduct is grossly disorderly and call on the House to judge the conduct of the member.

87   Member may be suspended
Whenever a member has been named, the Speaker forthwith puts a question, "That [*such member*] be suspended from the service of the House". There is no amendment or debate on this question.

88   Naming in committee of whole House
If a member is named in a committee of the whole House, the committee is suspended and the chairperson reports the matter to the House. The Speaker then puts the question for the member's suspension as provided in Standing Order 87.

89   **Time during which member is suspended**
      If any member is suspended under Standing Order 87, the suspension—
      (a)   on the first occasion is for 24 hours:
      (b)   on the second occasion during the same Parliament is for seven days, excluding the day of suspension:
      (c)   on the third or any subsequent occasion during the same Parliament is for 28 days, excluding the day of suspension.

90   **Refusal to obey Speaker's direction**
      If any member who is suspended under Standing Order 87 refuses to obey a direction of the Speaker to leave the Chamber, that member is, without any further question being put, suspended from the service of the House for the remainder of the calendar year.

91   **Rights forfeited by suspended member**
      A member who is suspended from the service of the House may not enter the Chamber, vote, serve on a committee or lodge questions or notices of motion.

92   **House's right to hold in contempt**
      The fact that a member has been suspended under Standing Orders 87 or 90 does not prevent the House also holding the member's conduct to be a contempt.

MOTIONS

93   **Notice necessary before motion moved**
      A motion may be moved only after notice of it is given and the notice appears on the Order Paper, unless a Standing Order or the practice of the House provides to the contrary.

94   **Giving of notice of motion**
(1)   Subject to paragraph (2), notice of a motion a member intends to move may be given by any member by delivering a signed copy to the Clerk between 9 am and 10 am on any sitting day.
(2)   Notice of a motion relating to a particular Supplementary Order Paper cannot be given unless that Supplementary Order Paper has been circulated to members.

95   **Examination of notices**
      The Speaker examines all notices of motion that have been given, and those that are accepted as being in order are made available at the Table when the House meets and are set down as Government or Members' orders of the day according to whether they are Government notices of motion or Members' notices of motion.

96   **Disposal of Members' notices of motion**
(1)   Subject to paragraph (2), all Members' notices of motion that have not been dealt with within one week of their first appearance on the Order Paper lapse and are struck off the Order Paper.
(2)   A notice of motion for the disallowance of a regulation given by a member who is, at the time of the giving of the notice, a member of the Regulations Review Committee does not lapse and is retained on the Order Paper until dealt with by the House.

97   **Form and content of notices**
(1)   A notice of motion must be expressed in a form and with content appropriate for a resolution of the House. It must clearly indicate the issue to be raised for debate and include only such material as may be necessary to identify the facts or matter to which the motion relates.
(2)   Notices of motion must not contain—
      (a)   unbecoming or offensive expressions or expressions or words that would not be permitted in debate:
      (b)   statements of fact or the names of persons unless they are strictly necessary to render the notice intelligible and can be authenticated.

98   **No seconder required**
      A seconder is not required for a motion.

99   **Question proposed on motion**
(1)   When a motion has been moved, the Speaker proposes the question that the motion be agreed to.
(2)   After the Speaker has proposed the question on the motion, the motion cannot be withdrawn without leave.

100 Rescission of resolution

A resolution of the House may be rescinded on motion with notice.

RULES OF DEBATE

101 Speaker calls upon member to speak

When two or more members rise together the member called upon by the Speaker is entitled to speak.

102 Factors to be taken into account by Speaker in calling members

In deciding whom to call, the Speaker takes account of the following factors:

(a) if possible, a member of each party should be able to speak in each debate:

(b) overall participation in a debate should be approximately proportional to party membership in the House:

(c) priority should be given to party spokespersons in order of size of party membership in the House:

(d) the seniority of members and the interests and expertise of individual members who wish to speak.

103 Members to address Speaker

A member on being called to speak addresses the Speaker and, through the Speaker, the House.

104 Speeches in English or Māori

A member may address the Speaker in English or in Māori.

105 Member may speak only once to question

Except as otherwise provided, a member may speak only once to a question before the House.

106 Misrepresentation

(1) A member who has spoken to a question may speak again to explain some material part of the member's speech which has been misquoted, misunderstood or misrepresented in the same debate.

(2) A member may not introduce any new matter or interrupt any member to explain a misquotation, misunderstanding or misrepresentation.

107 Relevancy

(1) All debate must be relevant to the question before the House.

(2) After having called the attention of the House to the conduct of a member who persists in irrelevance or tedious repetition either of the member's own arguments or of the arguments used by other members in debate, the Speaker may terminate that member's speech.

108 Visual aids

(1) A member may use an appropriate visual aid to illustrate a point being made during the member's speech, provided that the aid does not inconvenience other members or obstruct the proceedings of the House.

(2) Such an aid may be displayed only when the member is speaking to a question before the House and must be removed from the Chamber at the conclusion of the member's speech.

109 Anticipating discussion

(1) A member may not anticipate discussion of any general business or order of the day.

(2) In determining whether a discussion is out of order, the Speaker has regard to the probability of the matter anticipated being brought before the House within a reasonable time.

110 Proceedings of committees not to be referred to

A member may not refer to confidential proceedings of a select committee until those proceedings are reported to the House.

111 Matters awaiting judicial decision

Subject always to the discretion of the Speaker and to the right of the House to legislate on any matter, matters awaiting or under adjudication in any court of record may not be referred to—

(a) in any motion, or

(b) in any debate, or

(c) in any question, including a supplementary question,—

if it appears to the Speaker that there is a real and substantial danger of prejudice to the trial of the case.

112 Application of prohibition of reference to matters awaiting judicial decision

(1) Standing Order 111 has effect,—

(a) in relation to a criminal case, from the moment the law is set in motion by a charge being made:

(b)   in relation to cases other than criminal, from the time when proceedings have been initiated by the filing of the appropriate document in the registry or office of the court.

(2)   Standing Order 111 ceases to have effect in any case when the verdict and sentence have been announced or judgment given.

(3)   In any case where notice of appeal is given, Standing Order 111 has effect from the time when the notice is given until the appeal has been decided.

113   Offensive references to House or judiciary

A member may not use offensive words against the House or against any member of the judiciary.

114   References to Sovereign or Governor-General

A member may not refer to the Sovereign or the Governor-General disrespectfully in debate or for the purpose of influencing the House in its deliberations.

115   Offensive or disorderly words

If any offensive or disorderly words are used, whether by a member who is speaking or by a member who is present, the Speaker intervenes.

116   Personal reflections

A member may not make an imputation of improper motives against a member, an offensive reference to a member's private affairs or a personal reflection against a member.

117   Time limits of speeches and debates

(1)   The time limits for speeches and debates are set out in Appendix A.

(2)   An individual speaking time may be shared between two members of the same party or between two members of different parties if both parties agree.

RULES FOR AMENDMENTS

118   General rules

The general rules relating to amendments set out in Standing Orders 119 to 126 apply subject to any provision in the Standing Orders to the contrary.

119   Amendment to be relevant

An amendment must be relevant to the question that it proposes to amend.

120   Amendments to be in writing

An amendment must be put into writing, signed by the mover, and delivered to the Clerk at the Table.

121   Form of question on amendment

When an amendment has been moved, the Speaker proposes a question, "That the amendment be agreed to".

122   No amendment to be made to words already agreed to

An amendment (except an amendment to add further words) may not be moved to any words that the House has declined to omit, or which have been inserted in or added to a question.

123   Order of moving amendments

Each amendment is disposed of before another amendment to the same question may be moved.

124   Amendment to amendment

An amendment may be moved to a proposed amendment.

125   Withdrawal of amendment

After the Speaker has proposed the question on an amendment, the amendment cannot be withdrawn without leave.

126   Questions put

(1)   When amendments are agreed to, the question, as amended, is put.

(2)   When amendments are not agreed to, the question is put as originally proposed.

LIMITATIONS ON SPEAKING TO AND MOVING AMENDMENTS

127   Member who has spoken on main question may speak to new question arising

A member who has spoken to a question may speak to any new question that arises.

128   Debate on amendment confined to amendment

When an amendment is moved the debate must be confined to the amendment, unless it involves the consideration and decision of the main question, in which case both the main question and the amendment are open for discussion.

129   Member who has spoken to amendment involving main question may not speak to main question

A member who has spoken to any amendment that involves the consideration and decision of the main question may not subsequently speak to the main question, either as originally proposed or as amended.

130   Member who has moved or spoken to amendment may not move further amendment

A member who has moved or spoken to an amendment may not move a further amendment to the same question.

131   Member who has spoken to main question may not move amendment

A member who has spoken to the main question, or to any amendment that involves the consideration and decision of the main question, may not move an amendment, but may speak to any such amendment when moved by another member.

INTERRUPTION OF DEBATE

132   Interruption of member speaking

A member speaking may be interrupted—

(a)   by a point of order:

(b)   by the raising of a matter of privilege relating to the conduct of strangers present.

133   Interruption of debate

The debate on a question may be interrupted—

(a)   by a point of order:

(b)   by the raising of a matter of privilege relating to the conduct of strangers present:

(c)   by the suspension of a sitting:

(d)   by a message from the Governor-General:

(e)   by a member taking the oath or making the affirmation:

(f)   by a motion that strangers be ordered to withdraw:

(g)   by the making of a ministerial statement, a personal explanation or a maiden statement.

ADJOURNMENT OF DEBATE

134   Adjournment of debate

(1)   After a question has been proposed, any member, on being called to speak to that question, may move "That this debate be now adjourned" either to a later hour on the same day or to any other day. There is no amendment or debate on this question.

(2)   On the adjournment of the House any debate in progress is adjourned and set down for resumption on the next sitting day.

135   Member entitled to speak first on resumption

The member upon whose motion a debate is adjourned or who was speaking when the House adjourned may speak first on the resumption of the debate if the member claims that right.

136   If motion negatived mover may speak

If a motion for the adjournment of the debate is negatived, the member moving the motion for the adjournment may speak, otherwise the member's speech lapses.

CLOSURE OF DEBATE

137   Closure

(1)   After a question has been proposed, any member, on being called to speak to that question, may move, "That the question be now put". In all cases the speech of the member lapses on the moving of the closure motion.

(2)   The Speaker may not accept a closure motion if the time for the debate is prescribed by the Standing Orders or by a determination of the Business Committee.

(3)   The Speaker may accept a closure motion if, in the Speaker's opinion, it is reasonable to do so.

(4)   A temporary Speaker or, in committee, a temporary chairperson may not accept a closure motion.

138   Acceptance of closure motion

If the Speaker accepts a closure motion, a question is put on the closure and decided without amendment or debate.

139   Effect of carrying of closure
(1)   When the question for the closure is agreed to, the question under debate is put without further amendment or debate.
(2)   Any other question (including any proposed amendment that has been properly notified on a Supplementary Order Paper or handed in to the Table before the closure motion was accepted and that relates to the matter under consideration) is then put to allow the main question itself to be decided without further amendment or debate.

PUTTING THE QUESTION

140   Question is put when debate concluded
(1)   Except where otherwise provided, as soon as the debate upon a question is concluded the Speaker puts the question to the House.
(2)   Questions are determined by a majority of votes Aye or No. Every member is entitled to one vote or to abstain.

141   Voice vote
The Speaker asks members to answer "Aye" or "No" to the question and states the result of the voice vote. Any member present may then call for a further vote to be held.

142   Party vote
Where a further vote is called for, a party vote is held unless the subject of the vote is to be treated as a conscience issue.

143   Personal vote on conscience issue
Where the Speaker considers that the subject of a vote is to be treated as a conscience issue, the Speaker will permit a personal vote to be held instead of a party vote.

144   Procedure for party vote
(1)   In a party vote—
    (a)   the Clerk asks the leader of each party or a member authorised by the leader to cast the party's votes; parties are asked to vote in the order of the size of their parliamentary membership:
    (b)   a party's votes may be cast for the Ayes or for the Noes or recorded as an abstention and a party may cast some of its votes in one of these categories and some in another or others (a **split-party** vote):
    (c)   the total number of votes cast for each party may include only those members present within the parliamentary precincts together with any properly authorised proxy votes:
    (d)   after votes have been cast by parties, any Independent member and any member who is voting contrary to his or her party's vote may cast a vote; finally, any proxy vote for a member who is voting contrary to his or her party may be cast:
    (e)   the Speaker declares the result to the House.
(2)   If a party casts a split-party vote the member casting the vote must deliver to the Clerk at the Table, immediately after the vote, a list showing the names of the members of that party voting in the various categories.
(3)   Any member absent from the parliamentary precincts—
    (a)   attending a meeting of a select committee held outside the Wellington area with the agreement of the House or the Business Committee, or
    (b)   attending other official business approved by the Business Committee—
        is regarded as present for the purposes of paragraph (1)(c).
(4)   Subject to Standing Order 156, any party consisting of three or fewer members, and any Independent member, may cast their votes by proxy, otherwise a party may have votes cast on its behalf only if it has a member in the House at the time of the vote.
(5)   The number of votes cast for each party and the names of the members of a party voting in each category on a split-party vote are recorded in the Journals of the House and in *Hansard*.

145   Personal vote following party vote
A personal vote may be held following a party vote if a member requests one and the Speaker considers that the decision on the party vote is so close that a personal vote may make a material difference to the result.

146   Procedure for personal vote
(1)   In a personal vote—
    (a)   the bells are rung for seven minutes:
    (b)   the Speaker directs the Ayes to pass to the right, the Noes to the left and abstentions to the centre and appoints a teller for the Ayes and one for the Noes:

- (c) the doors are closed and locked as soon after the bells have stopped as the Speaker directs, and the Speaker then restates the question:
- (d) all members present within the Chamber or the lobbies when the doors are locked must vote or record their abstentions:
- (e) members' votes are counted by the tellers and their names recorded; members abstaining have their abstentions recorded by the Clerk at the Table:
- (f) the personal vote lists are signed by the tellers and returned to the Speaker, and the Speaker declares the result to the House.
- (2) Members may observe the voting in any part of the Chamber and in the lobbies.

147 Members to remain in Chamber
Members voting or abstaining on a personal vote must remain in the Chamber or in the lobbies until the declaration of the result by the Speaker; the vote or abstention of any member who does not remain in the Chamber or in the lobbies until the declaration of the result is disallowed.

148 One minute bell for personal votes in certain cases
In respect of any personal vote that is held without any debate or other proceeding occurring since the immediately preceding personal vote, the bells may be rung for one minute only.

149 Member acting as teller must continue to act unless excused by Speaker
A member who has begun to act as a teller must continue to act in that capacity unless excused by the Speaker.

150 If no teller no personal vote allowed
If there is no teller for the Ayes or for the Noes the Speaker immediately declares the result for the other side.

151 Records of personal votes
- (1) The names of members who have voted or abstained on a personal vote are recorded in the Journals.
- (2) The personal vote lists show where an individual's vote or abstention is by proxy.

152 Fewer than 20 members participating
Where fewer than 20 members vote or abstain on a personal vote, that vote is of no effect.

153 Errors and mistakes
- (1) In case of confusion or error concerning the result of a vote, the House, unless any error can be otherwise corrected, proceeds to a second vote.
- (2) If the result of a vote has been inaccurately reported, the Speaker may correct it.

154 Ties
In the case of a tie on a vote the question is lost.

155 Proxy voting
- (1) A member may give authority for a proxy vote to be cast in the member's name or for an abstention to be recorded.
- (2) A proxy must state the name of the member who is giving the authority, the date it is given and the period or business for which the authority is valid. It must be signed by the member giving it and indicate the member who is given authority to exercise it.
- (3) A member who has given a proxy may revoke or amend that proxy at any time before its exercise.
- (4) The leader or senior whip of each party, or a member acting as the leader or senior whip of the party in the House for the time being, may exercise a proxy vote for any member of the party, subject to any express direction from a member to the contrary.

156 Casting of proxy vote
- (1) A proxy vote may be cast or an abstention recorded on a party or personal vote only by the person who has authority to exercise it. In the case of any dispute, the member exercising a proxy must produce the authority to the Speaker.
- (2) In the case of a party vote, proxies may be exercised for a number equal to no more than 25 percent of a party's membership in the House, rounded upwards where applicable, but at least one proxy may be exercised for a party.
- (3) In the case of a party vote, proxy votes may be exercised for a party consisting of two or three members only if at least one of the members of that party is within the parliamentary precincts at the time.

(4)   In the case of a party vote, a proxy may be exercised for a party consisting of one member and for any Independent member only if the member concerned is—

    (a)   present within the parliamentary precincts, or

    (b)   absent from the parliamentary precincts attending a meeting of a select committee held outside the Wellington area with the agreement of the House or the Business Committee, or

    (c)   absent from the parliamentary precincts attending other official business approved by the Business Committee, or

    (d)   absent from the parliamentary precincts with the permission of the Speaker granted—

        (i)   for illness or other family cause of a personal nature, or

        (ii)   to enable the member to attend to other public business (whether in New Zealand or overseas).

EXAMINATION BY ORDER OF THE HOUSE

157   Issue and service of summons

(1)   The House may order that a summons be issued to any person—

    (a)   to attend at the bar of the House or before any committee of the House to be examined and give evidence:

    (b)   to produce papers and records in that person's possession, custody or control to the House or a committee.

(2)   Every summons issued at the direction of the House or a committee—

    (a)   must state the time and place at which it is to be complied with by the person to whom it is addressed, and

    (b)   is signed by the Speaker and served upon the person concerned under the Speaker's direction.

158   Examination on oath

(1)   The House may, on motion without notice, order that any person giving evidence before it be examined after taking an oath or making an affirmation.

(2)   When a person is examined on oath or affirmation, the oath or affirmation is administered by the Clerk.

159   Conduct of examination

(1)   The examination of witnesses before the House is conducted as the Speaker, with the approval of the House, directs.

(2)   The Speaker, and every member through the Speaker, may put questions to a witness.

RESPONSES

160   Application for response

(1)   A person (not a member) who has been referred to in the House by name, or in such a way as to be readily identifiable, may make a submission to the Speaker in writing—

    (a)   claiming to have been adversely affected by the reference or to have suffered damage to that person's reputation as a result of the reference, and

    (b)   submitting a response to the reference, and

    (c)   requesting that the response be incorporated in the parliamentary record.

(2)   A submission must be made within three months of the reference having been made.

(3)   Any response must be succinct and strictly relevant to the reference that was made. It must not contain anything offensive in character.

161   Consideration by Speaker

(1)   The Speaker considers whether in all the circumstances of the case the response should be incorporated in the parliamentary record.

(2)   In that consideration, the Speaker—

    (a)   may confer with the person who made the submission and with the member who referred to that person in the House, and

    (b)   takes account of the extent to which the reference is capable of adversely affecting, or damaging the reputation of, the person making the submission.

    (3)   The Speaker is not to consider or judge the truth of the reference made in the House or of the response to it.

162   Speaker decides against incorporation

If the Speaker decides that the response should not be incorporated in the parliamentary record, the Speaker must inform the person concerned that no further action will be taken.

163   Speaker decides response should be incorporated

(1)   A response that the Speaker determines should be incorporated in the parliamentary record is presented to

the House for publication by order of the House.

(2)   The Speaker may decide that a response should be incorporated in the parliamentary record after the person has amended it in a manner approved by the Speaker.

PECUNIARY INTERESTS

164   Pecuniary interests

(1)   Members must make returns of pecuniary interests in accordance with the provisions of Part 1 of Appendix B.

(2)   Returns of members' pecuniary interests are to be maintained in a register in accordance with the provisions of Part 2 of Appendix B.

DECLARATION OF FINANCIAL INTERESTS

165   Financial interests

(1)   A financial interest is a direct financial benefit that might accrue to a member personally, or to any trust, company or other business entity in which the member holds an appreciable interest, as a result of the outcome of the House's consideration of a particular item of business.

(2)   A financial interest—
   (a)   includes a financial interest held by a member's spouse or domestic partner or by any child of the member who is wholly or mainly dependent on the member for support, but
   (b)   does not include any interest held by a member or any other person as one of a class of persons who belong to a profession, vocation or other calling or who hold public offices or an interest held in common with the public.

166   Declaration of financial interest

(1)   A member must, before participating in the consideration of any item of business, declare any financial interest that the member has in that business.

(2)   Nothing in this Standing Order requires a member to declare an interest that is contained in the Register of Pecuniary Interests of Members of Parliament.

167   Speaker decides if interest held

If any dispute arises as to whether a member has a financial interest, the matter is referred to the Speaker, whose decision is final.

MESSAGES AND ADDRESSES

168   Messages from Governor-General

(1)   The Speaker announces to the House a message from the Governor-General.

(2)   The announcement of a message may interrupt a debate but may not interrupt a member who is speaking.

(3)   When the Speaker announces the receipt of a message from the Governor-General, members rise in their places in acknowledgement.

169   Preparation and adoption of addresses

(1)   The Speaker prepares any address agreed to by the House.

(2)   An address must contain any words ordered by the House to be part of the address. Otherwise an Address in Reply must not be controversial.

(3)   The Speaker reads any proposed address to the House and puts the question for its adoption forthwith. There is no amendment or debate on the question.

170   Presentation of addresses

(1)   The Speaker presents or transmits to the Governor-General all addresses adopted by the House.

(2)   An address is presented or transmitted in such manner as the Governor-General approves.

(3)   The Speaker reports to the House the Governor-General's answer to an address.

(4)   An address to the Sovereign may be presented or transmitted to the Governor-General for transmission to the Sovereign.

COMMITTEES OF THE WHOLE HOUSE

171   House resolves itself into committee

On the order of the day being called for going into committee for any purpose, the Speaker declares the House in committee and leaves the Chair without putting any question.

172   Mace placed under Table

When the Speaker has left the Chair, the Mace is placed under the Table.

173   Presiding officers

(1)   The Deputy Speaker or, in the Deputy Speaker's absence, an Assistant Speaker acts as chairperson in a committee of the whole House.

(2)   At any time during a sitting of a committee of the whole House, and without any formal communication to the committee, any member may, at the request of the chairperson, take the Chair as temporary chairperson.

174   Conduct of proceedings

Subject to the express provisions of the Standing Orders, the same rules for the conduct of proceedings are followed in a committee of the whole House as apply to the conduct of proceedings in the House itself.

175   Conduct of examination

(1)   The examination of witnesses is conducted before a committee of the whole House as the chairperson, with the approval of the committee, directs.

(2)   The chairperson, and every member through the chairperson, may put questions to a witness.

176   Committee to consider only matter referred

A committee of the whole House may consider only those matters referred to it by the House.

177   Instructions to a committee of the whole House

(1)   An instruction may be given to a committee of the whole House extending or restricting its powers in regard to consideration of the bill or other matter referred to it or requiring it to carry out that consideration in a particular manner.

(2)   An instruction is moved immediately after the order of the day for consideration in committee has been called.

(3)   There is no amendment or debate on the question for an instruction to a committee requiring it to consider a bill clause by clause. Any debate on the question for any other instruction is restricted to the subject-matter of the motion. It may not extend to the principles, objects or provisions of the bill or other matter to which the motion relates.

(4)   An instruction may not be moved that is the same in substance as an instruction that was agreed to or defeated in the same calendar year.

(5)   A committee may, by leave, vary the terms of any instruction that has been given to it.

178   Disorder in committee

(1)   In the case of any grave disorder arising in committee, the chairperson may temporarily suspend the proceedings of the committee.

(2)   Where the proceedings of a committee are temporarily suspended, the Speaker automatically resumes the Chair.

179   Report to take Speaker's ruling

A motion may be moved that the chairperson obtain the Speaker's ruling on a matter of procedure. There is no amendment or debate on the question.

180   Interruption of proceedings

Whenever the proceedings of a committee are suspended on account of disorder or for a Speaker's ruling to be taken, the Speaker may, after dealing with such matters as are necessary, declare the House in committee again and leave the Chair. In committee, business is resumed at the point of interruption.

181   Committee may not adjourn

A committee of the whole House may not adjourn its own sitting or the consideration of any matter to a future sitting.

182   Motions to report progress

(1)   A member may move, "That the committee report progress". On the report being agreed to by the House, the bill or other matter is set down for further consideration in committee on the next sitting day.

(2)   The member in charge of a bill may move, "That the committee report progress and sit again presently". On the report being agreed to by the House, the bill is set down for further consideration in committee later in the sitting.

(3)   There is no amendment or debate on a question to report progress.

183   Report

(1)   When all the matters referred to a committee of the whole House have been considered, the chairperson reports them to the House.

(2)   When all such matters have not been considered, the chairperson reports progress, or no progress, as the case may be.

184   Adoption of report
In reporting to the House, the chairperson moves that the report be adopted. There is no amendment or debate on the question.

CHAPTER IV

SELECT COMMITTEES

ESTABLISHMENT OF COMMITTEES
185   Establishment and life of select committees
(1)   The following select committees are established at the commencement of each Parliament:
    (a)   the subject select committees specified in Standing Order 189, and
    (b)   the Officers of Parliament Committee, the Privileges Committee, the Regulations Review Committee and the Standing Orders Committee.
(2)   The House may establish other select committees.
(3)   A select committee continues in existence for the duration of the Parliament unless the House provides otherwise or, in the case of a committee established for a particular purpose, until the committee makes its final report.

186   Membership of committees
(1)   The overall membership of select committees must, so far as reasonably practicable, be proportional to party membership in the House.
(2)   The Business Committee may determine the size of each committee.
(3)   The Business Committee may appoint members to serve on each committee and may fill a vacancy in the membership of a committee.

187   Non-voting members
(1)   The Business Committee may appoint a member to serve on a select committee but without the right to vote on any question put to the committee.
(2)   Such membership may be permanent, for a limited time or for consideration of a particular matter.
(3)   The Business Committee may end such an appointment.

188   Changes in membership
(1)   A change in the membership of a committee may be a permanent change for the life of the committee or a temporary change for a limited time or for consideration of a particular matter.
(2)   Changes which are in the nature of permanent replacements in the membership of a select committee may be made by the Business Committee and temporary replacements by the leader or a whip of the party or parties to which each member involved belongs.
(3)   A member may not be replaced on a committee during any period in which the member is suspended from the service of the House.

SUBJECT SELECT COMMITTEES
189   Subject select committees
The subject select committees and their subject areas are—
Commerce Committee: business development, commerce, communications, consumer affairs, energy, information technology, insurance and superannuation
Education and Science Committee: education, education review, industry training, research, science and technology
Finance and Expenditure Committee: audit of the financial statements of the Government and departments, Government finance, revenue and taxation
Foreign Affairs, Defence and Trade Committee: customs, defence, disarmament and arms control, foreign affairs, immigration and trade
Government Administration Committee: civil defence, cultural affairs, fitness, sport and leisure, internal affairs, Pacific Island affairs, Prime Minister and Cabinet, racing, services to Parliament, State services, statistics, tourism, women's affairs and youth affairs
Health Committee: health
Justice and Electoral Committee: Crown legal and drafting services, electoral matters, human rights and justice
Law and Order Committee: corrections, courts, criminal law, police and serious fraud

Local Government and Environment Committee: conservation, environment and local government
Māori Affairs Committee: Māori affairs
Primary Production Committee: agriculture, biosecurity, fisheries, forestry, lands and land information
Social Services Committee: housing, senior citizens, social development, veterans' affairs and work and income support
Transport and Industrial Relations Committee: accident compensation, industrial relations, labour, occupational health and safety, transport and transport safety.

190   Functions of subject select committees

(1)   The subject select committees specified in Standing Order 189 consider and report to the House on the following types of business referred by the House or otherwise under Standing Orders:
    (a)   bills:
    (b)   petitions:
    (c)   financial reviews:
    (d)   Estimates:
    (e)   Supplementary Estimates:
    (f)   international treaty examinations:
    (g)   any other matters.

(2)   The subject select committees may receive briefings on, or initiate inquiries into, matters related to their respective subject areas as specified in Standing Order 189.

(3)   Paragraph (2) does not allow a subject select committee to consider—
    (a)   a bill that has not been referred to it, except as provided in Standing Orders, or
    (b)   a Supplementary Order Paper relating to a bill that is not before the committee—
without the approval of the House or the Business Committee.

MEETINGS OF COMMITTEES

191   Time for meetings

(1)   The first meeting of a select committee is held at a time appointed by the Speaker.

(2)   A committee adjourns until the time it decides that it should next meet. In the absence of a time decided by the committee for its next meeting, the chairperson, by notice in writing, decides when it should next meet.

(3)   If there is no chairperson or deputy chairperson or if they are both absent from New Zealand, the Speaker may exercise the chairperson's power to decide when the committee should meet.

192   Meetings on Fridays

Except by leave of the committee, a select committee may not meet on a Friday in a week in which there has been a sitting of the House.

193   Place of meeting

A select committee may meet at any place within New Zealand. It must be authorised by the House before it can meet outside New Zealand.

194   Meetings outside Wellington area

A committee may meet outside the Wellington area,—
    (a)   during a sitting of the House, only with the agreement of the Business Committee, and
    (b)   otherwise than during a sitting of the House, only if the committee has itself agreed to the place for its meeting.

195   Meetings within Wellington area

(1)   When meeting within the Wellington area, a select committee may not meet—
    (a)   during questions for oral answer:
    (b)   during a sitting of the House, except by leave of the committee:
    (c)   during an evening (after 6 pm) on a day on which there has been a sitting of the House.

(2)   When a meeting within the Wellington area is in progress at 6 pm on a day on which there has been a sitting of the House, it may be continued while the leave of the committee is forthcoming in order to conclude business before the committee.

POWERS OF COMMITTEES

196   Seeking evidence

(1)   The chairperson of a select committee may, on behalf of the committee, request any person to attend and give evidence before the committee.

(2)   The chairperson may, on behalf of the committee, request that papers and records that are relevant to its proceedings be produced.

197   Exercise of power to send for persons, papers and records

(1)   A committee with the power to send for persons, papers and records may order that a summons be issued to any person—

   (a)   to attend before that committee to be examined and give evidence:

   (b)   to produce papers and records in that person's possession, custody or control to that committee.

(2)   Every summons issued under this Standing Order—

   (a)   must state the time and place at which it is to be complied with by the person to whom it is addressed, and

   (b)   is signed by the Speaker and served upon the person concerned under the Speaker's direction.

198   Application to Speaker for summons

(1)   A select committee without the power to send for persons, papers and records may apply to the Speaker, in writing, seeking the issue of a summons to any person—

   (a)   to attend and be examined and give evidence before the committee:

   (b)   to produce papers and records in that person's possession, custody or control to the committee.

(2)   When an application is received, a summons may be issued if the Speaker is satisfied that—

   (a)   the evidence, papers or records sought by the committee are necessary to its proceedings, and

   (b)   the committee has taken all reasonable steps to obtain the evidence, papers or records.

(3)   Every summons issued under this Standing Order—

   (a)   must state the time and place at which it is to be complied with by the person to whom it is addressed, and

   (b)   is signed by the Speaker and served upon the person concerned under the Speaker's direction.

199   Subcommittees

(1)   A select committee may appoint a subcommittee.

(2)   Committees may prescribe rules for the conduct of subcommittee proceedings provided that these rules are consistent with Standing Orders. Subject to any such rules, the same rules for the conduct of proceedings in a subcommittee apply as apply to a select committee.

200   Criminal wrongdoing

(1)   Without the express authority of the House, a select committee may not inquire into, or make findings in respect of, allegations of crime by persons who are named or otherwise identifiable.

(2)   A select committee is not prevented, by reason of paragraph (1), from conducting inquiries, and making findings, of a general nature into alleged criminal wrongdoing by persons who are not named or otherwise identifiable.

201   Charges against members

(1)   A select committee (except the Privileges Committee) may not enquire into, or make findings in respect of, the private conduct of any member of the House, unless it is specially directed by the House to do so.

(2)   If any information comes before a select committee or any allegation is made to a select committee (except the Privileges Committee) charging any member with reprehensible conduct, the committee must inform the member concerned of the details of the charge and give the member a reasonable opportunity to make any statement to it bearing on the matter. Otherwise the committee may not proceed further on that information or allegation without being specially directed by the House to do so.

CHAIRPERSON AND DEPUTY CHAIRPERSON

202   Chairperson and deputy chairperson

(1)   At its first meeting, or at its first meeting after a vacancy occurs in the office, a select committee must proceed to the election of a chairperson and the appointment of a deputy chairperson.

(2)   The chairperson and the deputy chairperson may be removed from office by the committee only at a meeting of which at least seven days' notice is given of a member's intention to move for such a removal.

(3)   The Speaker is the chairperson of the Officers of Parliament Committee.

203   Absence of chairperson

(1)   In the absence of the chairperson—

   (a)   during a meeting, or

   (b)   from New Zealand,—

   and during a vacancy in the office, the deputy chairperson may perform the duties and exercise the authority of the chairperson.

(2)   If the chairperson and the deputy chairperson are not present at the commencement of a meeting, the committee may elect a member of the committee to chair that meeting and perform the duties and exercise the authority of the chairperson in respect of the meeting.

(3)   The chairperson or the deputy chairperson may, while chairing a meeting, ask any member of the

committee to chair the meeting while the chairperson or deputy chairperson is absent. Any such member performs the duties and exercises the authority of the chairperson while chairing the meeting.

204   Transfer of powers of chairperson during meeting

(1)   The chairperson of a select committee may invite the committee to authorise the deputy chairperson or, in the absence of the deputy chairperson, any other member of the committee to chair meetings while a particular item of business is considered.

(2)   The chairperson may participate as a committee member when the deputy chairperson or another member is authorised to chair a meeting under this Standing Order.

(3)   A member who chairs a meeting under this Standing Order performs the duties and exercises the authority of the chairperson while chairing the meeting.

CONDUCT OF PROCEEDINGS

205   Conduct of proceedings

Subject to the express provisions of Standing Orders or any practice of the House to the contrary, the same rules for the conduct of proceedings are followed by select committees as apply to the conduct of proceedings in a committee of the whole House.

206   Notice of meeting

(1)   A written notice informing members of the committee of a meeting of the committee is to be circulated by the clerk of the committee no later than the day before the meeting. The notice must contain a summary of the items of business proposed to be dealt with at the meeting.

(2)   The requirement for a written notice to be circulated may be waived if all members of the committee, or the leaders or whips of their respective parties, agree. When a meeting has lapsed or been adjourned for lack of a quorum, agreement is required under this paragraph only from those members who were expected to attend that meeting.

207   Giving notice of business

(1)   Members of a committee may give notice of business or motions to be considered by the committee either orally at a meeting of the committee or in writing to the clerk of the committee.

(2)   Notices given at a meeting and notices given to the clerk of the committee before 2 pm on the day before a meeting are placed on the agenda for the next meeting of the committee or, where the Standing Orders prescribe a longer period of notice, for the first meeting at which the notice may be considered.

(3)   Nothing in this Standing Order affects the chairperson's power to rule on whether a proposed notice is in order.

208   Question previously decided

A motion or an amendment that is the same in substance as a motion or amendment that was agreed to or defeated in a select committee may be proposed again in that committee in the same calendar year only by leave or if notice has been given.

209   Names of members present

The names of the members of a select committee present at a meeting are recorded in the committee's minutes.

210   Quorum

(1)   The quorum of a select committee is half of the membership of the committee (rounded upwards where applicable).

(2)   A non-voting member is not counted as part of the membership of a committee for the purposes of determining the quorum.

(3)   If there is no quorum present within 10 minutes of the time for a meeting to commence, the meeting is adjourned. If there is no quorum present during a meeting, the meeting is suspended for up to 10 minutes and, if no quorum is formed, the meeting is adjourned.

211   Members may be present

(1)   Subject to this Standing Order, any member of the House (not being a member of the committee) may attend any meeting of a select committee but can participate in the proceedings only by leave of the committee.

(2)   The Minister or member in charge of a bill may take part in the proceedings of the committee even though not a member of the committee but may not vote on any question put to the committee.

(3)   Except by leave of the committee, only members of the Privileges Committee may attend any meeting of that committee while the committee is deliberating.

212   Advisers

(1)   A select committee may seek the assistance of persons as advisers to the committee during its consideration of a matter.

(2)   Advisers may remain present during relevant proceedings that are not open to the public, unless excluded by the committee.

213   Attendance by strangers

A select committee may—

(a)   invite any person to be present during relevant proceedings that are not open to the public to assist it in its consideration of any matter:

(b)   by leave, allow a stranger (not present to assist the committee) to be present during proceedings that are not open to the public.

214   Voting

A member may require that the respective votes or abstentions of each member present on a question put to a select committee be recorded in the committee's minutes.

215   Disorder

(1)   The chairperson may order any stranger to withdraw from a meeting if that person's conduct is disorderly.

(2)   The chairperson may order any member (not being a member of the committee) to withdraw from a meeting if that member's conduct is disorderly.

(3)   A select committee may resolve to exclude a member of the committee from its meeting if that member's conduct is highly disorderly. The member may be excluded for up to the remainder of the meeting held on that day.

GENERAL PROVISIONS FOR EVIDENCE

216   Written submissions

A witness will be given the opportunity to make a submission in writing before appearing to give oral evidence.

217   Return of evidence

A select committee may return, or expunge from any transcript of proceedings, any evidence or statement that it considers to be irrelevant to its proceedings, offensive or possibly defamatory.

218   Release of submissions

(1)   A select committee may make a written submission to it available to the public at any time after receiving it.

(2)   A submission (if not already made available) becomes available to the public on the committee hearing oral evidence from the witness who made the submission.

(3)   This Standing Order does not prevent the release of a submission by the person who submitted it.

219   Private evidence

(1)   Some or all of the evidence to be given to a select committee may, by leave, be heard or received in private.

(2)   The committee may require all strangers or any stranger to withdraw from a meeting while evidence is being heard in private.

(3)   Evidence heard or received in private is confidential to the committee until it reports to the House.

220   Secret evidence

(1)   A select committee may, by leave, declare evidence to be secret evidence where—

(a)   information that it wishes to obtain can be obtained only if it can assure a witness, or other person in possession of that information, that evidence given to it will remain confidential, or

(b)   it is satisfied that it is necessary to do so to protect the reputation of any person.

(2)   All strangers must withdraw from a meeting while secret evidence is being heard, unless leave is given for them to remain present.

(3)   Except to give effect to Standing Order 238, secret evidence may not be disclosed to any other person by the committee or by any member of the committee or by any other person, unless the House expressly authorises such disclosure. Following the committee's report to the House, secret evidence is delivered into the custody of the Clerk.

221   Application for evidence to be private or secret

(1)   Before providing written evidence to a select committee, a person may apply for that evidence to be received in private or in secret. Where practicable, witnesses are informed before providing written

evidence that such an application may be made.

(2) Before giving evidence, or at any time while being heard, a witness may apply for any or all of the evidence of that witness to be heard in private or in secret. All witnesses are informed before giving evidence that such an application may be made.

(3) A witness must give reasons for any such application.

(4) Before giving evidence in private, a witness will be informed that the evidence will become available when the committee reports to the House or, if it may seriously damage the reputation of any person, will be made available to that person. Before giving evidence in secret, a witness will be informed that secret evidence may be disclosed to give effect to Standing Order 238 and that the House has the power to order the disclosure of such evidence.

222   Access to information

A select committee will give a witness reasonable access to any material or other information that the witness has produced to the committee.

HEARING OF EVIDENCE

223   Public attendance at hearings

(1) The proceedings of any select committee during the hearing of evidence on a bill or other matter, which is the subject of consideration by the committee, are open to the public, unless the evidence is private or secret.

(2) A committee may require all strangers or any stranger to withdraw from a meeting while the committee is formally receiving a delegation that includes a member, or members, of another Parliament.

224   Matters of concern before giving evidence

A person who is to appear before a committee may raise any matters of concern relating to that evidence with the clerk of the committee before appearing before the committee. Any such matters will be brought to the attention of the committee.

225   Conduct of examination

(1) The examination of witnesses is conducted as the chairperson, with the approval of the select committee, directs.

(2) The chairperson, and every member through the chairperson, may put questions to a witness.

226   Relevance of questions

(1) The chairperson will take care to ensure that all questions put to a witness are relevant to the committee's proceedings and that the information sought by those questions is necessary for the purpose of those proceedings.

(2) A witness may object to a question on the ground that it is not relevant. The chairperson will then determine whether it is relevant to the committee's proceedings.

227   Objections to answer

Where a witness objects on any ground to answering a relevant question put to the witness, the witness will be invited to state the ground upon which objection to answering the question is taken.

228   Committee consideration of objections

(1) Where a witness objects to answering a question on any ground, the select committee, unless it decides immediately that the question should not be pressed, will then consider in private whether it will insist upon an answer to the question, having regard to the importance to the proceedings of the information sought by the question.

(2) If the committee decides that it requires an answer to the question, the witness will be informed of that decision, and is required to answer the question.

(3) The committee may decide that the public interest would best be served by hearing the answer in private or secret.

(4) Where a witness declines to answer a question to which the committee has required an answer, the committee may report this fact to the House.

229   Counsel

(1) A witness may be accompanied by counsel (of the witness's choice) and may consult counsel in the course of a meeting at which the witness appears.

(2) Counsel may—

    (a) make written submissions to the committee on the procedure to be followed by the committee:

    (b) with the committee's agreement, address the committee on the procedure to be followed by the committee before counsel's client is heard:

(c)   object to a question to counsel's client on the ground that it is not relevant:

(d)   object to counsel's client answering a question:

(e)   when the client's reputation may be seriously damaged by proceedings of a committee, ask that further witnesses give evidence in the client's interest.

230   Witnesses' expenses

(1)   No expenses may be paid to any witness or proposed witness except with the permission of the Speaker.

(2)   No select committee, chairperson, member or other person may give any undertaking, promise or assurance to any person that any expenses of a witness or proposed witness will be paid out of public money without first obtaining the authority of the Speaker.

231   Evidence on oath

(1)   A select committee may order any person to take an oath or make an affirmation before giving evidence to it.

(2)   When a person gives evidence on oath or affirmation, the oath or affirmation is administered by the clerk of the committee.

232   Transcripts of evidence

(1)   A select committee may decide to record and, if it thinks fit, transcribe evidence given to it.

(2)   Reasonable opportunity will be afforded to witnesses to make corrections of errors of transcription in any transcript of their evidence.

NATURAL JUSTICE

233   Disqualification for apparent bias

A member who has (whether in the House or outside the House) made an allegation of crime or expressed a concluded view on any conduct or activity of a criminal nature, identifying by name or otherwise a person as being responsible for or associated with that crime, conduct or activity (referred to as **apparent bias**), may not participate—

(a)   in any select committee inquiry into that person's responsibility for or association with that crime, conduct or activity, or

(b)   in any other proceedings in a select committee that may seriously damage the reputation of that person.

234   Complaints of apparent bias

(1)   A complaint of apparent bias on the part of a member of a select committee may be made by any member (whether or not a member of the committee) or by any person appearing or about to appear before the committee whose reputation may be seriously damaged by proceedings of the committee.

(2)   A complaint of apparent bias must be made, in writing, to the chairperson.

(3)   The chairperson, after considering any information or comment from the member against whom the complaint is made, decides whether the member is disqualified by reason of apparent bias.

(4)   Any member of a committee who is dissatisfied with the chairperson's decision on a complaint of apparent bias may refer the matter to the Speaker for decision. The Speaker's decision is final.

235   Evidence containing allegations

(1)   At any stage during a select committee's proceedings, the committee may consider hearing in private evidence that contains an allegation that may seriously damage the reputation of a person. The committee may also invite that person to be present during the hearing of such evidence.

(2)   A person who is to appear before a committee will be informed of or given a copy of any evidence (other than secret evidence) or material in the committee's possession that contains an allegation that may seriously damage the reputation of that person.

236   Access to information by person whose reputation may be seriously damaged

(1)   Any person whose reputation may be seriously damaged by proceedings of a select committee may request from the clerk of the committee a copy of all material, evidence (except secret evidence), records or other information that the committee possesses concerning that person.

(2)   The committee considers any such request and may, if it considers it to be necessary to prevent serious damage to that person's reputation, furnish such material.

(3)   The committee may furnish such material in a form different from that requested if to provide it in the form requested would impose undue difficulty, expense or delay.

237   Irrelevant or unjustified allegations

When a witness gives evidence that contains an allegation that may seriously damage the reputation of a person and the select committee is not satisfied that that evidence is relevant to its proceedings or is satisfied that the evidence creates a risk of harm to that person, which risk exceeds the benefit of the evidence, the committee will give consideration—

(a)   to returning any written evidence and requesting that it be resubmitted without the offending material:

(b)   to expunging that evidence from any transcript of evidence:

(c)   to seeking an order of the House preventing the disclosure of that evidence.

238   Information about allegation that may seriously damage reputation

(1)   When, in evidence heard or received in public or in private, an allegation is made against a person that may seriously damage the reputation of that person, the committee will—

(a)   apply Standing Order 237, and

(b)   if the evidence is not to be returned, resubmitted or expunged under that Standing Order, inform that person of the allegation.

(2)   When, in evidence heard or received in secret, an allegation is made against a person that may seriously damage the reputation of that person, the committee will—

(a)   apply Standing Order 237, and

(b)   if the evidence is not to be returned, resubmitted or expunged under that Standing Order, inform that person of the allegation if it appears to the committee that the possible damage to that person's reputation outweighs any detriment to the witness who gave the secret evidence.

(3)   When, in advice provided to a committee, an allegation is made against a person that may seriously damage the reputation of that person, the committee will—

(a)   return the advice (if it is in writing) after considering whether to request that it be provided again without the allegation, or

(b)   inform that person of the allegation.

239   Responding where allegation may seriously damage reputation

(1)   Any person against whom an allegation has been made that may seriously damage the reputation of that person, and who has been informed of that allegation under Standing Order 238,—

(a)   will be given a reasonable opportunity to respond to the allegation by written submission and appearance before the committee, and

(b)   may ask that further witnesses give evidence to the committee in that person's interest.

(2)   A response made or further evidence given under this Standing Order is received or heard—

(a)   in private, if the allegation was made in private evidence or in advice:

(b)   in secret, if the allegation was made in secret evidence.

INFORMATION ON PROCEEDINGS

240   Confidentiality of proceedings

(1)   The proceedings of a select committee or a subcommittee other than during the hearing of evidence are not open to the public and remain strictly confidential to the committee until it reports to the House.

(2)   Paragraph (1) does not prevent—

(a)   the disclosure, by the committee or by a member of the committee, of proceedings to a member of Parliament or to the Clerk or another officer of the House in the course of their duties:

(b)   the disclosure of proceedings in accordance with Standing Orders.

(3)   The following proceedings may be disclosed:

(a)   those proceedings that do not relate to any business or decision still before the committee:

(b)   those proceedings in respect of matters of process or procedure that do not—

(i)   relate to decisions on matters of process or procedure that are still before the committee, or

(ii)   include any substantive proceedings relating to business before the committee, or

(iii)   reflect, or divulge the contents of, a report or draft report or the committee's potential findings.

(4)   A committee making an interim report or a special report to the House may resolve that some or all proceedings relating to the report remain confidential to the committee until it reports finally to the House.

241   Confidentiality of reports

(1)   A report or a draft of the report of a select committee or a subcommittee is strictly confidential to the committee until it reports to the House.

(2)   Paragraph (1) does not prevent—

(a)   the disclosure, by the committee or by a member of the committee, of a report or a draft report to a member of Parliament or to the Clerk or another officer of the House in the course of their duties:

(b)   the disclosure of a report or a draft report in accordance with Standing Orders.

242 Confidentiality of lapsed business

(1) Any proceedings of a select committee or draft report that is confidential to the committee on the dissolution or expiration of Parliament remains confidential for nine sitting days in the new Parliament.

(2) If the business to which proceedings or a draft report relate is reinstated by the House or is readopted by the committee concerned within nine sitting days of the opening of the new Parliament, those proceedings or the draft report continue to remain confidential in accordance with Standing Orders 240 and 241.

243 Information on committee's proceedings

(1) The chairperson of a select committee or a subcommittee may, with the agreement of the committee, make a public statement to inform the public of the nature of the committee's consideration of a matter.

(2) The committee or subcommittee may make its proceedings available to any person for the purpose of assisting in the committee's consideration of a matter. When proceedings have been disclosed under this paragraph, any evidence provided in response to those proceedings is received in private, unless it is received in secret.

REPORTS

244 Interim reports

A select committee may from time to time make an interim report informing the House of some only of its conclusions on a bill or other matter before it or of the progress of its investigation into a bill or other matter.

245 Special reports

A select committee may from time to time make a special report to the House seeking authority from the House to do something, or seeking guidance from the House on some procedural question which has occurred in the committee, or informing the House of some other matter connected with its proceedings which it considers should be reported to the House.

246 Minority views

A select committee may, in its report, indicate the differing views of its members.

247 Findings

(1) As soon as practicable after a select committee has determined any findings to be included in a report to the House, and prior to the presentation of the report, any person named in the report whose reputation may be seriously damaged by those findings must be acquainted with any such findings and afforded a reasonable opportunity to respond to the committee on them. The committee will take such a response into account before making its report to the House.

(2) Any response made under this Standing Order is strictly confidential to the committee until it reports to the House.

248 Reports to be signed

When a select committee has adopted a report, the report is signed by the chairperson on behalf of the committee, or by some other member of the committee authorised to do so by the committee, and is presented to the House.

249 Day fixed for presentation of reports

When a day is fixed for the presentation of a select committee's report, the final report must be made on or before that day, unless the House grants further time.

250 Presentation of reports

(1) A report of a select committee is presented by delivering it to the Clerk on any working day but no later than 1 pm on a day on which the House sits.

(2) Once a report has been presented it is published under the authority of the House.

(3) The Clerk announces the presentation of reports of select committees at the time appointed by Standing Order 63.

251 Reports set down

(1) Following their presentation, reports of select committees are set down as follows—

   (a) a report from the Privileges Committee is set down for consideration as general business:

   (b) a report on a bill is set down as prescribed in Standing Order 292:

   (c) reports on the Budget policy statement, the fiscal strategy report and the economic and fiscal update, the financial statements of the Government, Estimates, Supplementary Estimates and financial reviews are considered as determined under Standing Orders 324, 332, 338 and 341:

   (d) a report on a notice of motion under Standing Order 317 is set down for consideration together with that notice of motion.

(2)   The Business Committee may direct that a report on a petition be set down as a Members' order of the day.

(3)   A report on a briefing, inquiry, international treaty examination or other matter, or a report of the Regulations Review Committee, is set down as a Members' order of the day.

252   Consideration of reports

(1)   On the consideration of any select committee report (other than a report on a bill or a report to which paragraph (2) applies), the chairperson of the select committee moves a motion to take note of the report. In the absence of the chairperson any other member of the committee may move the motion.

(2)   On the consideration of a report of the Privileges Committee containing a recommendation to the House, the chairperson or a member of that committee may move a motion that reflects that recommendation.

253   Government responses to select committee reports

(1)   The Government must, not more than 90 days after a select committee report has been presented, present a paper to the House responding to any recommendations of the committee which are addressed to it.

(2)   No response under this Standing Order is required in respect of select committee reports on bills, Supplementary Order Papers, questions of privilege, Estimates, Supplementary Estimates and financial reviews of departments, Offices of Parliament, Crown entities, public organisations or State enterprises.

CHAPTER V

LEGISLATIVE PROCEDURES

FORM OF BILLS

254   Classification of bills

(1)   A bill may be introduced as—

   (a)   a Government bill—a bill dealing with a matter of public policy introduced by a Minister, or

   (b)   a Member's bill—a bill dealing with a matter of public policy introduced by a member who is not a Minister, or

   (c)   a local bill—a bill promoted by a local authority and which affects a particular locality only, or

   (d)   a private bill—a bill promoted by a person or body of persons (whether incorporated or not) for the particular interest or benefit of that person or body of persons,—

   and a bill must show on its face which of these types it is.

(2)   If any question arises as to the classification of a bill, the Speaker decides the matter.

255   Enacting formula in bills

The enacting formula in bills introduced into the House is in the following form:

   "The Parliament of New Zealand enacts as follows:"

or, in the case of bills containing a preamble,—

   "The Parliament of New Zealand therefore enacts as follows:".

256   Title

(1)   The first clause of each bill is confined to stating the title by which the Act is to be known.

(2)   If the Act is to be part of another Act, the clause may also state that fact, and how that other Act is to be referred to.

257   Date of commencement

(1)   A bill must include a distinct clause stating when the bill comes into force.

(2)   If different provisions of a bill are to come into force on different dates, the distinct clause may refer to separate clauses or subclauses that state when each of those provisions comes into force.

258   Explanatory notes

Every bill as introduced must have an explanatory note that states the policy that the bill seeks to achieve, and may also explain the provisions of the bill.

259   Private bills

Every private bill must contain a preamble, setting out the facts on which the bill is founded and the circumstances giving rise to the necessity for it. If the objects of the bill could be attained otherwise than by legislation, the preamble must state why legislation is preferred.

260   Temporary law

(1)   If a bill for an Act provides that the whole of the Act itself is to be repealed or is to expire, that repeal or expiry must be provided for in a distinct clause in the bill.

(2) If a bill for an Act provides that a provision of the Act is to be repealed or is to expire, that repeal or expiry must be provided for in a distinct clause or a distinct subclause in the bill.

(3) This Standing Order does not apply in relation to a provision of a bill that is to be incorporated into another enactment, for example, a new section inserted into a principal Act.

OMNIBUS BILLS
261   Bills to relate to one subject area
(1) Except as otherwise permitted by Standing Orders, a bill must relate to one subject area only.

(2) A bill may make consequential amendments to a number of Acts affected by its provisions.

262   Speaker to scrutinise bills
The Speaker scrutinises each bill on its introduction to ensure that it complies with Standing Order 261. Any bill that does not comply is discharged or allowed to proceed with such amendments as the Speaker directs.

263   Types of omnibus bills that may be introduced
(1) The following types of bills may be introduced although they are omnibus in nature:
  (a) Finance bills or confirmation bills that validate or authorise action otherwise illegal or validate and confirm regulations:
  (b) Local Legislation bills that contain provisions affecting particular localities that otherwise would have been introduced as local bills:
  (c) Māori Purposes bills that—
    (i) amend one or more Acts relating to Māori affairs, or
    (ii) deal with authorisations, transfers and validations in respect of Māori land and property:
  (d) Reserves and Other Lands Disposal bills that—
    (i) deal only with authorisations, transfers and validations of matters relating to Crown land, reserves and other land held for public or private purposes, or
    (ii) amend a Reserves and Other Lands Disposal Act:
  (e) Statutes Amendment bills that consist entirely of amendments to Acts.

(2) Matter more appropriate for inclusion in a Local Legislation Bill, a Māori Purposes Bill, or a Reserves and Other Lands Disposal Bill is to be included in one of those types of bills rather than a Finance Bill.

264   Law reform or other omnibus bills
A law reform or other omnibus bill to amend more than one Act may be introduced if—
  (a) the amendments deal with an interrelated topic that can be regarded as implementing a single broad policy, or
  (b) the amendments to be effected to each Act are of a similar nature in each case, or
  (c) the Business Committee has agreed to the bill's introduction as a law reform or omnibus bill.

GENERAL PROVISIONS
265   Same bill or amendment not to be proposed
The following may not be proposed in the same calendar year:
  (a) a bill that is the same in substance as a bill that received, or was defeated on, a first, second or third reading:
  (b) an amendment to a bill that is the same in substance as an amendment that was agreed to or defeated in a committee of the whole House.

266   New Zealand Bill of Rights
(1) Whenever a bill contains any provision which appears to the Attorney-General to be inconsistent with any of the rights and freedoms contained in the New Zealand Bill of Rights Act 1990, the Attorney-General, before a motion for the bill's first reading is moved, must indicate to the House what that provision is and how it appears to be inconsistent with the New Zealand Bill of Rights Act 1990.

(2) An indication by the Attorney-General to the House concerning the New Zealand Bill of Rights Act 1990 is made by the presentation of a paper for publication by order of the House.

(3) Where the House has accorded urgency to the introduction of a bill, the Attorney-General may, on the bill's introduction, present a paper under this Standing Order and move, without notice, that the paper be published. There is no debate or amendment on the question.

267   Entrenched provisions
(1) A proposal for entrenchment must itself be carried in a committee of the whole House by the majority that it would require for the amendment or repeal of the provision to be entrenched.

(2) A **proposal for entrenchment** is any provision in a bill or amendment to a bill that would require that that provision or amendment or any other provision can be amended or repealed only by a majority of more than 50 percent plus one of all the members of the House.

268   Copies of bills

(1)   On the introduction of a bill, the member in charge must provide printed copies of the bill to the Clerk for circulation.

(2)   A bill must be reprinted when it is reported by a select committee or committee of the whole House if it is reported with amendment or is divided by the committee, except—

   (a)   a bill passed under urgency, or

   (b)   a bill that is set down for third reading forthwith, or

   (c)   as approved by the Speaker in respect of any minor textual amendment.

(3)   If a bill is reprinted,—

   (a)   the member in charge must provide printed copies of the reprinted bill to the Clerk for circulation, and

   (b)   the bill is not available for debate until copies of it, as reprinted, have been circulated to members.

269   Passing of bills

(1)   A bill must be read three times by order of the House to be passed by the House.

(2)   On every order for the reading of a bill the title only is read.

270   Special rules in respect of Appropriation and Imprest Supply bills

The procedures for passing Appropriation bills and Imprest Supply bills are subject to the special rules set out in Chapter VI.

271   Member's bill may be adopted by Government

(1)   The Government may, with the agreement of the member in charge, adopt a Member's bill.

(2)   The Minister adopting a bill for the Government must notify the Speaker in writing that the bill has been adopted by the Government.

(3)   A bill adopted by the Government is thereafter treated as a Government bill.

272   Private bill petitions

Before a petition for a private bill can be presented the bill must be endorsed as complying with Standing Orders as provided in Appendix C.

273   Local bills and Local Legislation bills

(1)   Legislation that would otherwise require to be introduced by means of a local bill may be included in a Local Legislation Bill.

(2)   Before a local bill or a Local Legislation Bill is introduced it must be endorsed as complying with Standing Orders as provided in Appendix C.

274   Withdrawal of local bills and private bills

(1)   The promoter of a local bill or a private bill may, in writing, notify the Speaker that the promoter withdraws the bill. The Speaker informs the House of any such notification.

(2)   A bill that has been withdrawn is discharged from further consideration by the House.

INTRODUCTION

275   Introduction of Government bills

A Government bill is introduced by the Leader of the House informing the Clerk on any working day or by 1 pm on any sitting day of the Government's intention to introduce the bill.

276   Introduction of Members' bills

(1)   A Member's bill is introduced after notice of intention to introduce it is given and the bill's introduction has been announced to the House. Notice is given by delivering a signed copy to the Clerk between 9 am and 10 am on a sitting day.

(2)   A fair copy of every Member's bill must be delivered to the Clerk no later than the time at which the member gives notice of intention to introduce it.

277   Ballot for Members' bills

(1)   There may not be more than four orders of the day for the first readings of Members' bills before the House at any one time. The Clerk rejects any notices that would lead to more than this number.

(2)   If two or more notices to introduce Members' bills are given on the same day, the Clerk conducts a ballot at midday on that day to determine which bills are to be introduced and the order in which they are to be introduced.

(3)   No member is to be entered in a ballot in respect of more than one notice and only one notice is to be entered in respect of any bills that are the same or substantially the same in substance. When members have, on the same day, given notices in respect of bills that are the same or substantially the same in

substance, the notice that is to be entered in the ballot is (in the absence of agreement among the members concerned) determined by a ballot conducted by the Clerk.

278   Introduction of local bills
A local bill is introduced when notice of intention to introduce it is given by any member by delivering a signed copy to the Clerk on any working day or by 1 pm on any sitting day.

279   Introduction of private bills
A private bill is introduced by presenting a petition for the bill to the House.

280   Announcement of introduction of bills
The Clerk announces the introduction of bills at the time appointed by Standing Order 63.

281   Introduction of Appropriation bills, Imprest Supply bills and bills under urgency
An Appropriation Bill, an Imprest Supply Bill and any bill to which the House has accorded urgency may be introduced and proceeded with at any time but not so as to interrupt a debate.

FIRST READING
282   Bills set down for first reading
After its introduction a bill is set down for first reading on the third sitting day following.

283   First reading
The motion on the order of the day for the first reading of a bill is that the bill be now read a first time.

284   Debate on first reading
(1)   The member moving the bill's first reading must indicate in that member's speech to which select committee it is proposed to refer the bill and whether it is proposed to move for any special powers or give an instruction in respect of the committee's consideration of the bill.
(2)   Following the member's speech, written notice of any special powers or instruction to be moved must be delivered to the Clerk at the Table.

SELECT COMMITTEE CONSIDERATION
285   Reference to a select committee
(1)   A bill stands referred to a select committee for consideration after its first reading unless the House has otherwise accorded urgency to it.
(2)   An Appropriation Bill and an Imprest Supply Bill do not stand referred to a committee.

286   Determination of committee to consider bill
(1)   After a bill's first reading the member in charge moves a motion nominating the committee to consider the bill. There is no debate on the question or on any amendment to the question.
(2)   The committee to consider the bill may be a committee to be specially established by motion with notice.
(3)   The member in charge may also include in the motion nominating the committee to consider the bill any special powers or instruction in respect of the committee's consideration of the bill that the mover has indicated in the first reading speech are to be proposed.
(4)   If notice of an amendment to substitute another committee or to alter any proposed special powers or instruction is delivered to the Clerk at the Table before the bill is read a first time, the question on such an amendment is put when the motion for the special powers or instruction is reached.

287   Select committee consideration of bills
(1)   Each select committee to which a bill is referred examines the bill and—
(a)   determines whether to recommend that the bill be passed, and
(b)   may recommend amendments in accordance with Standing Order 288.
(2)   In the case of a private bill, the committee also determines whether or not the statements in the preamble have been proved to the satisfaction of the committee.
(3)   In the case of a Local Legislation Bill, the committee also determines whether, in the committee's opinion, any clause or clauses should more properly be the subject of a local bill.
(4)   A report by a select committee on a bill indicates the committee's determinations on the matters set out in this Standing Order.

288   Recommendation of amendments
(1)   Except as otherwise provided in this Standing Order, a select committee may recommend only amendments that are relevant to the subject-matter of the bill, are consistent with the principles and objects of the bill and otherwise conform to Standing Orders and the practices of the House.

(2)   Further to paragraph (1), a committee may not recommend an amendment to a local bill or a private bill that is outside the scope of the notices advertising the intention to introduce or promote the bill.

(3)   Despite paragraph (1), a committee may, in the case of a Statutes Amendment Bill, recommend, by leave, a substantive amendment to an Act not amended by the bill as originally introduced.

(4)   In its report to the House recommending amendments to a bill, a committee must distinguish between those amendments adopted unanimously by the committee and those adopted by a majority of the committee.

289   Opinions from other committees

(1)   The select committee to which a bill is referred may ask any other committee for its opinion on the bill or on a part, clause, schedule or other provision of the bill.

(2)   For the purposes of giving its opinion, the other committee may call for submissions, hear evidence and generally consider the part, clause, schedule or other provision. In giving its opinion to the select committee on the bill, it may, if it thinks fit, recommend amendments to the part, clause, schedule or other provision.

290   Select committee may divide bill

(1)   A select committee may divide into two or more separate bills any bill which—
   (a)   is drafted in parts, or
   (b)   lends itself to division because it comprises more than one subject-matter,—
   and report such bills separately to the House.

(2)   A new bill must have inserted into it an enacting formula, title and commencement provision.

SELECT COMMITTEE REPORTS

291   Time for report

(1)   A select committee must finally report to the House on a bill within six months of the bill being referred to it or by such other time fixed by the House.

(2)   The Business Committee may extend the time for report for any bill.

(3)   If the committee has not reported within the time for report, the bill is discharged from further consideration by the committee and set down for its next stage in the House on the third sitting day following.

292   Select committee reports

Following the presentation of a select committee report on a bill,—
   (a)   in the case of a report other than an interim report or a special report, the bill is set down for second reading, or
   (b)   in the case of an interim report or a special report, the report is set down for consideration—
   on the third sitting day following, according to whether the bill is a Government bill, a Member's bill, a local bill or a private bill.

SECOND READING

293   Second reading

The motion on the order of the day for the second reading of a bill is that the bill be now read a second time.

294   Questions put at conclusion of debate

(1)   At the conclusion of the debate on the second reading of a bill the Speaker puts a question that the amendments recommended by the committee by majority be agreed to. There is no amendment or further debate on the question.

(2)   When this question is determined, the Speaker puts a further question, that the bill be now read a second time.

295   Next stage of bill

A bill that has been read a second time is set down for consideration in committee next sitting day. The Business Committee may decide that the bill does not require consideration in committee, in which case the order of the day is altered and the bill is set down for third reading.

296   Adoption of amendments

Amendments recommended by a committee by majority that are agreed to by the House and amendments recommended by the committee unanimously are adopted as part of the bill when the bill is read a second time.

COMMITTEE STAGE

297 Consideration in committee

(1) A committee of the whole House considers a bill to determine whether the bill properly incorporates the principles or objects of the bill as read a second time by the House.

(2) The committee may make amendments that are relevant to the subject-matter of the bill, are consistent with the principles and objects of the bill and otherwise conform to Standing Orders and the practices of the House.

(3) No amendment may be made to a local bill or a private bill that is outside the scope of the notices advertising the intention to introduce or promote the bill.

298 Order of considering bill

(1) Subject to this Standing Order, the committee considers a bill as set out in paragraph (2) unless—
    (a) the bill is not drafted in parts, or
    (b) the committee decides otherwise, or
    (c) the member in charge of the bill requires that consideration or further consideration of a part or other provision be postponed.

(2) When the committee considers a bill part by part, the committee considers the provisions of the bill as follows:
    (a) any preamble:
    (b) provisions contained in parts and other provisions that are not preliminary clauses:
    (c) for the purposes of debate, any schedules are considered together with the parts to which they principally relate:
    (d) questions on any schedules, which are put separately without further debate:
    (e) any preliminary clauses not in a part, which are considered together for the purposes of debate, and the questions on which are put separately without further debate.

(3) Where a bill is not drafted in parts,—
    (a) the committee considers its provisions in sequence, and
    (b) for the purposes of debate, any schedules are considered along with the clauses to which they relate, and
    (c) questions on any schedules are put separately without further debate.

(4) Unless otherwise specified, consideration or further consideration of—
    (a) any postponed clause or part is taken when all other clauses or parts have been dealt with, other than preliminary clauses that are considered together, and
    (b) any other postponed provision is taken when all other provisions have been dealt with.

299 Numbers only read

In reading the clauses or other provisions of a bill it is sufficient to read the numbers only.

300 Questions to be proposed in committee

(1) A question is proposed that each provision stand part of the bill or as amended stand part of the bill. In the case of a tie, the provision stands part of the bill.

(2) If any member objects to a clause standing part of a Statutes Amendment Bill (or of a bill that was formerly part of a Statutes Amendment Bill), the clause is struck out of the bill.

301 Amendments may be placed on Supplementary Order Paper

Any member intending to move an amendment to a bill may lodge a written copy of the amendment with the Clerk in time for the amendment to be printed on a Supplementary Order Paper and circulated to members.

302 Consideration of amendments

(1) Any relevant amendment that is on a Supplementary Order Paper that has been circulated to members, or which is delivered to the Clerk at the Table, can be referred to in the course of the debate on the provision proposed to be amended.

(2) If an amendment is not on a Supplementary Order Paper, six copies of the amendment must be delivered to the Clerk at the Table.

(3) At the conclusion of the debate on a provision, the question on any amendment or motion to change a Vote that is in order is put.

303 Amendments of member in charge

(1) The member in charge of a bill can require that any or all amendments in that member's name to a provision be put as one question.

(2) If two or more amendments occur at the same place in the bill, then, subject to paragraph (3),—
    (a) an amendment proposed by the member in charge of the bill is taken ahead of an amendment proposed by another member, and

(b)   amendments (not being amendments of the member in charge of the bill) are put in the order in which they were lodged with, or delivered to, the Clerk.

(3)   Amendments put as one question under paragraph (1) are taken after other amendments to the provision unless the member in charge of the bill requires otherwise.

304   Amendment of law reform or other omnibus bill

(1)   In considering a law reform or other omnibus bill, no substantive amendment to an Act not amended by the bill as originally introduced may be moved without the leave of the committee.

(2)   A consequential amendment to an Act not amended by the bill as originally introduced may be made.

305   Committee may divide bill

(1)   A committee of the whole House may divide into two or more separate bills any bill that—
(a)   is drafted in parts, or
(b)   lends itself to division because it comprises more than one subject-matter—
and in respect of which a Supplementary Order Paper notifying the intention to move for division of the bill into separate bills has been circulated.

(2)   The Supplementary Order Paper must show how it is proposed to divide the bill, setting out the enacting formula, title and commencement provision for each new bill.

(3)   A motion to divide a bill into separate bills, as set out on the Supplementary Order Paper, is moved after the bill has been fully considered by the committee.

306   Adoption of report on bill

If the report on a bill is adopted, the bill is set down for third reading or for further consideration in committee next sitting day, as the case may be.

THIRD READING AND PASSING

307   Recommittal

A motion to recommit a bill to a committee of the whole House may be moved after the order of the day for the third reading of the bill has been called. There is no amendment or debate on the question.

308   Third reading

(1)   The motion on the order of the day for the third reading of a bill is that the bill be now read a third time.

(2)   At the option of the member in charge, the third readings of each bill divided out of a bill during the committee stage may be taken together.

309   Members' bills, local bills and private bills affecting rights or prerogatives

No Member's bill, local bill or private bill that contains any provision affecting the rights or prerogatives of the Crown may be passed unless the Crown has, by message, indicated its consent to that provision.

310   Bill passed

When a bill has been read a third time, it has been passed by the House.

311   Bills passed to be printed fair, authenticated and presented for Royal assent

When a bill has been passed it is printed fair, by direction of the Clerk, who authenticates two prints of it and presents them for the Royal assent.

312   Verbal or formal amendments

In preparing the bill for the Royal assent, amendments of a verbal or formal nature may be made and clerical or typographical errors may be corrected in any part of the bill by the Clerk.

313   After Royal assent given

When the Royal assent to a bill has been given, the Clerk deposits one of the fair prints of the bill with the Registrar of the High Court at Wellington, and retains the second.

DELEGATED LEGISLATION

314   Functions of Regulations Review Committee

(1)   The Regulations Review Committee examines all regulations.

(2)   A Minister may refer draft regulations to the committee for consideration and the committee may report on the draft regulations to the Minister.

(3)   In respect of a bill before another committee, the committee may consider—
(a)   any regulation-making power,
(b)   any provision that contains a delegated power to make instruments of a legislative character, and
(c)   any matter relating to regulations,—
and report on it to the committee that is considering the bill.

(4)   The committee may consider any matter relating to regulations and report on it to the House.

(5)   The committee investigates complaints about the operation of regulations, in accordance with Standing Order 316, and may report on the complaints to the House.

315   Drawing attention to a regulation

(1)   In examining a regulation, the committee considers whether it ought to be drawn to the special attention of the House on one or more of the grounds set out in paragraph (2).

(2)   The grounds are, that the regulation—
    (a)   is not in accordance with the general objects and intentions of the statute under which it is made:
    (b)   trespasses unduly on personal rights and liberties:
    (c)   appears to make some unusual or unexpected use of the powers conferred by the statute under which it is made:
    (d)   unduly makes the rights and liberties of persons dependent upon administrative decisions which are not subject to review on their merits by a judicial or other independent tribunal:
    (e)   excludes the jurisdiction of the courts without explicit authorisation in the enabling statute:
    (f)   contains matter more appropriate for parliamentary enactment:
    (g)   is retrospective where this is not expressly authorised by the empowering statute:
    (h)   was not made in compliance with particular notice and consultation procedures prescribed by statute:
    (i)   for any other reason concerning its form or purport, calls for elucidation.

316   Procedure where complaint made concerning regulation

(1)   Where a complaint is made to the committee or to the chairperson of the committee by a person or organisation aggrieved at the operation of a regulation, the complaint must be placed before the committee at its next meeting for the committee to consider whether, on the face of it, the complaint relates to one of the grounds on which the committee may draw a regulation to the special attention of the House.

(2)   The person or organisation making the complaint is given an opportunity to address the committee on the regulation unless the committee agrees by unanimous resolution not to proceed with the complaint.

317   Affirmative resolution procedure

(1)   Any notice of a motion that the House approve a regulation, a proposed regulation, or an instruction under any statute stands referred to a select committee. The notice of motion is allocated by the Clerk to the most appropriate select committee for consideration.

(2)   The committee must report to the House on any notice of motion, which has been referred under this Standing Order, no later than the first working day 28 days after the day on which the notice of motion was lodged.

(3)   No motion to approve a regulation, a proposed regulation, or an instruction may be moved until—
    (a)   after the committee to which the notice of motion was referred reports, or
    (b)   the first working day after 28 days have passed since the day on which notice of motion was lodged,—
    whichever is the earlier.

CHAPTER VI

FINANCIAL PROCEDURES

CROWN'S FINANCIAL VETO

318   Financial veto

(1)   The House will not pass a bill, amendment or motion that the Government certifies it does not concur in because, in its view, the bill, amendment or motion would have more than a minor impact on the Government's fiscal aggregates if it became law.

(2)   In addition, the House will not make a change to a Vote that the Government certifies it does not concur in because, in its view, the change would, if made, have more than a minor impact on the composition of the Vote.

(3)   In this Standing Order, and in Standing Orders 319 and 320, **motion** means a motion that, if passed as a resolution of the House of Representatives, would have the force of law.

319   Financial veto certificates

(1)   A certificate by the Government not concurring in a bill, amendment or motion on the ground that, in its view, the bill, amendment or motion would have more than a minor impact on the Government's fiscal

aggregates must state with some particularity the nature of the impact on the fiscal aggregate or aggregates concerned and the reason why the Government does not concur in the bill, amendment or motion.

(2)   A certificate by the Government not concurring in a change to a Vote on the ground that, in its view, the change would have more than a minor impact on the composition of the Vote must state with some particularity the nature of the impact on the composition of the Vote and the reason why the Government does not concur in the change.

(3)   A certificate is given by delivering it to the Clerk.

(4)   Any certificate may be debated on the House's next consideration of the bill, amendment, motion or Vote.

(5)   The Government may withdraw a certificate at any time by notifying the Clerk in writing.

320   Application of financial veto rule to bills and motions

(1)   A certificate relating to a bill may be given only when the bill is awaiting its third reading.

(2)   The certificate may relate to the bill as a whole or to a particular provision or provisions of the bill.

(3)   The Speaker will not put any question for the third reading of a bill to which such a certificate relates unless the House has first amended the bill to remove any provision that the Government has certified that it does not concur in.

(4)   A certificate relating to a motion may be given before the motion is moved. Where a certificate is given, the motion is out of order and no question is put on it.

321   Application of financial veto rule to amendments to bills and changes to Votes

(1)   A certificate relating to amendments recommended to a bill by a select committee may be given before the House agrees to those amendments. Where a certificate is given, those amendments are omitted from the bill.

(2)   A certificate relating to an amendment to a bill or a change to a Vote to be proposed by a member in a committee of the whole House may be given before the question on the amendment or change is put. Where a certificate is given, the amendment or change is out of order and no question is put on it.

(3)   A certificate relating to amendments recommended to a bill by a select committee also applies to those amendments if proposed in a committee of the whole House.

322   Notice of amendment to bill or change to Vote

(1)   Any member intending to propose an amendment which may have an impact on the Government's fiscal aggregates or to move a change to a Vote must give notice of the amendment or change by lodging it with the Clerk at least 24 hours before the House meets on the day on which the amendment is to be proposed or the change is to be moved. In the case of a motion to change a Vote, 24 hours' notice is not required where the proposed change was recommended in the report of the select committee that examined the Vote.

(2)   If a member seeks to propose an amendment or move a change to a Vote without having given the required notice of it, the amendment or change is out of order and no question is put on it.

(3)   This Standing Order applies in respect of an amendment to a bill only when the bill is set down for consideration in committee on the next sitting day.

IMPREST SUPPLY

323   Imprest Supply bills

(1)   All stages of an Imprest Supply Bill may be taken on the same day within the normal hours of sitting.

(2)   There is no amendment or debate on the question for the first reading.

(3)   An amendment to the question for the second reading of the bill may relate to any matter concerning public affairs and is not required to be strictly relevant.

(4)   After the second reading of the bill the House proceeds to the third reading forthwith, unless the Minister in charge of the bill requires the House to resolve itself into committee to consider an amendment.

(5)   There is no amendment or debate on the question for the third reading.

THE BUDGET

324   Budget policy statement

(1)   The Budget policy statement stands referred to the Finance and Expenditure Committee.

(2)   The Finance and Expenditure Committee must report on the Budget policy statement within 40 working days of the presentation of that statement to the House.

(3)   The Minister of the Crown responsible for presenting the Budget policy statement to the House will attend the committee for consideration of the statement, if requested.

(4)   In place of the first general debate after the report of the Finance and Expenditure Committee on the Budget policy statement has been presented, a debate is held on the Budget policy statement and on the report of the Finance and Expenditure Committee on that statement. The chairperson of the Finance and Expenditure Committee (or, in the chairperson's absence, another member of the committee) may move a motion relevant to the report and speak first.

325   Delivery of the Budget

(1)   The main Appropriation Bill may be introduced only after the announcement of the introduction of bills on a Thursday on a day previously notified to the House by the Government. There is no amendment or debate on the question for its first reading and the House proceeds to the second reading forthwith.

(2)   A Minister delivers the Budget statement in moving the second reading of the main Appropriation Bill.

326   Budget debate

(1)   The debate on the Budget is taken ahead of all other Government orders of the day.

(2)   An amendment to the question for the second reading of the bill may relate to any matter concerning public affairs and is not required to be strictly relevant.

327   Fiscal strategy report and economic and fiscal update

(1)   The fiscal strategy report and the economic and fiscal update stand referred to the Finance and Expenditure Committee.

(2)   The Finance and Expenditure Committee must, within 2 months of the delivery of the Budget, report on the fiscal strategy report and the economic and fiscal update presented to the House on the day the Budget was delivered.

328   Half-year economic and fiscal updates and statement on long-term fiscal position

Half-year economic and fiscal updates and the statement on the long-term fiscal position stand referred to the Finance and Expenditure Committee.

ESTIMATES

329   Referral of Estimates

(1)   Following delivery of the Budget, the Estimates stand referred to the Finance and Expenditure Committee.

(2)   The Finance and Expenditure Committee may examine a Vote itself or refer it or some of the appropriations contained in the Vote to any subject select committee for examination.

330   Examination of Estimates

(1)   Each select committee to which a Vote is referred examines the Vote and—

(a)   determines whether to recommend that the appropriations in respect of the Vote be accepted, and

(b)   may recommend a change to the Vote.

(2)   All committees must report to the House on their examinations of the Estimates within two months of the delivery of the Budget.

331   Estimates debate

(1)   The consideration in committee of the main Appropriation Bill is the Estimates debate. The Estimates debate is a consideration of the appropriations being sought by the Government in each Vote in the main Appropriation Bill.

(2)   During the Estimates debate, Votes are considered as determined under Standing Order 341. As each Vote is reached, the question is proposed that the Vote stand part.

(3)   A motion may be moved to change a Vote. Such a motion must specify the appropriation or appropriations within the Vote that it proposes to alter.

(4)   At the conclusion of the total time for the Estimates debate the remaining Votes and provisions of the main Appropriation Bill and any amendments proposed by the Minister in charge of the bill that are notified on a Supplementary Order Paper are put as one question. There is no amendment or debate on the question.

332   Third reading of main Appropriation Bill

(1)   The debate on the question for the third reading of the main Appropriation Bill must be completed within three months of the delivery of the Budget.

(2)   The debate on the third reading of the main Appropriation Bill may include reference to the content of the fiscal strategy report and the economic and fiscal update laid before the House on the day when the Budget was delivered and the report of the Finance and Expenditure Committee on those documents.

(3)   The debate on the third reading of the main Appropriation Bill may be taken together with the debate on the second reading of an Imprest Supply Bill.

SUPPLEMENTARY ESTIMATES

333   Examination of Supplementary Estimates

(1)   Following the introduction of an Appropriation (Supplementary Estimates) Bill, the Supplementary Estimates stand referred to the Finance and Expenditure Committee. The committee may examine a Vote itself or refer it to any subject select committee for examination.

(2)   Each select committee to which a Vote is referred examines the Vote and—
    (a)   determines whether to recommend that the appropriations in respect of the Vote be accepted, and
    (b)   may recommend a change to the Vote.

334   Passing of bill
(1)   There is no amendment or debate on the question for the first reading of an Appropriation (Supplementary Estimates) Bill.
(2)   The debate on the second reading of an Appropriation (Supplementary Estimates) Bill may be taken together with the debate on the second reading of an Imprest Supply Bill.
(3)   After the second reading of an Appropriation (Supplementary Estimates) Bill, the House proceeds to the third reading forthwith, unless—
    (a)   the Minister in charge requires the House to resolve itself into committee to consider an amendment, or
    (b)   a change to a Vote has been recommended by a select committee and is in order, in which case the House resolves itself into committee to consider that change.
(4)   There is no amendment or debate on the question for the third reading.

FINANCIAL REVIEW
335   Allocation of responsibility for conducting financial reviews
(1)   As soon after the commencement of the financial year as it thinks fit, the Finance and Expenditure Committee allocates to a subject select committee (or retains for itself) the task of conducting a financial review of the performance in the previous financial year and the current operations of each individual department, Office of Parliament, Crown entity, public organisation or State enterprise.
(2)   When the annual report of each department, Office of Parliament, Crown entity, public organisation or State enterprise is presented to the House, its financial review stands referred to a select committee as allocated by the Finance and Expenditure Committee.

336   Select committees to conduct financial reviews
(1)   The Finance and Expenditure Committee must, within one week of the first sitting day in each year, report to the House on the annual financial statements of the Government as at the end of the previous financial year.
(2)   Each select committee must, within one week of the first sitting day in each year, conduct and finally report to the House on a financial review of the performance and current operations of every department and Office of Parliament allocated to it.
(3)   Each select committee must, within six months of the relevant annual report having been presented, conduct and finally report to the House on a financial review of the performance and current operations of every Crown entity, public organisation or State enterprise allocated to it.

337   Appropriation (Financial Review) Bill
(1)   An Appropriation (Financial Review) Bill is an Appropriation Bill containing provisions solely concerned with the sanctioning, confirming or validating of expenditure incurred in respect of any previous financial year.
(2)   There is no amendment or debate on the question for the first reading or the second reading of the bill.

338   Financial review debate
(1)   The consideration in committee of the Appropriation (Financial Review) Bill is the financial review debate. The financial review debate is the consideration of—
    (a)   the financial position as reflected in the report of the Finance and Expenditure Committee on the annual financial state-ments of the Government for the previous financial year, and
    (b)   the financial reviews of the performance in the previous financial year and the current operations of individual departments and Offices of Parliament.
(2)   When the financial review debate commences, the question is proposed that the report of the Finance and Expenditure Committee on the annual financial statements of the Government for the previous financial year be noted.
(3)   The committee then proceeds to consider financial reviews as determined under Standing Order 341. As each financial review is reached, the question is proposed that the report of the select committee on the financial review be noted.
(4)   At the conclusion of the total time for the financial review debate, the provisions of the bill and any amendments proposed by the Minister in charge of the bill that are notified on a Supplementary Order Paper are put as one question. There is no amendment or debate on the question.
(5)   The financial review debate must be held no later than 31 March.

339 Passing of Appropriation (Financial Review) Bill

(1) When the report of the committee of the whole House on the Appropriation (Financial Review) Bill is adopted, the bill is set down for third reading forthwith.

(2) There is no amendment or debate on the question for the third reading.

340 Debate on financial review of Crown entities, public organisations and State enterprises

(1) The debate on the financial review of Crown entities, public organisations and State enterprises may be set down as a Government order of the day in the charge of a Minister. This debate is the consideration in committee of the performance in the previous financial year and the current operations of Crown entities, public organisations and State enterprises.

(2) When the order of the day is reached, the House resolves itself into committee, and the committee considers financial reviews of Crown entities, public organisations and State enterprises as determined under Standing Order 341.

(3) As each financial review is reached, the question is proposed that the report of the select committee on the financial review be noted.

DETERMINATION OF VOTES AND FINANCIAL REVIEWS FOR DEBATE

341 Determination of Votes and financial reviews for debate

(1) The Government may select any day (other than a Wednesday on which Members' orders of the day take precedence) for the Estimates debate, the financial review debate or the debate on the financial review of Crown entities, public organisations and State enterprises.

(2) The Government determines which Votes or financial reviews are available for debate on a particular day and how long in total is to be spent on the debate that day. This information is to be included on the Order Paper.

(3) The Business Committee may determine the order in which the Votes or financial reviews are to be considered on a particular day and how long is available for considering each or any Vote or financial review.

CHAPTER VII

NON-LEGISLATIVE PROCEDURES

ADDRESS IN REPLY

342 Motion for Address in Reply

(1) The motion for an Address in Reply is in the following form:
"That a respectful Address be presented to [*His or Her*] Excellency the Governor-General in reply to [*His or Her*] Excellency's Speech."

(2) Such a motion may be seconded.

343 Amendment to motion

Any amendment to the motion for an Address in Reply may propose only to add words to the motion.

344 Debate takes precedence

The Address in Reply debate is taken ahead of all other Government orders of the day.

STATEMENTS

345 Prime Minister's statement

(1) On the first sitting day of each year, the Prime Minister must make a statement to the House reviewing public affairs and outlining the Government's legislative and other policy intentions for the next 12 months.

(2) No Prime Minister's statement is made—
(a) when the first sitting day of the year is the first day of the meeting of a new Parliament, or
(b) when the first sitting day of the year is the first day of a session of Parliament, or
(c) when the Address in Reply debate is in progress on the first sitting day of the year.

346 Timing of Prime Minister's statement

The Prime Minister's statement is made at 2 pm. The text of the statement that the Prime Minister is to make must be made available to each party leader no later than 10 am that day.

347 Debate on Prime Minister's statement

A debate is held immediately following the Prime Minister's statement on a motion moved by the Leader of the Opposition. The debate on the Prime Minister's statement is taken ahead of all other Government orders of the day.

348   Ministerial statements

(1)   A Minister may make a statement informing the House of some matter of significant public importance which requires to be brought to the House's attention immediately.

(2)   A ministerial statement may be made at any time, but not so as to interrupt a member who is speaking. If possible, a copy of the statement should be delivered to the leader of each party before it is made.

349   Comment on ministerial statement

The leader of each party with six members or a member authorised by the leader may comment on a ministerial statement. Following their comments, the Minister may reply.

350   Personal explanation

A member may explain matters of a personal nature with the leave of the House. A personal explanation may not be debated.

351   Maiden statements

A member who has not made a maiden speech during an Address in Reply debate may make a maiden statement. The maiden statement may interrupt a debate and is made at a time that the Speaker agrees is convenient.

PETITIONS

352   Addressed to House and contain request for action

A petition must be addressed to the House of Representatives and ask the House to take some action in respect of the subject-matter of the petition.

353   To be in English or Māori

A petition must be in English or in Māori.

354   Communications concerning petition

A petition must identify by name and address the person to whom communications concerning the petition should be addressed.

355   Signatures

A signatory to a petition must sign by his or her own hand except in the case of incapacity. A person signing on behalf of a person incapacitated must state this fact alongside the signature.

356   Signatures to be on sheet containing request

Every signature must be written upon the petition or upon pages on which the request to the House to take action is written in full. A signature may not be pasted upon or otherwise transferred to such petition or pages.

357   Petitions of corporations

A petition from a corporation must be signed by a duly authorised officer of the corporation. In the case of a body incorporated outside New Zealand, it may be signed by an authorised attorney.

358   Form of petition

(1)   A petition must be respectful and moderate in its language.

(2)   A petition must not contain irrelevant statements.

359   Members to examine and certify petitions

(1)   A member presenting a petition must take care that it conforms with the Standing Orders and must certify that the member is presenting it.

(2)   A member may not present a petition from himself or herself or a petition to which the member is a party.

360   Petitions to be delivered to Clerk

(1)   A petition is presented to the House by a member delivering it to the Clerk on any working day but not later than 1 pm on a sitting day.

(2)   The Clerk announces the presentation of petitions at the time appointed by Standing Order 63.

361   Petitions referred to select committees

When a petition (except a petition for a private bill) that conforms with the Standing Orders is presented, it stands referred to a select committee. The petition is allocated by the Clerk to the most appropriate select committee for consideration and report.

362   Petitions not in order

The following are not in order:

(a)   a petition (other than a petition for a private bill) in respect of a matter for which legal remedies have not been exhausted:

(b)   a petition on a matter within the competence of the Ombudsmen, if application has not been made to an Ombudsman:

(c)   a petition on the same matter as an earlier petition which was finally dealt with by the House during the term of that Parliament, unless substantial and material new evidence is available that was not available when the earlier petition was considered.

PAPERS AND PUBLICATIONS

363   Presentation of papers

(1)   A paper may be presented to the House by the Speaker or by a Minister by delivering it to the Clerk on any working day but not later than 1 pm on a sitting day.

(2)   Notwithstanding paragraph (1), the Speaker may present a paper to the House.

364   Publication of papers

(1)   In presenting a paper, the Minister may indicate that it is intended that it be published by order of the House. The Clerk announces the presentation of such papers at the time appointed by Standing Order 63.

(2)   Following the announcement of papers and the presentation of those papers the Speaker wishes to present, a Minister may move, without notice, that that paper or those papers be published. There is no debate or amendment on the question.

365   Speaker controls publication

The Speaker has control and direction of all matters which relate to printing and publication executed by order or under the authority of the House.

366   Translation of documents

The Speaker may order that bills introduced into the House and reports, petitions and papers presented to it are to be translated and printed in another language.

367   Budget papers and Estimates

After delivering the Budget or introducing an Appropriation Bill, a Minister may present any papers relating to the Budget or the bill and move, without notice, that those papers be published. There is no debate or amendment on the question.

368   Quoting documents

Whenever a Minister quotes from a document relating to public affairs a member may, on a point of order, require the Minister to lay the document on the Table. The Minister must then lay the document on the Table unless it is of a confidential nature.

QUESTIONS TO MINISTERS AND MEMBERS

369   Questions to Ministers

Questions may be put to a Minister relating to—

(a)   public affairs with which the Minister is officially connected, or

(b)   proceedings in the House or any matter of administration for which the Minister is responsible.

370   Questions to other members

(1)   Questions may be put to a member (not being a Minister or the Speaker) relating to any bill, motion or public matter connected with the business of the House, of which the member has charge.

(2)   Questions for written answer may be put to the Speaker relating to any matter of administration for which the Speaker is responsible.

(3)   Questions to other members are dealt with following questions addressed to Ministers and urgent questions.

371   Content of questions

(1)   Questions must be concise and not contain—

(a)   statements of facts and names of persons unless they are strictly necessary to render the question intelligible and can be authenticated, or

(b)   arguments, inferences, imputations, epithets, ironical expressions or expressions of opinion, or

(c)   discreditable references to the House or any member of Parliament or any offensive or unparliamentary expression.

(2)   Questions must not seek a legal opinion.

(3)   A question for written answer must not repeat the substance of a question already lodged in the same calendar year.

(4)   Questions must not refer to proceedings in committee at meetings closed to the public until those proceedings are reported to the House or (subject to Standing Order 111) to a case pending adjudication by a court.

(5)   Where the notice of a question does not comply with the provisions of the Standing Orders, it is not accepted. If, by inadvertence, such a notice is accepted it may be subsequently disallowed by the Speaker unless it is amended or revised so as to comply with the Standing Orders.

372   Lodging of oral questions

(1)   Notices of questions for oral answer are lodged by members in writing to the Clerk. A notice of a question for oral answer must be—

(a)   signed by the member or by another member on the member's behalf, and

(b)   delivered to the Clerk between 10 am and 10.30 am on the day the question is to be asked.

(2)   Twelve questions may be accepted for oral answer each day. Questions will be allocated on a basis that is proportional to party membership in the House. The Business Committee decides the weekly allocation and rotation of questions.

373   Lodging and publication of written questions and replies

(1)   Subject to paragraph (2), during a session of Parliament notices of questions for written answer may be lodged no later than 10.30 am on any working day.

(2)   Notices of questions for written answer may not be lodged after the last day on which the House sits in any calendar year or before the first day on which the House sits in the following year.

(3)   Notices of questions for written answer, and replies to them (including both interim and final replies, if applicable),—

(a)   may be lodged with the Clerk only in electronic form, and

(b)   must be signed by way of an electronic signature by a member of Parliament or by another member on the member's behalf, and

(c)   are published electronically,—

(i)   in the case of questions, on the day they are accepted:

(ii)   in the case of replies, on the third working day following the day on which they are lodged.

(4)   The reply to a question for written answer must be lodged no later than the sixth working day following the day on which the question is published.

(5)   The Speaker may, in exceptional circumstances arising from the operation of the electronic system for questions for written answer, authorise the lodging or publication of questions or replies in a form or within a time other than that specified in this Standing Order.

374   Time for oral questions

(1)   Subject to the Standing Orders, oral questions are taken at the time appointed by Standing Order 63.

(2)   The House deals with all questions for oral answer lodged each day.

375   Asking a question for oral answer

(1)   When a question for oral answer is called by the Speaker, the member in whose name it stands indicates the Minister or member to whom it is addressed and reads it to the House.

(2)   A member may ask a question for oral answer on behalf of a member who is absent when authorised by that member to do so.

376   Replying to a question for oral answer

(1)   When a question for oral answer has been asked, the Speaker then calls upon the Minister or member to give a reply.

(2)   A Minister or Parliamentary Under-Secretary may answer a question on behalf of another Minister who is not present when a question addressed to the Minister is asked.

377   Contents of replies

(1)   An answer that seeks to address the question asked must be given if it can be given consistently with the public interest.

(2)   The reply to any question must be concise and confined to the subject-matter of the question asked, and not contain—

(a)   statements of facts and the names of any persons unless they are strictly necessary to answer the question, or

(b)   arguments, inferences, imputations, epithets or ironical expressions, or

(c)   discreditable references to the House or any member of Parliament or any offensive or unparliamentary expression.

(3)   Replies shall not refer to proceedings in committee at meetings closed to the public that have not yet been reported to the House or (subject to Standing Order 111) to a case pending adjudication by a court.

378   Supplementary questions
(1)   At the discretion of the Speaker, a supplementary question may be asked by any member to elucidate or clarify a matter raised in a question for oral answer or in an answer given to a question.
(2)   Supplementary questions cannot be asked on behalf of another member.

379   Urgent questions
(1)   Any member desiring to ask a question on the ground of urgency in the public interest may give to the Clerk a copy of the proposed question marked "urgent question". The member must also give a copy to the Minister to whom it is intended to address the question.
(2)   After questions for oral answer addressed to Ministers have been taken the Speaker (if the proposed question is one which in the public interest the Speaker considers should be answered immediately) may call upon the member to ask the question.
(3)   The Speaker may permit the member asking an urgent question to ask one supplementary question.

DEBATE ON A MATTER OF URGENT PUBLIC IMPORTANCE
380   Application for debate
(1)   A member who wishes the House to debate a matter of urgent public importance must give the Speaker a written statement of the matter proposed to be debated. The written statement must be provided at least one hour before the time fixed for the House to sit or such lesser time as may be allowed by the Speaker.
(2)   The Speaker may allow the debate to be held if, in the Speaker's opinion, the matter—
      (a)   is a particular case of recent occurrence, and
      (b)   involves the administrative or ministerial responsibility of the Government, and
      (c)   requires the immediate attention of the House and the Government.

381   Announcement and debate
(1)   Immediately after questions for oral answer and before the next business of the day is entered upon, the Speaker announces what applications for debate that day have been received.
(2)   In announcing that a debate has been allowed, the Speaker calls on the member who submitted it to move that the House take note of the matter of urgent public importance. There is no amendment on the question. At the conclusion of the debate the motion lapses without any question being put.

382   Only one debate on same day
Only one debate on a matter of urgent public importance may be held on the same day. If more than one written statement is given for the same day and the Speaker considers that each would otherwise justify a debate, the Speaker gives priority to the matter which, in the Speaker's opinion, is the most urgent and important.

GENERAL DEBATE
383   General debate each Wednesday
(1)   Each Wednesday, after questions for oral answer, a general debate is held on a motion that the House take note of miscellaneous business. There is no amendment on the question.
(2)   During a general debate members may raise matters of concern to them. At the conclusion of the debate the motion lapses without any question being put.
(3)   No general debate is held in a week in which the debates on the Address in Reply, the Prime Minister's statement, the Budget or the Budget policy statement are held.

WHOLE OF GOVERNMENT DIRECTIONS
384   Whole of government directions
(1)   Any whole of government direction stands referred to the Finance and Expenditure Committee.
(2)   The Finance and Expenditure Committee will consider the subject area of the direction and,—
      (a)   if the direction's subject area is primarily within the committee's own terms of reference, retain it for examination, or
      (b)   if the direction's subject area is primarily within the terms of reference of another select committee, refer it to that committee for examination.
(3)   The Finance and Expenditure Committee, or any committee to which it has referred a direction for examination, must report to the House on the direction no later than 12 sitting days after its referral to the committee.

CIVIL DEFENCE
385   Civil defence
(1)   Any national civil defence emergency management strategy and any proposed civil defence emergency management plan stand referred to the Government Administration Committee.

(2)   The Government Administration Committee must report to the House on a national civil defence emergency management strategy no later than 12 sitting days after its referral to the committee.

OFFICERS OF PARLIAMENT
386   Functions of Officers of Parliament Committee
(1)   The Officers of Parliament Committee considers and recommends to the House,—
   (a)   in respect of each Office of Parliament, an estimate of appropriations for inclusion as a Vote in an Appropriation Bill, and any alteration to such a Vote:
   (b)   an auditor to be appointed by the House to audit the financial statements of each Office of Parliament:
   (c)   any proposal referred to it by a Minister for the creation of an Officer of Parliament:
   (d)   the appointment of persons as Officers of Parliament.

(2)   The committee may develop or review a code of practice applicable to any or all Officers of Parliament.

INTERNATIONAL TREATIES
387   Presentation and referral of treaties
(1)   The Government will present the following international treaties to the House:
   (a)   any treaty that is to be subject to ratification, accession, acceptance or approval by New Zealand:
   (b)   any treaty that has been subject to ratification, accession, acceptance or approval on an urgent basis in the national interest:
   (c)   any treaty that has been subject to ratification, accession, acceptance or approval and that is to be subject to withdrawal or denunciation by New Zealand:
   (d)   any major bilateral treaty of particular significance, not otherwise covered by subparagraph (a), that the Minister of Foreign Affairs and Trade decides to present to the House.

(2)   A national interest analysis for the treaty, which addresses all the matters set out in Standing Order 388, will be presented at the same time as the treaty.

(3)   Both the treaty and the national interest analysis stand referred to the Foreign Affairs, Defence and Trade Committee.

388   National interest analysis
(1)   A national interest analysis must address the following matters:
   (a)   the reasons for New Zealand becoming party to the treaty:
   (b)   the advantages and disadvantages to New Zealand of the treaty entering into force for New Zealand:
   (c)   the obligations which would be imposed on New Zealand by the treaty, and the position in respect of reservations to the treaty:
   (d)   the economic, social, cultural and environmental effects of the treaty entering into force for New Zealand, and of the treaty not entering into force for New Zealand:
   (e)   the costs to New Zealand of compliance with the treaty:
   (f)   the possibility of any subsequent protocols (or other amendments) to the treaty, and of their likely effects:
   (g)   the measures which could or should be adopted to implement the treaty, and the intentions of the Government in relation to such measures, including legislation:
   (h)   a statement setting out the consultations which have been undertaken or are proposed with the community and interested parties in respect of the treaty:
   (i)   whether the treaty provides for withdrawal or denunciation.

(2)   In the case of a treaty that has been subject to ratification, accession, acceptance or approval on an urgent basis in the national interest, the national interest analysis must also explain the reasons for the urgent action taken.

(3)   In the case of a treaty that has been subject to ratification, accession, acceptance or approval and that is to be subject to withdrawal or denunciation by New Zealand, the national interest analysis must address the matters set out in paragraph (1) to the full extent applicable to that proposed action.

389   Select committee consideration of treaties
(1)   The Foreign Affairs, Defence and Trade Committee considers the subject area of the treaty and,—
   (a)   if that subject area is primarily within the committee's own terms of reference, retains the treaty for examination, or
   (b)   if that subject area is primarily within the terms of reference of another select committee, refers the treaty to that committee for examination.

(2)   If the Foreign Affairs, Defence and Trade Committee is not due to meet within seven days of the

presentation of a treaty, and the subject area of the treaty is clearly within the terms of reference of another select committee, the chairperson may refer the treaty to that committee for examination.

390   Reports by select committees on treaties
(1)   A select committee must report to the House on any treaty that has been referred to it.
(2)   In examining a treaty and the accompanying national interest analysis, the committee considers whether the treaty ought to be drawn to the attention of the House—
    (a)   on any of the grounds covered by the national interest analysis, or
    (b)   for any other reason.
(3)   The committee must include the national interest analysis as an appendix to its report.

CHAPTER VIII

PARLIAMENTARY PRIVILEGE

391   Privileges Committee
(1)   The Privileges Committee considers and reports on any matter referred to it by the House relating to or concerning parliamentary privilege.
(2)   The committee has the power to send for persons, papers and records.

392   Raising a matter of privilege
(1)   A member may raise a matter of privilege with the Speaker in writing at the earliest opportunity.
(2)   In any case a matter of privilege must be raised before the next sitting of the House or, if the matter relates to the proceedings of a select committee, before the commencement of the sitting of the House following the day of the next meeting of the committee concerned.
(3)   A matter of privilege relating to the conduct of strangers present may be raised forthwith in the House and dealt with in such way as the Speaker determines.

393   Allegation of breach of privilege or contempt
An allegation of breach of privilege or of contempt must be formulated as precisely as possible so as to give any person against whom it is made a full opportunity to respond to it.

394   Consideration by Speaker
(1)   The Speaker considers a matter of privilege and determines if a question of privilege is involved.
(2)   In considering if a question of privilege is involved, the Speaker takes account of the degree of importance of the matter which has been raised.
(3)   No question of privilege is involved if the matter is technical or trivial and does not warrant the further attention of the House.

395   Members to be informed of allegations against them
Any member raising a matter of privilege which involves another member of the House must, as soon as reasonably practicable after raising the matter, forward to that other member a copy of the matter that has been raised with the Speaker.

396   Speaker's ruling
(1)   If the Speaker considers that a matter involves a question of privilege, this is reported to the House at the first opportunity.
(2)   The Speaker will not report to the House that a matter involving another member involves a question of privilege without first informing that member that it is intended to do so.

397   Question of privilege stands referred to Privileges Committee
Any matter reported to the House by the Speaker as involving a question of privilege stands referred to the Privileges Committee.

398   Maker of allegation not to serve on inquiry
A member who makes an allegation of breach of privilege or of contempt may not serve on an inquiry into that allegation.

399   Contempt of House
The House may treat as a contempt any act or omission which—
    (a)   obstructs or impedes the House in the performance of its functions, or
    (b)   obstructs or impedes any member or officer of the House in the discharge of the member's or officer's duty, or
    (c)   has a tendency, directly or indirectly, to produce such a result.

400 Examples of contempts

Without limiting the generality of Standing Order 399, the House may treat as a contempt any of the following:

(a) the breach of one of the privileges of the House:

(b) deliberately attempting to mislead the House or a committee (by way of statement, evidence or petition):

(c) serving legal process or causing legal process to be served within the parliamentary precincts, without the authority of the House or the Speaker, on any day on which the House sits or a committee meets:

(d) removing, without authority, any papers or records belonging to the House:

(e) falsifying or altering any papers or records belonging to the House:

(f) as a member, failing to declare, before participating in the consideration of any item of business, any financial interest that the member has in that business:

(g) as a member, knowingly failing to make a return of pecuniary interests by the due date:

(h) as a member, knowingly providing false or misleading information in a return of pecuniary interests:

(i) as a member, receiving or soliciting a bribe to influence the member's conduct in respect of proceedings in the House or at a committee:

(j) as a member, accepting fees for professional services rendered by the member in connection with proceedings in the House or at a committee:

(k) offering or attempting to bribe a member to influence the member's conduct in respect of proceedings in the House or at a committee:

(l) assaulting, threatening or intimidating a member or an officer of the House acting in the discharge of the member's or the officer's duty:

(m) obstructing or molesting a member or an officer of the House in the discharge of the member's or the officer's duty:

(n) reflecting on the character or conduct of the House or of a member in the member's capacity as a member of the House:

(o) misconducting oneself in the presence of the House or a committee:

(p) divulging the proceedings or the report of a select committee or a subcommittee contrary to Standing Orders:

(q) publishing a false or misleading account of proceedings before the House or a committee:

(r) failing to attend before the House or a committee after being ordered to do so:

(s) failing to obey an order of the House or a summons issued by order of the House or by the Speaker:

(t) intimidating, preventing or hindering a witness from giving evidence, or giving evidence in full, to the House or a committee:

(u) refusing to answer a question as ordered by the House or a committee:

(v) assaulting, threatening or disadvantaging a member on account of the member's conduct in Parliament:

(w) assaulting, threatening or disadvantaging a person on account of evidence given by that person to the House or a committee.

401 Reference to parliamentary proceedings before court

(1) Subject to this Standing Order, permission of the House is not required for reference to be made to proceedings in Parliament in any proceedings before a court.

(2) Reference to proceedings in Parliament is subject always to article 9 of section 1 of the Bill of Rights 1688, which prohibits the impeaching or calling into question in a court of such proceedings. Nothing in paragraph (1) is intended to derogate from the operation of article 9.

(3) Paragraph (1) does not authorise reference to proceedings in Parliament contrary to any Standing Order or other order of the House relating to the disclosure of proceedings of the House or of a committee of the House.

402 Evidence of proceedings not to be given

The Clerk and other officers of the House and any other person employed to make a transcript of proceedings of the House or of a committee may not give evidence of proceedings in Parliament without the authority of the House.

APPENDIX A

TIME LIMITS OF SPEECHES AND DEBATES

Item of business and member speaking	*Times for speeches or debates*

GENERAL PROCEDURES
Debates not otherwise provided for

Each member	10 minutes

Amendments

Each member	Same as on the original motion

Committees of the whole House
On questions not otherwise provided for—

Minister or member in charge of business	Multiple speeches of 5 minutes each, but normally not more than 2 consecutive speeches
Other members	Not more than 4 speeches of 5 minutes each

LEGISLATIVE PROCEDURES
First reading of Government bills

Each member	10 minutes
Whole debate	12 speeches

First reading of Members' bills, private bills and local bills

Each member	10 minutes
Member in reply	5 minutes
Whole debate (including reply)	7 speeches

Second reading of bills

Each member	10 minutes
Whole debate	12 speeches

Committee of the whole House
Title of bill—

Minister or member in charge of bill	Multiple speeches of 5 minutes each, but normally not more than 2 consecutive speeches
Other members	Not more than 3 speeches of 5 minutes each

Other clause or other provision—

Minister or member in charge of bill	Multiple speeches of 5 minutes each, but normally not more than 2 consecutive speeches
Other members	Not more than 4 speeches of 5 minutes each

Third reading of bills

Each member	10 minutes
Whole debate	12 speeches

FINANCIAL PROCEDURES
Imprest Supply Bill
On second reading—

Each member	10 minutes
Whole debate	3 hours

Budget policy statement debate

Each member	10 minutes
Whole debate	12 speeches

Budget debate (second reading of main Appropriation Bill)

Minister in charge of bill, on first speaking	Unlimited
Specified party leaders	20 minutes each
Other members	10 minutes
Minister in reply	10 minutes
Whole debate (excluding delivery of the Budget statement)	14 hours

Estimates debate (committee of the whole House stage of main Appropriation Bill)

Minister in charge of the Vote	Multiple speeches of 5 minutes each, but normally not more than 2 consecutive speeches
Other members speaking on each Vote	Not more than 2 speeches of 5 minutes each
Whole debate	8 hours

Third reading of main Appropriation Bill (including with second reading of an Imprest Supply Bill)

Each member	10 minutes
Whole debate	3 hours

Appropriation (Supplementary Estimates) Bill (including with second reading of an Imprest Supply Bill)

On second reading—	
Each member	10 minutes
Whole debate	3 hours

Financial review debate (committee of the whole House stage of Appropriation (Financial Review) Bill)

Minister in charge of the annual financial statements of the Government for the previous financial year or Minister responsible for department or Office of Parliament	Multiple speeches of 5 minutes each, but normally not more than 2 consecutive speeches
Other members speaking on each financial review	Not more than 2 speeches of 5 minutes each
Whole debate	4 hours

Debate on performance and current operations of Crown entities, public organisations and State enterprises

Minister responsible for Crown entity, public organisation or State enterprise	Multiple speeches of 5 minutes each, but normally not more than 2 consecutive speeches
Other members speaking on each financial review	Not more than 2 speeches of 5 minutes each
Whole debate	3 hours

NON-LEGISLATIVE PROCEDURES
Address in Reply

Specified party leaders	30 minutes each
Members making maiden speeches	15 minutes each
Other members	10 minutes each
Whole debate	19 hours

Prime Minister's statement and debate

Prime Minister	Unlimited
Specified party leaders	20 minutes each
Other members	10 minutes each
Whole debate (excluding delivery of the Prime Minister's statement)	14 hours

Ministerial statement and comment on it

Minister making statement and specified party leaders	5 minutes each
Minister in reply	2 minutes

Maiden statement

A member who has not made a maiden speech during the Address in Reply debate	15 minutes

Debate on motion to take note of matter of urgent public importance

Mover and next speaker	15 minutes each
Subsequent six members	10 minutes each

General debate each Wednesday

Each member	5 minutes each
Whole debate	12 speeches

NOTE:

The term specified party leader means a member who is the leader of a party represented in the House by 6 or more members (inclusive of the leader) or a member authorised by that leader.

APPENDIX B

PECUNIARY INTERESTS

DEFINITIONS

1   Definitions

(1)   For the purposes of the return and registration of pecuniary interests, unless the context otherwise requires,—

business entity means any body or organisation, whether incorporated or unincorporated, that carries on any profession, trade, manufacture, or undertaking for pecuniary profit, and includes a business activity carried on by a sole proprietor

company means—

(a)   a company registered under Part 2 of the Companies Act 1993:

(b)   a body corporate that is incorporated outside New Zealand

effective date of the return means the date as at which the return is effective as required by clause 2(1) or clause 3(1) (as the case may be)

employed—

(a)   means employed under a contract of service, but

(b)   does not include holding the position of a member of Parliament or any other position for which the person in question would not be qualified unless he or she had been elected a member of Parliament (for example, the position of Minister of the Crown, Parliamentary Under-Secretary, Leader of the Opposition, or Whip)

general election means the election that takes place after the dissolution or expiration of Parliament

Government funding means funding from any one or more of the following:

(a)   the Crown:

(b)   any Crown entity:

(c)   any State enterprise

polling day, in relation to any election, means the day appointed in the writ for that election for the polling to take place if a poll is required

register means the Register of Pecuniary Interests of Members of Parliament established by clause 11

registrar—

(a)   means the Deputy Clerk or a person appointed by the Clerk, with the agreement of the Speaker, to act as registrar, and

(b)   includes every person who has been authorised by the registrar to act on his or her behalf under the Standing Orders

registered superannuation scheme means any superannuation scheme that is registered under the Superannuation Schemes Act 1989 (including any scheme referred to in section 19H of the Government Superannuation Fund Act 1956)

voting right means a currently exercisable right to cast a vote at meetings of the owners or proprietors of a business entity, not being a right to vote that is exercisable only in relation to a special, immaterial, or remote matter that is inconsequential to control of the entity.

(2)   Every amount specified in this Appendix is inclusive of goods and services tax (if any).

(3)   Every reference in this Appendix to a person elected at an election includes a person elected as a consequence of a recount or an election petition relating to that election.

PART 1

2   Duty to make initial return of pecuniary interests

(1)   Every member must make an initial return of pecuniary interests as at the day that is 90 days after the date that the member takes the oath or makes the affirmation required by section 11(1) of the Constitution Act 1986.

(2)   Subclause (1) does not apply if,—

(a)   in the case of a member who is elected at an election, polling day for the election is after 1 July in the year of the election, or

(b)   in the case of a member who is declared to be elected under section 137 of the Electoral Act 1993, the date that the member's election is notified in the *Gazette* is after 1 July in the year that the member is declared to be elected.

(3)   An initial return must be transmitted by the member to the registrar within 30 days of the effective date of the return.

3   Duty to make annual return of pecuniary interests

(1)   Every member must make an annual return of pecuniary interests in each year as at 31 January.

(2)   The annual return must be transmitted by the member to the registrar by 28 February in each year in which an annual return must be made.

4   Contents of return relating to member's position as at effective date of return

(1)   Every return of pecuniary interests must contain the following information as at the effective date of the return:

(a)   the name of each company of which the member is a director or holds or controls more than 5 percent of the voting rights and a description of the main business activities of each of those companies, and

(b)   the name of every other company or business entity in which the member has a pecuniary interest and a description of the main business activities of each of those companies or entities, and

(c)   if the member is employed, the name of each employer of the member and a description of the main business activities of each of those employers, and

(d)   the name of each trust in which the member has a beneficial interest, and

(e)   if the member is a member of the governing body of an organisation or a trustee of a trust that receives, or has applied to receive, Government funding, the name of that organisation or trust and a description of the main activities of that organisation or trust, unless the organisation or trust is a Government department, a Crown entity, or a State enterprise, and

(f)   the location of each parcel of real property in which the member has a pecuniary interest, unless the member has no beneficial interest in the real property, and

(g)   the name of each registered superannuation scheme in which the member has a pecuniary interest, and

(h)   the name of each debtor of the member who owes more than $50,000 to the member and a description of each of the debts that are owed to the member by those debtors, and

(i)   the name of each creditor of the member to whom the member owes more than $50,000 and a description of each of the debts that are owed by the member to those creditors.

(2)   For the purposes of subclause (1)(b), a member does not have a pecuniary interest in a company or business entity (entity A) merely because the member has a pecuniary interest in another company or business entity that has a pecuniary interest in entity A.

(3)   The description of a debt under subclause (1)(h) and (i) must include disclosure of the rate of interest payable in relation to the debt if that rate of interest is less than the most recent rate of interest prescribed by regulations made under section ND 1F of the Income Tax Act 2004 (or any successor to that provision) as at the effective date of the return.

5   Debts owed by certain family members do not have to be disclosed

A member does not have to disclose the name of any debtor of the member and a description of the debt owed by that debtor if the debtor is the member's spouse or domestic partner or any parent, child, step-child, foster-child, or grandchild of the member.

6   Short-term debts for supply of goods or services do not have to be disclosed

A member does not have to disclose the name of any debtor or creditor of the member and a description of the debt owed by that debtor or to that creditor if the debt is for the supply of goods or services and payment is required—

(a)   within 90 days after the supply of the goods or services, or

(b)   because the supply of the goods or services is continuous and periodic invoices are rendered for the goods or services, within 90 days after the date of an invoice rendered for those goods or services.

7   Contents of return relating to member's activities for period ending on effective date of return

(1)   Every return must contain the following information for the period specified in clause 8:

(a)   for each country (other than New Zealand) that the member travelled to,—

(i)   the name of the country, and

(ii)   the purpose of travelling to the country, and

(iii)   the name of each person who contributed (in whole or in part) to the costs of the travel to and from the country, and

(iv)   the name of each person who contributed (in whole or in part) to the accommodation costs incurred by the member while in the country, and

    (b)   a description of each gift (including hospitality and donations in cash or kind but excluding any donation made to cover expenses in an electoral campaign) received by the member that has an estimated market value in New Zealand of more than $500 and the name of the donor of each of those gifts (if known or reasonably ascertainable by the member), and

    (c)   a description of all debts of more than $500 that were owing by the member that were discharged or paid (in whole or in part) by any other person and the names of each of those persons, and

    (d)   a description of each payment received by the member for activities in which the member is involved (other than the salary and allowances paid to that person under the Civil List Act 1979 and the Remuneration Authority Act 1977).

(2)   The information referred to in subclause (1)(a) does not have to be included in the return if the travel costs or accommodation costs (as the case may be) were paid in full by the following or any combination of the following:

    (a)   the member:

    (b)   the member's spouse or domestic partner:

    (c)   any parent, child, step-child, foster-child, or grandchild of the member:

    (d)   the Crown:

    (e)   any State government, if the primary purpose of the travel was in connection with an official parliamentary visit.

8   Period covered by return

(1)   The period for which the information specified in clause 7 must be provided is the 12-month period ending on the effective date of the return.

(2)   However,—

    (a)   a member does not have to include any information specified in clause 7 that has been included in a previous return:

    (b)   if the member is elected at an election and the member was not also a member of Parliament immediately before that election and the return is the first return required to be made by the member after that election, the period for which the information specified in clause 7 must be provided is the period beginning on polling day for that election and ending on the effective date of that return:

    (c)   if an initial return is required to be made by a member elected at a general election who was also a member of Parliament immediately before that general election, the period for which the information specified in clause 7 must be provided is the period beginning on 1 February in the year in which the general election is held and ending on the effective date of that return:

    (d)   if the member is declared to be elected under section 137 of the Electoral Act 1993 and the return is the first return required to be made by the member after being elected, the period for which the information specified in clause 7 must be provided is the period beginning on the date that the member's election is notified in the *Gazette* and ending on the effective date of that return:

    (e)   if the previous return that the member had a duty to make was an initial return, the period for which the information specified in clause 7 must be provided is the period beginning on the day after the effective date of that initial return and ending on the effective date of the return that must be made.

(3)   For the purposes of subclause (2)(b) and (d), the first return required to be made by a member may be either an initial return or an annual return.

9   Actual value, amount, or extent not required

Nothing in this Appendix requires the disclosure of the actual value, amount, or extent of any asset, payment, interest, gift, contribution, or debt.

10   Form of returns

Returns must be either—

    (a)   in a form specifically prescribed by the House, or

    (b)   in a form approved by the registrar.

PART 2

11   Register of Pecuniary Interests of Members of Parliament

(1)   A register called the Register of Pecuniary Interests of Members of Parliament is established.

(2)   The register comprises all returns transmitted by members under this Appendix.

12   Office of registrar

The office of registrar is held by the Deputy Clerk or a person appointed by the Clerk, with the agreement of the Speaker, to act as registrar.

13   Functions of registrar

The functions of the registrar are to—

    (a)   compile and maintain the register, and

    (b)   provide advice and guidance to members in connection with their obligations under this Appendix.

14 Registrar must supply returns to Auditor-General

The registrar must supply to the Controller and Auditor-General a copy of every return within 14 days of the date on which that return is received by the registrar.

15 Auditor-General's review and inquiry

(1) The Auditor-General will review the returns provided under clause 14 as soon as is reasonably practicable.

(2) The Auditor-General may inquire, either on request or on the Auditor-General's own initiative, into any issue as to whether—

(a) any member has complied, or is complying, with his or her obligations under this Appendix, or

(b) the registrar has complied, or is complying, with his or her obligations under this Appendix.

(3) The Auditor-General may, after he or she has completed an inquiry under subclause (2), report to the House the findings of the inquiry and any other matter that the Auditor-General considers it desirable to report on.

16 Registrar must publish summary of returns of current members of Parliament

(1) The registrar must, within 90 days of the due date for transmitting any initial returns that are required to be made following a general election, publish on a website and in booklet form a summary containing a fair and accurate description of the information contained in those initial returns that has been transmitted by persons who, at the date of publication, are members of Parliament.

(2) The registrar must, within 90 days of the due date for transmitting annual returns, publish on a website and in booklet form a summary containing a fair and accurate description of the information contained in those annual returns that has been transmitted by persons who, at the date of publication, are members of Parliament.

(3) The registrar must promptly provide a copy of the booklet to the Speaker.

(4) The registrar must ensure that a summary containing a fair and accurate description of information contained in all returns is—

(a) maintained on a website:

(b) available for inspection by any person at Parliament Buildings in Wellington on every working day between the hours of 10 am and 4 pm.

(5) A person may take a copy of any part of the summary referred to in subclause (4)(b) on the payment of a fee (if any) specified by the House.

17 Speaker must present copy of booklet to House of Representatives

The Speaker must, as soon as practicable after receipt of a copy of a booklet under clause 16(3), present a copy of the booklet to the House.

18 Information about register

(1) The registrar must disclose any information relating to the register that the Auditor-General requires for the purposes of reviewing and inquiring into the returns under clause 15.

(2) Subject to subclause (1), all returns and information held by the registrar relating to an individual member (other than information that is required to be disclosed under clause 16) are confidential until the dissolution or expiration of Parliament.

(3) On the dissolution or expiration of Parliament all returns and information held by the registrar relating to individual members are to be destroyed, except in respect of the return of any individual member which the Auditor-General requires to be retained for the purposes of a review or inquiry under clause 15.

19 Responsibilities of members and registrar

(1) It is the responsibility of each member to ensure that he or she fulfils the obligations imposed on the member by this Appendix.

(2) The registrar is not required to—

(a) notify any member of that member's failure to transmit a return by the due date or of any error or omission in that member's return, or

(b) obtain any return from a member.

APPENDIX C

PRELIMINARY PROCEDURES FOR PRIVATE BILLS AND LOCAL BILLS AND LOCAL LEGISLATION BILLS

PRIVATE BILLS AND LOCAL BILLS

1   Notice to be given

The promoter of a private bill or a local bill must give written notice of the intention to introduce the bill before the bill can be introduced.

2   Form and contents of notice

(1)   Every notice must be headed with the title by which the Act is to be known.

(2)   The notice must state—

(a)   that it is the intention of the promoter to promote the bill, and

(b)   the objects of the bill, and

(c)   the postal address of the promoter, or the promoter's solicitor or agent, to which communications may be sent, and

(d)   the address of the promoter, or other place specified in clause 7(2), at which a copy of the bill may be inspected, and

(e)   the address of the District Court at which a copy of the bill may be inspected, and

(f)   the dates of the period during which the bill will be available for inspection.

3   Publication of notice

(1)   A notice must be published at least once in each of two consecutive calendar weeks,—

(a)   if for a private bill, in a daily newspaper circulating in each of the cities of Auckland, Hamilton, Wellington, Christchurch, and Dunedin:

(b)   if for a private bill affecting any land or interest in land, also in a daily newspaper circulating in the locality in which the land is situated:

(c)   if for a local bill, in a daily newspaper circulating in the local authority district.

(2)   If subparagraph (b) or subparagraph (c) of paragraph (1) cannot be applied as no daily newspaper circulates in the locality or local authority district, then the notice is—

(a)   published in a daily newspaper circulating in an adjoining district, or

(b)   affixed to a noticeboard that is accessible to the public without charge.

4   Notice to persons with direct interest

(1)   The promoter of a private bill or local bill must give notice to every person who, to the knowledge of the promoter, has a direct interest in the subject-matter of the bill or in the exercise of any power proposed to be given by the bill.

(2)   Without limiting the generality of paragraph (1), notice must be given,—

(a)   if the bill may involve an appropriation or affect the public revenues or the rights and prerogatives of the Crown, to the Secretary to the Treasury and the Solicitor-General:

(b)   if the bill proposes to modify, restrict, repeal or amend the provisions of an Act of Parliament, to the chief executive of the Government department or agency charged with the administration of that Act:

(c)   if the bill may affect liability under an Inland Revenue Act, to the Commissioner of Inland Revenue:

(d)   if the bill may affect liability to excise duty or a related duty, to the chief executive of the New Zealand Customs Service:

(e)   if the bill involves the alienation or disposal of Crown land or the exchange of Crown land for other land, to the Commissioner of Crown Lands:

(f)   if the bill affects land administered under enactments for the time being relating to reserves, national parks, conservation areas, or otherwise for conservation purposes, to the chief executive of the responsible department:

(g)   if the bill relates to the transfer of title to land, to the Registrar-General of Land:

(h)   if the bill affects a charitable trust, to the Solicitor-General:

(i)   if the bill affects the incorporation or registration of any body corporate, to the relevant registering authority.

5   Notice to constituency members of Parliament

(1)   The promoter of a local bill must give notice to every member of Parliament for a General or Māori electoral district whose constituents may be affected by the provisions of the bill.

(2)   The chief executive of the promoter of a local bill must certify that each such member, by name, has been given notice, and the certificate must—

(a)   specify the date on which notice was given, and

(b)   be signed by the chief executive, and

(c)   be dated.

6 Delivery of notices

(1) Notice is given under clause 4 or clause 5 by—

(a) having it delivered to the person or the office of the department or agency concerned, or

(b) posting it, or delivering it by courier, to that person's last known address or address for service or to the chief executive of that department or agency at the department's or agency's official address, or delivering it to a document exchange which that person or department or agency uses, or

(c) sending it as an electronic communication (for example, by facsimile or e-mail message) to that person or the chief executive of that department or agency.

(2) Any notice delivered or sent may be included in or with any other document provided that it is given reasonable prominence.

7 Deposit and inspection of bill

(1) At the time of the first publication of notice of a bill a copy of the bill must be deposited,—

(a) in the case of a private bill, in the District Court in or nearest to the locality in which the promoter's residence or registered office is situated:

(b) in the case of—

(i) a private bill that affects any land or an interest in land, or

(ii) a local bill,—

in the District Court in or nearest to the locality or local authority district concerned.

(2) Another copy of the bill must be deposited in one of the following:

(a) the office of the promoter, or

(b) in the case of a private bill, in the office of the promoter's solicitor or agent, or

(c) in the case of a local bill, in a public library or a service centre.

(3) Each copy of the bill must be open to public inspection during the usual business hours of the place of deposit, without fee, for a period of not less than 15 whole working days.

8 Certification of deposit of bill

(1) The fact that a copy of the bill was deposited and remained open for public inspection must be certified,—

(a) in the case of the copy of the bill that was deposited in the District Court, by the District Court Judge or the Registrar or a Deputy Registrar of the District Court, and

(b) in the case of the copy of the bill that was deposited in the public office of the promoter or other place specified in clause 7(2), by—

(i) the promoter, or

(ii) the promoter's solicitor or agent, or

(iii) the promoter's chief executive.

(2) Each certificate must—

(a) state the first and last whole days on which the copy of the bill was open for public inspection, and

(b) be written directly on the copy of the bill and may not be separate from it, and

(c) be signed by the relevant person over his or her designation, and

(d) be dated.

9 Bills dealing with land

(1) Where it is intended in any private bill or local bill to take power to deal with any land, each deposited copy of the bill must be accompanied by a description of the land together with a true copy of the plan of the land, both certified to be correct by the chief executive of the department of State responsible for the administration of the Cadastral Survey Act 2002 (the **chief executive**) or by any other person to whom that power has been delegated by the chief executive.

(2) A true copy of the plan is not required if the chief executive or delegate certifies that the bill proposes to deal—

(a) with the whole or the residue of the land comprised in any certificate of title issued under the Land Transfer Act 1952 or any computer register created under that Act:

(b) with land previously dealt with and separately described in any statute, ordinance, Proclamation, declaration, notice or Order in Council:

(c) with the whole of the land comprised in a separate lot or other surveyed subdivision which is shown on a plan deposited in the relevant Land Information New Zealand office in accordance with the provisions of the Land Transfer Act 1952 or lodged with the chief executive or with any other person to whom the power to receive such a lodgement has been delegated by the chief executive.

(3) The plan is to be—

(a) in a form specified in rules made under the Cadastral Survey Act 2002:

(b) lodged in the relevant Land Information New Zealand office and endorsed by the chief executive, or by a person to whom that power has been delegated by the chief executive, with the words "approved for parliamentary purposes".

10   Certification of deposit of plans

All deposited descriptions and plans of the land dealt with in the bill must be certified in the same manner as for each deposited copy of the bill.

11   Forwarding of bills, plans, and other documents

(1)   Each deposited copy of the bill, together with each deposited copy of any descriptions of land and plans, as certified, copies of notices, and certificates are forwarded to the Clerk.

(2)   The documents are attached to the petition for a private bill or to the declaration for a local bill.

12   Currency of proposed bill

The copies of the bills and other documents referred to in clause 11 must be lodged with the Clerk within 6 months of the first publication of the notice of the bill.

13   Fees

(1)   The fee payable by the promoter of a bill is $2,000 (including goods and services tax) and accompanies the documents forwarded under clause 11.

(2)   The fee is,—

(a)   in the case of a private bill, made payable to the Speaker and held in a private bills fees account, and may be applied for such parliamentary purposes as the Speaker directs:

(b)   in the case of a local bill, made payable to the Clerk of the House of Representatives, and applied to defraying general administrative expenses incurred in respect of the promotion of local bills.

14   Refunds

(1)   If the select committee which considers a private bill recommends to the House that a refund be made on the ground of hardship, the House may direct that the whole or any part of the fee be refunded to the promoter.

(2)   Every refund directed by the House is made accordingly by the Speaker out of the private bills fees account.

15   Petition for private bill

The promoter of a private bill must petition the House for the introduction of the bill.

16   Form and content of petition for private bill

The petition must conform, in general, to the following form and contain all matters specified in it, and have attached to it the relevant notices:

PETITION FOR A PRIVATE BILL

To the House of Representatives

1   The petition of [*full name of individual(s) or corporation*] respectfully requests that [*title of bill*] (the deposited copies of which are attached) be introduced into the House.

2   [*If a corporation*] Your petitioner is represented by its duly authorised officer [*or authorised attorney, if a corporation incorporated outside New Zealand*], [*person's name*], of [*place of residence or headquarters*].

3   The reasons for the bill are—
[*list the reasons in the preamble of the bill*].

4   The objects of the bill are—
[*list the objects in the preamble or purpose clause*].

5   The objects of the bill cannot be attained otherwise than by legislation because [*give reasons*].
or
The objects of the bill can be attained otherwise than by legislation but [*give reasons why legislation sought*].

6   Notice of the bill has been published in two consecutive calendar weeks in issues of [*name(s) of newspaper(s)*] on [*dates*] on page(s) [*give numbers*] or on noticeboards at [*specify places*] (copies of which notices are attached).

7   Notice of the bill was given to the following persons who have a direct interest in the subject-matter of the bill or in the exercise of a power proposed to be given by the bill:
[*name and address of natural or legal person, including person specified in clause 4(2) of this Appendix*], who is affected by clause [*give reference*] of the bill because [*give reason*].
[*etc.*]
(copies of which notices are attached).

[*Signature*]
[*Name of signatory*]
[*Date*]

17   Declaration for local bill

The promoter of a local bill must make a declaration to the House relating to the bill for introduction.

18   Form and content of declaration for local bill

The declaration must conform, in general, to the following form and contain all matters specified in it, and have attached to it the relevant notices:

DECLARATION FOR A LOCAL BILL

To the House of Representatives

I, [*full name of representative, and position*] declare that—

1   The [*name of local authority*] respectfully requests that [*title of bill*] (the deposited copies of which are attached) be introduced into the House.

2   The reasons for the bill are—
      [*list the reasons*].

3   The objects of the bill are—
      [*list the objects, including any in a preamble or purpose clause*].

4   The objects of the bill cannot be attained otherwise than by legislation because [*give reasons*].
      or
      The objects of the bill can be attained otherwise than by legislation but [*give reasons why legislation sought*].

5   Notice of the bill has been published in two consecutive calendar weeks in issues of [*name(s) of newspaper(s)*] on [*dates*] on page(s) [*give numbers*] or on noticeboards at [*specify places*] (copies of which notices are attached).

6   Notice of the bill was given to the following persons who have a direct interest in the subject-matter of the bill or in the exercise of a power proposed to be given by the bill:
      [*name and address of natural or legal person, including person specified in clause 4(2) of this Appendix*], who is affected by clause [*give reference*] of the bill because [*give reason*].
      [*etc.*]
      (copies of which notices are attached).

      [*Signature*]
      [*Name of signatory*]
      [*Date*]

19   Examination and endorsement of bills and documents

(1)   The Clerk examines the bill and other documents required to be forwarded to the Clerk to ensure that the Standing Orders have been complied with.

(2)   If the Standing Orders appear to have been complied with, the Clerk—
      (a)   endorses the petition for a private bill or the declaration for a local bill "Standing Orders complied with", and
      (b)   signs and dates that endorsement.

(3)   If the Standing Orders appear not to have been complied with, the Clerk returns the documents and the fee to the promoter.

LOCAL LEGISLATION BILLS

20   Initiation of clauses in Local Legislation bills

(1)   Any local authority may apply to the Minister of Local Government for preliminary consideration and provisional approval of a clause or clauses to be included in a Local Legislation Bill.

(2)   Every application must be accompanied—
      (a)   by a draft of the proposed clause or clauses, and
      (b)   by a certificate signed by the chief executive of the local authority certifying that every member of Parliament, by name, for a General or Māori electoral district whose constituents may be affected by the proposed legislation, has been provided with a copy of the proposed clause or clauses, together with a notice in writing stating that it is the intention to apply for their inclusion in a Local Legislation Bill.

(3)   The certificate must—
      (a)   specify the date on which notice was given, and
      (b)   be signed by the chief executive, and
      (c)   be dated.

(4)   A copy of the proposed clause or clauses and the notice is given to such a member by—
      (a)   personal delivery, or
      (b)   post, or delivery by couriers, or delivery to a document exchange which the member uses, or
      (c)   sending as an electronic communication (for example, by facsimile or e-mail message) to the member.

21   Repeal of spent local legislation

The Minister may also include in a Local Legislation Bill a clause or clauses repealing any spent local Act, any spent Local Legislation Act, or any spent provisions contained in a Local Legislation Act.

22   Objections

The Minister must transmit to the select committee that considers a Local Legislation Bill a copy of any objection received by the Minister to any clause included in the bill.

23   Clauses provisionally approved by Minister may be included in bill

When the Minister has provisionally approved a clause or clauses these may be included in a Local Legislation Bill.

24   How further clauses dealt with

If a Local Legislation Bill is already before the House, a further clause or clauses for inclusion in the bill may, after being provisionally approved by the Minister, be placed upon a Supplementary Order Paper by the Minister, and may be considered by the select committee that is considering the bill.

25   Provisional approval by Minister and report by committee essential

(1)   No Local Legislation Bill may be passed by the House and no clause or clauses added to any Local Legislation Bill unless they have been provisionally approved by the Minister and reported on by a select committee.

(2)   Despite paragraph (1), a new clause may be inserted that is in substitution for, incidental to, or consequential upon a clause which has been provisionally approved by the Minister and reported on by a select committee.

INDEX

745

T